This Is Who We Were In The 1990s

This Is Who We Were
In The 1990s

Based on material from Grey House Publishing's
Working Americans Series by Scott Derks

Grey **H**ouse
Publishing

PUBLISHER: Leslie Mackenzie
EDITORIAL DIRECTOR: Laura Mars
EDITORIAL ASSISTANT: Ariel Picton
PRODUCTION MANAGER: Kristen Hayes
MARKETING DIRECTOR: Jessica Moody
COMPOSITION: David Garoogian

Grey House Publishing, Inc.
4919 Route 22
Amenia, NY 12501
518.789.8700
FAX 845.373.6390
www.greyhouse.com
e-mail: books @greyhouse.com

Publisher's Cataloging-In-Publication Data
(Prepared by The Donohue Group, Inc.)

ISBN 978-1-68217-379-4

TABLE OF CONTENTS

Section One: Profiles

This section contains 28 profiles of individuals and families living and working in the 1990s. It examines their lives at home, at work, and in their communities. Based upon historic materials, personal interviews, and diaries, the profiles give a sense of what it was like to live in the years 1990 to 1999.

Section Two: Historical Snapshots

This section includes lists of important "firsts" in America, from technical advances and political events to new products, books, and movies. Combining American history with fun facts, these snapshots present an easy-to-read overview of the 1990s.

Section Three: Economy of the Times

This section looks at a wide range of economic data, including prices for food, clothing, transportation, and housing, plus reprints of actual advertisements for products and services of the time. It includes comparable figures for expenditures, income, and prices, plus a valuable year-by-year listing of the value of a dollar.

Section Four: All Around Us—What We Saw, Wrote, Read & Listened To

This section offers reprints of newspaper and magazine articles, speeches, and other items designed to help readers focus on what was on the minds of Americans in the 1990s. These 50 original pieces show how popular opinion was formed, and how American life was affected.

Section Five: Census Data

This section includes state-by-state comparative tables, Census 2000 briefs and special reports.

ESSAY ON THE 1990S

The 1990s, called the "Era of Possibilities" by *Fortune* magazine, were dominated by an economic expansion that became the longest in the nation's history. Characterized by steady growth, low inflation, low unemployment and dramatic gains in technology-based productivity, particularly meaningful to computer companies and the emerging concept known as the Internet.

This robust economy also empowered and emboldened the nation's lower, middle, and minority classes. The ranks of the African American middle class swelled; women filled half of all seats at the nation's law and medical schools, and Hispanic workers immigrated in droves to chase the dream of economic prosperity in a foreign land. Predictably, this growing population of Spanish-speaking workers ignited raucous rounds of debate concerning America's immigration policy—especially as it related to immigrants arriving by way of Mexico.

America's disabled individuals gained new rights and more respect, and America's Christian fundamentalists found their political voice. As wealth grew, possibilities flourished: colleges became overcrowded; buying power of America's youth exploded; personal computers, on the cusp of competing with television's rapidly expanding array of specialized channels, became a fixture in millions of homes.

Current Events

The early 1990s faced an economic recession, ballooning national debt, and the collapse of much of the savings and loan industry. The automobile industry had record losses, while housing values plummeted and factory orders fell. Military operations involving American troops included Operation Desert Storm in response to Iraqi President Saddam Hussein's invasion of Kuwait; in a matter of weeks, an international coalition removed Iraqi troops from Kuwait, with estimates of Iraqi military deaths ranging from 8,000 to 100,000, while the allies lost about 300 troops. In 1995, President Bill Clinton, in concert with NATO, organized Operation Deliberate Force in Bosnia, to stop the Bosnian Serb's campaign of "ethnic cleansing" of the Muslim population. Media headlines were dominated by rising drug use, crime in the cities, racial tensions, and the rise of personal bankruptcies. Family values ranked high on the conservative agenda and despite efforts to limit Democrat Bill Clinton to one term as president, the strength of the economy played a critical role in his re-election in 1996. Most of the military campaigns during the period had been successful, and the last bastion of gender segregation—the all-male military college The Citadel—finally admitted its first female cadet.

Economy

Guided by Federal Reserve Chair Alan Greenspan's focus on inflation control and Clinton's early efforts to control the federal budget, the U.S. economy soared, producing its best economic indicators in three decades. By 1999 the stock market produced record returns, job creation was at a 10-year high, and the federal deficit was falling. Businesses nationwide hung "Help Wanted" signs outside their doors and even paid signing bonuses to acquire new workers. Crime rates, especially in urban areas, plummeted to levels unseen in three decades, illegitimacy rates fell, and every year business magazines marveled at the length of the recovery, asking, "can it last another year?"

The stock market broke several records throughout the decade, attracting thousands of first-time investors, especially enticed by high technology companies. From 1990 to the dawn of the 21st century, the Dow Jones Industrial Average rose 318 percent. This market boom eventually spawned unprecedented new wealth, encouraging early retirement to legions of baby boomers. The dramatic change in the cultural structure of corporations continued to threaten the job security of American workers, who were forced to learn new skills, try new jobs, and move from project to project. Profit sharing became more common, allowing workers to benefit from increased productivity. Retirement programs and pension plans became more flexible and transferable, serving the needs of a highly mobile work force. The emerging gap of the 1990s was not just between the rich and the poor, but also between the computer literate and the technically deficient. Symbolizing the changing role of women in the work force, cartoon character Dagwood Bumstead's wife, Blondie, opened her own successful catering business. Studies showed that, for the first time, 55 percent of women provided at least half of their household's income.

The 1990s give birth to $150 tennis shoes, condom boutiques, pre-ripped jeans, Motorola 7.7-ounce cell phones, rollerblading, TV home and Internet shopping, Java computer language, digital cameras, and DVD players. A 1960's fashion revival brought back miniskirts, pop art prints, pants suits, and the A-line dress. Black became popular regardless of time of day or occasion. Increasing consumer debt not only drove the American economy, but also produced increasing personal bankruptcy and less savings overall. rate. At the same time, mortgage interest rates hit 30-year lows during the decade, creating refinancing booms that pumped millions of dollars into the economy, further fueling a decade of consumerism.

Political and Social Change
In the media-obsessed 1990s, a main attraction was President Bill Clinton's affair with White House intern Monica Lewinsky. While American forces were attacking Iraq, the House of Representatives voted to impeach Clinton for perjury and obstruction of justice, but the Senate conducted an impeachment hearing and voted to acquit the president of the charges.

During the decade, America debated abortion, criminal sentencing, welfare, Affirmative Action, bilingual education, educational standards, rights of legal immigrants, and warnings on unsuitable material on the Internet, powered by 24-hour programming on television channels and the resurgence of talk radio. Nationwide, an estimated 15 million people, including smokers, cross-dressers, alcoholics, sexual compulsives, and gamblers attended weekly self-help support groups, and dieting became a $33 billion industry.

Education
The impact of the GI Bill's focus on education, rooted in the decade following World War II, flowered in the generation that followed that war. The number of Americans with a four-year college education rose from 6.2 percent in 1950 to 24 percent in 1997. Despite this impressive rise, the need for a more educated population and the rapidly rising expectations of the technology sector, the perception at the end of the century was that public education was declining, fueled by an increase in school violence.

By the 1990s, largely resulting from the Civil Rights Movement and increased immigration, the debate concerning multicultural education ranged from empowering oppressed people to creating national unity through the teaching common cultural values. The public schoolhouse became the battleground for those who wanted the 10 Commandments displayed and cable television to broadcast educational programs.

Music
The 1990s experienced a revival of the singer-songwriter movement of the 1970s, bringing artists like Norah Jones, Sarah McLachlan, and Alanis Morissette to the fore. Grunge remained a local phenomenon, and Nirvana's album *Nevermind*, led to the widespread popularization of alternative rock in the 1990s. Groups like the Red Hot Chili Peppers, Backstreet Boys, 'N Sync, 98 Degrees, and The Spice Girls were popular, as were Christina Aguilera, Britney Spears, Jennifer Lopez, and Destiny's Child, targeting younger members of Generation Y. Mariah Carey's duet with Boyz II Men "One Sweet Day," recorded in 1995, spent 16 weeks atop the Hot 100 and was pronounced song of the decade.

Sports

The business of sports exploded during the 1990s as the Michael Jordan-led Chicago Bulls won six championships in the National Basketball Association, steroid-influenced homerun hitting dominated major league baseball and the world came to Atlanta, Georgia, for the twenty-sixth Olympiad. There, Carl Lewis won his ninth Olympic gold medal and sprinter Michael Johnson made breaking records look easy. Free agency within the professional ranks, which enabled players to sign with any team, left fans confused as players moved from team to team. And in 1994, the first time since 1904, baseball's World Series was canceled, because striking players and owners couldn't agree about how to divide billions of dollars in revenue.

In the process, television's reach expanded exponentially: cable television carved out niches like the Golf Channel just in time for African American golfer Tiger Woods to burst onto the golf scene in 1996. The U.S. women's soccer team won the World Cup on American turf in 1999. The success of women athletes was best exemplified by the National Basketball Association's decision to create the Women's National Basketball Association in 1997, the excitement created by speed skater Bonnie Blair in the XVI Winter Olympics, and the three NCAA National Championships captured by the University of Tennessee's Lady Vols basketball team.

INTRODUCTION

This Is Who We Were In The 1990s is an offspring of our 14-volume *Working Americans* series, which is devoted, volume by volume, to Americans by class, occupation, or social cause. This new edition is devoted to the 1990s. It represents various economic classes, dozens of occupations, and all regions of the country. This comprehensive look at this decade is through the eyes and ears of everyday Americans, not the words of historians or politicians.

This Is Who We Were In The 1990s presents 28 profiles of individuals and families—their lives at home, on the job, and in their neighborhood—with lots of photos and historical images. These stories portray struggling and successful Americans, and capture a wide range of thoughts and emotions. With government surveys, economic data, family diaries and letters, and newspaper and magazine features, this unique reference assembles a remarkable personal and realistic look at the lives of a wide range of Americans between the years 1990-1999.

The profiles, together with additional sections outlined below, present a complete picture of what it was like to live in America in the 1990s.

Section One: Profiles

Each of the 28 profiles in Section One begins with a brief introduction. Each profile is arranged in three categories: Life at Home; Life at Work; Life in the Community. Photographs and original advertisements support each chapter, and many include industry or social timelines and contemporary articles.

Section Two: Historical Snapshots

Section Two is made up of three long, bulleted lists of significant events and milestones. In chronological order—Early 1990s, Mid 1990s, and Late 1990s—these offer an amazing range of firsts and turning points in American history, including a few "can you believe it?" facts.

Section Three: Economy of the Times

One of the most interesting things about researching an earlier time is learning how much things cost and what people earned. This section offers this information in three categories—Consumer Expenditures, Annual Income of Standard Jobs, and Selected Prices—with actual figures from three specific years for easy comparison and study.

At the end of Section Three is a Value of a Dollar Index that compares the buying power of $1.00 in 2016 to the buying power of $1.00 in every year prior, back to 1860, helping to put the economic data in *This Is Who We Were In The 1990s* into context.

Section Four: All Around Us

There is no better way to put your finger on the pulse of a country than to read its magazines and newspapers. This section offers 50 original articles, book excerpts, speeches, and advertising copy that influenced American thought from 1990-1999.

Section Five: Census Data

This section includes invaluable data to help define the 1990s such as State-by-State comparative tables, and actual reprints from the 2000 Census, including 27 Census Briefs and three Special Reports. Here you will find detailed population, social and economic characteristics. This section also includes dozens of maps and charts for easy analysis.

This Is Who We Were In The 1990s ends with a Further Reading section and detailed Index.

The editors thank all those who agreed to be interviewed and share their personal photos for this book. We also gratefully acknowledge the Prints & Photographs Collections of the Library of Congress.

1991: Airline Captain & Underwriting Manager

Ben and Bridget Nichols, of Chicago, began the year confident, excited, and at the peak of their earnings. Bridget had turned 40, Ben's daughter Meghan moved in with them, and they bought two new cars and an airplane. By the end of the year, however, Ben was out of work, the victim of a corporate bankruptcy.

Life at Home

- Bridget made $68,000 as the manager of underwriting with Chase Mortgage; Ben earned $64,000, despite the layoff.
- Bridget had just become an instant mother; Ben's 16-year-old daughter Meghan, who had been living with her natural grandmother in Charlotte, North Carolina, moved in with them.
- Married for the first time, Bridget was excited by the chance to help raise his middle daughter, and participate in her band competitions, homework, and dating.
- Active in band competitions, Meghan played the flute and captured second chair.
- The couple was married in 1988; this was his fourth marriage, and her first.
- He had just purchased his own airplane; life had never been better.
- At mid-year, in his new role of captain and instructor for Midway Airlines, he was on track to make $120,000 a year.
- They purchased their three bedroom, split level brick house in the suburbs the previous year for $176,000; they had a monthly mortgage payment of $1,100 per month.
- They paid $3,400 in property taxes each year.
- Their New Ford Tempo, bought that year, cost $8,000.
- On his days off, Ben flew a biplane at a crop-dusting school; when flying for Midway, he piloted a DC-9.
- He made $1.00 per acre, and earned up to $2,000 a weekend while crop dusting pesticides on corn and soybean fields.
- That year, they vacationed in Oshkosh, Wisconsin, where hundreds of home-built and antique airplane buffs camped out and socialized every year.
- Born in 1944 in Norfolk, Virginia, Ben grew up loving airplanes.
- He took his first airplane flight at two years old, spent his summers around airplanes, and by the time he was 14, his life revolved around flying.

One of Ben's three daughters, 16-year-old Meghan, moved in with the couple in Chicago.

Ben began flying when he was 14 years old.

- He learned to fly before he learned to drive.
- As a teenager, to get the $8 he needed for each flight lesson, he washed airplanes, swept hangars, and did odd jobs in his neighborhood.
- In 1961, using a technicality in the law, he joined the Marine Reserves on his seventeenth birthday so he would be eligible for a pilot's license without parental permission, which his father had refused to give. Otherwise, Ben would have had to wait until he was 21.
- His father worked for Remington Rand Typewriter Company.
- Following high school, Ben served in the Marines, training to become a flight engineer. He spent time in Vietnam, and then left the Marines to marry his first wife.
- As a couple, they attended an airplane dedication for missionaries in Africa; an event that changed Ben's life.
- After that day, he realized that it was God's will for him to be a missionary pilot.

The Nichols' home was in the suburbs of Chicago.

- The couple lived and worked in Liberia; his job was to fly missionaries into remote locations in the underdeveloped country.
- When he returned from Africa, he worked a variety of jobs, all relating to flying; he crop-dusted, flew helicopters, and worked as a pilot for a private development company.
- His wife died at age 32; he married twice more, both times briefly, before moving to Chicago in 1986, where he met Bridget.
- Born in Uniontown, Pennsylvania, Bridget grew up in the suburbs of

They attended the annual fly-in at Oshkosh, Wisconsin.

Chicago; when she was five, her parents divorced, after which she was raised by her mother and her grandfather.

- Her mother worked as a secretary for Ford Motor Company, and later for Clark Equipment.
- While her mother worked late, Bridget heated cans of Spaghettios and dreamed of having a mom who stayed home and baked cookies.
- After high school, she attended community college at night, working her way through school at the First National Bank of Chicago.
- As a part of the secretarial pool, she used manual typewriters and carbon paper to prepare the reports dictated by the male managers.
- In 1974, she joined Fannie Mae, a private investor in second mortgages, taking a job as a paralegal, though her bosses said they were unsure a woman could do that kind of work.
- In 1984, she became a lender representative at Fannie Mae, before moving to an aggressive savings and loan company, as the manager of underwriting.
- She quickly discovered the financial institution was more interested in increasing sales than in making quality loans, and shortly thereafter, Chase Manhattan acquired the company.
- By 1987, when the couple met, Bridget was vice president of underwriting for Chase; her lending authority was $750,000.

Life at Work

- Ben had been working for Midway Airlines, which served 40 cities nationwide. For the past four years he had worked as a pilot, instructor, and captain-the job he always wanted.
- He typically worked 17 days a month.
- That year, Midway struggled with rising fuel prices, tight credit, and escalating debt.
- Airline rate wars were producing tremendous consumer demand in the midst of a recession; and though airplanes were full, profits were still low.
- Northwest Airlines had planned to buy the discount airline, formed after deregulation of the airline industry.

- On his last day on the job with Midway, Ben flew from Chicago to Palm Springs, Florida, and then all the way to Nassau and back, not knowing if at the end of the day he would be a new employee of Northwest, or out of a job.
- After he landed his plane in Chicago, he learned the purchase had fallen through.
- Midway passengers were stranded at airports across the country.
- A friend called from Midway: "They are shutting the airline down, do you want me to get your flight bag out of the airport?"
- His next-door neighbor called after the 10 p.m. news announcement of the bankruptcy, and offered him a job with his company.
- For the last few months of the year, he learned about auto sprays and dreamt of ways to get back into the air.
- At Chase Manhattan Mortgage, Bridget spent much of her year traveling and training; it had been a creative, but difficult year.
- The economy was clearly slowing-its first major economic decline since 1982; unemployment was climbing.
- The year began with 30-year, fixed-rate mortgages hovering at 9.5 percent; during the year, driven by the recession, rates dropped steadily.

Ben was an instructor and a captain—the job he had always wanted.

Life in the Community: Chicago, Illinois

- Ben and Bridget lived in the suburbs of Chicago, the second-largest city and third-largest metropolitan area in the United States.
- 2,982,370 people worked in the Chicago area—more than the total population of the city.
- Chicago was the birthplace of the skyscraper; the first ten story skyscraper had been constructed in 1885.

Chicago was the nation's second-largest city.

- Afterwards, the 110-story Sears Tower and the 100-story John Hancock Center were built.
- Thanks in part to the World's Columbian Exposition, Chicago was home to the largest number of medical associations of any other American city, including the American Medical Association, The American Hospital Association, the American College of Surgeons, The American College of Radiology, the American Society of Anesthesiologists, the Association of American Physicians & Surgeons, the American Association of Industrial Physicians & Surgeons, and the College of American Pathologists.
- There were 19 million biological specimens—9.8 million of which were insects, in the Field Museum storage vault.
- The *Chicago Tribune* reported that Joseph "Pops" Panczko, dean of Chicago's trunk poppers and lock pickers, retired at the age of 72, after serving time for his 200th arrest.

- Two years earlier, the Chicago Cubs became the last major league team to introduce night baseball in their home field.
- The filming of the movie *Uncle Buck* was completed in Chicago, along with *Looking for Mr. Goodbar, The Blues Brothers, Ordinary People, Rich and Famous,* and *The Fury.*
- A three-bedroom, one-and-a-half-bath brick home in the Chicago Ridge section, featuring six rooms, a full basement with a recreation room and a workshop, a living room with a fireplace, and an updated kitchen sold for $99,000, with a qualifying income of $33,774, a down payment of $19,980, and a the monthly payment for the $79,020 loan at nine percent would be $788 per month.

The Nichols loved relaxing with friends at home, at the lake and at fly-ins.

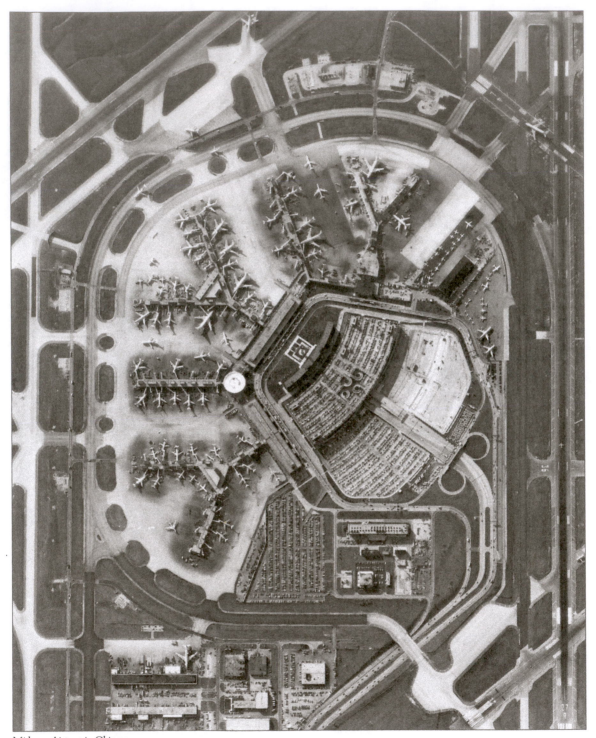

Midway Airport in Chicago.

1991: Lance Corporal, Operation Desert Storm

Lance Corporal Raul Hernandez was just as eager to enter Operation Desert Storm as he had been to join the Marines, which offered him an escape from poverty in Bronx, New York, and the chance for a better future.

Life at Home

- Raul Hernandez discovered his future while sitting on the steps of his apartment building.
- He grew up on the rough streets of the South Bronx, where hope was just an invitation to disaster.
- Few of the men could find jobs, and drug and alcohol abuse were as rampant as violent crime; every month or so, Raul learned of someone else he knew who had been killed.
- Then, on a Saturday morning, when Raul was sitting outside, his old friend Rafael, whom Raul had not seen in years, stepped from a cab.
- Rafael had completely changed.
- He stood ramrod straight, walked with a purpose, and his Marine uniform, which was graced by three stripes on its sleeve, was spotless and crisp.
- They spoke briefly, making arrangements to meet again.
- During the next few days, they talked about Rafael's experiences, his travels, plans, and expectations for the future.
- Raul decided the Marines were his answer—and his escape.
- Because he was unaccustomed to discipline, training at Parris Island was difficult, but for the first time, he made friends with non-Hispanics.
- He began to read the newspapers and explore the greater world around him.
- By the summer of 1990, it was obvious to him and his fellow trainees that trouble was brewing in the Middle East; Iraq had invaded Kuwait without provocation.
- American troops were joining military units from countries as diverse as Great Britain, France, Bangladesh, Pakistan and Egypt, among many others.
- President George Bush had issued an ultimatum to Iraq's leader Saddam Hussein: Get out of Kuwait or suffer the consequences.

Raul Hernandez joined the Marines for the chance at a better life.

Once in Saudi Arabia, Raul learned one of the lessons of military life: waiting.

- Raul was excited when orders arrived in August for his entire division to ship out for Saudi Arabia.
- His girlfriend cried, and his mother said she was proud.
- Most of the officers felt Saddam would back down in the face of the overwhelming coalition of forces mounted against him.
- Once he arrived in Saudi Arabia, Raul learned another lesson of military life: waiting.
- After the initial excitement of getting settled, the days became routine.
- In a nearby warehouse, a priest held mass, which Raul attended occasionally.
- A baptized Catholic, he knew that when the shooting started he was going to need all the help he could get.
- Besides, because the base was located in Saudi Arabia, no alcohol was allowed.
- This was a hardship; Raul had grown accustomed to ending his day with a few cold beers.
- As he waited, he checked his gear, took field exercise, played touch football, and feared a Dear John letter from his girlfriend.
- The few cards he got from home were displayed on the bed above his cot.
- When Christmas in the hot desert arrived on schedule, Raul joined his few Marines in what they were told would be a traditional Christmas meal.
- As expected, his fellow Marines complained about the chow and told stories about grand, wonderful Christmas celebrations back home.

- Raul was fascinated; he and his mother normally ate a simple meal on Christmas after mass, since it was all they could afford.

Life at Work

- As the New Year passed, Lance Corporal Raul Hernandez's anticipation began to grow.
- President George Bush had given Iraqi President Saddam Hussein until January 15, 1991, to get his forces out of Kuwait or be subject to attack.

Like most Marines, Raul was constantly hungry for news of the war and its progress.

- The coalition forces had amassed 500,000 troops, 3,300 tanks, 4,000 armored personnel carriers, 3,600 pieces of artillery, 1,900 helicopters and 2,600 combat aircraft in the region.
- More than 100 ships were stationed offshore.
- As the deadline passed, the air war began.
- Day after day, the Iraqi forces were pounded, while the Marines waited on ready.
- Raul knew the ground war was next, and that his time was coming.
- Like most Marines, he was constantly hungry for news of the war and its progress.
- After 38 days of air assaults, orders arrived to move out.
- Accompanied by a picture of his girlfriend, Raul climbed aboard a HUMVEE heading toward the Kuwait border.
- Now he could prove he was a soldier worthy of the Marine uniform.
- Raul was part of a recon force of three companies outfitted in light armored vehicles; their task was to determine the Iraqi position within Kuwait.
- The approximately 500 men were armed with M-16 rifles, machine guns, grenade launchers and antitank weapons.
- The first major battle of Raul's young life began around noon.

- The Iraqis attacked with mortars, artillery and machine-gun fire, then with T-55 tanks.
- To counter, the Marines' land-launched TOW missiles took out four Iraqi tanks, seven trucks and an BMP armored personnel carrier.
- Despite all his training, Raul felt unsure of his first burst of fire, but his confidence grew quickly.
- In the first wave, 73 prisoners were captured, with an additional 23 surrendering under fire early the following day.
- Raul was amazed at the fast appearance of white flags, but the officers explained that the Iraqi soldiers were eager to avoid being killed for Saddam.
- Most were not trained soldiers, and just wanted to go home.
- The next day presented Raul with a different picture of war.

- The battle unfolded against a surrealistic backdrop: more than two dozen burning Kuwaiti oil wells, each shooting orange jets of flame 50 or 60 feet into the air and throwing off vast clouds of black smoke that formed a thick curtain above the Iraqi positions.
- Both sides exchanged artillery and mortar fire, but the Iraqi fire came from a fixed position, so the Marines quickly calculated where it would land.
- Two Marines were wounded.
- During the battle, Raul and another Marine moved forward in a HUMVEE filled with ammunition.
- Only later did Raul learn that it was a mortar round which landed in the back and detonated, exploding the ordnance in the Hummer and blowing the entire vehicle to shreds.
- Both men were blasted out of the vehicle.
- The next thing Raul knew, he and the other Marine were lying on the ground.
- Both experienced ringing in their ears and a few bruises, but little else.
- The medics were amazed.
- Both Marines inscribed their helmets with "LUCKY AS HELL" and returned to battle.
- With his M-16 in hand, Raul felt like real Marine with a story to tell.
- But even though thousands of Iraqis were surrendering, the war was far from over.
- Kuwait City—and possibly Baghdad—were still ahead.
- Modern Warfare in Desert Storm The focus of high-tech conventional warfare had been to reduce general destruction.

Life in the Community: Desert Storm
- During the first five days of Desert Storm, the coalition air force delivered around 15 kilotons of high explosives—about the same as the blast power of the Hiroshima bomb—yet the civilian loss of life was considerably less and accuracy greater.

- In World War II, the typical allied bombing range was almost one mile, meaning nonmilitary targets were often hit when rail yards or airbases had been the real targets.
- By the Vietnam War, overall bombing accuracy had improved to roughly one quarter of a mile.
- Smart bombs used in the Desert Storm raids had an accuracy of within 100 feet or less, allowing three missiles to destroy the Iraqi Ministry of Defense, while leaving a nearby hospital untouched.
- Experts say a similar raid in World War II would have required 30 planes scattering bombs over an area of several miles.
- Most of the Desert Storm weapons were launched from maneuverable, fighter-type aircraft such as the F-15E or F/A-18.
- Unlike lumbering high-altitude bombers such as the B-52, these aircraft could draw close enough to the target for it to be seen—visually or electronically—before a weapon was released.
- Destruction was also decreased because of greater explosion control.
- Though new explosive compounds were more energetic than those of World War II, in many cases the warhead of a smart weapon was not very large.
- Huge warheads were not needed if the weapon found the target precisely.
- Now, the body of the device must accommodate engines, fuel and electronics, leaving less room for explosives.

1992: Daughter of Cattle Rancher

Fourth-grader Cordelia Dorffman lived a dream life on her family's Texas ranch, always aware that she was the rich kid, and often felt under attack due to her lifestyle and a changing world.

Life at Home

- Cordelia Dorffman and her family were close.
- She even liked her older sister, who attended a prep school in Houston. Both girls favored stuffed animals and frilly dresses.
- Her brothers were the most handsome men in the world, and surely would break many hearts before they married.
- Her oldest brother had already attended college and graduate school, and had taken his place among the corporate management of the increasingly diversified Two Crowns Ranch, Inc., in Houston.
- Her second brother was still in college; unlike his older brother, he was taking his time and enjoying every minute of his college experience, much to the frustration of their father.
- She also loved being with her mother and looking at pictures of her mother growing up, especially a picture taken years ago when she was a teen, dancing with Cordelia's grandfather.
- They were all dressed up in white gloves and enjoying themselves tremendously.
- But most of all, she loved going out to tour the ranch with her father.
- The ranch, which was pretty much the size of Rhode Island, was always a gumbo of activity.
- Every day, something new was happening—breaking new horses, castrating bulls or branding cows.
- Cordelia was convinced that there was no greater place to be in the entire world.
- The family lived in a modern split-level house, large enough to require a full-time maid and a live-in cook.
- Cordelia dreaded the cook's day off, since cooking was not among her mother's finest talents.

Cordelia Dorffman loved life on a Texas cattle ranch.

- Her father might have felt the same way; often on those nights, he took the family to a restaurant in Kingsville or brought home barbecue.
- Her mother absolutely refused to ride in the Ram Charger pickup truck her husband loved so dearly, so when they went out, they rode in her Suburban.
- In a large clearing near Cordelia's house stood the ranch hacienda, a 25-room Spanish-style manor with a bell tower, which served as the owner's house for the first half of the twentieth century.
- Now, it was carefully preserved in a museum-like state and used only by family members for very special occasions, such as the annual weeklong meeting of the Two Crowns Ranch, Inc., shareholders.
- All 60 stockholders were descendents of Julius and Cordelia Dorffman, although some kin were closer to the trunk of the family tree than others.
- Over the years, many branches of the family had moved away from the hot, heavy work of Texas ranch life, and today only a few direct descendents were still involved with any agricultural pursuits at all.

Every day something new happened on the ranch.

- That was only one of the reasons her father, as vice president for agriculture, dreaded the annual gathering of what he called "the sorta-clan."
- On more than one occasion, he had explained to Cordelia that his title means he "ran the ranches"—the 13 million acres of agricultural property owned around the world by Two Crowns, including cattle ranches in Brazil, Venezuela and Australia; citrus groves in Florida; and a large horse farm in Kentucky.

Cordelia's friends said she was rich; her father said they were comfortable.

- For the past several years, the other stockholders had been critical of the agricultural division's performance.
- This group of non-ranchers, who couldn't ride to save their necks, were city folk who always knew more about how to manage the ranches than he did.
- A handful even brought in articles from *The New York Times* (of all things!) on how to make money in ranching in the 1990s.
- Currently, there was a growing sentiment that the corporation needed a Harvard M.B.A. type who knew the "value of a dollar" to run this far-flung empire.
- The shareholders were convinced that the employee benefits were too generous, the return too small, and ranching, overall, too much trouble in this modern age.
- Last year, he was accused of being too sentimental, because he allowed retired

Exploring the cattle ranch was always a joy.

employees with 40 years of service to live out their lives in the company-provided homes built on the ranch.

- He was not about to change that, no matter what the absentee stockholders had to say; loyalty got Two Crowns where it was today.
- Cordelia found little to like about the cousins who showed up each summer; although a few had grown up around horses, most were city kids looking for a country adventure and ready—oh, so ready—to make fun of everything.
- Even cousin Lavinia, who was an excellent rider, looked down her nose at Two Crowns' horses because they didn't measure up to her standards.
- Lavinia, as she liked to mention in every other sentence, was a champion dressage rider.
- Cordelia's favorite visitors each summer were Davie and Daniel, whose father managed the Australian operations.
- They promised that if she would return with them to Australia one year she could see kangaroos and even pet a koala.
- They even worked out a secret code all their own so they could send messages back and forth.
- Most of the kids were from places like San Antonio, Houston or Dallas or, worse, "back East," where their parents bought them brand-new jeans and boots each year for their "ranching adventure."
- When the shareholder meetings got too bad or long or theatrical, Cordelia's father sought her out and they jumped into his pickup for a long ride around the ranch.
- Typically, they would pass herds of grazing cattle and miles of cotton, sorghum and sugar cane; often, they would run up on small parties of cowboys working the range as they had for hundreds of years.
- These days, he told his daughter, "It's good to get out in the open air with you, Cordelia."
- She hated stockholders and corporations and ranches that end in "Inc."

She had always loved horses.

- After the stockholders went home each year, her sister and mother immediately headed to the family beach house, where there were tons of boys, and that meant Cordelia and her dad could enjoy time together.
- The two often got up early, fixed a campfire breakfast, and then rode around the ranch supervising operations.
- At night, she tended to her filly, Heidi, and had dinner with her father and a few of her father's oldest friends—men who worked for him on the ranch.

Before she walked, she rode.

Life at School

- The fourth grade was a mixed bag of joy and disappointment.
- First of all, lots of what she was being taught felt like a review of the third grade and was not challenging at all.
- Second, it was sometimes hard to make friends because her name was Dorffman: Everyone thought she was rich, even though her father insisted they were simply a comfortable family that worked for what they had, and would have to work hard to keep it.
- Cordelia wanted to have friends because she was just "Cordelia."
- Sometimes, the girls would whisper about her and the size of her house, and then not talk with her at lunch, as though it was her fault her father worked hard.
- Cordelia loved the nuns because they were like her parents—strict, but fair—and she was often shocked by what the other children did when the nuns' backs were turned, even imitating the walk of one of the older nuns when she was right there in the room.

Heidi, the most beautiful filly in the world, was predestined to be Cordelia's very own horse.

- Some girls even made ugly remarks about Cordelia's name.
- She loved having a unique name, shared by both the good daughter of Shakespeare's play, *King Lear*, and the first white woman—her ancestor—to come to this semi-desert of the South Texas Coast 140 years earlier.
- The first Cordelia survived a harsh land of thorn bushes and tidal flats to raise 10 children on what was to become the largest ranch in the country.
- The favorite activity of her namesake was reading, especially about horses.
- Her father's sprawling library was packed with great books about horses of every type.
- He even took the time to find unique books, which Cordelia was allowed to keep in her room on a special bookshelf of her own.
- She had loved horses for as long as she could remember.
- Before she could walk, she would ride with her father on his big stallion, Anthracite; when she was four, she frequently rode Pepe, an old and gentle pony which she regularly fed and looked after.
- Recently, Heidi, the most beautiful filly in the world, was born—predestined to be Cordelia's very own horse.
- When Heidi got old enough, Cordelia is sure the two of them would be inseparable; at night, she dreamt of riding Heidi like the wind into the broad fields of the ranch.
- Even though she liked many of the girls at school, her real best friends were the children who lived in neat frame bungalows with shady yards on the ranch and went to the school on ranch property.

- Most were descendents of an entire Mexican village who were recruited years ago by Julius Dorffman to work for him on Two Crowns.
- Cordelia's father and Two Crowns, Inc., handled all their pay, health care and retirement.

Life in the Community: Houston, Texas

- The ranch covered 825,000 acres, or 1,289 square miles, and was crossed with so many fences that, if stretched end to end, they would run from the ranch headquarters in South Texas to Boston.
- The fences held 65,000 head of cattle, managed by riders using 550 quarter horses, a breed developed on the ranch.
- The dominant breed of cattle was the cherry-red Santa Gertrudis, a disease-resistant breed created to withstand the region's hot, arid conditions.
- It was the first breed of cattle produced in America.
- The ranch's diversified corporation included among its assets 630 oil and gas wells.
- Spanish colonists called this land El Desierto de los Muertos—the Desert of the Dead.

1992: High School Female Athlete and Scholar

Gayle Warwick was the first woman in her family to benefit by Title IX by participating in volleyball, track and softball, and by studying advanced science and math.

Life at Home

- Gayle Warwick had heard all the excuses before; they were disappointedly familiar to what her older sister, mother and grandmother had been told.
- "Playing sports with boys was not only unfeminine but proof of lesbianism."
- "Female athletes were physically unattractive and weren't asked out on dates."
- "Competitive sports would harm reproductive organs as well as a woman's chances of marriage."
- "Girls were too selfish to play team sports; their hearts were too small, tempers too short."
- Girls' teams had to raise their own money through bake sales or carwashes.
- Girls' teams could not afford new uniforms and could only practice when the boys did not "need" the gym.
- Only the newest and worst referees were assigned to the girls' games.
- Cheerleaders received more attention than female athletes.
- If the boys' program was cut so that girls could have a team, the entire school would be mad—any decline in the boys' achievements would be the girls' fault.
- Gayle Warwick bucked the trends by excelling in sports, science and math.
- Girls played in empty gymnasiums; even parents wouldn't watch their daughters compete.
- Born in 1972—the year Title IX of the Education Amendment was enacted—Gayle was a natural athlete who wanted to take advantage of the law that had changed women's athletics.
- Her older sister had helped blaze the trail in Tampa, Florida, by playing on the boys' soccer team and starring on the newly created girls' squads.
- When it was Gayle's turn to explore the various benefits of playing on girls-only soccer and field hockey teams, she chose to play them both.
- Her father understood; her mother was sure it would end badly.

Gayle Warwick bucked the trends by excelling in sports, science and math.

- In addition to soccer, Gayle wanted to participate in volleyball, track and softball.
- But as important, she also demanded a space in the advanced classes in science and math— avenues that had been considered "boys' activities" and discouraged for girls—prior to Title IX.
- Although Title IX had ushered in athletic opportunities for thousands of girls like Gayle, its impact was far wider, having erased the boys-only label that had been attached to certain academic disciplines, job opportunities and extracurricular activities.
- Hailed as one of the great achievements of the Women's Movement, Title IX states: "No person in the United States shall, on

the basis of sex, be excluded from participation in, be denied the benefits of, or be subjected to discrimination under any education program or activity receiving federal financial assistance."
- Gayle considered the law to be "gender-neutral" and not a "gift" to girls like some grown-ups liked to say.
- Title IX simply eliminated the special privileges historically given to boys by providing girls with equal access to higher education, career education, education for pregnant and parenting students, employment, a healthy learning environment, math and science, standardized testing, technology, and laws against sexual harassment.
- Title IX covered all state and local agencies that received federal education funds, including approximately 16,000 local school districts, and 3,200 colleges and universities.
- Prior to the passage of Title IX in 1972, some tax-supported colleges did not admit women, athletic scholarships were rare, and math and science were realms reserved for boys.
- Girls were encouraged to become teachers and nurses, but not doctors or principals; women rarely were awarded tenure and even more rarely appointed college presidents.
- Sexual harassment was excused because "boys will be boys," but if a student became pregnant, her formal education ended.
- Before Title IX, female athletes at the University of Michigan sold apples at football games so that they could compete for the school, which did not have a budget for women, and female gymnasts at

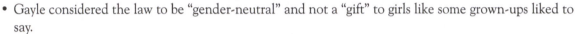

By the 1990s, more females were participating in organized sports.

the University of Minnesota had to rely on their male counterparts to provide them with leftover tape.

- Graduate professional schools openly discriminated against women; being female was seen as a pre-existing condition that made them unqualified.
- By the 1990s, more females were participating in organized sports.

Life at School

- Gayle Warwick was voted the school's most athletic student in her senior year, having earned letters in five different sports and earned three state championships.
- The athletic fields on which she played were considerably better than those provided to her older sister, and the referees who called the games actually liked working the girls' games, without considering it a "punishment."
- In 1972, fewer than 295,000 girls participated in high school varsity athletics, accounting for just 7 percent of all varsity athletes.
- In 1992, female participation exceeded one million, including the traditional male sports of wrestling, weightlifting, rugby, and boxing.
- Parents eagerly watched their daughters on the playing fields, courts, and on television; Gayle's father scheduled his work around her soccer and field hockey games.
- But as far as Gayle was concerned, her greatest achievement was a full-ride scholarship offer from Duke University in Durham, North Carolina, to study biochemistry, not to mention the scholarships offered to her by Florida State, Vanderbilt, and Virginia Tech to play field hockey.
- She had tried to do both sports and biochemistry, and played for Duke's field hockey team her freshman year, but realized that her real interest was in lab research.

Title IX gave girls an alternative to cheerleading.

21

- Now a junior with half a dozen science classes under her belt, she had fallen in love with the exploratory study of essential fatty acids such as omega-3s and the role they played in the human inflammatory system.
- Gayle loved to work in the science lab.
- Considerable information had already emerged concerning infant brain development and fatty acids.
- Now, if science could link omega-3s to the body's inflammatory receptors, Gayle was convinced the impact on medicine would be huge.
- She was convinced this opportunity would have passed her by without Title IX; her success was exactly the result the bill's sponsors had intended.

Gayle loved to work in the science lab.

- The first person to introduce Title IX in Congress was its author and chief Senate sponsor, Senator Birch Bayh of Indiana.
- At the time, Senator Bayh was working on numerous constitutional issues related to women's rights, including the Equal Rights Amendment, to build "a powerful constitutional base from which to move forward in abolishing discriminatory differential treatment based on sex."
- But he was struggling to get the ERA out of committee, and the Higher Education Act of 1965 was on the floor for reauthorization.
- On February 28, 1972, Senator Bayh introduced the ERA's equal education provision as an amendment.
- In his remarks on the Senate floor, he said, "We are all familiar with the stereotype of women as pretty things who go to college to find a husband, go on to graduate school because they want a more interesting husband, and finally marry, have children, and never work again. The desire of many schools not to waste a 'man's place' on a woman stems from such stereotyped notions. But the facts absolutely contradict these myths about the 'weaker sex' and it is time to change our operating assumptions.
- "While the impact of this amendment would be far reaching, it is not a panacea. It is, however, an important first step in the effort to provide for the women of America something that is rightfully theirs—an equal chance to attend the schools of their choice, to develop the skills they want, and to apply those skills with the knowledge that they will have a fair chance to secure the jobs of their choice with equal pay for equal work."
- When President Nixon signed the bill, he spoke mostly about desegregation through busing, which was also a focus of the signed bill, but did not mention the expansion of educational access for women he had enacted.
- Opposition from established men's athletics emerged quickly and powerfully,
- Senator Bayh spent the next three years keeping watch over Health, Education & Welfare (HEW) to formulate regulations that carried out its legislative intent of eliminating discrimination in education on the basis of sex.
- When the regulations were finally issued in 1975, they were contested, and hearings were held by the House Subcommittee on Equal Opportunities on the discrepancies between the regulations and the law.
- Senator John Tower had already tried to reduce the impact of Title IX in 1974 with the Tower Amendment, which would have exempted revenue-producing sports
- Title IX gave girls an alternative to cheerleading.

- More than 20 lawsuits had been filed challenging the law.
- When HEW published the final regulations in June 1975, the National Collegiate Athletic Association (NCAA) claimed that the implementation of Title IX was illegal, even though America's colleges and universities were given an additional three years to comply.
- Despite the regulatory delays, the concept behind Title IX began having an impact, even in sporting venues not under the aegis of Title IX.
- The Boston Marathon began officially accepting women contestants in 1972; in 1992, 1,893 entrants—nearly 20 percent—in the race were female.
- Women had hardly been welcomed with open arms.

- When Katherine Switzer, a 20-year-old Syracuse University junior, showed up to run the Boston Marathon in 1967, her goal was to prove to her coach that she was capable of running 26.2 miles.
- Women were not allowed to officially run the marathon, but no one had any reason to question "K. V. Switzer" as her name appeared on the application.
- In the middle of the race, Jock Semple, a Boston Marathon official, jumped off a truck, ran toward Switzer and shouted, "Get the hell out of my race."
- Another female athlete, Marge Snyder, said, "I played on my Illinois high school's first varsity tennis team from 1968 to 1970. We were 56-0 over my three years. We were permitted to compete as long as we made no efforts to publicize our accomplishments and personally paid for our uniforms and equipment."
- For Gayle, the celebration of Title IX also embraced a number of less tangible victories, including a study that showed a direct correlation between increased athletic participation and reduced obesity rates.
- In addition, athletics in high school had taught her how to be a member of a team—a valuable skill, for someone determined to collaborate on major science discoveries—and how to handle the personal disappointment of a bad game or a close loss.
- School athletics had given her a strong body frame, which added to her confidence and allowed her to take risks that translated into opportunities.
- "It's a different world now," Gayle told her parents, "and just imagine the opportunities that will be open to my children."

Life in the Community: Tampa, Florida
- Located on the Gulf of Mexico, Tampa, Florida, experienced dramatic growth during the second half of the twentieth century as both a retirement and vacation destination.
- Once inhabited by indigenous peoples, notably the Tocobaga and the Pohoy, Tampa was briefly explored by Spanish explorers in the early sixteenth century, but there were no permanent American or European settlements within the current city limits until after the United States had acquired Florida from Spain in 1819.
- "Tampa" may mean "sticks of fire" in the language of the Calusa, a Native American tribe, and be a reference to the many lightning strikes that the area receives during the summer months.
- Other historians claim the name means "the place to gather sticks."
- In 1824, the Army established a frontier outpost near the mouth of the Hillsborough River, which provided protection to pioneers from the nearby Seminole population.
- Tampa grew slowly until the 1880s, when railroad links, the discovery of phosphate, and the arrival of the cigar industry jumpstarted Tampa's development.
- In 1891, Henry B. Plant built a lavish 500+ room, quarter-mile long, $2.5 million eclectic/Moorish Revival-style luxury resort hotel called the Tampa Bay Hotel among 150 acres of manicured gardens along the banks of the Hillsborough River.
- The resort featured a race track, a heated indoor pool, a golf course, a 2,000-seat auditorium, tennis courts, stables, hunting and fishing tours, and electric lights and telephones in every
- Luxury hotel in Tampa emphasized the city's importance in the early 1900s.
- Tampa became an important city by the early 1900s and adopted the mantle of "Cigar Capital of the World" long before production peaked in 1929, when over 500 million cigars were hand-rolled in the city.
- During the Depression, profits from the bolita lotteries and Prohibition-era bootlegging led to the development of several organized crime factions in the city.
- The era of rampant and open corruption ended in the 1950s, when the Senator Kefauver's traveling organized crime hearings resulted in sensational misconduct trials of several local officials.

Luxury hotel in Tampa emphasized the city's importance in the early 1900s.

- During the 1950s and 1960s, Tampa saw record-setting population growth spurred by major expansion of the city's highways and bridges, bringing thousands into the city and spawning two of the most popular tourist attractions in the area—Busch Gardens and Lowry Park.
- In 1956, the University of South Florida was established in North Tampa, spurring major development in this section of the city.
- The biggest recent growth in the city was the development of New Tampa, which started in 1988 when the city annexed a mostly rural area of 24 square miles between I-275 and I-75.
- Tampa was part of the metropolitan area most commonly referred to as the Tampa Bay Area that was part of the Tampa-St. Petersburg-Clearwater, Florida Metropolitan Statistical Area (MSA) that embraced 2.7 million residents, making it the fourth-largest in the Southeastern United States, behind Miami, Washington, DC, and Atlanta.
- That population supported a number of sports teams, such as the Buccaneers of the National Football League, the Lightning of the National Hockey League, the Rowdies of the North American Soccer League and the Rays in Major League Baseball.

1992: Disabled Teenager and The Disability Act

Jordan Mitchell, a high school football jock, saw his whole world change when a car accident left him paralyzed from the waist down.

Life at Home

- Jordan Mitchell, the second of two children, was born on March 1, 1972, while his father was completing an internship at the University of Colorado Medical School.
- His mother taught math at a local middle school to help out financially.
- They did not have much money during the early years of Jordan's life.
- His father had recently received a Ph.D. in biochemistry and was hoping to work his way up the scientific research ladder.
- After a few years in Colorado, Jordan's father finished his postdoctoral training and was soon offered his first job in Baltimore, Maryland, at the prestigious Johns Hopkins Medical Center.
- The job allowed the family to move into their first home in a residential neighborhood.
- Jordan and his family lived there until he was five, when Wake Forest Medical University offered Jordan's father a position at the Medical Center in Winston-Salem, North Carolina, close to Jordan's extended family.
- As he grew, Jordan developed a passion for playing sports: baseball, soccer, basketball and football—he loved the competition.
- The sport that captured his focus was football, especially as a running back.
- Jordan enjoyed scoring touchdowns, but loved to run people over even more.
- The second year he played, the coaches switched him to linebacker, which allowed him to use what he had learned on offense to read the developing play on defense and then react.
- By the time Jordan reached high school, he had narrowed the number of sports he participated in down to one: football.
- His goal was to become a starter on the varsity team by the time he was a junior, even though he was undersized for a linebacker at just 5' 11" and only 185 pounds.

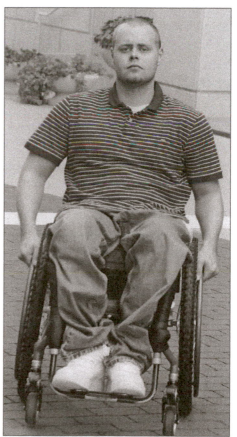

Jordan Mitchell refocused his energy from football to rights for the disabled.

- Relying on instincts and quickness, Jordan was soon one of the top players on the team and one of the most feared linebackers in the conference.
- When Jordan's team lost in the second round of the state playoffs his junior year, the team's rising seniors vowed to win a state championship.
- The next season got off to a terrific start with only one loss during the regular season and no defeats in their conference for the third straight year.
- When it was playoff time, Jordan and his teammates were thrilled to be the number one seed and breezed through the opening rounds.
- The state semifinal contest promised to be tremendous: Jordan's Mount Tabor Spartans against perennial powerhouse West Charlotte.
- On the day of the game, the team was scheduled to report to the gym at 3 o'clock.
- It was a messy day.
- Rain poured hard on this Friday after Thanksgiving, and Jordan was anxious to report, anxious to play, anxious to do well.
- On the way to the gym, Jordan lost control of his Honda Accord going around a turn.
- That was the last thing he could remember.
- Everything that happened during the next two weeks was a blur.
- Between the shock and the powerful painkillers, it became hard to sort things out.

Jordan was a top player on his HS team.

- He could remember parts of the ambulance ride to the hospital as well as talking to his girlfriend when he first arrived, but little else.
- The Spartans won the game that night for Jordan but lost a week later in the championship.
- During those two weeks, family members, teammates, and friends streamed in and out of his hospital room.
- The intensive care nurses said they had never seen so many people come to visit one person.
- The doctors told Jordan's parents that he had sustained a number of serious injuries, all of which would heal except for one.
- Jordan had broken his back in the accident and was paralyzed from the waist down.
- A week after his wreck, he had surgery to place five metal rods down his spinal cord.
- One morning, Jordan woke up and everything that had taken place suddenly seemed all too real.
- He was devastated, and scared about his future.
- When Jordan had recovered from his internal injuries, he was moved to the Shepherd Center, a top spinal cord rehabilitation facility in Atlanta, Georgia.
- There, Jordan began to learn the basics of living in a dramatically different body.
- The first step was simply to sit up straight.
- The interrupted blood flow in his body caused him to pass out every time he sat up.
- It took three weeks before he was finally sitting up for extended periods of time.
- Jordan felt like a newborn all over again; he could not control his bowels or bladder and was reduced to wearing a diaper.

- The muscles for which Jordan had worked so hard were gone; he lost 30 pounds in a little under a month.
- There was still no movement or sensation in his legs, but Jordan promised himself that he would do his best with what he still had.
- He learned how to transfer himself from his bed to a wheelchair.
- This was his first step toward independence, but certainly not his last.
- He lifted weights to regain some of his upper body strength.
- He learned how to get in and out of a car from his wheelchair, how to take a shower, and how to manage his bowels and bladder.
- The rehab experience proved to be extremely beneficial.
- While most patients needed three to four months to finish, Jordan took two.
- However, although he was ready physically, he was not mentally prepared to go out into a social environment.
- The first month was a learning experience.
- Accustomed to being the big "jock," he felt his self-confidence evaporate and struggled to look people in the face.
- While visiting a friend who lived in an older house, Jordan discovered that he could not even fit through the bathroom door.
- For the first time, he wondered how anyone could have built a house without thinking about the needs of someone in a wheelchair.
- Jordan decided to inform himself.

It took time for Jordan to feel comfortable at his university.

Jordan learned about his rights on campus.

- He had never thought about wheelchair barriers before, almost as if they did not exist.
- He remembered hearing about the Americans with Disabilities Act (ADA) that was passed in 1990 but was unclear of the details.
- The main objective of the ADA was to provide equal rights for disabled people to include job opportunities, Social Security benefits, building regulations, and health care.
- Jordan was amazed at the fact that it took until 1990 for a law like this to be passed, and wondered how disabled people had functioned before.

Life at School

- Although it had been over a year since the Americans with Disabilities Act was passed, the process of making facilities accessible to all was just starting.
- Private employers were required to make accommodations for future disabled employees.
- Public buildings were given 12 months to comply with accessibility regulations.
- Change was coming, but in baby steps.
- Jordan Mitchell graduated high school in 1991 by completing his remaining classes at home.
- He applied for and was accepted to a major university.
- During orientation Jordan felt out of place.
- Surrounded by people he did not know, he was unsure how to ask others for help.
- As they toured the campus, Jordan struggled to get up many of the hills.
- Because a number of buildings had no ramps, he could not even enter some parts of his own school.
- Before the start of the first semester, Jordan met with the school's disability office, still in its infancy.
- The staff handed Jordan a generic letter for his professors that explained that he might arrive late for class and may need special bathroom privileges.
- On the first day of classes, Jordan was up early to make sure he got to class on time.

Handicap seating was far removed from the action.

- As he rolled on to the main campus, a feeling of anxiety crashed over him.
- Jordan noticed people looked at him differently.
- Some were looks of curiosity; most seemed to be looks of sympathy.
- By the time Jordan made it to class, he was physically and emotionally worn out.
- He tried to concentrate on class work but found it hard to think about anything except how uncomfortable he was with his new life.

The school library was difficult to maneuver.

- As weeks progressed, so did Jordan.
- He learned campus shortcuts and which buildings provided quality access points; he even began to hold his head up a little more when he rolled, as a show of confidence.
- Jordan lived in an on-campus apartment with two of his friends from high school.
- It was important to live with people around whom he felt comfortable; living independently and being a paraplegic were challenges in and of themselves.
- Laundry was the toughest thing to do alone.

- Because his bladder still leaked on occasion in his sleep, Jordan had much more laundry than a normal college student would.
- It hurt his back to try to reach far enough into the washing machine to retrieve his clothes; it was the same with the dryer.
- After about a month of struggling, Jordan finally hired a laundry pick-up service to do his laundry every week for $30.00.
- He felt as if he had control of something for the first time since his accident.
- As late summer turned to fall, Jordan was excited about attending a university football game.
- He missed his favorite sport and could not wait to watch his new team perform.
- Jordan went to the ticket office intent on obtaining some of the best seats in the stadium that were accessible to the handicapped.
- The people there explained that good handicap access seats were limited: there was not yet a way for a wheelchair to get down to the lowest level near the field.
- He could only get a seat at the top of the deck.
- Jordan was infuriated but did not want to draw attention to himself until he had at least gone to the game to check the seats out.
- He and his father, who came with him to the game, were impressed by how close the handicap parking spots were to the stadium.
- The seats turned out to be terrible.
- Jordan was not close enough even to feel part of the game.
- He could not help but laugh and say that he would have been better off watching the game on TV.
- Afterwards, Jordan went to the library to do some further research on the Americans with Disabilities Act of 1990.

The ADA guaranteed the same rights for all Americans.

- If the disabled had rights, it was time he learned what they were.
- He found that under Section 302, Article IV states that no individual can be discriminated against on the basis of disability in the full and equal employment of public goods, services, facilities, advantages or accommodations that are not equally afforded to other individuals.
- He also learned that public places of entertainment and sporting events were definitely included.
- All public buildings were supposed to comply within 12 months of the act being passed.
- It had been 16 months and the stadium was clearly not up to par.
- This meant that if able-bodied people could purchase a ticket to sit in the front row, then so should someone in a wheelchair.
- So Jordan printed this information out and took it to the disability office on campus.
- They seemed impressed by his initiative and insistence and promised to present this information to the dean of the school.
- After a week the office finally called to say that the dean was concerned about the situation and had been totally unaware that this was a problem.
- He promised to inquire with the city as well as the North Carolina Department of Labor in Raleigh to see what could be done.
- The next month, Jordan checked by the office weekly to see if the school had made any progress.
- He also attended the games and continued to sit in the upper deck.
- Six weeks after he first asked about the situation, his persistence was rewarded.
- Jordan received a personal call from the dean of students telling him that because the team's stadium was owned by the city, it was responsible for fixing the problem.
- A decision had been made to install an elevator as well as make room for 20 new handicap seats in the lower deck.
- All the changes were completed for the start of the 1992 football season.
- By then Jordan had adjusted to his new life: he drove to school using hand controls affixed to a regular car, did all his own laundry, and held his head up high.
- Most of all, on Saturdays when he sat in the lower deck, he felt responsible for having done something positive.

The Americans with Disabilities Act

- The Americans with Disabilities Act, or ADA, was termed the most comprehensive federal civil rights statute protecting the rights of people with disabilities.
- It affected access to employment; state and local government programs and services; access to places of public accommodation such as businesses, transportation, and nonprofit service providers; and telecommunications.
- The scope of the ADA in addressing the barriers faced by people with disabilities was very broad.
- Advocates insisted that the Americans with Disabilities Act protections paralleled those that had previously been established by the federal government for women and racial, ethnic and religious minorities.
- Critics predicted that accommodating America's 54 million citizens with disabilities would bankrupt the economy.
- A critical aspect to the ADA's ability to bring about change was the practice of designing products, buildings, public spaces and programs to be usable by the greatest number of people.
- The Act helped create a society where curb cuts, ramps, lifts on buses, and other access designs are increasingly common.
- In the process, curb cuts designed for wheelchair users were also used by delivery people, people with baby carriages, and people on skateboards and roller blades.
- When the ADA was before Congress, members predicted a flood of lawsuits that would bankrupt or at least overburden business.

- One congressional leader characterized the ADA a "disaster" benefiting only "gold diggers" filing frivolous lawsuits.
- But adoption was less expensive than the doomsayers predicted.
- Many businesses found that compliance was often as easy as raising or lowering a desk, installing a ramp, or modifying a dress code.
- One survey found that three-quarters of all changes cost less than $100.

1993: College Campus Music Promoter

Anwar X. Holliday promoted popular New York City rap and hip-hop music to his fellow students at Howard University by organizing concerts on campus and encouraging students, especially New Yorkers, to attend.

Life at Home

- Anwar X. Holliday was born on a Monday in Queens, New York, October 16, 1971.
- His father John 23X Holliday immediately associated his son's Monday birth with the lead character in the 1970s blaxploitation film Black Caesar.
- Black Caesar starred ex-NFL player Fred "The Hammer" Williamson, who portrayed "Bumpy" Johnson's rise to the top of the Harlem numbers rackets.
- The theme song by soul singer James Brown began with the famous line "I was born in New York City on a Monday," hence, the connection between Anwar and his father's favorite song and favorite movie.
- She and several cousins had made the natural transition from church choir to performing covers of songs by popular girl groups of the 1960s, like the Supremes and Martha and the Vandellas at block parties and recreational halls around Queens.
- In 1969, Juanita and John Holliday met, and later that year the couple settled into a walk-up duplex in the Hollis section of Queens.
- When Anwar's grandparents migrated from the South in the 1950s, Queens was a magnet for blacks seeking upward mobility.
- Harlem had been the original black Mecca during the great South and North migration in the early part of the twentieth century.
- Due to deterioration and overcrowded conditions in Harlem, the focus shifted to Brooklyn during the 1930s and 1940s.
- By the 1950s, Queens had become home to jazz legends like Count Basie, Louis Armstrong, Ella Fitzgerald, and Dizzy Gillespie.
- By the 1960s, the tremendous influx of blacks and Latinos from the other boroughs triggered "white flight" from Queens to the more suburban Nassau and Suffolk County on Long Island.
- During the fall of 1978, eight-year-old Anwar started third grade at St. Pascal-Baylon Elementary School, a Catholic school that

While still a student, Anwar X. Holliday promoted music on the campus of Howard University.

required its students to wear a blue and yellow uniform every day.

- Anwar Holliday began promoting rap and hip-hop while still a student at Howard University.
- While raising Anwar within the Five Percent Nation at home, his parents felt that a Catholic school would provide their son with a better education than the public school system.
- Anwar quickly learned to avoid the older bullies who waited outside the school each day to rob the younger kids of their possessions.
- At the same time, the hip hop culture was forming in New York City as block parties became increasingly numerous, especially when they incorporated DJs who played popular genres of music, especially funk and soul music.

Anwar and his cousin Malik supported their way through Howard with a variety of entrepreneurial efforts.

- Soon DJs began isolating the percussion breaks of popular songs, a technique then common in Jamaican dub music, and developed turntable
- techniques, such as scratching, beat mixing/matching, and beat juggling that created a base that could be rapped over.
- Rapping was a vocal style in which the artist speaks lyrically, in rhyme and verse, generally to an instrumental or synthesized beat, which is almost always in 4/4 time.
- Anwar's father believed hip hop had emerged as a direct response to the watered-down, Europeanized disco music that permeated the airwaves.
- The first hip hop recording Anwar heard was The Sugarhill Gang's "Rapper's Delight," initially at home and then throughout the neighborhood.
- Hollis was a working middle-class neighborhood south of the Grand Central Parkway and east of 184th Street.
- Anwar grew into his teens in a neighborhood filled with private homes and busy main streets with stores and movie theaters.
- By the mid-1980s, a trend developed among black youngsters nationwide in which academic achievement lost its importance and was replaced by "street credibility," represented by various forms of thuggery in the pursuit of a cool image.
- Despite being from solid homes where good grades were expected, Anwar and his crew of friends shared many of the same ideas as their peers and allowed their grades to slip in solidarity.
- When the crew played basketball at 205th Street Park, they couldn't help noticing the drug dealers and other hustlers with their Mercedes and BMW cars, gold watch chains, and Movado watches.
- They also surrounded themselves with rap music.
- Anwar's infatuation with street life came to an abrupt end when his best friend's grandfather was abducted and shot in an attempted robbery and drug extortion scheme.
- In 1989, Anwar graduated from Harlem Brothers Rice Catholic High School with plans to attend Howard University in Washington, DC.

Life at Work

- The fall of 1989 found Anwar X. Holliday as a member of the freshman class at Howard University in Washington, DC.
- Howard was founded in 1867 to educate freed slaves and their descendents. Anwar was joined at Howard by his cousin Malik, who, like Anwar, had chosen radio and television media studies as a major.

Anwar and Malik worked distributing The Final Call *on campus.*

- Like most college students, Anwar and his cousin were plagued by cash flow shortages and were constantly brainstorming for a solution to this problem.
- They decided to be entrepreneurs, moving from project to project.
- Along with his brother Raymond, Malik's father had ridden the popularity wave of vinyl siding and window installation to achieve middle-class stability.
- So the two enterprising young men secured a $500 loan from their fathers to purchase the Supreme Bean Pies and Cookies concern from the Nation of Islam Bakery in Newark.
- They also arranged to distribute *The Final Call* newspaper, published by the Nation of Islam on campus.
- After that, the two young men roamed the campus selling pies, cookies and newspapers—it was a great education in business, human psychology and accounting.
- Not only did the venture provide snacks and much-needed income, but it gave the pair a high level of exposure and visibility.
- Then, when Anwar repaid the loan on time-with interest-he elicited a look of respect from his father that he had been seeking his entire life.
- Being a New Yorker, Anwar noted that the Howard student body included a substantial percentage of New Yorkers who missed the rap and hip hop performances so common in the city's parks and squares.

The cousins started a pie business with a loan from Anwar's father.

- So Anwar decided on his summer break that he would get into the promotion of music on campus.
- In the fall, when the pair returned to Howard with the summer money they had earned working with their fathers, they began to stage special events on campus, especially parties at the fraternity houses.
- With his Five Percent connections, Anwar was able to bring the highly popular Big Daddy Kane to Howard for his football homecoming party.
- From that point on, their parties and events became the most popular on campus; Anwar quickly learned to balance the risks associated with an event, such as a concert, with the financial rewards it might bring.
- After two years of working in special events, Anwar knew he wanted a career in music.
- In 1991, he got his start as an assistant to Dante Ross, who was an artists and repertoire (A&R) man for a group called Brand Nubian, a Five Percent group that came to prominence in the 1980s.
- The Five Percent belief that white men were devils while black men were gods echoed loudly in hip hop lyrics.
- A white man, Dante Ross, seemed highly unlikely to sponsor and support groups that espoused such beliefs.
- However, Ross was a professional, and Anwar took note of his dedication to the groups under his care.
- More than just talent scouts, A&Rs were responsible for shaping the artists' sound, finding material to record, and generally nurturing an artist's career.
- They also attempted to predict musical trends, discover new artists, and then mold them into the image that maximized their talent.
- At smaller labels, the job might consist of seeking out new talent the hard way: going to shows, scouring the Internet, sifting through endless demos, and then bringing the artists to the label, signing them, and bringing an album to fruition.
- Often, A&R professionals were a sort of liaison between the label and the artists.
- They oversaw most of the interaction between an artist's management and the label, lawyers, and publishing/distribution companies.
- It was the "Golden Age" in mainstream hip hop, characterized by its diversity, quality, innovation and influence.
- Its strong themes of Afrocentricity and political militancy blended well with music that was highly experimental and whose sampling was eclectic.
- "It seemed that every new single reinvented the genre," according to Rolling Stone.
- The artists most often associated with the period were Public Enemy, Boogie Down Productions, Eric B. & Rakim, De La Soul, A Tribe Called Quest, Gang Starr, Big Daddy Kane, and the Jungle Brothers.
- The freedom and creativity also spawned gangsta rap, a subgenre of hip hop that reflects the violent lifestyles of inner-city American black youths, best epitomized by rappers such as Schoolly D and Ice T.

The music of rapper Ice-T depicted the violent lifestyles of inner city youth.

- By the early 1990s, gangsta rap became the most commercially lucrative subgenre of hip hop.
- In 1992, Dr. Dre released *The Chronic*, an album that founded a style called G Funk, which was further developed and popularized by Snoop Dogg's 1993 album *Doggystyle*.
- The Wu-Tang Clan shot to fame around the same time and brought the East Coast back into the mainstream of rap, when the West Coast dominated.
- Another act Ross had worked with at Def Jam was 3rd Bass, one of the first successful interracial hip hop groups, featuring Michael Berrin, also known as MC Serch.
- Michael Berrin, who was raised in mostly black Far Rockaway, Queens, spent his teenage weekends facing initially hostile crowds at the Latin Quarter.
- Berrin continued getting to the mike and finally earned respect for his rhyme skills and give-no-quarter attitude.
- Through Dante Ross, Anwar met Michael Berrin.
- Ross, after his successful experience with 3rd Bass, had moved into management and production, while Anwar, following his internship under Ross of Def Jam, had moved into A&R with Sony.
- In his management and production capacity, Berrin came into contact with Nas, a young rapper with a reputation as one of the best lyricists ever.
- As Nas's manager, Berrin brought demos to Anwar's office.
- It was Anwar's first major signing.

Life in the Community: Queens, New York

- Hollis was a neighborhood within the southeastern section of the New York City borough of Queens.
- The boundaries of the predominantly African-American community were considered to be the Far Rockaway Branch of the Long Island Rail Road to the west, Hillside Avenue to the north, and Francis Lewis Boulevard to the east.
- The first European settlers were Dutch homesteaders in the seventeenth century.
- A century later, early in the American Revolutionary War, it was the site of part of the Battle of Long Island, a conflict in which the rebel Brigadier General Nathaniel Woodhull was captured at a tavern.
- The area remained rural until 1885, when developers built houses on 136 acres, and three years later it became a part of New York City with the rest of the borough of Queens.
- Since the end of the Korean War, the neighborhood had been settled primarily by African-American middle class families.
- Since the rise of hip hop, the neighborhood has been a hotbed of rap talent, sparked primarily by the fact that hip hop producer and icon Russell Simmons was from this community, as was his brother Joseph, who along with two other neighborhood residents, formed the rap group Run-D.M.C.
- Young MC—winner of the second and final Grammy Award for Best Rap Performance—Ja Rule, and DJ Hurricane were also from Hollis.
- LL Cool J was from nearby St. Albans.
- Anwar X. Holliday grew up in the Hollis community during a radical shift in the outlook of black youth.

Fab 5 Freddy hosted the highest rated MTV show in its history, Yo!MTV Raps.

- Although Hollis was a working middle-class neighborhood, its young people took on the attitudes of the more impoverished and crime-ridden areas like the Bronx.
- Hip hop's beginning flowed from the Bronx through people like Afrika Bambaataa a DJ known as the Amen Ra of Universal Hip Hop Culture as well as the Father of The Electro Funk Sound.
- Through his co-opting of the street gang the Black Spades into the music and culture-oriented Universal Zulu Nation, he was responsible for spreading hip hop culture.
- Zulu nation was a collective of DJs, break dancers and graffiti artists who filled the void once occupied by gang culture by de-emphasizing violence and crime in the mid-seventies.
- In the mid-1980s, when Anwar was in his teens, the crack cocaine epidemic emerged and changed the nation.
- Young men and women like Anwar were affected by the glamorization of the violent, cash-fueled cocaine culture glorified through hip hop music and images he saw on the streets of Hollis.
- The price of a kilo of cocaine dropped from $35,000 in 1982 to $12,000 in 1984, when it was estimated that 650,000 people were employed in New York City drug trade.
- In the fashion world, Run-D.M.C.'s My Adidas set the tone for a very high premium to be placed on the hippest sneakers and athletic wear.
- Michael Jordan was already on his way to revolutionizing sports apparel with his landmark Nike deal. By 1987, Run-D.M.C.
- Fab 5 Freddy hosted the highly rated MTV show, *Yo!MTV Raps*.

- had negotiated a $1.7 million sneaker deal with Adidas—the same shoes kids were fighting life-and-death battles over in the streets of Hollis.
- Many diverse influences affected the evolution of hip hop: cash, corporations, sampling, crime, violence, but none more important than the music video.
- As rap videos emerged as a viable business, two black-owned companies rose to prominence in New York: Atlantis and Classic Concept.
- *Yo! MTV Raps* debuted in September 1988 and scored the highest ratings of any show in MTV history.
- *Yo! MTV Raps* forced the more conservative Black Entertainment Television network to introduce Rap City a year later.
- Exposure and sales were increased dramatically by bringing the images of the clothes, cars, jewelry and attitudes into the average American home.

1993: Technology Business Owner

Harry deBoer hoped that his company would lead the rebirth of industry in Connecticut. As a partner in the firm, he was committed to employee ownership as the modern vehicle for managing people and making money.

Life at Home

- His annual salary was $95,000; the sale of a small portion of his stock options this year essentially resulted in a $41,000 bonus.
- Harry and Nicole moved from Detroit, Michigan, several years ago and purchased a 150-year-old home they fell in love with.
- The home, which had six fireplaces, tall ceilings, solid hand-made doors, and a steep roof, was built in three stages, each addition about 30 years apart, with the last addition in the 1930s.
- Nicole was going to New York City with a decorator each month to discover new treasures, as she carefully restored the home.
- She had completely modernized the bathrooms and kitchen, while the rest of the rooms she hoped to restore to their original look.
- Harry enjoyed watching the house being transformed; even though he had little time to pick colors and wallpaper for each room.
- On a few occasions, he assisted in the renovations, as he had established a full woodworking shop in a barn on the property.
- When time permitted, he slipped into the shop to work on a shaker-style clock, inspired by a story he read in *Fine Woodworking* magazine.
- Their youngest child attended prep school at Hotchkiss; Connecticut was renowned for its long tradition of excellent prep schools, including Taft, Choate, Loomis, Westminster, and Ethel Walker.
- His oldest son attended Yale, while their daughter, a junior at Northwestern, studied in France.

Harry deBoer moved to Connecticut from Detroit.

Their oldest son went to Yale.

Life at Work

- His small company had just weathered an economic downturn, by shifting gears quickly to keep profits steady.
- Sales in the past year were more than $31 million, an increase of 200 percent since 1986, and its work force had tripled to more than 300.
- Even though Harry's company competed with the giant 3M Corporation for customers, Reflective was bold enough to expand into Canada, Europe, and Mexico.
- Reflective was owned by its employees, who owned 59 percent of the company's stock.
- Harry had instituted an in-house technology-development capability, in order to stay ahead of the competition.
- Under this system, Reflective engineers and technicians designed and built the big multi-million-dollar machines that produced the prismatic material they needed. Some of their products required a complex blend of eight to 10 chemical layers.
- The company was started by two Connecticut-born brothers who both graduated from Yale in the 1940s.
- As engineers, they had always been fascinated by new products, particularly in the plastics industry.
- In the 1960s, one of the brothers invented a new method for producing material that was retro-reflective, meaning reflecting light back to its source; it was often used to coat highway signs and barricades.

Reflective was owned by its employees.

- The new method he created involved molding thousands of microscopic prisms onto every square inch of a plastic sheet.
- In the past, competitor 3M had attempted to buy the business, offering 42 times the earnings.
- The brothers would have made $5 million each; and would have resulted in the closing of the factory in New Britain, Connecticut.
- Harry was hired to make Reflective capable of competing worldwide against giants such as 3M, and find new applications for his company's technology, if it was to remain viable in the marketplace.
- He had previous experience in the corporate world, including stints with Anheuser-Busch and Container Corporation of America.
- The experience had crystallized a belief that traditional top-down management, left over from the days when immigrant workers might have no more than a strong back to offer an employer, was no longer the best way to run a company in the twentieth century.
- He believed that today's employee, because of education and background, had more to contribute than traditionally believed.
- He also believed employees wanted to be committed to something and to have some power over the decisions affecting their work lives.
- Creating an employee-owned company was more than a matter of altruism, Harry believed; it was smart business.
- The federally approved employee stock ownership plans (ESOPs) provided him with the way to convert the company from private ownership by a few to a company owned broadly by its workers.
- Economist Louis O. Kelso invented ESOPs in hopes of transforming society by making workers into capitalists.
- Most companies that created ESOPs experienced modest success.

- Harry believed an employee-owned company created a different kind of culture, where employees were more willing to move faster into new markets to protect themselves from competition.
- In addition, the longer employees stayed at Reflective, the more shares they would receive.
- They were also more willing to run leaner, thus more profitably, because they shared more equitably in the results.
- The median ESOP account contained more than $50,000; long-term employees' accounts were significantly higher.
- Employees also received a bonus once a month; three percent of the company's operating profit, divided up in shares.
- In a good month, the bonus added several hundred dollars to the average, experienced worker's paycheck; in a bad month, nothing at all was paid out.

Harry believed that employees had much to contribute.

- All shareholders, including employee shareholders, got annual dividends amounting to 20 percent of pretax earnings.
- A middle manager with an average number of shares received about $1,000 in dividends a year.
- Quarterly plant meetings were held to provide regular information about the company's performance and priorities.
- At the annual meeting, employees voted for the Board of Directors.
- Current products included reflective traffic cones that changed colors at night to provide a higher reflection value; they were also working with the Coast Guard on reflective buoys.
- Invention was only one part of the process; getting products into so many markets was both tricky and time-consuming.

- Reflective was able to adapt and expand rapidly by finding entrepreneurs in the host company who knew the industry, and then provide them with capital and technical expertise so they could run their own business; bonuses reflected how well they handled this responsibility.
- The business opportunities changed daily; Harry liked to tell his teammates that a weekend edition of *The New York Times* contained more information than the average person was likely to come across in a lifetime, during seventeenth-century England.
- He also reminded them that change was ever-present; during the 1980s, a total of 230 companies—46 percent—disappeared from the listing of the *Fortune 500*.

Life in the Community: New Britain, Connecticut

- New Britain was known as the Hardware City; during its early history, the city was a manufacturing center for sleigh bells, locks, and saddlery gear.
- In more recent years, tools, hardware, and machinery were manufactured in the community, though several factories had closed in recent years.
- The huge former home of New Britain Machine was now dark and silent, "a mute testament to the decline and fall of yesterday's industrial economy," one magazine proclaimed.
- The growth of Reflective was a point of community pride for many in New Britain. It symbolized the new economy of technology-based businesses competing for a place in the world economy.
- Many in the community now believe that knowledge was becoming America's most important "product"; the Industrial Age had given way to the Information Age.
- As recently as the 1960s, almost one half of all workers in the industrialized countries were involved in manufacturing; currently, only one sixth of the work force of industrialized countries was involved in the traditional role of making and moving goods.

The deBoers loved the older homes of the state.

- In 1991, for the first time ever, companies spent more money on computing and communications gear than the combined money spent on industrial, mining, and farm and construction equipment.
- The community was dotted with homes that dated to the days of the Declaration of Independence.
- The state was shaped by its early history; the lack of a major crop—such as cod, rice, cotton, or tobacco to trade with the Old World—and the absence of a deep-water port caused Connecticut to remain isolated for two centuries.
- Those who made money reinvested in Connecticut; absentee ownership had never been the tradition of the state.

Restoring a 150-year-old home was a painstaking and exacting task.

1993: Corporate Restructurer

Tim Harding was a corporate Mr. Fix-it; restructuring companies that didn't operate efficiently. He was well rewarded for his work, and owned three homes on the East coast.

Life at Home

- Tim and Louise enjoyed splitting their time among their island home off the coast of South Carolina, their home in Palm Beach and a Manhattan apartment in New York City.
- The South Carolina home was Louise's favorite; it could only be reached by boat, but included a tennis court, docks and a spectacular view of the ocean.
- Recently, she collected dozens of sand dollars that had been washed ashore during the night by a northeastern storm, and considered it a sign that more good fortune was in store for her family.
- Along the South Carolina coast, she felt free to be herself; currently, she was studying qigong with a mentor in Charleston.
- According to Chinese philosophy, there was qi in everything—in our bodies, our homes, and in the earth itself.
- Acupuncture needles were said to modulate the flow of qi in the body; a feng-shui makeover moved the qi of the home.
- When in South Carolina, Tim loved to go on dove shoots, often taking his grandchildren along.
- As he likes to tell friends, "I hunt deer, bear and woodcock, but when it comes to the twisting, turning rocketry of doves, I shoot."
- His favorite home was the house in Palm Beach—the 3.75-square-mile island in Florida, known alternately throughout the world as the most wealthy, glamorous, decadent, extravagant and self-indulgent spot on earth.
- Their first home in Palm Beach was a 3,000-square-foot apartment at the Biltmore, which overlooked both the Atlantic Ocean and the inland waterway.

When in South Carolina, Tim Harding went on dove shoots.

- About the same time, they bought a $1 million Picasso for their New York home. During their visits to Palm Beach, he fell in love with "the season," the social season of the very rich.

- During the week he wrestled with the turnaround of major corporations, often earning the label of "villain" for his propensity to cut costs; then on weekends he could be a hero to the wealthy stockholders of Palm Beach who understood his need to demand layoffs if companies were to produce good financial returns.

- Besides, Palm Beach parties were always done so well—with beluga caviar and Dom Perignon champagne.

- While on the island, he dressed like a resident in a blue blazer, open sport shirt and loafers with no socks; it's a look dating back to 1919 and Charles Munn, a descendant of Carrie Louise Gurnee Armour, widow of the meatpacking king.

Louise's favorite house of the three was along the South Carolina coast.

- Evening wear was often formal; for the season, Louise normally bought a dozen evening gowns, each costing more than $18,000, while Tim paid $2,500 for formal wear, $900 a pair for Ferragamo shoes and $2,500 each for Valentino suits.

- In recent years, using Louise's money, they purchased a 20,000-square-foot home with 15 bedrooms, 12 bathrooms, two libraries, a media room, sauna and a master bedroom closet that was almost 1,000 square feet.

Louise was studying qigong with a mentor.

- Their neighborhood included a poured cement, art deco home that won the House of the Future Award at the 1939 New York World's Fair and was now owned by the heir of a dog food fortune.

- Tim and Louise had been careful not to mention her Jewish father—the source of their inherited wealth—afraid it would affect their membership in the Everglades Club and the Bath & Tennis Club where she played tennis many afternoons.

- While living at Palm Beach during the season, she helped organize fundraisers as a way of meeting people; she had helped organize a ball for heart disease, and was now helping to raise money for a social disease called AIDS.

- Tim believed that being part of The Social Index-Directory would help him in business; like most of the families listed in the book, the Hardings' index item included addresses for additional homes.

- Some families listed up to five additional homes in places like Monte Carlo, Paris, London, New York and Newport, Rhode Island, in addition to the names of their planes and yachts.

Palm Beach, Florida garden fountain.

- Several of the jet set recently purchased expedition yachts, 184-foot boats capable of circumnavigating the globe on a single tank of gas; many came equipped with a 36-foot fishing boat and a personal submarine for times when the boat was in dock and located over an exciting wreck.
- A North Carolina real-estate developer bought an expedition yacht so he could take his family on a voyage to Indonesia, Australia and New Zealand.
- As Charles Dana, commodore of the New York Yacht Club, explained, "A lot of guys have worked too hard all their lives to spend time yoked in with 50 other gin palaces in a marina in St. Tropez. They want to go where no one has ever gone, in a tough boat that can take it."
- Tim recently got together with three other business associates and had a climbing wall constructed for their grandchildren to enjoy when they visited in Florida.
- The 16' x 24' tower was equipped with three different climbing paths, and was made of concrete and crushed granite to look like sandstone cliffs.

Life at Work

- As the current chief executive officer of a 1,300-hotel chain, Tim made more than $1 million a year.
- He was asked to head the company when the merger of two hotel chains ran into trouble, and quickly established himself as the leader, demanding total loyalty.
- During his three years on the job, dozens of key executives had been fired for questioning his leadership style—several were dismissed during a company meeting when they challenged one of his decisions.

- In each of his management roles designed to turn around a company, he had gained a reputation for freely handing out pink slips; he considered himself a head coach who seldom needed or wanted assistants, making decisions rapidly and rarely looking back.
- He was currently negotiating to sell the company to a larger, more stable hotel chain; if successful, he would earn a bonus of several million dollars.
- It was a pattern he had worked successfully before; previously, he arrived as head of a major insurance carrier which was nearing bankruptcy and whose stock was falling rapidly.
- He moved decisively—or as his critics claimed, ruthlessly—to save the company; under his direction, the insurance company cut its quarterly dividend from $0.75 per share to a nickel, and the work force of 5,000 was cut in half.
- Within 24 months the company's stock had rebounded and the firm was sold for $2.8 billion; when he left, his exit package totaled $43 million.
- He understood that bankrupt companies have little shareholder value, and that his job was to bring about change—quickly.
- A nameplate-sized sign made of flimsy plastic sits prominently on his desk and summarizes his philosophy of business: "Get the spectators off the field."
- He believes, "There are givers and takers in life. Givers contribute as much as they can. Takers are always trying to hang on to someone else's accomplishments."

Life in the Community: Palm Beach, Florida

- Eighty-seven percent of Palm Beachers were millionaires; megaresidents included John Kluge, worth $10.5 billion from Metromedia; Ronald O. Perelman, worth $4.2 billion from Revlon; Estée Lauder's sons, Ronald and Leonard, (each owning approximately $4 billion from cosmetics), and Diana Stawbridge Wister (owning $900 million from a Campbell Soup inheritance).
- By design, no signs along Interstate Route 95 pointed to Palm Beach, 65 miles north of Miami; if you had to ask where Palm Beach was, you shouldn't be there, residents liked to say.
- The coconut palm trees that dominated the island vegetation were the legacy of a Spanish ship called the *Providencia* which ran aground in 1878; bound for Barcelona from Havana, the ship carried hides, coconuts and wine.
- After the wreck, the crew and local settlers consumed the wine and the captain gave the Americans 20,000 coconuts; palms grew from the coconuts and the party was still going on, local wags enjoyed saying.
- In 1892, Henry Morrison Flagler decided to turn Palm Beach into America's Riviera—a playground for the rich and famous.
- To that end, he extended his Florida East Coast railway to the island and built the plush, 1,150-room Royal Poinciana Hotel, at that time, the world's largest hotel; after a few years he built the Palm Beach Inn, later named The Breakers, on the ocean side of the island.
- The hotel's cottages became the winter homes of John D. Rockefeller, John Jacob Astor, Andrew A. Carnegie and J.P. Morgan, who all traveled to the Florida resort in their own railroad cars.
- Flagler was so influential in the state, in 1901 he got the Florida legislature to legalize divorce on grounds of incurable insanity; after his divorce was granted, the law was rescinded.

- As a wedding present to his third wife, Flagler built Whitehall, a 55,000-square-foot marble beaux-arts palace that became the Henry Morrison Flagler Museum.
- Flagler helped establish entertaining as a sacred institution of Palm Beach; for a party in 1898 commemorating George Washington's birthday, the wealthiest men in America were invited to dress as famous women, including wigs, makeup and corsets under sequined gowns, with Flagler himself arriving as Martha Washington.
- However, it was Marjorie Merriweather Post who turned grand parties into a tradition; from her $8 million, 55,000-square-foot "cottage by the sea" built in 1827, post reigned as the queen of Palm Beach until her death in 1973.
- In more recent times, Sydell L. Miller, worth $1.3 billion from her hair-care company, Matrix Essentials, built a 37,000-square-foot home with 42 rooms and a basement garage for 17 cars.
- Most of the owners of the larger homes occupied them for only a few months during the season, even though the bills continued all year; electric bills were often $5,000 a month, property taxes could exceed $500,000 a year, the bill for landscape maintenance for a five acre estate was about $140,000, not to mention the cost of retaining a staff of chefs, butlers, maids, chauffeurs and gardeners.

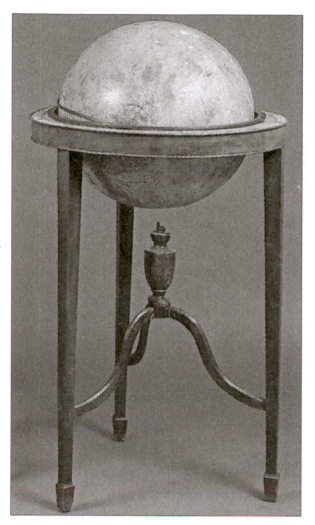

- Because of its privacy and tradition of wealth, the famous would often pop into Palm Beach knowing they would not be bothered; this season, celebrities included Elizabeth Taylor, Kim Basinger, Harrison Ford, Mike Wallace, Suzanne Somers and Ann-Margret.
- Worth Avenue was the primary shopping district, where Petrossian beluga caviar could sell for $1,173 a pound and residents, refreshed by an afternoon of tennis, could shop at Ferragamo, Armani, Cartier, Tiffany, Van Cleef & Arpels, Valentino and Saks.
- More exclusive than Rodeo Drive, Worth Avenue was often lined with Rolls-Royces, Jaguars, Ferraris and Bentleys, many driven by chauffeurs.
- At Mary Mahoney, a single cotton pillowcase—300-thread count with hand stitching made by Porthault in France—cost $390.
- Residents frequently shopped personally at the only supermarket on the island, Publix, often bringing along a butler to assist with pushing the cart and carrying out the groceries; the grocery store offered free valet parking.
- So customers could safely store their jewels after attending social functions, the local bank offered a special vault where valuables could be deposited after hours.
- City ordinances limited the size of all retail signs, tennis-ball machines were not to emit noises above prescribed decibel levels, the use of heavy construction machinery was banned during the season and employees were required to register with the police and submit to fingerprinting and photographing.

- The community of Palm Beach boasted 1,100 swimming pools and 100 tennis courts.
- Many people were excited about building environmentally sound homes; one family was constructing a 12,000-square-foot compound into a mountain in Colorado for natural cooling and insulation, and heating it with geothermal pumps.
- The home also featured a 900-square-foot living room with 21-foot glass windows; to further conserve energy, and the couple's five-car garage was equipped with solar panels.

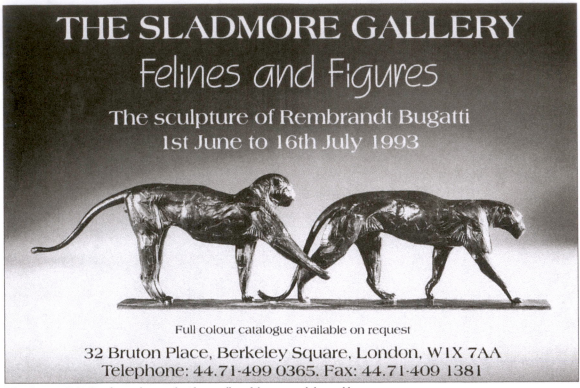

THE SLADMORE GALLERY
Felines and Figures
The sculpture of Rembrandt Bugatti
1st June to 16th July 1993

Full colour catalogue available on request
32 Bruton Place, Berkeley Square, London, W1X 7AA
Telephone: 44·71·499 0365. Fax: 44·71·409 1381

Their home in Palm Beach was decorated with art collected from around the world.

1994: Hydrogen Fuel Cell Visionary

Marie Moffett grew up in Atlanta, Georgia, attracted to theater and puppetry. She never dreamed that she would become a twenty-first-century hydrogen fuel cell visionary and investor.

Life at Home

- During Marie Moffett's sophomore year at Oglethorpe University in Atlanta, she applied for a summer job building theater sets; the only other position open required her to repair cars.
- Necessity followed form and function, and she soon became a mechanic who spent as much time as possible under the hood of a car, wistfully dreaming of how to make automobiles as efficient as possible.
- She imagined a car that didn't use vanishing fossil fuels to function, but was capable of fast starts, long-distance travel and high style.
- The car of the future should be both smart and sexy, she believed.
- A decade later—in 1990—she decided the answer was hydrogen fuel cells that emitted only vapor out the tailpipe.
- Hydrogen fuel cells made possible a car that was largely pollution-free, was not dependent on fossil fuels, was cheap to run, and most important—because it had no engine or traditional transmission—could be designed a million new and different ways.
- The car she envisioned wasn't exactly a car but the underpinnings of one, sort of a skateboard that encased the car's power and control system, which could be kept for decades while customers shuffled car bodies as tastes changed.
- And the bodies, too, would be radically different, with the windshield extending all the way down to the floor, if desired, because the car's essential systems are kept underfoot.
- The brake pedal and accelerator could be replaced with electronically controlled steering using hand grips on the wheel.
- Marie Moffett invested her time and money in her vision of a hydrogen-fueled car.
- The car of the future would have interchangeable bodies, and a power source that could last for decades.

Marie Moffett invested her time and money in her vision of a hydrogen-fueled car.

- The challenge was to efficiently and economically harness hydrogen as a fuel source.
- But it was not going to be easy: similar to the early days of autos in 1900, there was a race among France, Germany, and the United States; Japan had its own $11 billion initiative called New Sunshine to be the leader in hydrogen power.
- Marie fully expected that the blending of technologies would result in a hybrid using both hydrogen and electricity initially.
- She knew, taken together, the technologies would move the automobile from the machine age to the digital age and result in a car that emitted no carbon dioxide.

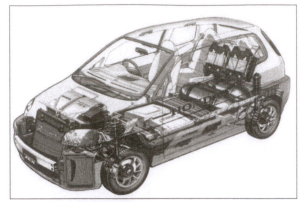

The car of the future would have interchangeable bodies, and a power source that could last for decades.

- By then, she had earned a master's degree in engineering and gone to work designing the car of the future—and repairing cars for her mechanically challenged brothers.
- Marie was the last of seven children; her older sister was 26 years old when she was born.
- She was so much younger, Marie was treated like a talkative house pet who could be dragged to every adult event without a thought; hers was a resource-filled childhood jammed with events and adventures that required Marie to grow up quickly if she wanted to keep up.
- As a result, she knew few children her age and joined an adult theater group when she was 12; at 16 she entered college, and at 26, she was convinced she was being called to help solve the world's energy crisis.
- Four years later, reports of acid rain, dying forests and global warming all cried out for a carbonless solution to America's energy needs.
- She first dabbled with the potential of solar energy, then thermal, then wind, before discovering the potential of hydrogen fuel cells.
- Hydrogen—an invisible, tasteless, colorless gas—is the most abundant element in the universe, and when combined with a fuel cell, highly efficient.

The challenge was to efficiently and economically harness hydrogen as a fuel source.

- Fuel cells are electrochemical engines that combine hydrogen and oxygen in a flameless process to produce electricity, heat and pure, distilled water.
- The hydrogen fuel cell operated similarly to a battery: it had two electrodes, an anode and a cathode, separated by a membrane; oxygen passed over one electrode and hydrogen over the other.
- The hydrogen reacted to a catalyst on the electrode anode that converted the hydrogen gas into negatively charged electrons (e-) and positively charged ions (H+).
- The electrons flowed out of the cell to be used as electrical energy.
- The hydrogen ions moved through the electrolyte membrane to the cathode electrode where they combined with oxygen and the electrons to produce water; unlike batteries, fuel cells never run out.
- The problem with hydrogen as an energy source was devising an economical way of making the fuel and how to efficiently store it in a tightly controlled container.

An electric car could be quickly recharged at stations across the country.

- The first fuel cell was conceived in 1839 by Sir William Robert Grove, a Welsh judge, inventor and physicist who mixed hydrogen and oxygen in the presence of an electrolyte and produced electricity and water.
- The invention, which later became known as a fuel cell, didn't produce enough electricity to be useful.
- In 1889, the term "fuel cell" was first coined by Ludwig Mond and Charles Langer, who attempted to build a working fuel cell using air and industrial coal gas.
- In the 1920s, fuel cell research in Germany paved the way to the development of the carbonate cycle and solid oxide fuel cells of today.
- In 1932, engineer Francis T. Bacon began his vital research into fuel cells.
- Early cell designers used porous platinum electrodes and sulfuric acid as the electrolyte bath.
- Using platinum was expansive, and sulfuric acid was corrosive.
- Bacon improved on the expensive platinum catalysts with a hydrogen and oxygen cell using a less corrosive alkaline electrolyte and inexpensive nickel electrodes.
- It took Bacon until 1959 to perfect his design, when he demonstrated a five-kilowatt fuel cell that could power a welding machine.
- In October of 1959, Harry Karl Ihrig, an engineer for the Allis-Chalmers Manufacturing Company, demonstrated a 20-horsepower tractor that was the first vehicle ever powered by a fuel cell.
- During the early 1960s, General Electric produced the fuel cell-based electrical power system for NASA's Gemini and Apollo space capsules.
- The Space Shuttle's electricity was provided by fuel cells, and the same fuel cells provided drinking water for the crew.
- NASA funded more than 200 research contracts exploring fuel cell technology, bringing the technology to a level now viable for the private sector.
- The first bus powered by a fuel cell was completed in 1993, and several fuel cell cars were being built in Europe and in the United States.

Life at Work

- For Marie Moffett, hydrogen represented the space-age fuel of the future, so drawing upon her theater experience and her passion for a new energy policy, she traveled the nation telling the hydrogen energy story and personally investing in ideas that excited her.
- "The Space Shuttle already used hydrogen fuel cells to provide onboard electricity and drinking water; BMW operated experimental buses using fuel cells.
- And one of the leading firms working on hydrogen-powered cars had developed its technology to provide energy underwater.

Unfortunately, hydrogen often was thought of in connection with the 1937 Hindenburg disaster.

- Energy Partners, based in West Palm Beach, Florida, was founded by John H. Perry, Jr., a former newspaper and cable television owner who introduced computerized typesetting into the newsroom.
- In the 1960s, Perry began producing small manned submarines for the offshore oil industry, eventually cornering 90 percent of the market.

Marie realized technology was not standing in her way, but marketing and economics were.

- He also built the hydrogen fuel cell-powered Hydrolab, in which astronauts trained underwater for the weightlessness of space, and began to experiment with fuel cells in submarines.
- "The fuel cell," he told Marie, "is the silicon chip of the hydrogen age."
- Speaking to college groups, business forums and economic developer conclaves on behalf of Energy Partners and hydrogen fuel cells became an all-consuming job.
- Unfortunately, hydrogen often was thought of in connection with the 1937 Hindenburg disaster.
- America needed to understand the potential of this energy source, she told her brothers and sisters when she moved back to Atlanta to take advantage of the city's airport, rail and road transportation.
- She quickly learned that the explosion of the Hindenburg cast a pall over hydrogen, and the words "fuel cell" caused considerable confusion.
- Fuel cells were bulky and very expensive, until the development of proton exchange membranes, or PEMs for short.
- A PEM was a type of Teflon that looked like a regular sheet of transparent plastic.
- When treated with platinum as a catalyst, it split hydrogen and separated out its electrons to form electricity.
- A series of PEM's stacked one on top of another like layers of meat in a sandwich produced a fuel cell that was light, small and potentially cheap enough to use in a car.
- After all, hydrogen can be burned in an internal-combustion engine.
- BMW, Mercedes-Benz, and Mazda all had prototype internal-combustion cars working on hydrogen fuel, but when used instead to produce electricity in a fuel cell, it will take that same car twice as far.
- A fuel cell in an electric car could increase its range to about 400 miles, and reduce its recharge time to two or three minutes.
- Energy Partners planned to build a "proof of concept" car, rather than a production prototype, running on two hydrogen fuel cells.
- With it, Marie hoped to demonstrate that such cars can be ready for the mass market by the end of the decade, rather than 20 years from then, as most experts predicted.

Marie's dream was that everyone would own a vehicle with a fuel cell engine.

- One of the many advantages of hydrogen as an energy carrier was fuel flexibility: hydrogen can be made from just about anything.
- It could be reformed either aboard the car or at the service station from methanol, ethanol or natural gas.
- It could even be produced by using solar power to electrolyze water.
- It seemed the perfect fantasy: a car running basically on sun and water.
- But outside Munich, Germany, an experimental power plant was already producing hydrogen from solar power and water.

- Solar technology may have been nowhere near the stage where it could power a family car directly, but its potential to power the car indirectly, by producing hydrogen, had now been established.
- The problem was building a market—at the right price—that was big enough to justify the large production runs that would make electric cars more economical.
- Marie came to realize it was economics, not science, that dominated this whole issue.
- The hydrogen-powered cars had to be affordable, which was even trickier when gasoline was cheaper than bottled water.
- Department of Energy studies indicated that fuel cells cost $141 per kilowatt; the car industry believed fuel cell engines couldn't compete with conventional ones until they cost less than $50 a kilowatt.
- Ford Motor Company said it could mass-produce hydrogen cars once 10,000 natural gas-reforming pumps at $250,000 to $1.5 million each were installed at filling stations around the country.
- Marie realized technology was not standing in her way, but marketing and economics were.
- Marie's dream is that everyone would own a vehicle with a fuel cell engine.
- Marie continued to bet on the future, making 50 speeches a year while investing $1.6 million of her own money.

Life in the Community: Atlanta, Georgia

- Atlanta, Georgia, the capital and most populous city in the state, with a metropolitan population approaching six million.
- Like many areas in the Sun Belt, the Atlanta region had experienced explosive growth since the 1970s, thanks to its role as a primary transportation hub of the Southeastern United States, including highways, railroads, and airports.
- It was an industrial legacy dating back to the Civil War, when Atlanta served as a vital nexus of the railroads and hence a hub for the distribution of military supplies.
- On September 7, 1864, Union General William T. Sherman ordered the city's civilian population to evacuate, then torched the buildings of Atlanta to the ground, sparing only the city's churches and hospitals.
- In 1868, the Georgia State Capital was moved from Milledgeville to Atlanta because of the latter's superior rail transportation network; it was the fifth location of the capital of the State of Georgia.
- On December 15, 1939, Atlanta hosted the film premiere of "Gone with the Wind," the epic film based on Atlanta's Margaret Mitchell's best-selling novel *Gone with the Wind.*
- Several stars of the film, including Clark Gable, Vivien Leigh, Olivia de Havilland, and its legendary producer, David O. Selznick, attended the gala event, which was held at Loew's Grand Theatre.

- When the date of the Atlanta premiere of "Gone with the Wind" approached, Hattie McDaniel, who had played Mammy, told director Victor Fleming she would not be able to go, when in actuality she did not want to cause trouble because of the violent racism in Atlanta at the time.
- During World War II, companies such as the Bell Aircraft Company and the manufacture of railroad cars were dedicated to the war effort.
- Shortly after the war, the Federal Centers for Disease Control and Prevention was founded in Atlanta.

- During the 1960s, Atlanta was a major organizing center of the Civil Rights Movement, with Dr. Martin Luther King, Jr., Ralph David Abernathy, and students from Atlanta's historically Black colleges and universities played major roles in the movement's leadership.
- Two of the most important civil rights organizations, the Southern Christian Leadership Conference and the Student Nonviolent Coordinating Committee, had their national headquarters in Atlanta.
- Despite racial tension during the Civil Rights era, Atlanta's political and business leaders labored to foster Atlanta's image as "the city too busy to hate."
- In 1961, Atlanta Mayor Ivan Allen, Jr., became one of the few Southern white mayors to support desegregation of his city's public schools.
- African-American Atlantans demonstrated their growing political influence with the election of the first African-American mayor, Maynard Jackson, in 1973.
- In 1990, Atlanta was selected as the site for the 1996 Summer Olympic Games, and undertook several major construction projects to improve the city's parks, sports facilities, and transportation.
- By the 1990s, Atlanta was so unruly it was considered to be an archetype for cities experiencing rapid growth and urban sprawl.
- Unlike most major cities, metropolitan Atlanta did not have any natural boundaries, such as an ocean, lakes, or mountains that might constrain growth.

EASY TO
ASSEMBLE PIECES

SANDPAPER AND
INSTRUCTIONS INCLUDED

PRECISION STAMPED

QUALITY
IMPORTED PLYWOOD

NO GLUE
NECESSARY

1995: High School Paperboy and Football Player

Fifteen-year-old John Pritich was the fifth of nine children. He attended a Jesuit high school in Cleveland, Ohio, where he thought about playing college football, maintained a paper route and helped his father paint houses on weekends.

Life at Home

- John Pritich was a 240-pound 15-year-old who attracted attention wherever he went because of his size and gentle nature.
- The fifth of nine children in a family that proudly identified itself with Croatia, John attended an all-male Jesuit high school in Cleveland, Ohio.
- The school had a reputation for being strict and academically challenging—just what his parents, Peter and Elizabeth, wanted for their son.
- He lived with his family in a neat bungalow in Eastlake, a suburb 20 miles east of downtown Cleveland.
- His entire family, on both sides, came from Croatia to Cleveland between 1880 and 1925.
- Croatia, formerly a district of Yugoslavia, was situated to the east of Italy across the narrow Adriatic Sea.
- Like most early Croatian male immigrants, they originally worked in the iron and steel industry, where big-boned, hardworking men were an asset.
- John's father, a member of the United Steel Workers of America, was now the foreman in a plant that made industrial hoses.
- His previous union, the United Rubber, Cork, Linoleum and Plastic Workers of America, merged with the Steel Workers earlier that year.
- He knew he would always be part of a union, but was unsure whether that was the way for his children to go, especially if they could get a college education.
- On weeknights and weekends, John's father painted houses to earn extra money, while his mother managed the

John Pritich attracted attention wherever he went.

The Pritich family was large and close.

books, bought the paints and handled the customers.
- During the week, John had little time to assist his father, but most Saturdays were spent on a ladder, swinging a paintbrush at someone's house.
- After three years of practice, he was very good at doing outdoor trim work and was proud of his skills.
- John's day began at 5:00 each morning, when he picked up the *Cleveland Plain Dealer* for house-to-house delivery in his own neighborhood and the surrounding area.
- Grounded in family history, he was allowed to keep all the extra money he made—if he was willing to save half of every paycheck.
- He usually made $75 to $85 a week on his route.
- Collecting payment from all his customers was still the hardest part of the job, but as he had grown bigger and more confident, the task had become easier.
- When the snow was especially deep or the winds stronger than 30 miles an hour, his father would help him peddle his papers.
- John couldn't wait until he was 16 and could drive one of the family cars; then he would be eligible for a larger, more lucrative paper route.
- After his delivery was complete at 7 a.m., John changed into school clothes and had breakfast with the entire family.
- Then, everyone piled into the station wagon for school; the four youngest children—aged seven, nine, 11 and 13—were dropped off at a Catholic grammar and middle school a few miles from their home.
- John was then taken to the Jesuit school in downtown Cleveland.
- Many Croatians were Roman Catholic, but John's family was Eastern Catholic and used the Byzantine Rite based on the Rite of St. James of Jerusalem.
- The Byzantine Rite was proper to the Church of Constantinople, and had a large following in Croatia.

- The Pritich family was extremely proud that John's oldest brother, Peter, was in his second year at a seminary in Pittsburgh, training to become a Byzantine Catholic priest.
- Many of the family's activities centered around the American Croatian Lodge near the family home.
- This complex housed the Croatian Museum, a large library, and a banquet hall for community dances and gatherings, plus an outdoor sports field for bocce and soccer.
- The building was also home to the Dubrovnik Garden Restaurant, which was open to the public, and often used for special occasions such as confirmations and graduations.
- The hall had become the central gathering place to discuss the progress of the war in the Balkans and the recently concluded Dayton peace talks.
- Since the country's break with Yugoslavia in May 1991, the lodge had been the best place in town to get the real inside story of what was happening, because the evening news was not always correct.
- For its part, the lodge was sponsoring an 18-year-old Croatian student named Mislava, whose home in Bosnia was destroyed and several members of her family killed.
- Lodge members contributed cash to pay for her immediate return from the war-torn country, while others were raising money to provide her with tuition to the State University in Cleveland.
- Since arriving in America, she had stayed with the Pritich family, sharing a bedroom with the two oldest girls, Mary and Anne.
- The four younger girls shared another bedroom; John and his 13-year-old brother Mike occupied a third bedroom.
- Mislava was grateful to be in America with a chance to attend college; she did chores around the house and got a job as a waitress in a restaurant to help with expenses.

- Twice a week she hung out with the more than five dozen kids, many still in high school, who left the Balkans and were now living in Cleveland's "Little Croatia."
- North High School at Eastlake had now added classes teaching English as a second language because of the sudden influx of new foreign students.
- According to the Croatian Consulate at Eastlake, the Croatian population in northeast Ohio now topped 35,000, up from 20,000 in 1980.
- Twenty years ago, when the family moved into their one-story home, built in 1960, it included three bedrooms, two baths, a kitchen, living room and dining room.
- When the seventh child was born, they added an extra bedroom, bath and small office, which now served as the family's part-time painting company.

- They had three cars—a 10-year-old station wagon, which was most often used to transport children, a four-year-old station wagon driven by John's mother, and a van used by his father to go to work and haul paint for his second business.
- When he was younger, John spent many a spring or summer day waiting for night to fall, so all the guys in the neighborhood could play hide-and-go-seek.
- Although he made jokes about his little sisters running willy-nilly about the grounds, he enjoyed watching them compete to see who could collect the most fireflies in a Mason jar.
- He loved being from a big family, and playing big brother to the little ones.
- Rarely a day went by that he didn't tease someone; his current victim was his young brother.
- In a loud voice, John told how his brother was too embarrassed to go to the bathroom around strangers; while attending his first summer camp at age nine, he got constipated and had to return to Cleveland homesick, humiliated and in great pain.
- Once he got home, he was fine—until the teasing began.
- His sisters were fascinated by the trial of actor and former football player O.J. Simpson, who was accused of brutally killing his estranged wife Nicole Brown Simpson, and her friend Ronald Goldman.
- Day after day, they stayed glued to the TV set; for his part, John had been convinced that Simpson was guilty since the day he ran away in his white Bronco to avoid being arrested.
- The youngest children were more interested in *The Lion King*; it seemed to John that everywhere he looked, something—whether it was a book, a record or a lunch box—had a *Lion King* character; even the thirty-fifth anniversary of the Barbie doll the last year didn't get that kind of play.

Life at School

- In school, regular classes had been set aside while everyone talked about the bombing of a federal office building in Oklahoma City.
- Students wondered, if it could happen in Oklahoma, could it happen here?
- John wanted to know how someone could hate enough to kill that many people; it didn't make sense, and he felt revenge was justified in this case.
- He was proud of the fact that he made good grades, thanks to hard work and solid organization; others were smarter, but few worked harder.
- This was especially true on the football field, where his coach had said repeatedly that John had the skills, dedication and size to win a scholarship to a Big Ten School—even Notre Dame.
- He was unsure whether he wanted to play college football; he was not sure what he wanted to do.
- A football scholarship would give him access to many fine schools, but the priests at school had convinced him that he should set his sights on Georgetown, the Jesuit University in Washington.
- The many family discussions around the dinner table concerning the Balkan War had

John's football skills had the coach talking about a college scholarship.

convinced him that a career in the Foreign Service was more important than playing football.

- His father hoped his son would become a certified public accountant, where the money was good and steady, and that he would then settle down in Cleveland and still come over to the house every Sunday.
- John had grown up in a family obsessed with the Cleveland Browns professional football team.
- During football season, Sunday afternoons after church and dinner were spent watching the Browns play.
- Once or twice a year, John's father snagged enough tickets to take the entire family to a home game.
- The Browns' recent decision to leave Cleveland for Baltimore had caused their loyal fans to mourn.
- John knew that when his entire extended family—grandparents, uncles, aunts and cousins—all gathered for the traditional Thanksgiving meal, the subject of owner Art Modell taking their beloved Browns away would come up again and again.
- At the community center, where he sometimes hung out to meet girls, the most popular theme seemed to be the song, "Shut Up and Kiss Me". Shy by nature, he was not sure how to take the laughter when the song was played.

OTTO GRAHAM
CLEVELAND BROWNS

- Another hot topic was whether the Grateful Dead would get back together now that Jerry Garcia had died, though John was not really interested one way or the other.
- Many of his friends were wild about the Rock and Roll Hall of Fame Museum opening in their city; since it cost $92 million, he figured he should go, but hadn't gotten up the energy yet.

Life in the Community: Cleveland, Ohio

- The people of Cleveland believed they had plenty to brag about.
- The Cleveland Museum of Art was second only to the Metropolitan in New York in the value of its collection.
- The city's 18,000-acre park system was considered one of the nations finest, and the Cleveland Playhouse was the oldest professional resident theater company in the United States.
- Cleveland was considered the melting pot for the Midwest, and enjoyed a long history of attracting immigrants eager for work.
- The city accounted for more than a third of all Croatians in the state.
- Ohio's first residents were the mysterious, prehistoric Indians known as the Mound Builders who left behind burial and effigy mounds.
- When white people arrived in Ohio in the seventeenth century, the land was populated by Shawnee, Miami, Wyandot and Delaware Indians.
- By 1788, settlers from the East were discovering a land said to be so fertile, a farmer only needed to "tickle the soil with a hoe to laugh with the harvest."
- In fits of "Ohio Fever," entire New England villages pulled up stakes to move west, followed by immigrants from Germany and Switzerland, who headed for Ohio right off the boat.
- So many Swiss came to the state that parts of Tuscarawas and Monroe counties, where they settled, were referred to as "little Switzerland."

- The factories of Cleveland, Toledo, Youngstown and Dayton brought even more diversity to the state.
- At the turn of the twentieth century, 63 different ethnicities and nationalities settled in Cleveland, giving the city a cosmopolitan character.
- After World War I, when stricter immigration laws slowed European movement, Ohio's factories began recruiting blacks from the South.
- From 1870 to 1970, the black population of Cleveland grew from 62,000 to 970,000.
- The need for manufacturing labor had been a magnet for immigrant groups ever since.

Winter sports were part of growing up in Cleveland, Ohio.

1995: Air Force Major, Operation Deliberate Force

For as long as he could remember, Major Jimmy Tittle, from Phoenix, Arizona, wanted to attend the Air Force Academy; when he did, they trained him to fly an F-16—straight into Operation Deliberate Force in Bosnia.

Life at Home

- Major Jimmy Tittle was a physical fitness machine; even the younger pilots were in awe of his conditioning and discipline.
- A native of Phoenix, Arizona, he had always taken great pride in his skills, precision and ability to perform under pressure.
- Early on, two things were clear: His older brother Matt was going to take over the family land surveying business, and Jimmy was obsessed with flying and physical fitness.
- While still in junior high school, he wrote an essay called, "Why I should attend the Air Force Academy."
- Privately, his father thought this obsession would pass; one tour of service duty and then his youngest son would enjoy a lifetime of good pay and good living as a commercial airline pilot.
- Upon graduating from the Air Force Academy in Colorado Springs, Jimmy got to live his real dream—a chance to train in jet fighters.
- At flight training school, he also found a wife; Kim, the daughter of a retired colonel, who fully understood the unconventional and transient life of an air force wife.
- Three daughters followed, and Jimmy was careful never to mention his hunger for a son.
- The Tittle family was stationed at Ramstein Air Force Base when he learned that his squadron would be shipped to Aviano, Italy.
- There, his F-16C fighters would be deployed to his new assignment: Bosnia.
- Four years earlier, in 1991, when he had flown in the Gulf War, he had seen relatively little actual combat.
- This time, after a dozen years in the air force, it looked as if he would be in the middle of a real shoot-out.
- Jimmy's family loved having a duty station in Europe and often took trips together; the girls were learning to speak German.
- Alex, the oldest, was mesmerized by the Alps and covered her bedroom walls with Alpine scenes.

Jimmy Tittle took pride in his skills, precision and coolness under fire.

Life at Work

- When Major Tittle's squadron arrived in Aviano, Italy, their mission was described as "routine patrols" over Bosnia.
- It did not work out that way.
- The flights were often harrowing and included hostile fire.
- In May, NATO planes returned fire, hitting a Serb ammo depot, just to prove that the patrols were not to be taken lightly.
- In June, Captain Scott O'Grady, a pilot in another air force squadron, was shot down by a Serb missile and forced to live off the land for several days until he was rescued by Marines.
- This highly publicized incident caused Kim and the girls considerable concern.
- Julia, who was too young to write, sent a smiling yellow sun to cheer up her dad.
- By the time NATO and the U.S. were prepared to make an aggressive commitment to peace by waging war on the Serbs, Jimmy had flown 50 peacekeeping missions over Bosnia.
- His F-16 squadron was called upon to play a lead role.
- He enjoys flying the F-16, which has a single seat, making the pilot alone responsible for all aspects of flight, from navigation to weapons systems.
- His adrenaline would pump his heart harder every time he entered Bosnian air space, even as he struggled to fully understand the conflict.
- After the death of the dictator Tito in 1980, the various nations of Yugoslavia dissolved into warring factions.
- Many ethnic groups saw this as an opportunity to reclaim land or capture power lost decades earlier.
- United Nations peacekeepers tried to keep order, but generally, they were ineffective—sometimes embarrassingly so.
- The Bosnian Serbs continued to be hostile; thousands of Muslims were murdered and the boundary line redrawn.

- After more than three and a half years of measures intended to resolve the fighting, President Bill Clinton felt the United States—acting in concert with NATO—had few options but to take charge.
- Peace would only come, he concluded, through the threat of war, to include a massive NATO bombing campaign against the Bosnian Serbs and a multilateral effort to arm and assist the Muslims.
- Led by American fighter planes, NATO launched its most massive military operation to date.

- This decision came after the Bosnian Serb Army captured the town of Srebrenica, 50 miles northeast of Sarajevo.
- Dutch peacekeepers were held at gunpoint while the Muslim population was brutalized by the Serbs, who murdered the men and raped the women.
- In all, 8,000 men were taken from the town and gunned down in a nearby field.
- The world was outraged, but little changed for another month.
- In late July, the Bosnian Serb Army fired a mortar shell into a marketplace in Sarajevo, a once-glorious city that had been under siege for three years.
- Over 37 people were killed and dozens wounded.
- Finally, NATO and the U.N. demanded retaliation against the Serbs; thus, Operation Deliberate Force was unleashed.
- In its first wave, U.S. F-15Es, F-16s and F/A-18s attacked the Serb air-defense installations in Mostar, Gorazde and Tuzla.
- In subsequent waves, the allies went after command and control centers, ammunition dumps and surface-to-air missile sites.
- At the same time, A-10 Warthogs and AC-130 gunships pounded heavy-artillery installations around Sarajevo.
- On the ground, four-star admiral Leighton Smith, Jr. led the 60,000-member NATO force in the Balkans.

- Jimmy was proud to be in the center of the assault.
- Before each flight, he read the latest letter from home.
- Over three days, the NATO allies—Spain, France, Britain, Germany, Turkey and the Netherlands—flew hundreds of sorties.
- During Jimmy's initial flight, he had a clear shot at his target and dropped his bomb accurately, helping eliminate an ammunition depot near Sarajevo.
- His squadron struck again the next night and the day after that, while the U.N.'s Rapid Reaction Force fired more than 1,000 shells on Serb positions near Sarajevo.
- On the fourth day, they stopped to assess the situation.
- Jimmy used that time to write home and thank little Julia for her picture.
- Unfortunately, the Bosnian Serb Army did not pull back, and he was in the air bombing targets again the next day.
- For days, the NATO force pounded the targets.
- Jimmy was beginning to wonder what kind of fanatical, stubborn force they were fighting, when word came that the Bosnian Serb Army had been broken.
- Two days later, when the siege of Sarajevo was lifted, thousands celebrated in the streets.
- Clearly, NATO was going to stop short of a full-scale military solution.
- Jimmy was pleased and disappointed; now, his life would become routine again.

Life in the Community: Yugoslavia

- As communism declined in the late 1980s, Yugoslavia was believed to be better positioned than any other communist state to make the transition to multiparty democracy.
- Below the surface lurked a problem, however: For decades under communism, ethnic grievances had been suppressed.
- Even as the presidents of Yugoslavia's six republics—Bosnia-Herzegovina, Croatia, Macedonia, Montenegro, Serbia, and Slovenia—quarreled in public about the country's future structure, some were plotting a path to disintegration.
- The most visible of these powers was Serbia's Slobodan Milosevic, who carefully used nationalism to strengthen his role, first over Serbia, then Yugoslavia.

- His dream was to step into the shoes of Josip Broz Tito as leader over all of Yugoslavia.
- By 1991, when he found this impossible, he focused on the creation of an enlarged Serbian state, encompassing as much of Yugoslavia as possible.
- This action helped convince the other states that the Yugoslav federation would fail and set them on the road to independence, and then war.
- The first Yugoslav state was created after World War I from the ruins of the Ottoman and Hapsburg empires.
- At its founding, it was called the Kingdom of Serbs, Croats and Slovenes, and only later rechristened Yugoslavia.
- The country embodied a dream of unity for southern Slavic people, and freedom from Austrian and Ottoman domination.
- In 1941, the Axis powers invaded the country, and communist Yugoslavia was founded in 1943 by Tito.
- When in 1945 the Soviet Army installed communist governments throughout Eastern Europe, Yugoslavia stood alone, already communist but not under the control of Russia.
- From Moscow's viewpoint, Tito and his country were dangerously independent and were expelled from the common institutions of the Eastern Bloc in 1948.
- After his split with Moscow, Tito used his country's unique position to secure backing from both the East and the West.
- Throughout his rule, Tito prevented the biggest faction—the Serbs—from dominating the Croats through constitutional balancing and brute force.
- For all its faults, Tito's Yugoslavia enabled the country's many peoples, cultures and traditions to live side-by-side.
- Upon Tito's death in 1980, the framework known as Yugoslavia began to disintegrate.

- Yugoslavia formally ceased to exist in January 1992 when all 12 members of the European Community (EC) officially recognized Slovenia and Croatia as independent states.
- Preoccupied with the Gulf War and the future of the former Soviet Union in 1991, the U.S. left the handling of the conflict to the EC.
- Several months later, as war engulfed Croatia, the United Nations entered the diplomatic search for peace.
- Reports of widespread killings, rapes and other atrocities, despite the presence of U.N. and European peacekeepers, captured worldwide attention.
- More than 300,000 people would die in the next three years.
- The U.S. entered the conflict as part of NATO in 1995.

1995: Cell Phone Entrepreneur

Jerry D. Neal's childhood interest in telephone communications had positioned him to be in the forefront of the cell phone revolution. Finding the capital to launch his company, RF Micro Devices, and keep it funded, was a challenge.

Life at Home

- Jerry D. Neal's fascination with telephone and radio began in elementary school when he checked out of the school library a book on inventor Alexander Graham Bell.
- The story of how the Scotsman, whose initial focus was on the deaf, transformed American communications inspired Jerry to build his own functioning telephone using coffee can lids.
- By the time he was 11, Jerry reconstructed Guglielmo Marconi's original experiments with the wireless telegraph and later built a primitive microphone transmitter that allowed him to create his own radio station in Greensboro, North Carolina, where he grew up.
- With his father's help, Jerry would load his high-stack 45 RPM record player with Conway Twitty, Brenda Lee, and the Everly Brothers, put a microphone beside the speaker and drive around the country roads to see how far the signal was reaching.
- He also devoured a radio repair correspondence course his father had ordered, which deepened his technical understanding.
- Bill Pratt was the general manager of Analog Devices, Jerry was a regional marketing manager reporting to Bill, and Powell Seymour was in charge of the team making the prototype parts.
- In 1991, in the midst of a management change, Bill and Powell left Analog Devices to form their own company, RF Micro Devices, with Jerry following a short time later.
- As part of the separation, Analog Devices agreed to give Bill the rights to the radio frequency chips he'd already developed, agreed to continue paying the rent on the lab until the lease expired, and offered to sell the equipment that Bill and Powell were using at the bargain price of $70,000, and then made Bill a loan for that amount with generous repayment provisions.

Jerry D. Neal longed to be a vanguard in the emerging cell phone and wireless telephone communications market.

- The plan was for Bill and Powell to take care of design, testing, and manufacturing while Jerry took care of marketing.
- But first, they had to raise money to launch the company.
- Before the new company was formed, several friends and business associates had indicated they were interested in investing in the startup, but when it came time to write checks, Jerry quickly encountered a plethora of creative reasons why "now" was not the right time to invest.
- The entire list of potential investors yielded not a single dollar, even though Analog Devices had spent $1.5 million developing the products RF Micro Devices planned to manufacture and sell.
- Many people had recently lost money on tech stocks and were loath to consider diving into the deep end again.
- Besides, few investors fully understood the potential commercial value of radio frequency integrated circuits.
- Even though RF Micro Devices held the rights to chips unlike anything the market had seen, people were reluctant to invest in unexplored new technology.
- Using his personal frequent flier points, in 1992 Jerry booked flights to California where he pitched the potential of the

company, demonstrated the chips and talked numbers—potential revenues, rate of growth, size of the potential market and possible investor return.
- Months later, still with no clear signs of success, RF Micro Devices turned to venture capital firms despite their reputations for demanding too much control, too much ownership and too little flexibility.
- After numerous grueling sessions with venture capital firms nationwide, the three partners were told they lacked passion, needed to live in a more exciting place than Greensboro, North Carolina, to get funding, and must give up 60 percent of the company to receive $1.5 million—most of which was conditioned on hitting very aggressive benchmarks.
- For Jerry, it was a bitter pill to swallow.
- When a manufacturer made a better offer, Jerry turned down the venture capital offer, but then had to beg that the deal be put in place when the "white knight" financing literally disappeared into Mexico.
- After more than a year of work, RF Micro Devices was just getting started.
- The three partners had not taken a paycheck from RF Micro Devices in 12 months.
- The new investors owned almost two-thirds of the company; Jerry and his two partners combined held 36 percent of the company they had conceived, built and grown.

Life at Work
- With money in hand, a sales team was recruited and a catalog of products set.
- Jerry Neal and RF Micro Devices had only one problem—making the chips work as promised.
- Even though Jerry had been taught by his father to "run toward problems," not away from them, the challenges at times appeared overwhelming.
- RF Micro Devices had signed two customers interested in radio frequency technology—only neither wanted existing products.
- The first, a Canadian company, wanted to manufacture wireless motion and smoke detectors and asked Jerry's firm to provide transmitter and receiver chips.

- They had been looking for a solution for two years and were willing to pay $185,000 in engineering fees to find a solution.
- The second was a Japanese company based in California which needed a power amplifier for an upscale phone.
- However, no power amplifier had ever been designed as an integrated circuit, and they were willing to pay $200,000 in engineering fees to make it happen.
- Suddenly, company projections of $1 million in first-year revenues looked promising.
- In reality, the path to making cell phones ubiquitous was littered with dozens of hard-fought failures alongside a handful of victories.
- In 1978, AT&T set up the first cellular phone system in Chicago with 2,000 subscribers; three years later Motorola established a trial system in Washington and Baltimore.
- By 1982, the Federal Communications Commission was ready to authorize commercial cellular service, mostly restricted to large cities where the huge, cumbersome "bag phones" could be serviced with towers.
- Despite the inconveniences, by 1987 a million subscribers had signed up for the service, outstripping capacity and transmission technology.

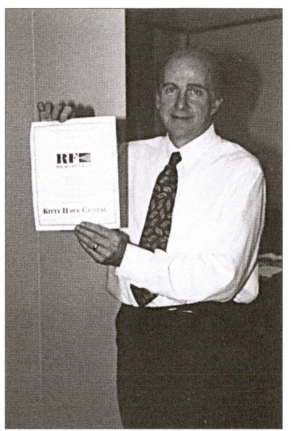

Two good-sized contracts helped Neal launch RF Micro Devices.

- Clearly, the future of wireless devices rested in digital technology in which the code of zeros and ones—which also operated computers—would convert and condense the voice signal to binary code, allowing a far greater number of calls to be transmitted over the same frequencies.
- RF Micro Devices believed that the semiconductor gallium arsenide, which conducts electricity six times faster than silicon, represented the future of power amplifiers even though the technology had never been used in a mass-market product.
- With one manufacturer, the price quotes were astronomically high; with another the chips failed to work.
- Customers were becoming impatient with the little startup from North Carolina that couldn't produce a workable prototype.
- Meanwhile, the venture-capital firm providing $1.5 million was demanding that the company hire a chief executive officer of their choosing.
- The staff had grown to 16—five times the size of the prior year—while revenues reached $212,000 in 1993, almost $800,000 short of the goal.
- Two good-sized contracts helped Neal launch RF Micro Devices.
- As Neal's company expanded, investors wanted more say in the decision-making.
- Just when RF Micro Devices needed new money, the company produced a working prototype that met all the criteria.
- Success was in the air: the chip was a powerhouse with a great potential for success—a real breakthrough in technology.
- It was Jerry's job to tell the world through advertisements in trade magazines, speeches and hundreds of presentations.

- Quickly it became clear that the industry didn't believe that gallium arsenide heterojunction bipolar transistor (HBT) could be reliable or produced at a reasonable cost.
- Most in the industry still saw it as flawed technology that only the government could afford to make work, and impractical for an integrated circuit power amplifier.
- So Jerry began giving chip samples to everyone who inquired.
- At the same time, the company had to return to its venture capital firm and ask for more money; the seed round of $1.5 million was spent.
- They asked for an extra $1.75 million and got it.
- The partners all gave up more equity in their creation, but they had little choice; they were dead in the water without new funding.
- To tell their success story, Jerry designed an advertising campaign featuring a levitating football field around the slogan "Optimum Technology Matching," with two-page advertisements that were headlined, "Unfortunately for Our Competition, We've Just Unleveled the Playing Field."

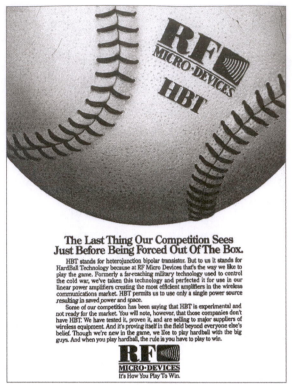

Neal's creative marketing approach brought in the sales.

- The company then designed a second advertisement featuring a baseball that appeared to be coming straight at the reader, accompanied by the words, "The Last Thing Our Competition Sees Just Before Being Forced Out of the Box."
- Jerry then mailed hundreds of specially designed baseballs to prospective customers with a letter that described RF Micro Devices' revolutionary new product.
- And it worked.
- AT&T signed on, ordered more than 150,000 chips, and even appeared at a press conference in Washington to promote the new technology.
- The company was jubilant.
- Then, just as Jerry was anticipating millions of dollars in new revenues, AT&T canceled the order, along with the phone they had planned to introduce.
- Neal's creative marketing approach brought in the sales.
- Next up was Motorola, which was selling one million emergency two-way radios worldwide every year and eventually redesigned their phone around the little company's microchip and saved $10 million a year.
- Then came Qualcomm/Sony with its next-generation cell phone, which offered call waiting, caller identification, and call answering.
- Qualcomm had a reputation for being tough; they proved tougher and signed a letter of intent.
- At the same time, RF Micro Devices was running out of money—again.
- The company's capital needs had grown from $3 million to $5.75 million; more investors were brought in, while more equity in the company was forfeited.
- Twelve-hour days had allowed Jerry to see his dreams coming into focus, while watching his ownership interest get smaller and smaller.
- By October 1994, RF Micro Devices had grown to 36 employees, 45 standard products, extensive quality monitoring program boundaries, and a greatly expanded lab.

RF Micro Devices continued to grow and to meet their own standards for quality products.

- As the year progressed, Motorola downsized its order, Nokia showed increased interest, Qualcomm/Sony was willing to be part of a joint advertisement, and the cell phone business was beginning to boom.
- Business was growing at 40-50 percent a year.
- Although few people had cell phones, most who knew about them were keen to have one.
- System providers could not set up systems fast enough; the demand for phones, base stations and other equipment was overwhelming.
- A maker of high-quality radar detectors, which had ordered 22,500 parts in the previous year, ordered 300,000 parts in 1995.
- That's when Jerry got a phone call from Motorola: the chips were failing in emergency radios that required a zero failure rate.
- Then, another complaint: a small company in Maryland that made tiny transmitters for tracking migratory birds had also received faulty chips; trackers' scientific studies, having lost contact with the birds, were ruined.
- A solution had to be found immediately or the company's entire reputation would be lost.
- Working with Motorola, the company frantically searched for a way to troubleshoot faulty chips, only to discover that a-wire-bond was causing the problem.
- Then, in conjunction with a Motorola vendor, RF Micro Devices began testing the chips, rejecting entire batches if a faulty wire was found.
- In all, 40,000 chips—$184,000 worth, or 10 percent of the previous year's sales—ended up in the dumpster.
- As that dilemma abated, Qualcomm began increasing the pressure for delivery of its new product.
- RF Micro Devices continued to grow and to meet their own standards for quality products.
- Changing one aspect of a chip could increase one function while lowering another.
- By midsummer, Qualcomm was ready to begin production, but habitually rejected RF Micro Devices' chips as unacceptable.
- Tension was enormously high; both companies had a great deal at stake.

As Neal's company expanded, investors wanted more say in the decision-making.

- Some meetings dissolved into screaming sessions.
- Jerry considered working with Qualcomm "one of the most difficult challenges of my career."
- New pricing and new testing procedures were arranged, but frustration remained high when the foundry was unable to meet the production.
- As production issues increased, the venture capitalists agreed to invest further, bringing their total commitment to $23.5 million.
- As a result, the portion of the company owned by Jerry and his two partners was down from 12 percent each at the initial investment to 2.63 percent per partner.
- The original plan, outlined by the venture capitalists, was to sell micro devices within five years and get a return on their money 10 times over.
- But RF Micro Devices' fantastic rate of growth had changed all that; as 1996 loomed, plans were underway to make the company publicly owned.
- RF Micro Devices needed to meet the exploding demands of its customers without losing its reputation for quality.

Life in the Community: Greensboro, North Carolina
- Greensboro, the third-largest city in North Carolina, was home to 223,891 residents one-third of the Piedmont Triad that embraced Greensboro–Winston-Salem–High Point, North Carolina, and counted $1 million residents.
- In 1808, Greensboro was created around a central courthouse square in the geographical center of the county, a location more easily reached by the majority of the county's citizens.
- The city was named for Major General Nathanael Greene, commander of the American forces at the Battle of Guilford Court House on March 15, 1781.
- Although the Americans lost the battle, Greene's forces inflicted such heavy casualties on the British Army that Lord Cornwallis chose to pull his battered army out of North Carolina and into Virginia.

White Oak Cotton Mill in Greensboro, N.C.

- This decision allowed a combined force of American and French troops to trap Cornwallis at Yorktown, Virginia, where the British were forced to surrender on October 19, 1781, thus ending the military phase of the American Revolution.
- In the early 1840s, after Greensboro was linked to a new railroad line, the community grew substantially in size and soon became known as the "Gate City" due to its role as a transportation hub for the state.
- The railroads transported goods to and from textile mills, which grew up with their own mill villages around the city.
- In the 1890s, the city continued to attract attention from northern industrialists, including Moses and Ceasar Cone White Oak Cotton Mill in Greensboro, N.C.
- The Cone brothers established large-scale textile plants, changing Greensboro from a village to a city within a decade.
- By 1900, Greensboro was considered a center of the Southern textile industry, with large factories producing denim, flannel and overalls.
- During the twentieth century, Greensboro continued to expand in wealth and population.
- The city remained a major textile headquarters with the main offices of Cone, Burlington Industries, Galey & Lord, Unifi, and VF Corporation, which sold Wrangler, Lee, North Face and Nautica.
- Other industries became established in the city, including Vicks Chemical Company, maker of over-the-counter cold remedies such as VapoRub and NyQuil; Carolina Steel Corporation; and Pomona Terra Cotta Works.
- On February 1, 1960, four black college students from North Carolina Agricultural and Technical College sat down at an all-white Woolworth's lunch counter and refused to leave after they were denied service.
- Hundreds of others soon joined in this sit-in, which lasted several months.
- Similar protests quickly spread across the South, ultimately leading to the desegregation of Woolworth's and other chains.

Wireless tower in Nome, Alaska, 1916.

1995: Professional Musician and Hootie & the Blowfish Member

After years on the road riding in the back of an Econo-line van, bandmember Soni Sonefeld and the ultimate bar band—Hootie & the Blowfish—became an overnight success.

Life at Home

- The big break for Hootie & the Blowfish came in 1994 when David Letterman, the late night talk show host, heard one of their songs on New York radio station KNEW-FM and directed his producer to book the four musicians on his top-rated show.
- Then, following a set featuring songs from their self-penned album, the band heard Letterman say to the national audience, "If you don't have this album, there's something wrong with you," and sales tripled overnight.
- More Letterman invites were accepted; the next stop was the recording of the number one album in the nation in 1995.
- Their first album, Cracked Rear View, would sell 13 million copies and go platinum 16 times.
- Drummer and backup singer Jim "Soni" Sonefeld had fantasized that one day the band would be famous.
- But he did not wish to lose what they had.
- Soni enjoyed creating the exuberant, no-nonsense melodic sets that framed lead singer Darius Rucker's powerful rock/soul voice. The band had formed in 1986, originally with Brantley Smith as drummer; Soni took his place in 1989.
- Born October 20, 1964, Soni started his music career playing drums in the basement of his childhood home near Chicago, Illinois.
- His musical influences embraced classic rock and R&B bands that included Marvin Gaye; Blood, Sweat, and Tears; Led Zeppelin; and even Elton John.
- He was a graduate of Naperville Central High School, one of the nation's top high schools, and then played soccer for the University of South Carolina in Columbia.
- Although intensely interested in music and drumming, Soni channeled his energy into sports, especially soccer, which kept him from playing in bands till he was well into college.

Jim "Soni" Sonefeld of the overnight success band, Hootie & the Blowfish.

Hootie & the Blowfish.

- At age 21, Soni joined his first band armed with his "flashy mullet and challenged fashion sense. " He played in various bands in Columbia, South Carolina, from the mid-to late 1980s until he met and then joined a couple of college friends who had a cover band called Hootie & the Blowfish.
- The band had toured bars and frat houses in the South for many years before creating a self-financed, six-song EP Kootchypop in July 1993, and recorded with the help of R. E. M. producer Don Dixon.
- Atlantic Records A&R scout Tim Sommer, who was impressed with both their on-the-road reputation and the sounds they produced, struck a record deal in October 1994.
- Then came Letterman, endless play on radio, and the fame they sought.
- Hootie & the Blowfish was simply one more harebrained idea spawned in the freshman dormitory, where three-digit heat was both common and fully capable of frying a college student's brain.
- Mark Bryan was playing his guitar and reminiscing about high school when he heard Darius Rucker down the hall warbling along with the radio in his room.
- The two met and had visions of grandeur that would not remotely approach the phenomenal success of Hootie & the Blowfish.
- Within a month they did a gig at a chicken wing joint, calling themselves the Wolf Brothers.
- Their opening song that first night was "Take It Easy" by the Eagles, which foreshadowed their record-breaking style.
- Soni joined Darius Rucker, Mark Bryan and Dean Felber in 1989, after they had adopted the Hootie & the Blowfish moniker borrowed from the nicknames of two college friends.
- It was a name that would delight and frustrate fans; they always wanted someone in the band to be named Hootie.
- By the time the four friends graduated, endless gigs at frat parties and local bars up and down the East Coast had created an enthusiastic following, so they started adding original material to their repertoire.

- When those songs went over well, the four decided to see if they could make a career out of it.
- "Even if we hadn't had a hit, I know we'd still be making music today, because it's exactly what we want to be doing," Mark Bryan said.
- The band's secret weapon, and the force that pulled all of its diverse influences together, was the voice of Darius Rucker, an expressive instrument brimming with gritty soul and subtle wit that connected with audiences on an almost spiritual level.
- Darius Rucker's voice allowed the band to experiment: funky, or rock, or bluegrass or a ballad, it didn't matter; the voice tied it all together.
- Their blend of pop, folk, blues, soul and rock made them hard to categorize, but it was easily accessible to anyone who loved good music.
- Atlantic Records, impressed by their regional draw, signed them and released Cracked Rear View in 1994.
- The album had been out for six months before the band played on the "Late Show with David Letterman."
- The day after the show aired, sales went from four or five thousand a week to 17,000 a week, and eventually to number one on the Billboard charts the following spring.
- That's when the "blur" began for four guys living in two vans accompanied by a goofy name.

Life at Work

- Soni Sonefeld and his bandmates were in Omaha, Nebraska, of all places, when a young woman began screaming, repeatedly, "I want to have your children!" just as Hootie & the Blowfish were transitioning from an a cappella verse of "Motherless Child" before launching into "I'm Going Home." After the concert was over, Soni didn't remember the incident; it happened too often.
- Life had changed dramatically since "Cracked Rear View" had been issued, illustrated by photographs of their home base in Columbia, South Carolina, including a dilapidated "Heart of Columbia Hotel" sign and an intentionally out-of-focus picture of a statue of a wealthy owner of a plantation and slaves.
- Since the album had been launched, Soni found he didn't mind parking the old band bus to ride in custom rental coaches driven by someone else, complete with Sega video games and dressing rooms that didn't smell.
- It was quite a ride.
- Fans loved them, critics panned them, their album was selling 200,000 copies a week and they were on the road performing nightly.
- Steven Wine of the Associated Press carped, "Talk about your one-note Band. Hootie & the Blowfish appear to draw most of their inspirational materials from Kleenex." But while complaining about the album sporting too many crying songs, he added, "The South Carolina quartet with the silly name but serious musical talent sounds almost ready for the big time on its major label debut." Folk-rock had always spanned rock's generation gap: Counting Crows certified the neo-folk-rock boom with its 1993 debut album, August and Everything After, which sold five million copies.
- The Gin Blossoms, Toad the Wet Sprocket, the Rembrandts, Deep Blue Something and a Hootie sound-alike, Dog's Eye View, had strummed their way onto the charts.

Playing to sold out, screaming fans was a bit disconcerting to a band who was "afraid of being rock stars."

- In the new folk-rock, Baby Boomers heard pleasant echoes of past favorites from Bob Dylan to the Allman Brothers; younger listeners connected via R. E. M. and its collegiate-rock disciples.
- Folk-rock easily straddled the evolving world of radio formats from classic rock to modern rock.
- As one critic said: "Amid the distortion of grunge and the claustrophobic crunch of hip hop, Hootie's basic three-chord harmonies and steady-strummed guitars seem comforting, and they never attack. In the word most often used by Hootie's fans and detractors alike, the band sounds "normal." Soni saw the band as just a group of hardworking regular guys who loved football and golf, beer drinking, fast food eating and playing music.

Monica, on the smash TV show Friends, spent an entire episode swooning over the Hootie & the Blowfish concert she went to.

- Guitarist Dean Felber, who majored in finance, set up the band as a corporate partnership, with tax withholding and health insurance like any other full-time job.
- "I guess we haven't let this thing sink in," Soni said, concerning the band's bestselling album, a hit song, the thrill of hearing their songs in constant radio rotation, and fans who could sing every word of every song.
- It was every bar band's dream and nightmare.
- "It's been this phantom thing that just caught up with us and we are still trying to figure out what it means," Soni said.
- "More than anything, we are afraid of being rock stars" Soni said.
- For years they had survived anonymity; the question now was, Could they survive fame? "We're breaking ground by being normal," Soni said. "In rock 'n' roll you got to do something whacked to be different. And now being ultra-normal is the most whacked thing of all." As one fan said after their show, "The music is happy, the songs make sense, you can understand the words." Even lead singer Darius Rucker's baseball cap and V-neck sweater communicated "normal," as did a clause in their contract that said the first 10 rows of any concert must be sold on a first come, first served basis to prevent institutional scalping of the best tickets.
- The "normal" band wanted "normal" people to get front-row tickets.
- Then they were paid the ultimate cultural compliment—next to being the answer to a Jeopardy question—when they were featured on the hit TV show Friends.
- During the episode, Monica, the character played by Courteney Cox, returned from a Hootie & the Blowfish concert with a hickey supposedly planted on her by a member of the band.
- What fun! When on the road touring, the band carried enough golf clubs to take impromptu trips to golf courses along the way or stop at the local YMCA to challenge all comers to a game of basketball.
- As the year ended, "Cracked Rear View" and the band won two Grammys—Best New Artist and Song of the Year by a duo or group for "Let Her Cry." They also took home an MTV Video Music Award for Best New Artist for "Hold My Hand"; also a Billboard Music Award for Album of the Year, a People's Choice Award for Album of the Year and a People's Choice Award for Best Selling Artist.

Life in the Community: Columbia, South Carolina

- The main campus of the University of South Carolina, located in downtown Columbia, covered over 359 acres and accommodated approximately 26,000 students.
- Founded in 1801, USC offered 350 programs of study leading to bachelor's, master's, and doctoral degrees.
- Professional schools on the Columbia campus included business, engineering, law, medicine, and pharmacy.
- The University was founded as South Carolina College on December 19, 1801, by an act initiated by Governor Drayton in an effort to promote harmony between the affluent low country and the untamed backcountry.
- The park-like area known as the Horseshoe was listed on the National Register of Historic Places, and most of its buildings reflect the federal style of architecture in vogue in the early days of the nation, including the Caroliniana Library, the first freestanding academic library in the United States.
- The urban campus had exerted considerable influence on the music, pace and party atmosphere of Columbia—especially in a section of town known as Five Points.
- The best-known rock band to hail from South Carolina was Hootie & the Blowfish, but others came from there too—Marshall Tucker Band, the Swinging Medallions, Maurice Williams and the Zodiacs, and Crossfade.
- Native musicians, singers, and other artists born or raised in the state include James Brown, Dizzy Gillespie, Chubby Checker, Eartha Kitt, Peabo Bryson, Nick Ashford, Teddy Pendergrass, Josh Turner, Bill Anderson, Edwin McCain, Duncan Sheik, Rob Thomas, and John Phillips.

Birds eye view of Columbia, South Carolina.

- The bluegrass scene has produced such bands as Hired Hands.
- South Carolina was known as the birthplace of three dances: the Shag; a product of early R&B and rock 'n' roll, the Charleston and the Big Apple, both popular in the Jazz Age.
- In the town of West Columbia, not far from the University of South Carolina, Bill Wells of the Blue Ridge Mountain Grass was the owner of a local music shop, next to which is held a weekly bluegrass show at the Pickin' Parlor.

1995: Professional Strongman Competitor

As a professional strongman, Mark Strahorn had done it all—often on national television. At six foot two inches and 300 compact pounds, Mark boasted the kind of body capable of wrestling an anchor chain to a standstill.

Life at Home

- In competition Mark Strahorn had dragged a Mack truck up a ramp, flipped an 800 pound tire a dozen times across a football field and lifted a 400-pound Atlas stone (a concrete ball with lead cores) and still failed to win America's Strongest Man Contest.
- On some cable channels—especially those in the high two figures, he was a regular at 2 a.m. when repeats of the World's Strongest Man Contests received their most consistent exposure.
- Despite years of competition and television publicity, Mark was best known as the friendly barkeeper at the Elk's Horn in Jackson Hole, Wyoming.
- The total earnings from strongman contests were less than $20,000.
- Growing up in upstate New York, Mark was the son of a welder and an emergency room nurse.
- His parents had a good marriage and liked, but did not worship, their three children.
- From an early age, Mark was expected to work beside his father, always relegated to grunt work and was ignored when he complained.
- His dad also built him his first set of weights from scrap metal.
- Only an average athlete growing up, Mark was too small to play football, weighing only 156 pounds in the 10th grade.
- And then, after graduating high school and working on construction, he began to grow.
- He also continued lifting weights.
- Three years later he entered a competitive bodybuilder contest long before made-for-TV strongman specials became a feature of late-night television.

Life at Work

- When he wasn't working, Mark Strahorn, 33, was training for the next strongman competition.
- Nearly everyone in the sport was required to hold a full-time job: in previous years the title of America's Strongest Man had been held by a

Too small to play football as a boy, Mark grew to a compact 300 pounds.

An 800-pound tire was no match for Mark.

cop, a salesman for a nutrient supplement company and a bartender.

- In Eastern Europe, stronger men were national celebrities; in America, most were just big, big guys.
- Mark figured, "That's life."
- There was no room for introspection in the midst of the dead lift when it felt like battery cables were hooked to his sciatic nerve.
- Or during a seated rope pull, when his vertebrae popped like firecrackers; deep down he knew he would pay for this abuse one day.
- Or even when he read about a fellow strongman—and friend—who had died suddenly in the midst of a strenuous workout.
- The media always blamed steroids.
- Mark understood that a gigantic dead lift could exert enough physical pressure to kill.
- It's also the point that the exhilaration of adrenaline kicked in.
- One strongman reported, "Six hundred seventy-five pounds for eight reps, last set was pretty cool, shins were bleeding, nose was bleeding, couldn't hear out of my right ear for 30 seconds, acid reflux, fun all the way around."
- In all, Mark lifted six days a week—anything that was heavy—Atlas stones, lead cylinders, barbells, cars, anything.
- Monday was bench/back, Tuesday was hips and thighs (squats), Wednesday was GPP/conditioning work, typically some sled-dragging or weighted walks.
- "I also hit my core hard on this day," he remarked.
- Thursday he did Olympic lifts: snatches/cleans and jerks, front squats in that order.
- Friday was more conditioning work, Saturday was event work; "Sunday I'm off completely."
- Strongman competition workouts legitimately took 45 minutes; shorter if he pushed his pace.
- "I just find that working more often helps my recovery, and I'm too obsessive-compulsive to just stay away," he explained.
- Strongman contests have their roots in early twentieth-century circuses, the American West, and stone lifting in ancient northern Spain.

- Modern strongman contests officially date to 1977 when Bruce Wilhelm won the first World's Strongest Man competition.
- Since then the strongest men on the planet have come together annually in a series of unique tests of strength to determine the World's Strongest Man.
- The competitions had been held in a variety of locations including Zambia, Iceland, Mauritius, Malaysia, Morocco, China and the U.S.
- Many of the gigantic competitors received their training as Olympic weightlifters or, as in the case of British champion Geoff Capes, an Olympic shot-putter.
- The reigning champions were both from Iceland: Jon-Pall Sigmarsson, who earned four championships between 1984 and 1990, and Magnus ver Magnusson, who had won in 1994 and was favored in 1995.
- Mark understood that at 33 he was running out of time; it's one of the reasons he became part owner of the bar in Jackson Hole.
- "I'll know when it's time," Mark said. "My back will tell me in a loud voice."

Life in the Community: Jackson Hole, Wyoming

- Jackson Hole, Wyoming, had become a tourist town.
- Archeologists claimed that people had been visiting the valley for 12,000 years.
- During those prehistoric times, no one tribe claimed ownership to Jackson Hole, but Blackfeet, Crow, Gros Ventre, Shoshone and other Native Americans used the valley during the warm months.
- Severe winters prevented habitation.
- Between 1810 and 1840, the area was a crossroads for the six main trapper trails that converged in Jackson Hole.
- Mountain men held annual summer rendezvous, or trade shows, there, where they sold their furs or traded them with companies like the Hudson Bay Company and the Astoria Fur Company for winter supplies.
- These gatherings also allowed the trail-weary mountain men a chance to eat, drink and exchange tales with other trappers.
- By 1845 the fur trade had ended, as the fashion of men's beaver hats back East gave way to silk hats.
- Then the passage of the Homestead Act of 1862, which allowed settlers to acquire land at the cost of improvement, attracted homesteading families along with a sizable influx of Mormon settlers.
- The inhospitable climate with its very limited growing season soon caused some homesteaders to sell out, while others grew hay and 90-day oats and raised beef cattle as cash crops.
- For many, outfitting and guiding became a means of supplementing family income as wealthy Eastern visitors traveled to the valley.

- Ranchers quickly determined that wrangling city dudes was easier and more profitable than wrangling cows.
- In the early twentieth century, economic downturns further encouraged the development of dude ranches.
- Tourism became a significant business in the valley after the formation of Grand Teton National Park and the designation of other federal lands, including Yellow-stone National Park.
- The expansion of Grand Teton National Park in 1929, 1943 and 1950 spawned a different type of tourism.
- Tourists from all over the world, numbering as many as three million annually, visited the area for the scenery, the wildlife, the recreational opportunities, the geographic features, and the romance of the American West.
- Through the years, the many movies made in Jackson Hole have added to the valley's fame, including an early version of Nanette of the North in 1921, Shane and Spencer's Mountain in 1963.

Geographic beauty attracted tourists to Jackson Hole.

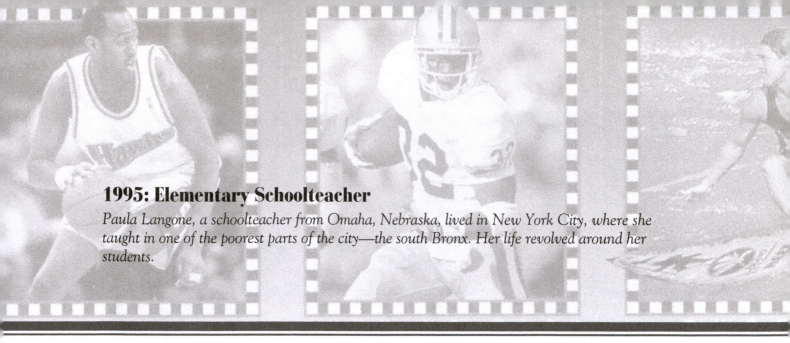

1995: Elementary Schoolteacher

Paula Langone, a schoolteacher from Omaha, Nebraska, lived in New York City, where she taught in one of the poorest parts of the city—the south Bronx. Her life revolved around her students.

Life at Home

- Paula lived in the Italian Williamsburg section of Brooklyn, New York.
- Her apartment, which sat right on the street, was built at the turn of the century to accommodate immigrant dock workers.
- Later, the building became a prosperous bar and brothel.
- Paula's third-floor, 900-square-foot apartment was created by combining two rooms.
- The apartment had a living room, bedroom, kitchen, and bathroom.
- The bathroom was added in the 1940s, when outhouses were removed from the area; the space occupied by the toilet and bathtub was once a closet. There was no room for a sink, so she washed her long hair in the kitchen sink.
- Heat, the cost of which was included in the $480.00 monthly rent, was provided by noisy steam radiators.
- Paula lived with her cat and hundreds of art and education books.
- The television set was eight years old and stayed unplugged.
- Her food expenses included eating at a deli twice a week near Columbia Teacher's College, where she was working on her master's degree in education.
- Her food consisted of vegetables from the Korean market, rice, pasta, and chicken; she spent $4.00 a week on cat food.
- She only ate pork, beef and fish on special occasions.
- A pack-a-day smoker, her tobacco bill ran $18 a week; she also occasionally bought beer and wine.
- She did not own a car, but she rode the subway to work and home every day, and twice a week to night classes at Columbia Teacher's College; she received scholarship money to attend the school.
- The subway stop was three blocks from her apartment; she never hesitated to ride the subway by herself, or late at night.
- A friend in Omaha, Nebraska, who worked at a major department store, was helping Paula build her work wardrobe.

Paula wanted to help these kids, and help save the world.

She put away clothing for her all year, so Paula could spend $600 on clothing that would have cost twice that in New York City.

- During her flight across the country to Nebraska to see her parents, she bought the clothes her friend had collected for her; she normally spent a total of $1,200 on trips out West.
- The bulk of her discretionary money went towards supplies for her classroom; however, the $125 "teachers choice" supply allowance only covered about one-third of her needs. In addition, she bought books and magazines for her use in the classroom.
- School supply buying trips included a visit to the New York City Library where she bought used paperback books for $0.25 and hardbacks for $0.50; friends often donated art supplies and magazines for her use in the classroom.
- Her personal care budget included perfume and normal toiletries; she did her own hair.
- On major holidays such as Easter, Christmas, and summer she escaped the city by traveling to a monastery in upstate New York, where her uncle was a monk.
- On Thanksgiving, she often slept late and ate Chinese takeout.

Life at Work
- Her fifth grade class in the south Bronx included 20 children.
- Approximately 40 percent were African-American and 60 percent Spanish, mostly from Puerto Rico.
- She always thought, "If I can help them, I can save the world."
- She believed that she was called to be a teacher of the disadvantaged.
- The parents of more than half the class were on welfare. Most have been in the United States all of their lives, and a few new immigrants were moving into the area.
- Three of the 20 children had both a mother and father in the home.
- The school where she taught was built in 1960 with sleek, modern lines; the janitorial service worked hard to maintain the facilities, despite declining funds.

- Most of her children had serious deficiencies in reading and English; many spoke only Spanish at home.
- Paula often used her own money to buy hands-on materials, such as puzzles, to help the children with their reading skills.
- Typically, the children scored closer to their expected age group in math.
- The school provided both breakfast and lunch; for most of the children in her class, these meals were important, because they guaranteed the children a meal, and were often the biggest meals of the day for them.
- A typical day included reading and writing exercises, sentence diagramming, and extensive work with grammar and math, through applied science exercises.

Science projects captivated the class.

- The class took a field trip once a month to art museums, zoos, the ballet, and parks.
- In the spring, much of the school curriculum revolved around teaching for the annual city and state tests that measured performance and determined funding.
- Test scores were declining; Paula believed it was a "forgotten school."
- Currently, the increasing use of crack was having an influence on her classroom; children came to school exhausted because their parents used the drug and were up all night.
- Some of her best students had the most isolated lives, she said.
- To protect their children from gangs and drugs, parents kept the children inside on weekends, often renting three of four movie videos on Friday afternoons, and watching them continuously until Sunday evening.
- Many of the children attended church on weekends, especially Jehovah's Witness and fundamental Baptist; many of the Spanish families were once Catholic.
- By her own description, Paula fell into teaching "backwards," after two decades in theater and set design.
- Originally from Omaha, Nebraska, where she attended an all girl's Catholic high school, her life revolved around the community theater where she both acted and worked in the make-up crew.
- After attending colleges in Nebraska, Florida, and New York, she went to work in theater in 1978.
- She worked primarily in set design, and finally left in 1991, at age 38, to begin substitute teaching, because she "didn't want to paint scenery anymore."

Field trips were welcomed events.

Life in the Community: The Bronx, New York

- The two most secure institutions in the south Bronx community were the police station and the schools; the community included few banks, grocery stores, or movie houses.

91

- Most services were available within the community, and more expensive than those in other sections of New York; many of the families had cars, often nice cars.
- Income was not the sole determinant of how children turn out, but many believed parental income was the single most important influence on a child's chances.
- Poor children tended to weigh less than rich children at birth, and die more often in their first year of life.
- When they entered school, poor children scored lower on standardized tests.
- Poor children were absent more often from school, and had more behavior problems.
- Poor teenagers were more likely than teenagers of affluent families to have a baby, drop out of school, and get in trouble with the law.
- Children raised in poverty were more likely to end up poor and in need of public assistance.
- From the Great Depression to the 1970s, U.S. policy was dominated by the theory that income support can cure many of the problems of poor children.
- Prior to the Great Depression, poverty was viewed as a sign of weak character.
- Aid to families with dependent children grew from 3.1 million families in 1960 to 6.1 million in 1969.

1995: Champion of the Arts in Schools

As a young woman who had grown up with a love for the arts, Scott Shanklin-Peterson became executive director of a South Carolina arts agency that expanded the arts curriculum in the schools.

Life at Home

- Scott Shanklin-Peterson was born June 10, 1944, at Eglin Army Air Corps base on the Florida Panhandle, the only child of Ferryle Yeager of Alabama and Edward Henry Shanklin of South Carolina.
- Henry Shanklin's parents died when he was young, so he and his other four siblings were parceled out to relatives; he grew up in Rocky Mount, North Carolina.
- In the mid-1930s, he went to Clemson College, located in the South Carolina countryside between the mid-sized cities of Anderson and Greenville.
- He went there, at least in part, because his older sister, Virginia Shanklin, had been working there since 1925 as secretary to the college's presidents.
- Henry graduated in the late 1930s with a degree in textiles.
- He went into the Army, and was serving as a major in the Army Air Corps when Scott was born.
- After World War II ended in 1945, he worked briefly at a cotton mill in Danville, Virginia, before returning to Clemson to work for the U.S. Department of Agriculture at its Cotton Quality Research Lab.
- Scott grew up in the small town by the Clemson campus.
- Her Aunt Virginia was still serving as a secretary to the Clemson president.
- Over her 41 years at the college, Virginia served four presidents; one of her jobs was to coordinate all arts activities on campus, including an annual schedule of visiting ballet companies and orchestras.
- Aunt Virginia made sure her niece had tickets, "and she made sure I got there," Scott said.
- "She was a great influence on me for the arts."
- Another influence was Sarah Waikart, an accomplished artist who returned to her hometown near Clemson in 1950.
- Public schools in the area didn't have art classes, but Waikart provided private lessons; Scott was one of her students for two years during elementary school.
- When Scott was a senior in high school, she and her best friend, who also wanted to study

Scott Shanklin-Peterson worked to expand the arts curriculum in South Carolina schools.

art in college, asked the principal to let them take drafting, also called mechanical drawing.

- "They wouldn't let us take it because we were girls," recalls Scott.
- The pair kept insisting, and finally the principal relented.
- Scott went to Columbia College, a small women's college in Columbia, South Carolina.
- She wanted to major in art and business.
- "They told me I couldn't because people who were good in art weren't good in business."
- After being sent to the school psychologist for aptitude tests, she tested fine for both and the college agreed to her request.
- Scott graduated in 1966 with a bachelor's degree in studio art, with minors in business and art education.
- She married Frank Buck Sanders in 1965 and had two children: Buck Henry Sanders, born in 1971, and Stacie Sanders, born in 1975.
- Although Scott and her husband later separated, she continued to use the name Scott Sanders until she

Scott encouraged creativity at a young age.

married Terry Peterson in the mid-1990s, who was then an advisor to U.S. Secretary of Education Richard W. Riley.
- After college, Scott worked for a few years with the state employment agency, counseling the jobless on how to find work.
- When her husband graduated from University of South Carolina Law School in 1969, Scott moved with him to the Rosebud Indian Reservation in South Dakota, where he provided legal assistance to members of the Sioux tribe.
- Scott helped the tribe set up a co-operative to sell crafts.
- After a year or so, she and Terry moved to Philadelphia, Mississippi, where her husband provided legal aid to the Mississippi band of the Choctaw tribe.
- They then moved to Columbia, South Carolina, in June 1971, shortly after their first child was born.
- When Scott took her baby down to the state employment agency to show him off to her former coworkers, someone remembered her interest in the arts, and mentioned that the South Carolina Arts Commission needed some help.
- The Arts Commission, then only four years old, was looking for someone to set up a program that would place poets into schools to work with students.
- Scott's job application process included being interviewed by three poets and writing several grant proposals.
- She got the job.
- It was considered part-time, and she was paid $3,000 a year—half the salary of an office secretary.
- Her enthusiasm made it full-time.
- Scott encouraged creativity at a young age.
- Scott initiated her arts education project in the schools with the help of the Springs Foundation, which was interested in the arts and was willing to provide grants for work in three counties.
- Starting in 1973, the program employed painters, poets, potters, printers, and musicians who would work in the schools to expose children to the arts.
- Some teachers' groups feared that employing artists in schools would discourage administrators from hiring full-time arts instructors.
- "The opposite was true," Scott said.

- "Artist residencies developed an interest in having more arts, and the number of art and music teachers expanded."
- It was a lesson that she would carry with her when she was promoted to executive director of the South Carolina Arts Commission in 1980, and over the next 13 years as South Carolina became a national petri dish for a new way of raising the profile and quality of arts in the classroom.

Life at Work

- When the national "Arts in Education" program began in 1986, Scott Shanklin-Peterson jumped at the opportunity to participate.
- The goal of the NEA-sponsored effort was that students would graduate high school with "with a general understanding of, and elementary literacy in, the major art forms."
- In March 1987, South Carolina was one of 16 states to receive planning grants.
- South Carolina was already ahead of many states in its approach to arts education.
- One reason: Arts educators became angry.
- In the late 1970s, the South Carolina Board of Education issued a regulation saying students in grades 9-12 could use no more than two credits earned in music and visual arts toward their graduation requirements.
- For the first time, visual arts and music educators joined forces through their professional organizations to "right this wrong," said educator Ray Doughty.
- Groups representing arts teachers and students "mounted an intensive campaign which ultimately resulted in the State Board rescinding the so-called two-unit regulation," Doughty said.
- Another factor was that arts education was becoming something students (and their parents) aspired to—at least in Greenville County.
- The county, which borders the mountains in the western end of South Carolina, had one of the state's largest school districts.
- In 1975, it established a Fine Arts Center where gifted high school students would spend half their day working within a given discipline from painting to violin.
- The other half of the day would be spent at their "home" high school, where they would study language, math, science and other required courses.
- This became so popular that a statewide version was established in 1980 as a summer program on the campus of Furman University in Greenville County.
- Then, the Ashley River Creative Arts Elementary School, founded in Charleston in 1984, captured attention by taking arts beyond the domain of the gifted.
- Gifted students thrived in the Fine Arts Center.
- The magnet school accepted all students in its district, regardless of their artistic abilities.
- While there were special arts classes, it also wove the arts into lessons from science to music; the school's waiting list would swell to 1,500 by 1994.
- Richard W. Riley was elected governor of South Carolina in 1978 on a campaign platform to improve education in the state.

Gifted students thrived in the Fine Arts Center.

- In 1980, the South Carolina legislature enacted a set of minimum requirements for schools that included arts instruction.
- For every 800 students, schools were supposed to have at least one full-time visual art teacher and one music teacher in grades one through six.
- With funding, an elementary school student spent 40 minutes each week on visual arts and another 40 minutes on music.
- These reforms laid a foundation that made it easier in South Carolina to roll out its proposed Arts in Basic Curriculum project in the late 1980s.

Art class in elementary school.

- Nationally, arts were being squeezed out of the schools by shrinking dollars and a clamor for more basics.
- Some educators and the public were concerned about the quality of education basics— reading, writing and arithmetic —being neglected.
- After the election of Ronald Reagan in 1980, newly appointed U.S. Education Secretary T.
- Bell ordered a study to "define the problems afflicting American education."
- In 1983, Bell released a report called "A Nation at Risk" that warned of "a rising tide of mediocrity that threatens our very future as a Nation and a people."
- The report detailed shortcomings in reading, writing and arithmetic.
- It mentioned the arts in a passage noting that some observers "are concerned that an overemphasis on technical and occupational skills will leave little time for studying the arts and humanities that so enrich daily life, help maintain civility, and develop a sense of community."
- But since the late 1950s, some psychologists, educators and artists had been forming a different way of looking at the place of arts—not just in society but within the human brain.
- One of these was Elliot W. Eisner.
- Growing up in Chicago in the 1930s and 1940s, Eisner had not done well in classes like math and English, but he flourished in the arts and became an art teacher, and then finished his doctoral degree in education.
- He was teaching at Stanford University in 1982 when he was asked to meet with directors from the J. Paul Getty Trust.
- The trust had been established six years after the death of its namesake, one of the nation's richest Americans and an art collector who had founded the Getty Oil Company.
- *The New York Times* reported that the J. Paul Getty Trust planned to establish, in early 1986, partnerships with state arts councils to make the arts an integral part of basic education, from the first to the twelfth grade.
- It was the first time the endowment had encouraged changes in curricula at local schools.
- In the past, the endowment presence in the schools was to provide small salaries for artists who worked within schools for several months.
- The money for the new program would come from cuts in these artists-in-residency programs.
- South Carolina was one of only eight states to win a three-year grant in 1988 to begin rolling out Arts in Basic Curriculum to its first group of 11 schools or school districts.
- "Dismissed as a luxury by school systems fighting even to keep enough textbooks in stock, arts studies have steadily dwindled in recent years," *The New York Times* reported.

- "The National Center for Education Statistics estimates that almost half of all American schools have no full-time arts staff members. The new standards will provide no immediate relief," the paper reported.
- "States or school districts that choose to adopt them will be eligible for some of the $700 million earmarked in the Clinton budget for its Goals 2000 legislation, a broad education bill stressing basic educational goals and including the adoption of voluntary national standards as a central feature."
- Because the goals were voluntary, any chance for implementation depended on cooperation.
- "Local and state arts agencies and organizations, schools and arts educators need to strengthen their partnerships to ensure that quality arts education becomes a reality in all schools," Riley said.
- Among the chief organizers of the partnerships had been Scott.
- Clinton appointed Scott as deputy chair of the NEA in January 1994 on the recommendation of Jane Alexander, Clinton's new NEA chair.
- Alexander was an award-winning actress who had co-starred with James Earl Jones in "The Great White Hope," an NEA-funded play that opened in 1968.
- It was the first time that a white woman and a black man had played bedroom scenes on stage, a first that brought death threats to both of them.
- "Because Jane's career began with an NEA-funded project, she understood the great value to our country of the NEA," Scott said.
- Meanwhile, Scott's mission was to adapt the model of cooperation from South Carolina to the national stage; her title was Deputy Chair for Partnerships.
- The task would be difficult, with more than 50 groups and agencies representing different segments of arts education, from administrators to teachers unions.
- The key was the support from both Riley and NEA Chair Jane Alexander.
- "People came together, stepped up and did it," Scott said.
- The group spent six months developing a national partnership and a plan to help make the arts part of basic education.
- The success was marked by the creation of the National Arts Education Partnership in 1995 through an unusual interagency agreement between the National Endowment for the Arts and the Department of Education.
- The partnership helps to provide a uniform voice for arts educators.
- Its mission is also to expand arts education to more students, improve arts education practices, and research how art influences and strengthens American education.
- "We created on the national level the same type of partnership we had created in South Carolina," Scott said.
- Elliot Eisner spearheaded Arts in Basic Curriculum.
- In November 1994, Americans elected more Republicans to the U.S. House than Democrats.
- House Speaker Newt Gingrich of Georgia; Representative Dick Armey of Texas, the majority leader; and Representative John A. Boehner of Ohio had all declared that the federal government had no business making grants to artists and arts organizations.
- "That," Scott said, "was the beginning of the culture wars."

Elliot Eisner spearheaded Arts in Basic Curriculum.

Life in the Community: South Carolina

- In 1995, South Carolina had 3.7 million people, making it the twenty-sixth-largest of the 50 states and Washington, DC.
- The state's population had grown 18 percent since 1980, slightly faster than the overall growth rate for the nation.
- South Carolina had 38,700 teachers for its 645,000 kindergarten through twelfth-grade public school students in 1995.
- The average class was about 17 students—slightly fewer than the national average.
- The average public schoolteacher earned $30,300 in the 1994-95 school year—18 percent less than the national average of $36,800.
- Taxpayers spent $912 per student per year in a typical district in South Carolina in 1995—21 percent less than the U.S. average.
- By 1990, the state's spending was $2,027 per student—only 6 percent under the national average.
- But the state's spending fell compared with other states through 1995.
- About 174,000 people were enrolled in college in South Carolina.
- That came out to 4.7 percent of the state's population, ranking South Carolina fortieth by that measure.

One of South Carolina's mobile arts centers.

Biscuitville

1996: Biscuitville Restaurant Chain Founder

Entrepreneur Maurice Jennings learned from his grandma how to make the big buttermilk biscuits that launched his restaurant chain, Biscuitville, Inc.

Life at Work

- Maurice Jennings spent summers with his grandmother in middle Tennessee, where she made biscuits, a Southern staple, and set the taste standard Maurice would use when he opened his restaurant.
- According to company legend, before she died, Erma Jennings gave her grandson Maurice a choice: inherit the family farm or her biscuit recipe.
- He took the recipe, using it to launch Biscuitville Inc., a chain of restaurants.
- A needlepoint at company headquarters in Burlington, North Carolina—and in each of the 43 restaurants—said so.
- It was a touching story if only it were true.
- Maurice cribbed the recipe from a flour sack.
- Or maybe it was a cookbook; he wasn't really sure.
- Wherever it came from, he tinkered with it until he found a taste and texture he liked.
- He ran his businesses much the same way—displaying a willingness to tinker with any idea and always remain flexible.
- Maurice started with a bread shop, then moved to pizzas before settling into a breakfast-biscuit niche.
- Maurice's biscuit-making education started when his father bought a bakery in Burlington, North Carolina, in 1941.
- There, the third-grader learned how to bake and set out carryout boxes for the wholesale operation; he also learned that if you eat three dozen doughnuts in one day when no one's looking, you won't want another doughnut for two years.
- As he grew up, Maurice worked in the bakery, played football and baseball and did everything he could to sneak into University North Carolina football games at Chapel Hill when running back Charlie "Choo Choo" Justice was playing.
- Maurice Jennings struck it big with biscuits.
- Maurice and his buddies also formed "The Blue Streak Boxing Club" to stage fight exhibitions in his basement; the club was named after the blue streak left by the printer on the event tickets.

Maurice Jennings struck it big with biscuits.

- When he was 12 years old, mornings before school were spent delivering the Greensboro newspaper starting at 5:30 a.m. and the Burlington paper in the afternoon.
- In 1950, when Maurice was 15, his father suffered a stroke and was less able to work after that.
- Maurice went to work for a movie theater, clothing store, radio stations and on a farm to help support the family.
- The summer he turned 18, Maurice thumbed a ride to Kansas to work the wheat harvest driving a truck; he slept wherever he could find a place, usually in the wheat truck, and earned $1.50 a hour—$1.00 in cash and $0.50 at the end of the season, if he stayed to the end of the harvest.

The key to success was fresh, warm biscuits.

- Then, after one semester at Elon College, Maurice joined the Air Force, only to return to Burlington in 1955 to help with the family bakery ingredient business.
- By then, his father, a flour merchant, was no longer able to talk, so Maurice traveled the region developing the wholesale flour part of the business while his mother stayed home and ran the office.
- Maurice found considerable success in the bakery flour business, enough to buy his first airplane, a Beechcraft Bonanza, and use it for business travel.
- During that time, he saved $30,000—enough to start another business.
- One of Maurice's flour customers in Memphis had opened a bread store he admired, so he tried the same concept in Burlington.
- Because there was extra space in the store, Maurice added pizza to the menu, a rare commodity at that time.
- Pizzas proved so popular that the bread concept disappeared and the pizza stayed, forming the basis for a small chain of carry-out places called Pizzaville.
- By the early 1970s, the chain had grown to 12 stores throughout north-central North Carolina.
- This was followed by a steakhouse that specialized in ribeye steaks cut to order.
- In 1972, the 37-year-old Maurice re-enrolled in Elon College and took every business course they offered.

Life at Work

- Maurice Jennings remembers the exact moment he conceived of Biscuitville.
- He was on the way to the company's Chapel Hill, North Carolina, Pizzaville when it occurred to him they could take the salad bar down at night and open the next morning with a jelly bar featuring freshly made buttermilk biscuits.

Bacon, egg, and cheese on a biscuit soon became a best-seller.

- "I love sweets and could see people taking their biscuits down the line getting all kinds of jams and jellies," Maurice said.
- So he put in a jelly bar with about 40 types of jams.
- The key to success was fresh, warm biscuits.
- "People would come in and look at the jelly bar and say, 'Now ain't that a cute idea? Gimme two ham biscuits and a cup of coffee,'" Maurice said. "That lasted about two weeks. We threw the jelly bar out and kept the biscuits."
- The first all-biscuit store opened in Danville, Virginia, in 1975 in an old Rich's hamburger building.

- "It was pretty efficient, and the biscuits were always warm."
- The biscuit store in North Asheboro grossed $12,000 a week.
- "I should have dropped everything else and concentrated on Biscuitville; instead, like a true entrepreneur, I tried about a dozen different things. No use listing them: the point is, when you stumble onto something that really works, you should concentrate on that almost single-minded, like you're running a straight line."
- Before long, customers could stuff the biscuits in two dozen ways.
- Within a few years, the company made $30 million annually, just on the biscuits.
- The recipe was simple—flour, buttermilk and shortening; in the early 1990s, shortening became all-vegetable for the health-conscious.
- "The secret in making good biscuits is in handling them right, which is a physical thing, and also in keeping them young. If you let them sit there and dry out, they are not going to be any good."
- Unlike its competitors, Biscuitville doesn't do franchises, stays close to its biscuit theme and doesn't tolerate downtime.
- For a long time, the stores stayed open until 8 p.m., serving up fried chicken, green beans and other Southern dishes to the dinner crowd.
- That brought in customers at night but left a quiet afternoon.
- So the company ditched dinner and closed every day at 2 p.m.
- It also simplified the menu, emphasizing biscuit breakfasts and lunches.
- By limiting its hours, Biscuitville cut its second-largest cost—labor.
- The new schedule needed only one shift of workers.
- It also meant less sales per restaurant compared with other fast food chains.
- Each Biscuitville brought in about $645,000 a year in sales.
- A typical Bojangles' pulled in $900,000, much of it during dinner.
- But since Biscuitville concentrated on carbohydrates rather than protein, its food costs were lower and margins higher.
- In 1991, Biscuitville created a profit-sharing plan to attract the best managerial talent.
- Biscuitville's high-carb, low protein menu kept food costs low.
- Part of each manager's pay was based on profit.
- Many managers didn't like the concept.
- Maurice found that profit-sharing required a different mentality; some managers would much rather know what they are going to make.
- Many of those who stayed turned the plan to their advantage; Biscuitville managers earned on average $70,000 a year.

Biscuitville's high-carb, low protein menu kept food costs low.

Biscuitville's managers made an average of $70,000 a year.

- Maurice also learned through the years that the mundane aspects of the business such as accounting were critical to understanding the profitability and reacting accordingly.
- "I strongly believe that if you're doing poorly, you want to know why; if you are doing well, you want to know why."
- When Maurice began Biscuitville, he bought and paid for his equipment and leased the land and buildings; with some experience, he learned to do just the opposite: he leased his equipment and bought—with financing—the land and buildings.
- But buy carefully, he learned.
- "Location is the most important decision an entrepreneur can make, and it's the hardest to change."
- In 1996, the Jennings family biscuit recipe and business were passed to a new generation.
- Jennings's son, Burney, took over as president and CEO.
- During the next five years, Burney Jennings wanted to build 27 more Biscuitvilles, a growth rate of more than 60 percent.
- Much of the growth was planned in Winston-Salem, which already had eight Bojangles', and Raleigh, home to 12 Hardee's.
- The growth carried risks.
- Attracting and keeping good help—always a struggle in the fast-food industry—was even tougher in a tight labor market; expand too fast and you end up with new managers training newer ones, and quality plummets.
- Biscuitville planned to finance its growth internally, without help from franchising, which would spread the investment risk and responsibility for finding good help to franchisees.
- Maurice, whose strong survival instinct built the chain, said his formula for success was simple: "We move like a river. We try to go wherever it is natural to go."
- Biscuitville's managers made an average of $70,000 a year.

Life in the Community: Burlington, North Carolina

- Burlington was born of the railroad, bred on the loom and built on an ability to turn adversity into opportunity.

- Alamance County, where Burlington was located, was settled by several groups of Quakers, German farmers, and Scots-Irish immigrants.
- It was the site of several American Revolutionary War battles, including the War of the Regulation, which took place prior to the actual Revolution, when citizens rebelled against the corrupt British Colonial Government.
- The Holt family was instrumental in building several different textile mills in Burlington and the surrounding towns; these textile mills provided much of the economic base on which the county would grow.

Burlington, N.C., 1943.

- The need of the North Carolina Railroad Company in the 1850s to locate land where it could build, repair and do maintenance on its track was the genesis of Burlington, North Carolina, which was originally dubbed "Company Shops."
- By the time the shops were completed in 1857, the village had grown to 27 buildings.
- Thirty-nine white men, 20 Negro slaves and two free Negroes were employed in or around the shops.
- In 1887, after the North Carolina Railroad Company transferred its operations to Manchester, Virginia, and the stores at Company Shops were closed, a committee of the town's leading citizens renamed the community "Burlington."
- The City of Burlington was incorporated and a charter was issued by the state legislature on February 14, 1893.
- Textiles, in particular, hosiery, took the place of the railroads and as the century turned, many new jobs were created, making Burlington "The Hosiery Center of the South."
- In the 1920s, with the financial support from the Chamber of Commerce, Burlington Mills was begun—which became the largest textile maker in the world.
- But that company faced adversity immediately.
- The market for its cotton goods fell into depression, so the mill switched to a new and untried manmade fiber—rayon.
- On that product, Burlington Mills would become an industrial giant.
- During World War II, an aircraft factory was opened, adding new citizens to Burlington's work force.
- After the war, Western Electric came, adding electronics to the city's economic base.
- After textiles suffered a severe decline in the 1970s, when unemployment rose to almost 20 percent, the local leadership embarked on a diversification campaign so Burlington would no longer rely on a single industry.

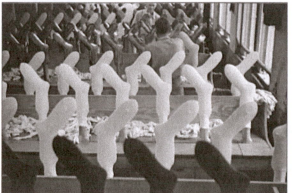

Burlington was unofficially called "The Hosiery Center of the South."

- The city's largest single employer in 1996 was a medical diagnostic company.
- Employing 3,000 people, LabCorp was one of the largest clinical laboratory companies in the world, had its headquarters and several testing facilities in Burlington, and was the county's largest employer.
- Burlington had a population of 40,000 in 1996 and was part of the Piedmont Triad region of the state.
- Biscuitville, a regional fast food chain, and Gold Toe Brands, a manufacturer of socks, were both based in Burlington.

1996: Immigrant Worker and Striker

Once Airto Escavedo left war-torn Guatemala for America to make a better life, he found himself in the midst of another battle—to make better working conditions in the North Carolina poultry processing plant where he was employed.

Life at Home

- Twenty-five-year-old Airto Escavedo grew up in the midst of war in Guatemala.
- Like most indigenous Guatemalans, Airto was of Mayan descent and traced his bloodline and language back to the ancient "corn people."
- He was the son of Soledad and Flora Escavedo, successful garlic farmers in Aguacatan.
- There, commercial agriculture was the main industry; crops consisted of tomatoes, onions, and especially garlic, which was the chief export to foreign markets.
- Perched between mountain ridges, Aguacatan had historically been a busy farming and commercial center because of its well-irrigated valley location.
- Size as well as its proximity to the provincial capital contributed to its prosperity.
- But Soledad's failing health and the disastrous effects of the war had all but eliminated the family business.
- For nearly 30 years, the Western Hemisphere's longest-running guerilla war between the armed left and the military-dominated government had ravaged Guatemala's economy in a Cold War conflict.
- The war had claimed an estimated 200,000 casualties in dead and disappeared; some 600 indigenous communities were eliminated by government-sponsored attacks, according to a United Nations Truth Commission.
- It was against this backdrop of economic stagnation that men like Airto Escavedo prepared to leave their homeland in the late 1980s, seeking the means in America to support their families.
- And Airto believed he possessed an advantage—an education.
- Education was more easily available in Aguacatan because of the efforts of Henry and Lucille McArthur.
- The McArthurs were Canadian-born missionaries, linguistic scholars and Wycliffe Bible translators, who did much to promote literacy and education among the Aguacatan people by cross-translating indigenous languages and Spanish.
- Through their efforts, thousands of children were enrolled in primary schools and more than 500 attended secondary schools.
- Newly married with a child on the way, Airto knew that he must leave Guatemala if he was to support his family.

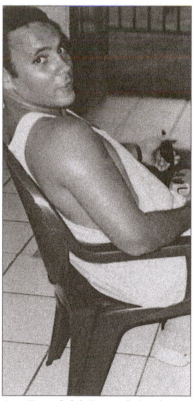

Airto Escavedo left Guatemala for a better life in the U.S.

105

- For prospective émigrés like Airto, survival in America would depend on locating job prospects, arranging transportation, successfully crossing the border, finding housing, actually getting a job, and then learning the ropes at work and outside work.
- To travel to the United States, it cost up to $3,000, which he borrowed from his parents.
- Airto walked, paid for van rides, and rode a bus through Mexico before crossing into the United States by way of Arizona.

Typical Guatemalan hut.

- Upon arrival in the U.S., Airto worked in agriculture and construction until he was advised by a family friend and fellow Aguacateco Francisco Fuentes of the opportunity for work at a poultry processing plant known as Case Farms.
- Airto was told that Case Farms was located in the more familiar mountain surroundings of Morganton, North Carolina, offered inside work, and steady pay.
- It was such a popular designation for Mayans that a regular van service from Indiantown, Florida, to Morganton had been established.
- Case Farms even rented public housing for its Guatemalan labor and provided bicycles as transportation to work.
- Fuentes charged Airto $20.00 for the trip and $30.00 as a referral fee for a job at the plant.
- Fuentes claimed to have transported over 300 workers to Morganton by the time Airto arrived in 1993.
- It was rumored that Fuentes received up to $50.00 from Case Farms for each worker he procured.

Life at Work

- Airto Escavedo's goal as an employee of Case Farms in Morganton, North Carolina, was simple: to make enough money to return to his pueblo and be with his family and community in Guatemala.
- By 1993, Airto was becoming familiar with his new surroundings.
- He noted three major differences between American life and what he had previously known.

Looking for work in Guatemala.

- One, he discovered the meaning of the weekend; two, he opened a bank account; and three, television became a part of his daily routine.
- Airto lived in a single male household with six other Aguacateco men in their twenties and thirties, who took turns cooking and cleaning for themselves.
- Eighty percent of Aguacateco male workers were married, but few had been able to bring their wives along.
- But the large Mayan population in Morganton meant he could routinely eat traditional foods, such as corn tortillas and beans, and use natural cures for minor ills.

- Upon arrival in Morganton, Airto started work in the "live bird" area of Case Farms, where workers pulled live, struggling birds from crates and hung them on hooks by their feet.
- He was paid $6.35 an hour, which was less than he had been promised.
- He found that work in a poultry plant, even under the best conditions, presented a demanding and unpleasant routine.
- His education concerning poultry processing and illegal immigrant labor started almost immediately upon arrival.

The Case Farms plant.

- The poultry industry provided the lowest pay in the food industry.
- Poultry plants were known for unreported accident claims: carpal tunnel syndrome was ranked the third-highest complaint among U.S. industries.
- One out of every six employees in the poultry industry suffered a work-related illness or injury every year, according to the U.S. Department of Labor.
- For employers, immigrant workers were a valuable commodity, who filled hard-tohire- for jobs at a low price.
- The first large-scale labor eruption at the Case Farms plant occurred in May 1993, just months before Airto arrived.
- Approximately 100 workers stood up in the plant cafeteria and refused to return to work unless the company addressed a list of grievances.
- The list included unpaid hours, unauthorized company deductions for safety equipment like smocks and gloves, the lack of bathroom breaks, poor working materials and inadequate pay.
- The plant manager summoned local police and 52 workers were charged with trespassing.
- Following mediation by lawyers from the local legal services office and state labor board officials, the workers agreed to return to work and the company dropped all legal charges.
- The disruption was also one of the reasons that Airto was able to get a job so easily: troublemakers were being moved out.
- But by early 1995, he was tired of handling chickens, angry with management, and nowhere close to having enough money to return to Guatemala.
- He desperately missed his wife and child.
- Airto's first confrontation with management occurred on May 11, 1995.
- By this time, of the 500 people employed at the Case Farms processing plant, 80 percent were Spanish-speaking, and of those, 80 to 90 percent were Guatemalan.
- The work protest began in Airto's "live bird" area.
- By prior agreement, everyone stopped work when a supervisor denied a bathroom break requested by one of the men.
- Once the workers had management's attention, three men were designated to approach the manager with their grievances: the arbitrary control of bathroom breaks, increasingly stressful line speed, eductions for safety equipment, and consistently low wages.
- Instead of giving the three young men a hearing, the manager had them arrested for trespassing.
- A plant-wide shutdown then began, immediately followed by a workers' rally outside the plant gates.
- The strike lasted 11 days.

- Following threats by the company to replace them, the workers returned to their jobs, having succeeded in getting a real response from the company and bringing the Mayan workers into contact with the American trade unions.
- As the strike proceeded through its first week, the chief organizer for the Laborers' International Union of North America arrived in Morganton.
- He was awestruck by the fact that the workers had organized this strike and demonstration with no help from any sort of institution except the church and a legal aid attorney in Morganton.
- He was also amazed that the workers self-organized so that the first union-organizing meeting could be translated into seven or eight dialects required by the Mayan workers.

Scenes of Case Farm, above and below.

- At meetings on the property of Francisco Fuentes, and later at St. Charles Catholic church, the movement gathered strength.
- The workers were ready to fight even if the company took their jobs and evicted them from their apartments.
- On July 12, 1995, after a heated campaign, the employees voted 238-183 to form a union and be represented by the Laborers' International Union of North America.
- The vote by the workers made the Case facility the only unionized chicken plant in the state.
- Nationally, the story of the Case Farms workers became a cause célèbre in labor circles.
- Union leaders saw it as a potential breakthrough in their drive to organize the lowwage poultry industry, which employed more than 21,000 people in North Carolina, many of them immigrants.
- But big victories took time.
- The national union win rate in National Labor Relations Board elections was less than 40 percent, a figure that dropped even further in "right to work" states like North Carolina.
- At the national level, fewer than 20 percent of private sector workers who attempted to organize were able to gain representation under a union contract.
- Airto had been told that even after winning an organizing drive, the Case Farms workers might not

get serious consideration of their desire to bargain for a union contract—and they didn't.
- The company's lawyers filed a variety of appeals.
- By delaying union recognition and serious contract bargaining, the company wanted to take advantage of worker turnover, fatigue, demoralization and the dwindling union organizing budget.
- In the 1990s, an estimated one-third of the workplaces where workers voted for a union never achieved a first contract.
- And Airto could only wait so long.

- He was not prepared to spend another Christmas without his family, and be too poor to send presents and be a good father.
- By February 1996, he had given up and journeyed back to Guatemala as poultry workers from North Carolina joined national religious and labor activists in demanding a "code of ethics" for an industry they branded as unsafe, unsanitary and inhumane.

Life in the Community: Morganton, North Carolina

- Prior to the arrival of the Maya in Morganton, North Carolina, the area had absorbed two extraordinary immigrant colonies in the past century.
- At the beginning of the 1900s, several hundred French-speaking Waldensians arrived in Burke County and settled in a nearby community named Valdesa.
- Beginning in the late 1970s, 500 Laotian Hmong refugee families settled in Morganton with help from area churches and the federal government.
- The gradual migration of hundreds of Mayan immigrants was largely ignored.

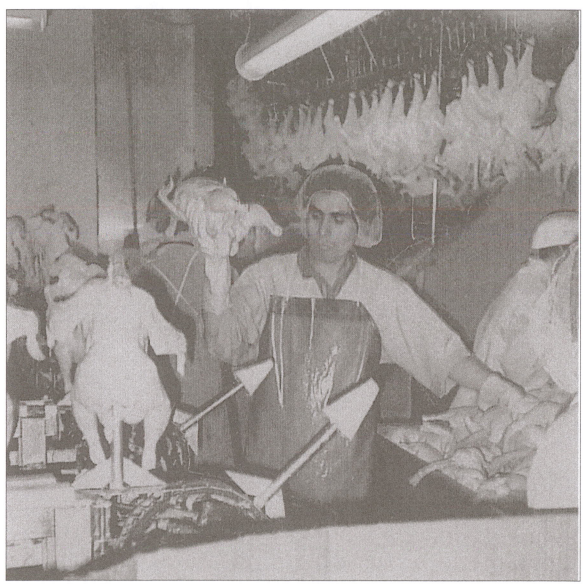

Immigrant poultry worker.

- The community of Morganton and the Guatemalan workers at Case Farms occupied different worlds.
- The workers used a self-created community to protect themselves and find comfort.
- Airto enrolled in a successful all-Hispanic soccer league, organized by town of origin.
- Religious life was directed with the establishment of two additional Hispanic evangelic churches.
- But the average Morganton resident did not welcome the new arrivals with open arms.
- They seemed to feel that eventually the newcomers would just disappear.
- Mayor Mel Cohen judged that the Mayan migration had a more negative than positive effect on Morganton.
- Cohen's observation was based on five points.
- First, the immigrants' inability to understand the language.
- Second, their inability to adhere to the local quality of life.
- Third, they sent most of their money back to Guatemala and did not spend it locally.
- Fourth, their lack of respect for community property.
- Fifth, their willingness to live in substandard habitation.
- The immigrants, for their part, held a residual distrust for anyone in uniform because of their experience with corrupt police and military in their own country.
- As the Mayan population grew, they became the victims of neglect more than hostility.
- Banished to the margins of town life, the Mayan presence took more than a decade to appear in the annual Morganton Historic Festival.
- Yet a small band of citizens helped to ease the migrants' acclimation.
- As early as 1992, National Red Cross agencies hired a Spanish-speaking teacher to direct Project Amigo, an outreach program, which provided the new Guatemalan community with health care and other services.
- Unquestionably, the center for Guatemalan socialization was St. Charles Catholic church.

1997: Department of Transportation Administrator

Dan Stevens was the division administrator for the Iowa Division of the Federal Highway Administration in the U.S. Department of Transportation. This was his eighth move in 21 years, and promised his family it would be their last.

Life at Home

- To move up in the organization, Dan had asked his family to move eight times; so this time he told the family they would stay in Ames, Iowa, where his current assignment was.
- They were particularly happy with the public schools and the friendly atmosphere of the community.
- He designed their new home in Ames himself, and was extremely pleased with the craftsmanship and skills of the workers who built his house.
- Generally, he found that workers in Iowa took great pride in their craftsmanship, whether they were building houses or roads.
- The home cost $280,000 to construct. The family had a $1,500 monthly house payment; for the first time he was using a 15-year mortgage to finance his home rather than a 30-year mortgage.
- The length of the winters, often seven months long, had surprised Dan; he enjoyed being around his wife and three children, but felt confined.
- On weekends, he coached youth soccer, which was in its infancy in the state; few of the parents played soccer as children, and struggled with the rules.
- Dan played soccer in high school and in a college intramural league at the Pennsylvania State University.
- His daughter's team traveled throughout Iowa and Nebraska to find competition.
- He was also spending time building a deck on his new home and finishing the landscaping; new homes always require lots of touch-ups to get them right, he had learned.
- Both he and his wife Maura earned civil engineering degrees from the Pennsylvania State University.
- They met in college and married after graduation, when they both got jobs with the Federal Highway Administration.
- Once they were married, they were not allowed to work in the same

Iowa's long winters encouraged family-oriented projects.

111

On weekends, he coached youth soccer.

Dan designed his new home in Ames himself.

Dan enjoyed coaching soccer and seeing young people learn the game.

office, but were assigned to areas near one another, particularly during the two-year training program.

- Maura worked for 10 years before electing to stay home with their two children.
- At the time, they were each making approximately $35,000 a year.
- The long winters gave her more time to cook; she had carefully designed the kitchen and often ordered specialty items from kitchen catalogs.

Life at Work

- Dan managed 17 employees in an office which handled approximately $200 million in Federal Highway Aid coming to Iowa.
- His role was to help highway projects move through their various stages to completion; from concept to completion nearly always took several years.
- A typical project moved from planning to environmental evaluation, right-of-way acquisition, to design, and then construction.

- He saw his principal role as creating an environment in which his engineers could make quality decisions, despite political pressures.
- Twenty years of experience had taught him that problems would arise on complex, expensive Interstate projects, and without a good working relationship, problems quickly turned to crises.
- He believed that open and honest communication was the best way to forge partnerships.
- He encouraged the people in his office to socialize with each other, and their counterparts with the Iowa DOT.
- Getting to know each other would make communication easier, he believed.

- He also believed in having fun on the job, because confident people made better decisions, he felt.
- He tried not to get involved in highway projects personally, unless his agency was preparing to say "no" or planning to withhold federal funds on a project.
- He believed his staff needed to be empowered to make decisions.
- Because his agency controlled millions of dollars, its decisions would often spark political debate and controversy.
- Much of his time was spent improving the relationship between the Federal Highway Administration and the Iowa Department of Transportation.
- When he arrived a year ago, an adversarial relationship existed; he was asked to move to Iowa to help breed a sense of partnership.
- Cooperation was especially critical now that the national staff of the Highway Administration had been cut from 5,500 employees to 2,800; without trust and a partnership, projects could not be easily completed.
- The local newspapers editorialized against his department shortly after his arrival, saying the Federal employees did little for the community.

- Since then, Dan had demonstrated the community spirit of the federal agency, showing its involvement in the local Multiple Sclerosis Society, his role as a soccer coach, and various other community activities by his staff.
- Although trained as a civil engineer, he most enjoyed his leadership role and working with people, projects, and problems.
- Unlike many engineers, he tested as an extrovert on the Myers Briggs Personality profile, while most engineers were more introverted.
- Recently, his department began working on widening the Interstate around Des Moines.
- His team was assisting with design and traffic analyses for the project, as well as traffic flow and safety during the construction phase.
- Managing existing traffic while building highways for future traffic had become increasingly important in recent years.
- The Federal Highway Department was also working on a new, four-lane bypass in Eddyville, Iowa.
- When designed several years earlier, planners failed to fully account for the environmental sensitivity of sand dunes in the area.
- Dan was now working with the Iowa DOT to review alternate routes for the highway without substantially increasing the cost of the project.
- To level the dunes would be environmentally controversial, as would changing the design plans at this stage.
- His staff was spending considerable time at public hearings and workshops looking for solutions.

- Normally, engineers involved with rights-of-way and property rights planned and attended public hearings to answer the public's questions.
- Gaining promotions and positions with greater authority in the Federal Highway Administration often required multiple moves.
- Dan had moved eight times, having lived in Massachusetts, Maryland, North Carolina, Georgia twice, Washington, DC, and now Iowa.
- In each location, he gained experience in state-federal relations, since each state's politics were unique.
- The Highway Department rarely promoted in place; to get promoted you had to move.
- He had held a wide variety of jobs, including pavement design and in safety, and manager of field offices; he had also served as a district engineer.
- While assigned to the national headquarters in Washington, DC, he came to appreciate the complexity of national politics surrounding the Federal-Aid Highway system and its funding.
- He was ready to leave Washington, its politics, and paperwork behind when he moved to Iowa.
- He enjoyed the day-to-day management of projects and seeing the results of his department; in Washington, it was more difficult to measure his progress each day.

Life in the Community: Ames, Iowa

- Many in the community had deep roots running back several generations; they grew up in the town and never saw a need or had a desire to move.
- Located in the center of the state, Ames still retained much of the ethnic flavor introduced by German, Dutch, and Scandinavian immigrants who first began arriving in large numbers in the 1850s.
- Small comments and reactions reminded him that he would always be considered an outsider no matter how long he lived in the state.

They were pleased with the schools in Ames.

- Friday nights in Ames were reserved for high school football; the stands were packed with adults who attended the school years before and whose children had long since graduated.
- Drug use within the community was beginning to rise; community leaders didn't like to discuss the problem, but believed they must find more for teenagers to do before drug use got worse.
- A socially conservative state, laws against Sunday dancing, hunting, and horse racing were not repealed until 1955.
- The flat, vast plains of Iowa, leveled off thousands of years ago by the glaciers of the Pleistocene epoch, were largely used for farming hogs, corn, and soybeans.
- Iowa was one of the few states in which the number of people still living on farms was equal to the number of city dwellers.
- The state raised seven percent of the nation's food supply, ranking second to California in agricultural output.
- Nearly 95 percent of Iowa's land was under cultivation—almost 34 million acres divided into more than 150,000 farms.

The Interstate System

- Created by Congress in 1956, the Interstate Highway System in America was now 41 years old.
- The Great Wall of China and the Interstate Highway System were among the only human creations that could be seen by astronauts from an orbiting spacecraft.
- The property that Highway authorities had acquired in order to site the Interstates equaled a land mass the size of Delaware.
- When created, politicians and writers celebrated the goal of "man's triumph over na ture."
- President Eisenhower passionately believed in the need for a modern, interstate highway system to ensure the "personal safety, the general prosperity, the national security of the American people."
- Before the passage of the Federal-Aid Highway Act of 1956, the Bureau of Public Roads produced a 100-page book designating the 2,175 miles of proposed interstate highways.
- Congressmen, businessmen, and local politicians could study and anticipate the impact the Interstate Highway System would have on their communities.

- The Federal-Aid Highway Act of 1956 was signed by Eisenhower in June 1956 while he was recovering from surgery in Walter Reed Army Medical Center.
- The bill authorized $25 billion for 12 years to accelerate construction of a National Sys tem of Interstate and Defense Highways.
- It also created a Highway Trust Fund supported by increasing the federal tax on gas and diesel fuel from $0.02 to $0.03 cents, and increased the federal portion of construction of interstate highways to 90 percent.
- All standards were based on meeting the needs of American traffic in 1972, the year the System was slated for completion.
- Editorials nationwide lauded the legislation, since Americans valued their mobility.
- At the time, 72 percent of American families owned an automobile; by 1970, the number would rise to 82 percent.
- Despite enthusiasm, early construction went slowly.
- Even though the federal government paid for 90 percent of the costs of the new highways and could veto expenditures, individual states had the responsibility of initiating construction projects and determining when and where to build particular sections of interstate.
- In many states, including Iowa, bid rigging was common enough that several county officials were convicted and sent to prison.
- Then, in the early 1960s, with the leadership of Rex Whitton, road construction was on schedule and honest.
- By the stated 1972 completion date for the Interstate System, enough roadways had been completed so that the wide bands of concrete were highly controversial.
- Mass transit advocates were lobbying for more mass tran sit dollars in the face of a gas crisis; many areas also feared that even more urban sprawl and white flight would result from building highly ef.cient and convenient Interstates from city to city.

- From the inception of the Highway Act, the control of ex penditures and handling of federal dollars within each state had caused numerous political and .nancial tug-of-wars; by mid-1975, the question of control caused out right warfare in many cities and states.
- Highways that cut through urban areas such as Boston or San Francisco were accused of destroying neighborhoods and dividing the city.
- Despite criticism, traffic on the nation's Interstates boomed; travel time from region to region dropped dramatically.
- Soon, skiers in St. Louis thought little of driving to Colorado for the weekend; winter-weary water lovers from Michigan shot down the Interstate to Florida in record time.
- By 1986, the building of 97 percent of the System had been completed.
- Even though the Interstate System accounted for about one percent of the nation's highways, it carried about 20 percent of the nation's traffic and 50 percent of its trucks.
- People and businesses placed their lives in relation to the highway, as in, "we are about three miles east of 77 on Highway 21."
- Relocating businesses began asking more about transportation routes than about labor forces; if the roads were available, the people would come.
- In 1990, there were 115 million workers in the United States age 16 and older; fully 99.8 million of those workers rode a car, motorcycle, or truck to work, while six million used public transit, and five million walked or road a bike.
- Yet, despite the frenzy of activity, Highway System accidents actually fell.
- In 1990, just 4,941 people lost their lives on the Interstate System, which carried cars, trucks, and business 479 billion miles; the death rate per 100 million vehicle miles was 1.03.

The opening of new Interstates created excitement in the 1950s.

1997: Machinery Company Owner

Eighty-year-old Spence Dowling believed that he was worth approximately $400 million, thanks to a machinery business he had run for 50 years. Despite his wealth, he lived in a mobile home located behind his factory.

Life at Home

- Since his divorce 33 years ago, Spence Dowling had been living in a double-wide mobile home located behind the flagship plant for his company.
- The trailer was furnished with hand-me-down furniture from his grandfather's estate, plus chairs and beds bought at Sears and Roebuck.
- The dinnerware was purchased 30 years ago from the Kress' Five and Dime, formerly in downtown Columbia.
- He owned one suit for attending funerals and weddings; otherwise, he dressed as he always has—in work clothes.
- His closet was filled with overalls and flannel shirts; his wristwatch—a 1950s gold Longines—was looped through a buttonhole.
- He rarely saw his only daughter, whom he had accused of stealing money from the company. She had tried to reunite with him, even running advertisements in the newspaper requesting that he contact her. He had declined.
- He had never met three of his six grandchildren, or any of his great-grandchildren.
- His entire life revolved around work; he was fond of saying, "As long as you have work to do, food to eat and a place to sleep, what else do you need?"
- During the past 50 years he had attempted to take only two vacations—and hated it both times; "To work is to breathe," he said.
- He belonged to no social clubs and rarely ate out; he encouraged his employees to support local charities, and he also participated in their fundraising activities.
- In the past decade, he had given away more than $2 million to the local community, anonymously.
- To protect his privacy, he carried thousands of dollars with him at all times so that he rarely had to write a check or give his name.

Spence took great satisfaction in putting in long days at his own plant.

119

- Now that he had turned 80, he was reviewing his will to determine where his money should go; he was considering a major gift to the local YMCA where he did a daily workout.
- Even though the YMCA was in the center of Columbia and required a commute down the interstate, Spence was a creature of habit, and would not shift his loyalty, despite the proliferation of private gyms that were now close to his home.
- He also planned to create a multimillion-dollar endowment for the school he attended for one year—the University of South Carolina, which now enrolled 25,000 students.
- During his stay there, he planned to major in business; his will, however, directed that his money be used for educating classroom teachers.
- He did not plan to provide any money to his former wife or to his daughter, although he was planning a $250,000 educational fund for his grandchildren, provided they graduate from college in four years.
- He had been told that his IQ topped 160, but he put little stock in tests that didn't measure real-life performance.

Trinity Cathedral anchored the religious community of the city.

Life at Work

- Spence's company, Dowling Machinery & Equipment, was a specialized heavy equipment manufacturing firm created by his grandfather in the late 1800s.
- A one-man operation, the company began with his grandfather traveling the countryside in a mule-drawn wagon, visiting textile plants to repair their equipment.
- Eventually, he came to understand which plants needed what equipment and began supplying them with machinery.
- Thanks to his close working relationship with plant owners, Dowling Machinery prospered, even during the Depression, when few companies were investing in new equipment.
- Due to a willingness to repair and renovate equipment to keep the plants going during hard times, his company earned the loyalty of many businessmen who became powerful in the years after the Depression and Second World War, when South Carolina began to gain some economic momentum.
- When the woolen and worsted industry migrated to the South from New England after World War II, business exploded.
- After his one year at the University of South Carolina, Spence joined his grandfather in the business, transforming Dowling Machinery into an international conglomerate which now controlled 70 percent of the world market for card combing—the teeth that combed fibers to make cloth.
- The company was listed among America's richest in Forbes 500 list of private companies—a fact Spence hated.
- Dowling Machinery had remained privately held, despite the temptation to sell stock and gain instant wealth; Spence didn't need the money and hated having to discuss his business with anyone, thus conducting much of his banking in New York so that no one in South Carolina would know about his private affairs.

- Over the years he had purchased more than 40,000 acres across South Carolina, leasing some of the land, or selling it to companies like Home Depot or developers of upscale subdivisions.
- Much of the land he owned was near the state's sprawling interstate highways, and had been purchased as sites for giant shopping centers; his holdings also included extensive amounts of timberland.
- For the past decade, he had avoided making sales calls, even to old friends, preferring to stay at the plant and direct operations.
- The company currently employed 1,200 people in plants in South Carolina, Massachusetts, Alabama, Texas, Brazil, Canada, France, Germany, Italy, Portugal, Spain and the United Kingdom.
- He was a hands-on boss, often on the machine floor at 5 a.m.; it was not unusual for him to put in 12-hour days, even at his age.
- Because he was fair and paid well, many of his employees had worked for him for decades; they understood that there was one way to do the job right—his way.

Life in the Community: Columbia, South Carolina

- Boasting a population of 450,000, Columbia was the capital of South Carolina—situated in the center of the state.
- Located at the confluence of the Broad and Saluda Rivers, it was nearly halfway between New York City and Miami, Florida.
- The city was bordered by Lake Murray, a manmade, 50,000-acre lake that extends 41 miles upstream.
- Lake Murray, originally created to supply hydropower to the South, was recognized as one of the nation's top black bass fishing spots, and was a popular site for camping, boating and skiing.

South Carolina's Governor's Mansion

Columbia, the capital of South Carolina, boasted 450,000 residents.

Columbia's Riverbanks Zoo attracted thousands of tourists annually.

- In addition to the University of South Carolina, the capital city had nine other universities and colleges, including the historically black college of Benedict and Columbia College, which focused on women's higher education.
- Currently, Columbia is focusing enormous energy on bringing back a dying Main Street, offering tax breaks for renovation projects to attract jobs and residents to the core of the city; according the mayor, "Main Street is everyone's neighborhood."
- The city prides itself on businesses like the Capitol Newsstand on Main Street; "The Times Square Newsstand in Manhattan offers a few more newspapers than we do," the owner claims, "but not many more."
- Author, poet and Columbia resident James Dickey held one of his first book signings at the Capitol Newsstand when *Deliverance* was published.

1998: Former Printer and Caretaker

Mike and Helen Howard were in their late 50s when a serious automobile accident turned Helen into an invalid. After 35 years as a printer, Mike left his job to care for his wife. However, healthcare costs were rapidly depleting their savings.

Life at Home

- Mike made $15,000 a year working for a Boy's Home near his house; the remainder of their income was produced by investments from Helen's retirement funds, their savings, and the proceeds from a legal settlement against the automobile manufacturer.
- Mike and Helen lived in an attractive, compact 1,200-square-foot house they designed themselves outside Rock Hill, South Carolina.
- Following Helen's accident, the entire house was renovated to accommodate a wheelchair.
- They lived seven miles from town on four acres of property, which she inherited from her mother.
- Both were married before, and each had two sons.
- Six years ago, while on the way to work, she was severely injured when her car skidded and crashed on a wet road, only a mile from their house.
- Following the accident, she was in a coma for seven months in another city; Mike visited her seven days a week, twice a day, travelling one hour each way, even though she did not recognize him.
- Afterwards, Helen's 24-hour care was provided by two nurses and her husband; the cost of nursing care was $800 a week-more if he left town for the weekend.
- She was unable to feed or dress herself. Intermittently, she engaged in witty conversation for short periods, but most of the time she slept or sat silently.
- Her ability to communicate and recognize her surroundings varied widely from day to day; even on good days, her speech was difficult to understand.
- Friends often came to the lake on Sunday afternoons to fish, drink beer, and socialize; one of the friends had supplied most of the metal foundation for the dock, while another did the electrical wiring so they would have lights.
- Her special diet required by her condition elevated the food bill to more than $100 a week.
- Her diapers cost $17 a pack; and she usually required three packs a week.
- Her routine medication, after health insurance, cost approximately $100 a month.

Mike and Helen, before Helen's debilitating accident.

- Her company's insurance covered many of the medical bills, but money was often tight.
- The cost of around-the-clock nursing care equaled three times his annual pay.
- She went to the doctor at least once a month, and had been in and out of the hospital throughout the past six years for severe headaches, infections, and bladder disorders.
- Insurance and the proceeds from a legal settlement with the automobile manufacturer allowed them to provide her with excellent care, and to avoid bankruptcy.
- Because his wife often slept for long periods, Mike worked on projects around the property; he was currently restoring a 1926 farm tractor he bought for $300, and had also built a dock on the small lake on their property so Helen could sit by the water.
- He planted large numbers of roses on the side of the house facing her bedroom window.
- For more than a year, he spent all of his time caring for his wife and redoing their home, including installing a bathroom capable of accepting a wheelchair.
- He had finally realized that she would never be better.
- They purchased a special van, fitted for her disabilities, so she could travel around the community comfortable; it cost $40,000 to equip.
- Before the accident, they spent weekends travelling to antique shows and markets where he bought and sold old bottles, while she looked for decorative pottery.

Having friends over took Helen's mind off of her struggles.

124

He collected 150-year-old bitters bottles.

- Mike's collected 150-year-old bitters bottles made in the shape of Indian squaws, an ear of corn, or log cabins.
- Occasionally he still attended antique shows, but rarely bought anything; he has lost much of his interest in fine antique bottles.

Life at Work

- Before the accident, he was working as a printer for 35 years, operating sophisticated, four-color printing presses, as well as supervising regular black and white print runs.
- He often went to work at 4 a.m. to meet deadlines or worked late at night; he was allowed to set his own schedules as long as deadlines were met.
- Three years ago, the company consolidated its operations in another city, and he was offered a job in the new location, but declined.
- To fill his time, he got a job as a facilities supervisor at a Boy's Home near his house, doing maintenance and helping the boys; the hours were flexible and management is supportive of his situation.
- He saw himself in many of the unfocused young men who were sent to the home; most repairs and construction projects were designed to include assistance from the boys.
- The 14 boys living in the home had all been expelled from school at least once before coming here, and most were sentenced by the courts to a home; most of the boys believed they had no future, and acted accordingly.

Mike enjoyed his time helping the young men find their skills.

- The Boy's Home was making plans to create a regular school for the boys in the home, as most found themselves expelled from the Rock Hill schools shortly after coming to the home.
- Thanks to friends willing to serve as volunteer teachers, Mike was now conducting classes in refrigerator repair and auto mechanics.

Life in the Community: Rock Hill, North Carolina

- Mike had lived in Rock Hill his entire life, and had many friends.
- His mother lived nearby, although she was not in good health.
- The members of the American Veterans of Foreign Wars had been very supportive; Mike's family had attended several dances at the VFW, and danced, despite the limited use of Helen's legs.
- He had served in the navy at the young age of 17, earning his place in the VFW while in a combat zone near Lebanon in the 1950s; he was stationed on a mine sweeper.
- Historically, Rock Hill was a textile town dominated by a few industries; textile villages, composed of hundreds of small houses, dominated the community.
- The city was proud of Winthrop University, which was in the center of town and had originally been established as a teacher's college.
- The largest garden in Rock Hill was the Glencairn Garden, opened by its owner, who donated the six-acre park after planting hundreds of azaleas, camellias, and other southern favorites.
- The city of Rock Hill was fast becoming a suburb of the rapidly growing city of Charlotte, North Carolina.
- Through a series of mergers, two Charlotte-based banks were now among the 10 largest in the nation, and combined, they employed 20,000 people in Charlotte.
- IBM, Microsoft, and other major corporations eventually established facilities in Charlotte, drawing workers from 10-counties, including Rock Hill.
- Every morning more than 22,000 Rock Hill residents traveled north on Interstate 77 for jobs in Charlotte; the roads were often jammed.

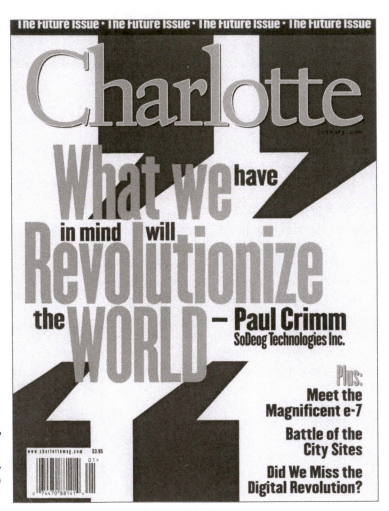

1998: High School Soccer Player and Coach

When Frankie Parsons did not make the high school varsity soccer team his junior year, he turned to coaching to stay involved with the game.

Life at Home

- Frankie Parsons began his soccer career at age six.
- He played for the Prince William County (Virginia) REC League; they were called the Skyrockets and wore royal blue shirts.
- Frankie mostly played defense; his main job was to stop the forward from scoring goals.
- After one season, his family moved to Summerville, South Carolina, and he began playing for the Summerville YMCA youth league, where he continued to stop the forwards from advancing to the goal.
- For six years he toiled in the YMCA league before being recruited by the Summerville Soccer Club.
- Three years later he made its Classic team, composed of the highest skilled players who traveled the southeast playing on weekends.
- During his junior year of high school, Frankie was recruited by the area rival Hungryneck Soccer Club, where he played marking back for the men's Under-19 team.
- But to his deep disappointment, he did not make the high school varsity team his junior year.
- Frankie turned to coaching to stay involved with soccer, taking on a coed under-10-years-old team for the Summerville Soccer Club.
- He earned his first coaching certification license that year: the US Soccer F license.
- He also began to draw on the coaching philosophy he learned at the Ralph Lundy summer soccer camp and applied it to his team.
- In addition, Frankie enrolled in the teacher cadet program, designed to get students interested in being teachers.
- Frankie taught fourth and eighth graders; the eighth grade class he taught reunited him with his own eighth grade teacher, Mr. Clark.
- His coaching career began in high school.
- The fall of his senior year, he was asked to coach the Summerville Soccer Club's boys REC U-12 team.

Frankie Parsons decided to coach soccer instead of play.

- During his search for colleges that year, he concentrated on quality schools where he might play soccer.
- He also wanted a small school, and mainly concentrated his search to Division III schools.
- He decided to go to Erskine College in Due West, South Carolina, because it was an in-state school where he could use a tuition grant that made the school affordable.

Life at Work

- Frankie Parsons was a walk-on for Erskine College's soccer team; his first year he compiled 35 minutes of playing time.
- After that, he returned to coaching.
- His training sessions (practices) were organized around the Ralph Lundy Method; the skill is displayed, then the players break into groups and practice the skill demonstrated.
- He worked to avoid unproductive habits such as singling out players, which can break down the team culture, allowing players to be apathetic.
- Frankie believed that quality team culture demanded that everyone respect one another.

His coaching career began in high school.

- Players didn't have to be friends, but they did have to respect every team member.
- It was the coach's job to teach the players how to be better and work their hardest at every task.
- As a coach, Frankie learned how to be a leader and a mentor, not a buddy, and not to acknowledge favorites, which fostered a poor team culture.
- After college Frankie moved to Columbia, South Carolina, for graduate school and continued his soccer coaching career.

Frankie made sure he treated all players the same.

- He was told by his new club that if he got his South Carolina Youth Soccer Association D Coaching license, he would be paid $750 per season.
- The first semester of graduate school, Frankie began coaching the U-12 Lightnings for the Irmo Soccer Association.
- It was the club's only girls' team.
- The assemblage of players was a hodgepodge of 8-12-year-olds of varying skill levels.
- He knew immediately he had his work cut out for him.

The Lightnings were a champion team.

- Frankie also quickly learned the difference between coaching boys and girls: boys you pushed, girls you guided—especially younger girls.
- Girls were also much more social and had to be guided to keep their focus; girls also wanted to develop personal friendships with the coach, which allowed Frankie to figure out the different motivators for each girl.
- At their first game, the Lightnings won 4-1.
- It was the first of many wins.
- In the spring of 1995, Frankie's team found themselves in the State Finals, in a strange twist of fate, against the Hungryneck Hurricanes.
- The game ended in a tie and was decided by penalty kicks; Frankie's team lost by one.
- After the game the goalkeeper and the player who had missed her penalty kick were inconsolable.
- Frankie and his assistant coach did their best to stay positive and felt it was time to lead by example.
- He told the team they played great and that they were champions, even though they'd not won their last game.
- Frankie reminded his girls how much they'd improved and how much fun they had all had together.
- He emphasized how impressed their parents were in the amount of progress they'd made in one season.
- Overall, it had been a great season.

Frankie coached the newly-named Nightmares.

- That fall, he was rehired to coach the U-12 girls' team; they renamed themselves the Nightmares.
- That year Frankie made another discovery: parents can be one of the worst parts of youth sports.
- One parent secretly paid his child to score goals, which disrupted the team mentality; another parent was loudly abusive to referees, opposing players and fans.
- And Frankie kept on winning, including a six-state tournament in Jacksonville, Florida.

- He also got a boost from the 1996 Summer Olympics and the U.S. Women's team gold medal win that significantly spurred interest by girls to the sport of soccer.
- In the spring of 1997, Frankie went to the next level and began coaching the junior varsity girls at Cardinal Newman, a small private school in Columbia.
- He was invited to coach the girls through a connection he'd made in the area's soccer network.
- Here, too, he had his work cut out for him; newly found enthusiasm for soccer did not necessarily equal skilled players with years of experience.

Cardinal Newman High School's JV team.

- By the spring of 1998, Frankie was coaching the Cardinal Newman JV team and the U-13 Nightmares.
- Older players did not play in the spring, as that is when high school soccer is in season.
- He was also helping two other coaches with a U-10 girls' advanced REC team, working to create a feeder system of talent.
- During the spring of 1998, Frankie took his U-13 girls to a tournament in Johnsonville, Tennessee, where they lost to a team from Ann Arbor, Michigan.
- One of the traditions at soccer tournaments was for each team to exchange club patches, embroidered with each club's logo.
- Although his girls had many patches from other teams in previous tournaments, the highlight of this one was to receive a patch from a team that was from so far away.
- The league also decided to pay for Frankie to get his National Soccer Association Class C coaching license: $1,000 dollars for an eight-day residential clinic at an out-of-state sports complex.
- The National Class C clinic consisted of morning classroom time and a field session, an afternoon classroom and field session, and an after-dinner two- to three-hour field session.

Frankie and his assistant coach were proud their team made it to the tournament.

- The last day of the clinic, the coaches were required to do a main field assessment, which was an assessment of tactical and technical training techniques and an oral and written exam.
- Not everyone who attended the clinic was certified as a Class C coach by the National Soccer Association.
- Frankie passed his exams and was certified by the reigning body of U.S. soccer as a National Class C coach.
- After he received his certification, he was asked to be the director of soccer for the club, giving him a $10,000 raise in addition to his $2,300 per team he coached.

Life in the Community: Columbia, South Carolina

- Columbia was home to the main campus of the University of South Carolina, which was chartered in 1801 as South Carolina College.
- The city itself had a population of 116,278.
- It was founded in 1786 as the site of South Carolina's new capital and was one of the first planned cities in the United States.
- Located at the confluence of two major rivers, Columbia grew rapidly with cotton as its economic lifeblood.
- Columbia's First Baptist Church hosted the South Carolina Secession Convention on December 17, 1860, where the delegates approved a resolution in favor of secession, 159-0.
- In February 1865, during the Civil War, much of Columbia was destroyed by fire while being occupied by Union troops under the command of General William Tecumseh Sherman.
- Frankie and his assistant coach were proud their team made it to the tournament.
- The National Soccer Association certified Frankie as a coach.
- According to legend, Columbia's First Baptist Church barely missed being torched by Sherman's troops.
- The soldiers marched up to the church and asked the groundskeeper if he could direct them to the church where the declaration of secession was signed.
- The loyal groundskeeper directed the men to a nearby Methodist church; thus, the historic landmark was saved from destruction.
- During Reconstruction, journalists, travelers and tourists flocked to South Carolina's capital city to witness a Southern state legislature whose members included ex-slaves.
- Columbia had no paved streets until 1908, when 17 blocks of Main Street were surfaced.
- There were, however, 115 publicly maintained street crossings at intersections to keep pedestrians from having to wade through a sea of mud between wooden sidewalks.

In 1865, fire destroyed much of Columbia.

- In 1917, the city was selected as the site of Camp Jackson, which grew into the U.S. Army's largest training facility.
- On August 21, 1962, eight downtown chain stores served blacks at their lunch counters for the first time.
- The University of South Carolina admitted its first black students in 1963.
- As many vestiges of segregation began to disappear from the city, blacks attained membership on various municipal boards and commissions, and a non-discriminatory hiring policy was adopted by the city.
- These and other such signs of racial progression helped earn the city the 1964 All-America City Award for the second time, and a 1965 article in Newsweek magazine lauded Columbia as a city that had "liberated itself from the plague of doctrinal apartheid."
- By 1990 the Columbia metropolitan population reached 470,000.

Columbia, South Carolina

1998: Young Indian Student in Transition

Emigration from India led Gashwin Gomes from a study of geology to one of theology when he settled at the University of South Carolina.

Life at Home

- Gashwin Gomes experienced a more advantageous childhood than most people in India.
- His father's occupation as an economist and his involvement in numerous business operations brought atypical opportunities, including a brief stay during Gashwin's early childhood in the United States.
- The family lived in Maryland, near where Manu Gomes, Gashwin's father, worked as an economist at the World Bank in Washington, DC.
- Some of his earliest childhood memories were of the United States—playing catch with his brother Gautam or chasing a neighbor's dog, Rusty, around in the backyard.
- When the U.S. assignment ended, his family returned to India; Gashwin was five years old.
- In his home country of India his father worked as an economic advisor for Merrill Lynch and oversaw its Indian mutual funds.
- Gashwin's mother held a position within the Indian Government's Administrative Service.
- Because Gashwin's parents both worked, a housekeeper took care of the home and watched after their two sons.
- The Gomes family grew up in a modest-sized residence: a four-bedroom condominium located in downtown Bombay.
- It was in an attractive location next to a nature sanctuary; thus, the area's beauty could be seen from the windows and balcony and would not be spoiled by the constant development in the city.
- To get around town, the family owned two Indian-made cars; one was a Fiat and the other an Ambassador.
- Academics were important to Gashwin's father.
- A graduate of the London School of Economics, he knew that education was imperative to success and economic stability for his children, a concept he constantly reinforced with his two sons.

Gashwin Gomes left India after college to further his studies in the United States.

- Gashwin struggled in school initially and would often cringe when bringing home scores below his father's expectations.
- He also heard a few taunts from his older brother, who did better academically.
- By high school Gashwin had discovered a strong interest in science.
- Learning about the formation of the natural world and its life fascinated him.
- He was especially interested in the physical environment; rocks and geography were his passions.
- Gashwin's bedroom shelves were covered with rocks that he discovered outside in the neighborhood or on family trips.
- His desire was to collect every known rock in the world, even the rarest forms created by volcanic activity.
- His father wished him the best of luck with this task, knowing full well that it was next to impossible.
- Education was not the only thing important to the Gomes family; religion held a special significance as well.
- Living in a Hindu household, the family made a point of practicing their beliefs, especially around the big festivals of Diwali, Dussera and Holi.
- These holy days included visits to the neighborhood temple, spending the occasions with relatives and eating wonderful family prepared meals.
- Often Gashwin and his cousins received lots of sweets from family members as part of these celebrations.
- With his success in high school, Gashwin was accepted into St. Xavier's University of Bombay, a private accredited university in Bombay administered by the Jesuits.
- It was here that he focused on his passion for geology.

A temple in Bombay.

Gashwin excelled at St. Xavier's.

- Gashwin's father retired from Merrill Lynch as soon as Gashwin received his acceptance to college.
- After Gashwin's parents moved to his father's hometown of Baroda, India, he remained in the family condo and attended to his university studies.
- The education system of India was strongly influenced by the British and still maintained striking similarities.
- When accepted to university, a student traditionally followed one of the three academic levels from high school—Humanities, Commerce or Science.
- The three-year program only focused on core studies based upon the program; thus, one would not traditionally see a student in the Commerce program taking a history course traditionally reserved for a Humanities student.

Gashwin's large extended family gathered during holy day festivals.

- However, coursework at St. Xavier's was untraditional.
- To Gashwin's surprise, he was required to take a select number of humanities courses outside of his academic tract of science.
- The experience exposed him to some history and foreign language studies; already fluent in Hindi and English, he also added the German language to his résumé.
- The university system in India traditionally required mostly rote memorization and less critical thinking; due to substantial government academic subsidies, the cost was approximately between US$300-$400 over the entire three years in school.
- Gashwin embraced his academic studies in geology and focused on petrology, the study of volcanic rocks.
- His scientific coursework required the least amount of mathematics and enabled him to conduct research in an outside environment.

With his godmother in India, before leaving for the United States.

- Socially, Gashwin spent time with friends, gathered at local dance clubs on the weekend, and watched sporting events, like soccer and cricket, on television.
- Students typically lived at home with their parents or in an apartment near school; the universities in India did not provide housing, neither dorms nor apartments, for students.
- Although like most of his friends, Gashwin was a practicing Hindu, he slowly became interested in Christianity and the teachings of Catholicism.

- This change happened gradually during his time learning from the priests at St. Xavier and becoming involved at St. Peter's Church in a suburb of Bombay.
- During his last year of university, Gashwin shared with his parents his desire to convert from Hinduism to a Christian faith.
- Though it caught his parents by surprise, they realized the decision was thought out and their son desired this conversion.
- Although bewildered at this spiritual change, they supported his decision.
- Between his academic coursework and his religious instruction at St. Peter's Church, the year was exceptionally busy for Gashwin.

Gashwin was baptized into the Catholic faith.

- Nonetheless, he excelled in his studies.
- By April of 1993, he graduated from St. Xavier's with his degree.
- It was also during this period that he applied to a number of universities in the United States to work on his graduate education.
- His older brother Gautam acquired his doctorate of computer science at Rensselaer Polytechnic Institute in New York.
- Upon completion, he accepted a professorship at the India Institute of Technology in Delhi.
- Gashwin applied to six universities in the United States, which included the University of South Carolina and the University of Rochester in New York.
- Both of these universities offered full scholarships in the field of geology.
- After serious contemplation and without visiting any of the options, he decided to attend the University of Rochester because his graduate advisor was receiving a grant in petrology research in India.
- It was an ideal opportunity—studying his passion and having the opportunity to return to India for research.
- Prior to his departure, Gashwin maintained strong ties with his new religious community and was baptized at St. Peter's in August.
- It was an important event and, though reluctant, his family attended the service.
- With graduation and his baptism behind him, he needed to prepare for his journey to the United States for graduate school.
- He packed two large suitcases and a few books—the sum of all he was taking with him from India.
- Outside of his belongings, his father stressed the importance of extended family.
- Family was not only the immediate relatives in India, but those he would meet and with whom he would share his life within the United States.

University of Rochester.

Life at Work

- Excitement was the initial emotion for Gashwin Gomes on his journey to the United States, but fatigue set in from the 20-hour flight on British Airways with layovers in London and Boston.
- By the time he arrived in Rochester, he was exhausted and ready for some sleep.
- Fortunately, his extended family network was already being formed.
- At the University of Rochester, the Indian Student Association sent members to greet arriving Indian students at the airport.
- Bhanu, an undergrad student, was there to meet and welcome Gashwin to Rochester and allowed him to stay at his apartment for a couple of days until he could find his own place.
- A couple of days of sleeping on a couch motivated Gashwin to find an apartment with another grad student and make contact with the Catholic community on campus.
- His father's advice on establishing an extended family was sound, Gashwin discovered, and made the transition into the United States culture less of a challenge.
- Gashwin's work-study job required him to assist his advisor with grading papers and course projects, conducting field work for research and instructing students on field assignments.
- Because his work was in geology, it was not uncommon for him to be lugging a lot of rocks around the university.
- His biggest learning curve was computers.
- Undergraduate students had no access to them in India; the only time he used his father's computer was to play video games.
- In the United States, all of his written assignments required that he fully understand Windows 3.1 and WordPerfect.
- It struck him as odd seeing everything printed using computer software on campus—flyers regarding fraternity parties, group meetings and university events.
- The university community was expressing that it was literate with software but using the technology on trivial matters—an observation he shared in handwritten letters to family and friends in India.
- His fellow graduate students were actively using a new and growing form of electronic communication, but few people in India used e-mail.
- Therefore, the number of computer messages he received was limited except for university matters such as student meetings or discovering information on the World Wide Web with Internet software GOPHER and Mosaic.
- His biggest concern was that his advisor "miscommunicated" the focus of his research when he recruited Gashwin to Rochester; the focus was not petrology research, but instead he had a grant to study water isotopes—a field that held no interest for Gashwin.
- With the support of the Catholic community on campus, where he developed a number of close friendships with people who were also Indians, Gashwin decided to transfer.
- He had no desire to spend four years studying in a field in which he had no interest and reporting to an uncommunicative advisor.
- He talked to his parents about the problem, but calls home were expensive and usually cost $1 per minute.

Outside his apartment in Rochester.

- Knowing he received a full scholarship at the University of South Carolina, he contacted the department in Columbia to see if there was an opportunity to transfer.
- After a tour and interviews with faculty, he was accepted at the beginning of the fall semester; his future advisor was able to maintain his offer of the scholarship.
- Upon his return to Rochester, Gashwin kept the exciting news quiet, telling only a small circle of friends, mostly those he knew within the Catholic community.

Life in the Community: Columbia, South Carolina

- Gashwin's ability to adapt to South Carolina was aided by his American-style accent which he had acquired early in his childhood.
- Therefore, he was more easily accepted by Americans than were his friends who had more of an "Indian English" accent.
- Upon arrival in Columbia, South Carolina, Gashwin established his extended community within the Catholic student center; he did make a few friends within the Indian community, but most Indians did not share his religious faith.
- Through an ad search he found an apartment a few blocks from the university with a master's in business student at USC.
- He quickly partook of one of the common activities during football season: tailgating outside the stadium with his girlfriend Sarah McClutchen and some of his classmates.
- He also started to define himself based upon his involvement at St. Thomas More, on the campus of USC, the Catholic student center that had become a second home.
- Even though he shared Christianity with his new American friends, his view of family relationships was different from theirs.
- Most openly discussed family problems with each other, the issues of divorces or dreading family visits due to the inconvenience.
- Divorce was uncommon in India, and the extended family based upon step-parents and siblings was most unusual.
- One of his most embarrassing moments was constantly confusing Sarah's mother and stepmother on a day they both were in town visiting on Parent's Weekend.
- Sarah, a child of a divorced family, often complained about her parents.
- When her folks visited for the weekends, she mentioned the inconvenience of having family in town.
- Within Gashwin's cultural perspective, family visits were typically long and a welcomed inconvenience instead of a burden on one's individual liberty.
- While working on his master's degree in the university's Geology Department was fulfilling for Gashwin, he felt a stronger calling in another direction—the religious life.
- When he shared this news with his girlfriend Sarah, the conversation did not go well; his faith would require him to enter

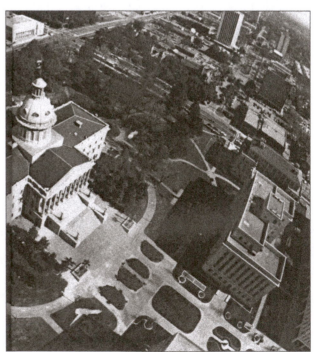

Columbia, South Carolina

the priesthood, which, in the Catholic Church, required men to be unmarried and celibate.

- As Gashwin began talking extensively with those in the Catholic diocese of Charleston and changing his academic focus to Religious Studies, Sarah realized he was serious.
- At first she thought it might be a phase and he would continue in geology.
- Numerous arguments ensued between Gashwin and Sarah during the next several months when this topic was discussed; over time she came to realize that her relationship with Gashwin would not lead to marriage but would remain only as a strong friendship.
- Gashwin's decision shocked his parents.
- Converting to another faith was challenging enough to understand, but for their son never to marry was almost unfathomable.
- The idea of their son's life without a wife or children was hard to accept for them.
- During the fall of 1995, Gashwin received a fellowship at USC under the university's Chaplains Association and completed his work in the spring of 1998.
- With a degree in hand, his visa expired and required to return to India, Gashwin had some decisions to make.
- The United States was Gashwin's new home, and he could work with the diocese to acquire his legal status there.
- Under U.S. law, one may acquire documentation for permanent residency if one spends two years as a religious worker.
- To delay entering the priesthood for two years and work for the Charleston diocese was required to

Gashwin and friends in South Carolina.

fulfill his dream if he wished to remain in America.

- An additional 24-month wait was required prior to any processing of a green card.

Columbia, South Carolina

1998: High School Soccer Player

As a high school sophomore, Robin Lye played on a basketball team that emerged second in the state, a soccer team that was state champion, and was named player of the year. Plus, she was a straight-A student.

Life at Home

- The past year had been rewarding.
- It began with the high school cross-county season last fall, when Robin finished eighth in the state of Georgia, and fifth in Atlanta.
- Soccer, however, was her real passion.
- During the same season, Robin played "club" soccer with girls aged 17 years and under, many actively recruited for the team from seven other high schools in the area.
- Each weekend they would travel as far as Jacksonville, Florida; Columbia, South Carolina; Washington, DC; or Raleigh, North Carolina, to play soccer against the region's best teams.
- They won more than half their games and were seen by a wide range of college recruiting coaches; because Robin was a sophomore, no coach was allowed to talk with her, but many asked questions of her coach.
- When basketball season arrived, the high school coach asked her if she would try out, and she became the only white girl on the squad.
- Her school, which was 50 percent African-American, generally observed clear dividing lines—black girls play basketball and white girls play soccer.
- Most of the teams they played reflected the same racial makeup; at most basketball games, 90 percent of the fans were African-American, while at the soccer games, less than five percent were black.
- Her primary job on the basketball team was playing defense, and she was only occasionally called upon for her skills.

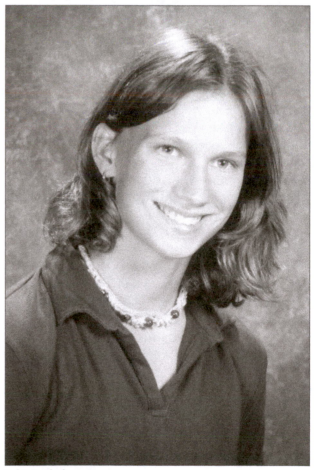

Robin Lye had a great year.

Robin travelled throughout the South and played soccer on weekends.

- Her jump shot was awkward, and the source of great amusement for her more experienced teammates.
- Before one important game, when the other members of the team decided to fashion their hair in cornrows, Robin wove her hair into French braids in a show of unity.
- Spanning two seasons, the team won 40 games in a row, before losing in the state finals.
- Because she never left the bench in the final game, she was unsure whether she would rejoin the basketball team next year, or simply focus on visiting colleges, rock climbing, water sports and soccer.
- Rock climbing was a particular attraction because her fellow athletes were so laid-back and supportive.
- She believed she could be less self-conscious while rock climbing than in any of the team sports she played.
- She especially enjoyed the fact that many of the indoor climbing walls in the area provided both physical and mental challenges.
- Several times, her athletic skills allowed her to reach places that turned into dead ends, but now she was learning to combine her strength with excellent planning.
- The highlight of the year was high school soccer, where she played with many of her best friends.
- Entering the season, she and her teammates knew the coach would be leaving in the fall to attend law school, so they wanted the year to be special.
- He delayed his entry into law school for one year so he could coach the team; he, too, wanted the year to be special.
- Robin played center forward, and was the leading scorer on the team.
- She believed her greatest skill was passing and creating good ball movement.
- The two-week buildup to the game was exciting, as they worked their way through the playoffs.

The fans were enthusiastic at the championship game.

- On the day of the championship, held at her high school's highly manicured, natural grass stadium, the student body arrived in force.
- For the first time all season, all seats were filled an hour before the game, and many of the fans had brought giant banners and horns.
- Having lived with the embarrassment of the basketball team's loss of its state championship game, Robin was focused on winning.
- The first half ended in a scoreless tie, and then the other team scored first to break the deadlock, 1-0.
- Late in the game, Robin sprinted past two defenders and drove the tying goal into the upper corner of the net, forcing the game into overtime.
- During the extra time period, with the crowd screaming, she contributed two additional assists, resulting in a 3-1 victory; it was the school's first state championship in women's soccer.
- Pandemonium reigned afterward.
- Following the game, a panel of coaches named her player of the year, even though she was only a sophomore, and the local sportswriters then bestowed on her the same honor, earning her a picture in the newspaper.
- The three local television stations showed her goal and assists over and over.
- She realized that the quality of her coaches, uniforms, fields and referees were a direct result of the 1972 Title IX law that required schools to provide equal opportunities for men and women.
- In 1972, females represented seven percent of high school varsity athletes, while now, they represented 42 percent.
- At the college level, the number of women athletes rose from 15 percent to 42 percent during the same period.
- Now that school was over, Robin was working at a summer camp in the mountains of North Carolina as a junior counselor.

- Her cabin was populated with nine-year-olds who had a fascination with her personal life, especially her boyfriend.
- Even the slightest tidbit of information would keep them up for hours giggling with each other.
- When the year began, she was dating a senior from a neighboring school, whom she could only see after school and on weekends.
- The relationship ended when she caught him with another girl.
- Within two months, she met a guy at a local gym, a college sophomore who was working his way through school.
- Her parents, who divorced eight years ago, were uncomfortable with the four-year age difference.

Robin scored during the championship game.

- Robin's mother, in particular, was concerned about the relationship, but her father made very few negative comments, and even invited her boyfriend to the house for meals and conversation.
- Since the divorce, Robin had lived with her mother, even though her parents had joint custody.
- Her parents lived only a few miles apart; she spent Wednesdays, Thursdays and every other weekend with her father, who remarried several years ago.
- Recently, as part of the divorce settlement, her mother sold the home in which Robin had grown up to help pay college tuition for her older brother.

Following the championship victory, pandemonium reigned.

- Robin still did not think it was fair that her mother and father waited six years until her brother graduated from high school to sell the family house, but could not wait three more years for her graduation.
- One of the hardest parts of living between two houses was telling friends where to find her on any given day.
- She also worried that if she left schoolbooks and notes she needed for homework at one house, someone would get mad.
- When she was in middle school, she felt different from other kids because of the divorce; everyone else's parents were married, and many had stay-at-home moms who could help with school projects.
- Now, though, it bothered her less, especially since she had a car and could drive where she needed to be.

Life at School

- Last year, in an attempt to raise standards and test scores, Robin's school adopted block scheduling, in which all classes were 93 minutes long, and last for only one semester.
- Robin took four classes per semester, 2 of which are AAP, or Advanced Academic Placement classes for college.
- She was also taking two AP, or advanced placement, classes, allowing her to earn college credit if she passed a nationally sanctioned exam at the end of the semester.
- She thought the longer classes were stupid, believing that the absorption rate of high school students—even smart ones—ended long before the 93 minutes are up.
- Besides, most of the teachers geared their lesson plans to 50-minute classes, and most had difficulty shifting to the longer format, resulting in wasted time.
- Last semester, she took Spanish 4, U.S. history, chemistry, and business computer applications.
- Her favorite was chemistry, because of both the subject and the entertaining way the teacher presented the material.
- This semester, she was taking anatomy and physiology, precalculus, history and English.
- Her English class, which included an intensive unit on writing, was taught by her favorite teacher.
- Unlike many of her other teachers, Ms. Haggett provided the freedom to learn; if you knew the material and didn't want to pay attention all the time, it was okay.
- Robin was preparing to take the SAT exam; her PSAT came in at 1260, but she wanted to break 1400 to ensure a good choice of colleges.
- Friends had repeatedly said she was a shoo-in to get a college soccer scholarship, but, having heard that college soccer was all-consuming and would dominate her life, she was unsure if she wanted to play in college.
- Besides, she dreamt of attending a college that would prepare her for a career in medicine, and though she had not yet chosen a school, her criteria included an out-of-state location and a pre-med course.

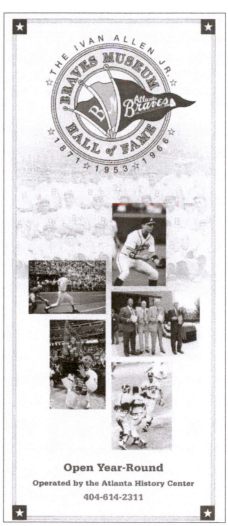

Open Year-Round
Operated by the Atlanta History Center
404-614-2311

Atlanta was known for its innovative educational programs.

- In class rank, she was now number five overall in a class of 350, having moved from the number eight slot as a freshman; in her high school career she had made one B out of all A's.
- She was also trying to decide how active she would like to be in her high school sorority.
- As a freshman, she was honored to be invited by the popular girls into the social club, which was banned by the school because of its exclusivity, but she was now wondering how much time she wanted to devote to it.
- Athletics and schoolwork allowed her only occasionally to attend the parties thrown by the group.
- Currently, the newspapers were replete with stories about high school drug use; when her father asked about marijuana, she readily admitted that a lot of people "smoke up" in the mornings.
- Acid and cocaine, she believed, were used primarily by the rich kids in school who could afford a more expensive high.
- Alcohol, especially beer, was the drug of choice at her school; it was readily available at parties, especially those that formed almost spontaneously at homes where parents had left for a weekend, trusting their children to do the right thing.

Life in the Community: Atlanta, Georgia

- The city of Atlanta, where the 1996 Olympics were held, was struggling with what to do with the Olympic caldron, the symbol of the summer games.
- Atlanta media mogul and billionaire Ted Turner, who recently pledged $1 billion to the United Nations, was being criticized because his foundation had only given $2.7 million to Atlanta-based charities.
- Atlanta ranked fifth among major American cities in the percentage of people living in poverty.
- The latest FBI statistics showed that the city's murder rate plunged to 36 murders per 100,000 residents, the lowest level in a decade.
- An intensive manhunt continued for Eric Rudolph, accused of three bombings in Atlanta, including a blast at Centennial Olympic Park during the Olympics.

Atlanta was the home of the 1996 Olympics.

1998: Professional Musician and Teacher

Zachary Alexander's French horn earned him a partial college scholarship, a fellowship to Europe, and his first job—not bad for a brass instrument consisting of about 12-13 feet of tubing wrapped into a coil with a flared bell.

Life at Home

- Zachary Alexander used to describe himself as a musician who played the French horn in a symphony orchestra.
- But now that the International Horn Society had recommended that the German-made horn no longer be attributed to the French, Zachary tells people that he is a hornist—a word that's sometimes misunderstood.
- And now that he was spending more time teaching children to love music of all kinds than he was playing his horn, he liked to consider himself a musical mentor.
- All he knew was that he loved his life; he was living the dream.
- Born in Belleville, Illinois, in August 1968, Zachary moved with his family a dozen times before he graduated from high school in Bloomington, Indiana.
- Every move was more difficult than the last, especially as the potential friends got older and their social engagements more complex.
- Outgoing and eager to have friends, Zachery relied on his sense of humor and his French horn.
- He learned early that one short tune with the French horn would transform him from the dorky new kid to the interesting horn player; he was never the most popular, but the French horn allowed him to develop solid friendships wherever he went.
- Of all the instruments, the French horn boasts a certain glamour that goes beyond the mystique of its rich tone, developed through its unusual length.
- The second-highest sounding instrument group in the brass family, French horns had a difficult mouthpiece that supported a wide usable range—approximately four octaves—depending on the ability of the player.
- To produce different notes on the horn, Zachary had to press the valves and hold the appropriate amount of lip tension while blowing air into the instrument and placing his hand in the bell.
- Zachary Alexander remained outgoing—and true to his French horn—during his dozen or so family moves.
- It wasn't for everyone.

Zachary Alexander remained outgoing—and true to his French horn—during his dozen or so family moves.

- More lip tension and faster air produced higher notes; the right hand, cupped at a "three o-clock" position in the bell, could lower the pitch.
- The limitations on the range of the instrument are primarily governed by the available valve combinations for the first four octaves of the overtone series, and after that by the ability of players to control the pitch through their air supply and embouchure.
- Many pieces from the Baroque to Romantic periods are written in keys other than F.
- Early horns were originally played on a hunt, often while mounted, and the sound they produced was called a recheat; the change of pitch was effected entirely by the lips.
- Around 1815, the use of valves opened up a great deal more flexibility for playing in different keys; in effect, the horn became an entirely different instrument—fully chromatic for the first time.
- Zachary's first love was the trumpet, which he played until he was seven when his older brother told him he wasn't any good at it and then proceeded to demonstrate the musical holes in Zachary's education.
- Zachary found his father's French horn in the back corner of his closet a few days later, and the boy and the instrument became inseparable.
- Following college graduation and a fellowship in Barcelona, Spain, Zachary was named to the position of Third Horn with the Oklahoma Symphony Orchestra, where he spent five years struggling to learn the music of the Masters and how to interpret the tonal shifts of modern composers.
- But it was in his next position as Principal Horn with the Savannah Symphony Orchestra, where he helped create a youth program, that he understood how to blend his musical side with his gregarious teaching side.
- The youth program was designed to make classical music fun.
- Zachary wanted to mold the musically intelligent audience of the future.

Life at Work

- Zachary Alexander understood that the field of music was competitive; only a tiny percentage of those who trained as musicians actually became employed as performers.
- Yet everyone had been issued two ears and the intellect—with a little training—to appreciate the sounds made by a well-coordinated orchestra.
- So when he left Savannah for the Pittsburgh Symphony Orchestra two years later, his goal was to divide his time equally between musician and educator.
- Zachary liked to think that every musician who had breathed through its brass was a genial soul.
- He also learned the amazing variety of questions children invariably asked: "They want to know what I do with my lips, why I put my hand in the bell, and how my horn works.
- I have even been asked why my eyebrows go up and down when I play," he said.
- Those were just the kind of conversations he liked to have with curious kids; as for the twitching of his eyebrows: "I have no idea. It just happens."
- Now, prior to designated concerts, families had an opportunity to meet guest artists and learn

Zachary developed and taught a youth program for young musicians.

Family Night Backstage introduced children of all ages to classical concerts—above are the Pittsburgh Symphony Horns.

more about the instrument and the music the musicians would be playing.

- "As musicians, we deal with communication through music," Zachary said.
- "This is an opportunity to use our mouths to explain how we make sounds come out of our instruments."
- The Family Night Backstage series was designed to introduce children of all ages to classical music and orchestral concerts in a non-threatening atmosphere.
- Zachary developed and taught a youth program for young musicians.
- "It's good to have a little taste of the music beforehand; they should also know something about the instruments they will be seeing."
- Family Night parties, however, were not designed to be hands-on experience for children.
- Professional musicians are understandably squeamish about anyone else touching the instruments with which they make their living, Zackary said "Little kids are wide open for the experience," he said.
- "More and more, we see families there with little kids wearing jackets and ties."
- For busy families seeking ways to spend quality time with the children, the Symphony Orchestra has many pluses.
- "This is more than a visit to the McDonald's Playground—we are looking for something that is a real growing experience for the child."
- There's nothing like going to a live concert, and that goes for any age.
- Zachary said it doesn't bother him when a youngster stands up in the middle of a symphony concert and announces, "'Look at that cool horn!' If I were playing the Brandenburg Concertos, it might be disruptive," he said.
- "But at the family concert, it's not out of place. Nothing delights me more."
- The modern orchestra has its historical roots in ancient Egypt, where the first orchestras were composed of small groups of musicians who gathered for festivals, holidays or funerals.

- True modern orchestras started in the late sixteenth century when composers started writing music for instrumental groups.
- In the sixteenth century, wealthy Italian households had musicians to provide music for dancing and the court, as well as the theater, particularly opera.
- In the seventeenth century and early eighteenth century, instrumental groups were recruited from the best available talent.
- As nobility began to build retreats away from towns, they hired musicians to form permanent ensembles.
- Composers such as the young Joseph Haydn would then have a fixed body of instrumentalists to work with, while traveling virtuoso performers such as the young Wolfgang Amadeus Mozart would write concerti that showed off their skills, and they would travel from town to town arranging concerts along the way.
- Gradually, the financial sponsorship of the symphony shifted from private patrons to a civic enterprise; this change placed a premium on music that was easy to learn, often with little or no rehearsal.
- In 1781, the Leipzig Gewandhaus Orchestra was organized from the Merchants Concert Society, and it began a trend towards the formation of civic orchestras that would accelerate into the nineteenth century.
- In 1815, Boston's Handel and Haydn Society was founded, and in 1842, the New York Philharmonic.
- The invention of the piston and rotary valve in 1815 was the first in a series of innovations, including the development of modern keywork for the flute and the innovations of Adolphe Sax in the woodwinds.
- These advances would lead Hector Berlioz to write a landmark book on instrumentation, which was the first systematic treatise on the use of instrumental sound as an expressive element of music.
- As the twentieth century dawned, symphony orchestras were larger, better funded, and better trained than ever before; consequently, composers could write larger and more ambitious works.
- With the beginning of the recording era, the standard of performance changed from simply "getting through" the music to a higher level of performances—now that a recording could be played repeatedly.
- Family Night Backstage introduced children of all ages to classical concerts—above are the Pittsburgh Symphony Horns.
- As sound was added to silent films, the virtuoso orchestra became critical to the establishment of motion pictures as mass-market entertainment.
- By the late twentieth century, dozens of public/private partnerships experienced a crisis of funding and support for orchestras.
- The size and cost of a symphony orchestra, compared to the size of the base of supporters, became an issue in city after city—encouraging symphonies of all sizes to rebuild their bases through educational programs.

Life in the Community:

- Pittsburgh, Pennsylvania Pittsburgh, the second-largest city in Pennsylvania, with a seven-county metropolitan area with a population of more than two million, was shaped by the confluence of the Allegheny and Monongahela rivers, which form the Ohio River.
- Known as "The Steel City" for its history of steel manufacturing, its economy had shifted to healthcare, education, technology, robotics, and financial services.
- No steel mills remained within the city of Pittsburgh, and only two mills remained in the county, while supporting 1,600 technology companies.

Pittsburgh steel mill, circa 1905.

- In 1895, the Pittsburgh Symphony Orchestra was founded by the Pittsburgh Arts Society with conductor Frederic Archer, who brought with him a number of musicians from the Boston Symphony Orchestra.
- Archer was replaced by Victor Herbert, who took the orchestra on several tours and greatly increased its presence.
- A number of prominent guest conductors were lured to Pittsburgh during these early years, including Edward Elgar and Richard Strauss, but the orchestra was dissolved in 1910 because of financial difficulties.
- In 1926, the orchestra was resurrected, with its members rehearsing for no fee and contributing money to make possible a new season the following year.
- In 1930, Antonio Modarelli was brought in as conductor, followed in 1937 by Otto Klemperer, who raised the orchestra to an international level.
- Since then, the orchestra has experienced ongoing growth and development, including building a substantial endowment fund.
- Fritz Reiner led the orchestra as Music Director for a decade (1938-1948), imposing his precise technical demands.

- He also made a number of recordings of a wide range of repertory, including music by Mozart, Richard Strauss, and Bela Bartók.
- From 1948-1952, a series of guest conductors led the orchestra, including Leonard Bernstein and Leopold Stokowski.
- André Previn (1976-1984) brought the Pittsburgh Symphony Orchestra to a national audience with a PBS television series, Previn and the Pittsburgh.
- Lorin Maazel, a Pittsburgh native, served as Music Consultant to the orchestra from 1984-1988, and Music Director from 1988-1996, followed by Mariss Jansons.

The Carnegie Library, Museums of Art and Natural History (foreground), Carnegie Mellon University (background)

1999: Advertising, Telemarketing, and Internet Entrepreneur

Chinese-born immigrant Liming Shao came to the United States in 1975 when he was 18 years old, with just $68 in his pocket. Now in his early forties, he was a multimillionaire, owning five different companies in New York City.

Life at Home

- His usual uniform was jeans, a polo shirt and cowboy boots; his black mane of hair was worn shoulder-length.
- He still shopped at the local Chinese open-air markets of New York for fruits native to his Chinese hometown, especially thick-skinned pears.
- When he first arrived in America, he shared a room with 16 other men in a rundown section of the city, dominated by prostitutes and drug dealers; the room was a good deal at $12 a month.
- He now drove a Mercedes-Benz and lived in a six-bedroom Victorian home in Greenwich, Connecticut, where the average home cost more than $1 million.
- His five-car garage also held two Harley-Davidsons—one vintage and one brand-new—plus a pickup truck and a BMW for Ping.
- After founding five companies that grossed more than $40 million this year, he now had a stock portfolio of more than $1 million and real-estate holdings of more than $5 million.
- He enjoyed flaunting his wealth and letting everyone know that Chinese immigrants were capable of more than running restaurants or dry-cleaning stores.
- Early on, he fell in love with wristwatches and now owned dozens, many of which cost $10,000 or more to buy; his favorite was a Chase-Durer Combat Command GMT, because of its expensively rugged look. When he went to parties, he enjoyed slipping on a Cartier Tank American watch.
- As a hobby, he loved to day trade stocks, often taking enormous risks; "I've already taken the greatest risk coming here," he told friends. "Why should the stock market scare me?"
- Born in a fishing village in the Fujian province of southern China, he was left by his parents when he was four years old so they could find work tapping rubber trees in Indonesia; they sent cash home whenever possible for Liming and his two brothers.
- As a child, he often robbed peach orchards and caught crabs for food.
- At age 13, he took a boat to Hong Kong with no papers and no money;

Liming thought he was setting an impressive example for Chinese immigrants.

153

His five-car garage held two Harley-Davidsons—one vintage and one brand-new.

- at the border, he dove into the bay and swam to the British colony.
- There he worked odd jobs and saved his money, until, at age 18, he had accumulated $2,000 for a phony visa and $800 for a plane ticket to America, which he believed was the land of opportunity, and "New York best of all. Best money, best job, best opportunity."
- Upon arrival, he worked as a dishwasher and waiter, soon marrying an American cook who also worked at the restaurant; he became a U.S. citizen shortly after and the couple had two children.
- Inspired one day by watching a professional photographer shoot photos, he bought a second-hand Nikon camera for $1,000 and began soliciting for freelance jobs.
- That first year, he made $30,000 shooting pictures, and by the late 1980s, he was earning $300,000 a year.
- In the early 1990s, he realized that no American advertising agency was addressing the growing needs of the Chinese market, so he created his own agency.

Life at Work
- His Manhattan office was painted red for luck, and prominently featured cutouts of the Chinese character for money.
- The Chinese symbolism was offset by a vintage Coke machine, a row of cowboy boots and a framed picture of a Harley-Davidson motorcycle.
- His advertising agency, which focused on selling to the affluent Chinese market, now had 75 employees in offices in New York City, Toronto and Los Angeles.
- He also operated a telemarketing company with 300 bilingual workers and a translation agency.
- His two newest companies were designed around the Internet, with one firm designing Asian-language Web sites, and the other serving as a liaison between Asian-owned companies in America and abroad.
- This budding empire was called the New A: New for New Economy, A for Asia.

- He had plans to buy an Internet company, a radio station, a newspaper and a magazine, believing that by owning various media outlets he could improve the image of Chinese immigrants.
- "Always I want to change that," he said proudly. "We are not all just sweatshops and laundromats and restaurants. They do dot-com. We do dot-com."
- He was not concerned about failure: "I never think about it. I come here with nothing. What have I got to lose?"
- He was, however, deeply concerned that the accusations of spying against Chinese scientist Wen Ho Lee at the Los Alamos National Laboratory would tarnish the reputation across America of Chinese leaders.
- More than three million Chinese now lived in America; approximately 60,000 arrived legally every year, along with another 20,000 illegal immigrants.
- Many were well-educated and highly computer-savvy, often earning more than the average American family within a few years of arriving.

Liming's advertising agency addressed the growing needs of the Chinese market in America.

- Eschewing the notion that immigrants must suffer a long period of hard work and poverty before they could succeed, many publicly announced they came to America to become rich immediately.
- The impact of Chinese wealth had not escaped Wall Street; Charles Schwab had a Chinese-language trading site, E-Trade and T.D. Waterhouse were launching sites for Chinese-speaking traders, and Yahoo! now let Chinese investors track stocks in their own language.
- Brokers reported that the Chinese craze for stocks was not confined to affluent professionals; the manager of Schwab's Chinatown branch had seen restaurant workers rush in with their first paycheck to buy stocks.

Life in the Community: New York, New York

- Many parts of New York City were undergoing massive renovation and change.
- In addition to the remarkable transformation of Grand Central Terminal, work was under way at TriBeCa.
- Once a manufacturing and downtown commercial area, it became a haven for artists in the 1970s; in the 1990s, it began attracting young affluent families looking for comfortable lofts.
- The area featured distinguished nineteenth-century architecture—much of it made of marble or cast iron—protected by historic-district designations.
- Today, these former warehousing sites had become a mecca for some of the city's finest restaurants.
- At 48 Wall Street, the former 36-story headquarters of Bank of New York were being transformed into 277 apartments; the renovation of the neo-Georgian landmark was costing $90 million.
- In Chelsea, at the other end of the economic scale, the 33 residents of the McBurney YMCA on West 23rd Street in Manhattan had been evicted; the YMCA of Greater New York, which operated

19 branches in the city and upstate, had decided to sell the 95-year-old structure and build a gym and health club at another location in the neighborhood—this time without residential apartments.

- *The New York Times* was editorializing against "Gridlock City," carping that "Manhattan's hottest piece of real estate, Times Square, had gotten so crowded lately that pedestrians often had to wait in line to cross the street. The newest arrival, Condé Nast Publications, planned to hold court in its icy tower by mid-August. ABC's *Good Morning, America* would settle nearby in September. The human gridlock could only get worse in November, when the World Wrestling Federation hunkered down in the Paramount Building to open a theme restaurant. The real theater that fall would unfold on Broadway, the street."
- The mayor's office recently won a legal fight to keep a Brooklyn artist from assembling 100 naked people in lower Manhattan for a photograph.
- City Hall was currently debating how to improve the health of the city's children by requiring landlords to remove lead paint from apartments.

1999: Mike Lincoln, Division I Basketball Player

Mike Lincoln was a basketball player from Indianapolis, Indiana, who walked-on to a basketball team in one of the most competitive conferences in the country—the Big Ten.

Life at Home

- Unlike the fairy tales of old, there was no magical moment when Mike Lincoln discovered basketball; he dreamed of playing Division One college basketball all the time.
- In school during math class, he daydreamed about hitting the winning shot just as the buzzer sounded; on the court after school, he carefully crafted the perfect pass, and in bed at night, he repeatedly executed a spectacular dunk before a roaring crowd.
- And when his mother needed Mike at suppertime, she always knew where to find him—on the basketball court behind the house.
- There he practiced constantly the skills needed in a game: squaring his shoulders before a leaping shot from the corner, dribbling confidently with his left hand as he exploded past a defender in the lane or shooting with consistency no matter the circumstance.
- One summer, on his way to basketball camp, Mike and his father even compiled a list of schools Mike dreamed of attending.
- When they reviewed the list, they discovered the colleges were all Division I schools and they were all in the Big Ten.
- Basketball was everything for Mike, whose parents were supportive of his every decision as long as his grades were solid.
- Spring meant one thing: the arrival of wall-to-wall televised games in an athletic festival of happiness known as March Madness.
- Over a matter of weeks, the nation's best teams would battle for the right to play for the national championship.
- The stated rules were simple: one loss and your tournament was over—no second chances, no voting, no appeals.
- Mike could not imagine a life better spent than watching the likes of Illinois, Indiana, Michigan, Northwestern, Purdue or Wisconsin in a battle for domination above the rim night after night.
- Mike's personal opportunity at greatness occurred after his sophomore year of high school, when he attended the Pittsburgh session of Five Star Basketball Camp.

Mike Lincoln grew up dreaming of playing Division I basketball.

A basketball court was Mike's favorite place to be.

- There, under the experienced gaze of Howard Garfinkle, for three minutes that July Mike played a perfect game.
- Howard Garfinkle was the director of the famed Five Star Basketball Camp.
- Employing a formula that had produced over 320 NBA players, his camps emphasized the fundamentals of the game and offered players the opportunity to play in front of college coaches.
- The daily schedule included stern lessons in everything from how to effectively handle a half-court trap to how to properly set up a defender before using a screen.
- Unaware that Garfinkle was watching, Mike played aggressive, smart basketball, drilling a series of mid-range jumpers.
- Garfinkle became a fan and remained one even after the country's Division I coaches did not bother to recruit Mike.
- Several small colleges invited Mike for visits that could have resulted in a basketball scholarship, but he wanted an academically challenging institution, preferably noted for its engineering program, where he could play basketball.
- The idea for Mike to walk-on to a college basketball team had come from Howard Garfinkle.
- He called Mike during his senior year of high school and asked if he was willing to walk-on to a team since no scholarships had come his way.
- Mike had no problem walking on, and the University of Illinois was selected as the perfect place; after Garfinkle placed a call to the coach, Mike was offered a spot.
- To prepare himself, the summer before his freshman year of college Mike worked out with several ex-college players who helped him prepare for the quickness and physicality of college basketball.
- In Division I everyone was fast, physical and fit; Mike learned there would be no rest breaks after a drill, and time in the weight room was intense.
- Before he ever set foot on the Illinois campus, he was exhausted.

Life at Work

- When Mike Lincoln arrived at the University of Illinois, he was a 6' 2", 175-pound shooting guard without a scholarship or reputation.
- Of the 14 players on the basketball team, only two were non-scholarship walk-ons; Mike had an immediate sense of being an outsider.
- In the immediate run-up to the basketball season, Mike participated with the rest of the squad in open gyms.
- Open gyms were run by the players without coaches present.
- Mike was told to pass the ball to gain respect from the older players, even though Mike had built his entire basketball repertoire around highly consistent, pinpoint shooting.
- But he quickly discovered that he had been given good advice.
- During the open gyms, Mike was startled by the speed of play and the size of the players.
- Everyone was bigger and quicker than he.
- He had to exert much more energy than the other players just to keep up.
- Some of his finest moves resulted in impressive blocks by his older teammates.
- There were no "gimmes" in Division I basketball.
- After being the go-to player in high school, Mike found it difficult to come to terms with his new role as a basketball player.
- After the acclaim of high school and numerous awards, Mike had to face the fact that he was smaller, slower and a non-scholarship player who was often overlooked and rarely a recipient of the perks of being a basketball player.
- Few of his teammates even bothered to learn his real name; he was habitually referred to by his teammates as Buddy.
- "Buddy, go rebound for those guys," or "You take Buddy on your team."
- Living hours away from his parents took an adjustment; they had attended every game he ever played.
- He was also challenged by the pressures of the classroom.
- The time demands of being a student-athlete were rigorous.
- To ensure that eligibility was not lost, the basketball players had an academic advisor who kept close tabs on the players, their grades and their attendance of classes.
- Some professors did not even understand that Mike was on the team—thus the reason for an absence.
- In a similar fashion, the first time Mike entered the team locker room he was dazzled, until he made his way to his locker.
- That's when he realized that, unlike the others, his locker did not have his name and number, only masking tape with the number 20 written on it.
- Walk-ons didn't always last, he was told; he would earn his name on the locker by and by.
- Mike needed to stay healthy, fast and fit.
- Sometimes Mark's role was to cheer his team-mates on from the bench.

Mike needed to stay healthy, fast and fit.

In high school Mike was one of the best players.

- Then, in October of Mike's freshman year, everyone in the basketball program met at the coliseum to have the team picture taken.
- It was an exciting time, marking the end of pre-season and the beginning of the regular season.
- When Mike walked into the locker room, there were only jerseys for the 12 scholarship players.
- His heart trembled as he walked out of the locker room without a jersey.
- It was a lesson in life as a walk-on.
- After games, the players would walk back out to the arena to meet friends and family.
- There were always kids waiting for autographs.
- Because Mike played so little, he often didn't have to shower after games and was the first out to the arena.
- There, kids would ask if he was a player, then ask for an autograph.
- Just as Mike would put the pen to paper, the kids would see one of the stars of the team and run to him instead.
- Hitting a game-winning shot was not even a possibility, Mike realized by mid-season.
- He was the one player on the team who could not dunk the basketball, but on occasion he would slap the backboard on the way in for a lay-up.
- He was the player at the end of the bench who always cheered on his teammates.
- If he checked in, the fans knew the game was over.
- Yet he stayed on the team, despite rumors of coaching changes, a severe case of shin splints, and the open disdain of one senior player who repeatedly challenged Mike's right to a place on the team.
- "It's about character, not points," Mike's father told him after freshman year ended.
- "No," Mike replied. "It's about proving points, playing time and proving everyone wrong about me."

Life in the Community: Urbana, Illinois

- The University of Illinois was created through the Morrill Act of 1862, which granted each state in the United States a portion of land on which to establish a major public state university, one that could teach agriculture, mechanic arts and military training "without excluding other scientific and classical studies."
- After a fierce bidding war among a number of Illinois cities, Urbana was selected as the site for the new "Illinois Industrial University" in 1867.
- The campus became known for its landscape and architecture and was identified as one of 50 college or university "works of art" by T.A. Gaines in his book The Campus as a Work of Art.
- The main research and academic facilities were divided almost exactly between the twin cities of Urbana and Champaign.
- The campus has four main quads, which compose the center of the university and are arranged from north to south and regarded as a world-leading magnet for engineering and sciences, both applied and basic.
- In 1952, the university built the Illinois Automatic Computer, the first computer built and owned entirely by an educational institution.
- Its reputation was such that the university recently celebrated January 12, 1997, as the "birthday" of HAL 9000, the fictional supercomputer from the novel and film *2001: A Space Odyssey*; in both works, HAL credited "Urbana, Illinois" as his place of operational origin.

- The University of Illinois was also the site of the Department of Energy's Center for the Simulation of Advanced Rockets, an institute which has employed graduate and faculty researchers in the physical sciences and mathematics.
- It performs materials science and condensed matter physics research, and is home to the Frederick Seitz Materials Research Laboratory.
- Since 1957, the Illinois Transportation Archaeological Research Program has conducted archaeological and historical compliance work for the Illinois Department of Transportation.
- It serves as a repository for a large collection of Illinois archaeological artifacts numbering over 17,000 boxes, including 550 boxes from the famous Cahokia Mounds, an ancient Indian city and the oldest archaeological site in the U.S.
- The university had also developed one of the largest Greek systems in the world by membership with 69 fraternities and 36 sororities on the campus.
- Of the approximately 30,000 undergraduates, about 3,330 were members of sororities and about 3,370 were members of fraternities.
- Among university libraries in North America, only the collections of Harvard, Yale, the University of California, Berkeley, and the University of Toronto were larger than those of the University of Illinois.
- These were the penalties, which restricted both the coaches and the university:
- The team could play in the March 1991 NCAA championship tournament.
- The university could offer more than two basketball scholarships in each of the 1991-92 and 1992-93 academic years.
- In calendar year 1991, basketball coaches were prohibited from recruiting off campus; no more than two basketball coaches would be permitted to recruit off campus the following year.
- The university was barred from paying for official campus visits by potential student athletes during 1991.

Foellinger Auditorium on the campus of the University of Illinois at Urbana–Champaign.

Lincoln the Lawyer by Lorado Taft

1999: Teacher and Skeptic of Standardized Testing

Viola Chadusky's job as a teacher had always been tough, but the challenges of new testing standards led her to wonder whether the stakes for testing were becoming too high.

Life at Home

- Viola Chadusky was born in Syracuse, New York, on September 17, 1959.
- She was a bright, vivacious girl who grew up wanting to make a difference in the world.
- As a college student, she chose the classroom as a place to start.
- Viola's mother, Anna Fisselbrand, was from nearby Manlius, where the family had lived for generations.
- Anna became a registered nurse and went to work in 1956 at the State University of New York's Upstate Medical Center, where she met Alfred Chadusky, an accountant at the hospital; they married in 1958.
- Al had grown up in Rochester and graduated from Columbia College in New York City in 1955.
- By the time Viola turned five, she had a sister, Anna, and a brother, Tom.
- Viola's parents sent her to a private kindergarten, then to a Catholic school in first grade.
- She was so excited before her first day at school she had trouble going to sleep.
- Girls wore a uniform consisting of a plaid, pleated skirt and a white blouse; boys wore black pants, a white shirt and a plaid bowtie.
- Viola was a good student and liked to play teacher with her siblings.
- Whenever she was alone, she read.
- When her friends came over, they played with Barbie dolls or talked about the Beatles; her best friend Marcia liked Paul, but Viola liked John.
- Soon their musical interests drifted to the Monkees, who had their own television show from 1966 to 1968.
- The intrigue of the made-for-television band was heightened by the fact that the show debuted in color.
- Until then, television shows were almost always in black and white, and color television sets were just becoming available.
- Marcia's parents were the first on the block to get a color TV, so Viola stopped by often.

Teacher Viola Chadusky questioned the value of standardized testing.

- Her parents decided in 1969 that it was too expensive to send their kids to Catholic schools, and enrolled them in public schools in the fall.
- For the first time, Viola had to choose what to wear to school each day.
- She didn't think much about "what she wanted to be when she grew up" as she moved from junior high into high school in 1973; she was more interested in hanging out with her friends.
- When they got together, she was often the one to steer them into their evening plans, and had a quick wit and a loud laugh.
- In a group, she wasn't always the one who talked the most, but when she spoke, people listened.
- Viola continued to read, and in tenth grade had an English teacher, Molly Peacock, who opened up her mind to authors new and old.
- When Viola first read Shakespeare, she was struck by the oddness of how words were spelled and strung together.
- But as Mrs. Peacock helped untangle the language, Viola marveled as she began to understand English as it was spoken in the 1600s.

In Catholic school, Viola didn't think about what to wear.

- She read John Steinbeck's The Grapes of Wrath, in which she saw stark choices faced by many in the Great Depression.
- Watching Mrs. Peacock orchestrating her classroom through lively discussions led Viola to consider teaching as a career.
- While Viola had always earned good grades, she didn't consider herself very smart.
- But when she took her college aptitude tests in her junior year, she was surprised at having scored near the top, with especially high marks in English. Everyone else seemed to be able to write their papers effortlessly, while her first drafts were as painful as pulling fingernails.
- Second and third drafts were another matter; by that point, she could whip her words into shape.
- Her high scores were a big help in getting her a scholarship to New York University, which her family would not have been able to afford otherwise.
- She decided to major in education.
- Some of her classes were extremely dull and filled with a mind-numbing amount of jargon that she believed was more a way of showing status than conveying ideas.
- Her classes became more interesting as she entered her junior year, and her ability to write, speak and use her natural leadership skills helped her excel.
- During her senior year, she did an internship in a third-grade classroom in a New York public elementary school.
- It was an eye-opening experience.
- She met students who couldn't read, some who couldn't even speak English.
- Many were being raised by single mothers, or grandparents, who lacked the skills or time to help them.
- "I'm not in Syracuse anymore," Viola said to herself.
- She was hired in the fall of 1981 to teach fourth grade at a public school in New York City.

- During her first year of teaching, she came home many days and cried.
- The range of students' backgrounds and abilities was dizzying.
- Some of the brightest seemed bored, and she felt she wasn't doing enough to help those who were struggling.
- Discipline problems were constant.
- Administrators didn't seem to care, except when they dropped in to observe her class.
- Many of her fellow education graduates dropped out after their first year of teaching, but Viola persevered.
- As she talked with other teachers, she learned to focus better on her students by not carrying the guilt of all their failings.
- She did the best she could, which turned out to be pretty good, indeed.
- Her writing talent was a help, but she listened closely to other teachers, and when she could, she watched their techniques.
- A few of the other teachers were mediocre, but despite the school's failings, most of the teachers were committed and effective.
- Viola emphasized reading in her classroom, especially nonfiction.
- She kept lists of all the books students were reading during the year, helped organize book clubs, and arranged reading partners so her students could talk about what they read.
- As the years passed, she gained the respect of her peers, and even the administrators.
- She received recognition for her work at the end of her fifth year of teaching in 1997, and also completed her master's degree at the Teachers College of Columbia University in 1998, bumping up her pay to about $35,000 a year.

Life at Work

- Viola Chadusky accepted that standardized testing had always been part of teaching.
- However, she felt truly challenged when a movement for higher standards and tougher tests gained momentum in New York City in the mid-1990s.
- Viola often thought the tests were measuring the wrong things.
- Worse, the results tended to be used in ways for which the tests were not designed.
- On the other hand, she had seen from her students' work the paucity of their knowledge and the weakness of their skills.
- And, if nothing else, Viola had learned to work within the system to get the job done.
- Whatever tests the administration wanted, she would prepare her students for them.
- Most of her colleagues felt about the same way.
- Elementary schools already were under pressure from the city, with new and more stringent tests that could be used to fire principals or reassign teachers.
- But teachers' concerns about testing increased when they learned the State Board of Regents were planning to introduce a new, more rigorous set of language and math tests in 1999.
- Principals held long meetings with teachers in the fall of 1998 on what the new tests would mean.
- The old fill-in-the-blank test about a passage students had read was intended to measure minimum adequacy.
- About two-thirds of Viola's class had passed the test the previous year.
- Fourth-graders across the state would be taking three 55-minute tests over the course of three days starting January 12, 1999.
- This test differed from the usual in that it had an essay component.
- In one segment, students would read an excerpt and write a short essay; in another, teachers would read them a story, after which students would write an essay.
- The January 1999 test would be a practice run for students, but the next year it could be used to flunk and hold back fourth- and eighth-grade students.

Standardized testing was becomming more important in 1999.

- Viola's principal estimated that about 25 percent of the school's fourth-graders were in danger of failing.
- Although Viola didn't show her concern with her fourth-graders, she began spending more time on punctuation, rules of grammar, and—in anticipation of the stress—deep breathing exercises.
- She waited until November to describe the tests to her students.
- "They were stunned," she recalled.
- In the teachers' lounge, one third-grade teacher recounted how one of his borderline students had vowed "from now on I'll study more and I won't talk in class."
- The other teachers at the table laughed, but they also knew how devastating being held back would be on a child.
- Viola remembered the sleepless nights she had in her first years when she knew one of her children was going to be held back.
- She practiced with "Amos and Boris," a story about a mouse who is saved from drowning and carried home by Boris, a whale; years later, Amos finds Boris beached on the seashore and finds a way to return him to the sea.
- After reading the story, she told her students to jot down what each character did, and then to some of those words to write sentences describing the personality traits of the mouse and the whale.
- Standardized testing was becoming more important in 1999.
- When two of her most worried students had done especially well, she praised them out loud.
- But many of her students didn't seem to grasp the task, and wrote garbled sentences.
- When Viola finally had a chance to retreat to the teachers' lounge, she could see that other teachers were worried, too.
- "They're not going to do their homework, and they know I can't make them," third-grade teacher Catherine Browne said. "I can't control what happens at home. I can't even reach a parent on the phone half the time."
- "Yeah," Viola said, "the public doesn't seem to get it. They look at our absentee rates and point their fingers at the schools. They wouldn't believe some of the reasons. I had one kid last year who skipped school so he could translate for his dad at the Immigration Office."
- The school remained open three hours in the mornings during most of the holiday break.
- About half the students attended the special sessions.
- In March, the results from the tests given back in January came in.

- Two-thirds of the fourth-graders at the school had flunked the English test, and it was only a small consolation to Viola that the failure rate in her classroom was 52 percent; she had hoped for at least a little more than that.
- She began thinking of new ways to teach that would strengthen her students' comprehension and writing skills.
- As much stress as the state test caused fourth-grade teachers, she heard even more complaints about the city's burgeoning schedule of multiple-choice tests.
- "And I don't know why they're so hot about these tests," a third-grade teacher said. "When was the last time anyone told kids to memorize the 50 states and their capitals? Not in the last 10 years. What's important is teaching the kids how to find the answers. Okay, they get them wrong half the time, but at least they're trying."
- At lunch, when fifth-grade teacher Henry Shekhanna said that the advocates of high-stakes testing would not be satisfied until they could put teachers' names and their performance scores on the school bulletin board, Viola said he was a crazy old man.
- "The union wouldn't stand for it," she said, "and even the regents would know it would backfire. People would never want to be teachers with that hanging over their heads."
- Henry, who was two years from retirement, had to have the last word: "That'll be yours to find out."

Life in the Community: New York City
- In 1995, big changes started happening in schools in New York City and across the state.
- By 1999, the number of tests students were required to take had increased, the tests became harder, and the stakes for failing higher.
- The changes started at the top.
- In 1995, the New York Board of Regents hired Richard P. Mills as its school superintendent, and Mayor Rudy Giuliani picked Rudy Crew as chancellor of New York City schools, the nation's largest school system, with more than one million students.
- Both Mills and Crew supported more stringent standards, more testing, and an end to "social promotion," the practice of promoting failing students from grade to grade so that they remain with their age group.
- New York became a leader in a national movement to set higher school standards and hold schools and students accountable to them through standardized tests.
- From 1993 to 1998, every state except Iowa had begun setting statewide standards.
- President Clinton wanted to create a national exam, and while states could use or ignore the federal test, it would set a national standard to allow parents, teachers and administrators to compare their schools with similar schools anywhere in the country where the national exam was adopted.
- Crew was able to convince the New York legislature to change a law to give him more power to appoint—and fire—superintendents of the system's 32 school districts—a move designed to curtail cronyism and make schools more accountable.
- He also negotiated a deal with the principals' union to end provisions providing lifetime job protection.
- But the biggest pressure on Crew was that New York City students weren't making the grade.
- They had lower test scores and higher dropout rates than students elsewhere in the state.
- And the pressure mounted.
- As Crew introduced new and tougher tests for students in the city, the state was imposing more stringent tests of its own.
- For Mills, a key piece for creating higher standards would be the New York State English Regents' Exam for seniors, who would have to hit a particular mark to graduate from high school.
- There were also new English tests for grades 4 and 8.

New York education leaders Rudy Crew, left, and Richard Mills supported stringent testing standards.

- "For teachers who have long been granted wide latitude in how they structured their lesson plans—especially those weaned on the flexible, child-centered approach popular since the 1960s—adapting to the new standards has required serious adjustment," *The New York Times* reported.
- The first round of the new state tests was set for Tuesday, January 12, 1999—one week after students returned from their holiday break.
- This would be a big change.
- With the old tests, fourth-graders read sentences or short passages, then filled in missing words from a list of multiple-choice answers.
- The new test, developed by a panel of 22 fourth-grade teachers, "moves from a focus on simple reading to an expectation that by the middle of fourth grade, pupils can understand and write about complex passages and about themselves, using correct spelling," *The New York Times* reported on the eve of testing.
- Mills expected the scores to be low because the standards were deliberately higher.
- Schools worked feverishly on writing exercises that fall, and offered special sessions during the holidays.
- The test's inauguration was inauspicious.
- There were complaints about late test deliveries and possible security breaches that might have given some schools an advantage.
- Also, bad weather closed dozens of schools.

- The test answers were scored by committees of teachers, after which the state released the results on May 25, 1999.
- Statewide, 48 percent of fourth-graders passed; in New York City only 33 percent passed.
- "This is an exercise in truth telling," Mills said. "Where do we go from here? We have to go up, obviously."
- An analysis by *The New York Times* showed that city students actually performed slightly better than others in the state when compared to similar groups based on poverty and homes where Spanish or another language other than English was used at home.
- Nevertheless, poor grades on the state test and city tests led Crew to send 35,000 failing students to summer school to give them another chance to pass their tests.
- The city's summer school program was strongly pushed by Mayor Giuliani, who argued that one way to improve schools was to get tough with failing students.
- But city officials flunked, too.
- The company that made the tests goofed in scoring them.
- In September 1999, the city announced that it had to revise results for citywide tests given in grades 3, 5, 6, and 7.
- The correct results showed higher scores, which meant the city had sent about 8,600 students to summer school by mistake.
- The display of incompetence in administering a student competency test was an embarrassment for Crew, even though the mistake was the vender's and was originally flagged by Crew's chief testing advisor.
- Relations between Giuliani and Crew had been worsening since April 1999, when the mayor proposed experimenting with school vouchers.
- Crew, who opposed vouchers because they diverted public money to private schools, fought the mayor's plan fiercely and defeated it.
- The testing problems and other issues made matters worse.
- On December 23, 1999, the city school board voted to end Crew's contract.

Since 2008, the former Tweed Courthouse in downtown Manhattan has served as the headquarters for the Department of Education.

SECTION TWO: HISTORICAL SNAPSHOTS

The 1990s was marked by steady economic growth, low inflation, low unemployment, dramatic gains in technology-based productivity and the emerging concept known as the Internet. Americans enjoyed, for the first time, lightweight cell phones, Internet shopping, and digital cameras. They wore ripped jeans and $150 tennis shoes. And the end of the century saw Y2K (Year 2000) worries escalate to doomsday proportions. These Historical Snapshots highlight significant firsts and milestones during the last decade of the 1900s.

Early 1990s

- A bomb blast injured hundreds in the World Trade Center bombing in New York City; Mohammed A. Salameh was arrested for the bombing when he attempted to reclaim his $400 car rental deposit
- A complete edition of John J. Audubon's book, *Birds of America*, sold for $3.96 million at auction
- A record 23,300 homicides were reported nationwide
- A single sheet of the first printing of the Declaration of Independence sold for $2,420,000; it was found at a flea market for $4 in the backing of a painting
- Allied forces attacked Iraq, dropping 2,232 tons of explosives the first day, the largest strike in history; all regular television programming was canceled for full coverage of the Gulf War
- An EPA report claimed that 3,800 people died annually from second-hand smoke
- An Oregon law permitted physician-assisted suicide; Michigan's Dr. Jack Kevorkian was jailed twice for assisting patients' suicides
- Arlette Schweitzer, 42, acted as surrogate mother for her daughter who was born without a uterus, giving birth to her own grandchildren—twins
- At the Olympic Summer Games in Barcelona, the U.S. basketball team included Larry Bird, Magic Johnson and Michael Jordan
- Bestsellers included Rush Limbaugh's *The Way Things Ought to Be*, H. Norman Schwarzkopf's *It Doesn't Take a Hero*, John Grisham's *The Pelican Brief* and Anne Rice's *The Tale of the Body Thief*
- Billy Joel released his final studio album before quitting music after 20 years
- Bobby Brown was arrested in Augusta, Georgia, for simulating a sex act onstage
- Boris Yeltsin announced that Russia would stop targeting cities in the U.S. and its allies with nuclear weapons, while George H. W. Bush announced that the U.S. and its allies would discontinue targeting Russia and the remaining communist states
- Both President Bush and Premier Gorbachev called for Iraqi withdrawal following its invasion of Kuwait
- Bureau of Alcohol, Tobacco and Firearms agents raided the Branch Davidian compound in Waco, Texas, with a warrant to arrest leader David Koresh on federal firearms violations; four agents and 81 Davidians died
- Census data showed that 25 percent of the population were members of a minority group; Asians and Pacific Islanders were the fastest-growing minorities
- Chicago Bulls basketball star Michael Jordan retired to play professional baseball
- Civil rights advocate Ruth Bader Ginsburg was named to the U.S. Supreme Court

- Congress approved family leave, allowing up to 12 weeks for family emergencies
- Congress halted a nationwide rail strike after one day
- Cosmologists discovered that stars and other observable matter occupied less than 10 percent of the universe
- *Dances with Wolves* was named the Academy Awards' best picture; *Pretty Woman, Total Recall, Goodfellas* and *Home Alone* were also released
- David Letterman was offered $16 million to move to CBS opposite late-night host Jay Leno; Johnny Carson's last night as host of *The Tonight Show* drew a record 55 million viewers
- Deadly rioting that killed 55 and injured 2,300 erupted in Los Angeles after a jury acquitted four Los Angeles police officers of state charges in the videotaped beating of Rodney King
- Dieting became a $33 billion industry
- Dr. Mae Jemison became the first African-American woman to travel into space, aboard the Space Shuttle *Endeavour*
- Airlines Eastern and Pan Am went into bankruptcy; Delta took over most Pan Am routes and became the leading carrier
- Eric Clapton won a Grammy award for his record "Tears in Heaven" and his album, *Unplugged*
- Extremist Hindu activists demolished Babri Masjid—a sixteenth-century mosque in Ayodhya, India—leading to widespread violence, including the Mumbai Riots
- First appearances included a McDonald's in Moscow and Beijing; the Infiniti, Saturn, and Lexus automobiles; gender-specific disposable diapers; Caller ID systems; and the contraceptive implant Norplant
- General Motors announced plans to close more than 20 plants over several years, eliminating more than 70,000 jobs
- Green tea was discovered to contain an important anti-cancer agent
- IBM announced an $8.9 billion restructuring of the world's largest computer maker; the firm eliminated 60,000 jobs
- In Kenya, Meave Leakey discovered the oldest hominid fossil to date, estimated to be 25 million years old and believed to be from the period of the ape-human divergence
- In Super Bowl XXVII the Buffalo Bills became the first team to lose three consecutive Super Bowls when they were defeated by the Dallas Cowboys, 52-17
- In Washington, DC, more than 500,000 people marched for abortion rights
- Janet Jackson's album *Janet* debuted at #1—the first to do so by a female artist based on Nielsen SoundScan, an information and sales tracking system; the album included the single "That's the Way Love Goes"
- Japan apologized for forcing tens of thousands of Korean women to serve as sex slaves
- *Jurassic Park* became the highest-grossing movie of all time
- Major League baseball owners announced new initiatives on minority hiring
- Michael Jackson signed a $1.1 billion multi-year contract with Sony
- Motorola introduced the 7.7-ounce cellular telephone
- Movie openings included *Unforgiven, The Crying Game, Scent of a Woman, Malcolm X, Aladdin, Sister Act, Basic Instinct, The Last of the Mohicans, A River Runs Through It* and *White Men Can't Jump*
- New-age clear beverages, mega CD video games, The Mall of America and the Intel 486 chip made their first appearance
- Nirvana's *Nevermind* album was No. 1 in the U.S. Billboard 200 chart, establishing the widespread popularity of the Grunge movement of the 1990s

- On his thirty-fifth birthday, Prince announced that he was changing his name to an unpronounceable symbol, which led to him being called The Artist Formerly Known as Prince
- One quarter of all newborns were born to single women
- Operation Julin was the last nuclear test conducted by the U.S. at the Nevada Test Site
- Oprah Winfrey interviewed Michael Jackson during a television prime time special; it was Jackson's first television appearance in 14 years
- Pearl Jam's second album *Vs.* sold 950,000 copies in one week to set a new record
- Poverty rose to 14.2 percent, the highest level since 1983
- President Bill Clinton promised "universal health coverage" comparable to that of *Fortune 500* companies; 64 million people lacked adequate coverage
- President Clinton supported easing a ban on homosexuals in the military
- President George H. W. Bush proposed tax breaks and business incentives to revive the economy, and announced dramatic cuts in the U.S. nuclear arsenal
- Royalties for Barbara and George Bush's dog's autobiography, *Millie's Book*, earned them $890,000
- Rudolph Marcus won the Nobel Prize in chemistry for his theory of electron-transfer reactions
- *Scarlett*, Alexandra Ripley's sequel to *Gone with the Wind*, sold a record 250,000 copies in one day
- School violence escalated; 25 percent of whites and 20 percent of blacks said they feared being attacked in school
- Sears department store ended its mail-order catalog business
- Simon LeVay's study showed anatomical hypothalamic differences in gay and heterosexual men, lending credibility to the biological origin of sexual orientation
- Singer Paul Simon toured South Africa
- The 10 most popular television shows were *60 Minutes*; *Roseanne*; *Murphy Brown*; *Cheers*; *Home Improvement*; *Designing Women*; *Coach*; *Full House*; *Murder, She Wrote*; and *Unsolved Mysteries*
- The 11-hour-long documentary *The Civil War* by Ken Burns was released on public television
- The average price of gas was $1.05 per gallon
- The brown uniform of the Girl Scout Brownies changed after 66 years to include pastel tops, culotte jumpers, and floral print vests
- The Church of England voted to allow women to become priests
- The Disney animated movie *Aladdin* was the highest-grossing picture of the year
- The economy officially went into a recession for the first time since 1982; disposable income fell as unemployment rose
- The FDA restricted the use of silicone-gel breast implants for reconstructive purposes
- The Federal Reserve slashed interest rates to spur the economy
- The first World Ocean Day was celebrated, coinciding with the Earth Summit held in Rio de Janeiro, Brazil
- The Ford Taurus topped the Honda Accord in total car sales
- The Hubble space telescope was launched into orbit
- The median age for first marriages was 26.3 years for men and 24.1 years for women
- The motion picture *Batman Returns* opened with the first weekend box office revenues of $47.7 million
- The Ms. Foundation began its "Take Our Daughters to Work Day"
- The number of single parents rose 41 percent from 1980, while the number of unmarried couples living together was up 80 percent
- The Senate voted to sharply restrict U.S. testing of nuclear weapons
- The Space Shuttle *Endeavour* made its maiden flight as a replacement for a lost Space Shuttle

- The Supreme Court ruled criminal defendants may not use race as a basis for excluding potential jurors from their trials
- The Supreme Court ruled prison guards who use unnecessary force against inmates may be violating the Constitution's ban on cruel and unusual punishment even if they inflict no serious injuries
- The Supreme Court ruled that cross-burning is protected under the First Amendment, and that prayer at public school graduations is unconstitutional
- The timber industry of the Pacific Northwest was outraged when the northwest spotted owl was declared an endangered species
- The U.S. Agriculture Department unveiled a pyramid-shaped recommended-diet chart, replacing the four food groups
- The U.S. began testing of RU-486, the French "morning after" pill
- The U.S. Postal Service increased the first-class postage stamp rate from $0.25 to $0.29
- The U.S. Supreme Court ended forced busing, originally ordered to end racial segregation
- The U.S. trade deficit hit an eight-year low
- Thirty-year mortgages dropped to 6.7 percent, the lowest in 25 years
- U.S. bombed Iraq for its failure to comply with United Nations-sponsored inspections
- U.S. pledged $1.6 billion in aid to assist in Russian reforms
- Unemployment topped 7.1 percent, the highest in five years
- Walter Annenberg donated more than 50 Impressionist paintings worth $1 billion to the Metropolitan Museum of Art in New York City
- Whitney Houston's single "I Will Always Love You" became the longest-running number one single of all time
- Willie Nelson, John Cougar Mellencamp, Neil Young and more than 30 other artists performed at Farm Aid 6 in Ames, Iowa, designed to bring attention to world hunger
- Women constituted 11 percent of U.S. troops, up from three percent in 1973, and received combat roles in aerial and naval warfare

Mid 1990s

- 25 percent of Americans continued to smoke cigarettes despite health warnings.
- A budget standoff between Democrats and Republicans forced the federal government to temporarily close national parks and museums, and operate with a skeleton staff
- A Unabomber bomb killed lobbyist Gilbert Murray in Sacramento, California
- About 55 percent of women provided half of more of household income.
- Actor Christopher Reeve was paralyzed from the neck down after falling from his horse in a riding competition
- After 139 years, Mississippi lawmakers ratified the 13th Amendment abolishing slavery
- Astronaut Norman Thagard became the first American aboard a Russian launch vehicle, the Soyuz TM-21
- *Braveheart* won Best Picture at the 68th Academy Awards, hosted by Whoopi Goldberg
- Ceremonies in Hiroshima, Nagasaki, Washington, DC, and Tokyo marked the fiftieth anniversary of the dropping of the atomic bombs
- Coffee bars, led by companies such as Starbucks, spread rapidly, providing an inexpensive, safe dating haven
- Congress passed the Child Protection and Obscenity Enforcement Act, requiring the producers of pornography to keep records of all models who were filmed or photographed

- Dolly the sheep, the first mammal to be successfully cloned from an adult cell, was born at the Roslin Institute in Midlothian, Scotland
- Dow Corning declared bankruptcy after failure of its silicone breast device
- Dr. Jack Kevorkian was acquitted of assisted suicide for helping two suffering patients kill themselves
- eBay was founded
- Federal Reserve Board Chairman Alan Greenspan gave a speech in which he suggested that "irrational exuberance" may have "unduly escalated asset values"
- For the first time, Ford sold more trucks than cars; demand for light trucks, like minivans and sports utility vehicles, increased in urban and rural areas.
- France detonated its sixth and most powerful nuclear bomb
- Guatemala's leftist guerrillas and the government signed an accord to end 35 years of civil war
- Hacker Kevin Mitnick was arrested by the FBI and charged with penetrating some of the country's most "secure" computer systems
- In Oklahoma City, 168 people were killed in the bombing of the Alfred P. Murrah Federal Building
- In Philadelphia, Pennsylvania, a panel of federal judges blocked a law against indecency on the internet
- In response to UNSCOM's evidence, Iraq admitted for first time the existence of an offensive biological weapons program
- Iraqi leader Saddam Hussein decreed economic austerity measures to cope with soaring inflation and widespread shortages caused by U.N. sanctions
- Jerry Garcia died of a heart attack; his band, the *Grateful Dead* broke up soon after
- Liggett became the first tobacco company to acknowledge that cigarettes are addictive and cause cancer
- Major League Soccer in America began
- Mars released a blue M&M candy for the first time.
- Martina Hingis became the youngest person in history at age 15 to win at Wimbledon in the Ladies' Doubles event
- Michael Jackson released his first double-album *HIStory*, which became the bestselling multiple album of all time, with 22 million copies sold worldwide
- Michael Johnson won the 200-meter finals of the 1996 Summer Olympics in Atlanta with a world-record time of 19.32 seconds
- Microsoft released Windows 95 The DVD, an optical disc computer storage media format, was announced
- More than 170 countries agree to extend the Nuclear Nonproliferation Treaty indefinitely
- More than seven million people subscribed to online computer services such as America Online, CompuServe and Prodigy
- Mother Teresa received honorary U.S. citizenship
- NASA announced that the ALH 84001 meteorite, thought to originate from Mars, contained evidence of primitive life forms
- New protease-blocking drugs were shown to be effective in combating AIDS
- New York became the 38th state to reinstate capital punishment.
- On television, *ER*, *Seinfeld*, *Friends*, *Caroline in the City*, NFL *Monday Night Football*, *Single Guy*, *Home Improvement*, *Boston Common*, *60 Minutes* and *NYPD Blue* led in the Nielsen ratings
- Osama bin Laden wrote "The Declaration of Jihad on the Americans Occupying the Country of the Two Sacred Places," a call for the removal of American military forces from Saudi Arabia

- Physicists discovered the mega-particle, predicted by Einstein and consisting of a few thousand atoms
- President Bill Clinton and Monica Lewinsky, a White House intern, engaged in a series of sexual encounters at the White House
- President Bill Clinton invoked emergency powers to extend a $20 billion loan to help Mexico avert financial collapse
- President Clinton signed the Comprehensive Nuclear-Test-Ban Treaty at the United Nations
- President Clinton signed the National Highway Designation Act, which ended the federal 55 mph speed limit
- Queen Elizabeth II advised "an early divorce" to Lady Diana Spencer and Prince Charles
- Rancid released their third studio album—*And Out Come the Wolves*—helping to revive mainstream interest in punk rock
- Research showed that three ounces of salmon a week reduced the risk of fatal heart arrhythmias
- Salt Lake City was selected to host the 2002 Winter Olympics
- San Francisco 49ers became the first NFL team to win five Super Bowls
- Sheik Omar Abdel-Rahman and nine followers were handed long prison sentences for plotting to blow up New York-area landmarks
- Singer Kurt Cobain's blood-stained guitar sold for $17,000 after his death by suicide
- Suspected "Unabomber" Theodore Kaczynski was arrested at his Montana cabin
- The 104th U. S. Congress was the first controlled by Republicans since 1953
- The 25th anniversary of Earth Day was celebrated.
- The all-male college, The Citadel, admitted its first female cadet, who withdrew after a few days
- The Beatles released "Free as a Bird" as their first new single in over 20 years
- The Centers for Disease Control reported a leveling-off of teen sexual activity; 52.8 percent used condoms.
- The Dayton Agreement to end the Bosnian War was reached at Wright-Patterson Air Force Base near Dayton, Ohio
- The Dow Jones Industrial Average closed above 4,000 and 5,000, the first time the Dow surpassed two millennium marks in a single year
- The FBI reported a sharp decline in crime rates.
- The federal government set aside 3.9 million acres of land in California, Oregon and Washington State for the endangered marbled murrelet
- The first full-length computer animated feature film, *Toy Story*, was released by Pixar Animation Studios and Walt Disney Pictures
- The first of the Nixon White House tapes concerning Watergate were released
- The first version of the Java programming language was released
- Canadian singer Alanis Morissette became the youngest person to win the top honor, Album of the Year, at the 38th Annual Grammy Awards
- The frozen body of a 500-year-old Inca girl was found bundled in fine wool in the Peruvian Andes
- The Hoover Institution released a report that global warming would reduce mortality in the United States and provide Americans with valuable benefits
- The Keck II telescope was dedicated in Hawaii
- The longest Major League Baseball strike in history—234 days—ended.
- The Million Man March was held in Washington, DC, conceived by Nation of Islam leader Louis Farrakhan

- The Minnesota Aid Project for Condoms advertised: "When you give the gift of love, make sure it's wrapped properly."
- The most distant galaxy yet discovered (an estimated 15 billion light years away) was found by scientists using the Keck telescope in Hawaii
- The movie *Forrest Gump* won Best Picture at the 67th Academy Awards
- The movies *Braveheart* with Mel Gibson, *Apollo 13* with Tom Hanks, *Leaving Las Vegas* with Nicolas Cage and *Dead Man Walking* with Susan Sarandon premiered
- The nation's 16,000 public companies were required to file their financial reports electronically with the Securities and Exchange Commission
- The Nintendo 64 video game system was released in Japan
- The Ramones released their final studio album, *Adios Amigos!*
- The Rock and Roll Hall of Fame opened in Cleveland, Ohio
- The Senate passed an immigration bill to tighten border controls, make it tougher for illegal immigrants to get U.S. jobs, and curtail legal immigrants' access to social services
- The Space Telescope Science Institute announced that photographs from the Hubble Space Telescope confirmed the existence of a "black hole" equal to the mass of two billion suns
- The Supreme Court ruled against a law that prevented cities in the state of Colorado from taking any action to protect the rights of homosexuals
- The U.S. Army disclosed that it had 30,000 tons of chemical weapons stored in Utah, Alabama, Maryland, Kentucky, Indiana, Arkansas, Colorado and Oregon
- The U.S. banned the manufacture of Freon because of its effect on the ozone layer
- The World Trade Organization (WTO) was established
- Top record singles for the year included "Can You Feel the Love Tonight" by Elton John, "Gangsta's Paradise" by Coolio and "Dear Mama" by Tupac Shakur
- Valeri Polyakov completed 366 days in space while aboard the *Mir* space station, breaking a duration record
- World chess champion Garry Kasparov beat IBM supercomputer "Deep Blue," winning a six-game match in Philadelphia
- Yahoo! was founded in Santa Clara, California
- Motorola introduced the Motorola StarTAC Wearable Cellular Telephone, the world's smallest and lightest mobile phone by 50 percent
- In the U.S. presidential election, Democratic incumbent Bill Clinton defeated Republican challenger Bob Dole to win his second term

Late 1990s

- 17 major newspapers called for President Bill Clinton's resignation after he admitted a sexual relationship with a White House intern
- A consortium of tobacco companies settled state health claims for $206 billion
- A New Jersey fertility clinic doubled its stipend to egg donors to $5,000 for a month's supply, igniting fears of a bidding war for human eggs
- A peace accord was reached in Northern Ireland
- A series of fatal shootings at high schools across the country revived the gun-control debate and prompted many to call for mandatory background checks for gun purchases
- Affirmative Action programs, designed to aid minorities, came under attack

- After 22 years of restoration work, Leonardo da Vinci's *The Last Supper* was placed on display in Milan, Italy
- After 442 years of Portuguese rule, the tiny island of Macao on the southeast coast of China got its first Chinese leader
- After Dr. Jack Kevorkian demonstrated patient-assisted suicide on the TV show *60 Minutes*, he was arrested for first-degree murder
- AIDS-related deaths fell nearly 50 percent
- Apple Computer released iBook, the first laptop designed specifically for consumers
- Archaeologists discovered a three million-year-old skeleton said to be the missing link in human evolution
- As obesity rates climbed dramatically, health food and vitamin supplement mania gripped the nation
- At the Academy Awards, the movie *Titanic* won a record 11 Oscars
- Bill Gates' personal fortune exceeded $100 billion, based on the increased value of Microsoft stock
- Biologists reported in the journal *Science* how they sequenced the genome of the bacterium that causes syphilis, *Treponema pallidum*
- Births to unwed mothers and infant mortality fell to 25-year lows
- Boris Yeltsin resigned as president of Russia, leaving Prime Minister Vladimir Putin as the acting President
- Britney Spears' debut single "Baby One More Time" sold over six million copies worldwide
- Cathy O'Dowd, a South African mountaineer, became the first woman to climb Mount Everest from both the north and south sides
- China announced that it had developed on its own the ability to make neutron bombs and miniature atomic weapons
- Citicorp and Travelers Group announced plans to merge, creating the largest financial-services conglomerate in the world, Citigroup
- Compaq bought Digital Equipment Corporation
- Computer giant Microsoft was accused of illegally seeking Internet control
- Congress passed the Sonny Bono Copyright Term Extension Act, which gave the entertainment industry 20 more years of exclusive rights to all works created since 1923
- Controversy erupted over allegations that large contributors were invited by President Bill Clinton to stay overnight in the White House Lincoln Bedroom
- Dale Earnhardt won the Daytona 500 on his twentieth attempt
- Data sent from the *Galileo* probe indicated that Jupiter's moon Europa had a liquid ocean under a thick crust of ice
- Digital cameras, DVD players, voice recognition software, and prosthetic knee joints all made their first appearances
- During the year, the Dow Jones Industrial Average closed above the 10,000 and 11,000 marks for the first time
- Flavored vodka, digital cameras, DVD players, voice recognition software and prosthetic knee joints all made their first appearance
- Ford Motor Company announced the buyout of Volvo Cars for $6.45 billion
- France defeated Brazil 3-0 to win the 1998 FIFA World Cup
- Georgia Governor Zell Miller proposed that newborns be sent home with a recording of Mozart and Bach to stimulate brain development
- Geraldo Rivera signed a six-year, $30 million contract with CNBC
- *Gotham: A History of New York to 1898* by Edwin G. Burrows won the Pulitzer Prize for U.S. History

- In Laramie, Wyoming, Russell Henderson pled guilty to kidnapping and felony murder for the hate crime killing of Matthew Shepard because he was gay
- In one of the largest drug busts in American history, the Coast Guard intercepted a ship with over 9,500 pounds of cocaine aboard, headed for Houston, Texas
- In the Columbine High School massacre two Littleton, Colorado teenagers opened fire on their teachers and classmates, killing 12 students and one teacher, and then themselves
- Jerry Seinfeld announced the last season for his television show, *Seinfeld*, despite a $5 million-per-episode offer to continue
- Ku Klux Klan leader Samuel Bowers was indicted in Mississippi in the 1966 murder of civil rights leader
- Lance Armstrong won his first Tour de France
- Major efforts began to avert a catastrophic "Y2K" blackout when computers may misread the year 2000 as 1900.
- Mattel introduced a new Barbie doll that had a larger waistline, smaller breasts and more modest clothing; she also had a friend in a wheelchair
- Media magnate Ted Turner donated $1 billion to the United Nations
- *Nancy Mace became the first female cadet to graduate from The Military College of South Carolina*
- Napster, a music downloading service, debuted
- NASA announced that the *Clementine* probe orbiting the moon had found enough water in polar craters to support a human colony and rocket fueling station
- NATO suspended its air strikes after Slobodan Miloševic agreed to withdraw Serbian forces from Kosovo
- NATO's mistaken bombing of the Chinese embassy in Belgrade caused further deterioration of U.S. and Chinese relations
- New York ticket scalpers demanded $1,000 per ticket for the Broadway play *The Lion King*
- Nineteen European nations agreed to forbid human cloning
- Of the original 30 companies in the 1896 Dow Jones Industrial Index, only General Electric has survived the Great Depression, two world wars and the terms of 20 U.S. presidents
- Off the coast of Martha's Vineyard, a plane piloted by John F. Kennedy, Jr. crashed, killing him, his wife Carolyn Bessette Kennedy and her sister Lauren Bessette
- On television, *Sports Night*, *Jesse*, *That '70s Show* and *Felicity* premiered
- Online birth, surgical glue, planets outside the solar system, a DNA database and drive-through cigar stores all made their first appearance
- Oprah Winfrey's support of reading through her Book Club created dozens of bestsellers as Americans followed her lead
- Osama bin Laden published a *fatwa*, declaring *jihad* against all Jews and Crusaders
- Paula Jones accused President Bill Clinton of sexual harassment
- Popular books included *Confederates in the Attic* by Tony Horwitz, *Pillar of Fire: America in the King Years* by Taylor Branch, *Slaves in the Family* by Edward Ball, *A Man in Full* by Tom Wolfe, *The Street Lawyer* by John Grisham, *Rainbow Six* by Tom Clancy, and *Tuesdays with Morrie* by Mitch Albom
- Popular movies included *Shakespeare in Love*, *Saving Private Ryan*, *The Thin Red Line*, *There's Something about Mary*, and *Godzilla*
- President Clinton became the first president to gain line-item veto power over the federal budget
- President Clinton ordered air attacks against Iraq's Saddam Hussein for obstructing the work of UN inspectors
- President Bill Clinton was impeached.

- Princess Diana's death generated more press coverage than any event in the century as millions watched her televised funeral
- Ramzi Yousef was sentenced to life in prison for planning the first World Trade Center bombing
- Researchers in Dallas, Texas, presented findings about an enzyme that slowed aging and cell death
- Russia began to circulate new rubles to stem inflation and promote confidence
- Scottish researchers announced the first cloning of an adult mammal, a sheep named Dolly
- Seventeen major newspapers called for President Bill Clinton's resignation following his admission to a grand jury that he had engaged in an extramarital affair and lied about the relationship
- Severe asthma, common in poor urban areas, was linked to cockroaches
- *Shakespeare in Love, Saving Private Ryan, Life Is Beautiful, A Bug's Life* and *Out of Sight* opened at movie theaters
- Singers Brandy and Monica dominated the Billboard charts with the duet, "The Boy Is Mine," holding the Billboard Hot 100 #1 spot for 13 weeks
- Sir Edward Elgar's unfinished third symphony was completed by Anthony Payne and performed for the first time at the Royal Festival Hall, London
- Smoking was banned in all California bars and restaurants
- *Star Wars Episode I: The Phantom Menace* was released in theaters and became the highest grossing Star Wars film
- Stevie Wonder was honored as the 1999 MusiCares Person of the Year
- Studies indicated that 50 percent of all Americans were overweight
- Suspected "Unabomber" Theodore Kaczynski pleaded guilty and accepted a sentence of life without the possibility of parole
- Television's top-rated shows included *ER, Frasier, Friends, Veronica's Closet, Jesse, NYPD Blue,* and *Touched by an Angel*
- Terrorist bombings of the United States embassies in Dar es Salaam, Tanzania, and Nairobi, Kenya, killed 224 people and injured over 4,500
- Texas Governor George W. Bush announced he would seek the Republican Party's nomination for president
- The 71st Academy Award for Best Picture went to *Shakespeare in Love*
- The annual reunion of Thomas Jefferson's descendents included, for the first time, the descendents of the children who claimed Jefferson as their father and his slave Sally Hemings as their mother
- The Chicago Bulls won their sixth NBA title in eight years, defeating the Utah Jazz 87-86 in Game 6 on a fadeaway jumper by Michael Jordan
- The combined stock market value of Microsoft and Intel was $274 billion, more than the combined market value of GM, Ford, Boeing, Eastman Kodak, Sears, J. P. Morgan, Caterpillar and Kellogg
- The cost of a 30-year mortgage fell to seven percent
- The Denver Broncos became the first American Football Conference (AFC) team in 14 years to win the Super Bowl, as they defeated the Green Bay Packers, 31-24
- The Detroit Red Wings swept the Washington Capitals in four games in the 1998 Stanley Cup finals
- The Exxon-Mobil Corporation merger was completed, forming the largest company in the world
- The final episode of *Seinfeld* was the fourth-highest-rated show in TV history
- The Food and Drug Administration approved Viagra for use as a treatment for male impotence, the first pill to be approved for this condition in the United States
- The Forbes 400 indicated that America's 400 richest families accounted for an estimated 2.6 percent of total personal net worth held by all Americans

- The Goo Goo Dolls single "Iris" set a new Billboard Hot 100 airplay record in the U.S. by achieving 18 weeks at number one
- The IRS Reform Bill passed by Congress shifted the burden of proof from the taxpayer to the IRS
- The last Checker taxicab was retired in New York City and auctioned off for approximately $135,000
- The last ice hockey game was played at the historic Maple Leaf Gardens in Toronto
- The leading tobacco companies made a $368 billion settlement with the states to settle smoking death claims
- The Modern Library's "100 Best Novels of the Century" listed *Ulysses*, *To the Lighthouse*, *A Portrait of the Artist as a Young Man*, *The Age of Innocence*, *Brave New World*, *The Sound and the Fury*, and *The Death of theHeart*
- The movie *Titanic* was the highest-grossing film in history, earning $850 million
- The National Distance Running Hall of Fame was established, inducting five members in its initial class
- The New York Yankees swept the Atlanta Braves to win their twenty-fifth World Series baseball championship
- The number of welfare recipients dropped below 4 percent, the lowest level in 25 years; unemployment, juvenile arrests and births to unwed mothers all fell to 25-year lows
- The price of personal computers (Compaq, Hewlett Packard, IBM) fell below $1,000
- The Roth IRA was introduced by Senator William V. Roth, Jr., as a retirement tool
- The Russian debt default set off a worldwide stock market plunge
- The second Terrastock Festival took place in San Francisco
- The Senate trial in the impeachment of President Clinton resulted in acquittal; he had been impeached by the House of Representatives
- The South Carolina legislature approved a constitutional amendment to remove from the state constitution a 103-year-old paragraph that made marriages between Blacks and Whites illegal.
- The Supreme Court upheld the murder convictions of Timothy McVeigh for the Oklahoma City bombing
- The U.S. defense budget, which was at $370 billion in 1987, fell to $260 billion
- The U.S. House of Representatives released the *Cox Report*, which details the People's Republic of China's nuclear espionage against the U.S. over the prior two decades
- The U.S. Senate rejected ratification of the Comprehensive Test Ban Treaty
- The U.S. Supreme Court ruled that federal laws banning on-the-job sexual harassment also applied when both parties were of the same sex
- The U.S. turned over complete administration of the Panama Canal to the Panamanian Government, as stipulated in the Torrijos-Carter Treaty of 1977
- The United Kingdom banned the importation of land mines
- The United States budget showed a $70 billion surplus, the first time it had been positive since 1969
- The United States claimed 274 of the world's 590 billionaires worldwide
- The United Way of Santa Clara County, California, home of Silicon Valley, collapsed as donations dropped from $32 million in 1990 to $20 million this year
- The World Trade Organization ruled in favor of the United States in its long-running trade dispute with the European Union over bananas
- Tobacco companies made a $260 billion settlement with states for smoking-related illnesses.
- Top albums of the year included the soundtrack from *Titanic*, Celine Dion's *Let's Talk about Love*, *Come On Over* by Shania Twain and *The Backstreet Boys* by the Backstreet Boys

- Two Libyans suspected of bringing down Pan Am flight 103 in 1988 were handed over to Scottish authorities for eventual trial in the Netherlands
- U.S. rockets were fired at Osama Bin Laden's terrorist network in Afghanistan and Sudan
- Undergraduate tuition including room and board at Harvard reached $30,000 a year
- USA soccer player Brandi Chastain scored the game-winning penalty kick against China in the FIFA Women's World Cup
- Veteran astronaut John Glenn returned to space aboard Space Shuttle *Discovery*
- Viacom and CBS merged
- Violent crime in New York City was down by 38 percent; the city's count of 981 homicides was the lowest since 1968
- *Voyager 1,* launched in 1977, was still transmitting from 6.5 billion miles from Earth
- White supremacist John William King was found guilty of kidnapping and killing African-American James Byrd, Jr. by dragging him behind a truck for two miles
- With the spread of cable television, the percentage of the TV viewing audience controlled by the three major networks fell to 49 percent from 75 percent a decade earlier
- *Worth* magazine declared Jupiter Island, Florida, the most expensive town in the country; the median home price was $3.9 million

SECTION THREE: ECONOMY OF THE TIMES

Despite a steady increase in the annual income of Americans from 1990 to 1999, there was also an increase in the cost of basic utilities and consumer goods due to inflation. Economy of the Times illustrates three economic elements: Consumer Expenditures, Annual Income of Standard Jobs, and Selected Prices. We highlighted three years for each category—1992, 1995, and 1998. The Value of a Dollar chart at the end of the section shows the change in the value of $1.00 yearly, from 1860 to 2016.

Consumer Expenditures

The numbers below are per capita expenditures in the years 1992, 1995, 1998 for all employees nationwide.

Category	1992	1995	1998
Auto Maintenance	$245.00	$254.00	$266.00
Auto Usage	$1,741.00	$1,943.00	$2,015.00
Entertainment	$566.00	$598.00	$644.00
Food	$2,651.00	$2,765.00	$2,803.00
Clothing	$514.00	$600.00	$681.00
Furniture	$113.00	$121.00	$130.00
Gas and Oil	$382.00	$393.00	$402.00
Health Care	$597.00	$655.00	$692.00
Health Insurance	$252.00	$305.00	$344.00
Housing	$1,996.00	$2156.00	$2,371.00
New Auto Purchase	$414.00	$445.00	$479.00
Per Capita Consumption	$11,390.00	$12,110	$12,905.00
Personal Business	$1,071.00	$1,130.00	$1,185.00
Personal Care	$153.00	$250.00	$348.00
Public Transportation	$116.00	$128.00	$142.00
Telephone	$237.00	$960.00	$283.00
Tobacco	$105.00	$106.00	$107.00
Utilities	$527.00	$556.00	$593.00

Annual Income of Standard Jobs

The numbers below are annual income for standard jobs across America in the years 1992, 1995, and 1998.

Category	1992	1995	1998
Bituminous Coal Mining	$39,988.00	$40,493.00	$42,711.00
Building Trades	$25,945.00	$26,739.00	$28,465.00
Domestics	$9,527.00	$10,854.00	$12,050.00
Farm Labor	$14,493.00	$15,019.00	$15,863.00
Finance, Insurance, and Real Estate	$31,008.00	$36,013.00	$38,577.00
Gas, Electricity, and Sanitation Workers	$33,940.00	$36,755.00	$38,936.00
Manufacturing, Durable Goods	$25,112.00	$26,992.00	$28,507.00
Manufacturing, Nondurable Goods	$21,823.00	$23,181.00	$24,387.00
Medical/Health Services Workers	$18,522.00	$20,091.00	$21,234.00
Miscellaneous Manufacturing	$19,107.00	$20,508.00	$21,798.00
Motion Picture Services	$35,152.00	$37,541.00	$39,585.00
Nonprofit Organization Workers	$13,368.00	$14,094.00	$15,016.00
Transportation Workers, Local and Highway	$16,770.00	$18,525.00	$20,010.00
Postal Employees	$33,210.00	$37,609.00	$35,797.00
Public School Teachers	$24,561.00	$25,816.00	$27,130.00
Radio Broadcasting and Television Workers	$28,455.00	$30,702.00	$32,223.00
Railroad Workers	$36,772.00	$40,672.00	$42,175.00
State and Local Government Workers	$25,863.00	$27,369.00	$29,023.00
Telephone and Telegraph Workers	$31,034.00	$33,871.00	$35,844.00
Wholesale and Retail Trade Workers	$12,930.00	$13,597.00	$14,412.00

Selected Prices

1992

Advil Caplets, 100-Count	$6.68
Alarm Clock	$9.99
American Museum of Natural History Tour	$10.00
Apple Macintosh Powerbook, 180 4/80	$3,799.00
Automobile, 1992 Miata	$14.978.00
Backpack, Leather	$29.95
Baseball Cap	$2.99
Bath Towel, J.C. Penney	$4.90
Bed, Cherrywood, Full-Size	$399.88
Blank Videotapes, Three-Pack	$8.49
Brother Intellifax-600 Fax Machine with Cutter	$353.43
Camcorder, RCA 8 mm	$699.00
Camel Genesis Sixty-Second Tent, 7' x 8'	$89.98
Canvas Pants	$19.99
Car Seat	$65.00
CD/Cassette Player, Sony	$166.00
Christmas Tree, Artificial	$124.99
Chrysler LeBaron, 1988	$8,495.00
Clothing	$667.00
Coffee Maker	$7.99
Columbia Bugaboo Parka	$119.00
Comforter	$26.88
Crackers, Ritz	$1.69
Cruise Ticket, Alaska, per Person	$2,395.00
Dishwasher, Whirlpool	$299.00
Duct Tape	$2.99
Easy Chair, La-Z-Boy	$599.00
Eggs, Dozen	$0.89

Etonic Stableair Base 11 Men's Running Shoes $49.96
Exercise Bicycle $249.99
Exercise Equipment, Nordic Track $399.95
Fax Machine $353.43
Gold Medal Flour, Five-Pound Bag $0.79
Goodyear 54S Tire $41.95
Hibachi Grill $6.99
High School Class Ring $69.95
Hose, 3-Gauge Sprinkler, 50' $7.99
Lawn Mower $289.00
Leggings $15.00
Light Bulb, Halogen $8.96
Loving Care Supreme Queen Size Mattress $189.95
Luggage, Garment Bag, American Tourister $39.96
Mardi Gras Paper Towels $0.50
Men's Tennis Shoes, Converse $24.00
Microwave Oven $99.00
Monsanto Round-Up Weed Killer $16.99
New Orleans Jazz and Heritage Festival Ticket $25.00
Nike Air Cross Trainer Shoes $58.99
Nissan Altima GXE, 1993 . . . .$14,484.00
Nyquil, 10-Ounce Bottle $4.93
Ointment, Preparation H $2.88
Oki-810 Car Phone with Antenna and Installation $149.00

Pager, Motorola, per Month $7.95
Philips Bag-A-Way, Two Bulbs $1.61
Pistol, Smith & Wesson, .38 Caliber $309.00
Plastic Reynolds Wrap $1.99
Raymond Weil Men's Watch $750.00
Rubbermaid Laundry Basket. $2.99
Sealy Queen Size Mattress $324.00
Sheet Set $17.96
Shelby Women's Leather Shoe $68.00
Sheraton New York Hotel Room, per Night $169.00
Shirt, Man's Spalding Golf Shirt. $14.98
Shower Curtain. $19.77
Smoke Detector $5.99
Television, Zenith 25-Inch $388.00
Tent, 7' x 8' $89.98
Turkey, per Pound $0.69
VCR, JVC $399.00
Vodka, Absolut, 750 ml $12.29
Wall Calendar $12.85
Washington State Delicious Apples, per Pound. $0.59
Wild Bird Food, 20 Pounds $2.99
Wilson Tennis Racket, 3.0 Tennis Frame $129.97
Women's Polo Shirt. $18.00
Work Shirt, Man's. $15.40
Xerox Personal Photocopier $899.99

1995

Advil, 50 Count $3.99

Airline Ticket, Los Angeles to Chicago $198.00

Answering Machine $250.00

Apple Personal Computer $1,099.00

Armoire $899.00

Art Exhibit, New York $8.00

Automobile, Lincoln Mark VIII $20,292.00

Bathroom Tissue, 12-Pack $5.49

Bathtub Reglazing $170.00

Battery, Two-pack $6.00

Bra, Maidenform $12.99

Breadmaker $100.00

Bridgestone High Performance 65 HR Tire $85.00

Camcorder $2,700.00

Carpet Deodorizer, Arm & Hammer $0.99

Cashmere-Blend Jacket $69.99

Cat Food $7.99

Cell Phone $49.99

Chair, Walnut $195.00

Comforter $160.00

Computer, Compaq Presario 1235 . . . . $1,199.00

Cordless Drill $129.00

Crest Gel Tartar Control Toothpaste, 6.4 Ounces $2.00

Cutlery Set $9.99

Dental Services, Tooth Extraction $25.00

Deodorant, Old Spice $1.79

Disney's Lion King Video $29.97

Everyday Battery, D-Size, Two-Pack $6.00
Exercise Equipment, Treadmill $299.96
Field Jacket $69.50
Fishing Reel $99.99
Food Processor, Cuisinart $139.00
Fur Coat, Russian Sable $7,995.00
Garage Door Opener $275.00
Gas Grill $259.00
Hotel Room, Chicago $160.00
Kirium Chronometer Men's Watch $1,695.00
Krazy Glue $1.00
Low Flush Toilet $270.00
Lubriderm Lotion, 16 Ounces $7.00
Luggage, Samsonite $399.99
Notebook Computer, Compaq Presario $1,199.00
Olive Oil, 23 Ounces $32.00
Organizer, Electronic Palm III $369.00
Piano, Yamaha, Digital $997.00
Pink/White Lily Flowering Tulip Bulbs, 100 . . . .$43.00
Pizza, Little Caesar's $12.95
Purse, Kenneth Cole $148.50
Rand Barbie 12" Girl's Bicycle $49.97
Roasting Pan, Calphalon $99.99
Robitussin DM Cough Suppressant, Four Ounces $3.00
Roller Blades $34.97
Scanner $49.00
Secret Deodorant, 1.7 Ounces $1.50
Shaving Cream $129.95
Sierra Four-Piece Setting; Bakelite Handles $40.00
Soccer Cleats $129.95
Sofa, Green Stripe Cover $999.00
SOLO Radar and Laser Cordless Detector $199.00
Studio Apartment, N.Y., Month $1,300.00
Television, Digital Home Theater $10,000
Tennis Racquet $79.99
Tire, Bridgestone High-Performance HR15 . . . .$85.00
Toilet $49.00

Fabric Softener, Ultra-Downy, 20 Ounces $2.00
Variflex Rollerblades $34.97
Vegetable Slicer $45.00
Videotape, Disney's Lion King $29.97
Videotape, Lethal Weapon $15.99
Water, 1.5 Liter $0.49
Whirlpool Tub $1,660.00
Wing Chair, Floral Cover $699.00
Zenith 19" Color Television $139.00
Zinsser's Blend & Glaze Decorative Paint, Gallon $25.00

1998

Amaretti Soft Almond Cookies in Tin $18.00
Answering Machine, Bank & Olufsen Beotalk 1100 . . . .$250.00
Audio Tape $5.00
Automobile, Volvo Sedan $26,895
Bath Towel $24.00
Bathtub Reglazing $170.00
Beer Mugs, Monogrammed $40.00
Belt, Fine-Grained Italian Leather $42.00
Blender $49.99
Book, Mediterranean Cooking $14.95
Breadmaker $129.99
Bulbs, 100 Tulips $43.00
Cabinet, 54" Utility, Ready to Finish $44.00
Camcorder $2,700.00
Camera, Canon, 35 mm $1,900.00
Carpet Deodorizer $0.99
Cat Food, Purina, 20 Pounds $7.99
Ceiling Fan $190.00
Cell Phone $199.00
Chair, La-Z-Boy $332.99
Cleanser, Mr. Clean $2.00
Computer, Apple MAC Performa $2,699.00
Computer, Compaq Presario $1,999.00
Cookware, All-Clad Soup Pot $230.00
Deodorant, Old Spice $1.79
Digital Camera $800.00
Electronic Organizer, Palm III $369.00
Envelopes, 100 9 x 12 Brown Kraft $4.65
Epson Stylus Color Printer $279.00
Fabric Softener, Downy, 20 Ounces $2.00
Field Jacket, Cotton Canvas with Corduroy Collar $69.50
Film, Kodak Gold, 24 Exposures $6.00
Flannel Pants by Diane Richard $28.00
Fur Coat $2,595.00
Garage Door Opener, Installed $275.00
Geometrics from Pakistan Rug, 9'1" x 12'1" $2,458.00
Hotel Room, South Carolina $260.00

Jacket, Adidas Polar Fleece $69.95
Ladderback Chair, Walnut Construction $195.00
Leather Chart Case, Willis & Geiger $470.00
Loafers of Flexible Nappa Leather $68.00
Luggage, Samsonite Hardside Cart $399.99
Mr. Potato Head Coin Bank $19.95
Admission for Museum for African Art $8.00
Necklace, Cultured Pearls, 18 . . . .$425.00
Olive Oil, 23 Ounces $32.00
Oriental Rug, 9' x 12' $2,458.00
Palm Pilot $369.00
Piano, Yamaha Digital $997.00
Pocketbook, Kenneth Cole $148.50
Pulsar Solar Watch, Man's $215.00
Purse, Kenneth Cole, Leather $148.50
Radar Detector $199.00
Roaster Pan, Calphalon $99.99
Shampoo, Vidal Sassoon $2.50
Shoes, Women's Hush Puppies $29.99
Soccer Ball $69.95
Soccer Cleats $129.95
Software, Microsoft Office 4.2 . . . .$248.99
Sterling Silver Ring with Cubic Zieconia, Woman's $40.00
Suit, Man's Hickey-Freeman $760.00
Tea, Tetley Ice Tea Mix $0.99
Television, Zenith 19" Digital Color $139.00
The Lion King $29.99

Tire, Bridgestone. $85.00
Tissue, Kleenex, 150-Count $0.99
Tuna, per Pound $2.06
Turtleneck Underwear, Pure Silk $32.50
VCR $240.00
Vegetable Slicer. $45.00
Viansa, 1997 Sauvignon Blanc $12.00
Volvo S70 Sedan, New $26,895.00
Water, Evian Pure Drinking Water, 1.5 Liter $0.49
Wine Bottle Holder. $150.00
Wine, 1994 Chardonnay Reserve $36.00

The Value of a Dollar, 1860-2016

Composite Consumer Price Index; 1860=1

Year	Amount	Year	Amount	Year	Amount	Year	Amount
1860	$1.00	1900	$1.01	1940	$1.69	1980	$9.97
1861	$1.06	1901	$1.02	1941	$1.77	1981	$10.94
1862	$1.22	1902	$1.04	1942	$1.96	1982	$11.62
1863	$1.52	1903	$1.06	1943	$2.08	1983	$11.99
1864	$1.89	1904	$1.07	1944	$2.12	1984	$12.50
1865	$1.96	1905	$1.06	1945	$2.17	1985	$12.95
1866	$1.92	1906	$1.08	1946	$2.35	1986	$13.20
1867	$1.78	1907	$1.13	1947	$2.68	1987	$13.67
1868	$1.71	1908	$1.11	1948	$2.90	1988	$14.24
1869	$1.64	1909	$1.10	1949	$2.87	1989	$14.92
1870	$1.58	1910	$1.14	1950	$2.90	1990	$15.72
1871	$1.47	1911	$1.14	1951	$3.13	1991	$16.38
1872	$1.47	1912	$1.17	1952	$3.19	1992	$16.88
1873	$1.45	1913	$1.19	1953	$3.22	1993	$17.38
1874	$1.37	1914	$1.20	1954	$3.24	1994	$17.83
1875	$1.32	1915	$1.22	1955	$3.23	1995	$18.33
1876	$1.29	1916	$1.31	1956	$3.28	1996	$18.88
1877	$1.26	1917	$1.54	1957	$3.39	1997	$19.32
1878	$1.20	1918	$1.82	1958	$3.48	1998	$19.63
1879	$1.20	1919	$2.08	1959	$3.50	1999	$20.06
1880	$1.23	1920	$2.41	1960	$3.56	2000	$20.74
1881	$1.23	1921	$2.16	1961	$3.60	2001	$21.32
1882	$1.23	1922	$2.02	1962	$3.64	2002	$21.66
1883	$1.22	1923	$2.06	1963	$3.68	2003	$22.16
1884	$1.18	1924	$2.06	1964	$3.73	2004	$22.76
1885	$1.17	1925	$2.11	1965	$3.79	2005	$23.53
1886	$1.13	1926	$2.13	1966	$3.90	2006	$24.29
1887	$1.14	1927	$2.09	1967	$4.02	2007	$24.97
1888	$1.14	1928	$2.06	1968	$4.19	2008	$25.91
1889	$1.11	1929	$2.06	1969	$4.42	2009	$25.81
1890	$1.09	1930	$2.01	1970	$4.67	2010	$26.22
1891	$1.09	1931	$1.83	1971	$4.88	2011	$27.06
1892	$1.09	1932	$1.65	1972	$5.03	2012	$27.63
1893	$1.08	1933	$1.57	1973	$5.35	2013	$28.05
1894	$1.04	1934	$1.61	1974	$5.93	2014	$28.49
1895	$1.01	1935	$1.65	1975	$6.47	2015	$28.54
1896	$1.01	1936	$1.67	1976	$6.85	2016	$28.90
1897	$1.00	1937	$1.73	1977	$7.30		
1898	$1.00	1938	$1.70	1978	$7.85		
1899	$1.00	1939	$1.67	1979	$8.74		

SECTION FOUR: ALL AROUND US

This section offers a ringside seat to the issues and attitudes that were 1990s America. These 50 documents, listed in chronological order below, come from newspapers and magazines of the time. They show how America's changing ideas on education, politics, music, sports, immigration, and health were shaped.

இல்லை

"Fast Food Industry Boxing Over Plastic Foam,"
Chicago Daily Herald, November 11, 1990

Call it the environmental burger war. Spurred on by a growing number of environmentally conscious customers, the fast food industry is getting into an argument about which company decided to make less trash first. The latest combatant is Burger King Corp., the Miami-based number two chain. Burger King burst forth Wednesday with newspaper advertisements implying that archrival McDonald's Corp. is a Johnny-come-lately to the world of environmental consciousness. "Welcome to the club," said Burger King ad. "We wonder what the planet would be like if you had joined us in 1955." At issue is a much publicized announcement by McDonald's on November 1 that they will no longer serve sandwiches in convenient but non-biodegradable plastic foam boxes.

Environmentalists have argued for some time that hamburger packaging of this sort is a waste and a hazard because it is used only briefly, then sits around making landfills full. In announcing the decision, Ed Rensi, president of U.S. operations at McDonald's, said that other fast food companies are likely to follow the lead set by McDonald's. But Burger King says it never used plastic foam to package its sandwiches. Instead, it packages its hamburger in paper boxes. Foodmaker Inc.'s Jack-in-the-Box chain, a smaller rival of McDonald's said it had already eliminated foam packaging from 93 percent of its menu items and hopes to drop all of it within the next few months.

இல்லை

"Legacy, Heirlooms from Seven Generations of One Southern Family,"
by Susan Stiles Dowell, *Southern Accents*, July-August, 1990

"Perhaps nowhere in America is a regional identity more strongly evident than in the South. In literature, lifestyle, historical perspective and even accent, southerners nurture a strong sense of place. Lest anyone overlook the alchemy of family and homeplace, consider the heirlooms of one southern family. Accumulated over two centuries, during seven generations, and by six branches of the family tree, they are a vivid reminder of place—a link with a past that gives continuity to the present. The owners represent the eighth and tenth generations of their families in America. Removed by less than a hundred miles from the original seventeenth-century land and manorial grants of their ancestors, they can visit many of their former family seats today. One such house, built in the eighteenth century, still serves as a residence for a branch of the family. And many of the stunning pieces of silver and porcelain in the owners' collection were originally bought for its seventeenth century predecessor, which stood nearby.

Few American families have memories beyond two or three former generations, never mind this personal link to the past. The husband explains that the generations became closer for having such tangible objects of connection. 'These possessions,' he says, 'knit the generations together. There's an awareness, through the pieces, of being part of a greater whole.' To illustrate this point, the wife tells a story about the matriarch who was left with her children and servants on the family plantation during the Civil War. Word came from town that Union troops bent on pillage were headed for the house, but the young lady kept her head. She had the family silver buried in the garden and sat on the portico to wait. When the Yankees marched up the long drive with an inebriated captain at their head, they were foiled in their attempt to get into the house and its liquor stores. This formidable young matron, so the story goes, was sitting on the keys to the house and would not move. 'She was my great-grandmother who died when I was three. Our generations touched and still do through these heirlooms we have in common.'

Some of the legends about the heirlooms bear repeating. The largest piece of silver in the collection, a massive three foot ovoid waiter made in London, was used during the twenty-first birthday festivities of an ancestor in 1800. It seems the master was celebrating not only his own birthday with a host of friends around the dining room table, but also the birth of his first son. In honor of both occasions, the baby boy was placed on the great waiter and passed around the table. The event was repeated in this century when another baby boy's advent into the family was celebrated with the same ceremony, around the same dining room table! The sentiments of both Tories and Patriots cling to many of the pieces, elucidating a tenor of the times undocumented by history books. The pair of miniature portraits on ivory surrounded by seed pearls, painted by celebrated miniaturist Richard Cosway circa 1774, depicts a bright young couple of London society who were collateral ancestors of the owners. On the eve of the Revolution, the gentleman of the pair gave up his position in the British Coldstream Guards to return to the family seat in America. When he subsequently died at home, she returned to England to live out her days. The husband comments, 'I always thought it remarkable that (our ancestors) weren't loyalists during the Revolution because they had so much to lose. There was only one loyalist I can think of, and his son was on George Washington's personal staff.' He speaks with familial experience when he says, 'There seemed to be an understanding of the problem of political loyalty back then and how people, even within the confines of a family, could go either way.'

During the War of 1812 when pirates and Tory sympathizers preyed upon unprotected American estates, some silver was stolen from the family's plantation. Records exist of a claim being made for the pieces, but no dramatic account of the outcome survives. One can always wonder if family member Francis Scott Key's celebrated verses and unbridled patriotism exacted some British retribution.

Perhaps the most stunning part of the family's collection is the tobacco leaf porcelain made in China circa 1860 for the Portuguese market. At least two hundred pieces were ordered by the family through London, and the extant bill of sale indicates that importation to be among the earliest for the pattern in the colonies. Roughly a quarter of the collection belongs to the present owners. The wife laughs when she remembers what she thought of the pattern as a child. 'It was everywhere in my grandmother's house, and I though it was gaudy,' she says. 'Children tend to be conservative in their tastes, and to me this was a weird pattern. Mother told me it had great value, and I don't think we understood why I thought it was hideous.'

Of course, the wife's regard for the tobacco leaf pattern changed as she matured and came to understand its significance to her family. As with most of the pieces, the owners are now of one mind and heart with the predilections of their ancestors and speak of this sentiment in terms of identity. Fortunately for us, that identity sheds a rare light on the too often impersonal documentation of history."

Editorial: "Caller ID Poses Invasion of Privacy," by Jeffrey M. Shaman, *Chicago Tribune*, May 18, 1990

"A new telephone device known as Caller ID is the latest technological innovation that at first blush seems to improve our lives, when in fact it may have disastrous consequences. Already available in a number of states, Caller ID is to be brought to Illinois if approved by the Commerce Commission. Caller ID operates by displaying the phone number of an incoming call on a screen at the recipient's phone while it is ringing. Without an implement that allows callers to selectively block the display of their telephone numbers, Caller ID automatically reveals them, and perhaps their identity and location as well. In the absence of a blocking implement, Caller ID deprives individuals of the ability to decide when and to whom to give their telephone numbers. This is an invasion of personal privacy and autonomy. Many individuals will be deterred from calling crisis centers that deal with suicide, rape, child abuse, or AIDS for fear of having their identities revealed. Psychiatrists, doctors, social workers, and lawyers will not be able to return emergency calls from home if they want to keep their numbers confidential."

๛๛๛๛๛๛๛

"Preface, A Parent's Guide to Coaching Soccer," by Jack McCarthy, 1990

"Hey, coach, I can't make baseball practice tomorrow because I have a soccer game, okay?" I looked down at the robust, freckle-faced kid, and remember wondering what this red-blooded American boy saw in soccer. It was 1978, not so long ago. My attitude reflected the ignorance of an entire generation of American parents. We grew up in a culture where football was the number one game. I had no idea what soccer was really about. I knew it was played all over Europe, and I figured Europe would come to our way of thinking sooner or later. It was a dark age here for soccer, and I was a dinosaur.

A few years later, my daughter developed an interest in playing sports. She tried a year of baseball, but never really got into it. Our town had just started a soccer team for girls a bit older than my daughter. I called the president of the local soccer club and asked why there was no team for younger girls. He said, "There is no coach." I answered, "You have a coach now; what do I do?" He said, "Get on the phone and put together a team." A month later we were on the field.

Fortunately for me, none of the girls had ever played soccer. They never knew how little I knew and neither did their parents. I had coached and played other sports before, so I could fake it, but I really knew nothing. Little did I know that I was on the threshold of my most rewarding coaching experience, and that I was about to become part of one of the greatest games in the world. The soccer explosion of the 1980s is a clear testimony to its growing popularity.

I figured the first step was to get a book on soccer. As I stated in my earlier book, A Parent's Guide to Coaching Baseball, there were plenty of baseball books, but none that really helped the novice. Well, what I found when looking for something on soccer was even worse. I couldn't find any books at all. Fortunately, there were coaching clinics available throughout our state soccer organization, and I learned the fundamentals. There just wasn't anything that really brought the concept of soccer home to me, or that clearly showed me how to develop a kid's skills. I felt very much alone. Most coaching materials assume the reader has played the game. But, like most American parents, I had not.... How did my girls do? We lost our first game 17-0 against a team that had been together for three years. So I set our goals realistically. The next game we decided to keep the other team below 10 goals, and we succeeded. Then our goal was to score, and we succeeded. Finally, our goal was to win a game, and we were successful in that, also. Two years later the girls went undefeated, and then became the first-ever girls' varsity team at Hillsboro High school in New Jersey. Then I dropped out to coach my younger son in soccer for a few years. During my years coaching soccer, I played the game myself on weekends, pickup games for coaches and parents at our high school field. It is hard to learn the sport as an adult, but the skills are slowly coming.

The Interstate System

- Created by Congress in 1956, the Interstate Highway System in America was now 41 years old.

- The Great Wall of China and the Interstate Highway System were among the only human creations that could be seen by astronauts from an orbiting spacecraft.

- The property that Highway authorities had acquired in order to site the Interstates equaled a land mass the size of Delaware.

- When created, politicians and writers celebrated the goal of "man's triumph over nature." President Eisenhower passionately believed in the need for a modern, interstate highway system to ensure the "personal safety, the general prosperity, the national security of the American people."

- Before the passage of the Federal-Aid Highway Act of 1956, the Bureau of Public Roads produced a 100-page book designating the 2,175 miles of proposed interstate highways.

- Congressmen, businessmen, and local politicians could study and anticipate the impact the Interstate Highway System would have on their communities.

- The Federal-Aid Highway Act of 1956 was signed by Eisenhower in June 1956 while he was recovering from surgery in Walter Reed Army Medical Center.

- The bill authorized $25 billion for 12 years to accelerate construction of a National System of Interstate and Defense Highways.

- It also created a Highway Trust Fund supported by increasing the federal tax on gas and diesel fuel from $0.02 to $0.03 cents, and increased the federal portion of construction of interstate highways to 90 percent.

- All standards were based on meeting the needs of American traffic in 1972, the year the System was slated for completion.

- Editorials nationwide lauded the legislation, since Americans valued their mobility.

- At the time, 72 percent of American families owned an automobile; by 1970, the number would rise to 82 percent.

- Despite enthusiasm, early construction went slowly.

- Even though the federal government paid for 90 percent of the costs of the new highways and could veto expenditures, individual states had the responsibility of initiating construction projects and determining when and where to build particular sections of interstate.

- In many states, including Iowa, bid rigging was common enough that several county officials were convicted and sent to prison.

- Then, in the early 1960s, with the leadership of Rex Whitton, road construction was on schedule and honest.

- By the stated 1972 completion date for the Interstate System, enough roadways had been completed so that the wide bands of concrete were highly controversial.

- Mass transit advocates were lobbying for more mass transit dollars in the face of a gas crisis; many areas also feared that even more urban sprawl and white flight would result from building highly efficient and convenient Interstates from city to city.

- From the inception of the Highway Act, the control of expenditures and handling of federal dollars within each state had caused numerous political and financial tug-of-wars; by mid-1975, the question of control caused outright warfare in many cities and states.

- Highways that cut through urban areas such as Boston or San Francisco were accused of destroying neighborhoods and dividing the city.

- Despite criticism, traffic on the nation's Interstates boomed; travel time from region to region dropped dramatically.

- Soon, skiers in St. Louis thought little of driving to Colorado for the weekend; winter-weary water lovers from Michigan shot down the Interstate to Florida in record time.

- By 1986, the building of 97 percent of the System had been completed.

- Even though the Interstate System accounted for about one percent of the nation's highways, it carried about 20 percent of the nation's traffic and 50 percent of its trucks.

- People and businesses placed their lives in relation to the highway, as in, "we are about three miles east of 77 on Highway 21."

- Relocating businesses began asking more about transportation routes than about labor forces; if the roads were available, the people would come.

- In 1990, there were 115 million workers in the United States age 16 and older; 99.8 million of those workers rode a car, motorcycle, or truck to work, while six million used public transit, and five million walked or road a bike.

- Yet, despite the frenzy of activity, Highway System accidents actually fell.

- In 1990, just 4,941 people lost their lives on the Interstate System, which carried cars, trucks, and business 479 billion miles; the death rate per 100 million vehicle miles was 1.03.

❧❧❧❧❧❧❧❧

"The Girls of Summer, The U.S. Women's Soccer Team and How It Changed the World," by Jere Longman

Like representative government, soccer has been imported from England and democratized in the United States. It has become the great social and athletic equalizer in suburban America. From kindergarten, girls are placed on an equal footing with boys. In the fall, weekend soccer games are as prevalent in suburbia as yard sales. Girls have their own leagues, or they play with boys, and they suffer from no tradition that says women will grow professionally to be less successful than men....

Soccer has become the fastest growing sport in the country in both high school and college. From 1981 through 1999, the number of women's collegiate soccer teams grew from 77 to 818, propelled by Title IX. There are now 93 more women's teams than men's teams at the university level. Soccer is serious enough now as a sport that coaches are fired for poor performance, the big football schools are showing increased interest, and a few of the top women's collegiate programs now use private planes for recruiting. Chris Petrucelli, who won a national championship for Notre Dame, was lured to Texas in early 1999 by a contract worth $180,000 annually and by a $28 million soccer and track facility. On the high school level, there were 257,586 girls registered to play soccer in 1998-1999, compared with 11,534 in 1976-77. Of the 18 million registered soccer players the United States, 7.5 million, or 40 percent, were girls and women, according to the Soccer Industry Council of America.

❧❧❧❧❧❧❧❧

"Just What Do Suburbs Want at O'Hare? Fewer Flights, Less Noise," by Patricia Szymczak, *Chicago Tribune*, May 20, 1990

"If suburbia had its way at O'Hare International Airport, it would put the world's busiest air transportation center on a diet. Here's the menu: Cut flights by 100,000 a year, put airlines on a noise budget to make them schedule their newest and quietest aircraft into O'Hare, impose a nighttime curfew, compensate homeowners nearest the airport for property value lost to jet noise and other pollution, phase all of the above in slowly and in coordination with the opening of a new third airport in 1995 Close O'Hare.

Park Ridge Mayor Martin Butler, one of the most militant suburban voices in the O'Hare noise controversy, gets accused, in jest, of wanting to do that sometimes. 'It's stupid. It's unthinkable,' Butler says. 'O'Hare has been a tremendous engine driving the area's economy,' he says. 'But it is an engine that's running wild. The question is, what is the balance between O'Hare's impact on livability and its impact on economic vitality?' Mary Rose Loney, Chicago's first deputy commissioner of aviation, estimates that O'Hare pumps $11 billion a year into the economy of the six-county region. There are 50,000 jobs on the field alone.... 'Noise is not just a product of volume,' Loney said. 'But volume, a noise budget, and a nighttime curfew are on the table as solutions to the noise problem,' she said. Yet she added, 'Before we leap in we need to look at the impact in terms of jobs and dollars.'

The suburbs couldn't agree more. In fact, they contend a smaller O'Hare would be better for the region so far as jobs and economic muscle are concerned, if its downsizing were completed in tandem with the opening of another airport as big or bigger. Consider this: The Federal Aviation Administration says O'Hare at its current size is inefficient and actually chases business away from Chicago if used by more than 700,000 flights a year. That's because above 700,000 flights, delays become so intolerable that air travelers who are only connecting in Chicago to another flight choose to connect in another city, FAA studies say."

༺⚬༺⚬༺⚬༺⚬༺

"EPA Unveils Plan to Reduce Acid Rain,"
Salina Journal, October 30, 1991

The Environmental Protection Agency on Tuesday unveiled its plan to curb acid rain by forcing utilities to cut sulfur oxide emissions by 40 percent this decade. EPA Administrator William Reilly estimated that the proposed rules would cost $4 billion annually by the year 2000. They will lead to sharp increases in electricity rates in the areas of the country that have the dirtiest coal-burning power plants, he said. The new rules are expected to push up electricity rates about 1.5 percent nationwide, but much higher in some areas, Reilly said. He maintained the higher cost "will be more than offset" by the environmental benefits from controlling acid rain. The proposed regulations, which are expected to be made final early next year, implement the Clean Air Act passed by Congress last year. Acid rain is the name given to the industrial pollution that may be carried long distances in the atmosphere before returning to the earth as rain, snow, or soot, killing aquatic life. Sulfur dioxide emissions, mainly from coal-burning power plants in the Midwest, are a major cause of acid rain.

༺⚬༺⚬༺⚬༺⚬༺

"Reshaping the Mideast: After the Fall of Saddam,"
by Eliahu Salpeter, *The New Leader*, January 28, 1991

Almost from the start of the fighting in the Persian Gulf, one could discern the outlines of major changes likely to result in the geopolitics of the Middle East, in relations between the region and the outside world, as well as in maneuverings among the U.S., Europe and the Soviet Union. For although technically the war was launched to liberate Kuwait, it soon became clear that the destruction of Saddam Hussein's regime in Iraq was Washington's ultimate objective—and that rarely, if ever, had the conduct of a military conflict been as strongly influenced by potential postwar policies.

President George Bush's firm insistence upon sticking to the January 15 United Nations deadline for Iraq to quit Kuwait or face the consequences sharply enhanced U.S. credibility in this part of the globe and beyond. So did his speedy dispatch of American-manned Patriot missile batteries to Israel after the first Scud attack. In part, this explains Jerusalem's willingness to go along with Washington's request that it exhibit restraint and not pursue its traditional practice of instant retaliation. It should quickly be noted, though, that the enthusiastic support of the Palestine Liberation Organization (PLO) for Saddam, and the cheers sent up by the Palestinians in Jordan and the occupied territories when Iraqi missiles began to come down on Israel, have reinforced the hawks' opposition to establishing a Palestinian state 20 miles from Tel Aviv.

What is probably more important, doves now have grave doubts about such an entity, too. The Scuds confirmed the feelings of many here that the refusal of most Arab countries to accept the Jewish State's existence is a greater threat than the intifada. Israelis will, in short, be much more reluctant than in the past to make groundbreaking concessions to the Palestinians. Most of them believe the experiences of the war will have a positive impact on Washington's attitude when attention turns to settling longstanding Middle East disputes, yet they may be deluding themselves because of their belief that relations with the U.S. are close again.

"The objective is not simply to retaliate for the barbaric attack on Sarajevo, but to send a very strong deterrent signal to the Bosnian Serbs that this time around, the international community means business."

—*NATO spokesman Jamie Shea*

"Suburban Growth Is Finding Wildlife to Be a Formidable Foe," *Chicago Tribune*, March 9, 1991

"After a platoon of raccoons invaded his attic last February, Burt Wright thought his Hinsdale home was becoming a barracks for wayward critters. The five masked marauders, who apparently decided to relocate to the Wright's home after a development cleared a nearby vacant lot, gnawed on the insulation surrounding the air-conditioning ducts and plundered the garbage.... Whether it's a raccoon in the attic, beavers building dams in the drainage ditches, or coyotes in a St. Charles subdivision, encounters with wildlife are becoming more common these days, according to state statistics. The primary reason, experts agree, is growth. Du Page County alone has grown in population by 100,000 in the last 10 years, with subdivisions sprawling into territory once the exclusive province of beavers, raccoons, and deer."

"Practice Kaizen, New Work Habits for a Radically Changing World," by Price Pritchett, 1991

"A strong organization is the best position to protect your career. If it's financially successful, your paycheck is more secure. If it keeps getting better and better in the way it does business, your future usually gets brighter. But the organization doesn't improve unless its people do. Continuous improvement—the Japanese call it kaizen—offers some of the best insurance for both your career and your organization. Kaizen is the relentless quest for a better way, for higher quality craftsmanship. Think of it as the daily pursuit of perfection. Kaizen keeps you reaching, stretching to outdo yesterday.

The continuous improvements may come bit by bit. But enough of these small, incremental gains will eventually add up to a valuable competitive advantage. Also, if every employee constantly keeps an eye out for improvements, major innovations are more likely to occur. The spirit of kaizen can trigger dramatic breakthroughs. Without kaizen, you and your employer will gradually lose ground. Eventually, you'll both be 'out of business,' because the competition never stands still. Tom Peters puts it this way: 'Good quality is a stupid idea. The only thing that counts is your quality getting better at a more rapid rate than your principal competitors. It's real simple. If we're not getting more, better, faster than they are getting more, better, faster, then we're getting less better or more worse.' Nobody can afford to rest on a reputation anymore. Circumstances change too quickly. Competition gets tougher and more global all the time. What we consider 'good' today is seen as 'so-so' by tomorrow."

"The Overworked American, The Unexpected Decline in Leisure," by Juliet B. Schor, *Basic Books*, 1992

"In the last 20 years the amount of time Americans have spent on their jobs has risen steadily. Each year the change is small, amounting to about nine hours, or slightly more than one additional day of work. In any given year, such a small increment has probably been imperceptible. But the accumulated increase over two decades is substantial. When surveyed, Americans report that they have only 16.5 hours of leisure a week, after the obligations of job and household are taken care of. Working hours are already longer than they were 40 years ago. If present trends continue, by the end of the century Americans will be spending as much time at their jobs as they did back in the 1920s.

The rise of worktime was unexpected. For nearly a hundred years, hours had been declining. When this decline abruptly ended in the late 1940s, it marked the beginning of a new era in worktime. But the change was barely noticed. Equally surprising, but also hardly recognized, has been the deviation from western Europe. After progressing in tandem for nearly a century, the United States veered off into a trajectory of declining leisure, while in Europe work has been disappearing. Forty years later, the differences are large. U.S. manufacturing employees currently work 320 more hours—the equivalent of over two months—than their counterparts in western Germany or France.

The decline in Americans' leisure time is in sharp contrast to the potential provided by the growth of productivity. Productivity measures the goods and services that result from each hour worked. When productivity rises, a worker can either produce the current output in less time, or remain at work the same amount of hours and produce more. Every time productivity increases, we are presented with the possibility of either more free time or more money. That's the productivity dividend.

Since 1948, productivity has failed to rise in only five years. The level of productivity of the U.S. worker has more than doubled. In other words, we could now produce our 1948 standard of living (measured in terms of marketed goods and services) in less than half the time it took in that year. We actually could have chosen the four-hour day. Or a working year of six months. Or, every worker in the United States could now be taking every other year off from work—with pay. Incredible as it may sound, this is just the simple arithmetic of productivity growth in operation.

But between 1948 and the present we did not use any of the productivity dividend to reduce hours. In the first two decades after 1948, productivity grew rapidly, at about three percent a year. During that period, worktime did not fall appreciably. Annual hours per labor force participant fell only slightly. And on a per-capita (rather than a labor force) basis, they even rose a bit. Since then productivity growth has been lower, but still positive, averaging just over one percent a year. Yet hours have risen steadily for two decades. In 1990, the average American owns and consumes more than twice as much as he or she did in 1948, but also has less free time.

How did this happen? Why has leisure been such a conspicuous casualty of prosperity? In part, the answer lies in the difference between the markets for consumer products and free time. Consider the former, the legendary American market. It is a veritable consumer's paradise, offering a dazzling array of products varying in style, design, quality, price, and country of origin.... In cross-country comparisons, Americans have been found to spend more time shopping than anyone else. They also spend a higher fraction of the money they earn. And with the explosion of consumer debt, many are now spending what they haven't earned. After four decades of this shopping spree, the American standard of living embodies a level of material comfort unprecedented in human history. The American home is more spacious and luxurious than the dwellings of any other nation. Food is cheap and abundant. The typical family owns a fantastic array of household and consumer appliances: we have machines to wash our clothes and dishes, mow our lawns, and blow away our snow. On a per-person basis, yearly income is nearly $22,000 a year—or 65 times the average income of half the world's population.

On the other hand, the 'market' for free time hardly even exists in America. With few exceptions, employers (the sellers) don't offer the chance to trade off income gains for a shorter workday or the occasional sabbatical. They just pass on income in the form of annual pay raises or bonuses, or, if granting increased vacation or personal days, usually do so unilaterally. Employees rarely have the chance to exercise an actual choice about how they will spend their productivity dividend. The closest substitute for a 'market in leisure' is the travel and other leisure industries that advertise products to occupy our free time. But this indirect effort has been weak, as consumers crowd increasingly expensive leisure spending into smaller periods of time.

❧❧❧❧❧❧❧

"High School Football: At Elizabeth High School, It's a Matter of Getting From Here to There," by Robert Lipsyte, *The New York Times*, November 27, 1992

ELIZABETH, N.J.—The sounds and rhythms change at Elizabeth High School as the squeaky slap of leather on hardwood replaces the meaty thud of colliding bodies. The football season ended yesterday and practice begins for the girls' and boys' basketball teams today. But for the coaches, the purpose of all this noise and sweat remains the same: keep the 4,300 students of New Jersey's largest high school interested and involved until they are prepared to escape this tough port city of 110,000, to college or to meaningful work.

Most coaches here believe, perhaps self-servingly, that a successful athletic program is the secular church of this predominately Hispanic and black school, even for those who only worship. And that the coaches, overwhelmingly white men, are the ministers of a higher order. Basketball brings particular promise and pressure. The boys' coach, Ben Candeloni, is routinely expected to field a powerhouse. He has sent players to major colleges and the National Basketball Association. The girls' coach, Shannon Luby, may have a harder job: persuading historically oppressed young women from minority groups to assert themselves, even as she fights her own Title IX battles in a department that would prefer a man in her job.

The pressure is still on the football coach, Jerry Moore, who must repay the kids from whom he demanded a season of intensity and pain. He has to help them get into colleges that will pay them to play. The recruiters have been lumbering through the halls all week. Of his 22 seniors, Moore figures he has six blue-chippers who will quickly go to major schools, another four or five who will be harder sells and another half-dozen who won't be placed, in prep schools or junior colleges, much before February.

The star, six-foot-five-inch linebacker DuLayne Morgan has already been offered admission by Duke, and may also consider North Carolina, U.C.L.A., Rutgers, Florida State, Syracuse, Michigan, and Notre Dame. DuLayne had 980 on the college boards as a junior and a 3.25 average in the advanced honors program. He was rated one of the top 25 prospects in the country. But there are young men who need Moore to persuade a college to take a chance, to understand that uneven play or erratic grades or low body weight reflects problems that may only be solved by being away at college, away from a violent home, a drunken mother, secure in a place offering three meals a day and a sense of worth.

Moore says that his team, which ended its season yesterday with an anticlimactic 13-12 loss to Cranford, was his most talented ever. So why did it end the season with a 5-4-1 record and two losses to archrival Union? "Could have been the coaching," snapped Moore, who was pleased to be reminded that he had lost his quarterback and his tailback before the season began and had to depend on the remarkable though raw gifts of a 14-year-old freshman, Al Hawkins. Quarterback Hawkins suffered a sprained shoulder in the next-to-last game, but should be ready to throw his 85-mile-per-hour fastball for the baseball coach, Ray Korn, this spring.

The school's brassy, classy marching band, which often gives the impression that it thinks football is the sideshow to its performance, didn't win the big one, either, finishing third overall in its group at a big competition three weeks ago at Giants Stadium. But its crowd pleasing "Carmen" routine won best music award. At Elizabeth, however, victory is often measured not by winning and losing, but by survival, what Jerry Moore calls "getting from here to there," a phrase that has informed his coaching for the past 20 years. In 1972, as a 30-year-old basketball coach at a suburban, predominately white Somerville High, Moore was far more authoritarian and his West Virginia twang was more pronounced.

When a group of black students defied the principal and stormed out of school to protest what they considered unequal racial treatment, Moore warned his basketball team that anyone who joined the demonstration would never again play for him. Moore's best player, a black guard named Ken Hayes, said: "Coach, I have to go out because those are the people I pass on the way home. You can help me here, but every day I got to get from here to there." When Moore hesitated, Hayes said, "If you let me go, I'll bring everybody back into school in 30 minutes." Moore says now: "I always reflect back on that day. Look at the decision I was forcing on those black players. Give up a shot at a major college scholarship or go against the people in their community. How can I do that? "My kids at Elizabeth, some of them walk two miles past shootings and drug deals, they have to go from here to there every day, and you got to be sure you don't make too many rules that get in the way of their survival." Twenty years ago, Moore defied his principal and sent Ken Hayes out to join the demonstration. Hayes, who went on to college ball and is now a law enforcement officer, brought the protesters back inside within 20 minutes. They met with the administration, and the conflict subsided. "To this day I don't know who was right in all that," says Moore. "I only know it turned me around. When I deal with a kid, I always think first, he's got to get from here to there. How can I stay out of his way? How can I help him get there?"

❧❧❧❧❧❧❧❧

Female athletes deserving "Should males be allowed to compete in primarily female sports and vice versa? If considered as a 'right,' there can be no doubt that the potential to ruin female sport dictates disapproval of any such mandate. In professional sports, male golfers and tennis players could dominate on the women's tour and this sort of thing should not be allowed. A better way to phrase the question: should upward mobility be allowed for female athletes? For the gifted and competitive-minded female athletes, often the outlets available are more recreational than competitive. Should the female athletes be allowed to test themselves by moving to more competitive levels? Of course they should. Males do not belong in women's sports, but allowing women to compete in men's sports is necessary, not only to provide outlets where none exist for female athletes, but also to allow females to test themselves through performance."

—*Don Gates, North Syracuse*

Stick to their own teams "Should boys be allowed to play on girls teams, and vice versa? Certainly NOT. Feminism or civil rights are not justifiable reasons in the world of sports from the amateur to the professional. Fifteen-year-old Greg Crumb playing for the Holland Patent High School field hockey team is absurd. It's happened in other school areas, but approval makes a mockery of sports. The object of varsity sports in schools is two divisions. How can one take pride in being, say, the best girls' team if a boy is on the team? Would you permit a girl in your school to wrestle against boys? Would there be different rules? How does a boy grasp a girl in the chest or crotch? And vice versa? Football? How can a girl compete against hulking 250-pounders? Boxing: Forget it. Girls would be cut to shreds. And in other contact sports—lacrosse, basketball and soccer—girls or women wouldn't stand a chance."

—*Lou Defichy*

૭ઙ૭ઙ૭ઙ૭ઙ૭ઙ

"The Good Life, The Meaning of Success for the American Middle Class," by Loren Baritz

"What the middle-class employee owns is his skill—what working people have always offered employers—but now with a computer, legal brief, or ledge, not with a lathe. Because corporate fortunes are seen to be more dependent on the judgment of such employees than on the individual workers on the factory floor, the bureaucrats command commensurately higher salaries. Throughout the twentieth century, and even earlier, the skills that create the financial strength of corporations have been changing, and such evolution has created the opportunity for larger numbers of people to work their way upward. Job descriptions in middle management require specific forms of specialized 'education' increasingly accessible to middle-class students. Training has replaced the capital once required to start a business. Those with vocational training— professionals, they are called—are paid accordingly, and the nature and the quality of their private lives depends on the degree of their perceived value to their superior."

૭ઙ૭ઙ૭ઙ૭ઙ૭ઙ

"Yugoslavia had tourism, heavy industry; it was a food-surplus nation. Its new freeways linked the rest of the European Community with Greece, Turkey, and the export markets of the Middle East. The totems of an emerging consumer society were everywhere: new gas stations, motels, housing developments, and discos and sidewalk cafés in the villages. Most impressive were the large private houses covering the roadside hills. Before the killing started practically everyone, it seems, was just finishing a new house, or had just bought a new car."

—*T. D. Allman,* Vanity Fair, *1992*

૭ઙ૭ઙ૭ઙ૭ઙ૭ઙ

"Next in Car Fuel: Hydrogen," Cedar Rapids Gazette, February 8, 1993

Hydrogen power is the Holy Grail of clean energy; it doesn't pollute and it's universally available. But until recently, it's been too expensive for widespread use. Now, a Florida company has invented a simplified fuel cell that can eliminate the internal combustion engine and run a car on hydrogen, and Energy Partners, Inc., says it's just the beginning. "We think we can have an economically competitive car by the end of the century," says owner John

Perry, Jr., who runs Perry Oceanographics. "Eventually this could replace all fossil fuels." The company's experimental hydrogen-fueled "Green Car" is scheduled to be unveiled in March.

Company vice president Mitch Ewan briefed this staff of environmentally oriented Vice President Al Gore before the election, he said, and the company has also worked closely with Sen. Tom Harkin, (D-Iowa), a strong supporter of hydrogen as a nonpolluting power source. A fuel cell, although it sounds like some type of battery, is actually an electrochemical engine. It takes a fuel, hydrogen in this case, and pumps it through a chemically impregnated plate, generating an electrical current and the system's only waste product—water vapor. And unlike internal combustion engines, it has no moving parts. Energy Partners has supplied NASA with material for its Space Shuttle fuel cells, but the technology used in space is too cumbersome for widespread use on Earth, Perry says.

So the company set out to design a fuel cell that could be mass-produced in a factory. The company's fuel cell eliminates heat and hard-to-handle chemicals that make fuel cells unsuitable for most mundane uses, replacing them with a simple plastic sheet impregnated with chemical chains and platinum. By the year 2000, Perry believes, the price of a fuel cell car engine could be down to about $3,000 and would last twice as long as gasoline engines. And cars are not the only use.

Eventually, a television-sized hydrogen fuel cell can supply all the power needed by an average home. There are several problems, Ewan says. To further reduce the size and weight, the company is working with the California designer to install fuel cells in a flying wing. The aircraft would use solar power to produce the hydrogen and could theoretically stay in the air for two years. Fuel cell production requires far tighter tolerances than current engines, which means the manufacturing process must have very high precision. Another problem is storing the hydrogen. The Green Car gets a respectable 120 miles per tank, but that's not enough for most consumers. So the company is working on techniques of absorption—adhesion to a surface that would bind the hydrogen gas to solid materials in the tank. If it works, a full-sized van could eventually get 1,500 miles per tank, says Ewan.

"Pact Called Key to Lower Imports," by Robert D. Hershey, Jr., *The New York Times*, October 17, 1993

President Clinton, in his most vigorous promotion of the North American Free Trade Agreement since the formal signing of labor and environmental safeguards in mid-September, warned today that failure to ratify the deal could isolate the United States and flood it with imported goods. 'Without Nafta, one of our best markets, Mexico, could turn to Japan and Europe to make a sweetheart deal for trade,' the President said in his weekly radio address. 'Without Nafta, Mexico could well become an export platform allowing more products from Japan and Europe into America. Why would we want that to happen?'

Critics of the agreement have repeatedly argued that it would be American companies that would use Mexico as a platform from which to export goods after they move factories there, causing a substantial loss of jobs. Mr. Clinton's renewed campaign for the agreement, which would gradually remove tariffs and other trade barriers among the United States, Mexico, and Canada, was the latest example of a shift in the drive to stress the consequences if it fails.

"Scientist Clones Human Embryos, and Creates an Ethical Challenge,"
by Gina Kolata, *The New York Times*, October 19, 1993

"A university researcher in Washington has, as an experiment, cloned human embryos, splitting single embryos into identical twins or triplets. This appears to be the first time such a feat has been reported. The scientist, Dr. Jerry L. Hall of George Washington University Medical Center, reported his work at a recent meeting of the American Fertility Society. The experiment was not a technical breakthrough, since he used methods that are commonly used to clone animal embryos, but it opens a rank of practical and ethical questions. For example, since human embryos can be frozen and used at a later date, parents could have a child and then years later, use a cloned embryo to give birth to an identical twin, possibly as an organ donor for the older child."

"Climbing the Walls,"
***Boys' Life*, March, 1993**

"John Omohundro looked like Spiderman climbing a building. His chalk-covered fingers grabbed at dents in the wall. His feet found tiny ledges. He inched his way up. 'Stay with it. Hold,' his friends on the ground shouted. John's buddy, Zack Horwitz, pulled the safety rope taut. With a final burst of energy, John reached the top. 'All right, dude!' yelled Zack. 'It's great when you get to the top,' panted John. 'Climbing gives me a rush.' John is an 18-year-old mountain climber from Buffalo, Wyoming. But this was not a mountain. John had just scaled an artificial climbing wall—indoors. Climbing the walls is a popular sport at the Colorado Rocky Mountain School (CRMS) that John attends in Carbondale, Colorado.

It's also popular at other schools, health clubs and Boy Scout summer camps across the country. Artificial wall climbing has certain advantages over mountain climbing. With indoor walls, you don't have to worry about bad weather, ice on the rocks, or darkness at night. Some climbing walls are set up outdoors. They also have advantages over mountains. Setting up safety ropes is easy, and the walls can be adjusted for different levels of climbing skills. 'Artificial walls are a good way for beginners to learn or for advanced climbers to refine their skills,' John says.

"The Globetrotters,"
***Art & Antiques*, Summer 1993**

Having the world at your fingertips is easily mastered with a standing library globe. The esteemed Adams Family, a London company which served as scientific instrument makers to George III, crafted these circa-1802 globes. English globes of this period were generally made of 12 engraved gores pasted to a hollow sphere of papier-mâché and plaster. As with most paired globes, one is terrestrial, the other celestial; in this case, the former is current with the political subdivisions of 1805. The pair had been in a private collection for 30 years before showing up for auction in March at Leslie Hindman in Chicago. Fresh to the market, they created quite a stir when they traveled well past their estimates of $5,000 to $7,000 to land at $19,800. Though globe sales hit a peak four years ago, this price may indicate that the globe market is turning again.

"Greater Columbia, Diversity Abounds,"
Columbia Chamber of Commerce Brochure

Many great American cities are best known for the towering absolutes: their moss-draped history, their unique ethnic heritage or even the industries that dominate their skylines and economic storehouses. Each image enriches the city, while also binding it—like a badly worn cliché—to a self-perpetuating stereotype of itself. These images may be one of the reasons that visitors to South Carolina's central city are often surprised to discover that Columbia's greatest strength is its unabashed diversity and overwhelming sense of place. As one longtime Columbia resident explained, 'There is a sense of community here, a chance to get involved and to get to know more people who are involved.' Then with a smile, he adds, 'When people move here, they begin to feel their roots sinking in; ours is a softer dirt with a humus of friendship.'

There is also an overwhelming sense in this sprawling metro community of 410,000 that something is happening, evolving as the natural course of things. It is not simply that the profile of a healthy, viable Main Street is changing to the tune of the IBMs and Marriotts. Or that on any given weekend as many as four open-air concerts—something for every taste—can be found. It's not even the way spring spreads through the midlands like a slow smile, whetting an artist's palette with its brilliant azalea and dogwood hues. It's more a feeling that in this city, totally planned 200 years ago and then burned to the ground 80 years later by General Sherman's Union Army, Columbia's third century is going to be an exciting time. Missing here—as you talk to residents—are the smugness and self-satisfaction that emerges when talking to people from so-called 'highbrow' cities. Columbia is a city without a convenient label, despite being the home of the University of South Carolina, the army's Fort Jackson training facility, major centers for banking and insurance, as well as the seat of South Carolina government. This is a community that has been pieced together from widely divergent parts of the country—and thus immensely accepting of others.

"Union Membership Declines:
Competing Theories and Economic Implications,"
by Gail McCallion, *Congressional Research Service,*
Library of Congress, August 20, 1993

In 1992, union members comprised only 15.8 percent of the workforce. Union membership, as a percent of the workforce, peaked at 34.7 percent in 1954, and has been declining since. Until 1978, the number of union members was continuing to grow, but was outpaced by the growth of the labor force. Since 1978, the absolute number of union members has been falling. In 1978, there were 20.2 million union members; by 1992, there were 16.4 million union members. These figures reflect the decline in total union membership (private and public sector). However, the decline in private sector union membership has been even more dramatic.

If current trends continue, some experts estimate that the private sector union membership could decline to as low as 10 percent of the labor force by 1995, and then continue to decline until it levels out at three percent of the labor force.

The decline in union membership can be examined by looking at changes in the demand for and supply of union services (the quantity of union membership). In the late 1970s, the absolute number of union members began to fall. This is a period marked by recession, increased foreign competition and the deregulation of many major industries such as trucking and aviation. The appreciation of the dollar between 1979 and 1985, which hurt U.S. exports, also resulted in employment losses in unionized manufacturing industries. These factors operated to make workers more vulnerable to the threat of job loss, thereby lowering the demand for union services. Other demand factors linked to the decline of union membership include a reduced need for union representation due to labor-management cooperation, and increased government regulation and statutory protection of individual worker rights, thus reducing the benefits of unions to potential members.

ॐॐॐॐॐॐॐ

"Made in North America—Still; How Delat, Powermatic, and General Have Dealt with the Taiwanese Challenge," by Vincent Laurence, *Fine Woodworking*, July/August, 1993

"The woodworking machinery market looked a lot different 15 years ago. A handful of European companies and a Japanese newcomer or two were all the competition North American manufacturers faced. Then, in the early 1980s, Taiwanese machines began to flow into the United States, and everything changed. Little more than a decade later, what at first was a trickle has long since become a torrent. Open any woodworking magazine and chances are you'll see more advertisements for Taiwanesemade machines than for American machines. Despite the fact that American machines frequently cost twice as much as their Taiwanese counterparts, the American companies are thriving, which means they must be doing something right. Because every day we hear from readers who want advice on buying machinery—should I buy American or Taiwanese?—we thought it was a good idea to get reacquainted with the American manufacturers of stationary woodworking power tools.

I wanted to know how the American companies have remained competitive, what they've had to do here and in some cases, overseas, and what it means to the average power-tool buyer like me.... One of the most important questions anyone running a business can ask is, 'What market am I serving?' General Manufacturing Co. asked that question in the early '80s, and the answer was, 'We're manufacturers of industrial-grade woodworking machinery.' Unfortunately, the industrial market wasn't growing, labor and material costs were rising, and Taiwanese machinery was on the streets for a fraction of what a comparable U.S. or Canadian machine cost. Disaster wasn't imminent, but the handwriting was on the wall. General's solution was two-fold: First, it was decided to continue building the same heavy-duty industrial equipment it has since 1946, but to market equipment to home-shop woodworkers as well as to professionals.

Second, General increased the efficiency of its Drummondville, Quebec, plant and foundry. General upgraded its foundry with an electric furnace, allowing smaller, more consistent batches of iron to be poured more quickly. The firm also began buying CNC (computer numerically controlled) equipment for its machining and assembly plant. CNC machines are flexible, programmable milling machines, capable of performing a whole spectrum of operations. They require far less monitoring than traditional machining stations, so one worker can operate a number of machines safely and effectively. Also, setup time for a new part or operation is all but eliminated because the bulk of setup is in the programming."

ॐॐॐॐॐॐॐ

"A Debt Repaid: Rescuing the Future, A Chance for Bosnian Students," by Harvey Fireside, *Commonwealth*, September 23, 1994

For me, what is happening now in Bosnia brings to mind memories of a time—54 years ago—when my parents and I waited in Vienna for relatives in the United States to rescue us from the Nazis. Because there was no way for Jews to earn a living, we relied on American soup kitchens for our one hot meal of the day. Finally, after 18 months, the treasured invitation came. But there were still anxious moments at the U.S. consulate, where we had to prove that we were in good health and could support ourselves. Because of childhood polio, my father walked with a pronounced limp. Fortunately, the doctors who examined us were interested in photography, my father's profession, so, in fluent English, my father explained to the doctor the features of a new camera, thereby demonstrating his ability to make a living. Finally, with tickets supplied by HIAS, an American relief organization, we three boarded the Italian ship that brought us to New York harbor and the welcoming torch of the Statue of Liberty.

Now, seeing something very close to a new holocaust taking place in Bosnia, it is frustrating to realize that the official U.S. reaction has been as grudging and skeptical as it was 50 years ago. Once more, I'm learning that bureaucracies lack empathy and respond poorly to crises; one must look to individuals and private groups to keep us human. In my own case it was the New School for Social Research in Manhattan where I took my Ph.D. In 1933 it had set up a "University in Exile" that saved some 100 European scholars from the Nazis.

A few months ago, I was offered a chance to repay my moral debt. I learned that there were nearly 600 Bosnian students hoping to continue their education in the United States. Stranded in Croatia, Slovenia, or Serbia, out of contact with their families, they were indubitably refugees, but U.S. embassies routinely denied them immigrant status. They could, however, obtain student visas, a chance to survive and study, if an American college or university would admit them, and if they could show they would not be dependent. A rescue operation was organized by the Fellowship of Reconciliation (FOR), an ecumenical antiwar group in Nyack, New York, and by the Jerrahi Order of America, a Sufi Muslim organization. In response to an appeal from FOR, I called friends who contacted others; each of us jumped at the chance to approach colleges in the area. One friend, a professor at Tompkins-Cortland Community College in Dryden, New York, was sure the college president would offer a scholarship. FOR had sent us the papers on Jasmina Burdzovic, a 22-year-old woman who had completed a year of university work before her family was forced to flee by Serbian soldiers. They had taken her Muslim father to a concentration camp. Sure enough, Eduardo Marti, the college president, immediately offered a tuition waiver. He had himself fled Cuba in 1960 as part of the "Peter Pan Brigade" that brought children to the United States. Catholic Charities had responded to his parents' call for help in getting an education; he became a biology teacher, then a college administrator. "Now it's my turn to help," he said. Jasmina would still need a place to stay, expense money, a network in the community. In less than a week, 20 people—from Jewish, Catholic, Protestant, and Muslim backgrounds—gelled into a cohesive support group: the Bosnian Student Project of Ithaca. Jerrahi supplied the airfare for Jasmina. One of our friends, a linguist fluent in Serbo-Croatian, offered temporary housing and an Affidavit of Support required by the U.S. consulate in Istanbul, where Jasmina's family had found refuge.

Six weeks later, on February 4, about 20 of us, including Dr. Marti, welcomed Jasmina at the Ithaca bus station. We knew her story: the confiscation of her family's house and possessions, the arrest and torture of her father, threats to abduct her and her sister, their hair's-breadth escape to Turkey. But what was most memorable was her refusal to fit the stereotype of a victim. "I am only part Muslim," she said. "My father is Bosnian, but my mother is a Christian Serb." She had no desire for revenge against all Serbs. Indeed, she said, it was a highly placed Serb officer, a friend of the family, who had gone the rounds of the concentration camps until he found Jasmina's father, whose breath rasped through crushed ribs. The officer brazened the father's release from his captors to his own custody, so that he could spirit him to a hospital in Belgrade. Jasmina confirmed that Bosnians had constituted one of Europe's most cosmopolitan societies. Jews, Christians and Muslims had lived close to one another for generations; something like a quarter of them had intermarried. Yet, the fanatic nationalists, mostly Serbian, had been able to whip up religious hatred against the Muslims, even those who were thoroughly secularized. Jasmina's home had been taken over by the family's Serbian maid, who just moved in because her family needed more room.

❧❧❧❧❧❧❧❧❧

"Texas Lutheran's Own 'Fab Five,' Players Have Bonded Like Sisters During Four Years at TLC," by Barry Halvorson, *The Sequin Gazette-Enterprise* (Texas), October 30, 1994

A handful of freshmen arrived together in Texas Lutheran College in the fall of 1991, coming into a tradition-rich volleyball program that was in need of a boost. Injecting the energy and enthusiasm of youth and a considerable amount of talent, Dana Krueger, Jessica Szymanski, Christy Clawson, Stacie Matheson and Natalie Rundell quickly became known as "The Fab Five." And what England's "Fab Four," the Beatles, did for rock 'n roll, these five players have done for volleyball in Sequin—made it a red hot product.

The success started almost from day one with two of the five—Krueger and Szymanski, who were in the starting lineup—and the rest seeing considerable playing time off the bench. The five also found a mentor that first year in former TLC All-American Michelle Henniger, then a senior on the team. That season the team finished 21-17, were Hearts of Texas co-champions, and finished one game short of returning TLC to the NAIA National Championship Tournament for the first time since 1985. They were on their way. "That first year, we were really just a scrappy bunch of players," Szymanski, a Sequin High graduate, said. "And Michelle made a big contribution to our development. She really showed us a lot about playing at the college level." Helping to ease the adjustments was the way their personalities blended immediately. Szymanski and Matheson are the most outgoing and quickest to respond to questions from the press.

Clawson, the setter, served much the same role in the interview, passing things around to make sure everyone got a chance to respond. Krueger and Rundell are two of the quietist players both on and off the court, but are also two of the most dangerous players. All five arrived literally at the same time, each attending the same tryout camp, each feeling confident she had made the team, and each ready to go to college. "We all came in together," Krueger said. "I think that helped us a lot because we could support each other." Such a verbal outburst brought jokes from her teammates. "One of the first things that I noticed," Szymanski said "was that while the rest of us like to talk, Dana didn't." "We lived together, ate together, just really hit it off from that first (tryout)," Matheson said. "I had a feeling right then that we were all going to make it."

Their second year was not quite as successful. They had some doubts about college and aspects of their personal lives, but they never questioned the support they would receive from the rest of their recruiting class. "After our freshman year there were some doubts about being here," Matheson admitted. "I considered going somewhere else, but personally I stuck it out for everyone else. I didn't want to let them down." "I had some questions, too," Clawson said. "I asked myself what I would do without volleyball and I couldn't come up with an answer, so I stayed." "These ladies are my sisters," Szymanski said. "I never had any doubts about becoming a close-knit family. During that year is when we really got to know each other. We learned about our weaknesses and our strengths and we learned to play to our strengths." "We have all had to lean on each other," Matheson adds. "They have leaned on me and I on them. One of the big advantages we have is that we are all strong in own own way so that no player has had to carry this team. If one person is having a bad night, the rest of us realize it and pick up our own games." Szymanski says each has her own understood role in helping to motivate the others. "I can't yell at Christy or she gets mad at me," she laughed. "We will just look at each other and touch hands. It's different with Stacie. She can yell at all of us. She's the one that gets us fired up on the court. She's got a way of yelling at you that doesn't get you mad at her, just gets you going."

Season three of the "Fab Five" in Texas Lutheran was the most successful as a group. They finished the season with a 41-10 record as they earned a return trip to the NAIA National Championship Tournament and finished the season as the number nine-ranked team in the NAIA. It was a big payoff for a group of girls who had a wide variety of interest only a few years earlier when they were starting out in high school. Krueger, whose mother is a highly successful high school coach at John Jay High School in San Antonio, was always a volleyball player. "Ever since I was real little, I've always been hanging around in gyms," she admitted. "My mother never pushed me into athletics; it was kind of expected of me. I enjoyed it so much that it really didn't matter."

Rundell and Matheson both preferred basketball to volleyball early and both admitted to missing the other game. Szymanski played both volleyball and basketball in high school, but always harbored a dream to be on the dance team, while Clawson preferred soccer and softball. Each admits they had to give up some of their other passions to make it in their chosen sport. "I never understood why they (sports and dancing) couldn't coexist," Szymanski said. "That's been one of the big changes ever since I graduated from high school. Today girls are getting to do both. "I was given a choice in high school of playing volleyball or basketball and eventually chose volleyball," she said. "But I never thought I should have had to (make that decision)." Teamwork is important in volleyball.

Another social change the five have observed is a newfound popularity as the girls that guys want to be with. Breaking a certain mold, all are attractive, but none allowed herself to be pigeonholed into the typical high school pastimes which were reserved for the "pretty girls." "We are the female jocks," Matheson laughed. "We're the ones without makeup. When you see us after practice you'd wonder why anyone would look at us. But back when we started, people were unfamiliar with that idea. In junior high, athletics were not for girls. You were kind of a social outcast because the boys wanted pretty girls." "Things have changed now, Clawson said, picking up the argument. "A lot of guys don't want 'prissy.' We have the guys from the soccer, basketball and baseball teams always coming up to us wanting to know how to set or spike or how to make a particular serve. They recognize us for being athletes as well as women." "I think some of it has to do with the fact that we are more fit than most," Krueger contributed. "In the U.S. there is more of an emphasis on healthy lifestyles and people now find it more attractive."

The trip to the national tournament has resulted in more interest in the TLC volleyball team this year, an attention that the "Five," now seniors, are relishing. "The effect of going to the national tournament has been fantastic," Matheson said. "With the coverage we got, people are more aware of what is going on. I have seen every professor I have at games this season and most have been very supportive. And that helps because the volleyball team at TLC has always been noted for staying eligible, and when they see us play, they understand that we are working hard. But we also don't skip any classes, because professors are going to notice that as well." Two the most outspoken members of the team on the extra attention are the two shy ones. "I like to know that people have an interest in what we are doing," Rundell said. "Before it would be people saying, 'Oh you had a game last night' to asking 'What was the score?' to now going to the match themselves." "There is a great deal of motivation for us in the fact that people were behind what we were trying to do," Krueger said. "It makes it feel not like we're doing it just for ourselves but for the school and all the graduates we have around the country. It's a real motivation." So far this season, the Lady Bulldogs are right on schedule to return to the national tournament and right on schedule to graduate as their sport has helped them gain the self confidence of winning, but also made them better overall students and people. "Athletics teaches you a lot about life," Rundell said. "To be able to combine volleyball with college, you have to be more responsible, more organized in your life and set priorities. I have benefited a lot in other areas because of playing volleyball."

Timeline of Cell Phones and Wireless Communications

1876   Alexander Graham Bell invented the telephone. By the end of 1880, 47,900 telephones were in use in the United States.

1895   Guglielmo Marconi, an Italian inventor, proved the feasibility of radio communications by sending and receiving the first radio signal. Four years later, Marconi flashed the first wireless signal across the English Channel.

1903   The first international wireless conference was held in Berlin.

1906   Reginald Fessenden successfully completed an 11-mile wireless telephone call from his laboratory in Brant Rock, Massachusetts.

1912   The Radio Act was the first domestic legislation to address radio spectrum allocation.

1921   The Detroit Police Department began one-way radio messaging.

1941   A Motorola two-way radio was installed in a police cruiser.

1946   The first commercial mobile radiotelephone service was introduced in St. Louis.

1965   AT&T's Improved Mobile Telephone Service (IMTS) eliminated the need for push-to-talk operation and offered automatic dialing.

1968   The Federal Communications Commission (FCC) opened Docket 18262 to address questions regarding spectrum reallocation.

1972   Bell Labs received a patent for its Mobile Communications System, which described and enabled handoffs between cells.

1977   Experimental cellular systems were launched in Chicago and the Washington, DC/Baltimore region.

1981   In May, the FCC announced the decision to award two cellular licenses per market—one for a wireline company and one for a non-wireline company.

1983   Advanced Mobile Phone Service (AMPS) was released using the 800 MHz to 900 MHz frequency band and the 30 kHz bandwidth for each channel as a fully automated mobile telephone service. AMPS was the first standardized cellular service in the world.

      Motorola introduced the DynaTAC mobile telephone unit, the first truly "mobile" radiotelephone. The phone, dubbed the "brick," had one hour of talk time and eight hours of standby.

      On October 13, the first commercial cellular system began operating in Chicago.

      In December, the second system was activated in the Baltimore/Washington, DC, corridor.

1984   The Cellular Telecommunications Industry Association was founded.

1985   The 100th cellular system was activated in New Bedford, Massachusetts.

1986   The FCC switched to a lottery system to license cellular markets. At the urging of the industry, the FCC allocated an additional 10 MHz of spectrum for cellular telecommunications; cellular subscribership topped two million with 1,000 cell sites across America. 1987 The industry topped $1 billion in revenues.

1988 CIBER Record for carriers was created, which allowed nationwide wireless services.

1989 Motorola announced the MicroTAC personal cellular phone, which used a flip-lid mouthpiece and retailed for an estimated $3,000.

1990s RAM Mobile Data Network was brought online. CDPD packet networks began deployment. GSM cellular systems supported circuit-switched data.

1990 Nextel Communications, Inc., filed a series of waivers with the FCC to set up low-power, multiple transmitter networks in six of the top U.S. markets. Cellular subscribership surpassed five million.

1992 The FCC allocated spectrum in the 2-GHz band for emerging technologies, including Personal Communications Services (PCS). The number of cellular users passed the 10 million milestone, served by 10,000 cell sites across America.

1992 The world's first commercial text message was sent by employees of Logica CMG.

1993 Bell Labs developed the DSP1616 chip, a digital signal processor used in millions of handsets.

1994 iDEN network technology, a packet-data network that integrates paging, data communications, voice dispatch and cellular capabilities, was unveiled.

ტ≪ტ≪ტ≪ტ≪

"Media Making Racket over Glen Ellyn's Dynamic Duo of Tennis," *Chicago Daily Herald*, September 28, 1995

If the name Engel sounds familiar lately, perhaps it is because of the mini-media blitz we have been seeing in recent weeks for the sibling tennis players Marty and Adria Engel of Glen Ellyn.

They have been featured in the media for their tennis prowess and it's doubtful the name will leave the public's eye anytime soon.

Marty, 22, a fifth-year senior at Northern Illinois University, appeared in a "Faces in the Crowd" segment of the September 18 issue of Sports Illustrated after winning the men's singles title at the Intercollegiate Tennis Association Summer Collegiate Championships. He also appeared in the September 21 issue of Tennis Week. The title also gave him an automatic berth in the U.S. Open tryouts.

While Marty was gracing the inside pages of national magazines, Adria, 15, was featured in a Sports Channel segment last Friday evening. It was Adria's first time on television, but it's doubtful it will be the last. This sophomore at Glenbard West is traveling down a path leading to professional tennis. And she's taking the scenic route.

"This year I started playing pro tennis just to see how I would do out there," she said. "In March I went to Mexico for a month. I played four tournaments there and the last tournament was the Masters. It's a lot of fun. A good experience and really good competition. I like it more than Juniors."

Although Adria has chosen not to play on her high school tennis team to concentrate on tournament play, she has also decided not to forsake her high school years as some aspiring players have done in the past. She's content to do it her way and is quite proud of her world ranking of 755. "The truly cool to see you have a professional ranking in the world," she said. "I think I'm really lucky to be able to be doing all that I'm doing. I'm just really excited."

"What Money Can't Buy, Family Income and Children's Life Changes"

"An assistant principal in a school in which nearly all the students are economically disadvantaged described it this way: 'A lot of time the parents want to have expectations for their kids. But they think it doesn't do any good to have expectations if you don't think it's ever going to be in the reach of the child. So they don't follow through. Lack of hope. That is one of the most profound things. Simply the lack of hope. You take most of the parents that we work with and they would like to hope that their child will go to college, but they don't really see a way that they are going to make that happen.'"

"A Happier Twist on Housing: From Bad Landlords to Co-ops," *The New York Times*, September 17, 1995

"When Robert Santiago moved into his apartment on Division Avenue in Williamsburg 20 years ago, it had no boiler, no heat, and few tenants, and the landlord did not pay property taxes. The city took over the building in the mid-1980s. Now, Mr. Santiago and the other tenants won the building: They bought it four years ago from the city for $250.00 an apartment to form a co-op. Every month, they meet to pay bills and discuss repairs. 'When I came here, it was the *Twilight Zone*,' said Mr. Santiago, 38. 'I can sleep now. I couldn't sleep before.' Weighed down by the costs of maintaining buildings it has seized, the city has increased its efforts to sell them—to private landlords, nonprofit groups, and tenant co-ops. And a survey released last week indicates that, among Brooklyn residents in current and former city-owned housing, tenant co-ops are by far the most popular. The co-ops scored highest in terms of services like heat and hot water, management, and safety; city-owned units came out last.

The city owns 2,885 occupied buildings seized for tax delinquency, 1,054 of them in Brooklyn. The survey, sponsored by a group of housing organizations, polled 3,000 residents in 500 Brooklyn buildings. Deborah C. Wright, Commissioner of the Department of Housing Preservation and Development, which oversees city-owned housing, said that when the city sells a building, tenants are given the option to form co-ops. But 60 percent of the residents must agree to do so and must take classes in management, budgets, and repairs. 'Some people are highly motivated and want to own and take responsibility for every aspect of their buildings,' she said. 'Other people just want to rent.' Ms. Wright said that she thought the survey's conclusions did not reflect recent changes in housing programs under the Giuliani administration. 'The one thing we agree on 100 percent is that the city is the worst landlord in the city,' she said. Standing in a newly painted hallway of his tenant co-op on Division Avenue, Santana Rosendo said taking on the responsibility was worth the effort. 'Everyone owns their apartment,' said Mr. Rosendo, 74. 'Everything is better because it is our own.'"

"What Makes Hootie Swim?" *Syracuse Herald Journal*, May 10, 1996

This is the central mystery of pop music: why Hootie & the Blowfish? If anyone really knew, of course, there'd be a lot more Hooties on the horizon. Atlantic records head Val Azzoli gave it a shot recently, describing the band's appeal as being based on "positive song-driven music in a world of angst-rock." Azzoli's clearly a big fan, humming music to the positive tune of almost $100,000,000, which is how much the band has brought to Atlantic in selling an unbelievable 13 million copies of Cracked Rear View.

Two years after its release, Hootie & the Blowfish's major-label debut is still selling 200,000 copies a month. At that rate it's likely to pass Boston's 20-year record to become the top-selling debut of all time, even with competition from the Hooties' new Fairweather Johnson. That album, not incidentally, was snatched up by 411,000 fans during its first weekend. In truth, neither Azzoli nor Atlantic—nor the band, come to think of it—had any idea of the potential booty in Hootie. Then the following happened and made all the difference: In October 1994, video network VH-1 was getting rid of its hyphen and trying to overcome its reputation as MTV's ugly older sister. VH-1 was the graying end of the MTV Experience when it decided to "re-position" through an image makeover.... Once the province of veteran acts, VH1 became home to up-and-coming acts that stayed safely away from the edge. And who better fit that category than Hootie & the Blowfish, a seemingly new band from a decidedly older sound rooted in familiar classic-rock and country-rock forms?

Actually, the Hooties had been together almost a decade and had released three independent albums before Atlantic noticed they were selling pretty well in the South. In February 1995, David Letterman, hardly known for musical hipness for some reason, anointed Hootie & the Blowfish as his "favorite band" and booked them almost as frequently as he did diet clown Richard Simmons.... The "runaway train" factor of popular culture took over from there. But is it a fluke or a phenomenon? Critics look at the songs and suggest a slick betrayal of pop craft. Critics, it should be noted, had nothing to do with the success of Hootie & the Blowfish. It's easy for them to slam the unbearable lightness of being Hootie. The music is often a bit sluggish, mostly medium tempo, mellow folk rock of no particular distinction. At worst: it's harmless.

American Soccer Timeline

1620 In the original Jamestown settlement, Native Americans played a game called Pasuckuakohowog, with goals one mile apart and as many as 1,000 people participating at a time.

1820 A form of soccer was played among the Northeastern universities and colleges of Harvard, Princeton, Amherst and Brown.

1830 The modern form of soccer originated among working-class communities and was seen as a way of keeping young and energetic kids out of trouble at home and in school.

1848 In England, the first Cambridge Rules were drawn up.

1862 The Oneida Football Club was formed in Boston, the first soccer club anywhere outside of England.

1883 The four British associations agreed on a uniform code and formed the International Football Association Board.

1885 The first international match was played between teams (U.S. vs. Canada) outside of Great Britain.

1888 The penalty kick was introduced.

1904 The Olympic Games of 1904 in St. Louis included soccer as an official Olympic sport where club teams competed under the national team banner.

Delegates from France, Belgium, Denmark, The Netherlands, Spain, Sweden and Switzerland established FIFA (The Federation Internationale de Football Association) at a meeting in Paris.

1914 The United States Football Association (USFA) was granted full membership in FIFA at the annual congress at Oslo.

1916 The first United States Football Association (USFA) Men's National Team traveled to Norway and Sweden; the Americans played six matches, finishing 3-1-2.

1920 The Dick-Kerr's Ladies Professional Team (England's unofficial team) spurred interest in the sport.

1921 The American Soccer League (ASL) was born when franchises were granted to Fall River (MA), Philadelphia, Jersey City Celtics, Todd Shipyard of Brooklyn, New York FC, Falcons FC of Holyoke (MA), and JP Coats of Pawtucket (RI).

1926 The Hakoah team from Israel played before 46,000 fans at the Polo Grounds against an ASL select team.

The U.S. was one of 13 nations to compete in the first FIFA World Cup competition in Montevideo, Uruguay. 1932 At the 10th Olympic Games in Los Angeles, soccer was eliminated due to a controversy between FIFA and the International Olympic Committee (IOC) over the definition of an amateur athlete.

1933 The National Collegiate Athletic Association (NCAA), the governing body of college athletics in the United States, released an official rulebook covering all intercollegiate soccer in the U.S.

1950 Joe Gaetjens' goal gave the USA the win over England, 1-0, at the World Cup in Brazil; it was called the biggest upset ever in international soccer.

The first college bowl game was played in St. Louis; Penn State tied the University of San Francisco 2-2. The Philadelphia Old-Timers Association organized the National Soccer Hall of Fame with 15 inaugural inductees.

1967 Two new major professional leagues in the U.S. began which became the North American Soccer League (NASL). The Hermann Trophy award for the college player of the year was initiated with. Dov Markus of Long Island University as the first recipient.

1975 The New York Cosmos of the NASL signed Pelé for a reported $4.5 million.

1977 The NASL signed a seven-game contract for national television.

1978 The New York Cosmos became the first NASL team to break one million in home and away attendance. The Major Indoor Soccer League (MISL) started with six franchises: Cincinnati Kids, Cleveland Force, Houston Summit, New York Arrows, Philadelphia Fever and Pittsburgh Spirit.

1981 The United States Under-20 National Team competed in its first World Youth Championship in Australia; the U.S. team lost to Uruguay 3-0, tied Qatar 1-1, and lost to Poland 4-0.

1982 The National Soccer Hall of Fame and Museum opened in the Wilber Mansion, Oneonta, New York.

1985 The first U.S. Women's National Team competed internationally in Italy.

1988 The United States was awarded the 1994 World Cup during the FIFA Congress in Zurich.

1989 For the first time since 1950, the U.S. Men's National Team qualified for the 1990 World Cup after a 1-0 victory over Trinidad and Tobago.

1990 The U.S. Men's National Team competed in the World Cup in Italy for the first time in 40 years. The U.S. Women's National Team qualified for the world championship. The WSL and the ASL merged to form the American Professional Soccer League.

1991 The U.S. Men's National Team won its first-ever regional championship. The U.S. Women's National Team won the first-ever FIFA Women's World Championship in China after beating Norway 2-1 in the final.

The United States Under-23 team won the gold medal at the Pan Am Games in Cuba.

1992 The U.S. Men's National Team won the inaugural U.S. Cup. The Major Indoor Soccer League folded after 15 years in existence. The U.S. Futsal Team won the silver medal at the FIFA World Championship in Hong Kong.

1994 The United States hosted the 1994 FIFA World Cup, attracting over 3.5 million in attendance, a World Cup record. The Women's National Team won the Chiquita Cup, an international tournament with four national teams of Germany, China, Norway and the United States.

1995 The U.S. Men's National Team won the U.S. Cup, defeating Nigeria, tying Colombia and outplaying Mexico to a 4-0 victory.

1996 FIFA awarded the 1999 Women's World Cup to the United States. The U.S. Women's National Team won the first-ever gold medal in the Olympic Games in Atlanta, defeating China 2-1 in the championship game.

Major League Soccer was launched, providing the United States with its first Division I outdoor pro league since the North American Soccer League folded in 1985.

సౌ-సౌ-సౌ-సౌ-సౌ-సౌ-సౌ-సౌ

"Gasoline Pollution Is Serious, Too,"
by Marvin Legator and Amanda Daniel,
Galveston Daily News, June 8, 1996

Question: How safe is our gasoline? It is my understanding that one of the major sources of pollution is gasoline. How dangerous is gasoline, and what can we do about it? Answer: Gasoline is a complex chemical mixture containing more than 1,000 possible substances. Gasoline vapors are released at bulking installations, refineries, during tank and barge transportation and when refueling automobiles at service stations. According to the U.S. Environmental Protection Agency, approximately 40 percent of all gasoline releases occur during refueling.

Gasoline represents a major source of exposure to the general population of toxic substances, including several known carcinogens such as benzene and butadiene. Most experts agree that it's likely gasoline will be the dominant motor vehicle fuel well into the next century, although General Motors has developed an electric vehicle that is currently showing at select stops throughout the country. This automobile uses no gasoline, no water and no spark plugs. It runs on a battery which remains charged for approximately 70 miles. This is a step in the right direction, and with further development may be the automobile of the future.

᪥᪥᪥᪥᪥᪥᪥᪥

"Steroids Don't Cause Rage Outbursts, Study Says,"
Syracuse Herald Journal, July 4, 1996

Body builders already believed it, and science has finally proved it: Steroids make big muscles. But researchers found no evidence that steroids make users prone to outbursts of anger known as "roid rage."

The carefully controlled study showed convincingly for the first time a few weeks of male sex hormone injections substantially beef up arms and legs and increase strength.

In addition, psychological tests and questioning of the men's spouses found no evidence that steroids made them angrier or more aggressive.

Steroids are widely thought to cause violent mood swings, and people charged with violent crimes have pleaded roid rage as a defense. But among steroid users who are mentally healthy, "testosterone doesn't turn men into beasts," said Dr. Shalender Bhasin of Charles H Drew University in Los Angeles. Bhasin left open the possibility that in people who are mentally unbalanced to begin with, steroids can make them worse.

Possession and distribution of steroids without a prescription is a federal crime, punishable by up to a year in prison and a fine of at least $1,000. Doctors have warned that potential side effects include sterility, testicular shrinkage, acne, abnormal liver function, baldness, high blood pressure and heart disease. Bhasin and his colleagues said the results in no way legitimize steroid use by athletes, but suggested steroids may be a good way to help AIDS patients and others whose muscles waste away because of disease.

᪥᪥᪥᪥᪥᪥᪥

"The Costs of Peace,"
Commonweal, January 12, 1996

Peacemaking is not peaceful. In Somalia, violence dogged every peacemaking step, finally driving the United States to withdraw from what began as a humanitarian mission to feed the hungry. Haiti has been more complicated and the outcome more ambiguous. Shortterm peace has prevailed—more or less: Political agreements have been kept and elections were quiet. Still, development and real peace exist only in an elusive future. No doubt sending U.S. troops to Bosnia is a risk, not the least because the very presence of Americans may invite terrorist attacks from all of the belligerents: recalcitrant Bosnian Serbs; the Islamic fighters whose presence helped to fortify the Bosnian army, but whose future plans remain obscure; the Croats, should their territorial hopes be thwarted; and the unofficial militias who have operated outside of official chains-of-command. As 60,000 NATO troops, including 20,000 Americans, move to impose a rough calm on a still-simmering Bosnia, simply enumerating the potential terrorists begins to suggest the explosive costs of peace.

In Bosnia, two million people are displaced from their homes, 250,000 killed, 200,000 wounded. Yielding, negotiating, repenting and reconciling all demand more of us humans—spiritually, psychologically and materially—than most of us have much experience at giving. How much more it asks of those who have raped, tortured, murdered, burnt and pillaged, those who have been victims, and those who have been witnesses of these crimes. Healing these wounds, of course, is not the mandate of NATO, which has been given a year to separate armies, patrol borders, provide security. Armies can only protect a peace that the belligerents themselves must pursue. This in the midst of a devastated economy in which infrastructure, homes, schools, businesses have been ruthlessly destroyed and international funds for resettlement and reconstruction are in short supply. A year seems pitifully brief. Thus, the chief source of uneasiness about NATO troops in Bosnia: Are they guarding a peace that will take hold or enforcing a cease-fire that Serbs and Croats will use to prepare a final offensive against the vulnerable remains of Bosnia? Neither Franjo Tudjman of Croatia nor Slobodan Milošević of Serbia, signers of the Dayton Peace Accord, is to be trusted.

Many Americans, certainly many in Congress, do not trust that President Bill Clinton and his chief negotiator Richard Holbrooke know what they are getting into—and more critically, know how to get out. Every possible argument against sending American soldiers to Bosnia has been made; some are plausible, some reek of mere political calculation. All things considered, one thing is clear: In Bosnia, a year of peace is better than another year of war. A cease-fire is better than slaughter. The Bosnians did not start this war; they resisted defeat and international indifference; now they are ready to pursue peace despite the looming threat of a greater Croatia and a greater Serbia. For them, the cost of war has been enormous, and peace, if it is achieved, will exact a further price. The cost to the United States, in contrast, seems relatively modest. We should pay it.

ᑭᗊᑭᗊᑭᗊᑭᗊ

"She Traded Cows for French Horn,"
David Abrams, *The Syracuse Post-Standard*, March 13, 1997

When you think of it, the French horn is a mighty piece of architecture: a long, sprawling brass highway that starts modestly at one end, then twists and turns its way until it flares into a glorious musical cornucopia. Which, coincidentally, describes the career path taken by hornist Gail Williams. The Western New York-bred and central New York-educated Williams is Associate Principal Horn with the renowned Chicago Symphony Orchestra. She comes to town this weekend as soloist in the Syracuse Symphony Orchestra's set of Classics Series concerts. Surprisingly, her journey to orchestral stardom began rather modestly, without fanfare. She was the typical "farmer's daughter," raised on the family farm near Rushford. "I spent half of my youth, summer after summer, showing cows at the state fair (in Syracuse)," Williams recalled during a recent phone interview from her home in Chicago. After bovines, the country girl preferred sports. The French horn, which she began playing in fifth grade, was a distant third. "I just didn't have any interests," she recalled.

While many young instrumentalists at her school took private music instruction to improve their playing skills, Williams refused, despite her mother's urging, and her mom was the school music teacher! By the time she entered Ithaca College, Williams, strong like a bull from milking cows every day, was in great shape, excelling in basketball, track, gymnastics and soccer. She decided to major in physical education. That is, until she bumped into Walter Beeler—the formidable former director of bands at the IC School of Music—who at the time was the school's assistant Dean. Beeler, who taught Williams' mother during her school days at IC, learned that the young hornist had been accepted into the prestigious All-Eastern Band while in high school. He insisted the young woman forget soccer and basketball and major in music. Williams studied with John Covert, the school's horn teacher, until his retirement in 1995. She never expected to play professionally in pursuit of degree in music education, following in the footsteps of her mother.

In 1972 she fulfilled her student teaching requirement at West Genesee High School in Camillus. It proved to be the turning point in her career. "The experience suggested to me that I didn't really have the patience necessary for teaching," she recalled. "Besides, right around that time I began to get the bug to play." The 'bug' grew into a full-fledged virus, thanks to a summer at the famous Tanglewood Institute in Massachusetts. Williams began to fine-tune her skills on the horn at Northwestern University and landed a job at the Chicago Lyric

Opera. The experience proved invaluable in preparing her for what was to be the biggest, most competitive audition of her life: the Chicago Symphony Orchestra, under Sir Georg Solti. When the smoke had cleared, she found herself the newest member of what is arguably the finest horn section of any orchestra in the world. After Solti appointed Williams in 1984 to the position of Associate Principal alongside the legendary horn virtuoso Dale Clevenger, Williams' career began to take off. Yet while her performances took her all around the world, Williams always managed to stay close to Ithaca College. She continues to participate in a variety of IC-sponsored events, and still uses as her accompanist Mary Ann Covert, Ithaca College professor of piano.

෨෧෨෧෨෧෨෧෨෧

"U.S. Posts 27% Rise in Legal Immigration, Almost 916,000 People Admitted Last Year," by William Branigin, *Washington Post*, April 23, 1997

The United States admitted nearly 916,000 legal immigrants last year, a sharp increase that appears likely to add fresh fuel to a national debate over the appropriate level of immigration. The Immigration and Naturalization Service, which released the figure yesterday, said it represents a 27 percent jump from fiscal 1995 and resulted from increases in the number of visas granted to relatives of U.S. citizens and employer-sponsored immigrants, plus a "carryover" of unused visas from 1995 that increased the availability of family-based immigrant visas in fiscal 1996. The higher admissions of U.S. citizens' immediate relatives, which rose 36 percent and have no numerical caps under the immigration law passed last year, were driven in part by increased processing of applications by illegal immigrants seeking to legalize their status, the INS said. The increase also reflected record levels of naturalization in the past couple of years.

෨෧෨෧෨෧෨෧෨෧

"Where's the Panic? The Global Crisis May Not Be Over. But It Sure Feels Like It," *Newsweek*, November 30, 1998

"Ahh, the sights and sounds of normalcy. On Wall Street, Internet stocks are again getting bid skyward—and deflating a week later like billion dollar party balloons. Traders puffing on Montecristos are packing into tiny steak-and-cigar saloons like Angelo & Maxie's and talking trash to each other over the din. 'I've never seen a mood change this dramatic,' said one trader, Ralph Kartzman of First New York Securities, as the Dow finished at near-record levels above 9,000 last week. 'You don't hear about Russia, Brazil. Nobody cares, not even a bump.' Downtown at the New York Fed, which only six weeks ago orchestrated the bailout of a giant hedge fund to prevent global panic, officials will admit only to breathing easier. But they point out that money is flowing back into corporate junk bonds from the high, safe ground of U.S. treasuries. 'Stability,' says a Federal Reserve official, 'may yet break out.'"

෨෧෨෧෨෧෨෧෨෧

"Accord Would Increase Cap on Visas for Skilled Workers," by Robert Pear, *The New York Times*, July 25, 1998

House and Senate Republican leaders reached agreement today on a bill to increase the number of foreign computer programmers, engineers and other skilled workers who can be admitted to the United States to fill job openings at high-technology companies. Under the agreement, the annual limit on the number of visas for such workers, now 65,000, would rise to 115,000 over three years, an increase of 77 percent. High-tech companies and their chief executives, including William H. Gates of the Microsoft Corporation, have lobbied heavily for an increase in the quota, saying that their industry suffers from shortages of qualified employees and that they desperately need skilled foreign workers to help develop new products.... Whether there is in fact a shortage of high-tech workers is a hotly debated question. An industry group, the Information Technology Association of America, says there are 346,000 openings, amounting to 10 percent of all American jobs for computer programmers, engineers and systems analysts. But the Labor Department, the A.F.L.-C.I.O. and several groups representing American engineers say the high-tech industry, trying to hold down its labor costs by hiring from abroad, has overstated the problem. India provides by far the largest number of skilled foreign workers under the special-visa program. Its citizens received 44 percent of the visas, known as H-1B visas, issued in the first half of the current fiscal year.

"Good Times Mask Concerns about Financing Retirement, College," *The Charlotte Observer,* March 7, 1998

"David Wheat is only 13 months old. But already his parents, Steve and Mary, worry about how they'll be able to send him to college. It's a common concern. College costs seem so high that many parents don't attempt to save for college, experts say. The average for a year's tuition and fees at public universities is $3,111, and $13,664 at private schools. By the time David Wheat is college-age, that's expected to more than double, according to the American Association of State Colleges and Universities. In a recent poll, *Money* magazine found that 47 percent of parents who expect to attempt college said they hadn't saved any money to cover the costs. Six months before David was born, the Wheats set up a college savings fund. But they want to buy a house. David was born three months premature, so there are still hospital bills. There are also payments for the new car. 'Paying for college is always in the back of my mind,' Steve Wheat says. 'We're not going to be able to afford Harvard or nothing...I'd like for him to go to the best place he could, but it will probably be the best place we can afford.'"

"How to Clone a Herd," *Time Magazine,* December 21, 1998

"First there was Dolly the Scottish sheep. Then, last July, came several litters of cloned mice. Now scientists at Japan's Kinki University have produced something even bigger and a good deal tastier: eight identical calves cloned from a single cow. Writing in last week's issue of *Science,* the Japanese researchers report that they achieved this feat of bovine photocopying using two different types of cells, taken from a single cow's ovaries and fallopian tubes. Those cells—all carrying the same genetic payload—were introduced into cow ova whose genes had been scooped away. Ten such identical embryos were then implanted in the wombs of surrogate cow mothers, and all but two came to term. No one knows why the Kinki team managed to bat .800 (while Dolly's creators needed 29 embryos to get one hit). Japanese scientists hope to learn more when other calves—cloned from liver, kidney, and heart cells—are born next spring. The beef industry is anxiously awaiting the answer: the clones come from a line of prize cows whose meat sells for $100.00 a pound."

Top Songs: 1998

"I Don't Want To Miss a Thing," Aerosmith

"Everybody (Backstreet's Back)," Backstreet Boys

"Jump Jive An' Wail," Brian Setzer Orchestra

"I Want You Back," N*Sync

"The Cup of Life," Ricky Martin

"Too Close," Next

"Good Riddance (Time Of Your Life)," Green Day

"From This Moment On," Shania Twain

"My Heart Will Go On," Celine Dion

"Suavemente," Elvis Crespo

"Nice & Slow," Usher

"Tearin' Up My Heart," *NSYNC

"A Song For Mama," Boyz II Men

"The Boy Is Mine," Brandy & Monica

"Ghetto Supastar (That Is What You Are)," Pras Michel

"Intergalactic," Beastie Boys

"Stay (Wasting Time)," Dave Matthews Band

"No, No, No part 2," Destiny's Child

"This Is How We Party," S.O.A.P.

"I'll Be," Edwin McCain

"Just The Two of Us," Will Smith

"Cruel Summer," Ace of Base

"Gettin' Jiggy Wit It," Will Smith

"Zoot Suit Riot," Cherry Poppin' Daddies

"Landslide," Fleetwood Mac

"Low Long-Distance Rates Go to Web Users," *The Charlotte Observer*, February 16, 1998

"Consumers looking for the cheapest long-distance telephone rates need only log on to the Internet, the newest arena of intense competition, where companies are offering special prices from $0.05 to $0.10 a minute. This week, AT&T Corp. is expected to start offering its Internet customers long-distance calls at just $0.09 a minute, matching new rates introduced recently by MCI Communication. Both giants are scrambling to respond to the initiative of a little player that had a big idea: Tel-Save Holdings, a long-distance provider in New Hope, Pennsylvania, that caters primarily to small- and medium-sized businesses. Since December 18, it has contracted with America Online to offer the $0.09-a-minute rate to the online services' 11 million subscribers. America Online has signed up almost 400,000 customers so far, and expects to have a million by the end of June."

"Jobless Rate Hits Low Again,"
The Charlotte Observer, March 7, 1998

"Surprisingly robust job growth pushed the nation's unemployment rate to a 24-year low of 4.6 percent in February, renewing concerns that the United States is running short of skilled workers.... Two temporary factors—unseasonably mild winter weather and historically low mortgage rates, which have risen a bit since—account for some of the job growth. But analysts attributed much of the advance to the strength of the U.S. economy, which at least so far is showing only modest signs of spillover from Asian financial turmoil.

Economist Mark Zandi of Regional Financial Associates in West Chester, Pennsylvania, said the unemployment rate could sink to four percent by late summer, a level unseen since the 1960s."

ঔ৵ঔ৵ঔ৵ঔ৵ঔ৵

"Bowater's Buy Is Big News,"
The Charlotte Observer, March 10, 1998

"By early summer York County can expect to have a new marketing plug to help attract new business: home to a plant of the second-largest newsprint company in the world. Greenville, South Carolina-based Bowater, Inc., said Monday it will buy Canadian papermaker Avenor Inc. for $2.5 billion in cash, stock, and assumed debt, substantially increasing its clout in the paper industry.... Analysts and local business leaders—who were surprised at Monday's announcement—predict the merger will mean good things for York County. 'It will only help the area,' said Clay Andrews, executive director of the Rock Hill Economic Development Corp."

ঔ৵ঔ৵ঔ৵ঔ৵ঔ৵

"Were You Born That Way? It's not just brown eyes. Your inheritance could also include insomnia, obesity and optimism. Yet scientists are saying that genes are not—quite—destiny,"
by George Howe Colt and Anne Hollister, *Life*, April 1998

In the debate over the relative power of nature and nurture, there may be no more devout believers than new parents. As my wife and I, suffused with a potent mix of awe, exhaustion and ego, gazed down at our newborn daughter in the hospital, it has hard not to feel like miniature gods with a squirming lump of figurative putty in our hands. We had long believed that people could make the world a better place, and now we firmly believed that we could make this a better baby. At home our bedside tables are swaybacked by towers of well-thumbed parents' manuals. A black-and-white Stim-Mobile, designed to sharpen visual acuity, hung over the crib. The shelves were lined with books, educational puzzles and IQ-boosting rattles. Down the line we envisioned museum visits, art lessons, ballet. And if someone had tapped us on the shoulder and told us that none of this would matter—that, in fact, if we could switch babies in the nursery and send our precious darling home with any other new parents in the hospital, as long as these parents weren't penniless, violent or drug addicted, our daughter would turn out pretty much the same...well, we would have thwacked that someone with a Stim-Mobile. Does the key to who we are lie in our genes or in our family, friends and experiences?

In one of the most bitter controversies of the twentieth century—the battle over nature and nurture—a wealth of new research has tipped the scales overwhelmingly toward nature. Studies of twins and advances in molecular biology have uncovered a more significant genetic component to personality than was previously known. Far from a piece of putty, say biologists, my daughter is more like a computer's motherboard, her basic personality hardwired into infinitesimal squiggles of DNA. As parents, we would have no more influence on some aspects of her behavior than we had on the color of her hair. And yet, new findings are also shedding light on how heredity and environment interact. Psychiatrists are using these findings to help patients overcome their genetic predispositions. Meanwhile, advances in genetic research and reproductive technology are leading us to the brink of some extraordinary—and terrifying—possibilities.

The moment the scales began to tip can be traced to a 1979 meeting between a steelworker named Jim Lewis and a clerical worker named Jim Springer. Identical twins separated five weeks after birth, they were raised by families 80 miles apart in Ohio. Reunited 39 years later, they would have strained the credulity of the editors of *Ripley's Believe It or Not*. Not only did both have dark hair, stand six feet tall and weigh 180 pounds, they spoke with the same inflections, moved with the same gait and made the same gestures. Both loved stock-car racing and hated baseball. Both married women named Linda, divorced them and married women named Betty. Both drove Chevrolets, drank Miller Lite, chainsmoked Salems and vacationed on the same halfmile stretch of a Florida beach. Both had elevated blood pressure, severe migraines and had undergone vasectomies. Both bit their nails. Their heart rates, brain waves and IQs were nearly identical. Their scores on personality tests were as close as if one person had taken the same test twice. Identical twins raised in different families are a built-in research lab for measuring the relative contributions of nature and nurture. The Jims became one of 7,000 sets of twins studied by the Minnesota Center for Twin and Adoption Research, one of a half-dozen such centers in this country. Using psychological and physiological tests to compare the relative similarities of identical and fraternal twins, these centers calculate the "inheritability" of behavioral traits—the degree to which a trait in a given population is attributable to a gene rather than to the environment. They have found, for instance, that "assertiveness" is 60 percent heritable, while "the ability to be enthralled by an aesthetic experience" is 55 percent heritable.... Studying adolescents adopted in infancy, University of Virginia psychologist Sandra Scarr was surprised to find that children adopted by well educated, professional parents performed no better in school or on intelligence tests than children who had been adopted into working-class homes. "Providing children with super environments—private schooling, museum visits, lessons and so on—makes no difference in their intelligence, adjustment or personality development," says Scarr. She concludes that if a child has "good enough parenting"—parents who aren't abusive or neglectful and provide a basic level of support— one set of parents is as good as another. "It doesn't matter whether you take the kids fishing or to a Mozart concert," says Scarr. "As long as you do it with love, almost anything you do is going to be fine and functionally equivalent."

"Musician Credits Sibling Rivalry With Instrument Choice,"
Kerrville Daily Times (Texas), January 6, 1999

Sibling rivalry played an important role in the life of a French horn player with Kerrville ties. "It's the only instrument I've ever played," said Jane Lehman, with a slight German accent. Jane is the daughter of Kerrville's Ray and Mary Louise Lehman, who moved to Kerr County more than 20 years ago. Jane began playing French horn at 13 while attending school in Florida. "My sister played the flute, and she didn't want me playing her instrument," she said. Using a little psychology, "she told me it looked like Christmas," and sister JoAnne convinced Jane to take up the French horn. And although the instrument was challenging, "I never wanted to put it down. "I started taking lessons and it was so interesting I did not notice that it was difficult," she said.

After graduating from Florida State University and the Curtis Institute of Music in Pennsylvania, she landed a job with the Savannah Symphony in Georgia. There she quickly learned that she would be hard-pressed to make a decent living playing the French horn. So she set off for Cologne, Germany, to take French horn lessons. "I started taking auditions and got a job real quick substituting in an orchestra," she said. A short time later, she landed a full-time position with the Radio Symphony Orchestra of Saarbrucken, a city of approximately 300,000 located near the German-French border. The town has two full-time orchestras and the job pays quite well. "It's like living in Kerrville, but you're taken care of as a musician, well taken care of," she said. "If you're going to make that kind of money playing in the States, you have to be in big-city Boston, Dallas. I prefer living out in the country," she said.

ᚠᚠᚠᚠᚠᚠᚠᚠ

Americans with Disabilities Timeline

1817 The American School for the Deaf was founded in Hartford, Connecticut, the first school for disabled children anywhere in the United States.

1848 The Perkins Institution in Boston, Massachusetts, became the first residential institution for people with mental retardation.

1864 The Columbia Institution for the Deaf and Dumb and Blind was authorized by the U.S. Congress to grant college degrees.

1927 The Supreme Court decision ruled that forced sterilization of people with disabilities was not a violation of their constitutional rights; nationally, 27 states began wholesale sterilization of "undesirables."

1935 The League for the Physically Handicapped in New York City was formed to protest discrimination by the Works Progress Administration. The Social Security Act established federally funded old-age benefits and funds to states for assistance to blind individuals and disabled children.

1943 The LaFollette-Barden Vocational Rehabilitation Act added physical rehabilitation to the goals of federally funded vocational rehabilitation programs and provided funding for certain health care services.

1945 President Harry Truman created an annual national "Employ the Handicapped Week."

1948 The National Paraplegia Foundation, founded by members of the Paralyzed Veterans of America as the civilian arm of their growing movement, began advocating for disability rights.

1956 Social Security Amendments created the Social Security Disability Insurance program for disabled workers aged 50 to 64.

1961 President John Kennedy appointed a special President's Panel on Mental Retardation.

1963 The Mental Retardation Facilities and Community Health Centers Construction Act authorized federal grants for the construction of public and private nonprofit community mental health centers.

1965 Medicare and Medicaid were established providing federally subsidized health care to disabled and elderly Americans covered by the Social Security program.

1968 The Architectural Barriers Act prohibited architectural barriers in all federally owned or leased buildings.

1973 The Rehabilitation Act prohibited discrimination in federal programs and services and all other programs or services receiving federal funds.

1974 A suit filed in Pennsylvania on behalf of the residents of the Pennhurst State School and Hospital became a precedent in the battle for de-institutionalization of the mentally handicapped.

1975 The Individuals with Disabilities Education Act required free, appropriate public education in the least restrictive setting.

1977 Demonstrations by disability advocates took place in 10 American cities after Joseph Califano, U.S. Secretary of Health, Education and Welfare, refused to sign meaningful regulations.

1978 The American Disabled for Public Transit staged a year-long civil disobedience campaign to force the Denver, Colorado Transit Authority to purchase wheelchair lift-equipped buses.

1981-1984 Disability Rights advocates generated more than 40,000 cards and letters to Congress to halt attempts by the Reagan Administration to amend regulations implementing the Rehabilitation Act of 1973 and the Education for All Handicapped Children Act of 1975.

The Reagan Administration terminated the Social Security benefits of hundreds of thousands of disabled recipients.

1985 The Mental Illness Bill of Rights Act required states to provide protection and advocacy services for people with psychological disabilities.

1986 Toward Independence, a report of the National Council on the Handicapped, outlined the legal status of Americans with disabilities and documented the existence of discrimination.

1988 The Air Carrier Access Act prohibited airlines from refusing to serve people simply because they were disabled and from charging people with disabilities more than non-disabled travelers for airfare.

1990 The Americans with Disabilities Act provided comprehensive civil rights protection for people with disabilities; it mandated that local, state and federal governments and programs be accessible, and that businesses with more than 15 employees make "reasonable accommodations" for disabled workers.

> "Disability, like race and gender, is a natural and normal part of the human experience that in no way diminishes a person's right to live a normal life and participate in mainstream activities."
>
> —*Professor Robert Silverstein, George Washington University*

"The Y2K Nightmare,"
Vanity Fair, January 1999

The nightmare scenario goes like this: It is an instant past midnight, January 1, 2000, and nothing works. Not ATMs, which have stopped dispensing cash; not credit cards, which are being rejected; not VCRs, which now really are impossible to program. The power in some cities isn't working, either, and that means no heat, lights, or coffee in the morning, not to mention no television, stereos, or phones, which even in places with power aren't working, either. Bank vaults and prison gates have swung open; so have valves on sewer lines. The 911 service isn't functioning but fire trucks are on the prowl (though the blaze had better be no higher than the second floor, since ladders won't lift). People in elevators are trapped, and those with electric hotel or office keys can't get anywhere, either. Hospitals have shut down because their ventilators and X-ray machines won't work and, in any case, it's impossible to bill the HMO....

Will it happen? "Yes," "No," and "Maybe," say the experts. And that's the most unnerving thing about the phenomenon that's been known as "Y2K," "The Year 2000 problem," or "The Millennium Bug": no one will know the extent of its consequences until after they occur. The one sure thing is that the wondrous machines that govern and ease our lives won't know what to do. Some will freeze, electronically paralyzed, as others will become imbecilic, giving idiot answers and issuing lunatic commands; still others, overwhelmed, will simply die, as will the blind faith the world has placed in them.

"The reason we are in this screw-up," says Paul Strassmann, who oversaw the Pentagon's vast computer operations during the Bush administration, "is that...Americans fell in love with computers and put up with...failures that they would not put up with in a crummy toaster or microwave." The product is a looming disaster with an immovable deadline that will touch the entire world. Its scale is unique, too: 1.2 billion lines of potentially lethal software code located in virtually every country, plus 30 billion microprocessors. Many are linked computer to computer, network to network, place to place and everywhere from birthing rooms to crematoriums. And if potential catastrophe is to be avoided, every line and chip must be checked, a task variously likened to building the pyramids, changing all the light bulbs in Las Vegas in an afternoon, or individually polishing enough marbles to fill the Grand Canyon.

ॐॐॐॐॐॐॐॐ

"Report Claims Hispanics Need College Opportunities,"
Seguin Gazette Enterprise (Texas), October 6, 1999

The price that America pays for shortchanging higher education opportunities for its growing Hispanic population is $130 million annually in salaries that would come from higher-paying jobs that require college.

Increasing the ranks of Hispanic college graduates has become a national priority in this knowledge-based economy, which increasingly relies on the skills of the country's fastest-growing minority group, according to a new study by the Educational Testing Service and Hispanic Association of Colleges and Universities. The report, "Education = Success: Empowering Hispanic Youth and Adults," was released recently during a seminar in Washington, DC, sponsored by the ETS/HACU collaboration.

"America loses billions by not improving education for Hispanics," said ETS president Nancy Cole. "But more importantly, it also loses fresh, diverse talents and perspectives."

"Education = Success" not only assesses the Hispanic education gap, but sets out solutions that have as their goal steady improvements in the number of Hispanics that gain college degrees.

"The good news is that Hispanic access to college is improving and that this trend will continue," said HACU president Antonio Flores. "The bad news is that Hispanic youth still trail non-Hispanic white youth in educational achievement."

The gap in Hispanic college attendance will grow from the current level of 430,000 to as many as 550,000 Hispanic students still missing out on a college education by the year 2015. According to the study, among Hispanics age 25 to 64, 13 percent have a post-secondary degree. Of those without a college degree, 18 percent are ready to enroll in a two-year or four-year college, while another 24 percent would be ready to enroll with about 200 hours of basic skills training. Increasing the number of 18- to 24-year-old Hispanic youth pursuing an undergraduate degree by 10 percentage points would result in Hispanic youth obtaining their proportional share of college enrollments.

That underrepresentation on campus also equals representation in good jobs. "Almost 60 percent of jobs today require college-level skills," said the study's author, Anthony P. Carnevale, ETS vice president for public leadership. "More Hispanic youth will need college to get their first jobs—and more Hispanic adults will need college to keep their current jobs or get better ones."

The Hispanic good-job gap translates to lower wages. On average, non-Hispanic white men earn $17,000 more a year than Hispanic men, and non-Hispanic women earn $6,700 year more than Hispanic women. "Evidence is mounting that linguistic, racial and class bias differences are limiting the job prospects and incomes of minority workers," said Flores. According to the study, the broader problem-solving and interpersonal skills demanded by the new information-based economy may be more culturally and class bound than the narrower technical and vocational skills characteristic of the old industrial economy. How do we get from here to there? Carnevale addresses issues ranging from money to Affirmative Action, testing and language skills—but notes that they are only part of the story.

Financial aid has not kept pace with increasing college costs. In addition, since a large number of young Hispanic students entering college are either first-generation Americans or first-generation college students, they need more social support, counseling, college and career planning than is currently available. Hispanic adult students also need more supportive services and flexible course offerings that allow them to meld schooling, work and family.

Carnevale added that to increase Hispanic participation in college through graduation, America needs to substantially expand its focus on college access policies. "We need affirmative development and affirmative outreach for all Hispanic students through the full 5-K system, not just college admissions information provided to relatively few students in the spring of their senior year of high school," he said.

"And better tests can be part of the solution," said Cole. "The ultimate goal is to create tests that establish the linkages of how to improve academic skills in preparation for college," she added.

The bottom line, according to the report, is that America needs to invest in Hispanic social capital to achieve the economic rewards possible. To combat prejudice and low expectations that face Hispanics, Carnevale advocates a strategy of engagement, encouragement, and social support. "Financial investment will be necessary, but even more essential is human investment—showing interest, defining and imparting values, and advising and caring," he said. "If we focus on these deeper causes of frustrated potential, our policies will be more surefooted," concluded Carnevale.

Immigrant Labor Timeline

1941 The Fair Employment Practices Act was passed to eliminate discrimination in employment.

1943 Prompted by the labor shortage in World War II, the U.S. government made an agreement with the Mexican government to supply temporary workers, known as *braceros*, for American agricultural work.

The so-called "Zoot Suit" riots took place in southern California, where hundreds of soldiers roamed Hispanic neighborhoods beating up Mexican American young men who were wearing zoot suits.

1945 The War Brides Act authorized the limited admission into the U.S. of the wives and children of military men without regard to quotas.

1948 The Displaced Persons Act permitted the immigration of 202,000 Europeans displaced as a result of political or racial persecution.

1950 Congress upgraded Puerto Rico's political status from protectorate to commonwealth.

1954 The Supreme Court recognized Hispanics as a separate class of people suffering profound discrimination, paving the way for Hispanic Americans to use legal means to attack all types of discrimination.

1954-1958 Operation Wetback, a government effort to locate and deport undocumented workers, resulted in the deportation of 3.8 million persons of Mexican descent.

1960s Young Mexican Americans created a new identity for themselves known as the Chicano Movement.

1962 The United Farm Workers Organizing Committee in California began as an independent organization led by César Chávez.

1964 Congress enacted the Civil Rights Act of 1964, which prohibited discrimination on the basis of gender, creed, race or ethnic background.

1965 Amendments to the Immigration and Nationality Act abolished the nation-origin quotas and established an annual limitation of 170,000 visas for immigrants in the Eastern Hemisphere.

The end of the *bracero* program forced many Mexicans to return to Mexico, with many settling near the U.S. border. When Fidel Castro allowed Cubans to leave the island nation if they had relatives in the United States, several hundred thousand emigrated to Florida.

1968 Chicano student organizations sprang up throughout the nation, as did barrio groups such as the Brown Berets. Immigration was limited to 120,000 persons annually from the Western Hemisphere.

1970 A Chicano Moratorium to protest the Vietnam War was organized in Los Angeles to draw attention to the disproportionately high number of Chicano casualties in that war.

1974 Congress passed the Equal Educational Opportunity Act that made bilingual public education available to Hispanic youth.

1970s-1980s The rise in politically motivated violence in Central America spurred a massive increase in undocumented immigration to the United States.

1977 The Immigration and Naturalization Service (INS) apprehended more than one million undocumented workers. An amendment to the Immigration and Nationality Act abolished separate quotas for the Western and Eastern Hemispheres, changing the quota to 290,000 immigrants worldwide annually with a maximum of 20,000 from any one country.

1980 The Refugees Act reduced the worldwide quota to 270,000 immigrants.

More than 125,000 Cuban "Marielito" refugees migrated to the United States.

1980s The rate of immigration approached the levels of the early 1900s as 6.3 million immigrants were granted permanent residence; Hispanic immigrants continued to account for more than 40 percent of the total.

1986 After more than a decade of debate, Congress enacted the Immigration Reform and Control Act which gave legal status to applicants who had been in the United States illegally since January 1, 1982.

1990 The Immigration Act of 1990 set an annual ceiling of 700,000 immigrants per year to enter the U.S. for the next three years and an annual ceiling of 675,000 per year for every year thereafter.

1994 The North American Free Trade Agreement (NAFTA) took effect to eliminate all tariffs among trading partners Canada, Mexico, and the United States within 15 years from this date. Californians passed Proposition 187, which banned undocumented immigrants from receiving public education and public benefits such as welfare and subsidized health care, except in emergency situations.

1996 The Illegal Immigration Reform and Immigrant Responsibility Act made it easier to deport aliens attempting to enter the U.S. without proper documents.

SECTION FIVE: CENSUS DATA

This section begins with eighteen state-by-state ranking tables from the 1990, 2000, and 2010 Census, designed to help define the times during which the families profiled in Section One lived. Table topics are listed below. Following the state-by-state tables are reprints from the special report series We the Americans *published in 1993 by the U.S. Census Bureau. Finally, data portrayed by maps, tables, graphs, charts and narrative from the 2000 Census, help to visualize the environment at that time.*

State-by-State Comparative Tables: 1990, 2000 and 2010

Note: When reviewing the ranking columns, be aware that the District of Columbia is included in the list of states.

Twenty-second Decennial Census of the United States (Census 2000)

Census 2000 Briefs

Total Population

Area	Population			1990		2000		2010	
	1990	2000	2010	Area	Rank	Area	Rank	Area	Rank
Alabama	4,040,587	4,447,100	4,779,736	California	1	California	1	California	1
Alaska	550,043	626,932	710,231	New York	2	Texas	2	Texas	2
Arizona	3,665,228	5,130,632	6,392,017	Texas	3	New York	3	New York	3
Arkansas	2,350,725	2,673,400	2,915,918	Florida	4	Florida	4	Florida	4
California	29,760,021	33,871,648	37,253,956	Pennsylvania	5	Illinois	5	Illinois	5
Colorado	3,294,394	4,301,261	5,029,196	Illinois	6	Pennsylvania	6	Pennsylvania	6
Connecticut	3,287,116	3,405,565	3,574,097	Ohio	7	Ohio	7	Ohio	7
Delaware	666,168	783,600	897,934	Michigan	8	Michigan	8	Michigan	8
D.C.	606,900	572,059	601,723	New Jersey	9	New Jersey	9	Georgia	9
Florida	12,937,926	15,982,378	18,801,310	North Carolina	10	Georgia	10	North Carolina	10
Georgia	6,478,216	8,186,453	9,687,653	Georgia	11	North Carolina	11	New Jersey	11
Hawaii	1,108,229	1,211,537	1,360,301	Virginia	12	Virginia	12	Virginia	12
Idaho	1,006,749	1,293,953	1,567,582	Massachusetts	13	Massachusetts	13	Washington	13
Illinois	11,430,602	12,419,293	12,830,632	Indiana	14	Indiana	14	Massachusetts	14
Indiana	5,544,159	6,080,485	6,483,802	Missouri	15	Washington	15	Indiana	15
Iowa	2,776,755	2,926,324	3,046,355	Wisconsin	16	Tennessee	16	Arizona	16
Kansas	2,477,574	2,688,418	2,853,118	Tennessee	17	Missouri	17	Tennessee	17
Kentucky	3,685,296	4,041,769	4,339,367	Washington	18	Wisconsin	18	Missouri	18
Louisiana	4,219,973	4,468,976	4,533,372	Maryland	19	Maryland	19	Maryland	19
Maine	1,227,928	1,274,923	1,328,361	Minnesota	20	Arizona	20	Wisconsin	20
Maryland	4,781,468	5,296,486	5,773,552	Louisiana	21	Minnesota	21	Minnesota	21
Massachusetts	6,016,425	6,349,097	6,547,629	Alabama	22	Louisiana	22	Colorado	22
Michigan	9,295,297	9,938,444	9,883,640	Kentucky	23	Alabama	23	Alabama	23
Minnesota	4,375,099	4,919,479	5,303,925	Arizona	24	Colorado	24	South Carolina	24
Mississippi	2,573,216	2,844,658	2,967,297	South Carolina	25	Kentucky	25	Louisiana	25
Missouri	5,117,073	5,595,211	5,988,927	Colorado	26	South Carolina	26	Kentucky	26
Montana	799,065	902,195	989,415	Connecticut	27	Oklahoma	27	Oregon	27
Nebraska	1,578,385	1,711,263	1,826,341	Oklahoma	28	Oregon	28	Oklahoma	28
Nevada	1,201,833	1,998,257	2,700,551	Oregon	29	Connecticut	29	Connecticut	29
New Hampshire	1,109,252	1,235,786	1,316,470	Iowa	30	Iowa	30	Iowa	30
New Jersey	7,730,188	8,414,350	8,791,894	Mississippi	31	Mississippi	31	Mississippi	31
New Mexico	1,515,069	1,819,046	2,059,179	Kansas	32	Kansas	32	Arkansas	32
New York	17,990,455	18,976,457	19,378,102	Arkansas	33	Arkansas	33	Kansas	33
North Carolina	6,628,637	8,049,313	9,535,483	West Virginia	34	Utah	34	Utah	34
North Dakota	638,800	642,200	672,591	Utah	35	Nevada	35	Nevada	35
Ohio	10,847,115	11,353,140	11,536,504	Nebraska	36	New Mexico	36	New Mexico	36
Oklahoma	3,145,585	3,450,654	3,751,351	New Mexico	37	West Virginia	37	West Virginia	37
Oregon	2,842,321	3,421,399	3,831,074	Maine	38	Nebraska	38	Nebraska	38
Pennsylvania	11,881,643	12,281,054	12,702,379	Nevada	39	Idaho	39	Idaho	39
Rhode Island	1,003,464	1,048,319	1,052,567	New Hampshire	40	Maine	40	Hawaii	40
South Carolina	3,486,703	4,012,012	4,625,364	Hawaii	41	New Hampshire	41	Maine	41
South Dakota	696,004	754,844	814,180	Idaho	42	Hawaii	42	New Hampshire	42
Tennessee	4,877,185	5,689,283	6,346,105	Rhode Island	43	Rhode Island	43	Rhode Island	43
Texas	16,986,510	20,851,820	25,145,561	Montana	44	Montana	44	Montana	44
Utah	1,722,850	2,233,169	2,763,885	South Dakota	45	Delaware	45	Delaware	45
Vermont	562,758	608,827	625,741	Delaware	46	South Dakota	46	South Dakota	46
Virginia	6,187,358	7,078,515	8,001,024	North Dakota	47	North Dakota	47	Alaska	47
Washington	4,866,692	5,894,121	6,724,540	D.C.	48	Alaska	48	North Dakota	48
West Virginia	1,793,477	1,808,344	1,852,994	Vermont	49	Vermont	49	Vermont	49
Wisconsin	4,891,769	5,363,675	5,686,986	Alaska	50	D.C.	50	D.C.	50
Wyoming	453,588	493,782	563,626	Wyoming	51	Wyoming	51	Wyoming	51
United States	248,709,873	281,421,906	308,745,538	United States	–	United States	–	United States	–

Source: U.S. Census Bureau, 1990, 2000, and 2010 Census

White Population

Area	Percent of Population			1990		2000		2010	
	1990	2000	2010	Area	Rank	Area	Rank	Area	Rank
Alabama	73.6	71.1	68.5	Vermont	1	Maine	1	Vermont	1
Alaska	75.5	69.3	66.6	Maine	2	Vermont	2	Maine	2
Arizona	80.8	75.5	73.0	New Hampshire	3	New Hampshire	3	West Virginia	3
Arkansas	82.7	80.0	77.0	Iowa	4	West Virginia	4	New Hampshire	4
California	68.9	59.5	57.5	West Virginia	5	Iowa	5	Iowa	5
Colorado	88.1	82.7	81.3	North Dakota	6	North Dakota	6	Wyoming	6
Connecticut	86.9	81.6	77.5	Idaho	7	Wyoming	7	North Dakota	7
Delaware	80.3	74.6	68.8	Minnesota	7	Idaho	8	Montana	8
D.C.	29.6	30.7	38.4	Wyoming	9	Montana	9	Idaho	9
Florida	83.0	77.9	75.0	Nebraska	10	Kentucky	10	Kentucky	10
Georgia	71.0	65.0	59.7	Utah	11	Nebraska	11	Wisconsin	11
Hawaii	33.3	24.2	24.7	Oregon	12	Minnesota	12	Nebraska	12
Idaho	94.4	90.9	89.0	Montana	13	Utah	13	Utah	13
Illinois	78.3	73.4	71.5	Wisconsin	14	Wisconsin	14	South Dakota	14
Indiana	90.5	87.4	84.3	Kentucky	15	South Dakota	15	Minnesota	15
Iowa	96.6	93.9	91.3	South Dakota	16	Indiana	16	Indiana	16
Kansas	90.0	86.0	83.8	Rhode Island	17	Oregon	17	Kansas	17
Kentucky	92.0	90.0	87.7	Indiana	18	Kansas	18	Oregon	18
Louisiana	67.2	63.9	62.5	Kansas	19	Pennsylvania	19	Missouri	19
Maine	98.4	96.9	95.2	Massachusetts	20	Rhode Island	20	Ohio	20
Maryland	70.9	64.0	58.1	Washington	21	Ohio	21	Pennsylvania	21
Massachusetts	89.8	84.5	80.4	Pennsylvania	21	Missouri	22	Rhode Island	22
Michigan	83.4	80.1	78.9	Colorado	23	Massachusetts	23	Colorado	23
Minnesota	94.4	89.4	85.3	Ohio	24	Colorado	24	Massachusetts	24
Mississippi	63.4	61.3	59.1	Missouri	25	Washington	25	Michigan	25
Missouri	87.6	84.8	82.8	Connecticut	26	Connecticut	26	Connecticut	26
Montana	92.7	90.5	89.4	Nevada	27	Tennessee	27	Tennessee	27
Nebraska	93.8	89.6	86.1	Michigan	28	Michigan	28	Washington	28
Nevada	84.2	75.1	66.1	Florida	29	Arkansas	29	Arkansas	29
New Hampshire	98.0	96.0	93.8	Tennessee	30	Florida	30	Florida	30
New Jersey	79.3	72.5	68.5	Arkansas	31	Oklahoma	31	Arizona	31
New Mexico	75.6	66.7	68.3	Oklahoma	32	Arizona	32	Oklahoma	32
New York	74.4	67.9	65.7	Arizona	33	Nevada	33	Illinois	33
North Carolina	75.5	72.1	68.4	Delaware	34	Delaware	34	Texas	34
North Dakota	94.5	92.3	90.0	New Jersey	35	Illinois	35	Delaware	35
Ohio	87.7	84.9	82.6	Illinois	36	New Jersey	36	New Jersey	36
Oklahoma	82.1	76.1	72.1	Virginia	37	Virginia	37	Virginia	36
Oregon	92.7	86.5	83.6	New Mexico	38	North Carolina	38	Alabama	38
Pennsylvania	88.5	85.3	81.9	North Carolina	39	Alabama	39	North Carolina	39
Rhode Island	91.4	85.0	81.4	Alaska	40	Texas	40	New Mexico	40
South Carolina	69.0	67.1	66.1	Texas	41	Alaska	41	Alaska	41
South Dakota	91.6	88.6	85.9	New York	42	New York	42	Nevada	42
Tennessee	83.0	80.2	77.5	Alabama	43	South Carolina	43	South Carolina	42
Texas	75.2	70.9	70.4	Georgia	44	New Mexico	44	New York	44
Utah	93.7	89.2	86.0	Maryland	45	Georgia	45	Louisiana	45
Vermont	98.6	96.7	95.2	South Carolina	46	Maryland	46	Georgia	46
Virginia	77.4	72.3	68.5	California	47	Louisiana	47	Mississippi	47
Washington	88.5	81.8	77.2	Louisiana	48	Mississippi	48	Maryland	48
West Virginia	96.2	95.0	93.9	Mississippi	49	California	49	California	49
Wisconsin	92.2	88.9	86.2	Hawaii	50	D.C.	50	D.C.	50
Wyoming	94.1	92.0	90.7	D.C.	51	Hawaii	51	Hawaii	51
United States	80.2	75.1	72.4	United States	–	United States	–	United States	–

Source: U.S. Census Bureau, 1990, 2000, and 2010 Census

Black Population

Area	Percent of Population			1990		2000		2010	
	1990	2000	2010	Area	Rank	Area	Rank	Area	Rank
Alabama	25.2	25.9	26.1	D.C.	1	D.C.	1	D.C.	1
Alaska	4.0	3.4	3.2	Mississippi	2	Mississippi	2	Mississippi	2
Arizona	3.0	3.1	4.0	Louisiana	3	Louisiana	3	Louisiana	3
Arkansas	15.9	15.6	15.4	South Carolina	4	South Carolina	4	Georgia	4
California	7.4	6.6	6.1	Georgia	5	Georgia	5	Maryland	5
Colorado	4.0	3.8	4.0	Alabama	6	Maryland	6	South Carolina	6
Connecticut	8.3	9.1	10.1	Maryland	7	Alabama	7	Alabama	7
Delaware	16.8	19.2	21.3	North Carolina	8	North Carolina	8	North Carolina	8
D.C.	65.8	60.0	50.7	Virginia	9	Virginia	9	Delaware	9
Florida	13.6	14.6	15.9	Delaware	10	Delaware	10	Virginia	10
Georgia	26.9	28.7	30.4	Tennessee	11	Tennessee	11	Tennessee	11
Hawaii	2.4	1.8	1.5	Arkansas	12	New York	12	Florida	12
Idaho	0.3	0.4	0.6	New York	13	Arkansas	13	New York	13
Illinois	14.8	15.1	14.5	Illinois	14	Illinois	14	Arkansas	14
Indiana	7.7	8.3	9.1	Michigan	15	Florida	15	Illinois	15
Iowa	1.7	2.1	2.9	Florida	16	Michigan	16	Michigan	16
Kansas	5.7	5.7	5.8	New Jersey	17	New Jersey	17	New Jersey	17
Kentucky	7.1	7.3	7.7	Texas	18	Texas	18	Ohio	18
Louisiana	30.7	32.4	32.0	Missouri	19	Ohio	19	Texas	19
Maine	0.4	0.5	1.1	Ohio	20	Missouri	20	Missouri	20
Maryland	24.8	27.8	29.4	Pennsylvania	21	Pennsylvania	21	Pennsylvania	21
Massachusetts	4.9	5.4	6.6	Connecticut	22	Connecticut	22	Connecticut	22
Michigan	13.9	14.2	14.1	Indiana	23	Indiana	23	Indiana	23
Minnesota	2.1	3.4	5.1	Oklahoma	24	Oklahoma	24	Nevada	24
Mississippi	35.5	36.3	37.0	California	25	Kentucky	25	Kentucky	25
Missouri	10.7	11.2	11.5	Kentucky	26	Nevada	26	Oklahoma	26
Montana	0.3	0.3	0.4	Nevada	27	California	27	Massachusetts	27
Nebraska	3.6	4.0	4.5	Kansas	28	Kansas	28	Wisconsin	28
Nevada	6.5	6.7	8.1	Wisconsin	29	Wisconsin	29	California	29
New Hampshire	0.6	0.7	1.1	Massachusetts	30	Massachusetts	30	Kansas	30
New Jersey	13.4	13.5	13.7	Alaska	31	Rhode Island	31	Rhode Island	31
New Mexico	1.9	1.8	2.0	Colorado	32	Nebraska	32	Minnesota	32
New York	15.8	15.8	15.8	Rhode Island	33	Colorado	33	Nebraska	33
North Carolina	21.9	21.5	21.4	Nebraska	34	Minnesota	34	Arizona	34
North Dakota	0.5	0.6	1.1	West Virginia	35	Alaska	35	Colorado	35
Ohio	10.6	11.4	12.2	Washington	36	Washington	36	Washington	36
Oklahoma	7.4	7.5	7.4	Arizona	37	West Virginia	37	West Virginia	37
Oregon	1.6	1.6	1.8	Hawaii	38	Arizona	38	Alaska	38
Pennsylvania	9.1	9.9	10.8	Minnesota	39	Iowa	39	Iowa	39
Rhode Island	3.8	4.4	5.7	New Mexico	40	New Mexico	40	New Mexico	40
South Carolina	29.8	29.5	27.9	Iowa	41	Hawaii	41	Oregon	41
South Dakota	0.4	0.6	1.2	Oregon	42	Oregon	42	Hawaii	42
Tennessee	15.9	16.4	16.6	Wyoming	43	Utah	43	South Dakota	43
Texas	11.9	11.5	11.8	Utah	44	Wyoming	44	North Dakota	44
Utah	0.6	0.7	1.0	New Hampshire	45	New Hampshire	45	Maine	44
Vermont	0.3	0.5	1.0	North Dakota	46	South Dakota	46	New Hampshire	46
Virginia	18.8	19.6	19.3	South Dakota	47	North Dakota	47	Utah	47
Washington	3.0	3.2	3.5	Maine	48	Maine	48	Vermont	48
West Virginia	3.1	3.1	3.4	Vermont	49	Vermont	49	Wyoming	49
Wisconsin	5.0	5.6	6.3	Idaho	50	Idaho	50	Idaho	50
Wyoming	0.7	0.7	0.8	Montana	51	Montana	51	Montana	51
United States	12.0	12.3	12.6	United States	–	United States	–	United States	–

Source: U.S. Census Bureau, 1990, 2000, and 2010 Census

American Indian/Alaska Native Population

Area	Percent of Population			1990		2000		2010	
	1990	2000	2010	Area	Rank	Area	Rank	Area	Rank
Alabama	0.4	0.5	0.5	Alaska	1	Alaska	1	Alaska	1
Alaska	15.5	15.6	14.7	New Mexico	2	New Mexico	2	New Mexico	2
Arizona	5.5	4.9	4.6	Oklahoma	3	South Dakota	3	South Dakota	3
Arkansas	0.5	0.6	0.7	South Dakota	4	Oklahoma	4	Oklahoma	4
California	0.8	0.9	0.9	Montana	5	Montana	5	Montana	5
Colorado	0.8	1.0	1.1	Arizona	6	Arizona	6	North Dakota	6
Connecticut	0.2	0.2	0.3	North Dakota	7	North Dakota	7	Arizona	7
Delaware	0.3	0.3	0.4	Wyoming	8	Wyoming	8	Wyoming	8
D.C.	0.2	0.3	0.3	Washington	9	Washington	9	Washington	9
Florida	0.2	0.3	0.3	Nevada	10	Idaho	10	Oregon	10
Georgia	0.2	0.2	0.3	Utah	11	Utah	11	Idaho	11
Hawaii	0.4	0.2	0.3	Idaho	12	Nevada	12	North Carolina	12
Idaho	1.3	1.3	1.3	Oregon	13	Oregon	12	Nevada	13
Illinois	0.1	0.2	0.3	North Carolina	14	North Carolina	14	Utah	13
Indiana	0.2	0.2	0.2	Minnesota	15	Minnesota	15	Minnesota	15
Iowa	0.2	0.3	0.3	Kansas	16	Colorado	16	Colorado	16
Kansas	0.8	0.9	0.9	Colorado	17	California	17	Nebraska	17
Kentucky	0.1	0.2	0.2	California	18	Kansas	18	Kansas	18
Louisiana	0.4	0.5	0.6	Wisconsin	18	Wisconsin	19	California	19
Maine	0.4	0.5	0.6	Nebraska	20	Nebraska	20	Wisconsin	20
Maryland	0.2	0.2	0.3	Michigan	21	Arkansas	21	Arkansas	21
Massachusetts	0.2	0.2	0.2	Arkansas	22	Michigan	22	Texas	22
Michigan	0.6	0.5	0.6	Maine	23	Texas	23	Louisiana	23
Minnesota	1.1	1.1	1.1	Hawaii	24	Louisiana	23	Maine	24
Mississippi	0.3	0.4	0.5	Louisiana	25	Maine	25	Michigan	25
Missouri	0.3	0.4	0.4	Rhode Island	26	Alabama	26	Alabama	26
Montana	5.9	6.2	6.3	Alabama	26	Rhode Island	27	Rhode Island	27
Nebraska	0.7	0.8	1.0	Texas	28	Missouri	28	New York	28
Nevada	1.6	1.3	1.1	Missouri	28	New York	29	Mississippi	29
New Hampshire	0.1	0.2	0.2	New York	30	Mississippi	30	Delaware	30
New Jersey	0.1	0.2	0.3	Mississippi	31	Vermont	31	Missouri	31
New Mexico	8.8	9.5	9.3	Delaware	32	Delaware	32	South Carolina	32
New York	0.3	0.4	0.5	Vermont	32	Florida	33	Florida	33
North Carolina	1.2	1.2	1.2	Florida	34	South Carolina	33	Virginia	34
North Dakota	4.0	4.8	5.4	Maryland	35	Iowa	35	Iowa	35
Ohio	0.1	0.2	0.2	Iowa	36	D.C.	36	D.C.	36
Oklahoma	8.0	7.9	8.5	Virginia	37	Virginia	36	Maryland	36
Oregon	1.3	1.3	1.3	D.C.	38	Hawaii	38	Vermont	36
Pennsylvania	0.1	0.1	0.2	South Carolina	38	Maryland	38	Illinois	39
Rhode Island	0.4	0.4	0.5	Indiana	40	Connecticut	40	New Jersey	40
South Carolina	0.2	0.3	0.4	Georgia	41	Georgia	41	Georgia	40
South Dakota	7.2	8.2	8.8	Tennessee	41	Tennessee	41	Tennessee	42
Tennessee	0.2	0.2	0.3	Connecticut	43	Indiana	43	Connecticut	43
Texas	0.3	0.5	0.6	Massachusetts	43	Illinois	44	Hawaii	43
Utah	1.4	1.3	1.1	New Jersey	45	Massachusetts	45	Massachusetts	45
Vermont	0.3	0.4	0.3	Illinois	45	New Hampshire	45	Indiana	46
Virginia	0.2	0.3	0.3	Ohio	45	New Jersey	47	New Hampshire	47
Washington	1.6	1.5	1.5	New Hampshire	45	Ohio	48	Kentucky	48
West Virginia	0.1	0.2	0.2	Kentucky	49	Kentucky	49	Ohio	49
Wisconsin	0.8	0.8	0.9	West Virginia	50	West Virginia	50	Pennsylvania	50
Wyoming	2.0	2.2	2.3	Pennsylvania	51	Pennsylvania	51	West Virginia	51
United States	0.7	0.9	0.9	United States	–	United States	–	United States	–

Source: U.S. Census Bureau, 1990, 2000, and 2010 Census

Asian Population

Area	Percent of Population 1990	2000	2010	1990 Area	Rank	2000 Area	Rank	2010 Area	Rank
Alabama	0.5	0.7	1.1	Hawaii	1	Hawaii	1	Hawaii	1
Alaska	3.5	4.0	5.3	California	2	California	2	California	2
Arizona	1.5	1.8	2.7	Washington	3	New Jersey	3	New Jersey	3
Arkansas	0.5	0.7	1.2	New York	4	New York	4	New York	4
California	9.5	10.9	13.0	Alaska	5	Washington	5	Nevada	5
Colorado	1.8	2.2	2.7	New Jersey	6	Nevada	6	Washington	6
Connecticut	1.5	2.4	3.7	Nevada	7	Alaska	7	Maryland	7
Delaware	1.3	2.0	3.1	Maryland	8	Maryland	8	Virginia	8
D.C.	1.8	2.6	3.5	Virginia	9	Massachusetts	9	Alaska	9
Florida	1.1	1.6	2.4	Illinois	10	Virginia	10	Massachusetts	10
Georgia	1.1	2.1	3.2	Oregon	11	Illinois	11	Illinois	11
Hawaii	61.8	41.5	38.6	Massachusetts	12	Oregon	12	Minnesota	12
Idaho	0.9	0.9	1.2	Utah	13	Minnesota	13	Texas	13
Illinois	2.5	3.4	4.5	Texas	14	Texas	14	Connecticut	14
Indiana	0.6	0.9	1.5	D.C.	15	D.C.	15	Oregon	15
Iowa	0.9	1.2	1.7	Rhode Island	16	Connecticut	16	D.C.	16
Kansas	1.2	1.7	2.3	Colorado	17	Rhode Island	17	Georgia	17
Kentucky	0.4	0.7	1.1	Minnesota	18	Colorado	18	Delaware	18
Louisiana	0.9	1.2	1.5	Connecticut	19	Georgia	19	Rhode Island	19
Maine	0.5	0.7	1.0	Arizona	20	Delaware	20	Arizona	20
Maryland	2.9	3.9	5.5	Delaware	21	Arizona	21	Colorado	20
Massachusetts	2.3	3.7	5.3	Kansas	22	Pennsylvania	22	Pennsylvania	22
Michigan	1.1	1.7	2.4	Florida	23	Michigan	23	Florida	23
Minnesota	1.7	2.8	4.0	Georgia	24	Kansas	24	Michigan	24
Mississippi	0.5	0.6	0.8	Pennsylvania	25	Florida	25	Kansas	25
Missouri	0.8	1.1	1.6	Michigan	26	Utah	26	Wisconsin	26
Montana	0.5	0.5	0.6	Wisconsin	27	Wisconsin	27	North Carolina	27
Nebraska	0.7	1.2	1.7	Oklahoma	28	North Carolina	28	New Hampshire	28
Nevada	3.1	4.5	7.2	Louisiana	29	Oklahoma	29	Utah	29
New Hampshire	0.8	1.2	2.1	New Mexico	30	New Hampshire	30	Nebraska	30
New Jersey	3.5	5.7	8.2	Idaho	30	Nebraska	31	Iowa	31
New Mexico	0.9	1.0	1.3	Iowa	32	Iowa	32	Oklahoma	32
New York	3.8	5.5	7.3	Ohio	33	Louisiana	33	Ohio	33
North Carolina	0.7	1.4	2.1	New Hampshire	33	Ohio	34	Missouri	34
North Dakota	0.5	0.5	1.0	Missouri	35	Missouri	35	Indiana	35
Ohio	0.8	1.1	1.6	Nebraska	36	New Mexico	36	Louisiana	36
Oklahoma	1.0	1.3	1.7	North Carolina	36	Tennessee	37	Tennessee	37
Oregon	2.4	2.9	3.6	Indiana	38	Indiana	38	New Mexico	38
Pennsylvania	1.1	1.7	2.7	Tennessee	39	Idaho	39	South Carolina	39
Rhode Island	1.8	2.2	2.8	South Carolina	40	South Carolina	40	Vermont	40
South Carolina	0.6	0.9	1.2	Wyoming	41	Vermont	41	Arkansas	41
South Dakota	0.4	0.5	0.9	Vermont	42	Arkansas	42	Idaho	42
Tennessee	0.6	1.0	1.4	North Dakota	43	Kentucky	43	Kentucky	43
Texas	1.8	2.7	3.8	Alabama	43	Maine	44	Alabama	44
Utah	1.9	1.6	2.0	Maine	43	Alabama	45	North Dakota	45
Vermont	0.5	0.8	1.2	Montana	46	Mississippi	46	Maine	46
Virginia	2.5	3.6	5.5	Arkansas	46	South Dakota	47	South Dakota	47
Washington	4.3	5.4	7.1	Mississippi	48	Wyoming	48	Mississippi	48
West Virginia	0.4	0.5	0.6	Kentucky	49	North Dakota	48	Wyoming	49
Wisconsin	1.1	1.6	2.2	South Dakota	50	Montana	50	West Virginia	50
Wyoming	0.6	0.5	0.7	West Virginia	51	West Virginia	50	Montana	51
United States	2.9	3.6	4.7	United States	–	United States	–	United States	–

Note: In the 1990 Census, the Asian category included Native Hawaiian/Other Pacific Islanders.
Source: U.S. Census Bureau, 1990, 2000, and 2010 Census

Hispanic Population

Area	Percent of Population			1990		2000		2010	
	1990	2000	2010	Area	Rank	Area	Rank	Area	Rank
Alabama	0.6	1.7	3.8	New Mexico	1	New Mexico	1	New Mexico	1
Alaska	3.2	4.1	5.5	California	2	California	2	California	2
Arizona	18.7	25.2	29.6	Texas	3	Texas	3	Texas	2
Arkansas	0.8	3.2	6.3	Arizona	4	Arizona	4	Arizona	4
California	25.8	32.3	37.6	Colorado	5	Nevada	5	Nevada	5
Colorado	12.8	17.1	20.6	New York	6	Colorado	6	Florida	6
Connecticut	6.4	9.4	13.4	Florida	7	Florida	7	Colorado	7
Delaware	2.3	4.7	8.1	Nevada	8	New York	8	New Jersey	8
D.C.	5.3	7.8	9.1	New Jersey	9	New Jersey	9	New York	9
Florida	12.1	16.7	22.4	Illinois	10	Illinois	10	Illinois	10
Georgia	1.6	5.3	8.8	Hawaii	11	Connecticut	11	Connecticut	11
Hawaii	7.3	7.2	8.8	Connecticut	12	Utah	12	Utah	12
Idaho	5.2	7.8	11.2	Wyoming	13	Rhode Island	13	Rhode Island	13
Illinois	7.9	12.3	15.8	D.C.	14	Oregon	14	Oregon	14
Indiana	1.7	3.5	6.0	Idaho	15	D.C.	15	Washington	15
Iowa	1.1	2.8	4.9	Utah	16	Idaho	15	Idaho	16
Kansas	3.7	7.0	10.5	Massachusetts	17	Washington	17	Kansas	17
Kentucky	0.6	1.4	3.0	Rhode Island	18	Hawaii	18	Massachusetts	18
Louisiana	2.2	2.4	4.2	Washington	19	Kansas	19	Nebraska	19
Maine	0.5	0.7	1.2	Oregon	20	Massachusetts	20	D.C.	20
Maryland	2.6	4.3	8.1	Kansas	21	Wyoming	21	Wyoming	21
Massachusetts	4.7	6.7	9.5	Alaska	22	Nebraska	22	Hawaii	22
Michigan	2.1	3.2	4.4	Oklahoma	23	Georgia	23	Oklahoma	23
Minnesota	1.2	2.9	4.7	Maryland	24	Oklahoma	24	Georgia	24
Mississippi	0.6	1.3	2.7	Virginia	25	Delaware	25	North Carolina	25
Missouri	1.2	2.1	3.5	Delaware	26	North Carolina	26	Delaware	26
Montana	1.5	2.0	2.8	Nebraska	27	Virginia	27	Maryland	26
Nebraska	2.3	5.5	9.1	Louisiana	28	Maryland	28	Virginia	28
Nevada	10.3	19.7	26.5	Michigan	29	Alaska	29	Arkansas	29
New Hampshire	1.0	1.6	2.7	Pennsylvania	30	Wisconsin	30	Indiana	30
New Jersey	9.5	13.2	17.6	Wisconsin	31	Indiana	31	Wisconsin	31
New Mexico	38.2	42.0	46.3	Indiana	32	Michigan	32	Pennsylvania	32
New York	12.3	15.1	17.6	Georgia	33	Arkansas	33	Alaska	33
North Carolina	1.1	4.7	8.3	Montana	34	Pennsylvania	34	South Carolina	34
North Dakota	0.7	1.2	2.0	Ohio	35	Minnesota	35	Iowa	35
Ohio	1.2	1.9	3.0	Minnesota	36	Iowa	36	Minnesota	36
Oklahoma	2.7	5.2	8.8	Missouri	37	Louisiana	37	Tennessee	37
Oregon	3.9	8.0	11.7	Iowa	38	South Carolina	38	Michigan	38
Pennsylvania	1.9	3.2	5.6	North Carolina	39	Tennessee	39	Louisiana	39
Rhode Island	4.5	8.6	12.4	New Hampshire	40	Missouri	40	Alabama	40
South Carolina	0.8	2.3	5.1	South Carolina	41	Montana	41	Missouri	41
South Dakota	0.7	1.4	2.7	Arkansas	42	Ohio	42	Ohio	42
Tennessee	0.6	2.1	4.5	South Dakota	43	Alabama	43	Kentucky	43
Texas	25.5	31.9	37.6	North Dakota	44	New Hampshire	44	Montana	44
Utah	4.9	9.0	12.9	Tennessee	45	Kentucky	45	New Hampshire	45
Vermont	0.6	0.9	1.4	Vermont	46	South Dakota	46	Mississippi	46
Virginia	2.5	4.6	7.9	Mississippi	47	Mississippi	47	South Dakota	47
Washington	4.4	7.4	11.2	Alabama	48	North Dakota	48	North Dakota	48
West Virginia	0.4	0.6	1.2	Kentucky	49	Vermont	49	Vermont	49
Wisconsin	1.9	3.6	5.9	Maine	50	Maine	50	Maine	50
Wyoming	5.6	6.4	8.9	West Virginia	51	West Virginia	51	West Virginia	51
United States	8.9	12.5	16.3	United States	–	United States	–	United States	–

Source: U.S. Census Bureau, 1990, 2000, and 2010 Census

Foreign-Born Population

Area	Percent of Population			1990		2000		2010	
	1990	2000	2010	Area	Rank	Area	Rank	Area	Rank
Alabama	1.1	2.0	3.4	California	1	California	1	California	1
Alaska	4.5	5.9	7.2	New York	2	New York	2	New York	2
Arizona	7.6	12.8	14.2	Hawaii	3	New Jersey	3	New Jersey	3
Arkansas	1.1	2.8	4.3	Florida	4	Hawaii	3	Nevada	4
California	21.7	26.2	27.2	New Jersey	5	Florida	5	Florida	5
Colorado	4.3	8.6	9.8	D.C.	6	Nevada	6	Hawaii	6
Connecticut	8.5	10.9	13.2	Massachusetts	7	Texas	7	Texas	7
Delaware	3.3	5.7	8.2	Rhode Island	7	D.C.	8	Massachusetts	8
D.C.	9.7	12.9	13.0	Texas	9	Arizona	9	Arizona	9
Florida	12.9	16.7	19.2	Nevada	10	Illinois	10	Illinois	10
Georgia	2.7	7.1	9.6	Connecticut	11	Massachusetts	11	Connecticut	11
Hawaii	14.7	17.5	17.7	Illinois	12	Rhode Island	12	Maryland	11
Idaho	2.9	5.0	5.9	Arizona	13	Connecticut	13	D.C.	13
Illinois	8.3	12.3	13.6	Washington	14	Washington	14	Washington	14
Indiana	1.7	3.1	4.4	Maryland	14	Maryland	15	Rhode Island	15
Iowa	1.6	3.1	4.1	New Mexico	16	Colorado	16	Virginia	16
Kansas	2.5	5.0	6.3	Virginia	17	Oregon	17	Colorado	17
Kentucky	0.9	2.0	3.1	Oregon	18	New Mexico	18	New Mexico	18
Louisiana	2.1	2.6	3.6	Alaska	19	Virginia	19	Oregon	18
Maine	3.0	2.9	3.3	Colorado	20	Utah	20	Georgia	20
Maryland	6.6	9.8	13.2	Michigan	21	Georgia	20	Utah	21
Massachusetts	9.5	12.2	14.5	New Hampshire	22	Alaska	22	Delaware	21
Michigan	3.8	5.3	5.9	Utah	23	Delaware	23	North Carolina	23
Minnesota	2.6	5.3	7.0	Delaware	24	North Carolina	24	Alaska	24
Mississippi	0.8	1.4	2.2	Pennsylvania	25	Michigan	24	Minnesota	25
Missouri	1.6	2.7	3.7	Vermont	25	Minnesota	24	Kansas	26
Montana	1.7	1.8	2.0	Maine	27	Idaho	27	Idaho	27
Nebraska	1.8	4.4	5.9	Idaho	28	Kansas	27	Nebraska	27
Nevada	8.7	15.8	19.3	Georgia	29	Nebraska	29	Michigan	27
New Hampshire	3.7	4.4	5.3	Minnesota	30	New Hampshire	29	Pennsylvania	30
New Jersey	12.5	17.5	20.3	Kansas	31	Pennsylvania	31	New Hampshire	31
New Mexico	5.3	8.2	9.7	Wisconsin	31	Oklahoma	32	Oklahoma	32
New York	15.9	20.4	21.7	Ohio	33	Vermont	32	South Carolina	33
North Carolina	1.7	5.3	7.4	Oklahoma	34	Wisconsin	34	Wisconsin	34
North Dakota	1.5	1.9	2.4	Louisiana	34	Indiana	35	Indiana	35
Ohio	2.4	3.0	3.8	Nebraska	36	Iowa	35	Tennessee	35
Oklahoma	2.1	3.8	5.2	Wyoming	37	Ohio	37	Arkansas	37
Oregon	4.9	8.5	9.7	Indiana	37	South Carolina	38	Iowa	38
Pennsylvania	3.1	4.1	5.6	Montana	37	Maine	38	Vermont	39
Rhode Island	9.5	11.4	12.6	North Carolina	37	Arkansas	40	Ohio	40
South Carolina	1.4	2.9	4.7	Missouri	41	Tennessee	40	Missouri	41
South Dakota	1.1	1.8	2.3	Iowa	41	Missouri	42	Louisiana	42
Tennessee	1.2	2.8	4.4	North Dakota	43	Louisiana	43	Alabama	43
Texas	9.0	13.9	16.1	South Carolina	44	Wyoming	44	Maine	44
Utah	3.4	7.1	8.2	Tennessee	45	Alabama	45	Wyoming	45
Vermont	3.1	3.8	4.0	Arkansas	46	Kentucky	45	Kentucky	45
Virginia	5.0	8.1	10.8	South Dakota	46	North Dakota	47	North Dakota	47
Washington	6.6	10.4	12.7	Alabama	46	Montana	48	South Dakota	48
West Virginia	0.9	1.1	1.3	Kentucky	49	South Dakota	48	Mississippi	49
Wisconsin	2.5	3.6	4.6	West Virginia	49	Mississippi	50	Montana	50
Wyoming	1.7	2.3	3.1	Mississippi	51	West Virginia	51	West Virginia	51
United States	7.9	11.1	12.7	United States	–	United States	–	United States	–

Source: U.S. Census Bureau, 1990, 2000, and 2010 Census

Urban Population

Area	Percent of Population			1990		2000		2010	
	1990	2000	2010	Area	Rank	Area	Rank	Area	Rank
Alabama	60.4	55.4	59.0	D.C.	1	D.C.	1	D.C.	1
Alaska	67.5	65.7	66.0	California	2	California	2	California	2
Arizona	87.5	88.2	89.8	New Jersey	3	New Jersey	3	New Jersey	3
Arkansas	53.5	52.4	56.2	Hawaii	4	Nevada	4	Nevada	4
California	92.6	94.5	95.0	Nevada	5	Hawaii	4	Massachusetts	5
Colorado	82.4	84.5	86.2	Arizona	6	Massachusetts	6	Hawaii	6
Connecticut	79.1	87.7	88.0	Utah	7	Rhode Island	7	Florida	7
Delaware	73.0	80.0	83.3	Rhode Island	8	Florida	8	Rhode Island	8
D.C.	100.0	100.0	100.0	Florida	9	Utah	9	Utah	9
Florida	84.8	89.3	91.2	Illinois	10	Arizona	10	Arizona	10
Georgia	63.2	71.7	75.1	New York	11	Illinois	11	Illinois	11
Hawaii	89.0	91.6	91.9	Massachusetts	11	Connecticut	12	Connecticut	12
Idaho	57.4	66.4	70.6	Colorado	13	New York	13	New York	13
Illinois	84.6	87.8	88.5	Maryland	14	Maryland	14	Maryland	14
Indiana	64.9	70.8	72.4	Texas	15	Colorado	15	Colorado	15
Iowa	60.6	61.1	64.0	Connecticut	16	Texas	16	Texas	16
Kansas	69.1	71.4	74.2	Washington	17	Washington	17	Washington	17
Kentucky	51.8	55.7	58.4	Ohio	18	Delaware	18	Delaware	18
Louisiana	68.1	72.7	73.2	New Mexico	19	Oregon	19	Oregon	19
Maine	44.6	40.2	38.7	Delaware	19	Ohio	20	Pennsylvania	20
Maryland	81.3	86.1	87.2	Oregon	21	Pennsylvania	21	Ohio	21
Massachusetts	84.3	91.4	92.0	Michigan	21	New Mexico	22	New Mexico	22
Michigan	70.5	74.7	74.6	Minnesota	23	Michigan	23	Virginia	23
Minnesota	69.9	70.9	73.3	Virginia	24	Virginia	24	Georgia	24
Mississippi	47.1	48.8	49.3	Kansas	25	Louisiana	25	Michigan	25
Missouri	68.7	69.4	70.4	Pennsylvania	26	Georgia	26	Kansas	26
Montana	52.5	54.0	55.9	Missouri	27	Kansas	27	Minnesota	27
Nebraska	66.1	69.7	73.1	Louisiana	28	Minnesota	28	Louisiana	28
Nevada	88.3	91.6	94.2	Oklahoma	29	Indiana	29	Nebraska	29
New Hampshire	51.0	59.2	60.3	Alaska	30	Nebraska	30	Indiana	30
New Jersey	89.4	94.3	94.7	Nebraska	31	Missouri	31	Idaho	31
New Mexico	73.0	75.0	77.4	Wisconsin	32	Wisconsin	32	Missouri	32
New York	84.3	87.5	87.9	Wyoming	33	Idaho	33	Wisconsin	33
North Carolina	50.4	60.2	66.1	Indiana	34	Alaska	34	Tennessee	34
North Dakota	53.3	55.8	59.9	Georgia	35	Oklahoma	35	South Carolina	35
Ohio	74.1	77.3	77.9	Tennessee	36	Wyoming	36	Oklahoma	36
Oklahoma	67.7	65.3	66.2	Iowa	37	Tennessee	37	North Carolina	37
Oregon	70.5	78.7	81.0	Alabama	38	Iowa	38	Alaska	38
Pennsylvania	68.9	77.0	78.7	Idaho	39	South Carolina	39	Wyoming	39
Rhode Island	86.0	90.9	90.7	South Carolina	40	North Carolina	40	Iowa	40
South Carolina	54.6	60.5	66.3	Arkansas	41	New Hampshire	41	New Hampshire	41
South Dakota	50.0	51.9	56.7	North Dakota	42	North Dakota	42	North Dakota	42
Tennessee	60.9	63.6	66.4	Montana	43	Kentucky	43	Alabama	43
Texas	80.3	82.5	84.7	Kentucky	44	Alabama	44	Kentucky	44
Utah	87.0	88.3	90.6	New Hampshire	45	Montana	45	South Dakota	45
Vermont	32.2	38.2	38.9	North Carolina	46	Arkansas	46	Arkansas	46
Virginia	69.4	73.0	75.5	South Dakota	47	South Dakota	47	Montana	47
Washington	76.4	82.0	84.0	Mississippi	48	Mississippi	48	Mississippi	48
West Virginia	36.1	46.1	48.7	Maine	49	West Virginia	49	West Virginia	49
Wisconsin	65.7	68.3	70.2	West Virginia	50	Maine	50	Vermont	50
Wyoming	65.0	65.2	64.8	Vermont	51	Vermont	51	Maine	51
United States	75.2	79.0	80.7	United States	–	United States	–	United States	–

Source: U.S. Census Bureau, 1990, 2000, and 2010 Census

Rural Population

Area	Percent of Population			1990		2000		2010	
	1990	2000	2010	Area	Rank	Area	Rank	Area	Rank
Alabama	39.6	44.6	41.0	Vermont	1	Vermont	1	Maine	1
Alaska	32.5	34.3	34.0	West Virginia	2	Maine	2	Vermont	2
Arizona	12.5	11.8	10.2	Maine	3	West Virginia	3	West Virginia	3
Arkansas	46.5	47.6	43.8	Mississippi	4	Mississippi	4	Mississippi	4
California	7.4	5.5	5.0	South Dakota	5	South Dakota	5	Montana	5
Colorado	17.6	15.5	13.8	North Carolina	6	Arkansas	6	Arkansas	6
Connecticut	20.9	12.3	12.0	New Hampshire	7	Montana	7	South Dakota	7
Delaware	27.0	20.0	16.7	Kentucky	8	Alabama	8	Kentucky	8
D.C.	n/a	n/a	n/a	Montana	9	Kentucky	9	Alabama	9
Florida	15.2	10.7	8.8	North Dakota	10	North Dakota	10	North Dakota	10
Georgia	36.8	28.3	24.9	Arkansas	11	New Hampshire	11	New Hampshire	11
Hawaii	11.0	8.4	8.1	South Carolina	12	North Carolina	12	Iowa	12
Idaho	42.6	33.6	29.4	Idaho	13	South Carolina	13	Wyoming	13
Illinois	15.4	12.2	11.5	Alabama	14	Iowa	14	Alaska	14
Indiana	35.1	29.2	27.6	Iowa	15	Tennessee	15	North Carolina	15
Iowa	39.4	38.9	36.0	Tennessee	16	Wyoming	16	Oklahoma	16
Kansas	30.9	28.6	25.8	Georgia	17	Oklahoma	17	South Carolina	17
Kentucky	48.2	44.3	41.6	Indiana	18	Alaska	18	Tennessee	18
Louisiana	31.9	27.3	26.8	Wyoming	19	Idaho	19	Wisconsin	19
Maine	55.4	59.8	61.3	Wisconsin	20	Wisconsin	20	Missouri	20
Maryland	18.7	13.9	12.8	Nebraska	21	Missouri	21	Idaho	21
Massachusetts	15.7	8.6	8.0	Alaska	22	Nebraska	22	Indiana	22
Michigan	29.5	25.3	25.4	Oklahoma	23	Indiana	23	Nebraska	23
Minnesota	30.1	29.1	26.7	Louisiana	24	Minnesota	24	Louisiana	24
Mississippi	52.9	51.2	50.7	Missouri	25	Kansas	25	Minnesota	25
Missouri	31.3	30.6	29.6	Pennsylvania	26	Georgia	26	Kansas	26
Montana	47.5	46.0	44.1	Kansas	27	Louisiana	27	Michigan	27
Nebraska	33.9	30.3	26.9	Virginia	28	Virginia	28	Georgia	28
Nevada	11.7	8.4	5.8	Minnesota	29	Michigan	29	Virginia	29
New Hampshire	49.0	40.8	39.7	Oregon	30	New Mexico	30	New Mexico	30
New Jersey	10.6	5.7	5.3	Michigan	30	Pennsylvania	31	Ohio	31
New Mexico	27.0	25.0	22.6	New Mexico	32	Ohio	32	Pennsylvania	32
New York	15.7	12.5	12.1	Delaware	32	Oregon	33	Oregon	33
North Carolina	49.6	39.8	33.9	Ohio	34	Delaware	34	Delaware	34
North Dakota	46.7	44.2	40.1	Washington	35	Washington	35	Washington	35
Ohio	25.9	22.7	22.1	Connecticut	36	Texas	36	Texas	36
Oklahoma	32.3	34.7	33.8	Texas	37	Colorado	37	Colorado	37
Oregon	29.5	21.3	19.0	Maryland	38	Maryland	38	Maryland	38
Pennsylvania	31.1	23.0	21.3	Colorado	39	New York	39	New York	39
Rhode Island	14.0	9.1	9.3	New York	40	Connecticut	40	Connecticut	40
South Carolina	45.4	39.5	33.7	Massachusetts	40	Illinois	41	Illinois	41
South Dakota	50.0	48.1	43.3	Illinois	42	Arizona	42	Arizona	42
Tennessee	39.1	36.4	33.6	Florida	43	Utah	43	Utah	43
Texas	19.7	17.5	15.3	Rhode Island	44	Florida	44	Rhode Island	44
Utah	13.0	11.7	9.4	Utah	45	Rhode Island	45	Florida	45
Vermont	67.8	61.8	61.1	Arizona	46	Massachusetts	46	Hawaii	46
Virginia	30.6	27.0	24.5	Nevada	47	Nevada	47	Massachusetts	47
Washington	23.6	18.0	16.0	Hawaii	48	Hawaii	47	Nevada	48
West Virginia	63.9	53.9	51.3	New Jersey	49	New Jersey	49	New Jersey	49
Wisconsin	34.3	31.7	29.8	California	50	California	50	California	50
Wyoming	35.0	34.8	35.2	D.C.	n/a	D.C.	n/a	D.C.	n/a
United States	24.8	21.0	19.3	United States	–	United States	–	United States	–

Source: U.S. Census Bureau, 1990, 2000, and 2010 Census

Males per 100 Females

Area	Males per 100 Females			1990		2000		2010	
	1990	2000	2010	Area	Rank	Area	Rank	Area	Rank
Alabama	92.0	93.3	94.3	Alaska	1	Alaska	1	Alaska	1
Alaska	111.4	107.0	108.5	Nevada	2	Nevada	2	Wyoming	2
Arizona	97.6	99.7	98.7	Hawaii	3	Colorado	3	North Dakota	3
Arkansas	93.1	95.3	96.5	California	4	Wyoming	4	Nevada	4
California	100.2	99.3	98.8	Wyoming	4	Hawaii	5	Utah	5
Colorado	98.1	101.4	100.5	North Dakota	6	Idaho	6	Montana	6
Connecticut	94.0	93.9	94.8	Idaho	7	Utah	7	Colorado	7
Delaware	94.1	94.4	93.9	Utah	8	Arizona	8	Idaho	8
D.C.	87.4	89.0	89.5	Washington	9	North Dakota	9	Hawaii	9
Florida	93.8	95.3	95.6	Colorado	10	California	10	South Dakota	10
Georgia	94.3	96.8	95.4	Montana	10	Montana	10	Washington	11
Hawaii	103.6	101.0	100.3	Arizona	12	Washington	12	California	12
Idaho	99.0	100.5	100.4	Texas	13	Texas	13	Arizona	13
Illinois	94.5	95.9	96.2	South Dakota	14	South Dakota	14	Nebraska	14
Indiana	94.1	96.3	96.8	New Mexico	15	Oregon	15	Wisconsin	14
Iowa	93.9	96.3	98.1	Oregon	16	Minnesota	16	Minnesota	14
Kansas	96.2	97.7	98.4	Kansas	17	Kansas	17	Texas	17
Kentucky	94.0	95.6	96.8	Virginia	17	Wisconsin	18	Kansas	17
Louisiana	92.8	93.8	95.9	Minnesota	17	Nebraska	19	Iowa	19
Maine	94.9	94.8	95.8	New Hampshire	20	Georgia	20	Oregon	20
Maryland	94.1	93.4	93.6	Vermont	21	New Hampshire	20	Oklahoma	20
Massachusetts	92.4	93.0	93.7	Wisconsin	22	New Mexico	22	New Mexico	22
Michigan	94.4	96.2	96.3	Nebraska	23	Oklahoma	23	New Hampshire	23
Minnesota	96.2	98.1	98.5	Maine	24	Virginia	24	West Virginia	23
Mississippi	91.7	93.4	94.4	Oklahoma	25	Indiana	24	Vermont	25
Missouri	92.9	94.6	96.0	Illinois	26	Iowa	24	Indiana	26
Montana	98.1	99.3	100.8	Michigan	27	Michigan	27	Kentucky	26
Nebraska	95.1	97.2	98.5	Georgia	28	Vermont	28	Arkansas	28
Nevada	103.7	103.9	102.0	Maryland	29	North Carolina	29	Virginia	29
New Hampshire	96.1	96.8	97.3	Delaware	29	Illinois	30	Michigan	29
New Jersey	93.5	94.3	94.8	Indiana	29	Kentucky	31	Illinois	31
New Mexico	96.8	96.7	97.7	North Carolina	29	Florida	32	Missouri	32
New York	92.1	93.1	93.8	Connecticut	33	Arkansas	32	Louisiana	33
North Carolina	94.1	96.0	95.0	Kentucky	33	Tennessee	34	Maine	34
North Dakota	99.3	99.6	102.1	Iowa	35	Maine	35	Florida	35
Ohio	93.0	94.4	95.4	South Carolina	35	Missouri	36	Georgia	36
Oklahoma	94.8	96.6	98.0	Florida	37	West Virginia	36	Ohio	36
Oregon	96.7	98.4	98.0	New Jersey	38	South Carolina	38	Pennsylvania	38
Pennsylvania	92.0	93.4	95.1	Arkansas	39	Delaware	39	Tennessee	38
Rhode Island	92.2	92.5	93.4	Ohio	40	Ohio	39	North Carolina	40
South Carolina	93.9	94.5	94.7	Missouri	41	New Jersey	41	New Jersey	41
South Dakota	96.9	98.5	100.1	Tennessee	41	Connecticut	42	Connecticut	41
Tennessee	92.9	94.9	95.1	Louisiana	43	Louisiana	43	South Carolina	43
Texas	97.0	98.6	98.4	Massachusetts	44	Maryland	44	Mississippi	44
Utah	98.7	100.4	100.9	West Virginia	44	Pennsylvania	44	Alabama	45
Vermont	95.9	96.1	97.1	Rhode Island	46	Mississippi	44	Delaware	46
Virginia	96.2	96.3	96.3	New York	47	Alabama	47	New York	47
Washington	98.4	99.1	99.3	Pennsylvania	48	New York	48	Massachusetts	48
West Virginia	92.4	94.6	97.3	Alabama	48	Massachusetts	49	Maryland	49
Wisconsin	95.8	97.6	98.5	Mississippi	50	Rhode Island	50	Rhode Island	50
Wyoming	100.2	101.2	104.1	D.C.	51	D.C.	51	D.C.	51
United States	95.1	96.3	96.7	United States	–	United States	–	United States	–

Source: U.S. Census Bureau, 1990, 2000, and 2010 Census

Median Age

Area	Years 1990	Years 2000	Years 2010	1990 Area	Rank	2000 Area	Rank	2010 Area	Rank
Alabama	32.9	35.8	37.9	Florida	1	West Virginia	1	Maine	1
Alaska	29.3	32.4	33.8	West Virginia	2	Florida	2	Vermont	2
Arizona	32.0	34.2	35.9	Pennsylvania	3	Maine	3	West Virginia	3
Arkansas	33.7	36.0	37.4	Oregon	4	Pennsylvania	4	New Hampshire	4
California	31.3	33.3	35.2	New Jersey	5	Vermont	5	Florida	5
Colorado	32.4	34.3	36.1	Connecticut	5	Montana	6	Pennsylvania	6
Connecticut	34.3	37.4	40.0	Iowa	7	Connecticut	7	Connecticut	7
Delaware	32.7	36.0	38.8	Rhode Island	8	New Hampshire	8	Montana	8
D.C.	33.2	34.6	33.8	Montana	8	New Jersey	9	Rhode Island	9
Florida	36.2	38.7	40.7	Maine	8	Rhode Island	9	Massachusetts	10
Georgia	31.4	33.4	35.3	New York	11	Iowa	11	New Jersey	11
Hawaii	32.5	36.2	38.6	Arkansas	11	Massachusetts	12	Michigan	12
Idaho	31.5	33.2	34.6	Tennessee	13	Oregon	13	Delaware	13
Illinois	32.7	34.7	36.6	Massachusetts	14	Hawaii	14	Ohio	13
Indiana	32.7	35.2	37.0	Missouri	14	Wyoming	14	Hawaii	15
Iowa	34.0	36.6	38.1	Ohio	16	Ohio	14	Wisconsin	16
Kansas	32.8	35.2	36.0	Nevada	17	North Dakota	14	Oregon	17
Kentucky	32.9	35.9	38.1	D.C.	17	Missouri	18	Iowa	18
Louisiana	30.9	34.0	35.8	Oklahoma	19	Delaware	19	Kentucky	18
Maine	33.8	38.6	42.7	Washington	20	Maryland	19	New York	20
Maryland	32.9	36.0	38.0	North Carolina	20	Wisconsin	19	Maryland	20
Massachusetts	33.4	36.5	39.1	Maryland	22	Arkansas	19	Tennessee	20
Michigan	32.5	35.5	38.9	Nebraska	22	New York	23	South Carolina	23
Minnesota	32.4	35.4	37.4	Vermont	22	Tennessee	23	Alabama	23
Mississippi	31.1	33.8	36.0	Alabama	22	Kentucky	23	Missouri	23
Missouri	33.4	36.1	37.9	Kentucky	22	Alabama	26	Virginia	26
Montana	33.8	37.5	39.8	Kansas	27	Virginia	27	North Carolina	27
Nebraska	32.9	35.3	36.2	Wisconsin	27	South Dakota	28	Arkansas	27
Nevada	33.2	35.0	36.3	Illinois	29	Oklahoma	29	Minnesota	27
New Hampshire	32.7	37.1	41.1	Delaware	29	Michigan	29	Washington	30
New Jersey	34.3	36.7	39.0	Indiana	29	Minnesota	31	Indiana	31
New Mexico	31.1	34.6	36.7	New Hampshire	29	South Carolina	31	North Dakota	31
New York	33.7	35.9	38.0	Hawaii	33	Washington	33	South Dakota	33
North Carolina	33.0	35.3	37.4	Virginia	33	Nebraska	33	Wyoming	34
North Dakota	32.3	36.2	37.0	Michigan	33	North Carolina	33	New Mexico	35
Ohio	33.3	36.2	38.8	Colorado	36	Kansas	36	Illinois	36
Oklahoma	33.1	35.5	36.2	Minnesota	36	Indiana	36	Nevada	37
Oregon	34.5	36.3	38.4	South Dakota	36	Nevada	38	Nebraska	38
Pennsylvania	34.9	38.0	40.1	North Dakota	39	Illinois	39	Oklahoma	38
Rhode Island	33.8	36.7	39.4	Arizona	40	New Mexico	40	Colorado	40
South Carolina	31.9	35.4	37.9	Wyoming	40	D.C.	40	Kansas	41
South Dakota	32.4	35.6	36.9	South Carolina	42	Colorado	42	Mississippi	41
Tennessee	33.5	35.9	38.0	Idaho	43	Arizona	43	Arizona	43
Texas	30.6	32.3	33.6	Georgia	44	Louisiana	44	Louisiana	44
Utah	26.2	27.1	29.2	California	45	Mississippi	45	Georgia	45
Vermont	32.9	37.7	41.5	New Mexico	46	Georgia	46	California	46
Virginia	32.5	35.7	37.5	Mississippi	46	California	47	Idaho	47
Washington	33.0	35.3	37.3	Louisiana	48	Idaho	48	D.C.	48
West Virginia	35.3	38.9	41.3	Texas	49	Alaska	49	Alaska	48
Wisconsin	32.8	36.0	38.5	Alaska	50	Texas	50	Texas	50
Wyoming	32.0	36.2	36.8	Utah	51	Utah	51	Utah	51
United States	32.8	35.3	37.2	United States	–	United States	–	United States	–

Source: U.S. Census Bureau, 1990, 2000, and 2010 Census

High School Graduates

Area	Percent of Population			1990		2000		2010	
	1990	2000	2010	Area	Rank	Area	Rank	Area	Rank
Alabama	66.9	75.3	82.1	Alaska	1	Alaska	1	Wyoming	1
Alaska	86.6	88.3	91.0	Utah	2	Minnesota	2	Minnesota	2
Arizona	78.7	81.0	85.6	Colorado	3	Wyoming	3	Montana	3
Arkansas	66.3	75.3	82.9	Washington	4	Utah	4	New Hampshire	4
California	76.2	76.8	80.7	Wyoming	5	New Hampshire	5	Alaska	5
Colorado	84.4	86.9	89.7	Minnesota	6	Montana	6	Vermont	5
Connecticut	79.2	84.0	88.6	New Hampshire	7	Washington	7	Utah	7
Delaware	77.5	82.6	87.7	Nebraska	8	Colorado	8	Iowa	7
D.C.	73.1	77.8	87.4	Oregon	9	Nebraska	9	Nebraska	9
Florida	74.4	79.9	85.5	Kansas	10	Vermont	10	North Dakota	10
Georgia	70.9	78.6	84.3	Montana	11	Iowa	11	Maine	10
Hawaii	80.1	84.6	89.9	Vermont	12	Kansas	12	Wisconsin	12
Idaho	79.7	84.7	88.3	Hawaii	13	Maine	13	Hawaii	13
Illinois	76.2	81.4	86.9	Iowa	13	Oregon	14	Washington	14
Indiana	75.6	82.1	87.0	Massachusetts	15	Wisconsin	14	Colorado	15
Iowa	80.1	86.1	90.6	Idaho	16	Massachusetts	16	South Dakota	16
Kansas	81.3	86.0	89.2	Connecticut	17	Idaho	17	Kansas	17
Kentucky	64.6	74.1	81.9	Nevada	18	Hawaii	18	Massachusetts	18
Louisiana	68.3	74.8	81.9	Maine	18	South Dakota	18	Oregon	19
Maine	78.8	85.4	90.3	Arizona	20	Connecticut	20	Michigan	20
Maryland	78.4	83.8	88.1	Wisconsin	21	North Dakota	21	Connecticut	21
Massachusetts	80.0	84.8	89.1	Maryland	22	Maryland	22	Pennsylvania	22
Michigan	76.8	83.4	88.7	Delaware	23	Michigan	23	Idaho	23
Minnesota	82.4	88.0	91.8	South Dakota	24	Ohio	24	Maryland	24
Mississippi	64.3	72.9	81.0	Michigan	25	Delaware	25	Ohio	24
Missouri	73.9	81.3	86.9	New Jersey	26	New Jersey	26	New Jersey	26
Montana	81.0	87.2	91.7	North Dakota	26	Indiana	26	Delaware	27
Nebraska	81.8	86.6	90.4	California	28	Pennsylvania	28	D.C.	28
Nevada	78.8	80.7	84.7	Illinois	28	Virginia	29	Indiana	29
New Hampshire	82.2	87.4	91.5	Ohio	30	Illinois	30	Illinois	30
New Jersey	76.7	82.1	88.0	Indiana	31	Missouri	31	Missouri	30
New Mexico	75.1	78.9	83.3	Virginia	32	Arizona	32	Virginia	32
New York	74.8	79.1	84.9	New Mexico	33	Nevada	33	Oklahoma	33
North Carolina	70.0	78.1	84.7	New York	34	Oklahoma	34	Arizona	34
North Dakota	76.7	83.9	90.3	Pennsylvania	35	Florida	35	Florida	35
Ohio	75.7	83.0	88.1	Oklahoma	36	New York	36	New York	36
Oklahoma	74.6	80.6	86.2	Florida	37	New Mexico	37	Nevada	37
Oregon	81.5	85.1	88.8	Missouri	38	Georgia	38	North Carolina	37
Pennsylvania	74.7	81.9	88.4	D.C.	39	North Carolina	39	Georgia	39
Rhode Island	72.0	78.0	83.5	Texas	40	Rhode Island	40	South Carolina	40
South Carolina	68.3	76.3	84.1	Rhode Island	41	D.C.	41	Tennessee	41
South Dakota	77.1	84.6	89.6	Georgia	42	California	42	Rhode Island	42
Tennessee	67.1	75.9	83.6	North Carolina	43	South Carolina	43	New Mexico	43
Texas	72.1	75.7	80.7	Louisiana	44	Tennessee	44	West Virginia	44
Utah	85.1	87.7	90.6	South Carolina	44	Texas	45	Arkansas	45
Vermont	80.8	86.4	91.0	Tennessee	46	Arkansas	46	Alabama	46
Virginia	75.2	81.5	86.5	Alabama	47	Alabama	46	Louisiana	47
Washington	83.8	87.1	89.8	Arkansas	48	West Virginia	48	Kentucky	47
West Virginia	66.0	75.2	83.2	West Virginia	49	Louisiana	49	Mississippi	49
Wisconsin	78.6	85.1	90.1	Kentucky	50	Kentucky	50	California	50
Wyoming	83.0	87.9	92.3	Mississippi	51	Mississippi	51	Texas	50
United States	75.2	80.4	85.6	United States	–	United States	–	United States	–

Source: U.S. Census Bureau, 1990, 2000, and 2010 Census

College Graduates

Area	Percent of Population			1990		2000		2010	
	1990	2000	2010	Area	Rank	Area	Rank	Area	Rank
Alabama	15.7	19.0	21.9	D.C.	1	D.C.	1	D.C.	1
Alaska	23.0	24.7	27.9	Connecticut	2	Massachusetts	2	Massachusetts	2
Arizona	20.3	23.5	25.9	Massachusetts	2	Colorado	3	Colorado	3
Arkansas	13.3	16.7	19.5	Colorado	4	Maryland	4	Maryland	4
California	23.4	26.6	30.1	Maryland	5	Connecticut	5	Connecticut	5
Colorado	27.0	32.7	36.4	New Jersey	6	New Jersey	6	New Jersey	6
Connecticut	27.2	31.4	35.5	Virginia	7	Virginia	7	Virginia	7
Delaware	21.4	25.1	27.8	New Hampshire	8	Vermont	7	Vermont	8
D.C.	33.3	39.1	50.1	Vermont	9	New Hampshire	9	New Hampshire	9
Florida	18.3	22.3	25.8	California	10	Washington	10	New York	10
Georgia	19.3	24.3	27.3	New York	11	New York	11	Minnesota	11
Hawaii	22.9	26.2	29.5	Alaska	12	Minnesota	11	Washington	12
Idaho	17.7	21.7	24.4	Hawaii	13	California	13	Illinois	13
Illinois	21.0	26.1	30.8	Washington	13	Hawaii	14	Rhode Island	14
Indiana	15.6	19.4	22.7	Utah	15	Illinois	15	California	15
Iowa	16.9	21.2	24.9	Minnesota	16	Utah	15	Kansas	16
Kansas	21.1	25.8	29.8	Delaware	17	Kansas	17	Hawaii	17
Kentucky	13.6	17.1	20.5	Rhode Island	18	Rhode Island	18	Utah	18
Louisiana	16.1	18.7	21.4	Kansas	19	Oregon	19	Oregon	19
Maine	18.8	22.9	26.8	Illinois	20	Delaware	19	Montana	19
Maryland	26.5	31.5	36.1	Oregon	21	Alaska	21	Nebraska	21
Massachusetts	27.2	33.2	39.0	New Mexico	22	Montana	22	Alaska	22
Michigan	17.4	21.8	25.2	Texas	23	Georgia	23	Delaware	23
Minnesota	21.8	27.4	31.8	Arizona	23	Nebraska	24	North Dakota	24
Mississippi	14.7	16.9	19.5	Montana	25	New Mexico	25	Georgia	25
Missouri	17.8	21.6	25.6	Georgia	26	Arizona	25	Pennsylvania	26
Montana	19.8	24.4	28.8	Nebraska	27	Texas	27	Maine	27
Nebraska	18.9	23.7	28.6	Wyoming	28	Maine	28	North Carolina	28
Nevada	15.3	18.2	21.7	Maine	28	North Carolina	29	Wisconsin	29
New Hampshire	24.4	28.7	32.8	Florida	30	Wisconsin	30	South Dakota	29
New Jersey	24.9	29.8	35.4	North Dakota	31	Pennsylvania	30	Texas	31
New Mexico	20.4	23.5	25.0	Pennsylvania	32	Florida	32	Arizona	31
New York	23.1	27.4	32.5	Oklahoma	33	North Dakota	33	Florida	33
North Carolina	17.4	22.5	26.5	Missouri	33	Wyoming	34	Missouri	34
North Dakota	18.1	22.0	27.6	Idaho	35	Michigan	35	Michigan	35
Ohio	17.0	21.1	24.6	Wisconsin	35	Idaho	36	New Mexico	36
Oklahoma	17.8	20.3	22.9	Michigan	37	Missouri	37	Iowa	37
Oregon	20.6	25.1	28.8	North Carolina	37	South Dakota	38	Ohio	38
Pennsylvania	17.9	22.4	27.1	South Dakota	39	Iowa	39	South Carolina	39
Rhode Island	21.3	25.6	30.2	Ohio	40	Ohio	40	Idaho	40
South Carolina	16.6	20.4	24.5	Iowa	41	South Carolina	41	Wyoming	41
South Dakota	17.2	21.5	26.3	South Carolina	42	Oklahoma	42	Tennessee	42
Tennessee	16.0	19.6	23.1	Louisiana	43	Tennessee	43	Oklahoma	43
Texas	20.3	23.2	25.9	Tennessee	44	Indiana	44	Indiana	44
Utah	22.3	26.1	29.3	Alabama	45	Alabama	45	Alabama	45
Vermont	24.3	29.5	33.6	Indiana	46	Louisiana	46	Nevada	46
Virginia	24.5	29.5	34.2	Nevada	47	Nevada	47	Louisiana	47
Washington	22.9	27.7	31.1	Mississippi	48	Kentucky	48	Kentucky	48
West Virginia	12.3	14.8	17.5	Kentucky	49	Mississippi	49	Arkansas	49
Wisconsin	17.7	22.4	26.3	Arkansas	50	Arkansas	50	Mississippi	49
Wyoming	18.8	21.9	24.1	West Virginia	51	West Virginia	51	West Virginia	51
United States	20.3	24.4	28.2	United States	–	United States	–	United States	–

Source: U.S. Census Bureau, 1990, 2000, and 2010 Census

One-Person Households

Area	Percent of Population			1990		2000		2010	
	1990	2000	2010	Area	Rank	Area	Rank	Area	Rank
Alabama	23.8	26.1	27.4	D.C.	1	D.C.	1	D.C.	1
Alaska	22.1	23.5	25.6	New York	2	North Dakota	2	North Dakota	2
Arizona	24.7	24.8	26.1	Colorado	3	Rhode Island	3	Montana	3
Arkansas	24.0	25.6	27.1	Nebraska	4	New York	4	Rhode Island	4
California	23.4	23.5	23.3	North Dakota	4	Massachusetts	5	South Dakota	5
Colorado	26.6	26.3	27.9	South Dakota	6	Pennsylvania	6	New York	6
Connecticut	24.2	26.4	27.3	Montana	7	Nebraska	7	Ohio	7
Delaware	23.2	25.0	25.6	Rhode Island	8	South Dakota	7	Massachusetts	8
D.C.	41.5	43.8	44.0	Missouri	9	Montana	9	Nebraska	8
Florida	25.5	26.6	27.2	Kansas	10	Missouri	10	Pennsylvania	10
Georgia	22.7	23.6	25.4	Iowa	10	Ohio	10	Maine	10
Hawaii	19.4	21.9	23.3	Massachusetts	12	Iowa	12	Iowa	12
Idaho	22.4	22.4	23.8	Nevada	13	West Virginia	13	West Virginia	12
Illinois	25.7	26.8	27.8	Illinois	13	Kansas	14	Missouri	14
Indiana	24.1	25.9	26.9	Oklahoma	15	Maine	14	Wisconsin	15
Iowa	25.9	27.2	28.4	Pennsylvania	15	Minnesota	16	Vermont	15
Kansas	25.9	27.0	27.8	Florida	17	Illinois	17	New Mexico	17
Kentucky	23.3	26.0	27.5	Washington	18	Wisconsin	17	Wyoming	17
Louisiana	23.7	25.3	26.9	Oregon	19	Oklahoma	19	Minnesota	17
Maine	23.3	27.0	28.6	Minnesota	20	Florida	20	Colorado	20
Maryland	22.6	25.0	26.1	Ohio	21	Connecticut	21	Michigan	20
Massachusetts	25.8	28.0	28.7	Arizona	22	Colorado	22	Illinois	22
Michigan	23.7	26.2	27.9	Wyoming	23	Wyoming	22	Kansas	22
Minnesota	25.1	26.9	28.0	West Virginia	23	Washington	24	Oklahoma	24
Mississippi	23.4	24.6	26.3	Wisconsin	25	Michigan	24	Kentucky	24
Missouri	26.0	27.3	28.3	Connecticut	26	Vermont	24	Oregon	26
Montana	26.3	27.4	29.7	Indiana	27	Oregon	27	Alabama	26
Nebraska	26.5	27.6	28.7	Arkansas	28	Alabama	27	Connecticut	28
Nevada	25.7	24.9	25.7	Texas	29	Kentucky	29	Florida	29
New Hampshire	22.0	24.4	25.6	Tennessee	29	Indiana	30	Washington	29
New Jersey	23.1	24.5	25.2	Alabama	31	Tennessee	31	Arkansas	31
New Mexico	23.0	25.4	28.0	Louisiana	32	Arkansas	32	North Carolina	32
New York	27.2	28.1	29.1	Michigan	32	New Mexico	33	Indiana	33
North Carolina	23.7	25.4	27.0	North Carolina	32	North Carolina	33	Tennessee	33
North Dakota	26.5	29.3	31.5	California	35	Louisiana	35	Louisiana	33
Ohio	25.0	27.3	28.9	Vermont	35	Virginia	36	South Carolina	36
Oklahoma	25.6	26.7	27.5	Mississippi	35	Delaware	37	Mississippi	37
Oregon	25.3	26.1	27.4	Kentucky	38	Maryland	37	Arizona	38
Pennsylvania	25.6	27.7	28.6	Maine	38	South Carolina	37	Maryland	38
Rhode Island	26.2	28.6	29.6	Delaware	40	Nevada	40	Virginia	40
South Carolina	22.4	25.0	26.5	New Jersey	41	Arizona	41	Nevada	41
South Dakota	26.4	27.6	29.4	New Mexico	42	Mississippi	42	Delaware	42
Tennessee	23.9	25.8	26.9	Virginia	43	New Jersey	43	Alaska	42
Texas	23.9	23.7	24.2	Georgia	44	New Hampshire	44	New Hampshire	42
Utah	18.9	17.8	18.7	Maryland	45	Texas	45	Georgia	45
Vermont	23.4	26.2	28.2	Idaho	46	Georgia	46	New Jersey	46
Virginia	22.9	25.1	26.0	South Carolina	46	California	47	Texas	47
Washington	25.4	26.2	27.2	Alaska	48	Alaska	47	Idaho	48
West Virginia	24.5	27.1	28.4	New Hampshire	49	Idaho	49	California	49
Wisconsin	24.3	26.8	28.2	Hawaii	50	Hawaii	50	Hawaii	49
Wyoming	24.5	26.3	28.0	Utah	51	Utah	51	Utah	51
United States	24.6	25.8	26.7	United States	–	United States	–	United States	–

Source: U.S. Census Bureau, 1990, 2000, and 2010 Census

Homeownership

Area	Percent of Population			1990		2000		2010	
	1990	2000	2010	Area	Rank	Area	Rank	Area	Rank
Alabama	70.5	72.5	69.7	West Virginia	1	West Virginia	1	West Virginia	1
Alaska	56.1	62.5	63.1	Minnesota	2	Minnesota	2	Minnesota	2
Arizona	64.2	68.0	66.0	Mississippi	3	Michigan	3	Iowa	3
Arkansas	69.6	69.4	66.9	Michigan	4	Alabama	4	Michigan	3
California	55.6	56.9	56.0	Pennsylvania	5	Idaho	5	Delaware	5
Colorado	62.2	67.3	65.5	Alabama	6	Delaware	6	Maine	6
Connecticut	65.6	66.8	67.5	Maine	6	Iowa	6	New Hampshire	7
Delaware	70.2	72.3	72.0	Delaware	8	Mississippi	6	Vermont	8
D.C.	38.9	40.8	42.0	Indiana	8	South Carolina	9	Utah	9
Florida	67.2	70.1	67.3	Idaho	10	Maine	10	Idaho	10
Georgia	64.9	67.5	65.7	Iowa	11	Utah	11	Indiana	11
Hawaii	53.9	56.5	57.7	South Carolina	12	Indiana	12	Alabama	12
Idaho	70.1	72.4	69.9	Arkansas	13	Pennsylvania	13	Pennsylvania	13
Illinois	64.2	67.3	67.4	Kentucky	13	Kentucky	14	Mississippi	13
Indiana	70.2	71.4	69.8	Vermont	15	Vermont	15	Wyoming	15
Iowa	70.0	72.3	72.1	Missouri	16	Missouri	16	South Carolina	15
Kansas	67.9	69.2	67.7	New Hampshire	17	Florida	17	Missouri	17
Kentucky	69.6	70.8	68.7	Utah	18	New Mexico	18	Kentucky	18
Louisiana	65.9	67.9	67.3	Oklahoma	18	Wyoming	18	New Mexico	19
Maine	70.5	71.6	71.3	North Carolina	20	Tennessee	20	Tennessee	20
Maryland	65.0	67.7	67.5	Tennessee	20	New Hampshire	21	Wisconsin	21
Massachusetts	59.3	61.7	62.3	Kansas	22	North Carolina	22	South Dakota	21
Michigan	71.0	73.8	72.1	Wyoming	23	Arkansas	22	Montana	23
Minnesota	71.8	74.6	73.1	Ohio	24	Kansas	24	Kansas	24
Mississippi	71.5	72.3	69.6	New Mexico	25	Montana	25	Ohio	25
Missouri	68.8	70.3	68.8	Montana	26	Ohio	25	Connecticut	26
Montana	67.3	69.1	68.0	Florida	27	Oklahoma	27	Maryland	26
Nebraska	66.5	67.4	67.2	Wisconsin	28	Wisconsin	27	Illinois	28
Nevada	54.8	60.9	58.8	Nebraska	29	South Dakota	29	Florida	29
New Hampshire	68.2	69.7	70.9	Virginia	30	Virginia	30	Oklahoma	29
New Jersey	64.9	65.6	65.4	South Dakota	31	Arizona	31	Louisiana	29
New Mexico	67.4	70.0	68.5	Louisiana	32	Louisiana	32	Nebraska	32
New York	52.2	53.0	53.3	Connecticut	33	Maryland	33	Virginia	32
North Carolina	68.0	69.4	66.7	North Dakota	33	Georgia	34	Arkansas	34
North Dakota	65.6	66.6	65.4	Maryland	35	Nebraska	35	North Carolina	35
Ohio	67.5	69.1	67.6	New Jersey	36	Colorado	36	Arizona	36
Oklahoma	68.1	68.4	67.3	Georgia	36	Illinois	36	Georgia	37
Oregon	63.1	64.3	62.1	Arizona	38	Connecticut	38	Colorado	38
Pennsylvania	70.6	71.3	69.6	Illinois	38	North Dakota	39	New Jersey	39
Rhode Island	59.5	60.0	60.7	Oregon	40	New Jersey	40	North Dakota	39
South Carolina	69.8	72.2	69.3	Washington	41	Washington	41	Washington	41
South Dakota	66.1	68.2	68.1	Colorado	42	Oregon	42	Texas	42
Tennessee	68.0	69.9	68.2	Texas	43	Texas	43	Alaska	43
Texas	60.9	63.8	63.7	Rhode Island	44	Alaska	44	Massachusetts	44
Utah	68.1	71.5	70.5	Massachusetts	45	Massachusetts	45	Oregon	45
Vermont	69.0	70.6	70.7	Alaska	46	Nevada	46	Rhode Island	46
Virginia	66.3	68.1	67.2	California	47	Rhode Island	47	Nevada	47
Washington	62.6	64.6	63.9	Nevada	48	California	48	Hawaii	48
West Virginia	74.1	75.2	73.4	Hawaii	49	Hawaii	49	California	49
Wisconsin	66.7	68.4	68.1	New York	50	New York	50	New York	50
Wyoming	67.8	70.0	69.3	D.C.	51	D.C.	51	D.C.	51
United States	64.2	66.2	65.1	United States	–	United States	–	United States	–

Source: U.S. Census Bureau, 1990, 2000, and 2010 Census

Median Home Value

Area	Median Home Value ($) 1990	2000	2010	1990 Area	Rank	2000 Area	Rank	2010 Area	Rank
Alabama	53,700	85,100	123,900	Hawaii	1	Hawaii	1	Hawaii	1
Alaska	94,400	144,200	241,400	California	2	California	2	D.C.	2
Arizona	80,100	121,300	168,800	Connecticut	3	Massachusetts	3	California	3
Arkansas	46,300	72,800	106,300	Massachusetts	4	New Jersey	4	New Jersey	4
California	195,500	211,500	370,900	New Jersey	5	Washington	5	Massachusetts	5
Colorado	82,700	166,600	236,600	Rhode Island	6	Connecticut	6	Maryland	6
Connecticut	177,800	166,900	288,800	New York	7	Colorado	7	New York	7
Delaware	100,100	130,400	243,600	New Hampshire	8	D.C.	8	Connecticut	8
D.C.	123,900	157,200	426,900	D.C.	9	Oregon	9	Washington	9
Florida	77,100	105,500	164,200	Maryland	10	New York	10	Rhode Island	10
Georgia	71,300	111,200	156,200	Delaware	11	Utah	11	Virginia	11
Hawaii	245,300	272,700	525,400	Nevada	12	Maryland	12	Oregon	12
Idaho	58,200	106,300	165,100	Vermont	13	Alaska	13	Delaware	13
Illinois	80,900	130,800	191,800	Alaska	14	Nevada	14	New Hampshire	14
Indiana	53,900	94,300	123,300	Washington	15	New Hampshire	15	Alaska	15
Iowa	45,900	82,500	123,400	Virginia	16	Rhode Island	16	Colorado	16
Kansas	52,200	83,500	127,300	Maine	17	Illinois	17	Utah	17
Kentucky	50,500	86,700	121,600	Colorado	18	Delaware	18	Vermont	18
Louisiana	58,500	85,000	137,500	Illinois	19	Virginia	19	Minnesota	19
Maine	87,400	98,700	179,100	Arizona	20	Minnesota	20	Illinois	20
Maryland	116,500	146,000	301,400	Florida	21	Arizona	21	Montana	21
Massachusetts	162,800	185,700	334,100	Minnesota	22	Michigan	22	Wyoming	22
Michigan	60,600	115,600	123,300	Georgia	23	Wisconsin	23	Maine	23
Minnesota	74,000	122,400	194,300	New Mexico	24	Vermont	24	Nevada	24
Mississippi	45,600	71,400	100,100	Pennsylvania	25	Georgia	25	Wisconsin	25
Missouri	59,800	89,900	139,000	Utah	26	North Carolina	26	Arizona	26
Montana	56,600	99,500	181,200	Oregon	27	New Mexico	27	Pennsylvania	27
Nebraska	50,400	88,000	127,600	North Carolina	28	Idaho	28	Idaho	28
Nevada	95,700	142,000	174,800	Ohio	29	Florida	29	Florida	29
New Hampshire	129,400	133,300	243,000	Wisconsin	30	Ohio	30	New Mexico	30
New Jersey	162,300	170,800	339,200	Wyoming	31	Montana	31	Georgia	31
New Mexico	70,100	108,100	161,200	South Carolina	32	Maine	32	North Carolina	32
New York	131,600	148,700	296,500	Michigan	33	Pennsylvania	33	Tennessee	33
North Carolina	65,800	108,300	154,200	Missouri	34	Wyoming	34	Missouri	33
North Dakota	50,800	74,400	123,000	Texas	35	South Carolina	35	South Carolina	35
Ohio	63,500	103,700	134,400	Louisiana	36	Indiana	36	Louisiana	36
Oklahoma	48,100	70,700	111,400	Tennessee	37	Tennessee	37	Ohio	37
Oregon	67,100	152,100	244,500	Idaho	38	Missouri	38	South Dakota	38
Pennsylvania	69,700	97,000	165,500	Montana	39	Nebraska	39	Texas	39
Rhode Island	133,500	133,000	254,500	Indiana	40	Kentucky	40	Nebraska	40
South Carolina	61,100	94,900	138,100	Alabama	41	Alabama	41	Kansas	41
South Dakota	45,200	79,600	129,700	Kansas	42	Louisiana	42	Alabama	42
Tennessee	58,400	93,000	139,000	North Dakota	43	Kansas	43	Iowa	43
Texas	59,600	82,500	128,100	Kentucky	44	Texas	44	Indiana	44
Utah	68,900	146,100	217,200	Nebraska	45	Iowa	44	Michigan	44
Vermont	95,500	111,500	216,800	Oklahoma	46	South Dakota	46	North Dakota	46
Virginia	91,000	125,400	249,100	West Virginia	47	North Dakota	47	Kentucky	47
Washington	93,400	168,300	271,800	Arkansas	48	Arkansas	48	Oklahoma	48
West Virginia	47,900	72,800	95,100	Iowa	49	West Virginia	48	Arkansas	49
Wisconsin	62,500	112,200	169,400	Mississippi	50	Mississippi	50	Mississippi	50
Wyoming	61,600	96,600	180,100	South Dakota	51	Oklahoma	51	West Virginia	51
United States	79,100	119,600	179,900	United States	–	United States	–	United States	–

Source: U.S. Census Bureau, 1990, 2000, and 2010 Census

Median Gross Rent

Area	Median Gross Rent ($/month)			1990		2000		2010	
	1990	2000	2010	Area	Rank	Area	Rank	Area	Rank
Alabama	325	447	667	Hawaii	1	Hawaii	1	Hawaii	1
Alaska	559	720	981	California	2	New Jersey	2	D.C.	2
Arizona	438	619	844	Connecticut	3	California	3	California	3
Arkansas	328	453	638	New Jersey	4	Alaska	4	Maryland	4
California	620	747	1,163	Massachusetts	5	Nevada	5	New Jersey	5
Colorado	418	671	863	Alaska	6	Maryland	6	New York	6
Connecticut	598	681	992	New Hampshire	7	Massachusetts	7	Virginia	7
Delaware	495	639	952	Maryland	8	Connecticut	8	Massachusetts	8
D.C.	479	618	1,198	Nevada	9	New York	9	Connecticut	9
Florida	481	641	947	Virginia	10	Colorado	10	Alaska	10
Georgia	433	613	819	Delaware	10	Washington	11	Nevada	11
Hawaii	650	779	1,291	Rhode Island	12	Virginia	12	Delaware	11
Idaho	330	515	683	New York	13	New Hampshire	13	New Hampshire	13
Illinois	445	605	848	Florida	14	Florida	14	Florida	14
Indiana	374	521	683	D.C.	15	Delaware	15	Washington	15
Iowa	336	470	629	Vermont	16	Oregon	16	Rhode Island	16
Kansas	372	498	682	Illinois	17	Arizona	17	Colorado	17
Kentucky	319	445	613	Washington	17	D.C.	18	Illinois	18
Louisiana	352	466	736	Arizona	19	Georgia	19	Arizona	19
Maine	419	497	707	Georgia	20	Illinois	20	Vermont	20
Maryland	548	689	1,131	Michigan	21	Utah	21	Georgia	21
Massachusetts	580	684	1,009	Minnesota	22	Texas	22	Oregon	22
Michigan	423	546	730	Maine	23	Minnesota	23	Texas	23
Minnesota	422	566	764	Colorado	24	Rhode Island	24	Utah	24
Mississippi	309	439	672	Oregon	25	Vermont	24	Minnesota	25
Missouri	368	484	682	Pennsylvania	26	North Carolina	26	Pennsylvania	26
Montana	311	447	642	Wisconsin	27	Michigan	27	Louisiana	27
Nebraska	348	491	669	Texas	28	Wisconsin	28	North Carolina	28
Nevada	509	699	952	North Carolina	29	Pennsylvania	29	Michigan	29
New Hampshire	549	646	951	Ohio	30	Indiana	30	South Carolina	30
New Jersey	592	751	1,114	South Carolina	31	Idaho	31	Wisconsin	31
New Mexico	372	503	699	Indiana	32	Ohio	31	Maine	32
New York	486	672	1,020	New Mexico	33	South Carolina	33	New Mexico	33
North Carolina	382	548	731	Kansas	33	Tennessee	34	Tennessee	34
North Dakota	313	412	583	Utah	35	New Mexico	35	Wyoming	35
Ohio	379	515	685	Missouri	36	Kansas	36	Ohio	36
Oklahoma	340	456	659	Tennessee	37	Maine	37	Idaho	37
Oregon	408	620	816	Louisiana	38	Nebraska	38	Indiana	37
Pennsylvania	404	531	763	Nebraska	39	Missouri	39	Kansas	39
Rhode Island	489	553	868	Oklahoma	40	Iowa	40	Missouri	39
South Carolina	376	510	728	Iowa	41	Louisiana	41	Mississippi	41
South Dakota	306	426	591	Wyoming	42	Oklahoma	42	Nebraska	42
Tennessee	357	505	697	Idaho	43	Arkansas	43	Alabama	43
Texas	395	574	801	Arkansas	44	Montana	44	Oklahoma	44
Utah	369	597	796	Alabama	45	Alabama	44	Montana	45
Vermont	446	553	823	Kentucky	46	Kentucky	46	Arkansas	46
Virginia	495	650	1,019	North Dakota	47	Mississippi	47	Iowa	47
Washington	445	663	908	Montana	48	Wyoming	48	Kentucky	48
West Virginia	303	401	571	Mississippi	49	South Dakota	49	South Dakota	49
Wisconsin	399	540	715	South Dakota	50	North Dakota	50	North Dakota	50
Wyoming	333	437	693	West Virginia	51	West Virginia	51	West Virginia	51
United States	447	602	855	United States	–	United States	–	United States	–

Source: U.S. Census Bureau, 1990, 2000, and 2010 Census

Households Lacking Complete Plumbing Facilities

Area	Percent of Households			1990		2000		2010	
	1990	2000	2010	Area	Rank	Area	Rank	Area	Rank
Alabama	1.6	0.6	0.5	Alaska	1	Alaska	1	Alaska	1
Alaska	12.5	6.3	5.0	Maine	2	New Mexico	2	New Mexico	2
Arizona	1.9	1.1	0.8	New Mexico	3	Arizona	3	Maine	3
Arkansas	1.8	0.8	0.6	West Virginia	3	Hawaii	4	Vermont	4
California	0.6	0.7	0.6	Kentucky	5	West Virginia	4	Arizona	5
Colorado	0.8	0.4	0.5	Vermont	6	D.C.	6	Nevada	5
Connecticut	0.4	0.5	0.4	Mississippi	7	Kentucky	6	Rhode Island	5
Delaware	0.6	0.4	0.8	South Dakota	8	Mississippi	6	Delaware	5
D.C.	0.8	0.9	0.7	North Dakota	8	Maine	6	Montana	5
Florida	0.5	0.5	0.4	Arizona	10	New York	10	Texas	10
Georgia	1.1	0.6	0.5	Montana	10	Arkansas	10	D.C.	10
Hawaii	1.1	1.0	0.7	Virginia	12	Montana	10	Hawaii	10
Idaho	1.5	0.6	0.5	Arkansas	12	California	13	Kentucky	10
Illinois	0.7	0.5	0.5	Wyoming	14	Texas	13	Mississippi	10
Indiana	0.7	0.5	0.4	Tennessee	14	Virginia	13	South Dakota	10
Iowa	0.9	0.4	0.4	Alabama	14	Idaho	16	West Virginia	10
Kansas	0.8	0.4	0.3	Idaho	17	Massachusetts	16	California	17
Kentucky	2.9	0.9	0.7	North Carolina	17	Georgia	16	New York	17
Louisiana	1.3	0.6	0.5	Wisconsin	19	Oklahoma	16	Oregon	17
Maine	3.5	0.9	1.1	South Carolina	19	North Carolina	16	Washington	17
Maryland	0.7	0.5	0.5	Louisiana	21	Louisiana	16	Oklahoma	17
Massachusetts	0.5	0.6	0.4	Minnesota	21	South Carolina	16	Virginia	17
Michigan	0.8	0.4	0.5	Texas	23	Tennessee	16	Arkansas	17
Minnesota	1.3	0.5	0.5	Missouri	23	Alabama	16	Wisconsin	17
Mississippi	2.2	0.9	0.7	New Hampshire	23	South Dakota	16	New Hampshire	17
Missouri	1.2	0.5	0.5	Hawaii	26	Vermont	16	Colorado	26
Montana	1.9	0.8	0.8	Georgia	26	Nevada	27	New Jersey	26
Nebraska	0.8	0.4	0.2	Utah	28	Florida	27	Illinois	26
Nevada	0.5	0.5	0.8	Oklahoma	28	New Jersey	27	Utah	26
New Hampshire	1.2	0.5	0.6	Pennsylvania	28	Illinois	27	Idaho	26
New Jersey	0.5	0.5	0.5	New York	31	Connecticut	27	Georgia	26
New Mexico	3.2	1.8	1.3	Washington	31	Rhode Island	27	North Carolina	26
New York	0.9	0.8	0.6	Oregon	31	Oregon	27	Maryland	26
North Carolina	1.5	0.6	0.5	Iowa	31	Washington	27	Pennsylvania	26
North Dakota	2.0	0.4	0.2	Colorado	35	Wyoming	27	South Carolina	26
Ohio	0.8	0.4	0.5	D.C.	35	Maryland	27	Minnesota	26
Oklahoma	1.0	0.6	0.6	Kansas	35	Wisconsin	27	Tennessee	26
Oregon	0.9	0.5	0.6	Nebraska	35	Indiana	27	Michigan	26
Pennsylvania	1.0	0.5	0.5	Michigan	35	Pennsylvania	27	Louisiana	26
Rhode Island	0.5	0.5	0.8	Ohio	35	Minnesota	27	Alabama	26
South Carolina	1.4	0.6	0.5	Illinois	41	Missouri	27	Missouri	26
South Dakota	2.0	0.6	0.7	Maryland	41	New Hampshire	27	Ohio	26
Tennessee	1.6	0.6	0.5	Indiana	41	Colorado	43	Florida	43
Texas	1.2	0.7	0.7	California	44	Utah	43	Connecticut	43
Utah	1.0	0.4	0.5	Delaware	44	Kansas	43	Massachusetts	43
Vermont	2.3	0.6	0.9	Florida	46	Nebraska	43	Wyoming	43
Virginia	1.8	0.7	0.6	Nevada	46	Delaware	43	Indiana	43
Washington	0.9	0.5	0.6	New Jersey	46	Michigan	43	Iowa	43
West Virginia	3.2	1.0	0.7	Massachusetts	46	Iowa	43	Kansas	49
Wisconsin	1.4	0.5	0.6	Rhode Island	46	Ohio	43	Nebraska	50
Wyoming	1.6	0.5	0.4	Connecticut	51	North Dakota	43	North Dakota	50
United States	1.1	0.6	0.6	United States	–	United States	–	United States	–

Note: The reader is cautioned against comparing values across decades as the definition of plumbing facilities has changed over time.
Source: U.S. Census Bureau, 1990 and 2000 Census; U.S. Census Bureau, American Community Survey, 2010 1-Year Estimate

255

Population Change and Distribution

Census 2000 Brief

1990 to 2000

Issued April 2001

C2KBR/01-2

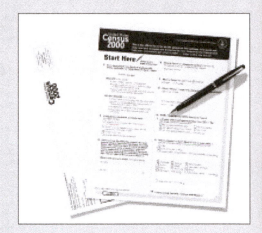

By
Marc J. Perry and
Paul J. Mackun

(With Josephine D. Baker,
Colleen D. Joyce,
Lisa R. Lollock, and
Lucinda S. Pearson)

In Census 2000, 281.4 million people were counted in the United States, a 13.2 percent increase from the 1990 census population of 248.7 million. Population growth from 1990 to 2000 varied geographically, with large population increases in some areas and little growth or decline in others. This report, part of a series that analyzes population and housing data collected from Census 2000, highlights population size and distribution changes between 1990 and 2000 in regions, states, metropolitan areas, counties, and large cities.[1]

The 1990 to 2000 population increase was the largest in American history.

The population growth of 32.7 million people between 1990 and 2000 represents the largest census-to-census increase in American history.[2] The previous record increase was 28.0 million people between 1950 and 1960, a gain fueled primarily by the post-World War II baby boom (1946 to 1964). Total decennial population growth declined steadily in the three decades following the 1950s' peak before rising again in the 1990s (see Figure 1).

---

[1] 1990 populations shown in this report were originally published in 1990 Census reports and do not include subsequent revisions resulting from boundary or other changes.

[2] This increase may be caused by changes in census coverage, as well as births, deaths, and net immigration.

Figure 1.
U.S. Population Growth: 1950-60 to 1990-2000
(For information on confidentiality protection, nonsampling error, and definitions, see *www.census.gov/prod/cen2000/doc/pl94-171.pdf*)

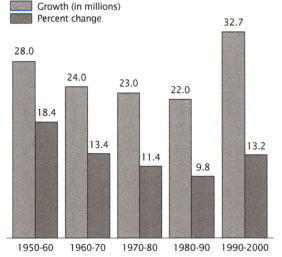

- Growth (in millions)
- Percent change

Source: U.S. Census Bureau, Census 2000; 1990 Census, *Population and Housing Unit Counts, United States* (1990 CPH-2-1).

USCENSUSBUREAU

Helping You Make Informed Decisions

U.S. Department of Commerce
Economics and Statistics Administration
U.S. CENSUS BUREAU

United States
Census 2000

In percentage terms, the population increase of 13.2 percent for the 1990s was higher than the growth rates of 9.8 percent for the 1980s and 11.4 percent for the 1970s. The 1990s growth rate was similar to the 13.4 percent growth in the 1960s and was well below the 18.4 percent growth for the 1950s.

West grew fastest in the 1990s; South reached 100 million.

Population growth varied significantly by region in the 1990s, with higher rates in the West (19.7 percent) and South (17.3 percent) and much lower rates in the Midwest (7.9 percent) and Northeast (5.5 percent).[3] The West increased by 10.4 million to reach 63.2 million people, while the South grew by 14.8 million to a population of 100.2 million people. The Midwest gained 4.7 million to reach 64.4 million people, and the Northeast's increase of 2.8 million brought it to 53.6 million people.

Because of differences in growth rates, the regional shares of the total population have shifted considerably in recent decades. Between 1950 and 2000, the South's share of the population increased from 31 to 36 percent and the West increased from 13 to 22 percent. Meanwhile, despite overall population growth in each of the past five decades, the Midwest's share of total population fell from 29 to 23 percent and the

[3] The Northeast region includes Connecticut, Maine, Massachusetts, New Hampshire, New Jersey, New York, Pennsylvania, Rhode Island, and Vermont. The Midwest includes Illinois, Indiana, Iowa, Kansas, Michigan, Minnesota, Missouri, Nebraska, North Dakota, Ohio, South Dakota, and Wisconsin. The South includes Alabama, Arkansas, Delaware, the District of Columbia, Florida, Georgia, Kentucky, Louisiana, Maryland, Mississippi, North Carolina, Oklahoma, South Carolina, Tennessee, Texas, Virginia, and West Virginia. The West includes Alaska, Arizona, California, Colorado, Hawaii, Idaho, Montana, Nevada, New Mexico, Oregon, Utah, Washington, and Wyoming.

Table 1.
U.S. Population Change for Regions, States, and Puerto Rico: 1990 to 2000

(For information on confidentiality protection, nonsampling error, and definitions, see www.census.gov/prod/cen2000/doc/pl94-171.pdf)

Area	Population April 1, 1990	Population April 1, 2000	Change, 1990 to 2000 Number	Percent
United States	248,709,873	281,421,906	32,712,033	13.2
Region				
Northeast	50,809,229	53,594,378	2,785,149	5.5
Midwest	59,668,632	64,392,776	4,724,144	7.9
South	85,445,930	100,236,820	14,790,890	17.3
West	52,786,082	63,197,932	10,411,850	19.7
State				
Alabama	4,040,587	4,447,100	406,513	10.1
Alaska	550,043	626,932	76,889	14.0
Arizona	3,665,228	5,130,632	1,465,404	40.0
Arkansas	2,350,725	2,673,400	322,675	13.7
California	29,760,021	33,871,648	4,111,627	13.8
Colorado	3,294,394	4,301,261	1,006,867	30.6
Connecticut	3,287,116	3,405,565	118,449	3.6
Delaware	666,168	783,600	117,432	17.6
District of Columbia	606,900	572,059	−34,841	−5.7
Florida	12,937,926	15,982,378	3,044,452	23.5
Georgia	6,478,216	8,186,453	1,708,237	26.4
Hawaii	1,108,229	1,211,537	103,308	9.3
Idaho	1,006,749	1,293,953	287,204	28.5
Illinois	11,430,602	12,419,293	988,691	8.6
Indiana	5,544,159	6,080,485	536,326	9.7
Iowa	2,776,755	2,926,324	149,569	5.4
Kansas	2,477,574	2,688,418	210,844	8.5
Kentucky	3,685,296	4,041,769	356,473	9.7
Louisiana	4,219,973	4,468,976	249,003	5.9
Maine	1,227,928	1,274,923	46,995	3.8
Maryland	4,781,468	5,296,486	515,018	10.8
Massachusetts	6,016,425	6,349,097	332,672	5.5
Michigan	9,295,297	9,938,444	643,147	6.9
Minnesota	4,375,099	4,919,479	544,380	12.4
Mississippi	2,573,216	2,844,658	271,442	10.5
Missouri	5,117,073	5,595,211	478,138	9.3
Montana	799,065	902,195	103,130	12.9
Nebraska	1,578,385	1,711,263	132,878	8.4
Nevada	1,201,833	1,998,257	796,424	66.3
New Hampshire	1,109,252	1,235,786	126,534	11.4
New Jersey	7,730,188	8,414,350	684,162	8.9
New Mexico	1,515,069	1,819,046	303,977	20.1
New York	17,990,455	18,976,457	986,002	5.5
North Carolina	6,628,637	8,049,313	1,420,676	21.4
North Dakota	638,800	642,200	3,400	0.5
Ohio	10,847,115	11,353,140	506,025	4.7
Oklahoma	3,145,585	3,450,654	305,069	9.7
Oregon	2,842,321	3,421,399	579,078	20.4
Pennsylvania	11,881,643	12,281,054	399,411	3.4
Rhode Island	1,003,464	1,048,319	44,855	4.5
South Carolina	3,486,703	4,012,012	525,309	15.1
South Dakota	696,004	754,844	58,840	8.5
Tennessee	4,877,185	5,689,283	812,098	16.7
Texas	16,986,510	20,851,820	3,865,310	22.8
Utah	1,722,850	2,233,169	510,319	29.6
Vermont	562,758	608,827	46,069	8.2
Virginia	6,187,358	7,078,515	891,157	14.4
Washington	4,866,692	5,894,121	1,027,429	21.1
West Virginia	1,793,477	1,808,344	14,867	0.8
Wisconsin	4,891,769	5,363,675	471,906	9.6
Wyoming	453,588	493,782	40,194	8.9
Puerto Rico	3,522,037	3,808,610	286,573	8.1

Source: U.S. Census Bureau, Census 2000; 1990 Census, *Population and Housing Unit Counts, United States* (1990 CPH-2-1).

Northeast's proportion declined from 26 to 19 percent.

Every state grew; Nevada's rate was fastest.

State population growth for the 1990s ranged from a high of 66 percent in Nevada to a low of 0.5 percent in North Dakota (see Table 1). This decade was the only one in the 20th Century in which all states gained population. Following Nevada, the fastest growing states were Arizona (40 percent), Colorado (31 percent), Utah (30 percent), and Idaho (29 percent). Following North Dakota, the slowest growing states were West Virginia (0.8 percent), Pennsylvania (3.4 percent), Connecticut (3.6 percent), and Maine (3.8 percent). Puerto Rico's population grew by 8.1 percent to reach 3.8 million, while the District of Columbia declined by 5.7 percent.

California had the largest population increase during the 1990s, adding 4.1 million people to its population. Texas (up 3.9 million), Florida (3.0 million), Georgia (1.7 million), and Arizona (1.5 million) rounded out the top five largest gaining states.

Within the Northeast, New Hampshire grew fastest for the fourth straight decade — up 11 percent since 1990. New York and New Jersey gained the most population, increasing by 986,000 and 684,000 respectively. In the Midwest, Minnesota was the fastest growing state for the third straight decade, growing by 12 percent since 1990. Illinois (up 989,000) and Michigan (up 643,000) had the largest numerical increases.

While no state in the Midwest grew faster than the U.S. rate of 13.2 percent, several states in the region had their fastest growth rates in many decades. Nebraska's 8 percent increase and Iowa's 5 percent increase were the highest growth rates for those states since their 1910 to 1920 increases of 9 percent and 8 percent, respectively. Missouri's 9 percent increase was its highest since a 16 percent increase from 1890 to 1900.

In the South, Georgia was the fastest growing state, up by 26 percent since 1990. This was Georgia's most rapid census-to-census population growth rate in the 20th Century, and the 1990s was the only decade in that century when Florida was not the South's fastest growing state.[4] Texas (up 3.9 million) and Florida (up 3.0 million) had the largest numerical increases.

Growth in the West was led by Nevada, now the country's fastest growing state for each of the past four decades. Of the 13 states in the region, only Wyoming (8.9 percent), Hawaii (9.3 percent), and Montana (12.9 percent) grew slower than the U.S. rate of 13.2 percent.

The majority of Americans lived in the ten most populous states.

The ten most populous states contained 54 percent of the population in 2000. California, with 33.9 million people, was the most populous one, accounting for 12 percent of the nation's population. The second and third most populous states — Texas, at 20.9 million people, and New York, at 19.0 million — together accounted for 14 percent of the U.S. population. The next seven most populous states — Florida, Illinois, Pennsylvania, Ohio, Michigan, New Jersey, and Georgia — contained an additional 28 percent of the population. The ten most populous states are distributed among all four regions: three each in the Northeast,

the Midwest, and the South, with one in the West.

The ten least populous states accounted for only 3 percent of the total population. Of the ten, three are in the Northeast (New Hampshire, Rhode Island, and Vermont), two in the Midwest (North Dakota and South Dakota), one in the South (Delaware) and four in the West (Hawaii, Montana, Alaska, and Wyoming).

Most counties grew, while some lost population.

Figure 2 shows population growth between 1990 and 2000 for the country's 3,141 counties and equivalent areas. Some broad patterns are immediately evident. A band of counties that lost population — in some cases declining more than 10 percent — stretches across the Great Plains states from the Mexican border to the Canadian border. A second band of slow growth counties includes much of the interior Northeast and Appalachia, extending from Maine through western Pennsylvania and West Virginia to eastern Kentucky. Rapid population growth occurred in the interior West and much of the South — particularly in counties in Florida, northern Georgia, North Carolina, Tennessee, southwestern Missouri, and eastern, central, and southern Texas.

Figure 2 underscores the continued concentration of population growth both within and adjacent to metropolitan areas.[5] In Texas, for

---

[4] Washington, DC, treated as a state equivalent for statistical purposes, had a larger percent gain than Florida in the 1910s and 1930s.

---

[5] This report uses the June 30, 1999, metropolitan areas as defined by the Office of Management and Budget for all 1990 and 2000 metropolitan area populations. All metropolitan areas in the text are either metropolitan statistical areas (MSAs) or consolidated metropolitan statistical areas (CMSAs). There are 276 metropolitan areas in the United States—258 MSAs and 18 CMSAs. In some cases, an abbreviated version of the full MSA or CMSA name was used in the text and tables.

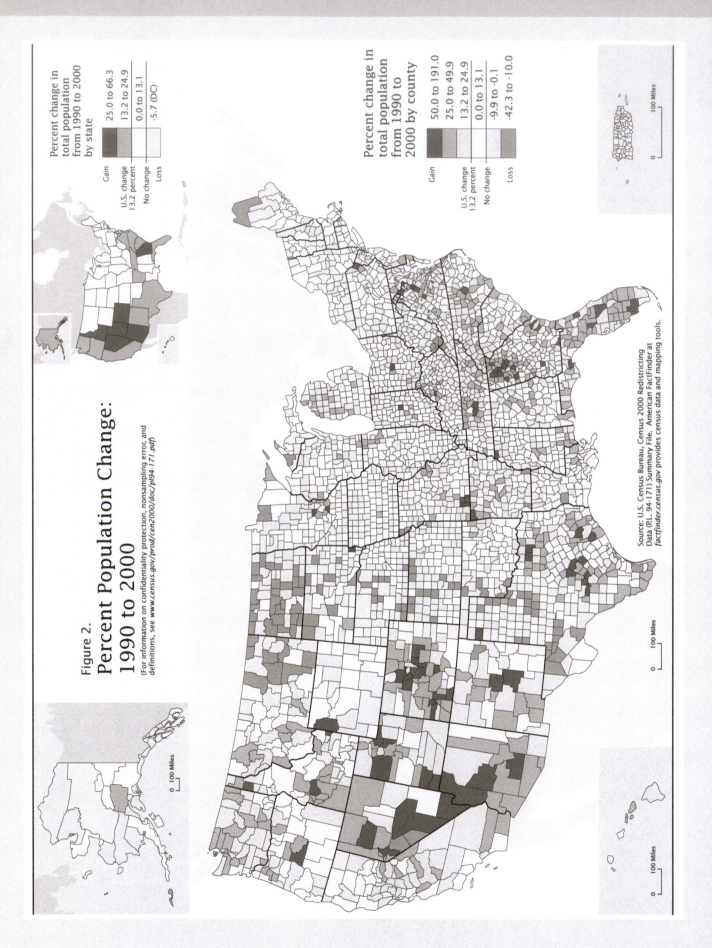

Figure 2.

Percent Population Change: 1990 to 2000

(For information on confidentiality protection, nonsampling error, and definitions, see *www.census.gov/prod/cen2000/doc/pl94-171.pdf*)

Percent change in total population from 1990 to 2000 by state

Gain
- 25.0 to 66.3
- 13.2 to 24.9

U.S. change 13.2 percent
- 0.0 to 13.1

No change

Loss
- -5.7 (DC)

Percent change in total population from 1990 to 2000 by county

Gain
- 50.0 to 191.0
- 25.0 to 49.9
- 13.2 to 24.9

U.S. change 13.2 percent
- 0.0 to 13.1

No change
- -9.9 to -0.1

Loss
- -42.3 to -10.0

Source: U.S. Census Bureau, Census 2000 Redistricting Data (P.L. 94-171) Summary File. American FactFinder at *factfinder.census.gov* provides census data and mapping tools.

Table 2.
Population Change and 2000 Share by Metropolitan Status and Size Category: 1990 to 2000

(For information on confidentiality protection, nonsampling error, and definitions, see www.census.gov/prod/cen2000/doc/pl94-171.pdf)

Population size category	Population		Percent change, 1990 to 2000	2000 share of U.S. total
	April 1, 1990	April 1, 2000		
United States	**248,709,873**	**281,421,906**	**13.2**	**100.0**
Total for all metropolitan areas	198,402,980	225,981,679	13.9	80.3
5,000,000 or more.........	75,874,152	84,064,274	10.8	29.9
2,000,000 - 4,999,999	33,717,876	40,398,283	19.8	14.4
1,000,000 - 1,999,999	31,483,749	37,055,342	17.7	13.2
250,000 - 999,999.........	39,871,391	45,076,105	13.1	16.0
Less than 250,000.........	17,455,812	19,387,675	11.1	6.9
Total nonmetropolitan	50,306,893	55,440,227	10.2	19.7

Source: U.S. Census Bureau, Census 2000; 1990 Census, *Population and Housing Unit Counts, United States* (1990 CPH-2-1).

instance, the Dallas, Houston, Austin, and San Antonio metropolitan areas show up as pockets of fast population growth, while most of the nonmetropolitan counties in the state recorded either slow growth or population decline.

In the slow growing upper Midwest, the rapid growth of counties in the Sioux Falls, South Dakota and Minneapolis-St. Paul, Minnesota metropolitan areas stands in sharp contrast to the population declines that occurred in most of the region's other counties. The Minneapolis-St. Paul metropolitan area has a common growth pattern: slow expansion in the central county or counties and faster growth in outlying counties. In the South, the Atlanta, Georgia metropolitan area also shows this pattern, with a large group of fast growing, primarily outlying, counties surrounding two slower growing central counties.

Population growth also differed between counties bordering Canada and those counties bordering

Mexico.[6] Between 1990 and 2000, the counties on the Mexican border grew rapidly, up 21 percent. In contrast, the population on the Canadian border remained stable over the period, increasing just 0.8 percent, with many counties experiencing population decline. In 2000, 6.3 million Americans lived in counties that bordered Mexico, while 5.0 million resided in counties bordering Canada.

Growth differences between coastal and noncoastal counties are also evident in Figure 2, particularly in the West, where coastal counties grew more slowly than noncoastal ones.[7] Nationwide, while some coastal counties grew rapidly in the 1990s, their overall growth rate of 11 percent was exceeded by that of noncoastal counties (up 15 percent). Over one half of all Americans (53 percent or 148.3 million people) lived in a coastal county in 2000.

Five counties more than doubled their populations during the 1990s.

Douglas County, Colorado (south of Denver) had the largest rate of population growth between 1990 and 2000, increasing by 191 percent. Following Douglas were Forsyth County, Georgia (north of Atlanta), up 123 percent; Elbert County, Colorado (southeast of Denver, adjacent to the metropolitan area), up 106 percent; Henry County, Georgia (east of Atlanta), 103 percent; and Park County, Colorado (southwest of Denver), up 102 percent.

Large metropolitan areas had strong growth in 1990s.

In 2000, 80.3 percent of Americans (226.0 million people) lived in metropolitan areas, up slightly from 79.8 percent (198.4 million people) in 1990 (see Table 2). The population within metropolitan areas increased by 14 percent, while the nonmetropolitan population grew by 10 percent.

Almost one-third of Americans (30 percent) lived in metropolitan areas of at least 5.0 million people, while those with populations between 2.0 million and 5.0 million contained 14 percent of the population. Metropolitan areas with populations between 1.0 million and 2.0 million contained 13 percent of the population, while those with populations between 250,000 and 1.0 million and those with populations less than 250,000 contained 16 percent and 7 percent of the population, respectively.

Metropolitan areas with populations of 2.0 million to 5.0 million in 2000 grew the fastest, up 20 percent. The largest and smallest metropolitan area size categories, those with populations of 5.0 million or more and those with populations less than 250,000, each grew by about 11 percent.

---

[6] The United States-Mexico county-based border region includes 25 counties in Texas, New Mexico, Arizona, and California. The United States-Canada county-based border region includes 64 counties in Maine, New Hampshire, Vermont, New York, Michigan, Minnesota, North Dakota, Montana, Idaho, Washington, and Alaska.

[7] Coastal areas as defined by the U.S. National Oceanic and Atmospheric Agency, 1992. Covers 673 counties and equivalent areas with at least 15 percent of their land area either in a coastal watershed (drainage area) or in a coastal cataloging unit (a coastal area between watersheds).

As shown in Table 3, New York was the most populous metropolitan area, surpassing the 20 million mark with a population of 21.2 million (7.5 percent of the total population). The Los Angeles metropolitan area was the second largest, with a population of 16.4 million (5.8 percent of the total). The third most populous was Chicago, with 9.2 million people and 3.3 percent of the population. The Washington, DC and San Francisco metropolitan areas ranked fourth and fifth – with 7.6 million and 7.0 million people, respectively. Philadelphia ranked sixth, with 6.2 million people. The seventh, eighth, and ninth largest metropolitan areas — Boston, Detroit, and Dallas — each had populations of between 5 million and 6 million. All of the metropolitan areas with populations of at least 5.0 million grew over the period, ranging from 29 percent for the Dallas metropolitan area to 5 percent for Philadelphia.

Between 1990 and 2000, Las Vegas, Nevada-Arizona was the fastest growing metropolitan area (83 percent), as shown in Table 4, followed by Naples, Florida, with a growth rate of 65 percent, and by seven other areas with growth rates between 44 percent and 50 percent: Yuma, Arizona; McAllen, Texas; Austin, Texas; Fayetteville, Arkansas; Boise City, Idaho; Phoenix, Arizona; and Laredo, Texas. The tenth fastest growing area, Provo, Utah, grew by almost 40 percent. Of the ten fastest growing metropolitan areas in 2000, one had a population

Table 3.
Population Change and 2000 Share for the Largest Metropolitan Areas: 1990 to 2000

(For information on confidentiality protection, nonsampling error, and definitions, see www.census.gov/prod/cen2000/doc/pl94-171.pdf)

Metropolitan area	Population		Percent change, 1990 to 2000	2000 share of U.S. total
	April 1, 1990	April 1, 2000		
Total for metropolitan areas of 5,000,000 or more	**75,874,152**	**84,064,274**	**10.8**	**29.9**
New York-Northern New Jersey-Long Island, NY-NJ-CT-PA	19,549,649	21,199,865	8.4	7.5
Los Angeles-Riverside-Orange County, CA	14,531,529	16,373,645	12.7	5.8
Chicago-Gary-Kenosha, IL-IN-WI......	8,239,820	9,157,540	11.1	3.3
Washington-Baltimore, DC-MD-VA-WV.	6,727,050	7,608,070	13.1	2.7
San Francisco-Oakland-San Jose, CA .	6,253,311	7,039,362	12.6	2.5
Philadelphia-Wilmington-Atlantic City, PA-NJ-DE-MD	5,892,937	6,188,463	5.0	2.2
Boston-Worcester-Lawrence, MA-NH-ME-CT....................	5,455,403	5,819,100	6.7	2.1
Detroit-Ann Arbor-Flint, MI............	5,187,171	5,456,428	5.2	1.9
Dallas-Fort Worth, TX................	4,037,282	5,221,801	29.3	1.9

Source: U.S. Census Bureau, Census 2000; 1990 Census, *Population and Housing Unit Counts, United States* (1990 CPH-2-1).

Table 4.
Population Change for the Ten Fastest Growing Metropolitan Areas: 1990 to 2000

(For information on confidentiality protection, nonsampling error, and definitions, see www.census.gov/prod/cen2000/doc/pl94-171.pdf)

Metropolitan area	Population		Change, 1990 to 2000	
	April 1, 1990	April 1, 2000	Number	Percent
Las Vegas, NV-AZ......................	852,737	1,563,282	710,545	83.3
Naples, FL	152,099	251,377	99,278	65.3
Yuma, AZ	106,895	160,026	53,131	49.7
McAllen-Edinburg-Mission, TX	383,545	569,463	185,918	48.5
Austin-San Marcos, TX	846,227	1,249,763	403,536	47.7
Fayetteville-Springdale-Rogers, AR	210,908	311,121	100,213	47.5
Boise City, ID	295,851	432,345	136,494	46.1
Phoenix-Mesa, AZ	2,238,480	3,251,876	1,013,396	45.3
Laredo, TX	133,239	193,117	59,878	44.9
Provo-Orem, UT	263,590	368,536	104,946	39.8

Source: U.S. Census Bureau, Census 2000; 1990 Census, *Population and Housing Unit Counts, United States* (1990 CPH-2-1).

between 2.0 million and 5.0 million; two had populations between 1.0 million and 2.0 million, five contained populations between 250,000 and 1.0 million, and two had populations less than 250,000.

ADDITIONAL TOPICS ON POPULATION CHANGE AND DISTRIBUTION

How did the population change in the ten largest American cities?

Eight of the ten largest cities in 2000 gained population in the 1990s; only Philadelphia and Detroit declined in size. New York remained the country's largest city, passing the 8 million threshold for the first time. Phoenix was the fastest growing of the 10 largest cities, up by 34 percent over the decade.

New York also had the largest numerical increase of any city, gaining 686,000 people. The 1990s was the first decade since the 1930s that New York City led in city population growth.

Los Angeles gained the most population in each of the decades from the 1940s through the 1980s, with the exception of the 1970s, when Houston gained the most.

Have any more counties crossed the 1 million population threshold?

Four counties exceeded the 1 million mark for the first time in Census 2000: Clark County, Nevada (1.4 million); Palm Beach County, Florida (1.1 million); Franklin County, Ohio (1.1 million); and St. Louis County, Missouri (1.0 million).

FOR MORE INFORMATION

Census 2000 data for state and local areas are available on the Internet via *factfinder.census.gov* and for purchase on CD-ROM and eventually on DVD. For information on population change and distribution, as well as information on the post-censal population estimates program, visit the U.S. Census Bureau's Internet site at *www.census.gov* and click on Estimates. For more information on metropolitan areas, including concepts, definitions, and maps, go to *www.census.gov/population/www/estimates/metroarea.html.*

Information on other population and housing topics will be presented in the Census 2000 Brief Series, located on the U.S. Census Bureau's Web site at *www.census.gov/population/www/cen2000/briefs.html.* This series will present information about race, Hispanic origin, age, sex, household type, housing tenure, and other social, economic, and housing characteristics.

For more information about Census 2000, including data products, call the Customer Services Center at 301-457-4100 or e-mail *webmaster@census.gov.*

Table 5.
Population Change for the Ten Largest Cities: 1990 to 2000

(For information on confidentiality protection, nonsampling error, and definitions, see *www.census.gov/prod/cen2000/doc/pl94-171.pdf*)

City and state	Population		Change, 1990 to 2000	
	April 1, 1990	April 1, 2000	Number	Percent
New York, NY.................	7,322,564	8,008,278	685,714	9.4
Los Angeles, CA	3,485,398	3,694,820	209,422	6.0
Chicago, IL...................	2,783,726	2,896,016	112,290	4.0
Houston, TX..................	1,630,553	1,953,631	323,078	19.8
Philadelphia, PA..............	1,585,577	1,517,550	−68,027	−4.3
Phoenix, AZ	983,403	1,321,045	337,642	34.3
San Diego, CA................	1,110,549	1,223,400	112,851	10.2
Dallas, TX....................	1,006,877	1,188,580	181,703	18.0
San Antonio, TX..............	935,933	1,144,646	208,713	22.3
Detroit, MI...................	1,027,974	951,270	−76,704	−7.5

Source: U.S. Census Bureau, Census 2000; 1990 Census, *Population and Housing Unit Counts, United States* (1990 CPH-2-1).

Gender: 2000

Census 2000 Brief

Issued September 2001

C2KBR/01-9

By Denise I. Smith and
Renee E. Spraggins

According to Census 2000, 281.4 million people were counted in the United States — 143.4 million of whom were female and 138.1 million male.[1] The former made up 50.9 percent of the population, compared with 51.3 percent in 1990.

Information on gender was derived from a question which was asked of all people (see Figure 1). A question on the sex of individuals was included in all censuses since the first one in 1790.

This report, part of a series that analyzes population and housing data collected by Census 2000, presents the number who are male and female in regions, states, counties, and places of 100,000 or more and highlights comparisons with data from the 1990 census.[2]

The male population continued to grow slightly faster than the female population.

Between 1990 and 2000, the male population grew slightly faster (13.9 percent) than the female population (12.5 percent). The excess of the female to male population dropped to 5.3 million in 2000, compared with 6.2 million in 1990. This resulted in the male-female ratio (the

Figure 1.

Reproduction of the Question on Sex From Census 2000

3. What is this person's sex? *Mark* ☒ *ONE box.*
☐ Male   ☐ Female

Source: U.S. Census Bureau, Census 2000 questionnaire.

number who were male times 100 divided by the number who were female) increasing from 95.1 in 1990 to 96.3 in 2000. The decline in the male-female ratio until 1980 resulted mainly from the relatively greater reduction in female mortality rates. The male-female ratio reversed its downward trend between 1980 and 1990 as male death rates declined faster than female rates and as immigration brought in more men.

Figure 2 shows how male-female ratios fluctuated for every decade since 1900. From 1900 to 1940, the male-female ratio was above 100, but beginning in 1950, it fell below. Between 1980 and 2000, the male-female ratio gradually increased.

The male-female ratio declined with age after age 24.

Up to age 24, the male-female ratios were about 105, reflecting the fact that more boys than girls are born every year and that boys continue to outnumber girls through early childhood and young adulthood. The male-female ratio dropped gradually in the working age groups, from 105.1 in the age group 15 to 24 years to

---

[1] The text of this report discusses data for the United States, including the 50 states and the District of Columbia. Data for the Commonwealth of Puerto Rico are shown in Table 1 and Figure 4.

[2] 1990 populations shown in this report were originally published in 1990 census reports and do not include subsequent revisions resulting from boundary or other changes.

USCENSUSBUREAU

Helping You Make Informed Decisions

U.S. Department of Commerce
Economics and Statistics Administration
U.S. CENSUS BUREAU

92.2 for the age group 55 to 64 (see Figure 3).[3] Among older adults, the male-female ratio fell rapidly, as women increasingly out-numbered men at older ages and by the age group 85 and over, the male-female ratio was 40.7.

Male-female ratios increased from 1990 to 2000.

Figure 3 also illustrates changes in the sex composition by age between 1990 and 2000. In 1990, the number who were male about equaled the number who were female (a ratio of 99.9) in the age group 25 to 34. In 2000, the male-female ratio in the age group 25 to 34 increased to 101.8. The age at which the number was almost equal shifted closer to the age group 35 to 44 in 2000. The largest increas-es in the male-female ratios from 1990 to 2000 occurred in the age group 55 and over. In 2000, the ratio was 92.2 in the age group 55 to 64 compared with 89.4 in 1990. In the age group 65 to 74, the ratio was 82.3 in 2000 compared with 78.1 in 1990. The greatest increase in the male-female ratio was in the age group 75 to 84, where the ratio increased from 59.9 in 1990 to 65.2 in 2000.

---

[3] Note that comparisons of census counts can be affected by differences in the complete-ness of census coverage between groups being compared. For example, men are usually cov-ered less completely in the census than women, which would lower the male-female ratio calcu-lated from census data. The male-female differ-ence in net coverage tends to be greatest for adults under age 65, particularly for Blacks or African Americans.

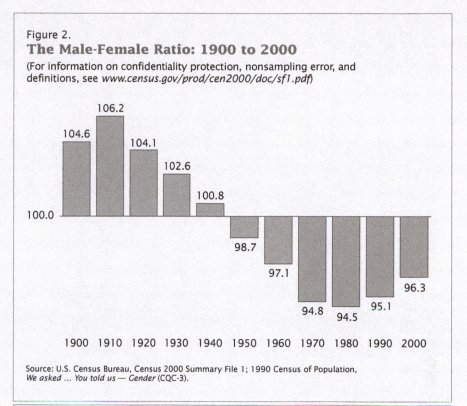

Figure 2.
The Male-Female Ratio: 1900 to 2000
(For information on confidentiality protection, nonsampling error, and definitions, see *www.census.gov/prod/cen2000/doc/sf1.pdf*)

Source: U.S. Census Bureau, Census 2000 Summary File 1; 1990 Census of Population, *We asked ... You told us — Gender* (CQC-3).

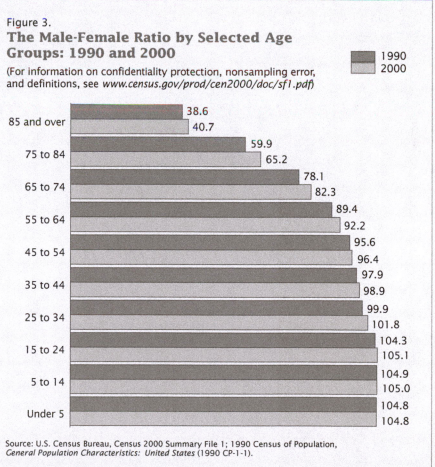

Figure 3.
The Male-Female Ratio by Selected Age Groups: 1990 and 2000
(For information on confidentiality protection, nonsampling error, and definitions, see *www.census.gov/prod/cen2000/doc/sf1.pdf*)

1990
2000

Source: U.S. Census Bureau, Census 2000 Summary File 1; 1990 Census of Population, *General Population Characteristics: United States* (1990 CP-1-1).

Table 1.
Population by Sex for the United States, Regions, and States, and for Puerto Rico: 1990 and 2000

(For information on confidentiality protection, nonsampling error, and definitions, see *www.census.gov/prod/cen2000/doc/sf1.pdf*)

Area	1990				2000				Percent change, 1990 to 2000		
	Total population	Male	Female	Male-female ratio	Total population	Male	Female	Male-female ratio	Total population	Male	Female
United States	248,709,873	121,239,418	127,470,455	95.1	281,421,906	138,053,563	143,368,343	96.3	13.2	13.9	12.5
Region											
Northeast	50,809,229	24,435,623	26,373,606	92.7	53,594,378	25,897,327	27,697,051	93.5	5.5	6.0	5.0
Midwest	59,668,632	28,971,653	30,696,979	94.4	64,392,776	31,555,438	32,837,338	96.1	7.9	8.9	7.0
South	85,445,930	41,491,327	43,954,603	94.4	100,236,820	49,057,320	51,179,500	95.9	17.3	18.2	16.4
West	52,786,082	26,340,815	26,445,267	99.6	63,197,932	31,543,478	31,654,454	99.6	19.7	19.8	19.7
State											
Alabama	4,040,587	1,936,162	2,104,425	92.0	4,447,100	2,146,504	2,300,596	93.3	10.1	10.9	9.3
Alaska	550,043	289,867	260,176	111.4	626,932	324,112	302,820	107.0	14.0	11.8	16.4
Arizona	3,665,228	1,810,691	1,854,537	97.6	5,130,632	2,561,057	2,569,575	99.7	40.0	41.4	38.6
Arkansas	2,350,725	1,133,076	1,217,649	93.1	2,673,400	1,304,693	1,368,707	95.3	13.7	15.1	12.4
California	29,760,021	14,897,627	14,862,394	100.2	33,871,648	16,874,892	16,996,756	99.3	13.8	13.3	14.4
Colorado	3,294,394	1,631,295	1,663,099	98.1	4,301,261	2,165,983	2,135,278	101.4	30.6	32.8	28.4
Connecticut	3,287,116	1,592,873	1,694,243	94.0	3,405,565	1,649,319	1,756,246	93.9	3.6	3.5	3.7
Delaware	666,168	322,968	343,200	94.1	783,600	380,541	403,059	94.4	17.6	17.8	17.4
District of Columbia	606,900	282,970	323,930	87.4	572,059	269,366	302,693	89.0	-5.7	-4.8	-6.6
Florida	12,937,926	6,261,719	6,676,207	93.8	15,982,378	7,797,715	8,184,663	95.3	23.5	24.5	22.6
Georgia	6,478,216	3,144,503	3,333,713	94.3	8,186,453	4,027,113	4,159,340	96.8	26.4	28.1	24.8
Hawaii	1,108,229	563,891	544,338	103.6	1,211,537	608,671	602,866	101.0	9.3	7.9	10.8
Idaho	1,006,749	500,956	505,793	99.0	1,293,953	648,660	645,293	100.5	28.5	29.5	27.6
Illinois	11,430,602	5,552,233	5,878,369	94.5	12,419,293	6,080,336	6,338,957	95.9	8.6	9.5	7.8
Indiana	5,544,159	2,688,281	2,855,878	94.1	6,080,485	2,982,474	3,098,011	96.3	9.7	10.9	8.5
Iowa	2,776,755	1,344,802	1,431,953	93.9	2,926,324	1,435,515	1,490,809	96.3	5.4	6.7	4.1
Kansas	2,477,574	1,214,645	1,262,929	96.2	2,688,418	1,328,474	1,359,944	97.7	8.5	9.4	7.7
Kentucky	3,685,296	1,785,235	1,900,061	94.0	4,041,769	1,975,368	2,066,401	95.6	9.7	10.7	8.8
Louisiana	4,219,973	2,031,386	2,188,587	92.8	4,468,976	2,162,903	2,306,073	93.8	5.9	6.5	5.4
Maine	1,227,928	597,850	630,078	94.9	1,274,923	620,309	654,614	94.8	3.8	3.8	3.9
Maryland	4,781,468	2,318,671	2,462,797	94.1	5,296,486	2,557,794	2,738,692	93.4	10.8	10.3	11.2
Massachusetts	6,016,425	2,888,745	3,127,680	92.4	6,349,097	3,058,816	3,290,281	93.0	5.5	5.9	5.2
Michigan	9,295,297	4,512,781	4,782,516	94.4	9,938,444	4,873,095	5,065,349	96.2	6.9	8.0	5.9
Minnesota	4,375,099	2,145,183	2,229,916	96.2	4,919,479	2,435,631	2,483,848	98.1	12.4	13.5	11.4
Mississippi	2,573,216	1,230,617	1,342,599	91.7	2,844,658	1,373,554	1,471,104	93.4	10.5	11.6	9.6
Missouri	5,117,073	2,464,315	2,652,758	92.9	5,595,211	2,720,177	2,875,034	94.6	9.3	10.4	8.4
Montana	799,065	395,769	403,296	98.1	902,195	449,480	452,715	99.3	12.9	13.6	12.3
Nebraska	1,578,385	769,439	808,946	95.1	1,711,263	843,351	867,912	97.2	8.4	9.6	7.3
Nevada	1,201,833	611,880	589,953	103.7	1,998,257	1,018,051	980,206	103.9	66.3	66.4	66.1
New Hampshire	1,109,252	543,544	565,708	96.1	1,235,786	607,687	628,099	96.8	11.4	11.8	11.0
New Jersey	7,730,188	3,735,685	3,994,503	93.5	8,414,350	4,082,813	4,331,537	94.3	8.9	9.3	8.4
New Mexico	1,515,069	745,253	769,816	96.8	1,819,046	894,317	924,729	96.7	20.1	20.0	20.1
New York	17,990,455	8,625,673	9,364,782	92.1	18,976,457	9,146,748	9,829,709	93.1	5.5	6.0	5.0
North Carolina	6,628,637	3,214,290	3,414,347	94.1	8,049,313	3,942,695	4,106,618	96.0	21.4	22.7	20.3
North Dakota	638,800	318,201	320,599	99.3	642,200	320,524	321,676	99.6	0.5	0.7	0.3
Ohio	10,847,115	5,226,340	5,620,775	93.0	11,353,140	5,512,262	5,840,878	94.4	4.7	5.5	3.9
Oklahoma	3,145,585	1,530,819	1,614,766	94.8	3,450,654	1,695,895	1,754,759	96.6	9.7	10.8	8.7
Oregon	2,842,321	1,397,073	1,445,248	96.7	3,421,399	1,696,550	1,724,849	98.4	20.4	21.4	19.3
Pennsylvania	11,881,643	5,694,265	6,187,378	92.0	12,281,054	5,929,663	6,351,391	93.4	3.4	4.1	2.7
Rhode Island	1,003,464	481,496	521,968	92.2	1,048,319	503,635	544,684	92.5	4.5	4.6	4.4
South Carolina	3,486,703	1,688,510	1,798,193	93.9	4,012,012	1,948,929	2,063,083	94.5	15.1	15.4	14.7
South Dakota	696,004	342,498	353,506	96.9	754,844	374,558	380,286	98.5	8.5	9.4	7.6
Tennessee	4,877,185	2,348,928	2,528,257	92.9	5,689,283	2,770,275	2,919,008	94.9	16.7	17.9	15.5
Texas	16,986,510	8,365,963	8,620,547	97.0	20,851,820	10,352,910	10,498,910	98.6	22.8	23.8	21.8
Utah	1,722,850	855,759	867,091	98.7	2,233,169	1,119,031	1,114,138	100.4	29.6	30.8	28.5
Vermont	562,758	275,492	287,266	95.9	608,827	298,337	310,490	96.1	8.2	8.3	8.1
Virginia	6,187,358	3,033,974	3,153,384	96.2	7,078,515	3,471,895	3,606,620	96.3	14.4	14.4	14.4
Washington	4,866,692	2,413,747	2,452,945	98.4	5,894,121	2,934,300	2,959,821	99.1	21.1	21.6	20.7
West Virginia	1,793,477	861,536	931,941	92.4	1,808,344	879,170	929,174	94.6	0.8	2.0	-0.3
Wisconsin	4,891,769	2,392,935	2,498,834	95.8	5,363,675	2,649,041	2,714,634	97.6	9.6	10.7	8.6
Wyoming	453,588	227,007	226,581	100.2	493,782	248,374	245,408	101.2	8.9	9.4	8.3
Puerto Rico	3,522,037	1,705,642	1,816,395	93.9	3,808,610	1,833,577	1,975,033	92.8	8.1	7.5	8.7

Source: U.S. Census Bureau, Census 2000 Summary File 1; 1990 Census of Population, *General Population Characteristics* (1990 CP-1).

The relative size of the male and female populations varied by geographic region.[4]

Table 1 shows that among regions in 2000, the Northeast had the lowest male-female ratio — 93.5. The Midwest and South had male-female ratios in 2000 of 96.1 and 95.9, respectively. The West had the highest male-female ratio, at 99.6, approaching parity between the sexes. The regional male-female ratios in 2000 follow the same pattern as in 1990.

At the state level in 2000, those who were female were more numerous than those who were male in all but seven states: Alaska led the states with the highest male-female ratio (107.0), followed by Nevada (103.9), Colorado (101.4), Wyoming (101.2), Hawaii (101.0), Idaho (101.0), and Utah (100.4). All of these states were in the West. In contrast, the lowest male-female ratios were recorded in Rhode Island (92.5), Massachusetts (93.0), and the District of Columbia (89.0).[5]

Over the decade, five states in the West grew at a faster rate than the other states, with the male population growing slightly faster than the female population.

Over the decade, the West experienced the fastest population growth at 19.7 percent followed by the South with 17.3 percent. In the

Table 2.
Ten Places of 100,000 or More Population With the Highest Male-Female Ratio: 2000

(For information on confidentiality protection, nonsampling error, and definitions, see www.census.gov/cen2000/doc/sf1.pdf)

Place	Total population	Male	Female	Male-female ratio
Salinas, CA.	151,060	80,361	70,699	113.7
Ft. Lauderdale, FL.	152,397	79,826	72,571	110.0
Paradise, NV*.	186,070	97,081	88,989	109.1
Santa Ana, CA	337,977	175,219	162,758	107.7
Tempe, AZ.	158,625	81,942	76,683	106.9
Wichita Falls, TX	104,197	53,657	50,540	106.2
Sunnyvale, CA	131,760	67,783	63,977	106.0
Austin, TX	656,562	337,569	318,993	105.8
Costa Mesa, CA.	108,724	55,694	53,030	105.0
Oxnard, CA.	170,358	87,090	83,268	104.6

*Paradise, Nevada is a census designated place and is not legally incorporated.

Source: U.S. Census Bureau, Census 2000 Summary File 1.

West, the male and female populations grew at about the same rate, 19.8 percent and 19.7 percent, respectively. In the South, the male population grew by 18.2 percent and the female population by 16.4 percent (see Table 1).

In the five states with the highest percent increase in total population (Nevada, Arizona, Colorado, Utah, and Idaho), the male population grew faster than the female population between 1990 and 2000. In the fastest growing state of Nevada, the male population grew by 66.4 percent and the female population by 66.1 percent. In the second fastest growing state of Arizona, the male and female populations grew by 41.4 percent and 38.6 percent, respectively. Between 1990 and 2000, the male population grew faster than the female population in 42 additional states.

There were only three states (Alaska, California, and Hawaii) where the female population grew at a faster rate than the male population. In Alaska, the female population grew by 16 percent compared with 12 percent for the male population. In California, the rate of growth was 14 percent for the

female population and 13 percent for the male population. In Hawaii, the rate of growth for the female and male populations were 11 percent and 8 percent, respectively.

The only decline in total population over the decade was in the District of Columbia. The population in the District of Columbia declined by 6 percent with the male population declining by 5 percent and the female population by 7 percent.

The female population outnumbered the male population in most counties in 2000.

At the county level, the female population outnumbered the male population in most counties. Of the 3,141 counties and equivalent areas, the number of counties with a greater female population was 2,305 representing 73 percent of all counties and equivalent areas. About 42 percent or 1,315 counties and equivalent areas had male-female ratios below the U.S. male-female ratio of 96.3.

The counties with low male-female ratios were concentrated in the Northeast and South. Most states in these regions predominantly had counties with low male-female

---

[4] The Northeast region includes Connecticut, Maine, Massachusetts, New Hampshire, New Jersey, New York, Pennsylvania, Rhode Island, and Vermont. The Midwest includes Illinois, Indiana, Iowa, Kansas, Michigan, Minnesota, Missouri, Nebraska, North Dakota, Ohio, South Dakota, and Wisconsin. The South includes Alabama, Arkansas, Delaware, the District of Columbia, Florida, Georgia, Kentucky, Louisiana, Maryland, Mississippi, North Carolina, Oklahoma, South Carolina, Tennessee, Texas, Virginia, and West Virginia. The West includes Alaska, Arizona, California, Colorado, Hawaii, Idaho, Montana, Nevada, New Mexico, Oregon, Utah, Washington, and Wyoming.

[5] Washington, DC is treated as a state equivalent for statistical purposes.

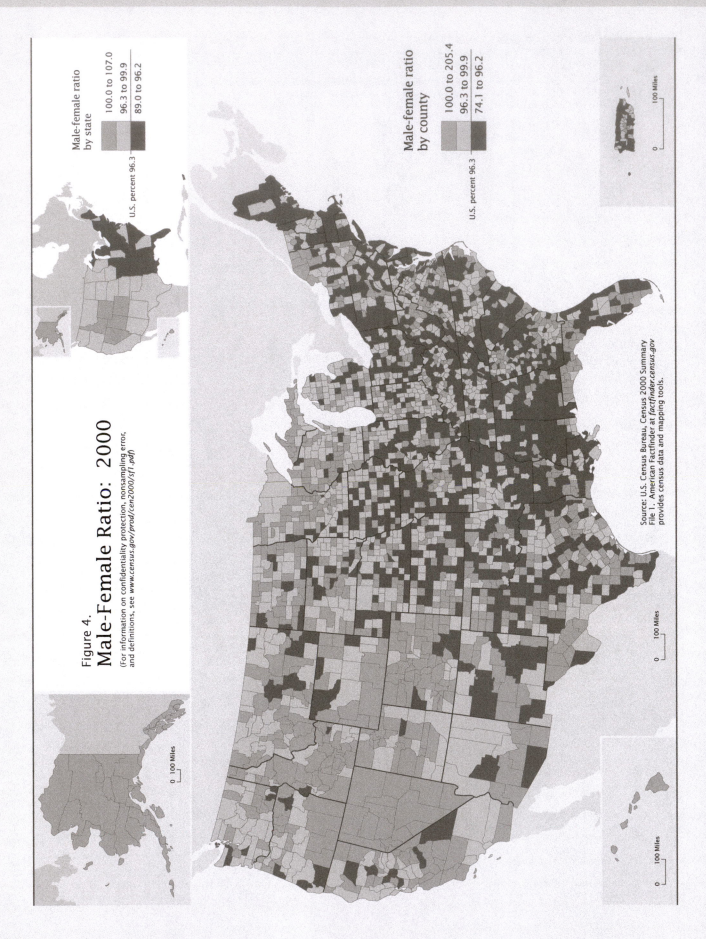

Figure 4.
Male-Female Ratio: 2000

(For information on confidentiality protection, nonsampling error,
and definitions, see *www.census.gov/prod/cen2000/sf1.pdf*)

Male-female ratio
by state

100.0 to 107.0
96.3 to 99.9
89.0 to 96.2

U.S. percent 96.3

Male-female ratio
by county

100.0 to 205.4
96.3 to 99.9
74.1 to 96.2

U.S. percent 96.3

0   100 Miles

Source: U.S. Census Bureau, Census 2000 Summary
File 1. American Factfinder at *factfinder.census.gov*
provides census data and mapping tools.

0   100 Miles

0   100 Miles

0   100 Miles

ratios, except for a few counties in upstate New York and the Florida panhandle. The female population exceeded the male population in all counties in Maine, New Hampshire, Massachusetts, and Delaware. The female population also exceeded the male population in most counties in Vermont, Rhode Island, New Jersey, Alabama, Mississippi, and South Carolina.

In contrast, counties with high male-female ratios were primarily in the West. All counties in Nevada, Alaska, and Hawaii had male-female ratios above 100. Other states with the majority of their counties with high male-female ratios were Idaho, Oregon, and Colorado.

Among the ten places of 100,000 or more with the highest male-female ratios, half were in California.

Seven of the places of 100,000 or more with the highest male-female ratios were in the West and three were in the South (see Table 2). Five of these places were in California: Salinas, Santa Ana, Sunnyvale, Costa Mesa, and Oxnard. Salinas, California had the highest male-female ratio (113.7), followed by Fort Lauderdale, Florida (110.0) and Paradise, Nevada (109.1).[6] Of the 245 places with a population of 100,000 or more, the male population exceeded the female population in 44 places.[7]

Table 3.
Ten Places of 100,000 or More Population With the Lowest Male-Female Ratio: 2000

(For information on confidentiality protection, nonsampling error, and definitions, see www.census.gov/cen2000/doc/sf1.pdf)

Place	Total population	Male	Female	Male-female ratio
Gary, IN	102,746	47,088	55,658	84.6
Birmingham, AL	242,820	112,046	130,774	85.7
Philadelphia, PA	1,517,550	705,107	812,443	86.8
Jackson, MS	184,256	85,656	98,600	86.9
Richmond, VA	197,790	92,068	105,722	87.1
Pembroke Pines, FL	137,427	64,044	73,383	87.3
Shreveport, LA	200,145	93,333	106,812	87.4
Baltimore, MD	651,154	303,687	347,467	87.4
Mobile, AL	198,915	93,015	105,900	87.8
New Orleans, LA	484,674	227,094	257,580	88.2

Source: U.S. Census Bureau, Census 2000 Summary File 1.

Table 4.
Male-Female Ratios of the Ten Largest Cities: 2000

(For information on confidentiality protection, nonsampling error, and definitions, see www.census.gov/prod/doc/sf1.pdf)

City	Total population	Male	Female	Male-female ratio
New York, NY	8,008,278	3,794,204	4,214,074	90.0
Los Angeles, CA	3,694,820	1,841,805	1,853,015	99.4
Chicago, IL	2,896,016	1,405,107	1,490,909	94.2
Houston, TX	1,953,631	975,551	978,080	99.7
Philadelphia, PA	1,517,550	705,107	812,443	86.8
Phoenix, AZ	1,321,045	671,760	649,285	103.5
San Diego, CA	1,223,400	616,884	606,516	101.7
Dallas, TX	1,188,580	598,991	589,589	101.6
San Antonio, TX	1,144,646	553,245	591,401	93.5
Detroit, MI	951,270	448,319	502,951	89.1

Source: U.S. Census Bureau, Census 2000 Summary File 1.

Eight of the places of 100,000 or more with the lowest male-female ratios were in the South.

Eight of the places of 100,000 or more with the lowest male-female ratios were in the South. They were New Orleans, Louisiana; Mobile, Alabama; Baltimore, Maryland; Shreveport, Louisiana; Pembroke Pines, Florida; Richmond, Virginia; Jackson, Mississippi; and Birmingham, Alabama. One place was in the Midwest (Gary, Indiana) and one place was in the Northeast (Philadelphia, Pennsylvania), as shown in Table 3. Gary, Indiana had the lowest male-female ratio with 84.6, followed by Birmingham,

Alabama (85.7); Philadelphia, Pennsylvania (86.8); and Jackson, Mississippi (86.9).

The male-female ratios of the ten most populous cities varied.

Table 4 illustrates the male-female ratio for the ten largest cities in 2000. Of the ten largest cities in 2000, the male population exceeded the female population in three cities: Phoenix, San Diego, and Dallas. The male and female populations were about equal in Los Angeles and Houston. Philadelphia and Detroit had the lowest male-female ratios, at 86.8 and 89.1, respectively.

[6] Paradise, Nevada is a census designated place and is not legally incorporated.
[7] Census 2000 showed 245 places in the United States with 100,000 or more population. They included 238 incorporated places (including 4 city-county consolidations) and 7 census designated places that were not legally incorporated. For a list of these places by state, see www.census.gov/population/www/cen2000/phc-t6.html.

ADDITIONAL FINDINGS ON GENDER

At what age were there almost twice as many women as men?

At age 85, there were about twice as many women as men in 2000 (485,320 compared with 244,874, respectively). This break-point is 2 years older than in 1990, when there were twice as many women than men at age 83.

What are the counties with the highest and lowest male-female ratios?

In 2000, Crowley County, Colorado led the counties with the highest ratio at 205.4, followed by West Feliciana Parish, Louisiana (191.1), and Aleutians-East Borough, Alaska (184.8). In contrast, the county equivalents with the lowest ratio were independent cities in Virginia. They included: Clifton Forge city (78.9), Franklin city (79.2), and Williamsburg city (81.4). All of these counties or county equivalents had populations less than 16,000.

ABOUT CENSUS 2000

People who answered the census help their communities obtain federal funds and valuable information for planning schools, hospitals, employment services, housing assistance, roads, and much more. All levels of government need information on sex to implement and evaluate programs, such as the Equal Employment Opportunity Act, the Civil Rights Act, the Women's Educational Equity Act, the Resource Conservation and Recovery Act, the Older Americans Act, the Juvenile Justice and Delinquency Prevention Act, and the Job Training Partnership Act.

FOR MORE INFORMATION

For more information on sex in the United States, visit the U.S. Census Bureau's Internet site at *www.census.gov/population/www/ socdemo/women02.html.*

Data on sex from the Census 2000 Summary File 1 were released on a state-by-state basis during the summer of 2001. Census 2000 data are available on the Internet via *factfinder.census.gov* and for purchase on CD-ROM and later on DVD.

For information on confidentiality protection, nonsampling error, and definitions, also see *www.census.gov/prod/cen2000/ doc/sf1.pdf* or contact Customer Services Center at 301-763-INFO (4636).

Information on other population and housing topics is presented in the Census 2000 Brief series, located on the U.S. Census Bureau's Web site at *www.census.gov/population/www/ cen2000/briefs.html.* This series presents information about race, Hispanic origin, age, sex, household type, housing tenure, and other social, economic, and housing characteristics.

For more information about Census 2000, including data products, call our Customer Services Center at 301-763-INFO (4636) or e-mail *webmaster@census.gov.*

The White Population: 2000

Census 2000 Brief

Issued August 2001

C2KBR/01-4

By
Elizabeth M. Grieco

Census 2000 showed that the United States population on April 1, 2000 was 281.4 million. Of the total, 216.9 million, or 77.1 percent, reported[1] White. This number includes 211.5 million people, or 75.1 percent, who reported only White in addition to 5.5 million people, or 1.9 percent, who reported White as well as one or more other races. Census 2000 asked separate questions on race and Hispanic or Latino origin. Hispanics who reported their race as White, either alone or in combination with one or more other races, are included in the numbers for Whites.

This report, part of a series that analyzes population and housing data collected from Census 2000, provides a portrait of the White population in the United States and discusses its distribution at both the national and subnational levels. It is based on the Census 2000 Redistricting Data (Public Law 94-171) Summary File, which was among the first Census 2000 data products to be released and is used by each state to draw boundaries for legislative districts.[2]

The term "White" refers to people having origins in any of the original peoples of Europe, the Middle East, or North Africa. It includes people who reported "White" or wrote in entries such as Irish, German, Italian, Lebanese, Near Easterner, Arab, or Polish.

Data on race has been collected since the first U.S. decennial census in 1790. Whites have been enumerated in every census.

Figure 1.

Reproduction of the Question on Race From Census 2000

6. **What is this person's race?** *Mark ☒ one or more races* to indicate what this person considers himself/herself to be.

☐ White
☐ Black, African Am., or Negro
☐ American Indian or Alaska Native — *Print name of enrolled or principal tribe.*

☐ Asian Indian   ☐ Japanese   ☐ Native Hawaiian
☐ Chinese   ☐ Korean   ☐ Guamanian or Chamorro
☐ Filipino   ☐ Vietnamese   ☐ Samoan
☐ Other Asian — *Print race.*   ☐ Other Pacific Islander — *Print race.*

☐ Some other race — *Print race.*

Source: U.S. Census Bureau, Census 2000 questionnaire.

---

[1] In this report, the term "reported" is used to refer to the answers provided by respondents, as well as responses assigned during the editing and imputation processes.

[2] This report discusses data for 50 states and the District of Columbia, but not Puerto Rico. The Census 2000 Redistricting Data (Public Law 94-171) Summary File was released on a state-by-state basis in March 2001.

USCENSUSBUREAU

Helping You Make Informed Decisions

U.S. Department of Commerce
Economics and Statistics Administration
U.S. CENSUS BUREAU

United States Census 2000

The question on race was changed for Census 2000.

For Census 2000, the question on race was asked of every individual living in the United States and responses reflect self-identification. Respondents were asked to report the race or races they considered themselves and other members of their households to be.

The question on race for Census 2000 was different from the one for the 1990 census in several ways. Most significantly, respondents were given the option of selecting one or more race categories to indicate their racial identities.[3]

Because of these changes, the Census 2000 data on race are not directly comparable with data from the 1990 census or earlier censuses. Caution must be used when interpreting changes in the racial composition of the United States population over time.

The Census 2000 question on race included 15 separate response categories and 3 areas where respondents could write in a more specific race (see Figure 1). The response categories and write-in answers were combined to create the five standard Office of Management and Budget race categories plus the Census Bureau category of "Some other race." The six race categories include:

- White;
- Black or African American;

- American Indian and Alaska Native;
- Asian;
- Native Hawaiian and Other Pacific Islander; and
- Some other race.

For a complete explanation of the race categories used in Census 2000, see the Census 2000 Brief, *Overview of Race and Hispanic Origin*.[4]

The data collected by Census 2000 on race can be divided into two broad categories: the race *alone* population and the race *in combination* population.

People who responded to the question on race by indicating only one race are referred to as the race *alone* population, or the group who reported *only one* race. For example, respondents who marked only the White category on the census questionnaire would be included in the White *alone* population.

Individuals who chose more than one of the six race categories are referred to as the race *in combination* population, or as the group who reported *more than one* race. For example, respondents who reported they were "White *and* Black or African American" or "White *and* Asian *and* American Indian and Alaska Native"[5] would be included in the White *in combination* population.

The maximum number of people reporting White is reflected in the White *alone* or *in combination* category.

One way to define the White population is to combine those respondents

who reported only White with those who reported White as well as one or more other races. This creates the White *alone or in combination* population. Another way to think of the White *alone or in combination* population is the total number of people who identified entirely or partially as White. This group is also described as people who reported White, whether or not they reported any other races.

The White population: a snapshot.

Table 1 shows the number and percentage of respondents to Census 2000 who reported White alone as well as those who reported White and at least one other race.

In the total population, 211.5 million people, or 75.1 percent, reported only White. An additional 5.5 million people reported White and at least one other race. Within this group, the most common combinations were "White *and* Some other race" (40 percent), followed by "White *and* American Indian and Alaska Native" (20 percent), "White *and* Asian" (16 percent), and "White *and* Black or African American" (14 percent). These four combination categories accounted for 90 percent of all Whites who reported two or more races. Thus 216.9 million, or 77.1 percent of the total population, reported White alone or in combination with one or more other races.

The White population increased slower than the total population between 1990 and 2000.

Because of the changes made to the question on race for Census 2000, there are at least two ways to present the change in the total number of Whites in the United States. The difference in the White population between 1990 and 2000 using the race alone concept for 2000 and the difference in the White

---

[3] Other changes included terminology and formatting changes, such as spelling out "American" instead of "Amer." for the American Indian and Alaska Native category and adding "Native" to the Hawaiian response category. In the layout of the Census 2000 questionnaire, the seven Asian response categories were alphabetized and grouped together, as were the four Pacific Islander categories after the Native Hawaiian category. The three separate American Indian and Alaska Native identifiers in the 1990 census (i.e., Indian (Amer.), Eskimo, and Aleut) were combined into a single identifier in Census 2000. Also, American Indians and Alaska Natives could report more than one tribe.

[4] *Overview of Race and Hispanic Origin: 2000*, U.S. Census Bureau, Census 2000 Brief, C2KBR/01-1, March 2001, is available on the U.S. Census Bureau's Internet site at *www.census.gov/population/www/cen2000/briefs.html*.

[5] The race in combination categories are denoted by quotations around the combinations with the conjunction *and* in bold and italicized print to indicate the separate races that comprise the combination.

Table 1.
White Population: 2000

(For information on confidentiality protection, nonsampling error, and definitions, see *www.census.gov/prod/cen2000/doc/pl94-171.pdf*)

Race	Number	Percent of total population
Total population.................................	281,421,906	100.0
White alone or in combination with one or more other races...	216,930,975	77.1
White alone...	211,460,626	75.1
White in combination with one or more other races...	5,470,349	1.9
White; Some other race.........................	2,206,251	0.8
White; American Indian and Alaska Native.......	1,082,683	0.4
White; Asian......................................	868,395	0.3
White; Black or African American...............	784,764	0.3
All other combinations including White..........	528,256	0.2
Not White alone or in combination with one or more other races...	64,490,931	22.9

Source: U.S. Census Bureau, Census 2000 Redistricting Data (Public Law 94-171) Summary File, Table PL1.

Figure 2.
Percent Distribution of the White Population by Region: 2000

(For information on confidentiality protection, nonsampling error, and definitions, see *www.census.gov/prod/cen2000/doc/pl94-171.pdf*)

Legend: ■ Northeast ■ Midwest ■ South ■ West

	Northeast	Midwest	South	West
White alone	19.6	25.5	34.4	20.5
White alone or in combination	19.5	25.2	34.3	21.0

Source: U.S. Census Bureau, Census 2000 Redistricting Data (Public Law 94-171) Summary File, Table PL1.

THE GEOGRAPHIC DISTRIBUTION OF THE WHITE POPULATION

The following discussion of the geographic distribution of the White population focuses on the White alone or in combination population. As the upper bound of the White population, this group includes all respondents who reported White, whether or not they reported any other race.[6] Hereafter in the text of this section, the term "White" will be used to refer to those who reported White, whether or not they reported any other race. However, in the tables and graphs, data for both the White alone and the White alone or in combination populations are shown.

The majority of the White population lived in the South and the Midwest.

According to Census 2000, of all respondents who reported White, 34 percent lived in the South, 25 percent lived in the Midwest, 21 percent lived in the West, and 20 percent lived in the Northeast (see Figure 2).[7]

[6] As a matter of policy, the Census Bureau does not advocate the use of the *alone or in combination* population over the *alone* population. The use of the *alone or in combination* population in this section does not imply that it is a preferred method of presenting or analyzing data. It is only one of many ways that the data on race from Census 2000 can be presented and discussed.

[7] The South region includes the states of Alabama, Arkansas, Delaware, Florida, Georgia, Kentucky, Louisiana, Maryland, Mississippi, North Carolina, Oklahoma, South Carolina, Tennessee, Texas, Virginia, and West Virginia and the District of Columbia. The Midwest region includes the states of Illinois, Indiana, Iowa, Kansas, Michigan, Minnesota, Missouri, Nebraska, North Dakota, Ohio, South Dakota, and Wisconsin. The West region includes the states of Alaska, Arizona, California, Colorado, Hawaii, Idaho, Montana, Nevada, New Mexico, Oregon, Utah, Washington, and Wyoming. The Northeast region includes the states of Connecticut, Maine, Massachusetts, New Hampshire, New Jersey, New York, Pennsylvania, Rhode Island, and Vermont.

population between 1990 and 2000 using the race alone or in combination concept for 2000 provides a "minimum-maximum" range for the change in the White population between 1990 and 2000.

The 1990 census showed there were 199.7 million Whites. Using the White alone population in 2000 shows an increase of 11.8 million, or 5.9 percent, in the total White

population between 1990 and 2000. If the White alone or in combination population is used, an increase of 17.2 million, or 8.6 percent, results. Thus, from 1990 to 2000, the minimum-maximum range for the increase in the White population was 5.9 percent to 8.6 percent. In comparison, the total population grew by 13.2 percent, from 248.7 million in 1990 to 281.4 million in 2000.

Table 2.
White Population for the United States, Regions, and States, and for Puerto Rico: 1990 and 2000

(For information on confidentiality protection, nonsampling error, and definitions, see *www.census.gov/prod/cen2000/doc/pl94-171.pdf*)

Area	1990 White population			2000 White alone population			White alone or in combination population		White in combination population only as a percent of White alone or in combination population
	Total population	Number	Percent of total population	Total population	Number	Percent of total population	Number	Percent of total population	
United States	**248,709,873**	**199,686,370**	**80.3**	**281,421,906**	**211,460,626**	**75.1**	**216,930,975**	**77.1**	**2.5**
Region									
Northeast	50,809,229	42,068,904	82.8	53,594,378	41,533,502	77.5	42,395,625	79.1	2.0
Midwest.	59,668,632	52,017,957	87.2	64,392,776	53,833,651	83.6	54,709,407	85.0	1.6
South	85,445,930	65,582,199	76.8	100,236,820	72,819,399	72.6	74,303,744	74.1	2.0
West	52,786,082	40,017,010	75.8	63,197,932	43,274,074	68.5	45,522,199	72.0	4.9
State									
Alabama	4,040,587	2,975,797	73.6	4,447,100	3,162,808	71.1	3,199,953	72.0	1.2
Alaska.	550,043	415,492	75.5	626,932	434,534	69.3	463,999	74.0	6.4
Arizona	3,665,228	2,963,186	80.8	5,130,632	3,873,611	75.5	3,998,154	77.9	3.1
Arkansas.	2,350,725	1,944,744	82.7	2,673,400	2,138,598	80.0	2,170,534	81.2	1.5
California.	29,760,021	20,524,327	69.0	33,871,648	20,170,059	59.5	21,490,973	63.4	6.1
Colorado	3,294,394	2,905,474	88.2	4,301,261	3,560,005	82.8	3,665,638	85.2	2.9
Connecticut.	3,287,116	2,859,353	87.0	3,405,565	2,780,355	81.6	2,835,974	83.3	2.0
Delaware.	666,168	535,094	80.3	783,600	584,773	74.6	594,425	75.9	1.6
District of Columbia. .	606,900	179,667	29.6	572,059	176,101	30.8	184,309	32.2	4.5
Florida.	12,937,926	10,749,285	83.1	15,982,378	12,465,029	78.0	12,734,292	79.7	2.1
Georgia.	6,478,216	4,600,148	71.0	8,186,453	5,327,281	65.1	5,412,371	66.1	1.6
Hawaii	1,108,229	369,616	33.4	1,211,537	294,102	24.3	476,162	39.3	38.2
Idaho.	1,006,749	950,451	94.4	1,293,953	1,177,304	91.0	1,201,113	92.8	2.0
Illinois	11,430,602	8,952,978	78.3	12,419,293	9,125,471	73.5	9,322,831	75.1	2.1
Indiana	5,544,159	5,020,700	90.6	6,080,485	5,320,022	87.5	5,387,174	88.6	1.2
Iowa	2,776,755	2,683,090	96.6	2,926,324	2,748,640	93.9	2,777,183	94.9	1.0
Kansas	2,477,574	2,231,986	90.1	2,688,418	2,313,944	86.1	2,363,412	87.9	2.1
Kentucky	3,685,296	3,391,832	92.0	4,041,769	3,640,889	90.1	3,678,740	91.0	1.0
Louisiana.	4,219,973	2,839,138	67.3	4,468,976	2,856,161	63.9	2,894,983	64.8	1.3
Maine	1,227,928	1,208,360	98.4	1,274,923	1,236,014	96.9	1,247,776	97.9	0.9
Maryland.	4,781,468	3,393,964	71.0	5,296,486	3,391,308	64.0	3,465,697	65.4	2.1
Massachusetts	6,016,425	5,405,374	89.8	6,349,097	5,367,286	84.5	5,472,809	86.2	1.9
Michigan	9,295,297	7,756,086	83.4	9,938,444	7,966,053	80.2	8,133,283	81.8	2.1
Minnesota	4,375,099	4,130,395	94.4	4,919,479	4,400,282	89.4	4,466,325	90.8	1.5
Mississippi.	2,573,216	1,633,461	63.5	2,844,658	1,746,099	61.4	1,761,658	61.9	0.9
Missouri.	5,117,073	4,486,228	87.7	5,595,211	4,748,083	84.9	4,819,487	86.1	1.5
Montana	799,065	741,111	92.7	902,195	817,229	90.6	831,978	92.2	1.8
Nebraska.	1,578,385	1,480,558	93.8	1,711,263	1,533,261	89.6	1,554,164	90.8	1.3
Nevada	1,201,833	1,012,695	84.3	1,998,257	1,501,886	75.2	1,565,866	78.4	4.1
New Hampshire	1,109,252	1,087,433	98.0	1,235,786	1,186,851	96.0	1,198,927	97.0	1.0
New Jersey	7,730,188	6,130,465	79.3	8,414,350	6,104,705	72.6	6,261,187	74.4	2.5
New Mexico	1,515,069	1,146,028	75.6	1,819,046	1,214,253	66.8	1,272,116	69.9	4.5
New York.	17,990,455	13,385,255	74.4	18,976,457	12,893,689	67.9	13,275,834	70.0	2.9
North Carolina.	6,628,637	5,008,491	75.6	8,049,313	5,804,656	72.1	5,884,608	73.1	1.4
North Dakota.	638,800	604,142	94.6	642,200	593,181	92.4	599,918	93.4	1.1
Ohio	10,847,115	9,521,756	87.8	11,353,140	9,645,453	85.0	9,779,512	86.1	1.4
Oklahoma	3,145,585	2,583,512	82.1	3,450,654	2,628,434	76.2	2,770,035	80.3	5.1
Oregon	2,842,321	2,636,787	92.8	3,421,399	2,961,623	86.6	3,055,670	89.3	3.1
Pennsylvania.	11,881,643	10,520,201	88.5	12,281,054	10,484,203	85.4	10,596,409	86.3	1.1
Rhode Island.	1,003,464	917,375	91.4	1,048,319	891,191	85.0	910,630	86.9	2.1
South Carolina	3,486,703	2,406,974	69.0	4,012,012	2,695,560	67.2	2,727,208	68.0	1.2
South Dakota	696,004	637,515	91.6	754,844	669,404	88.7	678,604	89.9	1.4
Tennessee.	4,877,185	4,048,068	83.0	5,689,283	4,563,310	80.2	4,617,553	81.2	1.2
Texas	16,986,510	12,774,762	75.2	20,851,820	14,799,505	71.0	15,240,387	73.1	2.9
Utah	1,722,850	1,615,845	93.8	2,233,169	1,992,975	89.2	2,034,448	91.1	2.0
Vermont	562,758	555,088	98.6	608,827	589,208	96.8	596,079	97.9	1.2
Virginia	6,187,358	4,791,739	77.4	7,078,515	5,120,110	72.3	5,233,601	73.9	2.2
Washington.	4,866,692	4,308,937	88.5	5,894,121	4,821,823	81.8	5,003,180	84.9	3.6
West Virginia.	1,793,477	1,725,523	96.2	1,808,344	1,718,777	95.0	1,733,390	95.9	0.8
Wisconsin	4,891,769	4,512,523	92.2	5,363,675	4,769,857	88.9	4,827,514	90.0	1.2
Wyoming.	453,588	427,061	94.2	493,782	454,670	92.1	462,902	93.7	1.8
Puerto Rico	**3,522,037**	**(X)**	**(X)**	**3,808,610**	**3,064,862**	**80.5**	**3,199,547**	**84.0**	**4.2**

X Not applicable.

Source: U.S. Census Bureau, Census 2000 Redistricting Data (Public Law 94-171) Summary File, Table PL1; 1990 Census of Population, *General Population Characteristics* (1990 CP-1).

Although the South and Midwest had the largest White populations, the Northeast and Midwest had the highest proportion of Whites in their total populations: 79 percent of all respondents in the Northeast and 85 percent in the Midwest reported White, compared with 74 percent in the South and 72 percent in the West.

Over half of all people who reported White lived in just ten states.

The ten states with the largest White populations in 2000 were California, Texas, New York, Florida, Pennsylvania, Ohio, Illinois, Michigan, New Jersey, and North Carolina (see Table 2). Combined, these states represented 52 percent of the total White population. These ten states were also the ten states with the largest total populations.

There were fourteen states where Whites represented 90 percent or more of the total population, led by the northeastern states of Vermont (98 percent), Maine (98 percent), and New Hampshire (97 percent). The other eleven states included the midwestern states of Iowa, North Dakota, Nebraska, Minnesota, and Wisconsin; the southern states of West Virginia and Kentucky; and the western states of Wyoming, Idaho, Montana, and Utah.

There were eight states where Whites represented less than 70 percent of the population, including Hawaii, Mississippi, California, Louisiana, Maryland, Georgia, South Carolina, and New Mexico. While California had the largest White population of all states, it ranked 48th among the 50 states in the proportion who reported White, with only 63 percent of respondents doing so. Hawaii (39 percent) was the only state in which the White population was less than one-half of the total population. Approximately one-third

(32 percent) of all respondents in the District of Columbia, a state equivalent, reported White.

The White population was concentrated in counties in the Northeast and Midwest.

Reflecting the fact that the White population represents about three-quarters of the United States population, the majority of all counties throughout the country had a high percentage of White respondents in their populations (see Figure 3). However, several distinct patterns can be seen in the national distribution of Whites.

The White population was generally most prevalent in counties across the northern half of the country with several southward projections: 1) along the boundary between the Appalachian/Upland South and Coastal/Lowland South; 2) throughout West Texas and the Rio Grande Valley; and 3) southern Arizona and New Mexico.

In addition, Whites were also concentrated in counties throughout Florida, representing a southern outlier of the more northerly concentration of Whites. Another distinctive boundary was across central Alaska, with Whites concentrated in the southeastern portion of the state.

Counties with percentages of Whites lower than the percentage for the country were concentrated across the Lowland and Coastal South. This band of counties extended from East Texas through Louisiana and southern Arkansas, across Mississippi, Alabama, and Georgia, then northward through the Piedmont and Coastal portions of the Carolinas, Virginia, Maryland, and Delaware. A northerly extension of this pattern included counties in New Jersey as well as in and around New York City.

Additional concentrations of counties with lower percentages of Whites were in New Mexico, northeastern Arizona, and a band of counties extending from southwestern Arizona through southern California, northward along the California coast, and through the Central Valley of California.

Elsewhere, counties with a low percentage of Whites were scattered but, in general, were found in large metropolitan areas, such as Chicago (Cook County, Illinois), Detroit (Wayne County, Michigan), Kansas City (Jackson County, Missouri and Wyandotte County, Kansas), and Miami (Miami-Dade County, Florida), as well as in nonmetropolitan counties in the Dakotas, Montana, and eastern Oklahoma. All counties in Hawaii had percentages of Whites lower than the national level.

The places with the largest White populations were New York, Los Angeles, Chicago, and Houston.

Census 2000 showed that, of all places[8] in the United States with populations of 100,000 or more, New York had the largest White population with over 3.8 million (see Table 3). Los Angeles, Chicago, and Houston each had White populations of between 1 and 2 million. These places were also the four largest places in the United States.

Although New York, Los Angeles, Chicago, and Houston had the largest White populations, only about half of all respondents in these places reported White, ranging from 44 percent in Chicago to

_____

[8] Census 2000 showed 245 places in the United States with 100,000 or more population. They included 238 incorporated places (including four city-county consolidations) and seven census designated places that were not legally incorporated. For a list of these places by state, see www.census.gov/population/www/cen2000/phc-t6.html.

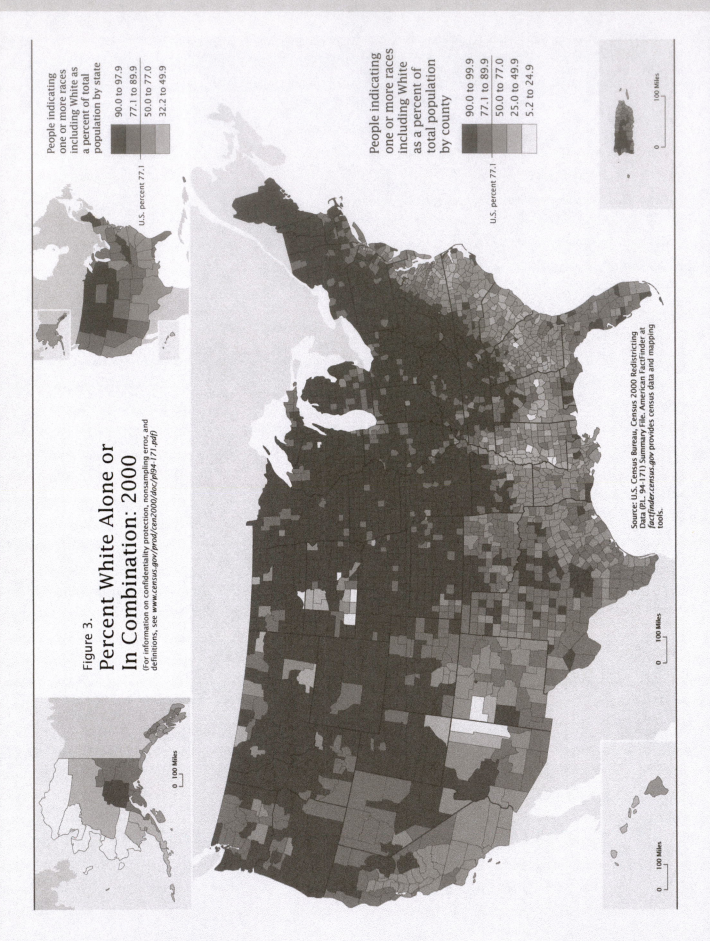

Figure 3.
Percent White Alone or In Combination: 2000

(For information on confidentiality protection, nonsampling error, and definitions, see *www.census.gov/prod/cen2000/doc/pl94-171.pdf*)

People indicating one or more races including White as a percent of total population by state

90.0 to 97.9
77.1 to 89.9
50.0 to 77.0
32.2 to 49.9

U.S. percent 77.1

People indicating one or more races including White as a percent of total population by county

90.0 to 99.9
77.1 to 89.9
50.0 to 77.0
25.0 to 49.9
5.2 to 24.9

U.S. percent 77.1

Source: U.S. Census Bureau, Census 2000 Redistricting Data (P.L. 94-171) Summary File. American FactFinder at *factfinder.census.gov* provides census data and mapping tools.

0   100 Miles

0   100 Miles

0   100 Miles

0   100 Miles

Table 3.
Ten Largest Places in Total Population and in White Population: 2000

(For information on confidentiality protection, nonsampling error, and definitions, see www.census.gov/prod/cen2000/doc/pl94-171.pdf)

Place	Total population		White alone		White alone or in combination		Percent of total population	
	Rank	Number	Rank	Number	Rank	Number	White alone	White alone or in combination
New York, NY.....	1	8,008,278	1	3,576,385	1	3,806,508	44.7	47.5
Los Angeles, CA ..	2	3,694,820	2	1,734,036	2	1,891,358	46.9	51.2
Chicago, IL	3	2,896,016	3	1,215,315	3	1,282,320	42.0	44.3
Houston, TX	4	1,953,631	4	962,610	4	1,012,413	49.3	51.8
Philadelphia, PA...	5	1,517,550	8	683,267	8	703,584	45.0	46.4
Phoenix, AZ	6	1,321,045	5	938,853	5	975,418	71.1	73.8
San Diego, CA....	7	1,223,400	7	736,207	7	781,652	60.2	63.9
Dallas, TX	8	1,188,580	9	604,209	9	630,419	50.8	53.0
San Antonio, TX...	9	1,144,646	6	774,708	6	810,913	67.7	70.8
Detroit, MI........	10	951,270	108	116,599	98	131,691	12.3	13.8
Indianapolis, IN ...	12	791,926	10	549,100	10	559,773	69.3	70.7

Source: U.S. Census Bureau, Census 2000 Redistricting Data (Public Law 94-171) Summary File, Table PL1.

Figure 4.
Ten Places of 100,000 or More Population With the Highest Percentage of Whites: 2000

(For information on confidentiality protection, nonsampling error, and definitions, see www.census/gov/prod/cen2000/doc/pl94-171.pdf)

Legend: White alone or in combination / White alone

Place	White alone or in combination	White alone
Livonia, MI	96.5	95.5
Cape Coral, FL	94.4	93.0
Boise City, ID	94.4	92.2
Independence, MO	94.0	91.9
Scottsdale, AZ	93.6	92.2
Springfield, MO	93.5	91.7
Cedar Rapids, IA	93.5	91.9
Sioux Falls, SD	93.4	91.9
Warren, MI	93.3	91.3
Manchester, NH	93.3	91.7

Source: U.S. Census Bureau, Census 2000 Redistricting Data (Public Law 94-171) Summary File, Table PL1.

52 percent in Houston. Of the ten largest places in the United States, Phoenix had the largest proportion of Whites with 74 percent, followed by 71 percent in San Antonio.

Although Detroit was ranked as the tenth largest place in the United States, it ranked 98th in the size of its White population, with only 14 percent of all respondents reporting White. Indianapolis, with 71 percent of its population report-ing White, had the tenth largest White population of all places.

Among places of 100,000 or more population, the highest proportion of Whites was in Livonia, Michigan, with 97 percent (see Figure 4). Each of the ten places with the highest proportion of Whites had popula-tions over 93 percent White. Six of these places were in the Midwest, two in the West, and one each in the South and Northeast.

ADDITIONAL FINDINGS ON THE WHITE POPULATION

What proportion of respondents reporting White also reported a Hispanic origin?

The Office of Management and Budget defines Hispanic or Latino as "a person of Cuban, Mexican, Puerto Rican, South or Central American, or other Spanish culture or origin, regardless of race." In data collection and presentation, federal agencies use two ethnicities: "Hispanic or Latino" and "Not Hispanic or Latino." Race and eth-nicity are considered two separate and distinct concepts by the federal system. Hispanics may be of any race, and Whites can be Hispanic or not Hispanic.

According to Census 2000, the overwhelming majority of the White population was non-Hispanic: 92 percent of those who reported only White and 91 percent of those

Table 4.
White Population by Hispanic or Latino Origin: 2000

(For information on confidentiality protection, nonsampling error, and definitions, see *www.census.gov/prod/cen2000/doc/pl94-171.pdf*)

Race and Hispanic or Latino origin	Alone			In combination with one or more other races			Alone or in combination with one or more other races		
	Number	Percent of total	Percent of White population	Number	Percent of total	Percent of White population	Number	Percent of total	Percent of White population
Total population....	274,595,678	100.0	(X)	6,826,228	100.0	(X)	281,421,906	100.0	(X)
White	211,460,626	77.0	100.0	5,470,349	80.1	100.0	216,930,975	77.1	100.0
Hispanic or Latino	16,907,852	6.2	8.0	1,845,223	27.0	33.7	18,753,075	6.7	8.6
Not Hispanic or Latino .	194,552,774	70.9	92.0	3,625,126	53.1	66.3	198,177,900	70.4	91.4

X Not applicable.

Source: U.S. Census Bureau, Census 2000 Redistricting Data (Public Law 94-171) Summary File, Tables PL1 and PL2.

Table 5.
Most Frequent Combinations of White With One or More Other Races by Hispanic or Latino Origin: 2000

(For information on confidentiality protection, nonsampling error, and definitions, see *www.census.gov/prod/cen2000/doc/pl94-171.pdf*)

White in combination	Total		Hispanic or Latino		Not Hispanic or Latino	
	Number	Percent	Number	Percent	Number	Percent
Total number reporting White and one or more other races.........................	5,470,349	100.0	1,845,223	100.0	3,625,126	100.0
White; Black or African American...............	784,764	14.3	87,687	4.8	697,077	19.2
White; American Indian and Alaska Native.......	1,082,683	19.8	113,445	6.1	969,238	26.7
White; Asian..................................	868,395	15.9	57,155	3.1	811,240	22.4
White; Some other race......................	2,206,251	40.3	1,474,532	79.9	731,719	20.2
All other combinations including White..........	528,256	9.7	112,404	6.1	415,852	11.5

Source: U.S. Census Bureau, Census 2000 Redistricting Data (Public Law 94-171) Summary File, Tables PL1 and PL2.

who reported White and at least one other race (see Table 4). However, only 66 percent of all respondents who reported White in combination with one or more other races were non-Hispanic.

The White non-Hispanic population represented 71 percent of people who reported exactly one race and 70 percent of the total population. Of the 6.8 million people who reported two or more races, 53 percent were non-Hispanics who included White as one of the races reported.

Which other races were White non-Hispanics most likely to report?

Among White non-Hispanics who reported more than one race, most indicated they were "White *and* American Indian and Alaska Native" (27 percent), followed by "White *and* Asian" (22 percent), "White *and* Some other race" (20 percent), and "White *and* Black or African American" (19 percent) as shown in Table 5. These four combination categories accounted for 88 percent of all White non-Hispanics who reported two or more races.

Which other races were White Hispanics most likely to report?

Among White Hispanics who reported more than one race, the majority indicated they were "White *and* Some other race" (80 percent), followed by "White *and* American Indian and Alaska Native" (6 percent), "White *and* Black or African American" (5 percent), and "White *and* Asian" (3 percent) as shown in Table 5.

Table 6.
People Who Reported White by Age and Hispanic or Latino Origin: 2000

(For information on confidentiality protection, nonsampling error, and definitions, see *www.census.gov/prod/cen2000/doc/pl94-171.pdf*)

Age and Hispanic or Latino origin	White alone or in combination with one or more races		White alone		White in combination with one or more other races	
	Number	Percent	Number	Percent	Number	Percent
Total	216,930,975	100.0	211,460,626	97.5	5,470,349	2.5
Hispanic or Latino	18,753,075	100.0	16,907,852	90.2	1,845,223	9.8
Not Hispanic or Latino	198,177,900	100.0	194,552,774	98.2	3,625,126	1.8
Under 18	51,963,909	100.0	49,598,289	95.4	2,365,620	4.6
Hispanic or Latino	6,347,306	100.0	5,571,202	87.8	776,104	12.2
Not Hispanic or Latino	45,616,603	100.0	44,027,087	96.5	1,589,516	3.5
18 and over	164,967,066	100.0	161,862,337	98.1	3,104,729	1.9
Hispanic or Latino	12,405,769	100.0	11,336,650	91.4	1,069,119	8.6
Not Hispanic or Latino	152,561,297	100.0	150,525,687	98.7	2,035,610	1.3

Source: U.S. Census Bureau, Census 2000 Redistricting Data (Public Law 94-171) Summary File, Tables PL1, PL2, PL3, and PL4.

Figure 5.
Percent Under Age 18 of People Who Reported White by Hispanic or Latino Origin: 2000

(For information on confidentiality protection, nonsampling error, and definitions, see *www.census.gov/prod/cen2000/doc/pl94-171.pdf*)

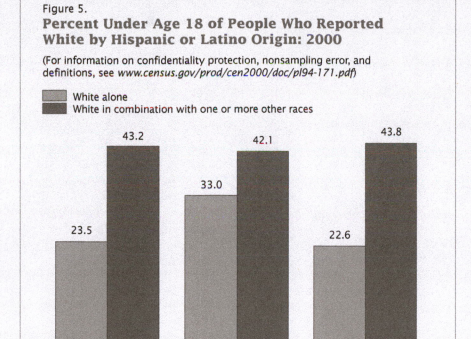

Source: U.S. Census Bureau, Census 2000 Redistricting Data (Public Law 94-171) Summary File, Tables PL3 and PL4.

Which group was more likely to report more than one race, White non-Hispanics or White Hispanics?

White Hispanics were more likely than White non-Hispanics to report two or more races. According to Census 2000, 18.8 million people reported White and Hispanic. Of those, 9.8 percent reported White with one or more other races (see Table 6). In contrast, of the 198.2 million Whites who reported as not Hispanic, only 1.8 percent reported at least one other race.

Were there differences in the age distribution between people who reported only White and people who reported White and one or more other races?

People who reported White as well as one or more other races were more likely to be under 18 than those reporting only White (see Figure 5). Of the 5.5 million people who reported White with at least one other race, 43 percent were under 18. This proportion is higher than the White alone population. Of the 211.5 million people who reported only White, 24 percent were under 18.

When the White population is cross-tabulated by Hispanic origin, this pattern persists. For both White non-Hispanics and White Hispanics, a higher proportion of those reporting more than one race was under 18 when compared with those reporting White alone. Among the 3.6 million White non-Hispanics who reported more than one race, 44 percent were under 18. Of the 194.6 million people who reported

White alone and not Hispanic, 23 percent were under 18. Similarly, among the 1.8 million White Hispanics who reported two or more races, 42 percent were under 18. Of the 16.9 million White Hispanics who reported one race, 33 percent were under 18.

ABOUT CENSUS 2000

Why did Census 2000 ask the question on race?

The Census Bureau collects data on race to fulfill a variety of legislative and program requirements. Data on race are used in the legislative redistricting process carried out by the States and in monitoring local jurisdictions' compliance with the Voting Rights Act. These data are also essential for evaluating Federal programs that promote equal access to employment, education, and housing and for assessing racial disparities in health and exposure to environmental risks. More broadly, data on race are critical for research that underlies many policy decisions at all levels of government.

How do data from the question on race benefit me, my family, and my community?

All levels of government need information on race to implement and evaluate programs, or enforce laws. Examples include: the Native American Programs Act, the Equal Employment Opportunity Act, the Civil Rights Act, the Voting Rights Act, the Public Health Act, the Healthcare Improvement Act, the Job Partnership Training Act, the Equal Credit Opportunity Act, the Fair Housing Act, and the Census Redistricting Data Program.

Both public and private organizations use race information to find areas where groups may need special services and to plan and implement education, housing, health, and other programs that address these needs. For example, a school system might use this information to design cultural activities that reflect the diversity in their community. Or a business could use it to select the mix of merchandise it will sell in a new store. Census information also helps identify areas where residents might need services of particular importance to certain racial or ethnic groups, such as screening for hypertension or diabetes.

FOR MORE INFORMATION

For more information on race in the United States, visit the U.S. Census Bureau's Internet site at *www.census.gov/population/ www/socdemo/race.html.*

Race data from the Census 2000 Redistricting Data (Public Law 94-171) Summary File were released on a state-by-state basis during March 2001. The Census 2000 Redistricting data are available on the Internet via *factfinder.census.gov* and for purchase on CD-ROM and later on DVD.

For information on confidentiality protection, nonsampling error, and definitions, also see *www.census.gov/prod/cen2000/doc/ pl94-171.pdf* or contact our Customer Services Center at 301-763-INFO (4636).

For more information on specific races in the United States, go to *www.census.gov* and click on "Minority Links." This Web page includes information about Census 2000 and provides links to reports based on past censuses and surveys focusing on the social and economic characteristics of the Black or African American, American Indian and Alaska Native, Asian, and Native Hawaiian and Other Pacific Islander populations.

Information on other population and housing topics is presented in the Census 2000 Brief series, located on the U.S. Census Bureau's Web site at *www.census.gov/ population/www/cen2000/briefs.html.* This series presents information about race, Hispanic origin, age, sex, household type, housing tenure, and other social, economic, and housing characteristics.

For more information about Census 2000, including data products, call our Customer Services Center at 301-763-INFO (4636), or e-mail *webmaster@census.gov.*

The Black Population: 2000

Issued August 2001

C2KBR/01-5

Census 2000 Brief

By
Jesse McKinnon

Census 2000 showed that the United States population on April 1, 2000 was 281.4 million. Of the total, 36.4 million, or 12.9 percent, reported[1] Black or African American. This number includes 34.7 million people, or 12.3 percent, who reported only Black in addition to 1.8 million people, or 0.6 percent, who reported Black as well as one or more other races. The term Black is used in the text of this report to refer to the Black or African American population, while Black or African American is used in the text tables and graphs. Census 2000 asked separate questions on race and Hispanic or Latino origin. Hispanics who reported their race as Black, either alone or in combination with one or more other races, are included in the numbers for Blacks.

This report, part of a series that analyzes population and housing data collected from Census 2000, provides a portrait of the Black population in the United States and discusses its distribution at both the national and subnational levels. It is based on the Census 2000 Redistricting Data (Public Law 94-171) Summary File, which was among the first Census 2000 data products to be released and is used by each state to draw boundaries for legislative districts.[2]

The term "Black or African American" refers to people having origins in any of the Black race groups of Africa. It includes people who reported "Black, African Am., or Negro" or wrote in entries such as African American, Afro American, Nigerian, or Haitian.

Data on race has been collected since the first U.S. decennial census in 1790.

Figure 1.
Reproduction of the Question on Race From Census 2000

6. What is this person's race? *Mark* ☒ *one or more races* to indicate what this person considers himself/herself to be.

☐ White
☐ Black, African Am., or Negro
☐ American Indian or Alaska Native — *Print name of enrolled or principal tribe.* ↘

☐ Asian Indian   ☐ Japanese   ☐ Native Hawaiian
☐ Chinese   ☐ Korean   ☐ Guamanian or Chamorro
☐ Filipino   ☐ Vietnamese   ☐ Samoan
☐ Other Asian — *Print race.* ↘   ☐ Other Pacific Islander — *Print race.* ↘

☐ Some other race — *Print race.* ↘

Source: U.S. Census Bureau, Census 2000 questionnaire.

---

[1] In this report, the term "reported" is used to refer to the answers provided by respondents, as well as responses assigned during the editing and imputation processes.

[2] This report discusses data for 50 states and the District of Columbia, but not Puerto Rico. The Census 2000 Redistricting Data (Public Law 94-171) Summary File was released on a state-by-state basis in March 2001.

USCENSUSBUREAU

Helping You Make Informed Decisions

U.S. Department of Commerce
Economics and Statistics Administration
U.S. CENSUS BUREAU

United States
Census
2000

Blacks have been enumerated in every census.

The question on race was changed for Census 2000.

For Census 2000, the question on race was asked of every individual living in the United States and responses reflect self-identification. Respondents were asked to report the race or races they considered themselves and other members of their households to be.

The question on race for Census 2000 was different from the one for the 1990 census in several ways. Most significantly, respondents were given the option of selecting one or more race categories to indicate their racial identities.[3]

Because of these changes, the Census 2000 data on race are not directly comparable with data from the 1990 census or earlier censuses. Caution must be used when interpreting changes in the racial composition of the United States population over time.

The Census 2000 question on race included 15 separate response categories and 3 areas where respondents could write in a more specific race (see Figure 1). The response categories and write-in answers were combined to create the five standard Office of Management and Budget race categories plus the Census Bureau category of "Some

other race." The six race categories include:

- White;
- Black or African American;
- American Indian and Alaska Native;
- Asian;
- Native Hawaiian and Other Pacific Islander; and
- Some other race.

For a complete explanation of the race categories used in Census 2000, see the Census 2000 Brief, *Overview of Race and Hispanic Origin*.[4]

The data collected by Census 2000 on race can be divided into two broad categories: the race *alone* population and the race *in combination* population.

People who responded to the question on race by indicating only one race are referred to as the race *alone* population, or the group who reported *only one* race. For example, respondents who marked only the Black, African American, or Negro category on the census questionnaire would be included in the Black *alone* population.

Individuals who chose more than one of the six race categories are referred to as the race *in combination* population, or as the group who reported *more than one* race. For example, respondents who reported they were "Black or African American *and* White" or "Black or African American *and* Asian *and* American Indian and Alaska Native"[5]

would be included in the Black *in combination* population.

The maximum number of people reporting Black is reflected in the Black *alone or in combination* category.

One way to define the Black population is to combine those respondents who reported only Black with those who reported Black as well as one or more other races. This creates the Black *alone or in combination* population. Another way to think of the Black *alone or in combination* population is the total number of people who identified entirely or partially as Black. This group is also described as people who reported Black, whether or not they reported any other races.

The Black population: a snapshot.

Table 1 shows the number and percentage of respondents to Census 2000 who reported Black alone as well as those who reported Black and at least one other race.

In the total population, 34.7 million people, or 12.3 percent, reported only Black. An additional 1.8 million people reported Black and at least one other race. Within this group, the most common combinations were "Black *and* White" (45 percent), followed by "Black *and* Some other race" (24 percent), "Black *and* American Indian and Alaska Native" (10 percent), and "Black *and* White *and* American Indian and Alaska Native" (6 percent). These four combination categories accounted for 85 percent of all Blacks who reported two or more races. Thus, 36.4 million, or 12.9 percent of the total population, reported Black alone or in combination with one or more other races.

---

[3] Other changes included terminology and formatting changes, such as spelling out "American" instead of "Amer." for the American Indian and Alaska Native category and adding "Native" to the Hawaiian response category. In the layout of the Census 2000 questionnaire, the seven Asian response categories were alphabetized and grouped together, as were the four Pacific Islander categories after the Native Hawaiian category. The three separate American Indian and Alaska Native identifiers in the 1990 census (i.e., Indian (Amer.), Eskimo, and Aleut) were combined into a single identifier in Census 2000. Also, American Indians and Alaska Natives could report more than one tribe.

---

[4] *Overview of Race and Hispanic Origin: 2000*, U.S. Census Bureau, Census 2000 Brief, C2KBR/01-1, March 2001, is available on the U.S. Census Bureau's Internet site at *www.census.gov/population/www/cen2000/briefs.html*.

[5] The race in combination categories are denoted by quotations around the combinations with the conjunction *and* in bold and italicized print to indicate the separate races that comprise the combination.

Table 1.
Black or African American Population: 2000

(For information on confidentiality protection, nonsampling error, and definitions, see
www.census.gov/prod/cen2000/doc/pl94-171.pdf)

Race	Number	Percent of total population
Total population	**281,421,906**	100.0
Black or African American alone or in combination with one or more other races	36,419,434	12.9
Black or African American alone	34,658,190	12.3
Black or African American in combination with one or more other races	1,761,244	0.6
Black or African American; White	784,764	0.3
Black or African American; Some other race	417,249	0.1
Black or African American; American Indian and Alaska Native	182,494	0.1
Black or African American; White; American Indian and Alaska Native	112,207	-
All other combinations including Black or African American	264,530	0.1
Not Black or African American alone or in combination with one or more other races	245,002,472	87.1

- Percentage rounds to 0.0.

Source: U.S. Census Bureau, Census 2000 Redistricting Data (Public Law 94-171) Summary File, Table PL1.

Figure 2.
Percent Distribution of the Black or African American Population by Region: 2000

(For information on confidentiality protection, nonsampling error, and definitions, see www.census.gov/prod/cen2000/doc/pl94-171.pdf)

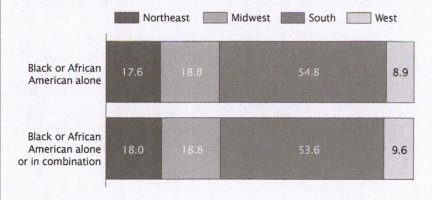

Source: U.S. Census Bureau, Census 2000 Redistricting Data (Public Law 94-171) Summary File, Table PL1.

The Black population increased faster than the total population between 1990 and 2000.

Because of the changes made to the question on race for Census 2000, there are at least two ways to present the change in the total number of Blacks in the United States. The difference in the Black population between 1990 and 2000 using the race alone concept for 2000 and the difference in the Black population between 1990 and 2000 using the race alone or in combination concept for 2000 provides a "minimum-maximum" range for the change in the Black population between 1990 and 2000.

The 1990 census showed there were 30.0 million Blacks. Using the Black alone population in 2000 shows an increase of 4.7 million, or 15.6 percent, in the total Black population between 1990 and 2000. If the Black alone or in combination population is used, an increase of 6.4 million, or 21.5 percent, results. Thus, from 1990 to 2000, the minimum-maximum range for the increase in the Black population was 15.6 percent to 21.5 percent. In comparison, the total population grew by 13.2 percent, from 248.7 million in 1990 to 281.4 million in 2000.

THE GEOGRAPHIC DISTRIBUTION OF THE BLACK POPULATION

The following discussion of the geographic distribution of the Black population focuses on the Black alone or in combination population. As the upper bound of the Black population, this group includes all respondents who reported Black, whether or not they reported any other race.[6] Hereafter in the text of this section, the term "Black" will be used to refer to those who reported Black, whether or not they reported any other race. However, in the tables and graphs, data for both the Black alone and the Black alone or in combination populations are shown.

The majority of the Black population lived in the South.

According to Census 2000, of all respondents who reported Black, 54 percent lived in the South (see Figure 2), 19 percent lived in the Midwest, 18 percent lived in the

---

[6] As a matter of policy, the Census Bureau does not advocate the use of the *alone or in combination* population over the *alone* population. The use of the *alone or in combination* population in this section does not imply that it is a preferred method of presenting or analyzing data. It is only one of many ways that the data on race from Census 2000 can be presented and discussed.

Table 2.
Black or African American Population for the United States, Regions, and States, and for Puerto Rico: 1990 and 2000

(For information on confidentiality protection, nonsampling error, and definitions, see *www.census.gov/prod/cen2000/doc/pl94-171.pdf*)

Area	1990			2000					
		Black or African American population			Black or African American alone population		Black or African American alone or in combination population		Black or African American in combination population only as a percent of Black or African American alone or in combination population
	Total population	Number	Percent of total population	Total population	Number	Percent of total population	Number	Percent of total population	
United States	248,709,873	29,980,996	12.1	281,421,906	34,658,190	12.3	36,419,434	12.9	4.8
Region									
Northeast	50,809,229	5,613,222	11.0	53,594,378	6,099,881	11.4	6,556,909	12.2	7.0
Midwest.	59,668,632	5,715,940	9.6	64,392,776	6,499,733	10.1	6,838,669	10.6	5.0
South	85,445,930	15,828,888	18.5	100,236,820	18,981,692	18.9	19,528,231	19.5	2.8
West	52,786,082	2,828,010	5.4	63,197,932	3,076,884	4.9	3,495,625	5.5	12.0
State									
Alabama	4,040,587	1,020,705	25.3	4,447,100	1,155,930	26.0	1,168,998	26.3	1.1
Alaska	550,043	22,451	4.1	626,932	21,787	3.5	27,147	4.3	19.7
Arizona	3,665,228	110,524	3.0	5,130,632	158,873	3.1	185,599	3.6	14.4
Arkansas.	2,350,725	373,912	15.9	2,673,400	418,950	15.7	427,152	16.0	1.9
California.	29,760,021	2,208,801	7.4	33,871,648	2,263,882	6.7	2,513,041	7.4	9.9
Colorado	3,294,394	133,146	4.0	4,301,261	165,063	3.8	190,717	4.4	13.5
Connecticut.	3,287,116	274,269	8.3	3,405,565	309,843	9.1	339,078	10.0	8.6
Delaware.	666,168	112,460	16.9	783,600	150,666	19.2	157,152	20.1	4.1
District of Columbia. .	606,900	399,604	65.8	572,059	343,312	60.0	350,455	61.3	2.0
Florida.	12,937,926	1,759,534	13.6	15,982,378	2,335,505	14.6	2,471,730	15.5	5.5
Georgia.	6,478,216	1,746,565	27.0	8,186,453	2,349,542	28.7	2,393,425	29.2	1.8
Hawai	1,108,229	27,195	2.5	1,211,537	22,003	1.8	33,343	2.8	34.0
Idaho.	1,006,749	3,370	0.3	1,293,953	5,456	0.4	8,127	0.6	32.9
Illinois	11,430,602	1,694,273	14.8	12,419,293	1,876,875	15.1	1,937,671	15.6	3.1
Indiana	5,544,159	432,092	7.8	6,080,485	510,034	8.4	538,015	8.8	5.2
Iowa	2,776,755	48,090	1.7	2,926,324	61,853	2.1	72,512	2.5	14.7
Kansas	2,477,574	143,076	5.8	2,688,418	154,198	5.7	170,610	6.3	9.6
Kentucky.	3,685,296	262,907	7.1	4,041,769	295,994	7.3	311,878	7.7	5.1
Louisiana.	4,219,973	1,299,281	30.8	4,468,976	1,451,944	32.5	1,468,317	32.9	1.1
Maine	1,227,928	5,138	0.4	1,274,923	6760	0.5	9,553	0.7	29.2
Maryland.	4,781,468	1,189,899	24.9	5,296,486	1,477,411	27.9	1,525,036	28.8	3.1
Massachusetts	6,016,425	300,130	5.0	6,349,097	343,454	5.4	398,479	6.3	13.8
Michigan.	9,295,297	1,291,706	13.9	9,938,444	1,412,742	14.2	1,474,613	14.8	4.2
Minnesota	4,375,099	94,944	2.2	4,919,479	171,731	3.5	202,972	4.1	15.4
Mississippi.	2,573,216	915,057	35.6	2,844,658	1,033,809	36.3	1,041,708	36.6	0.8
Missouri.	5,117,073	548,208	10.7	5,595,211	629,391	11.2	655,377	11.7	4.0
Montana	799,065	2,381	0.3	902,195	2,692	0.3	4,441	0.5	39.4
Nebraska.	1,578,385	57,404	3.6	1,711,263	68,541	4.0	75,833	4.4	9.6
Nevada	1,201,833	78,771	6.6	1,998,257	135,477	6.8	150,508	7.5	10.0
New Hampshire	1,109,252	7,198	0.6	1,235,786	9,035	0.7	12,218	1.0	26.1
New Jersey	7,730,188	1,036,825	13.4	8,414,350	1,141,821	13.6	1,211,750	14.4	5.8
New Mexico	1,515,069	30,210	2.0	1,819,046	34,343	1.9	42,412	2.3	19.0
New York.	17,990,455	2,859,055	15.9	18,976,457	3,014,385	15.9	3,234,165	17.0	6.8
North Carolina.	6,628,637	1,456,323	22.0	8,049,313	1,737,545	21.6	1,776,283	22.1	2.2
North Dakota.	638,800	3,524	0.6	642,200	3,916	0.6	5,372	0.8	27.1
Ohio	10,847,115	1,154,826	10.6	11,353,140	1,301,307	11.5	1,372,501	12.1	5.2
Oklahoma	3,145,585	233,801	7.4	3,450,654	260,968	7.6	284,766	8.3	8.4
Oregon	2,842,321	46,178	1.6	3,421,399	55,662	1.6	72,647	2.1	23.4
Pennsylvania	11,881,643	1,089,795	9.2	12,281,054	1,224,612	10.0	1,289,123	10.5	5.0
Rhode Island.	1,003,464	38,861	3.9	1,048,319	46,908	4.5	58,051	5.5	19.2
South Carolina	3,486,703	1,039,884	29.8	4,012,012	1,185,216	29.5	1,200,901	29.9	1.3
South Dakota	696,004	3,258	0.5	754,844	4,685	0.6	6,687	0.9	29.9
Tennessee.	4,877,185	778,035	16.0	5,689,283	932,809	16.4	953,349	16.8	2.2
Texas	16,986,510	2,021,632	11.9	20,851,820	2,404,566	11.5	2,493,057	12.0	3.5
Utah	1,722,850	11,576	0.7	2,233,169	17,657	0.8	24,382	1.1	27.6
Vermont	562,758	1,951	0.3	608,827	3,063	0.5	4,492	0.7	31.8
Virginia	6,187,358	1,162,994	18.8	7,078,515	1,390,293	19.6	1,441,207	20.4	3.5
Washington.	4,866,692	149,801	3.1	5,894,121	190,267	3.2	238,398	4.0	20.2
West Virginia.	1,793,477	56,295	3.1	1,808,344	57,232	3.2	62,817	3.5	8.9
Wisconsin	4,891,769	244,539	5.0	5,363,675	304,460	5.7	326,506	6.1	6.8
Wyoming.	453,588	3,606	0.8	493,782	3,722	0.8	4,863	1.0	23.5
Puerto Rico	3,522,037	(X)	(X)	3,808,610	302,933	8.0	416,296	10.9	27.2

X Not applicable.

Source: U.S. Census Bureau, Census 2000 Redistricting Data (Public Law 94-171) Summary File, Table PL1; 1990 Census of Population, *General Population Characteristics* (1990 CP-1).

Northeast, and 10 percent lived in the West.[7]

The South had the largest Black population, as well as the highest proportion of Blacks in its total population: 20 percent of all respondents in the South reported Black compared with 12 percent in the Northeast, 11 percent in the Midwest, and 6 percent in the West.

About three-fifths of all people who reported Black lived in ten states.

The ten states with the largest Black populations in 2000 were New York, California, Texas, Florida, Georgia, Illinois, North Carolina, Maryland, Michigan, and Louisiana (see Table 2). Combined, these states represented 58 percent of the total Black population, but only 49 percent of the total population. Five of these ten states had Black populations greater than 2 million: New York (3.2 million); California, Texas, and Florida (about 2.5 million each); and Georgia (2.4 million).

In the South, ten states (Texas, Florida, Georgia, North Carolina, Maryland, Louisiana, Virginia, South Carolina, Alabama, and Mississippi) had Black populations over one million and, when combined, they represented 47 percent of the Black population in the country.

[7] The South region includes the states of Alabama, Arkansas, Delaware, Florida, Georgia, Kentucky, Louisiana, Maryland, Mississippi, North Carolina, Oklahoma, South Carolina, Tennessee, Texas, Virginia, and West Virginia, and the District of Columbia. The Midwest region includes the states of Illinois, Indiana, Iowa, Kansas, Michigan, Minnesota, Missouri, Nebraska, North Dakota, Ohio, South Dakota, and Wisconsin. The Northeast region includes the states of Connecticut, Maine, Massachusetts, New Hampshire, New Jersey, New York, Pennsylvania, Rhode Island, and Vermont. The West region includes the states of Alaska, Arizona, California, Colorado, Hawaii, Idaho, Montana, Nevada, New Mexico, Oregon, Utah, Washington, and Wyoming.

In six states, Blacks represented over 25 percent of the total population, and all of them were located in the South — Mississippi (37 percent); Louisiana (33 percent); South Carolina (30 percent); Georgia and Maryland (29 percent) each; and Alabama (26 percent). The District of Columbia, a state equivalent, had the highest proportion of Blacks with 61 percent.

In 13 states, Blacks represented less than 3 percent of the total population. Seven of those states were located in the West — Hawaii, New Mexico, Oregon, Utah, Wyoming, Idaho, and Montana; three in the Midwest — Iowa, South Dakota, and North Dakota; and three in the Northeast — New Hampshire, Maine and Vermont.

The Black population was concentrated in counties in the South.

The Black population is still highly concentrated — 64 percent of all counties (3,141 counties) in the United States had fewer than 6 percent Black, but in 96 counties, Blacks comprised 50 percent or more of the total county population (see Figure 3). Ninety-five of those counties were located in the South and were distributed across the Coastal and Lowland South in a loose arc. With the notable exceptions of Baltimore city (a county equivalent) and Prince George's County, in Maryland, generally these counties were nonmetropolitan. St. Louis City, Missouri in the Midwest was the only county equivalent outside the South where Blacks exceeded 50 percent of the total population.

Concentrations of Blacks in the Midwest and West tended to be either in counties located within metropolitan areas or in counties containing universities or military bases or both. Metropolitan

concentrations tended to be in central counties containing older central cities.

Although Blacks were not as concentrated in Midwestern counties, in some metropolitan counties, such as around Chicago, Illinois; Gary, Indiana; and Detroit, Michigan, Blacks comprised a sizeable proportion of the population. In the Northeast, Blacks were concentrated in a band of counties extending from Philadelphia, Pennsylvania to Providence, Rhode Island and along the Hudson Valley northward from New York. Western counties with large concentrations of Blacks were located in Southern California, the San Francisco and Sacramento areas, around Denver and Colorado Springs, and in the Seattle and Tacoma area in Washington. Clark County, Nevada (Las Vegas area) also stood out distinctly from surrounding counties in Nevada, Utah, and Arizona.

The places with the largest Black populations were New York and Chicago.

Census 2000 showed that, of all places[8] in the United States with populations of 100,000 or more, New York had the largest Black population with 2.3 million, followed by Chicago (1.1 million) as shown in Table 3. Three other places — Detroit, Philadelphia, and Houston — had Black populations between 500,000 and 1 million. Five of the ten places with the largest Black population — Baltimore, Houston, Memphis, Washington, DC, and New Orleans — were in the South.

[8] Census 2000 showed 245 places in the United States with 100,000 or more population. They included 238 incorporated places (including four city-county consolidations) and seven census designated places that were not legally incorporated. For a list of these places by state, see www.census.gov/population/www/cen2000/phc-t6.html.

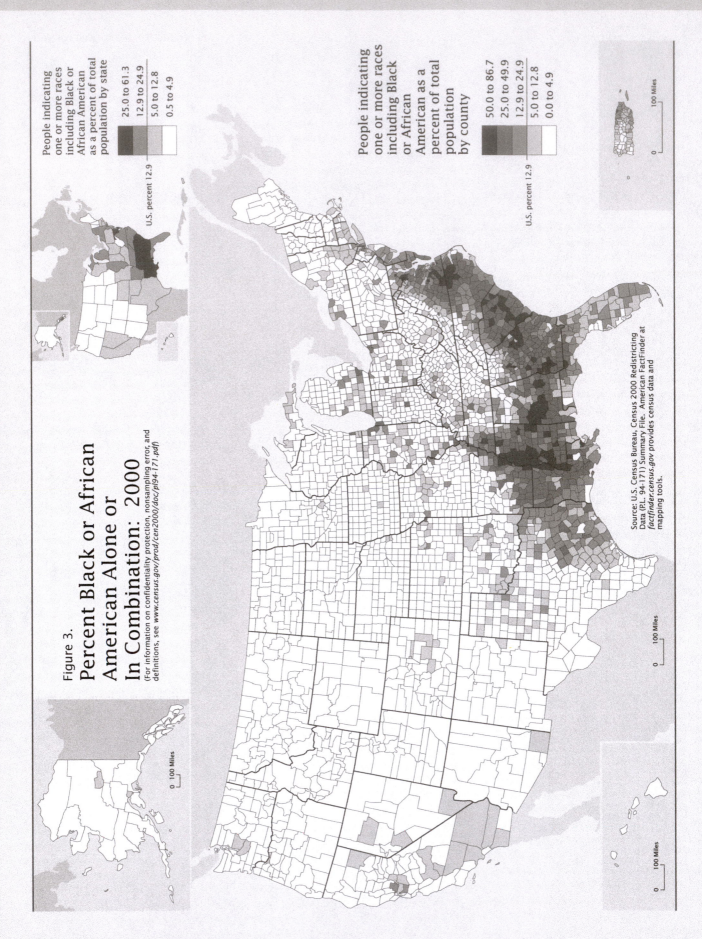

Figure 3.
Percent Black or African American Alone or In Combination: 2000

(For information on confidentiality protection, nonsampling error, and definitions, see *www.census.gov/prod/cen2000/doc/pl94-171.pdf*)

People indicating
one or more races
including Black or
African American
as a percent of total
population by state

U.S. percent 12.9

25.0 to 61.3
12.9 to 24.9
5.0 to 12.8
0.5 to 4.9

People indicating
one or more races
including Black
or African
American as a
percent of total
population
by county

U.S. percent 12.9

50.0 to 86.7
25.0 to 49.9
12.9 to 24.9
5.0 to 12.8
0.0 to 4.9

Source: U.S. Census Bureau, Census 2000 Redistricting
Data (P.L. 94-171) Summary File. American FactFinder at
factfinder.census.gov provides census data and
mapping tools.

Table 3.

Ten Largest Places in Total Population and in Black or African American Population: 2000

(For information on confidentiality protection, nonsampling error, and definitions, see *www.census.gov/prod/cen2000/doc/pl94-171.pdf*)

Place	Total population		Black or African American alone		Black or African American alone or in combination		Percent of total population	
	Rank	Number	Rank	Number	Rank	Number	Black or African American alone	Black or African American alone or in combination
New York, NY............	1	8,008,278	1	2,129,762	1	2,274,049	26.6	28.4
Los Angeles, CA........	2	3,694,820	7	415,195	6	444,635	11.2	12.0
Chicago, IL	3	2,896,016	2	1,065,009	2	1,084,221	36.8	37.4
Houston, TX	4	1,953,631	5	494,496	5	505,101	25.3	25.9
Philadelphia, PA.........	5	1,517,550	4	655,824	4	672,162	43.2	44.3
Phoenix, AZ	6	1,321,045	60	67,416	53	76,065	5.1	5.8
San Diego, CA..........	7	1,223,400	36	96,216	32	109,470	7.9	8.9
Dallas, TX	8	1,188,580	11	307,957	11	314,678	25.9	26.5
San Antonio, TX........	9	1,144,646	48	78,120	45	84,250	6.8	7.4
Detroit, MI..............	10	951,270	3	775,772	3	787,687	81.6	82.8
Baltimore, MD	17	651,154	6	418,951	7	424,449	64.3	65.2
Memphis, TN	18	650,100	8	399,208	8	402,367	61.4	61.9
Washington, DC........	21	572,059	9	343,312	9	350,455	60.0	61.3
New Orleans, LA........	31	484,674	10	325,947	10	329,171	67.3	67.9

Source: U.S. Census Bureau, Census 2000 Redistricting Data (Public Law 94-171) Summary File, Table PL1.

Figure 4.

Ten Places of 100,000 or More Population With the Highest Percentage of Blacks or African Americans: 2000

(For information on confidentiality protection, nonsampling error, and definitions, see *www.census.gov/prod/cen2000/doc/pl94-171.pdf*)

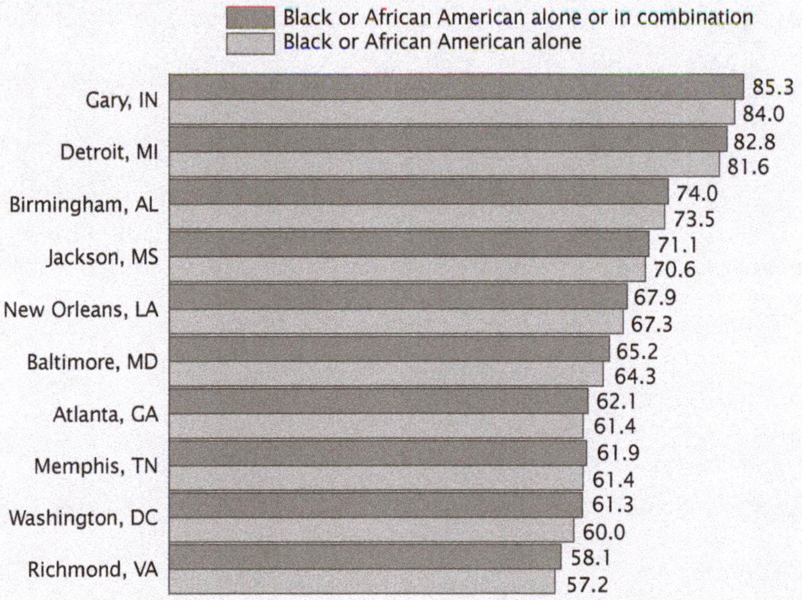

- ■ Black or African American alone or in combination
- ▨ Black or African American alone

Place	alone or in combination	alone
Gary, IN	85.3	84.0
Detroit, MI	82.8	81.6
Birmingham, AL	74.0	73.5
Jackson, MS	71.1	70.6
New Orleans, LA	67.9	67.3
Baltimore, MD	65.2	64.3
Atlanta, GA	62.1	61.4
Memphis, TN	61.9	61.4
Washington, DC	61.3	60.0
Richmond, VA	58.1	57.2

Source: U.S. Census Bureau, Census 2000 Redistricting Data (Public Law 94-171) Summary File, Table PL1.

Of the ten largest places in the United States, Detroit had the largest proportion of Blacks, 83 percent, followed by Philadelphia (44 percent), and Chicago (38 percent). Blacks represented less than 10 percent of the population in Phoenix (6 percent), San Antonio (7 percent), and San Diego (9 percent).

Two places — New York and Chicago — together accounted for 9 percent of the total Black population. The ten largest places for Blacks accounted for 20 percent of the total Black population.

Among places of 100,000 or more population, the highest proportion of Blacks was in Gary, Indiana, with 85 percent, followed by Detroit, Michigan with 83 percent (see Figure 4). The next eight places with the highest proportion of Blacks had populations over 58 percent Black. Of these 10 places,

Table 4.
Black or African American Population by Hispanic or Latino Origin: 2000

(For information on confidentiality protection, nonsampling error, and definitions, see *www.census.gov/prod/cen2000/doc/pl94-171.pdf*)

Race and Hispanic or Latino origin	Alone			In combination with one or more other races			Alone or in combination with one or more other races		
	Number	Percent of total	Percent of Black or African American population	Number	Percent of total	Percent of Black or African American population	Number	Percent of total	Percent of Black or African American population
Total population ..	274,595,678	100.0	(X)	6,826,228	100.0	(X)	281,421,906	100.0	(X)
Black or African American	34,658,190	12.6	100.0	1,761,244	25.8	100.0	36,419,434	12.9	100.0
Hispanic or Latino	710,353	0.3	2.0	325,330	4.8	18.5	1,035,683	0.4	2.8
Not Hispanic or Latino .	33,947,837	12.4	98.0	1,435,914	21.0	81.5	35,383,751	12.6	97.2

X Not applicable.

Source: U.S. Census Bureau, Census 2000 Redistricting Data (Public Law 94-171) Summary File, Tables PL1 and PL2.

Table 5.
Most Frequent Combinations of Black or African American With One or More Other Races by Hispanic or Latino Origin: 2000

(For information on confidentiality protection, nonsampling error, and definitions, see *www.census.gov/prod/cen2000/doc/pl94-171.pdf*)

Black or African American in combination	Total		Hispanic or Latino		Not Hispanic or Latino	
	Number	Percent	Number	Percent	Number	Percent
Total number reporting Black or African American and one or more other races	**1,761,244**	**100.0**	**325,330**	**100.0**	**1,435,914**	**100.0**
Black or African American; White	784,764	44.6	87,687	27.0	697,077	48.5
Black or African American; Some other race	417,249	23.7	161,283	49.6	255,966	17.8
Black or African American; American Indian and Alaska Native	182,494	10.4	14,472	4.4	168,022	11.7
Black or African American; White; American Indian and Alaska Native	112,207	6.4	18,046	5.5	94,161	6.6
Black or African American; Asian	106,782	6.1	7,269	2.2	99,513	6.9
Black or African American; White; Some other race.	43,172	2.5	15,481	4.8	27,691	1.9
All other combinations including Black or African American	114,576	6.5	21,092	6.5	93,484	6.5

Source: U.S. Census Bureau, Census 2000 Redistricting Data (Public Law 94-171) Summary File, Tables PL1 and PL2.

eight were in the South, and two were in the Midwest.

ADDITIONAL FINDINGS ON THE BLACK POPULATION

What proportion of respondents reporting Black also reported a Hispanic origin?

The Office of Management and Budget defines Hispanic or Latino as "a person of Cuban, Mexican, Puerto Rican, South or Central American, or other Spanish culture or origin, regardless of race." In data collection and presentation, federal agencies use two ethnicities: "Hispanic or Latino" and "Not Hispanic or Latino." Race and ethnicity are considered two separate and distinct concepts by the federal system. Hispanics may be of any race, and Blacks can be Hispanic or not Hispanic.

According to Census 2000, the overwhelming majority of the Black population was non-Hispanic: 98 percent of those who reported only Black and 97 percent of those who reported Black and at least one other race (see Table 4). However, only 82 percent of all respondents who reported Black in combination with one or more other races were non-Hispanic.

The Black non-Hispanic population represented 12.4 percent of people who reported exactly one race and about 12.6 percent of the total population. Of the 6.8 million people who reported two or more races, 21 percent were non-Hispanics who included Black as one of the races reported.

Table 6.
People Who Reported Black or African American by Age and Hispanic or Latino Origin: 2000

(For information on confidentiality protection, nonsampling error, and definitions, see *www.census.gov/prod/cen2000/doc/pl94-171.pdf*)

Age and Hispanic or Latino origin	Black or African American alone or in combination with one or more races		Black or African American alone		Black or African American in combination with one or more races	
	Number	Percent	Number	Percent	Number	Percent
Total............................	36,419,434	100.0	34,658,190	95.2	1,761,244	4.8
Hispanic or Latino................	1,035,683	100.0	710,353	68.6	325,330	31.4
Not Hispanic or Latino.............	35,383,751	100.0	33,947,837	95.9	1,435,914	4.1
Under 18........................	11,845,257	100.0	10,885,696	91.9	959,561	8.1
Hispanic or Latino................	442,970	100.0	275,432	62.2	167,538	37.8
Not Hispanic or Latino.............	11,402,287	100.0	10,610,264	93.1	792,023	6.9
18 and over	24,574,177	100.0	23,772,494	96.7	801,683	3.3
Hispanic or Latino................	592,713	100.0	434,921	73.4	157,792	26.6
Not Hispanic or Latino.............	23,981,464	100.0	23,337,573	97.3	643,891	2.7

Source: U.S. Census Bureau, Census 2000 Redistricting Data (Public Law 94-171) Summary File, Tables PL1, PL2, PL3, and PL4.

Figure 5.
Percent Under Age 18 of People Who Reported Black or African American by Hispanic or Latino Origin: 2000

(For information on confidentiality protection, nonsampling error, and definitions, see *www.census.gov/prod/cen2000/doc/pl94-171.pdf*)

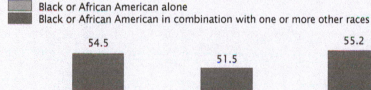
- Black or African American alone
- Black or African American in combination with one or more other races

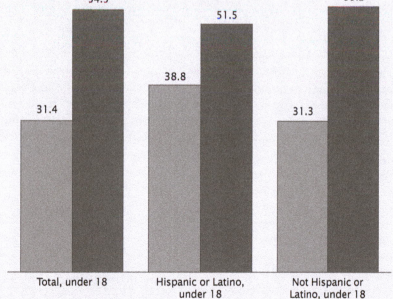

	Total, under 18	Hispanic or Latino, under 18	Not Hispanic or Latino, under 18
Black or African American alone	31.4	38.8	31.3
Black or African American in combination	54.5	51.5	55.2

Source: U.S. Census Bureau, Census 2000 Redistricting Data (Public Law 94-171) Summary File, Tables PL3 and PL4.

Which other races were Black non-Hispanics most likely to report?

Among Black non-Hispanics who reported more than one race, most indicated they were "Black or African American *and* White" (49 percent), followed by "Black or African American *and* Some other race" (18 percent), "Black or African American *and* American Indian and Alaska Native" (12 percent), and "Black or African American *and* Asian" (7 percent) as shown in Table 5. These four combination categories accounted for about 85 percent of all Black non-Hispanics who reported two or more races.

Which other races were Black Hispanics most likely to report?

Among Black Hispanics who reported more than one race, one-half indicated they were "Black or African American *and* Some other race," followed by "Black or African American *and* White" (27 percent), "Black or African American *and*

White **and** American Indian and Alaska Native" (6 percent), and "Black or African American **and** White **and** Some other race" (5 percent) as shown in Table 5.

Which group was more likely to report more than one race, Black non-Hispanics or Black Hispanics?

Black Hispanics were more likely than Black non-Hispanics to report two or more races. According to Census 2000, 1.0 million people reported Black and Hispanic. Of those, 31 percent reported Black with one or more other races (see Table 6). In contrast, of the 35.4 million Blacks who reported as not Hispanic, only 4.1 percent reported at least one other race.

Were there differences in the age distribution between people who reported only Black or African American and people who reported Black or African American and one or more other races?

People who reported Black as well as one or more other races were more likely to be under 18 than those reporting only Black (see Figure 5). Of the 1.8 million people who reported Black with at least one other race, 54 percent were under 18. This proportion is higher than the Black alone population. Of the 34.7 million people who reported only Black, 31 percent were under 18.

When the Black population is cross-tabulated by Hispanic origin, this pattern persists. For both Black non-Hispanics and Black Hispanics, a higher proportion of those reporting more than one race was under 18 when compared with those reporting Black alone. Among the 1.4 million Black non-Hispanics who reported more than one race, 55 percent were under 18. Of the 33.9 million people who reported

Black alone and not Hispanic, 31 percent were under 18. Similarly, among the 325,000 Black Hispanics who reported two or more races, 51 percent were under 18. Of the 710,000 Black Hispanics who reported one race, 39 percent were under 18.

ABOUT CENSUS 2000

Why did Census 2000 ask the question on race?

The Census Bureau collects data on race to fulfill a variety of legislative and program requirements. Data on race are used in the legislative redistricting process carried out by the States and in monitoring local jurisdictions' compliance with the Voting Rights Act. These data are also essential for evaluating Federal programs that promote equal access to employment, education, and housing and for assessing racial disparities in health and exposure to environmental risks. More broadly, data on race are critical for research that underlies many policy decisions at all levels of government.

How do data from the question on race benefit me, my family, and my community?

All levels of government need information on race to implement and evaluate programs, or enforce laws. Examples include: the Native American Programs Act, the Equal Employment Opportunity Act, the Civil Rights Act, the Voting Rights Act, the Public Health Act, the Healthcare Improvement Act, the Job Partnership Training Act, the Equal Credit Opportunity Act, the Fair Housing Act, and the Census Redistricting Data Program.

Both public and private organizations use race information to find areas where groups may need special services and to plan and

implement education, housing, health, and other programs that address these needs. For example, a school system might use this information to design cultural activities that reflect the diversity in their community. Or a business could use it to select the mix of merchandise it will sell in a new store. Census information also helps identify areas where residents might need services of particular importance to certain racial or ethnic groups, such as screening for hypertension or diabetes.

FOR MORE INFORMATION

For more information on race in the United States, visit the U.S. Census Bureau's Internet site at *www.census.gov/population/ www.socdemo/race.html.*

Race data from the Census 2000 Redistricting Data (Public Law 94-171) Summary File were released on a state-by-state basis during March 2001. The Census 2000 Redistricting data are available on the Internet via *factfinder.census.gov* and for purchase on CD-ROM and later on DVD.

For information on confidentiality protection, nonsampling error, and definitions, also see *www.census.gov/prod/cen2000/ doc/pl94-171.pdf* or contact our Customer Services Center at 301-763-INFO (4636).

For more information on specific races in the United States, go to *www.census.gov* and click on "Minority Links." This Web page includes information about Census 2000 and provides links to reports based on past censuses and surveys focusing on the social and economic characteristics of the Black or African American, American Indian and Alaska Native, Asian, and Native Hawaiian and Other Pacific Islander populations.

Information on other population and housing topics is presented in the Census 2000 Brief series, located on the U.S. Census Bureau's Web site at *www.census.gov/population/www/cen2000/briefs.html*. This series presents information about race, Hispanic origin, age, sex, household type, housing tenure, and other social, economic, and housing characteristics.

For more information about Census 2000, including data products, call our Customer Services Center at 301-763-INFO (4636), or e-mail *webmaster@census.gov*.

The Asian Population: 2000

Census 2000 Brief

Issued February 2002

C2KBR/01-16

By
Jessica S. Barnes and
Claudette E. Bennett

Census 2000 showed that the United States population was 281.4 million on April 1, 2000. Of the total, 11.9 million, or 4.2 percent, reported Asian.[1] This number included 10.2 million people, or 3.6 percent, who reported only Asian and 1.7 million people, or 0.6 percent, who reported Asian as well as one or more other races. Census 2000 asked separate questions on race and Hispanic or Latino origin. Hispanics who reported their race as Asian, either alone or in combination with one or more races, are included in the numbers for Asians.

This report, part of a series that analyzes population and housing data collected from Census 2000, provides a portrait of the Asian population in the United States and discusses its distribution at both the national and subnational levels. It begins by discussing the characteristics of the total Asian population and then focuses on the detailed groups, for example:

Figure 1.

Reproduction of the Question on Race From Census 2000

6. **What is this person's race?** *Mark* ☒ *one or more races* to indicate what this person considers himself/herself to be.
   ☐ White
   ☐ Black, African Am., or Negro
   ☐ American Indian or Alaska Native — *Print name of enrolled or principal tribe.*

   ☐ Asian Indian   ☐ Japanese   ☐ Native Hawaiian
   ☐ Chinese   ☐ Korean   ☐ Guamanian or Chamorro
   ☐ Filipino   ☐ Vietnamese ☐ Samoan
   ☐ Other Asian — *Print race.*   ☐ Other Pacific Islander — *Print race.*

   ☐ Some other race — *Print race.*

Source: U.S. Census Bureau, Census 2000 questionnaire.

Asian Indian, Chinese, and Japanese. This report is based on data from the Census 2000 Summary File 1.[2] The text of this report discusses data for the United States, including the 50 states and the District of Columbia.[3]

The term "Asian" refers to people having origins in any of the original peoples of the Far East, Southeast Asia, or the Indian subcontinent (for example, Cambodia, China, India, Japan, Korea, Malaysia, Pakistan, the Philippine Islands, Thailand, and Vietnam). Asian groups are not limited to nationalities, but include ethnic terms, as well.

---

[1] In this report, the term "reported" is used to refer to the answers provided by respondents, as well as responses assigned during the editing and imputation processes. The Asian population includes many groups who differ in language, culture, and length of residence in the United States. Some of the Asian groups, such as the Chinese and Japanese, have been in the United States for several generations. Other groups, such as the Hmong, Vietnamese, Laotians, and Cambodians, are comparatively recent immigrants.

[2] Data from the Census 2000 Summary File 1 were released on a state-by-state basis during the summer of 2001.

[3] Data for the Commonwealth of Puerto Rico are shown in Table 2 and Figure 3.

USCENSUSBUREAU

Helping You Make Informed Decisions

U.S. Department of Commerce
Economics and Statistics Administration
U.S. CENSUS BUREAU

United States
Census
2000

The first United States decennial census in 1790 collected data on race, but no distinction was made for people of Asian descent. Data have been collected on the Chinese population since the 1860 census and on the Japanese population since the 1870 census. The racial classification was expanded in the 1910 census to obtain separate figures on other groups such as Filipinos and Koreans. However, data on these other groups were collected on an intermittent basis through the 1970 census. Asian Indians were classified as White and the Vietnamese population was included in the "Other" race category in the 1970 census.

In the 1980 census, there were six separate response categories for Asians: Asian Indian, Chinese, Filipino, Japanese, Korean, and Vietnamese. These same six categories appeared on both the 1990 and Census 2000 questionnaires. Also, for Census 2000, a separate "Other Asian" response category was added with a write-in area for respondents to indicate specific Asian groups not included on the questionnaire.

The question on race was changed for Census 2000.

All U.S. censuses have obtained information on race for every individual, and for the past several censuses, the responses reflect self-identification. For Census 2000, however, respondents were asked to report *one or more* races they

considered themselves and other members of their households to be.[4]

Because of these changes, the Census 2000 data on race are not directly comparable with data from the 1990 census or earlier censuses. Caution must be used when interpreting changes in the racial composition of the United States population over time.

The Census 2000 question on race included 15 separate response categories and 3 areas where respondents could write in a more specific race (see Figure 1). For some purposes, including this report, the response categories and write-in answers were combined to create the five standard Office of Management and Budget race categories, plus the Census Bureau category of "Some other race." The six race categories include:

- White;

- Black or African American;

- American Indian and Alaska Native;

- Asian;

- Native Hawaiian and Other Pacific Islander; and

- Some other race.

---

[4] Other changes included terminology and formatting changes, such as spelling out "American" instead of "Amer." for the American Indian or Alaska Native category and adding "Native" to the Hawaiian response category. In the layout of the Census 2000 questionnaire, the seven Asian response categories were alphabetized and grouped together, as were the four Pacific Islander categories after the Native Hawaiian category. The three separate American Indian and Alaska Native identifiers in the 1990 census (i.e., Indian (Amer.), Eskimo, and Aleut) were combined into a single identifier in Census 2000. Also, American Indians and Alaska Natives could report more than one tribe.

For a complete explanation of the race categories used in Census 2000, see the Census 2000 Brief, *Overview of Race and Hispanic Origin.*[5]

The data collected by Census 2000 on race can be divided into two broad categories: the race *alone* population and the race *in combination* population.

People who responded to the question on race by indicating *only one* race are referred to as the race *alone* population. For example, respondents who reported their race as one or more Asian detailed groups, but no other race, would be included in the Asian *alone* population.[6]

Individuals who reported *more than one* of the six races are referred to as the race *in combination* population. For example, respondents who reported they were "Asian *and* Black or African American" or "Asian *and* White *and* American Indian and Alaska Native"[7] would be included in the Asian *in combination* population.

---

[5] *Overview of Race and Hispanic Origin: 2000*, U.S. Census Bureau, Census 2000 Brief, C2KBR/01-1, March 2001, is available on the U.S. Census Bureau's Internet site at *www.census.gov/population/www/cen2000/briefs.html.*

[6] Respondents reporting a single detailed Asian group, such as "Korean" or "Filipino," would be included in the Asian *alone* population. Respondents reporting more than one detailed Asian group, such as "Chinese and Japanese" or "Asian Indian and Chinese and Vietnamese" would also be included in the Asian *alone* population. This is because all of the detailed groups in these example combinations are part of the larger Asian race category.

[7] The race in combination categories are denoted by quotations around the combination with the conjunction *and* in bold and italicized print to indicate the separate races that comprise the combination.

Table 1.
Asian Population: 2000

(For information on confidentiality protection, nonsampling error, and definitions, see www.census.gov/prod/cen2000/doc/sf1.pdf)

Race	Number	Percent of total population
Total population	281,421,906	100.0
Asian alone or in combination with one or more other races	11,898,828	4.2
Asian alone	10,242,998	3.6
Asian in combination with one or more other races	1,655,830	0.6
Asian; White	868,395	0.3
Asian; Some other race	249,108	0.1
Asian; Native Hawaiian and Other Pacific Islander	138,802	-
Asian; Black or African American	106,782	-
All other combinations including Asian	292,743	0.1
Not Asian alone or in combination with one or more other races	269,523,078	95.8

- Percentage rounds to 0.0.

Source: U.S. Census Bureau, Census 2000 Summary File1.

The maximum number of people reporting Asian is reflected in the Asian *alone or in combination* population.

One way to define the Asian population is to combine those respondents who reported only Asian with those who reported Asian as well as one or more other races. This creates the Asian *alone or in combination* population. Another way to think of the Asian *alone or in combination* population is the total number of people who identified entirely or partially as Asian. This group is also described as people who reported Asian, whether or not they reported any other races.

Census 2000 provides a snapshot of the Asian population.

Table 1 shows the number and percentage of Census 2000 respondents who reported Asian alone as well as those who reported Asian and at least one other race.

Of the total United States population, 10.2 million people, or 3.6 percent, reported only Asian.

An additional 1.7 million people reported Asian and at least one other race. Within this group, the most common combinations were "Asian *and* White" (52 percent), followed by "Asian *and* Some other race" (15 percent), "Asian *and* Native Hawaiian and Other Pacific Islander" (8.4 percent) and "Asian *and* Black or African American" (6.4 percent). These four combination categories accounted for 82 percent of all Asians who reported two or more races. Thus, 11.9 million people, or 4.2 percent of the total population, reported Asian alone or in combination with one or more other races.

The Asian population increased faster than the total population between 1990 and 2000.

Because of the changes made to the question on race in Census 2000, there are at least two ways to present the change in the total number of Asians in the United States. They include: 1) the difference in the Asian population between 1990 and 2000 using the race alone concept for 2000, and 2) the difference in the Asian

population between 1990 and 2000 using the race alone or in combination concept for 2000. These comparisons provide a "minimum-maximum" range for the change in the Asian population between 1990 and 2000.

The 1990 census counted 6.9 million Asians. Using the Asian alone population in 2000, this population increased by 3.3 million, or 48 percent, between 1990 and 2000. If the Asian alone or in combination population is used, an increase of 5.0 million, or 72 percent, results. Thus, from 1990 to 2000, the range for the increase in the Asian population was 48 percent to 72 percent. In comparison, the total population grew by 13 percent, from 248.7 million in 1990 to 281.4 million in 2000.

THE GEOGRAPHIC DISTRIBUTION OF THE ASIAN POPULATION

The following discussion of the geographic distribution of the Asian population focuses on the Asian alone or in combination population in the text. As the upper bound of the Asian population, this group includes all respondents who reported Asian, whether or not they reported any other race.[8] Hereafter, in the text of this section, the term "Asian" will be used to refer to those who reported Asian whether they reported one or more than one race. However, in the tables and graphs, data for both the Asian alone and alone or in combination populations are shown.

_____

[8] The use of the *alone or in combination* population in this section does not imply that it is the preferred method of presenting or analyzing data. In general, either the *alone* population or the *alone or in combination* population can be used, depending on the purpose of the analysis. The Census Bureau uses both approaches.

About one-half of the Asian population lived in the West.[9]

According to Census 2000, of all respondents who reported Asian, 49 percent lived in the West, 20 percent lived in the Northeast, 19 percent lived in the South, and 12 percent lived in the Midwest (see Figure 2).

The West had the highest proportion of Asians in its total population as well as the largest total Asian population: 9.3 percent of all respondents in the West reported Asian, compared with 4.4 percent in the Northeast, 2.3 percent in the South, and 2.2 percent in the Midwest (see Table 2).

Over half of all people who reported Asian lived in just three states.

Over half (51 percent) of the Asian population lived in just three states: California, New York, and Hawaii, which accounted for 19 percent of the total population. California, by far, had the largest Asian population (4.2 million), followed by New York (1.2 million), and Hawaii (0.7 million). The ten states with the largest Asian populations in 2000 were: California, New York, Hawaii, Texas, New Jersey, Illinois, Washington, Florida, Virginia, and Massachusetts (see Table 2). Combined, these states represented 75 percent of the

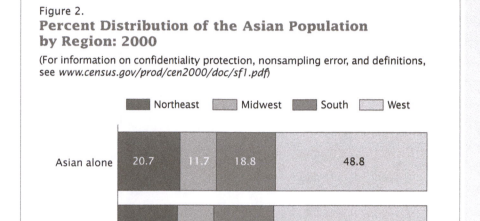

Figure 2.
Percent Distribution of the Asian Population by Region: 2000
(For information on confidentiality protection, nonsampling error, and definitions, see *www.census.gov/prod/cen2000/doc/sf1.pdf*)

Northeast | Midwest | South | West

Asian alone: 20.7 | 11.7 | 18.8 | 48.8

Asian alone or in combination: 19.9 | 11.7 | 19.1 | 49.3

Source: U.S. Census Bureau, Census 2000 Summary File 1.

Asian population, but only 47 percent of the total population in the United States.

The Asian population exceeded the U.S. level of 4.2 percent of the total population in nine states. Five states were in the West — Hawaii (58 percent), California (12 percent), Washington (6.7 percent), Nevada (5.6 percent), and Alaska (5.2 percent); two states were in the Northeast — New Jersey and New York (both 6.2 percent); and two states were in the South — Maryland (4.5 percent), and Virginia (4.3 percent). No states in the Midwest had Asian populations greater than the U.S. national average of 4.2 percent.

In nine states, Asians represented less than 1 percent of the total population. Four of those states were located in the South: Alabama, Kentucky, Mississippi, and West Virginia. Two were in the Midwest: North Dakota and South Dakota. Two were in the West: Montana and Wyoming. Maine was the only state in the Northeast with an Asian population less than 1 percent.

The Asian population was concentrated in counties in the West, especially in Hawaii and California.

Of the 3,141 counties in the United States, 122 counties had Asian populations greater than the national average of 4.2 percent, of which 39 counties had at least twice the national average. The overwhelming majority of counties (2,382) had lower concentrations of Asians (less than 1 percent).

Not surprisingly, the counties with the highest concentration of Asians (over 25 percent) were in Hawaii. Honolulu county, by far, had the highest proportion of Asians (62 percent). Three other counties in Hawaii were more than 47 percent Asian, followed by two counties each in Alaska, and the San Francisco Bay area in California.

Although Asians resided in an array of counties, the largest concentrations tended to be found in coastal and/or urban counties, while smaller concentrations were scattered throughout the United States (see Figure 3). The majority of the counties with Asian

___
[9] The West region includes the states of Alaska, Arizona, California, Colorado, Hawaii, Idaho, Montana, Nevada, New Mexico, Oregon, Utah, Washington, and Wyoming. The Northeast region includes the states of Connecticut, Maine, Massachusetts, New Hampshire, New Jersey, New York, Pennsylvania, Rhode Island, and Vermont. The South region includes the states of Alabama, Arkansas, Delaware, Florida, Georgia, Kentucky, Louisiana, Maryland, Mississippi, North Carolina, Oklahoma, South Carolina, Tennessee, Texas, Virginia, West Virginia, and the District of Columbia, a state equivalent. The Midwest region includes the states of Illinois, Indiana, Iowa, Kansas, Michigan, Minnesota, Missouri, Nebraska, North Dakota, Ohio, South Dakota, and Wisconsin.

Table 2.
Asian Population for the United States, Regions, and States, and for Puerto Rico: 1990 and 2000

(For information on confidentiality protection, nonsampling error, and definitions, see *www.census.gov/prod/cen2000/doc/sf1.pdf*)

Area	1990 Total population	1990 Asian population Number	1990 Percent of total population	2000 Total population	2000 Asian alone population Number	2000 Asian alone Percent of total population	2000 Asian alone or in combination population Number	Percent of total population	2000 Asian in combination population Number	Percent of Asian alone or in combination population
United States....	248,709,873	6,908,638	2.8	281,421,906	10,242,998	3.6	11,898,828	4.2	1,655,830	13.9
Region										
Northeast	50,809,229	1,324,865	2.6	53,594,378	2,119,426	4.0	2,368,297	4.4	248,871	10.5
Midwest	59,668,632	755,403	1.3	64,392,776	1,197,554	1.9	1,392,938	2.2	195,384	14.0
South	85,445,930	1,094,179	1.3	100,236,820	1,922,407	1.9	2,267,094	2.3	344,687	15.2
West	52,786,082	3,734,191	7.1	63,197,932	5,003,611	7.9	5,870,499	9.3	866,888	14.8
State										
Alabama	4,040,587	21,088	0.5	4,447,100	31,346	0.7	39,458	0.9	8,112	20.6
Alaska...........	550,043	17,814	3.2	626,932	25,116	4.0	32,686	5.2	7,570	23.2
Arizona..........	3,665,228	51,699	1.4	5,130,632	92,236	1.8	118,672	2.3	26,436	22.3
Arkansas.........	2,350,725	12,125	0.5	2,673,400	20,220	0.8	25,401	1.0	5,181	20.4
California.........	29,760,021	2,735,060	9.2	33,871,648	3,697,513	10.9	4,155,685	12.3	458,172	11.0
Colorado.........	3,294,394	57,122	1.7	4,301,261	95,213	2.2	120,779	2.8	25,566	21.2
Connecticut.......	3,287,116	50,078	1.5	3,405,565	82,313	2.4	95,368	2.8	13,055	13.7
Delaware.........	666,168	8,888	1.3	783,600	16,259	2.1	18,944	2.4	2,685	14.2
District of Columbia .	606,900	10,923	1.8	572,059	15,189	2.7	17,956	3.1	2,767	15.4
Florida...........	12,937,926	149,856	1.2	15,982,378	266,256	1.7	333,013	2.1	66,757	20.0
Georgia..........	6,478,216	73,764	1.1	8,186,453	173,170	2.1	199,812	2.4	26,642	13.3
Hawaii...........	1,108,229	522,967	47.2	1,211,537	503,868	41.6	703,232	58.0	199,364	28.3
Idaho............	1,006,749	8,492	0.8	1,293,953	11,889	0.9	17,390	1.3	5,501	31.6
Illinois	11,430,602	282,569	2.5	12,419,293	423,603	3.4	473,649	3.8	50,046	10.6
Indiana..........	5,544,159	36,660	0.7	6,080,485	59,126	1.0	72,839	1.2	13,713	18.8
Iowa.............	2,776,755	25,037	0.9	2,926,324	36,635	1.3	43,119	1.5	6,484	15.0
Kansas..........	2,477,574	30,708	1.2	2,688,418	46,806	1.7	56,049	2.1	9,243	16.5
Kentucky.........	3,685,296	16,983	0.5	4,041,769	29,744	0.7	37,062	0.9	7,318	19.7
Louisiana.........	4,219,973	40,173	1.0	4,468,976	54,758	1.2	64,350	1.4	9,592	14.9
Maine............	1,227,928	6,450	0.5	1,274,923	9,111	0.7	11,827	0.9	2,716	23.0
Maryland.........	4,781,468	138,148	2.9	5,296,486	210,929	4.0	238,408	4.5	27,479	11.5
Massachusetts	6,016,425	142,137	2.4	6,349,097	238,124	3.8	264,814	4.2	26,690	10.1
Michigan	9,295,297	103,501	1.1	9,938,444	176,510	1.8	208,329	2.1	31,819	15.3
Minnesota	4,375,099	76,952	1.8	4,919,479	141,968	2.9	162,414	3.3	20,446	12.6
Mississippi........	2,573,216	12,679	0.5	2,844,658	18,626	0.7	23,281	0.8	4,655	20.0
Missouri..........	5,117,073	39,271	0.8	5,595,211	61,595	1.1	76,210	1.4	14,615	19.2
Montana	799,065	3,958	0.5	902,195	4,691	0.5	7,101	0.8	2,410	33.9
Nebraska.........	1,578,385	11,945	0.8	1,711,263	21,931	1.3	26,809	1.6	4,878	18.2
Nevada..........	1,201,833	35,232	2.9	1,998,257	90,266	4.5	112,456	5.6	22,190	19.7
New Hampshire	1,109,252	9,121	0.8	1,235,786	15,931	1.3	19,219	1.6	3,288	17.1
New Jersey.......	7,730,188	270,839	3.5	8,414,350	480,276	5.7	524,356	6.2	44,080	8.4
New Mexico	1,515,069	13,363	0.9	1,819,046	19,255	1.1	26,619	1.5	7,364	27.7
New York.........	17,990,455	689,303	3.8	18,976,457	1,044,976	5.5	1,169,200	6.2	124,224	10.6
North Carolina	6,628,637	49,970	0.8	8,049,313	113,689	1.4	136,212	1.7	22,523	16.5
North Dakota	638,800	3,317	0.5	642,200	3,606	0.6	4,967	0.8	1,361	27.4
Ohio.............	10,847,115	89,723	0.8	11,353,140	132,633	1.2	159,776	1.4	27,143	17.0
Oklahoma	3,145,585	32,002	1.0	3,450,654	46,767	1.4	58,723	1.7	11,956	20.4
Oregon	2,842,321	64,232	2.3	3,421,399	101,350	3.0	127,339	3.7	25,989	20.4
Pennsylvania	11,881,643	135,784	1.1	12,281,054	219,813	1.8	248,601	2.0	28,788	11.6
Rhode Island	1,003,464	18,019	1.8	1,048,319	23,665	2.3	28,290	2.7	4,625	16.3
South Carolina	3,486,703	21,399	0.6	4,012,012	36,014	0.9	44,931	1.1	8,917	19.8
South Dakota	696,004	2,938	0.4	754,844	4,378	0.6	6,009	0.8	1,631	27.1
Tennessee........	4,877,185	30,944	0.6	5,689,283	56,662	1.0	68,919	1.2	12,257	17.8
Texas............	16,986,510	311,918	1.8	20,851,820	562,319	2.7	644,193	3.1	81,874	12.7
Utah.............	1,722,850	25,696	1.5	2,233,169	37,108	1.7	48,692	2.2	11,584	23.8
Vermont..........	562,758	3,134	0.6	608,827	5,217	0.9	6,622	1.1	1,405	21.2
Virginia..........	6,187,358	156,036	2.5	7,078,515	261,025	3.7	304,559	4.3	43,534	14.3
Washington........	4,866,692	195,918	4.0	5,894,121	322,335	5.5	395,741	6.7	73,406	18.5
West Virginia.......	1,793,477	7,283	0.4	1,808,344	9,434	0.5	11,873	0.7	2,439	20.5
Wisconsin	4,891,769	52,782	1.1	5,363,675	88,763	1.7	102,768	1.9	14,005	13.6
Wyoming..........	453,588	2,638	0.6	493,782	2,771	0.6	4,107	0.8	1,336	32.5
Puerto Rico.........	3,522,037	(X)	(X)	3,808,610	7,960	0.2	17,279	0.5	9,319	53.9

X Not applicable.

Source: U.S. Census Bureau, Census 2000 Summary File 1; 1990 Census of Population, *General Population Characteristics* (1990 CP-1).

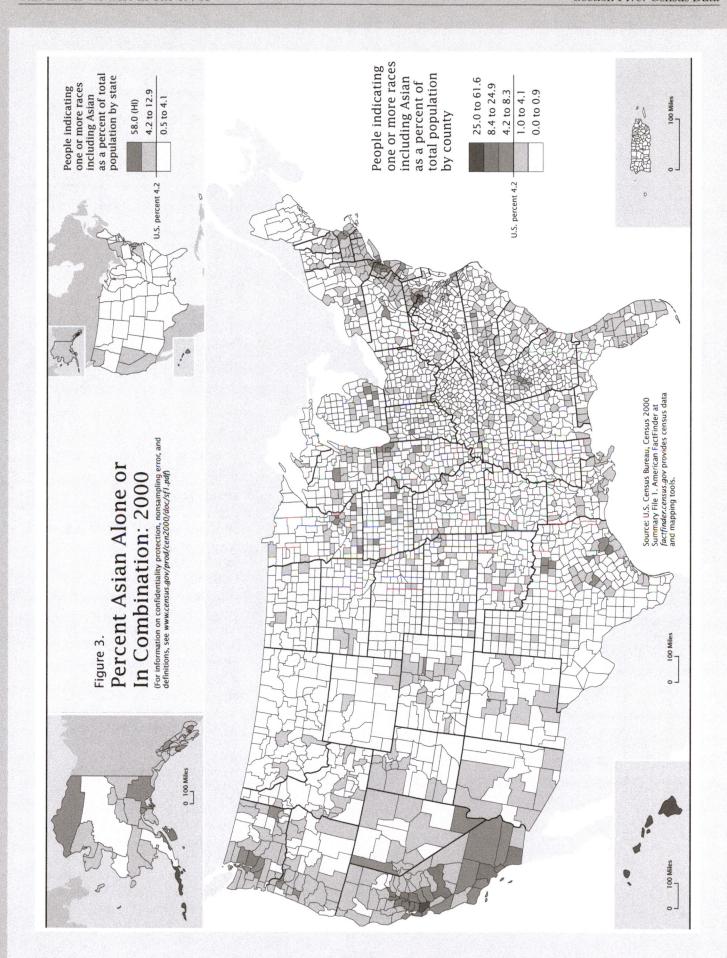

People indicating
one or more races
including Asian
as a percent of total
population by state

58.0 (HI)

4.2 to 12.9

0.5 to 4.1

U.S. percent 4.2

People indicating
one or more races
including Asian
as a percent of
total population
by county

25.0 to 61.6

8.4 to 24.9

4.2 to 8.3

1.0 to 4.1

0.0 to 0.9

U.S. percent 4.2

Figure 3.
Percent Asian Alone or
In Combination: 2000

(For information on confidentiality protection, nonsampling error, and
definitions, see *www.census.gov/prod/cen2000/doc/sf1.pdf*)

Source: U.S. Census Bureau, Census 2000
Summary File 1. American FactFinder at
factfinder.census.gov provides census data
and mapping tools.

100 Miles

0

100 Miles

0

100 Miles

0

100 Miles

0

Table 3.
Ten Largest Places in Total Population and in Asian Population: 2000

(For information on confidentiality protection, nonsampling error, and definitions, see www.census.gov/prod/cen2000/doc/sf1.pdf)

Place	Total population		Asian alone		Asian alone or in combination		Percent of total population	
	Rank	Number	Rank	Number	Rank	Number	Asian alone	Asian alone or in combination
New York, NY.............	1	8,008,278	1	787,047	1	872,777	9.8	10.9
Los Angeles, CA	2	3,694,820	2	369,254	2	407,444	10.0	11.0
Chicago, IL...............	3	2,896,016	7	125,974	7	140,517	4.3	4.9
Houston, TX	4	1,953,631	8	103,694	8	114,140	5.3	5.8
Philadelphia, PA...........	5	1,517,550	11	67,654	12	74,435	4.5	4.9
Phoenix, AZ	6	1,321,045	34	26,449	30	33,194	2.0	2.5
San Diego, CA.............	7	1,223,400	6	166,968	6	189,413	13.6	15.5
Dallas, TX................	8	1,188,580	27	32,118	27	36,665	2.7	3.1
San Antonio, TX...........	9	1,144,646	48	17,934	42	24,046	1.6	2.1
Detroit, MI................	10	951,270	94	9,268	84	12,361	1.0	1.3
San Jose, CA.............	11	894,943	3	240,375	3	257,571	26.9	28.8
San Francisco, CA	13	776,733	4	239,565	4	253,477	30.8	32.6
Seattle, WA..............	24	563,374	10	73,910	9	84,649	13.1	15.0
Honolulu, HI*..............	46	371,657	5	207,588	5	251,686	55.9	67.7
Fremont, CA..............	85	203,413	9	75,165	10	80,979	37.0	39.8

* Honolulu, HI, is a census designated place and is not legally incorporated. See footnote 10.

Source: U.S. Census Bureau, Census 2000 Summary File 1.

populations more than twice the national average were predominately concentrated in suburbs of large metropolitan areas such as Seattle, Washington; Los Angeles and the San Francisco Bay area of California; New York, New York; Newark, New Jersey; Washington, DC; Chicago, Illinois; Houston, Texas; and the Minneapolis-St.Paul, Minnesota, metropolitan area. Concentrations of Asians outside the suburbs of large metropolitan areas were typically located near colleges and universities.

Los Angeles county was the only county with over one million Asians. Honolulu county was the only other county with an Asian population over one-half million.

The two places with the largest Asian populations were New York and Los Angeles.[10]

Census 2000 showed that, of all places in the United States with 100,000 or more population, New York had the largest Asian population with 872,777, followed by Los Angeles with 407,444 (see Table 3). Eight places had Asian populations over 100,000: five in the West, and one each in the Northeast, Midwest, and the South.

Of the ten largest places in the United States, San Diego had the largest proportion of Asians (15 percent), followed by Los Angeles and New York with 11 percent each. Asians represented 1.3 percent of the total population in Detroit, the lowest percentage

[10] Census 2000 showed 245 places in the United States with 100,000 or more population. They included 238 incorporated places (including 4 city-county consolidations) and 7 census designated places that were not legally incorporated. For a list of these places by state, see www.census.gov/population/www/cen2000/phc-t6.html.

among the country's ten largest cities.

Among places of 100,000 or more population, the highest proportion of Asians was in Honolulu (68 percent) as shown in Figure 4. One additional place, Daly City, California, had over one-half of its population reporting Asian. The ten places with the highest proportion of Asians ranged from 29 percent in San Jose, California, to 68 percent in Honolulu, Hawaii. All ten places were in the West; nine of them were in California.

ADDITIONAL FINDINGS ON THE ASIAN POPULATION

Which Asian group was the largest?

According to Census 2000, Chinese was the largest detailed Asian group in the United States. This is true for both the alone and the alone or in combination populations. There were 2.3 million people who reported only Chinese and an additional 0.4 million people who reported Chinese with at least one other race or Asian group. A total of 2.7 million people reported Chinese alone or in combination with one or more other races or Asian groups (see Table 4).

Filipinos and Asian Indians were the next two largest specified Asian groups. There were 1.9 million people who reported Filipino alone and an additional 0.5 million who reported Filipino in combination with one or more other races or Asian groups. This gives a total of 2.4 million people who reported Filipino alone or in combination with at least one other race or Asian group. About 1.7 million people reported only Asian Indian and an additional 0.2 million reported Asian Indian in combination with one or more other races or Asian groups. A total of 1.9 million people reported Asian Indian alone or in combination with at least one other race or Asian group.

Combined, Chinese, Filipinos, and Asian Indians accounted for 58 percent of all respondents who reported a single Asian group. Of all Asian groups mentioned in race combinations, these three groups accounted for 57 percent of all responses.

Among the largest Asian groups, which was most likely to be in combination with one or more other races or Asian groups?

Of the six largest specified Asian groups, Japanese were most likely to report one or more other races or Asian groups. Of all respondents who reported Japanese, either alone or in combination, 31 percent reported one or more other races or Asian groups (see Figure 5). This included 4.8 percent who reported Japanese with one or more other

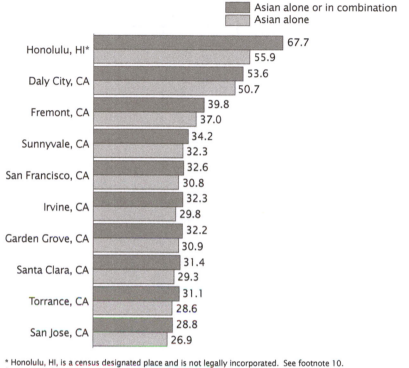

Figure 4.

Ten Places of 100,000 or More Population With the Highest Percentage of Asians: 2000

(For information on confidentiality protection, nonsampling error, and definitions, see www.census.gov/prod/cen2000/doc/sf1.pdf)

Legend:
- Asian alone or in combination
- Asian alone

Place	Asian alone or in combination	Asian alone
Honolulu, HI*	67.7	55.9
Daly City, CA	53.6	50.7
Fremont, CA	39.8	37.0
Sunnyvale, CA	34.2	32.3
San Francisco, CA	32.6	30.8
Irvine, CA	32.3	29.8
Garden Grove, CA	32.2	30.9
Santa Clara, CA	31.4	29.3
Torrance, CA	31.1	28.6
San Jose, CA	28.8	26.9

* Honolulu, HI, is a census designated place and is not legally incorporated. See footnote 10.
Source: U.S. Census Bureau, Census 2000 Summary File 1.

Asian groups, 21 percent who reported Japanese with one or more other races, and 4.8 percent who reported Japanese in addition to one or more other races and Asian groups (see Table 4). Vietnamese were least likely to be in combination with one or more other races or Asian groups. Of all respondents who reported Vietnamese, 8.3 percent reported one or more other races or Asian groups.

Were there differences in median age between the Asian alone and the Asian in combination populations and the total U.S. population?

The median age of the total U.S. population was 35.3 years. The overall median age for people who reported Asian alone was

32.7 years, which was 2.6 years younger than the total population. Those who reported Asian in combination with one or more races had a median age of 31.1 years, which was 4.2 years younger than the total.

ABOUT CENSUS 2000

Why did Census 2000 ask the question on race?

The Census Bureau collects data on race to fulfill a variety of legislative and program requirements. Data on race are used in the legislative redistricting process carried out by the states and in monitoring local jurisdictions' compliance with the Voting Rights Act. These data are also essential for evaluating federal programs that promote equal

Table 4.
Asian Population by Detailed Group: 2000

(For information on confidentiality protection, nonsampling error, and definitions, see *www.census.gov/prod/cen2000/doc/sf1.pdf*)

Detailed group	Asian alone		Asian in combination with one or more other races		Asian detailed group alone or in any combination[2]
	One Asian group reported[1]	Two or more Asian groups reported[2]	One Asian group reported	Two or more Asian groups reported[2]	
Total.....................	10,019,405	223,593	1,516,841	138,989	11,898,828
Asian Indian..................	1,678,765	40,013	165,437	15,384	1,899,599
Bangladeshi.................	41,280	5,625	9,655	852	57,412
Bhutanese..................	183	9	17	3	212
Burmese...................	13,159	1,461	1,837	263	16,720
Cambodian..................	171,937	11,832	20,830	1,453	206,052
Chinese, except Taiwanese.....	2,314,537	130,826	201,688	87,790	2,734,841
Filipino....................	1,850,314	57,811	385,236	71,454	2,364,815
Hmong....................	169,428	5,284	11,153	445	186,310
Indo Chinese	113	55	23	8	199
Indonesian	39,757	4,429	17,256	1,631	63,073
Iwo Jiman..................	15	3	60	-	78
Japanese...................	796,700	55,537	241,209	55,486	1,148,932
Korean....................	1,076,872	22,550	114,211	14,794	1,228,427
Laotian....................	168,707	10,396	17,914	1,186	198,203
Malaysian	10,690	4,339	2,837	700	18,566
Maldivian..................	27	2	22	-	51
Nepalese..................	7,858	351	1,128	62	9,399
Okinawan..................	3,513	2,625	2,816	1,645	10,599
Pakistani..................	153,533	11,095	37,587	2,094	204,309
Singaporean................	1,437	580	307	70	2,394
Sri Lankan.................	20,145	1,219	2,966	257	24,587
Taiwanese.................	118,048	14,096	11,394	1,257	144,795
Thai	112,989	7,929	27,170	2,195	150,283
Vietnamese.................	1,122,528	47,144	48,639	5,425	1,223,736
Other Asian, not specified[3]	146,870	19,576	195,449	7,535	369,430

- Represents zero.

[1]The total of 10,019,405 respondents categorized as reporting only one Asian group in this table is lower than the total of 10,019,410 shown in Table PCT5 (U.S. Census Bureau, Census 2000 Summary File 1 100-Percent Data, see *factfinder.census.gov*). This table includes more detailed groups than PCT5. This means that, for example, an individual who reported "Pakistani *and* Nepalese" is shown in this table as reporting two or more Asian groups. However, that same individual is categorized as reporting a single Asian group in PCT5 because both Pakistani and Nepalese are part of the larger Other specified Asian group.

[2]The numbers by detailed Asian group do not add to the total population. This is because the detailed Asian groups are tallies of the number of Asian *responses* rather than the number of Asian *respondents*. Respondents reporting several Asian groups are counted several times. For example, a respondent reporting "Korean *and* Filipino" would be included in the Korean as well as the Filipino numbers.

[3]Includes respondents who checked the "Other Asian" response category on the census questionnaire or wrote in a generic term such as "Asian" or "Asiatic."

Source: U.S. Census Bureau, Census 2000, special tabulations.

access to employment, education, and housing and for assessing racial disparities in health and exposure to environmental risks. More broadly, data on race are critical for research that underlies many policy decisions at all levels of government.

How do data from the question on race benefit me, my family, and my community?

All levels of government need information on race to implement and evaluate programs, or enforce laws. Examples include: the Native American Programs Act, the Equal Employment Opportunity Act, the Civil Rights Act, the Voting Rights Act, the Public Health Act, the Healthcare Improvement Act, the Job Partnership Training Act, the Equal Credit Opportunity Act, the Fair Housing Act, and the Census Redistricting Data Program.

Both public and private organizations use race information to find areas where groups may need special services and to plan and implement education, housing, health, and other programs that address these needs. For example, a school system might use this information to design cultural activities that reflect the diversity in their community. Or a business could use it to select the mix of merchandise it will sell in a new store. Census information also helps identify areas where residents might need services of particular importance to certain racial or ethnic groups, such as screening for hypertension or diabetes.

FOR MORE INFORMATION

For more information on race in the United States, visit the U.S. Census Bureau's Internet site at *www.census.gov/population/www/socdemo/race.html.*

Race data from the Census 2000 Summary File 1 were released on a state-by-state basis during the summer of 2001. The Census 2000 Summary File 1 data are available on the Internet via *factfinder.census.gov* and for purchase on CD-ROM and DVD.

For information on confidentiality protection, nonsampling error, and definitions, see *www.census.gov/prod/cen2000/doc/sf1.pdf* or contact our Customer Services Center at 301-763-INFO (4636).

For more information on specific races in the United States, go to *www.census.gov* and click on "Minority Links." This Web page includes information about Census 2000 and provides links to reports based on past censuses and surveys focusing on the social and economic characteristics of the

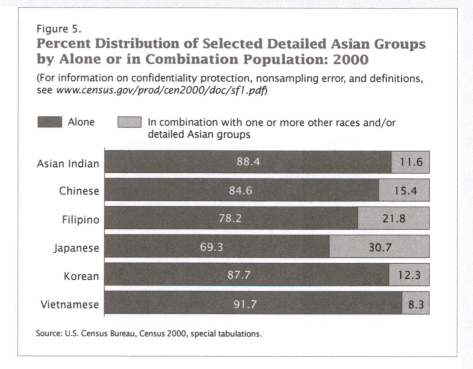

Figure 5.
Percent Distribution of Selected Detailed Asian Groups by Alone or in Combination Population: 2000
(For information on confidentiality protection, nonsampling error, and definitions, see *www.census.gov/prod/cen2000/doc/sf1.pdf*)

Alone ▮   In combination with one or more other races and/or detailed Asian groups ▮

Group	Alone	In combination
Asian Indian	88.4	11.6
Chinese	84.6	15.4
Filipino	78.2	21.8
Japanese	69.3	30.7
Korean	87.7	12.3
Vietnamese	91.7	8.3

Source: U.S. Census Bureau, Census 2000, special tabulations.

Black or African American, American Indian and Alaska Native, Asian, and Native Hawaiian and Other Pacific Islander populations.

Information on other population and housing topics is presented in the Census 2000 Brief series, located on the U.S. Census Bureau's Web site at *www.census.gov/population/www/cen2000/briefs.html.* This series presents

information on race, Hispanic origin, age, sex, household type, housing tenure, and other social, economic, and housing characteristics.

For more information about Census 2000, including data products, call our Customer Services Center at 301-763-INFO (4636), or e-mail *webmaster@census.gov.*

The American Indian and Alaska Native Population: 2000

Census 2000 Brief

Issued February 2002

C2KBR/01-15

By
Stella U. Ogunwole

Census 2000 showed that the United States population was 281.4 million on April 1, 2000. Of the total, 4.1 million, or 1.5 percent, reported[1] American Indian and Alaska Native. This number included 2.5 million people, or 0.9 percent, who reported only American Indian and Alaska Native in addition to 1.6 million people, or 0.6 percent, who reported American Indian and Alaska Native as well as one or more other races. The term American Indian is often used in the text of this report to refer to the American Indian and Alaska Native population, while American Indian and Alaska Native is used in the text tables and graphs. Census 2000 asked separate questions on race and Hispanic or Latino origin. Hispanics who reported their race as American Indian and Alaska Native, either alone or in combination with one or more races, are included in the number of American Indians.

This report, part of a series that analyzes population and housing data collected from Census 2000, provides a portrait of the American Indian population in the United States and discusses its distribution at both the national and subnational levels. It begins by discussing the characteristics of the total American Indian population and then focuses on selected tribal groupings,[2] for example, Navajo, Cherokee, or Eskimo. The report is based on data from the Census 2000 Summary File 1.[3] The text of this report discusses data for the United States, including the 50 states and the District of Columbia.[4]

Figure 1.

Reproduction of the Question on Race From Census 2000

6. **What is this person's race?** *Mark* ☒ *one or more races* to *indicate what this person considers himself/herself to be.*

☐ White
☐ Black, African Am., or Negro
☐ American Indian or Alaska Native — *Print name of enrolled or principal tribe.* ↗

☐ Asian Indian ☐ Japanese ☐ Native Hawaiian
☐ Chinese ☐ Korean ☐ Guamanian or Chamorro
☐ Filipino ☐ Vietnamese ☐ Samoan
☐ Other Asian — *Print race.* ↗ ☐ Other Pacific Islander — *Print race.* ↗

☐ Some other race — *Print race.* ↗

Source: U.S. Census Bureau, Census 2000 questionnaire.

---

[1] In this report, the term "reported" is used to refer to the answers provided by respondents, as well as responses assigned during the editing and imputation processes.

[2] Tribal grouping refers to the combining of individual American Indian tribes, such as Alamo Navajo, Tohajiileehee Navajo, and Ramah Navajo into the general Navajo tribe, or the combining of individual Alaska Native tribes such as American Eskimo, Eskimo and Greenland Eskimo into the general Eskimo tribe.

[3] Data from the Census 2000 Summary File 1 were released on a state-by-state basis during the summer of 2001.

[4] Data for the Commonwealth of Puerto Rico are shown in Table 2 and Figure 3.

USCENSUSBUREAU

Helping You Make Informed Decisions

U.S. Department of Commerce
Economics and Statistics Administration
U.S. CENSUS BUREAU

United States Census 2000

The term "American Indian and Alaska Native" refers to people having origins in any of the original peoples of North and South America (including Central America), and who maintain tribal affiliation or community attachment. It includes people who reported "American Indian and Alaska Native" or wrote in their principal or enrolled tribe.

Data on race have been collected since the first U.S. decennial census in 1790. American Indians were first enumerated as a separate group in the 1860 census. The 1890 census was the first to count American Indians throughout the country. Prior to 1890, enumeration of American Indians was limited to those living in the general population of the various states; American Indians in American Indian Territory and on American Indian reservations were not included.

Alaska Natives, in Alaska, have been counted since 1880, but until 1940, they were generally reported in the "American Indian" racial category. They were enumerated separately (as Eskimo and Aleut) in 1940 in Alaska. In the 1970 census, separate response categories were used to collect data on the Eskimo and Aleut population only in Alaska.

The 1980 census was the first in which data were collected separately for Eskimos and Aleuts in all states. The 1990 census used three separate response categories to collect data on the American Indian and Alaska Native population.

Census 2000 used a combined "American Indian or Alaska Native" response category to collect data on both the American Indian and Alaska Native population. Also, respondents were asked to provide the name of their enrolled or principal tribes. Previous decennial censuses collected data on both American Indian and Alaska Native tribes. However,

Census 2000 provides more extensive data for tribes than ever before.

The question on race was changed for Census 2000.

All U.S. censuses have obtained information on race for every individual and for the past several censuses, the responses reflect self-identification. For Census 2000, however, respondents were asked to report *one or more* races they considered themselves and other members of their households to be.[5]

Because of these changes, the Census 2000 data on race are not directly comparable with data from the 1990 census or earlier censuses. Caution must be used when interpreting changes in the racial composition of the United States population over time.

The Census 2000 question on race included 15 separate response categories and 3 areas where respondents could write in a more specific race (see Figure 1). For some purposes, including this report, the response categories and write-in answers were combined to create the five standard Office of Management and Budget race categories, plus the Census Bureau category of "Some other race." The six race categories include:

- White;
- Black or African American;

- American Indian and Alaska Native;
- Asian;
- Native Hawaiian and Other Pacific Islander; and
- Some other race

For a complete explanation of the race categories used in Census 2000, see the Census 2000 Brief, *Overview of Race and Hispanic Origin.*[6]

The data collected by Census 2000 on race can be divided into two broad categories: the race *alone* population and the race *in combination* population.

People who responded to the question on race by indicating *only one* race are referred to as the race *alone* population. For example, respondents who reported their race only as American Indian or Alaska Native on the census questionnaire would be included in the American Indian *alone* population.

Individuals who reported *more than one* of the six races are referred to as the race *in combination* population. For example, respondents who reported they were "American Indian *and* White" or "American Indian *and* Black or African American *and* Asian"[7] would be included in the American Indian *in combination* population.

---

[5] Other changes included terminology and formatting changes, such as spelling out "American" instead of "Amer." for the American Indian or Alaska Native category and adding "Native" to the Hawaiian response category. In the layout of the Census 2000 questionnaire, the seven Asian response categories were alphabetized and grouped together, as were the four Pacific Islander categories after the Native Hawaiian category. The three separate American Indian and Alaska Native identifiers in the 1990 census (i.e., Indian (Amer.), Eskimo, and Aleut) were combined into a single identifier in Census 2000. Also, American Indians and Alaska Natives could report more than one tribe.

---

[6] *Overview of Race and Hispanic Origin: 2000,* U.S. Census Bureau, Census 2000 Brief, C2KBR/01-1, March 2001, is available on the U.S. Census Bureau's Internet site at *www.census.gov/population/www/cen2000/briefs.html.*

[7] The race *in combination* categories are denoted by quotations around the combinations with the conjunction *and* in bold and italicized print to indicate the separate races that comprise the combination.

Table 1.
American Indian and Alaska Native Population: 2000

(For information on confidentiality protection, nonsampling error, and definitions, see www.census.gov/prod/cen2000/doc/sf1.pdf)

Race	Number	Percent of total population
Total population	281,412,906	100.0
American Indian and Alaska Native alone or in combination with one or more other races	4,119,301	1.5
American Indian and Alaska Native alone	2,475,956	0.9
American Indian and Alaska Native in combination with one or more other races	1,643,345	0.6
American Indian and Alaska Native; White	1,082,683	0.4
American Indian and Alaska Native; Black or African American	182,494	0.1
American Indian and Alaska Native; White; Black or African American	112,207	-
American Indian and Alaska Native; Some other race	93,842	-
All other combinations including American Indian and Alaska Native	172,119	0.1
Not American Indian and Alaska Native alone or in combination with one or more other races	277,293,605	98.5

- Percentage rounds to 0.0.

Source: U.S. Census Bureau, Census 2000 Summary File 1.

The American Indian population increased faster than the total population between 1990 and 2000.

Because of the changes made to the question on race for Census 2000, there are at least two ways to present the change in the total number of American Indians in the United States. They include: 1) the difference in the American Indian population between 1990 and 2000 using the race alone concept for 2000 and 2) the difference in the American Indian population between 1990 and 2000 using the race alone or in combination concept for 2000. These comparisons provide a "minimum-maximum" range for the change in the American Indian population between 1990 and 2000.

The 1990 census showed there were nearly 2 million American Indians. Using the American Indian alone population in 2000, this population increased by 516,722, or 26 percent, between 1990 and 2000. If the American Indian alone or in combination population is used, an increase of 2.2 million, or 110 percent, results. Thus, from 1990 to 2000, the range for the increase in the American Indian population was 26 percent to 110 percent. In comparison, the total population grew by 13 percent from 248.7 million in 1990 to 281.4 million in 2000.

THE GEOGRAPHIC DISTRIBUTION OF THE AMERICAN INDIAN POPULATION

The following discussion of the geographic distribution of the American Indian population focuses on the American Indian alone or in combination population in the text. As the upper bound of the American Indian population, this group includes all respondents who reported American Indian, whether or not

The maximum number of people reporting American Indian is reflected in the American Indian *alone or in combination* population.

One way to define the American Indian population is to combine those respondents who reported only American Indian with those who reported American Indian as well as one or more other races. This creates the American Indian *alone or in combination* population. Another way to think of the American Indian *alone or in combination* population is the total number of people who identified entirely or partially as American Indian. This group is also described as people who reported American Indian, whether or not they reported any other races.

Census 2000 provides a snapshot of the American Indian population.

Table 1 shows the number and percentage of Census 2000 respondents who reported American

Indian alone as well as those who reported American Indian and at least one other race.

Of the total United States population, 2.5 million people, or 0.9 percent, reported only American Indian. An additional 1.6 million people reported American Indian and at least one other race. Within this group, the most common combinations were "American Indian and Alaska Native *and* White" (66 percent), followed by "American Indian and Alaska Native *and* Black or African American" (11 percent), "American Indian and Alaska Native *and* White *and* Black or African American" (6.8 percent), and "American Indian and Alaska Native *and* Some other race" (5.7 percent). These four combination categories accounted for 90 percent of all American Indians who reported two or more races. Thus 4.1 million people, or 1.5 percent, of the total population, reported American Indian alone or in combination with one or more races.

they reported any other race.[8] Hereafter in the text of this section, the term "American Indian" will be used to refer to those who reported American Indian, whether they reported one race or more than one race. However, in the tables and graphs, data for both the American Indian alone and American Indian alone or in combination populations are shown.

Four out of ten American Indians lived in the West.[9]

According to Census 2000, of all respondents who reported American Indian, 43 percent lived in the West, 31 percent lived in the South, 17 percent lived in the Midwest, and 9 percent lived in the Northeast (see Figure 2).

The West had the largest American Indian population, as well as the highest proportion of American Indians in its total population: 2.8 percent of all respondents in the West and 1.3 percent in the South reported American Indian and Alaska Native, compared with 1.1 percent in the Midwest, and 0.7 percent in the Northeast.

---

[8] The use of the *alone* or *in combination* population in this section does not imply that it is the preferred method of presenting or analyzing data. In general, either the *alone* population or the *alone or in combination* population can be used, depending on the purpose of the analysis. The Census Bureau uses both approaches.

[9] The West region includes the states of Alaska, Arizona, California, Colorado, Hawaii, Idaho, Montana, Nevada, New Mexico, Oregon, Utah, Washington, and Wyoming. The South region includes the states of Alabama, Arkansas, Delaware, Florida, Georgia, Kentucky, Louisiana, Maryland, Mississippi, North Carolina, Oklahoma, South Carolina, Tennessee, Texas, Virginia, West Virginia, and the District of Columbia, a state equivalent. The Midwest region includes the states of Illinois, Indiana, Iowa, Kansas, Michigan, Minnesota, Missouri, Nebraska, North Dakota, Ohio, South Dakota, and Wisconsin. The Northeast region includes the states of Connecticut, Maine, Massachusetts, New Hampshire, New Jersey, New York, Pennsylvania, Rhode Island, and Vermont.

Over half of all people who reported American Indian lived in just ten states.

The ten states with the largest American Indian populations in 2000, in order, were California, Oklahoma, Arizona, Texas, New Mexico, New York, Washington, North Carolina, Michigan, and Alaska (see Table 2). Florida was the only other state with greater than 100,000 American Indian population. Combined, these 11 states included 62 percent of the total American Indian population, but only 44 percent of the total population. California (627,562) and Oklahoma (391,949) combined included about 25 percent of the total American Indian population.

There were 19 states where the American Indian population exceeded the U.S. proportion of 1.5 percent, led by the western state of Alaska (19 percent), followed by the southern state of Oklahoma (11 percent), and the western state of New Mexico (10 percent). The other 16 states included the western states of Arizona, California, Colorado, Idaho, Montana, Nevada, Hawaii, Oregon, Utah, Washington, and Wyoming; the midwestern states of Kansas, Minnesota, North Dakota, and South Dakota; and the southern state of North Carolina. No northeastern state had more than 1.5 percent of its population reporting as American Indian. Five states, Alaska, Oklahoma, New Mexico, Arizona, and Washington were represented in the top ten states in both number and percent reporting as American Indian.

American Indians were less than 1 percent of the total population in 21 states including Pennsylvania, New Jersey, West Virginia, Illinois, Massachusetts, Kentucky, Iowa, New Hampshire, Indiana, Georgia, Ohio, South Carolina, Mississippi, Tennessee, Connecticut, Florida,

Maryland, Virginia, Delaware, New York, and the District of Columbia, a state equivalent. While Texas had the fourth largest American Indian population of all states, it ranked 26th in percent of American Indian among the 50 states and the District of Columbia, with only 1 percent of respondents reporting American Indian. Wyoming had the 44th largest American Indian population, but ranked 8th in percent of the American Indian population among the 50 states and the District of Columbia.

The American Indian population was concentrated in counties in the West and Midwest.

American Indians were the majority of the population in 14 counties in the West and 12 counties in the Midwest (see Figure 3). In the West, the counties were in four states: Alaska, Arizona, Montana, and Utah. In the Midwest, the counties were also in four states: South Dakota, Wisconsin, North Dakota, and Nebraska.

Of the 3,141 counties or county equivalents in the United States, 786 counties met or exceeded the U.S. level of 1.5 percent of the total American Indian population, while the proportion reporting American Indian was below the national average in 2,355 counties.

The counties with their proportion reporting American Indian above the national average were located mostly west of the Mississippi River. Within this area, several clusters of counties with high percentages of American Indians were distinctly noticeable. Alaska Natives accounted for over 50 percent of the population in nearly all of the boroughs and census areas (county equivalents) in northern and western Alaska. In the Southwest, American Indians were represented in high percentages (and

Table 2.
American Indian and Alaska Native Population for the United States, Regions, and States, and for Puerto Rico: 1990 and 2000

(For information on confidentiality protection, nonsampling error, and definitions, see www.census.gov/prod/cen2000/doc/sf1.pdf)

Area	1990			2000						
		American Indian and Alaska Native population			American Indian and Alaska Native alone population		American Indian and Alaska Native alone or in combination population		American Indian and Alaska Native in combination population	
	Total population	Number	Percent of total population	Total population	Number	Percent of total population	Number	Percent of total population	Number	Percent of American Indian and Alaska Native alone or in combination population
United States	248,709,873	1,959,234	0.8	281,421,906	2,475,956	0.9	4,119,301	1.5	1,643,345	39.9
Region										
Northeast.	50,809,229	125,148	0.2	53,594,378	162,558	0.3	374,035	0.7	211,477	56.5
Midwest.	59,668,632	337,899	0.6	64,392,776	399,490	0.6	714,792	1.1	315,302	44.1
South	85,445,930	562,731	0.7	100,236,820	725,919	0.7	1,259,230	1.3	533,311	42.4
West.	52,786,082	933,456	1.8	63,197,932	1,187,989	1.9	1,771,244	2.8	583,255	32.9
State										
Alabama	4,040,587	16,506	0.4	4,447,100	22,430	0.5	44,449	1.0	22,019	49.5
Alaska.	550,043	85,698	15.6	626,932	98,043	15.6	119,241	19.0	21,198	17.8
Arizona	3,665,228	203,527	5.6	5,130,632	255,879	5.0	292,552	5.7	36,673	12.5
Arkansas	2,350,725	12,773	0.5	2,673,400	17,808	0.7	37,002	1.4	19,194	51.9
California	29,760,021	242,164	0.8	33,871,648	333,346	1.0	627,562	1.9	294,216	46.9
Colorado	3,294,394	27,776	0.8	4,301,261	44,241	1.0	79,689	1.9	35,448	44.5
Connecticut	3,287,116	6,654	0.2	3,405,565	9,639	0.3	24,488	0.7	14,849	60.6
Delaware	666,168	2,019	0.3	783,600	2,731	0.3	6,069	0.8	3,338	55.0
District of Columbia	606,900	1,466	0.2	572,059	1,713	0.3	4,775	0.8	3,062	64.1
Florida.	12,937,926	36,335	0.3	15,982,378	53,541	0.3	117,880	0.7	64,339	54.6
Georgia	6,478,216	13,348	0.2	8,186,453	21,737	0.3	53,197	0.6	31,460	59.1
Hawaii.	1,108,229	5,099	0.5	1,211,537	3,535	0.3	24,882	2.1	21,347	85.8
Idaho	1,006,749	13,780	1.4	1,293,953	17,645	1.4	27,237	2.1	9,592	35.2
Illinois	11,430,602	21,836	0.2	12,419,293	31,006	0.2	73,161	0.6	42,155	57.6
Indiana	5,544,159	12,720	0.2	6,080,485	15,815	0.3	39,263	0.6	23,448	59.7
Iowa	2,776,755	7,349	0.3	2,926,324	8,989	0.3	18,246	0.6	9,257	50.7
Kansas	2,477,574	21,965	0.9	2,688,418	24,936	0.9	47,363	1.8	22,427	47.4
Kentucky	3,685,296	5,769	0.2	4,041,769	8,616	0.2	24,552	0.6	15,936	64.9
Louisiana	4,219,973	18,541	0.4	4,468,976	25,477	0.6	42,878	1.0	17,401	40.6
Maine	1,227,928	5,998	0.5	1,274,923	7,098	0.6	13,156	1.0	6,058	46.0
Maryland	4,781,468	12,972	0.3	5,296,486	15,423	0.3	39,437	0.7	24,014	60.9
Massachusetts	6,016,425	12,241	0.2	6,349,097	15,015	0.2	38,050	0.6	23,035	60.5
Michigan	9,295,297	55,638	0.6	9,938,444	58,479	0.6	124,412	1.3	65,933	53.0
Minnesota	4,375,099	49,909	1.1	4,919,479	54,967	1.1	81,074	1.6	26,107	32.2
Mississippi	2,573,216	8,525	0.3	2,844,658	11,652	0.4	19,555	0.7	7,903	40.4
Missouri	5,117,073	19,835	0.4	5,595,211	25,076	0.4	60,099	1.1	35,023	58.3
Montana	799,065	47,679	6.0	902,195	56,068	6.2	66,320	7.4	10,252	15.5
Nebraska	1,578,385	12,410	0.8	1,711,263	14,896	0.9	22,204	1.3	7,308	32.9
Nevada	1,201,833	19,637	1.6	1,998,257	26,420	1.3	42,222	2.1	15,802	37.4
New Hampshire	1,109,252	2,134	0.2	1,235,786	2,964	0.2	7,885	0.6	4,921	62.4
New Jersey	7,730,188	14,970	0.2	8,414,350	19,492	0.2	49,104	0.6	29,612	60.3
New Mexico	1,515,069	134,355	8.9	1,819,046	173,483	9.5	191,475	10.5	17,992	9.4
New York.	17,990,455	62,651	0.3	18,976,457	82,461	0.4	171,581	0.9	89,120	51.9
North Carolina	6,628,637	80,155	1.2	8,049,313	99,551	1.2	131,736	1.6	32,185	24.4
North Dakota	638,800	25,917	4.1	642,200	31,329	4.9	35,228	5.5	3,899	11.1
Ohio	10,847,115	20,358	0.2	11,353,140	24,486	0.2	76,075	0.7	51,589	67.8
Oklahoma	3,145,585	252,420	8.0	3,450,654	273,230	7.9	391,949	11.4	118,719	30.3
Oregon	2,842,321	38,496	1.4	3,421,399	45,211	1.3	85,667	2.5	40,456	47.2
Pennsylvania	11,881,643	14,733	0.1	12,281,054	18,348	0.1	52,650	0.4	34,302	65.2
Rhode Island	1,003,464	4,071	0.4	1,048,319	5,121	0.5	10,725	1.0	5,604	52.3
South Carolina	3,486,703	8,246	0.2	4,012,012	13,718	0.3	27,456	0.7	13,738	50.0
South Dakota	696,004	50,575	7.3	754,844	62,283	8.3	68,281	9.0	5,998	8.8
Tennessee	4,877,185	10,039	0.2	5,689,283	15,152	0.3	39,188	0.7	24,036	61.3
Texas	16,986,510	65,877	0.4	20,851,820	118,362	0.6	215,599	1.0	97,237	45.1
Utah	1,722,850	24,283	1.4	2,233,169	29,684	1.3	40,445	1.8	10,761	26.6
Vermont	562,758	1,696	0.3	608,827	2,420	0.4	6,396	1.1	3,976	62.2
Virginia	6,187,358	15,282	0.2	7,078,515	21,172	0.3	52,864	0.7	31,692	60.0
Washington	4,866,692	81,483	1.7	5,894,121	93,301	1.6	158,940	2.7	65,639	41.3
West Virginia	1,793,477	2,458	0.1	1,808,344	3,606	0.2	10,644	0.6	7,038	66.1
Wisconsin	4,891,769	39,387	0.8	5,363,675	47,228	0.9	69,386	1.3	22,158	31.9
Wyoming	453,588	9,479	2.1	493,782	11,133	2.3	15,012	3.0	3,879	25.8
Puerto Rico	3,522,037	(X)	(X)	3,808,610	13,336	0.4	26,871	0.7	13,535	50.4

X Not applicable.

Source: U.S. Census Bureau, Census 2000 Summary File 1; 1990 Census of Population, *General Population Characteristics (1990 CP-1)*.

also in large numbers) in the counties in the Four Corners area of Arizona, New Mexico, Utah, and Colorado (where the boundaries of these four states meet). In the Great Plains, American Indians were concentrated in a cluster of counties in central and western South Dakota, southeastern Montana, and in several counties along the U.S.-Canadian border in Montana and North Dakota. In the southern Plains, American Indians accounted for relatively high percentages of the population in a cluster of counties in eastern Oklahoma. American Indians accounted for more than the U.S. level of 1.5 percent in all but one county (Harper County) in Oklahoma.

East of the Mississippi, counties in which American Indians were represented in percentages higher than the U.S. level of 1.5 percent were scattered throughout the South, Northeast, and upper Midwest. Two clusters of counties in North Carolina — one in the extreme southwest of the state and the other in the southeast — were evident; each cluster was anchored by a county in which American Indians accounted for over 25 percent of the population. Elsewhere in the South, groups of counties in which American Indians were represented at greater than the U.S. proportion were found in central Louisiana, portions of the Gulf Coast, northern Alabama, and in eastern Virginia.

In the Northeast, counties meeting or exceeding the national proportion of American Indians tended to be nonmetropolitan and along the U.S. and Canadian border of New York, Vermont, and Maine, although concentrations were found in the New York city area, metropolitan Rhode Island and Connecticut, and in western New York. In the Midwest, counties with high percentages of American Indians were located

Figure 2.

Percent Distribution of the American Indian and Alaska Native Population by Region: 2000

(For information on confidentiality protection, nonsampling error, and definitions, see *www.census.gov/prod/cen2000/doc/sf1.pdf*)

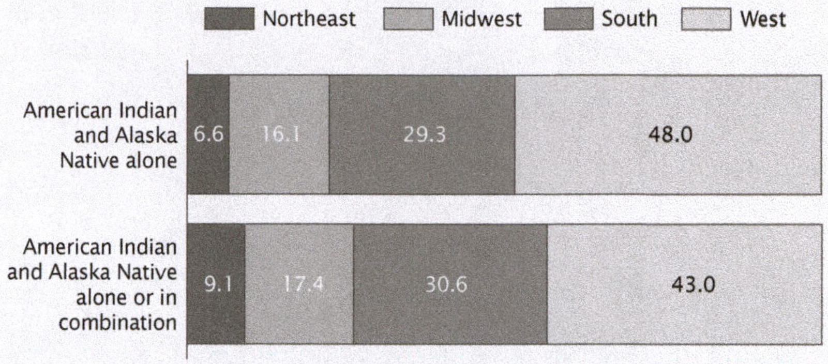

	Northeast	Midwest	South	West
American Indian and Alaska Native alone	6.6	16.1	29.3	48.0
American Indian and Alaska Native alone or in combination	9.1	17.4	30.6	43.0

Source: U.S. Census Bureau, Census 2000 Summary File 1.

primarily across northern Minnesota, Wisconsin, and Michigan. In general, counties throughout most of the lower Midwest, upper South, and Northeast were distinguished by very low percentages of American Indians.

The places with the largest American Indian populations were New York and Los Angeles.

Census 2000 showed that, of all places in the United States with 100,000 or more population,[10] New York and Los Angeles had the largest American Indian populations with 87,241 and 53,092, respectively (see Table 3). The next eight places with the largest American Indian populations had between 15,743 and 35,093 American Indians. Five of the top ten places — Los Angeles, Phoenix, San Diego, Anchorage, and Albuquerque — were in the West.

---

[10] Census 2000 showed 245 places in the United States with 100,000 or more population. They included 238 incorporated places (including 4 city-county consolidations) and 7 census designated places that are not legally incorporated. For a list of these places by state, see *www.census.gov/population/www/cen2000/phc-t6.html*.

The ten largest places for American Indians together accounted for 8.2 percent of the total U.S. American Indian population. New York and Los Angeles accounted for 3.4 percent of the total American Indian population (see Table 3). Of the ten largest places in the United States, Phoenix (2.7 percent) had the largest proportion of American Indians, followed by Los Angeles (1.4 percent), and San Diego and San Antonio, each with 1.3 percent.

Among places of 100,000 or more population, the highest proportion of American Indians was in Anchorage (10 percent) as shown in Figure 4. Tulsa was the second highest. Six of the top ten places with the highest proportion of American Indians were in the West, with two each in the Midwest and South.

ADDITIONAL FINDINGS ON THE AMERICAN INDIAN AND ALASKA NATIVE POPULATION

What proportion of American Indians and Alaska Natives reported a tribe?

In Census 2000, people who identified themselves as American Indian

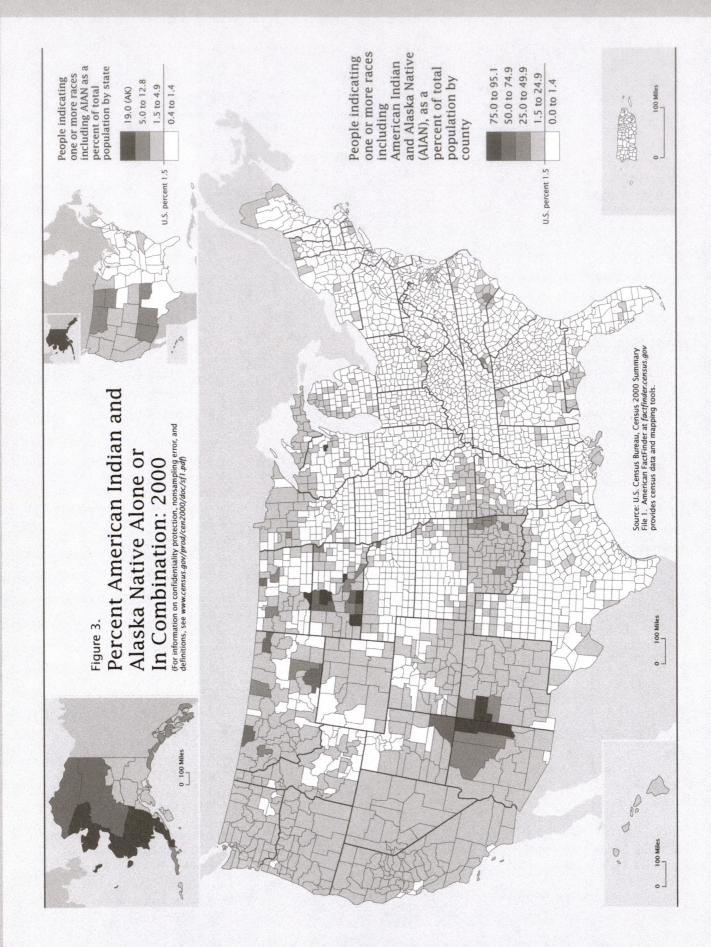

Figure 3.

Percent American Indian and Alaska Native Alone or In Combination: 2000

(For information on confidentiality protection, nonsampling error, and definitions, see *www.census.gov/prod/cen2000/doc/sf1.pdf*)

People indicating one or more races including AIAN as a percent of total population by state

19.0 (AK)
5.0 to 12.8
1.5 to 4.9
0.4 to 1.4

U.S. percent 1.5

People indicating one or more races including American Indian and Alaska Native (AIAN), as a percent of total population by county

75.0 to 95.1
50.0 to 74.9
25.0 to 49.9
1.5 to 24.9
0.0 to 1.4

U.S. percent 1.5

Source: U.S. Census Bureau, Census 2000 Summary File 1. American FactFinder at *factfinder.census.gov* provides census data and mapping tools.

Table 3.
Ten Largest Places in Total Population and in American Indian and Alaska Native Population: 2000

(For information on confidentiality protection, nonsampling error, and definitions, see *www.census.gov/prod/cen2000/doc/sf1.pdf*)

Place	Total population		American Indian and Alaska Native alone		American Indian and Alaska Native alone or in combination		Percent of total population	
	Rank	Number	Rank	Number	Rank	Number	American Indian and Alaska Native alone	American Indian and Alaska Native alone or in combination
New York, NY........	1	8,008,278	1	41,289	1	87,241	0.5	1.1
Los Angeles, CA	2	3,694,820	2	29,412	2	53,092	0.8	1.4
Chicago, IL	3	2,896,016	9	10,290	8	20,898	0.4	0.7
Houston, TX	4	1,953,631	11	8,568	10	15,743	0.4	0.8
Philadelphia, PA......	5	1,517,550	24	4,073	21	10,835	0.3	0.7
Phoenix, AZ	6	1,321,045	3	26,696	3	35,093	2.0	2.7
San Diego, CA.......	7	1,223,400	13	7,543	9	16,178	0.6	1.3
Dallas, TX...........	8	1,188,580	18	6,472	18	11,334	0.5	1.0
San Antonio, TX......	9	1,144,646	10	9,584	12	15,224	0.8	1.3
Detroit, MI	10	951,270	40	3,140	25	8,907	0.3	0.9
Oklahoma, OK.......	29	506,132	6	17,743	5	29,001	3.5	5.7
Tucson, AZ	30	486,699	8	11,038	11	15,358	2.3	3.2
Albuquerque, NM.....	35	448,607	7	17,444	7	22,047	3.9	4.9
Tulsa, OK	43	393,049	5	18,551	4	30,227	4.7	7.7
Anchorage, AK.......	65	260,283	4	18,941	6	26,995	7.3	10.4

Source: U.S. Census Bureau, Census 2000 Summary File 1.

or Alaska Native on the questionnaire were asked to report their enrolled or principal tribe. Additionally, respondents could report one or more tribes (see Table 4). Among respondents who reported as American Indian, 79 percent, or 2.0 million people, specified a tribe. For those who reported American Indian in any combination, 67 percent, or 1.1 million people, reported a tribe. For all people reporting American Indian either alone or in any combination, 74 percent, or 3.1 million people, identified a tribe.

Which American Indian tribal groupings were the largest?

According to Census 2000, the American Indian tribal groupings with 100,000 or more people or responses were Cherokee, Navajo, Latin American Indian,[11] Choctaw,

Sioux, and Chippewa (see Figure 5 and Table 5).[12] These six tribal groups accounted for 40 percent of all respondents who reported a single grouping or race. Of all American Indian tribal groupings in any combination, these six tribal groups accounted for 42 percent of all responses. There were 281,069 respondents who reported Cherokee alone and an additional 448,464 who reported Cherokee with at least one other race or American Indian tribal grouping. A total of 729,533 people reported Cherokee alone or in combination with one or more other race or American Indian tribal groupings.

Navajo and Latin American were the next two largest specified American Indian tribal groupings. There were 269,202 people who reported Navajo alone and an additional

28,995 people who reported Navajo in combination with one or more other races or American tribal groupings. This gives a total of 298,197 people who reported Navajo alone or in combination with at least one other race or American Indian tribal groupings. There were 104,354 people who reported only Latin American Indian and an additional 76,586 who reported Latin American in combination with one or more other races or American Indian tribal groupings. A total of 180,940 people reported Latin American Indian alone or in combination with at least one other race or American Indian tribal groupings.

Which Alaska Native tribal groupings were the largest?

In 2000, Eskimo was the largest Alaska Native tribal grouping alone or in any combination, followed by Tlingit-Haida, Alaska Athabascan, and Aleut. These four tribal groupings combined accounted for 3.6 percent of all American Indian

---

[11] In 1997, the Office of Management and Budget definition of American Indian or Alaska Native included the original peoples of North and South America (including Central America).

[12] Table 5 contains all American Indian and Alaska Native tribal groupings that contained at least 7,000 people according to the 1990 census. Additional information on individual tribes is forthcoming.

307

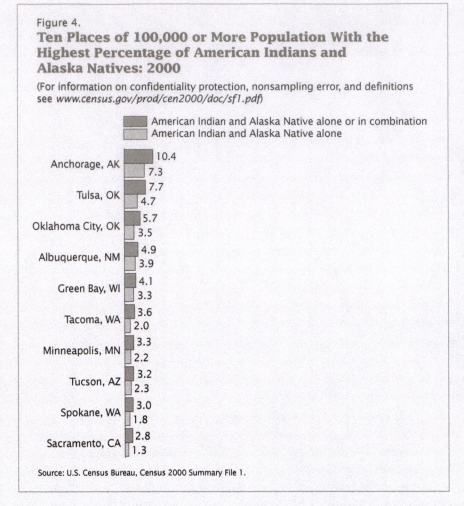

Figure 4.

Ten Places of 100,000 or More Population With the Highest Percentage of American Indians and Alaska Natives: 2000

(For information on confidentiality protection, nonsampling error, and definitions see *www.census.gov/prod/cen2000/doc/sf1.pdf*)

■ American Indian and Alaska Native alone or in combination
□ American Indian and Alaska Native alone

Place	alone or in combination	alone
Anchorage, AK	10.4	7.3
Tulsa, OK	7.7	4.7
Oklahoma City, OK	5.7	3.5
Albuquerque, NM	4.9	3.9
Green Bay, WI	4.1	3.3
Tacoma, WA	3.6	2.0
Minneapolis, MN	3.3	2.2
Tucson, AZ	3.2	2.3
Spokane, WA	3.0	1.8
Sacramento, CA	2.8	1.3

Source: U.S. Census Bureau, Census 2000 Summary File 1.

and Alaska Native tribal responses alone and 2.7 percent alone or in any combination (see Figure 6 and Table 5).

There were 45,919 respondents who reported Eskimo alone and an additional 8,842 who reported Eskimo with at least one other race or American Indian or Alaska Native tribal grouping. A total of 54,761 people reported Eskimo alone or in combination with one or more other races or American Indian or Alaska Native tribal groupings.

Tlingit-Haida, Alaska Athabascan, and Aleut were the next three largest specified Alaska Native tribal groupings. There were 14,825 people who reported Tlingit-Haida alone and an additional 7,540 who reported Tlingit-Haida with at least

one other race or American Indian or Alaska Native tribal groupings. A total of 22,365 people reported Tlingit-Haida alone or in combination with one or more other races or American Indian or Alaska Native tribal groupings.

There were 14,520 people who reported only Alaska Athabascan and an additional 4,318 people who reported Alaska Athabascan with one or more other races or American Indian or Alaska Native tribal groupings. A total of 18,838 people reported Alaska Athabascan alone or in combination with at least one or more other races or American Indian or Alaska Native tribal groupings.

Also, there were 11,941 people who reported only Aleut and an addition-

al 5,037 people who reported Aleut with one or more other races or American Indian or Alaska Native tribal groupings. A total of 16,978 people reported Aleut alone or in combination with at least one or more other races or American Indian or Alaska Native tribal groupings.

What proportion of American Indians and Alaska Natives reported more than one tribal grouping?

The proportion of respondents reporting a tribe with at least one other race or American Indian tribal grouping varied among the ten largest American Indian tribal groupings (see Table 5). Of all the respondents who reported more than one race or American Indian tribal grouping, the Blackfeet tribal grouping had the highest proportion, with 68 percent. The next two tribal groupings with the highest proportion of respondents reporting at least one other race or American Indian tribal grouping were Cherokee (62 percent) and Choctaw (45 percent). Of the ten largest American Indian tribal groupings, the Navajo had the lowest proportion (9.7 percent) reporting more than one race or American Indian tribal grouping, followed by Pueblo (19.6 percent).

Among the largest Alaska Native tribal groupings, the highest proportion of all respondents who reported more than one race or American Indian or Alaska Native tribal groupings was the Tlingit-Haida with 34 percent. The other tribal groupings with respondents reporting at least one other race or American Indian or Alaska Native tribal grouping were Aleut (30 percent) and Alaska Athabascan (23 percent). The Eskimo had the lowest proportion of respondents (16 percent) reporting more than one race or American Indian tribal grouping.

ABOUT CENSUS 2000

Why did Census 2000 ask the question on race?

The Census Bureau collects data on race to fulfill a variety of legislative and program requirements. Data on race are used in the legislative redistricting process carried out by the states and in monitoring local jurisdictions' compliance with the Voting Rights Act. These data are also essential for evaluating federal programs that promote equal access to employment, education, and housing and for assessing racial disparities in health and exposure to environmental risks. More broadly, data on race are critical for research that underlies many policy decisions at all levels of government.

How do data from the question on race benefit me, my family, and my community?

All levels of government need information on race to implement and evaluate programs or enforce laws. Examples include: the Native American Programs Act, the Equal Employment Opportunity Act, the Civil Rights Act, the Voting Rights Act, the Public Health Act, the Healthcare Improvement Act, the Job Partnership Training Act, the Equal Credit Opportunity Act, the Fair Housing Act, and the Census Redistricting Data Program.

Both public and private organizations use race information to find areas where groups may need special services and to plan and implement education, housing, health, and other programs that address these needs. For example, a school system might use this information to design cultural activities that reflect the diversity in their community. Or a business could use it to select the mix of merchandise it will sell in a new store. Census information also helps identify areas where residents might need services of particular importance to certain racial or ethnic groups, such as screening for hypertension or diabetes.

Table 4.
Specified Tribe Reported by American Indians and Alaska Natives: 2000

(For information on confidentiality protection, nonsampling error, and definitions, see *www.census.gov/prod/cen2000/doc/sf1.pdf*)

Whether or not tribe specified	American Indian and Alaska Native					
	Total		Alone		In combination	
	Number	Percent	Number	Percent	Number	Percent
Total..............	**4,119,301**	**100.0**	**2,475,956**	**100.0**	**1,643,345**	**100.0**
Tribe specified	3,062,844	74.4	1,963,996	79.3	1,098,848	66.9
Tribe not specified.	1,056,457	25.6	511,960	20.7	544,497	33.1

Source: U.S. Census Bureau, Census 2000 Summary File 1.

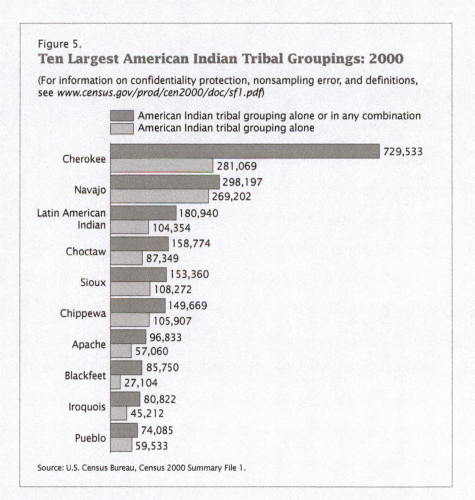

Figure 5.
Ten Largest American Indian Tribal Groupings: 2000

(For information on confidentiality protection, nonsampling error, and definitions, see *www.census.gov/prod/cen2000/doc/sf1.pdf*)

■ American Indian tribal grouping alone or in any combination
▢ American Indian tribal grouping alone

Tribe	Alone or in any combination	Alone
Cherokee	729,533	281,069
Navajo	298,197	269,202
Latin American Indian	180,940	104,354
Choctaw	158,774	87,349
Sioux	153,360	108,272
Chippewa	149,669	105,907
Apache	96,833	57,060
Blackfeet	85,750	27,104
Iroquois	80,822	45,212
Pueblo	74,085	59,533

Source: U.S. Census Bureau, Census 2000 Summary File 1.

FOR MORE INFORMATION

For more information on race in the United States, visit the U.S. Census Bureau's Internet site at *www.census.gov/population/www/socdemo/race.html*.

Table 5.
American Indian and Alaska Native Population by Selected Tribal Grouping: 2000

(For information on confidentiality protection, nonsampling error, and definitions, see www.census.gov/prod/cen2000/doc/sf1.pdf)

Tribal grouping	American and Alaska Native alone		American Indian and Alaska Native in combination with one or more races		American Indian and Alaska Native tribal grouping alone or in any combination[1]
	One tribal grouping reported	More than one tribal grouping reported[1]	One tribal grouping reported	More than one tribal grouping reported[1]	
Total..........................	2,423,531	52,425	1,585,396	57,949	4,119,301
Apache	57,060	7,917	24,947	6,909	96,833
Blackfeet	27,104	4,358	41,389	12,899	85,750
Cherokee.....................	281,069	18,793	390,902	38,769	729,533
Cheyenne	11,191	1,365	4,655	993	18,204
Chickasaw....................	20,887	3,014	12,025	2,425	38,351
Chippewa	105,907	2,730	38,635	2,397	149,669
Choctaw	87,349	9,552	50,123	11,750	158,774
Colville......................	7,833	193	1,308	59	9,393
Comanche....................	10,120	1,568	6,120	1,568	19,376
Cree........................	2,488	724	3,577	945	7,734
Creek.......................	40,223	5,495	21,652	3,940	71,310
Crow........................	9,117	574	2,812	891	13,394
Delaware.....................	8,304	602	6,866	569	16,341
Houma.......................	6,798	79	1,794	42	8,713
Iroquois	45,212	2,318	29,763	3,529	80,822
Kiowa.......................	8,559	1,130	2,119	434	12,242
Latin American Indian..............	104,354	1,850	73,042	1,694	180,940
Lumbee......................	51,913	642	4,934	379	57,868
Menominee....................	7,883	258	1,551	148	9,840
Navajo.......................	269,202	6,789	19,491	2,715	298,197
Osage	7,658	1,354	5,491	1,394	15,897
Ottawa......................	6,432	623	3,174	448	10,677
Paiute.......................	9,705	1,163	2,315	349	13,532
Pima........................	8,519	999	1,741	234	11,493
Potawatomi	15,817	592	8,602	584	25,595
Pueblo.......................	59,533	3,527	9,943	1,082	74,085
Puget Sound Salish	11,034	226	3,212	159	14,631
Seminole.....................	12,431	2,982	9,505	2,513	27,431
Shoshone	7,739	714	3,039	534	12,026
Sioux.......................	108,272	4,794	35,179	5,115	153,360
Tohono O'odham.................	17,466	714	1,748	159	20,087
Ute.........................	7,309	715	1,944	417	10,385
Yakama	8,481	561	1,619	190	10,851
Yaqui	15,224	1,245	5,184	759	22,412
Yuman.......................	7,295	526	1,051	104	8,976
Other specified American Indian tribes .	240,521	9,468	100,346	7,323	357,658
American Indian tribe, not specified[2]...	109,644	57	86,173	28	195,902
Alaska Athabascan	14,520	815	3,218	285	18,838
Aleut.......................	11,941	832	3,850	355	16,978
Eskimo.......................	45,919	1,418	6,919	505	54,761
Tlingit-Haida...................	14,825	1,059	6,047	434	22,365
Other specified Alaska Native tribes ...	2,552	435	841	145	3,973
Alaska Native tribe, not specified[2]	6,161	370	2,053	118	8,702
American Indian or Alaska Native tribes, not specified[3]	511,960	(X)	544,497	(X)	1,056,457

X Not applicable.

[1]The numbers by American Indian and Alaska Native tribal grouping do not add to the total population. This is because the American Indian and Alaska Native tribal groupings are tallies of the number of American Indian and Alaska Native **responses** rather than the number of American Indian and Alaska Native **respondents.** Respondents reporting several American Indian and Alaska Native tribes are counted several times. For example, a respondent reporting "Apache and Blackfeet" would be included in the Apache as well as Blackfeet numbers.

[2]Includes respondents who checked the "American Indian or Alaska Native" response category on the census questionnaire or wrote in a tribe not specified in the American Indian and Alaska Native Tribal Detailed Classification List for Census 2000.

[3]Includes respondents who checked the "American Indian or Alaska Native" response category on the census questionnaire or wrote in the generic term "American Indian" or "Alaska Native," or tribal entries not elsewhere classified.

Source: U.S. Census Bureau, Census 2000, special tabulations.

Race data from Census 2000 Summary File 1 were released on a state-by-state basis during the summer of 2001, including data for selected American and Alaska Native tribal groupings.

The Census 2000 Summary File 1 data are available on the Internet via *factfinder.census.gov* and for purchase on CD-ROM and on DVD.

For information on confidentiality protection, nonsampling error, and definitions, also see *www.census.gov/prod/cen2000/doc/sf1.pdf* or contact our Customer Services Center at 301-763-INFO (4636).

For more information on specific races in the United States, go to *www.census.gov* and click on "Minority Links." This Web page includes information about Census 2000 and provides links to reports based on past censuses and surveys focusing on the social and economic characteristics of the Black or African American, American Indian and Alaska Native, Asian, and Native Hawaiian and Other Pacific Islander populations.

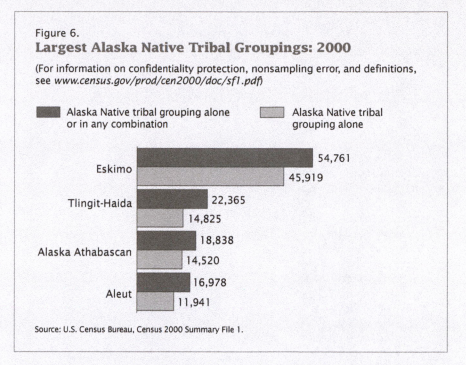

Figure 6.

Largest Alaska Native Tribal Groupings: 2000

(For information on confidentiality protection, nonsampling error, and definitions, see *www.census.gov/prod/cen2000/doc/sf1.pdf*)

■ Alaska Native tribal grouping alone or in any combination   ▢ Alaska Native tribal grouping alone

Eskimo — 54,761 / 45,919

Tlingit-Haida — 22,365 / 14,825

Alaska Athabascan — 18,838 / 14,520

Aleut — 16,978 / 11,941

Source: U.S. Census Bureau, Census 2000 Summary File 1.

Information on other population and housing topics is presented in the Census 2000 Brief series, located on the U.S. Census Bureau's Web site at *www.census.gov/population/www/cen2000/briefs.html*. This series presents information on race, Hispanic origin, age, sex, household type, housing tenure, and other social, economic, and housing characteristics.

For more information about Census 2000, including data products, call our Customer Services Center at 301-763-INFO (4636), or e-mail *webmaster@census.gov*.

The Hispanic Population

Census 2000 Brief

2000

Issued May 2001

C2KBR/01-3

By
Betsy Guzmán

In Census 2000, 281.4 million residents were counted in the United States (excluding the Commonwealth of Puerto Rico and the U.S. Island Areas[1]), of which 35.3 million (or 12.5 percent) were Hispanic. Mexicans represented 7.3 percent, Puerto Ricans 1.2 percent, Cubans 0.4 percent, and other Hispanics 3.6 percent of the total population.[2] An additional 3.8 million Hispanics were enumerated in the Commonwealth of Puerto Rico. This report, part of a series that analyzes population and housing data collected by Census 2000, provides a profile of the Hispanic population in the United States.

The concept and measurement of Hispanic origin have evolved across several censuses.[3]

In Census 2000, people of Spanish/Hispanic/Latino origin could identify as Mexican, Puerto Rican, Cuban, or other Spanish/Hispanic/Latino.[4] The term "Latino" appeared on the census form for

Figure 1.
Reproduction of the Question on Hispanic Origin From Census 2000

5. **Is this person Spanish/Hispanic/Latino?** *Mark* ☒ *the "No" box if not Spanish/Hispanic/Latino.*
☐ **No,** not Spanish/Hispanic/Latino ☐ Yes, Puerto Rican
☐ Yes, Mexican, Mexican Am., Chicano ☐ Yes, Cuban
☐ Yes, other Spanish/Hispanic/Latino — *Print group.* ↘

Source: U.S. Census Bureau, Census 2000 questionnaire.

the first time in 2000 (see Figure 1). People who marked "other Spanish/Hispanic/Latino" had additional space to write Hispanic origins, such as Salvadoran or Dominican, a practice started in the 1990 census. The 1990 and 1980 censuses asked people if they were of "Spanish/Hispanic origin or descent" and if so, to choose Mexican, Puerto Rican, Cuban, or other Spanish/Hispanic.

The census in 1970 was the first to include a separate question specifically on Hispanic origin, although it was only asked of a 5-percent sample of households. In 1970, respondents were asked to choose whether their origin or descent was Mexican, Puerto Rican, Cuban, Central or South American, or other Spanish. Prior to 1970, Hispanic origin was determined only indirectly; for example, the 1960 and 1950 censuses collected and published data for "persons of Spanish surname" in five southwestern states,[5] whereas the 1940 census identified

---

[1] The U.S. Island Areas include U.S. Virgin Islands, Guam, American Samoa, and the Commonwealth of the Northern Mariana Islands.

[2] The population universe for the size and distribution of the Hispanic population does not include data for the Commonwealth of Puerto Rico. Data for Puerto Rico are shown and discussed separately.

[3] People of Hispanic origin, in particular, were those who indicated that their origin was Mexican, Puerto Rican, Cuban, Central or South American, or some other Hispanic origin. For example, people who indicate that they are of Mexican origin may be either born in Mexico or of Mexican heritage. People of Hispanic origin may be of any race.

[4] The terms "Hispanic" and "Latino" may be used interchangeably to reflect the new terminology in the standards issued by the Office of Management and Budget in 1997 that are to be implemented by January 1, 2003.

[5] These states included Arizona, California, Colorado, New Mexico, and Texas.

USCENSUSBUREAU

Helping You Make Informed Decisions

U.S. Department of Commerce
Economics and Statistics Administration
U.S. CENSUS BUREAU

United States
Census 2000

people who reported Spanish as their "mother tongue." Mexican was included as a category within the race question only in the 1930 census.[6]

The Hispanic population increased by more than 50 percent since 1990.

The Hispanic population increased by 57.9 percent, from 22.4 million in 1990 to 35.3 million in 2000, compared with an increase of 13.2 percent for the total U.S. population. Population growth varied by group. Mexicans increased by 52.9 percent, from 13.5 million to 20.6 million. Puerto Ricans increased by 24.9 percent, from 2.7 million to 3.4 million. Cubans increased by 18.9 percent, from 1.0 million to 1.2 million. Hispanics who reported other origins increased by 96.9 percent, from 5.1 million to 10.0 million.[7]

As a result of these different growth rates, the proportionate distribution of Hispanics by type changed between 1990 and 2000. In 2000, Mexicans were 58.5 percent of all Hispanics (down from 60.4 percent in 1990), Puerto Ricans were 9.6 percent (down from 12.2 percent), Cubans were 3.5 percent (down from 4.7 percent), and the remaining 28.4 percent were of other Hispanic origins (up from 22.8 percent) as shown in Figure 2.

Other Hispanic origins refer to a variety of identifications.

Among the 10.0 million other Hispanics in 2000, 1.7 million were

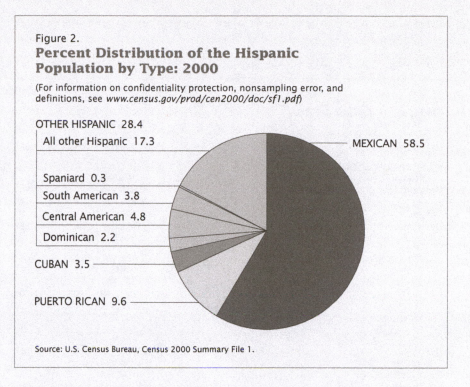

Figure 2.
Percent Distribution of the Hispanic Population by Type: 2000

(For information on confidentiality protection, nonsampling error, and definitions, see *www.census.gov/prod/cen2000/doc/sf1.pdf*)

OTHER HISPANIC 28.4
All other Hispanic 17.3

Spaniard 0.3
South American 3.8
Central American 4.8
Dominican 2.2
CUBAN 3.5
PUERTO RICAN 9.6
MEXICAN 58.5

Source: U.S. Census Bureau, Census 2000 Summary File 1.

Central American, 1.4 million were South American, and 765,000 were Dominican.

Most other Hispanics did not specify a detailed Hispanic origin, but either checked the Spanish/Hispanic/Latino box without providing any additional information or wrote in answers such as "Hispanic" or "Latino" or "Spanish" (see Table 1). At 17.3 percent (6.1 million) of the total Hispanic population, Hispanic respondents who did not give a detailed origin answer were second in size only to the Mexican origin group.

Salvadorans were the largest Central American group.

Central Americans represented 4.8 percent of the total Hispanic population. There were 655,000 Salvadorans (1.9 percent of the total Hispanic population), 372,000 Guatemalans (1.1 percent), and 218,000 Hondurans (0.6 percent).

South Americans represented 3.8 percent of the total Hispanic population. There were 471,000

Colombians (1.3 percent of the total Hispanic population), 261,000 Ecuadorians (0.7 percent), and 234,000 Peruvians (0.7 percent).

More than three-quarters of Hispanics lived in the West or South.[8]

In 2000, 43.5 percent of Hispanics lived in the West and 32.8 percent lived in the South. The Northeast and Midwest accounted for 14.9 percent and 8.9 percent, respectively, of the Hispanic population.

Hispanics accounted for 24.3 percent of the population in the West,

---

[6] For further information on the history of Hispanic origin in the census, see Chapa, Jorge, 2000, "Hispanic/Latino ethnicity and identifiers," in *Encyclopedia of the U.S. Census*, editor Margo J. Anderson, Congressional Quarterly Press, Washington, DC.

[7] This increase may be caused by a change in census coverage, as well as by a change in the question format (the question on Hispanic origin in 2000 did not include examples for the "Other Hispanic" category while the 1990 question did), or by a change in identification among Hispanics and non-Hispanics.

[8] The Northeast region includes Connecticut, Maine, Massachusetts, New Hampshire, New Jersey, New York, Pennsylvania, Rhode Island, and Vermont. The Midwest region includes Illinois, Indiana, Iowa, Kansas, Michigan, Minnesota, Missouri, Nebraska, North Dakota, Ohio, South Dakota, and Wisconsin. The South region includes Alabama, Arkansas, Delaware, the District of Columbia, Florida, Georgia, Kentucky, Louisiana, Maryland, Mississippi, North Carolina, Oklahoma, South Carolina, Tennessee, Texas, Virginia, and West Virginia. The West region includes Alaska, Arizona, California, Colorado, Hawaii, Idaho, Montana, Nevada, New Mexico, Oregon, Utah, Washington, and Wyoming.

Table 1.
Hispanic Population by Type: 2000

(For information on confidentiality protection, nonsampling error, and definitions, see www.census.gov/prod/cen2000/doc/sf1.pdf)

Subject	Number	Percent
HISPANIC OR LATINO ORIGIN		
Total population	281,421,906	100.0
Hispanic or Latino (of any race)	35,305,818	12.5
Not Hispanic or Latino	246,116,088	87.5
HISPANIC OR LATINO BY TYPE		
Hispanic or Latino (of any race)	35,305,818	100.0
Mexican	20,640,711	58.5
Puerto Rican	3,406,178	9.6
Cuban	1,241,685	3.5
Other Hispanic or Latino	10,017,244	28.4
Dominican (Dominican Republic)	764,945	2.2
Central American (excludes Mexican)	1,686,937	4.8
Costa Rican	68,588	0.2
Guatemalan	372,487	1.1
Honduran	217,569	0.6
Nicaraguan	177,684	0.5
Panamanian	91,723	0.3
Salvadoran	655,165	1.9
Other Central American	103,721	0.3
South American	1,353,562	3.8
Argentinean	100,864	0.3
Bolivian	42,068	0.1
Chilean	68,849	0.2
Colombian	470,684	1.3
Ecuadorian	260,559	0.7
Paraguayan	8,769	0.0
Peruvian	233,926	0.7
Uruguayan	18,804	0.1
Venezuelan	91,507	0.3
Other South American	57,532	0.2
Spaniard	100,135	0.3
All other Hispanic or Latino	6,111,665	17.3
Checkbox only, other Hispanic	1,733,274	4.9
Write-in Spanish	686,004	1.9
Write in Hispanic	2,454,529	7.0
Write-in Latino	450,769	1.3
Not elsewhere classified	787,089	2.2

Source: U.S. Census Bureau, Census 2000 Summary File 1.

the only region in which Hispanics exceeded the national level of 12.5 percent (see Table 2). Hispanics accounted for 11.6 percent of the population in the South, 9.8 percent in the Northeast, and 4.9 percent in the Midwest.

Mexicans, Puerto Ricans, and Cubans were concentrated in different regions. Among Mexicans, 55.3 percent lived in the West, 31.7 percent in the South, 10.7 percent in the Midwest, and 2.3 percent in the Northeast. Among Puerto Ricans, 60.9 percent lived in the Northeast, 22.3 percent in the South, 9.6 percent in the Midwest, and 7.2 percent in the West. Among Cubans, 74.2 percent lived in the South, 13.6 percent in the Northeast, 8.5 percent in the West, and 3.6 percent in the Midwest.

Half of all Hispanics lived in just two states: California and Texas.

In 2000, 27.1 million, or 76.8 percent, of Hispanics lived in the seven states with Hispanic populations of 1.0 million or more (California, Texas, New York, Florida, Illinois, Arizona, and New Jersey). Hispanics in California accounted for 11.0 million (31.1 percent) of the total Hispanic population, while the Hispanic population in Texas accounted for 6.7 million (18.9 percent). Hispanics numbered between 500,000 and 999,999 in only two states (Colorado and New Mexico). Hispanics in 22 states were between 100,000 and 499,999. Hispanics were less than 100,000 in 19 states and the District of Columbia.

Hispanics in New Mexico were 42.1 percent of the total state population, the highest proportion for any state. Hispanics were 12.5 percent (the national level) or more of the state population in eight other states (California, Texas, Arizona, Nevada, Colorado, Florida, New York, and New Jersey). Mexicans were the largest Hispanic group in five of these states (California, Texas, Arizona, Nevada, and Colorado), while Hispanics of other Hispanic origins were the largest group in the remaining states (New Mexico, Florida, New York, and New Jersey). Hispanics accounted for less than 12.5 percent of the population in 41 states and the District of Columbia.

Hispanic origin groups were concentrated in different states. The largest Mexican populations (more than a million) were in California, Texas, Illinois and Arizona, mostly southwestern states. The largest Puerto Rican populations (more than 250,000) were in New York, Florida, New Jersey, and Pennsylvania, mostly northeastern states. About two-thirds of all Cubans were in Florida.

Table 2.
Hispanic Population by Type for Regions, States, and Puerto Rico: 1990 and 2000

(For information on confidentiality protection, nonsampling error, and definitions, see *www.census.gov/prod/cen2000/doc/sf1.pdf*)

Area	1990			2000						
		Hispanic population			Hispanic population			Hispanic type		
	Total population	Number	Percent	Total population	Number	Percent	Mexican	Puerto Rican	Cuban	Other Hispanic
United States	**248,709,873**	**22,354,059**	**9.0**	**281,421,906**	**35,305,818**	**12.5**	**20,640,711**	**3,406,178**	**1,241,685**	**10,017,244**
Region										
Northeast	50,809,229	3,754,389	7.4	53,594,378	5,254,087	9.8	479,169	2,074,574	168,959	2,531,385
Midwest..........	59,668,632	1,726,509	2.9	64,392,776	3,124,532	4.9	2,200,196	325,363	45,305	553,668
South	85,445,930	6,767,021	7.9	100,236,820	11,586,696	11.6	6,548,081	759,305	921,427	3,357,883
West	52,786,082	10,106,140	19.1	63,197,932	15,340,503	24.3	11,413,265	246,936	105,994	3,574,308
State										
Alabama	4,040,587	24,629	0.6	4,447,100	75,830	1.7	44,522	6,322	2,354	22,632
Alaska...........	550,043	17,803	3.2	626,932	25,852	4.1	13,334	2,649	553	9,316
Arizona..........	3,665,228	688,338	18.8	5,130,632	1,295,617	25.3	1,065,578	17,587	5,272	207,180
Arkansas.........	2,350,725	19,876	0.8	2,673,400	86,866	3.2	61,204	2,473	950	22,239
California.........	29,760,021	7,687,938	25.8	33,871,648	10,966,556	32.4	8,455,926	140,570	72,286	2,297,774
Colorado.........	3,294,394	424,302	12.9	4,301,261	735,601	17.1	450,760	12,993	3,701	268,147
Connecticut.......	3,287,116	213,116	6.5	3,405,565	320,323	9.4	23,484	194,443	7,101	95,295
Delaware.........	666,168	15,820	2.4	783,600	37,277	4.8	12,986	14,005	932	9,354
District of Columbia..	606,900	32,710	5.4	572,059	44,953	7.9	5,098	2,328	1,101	36,426
Florida..........	12,937,926	1,574,143	12.2	15,982,378	2,682,715	16.8	363,925	482,027	833,120	1,003,643
Georgia..........	6,478,216	108,922	1.7	8,186,453	435,227	5.3	275,288	35,532	12,536	111,871
Hawaii...........	1,108,229	81,390	7.3	1,211,537	87,699	7.2	19,820	30,005	711	37,163
Idaho............	1,006,749	52,927	5.3	1,293,953	101,690	7.9	79,324	1,509	408	20,449
Illinois	11,430,602	904,446	7.9	12,419,293	1,530,262	12.3	1,144,390	157,851	18,438	209,583
Indiana	5,544,159	98,788	1.8	6,080,485	214,536	3.5	153,042	19,678	2,754	39,062
Iowa	2,776,755	32,647	1.2	2,926,324	82,473	2.8	61,154	2,690	750	17,879
Kansas	2,477,574	93,670	3.8	2,688,418	188,252	7.0	148,270	5,237	1,680	33,065
Kentucky.........	3,685,296	21,984	0.6	4,041,769	59,939	1.5	31,385	6,469	3,516	18,569
Louisiana.........	4,219,973	93,044	2.2	4,468,976	107,738	2.4	32,267	7,670	8,448	59,353
Maine	1,227,928	6,829	0.6	1,274,923	9,360	0.7	2,756	2,275	478	3,851
Maryland.........	4,781,468	125,102	2.6	5,296,486	227,916	4.3	39,900	25,570	6,754	155,692
Massachusetts	6,016,425	287,549	4.8	6,349,097	428,729	6.8	22,288	199,207	8,867	198,367
Michigan	9,295,297	201,596	2.2	9,938,444	323,877	3.3	220,769	26,941	7,219	68,948
Minnesota	4,375,099	53,884	1.2	4,919,479	143,382	2.9	95,613	6,616	2,527	38,626
Mississippi........	2,573,216	15,931	0.6	2,844,658	39,569	1.4	21,616	2,881	1,508	13,564
Missouri..........	5,117,073	61,702	1.2	5,595,211	118,592	2.1	77,887	6,677	3,022	31,006
Montana	799,065	12,174	1.5	902,195	18,081	2.0	11,735	931	285	5,130
Nebraska.........	1,578,385	36,969	2.3	1,711,263	94,425	5.5	71,030	1,993	859	20,543
Nevada	1,201,833	124,419	10.4	1,998,257	393,970	19.7	285,764	10,420	11,498	86,288
New Hampshire	1,109,252	11,333	1.0	1,235,786	20,489	1.7	4,590	6,215	785	8,899
New Jersey........	7,730,188	739,861	9.6	8,414,350	1,117,191	13.3	102,929	366,788	77,337	570,137
New Mexico.......	1,515,069	579,224	38.2	1,819,046	765,386	42.1	330,049	4,488	2,588	428,261
New York.........	17,990,455	2,214,026	12.3	18,976,457	2,867,583	15.1	260,889	1,050,293	62,590	1,493,811
North Carolina......	6,628,637	76,726	1.2	8,049,313	378,963	4.7	246,545	31,117	7,389	93,912
North Dakota.......	638,800	4,665	0.7	642,200	7,786	1.2	4,295	507	250	2,734
Ohio.............	10,847,115	139,696	1.3	11,353,140	217,123	1.9	90,663	66,269	5,152	55,039
Oklahoma	3,145,585	86,160	2.7	3,450,654	179,304	5.2	132,813	8,153	1,759	36,579
Oregon	2,842,321	112,707	4.0	3,421,399	275,314	8.0	214,662	5,092	3,091	52,469
Pennsylvania.......	11,881,643	232,262	2.0	12,281,054	394,088	3.2	55,178	228,557	10,363	99,990
Rhode Island.......	1,003,464	45,752	4.6	1,048,319	90,820	8.7	5,881	25,422	1,128	58,389
South Carolina	3,486,703	30,551	0.9	4,012,012	95,076	2.4	52,871	12,211	2,875	27,119
South Dakota	696,004	5,252	0.8	754,844	10,903	1.4	6,364	637	163	3,739
Tennessee.........	4,877,185	32,741	0.7	5,689,283	123,838	2.2	77,372	10,303	3,695	32,468
Texas	16,986,510	4,339,905	25.5	20,851,820	6,669,666	32.0	5,071,963	69,504	25,705	1,502,494
Utah	1,722,850	84,597	4.9	2,233,169	201,559	9.0	136,416	3,977	940	60,226
Vermont	562,758	3,661	0.7	608,827	5,504	0.9	1,174	1,374	310	2,646
Virginia	6,187,358	160,288	2.6	7,078,515	329,540	4.7	73,979	41,131	8,332	206,098
Washington........	4,866,692	214,570	4.4	5,894,121	441,509	7.5	329,934	16,140	4,501	90,934
West Virginia	1,793,477	8,489	0.5	1,808,344	12,279	0.7	4,347	1,609	453	5,870
Wisconsin	4,891,769	93,194	1.9	5,363,675	192,921	3.6	126,719	30,267	2,491	33,444
Wyoming..........	453,588	25,751	5.7	493,782	31,669	6.4	19,963	575	160	10,971
Puerto Rico[1]	**3,522,037**	**(NA)**	**(NA)**	**3,808,610**	**3,762,746**	**98.8**	**11,546**	**3,623,392**	**19,973**	**107,835**

NA Not available.

[1]Census 2000 was the first to ask a separate question on Hispanic origin in Puerto Rico.

Source: U.S. Census Bureau, Census 2000 Summary File 1; 1990 Census of Population, *General Population Characteristics* (CP-1-1).

Counties with the highest proportions of Hispanics were along the southwestern border of the United States.

In 2000, the proportion of Hispanics within a county exceeded the national level (12.5 percent) most often in the counties of the South and West, especially in counties along the border with Mexico (see Figure 3).

Hispanics were the majority of the population in 50 counties, accounting for 13.5 percent of the total Hispanic population. Of these counties, 35 are in the South and 15 are in the West. In the South, Hispanics were the majority in 34 counties in Texas and one in Florida. In the West, Hispanics were the majority in nine counties in New Mexico, and two counties in each of the following states: Arizona, California, and Colorado.

Hispanics also were concentrated in groupings of counties outside of the four states bordering Mexico. In particular, Hispanic concentrations occurred in counties within central Washington, in counties within the mountain states of Idaho, Wyoming, Utah, and Colorado, in counties around Chicago, New York, and the District of Colombia, and in counties within southern Florida.

Hispanics represented more than one-quarter but less than half of the county population in 152 counties. The percent Hispanic exceeded the national level of 12.5 percent but was less than 25.0 percent of the population in 181 counties. The percent Hispanic ranged from 6.0 percent to just under the national level in 311 counties. Hispanics represented less than 6.0 percent of the county's population in 2,447 counties. Furthermore, Hispanics represented less than 1.0 percent of a county's population in 899 counties.

Hispanics were also present in some counties within nontraditional states.

While most Hispanics lived in the South or West, some counties in nontraditional Hispanic states such as Georgia and North Carolina had sizable proportions of Hispanic populations.[9] Hispanics within some counties in North Carolina, Georgia, Iowa, Arkansas, Minnesota, and Nebraska represented between 6.0 percent and 24.9 percent of the county's total population. The percent Hispanic within these counties exceeded the percent Hispanic (less than 6.0 percent) for these states.

More than 4 million Hispanics lived in Los Angeles County, California.

In 2000, Hispanics in four counties accounted for 21.9 percent of the total Hispanic population. There were 4.2 million Hispanics in Los Angeles County, California, 1.3 million in Miami-Dade County, Florida, 1.1 million in Harris County, Texas, and 1.1 million in Cook County, Illinois.

Hispanic origin groups were concentrated in different counties. The largest Mexican populations lived in counties that had large Hispanic populations, including Los Angeles County, California (3.0 million), Harris County, Texas (815,000), and Cook County, Illinois (786,000). The two largest Puerto

Rican populations lived in two New York counties: Bronx County (319,000), and Kings County (213,000). More than half (651,000 or 52.4 percent) of all Cubans lived in Miami-Dade County, Florida.

The Commonwealth of Puerto Rico was 98.8 percent Hispanic.[10]

Of all Hispanics in Puerto Rico, 96.3 percent were of Puerto Rican origin. The second largest Hispanic population in Puerto Rico was Dominican, accounting for 1.5 percent of all Hispanics there.

The proportion Hispanic ranges from 97 percent to 99 percent in the four places[11] in Puerto Rico with 100,000 or more population (Ponce, Bayamón, Carolina, and San Juan).

In 2000, more than a million Hispanics lived in New York and in Los Angeles.[12]

More than 500,000 Hispanics resided in Chicago, Houston, and San Antonio (see Table 3). Among the ten places[13] with the largest Hispanic populations, Puerto Ricans represented the largest

---

[9] For further discussion of change in the Hispanic population between 1990 and 2000, see Brewer, Cynthia A., and Trudy A. Suchan, 2001, *Mapping Census 2000: The Geography of U.S. Diversity*, Census 2000 Special Reports, CENSR/01-1, U.S. Census Bureau, Washington, DC.

[10] Census 2000 was the first to ask a separate question on Hispanic origin in Puerto Rico.

[11] For further explanation of geographic entities in Puerto Rico, see Appendix A in U.S. Census Bureau, 1993, *Population and Housing Unit Counts: Puerto Rico*, 1990 Census of Population and Housing, CPH-2-53, Washington, DC.

[12] Three in four (75.3 percent) Hispanics in the state of New York resided in the five boroughs that make up New York City: 645,000 in the Bronx, 557,000 in Queens, 488,000 in Brooklyn, 418,000 in Manhattan, and 54,000 in Staten Island.

[13] In Census 2000, there were 245 places in the United States (excluding the Commonwealth of Puerto Rico) with 100,000 or more population. These included 238 incorporated places (including 4 city-county consolidations) and included 7 census designated places (CDPs) that were not legally incorporated. For a list of places by state, see Table 4 or Table 5 in *www.census.gov/population/ www.cen2000phc-t6.html.*

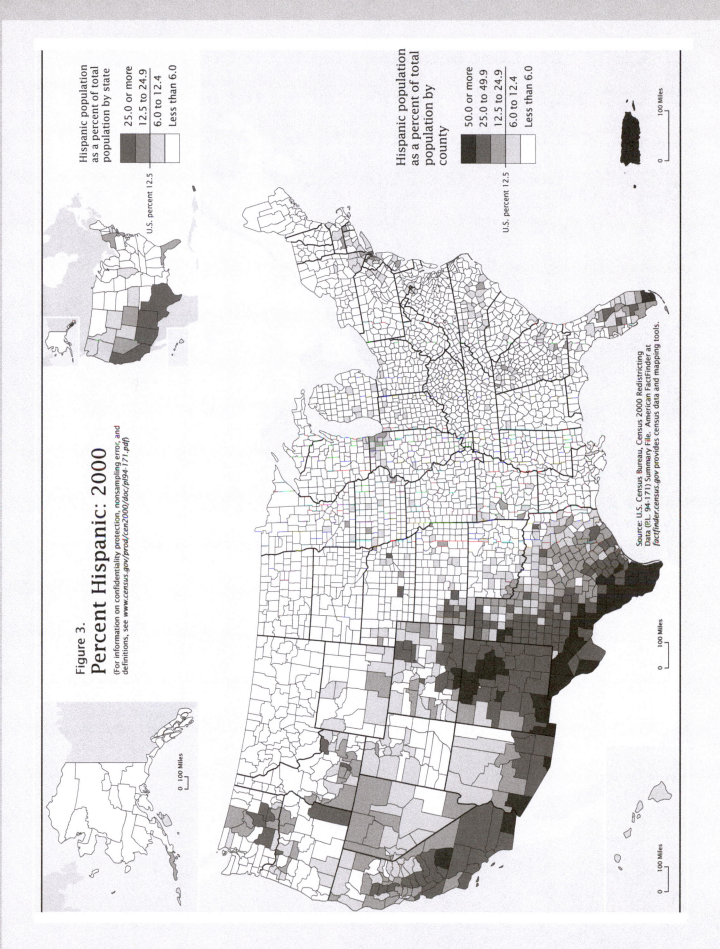

Figure 3.

Percent Hispanic: 2000

(For information on confidentiality protection, nonsampling error, and
definitions, see *www.census.gov/prod/cen2000/doc/pl94-171.pdf*)

Hispanic population
as a percent of total
population by state

25.0 or more
12.5 to 24.9
6.0 to 12.4
Less than 6.0

U.S. percent 12.5

Hispanic population
as a percent of total
population by
county

50.0 or more
25.0 to 49.9
12.5 to 24.9
6.0 to 12.4
Less than 6.0

U.S. percent 12.5

Source: U.S. Census Bureau, Census 2000 Redistricting
Data (P.L. 94-171) Summary File. American FactFinder at
factfinder.census.gov provides census data and mapping tools.

0   100 Miles

0   100 Miles

0   100 Miles

Table 3.
Ten Largest Places in Total Population and in Hispanic Population: 2000

(For information on confidentiality protection, nonsampling error, and definitions, see www.census.gov/prod/cen2000/doc/sf1.pdf)

Place and state	Total population		Hispanic population		Percent Hispanic of total population
	Number	Rank	Number	Rank	
New York, NY..........	8,008,278	1	2,160,554	1	27.0
Los Angeles, CA	3,694,820	2	1,719,073	2	46.5
Chicago, IL..............	2,896,016	3	753,644	3	26.0
Houston, TX.............	1,953,631	4	730,865	4	37.4
Philadelphia, PA.........	1,517,550	5	128,928	24	8.5
Phoenix, AZ.............	1,321,045	6	449,972	6	34.1
San Diego, CA..........	1,223,400	7	310,752	9	25.4
Dallas, TX..............	1,188,580	8	422,587	8	35.6
San Antonio, TX........	1,144,646	9	671,394	5	58.7
Detroit, MI..............	951,270	10	47,167	72	5.0
El Paso, TX	563,662	23	431,875	7	76.6
San Jose, CA...........	894,943	11	269,989	10	30.2

Source: U.S. Census Bureau, Census 2000 Summary File 1.

Table 4.
Ten Places of 100,000 or More Population With the Highest Percent Hispanic: 2000

(For information on confidentiality protection, nonsampling error, and definitions, see www.census.gov/prod/cen2000/doc/sf1.pdf)

Place and state	Total population	Hispanic population	Percent Hispanic of total population
East Los Angeles, CA*.......	124,283	120,307	96.8
Laredo, TX	176,576	166,216	94.1
Brownsville, TX	139,722	127,535	91.3
Hialeah, FL.................	226,419	204,543	90.3
McAllen, TX	106,414	85,427	80.3
El Paso, TX	563,662	431,875	76.6
Santa Ana, CA..............	337,977	257,097	76.1
El Monte, CA	115,965	83,945	72.4
Oxnard, CA.................	170,358	112,807	66.2
Miami, FL	362,470	238,351	65.8

*East Los Angeles, California is a census designated place and is not legally incorporated.

Source: U.S. Census Bureau, Census 2000 Summary File 1.

share (36.5 percent) of all Hispanics in New York, while Mexicans represented the largest share (varying from 63.5 percent in Los Angeles to 83.4 percent in San Diego) of all Hispanics in the nine other places.[14]

[14] Mexicans accounted for the majority of Hispanics in the remaining seven places (see Table 3): Phoenix (83.4 percent), El Paso (83.3 percent), Dallas (82.9 percent), San Jose (81.9 percent), Houston (72.2 percent), San Antonio (70.5 percent), and Chicago (70.4 percent).

ADDITIONAL FINDINGS ON THE HISPANIC POPULATION

Was the Hispanic population younger than the U.S. population?

The relative youthfulness of the Hispanic population is reflected in its population under age 18 and in its median age. While 25.7 percent of the U.S. population was under 18 years of age in 2000, 35.0 percent of Hispanics were less than

age 18. The median age for Hispanics was 25.9 years while the median age for the entire U.S. population was 35.3 years. Mexicans had a median age of 24.2 years, Puerto Ricans 27.3 years, Central Americans 29.2 years, Dominicans 29.5 years, South Americans 33.1 years, Spaniards 36.4 years, Cubans 40.7 years, and all other Hispanics had a median age of 24.7 years.

In what places were Hispanics the majority?

Hispanics in East Los Angeles[15] were 96.8 percent (120,000) of the population, the highest for any place outside the Commonwealth of Puerto Rico with 100,000 or more total population (see Table 4). Hispanics were the majority of the population in eighteen other places.[16] Two of the top ten places in terms of numbers of Hispanics, El Paso and San Antonio, also had a majority who were Hispanic (76.6 percent and 58.7 percent, respectively).

What were the top places for different Hispanic groups, by size?

Most, but not all, of the places with the largest specific Hispanic group populations were among the ten places with the largest Hispanic populations. The largest Mexican populations lived in Los Angeles, Chicago, Houston, San Antonio, and Phoenix. The largest Puerto Rican populations lived in New York, Chicago, and Philadelphia. The largest

[15] East Los Angeles, California is a census designated place and is not legally incorporated.
[16] Hispanics were the majority of the population in the ten places shown in Table 4 as well as in these nine additional places: Pomona, California (64.5), Salinas, California (64.1 percent), Norwalk, California (62.9 percent), Ontario, California (59.9 percent), San Antonio, Texas (58.7 percent), Downey, California (57.9 percent), Fontana, California (57.7 percent), Corpus Christi, Texas (54.3 percent), and Paterson, New Jersey (50.1 percent).

Cuban populations lived in Hialeah, Miami, New York, Tampa, and Los Angeles.

The largest Central American populations lived in the following places: Los Angeles, New York, Houston, Miami, and San Francisco, while the largest South American populations lived in New York, Los Angeles, Chicago, and Miami.

ABOUT CENSUS 2000

The Census Bureau is required by federal directive to collect data on Hispanic origin. For additional information on the legal basis for the question on Hispanic origin included in Census 2000, see *Revisions to the Standards for the Classification of Federal Data on Race and Ethnicity,* Federal Register Notice, October 30, 1997, Volume 62, Number 210. This document is available on the Census Internet site at: *www.census.gov/population/www/socdemo/race/Ombdir15.html.*

All levels of government need information on Hispanic origin to implement and evaluate programs, such as the Equal Employment Opportunity Act, Civil Rights Act, Voting Rights Act, Public Health Act, Healthcare Improvement Act, Job Partnership Training Act, Equal Credit Opportunity Act, Fair Housing Act, Census Redistricting Data Program, and others.

FOR MORE INFORMATION

For more information on Hispanic origin in the United States, visit the U.S. Census Bureau's Internet site at *www.census.gov/population/www/socdemo/hispanic.html.*

Data on Hispanic origin from the Census 2000 Summary File 1 are planned for release on a state-by-state basis during June and July of 2001. The Census 2000 Redistricting data are available on the Internet via *factfinder.census.gov* and for purchase on CD-ROM and later on DVD.

For information on confidentiality protection, nonsampling error, and definitions, also see

www.census.gov/prod/cen2000/doc/sf1.pdf or contact our Customer Services Center at 301-457-4100.

For more information on specific ethnic and race groups in the United States, go to *www.census.gov* and click on "Minority Links." This Web page includes information about Census 2000 and provides links to reports based on past censuses and surveys focusing on social and economic characteristics.

Information on other population and housing topics will be presented in the Census 2000 Brief series, located on the U.S. Census Bureau's Web site at *www.census.gov/population/www/cen2000/briefs.html.* This series will present information about race, Hispanic origin, age, sex, household type, housing tenure, and other social, economic, and housing characteristics.

For more information about Census 2000, including data products, call our Customer Services Center at 301-457-4100 or e-mail *webmaster@census.gov.*

The Arab Population: 2000

Census 2000 Brief

Issued December 2003

C2KBR-23

By
G. Patricia de la Cruz
and
Angela Brittingham

Census 2000 measured a U.S. population of 281.4 million, including 1.2 million who reported an Arab ancestry.[1] Arabs were 1 of 33 ancestry groups with populations over 1 million.[2] This is the first report the U.S. Census Bureau has produced on the population of Arab ancestry. In 1997, the Office of Management and Budget revised the federal standard for the classification of race and ethnicity, noting the lack of consensus about the definition of an Arab ethnic category and suggesting that further research be done in order to improve data on this population group.[3] This report contributes to ongoing research about people in the United States who identify an Arab ancestry and reflects the Census Bureau's consultation and collaboration with experts within the Arab community.

Figure 1.

Reproduction of the Question on Ancestry From Census 2000

🔟 **What is this person's ancestry or ethnic origin?**

(For example: Italian, Jamaican, African Am., Cambodian, Cape Verdean, Norwegian, Dominican, French Canadian, Haitian, Korean, Lebanese, Polish, Nigerian, Mexican, Taiwanese, Ukrainian, and so on.)

Source: U.S. Census Bureau, Census 2000 questionnaire.

For the purposes of this report, most people with ancestries originating from Arabic-speaking countries or areas of the world are categorized as Arab. For example, a person is included in the Arab ancestry category if he or she reported being Arab, Egyptian, Iraqi, Jordanian, Lebanese, Middle Eastern, Moroccan, North African, Palestinian, Syrian, and so on. It is important to note, however, that some people from these countries may not consider themselves to be Arab, and conversely, some people who consider themselves Arab may not be included in this definition. More specifically, groups such as Kurds and Berbers who are usually not considered Arab were included in this definition for consistency with 1990 census and Census 2000 data products. In the same manner, some groups such as Mauritanian, Somalian, Djiboutian, Sudanese, and Comoros Islander who may consider themselves Arab were not included, again for consistency. (For more information, see Table 1.)

[1] The text of this report discusses data for the United States, including the 50 states and the District of Columbia. Data for the Commonwealth of Puerto Rico are shown in Table 2 and Figure 2.
[2] Census 2000 Summary File 4 shows that the largest ancestry groups reported were German (42.9 million), Irish (30.5 million), and English (24.5 million). Ancestry groups similar in size to the Arab population included Greek, Czech, and Portuguese (approximately 1.2 million each).
[3] Office of Management and Budget. 1997. "Revisions to the Standards for the Classification of Federal Data on Race and Ethnicity." *Federal Register*, Vol. 62, No. 210, p. 58787.

USCENSUSBUREAU

Helping You Make Informed Decisions

U.S. Department of Commerce
Economics and Statistics Administration
U.S. CENSUS BUREAU

United States Census 2000

The information on ancestry was collected on the "long form" of the census questionnaire, which was sent to approximately one-sixth of all households. Item 10 on the questionnaire asked respondents to identify their ancestry or ethnic origin (see Figure 1).[4] As many as two ancestries were tabulated per respondent; if either response was included in the definition of Arab used here, the person is included in this analysis. Around 19 percent of the U.S. population provided no response to the ancestry question.

Ancestry refers to ethnic origin, descent, "roots," heritage, or place of birth of the person or of the person's ancestors. The ancestry question was not intended to measure the degree of attachment to a particular ethnicity, but simply to establish that the respondent had a connection to and self-identified with a particular ethnic group. For example, a response of "Lebanese" might reflect involvement in a Lebanese community or only a memory of Lebanese ancestors several generations removed.

The data in this report are based solely on responses to the Census 2000 ancestry question. Questions that were positioned before the ancestry question where respondents might have indicated an Arab origin (namely race, Hispanic origin, and place of birth) were not considered.

Although religious affiliation can be a component of ethnic identity, neither the ancestry question nor any other question on the decennial census form was designed to collect information about religion. No religious information was tabulated from Census 2000. Religious

responses were all reclassified as "Other groups."

This report presents national, regional, state, county, and selected place-level information for the total Arab population, as well as additional detailed information for the three largest Arab groups: Lebanese, Syrian, and Egyptian. Smaller groups are shown only at the national level.

The Arab population, which numbered over 1 million in 2000, increased by nearly 40 percent during the 1990s.

In 2000, 1.2 million people reported an Arab ancestry in the United States, up from 610,000 in 1980 (when data on ancestry were first collected in the decennial census) and 860,000 in 1990. The Arab population increased over the last two decades: 41 percent in the 1980s and 38 percent in the 1990s.[5] Arabs represented 0.42 percent of the U.S. population in 2000, compared with 0.27 percent in 1980.

People of Lebanese, Syrian, and Egyptian ancestry accounted for about three-fifths of the Arab population.

In 2000, more than one-third of those reporting an Arab ancestry were Lebanese (37 percent, see Table 1), including both people who indicated that they were only Lebanese and those who reported being both Lebanese and another ancestry, which might or might not also be Arab.[6] The next largest specific groups were Syrian and Egyptian (12 percent each).

Among the nearly half-million people who reported other specific Arab ancestries, the largest proportion was Palestinian (6.1 percent of the total Arab population). The Jordanian, Moroccan, and Iraqi populations were also sizable (3.3 percent, 3.3 percent, and 3.2 percent, respectively).[7] An additional 4.3 percent of the Arab population identified themselves as Yemeni, Kurdish, Algerian, Saudi Arabian, Tunisian, Kuwaiti, Libyan, Berber, or other specific Arab ancestries, each of which accounted for 1 percent or less of the total Arab population.[8]

A substantial portion of the Arab population (20 percent) identified with general Arab ancestries, such as "Arab" or "Arabic" (17 percent), "Middle Eastern" (2.4 percent), or "North African" (0.3 percent). This population was second in size only to the Lebanese ancestry group.

During the 1990s, the Egyptian population increased numerically more than any other group.

The number of people with Egyptian ancestry grew by 64,000, the most of any specific Arab ancestry group (see Table 1), increasing from 79,000 in 1990 to 143,000 in 2000 (growing by 82 percent). The number of people who identified as Lebanese also grew substantially, but by a smaller proportion, from 394,000 to 440,000 over the decade, an increase of 12 percent. Syrians, who numbered 130,000 in 1990, grew to 143,000 in 2000 (or by 10 percent).[9]

---

[4] The term respondent is used here to refer to all individuals for whom one or more ancestries were reported, whether or not one person answered the question for all household members.

[5] The estimates in this report are based on responses from a sample of the population. As with all surveys, estimates may vary from the actual values because of sampling variation or other factors. All statements made in this report have undergone statistical testing and are significant at the 90-percent confidence level unless otherwise noted.

[6] Hereafter, estimates of specific ancestry groups include people who reported solely that ancestry or who reported it in combination with another one.

[7] The proportions of the population who were Jordanian, Moroccan, or Iraqi were not statistically different.

[8] The proportion of the population that was Yemeni was not statistically less than 1 percent.

[9] The growth in the Syrian population from 1990 to 2000 was not statistically different from the growth in the Lebanese population.

Table 1.
Arab Population by Ancestry: 2000

(Data based on sample. For information on confidentiality protection, sampling error, nonsampling error, and definitions, see www.census.gov/prod/cen2000/doc/sf4.pdf)

Subject	1990		2000		Change, 1990 to 2000	
	Number	Percent	Number	Percent	Number	Percent
Total population	248,709,873	100.00	281,421,906	100.00	32,712,033	13.2
TOTAL ARAB POPULATION AND ANCESTRY[1]						
Total Arab population	860,354	0.35	1,189,731	0.42	329,377	38.3
Lebanese	394,180	45.82	440,279	37.01	46,099	11.7
Syrian................................	129,606	15.06	142,897	12.01	13,291	10.3
Egyptian	78,574	9.13	142,832	12.01	64,258	81.8
All other Arab reports	268,378	31.19	476,863	40.08	208,485	77.7
Specific Arab ancestry	132,066	15.35	239,424	20.12	107,358	81.3
Palestinian	48,019	5.58	72,112	6.06	24,093	50.2
Jordanian	20,656	2.40	39,734	3.34	19,078	92.4
Moroccan	19,089	2.22	38,923	3.27	19,834	103.9
Iraqi	23,212	2.70	37,714	3.17	14,502	62.5
Yemeni............................	4,093	0.48	11,683	0.98	7,590	185.4
Kurdish	2,181	0.25	9,423	0.79	7,242	332.0
Algerian	3,215	0.37	8,752	0.74	5,537	172.2
Saudi Arabian......................	4,486	0.52	7,419	0.62	2,933	65.4
Tunisian...........................	2,376	0.28	4,735	0.40	2,359	99.3
Kuwaiti............................	1,306	0.15	3,162	0.27	1,856	142.1
Libyan	2,172	0.25	2,979	0.25	807	37.2
Berber	530	0.06	1,327	0.11	797	150.4
Other specific Arab ancestry[2]	731	0.08	1,461	0.12	730	99.9
General Arab ancestry.................	136,312	15.84	237,439	19.96	101,127	74.2
Arab or Arabic	127,364	14.80	205,822	17.30	78,458	61.6
Middle Eastern......................	7,656	0.89	28,400	2.39	20,744	271.0
North African.......................	1,292	0.15	3,217	0.27	1,925	149.0

[1] Because respondents could list up to two ancestries, the total number of ancestries reported will sum to more than the total number of people.

[2] Groups whose population was less than 1,000 in 2000, including Emirati (United Arab Emirates), Omani, Qatari, Bahraini, Alhuceman, Bedouin, and Rio de Oro.

Source: 2000 data from U.S. Census Bureau, Census 2000, Summary File 4 and Sample Edited Detail File; 1990 data from U.S. Census Bureau, 1990 Census, Sample Edited Detail File.

Among the smaller Arab ancestry groups, the Moroccan, Jordanian, and Palestinian populations grew the most numerically over the decade. Proportionally, each of those groups experienced substantial growth as well, increasing by at least half. The number of Moroccans doubled (104 percent increase) to 39,000. People who identified as Jordanian increased 92 percent to 40,000, and the number who reported they were Palestinian increased by 50 percent to 72,000.[10]

The Yemeni-ancestry population tripled between 1990 and 2000.

People with Yemeni ancestry increased from 4,000 in 1990 to 12,000 in 2000. In addition, the Kurdish and Algerian populations also experienced a high growth rate over the decade, from 2,000 and 3,000 respectively in 1990 to 9,000 each in 2000.

[10] The growth in the Moroccan population from 1990 to 2000 was not statistically different from the growth in the Jordanian population.

The number of people who responded as "Arab" or "Middle Eastern" to the ancestry question increased over the decade.

Between 1990 and 2000, an increasing share of the Arab population identified themselves by a general term such as Arab or Middle Eastern and gave no other specific Arab ancestry. The population who identified as "Arab" or "Arabic" increased by 62 percent, reaching 206,000 in 2000. The number of people who reported being "Middle Eastern" was much smaller, but quadrupled to 28,000.

THE GEOGRAPHIC DISTRIBUTION OF PEOPLE OF ARAB ANCESTRY

People of Arab ancestry were fairly evenly distributed among the four regions of the United States.

In 2000, 27 percent of the Arab population lived in the Northeast, while 26 percent lived in the South, 24 percent in the Midwest, and 22 percent in the West (see Table 2).[11] Arabs accounted for 0.6 percent of the total population in the Northeast but for only 0.3 percent of the total population in the South.

About half of the Arab population was concentrated in only five states.

In 2000, 576,000 Arabs (or 48 percent of the Arab population) lived in just five states: California, Florida, Michigan, New Jersey, and New York. These states contained 31 percent of the total U.S. population. People reporting an Arab ancestry also numbered over 40,000 in five other states (Illinois, Massachusetts, Ohio, Pennsylvania, and Texas).[12]

Over the last decade, the Arab population increased in almost every state.

From 1990 to 2000, the number of people with Arab ancestry increased in most states.[13] The Arab population in California increased by 48,000, more than in any other state. The Arab population increased by 39,000 in Michigan and by 28,000 in Florida.

The Arab population grew by about half in several states.

The Arab population doubled in Tennessee (102 percent increase) since 1990.[14] However, the number of people who identified as Arab in that state was relatively small, increasing from 6,000 in 1990 to 13,000 in 2000. The Arab population also increased by over 50 percent in North Carolina, Washington, Colorado, and Virginia.[15] The Arab populations in Florida and Michigan experienced high growth rates as well as large numerical increases. The Arab population in Florida grew by 57 percent, from 49,000 to 77,000 between 1990 and 2000; the Arab population in Michigan grew by 51 percent, from 77,000 in 1990 to 115,000 in 2000.[16]

The proportion of the population that was Arab was highest in Michigan.

Arabs accounted for 1.2 percent of the total population in Michigan in 2000. Arabs comprised nearly 1 percent of the state populations in New Jersey and Massachusetts, which were 0.9 percent and 0.8 percent Arab, respectively.

Arabs represented a higher proportion of the population in 2000 than they did in 1990 in a large majority of states. The proportion of the population that was Arab grew from 0.8 percent in 1990 to 1.2 percent in 2000 in Michigan, and from 0.6 percent to 0.9 percent in New Jersey.[17]

The counties with the highest proportion of people who were Arab were in the Northeast and the Midwest.

The proportion of people who identified with an Arab ancestry by county is shown in Figure 2. The counties with the highest proportions of Arabs in 2000 were in Massachusetts, New York, New Jersey, Pennsylvania, Virginia, West Virginia, Ohio, Michigan, and California. The proportion of the population that was Arab in Wayne County, Michigan, was 2.7 percent.[18] In addition, at least 1.2 percent of the population was Arab in Macomb, Oakland, and Washtenaw Counties, Michigan; Bergen, Hudson, Middlesex, and Passaic Counties, New Jersey; Fairfax, Arlington, and Alexandria Counties, Virginia; Norfolk County, Massachusetts; Kings, Richmond,

---

[11] The Northeast region includes the states of Connecticut, Maine, Massachusetts, New Hampshire, New Jersey, New York, Pennsylvania, Rhode Island, and Vermont. The Midwest region includes the states of Illinois, Indiana, Iowa, Kansas, Michigan, Minnesota, Missouri, Nebraska, North Dakota, Ohio, South Dakota, and Wisconsin. The South region includes the states of Alabama, Arkansas, Delaware, Florida, Georgia, Kentucky, Louisiana, Maryland, Mississippi, North Carolina, Oklahoma, South Carolina, Tennessee, Texas, Virginia, West Virginia, and the District of Columbia, a state equivalent. The West region includes the states of Alaska, Arizona, California, Colorado, Hawaii, Idaho, Montana, Nevada, New Mexico, Oregon, Utah, Washington, and Wyoming.

[12] Although the estimated size of the Arab population in Virginia was more than 40,000, it was not statistically larger than 40,000.

[13] The Arab population did not change statistically in the following states: Hawaii, Iowa, Maine, Mississippi, Montana, North Dakota, Rhode Island, South Dakota, West Virginia, and Wyoming.

[14] The growth rate of the Arab population in Tennessee was not statistically different from the corresponding growth rates in Alaska, Idaho, Nevada, North Carolina, and Utah.

[15] Although the estimated increases in the Arab populations in Alaska, Florida, Georgia, Idaho, Illinois, Michigan, Nebraska, New Jersey, Nevada, and Utah were more than 50 percent, the increases were not statistically different from 50 percent.

[16] There was no statistical difference between the growth rates of the Arab populations in Florida and Michigan.

[17] The increase in the proportion of Arabs in Michigan was not statistically different from the increase in the proportion of Arabs in New Jersey.

[18] The proportion of the Arab population in Wayne County, Michigan was not statistically different from Passaic and Hudson Counties in New Jersey; Oakland and Macomb Counties, Michigan; Lehigh County, Pennsylvania; Fairfax, Arlington, and Alexandria Counties in Virginia.

Table 2.
Arab Population by Ancestry for the United States, Regions, States, and for Puerto Rico: 1990 and 2000

(Data based on sample. For information on confidentiality protection, sampling error, nonsampling error, and definitions, see www.census.gov/prod/cen2000/doc/sf4.pdf)

Area	1990			2000					
	Total population	Arab population[1]		Total population	Arab population[1]		Selected Arab groups[2]		
		Number	Percent		Number	Percent	Lebanese	Syrian	Egyptian
United States	248,709,873	860,354	0.35	281,421,906	1,189,731	0.42	440,279	142,897	142,832
Region									
Northeast...........	50,809,229	254,411	0.50	53,594,378	327,090	0.61	115,809	57,075	59,184
Midwest...........	59,668,632	203,549	0.34	64,392,776	286,537	0.44	120,172	27,448	16,756
South...........	85,445,930	211,103	0.25	100,236,820	309,924	0.31	121,534	30,825	29,849
West.............	52,786,082	191,291	0.36	63,197,932	266,180	0.42	82,764	27,549	37,043
State									
Alabama..........	4,040,587	5,839	0.14	4,447,100	6,634	0.15	3,769	444	361
Alaska	550,043	541	0.10	626,932	817	0.13	329	178	77
Arizona..........	3,665,228	11,796	0.32	5,130,632	17,111	0.33	6,388	1,849	1,253
Arkansas	2,350,725	1,854	0.08	2,673,400	2,397	0.09	969	403	214
California	29,760,021	142,805	0.48	33,871,648	190,890	0.56	53,286	19,553	30,959
Colorado	3,294,394	7,541	0.23	4,301,261	12,421	0.29	4,886	1,120	939
Connecticut	3,287,116	12,783	0.39	3,405,565	14,671	0.43	8,131	1,730	1,365
Delaware	666,168	1,443	0.22	783,600	1,766	0.23	468	156	448
District of Columbia ...	606,900	2,741	0.45	572,059	3,082	0.54	747	109	526
Florida	12,937,926	49,206	0.38	15,982,378	77,461	0.48	30,115	9,925	6,759
Georgia	6,478,216	10,357	0.16	8,186,453	17,110	0.21	7,823	1,549	1,731
Hawaii	1,108,229	1,149	0.10	1,211,537	1,622	0.13	651	115	159
Idaho	1,006,749	730	0.07	1,293,953	1,446	0.11	703	124	65
Illinois...........	11,430,602	34,747	0.30	12,419,293	52,191	0.42	10,542	4,295	3,794
Indiana...........	5,544,159	8,368	0.15	6,080,485	11,594	0.19	4,090	1,965	1,338
Iowa.............	2,776,755	3,965	0.14	2,926,324	4,365	0.15	2,057	590	319
Kansas...........	2,477,574	4,846	0.20	2,688,418	6,722	0.25	2,984	730	438
Kentucky	3,685,296	5,091	0.14	4,041,769	7,137	0.18	3,431	712	307
Louisiana	4,219,973	10,780	0.26	4,468,976	13,445	0.30	6,561	1,821	608
Maine...........	1,227,928	3,365	0.27	1,274,923	2,990	0.23	1,959	487	166
Maryland	4,781,468	15,683	0.33	5,296,486	20,224	0.38	6,608	2,201	3,246
Massachusetts.......	6,016,425	44,773	0.74	6,349,097	52,756	0.83	32,072	7,123	3,238
Michigan..........	9,295,297	76,504	0.82	9,938,444	115,284	1.16	54,363	8,876	3,310
Minnesota	4,375,099	9,732	0.22	4,919,479	13,795	0.28	6,806	923	2,269
Mississippi	2,573,216	4,063	0.16	2,844,658	4,185	0.15	2,785	329	237
Missouri	5,117,073	9,079	0.18	5,595,211	12,626	0.23	5,381	1,348	687
Montana..........	799,065	1,155	0.14	902,195	1,153	0.13	699	239	21
Nebraska	1,578,385	3,072	0.19	1,711,263	4,657	0.27	2,141	782	328
Nevada	1,201,833	4,176	0.35	1,998,257	7,188	0.36	2,897	997	772
New Hampshire......	1,109,252	4,953	0.45	1,235,786	6,767	0.55	4,706	801	454
New Jersey	7,730,188	46,381	0.60	8,414,350	71,770	0.85	13,353	12,624	25,170
New Mexico........	1,515,069	3,464	0.23	1,819,046	4,271	0.23	2,373	206	206
New York	17,990,455	94,319	0.52	18,976,457	120,370	0.63	31,083	17,685	23,661
North Carolina	6,628,637	10,551	0.16	8,049,313	19,405	0.24	6,998	1,584	2,076
North Dakota	638,800	975	0.15	642,200	1,042	0.16	546	199	40
Ohio.............	10,847,115	44,405	0.41	11,353,140	54,014	0.48	27,361	6,519	3,210
Oklahoma..........	3,145,585	6,859	0.22	3,450,654	8,090	0.23	4,408	608	331
Oregon...........	2,842,321	6,164	0.22	3,421,399	9,316	0.27	3,148	1,657	850
Pennsylvania	11,881,643	39,842	0.34	12,281,054	48,678	0.40	19,889	13,392	4,718
Rhode Island	1,003,464	6,342	0.63	1,048,319	7,012	0.67	3,016	3,089	338
South Carolina.......	3,486,703	5,702	0.16	4,012,012	6,423	0.16	3,573	594	547
South Dakota........	696,004	1,237	0.18	754,844	1,405	0.19	730	294	85
Tennessee	4,877,185	6,381	0.13	5,689,283	12,882	0.23	3,194	773	1,569
Texas	16,986,510	44,256	0.26	20,851,820	63,046	0.30	23,652	5,866	5,132
Utah.............	1,722,850	2,703	0.16	2,233,169	4,569	0.20	1,995	238	280
Vermont	562,758	1,653	0.29	608,827	2,076	0.34	1,600	144	74
Virginia...........	6,187,358	24,795	0.40	7,078,515	41,230	0.58	12,870	2,909	5,586
Washington	4,866,692	8,811	0.18	5,894,121	15,016	0.25	5,226	1,261	1,407
West Virginia	1,793,477	5,502	0.31	1,808,344	5,407	0.30	3,563	842	171
Wisconsin..........	4,891,769	6,619	0.14	5,363,675	8,842	0.16	3,171	927	938
Wyoming	453,588	256	0.06	493,782	360	0.07	183	12	55
Puerto Rico	3,522,037	(NA)	(NA)	3,808,610	2,633	0.07	828	66	56

NA Not available; the ancestry question was not asked in Puerto Rico during the 1990 census.
[1] Respondents who reported either one or two Arab ancestries were tabulated exactly once to calculate the Arab population by region and state.
[2] For selected Arab groups, the columns reflect the designated Arab ancestry regardless of whether or not another Arab ancestry was also reported; that is, someone who reported Lebanese and Syrian would be tabulated in each column. Hence, it is not appropriate to sum the columns.
Source: U.S. Census Bureau, Census 2000 Summary File 4 (SF4), 1990 Census Sample Edited Detail File.

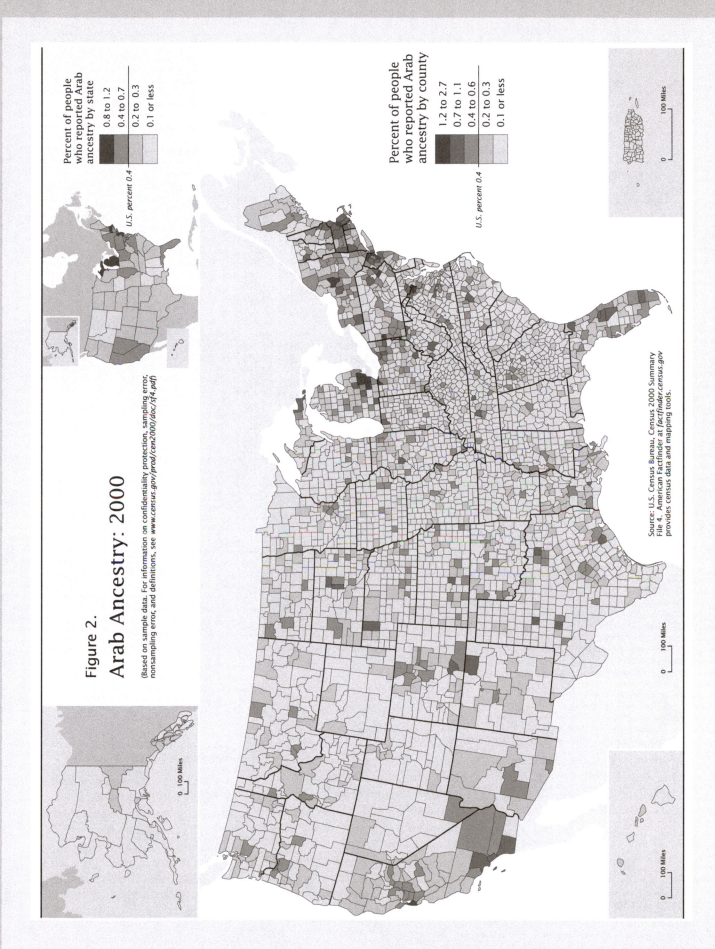

Figure 2.

Arab Ancestry: 2000

(Based on sample data. For information on confidentiality protection, sampling error, nonsampling error, and definitions, see *www.census.gov/prod/cen2000/doc/sf4.pdf*)

Percent of people who reported Arab ancestry by state

0.8 to 1.2
0.4 to 0.7
0.2 to 0.3
0.1 or less

U.S. percent 0.4

Percent of people who reported Arab ancestry by county

1.2 to 2.7
0.7 to 1.1
0.4 to 0.6
0.2 to 0.3
0.1 or less

U.S. percent 0.4

Source: U.S. Census Bureau, Census 2000 Summary File 4. American Factfinder at *factfinder.census.gov* provides census data and mapping tools.

Table 3.
Arab Population in Selected Places: 2000

(Data based on sample. For information on confidentiality protection, sampling error, nonsampling error, and definitions, see www.census.gov/prod/cen2000/doc/sf4.pdf)

Place	Total population	Arab population			
		Number	90-percent confidence interval	Percent Arab	90-percent confidence interval
Ten Largest Places					
New York, NY..............	8,008,278	69,985	68,241 - 71,729	0.87	0.85 - 0.90
Los Angeles, CA............	3,694,834	25,673	24,557 - 26,789	0.69	0.66 - 0.73
Chicago, IL................	2,895,964	14,777	14,108 - 15,446	0.51	0.49 - 0.53
Houston, TX	1,954,848	11,128	10,393 - 11,863	0.57	0.53 - 0.61
Philadelphia, PA...........	1,517,550	5,227	4,829 - 5,625	0.34	0.32 - 0.37
Phoenix, AZ	1,320,994	5,098	4,600 - 5,596	0.39	0.35 - 0.42
San Diego, CA.............	1,223,341	7,357	6,759 - 7,955	0.60	0.55 - 0.65
Dallas, TX................	1,188,204	4,077	3,632 - 4,522	0.34	0.31 - 0.38
San Antonio, TX...........	1,144,554	3,748	3,321 - 4,175	0.33	0.29 - 0.36
Detroit, MI................	951,270	8,287	7,787 - 8,787	0.87	0.82 - 0.92
Ten Places With Largest Arab Population					
New York, NY..............	8,008,278	69,985	68,241 - 71,729	0.87	0.85 - 0.90
Dearborn, MI	97,775	29,181	28,392 - 29,970	29.85	29.04 - 30.65
Los Angeles, CA	3,694,834	25,673	24,557 - 26,789	0.69	0.66 - 0.73
Chicago, IL................	2,895,964	14,777	14,108 - 15,446	0.51	0.49 - 0.53
Houston, TX	1,954,848	11,128	10,393 - 11,863	0.57	0.53 - 0.61
Detroit, MI................	951,270	8,287	7,787 - 8,787	0.87	0.82 - 0.92
San Diego, CA.............	1,223,341	7,357	6,759 - 7,955	0.60	0.55 - 0.65
Jersey City, NJ............	240,055	6,755	6,219 - 7,291	2.81	2.59 - 3.04
Boston, MA...............	589,141	5,845	5,341 - 6,349	0.99	0.91 - 1.08
Jacksonville, FL............	735,503	5,751	5,251 - 6,251	0.78	0.71 - 0.85
Ten Places of 100,000 or More Population With Highest Percent Arab					
Sterling Heights, MI.........	124,471	4,598	4,157 - 5,039	3.69	3.34 - 4.05
Jersey City, NJ.............	240,055	6,755	6,219 - 7,291	2.81	2.59 - 3.04
Warren, MI...............	138,276	3,470	3,149 - 3,791	2.51	2.28 - 2.74
Allentown, PA..............	106,632	2,613	2,279 - 2,947	2.45	2.14 - 2.76
Burbank, CA..............	100,316	2,395	2,057 - 2,733	2.39	2.05 - 2.72
Glendale, CA	195,047	4,028	3,589 - 4,467	2.07	1.84 - 2.29
Livonia, MI	100,545	1,953	1,712 - 2,194	1.94	1.70 - 2.18
Arlington, VA..............	189,453	3,352	2,972 - 3,732	1.77	1.57 - 1.97
Paterson, NJ..............	149,222	2,634	2,297 - 2,971	1.77	1.54 - 1.99
Daly City, CA	103,549	1,752	1,462 - 2,042	1.69	1.41 - 1.97

Note: Because of sampling error, the estimates in this table may not be statistically different from one another or from rates for other geographic areas not listed in this table.

Source: U.S. Census Bureau, Census 2000 Summary File 4.

and Oneida Counties, New York; Lehigh and Lawrence Counties, Pennsylvania; Ohio County, West Virginia; Lucas County, Ohio; and San Mateo County, California.[19]

_____
[19] The 90-percent confidence interval fell below 1.2 percent for all counties except for Wayne and Macomb Counties, Michigan; Passaic and Hudson Counties, New Jersey; and Fairfax County, Virginia.

Elsewhere in the country, the proportion of Arabs at the county level was more dispersed. The Arab population represented between 0.7 and 1.1 percent of the population in one or more counties in many states across the nation. However, more than half the counties in the United States had a low percentage of people who reported an Arab ancestry (0.1 or less).

The largest number of Arabs lived in New York City.

In 2000, 70,000 people of Arab ancestry lived in New York, making it the city with the largest number of Arabs (see Table 3). Six of the ten largest cities in the United States were also among the ten places with the largest Arab populations (New York, Los Angeles, Chicago, Houston, Detroit, and

San Diego). Although these cities were among those with the largest number of Arabs, their proportions Arab were relatively low (less than 1 percent).

Arabs were 30 percent of the population in Dearborn, Michigan.

Among places with 100,000 or more population, the highest proportion of Arabs lived in Sterling Heights, Michigan (3.7 percent).[20] Additionally, relatively high percentages of Arabs also lived in Warren and Livonia, Michigan. However, Dearborn, Michigan, which fell just below the 100,000 population threshold, had an Arab population of 30 percent, by far the largest proportion among places of similar size. California, (with Burbank, Glendale, and Daly City), and New Jersey, (with Jersey City and Paterson), also had more than one city of 100,000 or more population among the places with the highest proportion Arab.

ADDITIONAL FINDINGS ON THE ARAB POPULATION

Where are the Lebanese, Syrians, and Egyptians concentrated?

The largest specific Arab ancestries reported in Census 2000 were Lebanese, Syrian, and Egyptian. People reporting Lebanese ancestry lived predominately in Michigan, California, Massachusetts, and New York.[21] The largest groups with Syrian ancestry were in California,

New York, Pennsylvania, and New Jersey.[22] Those with Egyptian ancestry lived predominately in California, New Jersey, New York, and Florida.[23]

People of Arab ancestry also report other non-Arab ancestries, races, and Hispanic origins.

The Arab population in the United States is composed of people with many different ethnic backgrounds. More than one-quarter of the Arab population (29 percent) reported two ancestries: 28 percent reported one Arab and one non-Arab ancestry and 1.1 percent reported two Arab ancestries. Among Arabs who also reported a non-Arab ancestry, 14.7 percent reported Irish, 13.6 percent reported Italian, and 13.5 percent reported German.[24] Among the 13,000 people who reported two Arab ancestries, one-half reported Lebanese and Syrian.

In Census 2000, the vast majority of Arabs reported their race as White and no other race (80 percent), or as Two or more races (17 percent).[25] Small proportions

reported a single race of Black (1.1 percent), Asian (0.7 percent), American Indian and Alaska Native (0.07 percent), Native Hawaiian and Other Pacific Islander (0.03 percent), or Some other race (1.0 percent). In addition, 3.2 percent of the Arab population reported as Hispanic (of any race).

ABOUT CENSUS 2000

Why Census 2000 asked about ancestry.

Ancestry data are required to enforce provisions under the Civil Rights Act that prohibit discrimination based upon race, sex, religion, and national origin. More generally, these data are needed to measure the social and economic characteristics of ethnic groups and to tailor services to accommodate cultural differences.

Data about ancestry assist states and local agencies to develop health care and other services tailored to meet the language and cultural diversity of various groups.

Under the Public Health Service Act, ancestry is one of the factors used to identify segments of the population who may not be receiving medical services.

Accuracy of the Estimates

The data contained in this report are based on the sample of households who responded to the Census 2000 long form. Nationally, approximately 1 out of every 6 housing units was included in this sample. As a result, the sample estimates may differ somewhat from the 100-percent figures that would have been obtained if all housing units, people within those housing units, and people living in group quarters had been enumerated using the same questionnaires, instructions, enumerators, and so forth. The sample

---

[20] Census 2000 showed 245 places in the United States with 100,000 or more population. They included 238 incorporated places (including 4 city-county consolidations) and 7 census designated places that were not legally incorporated. For a list of these places by state, see www.census.gov /population/www/cen2000/phc-t6.html.

[21] The size of the Lebanese population in Michigan was not statistically different from that of the Lebanese population in California, nor was there a statistical difference between the Lebanese populations in Massachusetts and New York.

[22] The size of the Syrian population in California was not statistically different from that of the Syrian population in New York. Additionally, there was no statistical difference in size between the Syrian populations in Pennsylvania and New Jersey.

[23] There was no statistical difference between the size of the Egyptian populations in New Jersey and New York.

[24] Italian was not statistically different from German as another non-Arab ancestry reported by Arabs.

[25] Census 2000 allowed respondents to choose more than one race. In this report, a "single race" category refers to people who indicated exactly one racial identity among the six primary categories: White, Black or African American, American Indian and Alaska Native, Asian, Native Hawaiian and Other Pacific Islander, and Some other race. The "single race" or "alone" category is used for all of the racial groups in this brief except for the Two or more races category. The use of the alone population in this section does not imply that it is the preferred method of presenting or analyzing data. In general, either the alone population or the alone or in combination population can be used, depending on the purpose of the analysis. The Census Bureau uses both approaches.

estimates also differ from the values that would have been obtained from different samples of housing units, and hence of people living in those housing units, and people living in group quarters. The deviation of a sample estimate from the average of all possible samples is called the sampling error.

In addition to the variability that arises from the sampling procedures, both sample data and 100-percent data are subject to nonsampling error. Nonsampling error may be introduced during any of the various complex operations used to collect and process data. Such errors may include: not enumerating every household or every person in the population, failing to obtain all required information from the respondents, obtaining incorrect or inconsistent information, and recording information incorrectly. In addition, errors can occur during the field review of the enumerators' work, during clerical handling of the census questionnaires, or during the electronic processing of the questionnaires.

While it is impossible to completely eliminate error from an operation as large and complex as the decennial census, the Census Bureau attempts to control the sources of such error during the data collection and processing operations. The primary sources of error and the programs instituted to control error in Census 2000 are described in detail in *Summary File 3 Technical Documentation* under Chapter 8, "Accuracy of the Data,"

located at *www.census.gov/prod /cen2000/doc/sf3.pdf.*

Nonsampling error may affect the data in two ways: (1) errors that are introduced randomly will increase the variability of the data and, therefore, should be reflected in the standard errors; and (2) errors that tend to be consistent in one direction will bias both sample and 100-percent data in that direction. For example, if respondents consistently tend to underreport their incomes, then the resulting estimates of households or families by income category will tend to be understated for the higher income categories and overstated for the lower income categories. Such biases are not reflected in the standard errors.

All statements in this Census 2000 Brief have undergone statistical testing and all comparisons are significant at the 90-percent confidence level, unless otherwise noted. The estimates in tables, maps, and other figures may vary from actual values due to sampling and nonsampling errors. As a result, estimates in one category used to summarize statistics in the maps and figures may not be significantly different from estimates assigned to a different category. Further information on the accuracy of the data is located at *www.census.gov/prod/cen2000 /doc/sf3.pdf.* For further information on the computation and use of standard errors, contact the Decennial Statistical Studies Division at 301-763-4242.

For More Information

The Census 2000 Summary File 3 and Summary File 4 data are available from the American Factfinder on the Internet (*factfinder.census.gov*). They were released on a state-by-state basis during 2002. For information on confidentiality protection, nonsampling error, sampling error, and definitions, also see *www.census.gov /prod/cen2000/doc/sf4.pdf* or contact the Customer Services Center at 301-763-INFO (4636).

Information on population and housing topics is presented in the Census 2000 Brief series, located on the Census Bureau's Web site at *www.census.gov/population/www /cen2000/briefs.html*. This series presents information on race, Hispanic origin, age, sex, household type, housing tenure, and social, economic, and housing characteristics, such as ancestry, income, and housing costs.

For additional information on the Arab population, including reports and survey data, visit the Census Bureau's Internet site at *www.census.gov/population/www /ancestry.html*. To find information about the availability of data products, including reports, CD-ROMs, and DVDs, call the Customer Services Center at 301-763-INFO (4636), or e-mail *webmaster@census.gov*.

Ancestry: 2000

Census 2000 Brief

Issued June 2004

C2KBR-35

By
Angela Brittingham
and
G. Patricia de la Cruz

Ancestry is a broad concept that can mean different things to different people; it can be described alternately as where their ancestors are from, where they or their parents originated, or simply how they see themselves ethnically. Some people may have one distinct ancestry, while others are descendants of several ancestry groups, and still others may know only that their ancestors were from a particular region of the world or may not know their ethnic origins at all. The Census Bureau defines ancestry as a person's ethnic origin, heritage, descent, or "roots," which may reflect their place of birth, place of birth of parents or ancestors, and ethnic identities that have evolved within the United States.

This report is part of a series that presents population and housing data collected by Census 2000, where 80 percent of respondents to the long form specified at least one ancestry. (About one-sixth of households received the long form.) It presents data on the most frequently reported ancestries and describes population distributions for the United States, including regions, states, counties, and selected cities.[1] The listed ancestries

---

Figure 1.
Reproduction of the Question on Ancestry From Census 2000

10 What is this person's ancestry or ethnic origin?

(For example: Italian, Jamaican, African Am., Cambodian, Cape Verdean, Norwegian, Dominican, French Canadian, Haitian, Korean, Lebanese, Polish, Nigerian, Mexican, Taiwanese, Ukrainian, and so on.)

Source: U.S. Census Bureau, Census 2000 questionnaire.

---

were reported by at least 100,000 people, and the numbers cited in this report represent the number of people who reported each ancestry either as their first or second response.

The question on ancestry first appeared on the census questionnaire in 1980, replacing a question on where a person's parents were born. The question on parental birthplace provided foreign-origin data only for people with one or both parents born outside the United States. The current ancestry question allows everyone to give one or two attributions of their "ancestry or ethnic origin" (Figure 1), and in doing so, enables people to identify an ethnic background, such as German, Lebanese, Nigerian, or Portuguese, which was not otherwise identified in the race or Hispanic-origin questions.

The ancestries in this report also include the groups covered in the questions on race and Hispanic origin, such as

[1] The text of this report discusses data for the United States, including the 50 states and the District of Columbia. Data for the Commonwealth of Puerto Rico are shown in Table 3 and Figure 3.

USCENSUSBUREAU

Helping You Make Informed Decisions

U.S. Department of Commerce
Economics and Statistics Administration
U.S. CENSUS BUREAU

United States Census 2000

Table 1.
Ancestry Reporting: 1990 and 2000

(Data based on sample. For information on confidentiality protection, sampling error, nonsampling error, and definitions, see www.census.gov/prod/cen2000/doc/sf3.pdf)

Ancestry	1990[1]		2000		Change, 1990 to 2000	
	Number	Percent	Number	Percent	Numerical	Percent
Total population......................	248,709,873	100.0	281,421,906	100.0	32,712,033	13.2
Ancestry specified.........................	222,608,257	89.5	225,310,411	80.1	2,702,154	1.2
Single ancestry	148,836,950	59.8	163,315,936	58.0	14,478,986	9.7
Multiple ancestry	73,771,307	29.7	61,994,475	22.0	−11,776,832	−16.0
Ancestry not specified	26,101,616	10.5	56,111,495	19.9	30,009,879	115.0
Unclassified	2,180,245	0.9	2,437,929	0.9	257,684	11.8
Not reported..........................	23,921,371	9.6	53,673,566	19.1	29,752,195	124.4

[1]1990 estimates in this table differ slightly from 1990 Summary Tape File 3 in order to make them fully consistent with data from Census 2000.

Source: U.S. Census Bureau, Census 2000 Summary File 3 and 1990 special tabulation.

African American, Mexican, American Indian, and Chinese. For these groups, the results from the ancestry question and the race and Hispanic-origin questions differ, but the latter are the official sources of data for race and Hispanic groups. In some cases, the totals reported on the ancestry question are lower than the numbers from the race or Hispanic-origin question. For instance, nearly 12 million fewer people specified "African American" as their ancestry than gave that response to the race question. One reason for this large difference is that some people who reported Black or African American on the race question reported their ancestry more specifically, such as Jamaican, Haitian, or Nigerian, and thus were not counted in the African American ancestry category. Similarly, more than 2 million fewer people reported Mexican ancestry than gave that answer to the Hispanic-origin question.[2] In other cases, the ancestry question produced higher numbers, such as for Dominicans, whose estimated totals from the ancestry question were over 100,000 higher than from the Hispanic-origin question, where many Dominicans may have reported a general term (like Hispanic) or checked "other" without writing in a detailed response.[3]

More than four out of five people specified at least one ancestry.

In 2000, 58 percent of the population specified only one ancestry, 22 percent provided two ancestries, and 1 percent reported an unclassifiable ancestry such as "mixture" or "adopted." Another 19 percent did not report any ancestry at all, a substantial increase from 1990, when 10 percent of the population left the ancestry question blank (Table 1).

Nearly one of six people reported their ancestry as German.

In 2000, 42.8 million people (15 percent of the population) considered themselves to be of German (or part-German) ancestry, the most frequent response to the census question (Figure 2).[4] Other ancestries with over 15 million people in 2000 included Irish (30.5 million, or 11 percent), African American (24.9 million, or 9 percent), English (24.5 million, or 9 percent), American (20.2 million, or 7 percent), Mexican (18.4 million, or 7 percent), and Italian (15.6 million, or 6 percent).

Other ancestries with 4 million or more people included Polish, French, American Indian, Scottish, Dutch, Norwegian, Scotch-Irish, and Swedish.

In total, 7 ancestries were reported by more than 15 million people in 2000, 37 ancestries were reported by more than 1 million people, and

[2] The estimates in this report are based on responses from a sample of the population. As with all surveys, estimates may vary from the actual values because of sampling variation or other factors. All statements made in this report have undergone statistical testing and are significant at the 90-percent confidence level unless otherwise noted.

[3] For more information about race and Hispanic groups, see Census 2000 Briefs on Hispanic, American Indian and Alaska Native, Asian, Black, Native Hawaiian and Pacific Islander, White, and Two or More Races populations, available on the Census Bureau Web site at www.census.gov/prod/cen2000/index.html.

[4] The estimates in Figure 2 and Table 2 in some cases differ slightly from the estimates in other data products due to the collapsing schemes used. For example, here German does not include Bavarian.

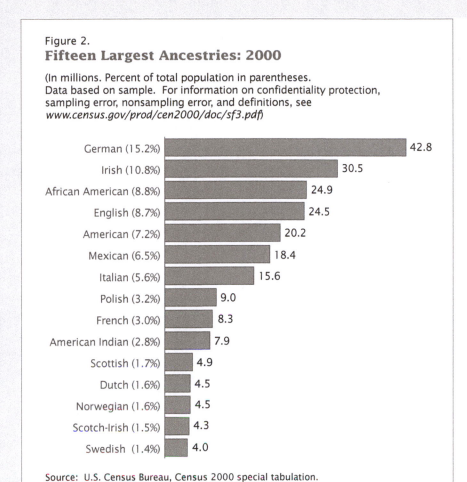

Figure 2.
Fifteen Largest Ancestries: 2000

(In millions. Percent of total population in parentheses.
Data based on sample. For information on confidentiality protection,
sampling error, nonsampling error, and definitions, see
www.census.gov/prod/cen2000/doc/sf3.pdf)

Ancestry	Millions
German (15.2%)	42.8
Irish (10.8%)	30.5
African American (8.8%)	24.9
English (8.7%)	24.5
American (7.2%)	20.2
Mexican (6.5%)	18.4
Italian (5.6%)	15.6
Polish (3.2%)	9.0
French (3.0%)	8.3
American Indian (2.8%)	7.9
Scottish (1.7%)	4.9
Dutch (1.6%)	4.5
Norwegian (1.6%)	4.5
Scotch-Irish (1.5%)	4.3
Swedish (1.4%)	4.0

Source: U.S. Census Bureau, Census 2000 special tabulation.

92 ancestries were reported by more than 100,000 people (Table 2).

The largest European ancestries have decreased in population, while African American, Hispanic, and Asian ancestries have increased.

The highest growth rates between 1990 and 2000 occurred in groups identified by a general heritage rather than a particular country of ancestry. For example, the number of people who reported Latin American, African, or European all more than quadrupled (Latin American increased from 44,000 in 1990 to 250,000 in 2000, African grew from 246,000 to 1.2 million, and European rose from 467,000 to 2.0 million). Other general-heritage groups that at least doubled in size included Western European, Northern European, Asian, Hispanic, and White.

The three largest ancestries in 1990 were German, Irish, and English. In 2000, these groups were still the largest European ancestries, but each had decreased in size by at least 8 million and by more than 20 percent (Table 2). As a proportion of the population, German decreased from 23 percent in 1990 to 15 percent in 2000, while Irish and English decreased from 16 percent to 11 percent, and from 13 percent to 9 percent, respectively. Several other large European ancestries also decreased over the decade, including Polish, French, Scottish, Dutch, and Swedish.

The number of people who reported African American ancestry increased by nearly 1.2 million, or 4.9 percent, between 1990 and 2000, making this group the third largest ancestry. However, the proportion of African Americans decreased slightly over the decade, from 9.5 percent to 8.8 percent.

The population of many ancestries, such as Mexican, Chinese, Filipino, and Asian Indian, increased during the decade, reflecting sizable immigration, especially from Latin America and Asia. Several small ancestry populations, including Brazilian, Pakistani, Albanian, Honduran, and Trinidadian and Tobagonian, at least doubled.

Seven percent of the U.S. population reported their ancestry as American.

The number who reported American and no other ancestry increased from 12.4 million in 1990 to 20.2 million in 2000, the largest numerical growth of any group during the 1990s.[5] This figure represents an increase of 63 percent, as the proportion rose from 5.0 percent to 7.2 percent of the population.

THE GEOGRAPHIC DISTRIBUTION OF ANCESTRIES

In each of the four regions, a different ancestry was reported as the largest.

Among the four regions, the largest ancestries in 2000 were Irish in the

[5] American was considered a valid ancestry response when it was the only ancestry provided by a respondent.

Table 2.
Ancestries With 100,000 or More People in 2000: 1990 and 2000

(Data based on sample. For information on confidentiality protection, sampling error, nonsampling error, and definitions, see www.census.gov/prod/cen2000/doc/sf3.pdf)

Ancestry	1990		2000		Change, 1990 to 2000	
	Number	Percent of total population	Number	Percent of total population	Numerical	Percent
Total population........................	248,709,873	100.0	281,421,906	100.0	32,712,033	13.2
African[*]	245,845	0.1	1,183,316	0.4	937,471	381.3
African American[*,1,2]	23,750,256	9.5	24,903,412	8.8	1,153,156	4.9
Albanian	47,710	-	113,661	-	65,951	138.2
American[*]	12,395,999	5.0	20,188,305	7.2	7,792,306	62.9
American Indian[*]	8,689,344	3.5	7,876,568	2.8	-812,776	-9.4
Arab[*]	127,364	0.1	205,822	0.1	78,458	61.6
Armenian........................	308,096	0.1	385,488	0.1	77,392	25.1
Asian[*]	107,172	-	238,960	0.1	131,788	123.0
Asian Indian	569,338	0.2	1,546,703	0.5	977,365	171.7
Austrian........................	864,783	0.3	730,336	0.3	-134,447	-15.5
Belgian........................	380,403	0.2	348,531	0.1	-31,872	-8.4
Brazilian........................	65,875	-	181,076	0.1	115,201	174.9
British........................	1,119,140	0.4	1,085,718	0.4	-33,422	-3.0
Cambodian[2]	134,955	0.1	197,093	0.1	62,138	46.0
Canadian........................	549,990	0.2	638,548	0.2	88,558	16.1
Chinese........................	1,505,229	0.6	2,271,562	0.8	766,333	50.9
Colombian........................	351,717	0.1	583,986	0.2	232,269	66.0
Croatian[1]	544,270	0.2	374,241	0.1	-170,029	-31.2
Cuban	859,739	0.3	1,097,594	0.4	237,855	27.7
Czech........................	1,296,369	0.5	1,258,452	0.4	-37,917	-2.9
Czechoslovakian	315,285	0.1	441,403	0.2	126,118	40.0
Danish........................	1,634,648	0.7	1,430,897	0.5	-203,751	-12.5
Dominican[1,2]........................	505,690	0.2	908,531	0.3	402,841	79.7
Dutch........................	6,226,339	2.5	4,541,770	1.6	-1,684,569	-27.1
Ecuadorian[1]	197,374	0.1	322,965	0.1	125,591	63.6
Egyptian........................	78,574	-	142,832	0.1	64,258	81.8
English........................	32,651,788	13.1	24,509,692	8.7	-8,142,096	-24.9
European[*]........................	466,718	0.2	1,968,696	0.7	1,501,978	321.8
Filipino........................	1,450,512	0.6	2,116,478	0.8	665,966	45.9
Finnish........................	658,854	0.3	623,559	0.2	-35,295	-5.4
French........................	10,320,656	4.1	8,309,666	3.0	-2,010,990	-19.5
French Canadian[1,2]........................	2,167,127	0.9	2,349,684	0.8	182,557	8.4
German[1]	57,947,171	23.3	42,841,569	15.2	-15,105,602	-26.1
Greek........................	1,110,292	0.4	1,153,295	0.4	43,003	3.9
Guatemalan	241,559	0.1	463,502	0.2	221,943	91.9
Guyanese	81,665	-	162,425	0.1	80,760	98.9
Haitian[1,2]........................	289,521	0.1	548,199	0.2	258,678	89.3
Hawaiian........................	256,081	0.1	334,858	0.1	78,777	30.8
Hispanic[*]........................	1,113,259	0.4	2,451,109	0.9	1,337,850	120.2
Hmong........................	84,823	-	140,528	-	55,705	65.7
Honduran	116,635	-	266,848	0.1	150,213	128.8
Hungarian........................	1,582,302	0.6	1,398,702	0.5	-183,600	-11.6
Iranian	235,521	0.1	338,266	0.1	102,745	43.6
Irish[1]........................	38,735,539	15.6	30,524,799	10.8	-8,210,740	-21.2
Israeli........................	81,677	-	106,839	-	25,162	30.8
Italian[1,2]........................	14,664,189	5.9	15,638,348	5.6	974,159	6.6
Jamaican[1,2]........................	435,024	0.2	736,513	0.3	301,489	69.3
Japanese........................	1,004,622	0.4	1,103,325	0.4	98,703	9.8
Korean[1,2]........................	836,987	0.3	1,190,353	0.4	353,366	42.2
Laotian........................	146,947	0.1	179,866	0.1	32,919	22.4
Latin American[*]	43,521	-	250,052	0.1	206,531	474.6
Lebanese[1,2]........................	394,180	0.2	440,279	0.2	46,099	11.7
Lithuanian	811,865	0.3	659,992	0.2	-151,873	-18.7
Mexican[1,2]........................	11,580,038	4.7	18,382,291	6.5	6,802,253	58.7
Nicaraguan	177,077	0.1	230,358	0.1	53,281	30.1
Nigerian[1,2]........................	91,499	-	164,691	0.1	73,192	80.0

(see footnotes on next page)

Table 2.
Ancestries With 100,000 or More People in 2000: 1990 and 2000—Con.

(Data based on sample. For information on confidentiality protection, sampling error, nonsampling error, and definitions, see www.census.gov/prod/cen2000/doc/sf3.pdf)

Ancestry	1990		2000		Change, 1990 to 2000	
	Number	Percent of total population	Number	Percent of total population	Numerical	Percent
Northern European[*]	65,993	-	163,657	0.1	97,664	148.0
Norwegian[2]	3,869,395	1.6	4,477,725	1.6	608,330	15.7
Pakistani	99,974	-	253,193	0.1	153,219	153.3
Panamanian	88,649	-	119,497	-	30,848	34.8
Pennsylvania German	305,841	0.1	255,807	0.1	-50,034	-16.4
Peruvian	161,866	0.1	292,991	0.1	131,125	81.0
Polish[1,2]	9,366,051	3.8	8,977,235	3.2	-388,816	-4.2
Portuguese	1,148,857	0.5	1,173,691	0.4	24,834	2.2
Puerto Rican	1,955,323	0.8	2,652,598	0.9	697,275	35.7
Romanian	365,531	0.1	367,278	0.1	1,747	(NS)
Russian	2,951,373	1.2	2,652,214	0.9	-299,159	-10.1
Salvadoran	499,153	0.2	802,743	0.3	303,590	60.8
Scandinavian	678,880	0.3	425,099	0.2	-253,781	-37.4
Scotch-Irish	5,617,773	2.3	4,319,232	1.5	-1,298,541	-23.1
Scottish	5,393,581	2.2	4,890,581	1.7	-503,000	-9.3
Serbian	116,795	-	140,337	-	23,5422	0.2
Slavic	76,923	-	127,136	-	50,213	65.3
Slovak[1]	1,882,897	0.8	797,764	0.3	-1,085,133	-57.6
Slovene	124,437	0.1	176,691	0.1	52,254	42.0
Spaniard	360,858	0.1	299,948	0.1	-60,910	-16.9
Spanish	2,024,004	0.8	2,187,144	0.8	163,140	8.1
Swedish	4,680,863	1.9	3,998,310	1.4	-682,553	-14.6
Swiss	1,045,492	0.4	911,502	0.3	-133,990	-12.8
Syrian	129,606	0.1	142,897	0.1	13,291	10.3
Taiwanese[1,2]	192,973	0.1	293,568	0.1	100,595	52.1
Thai[1]	112,11	-	146,577	0.1	34,460	30.7
Trinidadian and Tobagonian	76,270	-	164,738	0.1	88,468	116.0
Turkish	83,850	-	117,575	-	33,725	40.2
Ukrainian[1,2]	740,723	0.3	892,922	0.3	152,199	20.5
United States[*]	643,561	0.3	404,328	0.1	-239,233	-37.2
Vietnamese	535,825	0.2	1,029,420	0.4	493,595	92.1
Welsh	2,033,893	0.8	1,753,794	0.6	-280,099	-13.8
West Indian[*]	159,167	0.1	147,222	0.1	-11,945	-7.5
Western European[*]	42,409	-	125,300	-	82,891	195.5
White[*]	1,799,711	0.7	3,834,122	1.4	2,034,411	113.0
Yugoslavian	257,986	0.1	328,547	0.1	70,561	27.4
Other ancestries	3,989,728	1.6	4,380,380	1.6	390,652	9.8

- Rounds to 0.0.
* General response which may encompass several ancestries not listed separately (i.e., African American includes Black and Negro). NS Not statistically different from zero at the 90-percent confidence level.

[1] Included in the list of examples on the census questionnaire in 1990.
[2] Included in the list of examples on the census questionnaire in 2000.

Notes: Because of sampling error, the estimates in this table may not be significantly different from one another or from other ancestries not listed in this table.

People who reported two ancestries were included once in each category. The estimates in this table differ slightly in some cases from the estimates in other data products due to the collapsing schemes used. For example, here German does not include Bavarian. Some groups correspond to groups identified separately in the race and Hispanic-origin questions. The race item provides the primary source of data for White, Black, American Indian, Alaska Native, Asian groups, Native Hawaiian, and Pacific Islander groups. The Hispanic-origin question is the primary identifier for Mexican, Puerto Rican, Cuban, and other Hispanic groups.

Source: U.S. Census Bureau, 1990 Census and Census 2000 special tabulations.

Table 3.
Largest Ancestries for the United States, Regions, States, and for Puerto Rico: 2000

(Data based on sample. For information on confidentiality protection, sampling error, nonsampling error, and definitions, see www.census.gov/prod/cen2000/doc/sf3.pdf)

Ancestry	Total population	Ancestry	Per-cent	Ancestry	Per-cent	Ancestry	Per-cent	Ancestry	Per-cent	Ancestry	Per-cent
United States	**281,421,906**	**German**	**15.2**	**Irish**	**10.8**	**African Am.**	**8.8**	**English**	**8.7**	**American**	**7.2**
Region											
Northeast	53,594,378	Irish	15.8	Italian	14.1	German	13.6	English	8.3	African Am.	6.5
Midwest	64,392,776	German	26.6	Irish	11.8	English	8.4	African Am.	7.8	American	6.5
South	100,236,820	African Am.	14.0	American	11.2	German	10.0	Irish	8.8	English	8.4
West.	63,197,932	Mexican	16.0	German	13.3	English	9.9	Irish	9.0	American	4.1
State											
Alabama	4,447,100	African Am.	19.9	American	16.8	English	7.8	Irish	7.7	German	5.7
Alaska.	626,932	German	16.6	Irish	10.8	Am. Indian	10.5	English	9.6	Eskimo	6.1
Arizona	5,130,632	Mexican	18.0	German	15.6	English	10.4	Irish	10.2	Am. Indian	6.1
Arkansas	2,673,400	American	15.7	African Am.	11.9	Irish	9.5	German	9.3	English	7.9
California	33,871,648	Mexican	22.2	German	9.8	Irish	7.7	English	7.4	African Am.	5.1
Colorado.	4,301,261	German	22.0	Irish	12.2	English	12.0	Mexican	9.0	American	5.0
Connecticut.	3,405,565	Italian	18.6	Irish	16.6	English	10.3	German	9.8	Polish	8.3
Delaware	783,600	Irish	16.6	German	14.3	African Am.	14.0	English	12.1	Italian	9.3
District of Columbia	572,059	African Am.	43.4	Irish	4.9	German	4.8	English	4.4	Salvadoran	2.3
Florida	15,982,378	German	11.8	Irish	10.3	English	9.2	African Am.	8.6	American	7.8
Georgia.	8,186,453	African Am.	21.6	American	13.3	English	8.1	Irish	7.8	German	7.0
Hawaii.	1,211,537	Japanese	20.7	Filipino	17.7	Hawaiian	16.3	Chinese	8.3	German	5.8
Idaho	1,293,953	German	18.8	English	18.1	Irish	10.0	American	8.1	Mexican	5.5
Illinois.	12,419,293	German	19.6	Irish	12.2	African Am.	11.5	Mexican	8.2	Polish	7.5
Indiana	6,080,485	German	22.6	American	11.8	Irish	10.8	English	8.9	African Am.	6.5
Iowa	2,926,324	German	35.7	Irish	13.5	English	9.5	American	6.6	Norwegian	5.7
Kansas	2,688,418	German	25.8	Irish	11.5	English	10.8	American	8.7	Mexican	4.7
Kentucky.	4,041,769	American	20.7	German	12.7	Irish	10.5	English	9.7	African Am.	5.7
Louisiana	4,468,976	African Am.	25.5	French	12.2	American	10.0	German	7.0	Irish	7.0
Maine	1,274,923	English	21.5	Irish	15.1	French	14.2	American	9.3	Fr. Canadian	8.6
Maryland.	5,296,486	African Am.	20.5	German	15.7	Irish	11.7	English	9.0	American	5.6
Massachusetts . .	6,349,097	Irish	22.5	Italian	13.5	English	11.4	French	8.0	German	5.9
Michigan.	9,938,444	German	20.4	African Am.	11.0	Irish	10.7	English	9.9	Polish	8.6
Minnesota.	4,919,479	German	36.7	Norwegian	17.3	Irish	11.2	Swedish	9.9	English	6.3
Mississippi	2,844,658	African Am.	28.3	American	14.0	Irish	6.9	English	6.1	German	4.5
Missouri	5,595,211	German	23.5	Irish	12.7	American	10.4	English	9.5	African Am.	8.8
Montana.	902,195	German	27.0	Irish	14.8	English	12.6	Norwegian	10.6	Am. Indian	7.4
Nebraska.	1,711,263	German	38.6	Irish	13.4	English	9.6	Swedish	4.9	Czech	4.9
Nevada.	1,998,257	German	14.1	Mexican	12.7	Irish	11.0	English	10.1	Italian	6.6
New Hampshire .	1,235,786	Irish	19.4	English	18.0	French	14.6	Fr. Canadian	10.3	German	8.6
New Jersey.	8,414,350	Italian	17.8	Irish	15.9	German	12.6	African Am.	8.8	Polish	6.9
New Mexico	1,819,046	Mexican	16.3	Am. Indian	10.3	German	9.8	Hispanic	9.4	Spanish	9.3
New York	18,976,457	Italian	14.4	Irish	12.9	German	11.2	African Am.	7.7	English	6.0
North Carolina . .	8,049,313	African Am.	16.6	American	13.7	English	9.5	German	9.5	Irish	7.4
North Dakota . . .	642,200	German	43.9	Norwegian	30.1	Irish	7.7	Am. Indian	5.1	Swedish	5.0
Ohio	11,353,140	German	25.2	Irish	12.7	English	9.2	African Am.	9.1	American	8.5
Oklahoma.	3,450,654	German	12.6	Am. Indian	12.1	American	11.2	Irish	10.3	English	8.4
Oregon	3,421,399	German	20.5	English	13.2	Irish	11.9	American	6.2	Mexican	5.5
Pennsylvania . . .	12,281,054	German	25.4	Irish	16.1	Italian	11.5	English	7.9	African Am.	7.4
Rhode Island . . .	1,048,319	Italian	19.0	Irish	18.4	English	12.0	French	10.9	Portuguese	8.7
South Carolina . .	4,012,012	African Am.	22.8	American	13.7	German	8.4	English	8.2	Irish	7.9
South Dakota . . .	754,844	German	40.7	Norwegian	15.3	Irish	10.4	Am. Indian	8.2	English	7.1
Tennessee	5,689,283	American	17.3	African Am.	13.0	Irish	9.3	English	9.1	German	8.3
Texas	20,851,820	Mexican	22.6	German	9.9	African Am.	8.7	Irish	7.2	American	7.2
Utah	2,233,169	English	29.0	German	11.5	American	6.6	Danish	6.5	Irish	5.9
Vermont	608,827	English	18.4	Irish	16.4	French	14.5	German	9.1	Fr. Canadian	8.8
Virginia.	7,078,515	African Am.	14.9	German	11.7	American	11.2	English	11.1	Irish	9.8
Washington.	5,894,121	German	18.7	English	12.0	Irish	11.4	Norwegian	6.2	American	5.2
West Virginia . . .	1,808,344	American	18.7	German	14.0	Irish	11.0	English	9.7	Am. Indian	4.4
Wisconsin.	5,363,675	German	42.6	Irish	10.9	Polish	9.3	Norwegian	8.5	English	6.5
Wyoming	493,782	German	25.9	English	15.9	Irish	13.3	American	6.4	Am. Indian	4.7
Puerto Rico.	**3,808,610**	**Puerto Rican**	**69.0**	**American**	**2.5**	**Spaniard**	**2.1**	**Dominican**	**1.7**	**Hispanic**	**0.8**

Notes: Because of sampling error, the estimates in this table may not be significantly different from one another or from other ancestries not listed in this table.

People who reported two ancestries were included once in each category. Some groups correspond to groups identified separately in the race and Hispanic-origin questions. The race item provides the primary source of data for White, Black, American Indian, Alaska Native, Asian groups, Native Hawaiian, and Pacific Islander groups. The Hispanic-origin question is the primary identifier for Mexican, Puerto Rican, Cuban, and other Hispanic groups.

Northeast (16 percent), African American in the South (14 percent), German in the Midwest (27 percent), and Mexican in the West (16 percent, see Table 3).[6]

At the state level, 8 different ancestries were each the largest reported in 1 or more states. German led in 23 states, including every state in the Midwest, the majority of states in the West, and 1 state in the South (Figure 3). In 3 of those states, German was reported by more than 40 percent of the population: North Dakota (44 percent), Wisconsin (43 percent), and South Dakota (41 percent).

The other leading ancestries at the state level were African American in 7 contiguous states from Louisiana to Maryland and in the District of Columbia (also notably high at 43 percent); American in Arkansas, Tennessee, Kentucky, and West Virginia; Italian in Connecticut, New Jersey, New York, and Rhode Island; Mexican in 4 states from California to Texas; English in Maine, Utah and Vermont; Irish in Delaware, Massachusetts and New Hampshire; and Japanese in Hawaii.

Many other ancestries were not the largest ancestry in any state but represented more than 10 percent of a state's population, including American Indian in Oklahoma (12 percent) and Alaska

(11 percent); Filipino (18 percent) and Hawaiian (16 percent) in Hawaii; French in Maine (14 percent), Vermont (15 percent), and Rhode Island (11 percent); French Canadian in New Hampshire (10 percent); and Norwegian in North Dakota (30 percent), Minnesota (17 percent), South Dakota (15 percent), and Montana (11 percent, see Table 3).

Other ancestries not noted above were among the 5 largest in a state but represented less than 10 percent of the state's population. Examples include Chinese in Hawaii (8.3 percent), Czech in Nebraska (4.9 percent), Danish in Utah (6.5 percent), Eskimo in Alaska (6.1 percent), Polish in Michigan (8.6 percent), Portuguese in Rhode Island (8.7 percent), Spanish in New Mexico (9.3 percent), and Swedish in Minnesota (9.9 percent).

Twenty-four different ancestries were the largest in at least one county in the United States.

Ancestry patterns by county in 2000 are shown in Figure 3. German was the leading ancestry reported in many counties across the northern half of the United States, from Pennsylvania to Washington, as well as some counties in the southern half. Mexican was the leading ancestry along the southwestern border of the United States, and American and African American were the most commonly reported ancestries in many southern counties, from Virginia to eastern Texas.

Several ancestries that did not predominate in any state were the most common within one or more counties. Examples include Aleut and Eskimo in some counties of Alaska; American Indian in counties in Alaska, Arizona, California,

Montana, Nebraska, Nevada, New Mexico, North Carolina, Oklahoma, Oregon, South Dakota, Washington, and Wisconsin; Finnish in several counties in the Upper Peninsula of Michigan; French in counties in Connecticut, New York, Maine, New Hampshire, Vermont, and Louisiana; French Canadian in counties in Maine; Dutch in several counties in Michigan and Iowa; Norwegian in counties in Iowa, Minnesota, Montana, North Dakota, and Wisconsin; Polish in one county in Pennsylvania; and Portuguese in one county each in Massachusetts and Rhode Island.

African American and Mexican were the most commonly reported ancestries in the ten largest cities in the United States.

In 2000, African American was the most frequently reported ancestry in New York City, Chicago, Philadelphia, and Detroit (Table 4).[7] Mexican was the leading ancestry in Los Angeles, Houston, Phoenix, San Diego, Dallas, and San Antonio.

ADDITIONAL FINDINGS

What combinations were the most common among respondents who reported two ancestries?

The most common ancestry combinations in 2000 were German and Irish (2.7 percent of the population), German and English (1.7 percent), and Irish and English (1.4 percent).

---

[6] The Northeast region includes the states of Connecticut, Maine, Massachusetts, New Hampshire, New Jersey, New York, Pennsylvania, Rhode Island, and Vermont. The Midwest region includes the states of Illinois, Indiana, Iowa, Kansas, Michigan, Minnesota, Missouri, Nebraska, North Dakota, Ohio, South Dakota, and Wisconsin. The South region includes the states of Alabama, Arkansas, Delaware, Florida, Georgia, Kentucky, Louisiana, Maryland, Mississippi, North Carolina, Oklahoma, South Carolina, Tennessee, Texas, Virginia, West Virginia, and the District of Columbia, a state equivalent. The West region includes the states of Alaska, Arizona, California, Colorado, Hawaii, Idaho, Montana, Nevada, New Mexico, Oregon, Utah, Washington, and Wyoming.

[7] Census 2000 showed 245 places in the United States with 100,000 or more population. They included 238 incorporated places (including 4 city-county consolidations) and 7 census designated places that were not legally incorporated. For a list of places by state, see www.census.gov/population/www/cen2000/phc-t6.html

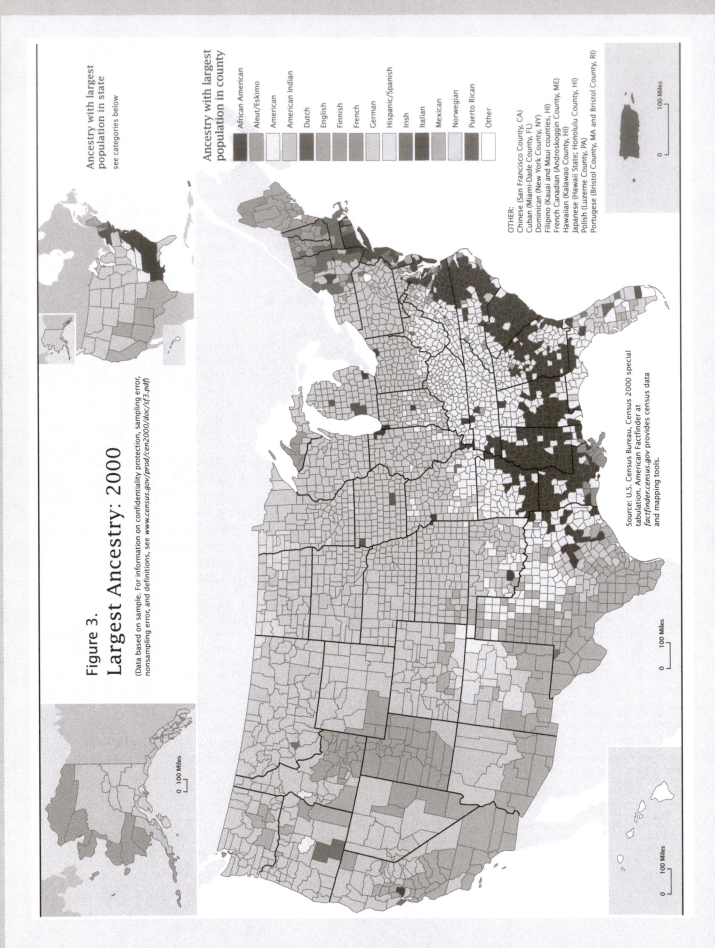

Figure 3.
Largest Ancestry: 2000

(Data based on sample. For information on confidentiality protection, sampling error, nonsampling error, and definitions, see *www.census.gov/prod/cen2000/doc/sf3.pdf*)

Ancestry with largest population in state
see categories below

Ancestry with largest population in county

African American
Aleut/Eskimo
American
American Indian
Dutch
English
Finnish
French
German
Hispanic/Spanish
Irish
Italian
Mexican
Norwegian
Puerto Rican
Other

OTHER:
Chinese (San Francisco County, CA)
Cuban (Miami-Dade County, FL)
Dominican (New York County, NY)
Filipino (Kauai and Maui counties, HI)
French Canadian (Androskoggin County, ME)
Hawaiian (Kalawao County, HI)
Japanese (Hawaii State; Honolulu County, HI)
Polish (Luzerne County, PA)
Portugese (Bristol County, MA and Bristol County, RI)

Source: U.S. Census Bureau, Census 2000 special tabulation. American Factfinder at *factfinder.census.gov* provides census data and mapping tools.

0   100 Miles

Table 4.
Largest Ancestry for the Ten Cities With the Highest Population: 2000

(Data based on sample. For information on confidentiality protection, sampling error, nonsampling error, and definitions, see www.census.gov/prod/cen2000/doc/sf3.pdf)

City	Total population	Largest ancestry			
		Ancestry	Number of people	Percent of population	90-percent confidence interval
New York, NY............................	8,008,278	African American	922,116	11.5	11.4 - 11.6
Los Angeles, CA	3,694,834	Mexican	983,157	26.6	26.5 - 26.8
Chicago, IL...............................	2,895,964	African American	804,053	27.8	27.6 - 27.9
Houston, TX	1,954,848	Mexican	467,213	23.9	23.7 - 24.1
Philadelphia, PA.........................	1,517,550	African American	493,177	32.5	32.3 - 32.8
Phoenix, AZ	1,320,994	Mexican	320,092	24.2	24.0 - 24.5
San Diego, CA...........................	1,223,341	Mexican	237,867	19.9	19.2 - 19.7
Dallas, TX.................................	1,188,204	Mexican	306,072	25.8	25.5 - 26.0
San Antonio, TX	1,144,554	Mexican	472,324	41.3	41.0 - 41.6
Detroit, MI.................................	951,270	African American	599,667	63.0	62.7 - 63.4

Notes: Because of sampling error, the estimates in this table may not be significantly different from one another or from other ancestries not listed in this table.

People who reported two ancestries were included once in each category. Some groups correspond to groups identified separately in the race and Hispanic-origin questions. The race item provides the primary source of data for White, Black, American Indian, Alaska Native, Asian groups, Native Hawaiian, and Pacific Islander groups. The Hispanic-origin question is the primary identifier for Mexican, Puerto Rican, Cuban, and other Hispanic groups.

Source: U.S. Census Bureau, Census 2000 special tabulation.

What other ancestries were reported?

Overall, about 500 different ancestries were reported during Census 2000. The category "Other ancestries" in Table 2 consists of all ancestries with fewer than 100,000 people (such as Venezuelan, Samoan, or Latvian) as well as all religious identifications (which are not tabulated).[8]

ABOUT CENSUS 2000

Why Census 2000 Asked About Ancestry

Information about ancestry is required to enforce provisions under the Civil Rights Act that prohibit discrimination based upon race, sex, religion, and national origin. More generally, these data are needed to measure the social and economic characteristics of ethnic groups and to tailor services to accommodate cultural differences.

Data about ancestry assist states and local agencies on aging to develop health care and other services tailored to address the language and cultural diversity of various groups.

Under the Public Health Service Act, ancestry is one of the factors used to identify segments of the population who may not be receiving medical services.

Accuracy of the Estimates

The data contained in this report are based on the sample of households who responded to the Census 2000 long form. Nationally, approximately 1 out of every 6 housing units was included in this sample. As a result, the sample estimates may differ somewhat from the 100-percent figures that would have been obtained if all housing units, people within those housing units, and people living in group quarters had been enumerated using the same questionnaires, instructions, enumerators, and so forth. The sample estimates also differ from the values that would have been obtained from different samples of housing units, people within those housing units, and people living in group quarters. The deviation of a sample estimate from the average of all possible samples is called the sampling error.

In addition to the variability that arises from the sampling procedures, both sample data and 100-percent data are subject to nonsampling error. Nonsampling error may be introduced during any of the various complex operations used to collect and process data. Such errors may include: not enumerating every household or every person in the population, failing to obtain all required information from the respondents, obtaining incorrect or inconsistent information, and recording information incorrectly.

[8] Smaller groups are listed at www.census.gov/population/www/ancestry.html.

In addition, errors can occur during the field review of the enumerators' work, during clerical handling of the census questionnaires, or during the electronic processing of the questionnaires.

Nonsampling error may affect the data in two ways: (1) errors that are introduced randomly will increase the variability of the data and, therefore, should be reflected in the standard errors; and (2) errors that tend to be consistent in one direction will bias both sample and 100-percent data in that direction. For example, if respondents consistently tend to underreport their incomes, then the resulting estimates of households or families by income category will tend to be understated for the higher income categories and overstated for the lower income categories. Such biases are not reflected in the standard errors.

While it is impossible to completely eliminate error from an operation as large and complex as the decennial census, the Census Bureau attempts to control the sources of such error during the data collection and processing operations.

The primary sources of error and the programs instituted to control error in Census 2000 are described in detail in *Summary File 3 Technical Documentation* under Chapter 8, "Accuracy of the Data," located at *www.census.gov/prod /cen2000/doc/sf3.pdf.*

All statements in this Census 2000 Brief have undergone statistical testing and all comparisons are significant at the 90-percent confidence level, unless otherwise noted. The estimates in tables, maps, and other figures may vary from actual values due to sampling and nonsampling errors. As a result, estimates in one category may not be significantly different from estimates assigned to a different category. Further information on the accuracy of the data is located at *www.census.gov/prod /cen2000/doc/sf3.pdf.* For further information on the computation and use of standard errors, contact the Decennial Statistical Studies Division at 301-763-4242.

For More Information

The Census 2000 Summary File 3 data are available from the American Factfinder on the Internet (*factfinder.census.gov*). They were released on a state-by-state basis during 2002. For information on confidentiality protection, nonsampling error, sampling error, and definitions, also see *www.census.gov /prod/cen2000/doc/sf3.pdf* or contact the Customer Services Center at 301-763-INFO (4636).

Information on population and housing topics is presented in the Census 2000 Brief series, located on the Census Bureau's Web site at *www.census.gov/population/www /cen2000/briefs.html.* This series presents information on race, Hispanic origin, age, sex, household type, housing tenure, and social, economic, and housing characteristics, such as ancestry, income, and housing costs.

For additional information on ancestry, including reports and survey data, visit the Census Bureau's Web site on at *www.census.gov /population/www/ancestry.html.* To find information about the availability of data products, including reports, CD-ROMs, and DVDs, call the Customer Services Center at 301-763-INFO (4636), or e-mail *webmaster@census.gov.*

The Foreign-Born Population: 2000

Census 2000 Brief

Issued December 2003

C2KBR-34

By
Nolan Malone
Kaari F. Baluja
Joseph M. Costanzo
Cynthia J. Davis

Census 2000 measured a population of 281.4 million, 31.1 million (or 11.1 percent) of whom were foreign born.[1] Individuals from Latin America represented 52 percent, Asia 26 percent, Europe 16 percent, and other areas of the world 6.0 percent of the foreign-born population. This report, part of a series that presents population and housing data collected by Census 2000, describes the distribution of the foreign-born population in the United States, regions, states, counties, and places with populations of 100,000 or more.[2]

The concept and measurement of the foreign-born population and its characteristics have evolved across several censuses.

Nativity is determined by U.S. citizenship status and place of birth (see Figure 1).

Figure 1.

Reproduction of the Questions on Place of Birth, Citizenship Status, and Year of Entry From Census 2000

12 **Where was this person born?**

☐ In the United States — *Print name of state.*

☐ Outside the United States — *Print name of foreign country, or Puerto Rico, Guam, etc.*

13 **Is this person a CITIZEN of the United States?**

☐ Yes, born in the United States → *Skip to 15a*
☐ Yes, born in Puerto Rico, Guam, the U.S. Virgin Islands, or Northern Marianas
☐ Yes, born abroad of American parent or parents
☐ Yes, a U.S. citizen by naturalization
☐ No, not a citizen of the United States

14 **When did this person come to live in the United States?** *Print numbers in boxes.*

Year

Source: U.S. Census Bureau, Census 2000 questionnaire.

The Census Bureau considers anyone who is not born a U.S. citizen to be foreign born. Conversely, natives are those born in the United States, Puerto Rico, or a U.S. Island Area, or born abroad of a U.S. citizen parent.[3] Because a person may be born outside the United States and be a U.S. citizen at birth (i.e., they were born abroad to a U.S. citizen parent), information on place of birth cannot

---

[1] The estimates in this report are based on responses from a sample of the population. As with all surveys, estimates may vary from the actual values because of sampling variation or other factors. All statements made in this report have undergone statistical testing and are significant at the 90-percent confidence level unless otherwise noted.

[2] The text of this report discusses data for the United States, including the 50 states and the District of Columbia. Data for the Commonwealth of Puerto Rico are shown in Tables 1 and 4, and Figure 4.

[3] The U.S. Island Areas include U.S. Virgin Islands, Guam, American Samoa, and the Commonwealth of the Northern Mariana Islands.

USCENSUSBUREAU

Helping You Make Informed Decisions

U.S. Department of Commerce
Economics and Statistics Administration
U.S. CENSUS BUREAU

United States
Census
2000

be used alone to determine whether an individual is native or foreign born and must be used in conjunction with information on citizenship status.

Information on nativity and the foreign-born population is used by researchers, federal agencies, and policy makers for many purposes, including determination of eligibility for certain government programs, examination of trends in net international migration, and analysis of the changing composition of the U.S. population.

In the 1820 and 1830 decennial censuses, enumerators were asked to "note" individuals who were aliens (foreigners not naturalized), although no specific questions on citizenship status were asked. In 1890, explicit measures of citizenship status were added to the census and have remained with some variations except in 1960.

Questions concerning an individual's place of birth have appeared in the decennial censuses since 1850.[4] From 1870 to 1970, parental nativity (place of birth of the individual's father and mother) was also asked. Census 2000 asked, "Where was this person born?," asking for the name of the state for those born within the United States or the country name for those born elsewhere.[5]

In many decennial censuses, an additional question asked the year in which a person born outside the United States (whether native or foreign born) came to live in the United States.[6]

Census 2000 asked, "Is this person a citizen of the United States?" Answers to this question categorized respondents into various citizenship groups based on the manner in which U.S. citizenship was obtained (for example, born in the U.S., Puerto Rico, or a U.S. Island Area; or born abroad to a U.S. citizen parent), or into a residual non-citizen group.[7]

The foreign-born population in the United States increased by more than half between 1990 and 2000.

Between 1990 and 2000, the foreign-born population increased by 57 percent, from 19.8 million to 31.1 million, compared with an increase of 9.3 percent for the native population and 13 percent for the total U.S. population (see Table 1). The foreign born who were naturalized citizens of the United States increased by 56 percent (from 8.0 million to 12.5 million), compared with an increase of 58 percent for those who were not U.S. citizens (from 11.8 million to 18.6 million).

In 2000, 40.3 percent of the foreign born were naturalized U.S. citizens, down slightly from 40.5 percent in 1990. The percentage naturalized varied by period of entry: while 82 percent of the foreign born who entered the United States prior to 1970 were naturalized U.S. citizens in 2000, only 13 percent of those who entered in 1990 or later were (see Figure 2).[8]

Over half of the foreign-born population were from Latin America.

In 2000, over 16 million foreign born were from Latin America, representing 52 percent of the total foreign-born population (see Figure 3).[9] Of the foreign born from Latin America, 11.2 million people (36 percent of all foreign born) were from Central America (including Mexico), 3.0 million people (10 percent) from the Caribbean, and 1.9 million people (6.2 percent) from South America.

The foreign born from Asia and Europe accounted for 26 percent (8.2 million) and 16 percent (4.9 million) of the total foreign-born population, respectively. The foreign born from Africa, Northern America, and Oceania each composed 3 percent or less of the total foreign-born population.[10]

Foreign born from Mexico accounted for 9.2 million people, or 30 percent of the total U.S. foreign-born population (see Table 2), making Mexico the leading country of birth. China (1.5 million) and the Philippines (1.4 million) were the next largest sources, providing 4.9 percent and 4.4 percent of the total foreign born, respectively.[11]

---

[4] For further discussion of the evolution of place of birth, year of entry, and citizenship questions in the decennial census, see Gauthier, Jason G., 2002, Measuring America: The Decennial Censuses From 1790 to 2000, POL/02-MA, U.S. Census Bureau, Washington, DC.

[5] Although a foreign-born respondent may indicate a place of birth that is more precise than a foreign country of birth (e.g., Bavaria), this information is categorized under the country name and is neither tabulated nor shown in such detail in U.S. Census Bureau data products.

[6] Questions on period of entry appeared from 1890 to 1930 and from 1970 to 2000 in various forms.

[7] No information about dual citizenship, citizenship other than U.S., or legal (migrant) status is collected in the decennial census.

[8] The naturalization process requires that the foreign-born applicant reside continuously in the United States for 5 years (or less for special categories of migrants) following admission as a lawful permanent resident. Therefore, most of the foreign born who arrived between 1995 and 2000 are not yet eligible to become U.S. citizens, resulting in a lower overall percentage naturalized of the foreign born who arrived in the last 10 years.

[9] Latin America encompasses Central America (including Mexico), the Caribbean, and South America.

[10] The Northern America region includes the foreign countries of Canada, Bermuda, Greenland, and St. Pierre and Miquelon. The Oceania region includes Australia, New Zealand, and island countries in Melanesia, Micronesia, and Polynesia.

[11] China includes those who responded China, Hong Kong, Taiwan, and the Paracel Islands.

Table 1.
Foreign-Born Population by Citizenship Status for the United States, Regions, States, and for Puerto Rico: 1990 and 2000

(Data based on sample. For information on confidentiality protection, sampling error, nonsampling error, and definitions, see www.census.gov/prod/cen2000/doc/sf3.pdf)

Area	1990 Total population	1990 Foreign born Total Number	1990 Foreign born Total Percent of total population	1990 Naturalized citizens as a percent of the foreign-born population	2000 Total population	2000 Foreign born Total Number	2000 Foreign born Total Percent of total population	2000 Naturalized citizens as a percent of the foreign-born population	Percent change in the foreign-born population: 1990-2000
United States.......	248,709,873	19,767,316	7.9	40.5	281,421,906	31,107,889	11.1	40.3	57.4
Region									
Northeast	50,809,229	5,231,024	10.3	47.6	53,594,378	7,229,068	13.5	46.4	38.2
Midwest	59,668,632	2,131,293	3.6	49.7	64,392,776	3,509,937	5.5	40.7	64.7
South	85,445,930	4,582,293	5.4	39.6	100,236,820	8,608,441	8.6	37.4	87.9
West..............	52,786,082	7,822,706	14.8	33.6	63,197,932	11,760,443	18.6	38.6	50.3
State									
Alabama...........	4,040,587	43,533	1.1	49.1	4,447,100	87,772	2.0	36.7	101.6
Alaska	550,043	24,814	4.5	53.9	626,932	37,170	5.9	53.8	49.8
Arizona...........	3,665,228	278,205	7.6	39.1	5,130,632	656,183	12.8	29.6	135.9
Arkansas..........	2,350,725	24,867	1.1	48.7	2,673,400	73,690	2.8	29.9	196.3
California.........	29,760,021	6,458,825	21.7	31.2	33,871,648	8,864,255	26.2	39.2	37.2
Colorado..........	3,294,394	142,434	4.3	47.2	4,301,261	369,903	8.6	31.6	159.7
Connecticut........	3,287,116	279,383	8.5	52.0	3,405,565	369,967	10.9	48.7	32.4
Delaware	666,168	22,275	3.3	55.8	783,600	44,898	5.7	42.4	101.6
Dist. of Columbia........	606,900	58,887	9.7	29.3	572,059	73,561	12.9	30.0	24.9
Florida...........	12,937,926	1,662,601	12.9	42.9	15,982,378	2,670,828	16.7	45.2	60.6
Georgia...........	6,478,216	173,126	2.7	38.9	8,186,453	577,273	7.1	29.3	233.4
Hawaii	1,108,229	162,704	14.7	55.3	1,211,537	212,229	17.5	60.1	30.4
Idaho	1,006,749	28,905	2.9	41.0	1,293,953	64,080	5.0	33.1	121.7
Illinois...........	11,430,602	952,272	8.3	44.5	12,419,293	1,529,058	12.3	39.5	60.6
Indiana...........	5,544,159	94,263	1.7	52.9	6,080,485	186,534	3.1	38.1	97.9
Iowa..............	2,776,755	43,316	1.6	46.2	2,926,324	91,085	3.1	32.9	110.3
Kansas............	2,477,574	62,840	2.5	43.3	2,688,418	134,735	5.0	33.2	114.4
Kentucky..........	3,685,296	34,119	0.9	46.6	4,041,769	80,271	2.0	34.3	135.3
Louisiana	4,219,973	87,407	2.1	43.6	4,468,976	115,885	2.6	48.4	32.6
Maine	1,227,928	36,296	3.0	58.6	1,274,923	36,691	2.9	55.2	NS
Maryland..........	4,781,468	313,494	6.6	40.5	5,296,486	518,315	9.8	45.3	65.3
Massachusetts	6,016,425	573,733	9.5	45.7	6,349,097	772,983	12.2	43.7	34.7
Michigan..........	9,295,297	355,393	3.8	55.7	9,938,444	523,589	5.3	45.8	47.3
Minnesota..........	4,375,099	113,039	2.6	44.9	4,919,479	260,463	5.3	37.4	130.4
Mississippi	2,573,216	20,383	0.8	46.7	2,844,658	39,908	1.4	40.3	95.8
Missouri	5,117,073	83,633	1.6	54.6	5,595,211	151,196	2.7	40.9	80.8
Montana...........	799,065	13,779	1.7	62.6	902,195	16,396	1.8	57.8	19.0
Nebraska	1,578,385	28,198	1.8	54.3	1,711,263	74,638	4.4	32.0	164.7
Nevada	1,201,833	104,828	8.7	41.4	1,998,257	316,593	15.8	36.9	202.0
New Hampshire........	1,109,252	41,193	3.7	55.5	1,235,786	54,154	4.4	47.6	31.5
New Jersey.........	7,730,188	966,610	12.5	48.7	8,414,350	1,476,327	17.5	46.2	52.7
New Mexico	1,515,069	80,514	5.3	39.6	1,819,046	149,606	8.2	34.8	85.8
New York	17,990,455	2,851,861	15.9	45.5	18,976,457	3,868,133	20.4	46.1	35.6
North Carolina.........	6,628,637	115,077	1.7	43.1	8,049,313	430,000	5.3	26.2	273.7
North Dakota..........	638,800	9,388	1.5	60.2	642,200	12,114	1.9	42.6	29.0
Ohio..............	10,847,115	259,673	2.4	59.8	11,353,140	339,279	3.0	49.9	30.7
Oklahoma...........	3,145,585	65,489	2.1	44.1	3,450,654	131,747	3.8	34.7	101.2
Oregon	2,842,321	139,307	4.9	42.5	3,421,399	289,702	8.5	33.6	108.0
Pennsylvania..........	11,881,643	369,316	3.1	59.1	12,281,054	508,291	4.1	50.6	37.6
Rhode Island..........	1,003,464	95,088	9.5	44.9	1,048,319	119,277	11.4	47.1	25.4
South Carolina	3,486,703	49,964	1.4	50.9	4,012,012	115,978	2.9	37.1	132.1
South Dakota	696,004	7,731	1.1	61.0	754,844	13,495	1.8	40.4	74.6
Tennessee	4,877,185	59,114	1.2	45.0	5,689,283	159,004	2.8	33.4	169.0
Texas.............	16,986,510	1,524,436	9.0	33.8	20,851,820	2,899,642	13.9	31.5	90.2
Utah	1,722,850	58,600	3.4	44.1	2,233,169	158,664	7.1	30.4	170.8
Vermont	562,758	17,544	3.1	60.7	608,827	23,245	3.8	53.6	32.5
Virginia...........	6,187,358	311,809	5.0	40.3	7,078,515	570,279	8.1	40.8	82.9
Washington.........	4,866,692	322,144	6.6	46.3	5,894,121	614,457	10.4	41.9	90.7
West Virginia........	1,793,477	15,712	0.9	59.0	1,808,344	19,390	1.1	53.9	23.4
Wisconsin..........	4,891,769	121,547	2.5	52.3	5,363,675	193,751	3.6	39.3	59.4
Wyoming...........	453,588	7,647	1.7	51.9	493,782	11,205	2.3	45.7	46.5
Puerto Rico	3,522,037	79,804	2.3	45.5	3,808,610	109,581	2.9	42.2	37.3

NS: Not significantly different from zero at the 90-percent confidence level.

Source: U.S. Census Bureau, Census 2000 Summary File 1 and Summary File 3; 1990 Census of Population, General Population Characteristics (CP-2-1).

THE GEOGRAPHIC DISTRIBUTION OF THE FOREIGN BORN

The foreign-born population in the South experienced the most rapid growth rate.[12]

The number of foreign born increased by 88 percent in the South between 1990 and 2000, followed by 65 percent in the Midwest, 50 percent in the West, and 38 percent in the Northeast. The West had the largest foreign-born population in 2000 (11.8 million), followed by the South (8.6 million), the Northeast (7.2 million), and the Midwest (3.5 million).

More than one-third of the foreign born lived in the West.

In 2000, 38 percent of the foreign-born population lived in the West, 28 percent in the South, and 23 percent in the Northeast. Only 11 percent lived in the Midwest. In comparison, the distribution of the total population was 22 percent in the West, 36 percent in the South, 19 percent in the Northeast, and 23 percent in the Midwest.

Foreign-born residents accounted for 19 percent of the population in the West and 14 percent of the population in the Northeast, exceeding the national level of 11.1 percent. The proportion was below the national level in the South (8.6 percent) and the Midwest (5.5 percent).

_____

[12] The South region includes the states of Alabama, Arkansas, Delaware, Florida, Georgia, Kentucky, Louisiana, Maryland, Mississippi, North Carolina, Oklahoma, South Carolina, Tennessee, Texas, Virginia, West Virginia, and the District of Columbia, a state equivalent. The West region includes the states of Alaska, Arizona, California, Colorado, Hawaii, Idaho, Montana, Nevada, New Mexico, Oregon, Utah, Washington, and Wyoming. The Northeast region includes the states of Connecticut, Maine, Massachusetts, New Hampshire, New Jersey, New York, Pennsylvania, Rhode Island, and Vermont. The Midwest region includes the states of Illinois, Indiana, Iowa, Kansas, Michigan, Minnesota, Missouri, Nebraska, North Dakota, Ohio, South Dakota, and Wisconsin.

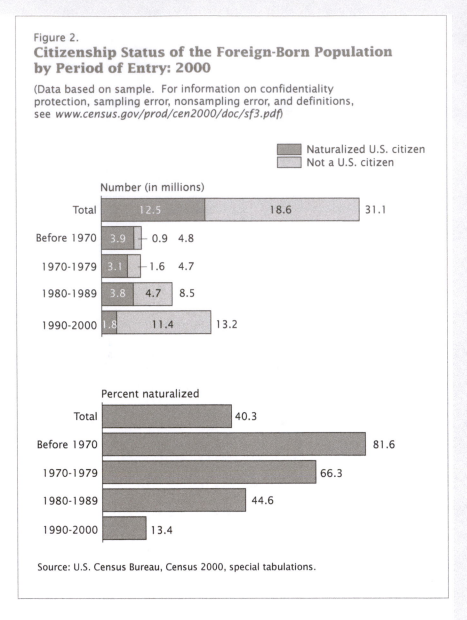

Figure 2.

Citizenship Status of the Foreign-Born Population by Period of Entry: 2000

(Data based on sample. For information on confidentiality protection, sampling error, nonsampling error, and definitions, see *www.census.gov/prod/cen2000/doc/sf3.pdf*)

Legend: ■ Naturalized U.S. citizen □ Not a U.S. citizen

Number (in millions)

Period	Naturalized	Not citizen	Total
Total	12.5	18.6	31.1
Before 1970	3.9	0.9	4.8
1970-1979	3.1	1.6	4.7
1980-1989	3.8	4.7	8.5
1990-2000	1.8	11.4	13.2

Percent naturalized

Period	Percent
Total	40.3
Before 1970	81.6
1970-1979	66.3
1980-1989	44.6
1990-2000	13.4

Source: U.S. Census Bureau, Census 2000, special tabulations.

The patterns of distribution by world region of birth show where various groups resided in 2000 (see Table 3). In 2000, 45 percent of the foreign born from Asia, 34 percent from Northern America, and 66 percent from Oceania lived in the West, home to the largest concentrations of these populations in the United States. Individuals from Europe were most likely to live in the Northeast (38 percent), while the foreign born from Africa were primarily in the South (35 percent) and the Northeast (31 percent).

The proportion of foreign born who were from Latin America ranged from 63 percent in the South to 36 percent in the Midwest (see Table 4). The proportion of foreign born from Asia ranged from 32 percent in the West to 19 percent in the South, and those from Europe ranged from 26 percent in the Midwest and Northeast to 10 percent in the West.

More than one-half of the foreign-born population lived in three states: California, New York, and Texas.

In 2000, 15.6 million foreign-born residents (50 percent of the total

Figure 3.
Percent Distribution of the Foreign-Born Population by World Region of Birth: 2000

(Data based on sample. For information on confidentiality protection, sampling error, nonsampling error, and definitions, see *www.census.gov/prod/cen2000/doc/sf3.pdf*)

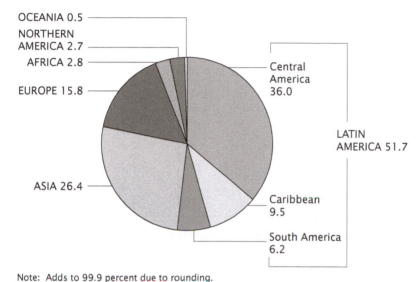

OCEANIA 0.5
NORTHERN AMERICA 2.7
AFRICA 2.8
EUROPE 15.8
ASIA 26.4
Central America 36.0
LATIN AMERICA 51.7
Caribbean 9.5
South America 6.2

Note: Adds to 99.9 percent due to rounding.
Source: U.S. Census Bureau, Census 2000, Summary File 3.

Table 2.
Top Ten Countries of Birth of the Foreign-Born Population: 2000

(Data based on sample. For information on confidentiality protection, sampling error, nonsampling error, and definitions, see *www.census.gov/prod/cen2000/doc/sf3.pdf*)

Country of birth	Number	Percent of foreign-born population	90-percent confidence interval on number
Total foreign born	31,107,889	100.0	31,080,801 - 31,134,977
Top ten countries	18,157,587	58.4	18,143,429 - 18,171,745
Mexico	9,177,487	29.5	9,164,388 - 9,190,586
China[1]	1,518,652	4.9	1,512,463 - 1,524,841
Philippines	1,369,070	4.4	1,363,179 - 1,374,961
India	1,022,552	3.3	1,017,431 - 1,027,673
Vietnam	988,174	3.2	983,137 - 993,211
Cuba[2]	872,716	2.8	867,973 - 877,459
Korea[3]	864,125	2.8	859,405 - 868,845
Canada[4]	820,771	2.6	816,168 - 825,374
El Salvador	817,336	2.6	812,742 - 821,930
Germany	706,704	2.3	702,424 - 710,984
All other countries	12,950,302	41.6	12,936,144 - 12,964,460

[1] Includes those who responded China, Hong Kong, Taiwan, and the Paracel Islands.
[2] The estimated foreign-born population from Cuba does not statistically differ from that of Korea.
[3] Includes those who responded Korea, North Korea, and South Korea.
[4] The estimated foreign-born population from Canada does not statistically differ from that of El Salvador.

Source: U.S. Census Bureau, Census 2000, Summary File 3.

foreign born) lived in these three states, and 21.3 million foreign-born residents (68 percent) lived in the six states with foreign-born populations of 1.0 million or more: California, Florida, Illinois, New Jersey, New York, and Texas. In contrast, these six states were home to 39 percent of all U.S. residents in 2000. The foreign born in California accounted for 8.9 million (29 percent of the total), followed by New York with 3.9 million (12 percent), and Texas with 2.9 million (9.3 percent). The foreign-born population ranged from 500,000 up to 1 million in 8 states and from 100,000 up to 500,000 in 19 states. The foreign born numbered fewer than 100,000 in the 17 remaining states and the District of Columbia.

The foreign born in North Carolina, Georgia, and Nevada grew by 200 percent or more.

From 1990 to 2000, the foreign born increased by 200 percent or more in three states: North Carolina, 274 percent; Georgia, 233 percent; and Nevada, 202 percent.[13] In 16 states, this group grew by 100 percent to 199 percent; in 12 states by 57 percent (the national average) to 100 percent, and by less than 57 percent in the remaining 19 states and the District of Columbia. The only growth rate below 10 percent occurred in Maine (1.1 percent).

The foreign born accounted for over one-quarter of the population in California.

The foreign born represented 26 percent of the population in California in 2000, the highest proportion in any state. The percentage also surpassed the national average (11.1 percent) in nine

[13] Although the point estimate for the increase in the foreign-born population in Arkansas (196 percent) appears to be less than 200 percent, no statistical difference exists between the two percentages.

Table 3.
Foreign-Born Population by World Region of Birth for the United States and Regions: 2000

(Data based on sample. For information on confidentiality protection, sampling error, nonsampling error, and definitions, see www.census.gov/prod/cen2000/doc/sf3.pdf)

Area	Total foreign-born popu-lation[1]	Europe	Asia	Africa	Oceania	Northern America[2]	Latin America		
							Total	Mexico	Other Latin America
NUMBER									
United States ...	31,107,573	4,915,557	8,226,254	881,300	168,046	829,442	16,086,974	9,177,487	6,909,487
Northeast...........	7,229,001	1,882,083	1,825,904	275,292	17,276	188,152	3,040,294	278,640	2,761,654
Midwest.............	3,509,895	915,328	1,053,950	132,542	13,041	132,648	1,262,386	1,000,394	261,992
South..............	8,608,363	991,351	1,634,826	307,324	26,937	223,174	5,424,751	2,717,612	2,707,139
West...............	11,760,314	1,126,795	3,711,574	166,142	110,792	285,468	6,359,543	5,180,841	1,178,702
PERCENT									
United States ...	100.0	100.0	100.0	100.0	100.0	100.0	100.0	100.0	100.0
Northeast...........	23.2	38.3	22.2	31.2	10.3	22.7	18.9	3.0	40.0
Midwest.............	11.3	18.6	12.8	15.0	7.8	16.0	7.8	10.9	3.8
South..............	27.7	20.2	19.9	34.9	16.0	26.9	33.7	29.6	39.2
West...............	37.8	22.9	45.1	18.9	65.9	34.4	39.5	56.5	17.1

[1] Does not include the foreign-born population "born at sea".
[2] The region Northern America includes the foreign countries of Canada, Bermuda, Greenland, and St. Pierre and Miquelon.

Source: U.S. Census Bureau, Census 2000, Summary File 3.

other states and the District of Columbia: New York (20 percent), New Jersey and Hawaii (18 percent each), Florida (17 percent), Nevada (16 percent), Texas (14 percent), the District of Columbia and Arizona (13 percent each), and Illinois and Massachusetts (12 percent each).

In 2000, 36 percent of the foreign born from Asia, 31 percent from Latin America, 17 percent from Northern America, and 40 percent from Oceania resided in California, accounting for the highest proportions of people from each of these regions of birth. Eighteen percent of the foreign born from Europe and 13 percent from Africa lived in New York.

The foreign born from Latin America, Asia, and Europe were concentrated in different states. The foreign born from Latin America constituted over 70 percent of the foreign-born populations in four states: Arizona (72 percent), Florida (73 percent), New Mexico (77 percent), and Texas (75 percent). Those from Asia accounted for 40 percent or more of the foreign-born

population in six states: Alaska (51 percent), Hawaii (83 percent), Michigan (40 percent), Minnesota (40 percent), Virginia (41 percent), and West Virginia (43 percent). Those from Europe composed over 35 percent in five states: Connecticut (38 percent), Montana (40 percent), Ohio (39 percent), Pennsylvania (36 percent), and Vermont (39 percent).

The foreign born who were naturalized U.S. citizens (40 percent nationally) outnumbered those who were not U.S. citizens in only seven states: Alaska, Hawaii, Maine, Montana, Pennsylvania, Vermont, and West Virginia. The proportion naturalized ranged from 60 percent in Hawaii to 26 percent in North Carolina.

High concentrations of the foreign born lived in counties in traditional "gateway" areas of the United States.

In 2000, the percentage foreign-born was at or above the national average (11.1 percent) in only 199 of the 3,141 counties (and county equivalents) in the United States. Many of these counties are in

traditional receiving areas for immigrants: southwestern border states (California to Texas) and the New York City and Miami metropolitan areas. Additional areas with high concentrations of the foreign-born population included the Pacific Northwest and the Washington, DC metropolitan area.

The foreign born were the majority of the population in only one U.S. county: Miami-Dade County, Florida, which was home to 1.1 million foreign born (51 percent of the county's population).

The foreign born represented 20 percent or more in 60 additional counties, some of which are far from the "gateway" areas noted earlier: Clark County, Idaho; Seward County, Finney County and Ford County, Kansas; Franklin County and Adams County, Washington; and Aleutians West Census Area, Alaska.

The proportion foreign-born ranged from 11.1 percent (the national average) to 19.9 percent of the population in 138 counties, from 7.5 percent to 11.0 percent in 141 counties, and from 3.0 percent

Table 4.
Percent Distribution of the Foreign-Born Population by World Region of Birth for the United States, Regions, States, and Puerto Rico: 2000

(Data based on sample. For information on confidentiality protection, sampling error, nonsampling error, and definitions, see www.census.gov/prod/cen2000/doc/sf3.pdf)

Area	Total foreign-born popula-tion[1]	Percent distribution					Latin America		
		Europe	Asia	Africa	Oceania	Northern America[2]	Total	Mexico	Other Latin America
United States......	31,107,573	15.8	26.4	2.8	0.5	2.7	51.7	29.5	22.2
Region									
Northeast	7,229,001	26.0	25.3	3.8	0.2	2.6	42.1	3.9	38.2
Midwest	3,509,895	26.1	30.0	3.8	0.4	3.8	36.0	28.5	7.5
South	8,608,363	11.5	19.0	3.6	0.3	2.6	63.0	31.6	31.4
West.............	11,760,314	9.6	31.6	1.4	0.9	2.4	54.1	44.1	10.0
State									
Alabama	87,767	21.0	29.9	4.2	0.6	3.8	40.5	26.6	14.0
Alaska	37,170	20.0	50.6	1.0	2.7	7.8	17.9	7.4	10.5
Arizona...........	656,183	10.9	11.8	1.3	0.5	4.0	71.5	66.4	5.0
Arkansas........	73,690	13.6	21.5	2.0	1.6	2.5	58.8	45.7	13.0
California	8,864,188	7.9	32.9	1.3	0.8	1.6	55.6	44.3	11.3
Colorado...........	369,894	17.6	19.6	2.6	0.8	3.7	55.6	49.1	6.5
Connecticut........	369,961	38.2	19.0	2.6	0.4	5.2	34.7	3.6	31.1
Delaware	44,898	22.1	30.1	5.0	0.2	3.6	39.0	17.5	21.5
Dist. of Columbia........	73,555	17.6	17.0	12.5	0.8	1.7	50.4	2.7	47.7
Florida	2,670,794	13.3	8.7	1.3	0.2	3.8	72.8	7.1	65.7
Georgia............	577,273	12.9	25.2	7.0	0.4	2.5	52.0	33.0	19.0
Hawaii	212,229	4.9	83.3	0.5	6.3	1.8	3.2	1.3	1.9
Idaho	64,080	18.8	12.6	0.9	0.8	7.1	59.8	55.3	4.6
Illinois............	1,529,058	25.5	23.5	1.7	0.2	1.3	47.8	40.4	7.4
Indiana...........	186,529	23.2	26.6	3.9	0.5	4.2	41.5	33.3	8.2
Iowa...........	91,083	22.3	33.1	4.4	0.6	3.6	36.0	27.7	8.3
Kansas	134,733	11.2	28.2	2.7	0.5	2.7	54.7	47.0	7.7
Kentucky...........	80,265	25.6	33.4	4.0	0.6	4.4	31.9	19.3	12.6
Louisiana	115,880	15.6	37.5	3.5	0.5	2.8	40.2	8.0	32.1
Maine	36,689	30.0	18.9	2.9	0.7	41.5	6.0	0.9	5.1
Maryland...........	518,315	16.8	35.0	12.1	0.4	1.8	34.0	3.7	30.2
Massachusetts	772,972	32.2	26.1	6.2	0.3	5.3	30.0	1.0	29.0
Michigan...........	523,585	30.0	40.0	3.2	0.4	9.5	16.9	11.2	5.8
Minnesota...........	260,454	16.8	40.4	13.2	0.5	5.1	24.0	16.0	8.0
Mississippi	39,904	19.2	36.2	3.2	0.6	4.3	36.5	23.8	12.8
Missouri	151,195	28.5	34.9	5.6	1.0	4.2	25.8	16.7	9.2
Montana	16,396	39.8	20.2	1.1	1.6	27.8	9.5	5.4	4.2
Nebraska	74,638	14.5	25.7	3.5	0.5	2.2	53.6	40.8	12.8
Nevada...........	316,593	10.2	22.9	1.6	0.7	3.4	61.4	48.6	12.7
New Hampshire........	54,154	33.7	24.9	3.4	0.6	23.0	14.3	2.6	11.7
New Jersey...........	1,476,327	23.9	27.8	4.1	0.2	1.1	43.0	4.6	38.4
New Mexico	149,606	10.2	9.6	0.7	0.4	2.2	76.8	71.7	5.1
New York	3,868,094	22.7	23.7	3.0	0.2	1.4	48.9	4.2	44.7
North Carolina........	430,000	14.0	21.7	4.7	0.4	3.4	55.8	40.0	15.8
North Dakota...........	12,114	33.1	23.1	6.5	1.0	25.0	11.3	4.8	6.5
Ohio...........	339,267	38.8	35.4	6.5	0.5	4.9	13.9	6.1	7.8
Oklahoma...........	131,739	12.2	30.2	3.5	0.6	2.8	50.6	42.5	8.1
Oregon...........	289,699	18.8	27.3	1.7	1.6	5.9	44.6	39.0	5.6
Pennsylvania...........	508,282	35.9	36.0	5.0	0.4	3.1	19.6	4.8	14.8
Rhode Island........	119,277	32.9	16.4	10.1	0.3	3.5	36.8	2.1	34.7
South Carolina........	115,978	23.4	25.4	2.8	0.7	4.9	42.8	27.3	15.4
South Dakota	13,495	31.5	30.1	11.6	0.7	7.6	18.5	10.4	8.2
Tennessee	159,004	17.7	31.8	5.5	0.6	4.5	39.9	28.1	11.8
Texas...........	2,899,640	5.3	16.1	2.2	0.2	1.3	74.9	64.8	10.1
Utah...........	158,657	16.2	17.9	1.5	4.2	4.9	55.4	41.9	13.5
Vermont	23,245	38.6	19.2	2.2	0.7	34.1	5.2	0.6	4.6
Virginia...........	570,271	15.2	41.3	7.5	0.5	2.3	33.3	5.7	27.6
Washington...........	614,414	20.6	39.0	3.1	1.3	7.8	28.3	24.1	4.2
West Virginia...........	19,390	34.5	43.2	3.4	0.8	5.6	12.4	5.3	7.1
Wisconsin...........	193,744	26.9	32.4	2.5	0.5	3.7	33.9	27.7	6.2
Wyoming...........	11,205	26.2	19.4	2.3	1.7	10.1	40.3	34.9	5.4
Puerto Rico	109,581	6.0	2.8	0.1	0.1	0.2	90.7	2.5	88.3

[1] Does not include the foreign-born population "born at sea."
[2] The region Northern America includes the foreign countries of Canada, Bermuda, Greenland, and St. Pierre and Miquelon.
Source: U.S. Census Bureau, Census 2000, Summary File 3.

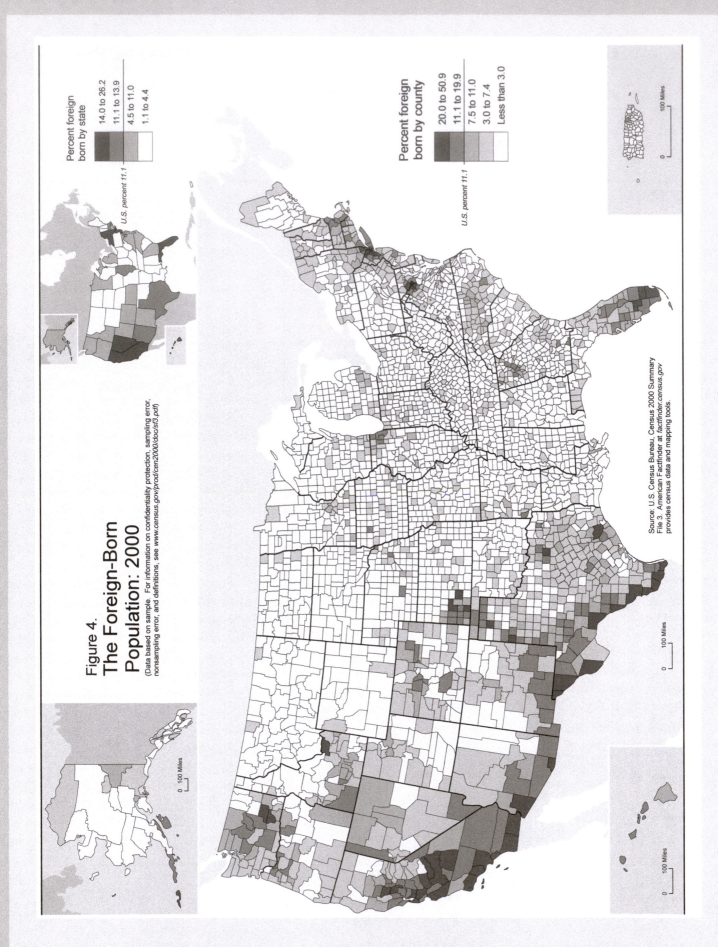

Figure 4.
The Foreign-Born
Population: 2000

(Data based on sample. For information on confidentiality protection, sampling error, nonsampling error, and definitions, see *www.census.gov/prod/cen2000/doc/sf3.pdf*)

Percent foreign
born by state

14.0 to 26.2
11.1 to 13.9
4.5 to 11.0
1.1 to 4.4

U.S. percent 11.1

Percent foreign
born by county

20.0 to 50.9
11.1 to 19.9
7.5 to 11.0
3.0 to 7.4
Less than 3.0

U.S. percent 11.1

Source: U.S. Census Bureau, Census 2000 Summary File 3. American Factfinder at *factfinder.census.gov* provides census data and mapping tools.

0   100 Miles

to 7.4 percent in 680 counties. The remaining 2,121 counties, where the foreign born accounted for less than 3.0 percent of the population, were concentrated in the Midwest and in several states in the South (Kentucky, Tennessee, Alabama, and Mississippi).

More than 3 million foreign born lived in Los Angeles County, California.

In 2000, four counties encompassed 22 percent of the total U.S. foreign-born population: Los Angeles County, California (3.4 million); Miami-Dade County, Florida (1.1 million); Cook County, Illinois (1.1 million); and Queens County, New York (1.0 million).[14]

The foreign-born population numbered from 100,000 to 1.0 million in 56 counties, from 10,000 to 99,999 in 224 counties, from 1,000 to 9,999 in 789 counties, and from 100 to 999 in 1,409 counties. It was below 100 in 659 counties.

_____

[14] These four counties were home to 6.8 percent of all U.S. residents in 2000.

The foreign born composed over one-half of the population in six large places.

In 2000, 163,000 foreign born lived in Hialeah, Florida, constituting 72 percent of the population (see Table 5). The foreign born were the majority in five additional places with 100,000 or more population (Miami, Florida; Glendale, California; Santa Ana, California; Daly City, California; and, El Monte, California) and constituted 41 percent to 50 percent in the four other places in the top ten (East Los Angeles, California; Elizabeth, New Jersey; Garden Grove, California; and Los Angeles, California).[15]

_____

[15] Census 2000 showed 245 places in the United States with 100,000 or more population. They included 238 incorporated places (including 4 city-county consolidations) and 7 census designated places (CDPs) that were not legally incorporated. For a list of these places by state, see *www.census.gov/population/www/cen2000/phc-t6.html*.

The largest foreign-born populations in 2000 were found in the four largest cities in the United States.

The largest foreign-born populations were in New York, New York (2.9 million); Los Angeles, California (1.5 million); Chicago, Illinois (629,000); and Houston, Texas (516,000) (see Table 6). The 5.5 million foreign born in these four cities represented 18 percent of the total, yet these four cities were home to only 5.9 percent of all U.S. residents in 2000. Three cities whose total populations were not among the top ten had foreign-born populations in the top ten: San Jose, California (330,000); San Francisco, California (286,000); and Miami, Florida (216,000).

ADDITIONAL FINDINGS ON THE FOREIGN BORN

How did the racial and Hispanic-origin compositions of the foreign born contrast with those of natives?

Census 2000 asked respondents to choose one or more races. With the exception of the Two or more races group, all race groups discussed in this report refer to people who indicated only one racial identity among the six major categories: White, Black or African American, American Indian and Alaska Native, Asian, Native Hawaiian and Other Pacific

Table 5.
Ten Places of 100,000 or More Population With the Highest Percentage Foreign Born: 2000[1]

(Data based on sample. For information on confidentiality protection, sampling error, nonsampling error, and definitions, see *www.census.gov/prod/cen2000/doc/sf3.pdf*)

Place and state	Total population	Foreign born		
		Number	Percent of total population	90-percent confidence interval on percent
United States	281,421,906	31,107,889	11.1	11.09 - 11.11
Hialeah, Florida	226,419	163,256	72.1	71.5 - 72.7
Miami, Florida.................	362,470	215,739	59.5	59.0 - 60.0
Glendale, California............	194,973	106,119	54.4	53.7 - 55.1
Santa Ana, California	337,977	179,933	53.2	52.8 - 53.8
Daly City, California............	103,621	54,213	52.3	51.4 - 53.2
El Monte, California............	115,965	59,589	51.4	50.5 - 52.3
East Los Angeles, California[2] ...	124,283	60,605	48.8	48.0 - 49.6
Elizabeth, New Jersey	120,568	52,975	43.9	43.0 - 44.8
Garden Grove, California.......	165,196	71,351	43.2	42.5 - 43.9
Los Angeles, California.........	3,694,820	1,512,720	40.9	40.7 - 41.1

[1] Although the point estimates shown appear to differ, no statistical difference exists between the percentages foreign born in Glendale and Santa Ana, Santa Ana and Daly City, Daly City and El Monte, and Elizabeth and Garden Grove.

[2] East Los Angeles, California is a census designated place and is not legally incorporated.

Source: U.S. Census Bureau, Census 2000, Summary File 1 and Summary File 3.

Islander, and Some other race.[16] The use of the single-race population in this report does not imply that it is the preferred method of presenting or analyzing data. The

[16] For further information on each of the six major race groups and the Two or more races population, see reports from the Census 2000 Brief series (C2KBR/01), available on the Census 2000 Web site at *http://www.census.gov/population/www /cen2000/briefs.html.*

Hereafter, this report uses the term Black to refer to people who are Black or African American, the term Pacific Islander to refer to people who are Native Hawaiian and Other Pacific Islander, and the term Hispanic to refer to people who are Hispanic or Latino. Because Hispanics may be of any race, data in this report for Hispanics overlap with data for racial groups. Based on Census 2000 sample data, the proportion Hispanic was 8.0 percent for Whites, 1.9 percent for Blacks, 14.6 percent for American Indians and Alaska Natives, 1.0 percent for Asians, 9.5 percent for Pacific Islanders, 97.1 percent for those reporting Some other race, and 31.1 percent for those reporting Two or more races.

Census Bureau uses a variety of approaches.[17]

In 2000, the foreign born were less likely than natives to report that they were non-Hispanic Whites (43 percent compared with 79 percent), but more likely than natives to report being Asian (23 percent compared with 1.3 percent). Almost half of the foreign-born population was Hispanic (46 percent), compared with 8.4 percent of natives.

Within separate race and Hispanic-origin categories, the foreign born represented the majority in only one group: 69 percent of those who responded Asian were foreign-

[17] This report draws heavily on Summary File 3, a Census 2000 product that can be accessed through American FactFinder, available from the Census Bureau's Web site, www.census.gov. Information on people who reported more than one race, such as "White and American Indian and Alaska Native" or "Asian and Black or African American," is available in Summary File 4, which is available through American FactFinder. About 2.6 percent of people reported more than one race.

born (see Figure 5). The foreign born accounted for 24 percent of Two or more races respondents, 20 percent of Pacific Islander respondents, 6.1 percent of Black respondents, and 3.5 percent of non-Hispanic White respondents. Among Hispanics, 40 percent were foreign born.

Did the age structure of the foreign born differ from that of the native population in 2000?

Figure 6 shows that the percentage of foreign born under 25 was less than that of natives (22 percent and 37 percent, respectively). The foreign-born population was concentrated in prime working ages, 25 to 54 years: 59 percent compared with 42 percent of natives.[18] The proportion 55 and older among the foreign born was only

[18] The 25 to 54 age group is important for labor force analysis because most are full-time workers, most have completed schooling, and most are not eligible to retire.

Table 6.
Ten Places of 100,000 or More Population With the Largest Total Population and Foreign-Born Population: 2000[1]

(Data based on sample. For information on confidentiality protection, sampling error, nonsampling error, and definitions, see www.census.gov/prod/cen2000/doc/sf3.pdf)

Place and state	Total population	Foreign born		
		Number	Percent of total population	90-percent confidence interval on number
United States....................	281,421,906	31,107,889	11.1	31,080,801 - 31,134,977
New York, New York...........................	8,008,278	2,871,032	35.9	2,860,937 - 2,881,127
Los Angeles, California.........................	3,694,820	1,512,720	40.9	1,505,660 - 1,519,780
Chicago, Illinois	2,896,016	628,903	21.7	623,994 - 633,812
Houston, Texas.............................	1,953,631	516,105	26.4	511,650 - 520,560
Philadelphia, Pennsylvania........................	1,517,550	137,205	9.0	135,030 - 139,380
Phoenix, Arizona	1,321,045	257,325	19.5	254,166 - 260,484
San Diego, California	1,223,400	314,227	25.7	310,945 - 317,509
Dallas, Texas..............................	1,188,580	290,436	24.4	287,082 - 293,790
San Antonio, Texas	1,144,646	133,675	11.7	131,394 - 135,956
Detroit, Michigan	951,270	45,541	4.8	44,286 - 46,796
San Jose, California	894,943	329,757	36.8	326,395 - 333,119
San Francisco, California.......................	776,733	285,541	36.8	282,411 - 288,671
Miami, Florida.............................	362,470	215,739	59.5	212,845 - 218,633

[1] Although the point estimates shown appear to differ, no statistical difference exists between the foreign-born totals in Dallas and San Francisco, and in Philadelphia and San Antonio.

Source: U.S. Census Bureau, Census 2000, Summary File 1 and Summary File 3.

slightly smaller than that of natives (20 percent and 21 percent, respectively).

ABOUT CENSUS 2000

Why did Census 2000 ask about place of birth, citizenship status, and year of entry?

The questions on place of birth, citizenship status, and year of entry provide essential data for setting and evaluating U.S. immigration policies and laws and for monitoring civil rights compliance. For example, under the Refugee Education Assistance Act, these data are used to allocate funds to public and private nonprofit organizations that provide employment resources aimed at making foreign-born residents economically self-sufficient. Knowing the characteristics of migrants, particularly their citizenship status, length of residence, and employment status, helps legislators and others understand how different migrant groups are integrated into society.

ACCURACY OF THE ESTIMATES

The data contained in this report are based on the sample of households who responded to the Census 2000 long form. Nationally, approximately one out of every six housing units was included in this sample. As a result, the sample estimates may differ somewhat from the 100-percent figures that would have been obtained if all housing units, people within those housing units, and people living in group quarters had been enumerated using the same questionnaires, instructions, enumerators, and so forth. The sample estimates also differ from the values that would have been obtained from different samples of housing units, and hence of people living in those housing units, and people living in group quarters. The deviation of a sample estimate from the average of all possible samples is called the sampling error.

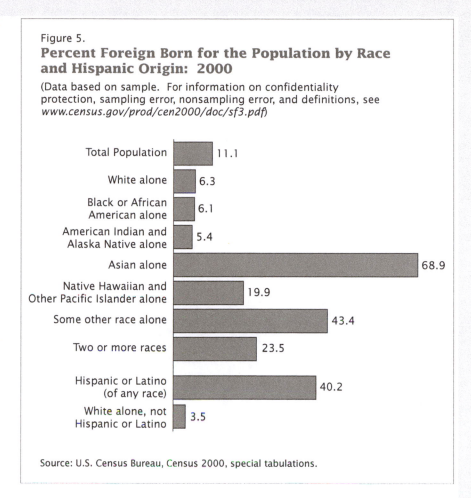

Figure 5.

Percent Foreign Born for the Population by Race and Hispanic Origin: 2000

(Data based on sample. For information on confidentiality protection, sampling error, nonsampling error, and definitions, see *www.census.gov/prod/cen2000/doc/sf3.pdf*)

Total Population	11.1
White alone	6.3
Black or African American alone	6.1
American Indian and Alaska Native alone	5.4
Asian alone	68.9
Native Hawaiian and Other Pacific Islander alone	19.9
Some other race alone	43.4
Two or more races	23.5
Hispanic or Latino (of any race)	40.2
White alone, not Hispanic or Latino	3.5

Source: U.S. Census Bureau, Census 2000, special tabulations.

In addition to the variability that arises from the sampling procedures, both sample data and 100-percent data are subject to nonsampling error. Nonsampling error may be introduced during any of the various complex operations used to collect and process data. Such errors may include: not enumerating every household or every person in the population, failing to obtain all required information from the respondents, obtaining incorrect or inconsistent information, and recording information incorrectly. In addition, errors can occur during the field review of the enumerators' work, during clerical handling of the census questionnaires, or during the electronic processing of the questionnaires.

While it is impossible to completely eliminate error from an operation as large and complex as the decennial census, the Census Bureau attempts to control the sources of such error during the data collection and processing operations. The primary sources of error and the programs instituted to control error in Census 2000 are described in detail in Summary File 3 Technical Documentation under Chapter 8, "Accuracy of the Data," located at *www.census.gov/prod/cen2000/doc/sf3.pdf*.

Nonsampling error may affect the data in two ways: (1) errors that are introduced randomly will increase the variability of the data and, therefore, should be reflected in the standard errors; and (2) errors that tend to be consistent in one direction will bias both sample and 100-percent data in that direction. For example, if respondents consistently tend to underreport their incomes, then the resulting estimates of households or families by income category will tend to be

Figure 6.
Age and Sex by Nativity: 2000

(Data based on sample. For information on confidentiality protection, sampling error, nonsampling error, and definitions, see *www.census.gov/prod/cen2000/doc/sf3.pdf*)

(In percent)[1]

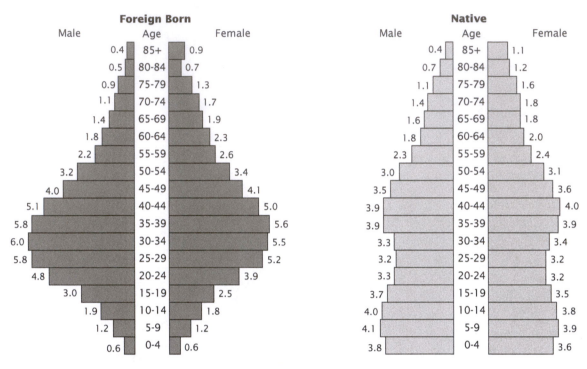

[1] Each bar represents the percent of the population (foreign-born or native) who were in the specified age-sex group.
Source: U.S. Census Bureau, Census 2000, special tabulations.

understated for the higher income categories and overstated for the lower income categories. Such biases are not reflected in the standard errors.

All statements in this Census 2000 Brief have undergone statistical testing and all comparisons are significant at the 90-percent confidence level, unless otherwise noted. The estimates in tables, maps, and other figures may vary from actual values due to sampling and nonsampling errors. As a result, estimates in one category used to summarize statistics in the maps and figures may not be significantly different from estimates assigned to a different cate-

gory. Further information on the accuracy of the data is located at *www.census.gov/prod/cen2000/doc/sf3.pdf*. For further information on the computation and use of standard errors, contact the Decennial Statistical Studies Division at 301-763-4242.

FOR MORE INFORMATION

The Census 2000 Summary File 3 data are available from the American Factfinder on the Internet *(factfinder.census.gov)*. They were released on a state-by-state basis during 2002. For information on confidentiality protection, nonsampling error, sampling error, and definitions, also see

www.census.gov/prod/cen2000/doc/sf3.pdf or contact the Customer Services Center at 301-763-INFO (4636).

Information on population and housing topics is presented in the Census 2000 Brief series, located on the Census Bureau's Web site at *www.census.gov/population/www/cen2000/briefs.html*. This series presents information on race, Hispanic origin, age, sex, household type, housing tenure, and social, economic, and housing characteristics, such as ancestry, income, and housing costs.

Language Use and English-Speaking Ability: 2000

Census 2000 Brief

Issued October 2003

C2KBR-29

By
Hyon B. Shin
with
Rosalind Bruno

The ability to communicate with government and private service providers, schools, businesses, emergency personnel, and many other people in the United States depends greatly on the ability to speak English.[1] In Census 2000, as in the two previous censuses, the U.S. Census Bureau asked people aged 5 and over if they spoke a language other than English at home. Among the 262.4 million people aged 5 and over, 47.0 million (18 percent) spoke a language other than English at home.

Figure 1.
Reproduction of the Questions on Language From Census 2000

11 a. Does this person speak a language other than English at home?

☐ Yes
☐ No → *Skip to 12*

b. What is this language?

(For example: Korean, Italian, Spanish, Vietnamese)

c. How well does this person speak English?

☐ Very well
☐ Well
☐ Not well
☐ Not at all

Source: U.S. Census Bureau, Census 2000 questionnaire.

This report, part of a series that presents population and housing data collected in Census 2000, presents data on language spoken at home and the ability to speak English of people aged 5 and over. It describes population distributions and characteristics for the United States, including regions, states, counties, and selected places with populations of 100,000 or more.

The questions illustrated in Figure 1 were asked in the census in 1980, 1990, and 2000. Various questions on language were asked in the censuses from 1890 to 1970, including a question on "mother tongue" (the language spoken in the person's home when he or she was a child).

The first language question in Census 2000 asked respondents whether they spoke a language other than English at home. Those who responded "Yes" to Question 11a were asked what language they spoke. The write-in answers to Question 11b (specific language spoken) were optically scanned and coded. Although linguists recognize several thousand languages in the world, the coding operation used by the Census Bureau put the reported languages into

---

[1] The text of this report discusses data for the United States, including the 50 states and the District of Columbia. Data for the Commonwealth of Puerto Rico are shown in Table 2 and Figure 5.

U S C E N S U S B U R E A U

Helping You Make Informed Decisions

U.S. Department of Commerce
Economics and Statistics Administration
U.S. CENSUS BUREAU

United States
Census 2000

351

about 380 categories of single languages or language families.[2]

For people who answered "Yes" to Question 11a, Question 11c asked respondents to indicate how well they spoke English. Respondents who said they spoke English "Very well" were considered to have no difficulty with English. Those who indicated they spoke English "Well," "Not well," or "Not at all" were considered to have difficulty with English — identified also as people who spoke English less than "Very well."

The number and percentage of people in the United States who spoke a language other than English at home increased between 1990 and 2000.

In 2000, 18 percent of the total population aged 5 and over, or 47.0 million people, reported they spoke a language other than English at home.[3] These figures were up from 14 percent (31.8 million) in 1990 and 11 percent (23.1 million) in 1980. The number of people who spoke a language other than English at home grew by 38 percent in the 1980s and by 47 percent in the 1990s. While the population aged 5 and over grew by one-fourth from 1980 to 2000, the number who spoke a language other than English at home more than doubled.

In 2000, most people who spoke a language other than English at home reported they spoke English "Very well" (55 percent or

---

[2] More detailed information on languages and language coding can be found in "Summary File 3: 2000 Census of Population and Housing Technical Documentation" issued December 2002 (*www.census.gov/prod /cen2000/doc/sf3.pdf*).

[3] The estimates in this report are based on responses from a sample of the population. As with all surveys, estimates may vary from the actual values because of sampling variation or other factors. All statements made in this report have undergone statistical testing and are significant at the 90-percent confidence level unless otherwise noted.

Figure 2.

Speakers of Languages Other Than English at Home and English Ability by Language Group: 2000

(Population 5 years and over, in millions. Data based on sample. For information on confidentiality protection, nonsampling error, sampling error, and definitions, see *www.census.gov/prod/cen2000/doc/sf3.pdf*)

Legend:
- Spoke English "Very well"
- Spoke English less than "Very well"

Language Group	Very well	Less than very well	Total
Spanish	14.3	13.8	28.1
Other Indo-European languages	6.6	3.4	10.0
Asian and Pacific Island languages	3.4	3.6	7.0
All other languages	1.3	0.6	1.9

Source: U.S. Census Bureau, Census 2000 Summary File 3.

Figure 3.

Ten Languages Most Frequently Spoken at Home Other Than English and Spanish: 2000

(Population 5 years and over, in millions. Data based on sample. For information on confidentiality protection, nonsampling error, sampling error, and definitions, see *www.census.gov/prod/cen2000/doc/sf3.pdf*)

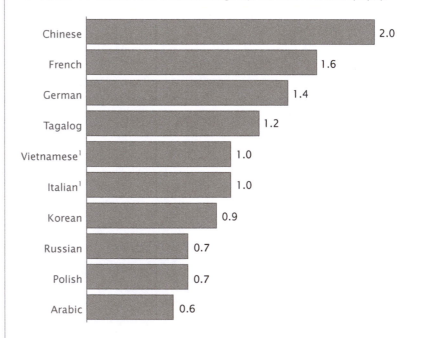

Language	Millions
Chinese	2.0
French	1.6
German	1.4
Tagalog	1.2
Vietnamese[1]	1.0
Italian[1]	1.0
Korean	0.9
Russian	0.7
Polish	0.7
Arabic	0.6

[1] The number of Vietnamese speakers and the number of Italian speakers were not statistically different from one another.

Note: The estimates in this figure vary from actual values due to sampling errors. As a result, the number of speakers of some languages shown in this figure may not be statistically different from the number of speakers of languages not shown in this figure.

Source: U.S. Census Bureau, Census 2000 Summary File 3.

Four Major Language Groups

Spanish includes those who speak Ladino.

Other Indo-European languages include most languages of Europe and the Indic languages of India. These include the Germanic languages, such as German, Yiddish, and Dutch; the Scandinavian languages, such as Swedish and Norwegian; the Romance languages, such as French, Italian, and Portuguese; the Slavic languages, such as Russian, Polish, and Serbo-Croatian; the Indic languages, such as Hindi, Gujarathi, Punjabi, and Urdu; Celtic languages; Greek; Baltic languages; and Iranian languages.

Asian and Pacific Island languages include Chinese; Korean; Japanese; Vietnamese; Hmong; Khmer; Lao; Thai; Tagalog or Pilipino; the Dravidian languages of India, such as Telegu, Tamil, and Malayalam; and other languages of Asia and the Pacific, including the Philippine, Polynesian, and Micronesian languages.

All other languages include Uralic languages, such as Hungarian; the Semitic languages, such as Arabic and Hebrew; languages of Africa; native North American languages, including the American Indian and Alaska native languages; and some indigenous languages of Central and South America.

25.6 million people). When they are combined with those who spoke only English at home, 92 percent of the population aged 5 and over had no difficulty speaking English. The proportion of the population aged 5 and over who spoke English less than "Very well" grew from 4.8 percent in 1980, to 6.1 percent in 1990, and to 8.1 percent in 2000.

In Figure 2, the number of speakers of the four major language groups (Spanish, Other Indo-European languages, Asian and Pacific Island languages, and All other languages) are shown by how well they spoke English (see text box above). Spanish was the largest of the four major language groups, and just over half of the 28.1 million Spanish speakers spoke English "Very well."

Other Indo-European language speakers composed the second largest group, with 10.0 million speakers, almost two-thirds of whom spoke English "Very well." Slightly less than half of the

7.0 million Asian and Pacific Island-language speakers spoke English "Very well" (3.4 million). Of the 1.9 million people who composed the All other language category, 1.3 million spoke English "Very well."

After English and Spanish, Chinese was the language most commonly spoken at home (2.0 million speakers), followed by French (1.6 million speakers) and German (1.4 million speakers, see Figure 3). Reflecting historical patterns of immigration, the numbers of Italian, Polish, and German speakers fell between 1990 and 2000, while the number of speakers of many other languages increased.

Spanish speakers grew by about 60 percent and Spanish continued to be the non-English language most frequently spoken at home in the United States. The Chinese language, however, jumped from the fifth to the second most widely spoken non-English language, as the number of Chinese speakers rose from 1.2 to 2.0 million people (see

Table 1).[4] The number of Vietnamese speakers doubled over the decade, from about 507,000 speakers to just over 1 million speakers.

Of the 20 non-English languages most frequently spoken at home shown in Table 1, the largest proportional increase was for Russian speakers, who nearly tripled from 242,000 to 706,000. The second largest increase was for French Creole speakers (the language group that includes Haitian Creoles), whose numbers more than doubled from 188,000 to 453,000.

THE GEOGRAPHIC DISTRIBUTION OF PEOPLE WHO SPOKE A LANGUAGE OTHER THAN ENGLISH AT HOME

This section discusses the geographic distribution of the population aged 5 and over who stated in Census 2000 that they spoke a language other than English at home.

The West had the greatest number and proportion of non-English-language speakers.[5]

People who spoke languages other than English at home were not distributed equally across or within regions in 2000.[6] While the West

---

[4] The changes in ranks between 1990 and 2000 have not been tested and may not be statistically significant.

[5] Hereafter, this report uses the term "non-English-language speakers" to refer to people who spoke a language other than English at home, regardless of their ability to speak English (see Table 1).

[6] The Northeast region includes the states of Connecticut, Maine, Massachusetts, New Hampshire, New Jersey, New York, Pennsylvania, Rhode Island, and Vermont. The Midwest region includes the states of Illinois, Indiana, Iowa, Kansas, Michigan, Minnesota, Missouri, Nebraska, North Dakota, Ohio, South Dakota, and Wisconsin. The South region includes the states of Alabama, Arkansas, Delaware, Florida, Georgia, Kentucky, Louisiana, Maryland, Mississippi, North Carolina, Oklahoma, South Carolina, Tennessee, Texas, Virginia, West Virginia, and the District of Columbia, a state equivalent. The West region includes the states of Alaska, Arizona, California, Colorado, Hawaii, Idaho, Montana, Nevada, New Mexico, Oregon, Utah, Washington, and Wyoming.

Table 1.
Twenty Languages Most Frequently Spoken at Home by English Ability for the Population 5 Years and Over: 1990 and 2000

(Data based on sample. For information on confidentiality protection, sampling error, nonsampling error, and definitions, see www.census.gov/prod/cen2000/doc/sf3.pdf)

Language spoken at home	1990		2000					
				Number of speakers				
				Total	English-speaking ability			
	Rank	Number of speakers	Rank	Total	Very well	Well	Not well	Not at all
United States	(X)	230,445,777	(X)	262,375,152	(X)	(X)	(X)	(X)
English only	(X)	198,600,798	(X)	215,423,557	(X)	(X)	(X)	(X)
Total non-English	(X)	31,844,979	(X)	46,951,595	25,631,188	10,333,556	7,620,719	3,366,132
Spanish	1	17,339,172	1	28,101,052	14,349,796	5,819,408	5,130,400	2,801,448
Chinese..............	5	1,249,213	2	2,022,143	855,689	595,331	408,597	162,526
French	2	1,702,176	3	1,643,838	1,228,800	269,458	138,002	7,578
German	3	1,547,099	4	1,382,613	1,078,997	219,362	79,535	4,719
Tagalog	6	843,251	5	1,224,241	827,559	311,465	79,721	5,496
Vietnamese[1]	9	507,069	6	1,009,627	342,594	340,062	270,950	56,021
Italian[1]	4	1,308,648	7	1,008,370	701,220	195,901	99,270	11,979
Korean..............	8	626,478	8	894,063	361,166	268,477	228,392	36,028
Russian	15	241,798	9	706,242	304,891	209,057	148,671	43,623
Polish..............	7	723,483	10	667,414	387,694	167,233	95,032	17,455
Arabic..............	13	355,150	11	614,582	403,397	140,057	58,595	12,533
Portuguese[2]	10	429,860	12	564,630	320,443	125,464	90,412	28,311
Japanese[2]..............	11	427,657	13	477,997	241,707	146,613	84,018	5,659
French Creole	19	187,658	14	453,368	245,857	121,913	70,961	14,637
Greek..............	12	388,260	15	365,436	262,851	65,023	33,346	4,216
Hindi[3]..............	14	331,484	16	317,057	245,192	51,929	16,682	3,254
Persian	18	201,865	17	312,085	198,041	70,909	32,959	10,176
Urdu[3]	(NA)	(NA)	18	262,900	180,018	56,736	20,817	5,329
Gujarathi	26	102,418	19	235,988	155,011	50,637	22,522	7,818
Armenian..............	20	149,694	20	202,708	108,554	48,469	31,868	13,817
All other languages	(X)	3,182,546	(X)	4,485,241	2,831,711	1,060,052	479,969	113,509

NA Not available.   X Not applicable.

[1] In 2000, the number of Vietnamese speakers and the number of Italian speakers were not statistically different from one another.
[2] In 1990, the number of Portuguese speakers and the number of Japanese speakers were not statistically different from one another.
[3] In 1990, Hindi included those who spoke Urdu.

Note: The estimates in this table vary from actual values due to sampling errors. As a result, the number of speakers of some languages shown in this table may not be statistically different from the number of speakers of languages not shown in this table.

Source: U.S. Census Bureau, Census 2000 Summary File 3.

had only slightly more than one-fifth of the U.S. population aged 5 and over, it was home to more than one-third (37 percent) of all non-English-language speakers, the highest proportion of any region (see Table 2). Within regions, the proportion who spoke a non-English language at home was 29 percent in the West, 20 percent in the Northeast, 15 percent in the South, and only 9 percent in the Midwest.

Reflecting the higher proportion of speakers of non-English languages

in the West, people in that region were more likely than those in the other regions to have difficulty with English. In 2000, 14 percent of all people aged 5 and over in the West spoke English less than "Very well" — compared with 9 percent in the Northeast, 7 percent in the South, and 4 percent in the Midwest.

Figure 4 illustrates the prevalence of the four major non-English-language groups spoken in each region. Spanish was spoken more than any other language group in

all regions. The West and the South combined had about three times the number of Spanish speakers (21.0 million) as the Northeast and the Midwest combined (7.1 million). In the Northeast and the Midwest, Spanish speakers composed slightly less than half of all non-English-language speakers, while in the South and the West, they represented around two-thirds (71 percent and 64 percent, respectively), in large part because of the geographic proximity to Mexico and other Spanish-speaking countries.

Table 2.
Language Use and English-Speaking Ability for the Population 5 Years and Over for the United States, Regions, and States and for Puerto Rico: 1990 and 2000

(Data based on sample. For information on confidentiality protection, sampling error, nonsampling error, and definitions, see www.census.gov/prod/cen2000/doc/sf3.pdf)

Area	1990			2000					1990 and 2000 percent change in "Spoke a language other than English at home"
	Population 5 years and over	Spoke a language other than English at home	Percent	Population 5 years and over	Spoke a language other than English at home	Percent	Spoke English less than "Very well"	Percent	
United States	230,445,777	31,844,979	13.8	262,375,152	46,951,595	17.9	21,320,407	8.1	47.4
Region									
Northeast	47,319,352	7,824,285	16.5	50,224,209	10,057,331	20.0	4,390,538	8.7	28.5
Midwest	55,272,756	3,920,660	7.1	60,054,144	5,623,538	9.4	2,398,120	4.0	43.4
South	79,248,852	8,669,631	10.9	93,431,879	14,007,396	15.0	6,149,756	6.6	61.6
West	48,604,817	11,430,403	23.5	58,664,920	17,263,330	29.4	8,381,993	14.3	51.0
State									
Alabama	3,759,802	107,866	2.9	4,152,278	162,483	3.9	63,917	1.5	50.6
Alaska	495,425	60,165	12.1	579,740	82,758	14.3	30,842	5.3	37.6
Arizona	3,374,806	700,287	20.8	4,752,724	1,229,237	25.9	539,937	11.4	75.5
Arkansas	2,186,665	60,781	2.8	2,492,205	123,755	5.0	57,709	2.3	103.6
California	27,383,547	8,619,334	31.5	31,416,629	12,401,756	39.5	6,277,779	20.0	43.9
Colorado	3,042,986	320,631	10.5	4,006,285	604,019	15.1	267,504	6.7	88.4
Connecticut	3,060,000	466,175	15.2	3,184,514	583,913	18.3	234,799	7.4	25.3
Delaware	617,720	42,327	6.9	732,378	69,533	9.5	28,380	3.9	64.3
District of Columbia. . . .	570,284	71,348	12.5	539,658	90,417	16.8	38,236	7.1	26.7
Florida	12,095,284	2,098,315	17.3	15,043,603	3,473,864	23.1	1,554,865	10.3	65.6
Georgia	5,984,188	284,546	4.8	7,594,476	751,438	9.9	374,251	4.9	164.1
Hawaii	1,026,209	254,724	24.8	1,134,351	302,125	26.6	143,505	12.7	18.6
Idaho	926,703	58,995	6.4	1,196,793	111,879	9.3	46,539	3.9	89.6
Illinois	10,585,838	1,499,112	14.2	11,547,505	2,220,719	19.2	1,054,722	9.1	48.1
Indiana	5,146,160	245,826	4.8	5,657,818	362,082	6.4	143,427	2.5	47.3
Iowa	2,583,526	100,391	3.9	2,738,499	160,022	5.8	68,108	2.5	59.4
Kansas	2,289,615	131,604	5.7	2,500,360	218,655	8.7	98,207	3.9	66.1
Kentucky	3,434,955	86,482	2.5	3,776,230	148,473	3.9	58,871	1.6	71.7
Louisiana	3,886,353	391,994	10.1	4,153,367	382,364	9.2	116,907	2.8	−2.5
Maine	1,142,122	105,441	9.2	1,204,164	93,966	7.8	24,063	2.0	−10.9
Maryland	4,425,285	395,051	8.9	4,945,043	622,714	12.6	246,287	5.0	57.6
Massachusetts	5,605,751	852,228	15.2	5,954,249	1,115,570	18.7	459,073	7.7	30.9
Michigan	8,594,737	569,807	6.6	9,268,782	781,381	8.4	294,606	3.2	37.1
Minnesota	4,038,361	227,161	5.6	4,591,491	389,988	8.5	167,511	3.6	71.7
Mississippi	2,378,805	66,516	2.8	2,641,453	95,522	3.6	36,059	1.4	43.6
Missouri	4,748,704	178,210	3.8	5,226,022	264,281	5.1	103,019	2.0	48.3
Montana	740,218	37,020	5.0	847,362	44,331	5.2	12,663	1.5	19.7
Nebraska	1,458,904	69,872	4.8	1,594,700	125,654	7.9	57,772	3.6	79.8
Nevada	1,110,450	146,152	13.2	1,853,720	427,972	23.1	207,687	11.2	192.8
New Hampshire	1,024,621	88,796	8.7	1,160,340	96,088	8.3	28,073	2.4	8.2
New Jersey	7,200,696	1,406,148	19.5	7,856,268	2,001,690	25.5	873,088	11.1	42.4
New Mexico	1,390,048	493,999	35.5	1,689,911	616,964	36.5	201,055	11.9	24.9
New York	16,743,048	3,908,720	23.3	17,749,110	4,962,921	28.0	2,310,256	13.0	27.0
North Carolina	6,172,301	240,866	3.9	7,513,165	603,517	8.0	297,858	4.0	150.6
North Dakota	590,839	46,897	7.9	603,106	37,976	6.3	11,003	1.8	−19.0
Ohio	10,063,212	546,148	5.4	10,599,968	648,493	6.1	234,459	2.2	18.7
Oklahoma	2,921,755	145,798	5.0	3,215,719	238,532	7.4	98,990	3.1	63.6
Oregon	2,640,482	191,710	7.3	3,199,323	388,669	12.1	188,958	5.9	102.7
Pennsylvania	11,085,170	806,876	7.3	11,555,538	972,484	8.4	368,257	3.2	20.5
Rhode Island	936,423	159,492	17.0	985,184	196,624	20.0	83,624	8.5	23.3
South Carolina	3,231,539	113,163	3.5	3,748,669	196,429	5.2	82,279	2.2	73.6
South Dakota	641,226	41,994	6.5	703,820	45,575	6.5	16,376	2.3	(NS)
Tennessee	4,544,743	131,550	2.9	5,315,920	256,516	4.8	108,265	2.0	95.0
Texas	15,605,822	3,970,304	25.4	19,241,518	6,010,753	31.2	2,669,603	13.9	51.4
Utah	1,553,351	120,404	7.8	2,023,875	253,249	12.5	105,691	5.2	110.3
Vermont	521,521	30,409	5.8	574,842	34,075	5.9	9,305	1.6	(NS)
Virginia	5,746,419	418,521	7.3	6,619,266	735,191	11.1	303,729	4.6	75.7
Washington	4,501,879	403,173	9.0	5,501,398	770,886	14.0	350,914	6.4	91.2
West Virginia	1,686,932	44,203	2.6	1,706,931	45,895	2.7	13,550	0.8	3.8
Wisconsin	4,531,134	263,638	5.8	5,022,073	368,712	7.3	148,910	3.0	39.9
Wyoming	418,713	23,809	5.7	462,809	29,485	6.4	8,919	1.9	23.8
Puerto Rico	3,522,037	(NA)	(NA)	3,515,228	3,008,567	85.6	2,527,156	71.9	(NA)

NA Not available.   NS Not statistically different from zero at the 90-percent confidence level.

Source: U.S. Census Bureau, Census 2000 Summary File 3 and 1990 Census Summary Tape File 3.

In the Northeast, the Midwest, and the South, speakers of Other Indo-European languages made up the second largest non-English-language speaking group, while in the West, the second largest group was speakers of Asian and Pacific Island languages. Half of Asian and Pacific Island-language speakers lived in the West in 2000.

Table 3 shows the change in the number of speakers of Spanish, Other Indo-European languages, Asian and Pacific Island languages, and All other languages between 1990 and 2000. The largest percentage increase of Spanish speakers was in the Midwest. Asian and Pacific Island-language speakers increased most rapidly in the South and the Midwest. Although the number of Spanish speakers grew in all regions, more than three-fourths of that growth was in the West and the South. The number of Asian and Pacific Island-language speakers grew substantially in all regions, with the greatest numerical increase in the West, which was home to more than half of all Asian and Pacific Island-language speakers in both years.

Figure 4.

Non-English Languages Spoken at Home, by Region: 2000

(Population 5 years and over, in millions. Data based on sample. For information on confidentiality protection, nonsampling error, sampling error, and definitions, see *www.census.gov/prod/cen2000/doc/sf3.pdf*)

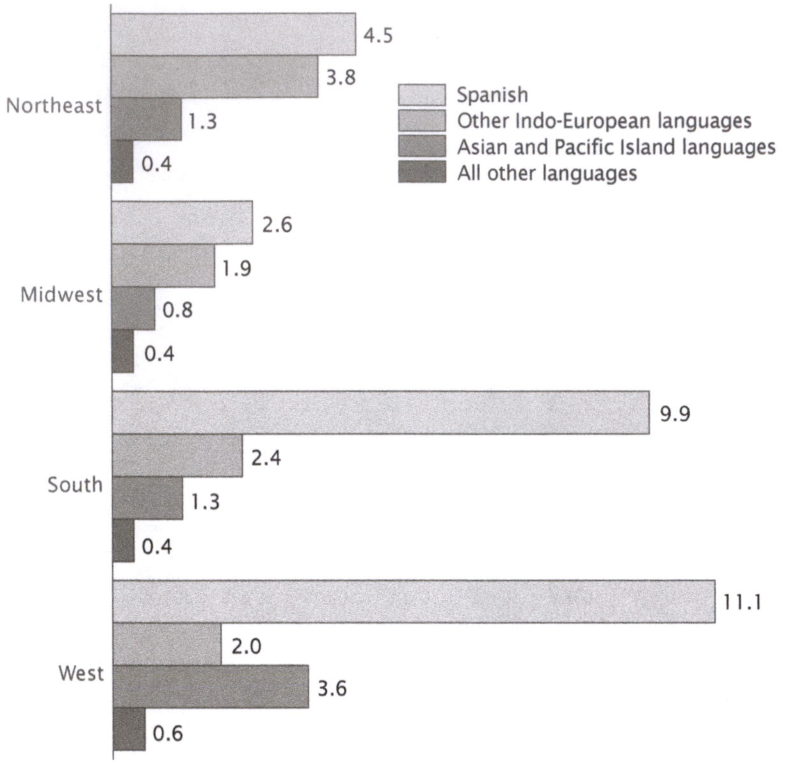

Source: U.S. Census Bureau, Census 2000 Summary File 3.

More than one-quarter of the population in seven states spoke a language other than English at home in 2000.

California had the largest percentage of non-English-language speakers (39 percent), followed by New Mexico (37 percent), Texas (31 percent), New York (28 percent), Hawaii (27 percent), Arizona, and New Jersey (each about 26 percent, see Table 2). The five states with fewer than 5 percent of the population who spoke a language other than English at home were all in the South — Tennessee (4.8 percent), Alabama and Kentucky (each 3.9 percent), Mississippi

(3.6 percent), and West Virginia (2.7 percent).

Eight states had over 1 million non-English-language speakers in 2000, led by California (12.4 million) with more than twice the number of any other state. Texas had the second largest number of non-English-language speakers (6.0 million), followed by New York (5.0 million), Florida (3.5 million), Illinois (2.2 million), New Jersey (2.0 million), Arizona (1.2 million), and Massachusetts (1.1 million).

During the 1990s, California surpassed New Mexico as the state with the largest proportion of

non-English-language speakers. While the proportion of non-English-language speakers in New Mexico increased slightly from 36 percent to 37 percent, the proportion in California jumped from 31 percent to 39 percent.

The number of non-English-language speakers at least doubled in six states from 1990 to 2000. The largest percentage increase occurred in Nevada, where the number increased by 193 percent. Nevada also had the highest rate of population increase during the decade. Georgia's non-English-language-speaking residents

Table 3.
Language Spoken at Home for the Population 5 Years and Over Who Spoke a Language Other Than English at Home for the United States and Regions: 1990 and 2000

(Data based on sample. For information on confidentiality protection, sampling error, nonsampling error, and definitions, see www.census.gov/prod/cen2000/doc/sf3.pdf)

Area	Spanish			Other Indo-European languages			Asian and Pacific Island languages			All other languages		
	1990	2000	Percent change	1990	2000	Percent change	1990	2000	Percent change	1990	2000	Percent change
United States ..	17,345,064	28,101,052	62.0	8,790,133	10,017,989	14.0	4,471,621	6,960,065	55.6	1,238,161	1,872,489	51.2
Region												
Northeast	3,133,043	4,492,168	43.4	3,547,154	3,778,958	6.5	845,442	1,348,621	59.5	298,646	437,584	46.5
Midwest	1,400,651	2,623,391	87.3	1,821,772	1,861,729	2.2	459,524	760,107	65.4	238,713	378,311	58.5
South	5,815,486	9,908,653	70.4	1,909,179	2,390,266	25.2	715,235	1,277,618	78.6	229,731	430,859	87.5
West.	6,995,884	11,076,840	58.3	1,512,028	1,987,036	31.4	2,451,420	3,573,719	45.8	471,071	625,735	32.8

Source: U.S. Census Bureau, Census 2000 Summary File 3 and 1990 Census Summary Tape File 3.

increased by 164 percent, followed by North Carolina (151 percent), Utah (110 percent), Arkansas (104 percent), and Oregon (103 percent).[7]

Since 1990, the proportion of people who spoke a language other than English at home decreased in three states. North Dakota had the largest decrease (19 percent), followed by Maine (11 percent) and Louisiana (2 percent). These three states also had low rates of population growth from 1990 to 2000.

Counties with a large proportion of the population who spoke a language other than English at home were concentrated in border states.

Figure 5 illustrates the high proportions of people who spoke a language other than English at home in 2000 in the states that border Mexico, the Pacific Ocean, or the Atlantic Ocean. Some of these "border states" were entry points for many immigrants.

In 2000, in about 1 percent of the 3,141 counties in the United States, more than 60 percent of

the population spoke a language other than English at home. In seven counties, more than 80 percent of the population spoke a non-English language at home — Maverick, Webb, Starr, Kenedy, Zavala, Presidio, and Hidalgo — all in Texas. All but one of the 20 counties with the highest proportions of non-English-language speakers were located in Texas (Santa Cruz County, Arizona being the exception).

Figure 5 shows the high proportion of non-English-language speakers in counties with large cities, such as Atlanta, Chicago, Miami, and New York City. Other counties with relatively high proportions of non-English-language speakers included concentrations of people who spoke Native American languages.[8] For example, in Bethel Census Area, Alaska, 66 percent of the population spoke a language other than English at home, and 97 percent of the non-English-language speakers spoke a Native North American language. The Navajo speakers in the Navajo Nation Indian Reservation, which spanned several counties throughout Arizona, New Mexico,

and Utah, accounted for a large proportion of the population who spoke a language other than English at home in these counties.

In some counties, relatively high proportions of non-English-language speakers are found in small, rural populations. For example, the proportions of non-English-language speakers were 25 percent in Logan County and 36 percent in McIntosh County in North Dakota and 33 percent in McPherson County in South Dakota.[9] In these three counties, each with a population of fewer than 4,000, German speakers were predominant among non-English-language speakers: 95.3 percent, 98.1 percent, and 99.6 percent, respectively.[10]

Among all counties, the median percentage of the population who spoke a language other than English at home was 4.6 percent.[11] The fact that the proportion was

---

[7] The percentage increases between Arkansas and Utah and between Arkansas and Oregon were not statistically different from one another.

[8] For more detailed information on language use and English-speaking ability, see Summary File 3.

[9] The proportions of non-English-language speakers in McIntosh County, North Dakota, and McPherson County, South Dakota, were not statistically different from each other.
[10] The proportions of German speakers among non-English-language speakers in Logan County and McIntosh County, North Dakota, were not statistically different from each other.
[11] The median percentage is a point estimate based on a sample.

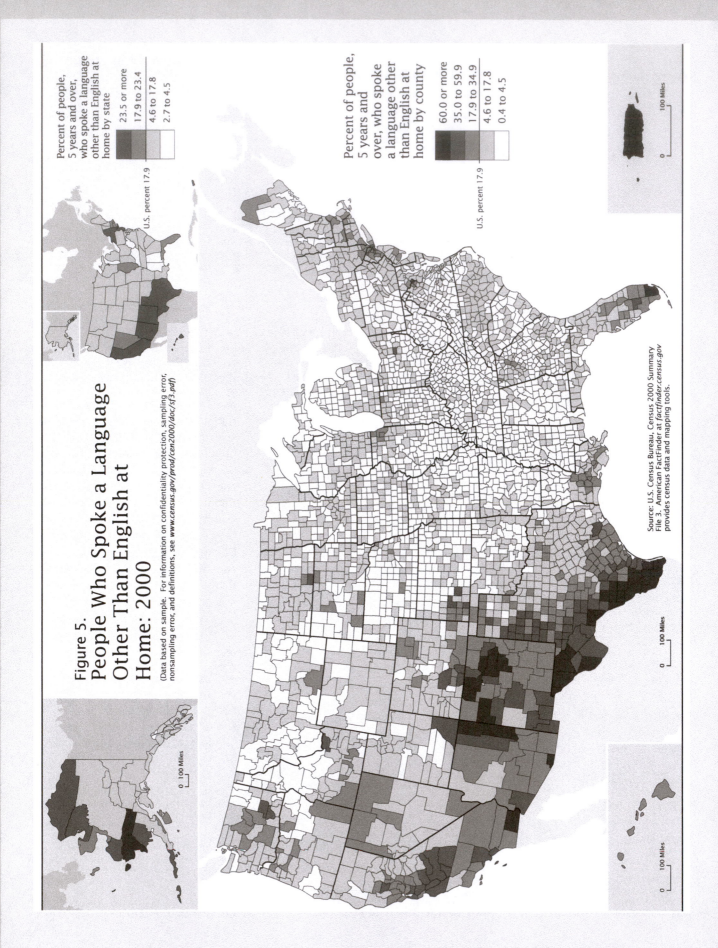

Figure 5.
People Who Spoke a Language
Other Than English at
Home: 2000

(Data based on sample. For information on confidentiality protection, sampling error, nonsampling error, and definitions, see *www.census.gov/prod/cen2000/doc/sf3.pdf*)

Percent of people,
5 years and over,
who spoke a language
other than English at
home by state

23.5 or more
17.9 to 23.4
4.6 to 17.8
2.7 to 4.5

U.S. percent 17.9

Percent of people,
5 years and
over, who spoke
a language other
than English at
home by county

60.0 or more
35.0 to 59.9
17.9 to 34.9
4.6 to 17.8
0.4 to 4.5

U.S. percent 17.9

Source: U.S. Census Bureau, Census 2000 Summary
File 3. American FactFinder at *factfinder.census.gov*
provides census data and mapping tools.

Table 4.
Ten Places of 100,000 or More Population With the Highest Percentage of People 5 Years and Over Who Spoke a Language Other Than English at Home, Who Spoke Spanish at Home, and Who Spoke English Less Than "Very Well": 2000

(Data based on sample. For information on confidentiality protection, sampling error, nonsampling error, and definitions, see *www.census.gov/prod/cen2000/doc/sf3.pdf*)

Place	Number	Percent	90-percent confidence interval
Spoke a Language Other Than English			
Hialeah, FL	197,504	92.6	92.3 - 92.9
Laredo, TX	145,510	91.8	91.4 - 92.2
East Los Angeles, CA[1]	97,645	87.4	86.8 - 88.0
Brownsville, TX	110,003	87.2	86.7 - 87.7
El Monte, CA	84,834	80.7	80.0 - 81.4
Santa Ana, CA	241,303	79.6	79.2 - 80.0
McAllen, TX	73,882	76.1	75.3 - 76.9
Miami, FL	254,536	74.6	74.2 - 75.0
El Paso, TX	369,000	71.3	70.9 - 71.7
Elizabeth, NJ	75,305	67.5	66.7 - 68.3
Spoke Spanish			
Hialeah, FL	195,884	91.9	91.6 - 92.2
Laredo, TX	144,633	91.3	90.9 - 91.7
Brownsville, TX	109,153	86.6	86.1 - 87.1
East Los Angeles, CA[1]	96,525	86.4	85.8 - 87.0
McAllen, TX	71,800	74.0	73.2 - 74.8
Santa Ana, CA	211,276	69.7	69.2 - 70.2
El Paso, TX	356,558	68.9	68.5 - 69.3
Miami, FL	227,293	66.6	66.1 - 67.1
El Monte, CA	64,889	61.8	61.0 - 62.6
Pomona, CA	74,557	55.0	54.2 - 55.8
Spoke English Less Than "Very Well"			
Hialeah, FL	126,358	59.3	58.7 - 59.9
East Los Angeles, CA[1]	57,966	51.9	51.1 - 52.7
Santa Ana, CA	156,692	51.7	51.2 - 52.2
El Monte, CA	53,662	51.1	50.2 - 52.0
Miami, FL	160,790	47.1	46.6 - 47.6
Laredo, TX	69,071	43.6	42.9 - 44.3
Brownsville, TX	52,970	42.0	41.2 - 42.8
Garden Grove, CA	57,313	37.6	36.9 - 38.3
Elizabeth, NJ	41,068	36.8	36.0 - 37.6
Salinas, CA	49,099	35.9	35.2 - 36.6

[1] East Los Angeles, CA, is a census designated place and is not legally incorporated.

Note: Because of sampling error, the estimates in this table may not be significantly different from one another or from rates for other places not listed in this table.

Source: U.S. Census Bureau, Census 2000 Summary File 3.

Places with the highest percentages of non-English-language speakers, Spanish speakers, and people who spoke English less than "Very well" were concentrated in California, Florida, and Texas.

Of the 245 places with 100,000 or more population in 2000, Hialeah, Florida, topped the list with 93 percent of the population aged 5 and over who spoke a language other than English at home in 2000.[12] In addition, 92 percent spoke Spanish and 59 percent spoke English less than "Very well" in Hialeah (see Table 4).[13] Six additional places were included in all three categories in Table 4: Laredo and Brownsville, Texas; East Los Angeles, El Monte, and Santa Ana, California; and Miami, Florida.

McAllen and El Paso, Texas, and Elizabeth, New Jersey, were included in two of the three categories. Pomona, Garden Grove, and Salinas, all in California, were included in one of the three categories.

ADDITIONAL FINDINGS

How many people were linguistically isolated?

In the United States, the ability to speak English plays a large role in how well people can perform daily activities. How well a person speaks English may indicate how well he or she communicates with public officials, medical personnel, and other service providers. It

[12] Census 2000 showed 245 places in the United States with 100,000 or more population. They included 238 incorporated places (including 4 city-county consolidations) and 7 census designated places that were not legally incorporated. For a list of these places by state, see *www.census.gov/population/www/cen2000/phc-t6.html*.
[13] The percentages of people who spoke English less than "Very well" in Hialeah, Florida, and Laredo, Texas, were not statistically different from each other. The percentages of people who spoke Spanish in Hialeah, Florida, and Laredo, Texas, were also not statistically different from each other.

below 4.6 percent in one-half of all counties, while the national average was 17.9 percent, reflects the large number of counties (primarily non-metropolitan counties in the Midwest and the South) with relatively small populations and with low proportions of non-English-language speakers.

Figure 5 illustrates the low proportions of non-English-language speakers in many counties in the South and the Midwest, including Alabama, Arkansas, Iowa, Kentucky, Michigan, Mississippi, Missouri, Tennessee, West Virginia, and Wisconsin. In West Virginia, all but 2 of the 55 counties had a proportion of non-English-language speakers below 4.6 percent.

Linguistically Isolated Households

A linguistically isolated household is one in which no person aged 14 or over speaks English at least "Very well." That is, no person aged 14 or over speaks only English at home, or speaks another language at home and speaks English "Very well."

A linguistically isolated person is any person living in a linguistically isolated household. All the members of a linguistically isolated household are tabulated as linguistically isolated, including members under 14 years old who may speak only English.

could also affect other activities outside the home, such as grocery shopping or banking. People who do not have a strong command of English and who do not have someone in their household to help them on a regular basis are at even more of a disadvantage. They are defined here as "linguistically isolated" (see text box above).

In 2000, 4.4 million households encompassing 11.9 million people were linguistically isolated. These numbers were significantly higher than in 1990, when 2.9 million households and 7.7 million people lived in those households.

ABOUT CENSUS 2000

Why Census 2000 Asked About Language Use and English-Speaking Ability

The question on language use and English-speaking ability provides government agencies with information for programs that serve the needs of people who have difficulty speaking English. Under the Voting Rights Act, information about language ability is needed to meet statutory requirements for making voting materials available in minority languages.

The Bilingual Education Program uses data on language to allocate grants to school districts for children with limited English proficiency. These data also are needed for local agencies developing services for the elderly under the Older Americans Act.

Accuracy of the Estimates

The data contained in this report are based on the sample of households who responded to the Census 2000 long form. Nationally, approximately 1 out of every 6 housing units was included in this sample. As a result, the sample estimates may differ somewhat from the 100-percent figures that would have been obtained if all housing units, people within those housing units, and people living in group quarters had been enumerated using the same questionnaires, instructions, enumerators, and so forth. The sample estimates also differ from the values that would have been obtained from different samples of housing units, people within those housing units, and people living in group quarters. The deviation of a sample estimate from the average of all possible samples is called the sampling error.

In addition to the variability that arises from the sampling procedures, both sample data and 100-percent data are subject to nonsampling error. Nonsampling error may be introduced during any of the various complex operations used to collect and process data. Such errors may include: not enumerating every household or every person in the population, failing to obtain all required information from the respondents, obtaining incorrect or inconsistent information, and recording information incorrectly. In addition, errors can occur during the field review of the enumerators' work, during clerical handling of the census questionnaires, or during the electronic processing of the questionnaires.

Nonsampling error may affect the data in two ways: (1) errors that are introduced randomly will increase the variability of the data and, therefore, should be reflected in the standard errors; and (2) errors that tend to be consistent in one direction will bias both sample and 100-percent data in that direction. For example, if respondents consistently tend to underreport their incomes, then the resulting estimates of households or families by income category will tend to be understated for the higher income categories and overstated for the lower income categories. Such biases are not reflected in the standard errors.

While it is impossible to completely eliminate error from an operation as large and complex as the decennial census, the Census Bureau attempts to control the sources of such error during the data collection and processing operations. The primary sources of error and the programs instituted to control error in Census 2000 are described in detail in *Summary File 3 Technical Documentation* under Chapter 8, "Accuracy of the Data," located at *www.census.gov/prod/cen2000/doc/sf3.pdf*.

All statements in this Census 2000 Brief have undergone statistical testing and all comparisons are significant at the 90-percent confidence level, unless otherwise noted. The estimates in tables, maps, and other figures may vary from actual values due to sampling and nonsampling errors. As a result, estimates in one category may not be significantly different from estimates assigned to a different category. Further information on the accuracy of the data is located at *www.census.gov /prod/cen2000/doc/sf3.pdf.* For further information on the computation and use of standard errors, contact the Decennial Statistical Studies Division at 301-763-4242.

For More Information

The Census 2000 Summary File 3 data are available from the American FactFinder on the Internet (*factfinder.census.gov*).

They were released on a state-by-state basis during 2002. For information on confidentiality protection, nonsampling error, sampling error, and definitions, also see *www.census.gov/prod/cen2000 /doc/sf3.pdf* or contact the Customer Services Center at 301-763-INFO (4636).

Information on population and housing topics is presented in the Census 2000 Brief series, located on the Census Bureau's Web site at *www.census.gov/population/www /cen2000/briefs.html.* This series presents information on race, Hispanic origin, age, sex, household type, housing tenure, and

social, economic, and housing characteristics, such as ancestry, income, and housing costs.

For additional information on language use and English-speaking ability, including reports and survey data, visit the Census Bureau's Internet site at *www.census.gov /population/www/socdemo /lang_use.html.* To find information about the availability of data products, including reports, CD-ROMs, and DVDs, call the Customer Services Center at 301-763-INFO (4636), or e-mail *webmaster@census.gov.*

Marital Status: 2000

Census 2000 Brief

Issued October 2003

C2KBR-30

By
Rose M. Kreider
and
Tavia Simmons

INTRODUCTION

Among the 221.1 million people aged 15 and over in the United States in 2000:

- 120.2 million, or 54.4 percent, were now married;

- 41.0 million, or 18.5 percent, were widowed, divorced or separated; and

- 59.9 million, or 27.1 percent, were never married.

This report, part of a series that presents population and housing data collected by Census 2000, presents data on the marital status of people aged 15 and over. It describes marital status distributions for the United States, including regions, states, counties, and places with populations of 100,000 or more.[1] Highlights include marital status patterns by age, sex, race and Hispanic origin, ratios of unmarried men to unmarried women, and changes in marital status distributions observed since the 1950 census.

Figure 1.

Reproduction of the Question on Marital Status From Census 2000

7 What is this person's marital status?

- ☐ Now married
- ☐ Widowed
- ☐ Divorced
- ☐ Separated
- ☐ Never married

Source: U.S. Census Bureau, Census 2000 questionnaire.

The data on marital status were derived from answers to question 7 on the Census 2000 long form, "What is this person's marital status?" (Figure 1). The resulting classification refers to the person's status at the time of enumeration. Marital status was reported for each person as either "now married," "widowed," "divorced," "separated," or "never married." Individuals who were living together (unmarried people, people in common-law marriages) reported the marital status which they considered most appropriate. Data on marital status were tabulated only for people aged 15 and over.

The decennial census has asked about the marital status of the population since 1880. From 1880 through 1940, marital status was categorized as "single," "married," "widowed," or "divorced." "Separated" was added as a category in 1950. In various years, additional related questions were asked, including age at first marriage, whether the person was married in the last year, whether

[1] The text of this report discusses data for the United States, including the 50 states and the District of Columbia. Data for the Commonwealth of Puerto Rico are shown in Table 2. The states in each region are shown in Figure 4.

The estimates in this report are based on responses from a sample of the population. As with all surveys, estimates may vary from the actual values because of sampling variation or other factors. All statements made in this report have undergone statistical testing and are significant at the 90-percent confidence interval unless otherwise noted.

USCENSUSBUREAU

Helping You Make Informed Decisions

U.S. Department of Commerce
Economics and Statistics Administration
U.S. CENSUS BUREAU

United States
Census
2000

ever-married people had married more than once, and the dates of current and first marriages, but these detailed questions were not asked in Census 2000. While in previous censuses, the marital status item appeared on the short-form questionnaire and was asked of the entire population; in Census 2000, the marital-status item appeared only on the long form, which was given to approximately 1 in every 6 households.[2]

NATIONAL DISTRIBUTIONS

Over half of all people aged 15 and over were now married.

Marital patterns vary by age, as shown in Table 1. While the majority of both men and women in the age groups 15 to 19 years and 20 to 24 years were never married in 2000, the majority of men aged 25 and over were now married, as were the majority of women aged 25 to 74. The percentage never married was lowest for men aged 75 and over (4 percent) and for women 65 to 84 years (also about 4 percent). These individuals likely married for the first time in the late 1940s and 1950s when people generally married very young and nearly everyone married. Since men have higher mortality rates, a lower percentage of women aged 85 and over in 2000 were now married (19 percent) than were men of that age (56 percent). The percentage of men and women aged 85 and over who were "married, spouse absent" was the

---

> **Marital status**: The marital status classification refers to the status on the census date, April 1, 2000. The "now married" category includes those who were "married, spouse present" and those who were "married, spouse absent." These latter two subcategories were determined in the processing and editing steps by the presence or absence of a spouse in the household as ascertained from the relationship-to-householder question on the long form and the assignment of people to related subfamilies. "Married, spouse present" applies to husbands and wives if both were living in the same household. "Married, spouse absent" applies to husbands and wives who answered that they were "Now married" on the census form but no spouse could be found who could be linked to them in the editing stages. Since people in group quarters housing (for example, institutions or shelters) were not asked the relationship item, all people in group quarters housing who reported that they were "Now married" were subsequently assigned to the "Married, spouse absent" category in the recoding steps.
>
> "**Separated**" refers to people who were not living with their spouse due to marital discord. "**Divorced**" indicates people who reported being divorced and had not remarried. "**Widowed**" indicates people whose last marriage ended with the death of their spouse and they had not remarried. The term "**Never married**" applies to those who had never been legally married or people whose only marriage ended in an annulment. All of the statistics in this report refer to the total population aged 15 and over living in both households and groups quarters.

---

same — 11 percent. It is likely that many of the absent spouses were in nursing homes.

The 45-to-54 age group had the highest percentage divorced for both men (15 percent) and women (18 percent). The percentage is slightly higher for women, which may be because women tend to remarry somewhat less often than men.[3] (As this item relates only to the marital status of the respondent at the time of the interview, information on the relative proportion of men and women who have ever been divorced is not available from Census 2000.) People aged

45 to 54 in 2000 were born from 1946 to 1955 and likely married for the first time in the 1970s, when divorce rates were climbing steadily (before leveling off in the late 1980s and 1990s), many divorce laws were liberalized, and no-fault divorce legislation was enacted in many states.

Asians had the lowest proportion separated or divorced.

Marital patterns often differ by race and Hispanic origin (Table 1). Census 2000 allowed respondents to choose more than one race. With the exception of the Two or more races group, all race groups discussed in this report refer to people who indicated *only one* racial identity among the six major categories: White, Black or African American,

---

[2] In 1990, data on marital status and relationship to reference person were edited simultaneously. Since information on marital status was only available in the sample data in 2000, data on marital status were edited independently, after the relationship item was edited. Small differences in marital status data between 1990 and 2000 should be treated with caution given these differences in editing procedures.

[3] Rose M. Kreider and Jason M. Fields, *Number, Timing, and Duration of Marriages and Divorces: 1996*, Current Population Reports, P70-80, U.S. Census Bureau, Washington, DC, 2002.

Table 1.
Marital Status of the Population Aged 15 and Over by Sex, Age, Race, and Hispanic Origin: 2000

(Data based on sample. For information on confidentiality protection, sampling error, nonsampling error, and definitions, see www.census.gov/prod/cen2000/doc/sf3.pdf)

Characteristic	Population aged 15 and over	Percent distribution						
		Total	Now married		Widowed	Divorced	Separated	Never married
			Spouse present	Spouse absent				
Total..........................	221,148,671	100.0	51.1	3.2	6.6	9.7	2.2	27.1
Men	107,027,405	100.0	52.9	3.9	2.5	8.6	1.8	30.3
15 to 19 years	10,243,740	100.0	0.7	3.1	0.1	0.1	0.2	95.8
20 to 24 years	9,705,979	100.0	12.9	6.0	0.2	1.2	0.9	78.8
25 to 29 years	9,682,926	100.0	38.6	5.5	0.2	4.6	1.9	49.2
30 to 34 years	10,219,811	100.0	55.0	4.9	0.3	8.0	2.3	29.6
35 to 44 years	22,797,615	100.0	63.3	3.8	0.5	12.0	2.6	17.9
45 to 54 years	18,425,577	100.0	69.4	2.8	1.0	14.7	2.4	9.7
55 to 64 years	11,569,387	100.0	74.6	2.4	2.8	12.6	1.9	5.6
65 to 74 years	8,355,575	100.0	74.9	2.5	8.3	8.3	1.4	4.6
75 to 84 years	4,823,419	100.0	67.3	4.6	18.2	4.9	0.9	4.1
85 years and over	1,203,376	100.0	45.4	10.9	35.3	3.3	0.8	4.3
Women	114,121,266	100.0	49.5	2.7	10.5	10.8	2.5	24.1
15 to 19 years	9,667,312	100.0	2.4	2.9	0.2	0.2	0.3	94.1
20 to 24 years	9,320,001	100.0	22.5	4.2	0.2	2.2	1.8	69.1
25 to 29 years	9,529,318	100.0	49.1	3.0	0.3	6.6	3.0	38.1
30 to 34 years	10,145,302	100.0	61.4	2.4	0.6	10.3	3.6	21.9
35 to 44 years	23,107,856	100.0	65.1	2.0	1.3	14.5	3.8	13.4
45 to 54 years	19,153,032	100.0	65.4	1.7	3.7	18.0	3.1	8.0
55 to 64 years	12,601,843	100.0	62.7	1.8	11.9	16.3	2.3	5.0
65 to 74 years	10,145,574	100.0	51.7	2.0	30.8	10.1	1.3	4.1
75 to 84 years	7,493,843	100.0	30.5	4.3	54.6	5.8	0.7	4.3
85 years and over	2,957,185	100.0	8.5	10.9	71.6	3.3	0.5	5.2
Men	107,027,405	100.0	52.9	3.9	2.5	8.6	1.8	30.3
White alone......................	82,527,456	100.0	56.8	2.8	2.6	9.0	1.4	27.3
Black or African American alone.....	11,691,001	100.0	34.2	7.3	3.0	9.5	4.4	41.6
American Indian and Alaska Native alone	870,020	100.0	40.1	5.3	2.2	11.3	2.7	38.5
Asian alone......................	3,862,972	100.0	53.3	6.4	1.3	3.3	1.1	34.6
Native Hawaiian and Other Pacific Islander alone	140,583	100.0	44.0	7.5	1.7	6.8	2.0	38.0
Some other race alone............	5,607,344	100.0	40.6	9.8	1.1	5.2	2.8	40.5
Two or more races	2,328,029	100.0	41.0	5.4	1.7	8.5	2.4	41.0
Hispanic or Latino (of any race).....	12,682,318	100.0	42.7	9.0	1.3	6.0	2.7	38.3
White alone, not Hispanic or Latino..	76,405,470	100.0	57.7	2.4	2.7	9.2	1.3	26.7
Women	114,121,266	100.0	49.5	2.7	10.5	10.8	2.5	24.1
White alone......................	87,653,093	100.0	53.2	2.2	11.2	10.9	1.8	20.8
Black or African American alone.....	13,626,532	100.0	27.5	3.7	10.4	12.8	5.9	39.7
American Indian and Alaska Native alone	901,416	100.0	40.0	3.5	7.4	13.7	3.7	31.7
Asian alone......................	4,293,154	100.0	55.8	4.8	7.0	5.1	1.5	25.8
Native Hawaiian and Other Pacific Islander alone	138,302	100.0	45.1	5.8	6.1	8.4	3.0	31.7
Some other race alone............	5,131,029	100.0	45.0	5.3	4.4	7.7	5.0	32.6
Two or more races	2,377,740	100.0	41.2	3.5	6.6	11.1	3.7	33.8
Hispanic or Latino (of any race).....	12,068,400	100.0	46.2	4.7	5.6	8.8	4.6	30.0
White alone, not Hispanic or Latino..	81,665,080	100.0	53.5	2.0	11.5	11.0	1.6	20.3

Source: U.S. Census Bureau, Census 2000 special tabulation.

American Indian and Alaska Native, Asian, Native Hawaiian or Other Pacific Islander, and Some other race.[4] The use of the single-race population in this report does not imply that it is the preferred method of presenting or analyzing data. The Census Bureau uses a variety of approaches.[5]

Asians had one of the highest percentages now married (60 percent for men; 61 percent for women) and the lowest proportion separated or divorced (4 percent for men; 7 percent for women), reflecting the lower incidence of divorce among Asians.[6]

Black men and women had the lowest percentages now married, and this percentage differed by sex. While 42 percent of Black men were now married, just 31 percent of Black women were married when Census 2000 was taken, the lowest proportion for women of any of the race or origin groups. The 10 percentage-point difference in the percentage of Black men and Black women who were now

married was the largest difference between men and women in any of the groups. Factors which might contribute to this difference include higher mortality among men than women, as well as differences in the incidence of intermarriage with other race/origin groups. Black men tend to marry non-Blacks more often than Black women do, resulting in a larger population of potential spouses for Black men. While 10 percent of married Black men had a spouse who was of a different race or origin than themselves, this was true for only 5 percent of married Black women.[7]

Overall, about 4 out of every 10 Black men and Black women had never been married, the highest proportion of any racial category. However, the difference between the percentage of Black men and Black women who had never been married was the smallest within any of the race/origin groups (2 percentage points). A slightly higher percentage of Black men than Black women were never married, mainly because these men marry later and, on average, marry women who are 2 to 3 years younger than they are.[8]

American Indians and Alaska Natives had the highest percentage divorced (11 percent for men; 14 percent for women). Among women, Blacks and Hispanics had the highest percentages separated: 6 percent and 5 percent,

respectively.[9] Research has shown that Black and Hispanic women are more likely to remain separated without getting a legal divorce than are women of other groups.[10]

REGIONAL AND STATE PATTERNS

The Northeast had the lowest percentage now married and the highest percentage never married.

Regional variations in the marital status distribution for the adult population aged 15 and over are relatively small; the estimates were no more than a few percentage points from the national averages (Table 2). People in the Northeast had the highest percentage never married (29 percent) and, correspondingly, had the lowest proportions who were now married (53 percent) and divorced (8 percent). People in the South had the lowest percentage never married (25 percent). The Midwest had the lowest percentage separated (2 percent), while the West had the lowest percentage widowed (6 percent). The Northeast, which had an older age structure than the West, had the highest proportion widowed (7 percent).

Geographic differences in marital status are related to many factors,

---

[4] Hereafter this report uses the term Black to refer to people who are Black or African American, the term Pacific Islander to refer to people who are Native Hawaiian and Other Pacific Islander, and the term Hispanic to refer to people who are Hispanic or Latino. For further information on each of the six major race groups and the Two or more races population, see reports from the Census 2000 Brief series (C2KBR/01), available on the Census 2000 Web site at *www.census.gov/population/www/cen2000 /briefs.html.*

[5] This report draws heavily on Summary File 3, a Census 2000 product that can be accessed through American FactFinder, available from the Census Bureau's Web site, *www.census.gov*. Information on people who reported more than one race, such as "White *and* American Indian and Alaska Native" or Asian *and* Black or African American," is available on Summary File 4, which can also be accessed through American FactFinder. About 2.6 percent of people reported more than one race.

[6] Rose M. Kreider and Jason M. Fields, *Number, Timing, and Duration of Marriages and Divorces: 1996,* Current Population Reports, P70-80, U.S. Census Bureau, Washington, DC, 2002.

[7] Tavia Simmons and Martin O'Connell, *Table 1, Hispanic Origin and Race of Wife and Husband for Married-Couple Households in the United States: 2000*, PHC-T-19, U.S. Census Bureau, *www.census.gov /population/www/cen2000/phc-t19.html*

[8] Rose M. Kreider and Jason M. Fields, *Number, Timing, and Duration of Marriages and Divorces: 1996,* Current Population Reports, P70-80, U.S. Census Bureau, Washington, DC, 2002.

[9] Because Hispanics may be of any race, data in this report for Hispanics overlap with data for racial groups. Based on Census 2000 sample data, the proportion Hispanic was 8.0 percent for Whites, 1.9 percent for Blacks, 14.6 percent for American Indians and Alaska Natives, 1.0 percent for Asians, 9.5 percent for Pacific Islanders, 97.1 percent for those reporting Some other race, and 31.1 percent for those reporting Two or more races.

Note that the percentage of Some other race women who were separated (5.0 percent) is greater than that for Hispanic women (4.6 percent).

[10] Matthew D. Bramlett and William D. Mosher, "Cohabitation, Marriage, Divorce and Remarriage in the United States," *Vital Health Statistics* 23:22, National Center for Health Statistics, Hyattsville, Maryland, 2002.

Table 2.
Marital Status of the Population Aged 15 and Over for the United States, Regions, and States and for Puerto Rico: 2000

(Data based on sample. For information on confidentiality protection, sampling and nonsampling error, and definitions, see www.census.gov/prod/cen2000/doc/sf3.pdf)

Area	Population aged 15 and over	Precent distribution						
		Total	Now married		Widowed	Divorced	Separated	Never married
			Spouse present	Spouse absent				
United States	221,148,671	100.0	51.1	3.2	6.6	9.7	2.2	27.1
Region								
Northeast.	42,697,789	100.0	49.3	3.4	7.4	8.2	2.5	29.3
Midwest.	50,588,742	100.0	52.7	2.5	6.7	9.8	1.5	26.8
South.	78,924,732	100.0	51.8	3.3	6.9	10.2	2.5	25.3
West	48,937,408	100.0	50.0	3.8	5.5	10.3	2.1	28.3
State								
Alabama	3,514,199	100.0	53.0	2.5	7.8	10.6	2.2	23.9
Alaska.	468,861	100.0	51.3	3.2	3.4	11.7	2.0	28.4
Arizona	3,979,336	100.0	51.6	3.4	6.0	11.1	1.8	26.1
Arkansas	2,111,663	100.0	55.1	3.2	7.6	11.0	1.9	21.2
California.	26,076,163	100.0	47.8	4.5	5.6	9.5	2.5	30.1
Colorado	3,385,369	100.0	52.5	3.1	4.7	11.0	1.6	27.0
Connecticut.	2,696,250	100.0	51.9	3.1	7.0	9.3	1.6	27.2
Delaware.	620,661	100.0	51.0	3.0	6.9	9.8	2.0	27.2
District of Columbia	474,417	100.0	24.9	5.0	7.8	9.7	4.2	48.4
Florida.	12,946,990	100.0	51.1	3.2	7.9	11.6	2.4	23.8
Georgia.	6,366,625	100.0	50.5	3.5	6.1	10.3	2.3	27.3
Hawaii	965,875	100.0	48.9	4.2	6.0	9.0	1.6	30.3
Idaho	991,624	100.0	57.3	2.7	5.3	10.6	1.2	22.8
Illinois	9,707,837	100.0	50.3	3.3	6.7	8.9	1.8	28.9
Indiana	4,771,040	100.0	53.9	2.5	6.6	10.9	1.3	24.8
Iowa.	2,324,863	100.0	55.6	2.2	7.2	9.1	1.0	24.9
Kansas	2,100,656	100.0	55.5	2.6	6.6	10.1	1.2	24.1
Kentucky	3,217,167	100.0	54.8	2.6	7.2	11.0	1.8	22.7
Louisiana.	3,466,380	100.0	48.1	3.1	7.4	10.2	2.6	28.6
Maine	1,028,823	100.0	54.2	2.1	7.1	11.5	1.2	23.9
Maryland	4,159,636	100.0	49.8	3.1	6.5	8.8	3.1	28.8
Massachusetts	5,091,369	100.0	48.9	2.8	7.0	8.3	2.0	31.1
Michigan	7,775,603	100.0	51.5	2.3	6.6	10.3	1.4	27.8
Minnesota	3,857,755	100.0	54.1	2.2	5.8	8.7	1.0	28.1
Mississippi.	2,203,615	100.0	48.8	2.7	7.9	10.1	2.9	27.7
Missouri.	4,414,391	100.0	53.0	2.4	7.1	10.8	1.8	24.8
Montana	715,915	100.0	54.7	2.6	6.5	10.9	1.3	24.0
Nebraska.	1,342,422	100.0	54.9	2.5	6.7	9.0	1.1	25.8
Nevada	1,563,580	100.0	49.9	3.5	5.5	13.8	2.3	24.9
New Hampshire	978,641	100.0	55.2	2.1	5.9	10.5	1.4	24.9
New Jersey.	6,655,333	100.0	51.4	3.3	7.4	7.5	2.4	28.1
New Mexico	1,398,496	100.0	50.5	2.5	6.1	11.6	1.8	27.5
New York.	15,055,876	100.0	45.8	4.2	7.2	7.8	3.2	31.7
North Carolina.	6,393,707	100.0	53.0	3.3	6.8	9.0	3.0	25.0
North Dakota.	512,281	100.0	54.5	2.3	7.2	7.8	0.7	27.6
Ohio.	8,952,721	100.0	52.4	2.0	7.1	10.6	1.6	26.2
Oklahoma	2,717,552	100.0	54.4	2.9	7.0	11.6	1.7	22.4
Oregon	2,722,134	100.0	52.9	2.6	6.1	11.6	1.7	25.1
Pennsylvania.	9,861,713	100.0	51.4	2.9	8.2	8.1	2.2	27.2
Rhode Island.	841,503	100.0	48.6	2.9	7.5	9.4	1.9	29.7
South Carolina	3,168,918	100.0	50.9	3.3	7.3	9.2	3.3	26.0
South Dakota	589,612	100.0	54.5	2.6	7.0	8.8	1.0	26.1
Tennessee.	4,522,630	100.0	53.5	2.6	7.0	11.3	2.0	23.5
Texas.	15,937,643	100.0	52.3	4.2	5.7	9.8	2.5	25.6
Utah.	1,639,688	100.0	56.3	2.4	4.1	8.1	1.2	27.9
Vermont.	488,281	100.0	53.2	2.0	6.3	10.6	1.3	26.7
Virginia	5,623,628	100.0	52.4	3.3	6.2	9.0	2.9	26.2
Washington	4,639,522	100.0	52.6	2.7	5.4	11.4	1.6	26.3
West Virginia.	1,479,301	100.0	55.1	2.1	8.8	10.4	1.5	22.1
Wisconsin	4,239,561	100.0	53.6	2.6	6.4	9.0	1.2	27.2
Wyoming.	390,845	100.0	55.6	2.5	5.7	11.6	1.2	23.3
Puerto Rico	2,903,329	100.0	49.4	2.6	6.8	9.6	3.6	28.0

Source: US Census Bureau, Census 2000 Summary File 3.

ranging from religious, cultural, and ethnic patterns to current social and economic circumstances. For example, some areas may attract younger single people because of jobs or educational opportunities, while other areas may attract older people because of climate and amenities for the retired population.

As was true for regional variation, marital status by state showed relatively little variation. The largest variations were observed among the now married and the never married categories. Idaho had the highest percentage of people now married (60 percent), followed by Utah (59 percent). Excluding the District of Columbia with 30 percent, New York had the lowest proportion now married (50 percent). Corresponding with the lower percentage now married, the percentage of people in the District of Columbia who were never married was 48 percent. The state with the highest percentage never married was New York (32 percent), followed by Massachusetts (31 percent). In contrast, 21 percent of the adult population in Arkansas in 2000 had never been married.

State estimates of the percentages widowed, divorced, and separated deviated only a few percentage points from the national averages. West Virginia had the highest percentage of people who were widowed (9 percent), followed by Pennsylvania (8 percent). Alaska (3 percent) had the lowest proportion widowed, followed by Utah (4 percent), reflecting the younger age structure in these states. Nevada had the highest proportion of divorced adults (14 percent). New Jersey (7.5 percent) had the lowest proportion of divorced adults. No state differed more than 2 percentage points from the

national average of 2 percent of adults who were separated.

The overall distributions shown in Table 2, however, mask some important differences among the states in the timing of marriage if the data are examined by age. For example, Table 2 shows that only 1 percentage point separated Arkansas and New Hampshire in the proportion of adults in each state who were now married (58 percent and 57 percent, respectively). However, among young adults aged 15 to 24 years, more than twice the percentage in Arkansas were now married (20 percent) compared with young adults in New Hampshire (8 percent).[11]

COUNTY PATTERNS

In the United States, there were 86 unmarried men per 100 unmarried women.

While no single indicator can capture the marital status profile of an area, a frequently used index, the ratio of unmarried men to unmarried women aged 15 and over, shown in Figure 2, summarizes the potential numbers of men and women available for marriage. This measure indicates how many widowed, divorced, and never married men live in an area per 100 women of the same age range and marital status.[12] A ratio of 100 means the numbers of unmarried men and women are equal.

Nationally, there were 86 unmarried men for every 100 unmarried women in 2000. The ratio of unmarried men per 100 unmarried

women by state shows a general pattern of higher ratios in the West than in other regions (see Figure 3). Of the states, Alaska had the highest ratio (114).[13] However, the county-level map shows that high-ratio areas are sprinkled throughout the United States. Many of these counties contain or are near Armed Forces installations, or other institutions that affect the characteristics of the area (for example, correctional facilities, retirement communities, or colleges). Alaska is an exception to this generalization: most of its counties have higher ratios than are found in most of the lower 48 states, but it does not have large military installations or prisons throughout the state. More likely, the forestry, fishing, hunting, mining, and construction industries, which involve a higher percentage of the workforce in Alaska than in the United States as a whole, attract young men as workers, creating unusually high ratios of unmarried men to unmarried women. Lower ratios appear more prevalent in the southern part of the United States. However, areas of New England also appear to have clusters of relatively lower-than-average ratios.

Suburbs of larger cities tend to have the highest percentage of people now married.

Table 3 shows differences in marital status among places of 100,000 or more population,[14] using three indicators for the population aged 15 and over: the ratio of unmarried men per 100 unmarried women, the percentage now married, and the

---

[11] See Table 1 in PHC-T-27, "Marital Status for the Population 15 Years and Over for the United States, Regions, States, Puerto Rico, and Metropolitan Areas: 2000."

[12] For this particular index, separated people are not included in the unmarried population since they are currently married and not available legally to be married to someone else.

[13] See Table 4 in PHC-T-27, "Marital Status..."

[14] Census 2000 shows 245 places in the United States with 100,000 or more population. They include 238 incorporated places (including 4 city-county consolidations) and 7 census designated places that are not legally incorporated. For a list of these places by state, see www.census.gov /population/www/cen2000/phc-t6.html.

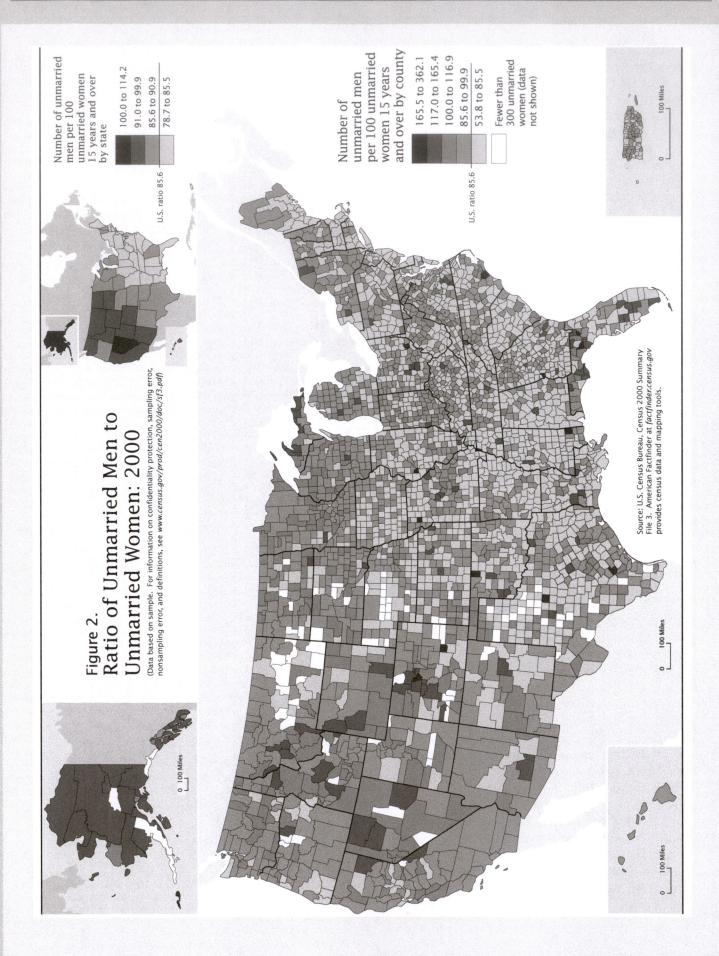

Figure 2.
Ratio of Unmarried Men to
Unmarried Women: 2000

(Data based on sample. For information on confidentiality protection, sampling error, nonsampling error, and definitions, see www.census.gov/prod/cen2000/doc/sf3.pdf)

Number of unmarried
men per 100
unmarried women
15 years and over
by state

100.0 to 114.2
91.0 to 99.9
85.6 to 90.9
78.7 to 85.5

U.S. ratio 85.6

Number of
unmarried men
per 100 unmarried
women 15 years
and over by county

165.5 to 362.1
117.0 to 165.4
100.0 to 116.9
85.6 to 99.9
53.8 to 85.5
Fewer than
300 unmarried
women (data
not shown)

U.S. ratio 85.6

Source: U.S. Census Bureau, Census 2000 Summary File 3. American Factfinder at factfinder.census.gov provides census data and mapping tools.

Table 3.
Top Places of 100,000 or More Population for Selected Marital Status Indicators: 2000

(Data based on sample. For information on confidentiality protection, sampling and nonsampling error, and definitions, see www.census.gov/prod/cen2000/doc/sf3.pdf)

Place	Population aged 15 and over	Indicator	90-percent confidence interval
Ratio of unmarried men per 100 unmarried women[1]			
Paradise, NV*..	152,439	118	115 - 121
Fort Lauderdale, FL	127,704	115	112 - 118
Tempe, AZ..	132,180	114	111 - 117
Sunnyvale, CA..	108,569	113	109 - 117
Santa Ana, CA..	238,293	113	110 - 116
Salinas, CA...	109,822	111	107 - 114
Oxnard, CA...	125,006	109	106 - 113
Costa Mesa, CA	87,017	106	103 - 110
North Las Vegas, NV	81,204	106	102 - 110
Austin, TX..	530,599	104	103 - 106
Percent now married[2]			
Naperville, IL	93,332	67.7	67.3 - 68.2
Gilbert, AZ..	77,383	66.7	66.0 - 67.4
Plano, TX	168,437	66.5	66.0 - 67.0
Cape Coral, FL	83,133	63.2	62.5 - 63.9
Carrollton, TX...	83,329	61.4	60.7 - 62.1
Overland Park, KS	116,721	61.2	60.7 - 61.7
Thousand Oaks, CA	91,562	61.2	60.6 - 61.9
Livonia, MI	80,932	61.1	60.5 - 61.7
Fremont, CA..	158,764	61.1	60.6 - 61.6
Corona, CA...	88,878	60.3	59.6 - 61.0
Percent formerly married[3]			
Gary, IN..	77,131	27.2	26.6 - 27.9
Clearwater, FL..	90,616	26.8	26.2 - 27.4
Birmingham, AL..	192,220	26.8	26.4 - 27.2
St. Petersburg, FL....................................	202,979	26.7	26.3 - 27.1
Hollywood, FL	114,192	26.6	26.1 - 27.1
Louisville, KY	205,336	26.3	26.0 - 26.6
Cleveland, OH	361,237	26.2	25.9 - 26.5
St. Louis, MO..	272,873	25.9	25.6 - 26.2
Miami, FL	297,081	25.7	25.4 - 26.0
Chattanooga, TN.......................................	126,215	25.6	25.2 - 26.1

* Paradise, NV, is a census designated place and is not legally incorporated.

[1] Unmarried includes widowed, divorced and never married.

[2] Now married includes married spouse present and married spouse absent.

[3] Formerly married includes widowed, divorced, and separated.

Note: Because of sampling error, the estimates in this table may not be significantly different from one another or from rates for other geographic areas not listed in this table.

Note: In Census 2000, there were 245 places in the United States with 100,000 or more population. They included 238 incorporated places (including 4 city-county consolidations) and 7 census designated places (CDPs) that were not legally incorporated. For a list of these places by state, see the footnote in the table at www.census.gov/population/www/cen2000/phc-t6/tab04.pdf.

Source: U.S. Census Bureau, Census 2000 Summary File 3.

percentage formerly married. Paradise, Nevada (an unincorporated suburb of Las Vegas); Fort Lauderdale, Florida; Tempe, Arizona; Sunnyvale and Santa Ana, California, had ratios of unmarried men per 100 unmarried women which were above the national average.

Naperville, Illinois; Gilbert, Arizona; and Plano, Texas, had the highest percentages of married people

(above 65 percent). Some of the top places for the percentage married are suburbs of larger cities, which may attract married-couple families with children.

Places with a high percentage of formerly married people (those widowed, separated, or divorced) included Gary, Indiana; Clearwater, Florida; Birmingham, Alabama; St. Petersburg, Florida; and Hollywood,

Florida (27 percent). The high rates in Clearwater, Hollywood, and St. Petersburg probably reflect the older age structure in these cities, which means a higher proportion of people likely to have been divorced and widowed. Meanwhile, the high percentage of formerly married people in Gary, Indiana, and Birmingham, Alabama, is partly the result of a relatively high proportion of Blacks in these places (over

Table 4.
Percent of the Population Aged 15 and Over by Sex and Age in Specified Marital Status: 1950 to 2000

(Data based on sample. For information on confidentiality protection, sampling and nonsampling error, and definitions, see www.census.gov/prod/cen2000/doc/sf3.pdf)

Sex and year	15 to 24 years, never married	25 to 34 years			35 to 59 years		60 years and over		
		Never married	Divorced	Separated	Divorced	Separated	Married	Divorced or separated	Widowed
Men									
1950.............	77.4	18.7	1.9	1.6	2.7	2.0	68.6	3.8	19.1
1960.............	77.2	16.2	2.0	1.6	2.9	1.8	73.1	4.1	15.1
1970.............	77.9	15.5	3.1	1.9	3.7	1.9	74.8	4.8	13.2
1980.............	82.8	23.9	7.6	2.7	7.4	2.4	79.1	5.5	11.4
1990.............	88.0	36.1	7.3	2.5	11.8	2.7	76.3	7.1	11.4
2000.............	87.5	39.1	6.4	2.1	13.2	2.5	74.9	9.3	11.2
Women									
1950.............	56.4	11.3	2.8	2.5	3.4	2.5	42.2	2.7	46.5
1960.............	58.6	8.6	2.9	2.8	4.0	2.5	43.3	3.6	44.8
1970.............	63.8	10.0	4.6	3.4	5.4	2.9	42.7	4.9	44.5
1980.............	70.9	16.3	10.1	3.9	10.0	3.3	44.9	6.0	44.1
1990.............	78.9	25.0	9.8	3.8	15.0	3.5	44.5	7.7	42.5
2000.............	81.8	29.7	8.5	3.3	16.3	3.4	46.4	10.3	38.9

Source: U.S. Census Bureau, Census 2000 Summary File 3; U.S. Bureau of the Census, 1990 Census of Population, *General Population Characteristics,* United States (1990 CP-1-1); 1980 Census of Population, *Characteristics of the Population,* United States Summary (PC80-1-D1-A); U.S. Census of Population: 1970, Detailed Characteristics Final Report PC(1)-D1, United States Summary; U.S. Census of Population: 1960, Vol. I. Characteristics of the Population, Part 1, United States Summary; U.S. Census of Population: 1950, Vol. II. Characteristics of the Population, Part 2, United States Summary.

70 percent of the total population), since nationally, of all races, Blacks had the highest proportion formerly married (Table 1).

ADDITIONAL FINDINGS

This section discusses several topics related to changes in the distribution of marital status from 1950 to 2000 for different age groups (see Table 4), and the connection between the ratio of unmarried men to women and the different life expectancies of men and women.

A smaller gap in life expectancy between men and women is associated with a higher ratio of unmarried men to unmarried women.

While sharp differences in the ratio of unmarried men per 100 unmarried women from area to area may be explained by place characteristics or migration patterns, at the national level, the ratio is affected

by changes in the gap between men and women in life expectancy.[15] During periods when women live significantly longer than men, the ratio of unmarried men to women tends to be lower than when the gap in life expectancy narrows. Then the ratio tends to be higher as more men survive throughout the life span of their wives, resulting in fewer widowed spouses. For example, in 1950 and in 2000, the gap in years between men's and women's average remaining life expectancy at age 15 was 5.0 years and 5.3 years, respectively, that is, women were expected to live about 5 years longer than men once they attained age 15.[16] The ratio of

[15] The ratio of unmarried men per 100 unmarried women may also be affected by the sex ratio at birth, the proportion ever married, and international migration.

[16] The life expectancy at age 15 for the years 1949-1951, 1959-1961, 1969-1971, 1979-1981, 1990, and 2000 is from: Elizabeth Arias, United States Life Tables, 2000, *National Vital Statistics Reports;* Vol. 51, No. 3, National Center for Health Statistics, Hyattsville, Maryland, 2002.

unmarried men per 100 unmarried women was 91 in 1950 and 86 in 2000.[17] But in 1970 and 1980, when the gap between men and women's life expectancy was 7.3 years, the ratio was lower, at 81 unmarried men per 100 women.

Have people increasingly delayed marriage since 1950?

In both 1950 and 2000, the majority of men and women aged 15 to 24 had never married, but the percentage increased during this time period by 11 percentage points for men (from 77 percent to 88 percent) and by 25 percentage points for women (from 56 percent to 82 percent). Most of the change occurred between 1970 and 1990 for both men and women.

[17] The ratios of unmarried men per 100 unmarried women were calculated using decennial census data tabulated by age, sex, and marital status for 1950 through 2000.

The percentage of people aged 25 to 34 who were never married also increased from 1950 to 2000, from 19 percent to 39 percent for men and from 11 percent to 30 percent for women. Most of these increases occurred in the 1970s and 1980s.

The percentage of both men and women aged 25 to 34 who were never married declined during the 1950s (the peak of the 1946 - 1964 Baby Boom), meaning that on average, people married earlier in 1960 than in 1950. Indeed, the median age at first marriage had been higher prior to the 1950s: for 1890, it was calculated at 26 years for men and 22 years for women, whereas in 1950, it was 23 years for men and 20 years for women.[18]

Were higher percentages of men and women aged 25 to 59 separated and divorced in 2000 than in 1950?

From 1950 to 2000, the percentage of people aged 25 to 34 who were divorced increased from 2 percent to 6 percent for men and from 3 percent to 9 percent for women. The corresponding increases for people aged 35 to 59 were from 3 percent to 13 percent for men and from 3 percent to 16 percent for women.

For those aged 25 to 34, the percentage divorced increased from 1950 to 1980, but subsequently decreased by several percentage points between 1980 and 2000 for both men and women. However, for both men and women aged 35 to 59, the percentages divorced increased by about 6 percentage points during the later period.

The small percentage-point decline in the percentage divorced among those aged 25 to 34 from 1980 to 2000 reflects the fact that people now marry later, thus reducing the possibility of a divorce during this age span. The increase in the median age at first marriage since 1980 has pushed the married population who might experience a first divorce into older age groups, resulting in an increased percentage of those aged 35 to 59 years who were divorced. The percentage of adults who are currently divorced is related also to recent declines in the likelihood of remarriage.[19]

Changes in the percentage of adults by age group who were separated show a similar pattern. The percentage of adults aged 25 to 34 who were separated declined slightly from 1980 to 2000, while the percentage of separated adults aged 35 to 59 remained roughly the same.

How has the percentage of people in various marital statuses changed among people aged 60 and over?

The percentage of men aged 60 and over who were widowed declined steadily from 19 percent in 1950 to 11 percent in 1980 and has remained at this level. The corresponding percentage of women also declined, from 47 percent in 1950 to 39 percent in 2000. Men's increased life expectancy may help explain both the decrease in the percentage of women aged 60 and over who were widowed (since their husbands were living longer) and the increase since 1970 in the percentage who were married.

In this same age group, the percentage of men who were married increased from 69 percent in 1950 to a high of 79 percent in 1980, before decreasing to 75 percent in 2000, the same level as in 1970. In contrast, for women aged 60 and over, the percentage who were married increased from 42 percent in 1950 to 46 percent in 2000.

What is the ratio of wives to partners among women aged 15 to 24?

Cohabitation is often a precursor to marriage, but on other occasions it is a short-term living arrangement. As the age at first marriage has risen, the likelihood that a woman will live with a partner before she marries also has increased. Survey data in 1995 indicated that a higher percentage of women aged 15 to 24 had ever cohabited than had ever married.[20]

In order to portray the current marital status of young people living together as couples who are maintaining their own households, Figure 3 shows, by state, the ratio of wives to unmarried partners for women aged 15 to 24.[21] The data are limited to couples maintaining their own households, and thus do not include married or unmarried couples living in other people's households.[22] Ratios greater than 1.0 indicate more women are living with men as wives than as their unmarried partners. However,

---

[18] This median is estimated based on ever married men and women. See Table MS-2, Estimated Median Age at First Marriage, by Sex, 1890 to the Present at www.census.gov /population/socdemo/hh-fam/tabMS-2.txt.

[19] Analysis of the National Survey of Family Growth, Cycle 2 (1976) compared with Cycle 5 (1995) indicates a decreasing probability that a woman will remarry within 5 years of divorce. Matthew D. Bramlett and William D. Mosher, "Cohabitation, Marriage, Divorce and Remarriage in the United States," *Vital Health Statistics* 23:22, National Center for Health Statistics, Hyattsville, Maryland, 2002.

[20] Matthew D. Bramlett and William D. Mosher, "Cohabitation, Marriage, Divorce and Remarriage in the United States," *Vital Health Statistics* 23:22, National Center for Health Statistics, Hyattsville, Maryland, 2002.
[21] Unmarried partners may have a marital status of widowed, divorced, separated, or never married.
[22] Although Census 2000 data permit the identification of "wives" in related subfamilies, it is not possible to estimate, in a similar fashion, the number of unmarried partners in a household unless one partner is the householder. For comparability reasons, only spouses and partners of the householder or the female householders themselves are used in this measure.

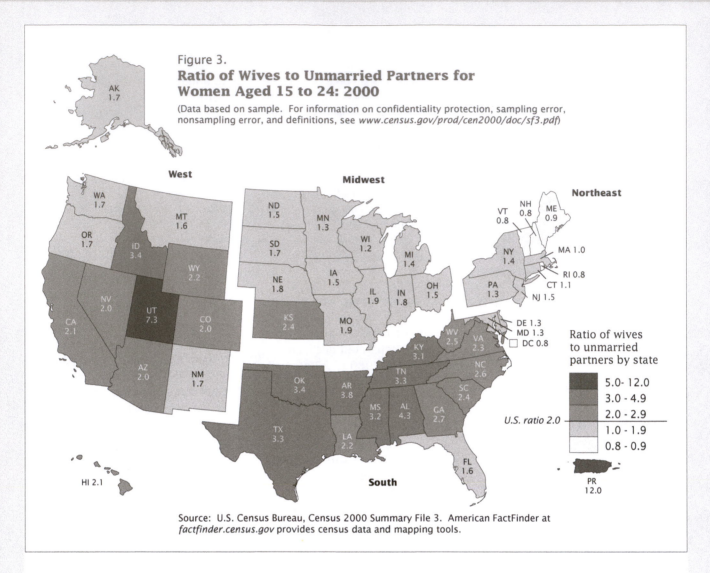

Figure 3.
Ratio of Wives to Unmarried Partners for Women Aged 15 to 24: 2000

(Data based on sample. For information on confidentiality protection, sampling error, nonsampling error, and definitions, see *www.census.gov/prod/cen2000/doc/sf3.pdf*)

Ratio of wives to unmarried partners by state

5.0- 12.0	
3.0 - 4.9	
2.0 - 2.9	
U.S. ratio 2.0	
1.0 - 1.9	
0.8 - 0.9	

Source: U.S. Census Bureau, Census 2000 Summary File 3. American FactFinder at *factfinder.census.gov* provides census data and mapping tools.

since the duration of cohabitations is shorter on average than that of marriages, and because many cohabitations become marriages, the point in time estimates shown in Census 2000 are likely to count more wives than unmarried partners since women who have been partners may have already married their partners, or may have ended the partnerships.

Overall, the national average ratio of wives to unmarried partners for women aged 15 to 24 was 2.0 in 2000. Only four states had ratios under 1.0: Maine, New Hampshire, Rhode Island, and Vermont. A ratio under 1.0 was also recorded for the District of Columbia. Utah

recorded the highest ratio, with more than 7 times as many wives as partners in this age group. Utah also had the highest proportion of people aged 15 to 24 who were married. The regional pattern is also consistent with marital patterns which indicate that women 15 to 24 years in the South and the West had higher proportions who were now married (20 percent and 18 percent, respectively) than did women in the Northeast and the Midwest (11 percent and 14 percent, respectively).[23]

_____
[23] See Table 3 in PHC-T-27, "Marital Status...," *www.census.gov/population/www /cen2000/phc-t27.html.*

ABOUT CENSUS 2000

Why Census 2000 asked about marital status.

Planning and implementing many government programs calls for accurate information on marital status, including the numbers of employed married women, elderly widows living alone, and single young people who may soon establish homes of their own. Data about marital status are used for budget and resource planning to identify the number of children needing special services, such as children in single-parent households. Local governments need data about marital status to assess the need for housing and services under Community Development Block Grant Evaluation. Other examples of statutory applications include the Public Health Service Act, Child Welfare Act, Adolescent Family Life Projects, and Low-Income Tax Credits.

Accuracy of the Estimates

The data contained in this report are based on the sample of households who responded to the Census 2000 long form. Nationally, approximately 1 out of every 6 housing units was included in this sample. As a result, the sample estimates may differ somewhat from the 100- percent figures that would have been obtained if all housing units, people within those housing units, and people living in group quarters had been enumerated using the same questionnaires, instructions, enumerators, and so forth. The sample estimates also differ from the values that would have been obtained from different samples of housing units, people within those housing units, and people living in group quarters. The deviation of a sample estimate from the average of all possible samples is called the sampling error.

In addition to the variability that arises from the sampling procedures, both sample data and 100-percent data are subject to nonsampling error. Nonsampling error may be introduced during any of the various complex operations used to collect and process data. Such errors may include: not enumerating every household or every person in the population, failing to obtain all required information from the respondents, obtaining incorrect or inconsistent information, and recording information incorrectly. In addition, errors can occur during the field review of the enumerators' work, during clerical handling of the census questionnaires, or during the electronic processing of the questionnaires.

Nonsampling error may affect the data in two ways: (1) errors that are introduced randomly will increase the variability of the data and, therefore, should be reflected in the standard errors; and (2) errors that tend to be consistent in one direction will bias both sample and 100-percent data in that direction. For example, if respondents consistently tend to underreport their incomes, then the resulting estimates of households or families by income category will tend to be understated for the higher income categories and overstated for the lower income categories. Such biases are not reflected in the standard errors.

While it is impossible to completely eliminate error from an operation as large and complex as the decennial census, the Census Bureau attempts to control the sources of such error during the data collection and processing operations. The primary sources of error and the programs instituted to control error in Census 2000 are described in detail in *Summary File 3 Technical Documentation* under Chapter 8, "Accuracy of the Data," located at *www.census.gov /prod/cen2000/doc/sf3.pdf*.

All statements in this Census 2000 Brief have undergone statistical testing and all comparisons are significant at the 90-percent confidence level, unless otherwise noted. The estimates in tables, maps, and other figures may vary from actual values due to sampling and nonsampling errors. As a result, estimates in one category may not be significantly different from estimates assigned to a different category. Further information on the accuracy of the data is located at *www.census.gov/prod /cen2000/doc/sf3.pdf*. For further information on the computation and use of standard errors, contact the Decennial Statistical Studies Division at 301-763-4242.

For More Information

The Census 2000 Summary File 3 data are available from the American FactFinder on the Internet (*factfinder.census.gov*). They were released on a state-by-state basis during 2002. For information on confidentiality protection, nonsampling error, sampling error, and definitions, also see *www.census.gov/prod/cen2000 /doc/sf3.pdf* or contact the Customer Services Center at 301-763-INFO (4636).

Information on population and housing topics is presented in the Census 2000 Brief series, located on the Census Bureau's Web site at *www.census.gov/population/www /cen2000/briefs.html*. This series presents information on race, Hispanic origin, age, sex, household type, housing tenure, and social, economic, and housing characteristics, such as ancestry, income, and housing costs.

For additional information on marital status, including reports and survey data, visit the Census Bureau's Internet site at *www.census.gov/population /www/socdemo/ms-la.html* or *www.census.gov/population/www /socdemo/marr-div.html*. To find information about the availability of data products, including reports, CD-ROMs, and DVDs, call the Customer Services Center at 301-763-INFO (4636), or e-mail *webmaster@census.gov*.

Educational Attainment: 2000

Issued August 2003

Census 2000 Brief

C2KBR-24

By
Kurt J. Bauman
and
Nikki L. Graf

The education levels of the United States population reached an all-time high, according to Census 2000.[1] Of the 182.2 million people aged 25 and over on April 1, 2000, 80 percent had a high school diploma or more, and 24 percent had completed at least a bachelor's degree.

Education has been included in the United States census questionnaire since 1840, when information was collected on literacy of the population 20 years and over. Since that time, questions on education have become more complex. From 1940 to 1980, the census inquired about the number of years of school each person had completed. In 1990 and 2000, the question was updated to reflect current interest in both level of school completed and the types of degrees (if any) people had received. The Census 2000 question allowed respondents to choose from a list of 16 educational levels, ranging from no schooling completed to professional or doctoral degrees (see Figure 1).

This report, part of a series that presents population and housing data collected by

Figure 1.
Reproduction of the Question on Educational Attainment From Census 2000

9 What is the highest degree or level of school this person has COMPLETED? *Mark* [x] *ONE box.*
If currently enrolled, mark the previous grade or highest degree received.

- ☐ No schooling completed
- ☐ Nursery school to 4th grade
- ☐ 5th grade or 6th grade
- ☐ 7th grade or 8th grade
- ☐ 9th grade
- ☐ 10th grade
- ☐ 11th grade
- ☐ 12th grade, **NO DIPLOMA**
- ☐ **HIGH SCHOOL GRADUATE —** high school DIPLOMA or the equivalent *(for example: GED)*
- ☐ Some college credit, but less than 1 year
- ☐ 1 or more years of college, no degree
- ☐ Associate degree *(for example: AA, AS)*
- ☐ Bachelor's degree *(for example: BA, AB, BS)*
- ☐ Master's degree *(for example: MA, MS, MEng, MEd, MSW, MBA)*
- ☐ Professional degree *(for example: MD, DDS, DVM, LLB, JD)*
- ☐ Doctorate degree *(for example: PhD, EdD)*

Source: U.S. Census Bureau, Census 2000 questionnaire.

[1] Comparison with the 1990 census shows a significantly higher proportion of the population 25 and over in 2000 completing each of the following thresholds or more: 5th, 9th, 10th, 11th, and 12th grade without a diploma, high school diploma, some college, associate degree, bachelor's degree, master's degree, professional degree, and doctoral degree. Censuses from 1940 through 1980 showed even lower levels of education at the high school and bachelor's degree level (see Figure 3). The text of this report discusses data for the United States, including the 50 states and the District of Columbia. Data for the Commonwealth of Puerto Rico are shown in Table 1 and Figure 4.

USCENSUSBUREAU
Helping You Make Informed Decisions

U.S. Department of Commerce
Economics and Statistics Administration
U.S. CENSUS BUREAU

United States Census 2000

Census 2000, presents data on the educational attainment of people 25 years and over in the United States. This report describes education distributions for the United States, including regions, states, counties, and places with populations of 100,000 or more.

Education levels in the United States were high and rising.

In 2000, most people 25 years and over in the United States had earned a high school diploma or higher degree (Figure 2).[2] The three most commonly achieved education levels were high school graduate (29 percent), bachelor's degree (16 percent), and 1 or more years of college, but no degree (14 percent). More than 1 in 20 people had obtained a master's degree (6 percent), an associate degree (6 percent), or completed some college, but less than 1 year (7 percent). Professional and doctoral degrees were relatively rare, as were the categories of education below high school. No one of these education levels accounted for as much as 4 percent of the population 25 and over.

More than half the U.S. population 25 and over in 2000 (52 percent) had completed at least some college education (Table 1). Just under one quarter (24 percent) had a bachelor's degree or more. Nine percent had an advanced degree (master's degree, professional degree, or doctoral degree).

Growth in the population 25 and over contributed to an increase in the number of people with high school or more education: 146.5 million in 2000, an increase of 27.0 million over 1990. The

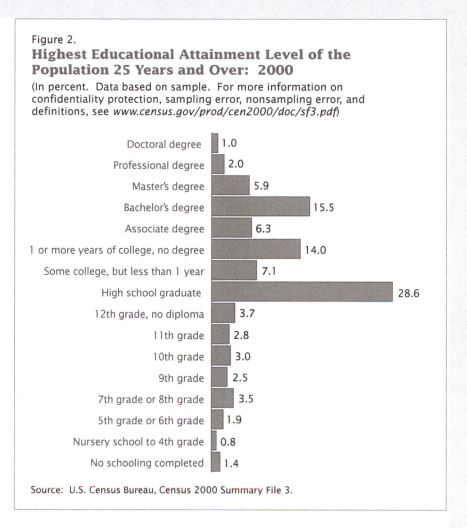

Figure 2.

Highest Educational Attainment Level of the Population 25 Years and Over: 2000

(In percent. Data based on sample. For more information on confidentiality protection, sampling error, nonsampling error, and definitions, see *www.census.gov/prod/cen2000/doc/sf3.pdf*)

Category	Percent
Doctoral degree	1.0
Professional degree	2.0
Master's degree	5.9
Bachelor's degree	15.5
Associate degree	6.3
1 or more years of college, no degree	14.0
Some college, but less than 1 year	7.1
High school graduate	28.6
12th grade, no diploma	3.7
11th grade	2.8
10th grade	3.0
9th grade	2.5
7th grade or 8th grade	3.5
5th grade or 6th grade	1.9
Nursery school to 4th grade	0.8
No schooling completed	1.4

Source: U.S. Census Bureau, Census 2000 Summary File 3.

number with a bachelor's degree or more increased by 12.2 million to 44.5 million, while the population with less than a high school diploma actually decreased during the decade from 1990 to 2000, falling by 3.6 million to 35.7 million.

The high levels of education observed in 2000 reflect a steady increase in educational attainment that took place over much of the preceding century. Figure 3 shows the levels of high school and college completion for the 25-and-over population from the censuses of 1940 to 2000.[3] In 1940, only

24 percent of the population 25 and over had completed high school. During a span of 60 years, high school has gone from being the mark of the educated minority of the population to the minimum education level for 4 out of 5 adults.

College completion rates also increased from 1940 to 2000. While just under 1 adult in 20 held a bachelor's degree in 1940, almost 1 adult in 4 had attained this educational level in 2000. For both levels of schooling recorded here (high school or more, and

---

[2] The estimates in this report are based on responses from a sample of the population. As with all surveys, estimates may vary from the actual values because of sampling variation or other factors. All statements made in this report have undergone statistical testing and are significant at the 90-percent confidence level unless otherwise noted.

[3] From 1940 to 1980, the census question on educational attainment asked about years of school completed, rather than about completion of degrees. For the purposes of this comparison, people with 12 or more years of education were considered high school graduates, while those with 16 or more years of

education were considered college graduates. For further discussion of the difference between asking about years and about degrees see Robert Kominski and Paul Siegel, "Measuring Education in the Current Population Survey," *Monthly Labor Review*, September 1993, pp. 34-38.

Table 1.
Educational Attainment of the Population 25 Years and Over for the United States, Regions, and States, and for Puerto Rico: 1990 and 2000

(Data based on sample. For information on confidentiality protection, sampling error, nonsampling error, and definitions, see www.census.gov/prod/cen2000/doc/sf3.pdf)

Area	1990					2000				
		Percent					Percent			
	Population 25 and over	High school graduate or more	Some college or more	Bachelor's degree or more	Advanced degree	Population 25 and over	High school graduate or more	Some college or more	Bachelor's degree or more	Advanced degree
United States.	158,868,436	75.2	45.2	20.3	7.2	182,211,639	80.4	51.8	24.4	8.9
Region										
Northeast.	33,544,628	76.2	44.0	22.8	9.0	35,828,187	81.6	50.9	27.5	11.0
Midwest.	37,873,006	77.1	43.1	18.4	6.3	41,537,007	83.5	51.1	22.9	7.9
South.	54,335,585	71.3	42.3	18.7	6.5	64,921,533	77.7	49.0	22.5	8.1
West	33,115,217	78.6	53.7	22.7	7.7	39,924,912	80.5	57.7	26.2	9.2
State										
Alabama	2,545,969	66.9	37.4	15.7	5.5	2,887,400	75.3	44.9	19.0	6.9
Alaska	323,429	86.6	57.9	23.0	8.0	379,556	88.3	60.5	24.7	8.6
Arizona	2,301,177	78.7	52.5	20.3	7.0	3,256,184	81.0	56.7	23.5	8.4
Arkansas	1,496,150	66.3	33.6	13.3	4.5	1,731,200	75.3	41.2	16.7	5.7
California.	18,695,499	76.2	53.9	23.4	8.1	21,298,900	76.8	56.7	26.6	9.5
Colorado	2,107,072	84.4	57.9	27.0	9.0	2,776,632	86.9	63.7	32.7	11.1
Connecticut	2,198,963	79.2	49.7	27.2	11.0	2,295,617	84.0	55.5	31.4	13.3
Delaware	428,499	77.5	44.8	21.4	7.7	514,658	82.6	51.2	25.0	9.4
District of Columbia	409,131	73.1	51.9	33.3	17.2	384,535	77.8	57.2	39.1	21.0
Florida	8,887,168	74.4	44.3	18.3	6.3	11,024,645	79.9	51.1	22.3	8.1
Georgia	4,023,420	70.9	41.3	19.3	6.4	5,185,965	78.6	49.9	24.3	8.3
Hawaii	709,820	80.1	51.3	22.9	7.1	802,477	84.6	56.1	26.2	8.4
Idaho	601,292	79.7	49.3	17.7	5.3	787,505	84.7	56.2	21.7	6.8
Illinois	7,293,930	76.2	46.2	21.0	7.5	7,973,671	81.4	53.7	26.1	9.5
Indiana.	3,489,470	75.6	37.4	15.6	6.4	3,893,278	82.1	44.9	19.4	7.2
Iowa.	1,776,798	80.1	41.6	16.9	5.2	1,895,856	86.1	50.0	21.2	6.5
Kansas	1,565,936	81.3	48.4	21.1	7.0	1,701,207	86.0	56.2	25.8	8.7
Kentucky	2,333,833	64.6	32.9	13.6	5.5	2,646,397	74.1	40.6	17.1	6.9
Louisiana.	2,536,994	68.3	36.6	16.1	5.6	2,775,468	74.8	42.4	18.7	6.5
Maine.	795,613	78.8	41.7	18.8	6.1	869,893	85.4	49.2	22.9	7.9
Maryland	3,122,665	78.4	50.3	26.5	10.9	3,495,595	83.8	57.1	31.4	13.4
Massachusetts.	3,962,223	80.0	50.3	27.2	10.6	4,273,275	84.8	57.5	33.2	13.7
Michigan	5,842,642	76.8	44.5	17.4	6.4	6,415,941	83.4	52.1	21.8	8.1
Minnesota	2,770,562	82.4	49.4	21.8	6.3	3,164,345	87.9	59.1	27.4	8.3
Mississippi	1,538,997	64.3	36.8	14.7	5.1	1,757,517	72.9	43.5	16.9	5.8
Missouri	3,291,579	73.9	40.8	17.8	6.1	3,634,906	81.3	48.6	21.6	7.6
Montana	507,851	81.0	47.5	19.8	5.7	586,621	87.2	55.9	24.4	7.2
Nebraska.	996,049	81.8	47.1	18.9	5.9	1,087,241	86.6	55.3	23.7	7.3
Nevada	789,638	78.8	47.2	15.3	5.2	1,310,176	80.7	51.3	18.2	6.1
New Hampshire.	713,894	82.2	50.5	24.4	7.9	823,987	87.4	57.3	28.7	10.0
New Jersey	5,166,233	76.7	45.6	24.9	8.8	5,657,799	82.1	52.7	29.8	11.0
New Mexico.	922,590	75.1	46.4	20.4	8.3	1,134,801	78.9	52.3	23.5	9.8
New York	11,818,569	74.8	45.3	23.1	9.9	12,542,536	79.1	51.3	27.4	11.8
North Carolina	4,253,494	70.0	41.0	17.4	5.4	5,282,994	78.1	49.7	22.5	7.2
North Dakota	396,550	76.7	48.6	18.1	4.5	408,585	83.9	56.0	22.0	5.5
Ohio.	6,924,764	75.7	39.3	17.0	5.9	7,411,740	83.0	46.9	21.1	7.4
Oklahoma	1,995,424	74.6	44.1	17.8	6.0	2,203,173	80.6	49.1	20.3	6.8
Oregon	1,855,369	81.5	52.6	20.6	7.0	2,250,998	85.1	58.9	25.1	8.7
Pennsylvania.	7,872,932	74.7	36.1	17.9	6.6	8,266,284	81.9	43.8	22.4	8.4
Rhode Island	658,956	72.0	42.6	21.3	7.8	694,573	78.0	50.2	25.6	9.7
South Carolina.	2,167,590	68.3	38.8	16.6	5.4	2,596,010	76.3	46.4	20.4	6.9
South Dakota.	430,500	77.1	43.4	17.2	4.9	474,359	84.6	51.7	21.5	6.0
Tennessee.	3,139,066	67.1	37.0	16.0	5.4	3,744,928	75.9	44.3	19.6	6.8
Texas.	10,310,605	72.1	46.5	20.3	6.5	12,790,893	75.7	50.8	23.2	7.6
Utah.	897,321	85.1	57.9	22.3	6.8	1,197,892	87.7	63.1	26.1	8.3
Vermont	357,245	80.8	46.2	24.3	8.9	404,223	86.4	54.1	29.4	11.1
Virginia	3,974,814	75.2	48.5	24.5	9.1	4,666,574	81.5	55.5	29.5	11.6
Washington	3,126,390	83.8	55.9	22.9	7.0	3,827,507	87.1	62.2	27.7	9.3
West Virginia	1,171,766	66.0	29.4	12.3	4.8	1,233,581	75.2	35.8	14.8	5.9
Wisconsin	3,094,226	78.6	41.5	17.7	5.6	3,475,878	85.1	50.5	22.4	7.2
Wyoming	277,769	83.0	49.9	18.8	5.7	315,663	87.9	56.9	21.9	7.0
Puerto Rico	1,952,297	49.7	28.7	14.3	3.6	2,288,326	60.0	37.7	18.3	4.7

Source: U.S. Census Bureau, Census 2000 Summary File 3; 1990 Census of Population.

college or more), the largest rate of growth was in the period 1960 to 1980. From 1990 to 2000, the increase in the percentage of people completing a bachelor's or higher degree was about the same as the percentage-point increase for the previous decade, and only slightly below the rate from 1970 to 1980.

Age differences in educational attainment were large.

In 2000, the middle-aged population had the highest levels of education—45- to 49-year-olds were highest in high school graduation and some college or more; 50- to 54-year-olds were highest at bachelor's and advanced degree attainment (Table 2). People 75 years and older had lower education levels (among those measured here) than any other age group. The differences between the highest and lowest age groups were often quite substantial. Among the 45- to 49-year-old group, 86 percent had a high school or greater education, compared with only 61 percent of people 75 and over. In these two age groups, completion of some college or more was reported by 59 percent and 30 percent, respectively. The 50- to 54-year-old group recorded a 29 percent rate of bachelor's or higher degree attainment, while only 13 percent of the population 75 years or older had that level of education. Advanced degrees were obtained by 13 percent of the 50- to 54-year-old population, but only 5 percent of the population 75 and older.

The youngest age group (25 to 29 years) had rates of educational attainment slightly lower than people aged 45 to 54. For example, 86 percent of people aged 45 to 49 had completed high school, compared with 84 percent of those aged 25 to 29. The largest gap was at the advanced degree level, where

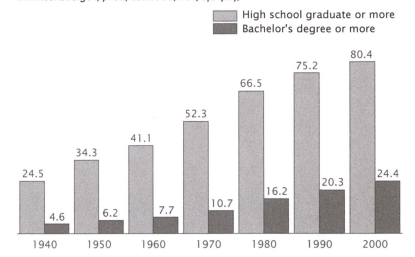

Figure 3.

Population 25 Years and Over Who Have Completed High School or College: 1940 to 2000

(In percent. Data based on sample. For information on confidentiality protection, nonsampling error, sampling error, and definitions, see *www.census.gov/prod/cen2000/doc/sf3.pdf*)

■ High school graduate or more
■ Bachelor's degree or more

Year	High school graduate or more	Bachelor's degree or more
1940	24.5	4.6
1950	34.3	6.2
1960	41.1	7.7
1970	52.3	10.7
1980	66.5	16.2
1990	75.2	20.3
2000	80.4	24.4

Note: Prior to 1990, educational attainment was measured by years of completed schooling.
Source: U.S. Census Bureau, Census 2000 Summary File 3; previous censuses.

13 percent of 50- to 54-year-olds had received an advanced degree, compared with only 6 percent of 25- to 29-year-olds. However, if 25- to 29-year-olds in 2000 were like those observed in previous censuses, many had not yet completed advanced education.[4]

The 25- to 29-year-old population was more likely to have completed some college or more, and was more likely to have earned a bachelor's degree than people 10 to 15 years their senior. The rate of completion of some college was 58 percent among those in the 25- to 29-year age group, while it was 56 percent among those in the 35- to 39-year age group, and 57 percent among those in the 40- to 44-year age group. Similarly, 27 percent of 25- to 29-year-olds had completed a

bachelor's degree or more, while 26 percent of those in the older groups (35 to 39 and 40 to 44) had reached this educational level.

Women's educational levels were close to those of men.

Sex differences in educational attainment were not as large as the range of disparities by age.[5] Men and women had nearly equal rates of high school completion in 2000, with women having the slight edge, 81 percent compared with 80 percent. At higher levels of education, men had higher completion rates. For example, among people 25 years or older in 2000, 26 percent of men had bachelor's degrees or more, compared with 23 percent of women. Men also led women in holding advanced degrees, 10 percent to 8 percent.

[4] In 1990, for example, 4.1 percent of the 25- to 29-year-old population held advanced degrees. Ten years later, 8.4 percent of the 35- to 39-year-old population held advanced degrees.

[5] The gap in educational attainment between people aged 50 to 54 and those aged 75 or older was significantly greater than the gap between men and women at each level of education.

Table 2.

Educational Attainment of the Population 25 Years and Over by Age, Sex, Race, and Hispanic or Latino Origin: 2000

(Data based on sample. For information on confidentiality protection, sampling error, nonsampling error, and definitions, see www.census.gov/prod/cen2000/doc/sf3.pdf)

Characteristic	Population 25 and over	Percent			
		High school graduate or more	Some college or more	Bachelor's degree or more	Advanced degree
Total..	182,211,639	80.4	51.8	24.4	8.9
Age					
25 to 29 years	19,212,244	83.6	58.3	27.2	5.9
30 to 34 years	20,365,113	84.2	57.9	27.9	8.4
35 to 39 years	23,083,337	84.7	56.5	25.9	8.4
40 to 44 years	22,822,134	85.4	56.7	25.9	9.1
45 to 49 years	20,181,127	86.4	59.5	28.5	11.3
50 to 54 years	17,397,482	85.4	58.5	29.1	12.7
55 to 59 years	13,383,251	81.1	50.6	24.6	11.5
60 to 64 years	10,787,979	76.1	43.5	20.3	9.3
65 to 69 years	9,569,199	72.1	38.9	18.3	8.0
70 to 74 years	8,931,950	67.3	34.9	16.2	6.7
75 years and over	16,477,823	60.7	29.6	13.3	5.4
Sex					
Men..	87,077,686	80.1	52.5	26.1	10.0
Women......................................	95,133,953	80.7	51.1	22.8	7.8
Race and Hispanic or Latino Origin					
White alone.................................	143,085,659	83.6	54.1	26.1	9.5
Black or African American alone..............	19,858,095	72.3	42.5	14.3	4.8
American Indian and Alaska Native alone	1,350,998	70.9	41.7	11.5	3.9
Asian alone.................................	6,640,671	80.4	64.6	44.1	17.4
Native Hawaiian and Other Pacific Islander alone ..	206,675	78.3	44.6	13.8	4.1
Some other race alone	7,611,121	46.8	25.0	7.3	2.3
Two or more races...........................	3,458,420	73.3	48.1	19.6	7.0
Hispanic or Latino (of any race).............	18,270,377	52.4	30.3	10.4	3.8
White alone, not Hispanic or Latino..........	133,786,263	85.5	55.4	27.0	9.8

Source: U.S. Census Bureau, Census 2000 Summary File 3.

The "Asian alone" race group led in attaining bachelor's and advanced degrees.

Census 2000 allowed respondents to choose more than one race. With the exception of the Two or more races group, all race groups discussed in this report refer to people who indicated *only one* racial identity among the six major categories: White, Black or African American, American Indian and Alaska Native, Asian, Native Hawaiian and Other Pacific Islander, and Some other race.[6] The use of the single-race

population in this report does not imply that it is the preferred method of presenting or analyzing data. The Census Bureau uses a variety of approaches.[7]

Large differences among races existed at all levels of education. In 2000, the proportion of people aged 25 and over who had completed high school or more education ranged from 84 percent of

those who reported they were White (and no other race), to 47 percent of people who reported Some other race only.[8] People who reported they were Asian (and no other race) were most likely to report having completed higher

[6] For further information on each of the six major race groups and the Two or more races population, see reports from the Census 2000 Brief series (C2KBR/01), available on the Census 2000 Web site at www.census.gov/population/www/cen2000/briefs.html.

[7] This report draws heavily on Summary File 3, a Census 2000 product that can be accessed through American FactFinder, available from the Census Bureau's Web site, www.census.gov. Information on people who reported more than one race, such as "White *and* American Indian and Alaska Native" or "Asian *and* Black or African American," is available in Summary File 4, also available through American FactFinder. About 2.6 percent of people reported more than one race.

[8] Hereafter this report uses the term Black to refer to people who are Black or African American, the term Pacific Islander to refer to people who are Native Hawaiian and Other Pacific Islander, and the term Hispanic to refer to people who are Hispanic or Latino.

Because Hispanics may be of any race, data in this report for Hispanics overlap with data for racial groups. Based on Census 2000 sample data, the proportion Hispanic was 8.0 percent for Whites, 1.9 percent for Blacks, 14.6 percent for American Indians and Alaska Natives, 1.0 percent for Asians, 9.5 percent for Pacific Islanders, 97.1 percent for those reporting Some other race, and 31.1 percent for those reporting Two or more races.

levels of education (some college, bachelor's or advanced degrees). Among the Asian population, 44 percent had a bachelor's degree, compared with 26 percent of the White population, 20 percent of people who reported two or more races, 14 percent of the Black population, 14 percent of the Pacific Islander population, 11 percent of the American Indian and Alaska Native population, and 7 percent of the Some other race population.

The percentage of Hispanics completing high school or more was 52 percent, compared with 85 percent of non-Hispanic Whites (single race). A large gap between the Hispanic population and the non-Hispanic White population is also seen at other levels of education. While 27 percent of non-Hispanic Whites had a bachelor's degree or more, only 10 percent of Hispanics had reached this education level.

GEOGRAPHIC DISTRIBUTION OF PEOPLE BY EDUCATIONAL ATTAINMENT

Regional education differentials shifted during the 1990s.

No one region can lay claim to having the best-educated population.[9] The rank depended on the level of education being examined (Table 1).

_____

[9] The Northeast region includes the states of Connecticut, Maine, Massachusetts, New Hampshire, New Jersey, New York, Pennsylvania, Rhode Island, and Vermont. The Midwest region includes the states of Illinois, Indiana, Iowa, Kansas, Michigan, Minnesota, Missouri, Nebraska, North Dakota, Ohio, South Dakota, and Wisconsin. The South region includes the states of Alabama, Arkansas, Delaware, Florida, Georgia, Kentucky, Louisiana, Maryland, Mississippi, North Carolina, Oklahoma, South Carolina, Tennessee, Texas, Virginia, West Virginia, and the District of Columbia, a state equivalent. The West region includes the states of Alaska, Arizona, California, Colorado, Hawaii, Idaho, Montana, Nevada, New Mexico, Oregon, Utah, Washington, and Wyoming.

The Midwest had the largest percentage of its population 25 and over holding a high school diploma or more (83 percent), while the West had the largest percentage having completed at least some college (58 percent). The population in the Northeast had the highest bachelor's degree and advanced degree levels, 27 percent and 11 percent, respectively. The South had the lowest completion rates from high school through college, but the Midwest had the lowest advanced degree completion rate, at 8 percent.[10]

Growth in educational attainment from 1990 to 2000 occurred in all four United States regions. In the West, which started the decade as one of the leaders at every level of education, growth was slower than in other regions.

The South and the Midwest jointly had the largest growth in the percentage with high school or more education, both growing by 6 percentage points between 1990 and 2000. The lowest growth was in the West, which saw only a 2 percentage-point increase over the decade. The percentage with some college or more education grew by 8 percentage points in the Midwest, but 4 percentage points in the West.

The net effect of these changes was to narrow differences across regions in the percentage holding high school diplomas or higher degrees. In 1990 the West led this category, with 79 percent, and the South trailed with 71 percent, a difference of 7 percentage points. In 2000, the difference between the leading region, the Midwest,

_____

[10] The percentage with advanced degrees in the Midwest was 7.9 percent, the percentage in the South was 8.1 percent. This difference is small, but statistically significant.

and the lowest region, the South, was only 6 percentage points.

A different pattern was observed at the high end of the educational range, due to growth in the percentage with bachelor's and advanced degrees in the Northeast, which was already the leading region on these measures. The percentage with bachelor's or higher degrees increased by 5 points in the Northeast, compared with 4 points in the West. In 1990, a gap of 2.6 points in the percentage with advanced degrees existed between the Northeast (which was highest in both censuses) and the Midwest (the lowest in both censuses). In 2000, the gap between these two regions had grown to 3.1 percentage points.

States with low high school completion rates were catching up.

Alaska, Minnesota, Wyoming, Utah, New Hampshire, Montana, Washington, and Colorado were among the highest in percentage of people 25 and over with high school or more education, while Mississippi had the lowest percentage, 73 percent.[11] As with the regions, however, differences among states narrowed from 1990 to 2000. The six states with the lowest percentage having high school or more education in 1990 (Mississippi, Kentucky, West Virginia, Arkansas, Alabama, and Tennessee) were among the states with the largest growth over the next decade. Mississippi's rate of high school completion grew by

_____

[11] While any of Alaska, Minnesota or Wyoming could have ranked number 1, given the margin of measurement error, they could have ranked as low as number 3, number 4 or number 5, respectively. That means that Utah or New Hampshire might rank in the top three states. All five states had high school graduation rates that might have fallen at 88 percent or above, given statistical error and rounding.

8.6 percentage points.[12] Kentucky had a more than 9 percentage-point increase in high school completion from 1990 to 2000 (West Virginia's growth was not statistically different).

The state with the highest proportion of people 25 and over having at least some college education was Colorado, at 64 percent. The largest growth in the percentage at this education level occurred in Minnesota.

The District of Columbia had the highest percentage of its population holding bachelors or higher degrees and also had the highest percentage with advanced degrees. In 2000, 39 percent of District residents had a bachelor's degree or more, and 21 percent had advanced degrees. Unlike the 50 states, Washington, DC, is entirely urban, and this urban population had high percentages at both ends of the educational scale. In contrast to its high ranking in bachelor's and advanced degrees, the District of Columbia ranked in the bottom third in the percentage with a high school diploma or more.

The state with the second highest percentage of its 25-and-over population holding bachelors and advanced degrees was Massachusetts. In 2000, 33 percent of Massachusetts' residents 25 and over had at least a bachelor's degree, and 14 percent had advanced degrees. Massachusetts also had the highest growth in percentage with bachelor's degrees from 1990 to 2000. Although Massachusetts' growth in percentage with advanced degrees trailed the District of Columbia's growth, it was a strong second place,

allowing it to bypass Connecticut and Maryland in the ranking of advanced degrees.

College graduates lived in suburban counties and counties with colleges.

The geographic distribution of college completion rates by United States county can be seen in Figure 4. High percentages of college graduates were found in metropolitan counties on the East and West coasts. A large concentration of high education counties formed a band from Albemarle County, Virginia, to Middlesex County, Massachusetts. Other counties included part of the San Francisco area, and King County, Washington, containing the city of Seattle.

Counties with high percentages of college graduates were also scattered across much of the central part of the country, around metropolitan areas and in college towns. For example, a cluster of high-education counties was found near Atlanta, Georgia, complemented by Clarke and Oconee counties, east of Atlanta, which contain a major university. Similar patterns of suburban and college-town concentrations of college graduates can be seen in states such as Colorado, Illinois, Indiana, Iowa, Kansas, Massachusetts, New York, North Carolina, Pennsylvania, Texas, Virginia, Washington, and Wisconsin. The metropolitan counties with high college education levels often exclude the county with a central city. For example, 49 percent of the 25-and-over population of Hamilton County, Indiana, had bachelor's degrees. This county is just north of Marion county, which contains the city of Indianapolis. The proportion with bachelor's degrees in Marion County was only 25 percent, significantly lower than Hamilton County but above the national average.

The Western states have many counties with large geographic size but sparse populations. Areas with highly college-educated populations in Colorado and nearby mountain states included three types of counties: suburban counties around Denver, several counties with large universities, and a number of counties with resort and vacation areas.

Places with universities attracted the greatest concentration of people with doctoral degrees.

The places most likely to have people with doctoral degrees are university towns like Cambridge, Massachusetts, Ann Arbor, Michigan, and Berkeley, California (Table 3).[13] In Cambridge, Massachusetts, nearly 1 in 10 residents 25 and over had a doctorate. All the other places with the highest percentage holding doctoral degrees were cities with universities enrolling at least 20,000 students, with the exception of Durham, North Carolina.[14] Durham, however, has a major university nearby, along with a large concentration of companies performing scientific research and related activities.

---

[12] Kentucky, West Virginia, Arkansas, Tennessee, Mississippi, Alabama, North Carolina, and South Carolina all experienced growth in high school completion of 8 percentage points or more.

[13] Census 2000 showed 245 places in the United States with 100,000 or more population. They included 238 incorporated places (including 4 city-county consolidations) and 7 census designated places that were not legally incorporated. For a list of these places by state, see www.census.gov/population/www/cen2000/phc-t6.html.
The percentage with doctorates in Cambridge is not significantly higher than that in Ann Arbor but is significantly higher than Berkeley. Ann Arbor and Berkeley are not significantly different. Cambridge, Ann Arbor, and Berkeley are all significantly higher than the other places listed in Table 3.

[14] Enrollment statistics for individual universities were obtained from the National Center for Education Statistics "College Opportunities On-Line" database, http://nces.ed.gov/ipeds/cool/.

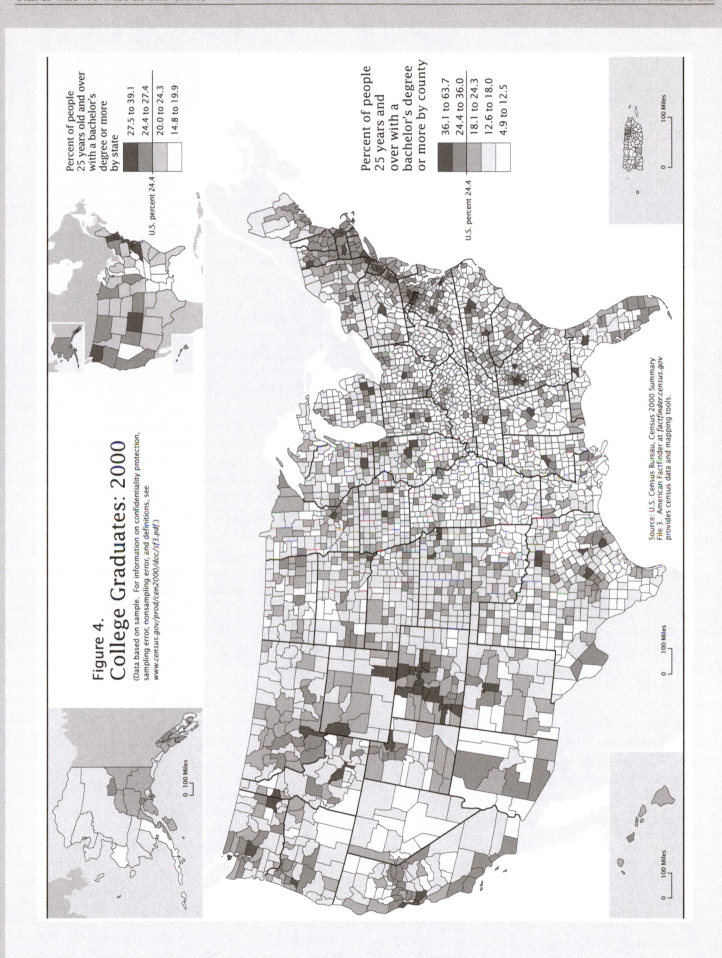

Figure 4.
College Graduates: 2000

(Data based on sample. For information on confidentiality protection, sampling error, nonsampling error, and definitions, see *www.census.gov/prod/cen2000/doc/sf3.pdf*.)

Percent of people 25 years old and over with a bachelor's degree or more by state

- 27.5 to 39.1
- 24.4 to 27.4
- 20.0 to 24.3
- 14.8 to 19.9

U.S. percent 24.4

Percent of people 25 years and over with a bachelor's degree or more by county

- 36.1 to 63.7
- 24.4 to 36.0
- 18.1 to 24.3
- 12.6 to 18.0
- 4.9 to 12.5

U.S. percent 24.4

Source: U.S. Census Bureau, Census 2000 Summary File 3. American Factfinder at *factfinder.census.gov* provides census data and mapping tools.

Table 3.
Ten Places of 100,000 or More Population With the Highest Percentage of People 25 and Over With Doctoral Degrees: 2000

(Data based on sample. For information on confidentiality protection, sampling error, nonsampling error, and definitions, see www.census.gov/prod/cen2000/doc/sf3.pdf)

Place	People with doctoral degrees		
	Number	Percent of population 25 and over	90-percent confidence interval
Cambridge, MA	6,370	9.6	9.1 - 10.1
Ann Arbor, MI	6,045	9.3	8.8 - 9.9
Berkeley, CA	5,347	8.1	7.6 - 8.6
Athens-Clarke County, GA*	3,015	5.8	5.3 - 6.3
Madison, WI	5,386	4.2	4.0 - 4.5
Durham, NC	4,784	4.1	3.8 - 4.3
Irvine, CA	3,589	4.0	3.7 - 4.4
Tallahassee, FL	3,002	3.8	3.4 - 4.1
Fort Collins, CO	2,506	3.7	3.4 - 4.1
New Haven, CT	2,473	3.4	3.1 - 3.7

*Athens-Clarke County, Georgia, is a census designated place (CDP). CDPs comprise densely settled concentrations of population that are identifiable by name but are not legally incorporated places.

Note: Doctoral degrees include PhD and EdD degrees. Because of sampling error, the estimates in this table may not be significantly different from one another or from rates for other geographic areas not listed in this table.

Source: U.S. Census Bureau, Census 2000 Summary File 3.

Table 4.
Ten Places of 100,000 or More Population With the Highest Percentage of People 25 and Over With Less Than a High School Diploma: 2000

(Data based on sample. For information on confidentiality protection, sampling error, nonsampling error, and definitions, see www.census.gov/prod/cen2000/doc/sf3.pdf)

Place	People with less than a high school diploma		
	Number	Percent of population 25 and over	90-percent confidence interval
East Los Angeles, CA*	43,452	66.3	65.5 - 67.2
Santa Ana, CA	101,475	56.8	56.2 - 57.3
El Monte, CA	34,813	55.8	54.8 - 56.7
Hialeah, FL	78,059	50.2	49.6 - 50.8
Brownsville, TX	36,762	48.3	47.5 - 49.1
Miami, FL	119,435	47.3	46.8 - 47.8
Laredo, TX	42,426	45.2	44.5 - 45.9
Pomona, CA	35,529	45.1	44.2 - 45.9
Salinas, CA	37,185	44.0	43.2 - 44.8
Newark, NJ	69,135	42.1	41.5 - 42.6

* East Los Angeles, California, is a census designated place (CDP) and is not legally incorporated.

Note: Because of sampling error, the estimates in this table may not be significantly different from one another or from rates for other geographic areas not listed in this table.

Source: U.S. Census Bureau, Census 2000 Summary File 3.

California, Texas, Florida, and New Jersey were home to places with a large percentage of people with less than a high school diploma.

The ten places of 100,000 or more with the highest percentages of people aged 25 and over who had not completed high school were certain urban areas in California, Texas, Florida, and New Jersey (Table 4). One characteristic shared by many of these places was a high percentage of Hispanics in the population. However, Newark's Hispanic population was relatively small. Five of the ten had a large percentage of foreign born (East Los Angeles, Santa Ana, and El Monte in California; Hialeah and Miami in Florida). Six of the places were high poverty areas, with over 20 percent of families in poverty (East Los Angeles and El Monte, California; Brownsville and Laredo, Texas; Miami, Florida; and Newark, New Jersey).

ADDITIONAL FINDINGS

Do younger and older men and women have the same educational differences?

According to results of Census 2000 discussed earlier, women were more likely to have a high school diploma, while men were more likely to have a bachelor's or higher degree. However, sex differences in education varied along the age spectrum (Figure 5). Completion of high school became increasingly common moving from the over-75 age group, in which women and men had graduation rates of 60 percent and 61 percent, respectively, to the 50- to 54-age group, in which 86 percent of women and 85 percent of men completed high school. For each age group 50 years and over, the percentages of men and women completing high school were close, with the difference never reaching more than 2 percentage points.

Among younger men and women, under the age of 50, high school graduation rates diverged. Younger men aged 25 to 29 were less likely to complete high school than men aged 50 to 54, while younger women were slightly more likely to complete high school than 50- to 54-year-old women. Women below the age of 50 were also more likely than men of the same age to graduate from high school.

As with high school graduation, bachelor's degree completion showed a change between those above and below the age of 50. Both men and women aged 75 and over (born in 1925 or earlier), had low rates of college completion, while those aged 50 to 54 (born between 1945 and 1950) had much higher rates. However, across all age groups from 50 on up, men maintained a fairly stable 7 to 10 percentage point advantage over women in college completion.

Those younger than 50 (born since 1950) showed a much different pattern. College graduation rates were lower among younger men (age 25 to 44) born later in the twentieth century than they were for men born just after 1950 (age 45 to 49). By contrast, younger women aged 25 to 34 increased their rate of college completion above and beyond the level of their elders in the 45- to 49-year-old age group. In the 25- to 39-age ranges, women surpassed men in college completion as well.

ABOUT CENSUS 2000

Why Census 2000 asked about educational attainment.

Government agencies require data on educational attainment for funding allocations and program planning and implementation. The Voting Rights Act requires information on education to determine the extent of illiteracy among language minorities. In addition, funding for school districts that provide classes to adults who have not completed high school is based on these data. Other federal applications include: the Community Development Block Grant (CDBG) Evaluation, the Americans With Disabilities Act, the National Science Foundation Biennial Report, the Bilingual Education Act, and the Older Americans Act. Local

Figure 5.

Differences in Educational Attainment by Sex and Age: 2000

(Data based on sample. For information on confidentiality protection, nonsampling error, sampling error, and definitions, see *www.census.gov/prod/cen2000/doc/sf3.pdf*)

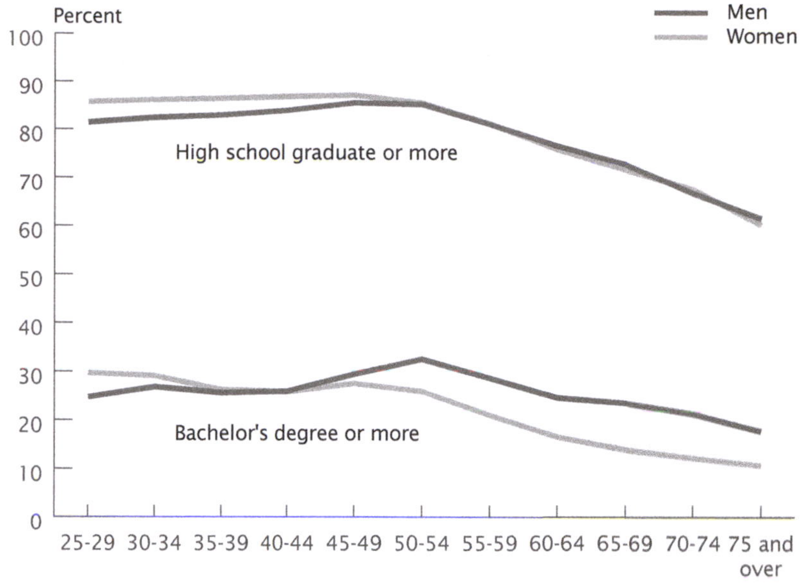

Source: U.S. Census Bureau, Census 2000 Summary File 3.

governments use information on educational attainment to attract potential employers to their areas.

ACCURACY OF THE ESTIMATES

The data contained in this report are based on the sample of households who responded to the Census 2000 long form. Nationally, approximately 1 out of every 6 housing units was included in this sample. As a result, the sample estimates may differ somewhat from the100-percent figures that would have been obtained if all housing units, people within those housing units, and people living in group quarters had been enumerated using the same questionnaires, instructions, enumerators, and so forth. The sample estimates also differ from the values that would have been obtained from different samples of housing

units, people within those housing units, and people living in group quarters. The deviation of a sample estimate from the average of all possible samples is called the sampling error.

In addition to the variability that arises from the sampling procedures, both sample data and 100-percent data are subject to nonsampling error. Nonsampling error may be introduced during any of the various complex operations used to collect and process data. Such errors may include: not enumerating every household or every person in the population, failing to obtain all required information from the respondents, obtaining incorrect or inconsistent information, and recording information incorrectly. In addition, errors can occur during the field review of the enumerators' work, during clerical handling of the census questionnaires, or during the electronic processing of the questionnaires.

Nonsampling error may affect the data in two ways: (1) errors that are introduced randomly will increase the variability of the data and, therefore, should be reflected in the standard errors; and (2) errors that tend to be consistent in one direction will bias both sample and 100-percent data in that direction. For example, if respondents consistently tend to underreport their incomes, then the resulting estimates of households or families by income category will tend to be understated for the higher income categories and overstated for the lower income categories. Such biases are not reflected in the standard errors.

While it is impossible to completely eliminate error from an operation as large and complex as the decennial census, the Census Bureau attempts to control the sources of such error during the data collection and processing operations. The primary sources of error and the programs instituted to control error in Census

2000 are described in detail in *Summary File 3 Technical Documentation* under Chapter 8, "Accuracy of the Data," located at *www.census.gov/prod/cen2000 /doc/sf3.pdf.*

All statements in this Census 2000 Brief have undergone statistical testing and all comparisons are significant at the 90-percent confidence level, unless otherwise noted. The estimates in tables, maps, and other figures may vary from actual values due to sampling and nonsampling errors. As a result, estimates in one category may not be significantly different from estimates assigned to a different category. Further information on the accuracy of the data is located at *www.census.gov /prod/cen2000/doc/sf3.pdf.* For further information on the computation and use of standard errors, contact the Decennial Statistical Studies Division at 301-763-4242.

FOR MORE INFORMATION

The Census 2000 Summary File 3 data are available from the American Factfinder on the Internet (*factfinder.census.gov*). They were released on a state-by-state basis

during 2002. For information on confidentiality protection, nonsampling error, sampling error, and definitions, also see *www.census.gov /prod/cen2000/doc/sf3.pdf* or contact the Customer Services Center at 301-763-INFO (4636).

Information on population and housing topics is presented in the Census 2000 Brief series, located on the Census Bureau's Web site at *www.census.gov/population/www /cen2000/briefs.html.* This series presents information on race, Hispanic origin, age, sex, household type, housing tenure, and social, economic, and housing characteristics, such as ancestry, income, and housing costs.

For additional information on educational attainment in the United States, including reports and survey data, visit the Census Bureau's Internet site at *www.census.gov /population/www/socdemo /educ-attn.html.* To find information about the availability of data products, including reports, CD-ROMs, and DVDs, call the Customer Services Center at 301-763-INFO (4636), or e-mail *webmaster@census.gov.*

Age: 2000

Census 2000 Brief

Issued October 2001

C2KBR/01-12

By
Julie Meyer

In 2000, the U.S. Census Bureau counted 281.4 million people in the United States.[1] Of this number;

- 72.3 million, or 26 percent of the U.S. population, were under age 18;

- 174.1 million, or 62 percent, were age 18 to 64; and

- 35.0 million, or 12 percent, were age 65 and over.

The age groups under 18 years, 18 to 64 years, and 65 years and over experienced similar growth rates over the past decade — 13.7 percent, 13.2 percent, and 12.0 percent, respectively. Median age increased from 32.9 in 1990 to 35.3 in 2000, reflecting a change in age distribution toward the older ages within the age range 18 to 64.[2]

This report, part of a series that analyzes population and housing data collected from Census 2000, provides a portrait of the age structure of people in the United States. It highlights information about various age groups in the country as a whole, the four regions, states, counties, and places with populations of 100,000

Figure 1.

Reproduction of the Question on Age From Census 2000

4. **What is this person's age and what is this person's date of birth?** *Print numbers in boxes.*
Age on April 1, 2000   Month   Day   Year of birth

Source: U.S. Census Bureau, Census 2000 questionnaire.

or more. It also includes comparisons with data from the 1990 census.[3]

A question on age has been asked since the first census of the population in 1790. The Census 2000 age data were derived from a two-part question that was asked of all people. The first part asked for the age of the person, and the second part asked for the date of birth (see Figure 1).

The Census 2000 age question added month and day of birth.

The Census 2000 age question differs slightly from the 1990 question. In the 1990 census, the question asked for a respondent's age and **year** of birth. In contrast, the Census 2000 age question asked respondents to report their age and date of birth, which included **month**, **day**, and year of birth.

[1] The text of this report discusses data for the United States, including the 50 states and the District of Columbia. Data for the Commonwealth of Puerto Rico are shown in Table 2 and Figure 6.
[2] Median age splits the population into halves. One-half of the population is older than the median age and the other half is younger.

[3] 1990 populations shown in this report were originally published in 1990 census reports and do not include subsequent revisions resulting from boundary or other changes.

USCENSUSBUREAU

Helping You Make Informed Decisions

U.S. Department of Commerce
Economics and Statistics Administration
U.S. CENSUS BUREAU

United States Census 2000

The figure below is a snapshot of the population in 1990 and 2000. It presents age information in 5-year age groups by sex.

In 2000, the largest 5-year age group was 35-to-39 year olds with 22.7 million people, representing 8.1 percent of the total population. The second largest 5-year age group was 40-to-44 year olds with 22.4 million people, representing 8.0 percent of the population. The relatively large number in these two age groups is represented in Figure 2 by a bulge in the age distribution. People in these two age groups were primarily born during the post-World War II "Baby Boom" (those born from 1946 through 1964). In Census 2000, the baby-boom cohort was age 36 to 54 and represented 28 percent of the total U.S. population.

The 50-to-54-year age group experienced the largest percentage growth.[4]

Of the 5-year age groups, 50-to-54 year olds experienced the largest percentage growth in population over the past decade, 55 percent (see Figure 3 and Table 1). The second fastest-growing group was the age group 45 to 49, which experienced a 45-percent increase. The baby-boom cohort entered these two

_____

[4]The changes in age structure between 1990 and 2000 may reflect changes in census coverage, as well as births, deaths, and net immigration.

age groups during the past decade. The third fastest-growing group in the past decade was 90-to-94 year olds, which increased by 45 percent.

Some of the younger age groups also grew. The 10-to-14-year group gained almost 20 percent, while 5-to-9 year olds and 15-to-19 year olds each increased by almost 14 percent.

Four age groups shown in the figure and table declined over the past decade: 25-to-29 year olds (9-percent decrease), 30-to-34 year olds (6-percent decrease), 65-to-69 year olds (6-percent decrease), and 20-to-24 year olds (0.3-percent decrease). The number of people in the younger age groups, especially

Figure 2.
Population by Age and Sex: 1990 and 2000

(For information on confidentiality protection, nonsampling error, and definitions, see *www.census.gov/prod/cen2000/doc/sf1.pdf*.)

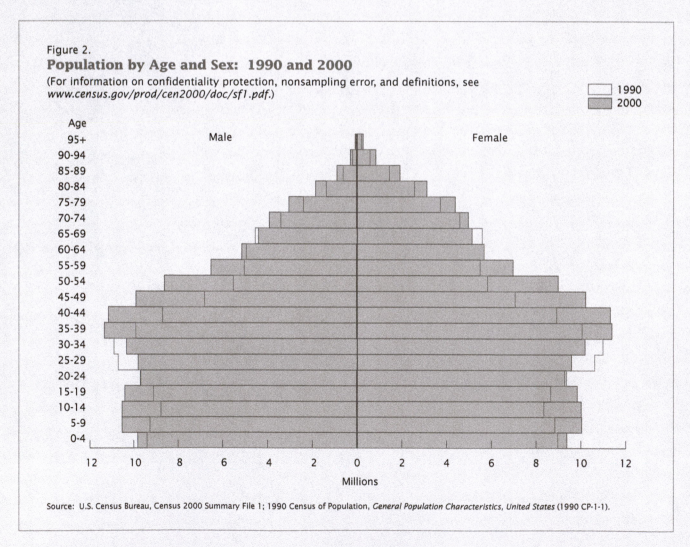

Source: U.S. Census Bureau, Census 2000 Summary File 1; 1990 Census of Population, *General Population Characteristics, United States* (1990 CP-1-1).

those age 25 to 34, fell as the baby-boom cohort aged into older age groups. The decline in 65-to-69 year olds is associated with a relatively low number of births during the early 1930s.

There were more older women than older men.

In general, the ratio of the male population to the female population declined with age. That is, the female population exceeded the male population at older ages, but the reverse was true at younger ages. In 2000, there were

20.6 million women aged 65 and over compared with only 14.4 million men. In contrast, there were 37.1 million males under 18 while there were 35.2 million females. The balance shifted toward more women at age 36.[5]

---

[5] For more Census 2000 information about the male and female populations, see Smith, Denise I. and Reneé E. Spraggins, 2001, *Gender: 2000*, Census 2000 Brief, C2KBR/01-9, U.S. Census Bureau, Washington, DC, *www.census.gov/prod/2001pubs/c2kbr01-9.pdf*.

The median age for people of Two or more races was nearly 13 years younger than the median age for people of one race.

Figure 4 shows age information by race using two ways to summarize race data. In Census 2000, individuals could report more than one race. For a detailed discussion on race reporting, see the Census 2000 Brief, *Overview of Race and Hispanic Origin*.[6] People who responded to the question on race by indicating only one race are referred to as the race *alone* population, or the group who reported *only one* race. For example, respondents who marked only the White category on the census questionnaire would be included in the White *alone* population. Six categories make up the population reporting *only one* race: White *alone*, Black or African American *alone*, American Indian and Alaska Native *alone*, Asian *alone*, Native Hawaiian and Other Pacific Islander *alone*, and Some other race *alone*.[7]

Individuals who chose more than one of the six race categories are referred to as the race *in combination* population, or as the group who reported Two or more races. For example, respondents who reported they were "White **and** Black or African American" or "White **and** Asian **and** American Indian and Alaska Native"[8] would be

---

[6] Grieco, Elizabeth M. and Rachel C. Cassidy, 2001, *Overview of Race and Hispanic Origin*, Census 2000 Brief, C2KBR/01-1, U.S. Census Bureau, Washington, DC, *www.census.gov/prod/2001pubs/c2kbr01-1.pdf*.
[7] Some other race is not a standard Office of Management and Budget race category.
[8] The race *in combination* categories are denoted by quotations around the combinations with the conjunction **and** in bold and italicized print to indicate the separate race groups that comprise the combination.

Figure 3.
Percent Change by Age: 1990 to 2000

(For information on confidentiality protection, nonsampling error, and definitions, see *www.census.gov/prod/cen2000/doc/sf1.pdf*)

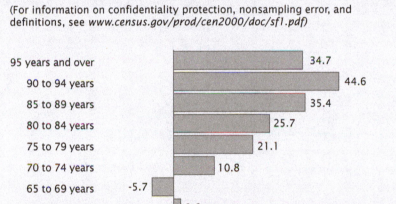

Age	Percent Change
95 years and over	34.7
90 to 94 years	44.6
85 to 89 years	35.4
80 to 84 years	25.7
75 to 79 years	21.1
70 to 74 years	10.8
65 to 69 years	-5.7
60 to 64 years	1.8
55 to 59 years	27.9
50 to 54 years	54.9
45 to 49 years	44.8
40 to 44 years	27.4
35 to 39 years	13.7
30 to 34 years	-6.2
25 to 29 years	-9.1
20 to 24 years	-0.3
15 to 19 years	13.9
10 to 14 years	19.9
5 to 9 years	13.5
Under 5 years	4.5

Source: U.S. Census Bureau, Census 2000 Summary File 1; 1990 Census of Population, *General Population Characteristics, United States* (1990 CP-1-1).

Table 1.
Population Change by Age: 1990 to 2000

(For information on confidentiality protection, nonsampling error, and definitions, see *www.census.gov/prod/cen2000/doc/sf1.pdf*)

Age	1990		2000		Change, 1990 to 2000	
	Number	Percent	Number	Percent	Number	Percent
Total...................................	248,709,873	100.0	281,421,906	100.0	32,712,033	13.2
Under 5 years	18,354,443	7.4	19,175,798	6.8	821,355	4.5
5 to 9 years	18,099,179	7.3	20,549,505	7.3	2,450,326	13.5
10 to 14 years	17,114,249	6.9	20,528,072	7.3	3,413,823	19.9
15 to 19 years	17,754,015	7.1	20,219,890	7.2	2,465,875	13.9
20 to 24 years	19,020,312	7.6	18,964,001	6.7	−56,311	−0.3
25 to 29 years	21,313,045	8.6	19,381,336	6.9	−1,931,709	−9.1
30 to 34 years	21,862,887	8.8	20,510,388	7.3	−1,352,499	−6.2
35 to 39 years	19,963,117	8.0	22,706,664	8.1	2,743,547	13.7
40 to 44 years	17,615,786	7.1	22,441,863	8.0	4,826,077	27.4
45 to 49 years	13,872,573	5.6	20,092,404	7.1	6,219,831	44.8
50 to 54 years	11,350,513	4.6	17,585,548	6.2	6,235,035	54.9
55 to 59 years	10,531,756	4.2	13,469,237	4.8	2,937,481	27.9
60 to 64 years	10,616,167	4.3	10,805,447	3.8	189,280	1.8
65 to 69 years	10,111,735	4.1	9,533,545	3.4	−578,190	−5.7
70 to 74 years	7,994,823	3.2	8,857,441	3.1	862,618	10.8
75 to 79 years	6,121,369	2.5	7,415,813	2.6	1,294,444	21.1
80 to 84 years	3,933,739	1.6	4,945,367	1.8	1,011,628	25.7
85 to 89 years	2,060,247	0.8	2,789,818	1.0	729,571	35.4
90 to 94 years	769,481	0.3	1,112,531	0.4	343,050	44.6
95 years and over	250,437	0.1	337,238	0.1	86,801	34.7

Source: U.S. Census Bureau, Census 2000 Summary File 1; 1990 Census of Population, *General Population Characteristics, United States (1990 CP-1-1).*

included in the *in combination* population of each race.[9]

In 2000, median age varied significantly by race. People who reported Two or more races had a significantly younger median age (22.7) than the population reporting one race (35.6). The difference between the races with the youngest and oldest median ages was about 13 years. Of those respondents reporting only one race, individuals who reported Some other race had the youngest median age (24.6), which reflects the fact that 97 percent of people choosing this race were Hispanic[10] and people reporting Hispanic origin, who may be of any race, had a relatively young median age. The

next youngest group was Native Hawaiian and Other Pacific Islander *alone* (27.5), followed by American Indian and Alaska Native *alone* (28.0), Black or African American *alone* (30.2), Asian *alone* (32.7), and White *alone* (37.7).

Across all races, people who reported more than one race tended to be younger than those who reported only one race. Figure 4 shows that 42 percent of people who reported Two or more races were under age 18 compared with 25 percent of people who reported one race.

GEOGRAPHIC DISTRIBUTION OF PEOPLE IN THREE BROAD AGE CATEGORIES

Median age was highest in the Northeast and lowest in the West.

In 2000, the Northeast had the highest median age (36.8) followed by the Midwest (35.6), and the

South (35.3) as shown in Table 2.[11] The West had the youngest median age, 33.8. This ranking reflects the relative proportions of population in the broad age groups for each region. The Northeast had the largest proportion of people age 65 and over, while it had the smallest proportion of people under age 18. The West had the opposite situation. More specifically, the 65-and-over population made up 14 percent of the population in the Northeast, 13 percent in the

[9]See Grieco, Elizabeth M. and Rachel C. Cassidy, 2001, *Overview of Race and Hispanic Origin*, Census 2000 Brief, C2KBR/01-1, U.S. Census Bureau, Washington, DC, *www.census.gov/prod/2001pubs/c2kbr01-1.pdf.*
[10]Ibid.

[11]The Northeast region includes Connecticut, Maine, Massachusetts, New Hampshire, New Jersey, New York, Pennsylvania, Rhode Island, and Vermont. The Midwest includes Illinois, Indiana, Iowa, Kansas, Michigan, Minnesota, Missouri, Nebraska, North Dakota, Ohio, South Dakota, and Wisconsin. The South includes Alabama, Arkansas, Delaware, the District of Columbia, Florida, Georgia, Kentucky, Louisiana, Maryland, Mississippi, North Carolina, Oklahoma, South Carolina, Tennessee, Texas, Virginia, and West Virginia. The West includes Alaska, Arizona, California, Colorado, Hawaii, Idaho, Montana, Nevada, New Mexico, Oregon, Utah, Washington, and Wyoming.

Midwest, 12 percent in the South, and 11 percent in the West. In contrast, children made up 27 percent of the population in the West followed by 26 percent in both the Midwest and South. The Northeast had 24 percent. All four regions had roughly the same proportion of people age 18 to 64 (61 or 62 percent).

The West had the highest growth rates in all three age groups.

Growth rates for each age group varied significantly by region (see Figure 5). For children, the growth rate in the West (21 percent) was more than three times that in the Midwest and more than twice that in the Northeast.

For the population age 18 to 64, the growth rates in the South and West (18 percent and 19 percent,

Figure 4.
Percent of Population by Selected Age Groups, Race, and Hispanic or Latino Origin: 2000

(For information on confidentiality protection, nonsampling error, and definitions, see www.census.gov/prod/cen2000/doc/sf1.pdf)

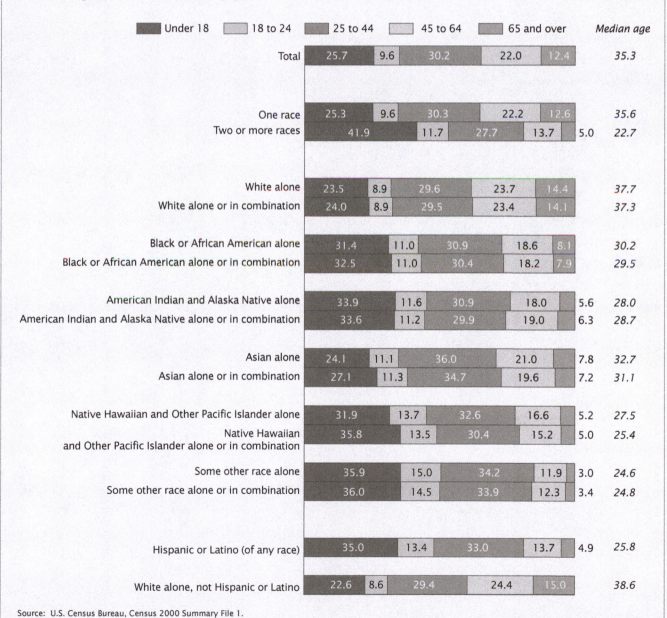

	Under 18	18 to 24	25 to 44	45 to 64	65 and over	Median age
Total	25.7	9.6	30.2	22.0	12.4	35.3
One race	25.3	9.6	30.3	22.2	12.6	35.6
Two or more races	41.9	11.7	27.7	13.7	5.0	22.7
White alone	23.5	8.9	29.6	23.7	14.4	37.7
White alone or in combination	24.0	8.9	29.5	23.4	14.1	37.3
Black or African American alone	31.4	11.0	30.9	18.6	8.1	30.2
Black or African American alone or in combination	32.5	11.0	30.4	18.2	7.9	29.5
American Indian and Alaska Native alone	33.9	11.6	30.9	18.0	5.6	28.0
American Indian and Alaska Native alone or in combination	33.6	11.2	29.9	19.0	6.3	28.7
Asian alone	24.1	11.1	36.0	21.0	7.8	32.7
Asian alone or in combination	27.1	11.3	34.7	19.6	7.2	31.1
Native Hawaiian and Other Pacific Islander alone	31.9	13.7	32.6	16.6	5.2	27.5
Native Hawaiian and Other Pacific Islander alone or in combination	35.8	13.5	30.4	15.2	5.0	25.4
Some other race alone	35.9	15.0	34.2	11.9	3.0	24.6
Some other race alone or in combination	36.0	14.5	33.9	12.3	3.4	24.8
Hispanic or Latino (of any race)	35.0	13.4	33.0	13.7	4.9	25.8
White alone, not Hispanic or Latino	22.6	8.6	29.4	24.4	15.0	38.6

Source: U.S. Census Bureau, Census 2000 Summary File 1.

Table 2.
Population by Selected Age Groups for the United States, Regions, and States, and for Puerto Rico: 1990 and 2000

(For information on confidentiality protection, nonsampling error, and definitions, see *www.census.gov/prod/cen2000/doc/sf1.pdf*)

| Area | 1990 | | | | | | 2000 | | | | | |
| | | Under 18 | | 65 and over | | | | Under 18 | | 65 and over | | |
	Total	Number	Percent	Number	Percent	Median age	Total	Number	Percent	Number	Percent	Median age
United States	248,709,873	63,604,432	25.6	31,241,831	12.6	32.9	281,421,906	72,293,812	25.7	34,991,753	12.4	35.3
Region												
Northeast	50,809,229	11,913,007	23.4	6,995,156	13.8	34.2	53,594,378	13,047,783	24.3	7,372,282	13.8	36.8
Midwest	59,668,632	15,614,783	26.2	7,749,130	13.0	32.9	64,392,776	16,647,666	25.9	8,259,075	12.8	35.6
South	85,445,930	22,008,378	25.8	10,724,182	12.6	32.7	100,236,820	25,566,903	25.5	12,438,267	12.4	35.3
West	52,786,082	14,068,264	26.7	5,773,363	10.9	31.8	63,197,932	17,031,460	26.9	6,922,129	11.0	33.8
State												
Alabama	4,040,587	1,058,788	26.2	522,989	12.9	33.0	4,447,100	1,123,422	25.3	579,798	13.0	35.8
Alaska	550,043	172,344	31.3	22,369	4.1	29.4	626,932	190,717	30.4	35,699	5.7	32.4
Arizona	3,665,228	981,119	26.8	478,774	13.1	32.2	5,130,632	1,366,947	26.6	667,839	13.0	34.2
Arkansas	2,350,725	621,131	26.4	350,058	14.9	33.8	2,673,400	680,369	25.4	374,019	14.0	36.0
California	29,760,021	7,750,725	26.0	3,135,552	10.5	31.4	33,871,648	9,249,829	27.3	3,595,658	10.6	33.3
Colorado	3,294,394	861,266	26.1	329,443	10.0	32.5	4,301,261	1,100,795	25.6	416,073	9.7	34.3
Connecticut	3,287,116	749,581	22.8	445,907	13.6	34.4	3,405,565	841,688	24.7	470,183	13.8	37.4
Delaware	666,168	163,341	24.5	80,735	12.1	32.8	783,600	194,587	24.8	101,726	13.0	36.0
District of Columbia	606,900	117,092	19.3	77,847	12.8	33.4	572,059	114,992	20.1	69,898	12.2	34.6
Florida	12,937,926	2,866,237	22.2	2,369,431	18.3	36.3	15,982,378	3,646,340	22.8	2,807,597	17.6	38.7
Georgia	6,478,216	1,727,303	26.7	654,270	10.1	31.5	8,186,453	2,169,234	26.5	785,275	9.6	33.4
Hawaii	1,108,229	280,126	25.3	125,005	11.3	32.6	1,211,537	295,767	24.4	160,601	13.3	36.2
Idaho	1,006,749	308,405	30.6	121,265	12.0	31.5	1,293,953	369,030	28.5	145,916	11.3	33.2
Illinois	11,430,602	2,946,366	25.8	1,436,545	12.6	32.8	12,419,293	3,245,451	26.1	1,500,025	12.1	34.7
Indiana	5,544,159	1,455,964	26.3	696,196	12.6	32.8	6,080,485	1,574,396	25.9	752,831	12.4	35.2
Iowa	2,776,755	718,880	25.9	426,106	15.3	34.0	2,926,324	733,638	25.1	436,213	14.9	36.6
Kansas	2,477,574	661,614	26.7	342,571	13.8	32.9	2,688,418	712,993	26.5	356,229	13.3	35.2
Kentucky	3,685,296	954,094	25.9	466,845	12.7	33.0	4,041,769	994,818	24.6	504,793	12.5	35.9
Louisiana	4,219,973	1,227,269	29.1	468,991	11.1	31.0	4,468,976	1,219,799	27.3	516,929	11.6	34.0
Maine	1,227,928	309,002	25.2	163,373	13.3	33.9	1,274,923	301,238	23.6	183,402	14.4	38.6
Maryland	4,781,468	1,162,241	24.3	517,482	10.8	33.0	5,296,486	1,356,172	25.6	599,307	11.3	36.0
Massachusetts	6,016,425	1,353,075	22.5	819,284	13.6	33.5	6,349,097	1,500,064	23.6	860,162	13.5	36.5
Michigan	9,295,297	2,458,765	26.5	1,108,461	11.9	32.6	9,938,444	2,595,767	26.1	1,219,018	12.3	35.5
Minnesota	4,375,099	1,166,783	26.7	546,934	12.5	32.4	4,919,479	1,286,894	26.2	594,266	12.1	35.4
Mississippi	2,573,216	746,761	29.0	321,284	12.5	31.1	2,844,658	775,187	27.3	343,523	12.1	33.8
Missouri	5,117,073	1,314,826	25.7	717,681	14.0	33.5	5,595,211	1,427,692	25.5	755,379	13.5	36.1
Montana	799,065	222,104	27.8	106,497	13.3	33.8	902,195	230,062	25.5	120,949	13.4	37.5
Nebraska	1,578,385	429,012	27.2	223,068	14.1	33.0	1,711,263	450,242	26.3	232,195	13.6	35.3
Nevada	1,201,833	296,948	24.7	127,631	10.6	33.3	1,998,257	511,799	25.6	218,929	11.0	35.0
New Hampshire	1,109,252	278,755	25.1	125,029	11.3	32.8	1,235,786	309,562	25.0	147,970	12.0	37.1
New Jersey	7,730,188	1,799,462	23.3	1,032,025	13.4	34.4	8,414,350	2,087,558	24.8	1,113,136	13.2	36.7
New Mexico	1,515,069	446,741	29.5	163,062	10.8	31.2	1,819,046	508,574	28.0	212,225	11.7	34.6
New York	17,990,455	4,259,549	23.7	2,363,722	13.1	33.8	18,976,457	4,690,107	24.7	2,448,352	12.9	35.9
North Carolina	6,628,637	1,606,149	24.2	804,341	12.1	33.1	8,049,313	1,964,047	24.4	969,048	12.0	35.3
North Dakota	638,800	175,385	27.5	91,055	14.3	32.4	642,200	160,849	25.0	94,478	14.7	36.2
Ohio	10,847,115	2,799,744	25.8	1,406,961	13.0	33.3	11,353,140	2,888,339	25.4	1,507,757	13.3	36.2
Oklahoma	3,145,585	837,007	26.6	424,213	13.5	33.1	3,450,654	892,360	25.9	455,950	13.2	35.5
Oregon	2,842,321	724,130	25.5	391,324	13.8	34.6	3,421,399	846,526	24.7	438,177	12.8	36.3
Pennsylvania	11,881,643	2,794,810	23.5	1,829,106	15.4	35.0	12,281,054	2,922,221	23.8	1,919,165	15.6	38.0
Rhode Island	1,003,464	225,690	22.5	150,547	15.0	33.9	1,048,319	247,822	23.6	152,402	14.5	36.7
South Carolina	3,486,703	920,207	26.4	396,935	11.4	32.0	4,012,012	1,009,641	25.2	485,333	12.1	35.4
South Dakota	696,004	198,462	28.5	102,331	14.7	32.5	754,844	202,649	26.8	108,131	14.3	35.6
Tennessee	4,877,185	1,216,604	24.9	618,818	12.7	33.5	5,689,283	1,398,521	24.6	703,311	12.4	35.9
Texas	16,986,510	4,835,839	28.5	1,716,576	10.1	30.7	20,851,820	5,886,759	28.2	2,072,532	9.9	32.3
Utah	1,722,850	627,444	36.4	149,958	8.7	26.3	2,233,169	718,698	32.2	190,222	8.5	27.1
Vermont	562,758	143,083	25.4	66,163	11.8	33.0	608,827	147,523	24.2	77,510	12.7	37.7
Virginia	6,187,358	1,504,738	24.3	664,470	10.7	32.6	7,078,515	1,738,262	24.6	792,333	11.2	35.7
Washington	4,866,692	1,261,387	25.9	575,288	11.8	33.1	5,894,121	1,513,843	25.7	662,148	11.2	35.3
West Virginia	1,793,477	443,577	24.7	268,897	15.0	35.4	1,808,344	402,393	22.3	276,895	15.3	38.9
Wisconsin	4,891,769	1,288,982	26.4	651,221	13.3	32.9	5,363,675	1,368,756	25.5	702,553	13.1	36.0
Wyoming	453,588	135,525	29.9	47,195	10.4	32.1	493,782	128,873	26.1	57,693	11.7	36.2
Puerto Rico	3,522,037	1,154,527	32.8	340,884	9.7	28.4	3,808,610	1,092,101	28.7	425,137	11.2	32.1

Source: U.S. Census Bureau, Census 2000 Summary File 1; 1990 Census of Population, *General Population Characteristics, United States (1990 CP-1-1) and Puerto Rico (1990 CP-1-53).*

respectively) were more than four times that in the Northeast for the same age group and more than twice that in the Midwest in this age group.

For the population 65 years and over, the growth rate in the South (16 percent) was nearly three times the growth rate in the Northeast. And the growth rate in the West (20 percent) was more than three times that of both the Northeast and the Midwest for this age group.

In the Northeast and West, the population under age 18 grew the fastest; in the Midwest and South, the 18-to-64-year age group grew the fastest.

A comparison of growth rates for each age group within each region showed differences. In the Northeast and West, the population under 18 grew the fastest of the three age groups. More specifically, the population under 18 years in the Northeast grew at a rate of 10 percent, compared with the lower growth rates of 5 percent for those 65 years and over and 4 percent for those 18 to 64. In the West, the population under 18 years old also grew the fastest of the three age groups between 1990 and 2000, although the other two groups grew quickly as well.

The fastest growing age group in both the Midwest and South was 18-to-64 year olds. In the Midwest, this age group grew 9 percent, a slightly higher growth rate than for the other two broad age groups, each with 7 percent. In the South, the age group 18 to 64 also grew the fastest of the three age groups, 18 percent during the decade. Both the population under age 18 and the population age 65 and over

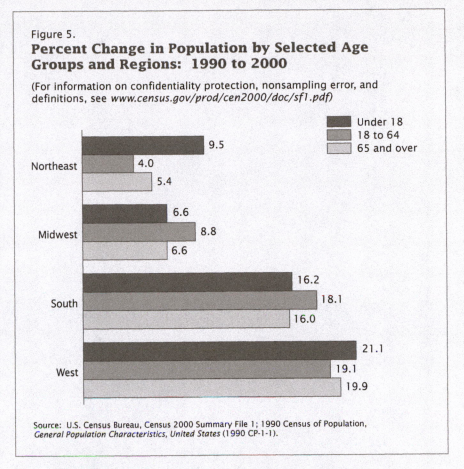

Figure 5.

Percent Change in Population by Selected Age Groups and Regions: 1990 to 2000

(For information on confidentiality protection, nonsampling error, and definitions, see *www.census.gov/prod/cen2000/doc/sf1.pdf*)

Legend:
- Under 18
- 18 to 64
- 65 and over

Northeast: 9.5, 4.0, 5.4
Midwest: 6.6, 8.8, 6.6
South: 16.2, 18.1, 16.0
West: 21.1, 19.1, 19.9

Source: U.S. Census Bureau, Census 2000 Summary File 1; 1990 Census of Population, *General Population Characteristics, United States* (1990 CP-1-1).

increased at a slightly lower rate of 16 percent.

West Virginia had the highest median age.

The Northeast was the only region where all states had median ages above the national level. In contrast, the West was the only region where states with median ages below the U.S. median outnumbered states with older median ages (see Figure 6).

The states with the highest median ages were West Virginia (38.9), Florida (38.7), Maine (38.6), and Pennsylvania (38.0). Utah had the youngest population and was the only state with a median age below 30 years (27.1). Other

states with low median ages were Texas (32.3) and Alaska (32.4) as shown in Table 2.

Florida had the highest proportion 65 years and over.

The proportion 65 years and over ranged from a low of 6 percent in Alaska to 18 percent in Florida.[12] In addition to Alaska, states that had a relatively low percentage of older adults were Utah (9 percent) and Georgia, Colorado, and Texas (each 10 percent). States along with

_____

[12]For more Census 2000 information about the population 65 years and over, see Hetzel, Lisa and Annetta Smith, 2001, *The 65 Years and Over Population: 2000*, Census 2000 Brief, C2KBR/01-10, U.S. Census Bureau, Washington, DC, *www.census.gov/prod/2001pubs/c2kbr01-10.pdf*.

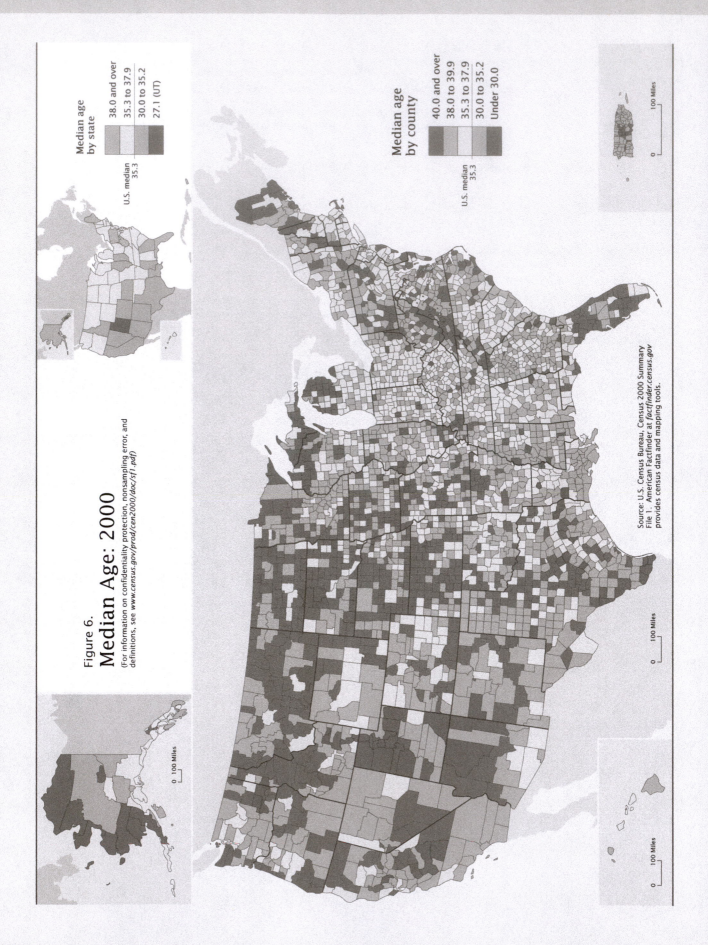

Figure 6.
Median Age: 2000
(For information on confidentiality protection, nonsampling error, and definitions, see *www.census.gov/prod/cen2000/doc/sf1.pdf*)

Median age
by state

U.S. median
35.3

38.0 and over
35.3 to 37.9
30.0 to 35.2
27.1 (UT)

Median age
by county

U.S. median
35.3

40.0 and over
38.0 to 39.9
35.3 to 37.9
30.0 to 35.2
Under 30.0

Source: U.S. Census Bureau, Census 2000 Summary File 1. American Factfinder at *factfinder.census.gov* provides census data and mapping tools.

0   100 Miles

0   100 Miles

0   100 Miles

0   100 Miles

Florida that had a relatively high percentage of older adults were Pennsylvania (16 percent) and West Virginia, Iowa, North Dakota, and Rhode Island (each 15 percent).

In 14 states, the older population[13] grew by more than 20 percent relative to the U.S. rate of 12 percent. Nevada had the highest growth rate for this age group (72 percent).[14] Alaska also experienced a large percentage increase (60 percent). Only the District of Columbia experienced a decline in the number of older adults (10-percent decrease).

The District of Columbia still had the largest proportion of people age 18 to 64 (67.7 percent), although this proportion was even higher in 1990 (67.9 percent). The proportion of people in this age group ranged from 59 percent to 65 percent across states. The states with the highest proportions (64 or 65 percent) were Colorado, Virginia, Georgia, Alaska, and North Carolina. The states with the lowest proportions (59 or 60 percent) were South Dakota, Utah, Florida, Iowa, and Nebraska.

The number of children grew by more than 25 percent in five states; five states experienced a percentage decline.

In five states, the population under 18 years grew by more than 25 percent, much higher than the U.S. increase of 14 percent. Those five states were Nevada (72 percent), Arizona (39 percent), Colorado (28 percent), Florida (27 percent), and Georgia (26 percent).

[13]For this report, the older population is defined as people 65 years and over.
[14]Nevada had the highest growth rate for all three age groups.

Five states and the District of Columbia experienced a decline in the population under age 18 between 1990 and 2000 — West Virginia (9-percent decrease), North Dakota (8-percent decrease), Wyoming (5-percent decrease), Maine (3-percent decrease), and Louisiana (1-percent decrease). The District of Columbia experienced a decrease of 2 percent.

Counties with low median ages were mostly in the southern and western portions of the country.

Median age varied among counties in the United States. Figure 6 shows median age for the country's 3,141 counties and equivalent areas. There were 734 counties with median age 40.0 and over and 131 counties with median age under 30.0. The areas with median age generally at the U.S. median or younger were in the southwest border region. In contrast, two bands of counties had older median ages — in the interior Northeast and Appalachia, and across the Great Plains states from the Mexican border to the Canadian border.

The Midwest had the highest percentage of counties with older median ages.

In terms of proportion, the Midwest had the largest percentage of its counties with median ages 40.0 and over (31 percent), followed by the West (29 percent), Northeast (19 percent), and South (17 percent). In contrast, the West had the largest proportion of counties with median ages less than 30.0 (10 percent), followed by the Midwest (4 percent), the South (3 percent), and the Northeast (1 percent).

There were three counties with 100,000 or more population where

median ages were very high (50.0 and over). All of them — Charlotte County (54.3), Citrus County (52.6), and Sarasota County (50.5) — were in Florida.

In contrast, four counties with 100,000 or more population had median ages below 26.0: Utah County, Utah (23.3); Brazos County, Texas (23.6); Onslow County, North Carolina (25.0); and Clarke County, Georgia (25.4).

In four states, all the counties in the state had median ages at or above the national median of 35.3. Those states were: Connecticut, Maine, Rhode Island, and Hawaii. There were no states where all the counties had median ages less than the national median. Utah came closest with 86 percent of its counties having median ages below the national median.

The places with the oldest populations (in terms of median age) were in the regions with the youngest median ages.

Five of the ten places (population of 100,000 or more) with the lowest median ages in 2000 were in California, and all were either in the South or West. Provo, Utah, had the lowest median age (22.9) as shown in Table 3. Although the South and West were the regions with the lowest median ages, all but one of the top ten places with the highest median ages were also in these two regions (see Table 4). The one exception was Livonia, Michigan (40.2). Five of the ten places with the highest median ages were in Florida, where Clearwater, Florida, had the highest (41.8). All of the ten largest cities had median ages below the national median (see Table 5).

Table 3.
Ten Places of 100,000 or More Population With the Lowest Median Age: 2000

(For information on confidentiality protection, nonsampling error, and definitions, see *www.census.gov/prod/cen2000/doc/sf1.pdf*)

Place[1]	Total population	Median age	Percent under 18	Percent 65 and over
Provo, UT	105,166	22.9	22.3	5.7
Athens-Clarke County, GA*	101,489	25.4	17.8	8.1
Fontana, CA	128,929	26.2	37.8	4.7
Tallahassee, FL	150,624	26.3	17.4	8.2
East Los Angeles, CA*	124,283	26.5	34.6	7.9
Pomona, CA	149,473	26.5	34.6	6.4
Santa Ana, CA	337,977	26.5	34.2	5.5
West Valley City, UT	108,896	26.8	33.7	5.4
Laredo, TX	176,576	26.9	35.5	7.8
El Monte, CA	115,965	27.1	34.1	6.9

*Athens-Clarke County, GA, is a city-county consolidation. East Los Angeles, CA, is a census desigated place and is not legally incorporated.

[1]Census 2000 showed 245 places in the United States with 100,000 or more population. They included 238 incorporated places (including 4 city-county consolidations) and 7 census designated places that were not legally incorporated. For a list of these places by state, see *www.census.gov/population/www/cen2000/phc-t6.html*.

Source: U.S. Census Bureau, Census 2000 Summary File 1.

Table 4.
Ten Places of 100,000 or More Population With the Highest Median Age: 2000

(For information on confidentiality protection, nonsampling error, and definitions, see *www.census.gov/prod/cen2000/doc/sf1.pdf*)

Place[1]	Total population	Median age	Percent under 18	Percent 65 and over
Clearwater, FL	108,787	41.8	19.1	21.5
Cape Coral, FL	102,286	41.6	22.6	19.6
Scottsdale, AZ	202,705	41.0	19.3	16.7
Livonia, MI	100,545	40.2	23.8	16.9
Honolulu, HI*	371,657	39.7	19.2	17.8
Metairie, LA*	146,136	39.5	20.6	16.4
St. Petersburg, FL	248,232	39.3	21.5	17.4
Fort Lauderdale, FL	152,397	39.3	19.4	15.3
Hollywood, FL	139,357	39.2	21.3	17.3
Torrance, CA	137,946	38.7	23.0	14.1

*Honolulu, HI, and Metairie, LA, are census designated places and are not legally incorporated.

[1]Census 2000 showed 245 places in the United States with 100,000 or more population. They included 238 incorporated places (including 4 city-county consolidations) and 7 census designated places that were not legally incorporated. For a list of these places by state, see *www.census.gov/population/www/cen2000/phc-t6.html*.

Source: U.S. Census Bureau, Census 2000 Summary File 1.

ADDITIONAL QUESTIONS ON AGE

Which states had the highest concentration of baby boomers?

Earlier in this report, the baby-boom cohort (people ages 36 to 54 in 2000) was shown to make up a large share of the total U.S. population. In 2000, the proportion of baby boomers in the states ranged from 23 percent to 32 percent. The states where baby boomers made up 30 percent or more of their populations were Alaska (32 percent), New Hampshire (31 percent), Vermont (31 percent), and Maine (30 percent). In contrast, Utah (23 percent) was the only state where baby boomers constituted less than 25 percent.

How many school-age children were there in 2000?

In 2000, there were 53.1 million elementary- and high school-age children (5-to-17 year olds), 73 percent of the population under age 18. There were 7.8 million pre-school-age children (3-to-4 year olds). Infants and toddlers (0-to-2 year olds) represented 16 percent of the population under age 18.

Table 5.
Ten Largest Cities by Age: 2000

(For information on confidentiality protection, nonsampling error, and definitions, see *www.census.gov/prod/cen2000/doc/sf1.pdf*)

City	Total population	Median age	Percent under 18	Percent 65 and over
New York, NY	8,008,278	34.2	24.2	11.7
Los Angeles, CA	3,694,820	31.6	26.6	9.7
Chicago, IL	2,896,016	31.5	26.2	10.3
Houston, TX	1,953,631	30.9	27.5	8.4
Philadelphia, PA	1,517,550	34.2	25.3	14.1
Phoenix, AZ	1,321,045	30.7	28.9	8.1
San Diego, CA	1,223,400	32.5	24.0	10.5
Dallas, TX	1,188,580	30.5	26.6	8.6
San Antonio, TX	1,144,646	31.7	28.5	10.4
Detroit, MI	951,270	30.9	31.1	10.4

Source: U.S. Census Bureau, Census 2000 Summary File 1.

ABOUT CENSUS 2000

Why did Census 2000 ask the question on age?

The Census Bureau collects age data to support two basic activities:

- Legislative redistricting and

- Allocating funds from federal programs to targeted age groups.

For example, age data are used in calculating the proportion of school-age children in poverty for each school district for allocating federal funds to assist educationally disadvantaged children. The Department of Veterans Affairs uses age data to develop state projections on the need for hospitals, nursing homes, cemeteries, and other services for veterans.

Communities can use census age data to aid them in making informed decisions about how to meet the needs of their older and their younger citizens. Researchers can use these data in their research on school-age children and many other age-related topics. Business owners can use these data in planning a new business around the needs of a certain age group in the community.

FOR MORE INFORMATION

More information on age data is available by visiting the U.S. Census Bureau's Web site at *www.census.gov* (click "A" for Age Data in the Subjects A to Z list).

Data on age from the Census 2000 Summary File 1 were released on a state-by-state basis during the summer of 2001 and are available via *factfinder.census.gov* and for purchase on DVD.

For information on confidentiality protection, nonsampling error, and definitions, see *www.census.gov/prod/cen2000/doc/sf1.pdf*, or contact our Customer Services Center at 301-763-INFO (4636).

Information on other population and housing topics is presented in the Census 2000 Brief series, located on the U.S. Census Bureau's Web site at *www.census.gov/population/www/cen2000/briefs.html*. This series presents information about race, Hispanic origin, age, sex, household type, housing tenure, and other social, economic, and housing characteristics.

For more information about Census 2000, including data products, call our Customer Services Center at 301-763-INFO (4636) or e-mail *webmaster@census.gov*.

The 65 Years and Over Population: 2000

Census 2000 Brief

Issued October 2001

C2KBR/01-10

By
Lisa Hetzel and
Annetta Smith

In 2000, 35.0 million people 65 years of age and over were counted in the United States.[1] This represents a 12.0-percent increase since 1990, when 31.2 million older people were counted.[2] Although the number of people 65 years and over increased between 1990 and 2000, their proportion of the total population dropped from 12.6 percent in 1990 to 12.4 percent in 2000.

This report, part of a series that analyzes population and housing data collected from Census 2000, provides a portrait of the 65 years and over population in the United States and discusses its distribution at the national and subnational levels. The report also highlights comparisons with data from the 1990 census.[3]

A question on age has been asked since the first census of the population in 1790, and data on the 65 years and over population was first published in 1870. The Census 2000 age data were derived from a two-part question that was asked of all people. The first part asked for the age

Figure 1.

Reproduction of the Question on Age From Census 2000

4. What is this person's age and what is this person's date of birth? *Print numbers in boxes.*
Age on April 1, 2000   Month   Day   Year of birth

Source: U.S. Census Bureau, Census 2000 questionnaire.

of the person, and the second part asked for the date of birth (see Figure 1).[4]

The 65 years and over population grew slower than the total population.

Census 2000 was the first time in the history of the census that the 65 years and over population did not grow faster than the total population. Between 1990 and 2000, the total population increased by 13.2 percent, from 248.7 million to 281.4 million people. In contrast, the population 65 years and over increased by only 12.0 percent.

Among the older population, those 85 years and over showed the highest percentage increase.

In 2000, there were 18.4 million people ages 65 to 74 years old, representing 53 percent of the older population

---

[1] The text of this report discusses data for the 50 states and the District of Columbia, but not the Commonwealth of Puerto Rico and the U.S. Island Areas.
[2] For this brief, the older population is defined as people 65 years and over.
[3] 1990 populations shown in this report were originally published in 1990 census reports and do not include subsequent revisions resulting from boundary or other changes.

[4] For more Census 2000 age information, see U.S. Census Bureau, 2001, *Age: 2000*, by Julie Meyer, Census 2000 Brief, C2KBR/01-12, Washington, DC.

USCENSUSBUREAU

Helping You Make Informed Decisions

U.S. Department of Commerce
Economics and Statistics Administration
U.S. CENSUS BUREAU

Table 1.
Population 65 Years and Over by Age: 1990 and 2000

(For information on confidentiality protection, nonsampling error, and definitions, see *www.census.gov/prod/cen2000/doc/sf1.pdf*)

Age	1990		2000		Percent of U.S. total		Percent change, 1990 to 2000
	Number	Percent	Number	Percent	1990	2000	
65 years and over	**31,241,831**	**100.0**	**34,991,753**	**100.0**	**12.6**	**12.4**	**12.0**
65 to 74 years	18,106,558	58.0	18,390,986	52.6	7.3	6.5	1.6
65 to 69 years	10,111,735	32.4	9,533,545	27.2	4.1	3.4	-5.7
70 to 74 years	7,994,823	25.6	8,857,441	25.3	3.2	3.1	10.8
75 to 84 years	10,055,108	32.2	12,361,180	35.3	4.0	4.4	22.9
75 to 79 years	6,121,369	19.6	7,415,813	21.2	2.5	2.6	21.1
80 to 84 years	3,933,739	12.6	4,945,367	14.1	1.6	1.8	25.7
85 to 94 years	2,829,728	9.1	3,902,349	11.2	1.1	1.4	37.9
85 to 89 years	2,060,247	6.6	2,789,818	8.0	0.8	1.0	35.4
90 to 94 years	769,481	2.5	1,112,531	3.2	0.3	0.4	44.6
95 years and over	250,437	0.8	337,238	1.0	0.1	0.1	34.7

Source: U.S. Census Bureau, Census 2000 Summary File 1; 1990 Census of Population, *General Population Characteristics, United States* (1990 CP-1-1).

(see Table 1). The 75-to-84-year-olds numbered 12.4 million people (35 percent of the older population), and those ages 85 and over numbered 4.2 million people (12 percent of the older population). These age groups represented 6.5 percent, 4.4 percent, and 1.5 percent of the total population, respectively.

During the 1990s, the most rapid growth of the older population occurred in the oldest age groups. The population 85 years and over increased by 38 percent, from 3.1 million to 4.2 million. In contrast, the population 75 to 84 years old increased by 23 percent, and the population 65 to 74 years old increased by less than 2 percent, from 18.1 million to 18.4 million. Within the 65-to-74 age group, the number of people 65 to 69 years old declined by 6 percent, compared with an increase of 11 percent in the number of people 70 to 74 years old. The changes in the 65-to-74 age group reflect the relatively low number of births in the

Figure 2.
Population 65 Years and Over by Age and Sex: 1990 and 2000

(Numbers in thousands. For information on confidentiality protection, nonsampling error, and definitions, see *www.census.gov/prod/cen2000/doc/sf1.pdf*)

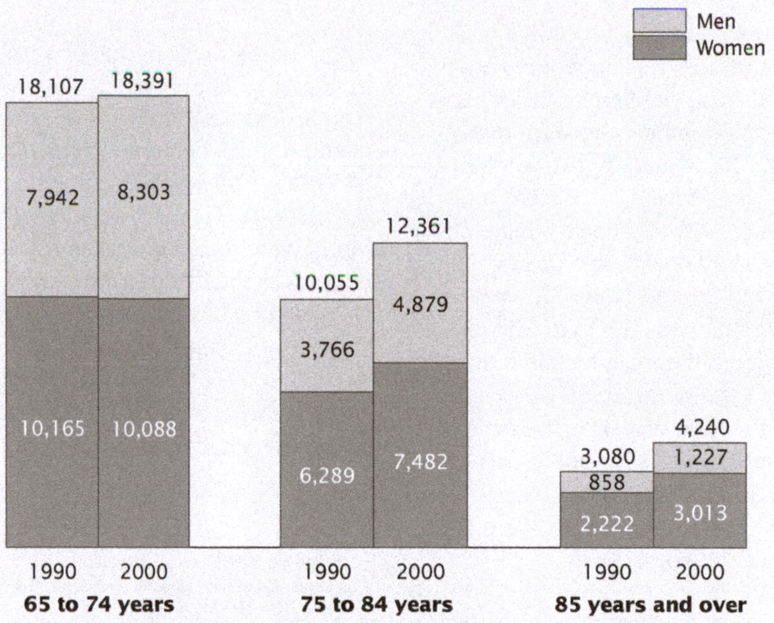

Legend: Men, Women

Source: U.S. Census Bureau, Census 2000 Summary File 1; 1990 Census of Population, *General Population Characteristics, United States* (1990 CP-1-1).

Table 2.
Number of Men per 100 Women by Age, for the 65 Years and Over Population: 1990 and 2000

(For information on confidentiality protection, nonsampling error, and definitions, see www.census.gov/prod/cen2000/doc/sf1.pdf)

Age	1990	2000
65 years and over	67	70
65 to 74 years	78	82
75 to 84 years.................................	60	65
85 years and over	39	41

Source: U.S. Census Bureau, Census 2000 Summary File 1; 1990 Census of Population, *General Population Characteristics, United States* (1990 CP-1-1).

late 1920s and early 1930s, which in turn led to a relatively small number of people reaching age 65 during the decade of 1990 to 2000. This trend is expected to reverse as baby boomers (born from 1946 through 1964) reach age 65, starting in 2011.

Women outnumbered men in the 65 years and over population.

In 2000, there were 14.4 million men and 20.6 million women aged 65 and over, yielding a male-female ratio (the number who were male times 100 divided by the number who were female) of 70 (see Figure 2 and Table 2).[5] The male-female ratio drops steadily with age group. In the 65-to-74 age group, the male-female ratio was 82; in the 75-to-84 age group, the male-female ratio was 65, and in the group 85 years and over, the ratio was 41. The male-female ratio for each age group in the older population has risen since 1990. In 1990, the ratios were 78, 60, and 39, respectively.

The West and South regions had the most growth in the total population and in the older population.

The regional pattern of growth of the older population matched the

regional growth of the total population. Between 1990 and 2000, the West and South regions grew the fastest (see Table 3).[6] The West experienced the highest percent increase of the older population, at 20 percent, and the South's older population grew by 16 percent. In contrast, the older population grew at a much lower rate in the Midwest (7 percent) and Northeast (5 percent).

Every state's older population grew between 1990 and 2000, ranging from a 1-percent increase in Rhode Island to a 72-percent increase in Nevada. After Nevada, the next highest increases in the older population were found in Alaska (60 percent), Arizona (39 percent), and New Mexico (30 percent). Only the District of Columbia showed a decline in the 65-years-and-over population.[7] Between 1990 and 2000, the older population in the

District of Columbia decreased by 10 percent, or 8,000 people.

People 65 years and over represented a smaller proportion of the total population in 2000 than in 1990.

Unlike previous decades, during the 1990s, the proportion of the population composed of people 65 years and over declined nationally, in two regions of the country, and in over half of the states. In the Midwest, the proportion 65 years and over declined from 13.0 percent of its total population in 1990 to 12.8 percent in 2000, and the proportion in the South declined from 12.6 percent to 12.4 percent. This proportion remained at 13.8 percent in the Northeast, but in the West, the proportion of people 65 years and over increased slightly from 10.9 percent in 1990 to 11.0 percent in 2000.

In over half of the states (29, including the District of Columbia), the proportion 65 years and over of the total population declined. Nineteen of these states are in the Midwest and South. The states with the largest declines in the proportion 65 years and over were Oregon, Arkansas, and Idaho, which each declined about 1 percentage point between 1990 and 2000 to proportions of 12.8 percent, 14.0 percent, and 11.3 percent, respectively. Although Florida continued to have the highest proportion 65 years and over (17.6 percent), Florida experienced a similar decline in this proportion since 1990.

A total of 29 states had a proportion of population 65 years and over that equaled or exceeded the national value of 12.4 percent. Florida's high proportion of population 65 years and over was followed by Pennsylvania and

[5] For more Census 2000 information about the male and female populations, see U.S. Census Bureau, 2001, *Gender: 2000*, by Denise I. Smith and Reneé E. Spraggins, Census 2000 Brief, C2KBR/01-9, Washington, DC.

[6] The West includes Alaska, Arizona, California, Colorado, Hawaii, Idaho, Montana, Nevada, New Mexico, Oregon, Utah, Washington, and Wyoming. The South includes Alabama, Arkansas, Delaware, the District of Columbia, Florida, Georgia, Kentucky, Louisiana, Maryland, Mississippi, North Carolina, Oklahoma, South Carolina, Tennessee, Texas, Virginia, and West Virginia. The Midwest includes Illinois, Indiana, Iowa, Kansas, Michigan, Minnesota, Missouri, Nebraska, North Dakota, Ohio, South Dakota, and Wisconsin. The Northeast region includes Connecticut, Maine, Massachusetts, New Hampshire, New Jersey, New York, Pennsylvania, Rhode Island, and Vermont.

[7] Washington, DC, is treated as a state equivalent for statistical purposes.

Table 3.
Population 65 Years and Over for the United States, Regions, and States, and for Puerto Rico: 1990 and 2000

(For information on confidentiality protection, nonsampling error, and definitions, see *www.census.gov/prod/cen2000/doc/sf1.pdf*)

Area	1990 Total population	1990 Population 65 years and over Number	1990 Population 65 years and over Percent	2000 Total population	2000 Population 65 years and over Number	2000 Population 65 years and over Percent	Change, 1990 to 2000 Number	Change, 1990 to 2000 Percent
United States	248,709,873	31,241,831	12.6	281,421,906	34,991,753	12.4	3,749,922	12.0
Region								
Northeast	50,809,229	6,995,156	13.8	53,594,378	7,372,282	13.8	377,126	5.4
Midwest	59,668,632	7,749,130	13.0	64,392,776	8,259,075	12.8	509,945	6.6
South	85,445,930	10,724,182	12.6	100,236,820	12,438,267	12.4	1,714,085	16.0
West	52,786,082	5,773,363	10.9	63,197,932	6,922,129	11.0	1,148,766	19.9
State								
Alabama	4,040,587	522,989	12.9	4,447,100	579,798	13.0	56,809	10.9
Alaska	550,043	22,369	4.1	626,932	35,699	5.7	13,330	59.6
Arizona	3,665,228	478,774	13.1	5,130,632	667,839	13.0	189,065	39.5
Arkansas	2,350,725	350,058	14.9	2,673,400	374,019	14.0	23,961	6.8
California	29,760,021	3,135,552	10.5	33,871,648	3,595,658	10.6	460,106	14.7
Colorado	3,294,394	329,443	10.0	4,301,261	416,073	9.7	86,630	26.3
Connecticut	3,287,116	445,907	13.6	3,405,565	470,183	13.8	24,276	5.4
Delaware	666,168	80,735	12.1	783,600	101,726	13.0	20,991	26.0
District of Columbia ...	606,900	77,847	12.8	572,059	69,898	12.2	-7,949	-10.2
Florida	12,937,926	2,369,431	18.3	15,982,378	2,807,597	17.6	438,166	18.5
Georgia	6,478,216	654,270	10.1	8,186,453	785,275	9.6	131,005	20.0
Hawaii	1,108,229	125,005	11.3	1,211,537	160,601	13.3	35,596	28.5
Idaho	1,006,749	121,265	12.0	1,293,953	145,916	11.3	24,651	20.3
Illinois	11,430,602	1,436,545	12.6	12,419,293	1,500,025	12.1	63,480	4.4
Indiana	5,544,159	696,196	12.6	6,080,485	752,831	12.4	56,635	8.1
Iowa	2,776,755	426,106	15.3	2,926,324	436,213	14.9	10,107	2.4
Kansas	2,477,574	342,571	13.8	2,688,418	356,229	13.3	13,658	4.0
Kentucky	3,685,296	466,845	12.7	4,041,769	504,793	12.5	37,948	8.1
Louisiana	4,219,973	468,991	11.1	4,468,976	516,929	11.6	47,938	10.2
Maine	1,227,928	163,373	13.3	1,274,923	183,402	14.4	20,029	12.3
Maryland	4,781,468	517,482	10.8	5,296,486	599,307	11.3	81,825	15.8
Massachusetts	6,016,425	819,284	13.6	6,349,097	860,162	13.5	40,878	5.0
Michigan	9,295,297	1,108,461	11.9	9,938,444	1,219,018	12.3	110,557	10.0
Minnesota	4,375,099	546,934	12.5	4,919,479	594,266	12.1	47,332	8.7
Mississippi	2,573,216	321,284	12.5	2,844,658	343,523	12.1	22,239	6.9
Missouri	5,117,073	717,681	14.0	5,595,211	755,379	13.5	37,698	5.3
Montana	799,065	106,497	13.3	902,195	120,949	13.4	14,452	13.6
Nebraska	1,578,385	223,068	14.1	1,711,263	232,195	13.6	9,127	4.1
Nevada	1,201,833	127,631	10.6	1,998,257	218,929	11.0	91,298	71.5
New Hampshire	1,109,252	125,029	11.3	1,235,786	147,970	12.0	22,941	18.3
New Jersey	7,730,188	1,032,025	13.4	8,414,350	1,113,136	13.2	81,111	7.9
New Mexico	1,515,069	163,062	10.8	1,819,046	212,225	11.7	49,163	30.1
New York	17,990,455	2,363,722	13.1	18,976,457	2,448,352	12.9	84,630	3.6
North Carolina	6,628,637	804,341	12.1	8,049,313	969,048	12.0	164,707	20.5
North Dakota	638,800	91,055	14.3	642,200	94,478	14.7	3,423	3.8
Ohio	10,847,115	1,406,961	13.0	11,353,140	1,507,757	13.3	100,796	7.2
Oklahoma	3,145,585	424,213	13.5	3,450,654	455,950	13.2	31,737	7.5
Oregon	2,842,321	391,324	13.8	3,421,399	438,177	12.8	46,853	12.0
Pennsylvania	11,881,643	1,829,106	15.4	12,281,054	1,919,165	15.6	90,059	4.9
Rhode Island	1,003,464	150,547	15.0	1,048,319	152,402	14.5	1,855	1.2
South Carolina	3,486,703	396,935	11.4	4,012,012	485,333	12.1	88,398	22.3
South Dakota	696,004	102,331	14.7	754,844	108,131	14.3	5,800	5.7
Tennessee	4,877,185	618,818	12.7	5,689,283	703,311	12.4	84,493	13.7
Texas	16,986,510	1,716,576	10.1	20,851,820	2,072,532	9.9	355,956	20.7
Utah	1,722,850	149,958	8.7	2,233,169	190,222	8.5	40,264	26.9
Vermont	562,758	66,163	11.8	608,827	77,510	12.7	11,347	17.2
Virginia	6,187,358	664,470	10.7	7,078,515	792,333	11.2	127,863	19.2
Washington	4,866,692	575,288	11.8	5,894,121	662,148	11.2	86,860	15.1
West Virginia	1,793,477	268,897	15.0	1,808,344	276,895	15.3	7,998	3.0
Wisconsin	4,891,769	651,221	13.3	5,363,675	702,553	13.1	51,332	7.9
Wyoming	453,588	47,195	10.4	493,782	57,693	11.7	10,498	22.2
Puerto Rico	3,522,037	340,884	9.7	3,808,610	425,137	11.2	84,253	24.7

Source: U.S. Census Bureau, Census 2000 Summary File 1; 1990 Census of Population, *General Population Characteristics,* (1990 CP-1).

Figure 3.

Percent 65 Years and Over: 2000

(For information on confidentiality protection, nonsampling error, and definitions, see *www.census.gov/prod/cen2000/doc/sf1.pdf*)

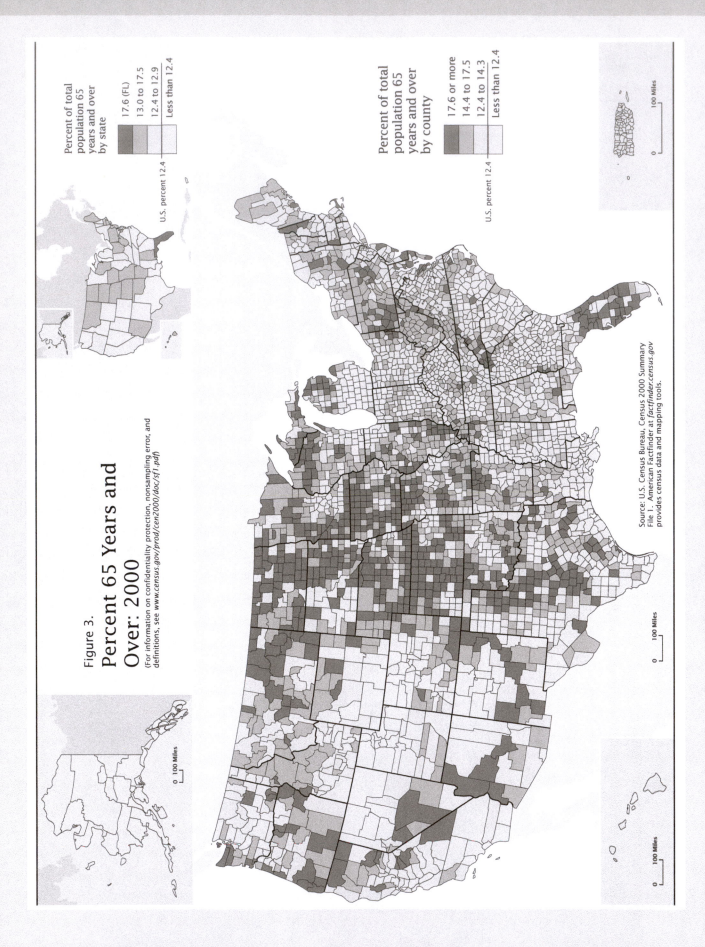

Percent of total population 65 years and over by state

17.6 (FL)
13.0 to 17.5
12.4 to 12.9
Less than 12.4

U.S. percent 12.4

Percent of total population 65 years and over by county

17.6 or more
14.4 to 17.5
12.4 to 14.3
Less than 12.4

U.S. percent 12.4

Source: U.S. Census Bureau, Census 2000 Summary File 1. American Factfinder at *factfinder.census.gov* provides census data and mapping tools.

West Virginia, which had proportions of 15.6 percent and 15.3 percent of their respective total populations. Alaska had the lowest proportion 65 years and over (5.7 percent). Four other states had proportions less than 10 percent — Texas (9.9 percent), Colorado (9.7 percent), Georgia (9.6 percent), and Utah (8.5 percent).

California, the most populous state, was also the state with the largest number of people 65 years and over (3.6 million people). Following California were Florida and New York, with 2.8 million and 2.4 million older people, respectively. Alaska had the fewest number of people 65 years and over, with 36,000 people.

The proportion 65 years and over in counties followed regional trends.

Figure 3 shows the proportion 65 years and over of each of the country's 3,141 counties and equivalent areas. The broad patterns evident on the map include a high proportion of people 65 years and over in counties extending through the Great Plains and south into central Texas. Many of these counties had a proportion of people 65 years and over that equaled or exceeded the proportion of the older population in the state of Florida (17.6 percent). The presence of this band in the Midwest suggests that the trends of outmigration of the young and aging-in-place have continued in this region. A similar band of counties with high proportions of older people is found in the Northeast region, stretching along Appalachia. By contrast, much of the West region consists of counties with lower proportions 65 years and over than the U.S. proportion of 12.4 percent, in part a result of higher net immigration and fertility.

Table 4.

Counties Exceeding the U.S. Proportion 65 Years and Over by Region: 2000

(For information on confidentiality protection, nonsampling error, and definitions, see www.census.gov/prod/cen2000/doc/sf1.pdf)

Region	Total counties	Counties exceeding U.S. proportion[1]	
		Number	Percent
United States	**3,141**	**2,263**	**72.0**
Northeast.................	217	170	78.3
Midwest..................	1,055	869	82.4
South....................	1,424	980	68.8
West.....................	445	244	54.8

[1]U.S. proportion 65 years and over was 12.4 percent.

Source: U.S. Census Bureau, Census 2000 Summary File 1.

Table 5.

Ten Places of 100,000 or More Population With the Highest Proportion of Their Population 65 Years and Over: 2000

(For information on confidentiality protection, nonsampling error, and definitions, see www.census.gov/prod/cen2000/doc/sf1.pdf)

Place[1]	Total population	Population 65 years and over	
		Number	Percent
Clearwater, FL	108,787	23,357	21.5
Cape Coral, FL	102,286	20,020	19.6
Honolulu, HI [2].............	371,657	66,257	17.8
St. Petersburg, FL..........	248,232	43,173	17.4
Hollywood, FL	139,357	24,159	17.3
Warren, MI	138,247	23,871	17.3
Miami, FL	362,470	61,768	17.0
Livonia, MI	100,545	16,988	16.9
Scottsdale, AZ	202,705	33,884	16.7
Hialeah, FL................	226,419	37,679	16.6

[1]Census 2000 showed 245 places in the United States with 100,000 or more population. They included 238 incorporated places (including 4 city-county consolidations) and 7 census designated places that were not legally incorporated. For a list of these places by state, see www.census.gov/population/www/cen2000/phc-t6.html.
[2]Honolulu, Hawaii, is a census designated place and is not legally incorporated.

Source: U.S. Census Bureau, Census 2000 Summary File 1.

The proportion 65 years and over of each county's population ranged from a low of 2 percent in Chattahoochee County, Georgia, which has a large military presence, to a high of 35 percent in Charlotte County, Florida. The older population represented 20 percent or more of the total population in 381 counties of the United States, and 30 percent or more of the total population in 10 counties, half of which were in Florida.

Of all 3,141 counties, 2,263 counties (or 72 percent) had a proportion of people 65 years and over that exceeded the national value of 12.4 percent (see Table 4). The Midwest had the highest percent of counties that exceeded this value (82 percent), followed by the Northeast (78 percent), the South (69 percent), and the West (55 percent).

Table 6.
Ten Places of 100,000 or More Population With the Lowest Proportion of Their Population 65 Years and Over: 2000

(For information on confidentiality protection, nonsampling error, and definitions, see www.census.gov/prod/cen2000/doc/sf1.pdf)

| Place[1] | Total population | Population 65 years and over | |
		Number	Percent
Gilbert, AZ	109,697	4,118	3.8
Fontana, CA...............	128,929	6,113	4.7
Plano, TX	222,030	10,911	4.9
Carrollton, TX.............	109,576	5,711	5.2
West Valley City, UT........	108,896	5,858	5.4
Anchorage, AK.............	260,283	14,242	5.5
Moreno Valley, CA..........	142,381	7,809	5.5
Santa Ana, CA.............	337,977	18,565	5.5
Palmdale, CA..............	116,670	6,520	5.6
Provo, UT	105,166	6,020	5.7

[1]Census 2000 showed 245 places in the United States with 100,000 or more population. They included 238 incorporated places (including 4 city-county consolidations) and 7 census designated places that were not legally incorporated. For a list of these places by state, see www.census.gov/population/www/cen2000/phc-t6.html.

Source: U.S. Census Bureau, Census 2000 Summary File 1.

Table 7.
Percent 65 Years and Over of the Ten Largest Cities: 2000

(For information on confidentiality protection, nonsampling error, and definitions, see www.census.gov/prod/cen2000/doc/sf1.pdf)

| City | Total population | Population 65 years and over | |
		Number	Percent
New York, NY	8,008,278	937,857	11.7
Los Angeles, CA	3,694,820	357,129	9.7
Chicago, IL................	2,896,016	298,803	10.3
Houston, TX	1,953,631	164,065	8.4
Philadelphia, PA............	1,517,550	213,722	14.1
Phoenix, AZ	1,321,045	106,795	8.1
San Diego, CA.............	1,223,400	128,008	10.5
Dallas, TX	1,188,580	102,301	8.6
San Antonio, TX............	1,144,646	119,362	10.4
Detroit, MI.................	951,270	99,056	10.4

Source: U.S. Census Bureau, Census 2000 Summary File 1.

A majority of the counties in most states (43) had a proportion of people 65 years and over that exceeded the national value of 12.4 percent. In seven states, more than 90 percent of the counties had proportions 65 years and over that were greater than 12.4 percent. In Rhode Island, all 5 counties had proportions that exceeded 12.4 percent, while in Maine, 15 of 16 counties had proportions exceeding 12.4 percent. The other states were Nebraska, Iowa, West Virginia, Pennsylvania, and North Dakota. In contrast, in only seven states did the majority of counties have proportions 65 years and over that were less than 12.4 percent. These states were Alaska (in which there were no counties that exceeded the national percentage), Delaware, Utah, New Mexico, Colorado, Georgia, and Louisiana.

Table 5 lists the ten places with populations over 100,000 that had the highest proportion of their total population 65 years and over. Six of these places are located in Florida, while two are in Michigan, one is in Hawaii, and one is in Arizona. Clearwater, Florida, had the highest proportion 65 years and over, at 21 percent, followed by Cape Coral, Florida (20 percent) and Honolulu, Hawaii (18 percent).

Eight of the ten places with the lowest proportion 65 years and over are located in the West; the remaining two places are located in the South (see Table 6). Gilbert, Arizona, had the lowest proportion 65 years and over (3.8 percent), followed by Fontana, California (4.7 percent) and Plano, Texas (4.9 percent).

Table 7 lists the proportion 65 years and over of the ten largest cities. Of these cities, only Philadelphia, Pennsylvania, at 14.1 percent, had a proportion that exceeded the national level of 12.4 percent.

ADDITIONAL TOPICS ON THE 65 YEARS AND OVER POPULATION

What proportion of the older population lived in nursing homes in 2000?

The percent of people 65 years and over living in nursing homes declined from 5.1 percent in 1990 to 4.5 percent in 2000 (see Table 8). This percent decline occurred for people 65 to 74 years, 75 to 84 years, and especially in the population 85 years and over, where only 18.2 percent lived in nursing homes in 2000, compared with 24.5 percent in 1990. Ninety-one percent of the nursing home population was 65 years and over in 2000, compared with 90 percent in 1990.

How many centenarians lived in the United States in 2000?

In 2000, there were 50,454 centenarians (people age 100 or over), representing only 1 out of every

Table 8.
Population 65 Years and Over in Nursing Homes by Age: 1990 and 2000

(For information on confidentiality protection, nonsampling error, and definitions, see www.census.gov/prod/cen2000/doc/sf1.pdf)

Age	Percent of age group		2000
	1990	2000	2000
65 years and over	**5.1**	**4.5**	**1,557,800**
65 to 74 years	1.4	1.1	210,159
75 to 84 years	6.1	4.7	574,908
85 years and over	24.5	18.2	772,733

Source: U.S. Census Bureau, Census 2000 special tabulation; 1990 Census of Population, *Nursing Home Population: 1990* (CPH-L-137).

5,578 people. In 1990, centenarians numbered 37,306 people (1 out of every 6,667 people). The greatest number of centenarians (5,341) lived in California in 2000, followed by 3,997 centenarians in New York. South Dakota, with 247 centenarians (1 out of every 3,056 people), and Iowa, with 941 centenarians (1 out of every 3,110 people), had the highest proportion of their population 100 years and over.

WHY DID CENSUS 2000 ASK THE QUESTION ON AGE?

People who answered the census help their communities obtain federal funds as well as valuable information for planning hospitals, roads, and housing assistance. Many government agencies use data on the older population to implement and evaluate programs and policies. For example, the Department of Veterans Affairs must plan for nursing homes, hospitals, and veterans' benefits; the Department of Health and Human Services monitors compliance with the Older Americans Act, and the Equal Employment Opportunity Commission uses data on age in order to enforce the Age Discrimination in Employment Act. The data are also used to forecast the use of social security and medicare benefits.

Private organizations and communities also value data on age for the purposes of planning and assessment. Knowledge about the characteristics of the older population helps businesses select an appropriate mix of merchandise and plan advertising campaigns. Communities also use this information in order to design needed health services and living facilities for the older population.

FOR MORE INFORMATION

For more information on the older population in the United States, visit the U.S. Census Bureau's Internet site at *www.census.gov/population/ www/socdemo/age.html#older.*

Data on age from the Census 2000 Summary File 1 were released on a state-by-state basis during the summer of 2001. Census 2000 data are available on the Internet via *factfinder.census.gov* and for purchase on CD-ROM and later on DVD.

For information on confidentiality protection, nonsampling error, and definitions, see *www.census.gov/ prod/cen2000/doc/sf1.pdf* or contact our Customer Services Center at 301-763-INFO (4636).

Information on other population and housing topics is presented in the Census 2000 Brief series, located on the U.S. Census Bureau's Web site at *www.census.gov/population/ www/cen2000/briefs.html.* This series presents information about race, Hispanic origin, age, sex, household type, housing tenure, and other social, economic, and housing characteristics.

For more information about Census 2000, including data products, call our Customer Services Center at 301-763-INFO (4636) or e-mail *webmaster@census.gov.*

Disability Status: 2000

Census 2000 Brief

Issued March 2003

C2KBR-17

By
Judith Waldrop
and
Sharon M. Stern

Census 2000 counted 49.7 million people with some type of long lasting condition or disability.[1] They represented 19.3 percent of the 257.2 million people who were aged 5 and older in the civilian non-institutionalized population — or nearly one person in five (see Table 1).[2] Within this population, Census 2000 found:

- 9.3 million (3.6 percent) with a sensory disability involving sight or hearing.

- 21.2 million (8.2 percent) with a condition limiting basic physical activities, such as walking, climbing stairs, reaching, lifting, or carrying.

- 12.4 million (4.8 percent) with a physical, mental, or emotional condition causing difficulty in learning, remembering, or concentrating.

- 6.8 million (2.6 percent) with a physical, mental, or emotional condition causing difficulty in dressing, bathing, or getting around inside the home.

- 18.2 million of those aged 16 and older with a condition that made it difficult to go outside the home to shop or visit a doctor (8.6 percent of

Figure 1.

Reproduction of the Questions on Disability From Census 2000

16 **Does this person have any of the following long-lasting conditions:**

	Yes	No
a. Blindness, deafness, or a severe vision or hearing impairment?	☐	☐
b. A condition that substantially limits one or more basic physical activities such as walking, climbing stairs, reaching, lifting, or carrying?	☐	☐

17 **Because of a physical, mental, or emotional condition lasting 6 months or more, does this person have any difficulty in doing any of the following activities:**

	Yes	No
a. Learning, remembering, or concentrating?	☐	☐
b. Dressing, bathing, or getting around inside the home?	☐	☐
c. (Answer if this person is 16 YEARS OLD OR OVER.) Going outside the home alone to shop or visit a doctor's office?	☐	☐
d. (Answer if this person is 16 YEARS OLD OR OVER.) Working at a job or business?	☐	☐

Source: U.S. Census Bureau, Census 2000 questionnaire.

---

[1] The estimates in this report are based on responses from a sample of the population. As with all surveys, estimates may vary from the actual values because of sampling variation or other factors. All statements made in this report have undergone statistical testing and are significant at the 90-percent confidence level, unless otherwise noted.

[2] In this report, the population universe for people with disabilities excludes people in the military and people who are in institutions.

USCENSUSBUREAU

Helping You Make Informed Decisions

U.S. Department of Commerce
Economics and Statistics Administration
U.S. CENSUS BUREAU

United States
Census 2000

Table 1.
Characteristics of the Civilian Noninstitutionalized Population by Age, Disability Status, and Type of Disability: 2000

(For information on confidentiality protection, sampling error, nonsampling error, and definitions, see www.census.gov/prod/cen2000/doc/sf3.pdf)

Characteristic	Total		Male		Female	
	Number	Percent	Number	Percent	Number	Percent
Population 5 and older	257,167,527	100.0	124,636,825	100.0	132,530,702	100.0
With any disability	49,746,248	19.3	24,439,531	19.6	25,306,717	19.1
Population 5 to 15	45,133,667	100.0	23,125,324	100.0	22,008,343	100.0
With any disability	2,614,919	5.8	1,666,230	7.2	948,689	4.3
Sensory	442,894	1.0	242,706	1.0	200,188	0.9
Physical	455,461	1.0	251,852	1.1	203,609	0.9
Mental	2,078,502	4.6	1,387,393	6.0	691,109	3.1
Self-care	419,018	0.9	244,824	1.1	174,194	0.8
Population 16 to 64	178,687,234	100.0	87,570,583	100.0	91,116,651	100.0
With any disability	33,153,211	18.6	17,139,019	19.6	16,014,192	17.6
Sensory	4,123,902	2.3	2,388,121	2.7	1,735,781	1.9
Physical	11,150,365	6.2	5,279,731	6.0	5,870,634	6.4
Mental	6,764,439	3.8	3,434,631	3.9	3,329,808	3.7
Self-care	3,149,875	1.8	1,463,184	1.7	1,686,691	1.9
Difficulty going outside the home	11,414,508	6.4	5,569,362	6.4	5,845,146	6.4
Employment disability	21,287,570	11.9	11,373,786	13.0	9,913,784	10.9
Population 65 and older	33,346,626	100.0	13,940,918	100.0	19,405,708	100.0
With any disability	13,978,118	41.9	5,634,282	40.4	8,343,836	43.0
Sensory	4,738,479	14.2	2,177,216	15.6	2,561,263	13.2
Physical	9,545,680	28.6	3,590,139	25.8	5,955,541	30.7
Mental	3,592,912	10.8	1,380,060	9.9	2,212,852	11.4
Self-care	3,183,840	9.5	1,044,910	7.5	2,138,930	11.0
Difficulty going outside the home	6,795,517	20.4	2,339,128	16.8	4,456,389	23.0

Source: U.S. Census Bureau, Census 2000 Summary File 3.

the 212.0 million people this age).

- 21.3 million of those aged 16 to 64 with a condition that affected their ability to work at a job or business (11.9 percent of the 178.7 million people this age).

This report is part of a series that presents population and housing data collected by Census 2000. It presents data on the disability status of people aged 5 and older in the civilian noninstitutionalized population, and describes the geographic distribution of people with disabilities for the United States,[3]

[3] The text of this report discusses data for the United States, including the 50 states and the District of Columbia. Data for the Commonwealth of Puerto Rico are shown in Table 3 and Figure 5.

including regions, states, counties, and places with populations of 100,000 or more.

Information on disability was first collected in the 1830 census and the questions have evolved over the decades. Census 2000 asked two questions (see Figure 1) about long-lasting conditions among the population aged 5 and older. The first question, with two subparts, focused on long-lasting impairments involving vision or hearing (sensory disability) and certain physical limitations, such as difficulty walking or climbing stairs (physical disability). The second question, with four subparts, concentrated on difficulty performing certain activities due to a physical, mental, or emotional condition. People aged 5

and older were asked if they experienced difficulty with cognitive tasks such as learning, remembering, and concentrating (mental disability). They were also asked about difficulty in taking care of personal needs like dressing and bathing (self-care disability). People aged 16 and older were asked if they experienced difficulty going outside the home to shop or visit the doctor. Additionally, people in this group were asked if a physical, mental, or emotional condition caused them difficulty working at a job or business (employment disability).

This report uses a disability status indicator to present estimates of the number and percentage of people with disabilities. People were defined as having a disability if

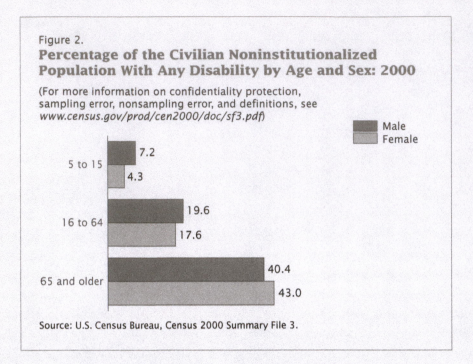

Figure 2.

Percentage of the Civilian Noninstitutionalized Population With Any Disability by Age and Sex: 2000

(For more information on confidentiality protection, sampling error, nonsampling error, and definitions, see *www.census.gov/prod/cen2000/doc/sf3.pdf*)

- Male
- Female

5 to 15: 7.2 / 4.3

16 to 64: 19.6 / 17.6

65 and older: 40.4 / 43.0

Source: U.S. Census Bureau, Census 2000 Summary File 3.

one or more of the following conditions were true:

- They were aged 5 or older and responded "yes" to a sensory, physical, mental, or self-care disability.

- They were aged 16 years or older and responded "yes" to a disability affecting going outside the home.

- They were between the ages of 16 and 64 and responded "yes" to an employment disability.

When referring to people with disabilities, this report does not distinguish between people who responded positively to only one of the subparts and those who responded positively to more than one. As a result, the terms "with a disability," "with any disability," and "with one or more disabilities" are used interchangeably throughout the report.

Census 2000 asked for disability information from all people aged 5 and older, except those responding to special military or shipboard questionnaires. This report consid-

ers only the civilian noninstitutionalized population.

As a result of extensive discussions with the disability and policy research communities, the Census 2000 questions on disability were substantially different from the 1990 questions on this topic. While Census 2000 gathered data from the population aged 5 and older, data collected in 1990 came only from the population aged 15 and older. The 1990 questions focused on conditions limiting work, going outside the home, and self-care, but did not specify sensory impairments or conditions restricting walking, climbing stairs, reaching, lifting, or carrying. Because of the major differences between the disability questions in 1990 and 2000, comparisons between the two censuses are not recommended.

Census 2000 showed disability rising with age.

Disability rates rose with age for both sexes, but significant differences existed between men and women, as illustrated in Figure 2. For people under 65 years old, the

prevalence of disability among men and boys was higher than among women and girls. In contrast, disability rates were higher for women than men aged 65 and older.

Specifically, in 2000, the disability rate was 7.2 percent for boys 5 to 15 years old and 4.3 percent for girls the same age. Nearly two-thirds of all children with disabilities were boys. Census 2000 found 1.7 million boys this age with one or more disabilities, compared with 949,000 girls this age.

Among people aged 16 to 64 in the civilian noninstitutionalized population, 19.6 percent of men and 17.6 percent of women reported one or more disabilities. Among people 65 and older, the disability rate was 43.0 percent for women and 40.4 percent for men. In this age group, 59.7 percent of people with disabilities were women. However, 58.2 percent of all people aged 65 and older were women.

In the civilian noninstitutionalized population, people 65 and older were much more likely than people of working age (16 to 64) to report a sensory, physical, mental, or self-care disability, or a disability causing difficulty going outside the home (see Figure 3). While only 6.4 percent of working-age adults experienced difficulty going outside the home alone to shop or visit the doctor, 20.4 percent of older adults reported these problems. Physical disabilities affected 6.2 percent of the working-age population and 28.6 percent of older adults. About 3.8 percent of working-age adults reported difficulties in learning, remembering, or concentrating (a mental disability), compared with 10.8 percent of older adults. The prevalence of a self-care disability was more than 5 times greater among older adults

(9.5 percent) than among people of working age (1.8 percent). Also, the occurrence of sensory disabilities was more than 6 times greater among older adults than working-age people, 14.2 percent compared with 2.3 percent.

Disability rates varied among the major racial and ethnic groups.

Census 2000 allowed respondents to choose more than one race. With the exception of the Two or more races group, all race groups discussed in this report refer to people who indicated *only one* racial identity among the six major categories: White, Black or African American, American Indian and Alaska Native, Asian, Native Hawaiian and Other Pacific Islander, and Some other race.[4] The use of the single-race population in this report does not imply that it is the preferred method of presenting or analyzing data. The Census Bureau uses a variety of approaches.[5]

Interestingly, people who indicated that they were White (and no other race) and were not of Hispanic or Latino origin had a low overall disability rate despite the fact that their median age was higher than for other racial and ethnic groups

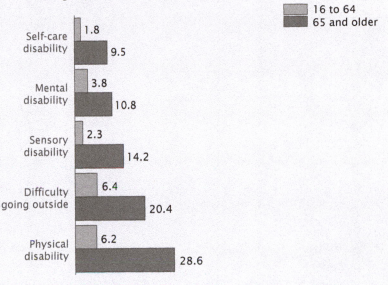

Figure 3.

Percentage of the Civilian Noninstitutionalized Population With a Disability by Age and Type of Disability: 2000

(For more information on confidentiality protection, sampling error, nonsampling error, and definitions, see *www.census.gov/prod/cen2000/doc/sf3.pdf*)

Legend: 16 to 64 / 65 and older

Self-care disability: 1.8 / 9.5
Mental disability: 3.8 / 10.8
Sensory disability: 2.3 / 14.2
Difficulty going outside: 6.4 / 20.4
Physical disability: 6.2 / 28.6

Source: U.S. Census Bureau, Census 2000 Summary File 3.

examined in this brief.[6] In Census 2000, they reported a disability rate of 18.3 percent, compared with 19.3 percent for all noninstitutionalized civilians aged 5 and older, as shown in Table 2.[7]

Among the racial and ethnic groups examined in this report, the highest overall estimated disability rate, 24.3 percent, was shared by two groups — people

who reported Black and people who reported American Indian and Alaska Native. The disability rates for these two groups were higher than the rates for non-Hispanic Whites in each of the broad age groups investigated in this report (see Table 2). Among children 5 to 15 years old, the disability rate was 5.7 percent for non-Hispanic Whites, but 7.0 percent for Black children and 7.7 percent for American Indian and Alaska Native children. Although the disability rate was 16.2 percent for non-Hispanic Whites of working age (16 to 64), it was 26.4 percent for Blacks and 27.0 percent for American Indians and Alaska Natives. Among people 65 and older, the rates were 40.4, 52.8, and 57.6 percent, respectively.

Asians who reported only one race had the lowest overall disability

---

[4] For further information on each of the 6 major race groups and the Two or more races population, see reports from the Census 2000 Brief series (C2KBR/01), available on the Census 2000 Web site at *www.census.gov/population/www/cen2000/briefs.html.*

[5] This report draws heavily on Summary File 3, a Census 2000 product that can be accessed through American FactFinder, available from the Census Bureau's Web site, *www.census.gov.* Information on people who reported more than one race, such as "White *and* American Indian and Alaska Native" or "Asian *and* Black or African American," is forthcoming in Summary File 4, which will also be available through American FactFinder in 2003. About 2.6 percent of people reported more than one race.

[6] For information on median age, see Age: 2000 (C2KBR/01-12).

[7] Hereafter this report uses the term Black to refer to people who are Black or African American, the term Pacific Islander to refer to people who are Native Hawaiian and Other Pacific Islander, and the term Hispanic to refer to people who are Hispanic or Latino.

Because Hispanics may be of any race, data in this report for Hispanics overlap with data for racial groups. Based on Census 2000 sample data, the proportion Hispanic was 8.0 percent for Whites, 1.9 percent for Blacks, 14.6 percent for American Indians and Alaska Natives, 1.0 percent for Asians, 9.5 percent for Pacific Islanders, 97.1 percent for those reporting Some other race, and 31.1 percent for those reporting Two or more races.

Table 2.
Percentage of the Civilian Noninstitutionalized Population With Any Disability by Age and Selected Race and Hispanic Origin Groups: 2000

(For information on confidentiality protection, sampling error, nonsampling error, and definitions, see www.census.gov/prod/cen2000/doc/sf3.pdf)

Race and Hispanic or Latino origin	Total population aged 5 and older	Percent with a disability			
		5 and older	5 to 15	16 to 64	65 and older
Total.......................................	257,167,527	19.3	5.8	18.6	41.9
White alone.............................	195,100,538	18.5	5.6	16.8	40.6
Black or African American alone.................	30,297,703	24.3	7.0	26.4	52.8
American Indian and Alaska Native alone	2,187,507	24.3	7.7	27.0	57.6
Asian alone.............................	9,455,058	16.6	2.9	16.9	40.8
Native Hawaiian and Other Pacific Islander alone ..	337,996	19.0	5.1	21.0	48.5
Some other race alone........................	13,581,921	19.9	5.2	23.5	50.4
Two or more races...........................	6,206,804	21.7	7.1	25.1	51.8
Hispanic or Latino (of any race)	31,041,269	20.9	5.4	24.0	48.5
White alone, not Hispanic or Latino...............	180,151,084	18.3	5.7	16.2	40.4

Source: U.S. Census Bureau, Census 2000 Summary File 3.

rate of any of the racial and ethnic groups examined in this report: 16.6 percent. Their child disability rate, 2.9 percent, was also the lowest. The disability rate for working-age Asians (16.9 percent) was slightly higher than the rate for working-age non-Hispanic Whites, whereas the rates for those 65 and older were not significantly different.

The overall disability rate for single-race Pacific Islanders (19.0 percent) and their child disability rate (5.1 percent) were both slightly higher than the corresponding rates for Asians, but not statistically different from the rates for non-Hispanic Whites. However, the rates for Pacific Islander working-age adults (21.0 percent) and older adults (48.5 percent) were higher than the rates for Asians and non-Hispanic Whites in these same age groups.

Even though people reporting two or more races had the lowest median age among the racial or ethnic groups examined in this

report, their disability rates were among the highest in 2000 — 21.7 percent overall. Among those reporting two or more races, 7.1 percent of children, 25.1 percent of working-age adults, and 51.8 percent of older adults reported at least one disability.

The overall disability rate was higher for Hispanics (20.9 percent) than for non-Hispanic Whites (18.3 percent). However, their child disability rate was lower — (5.4 percent compared with 5.7 percent). Still, the disability rates for Hispanics of working-age (24.0 percent) and older (48.5 percent) exceeded the rates for non-Hispanic Whites.

GEOGRAPHIC DISTRIBUTION OF PEOPLE WITH DISABILITIES

The following discussion on the geographic distribution of people with disabilities is based on the civilian noninstitutionalized population aged 5 and older.

Almost two out of every five people with a disability lived in the South, while about one in five lived in each of the other three regions of the United States.[8]

Even though 35.5 percent of the civilian noninstitutionalized population 5 and older lived in the South in 2000, this region was home to 38.3 percent of people with disabilities, as shown in Figure 4. The 20.9-percent disability rate in the South was higher than the rate in any other region. This high rate, coupled with the

[8] The Northeast region includes the states of Connecticut, Maine, Massachusetts, New Hampshire, New Jersey, New York, Pennsylvania, Rhode Island, and Vermont. The Midwest region includes the states of Illinois, Indiana, Iowa, Kansas, Michigan, Minnesota, Missouri, Nebraska, North Dakota, Ohio, South Dakota, and Wisconsin. The South region includes the states of Alabama, Arkansas, Delaware, Florida, Georgia, Kentucky, Louisiana, Maryland, Mississippi, North Carolina, Oklahoma, South Carolina, Tennessee, Texas, Virginia, West Virginia, and the District of Columbia, a state equivalent. The West region includes the states of Alaska, Arizona, California, Colorado, Hawaii, Idaho, Montana, Nevada, New Mexico, Oregon, Utah, Washington, and Wyoming.

fact that the South contained the largest total population among the four regions, accounted for the fact that the South recorded the largest disabled population in 2000 — 19.1 million people.

The West and the Midwest had the second and third largest disabled populations — 10.8 million and 10.5 million, respectively. However, the percentage of people with disabilities was low in both these regions — 18.7 percent in the West and 17.7 percent in the Midwest. Among the four regions, the Northeast had the fewest people with disabilities — 9.5 million or 19.2 percent of its total population — but it also had the smallest total population.

Among the states, the disability rate was highest in West Virginia.

Among the 50 states and the District of Columbia, the highest disability rates were in the South, as shown in Table 3. West Virginia, the state with the highest median age in the United States, also recorded the highest disability rate, 24.4 percent. It was followed closely by four other southern states: Kentucky (23.7 percent), Arkansas (23.6 percent), Mississippi (23.6 percent), and Alabama (23.2 percent).[9] Not all states in the South had high disability rates. In fact, Delaware, Maryland, and Virginia had disability rates that were significantly below the national rate.

Alabama, Arkansas, Kentucky, Mississippi, and West Virginia — the states with highest overall disability rates — also registered high rates for each of the individual

Figure 4.

Percent Distribution of All Noninstitutionalized Civilians Aged 5 and Older and All People With Disabilities by Region: 2000

(For information on confidentiality protection, sampling error, nonsampling error, and definitions, *www.census.gov/prod/cen2000/doc/sf3.pdf*)

	Northeast	Midwest	South	West
Percentage of total	19.2	22.9	35.5	22.4
Percentage of people with disabilities	19.0	21.0	38.3	21.6

Note: Numbers may not add to 100 percent due to rounding.
Source: U.S. Census Bureau, Census 2000 Summary File 3.

measures. For example, in Mississippi 4.8 percent of people reported a sensory disability, 11.3 percent reported a physical disability, and 6.4 percent reported a mental disability. These rates exceeded the national rates of 3.6 percent, 8.2 percent, and 4.8 percent, respectively.[10]

The states with the lowest disability rates were in the West and Midwest. Alaska (14.9 percent), Utah (14.9 percent), and Minnesota (15.0 percent) topped the list of states with the lowest disability rates.[11] Wisconsin and Nebraska, both of which had an estimated disability rate of 16.0 percent, followed.[12]

Minnesota and Utah registered low rates by every measure. Even so, low disability rates by one measure did not guarantee low rates by every measure. For example, Nevada had one of the lowest

percentages of the civilian noninstitutionalized population with difficulty learning, remembering, or concentrating (mental disability), 3.8 percent compared with 4.8 percent nationwide. However, among the civilian noninstitutionalized population 16 to 64 years old, the percentage of Nevadans who reported difficulty working at a job or business was high, 14.5 percent compared with 11.9 percent, nationally.

In 2000, counties with very high disability rates were clustered in the coal mining areas of Kentucky, West Virginia, and Virginia.[13]

Included in this group of counties were Bell, Breathitt, Clay, Harlan, Leslie, Martin, and Owsley counties in Kentucky; Buchanan County, Virginia; and McDowell County,

---

[9] The disability rate for Kentucky was not significantly different than the rates for Arkansas or Mississippi, and the rate for Arkansas is not significantly different than the rate for Mississippi.

[10] The rate of sensory disability in Mississippi and the rate of mental disability in the United States are not significantly different.

[11] The disability rates in Alaska, Utah, and Minnesota were not significantly different from one another.

[12] The disability rate in Nebraska was not significantly different from the rate for Colorado (16.3 percent).

[13] Although the point estimate for the disability rate in Kalawao county, Hawaii, (60 percent) was the highest, it was not statistically different from high disability rates in other counties. Kalawao County registered a high disability rate in Census 2000 in part because of its charter. According to Hawaii state law (§324-34(b)), it is "under the jurisdiction and control of the [state] department of health and is governed by the laws and rules relating to the department and the care and treatment of persons affected with Hansen's disease." Hansen's disease is also called leprosy.

Table 3.
Disability Status of the Civilian Noninstitutionalized Population of the United States, Regions, States, and for Puerto Rico: 2000

(For information on confidentiality protection, sampling error, nonsampling error, and definitions, *www.census.gov/prod/cen2000/doc/sf3.pdf*)

Area	Population 5 and older						Population 16 and older		Population 16 to 64	
		Percentage with selected disabilities						Percentage with difficulty going outside the home		Percentage with employment disability
	Number	Any disability	Sensory disability	Physical disability	Mental disability	Self-care disability	Number		Number	
United States ..	**257,167,527**	**19.3**	**3.6**	**8.2**	**4.8**	**2.6**	**212,033,860**	**8.6**	**178,687,234**	**11.9**
Region										
Northeast..........	49,386,446	19.2	3.3	7.7	4.6	2.6	41,161,934	8.8	34,177,140	11.9
Midwest...........	59,017,677	17.7	3.5	7.8	4.6	2.4	48,620,454	7.4	40,836,120	10.3
South.............	91,179,367	20.9	4.0	9.2	5.2	2.9	75,292,633	9.3	63,405,874	13.0
West.............	57,584,037	18.7	3.5	7.5	4.6	2.4	46,958,839	8.5	40,268,100	11.9
State										
Alabama	4,071,185	23.2	4.7	11.0	6.2	3.6	3,370,738	10.6	2,815,333	13.7
Alaska...........	557,705	14.9	3.8	6.6	4.4	1.9	436,142	5.3	401,841	8.3
Arizona	4,667,187	19.3	3.8	8.2	4.6	2.4	3,822,951	8.0	3,169,173	12.2
Arkansas.........	2,440,964	23.6	5.1	11.8	6.5	3.7	2,021,501	9.9	1,666,895	13.8
California.........	30,853,063	19.2	3.2	7.2	4.6	2.5	25,039,958	9.7	21,570,148	12.8
Colorado	3,926,325	16.3	3.3	6.7	4.2	1.9	3,246,486	6.1	2,847,842	9.9
Connecticut	3,120,953	17.5	3.1	6.9	4.2	2.3	2,589,549	7.6	2,149,614	11.0
Delaware.........	716,691	18.4	3.2	8.0	4.6	2.3	594,673	7.2	497,601	11.2
District of Columbia ..	528,933	21.9	3.2	8.0	4.9	3.0	458,424	11.0	391,946	13.5
Florida............	14,730,208	22.2	4.1	9.6	5.1	2.9	12,435,261	9.8	9,715,134	14.2
Georgia	7,402,293	19.7	3.4	8.2	4.8	2.6	6,061,272	9.2	5,306,618	12.6
Hawaii	1,087,490	18.4	3.5	7.2	4.6	2.3	903,314	8.9	745,317	11.4
Idaho............	1,174,093	17.1	4.2	7.9	4.9	2.1	947,715	6.0	807,071	9.4
Illinois	11,350,345	17.6	3.1	7.2	4.1	2.4	9,336,005	8.3	7,919,587	10.8
Indiana...........	5,563,619	19.0	3.8	8.3	4.8	2.5	4,591,434	7.5	3,884,065	11.3
Iowa.............	2,686,760	16.6	3.5	7.5	4.2	2.1	2,230,430	6.2	1,826,699	9.3
Kansas	2,440,373	17.6	3.7	8.0	4.3	2.3	1,999,749	6.9	1,669,088	10.2
Kentucky	3,695,005	23.7	5.1	12.2	6.9	3.6	3,081,517	9.7	2,604,977	13.9
Louisiana.........	4,045,963	21.8	4.3	9.8	5.9	3.3	3,288,622	9.5	2,799,048	12.9
Maine............	1,187,124	20.0	4.4	9.5	5.8	2.5	993,421	6.5	818,423	11.7
Maryland	4,843,046	17.6	3.0	7.0	4.3	2.2	3,985,174	7.9	3,412,197	10.8
Massachusetts......	5,860,845	18.5	3.2	7.1	4.7	2.4	4,918,464	7.9	4,111,458	11.8
Michigan	9,138,340	18.7	3.5	8.3	5.2	2.7	7,503,217	8.0	6,332,137	10.7
Minnesota	4,526,211	15.0	3.0	6.4	4.1	1.9	3,717,854	5.8	3,163,716	8.6
Mississippi	2,575,139	23.6	4.8	11.3	6.4	3.8	2,093,773	11.1	1,767,972	14.4
Missouri..........	5,120,568	19.0	3.9	9.1	5.2	2.7	4,227,906	7.9	3,516,489	10.8
Montana	831,694	17.5	4.4	8.6	4.9	2.1	685,843	5.7	571,484	9.3
Nebraska.........	1,561,301	16.0	3.4	7.0	3.8	2.0	1,283,164	6.3	1,066,390	9.4
Nevada	1,823,351	20.6	3.5	7.9	3.8	2.2	1,508,632	8.3	1,294,567	14.5
New Hampshire.....	1,145,557	16.9	3.4	7.2	4.6	2.0	946,154	5.6	807,076	10.1
New Jersey	7,735,218	18.0	2.9	6.9	4.0	2.4	6,426,224	8.8	5,362,242	11.6
New Mexico	1,659,502	20.4	4.5	9.0	5.4	2.7	1,339,155	8.6	1,133,564	12.3
New York.........	17,464,264	20.6	3.2	8.0	4.7	2.8	14,526,599	10.5	12,193,044	13.2
North Carolina	7,316,733	21.1	3.9	9.3	5.1	2.9	6,096,197	9.2	5,172,069	13.3
North Dakota	586,289	16.7	3.7	7.1	4.2	1.9	485,666	6.4	398,305	9.3
Ohio.............	10,417,902	18.3	3.6	8.5	5.0	2.6	8,608,703	7.6	7,186,632	10.3
Oklahoma	3,124,998	21.6	5.0	10.7	5.7	3.1	2,577,036	8.6	2,147,470	12.5
Oregon	3,158,684	18.8	4.1	8.7	5.5	2.5	2,634,072	6.8	2,210,613	10.6
Pennsylvania	11,336,483	18.6	3.7	8.4	4.8	2.7	9,478,129	7.9	7,668,809	10.6
Rhode Island	967,557	20.2	3.5	7.8	5.1	2.4	810,601	8.6	667,036	12.7
South Carolina	3,652,809	22.2	4.1	9.6	5.6	3.2	3,019,142	9.9	2,553,295	14.3
South Dakota......	686,094	16.7	3.8	7.6	3.9	1.9	560,279	6.2	459,778	9.4
Tennessee	5,214,986	22.0	4.5	10.6	6.2	3.3	4,346,553	9.4	3,678,482	13.2
Texas............	18,761,475	19.2	3.5	7.6	4.4	2.6	15,142,480	9.0	13,176,208	12.5
Utah.............	1,998,373	14.9	3.1	5.9	4.2	1.7	1,575,354	5.8	1,391,541	8.9
Vermont..........	568,445	17.1	3.8	7.7	5.1	2.1	472,793	5.5	399,438	9.7
Virginia	6,377,588	18.1	3.3	7.8	4.7	2.4	5,290,221	7.7	4,536,339	10.9
Washington	5,395,395	18.2	4.1	8.1	5.1	2.4	4,448,728	6.9	3,809,080	10.6
West Virginia	1,681,351	24.4	5.8	13.5	7.7	4.1	1,430,049	10.1	1,164,290	13.2
Wisconsin	4,939,875	16.0	3.1	6.9	4.2	2.1	4,076,047	6.4	3,413,234	9.1
Wyoming	451,175	17.1	4.2	7.7	4.4	1.8	370,489	5.3	315,859	9.8
Puerto Rico	3,482,047	26.8	7.1	11.2	7.8	4.6	2,810,111	17.3	2,392,893	15.0

Source: U.S. Census Bureau, Census 2000 Summary File 3.

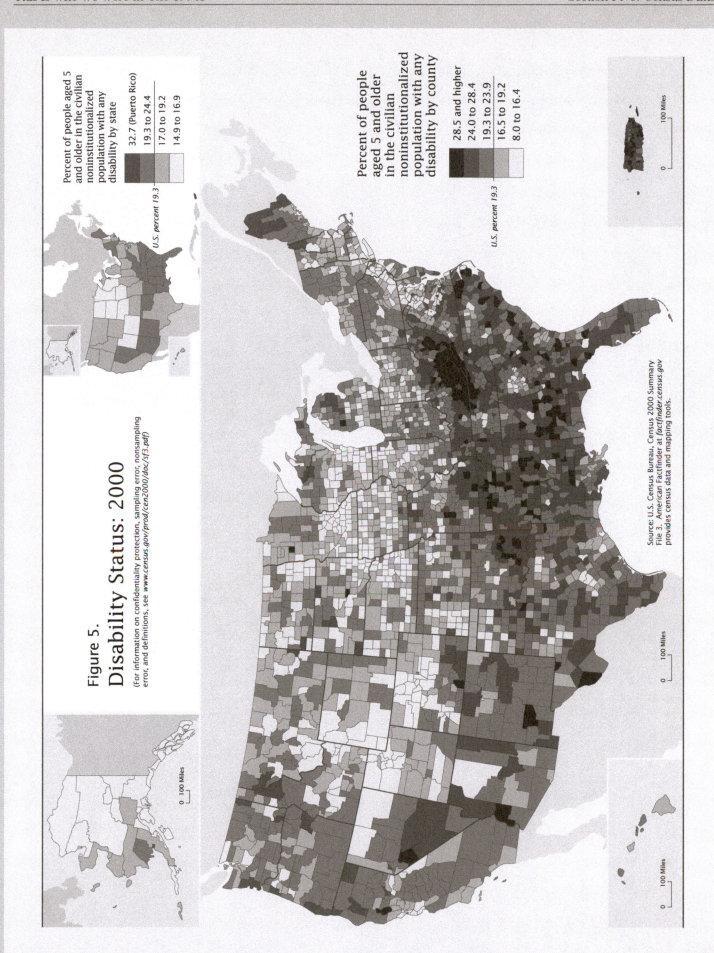

Figure 5.
Disability Status: 2000

(For information on confidentiality protection, sampling error, nonsampling error, and definitions, see *www.census.gov/prod/cen2000/doc/sf3.pdf*)

Percent of people aged 5 and older in the civilian noninstitutionalized population with any disability by state

32.7 (Puerto Rico)
19.3 to 24.4
17.0 to 19.2
14.9 to 16.9

U.S. percent 19.3

Percent of people aged 5 and older in the civilian noninstitutionalized population with any disability by county

28.5 and higher
24.0 to 28.4
19.3 to 23.9
16.5 to 19.2
8.0 to 16.4

U.S. percent 19.3

Source: U.S. Census Bureau, Census 2000 Summary File 3. American Factfinder at *factfinder.census.gov* provides census data and mapping tools.

Table 4.

Ten Places of 100,000 or More With the Highest Percentage of People Aged 5 and Older With Disabilities in the Civilian Noninstitutionalized Population: 2000

(For information on confidentiality protection, sampling error, nonsampling error, and definitions, see www.census.gov/prod/cen2000/sf3.pdf)

Place	Number with disabilities	Percent	Margin of error*
Paterson, NJ	40,068	29.8	0.4
Miami, FL	97,782	29.4	0.2
Newark, NJ	71,291	29.0	0.3
Detroit, MI	244,893	28.3	0.1
Birmingham, AL	61,421	27.6	0.3
Springfield, MA	38,264	27.6	0.4
Hartford, CT	29,669	27.2	0.4
Baltimore, MD	162,044	27.2	0.2
Gary, IN	25,182	26.9	0.4
Buffalo, NY	69,927	26.2	0.3

* When the margin of error is added to or subtracted from the estimate, it produces a 90-percent confidence interval.

Note: Because of sampling error, the estimates in this table may not be significantly different from one another or from other places not listed in this table.

Source: U.S. Census Bureau, Census 2000 Summary File 3.

West Virginia, as shown in Figure 5. Counties with high disability rates covered most of the South, with the exception of the Atlanta metropolitan area and a few counties scattered around the region.

The West, especially Colorado, contained many of the counties with the lowest disability rates. The disability rate was about 10 percent or less in Yakutat City and Borough in Alaska; Douglas, Gunnison, Routt, and San Miguel counties in Colorado; Madison County, Idaho, Summit County, Utah, and Teton County, Wyoming.

Counties with disability rates below the national rate distinguished the upper Midwest, especially the Minneapolis-St. Paul metropolitan area. Grant County, Nebraska, had a disability rate of about 10 percent. In fact, only a handful of counties in either the Midwest or the Northeast exhibited extremely high rates of disability. Many counties with low rates were found in the high-density area that stretched from New York City to Richmond, Virginia.

More than one person in four reported a disability in each of the ten places with the highest disability rates.

Among places with populations of 100,000 or more,[14] Paterson, New Jersey; Miami, Florida; and Newark, New Jersey, registered the highest proportions of people with disabilities, as shown in Table 4.[15] At least one person in four experienced some type of disability in each of the ten places with the highest point estimates for disability. Most of these places were older industrial cities. High concentrations of Blacks, Hispanics, and other populations exhibiting high disability rates were also common in these areas.

In 2000, many of the places with the lowest disability rates were

[14] Census 2000 shows 245 places in the United States with 100,000 or more population. They include 238 incorporated places (including 4 city-county consolidations) and 7 census designated places that are not legally incorporated. For a list of these places by state, see www.census.gov/population/www/cen2000/phc-t6.html.
[15] The disability rates in Paterson, Miami, and Newark were not significantly different from one another. The percentage in Newark was not significantly different than Detroit.

fast growing areas on the outskirts of metropolitan areas — places with high concentrations of families with children (see Table 5). Naperville, Illinois, was the place with the lowest percentage of people with disabilities, 7.9 percent. One of the reasons why some places had low disability rates may be that only a small proportion of residents were aged 65 and older. Provo, Utah; Gilbert, Arizona; Plano, Texas; and Carrollton, Texas, were among the ten places with the lowest disability rates and the lowest percentage of older residents.[16]

ADDITIONAL FINDINGS ON PEOPLE WITH DISABILITIES

How many people had more than one disability in 2000?

Disability measures from Census 2000 were not mutually exclusive and 46.3 percent of people with any disability reported more than one. A person with a single condition might report both a physical disability and an employment disability. For example, a person with severe asthma may have also experienced difficulty climbing stairs and difficulty working at a job or business. The people who responded positively to more than one of the Census 2000 disability questions demonstrated the degree to which a long-lasting physical, mental, or emotional condition could affect more than one aspect of a person's life.

Of the people who reported an employment disability, 56.4 percent also reported at least one other type of condition. (See Figure 6.) Additionally, 63.7 percent of people

[16] The disability rates in Provo, Gilbert, and Plano were not significantly different from one another. For more information on the population aged 65 and over, see The 65 Years and Over Population: 2000 (C2KBR/01-10).

with a sensory disability, 67.6 percent of people with a physical disability, and 70.9 percent of people with a mental disability reported more than one condition. Among people with difficulty going outside the home, 81.5 percent indicated at least one other measure of disability. The disability most likely to be linked to multiple conditions was the self-care measure — 97.0 percent of people who marked this type of condition also reported one or more of the other measures of disability.

Were people with disabilities less likely to be employed than others?

Census 2000 showed that people between the ages of 16 and 64 were less likely to be employed if they were disabled (see Figure 7). While 79.9 percent of working-age men without a disability were employed, only 60.1 percent of those with a disability worked. Among women of working age, the respective employment rates were 67.3 percent and 51.4 percent. Altogether, 10.4 million men and 8.2 million women with disabilities were employed.

How many people with disabilities lived in poverty in 2000?[17]

In 2000, 8.7 million people with disabilities were poor — a substantially higher proportion (17.6 percent) than was found among people aged 5 and older without disabilities (10.6 percent). However, the pattern of poverty by age was similar for both groups, with the highest poverty rates found among children aged 5 to 15 (see Figure 8). The

---

[17] Poverty status was determined for all noninstitutionalized civilians, except those in military group quarters and dormitories, and unrelated individuals under age 15. For more information on poverty, see www.census.gov/hhes/www/poverty.html.

Table 5.

Ten Places of 100,000 or More With the Lowest Percentage of People Aged 5 and Older With Disabilities in the Civilian Noninstitutionalized Population: 2000

(For information on confidentiality protection, sampling error, nonsampling error, and definitions, see www.census.gov/prod/cen2000/sf3.pdf)

Place	Number with disabilities	Percent	Margin of error*
Naperville, IL	9,261	7.9	0.2
Provo, UT	9,823	10.3	0.3
Gilbert, AZ.................	10,598	10.8	0.3
Plano, TX	22,233	10.9	0.2
Irvine, CA	14,985	11.1	0.3
Ann Arbor, MI.............	12,062	11.2	0.3
Fort Collins, CO............	12,727	11.5	0.3
Overland Park, KS	16,252	11.9	0.3
Carrollton, TX..............	12,338	12.3	0.3
Santa Clarita, CA..........	18,242	13.1	0.3

* When the margin of error is added to or subtracted from the estimate, it produces a 90-percent confidence interval.

Note: Because of sampling error, the estimates in this table may not be significantly different from one another or from other places not listed in this table.

Source: U.S. Census Bureau, Census 2000 Summary File 3.

Figure 6.

Percent Distribution of People With Disabilities in the Noninstitutionalized Civilian Population by Type and Number of Disabilities: 2000

(For more information on confidentiality protection, sampling error, nonsampling error, and definitions, see www.census.gov/prod/cen2000/doc/sf3.pdf)

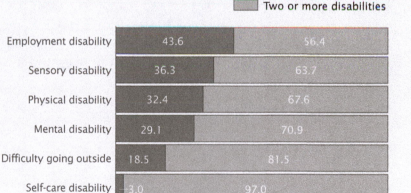

One disability only
Two or more disabilities

	One disability only	Two or more disabilities
Employment disability	43.6	56.4
Sensory disability	36.3	63.7
Physical disability	32.4	67.6
Mental disability	29.1	70.9
Difficulty going outside	18.5	81.5
Self-care disability	3.0	97.0

Note: The statistics for difficulty going outside the home are only for people aged 16 and older. The statistics on employment disability are only for people 16 to 64. All other disability estimates include people 5 and older.
Source: U.S. Census Bureau, Census 2000 Summary File 3.

---

poverty rate for young people with disabilities was 25.0 percent, compared with 15.7 percent for those without disabilities. The next highest poverty rates for both groups were found among people 16 to 64 years old — 18.8 percent for those with disabilities, nearly double the rate for those without (9.6 percent). Among people 65 years old and over, the respective proportions were 13.2 percent and 7.4 percent.

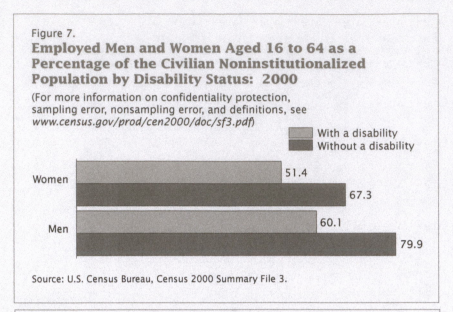

Figure 7.

Employed Men and Women Aged 16 to 64 as a Percentage of the Civilian Noninstitutionalized Population by Disability Status: 2000

(For more information on confidentiality protection, sampling error, nonsampling error, and definitions, see *www.census.gov/prod/cen2000/doc/sf3.pdf*)

■ With a disability
■ Without a disability

Women 51.4 / 67.3

Men 60.1 / 79.9

Source: U.S. Census Bureau, Census 2000 Summary File 3.

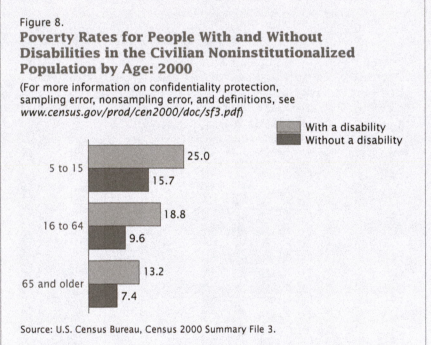

Figure 8.

Poverty Rates for People With and Without Disabilities in the Civilian Noninstitutionalized Population by Age: 2000

(For more information on confidentiality protection, sampling error, nonsampling error, and definitions, see *www.census.gov/prod/cen2000/doc/sf3.pdf*)

■ With a disability
■ Without a disability

5 to 15 25.0 / 15.7

16 to 64 18.8 / 9.6

65 and older 13.2 / 7.4

Source: U.S. Census Bureau, Census 2000 Summary File 3.

ABOUT CENSUS 2000

Why Census 2000 Asked About Disability

Information on disability is used by a number of federal agencies to distribute funds and develop programs for people with disabilities and the elderly. Among these are the Carl D. Perkins Vocational and Applied Technology Training Act, the School Dropout Demonstration Assistance Act, and State Literacy Initiatives. Data about the number, distribution, and needs of people with disabilities are essential under the Rehabilitation Act, which guarantees benefits to qualified people with disabilities. Data about difficulties going outside the home and work disabilities are important to ensure comparable public transportation services for all segments of the population, according to the goals of the Americans With Disabilities Act. Disability data also are used to allocate funds for employment and job training programs for veterans under the Disabled Veterans Outreach Program. Under the Older Americans Act, federal grants are awarded based on the number of elderly people with physical and mental disabilities. Medicare and medicaid programs and federal education programs also use data on people with disabilities.

Accuracy of the Estimates

The data contained in this report are based on the sample of households who responded to the Census 2000 long form. Nationally, approximately one out of every six housing units was included in this sample. As a result, the sample estimates may differ somewhat from the 100-percent figures that would have been obtained if all housing units, people within those housing units, and people living in group quarters had been enumerated using the same questionnaires, instructions, enumerators, and so forth. The sample estimates also differ from the values that would have been obtained from different samples of housing units, people within those housing units, and people living in group quarters. The deviation of a sample estimate from the average of all possible samples is called the sampling error.

In addition to the variability that arises from the sampling procedures, both sample data and 100-percent data are subject to nonsampling error. Nonsampling error may be introduced during any of the various complex operations used to collect and process data. Such errors may include: not enumerating every household or every person in the population, failing to obtain all required information from the respondents, obtaining incorrect or inconsistent information, and recording information incorrectly. In addition, errors can occur during the field review of the enumerators' work, during clerical handling of the census questionnaires, or during the electronic processing of the questionnaires.

Nonsampling error may affect the data in two ways: (1) errors that are introduced randomly will increase the variability of the data and, therefore, should be reflected in the standard errors; and (2) errors that tend to be consistent in one direction will bias both sample and 100-percent data in that direction. For example, if respondents consistently tend to underreport their incomes, then the resulting estimates of households or families by income category will tend to be understated for the higher income categories and overstated for the lower income categories. Such biases are not reflected in the standard errors.

While it is impossible to completely eliminate error from an operation as large and complex as the decen-

nial census, the Census Bureau attempts to control the sources of such error during the data collection and processing operations. The primary sources of error and the programs instituted to control error in Census 2000 are described in detail in *Summary File 3 Technical Documentation* under Chapter 8, "Accuracy of the Data," located at *www.census.gov/prod/ cen2000/doc/sf3.pdf.*

All statements in this Census 2000 Brief have undergone statistical testing and all comparisons are significant at the 90-percent confidence level, unless otherwise noted. Further information on the accuracy of the data is located at *www.census.gov/prod/cen2000/ doc/sf3.pdf.* For further information on the computation and use of standard errors, contact the Decennial Statistical Studies Division at 301-763-4242.

For More Information

For more information on people with disabilities in the United States, visit the U.S. Census Bureau's Internet site on disability at *www.census.gov/hhes/www/ disability.html.* Data on people with

disabilities from Census 2000 Summary File 3 were released on a state-by-state basis during the summer of 2002. The Census 2000 Summary File 3 data are available on the Internet via *factfinder.census.gov* and for purchase on CD-ROM and on DVD.

For information on confidentiality protection, nonsampling error, sampling error, and definitions, also see *www.census.gov/prod/ cen2000/doc/sf3.pdf* or contact our Customer Services Center at 301-763-INFO (4636).

Information on other population and housing topics is presented in the Census 2000 Brief series, located on the U.S. Census Bureau's Web site at *www.census.gov/population/ www/cen2000/briefs.html.* This series presents information on race, Hispanic origin, age, sex, household type, housing tenure, and other social, economic, and housing characteristics.

For more information about Census 2000, including data products, call our Customer Services Center at 301-763-INFO (4636), or e-mail *webmaster@census.gov.*

Veterans: 2000

Census 2000 Brief

Issued May 2003

C2KBR-22

By
Christy Richardson
and
Judith Waldrop

Census 2000 counted 208.1 million civilians 18 and older in the United States.[1] Within this population, approximately 26.4 million or 12.7 percent were veterans. Census data define a civilian veteran as someone 18 and older who is not currently on active duty, but who once served on active duty in the United States Army, Navy, Air Force, Marine Corps, or Coast Guard, or who served in the Merchant Marine during World War II.[2] This definition includes people who served for even a short time. Census 2000 collected data about the periods and length of service for veterans. Period of military service data distinguish veterans who

Figure 1.

Reproduction of the Questions on Veterans Status From Census 2000

20 a. Has this person ever served on active duty in the U.S. Armed Forces, military Reserves, or National Guard? *Active duty does not include training for the Reserves or National Guard, but DOES include activation, for example, for the Persian Gulf War.*

☐ Yes, now on active duty
☐ Yes, on active duty in past, but not now
☐ No, training for Reserves or National Guard only → *Skip to 21*
☐ No, never served in the military → *Skip to 21*

b. When did this person serve on active duty in the U.S. Armed Forces? *Mark* ☒ *a box for EACH period in which this person served.*

☐ April 1995 or later
☐ August 1990 to March 1995 (including Persian Gulf War)
☐ September 1980 to July 1990
☐ May 1975 to August 1980
☐ Vietnam era (August 1964—April 1975)
☐ February 1955 to July 1964
☐ Korean conflict (June 1950—January 1955)
☐ World War II (September 1940—July 1947)
☐ Some other time

c. In total, how many years of active-duty military service has this person had?

☐ Less than 2 years
☐ 2 years or more

Source: U.S. Census Bureau, Census 2000 questionnaire.

[1] The text of this report discusses data for the United States, including the 50 states and the District of Columbia. Data for the Commonwealth of Puerto Rico are shown in Table 2 and Figure 4.

[2] Active duty does not include active duty for training in the military Reserves or National Guard, such as the 4 to 6 months of initial training or yearly summer camps.

served during wartime from those who served during peacetime. Questions about period and length of military service provide information necessary to estimate the number of veterans who are

USCENSUSBUREAU

Helping You Make Informed Decisions

U.S. Department of Commerce
Economics and Statistics Administration
U.S. CENSUS BUREAU

United States
**Census
2000**

eligible to receive specific benefits.[3]

Decennial censuses have included a question on veterans since 1840. In the 1990 census, veterans data were collected from the population 15 and older, and data were released for those 16 and older. Veteran status information was also collected from people 15 and older in Census 2000, but the Census 2000 data are reported here only for the population 18 and older.

The Census 2000 long form was distributed to 1 in 6 households in the United States. Question 20, the veterans item on this form, asked respondents about any active-duty service in the U.S. Armed Forces, military Reserves, or National Guard; about periods of service; and about the number of years of active-duty military service (see Figure 1).

The 1990 census and Census 2000 questions asked about different periods of service. The most recent period on the Census 2000 questionnaire was April 1995 or later, while in 1990 it was September 1980 or later. The 1990 census provided a separate category for World War I service; Census 2000 asked people with such service to mark the "Some other time" category. In both 1990 and 2000, respondents could indicate that they served during more than one period.

This report is part of a series that presents population and housing data collected by Census 2000. It contains data on the veteran status of the civilian population 18 and

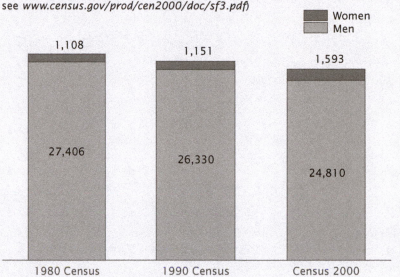

Figure 2.
Number of Male and Female Civilian Veterans Aged 18 and Over: 1980, 1990, and 2000

(In thousands. Data based on sample. For more information on confidentiality protection, sampling error, nonsampling error, and definitions, see *www.census.gov/prod/cen2000/doc/sf3.pdf*)

Women
Men

1980 Census: 1,108 / 27,406
1990 Census: 1,151 / 26,330
Census 2000: 1,593 / 24,810

Note: Individuals may be included in more than one period of service. The 1980 and 1990 veteran populations may include a small number of people who were 16 and 17 years old. Source: U.S. Census Bureau, 1980 and 1990 censuses and Census 2000 Summary File 3.

older. It highlights the size of the veteran population, changes between 1990 and 2000, the distribution of the population by periods of service, and the distribution of the population in regions, states, counties, and places with populations of 100,000 or more.

The total number of civilian veterans in the United States has been decreasing, but the number of female veterans has been increasing.

During the last 20 years of the 20th Century, the veteran population declined as older veterans, particularly Korean War, World War II, and World War I veterans, aged and died. In 1980, 28.5 million civilian veterans lived in the United States, but the number dropped to 27.5 million in 1990, and to 26.4 million in 2000.[4] The

declines occurred exclusively among the male veteran population, which fell from 27.4 million in 1980 to 24.8 million in 2000. Although women made up only 6.0 percent of the total veteran population in 2000, their numbers have steadily increased, as shown in Figure 2. Of the 26.4 million veterans in the United States in 2000, 24.8 million were men and 1.6 million were women.

Vietnam era veterans accounted for the largest veteran population in 2000.

Vietnam era veterans constituted the largest group of veterans in Census 2000, accounting for 8.4 million people or 31.7 percent of the total veteran population (see Table 1 and Figure 3).[5] World War II veterans made up the next largest group, 5.7 million people or

---

[3] The estimates in this report are based on responses from a sample of the population. As with all surveys, estimates may vary from the actual values because of sampling variation or other factors. All statements made in this report have undergone statistical testing and are significant at the 90-percent confidence level unless otherwise noted.

[4] The 1980 and 1990 veteran populations may include a small number of people who were 16 and 17 years old.

[5] Veterans may have served during more than one period of service.

Table 1.
Number and Percentage of Civilian Veterans Aged 18 and Over by Period of Service and Other Characteristics: 2000

(Data based on sample. For information on confidentiality protection, sampling error, nonsampling error, and definitions, see www.census.gov/prod/cen2000/doc/sf3.pdf)

Period of service	Number in 2000	Percentage of all veterans	Median age	Percentage women	Percentage employed	Percentage in poverty in 1999	Percentage disabled
All veterans 18 years and over	**26,403,703**	**100.0**	**57.4**	**6.0**	**54.7**	**5.6**	**29.1**
August 1990 or later (including Gulf War)	3,024,503	11.5	33.3	15.7	81.4	6.2	16.3
September 1980 to July 1990..............	3,806,602	14.4	38.8	13.0	82.7	5.5	18.2
May 1975 to August 1980	2,775,492	10.5	45.5	9.9	78.0	5.6	22.7
Vietnam era (August 1964 to April 1975)	8,380,356	31.7	53.2	3.2	75.4	5.1	24.8
February 1955 to July 1964	4,355,323	16.5	62.8	2.4	51.4	4.9	29.4
Korean War (June 1950 to January 1955)....	4,045,521	15.3	70.1	2.2	24.6	4.5	33.6
World War II (September 1940 to July 1947) .	5,719,898	21.7	76.7	4.2	11.6	4.8	45.2
Some other time	323,785	1.2	74.3	4.5	16.1	6.6	46.4

Note: The figures do not add to 100 percent because veterans may have served in more than one time period.

Source: U.S. Census Bureau, Census 2000 Summary File 3 and special tabulations.

Figure 3.
Number of Civilian Veterans Aged 18 and Over by Period of Service: 2000

(In millions. Data based on sample. For more information on confidentiality protection, sampling error, nonsampling error, and definitions, see *www.census.gov/prod/cen2000/doc/sf3.pdf*)

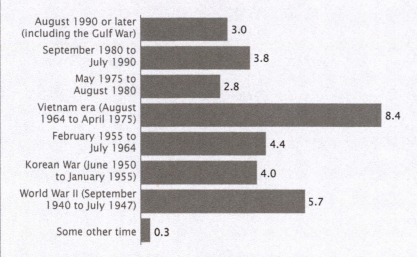

Note: Individuals may be included in more than one period of service.
Source: U.S. Census Bureau, Census 2000 Summary File 3.

21.7 percent of all veterans, followed by veterans who served from February 1955 to July 1964 (4.4 million or 16.5 percent) and those who served during the Korean War (4.0 million or 15.3 percent). Veterans who served from September 1980 to July 1990 accounted for 3.8 million or 14.4 percent of the veteran population. Finally, those who served from May 1975 to August 1980 (2.8 million or 10.5 percent) and those who served in August 1990 or later (3.0 million or 11.5 percent) made up the smallest percentages

of the total veteran population, respectively. This last group includes Gulf War veterans.[6]

Table 1 shows selected characteristics of the veteran population by period of service. In 2000, the median age of all veterans living in the United States was 57.4. Both age and period of service are time-dependent and closely related to each other. The median age ranged from 33.3 years for those serving since August 1990 to 76.7 years for World War II veterans. In total, 16.7 million veterans were under the age of 65 and 9.7 million were 65 and over.

Table 1 also shows the percentage of veterans who were women by period of service. Nearly 10.0 percent of veterans who served from May 1975 to August 1980 and 13.0 percent of those who served from September 1980 to July 1990 were women. In the most recent period of service, August 1990 or later, 15.7 percent were women. These numbers at least partially reflect the growing involvement of women in the military. Women

---

[6] "Gulf War" refers to active-duty service at any time in August 1990 or later, until the time of Census 2000.

made up 4.2 percent of the World War II veteran population and 2.2 percent of the Korean War veteran population.

A large percentage of U.S. veterans were employed.

The majority of U.S. veterans (54.7 percent) were employed in 2000, as shown in Table 1.[7] Reflecting the ties between age and period of service, and age and employment, veterans who served most recently were most likely to be employed in 2000. Among veterans serving in August 1990 or later, 81.4 percent were employed, while 82.7 percent of those who served from September 1980 to July 1990 were employed. They were closely followed by veterans who served from May 1975 to August 1980 (78.0 percent). More than three quarters (75.4 percent) of veterans of the Vietnam era were employed in 2000, and more than half (51.4 percent) of those who served from February 1955 to July 1964 were employed. The percentage employed was low for Korean War veterans (24.6 percent) and World War II veterans (11.6 percent), many of whom were likely to be retired.

Poverty rates were low among veterans for every period of service.

Overall, 5.6 percent of veterans lived in poverty in 1999, as shown in Table 1, compared with 10.9 percent of the U.S. adult population in general. The youngest veterans, those who served in August 1990 or later, were among the most likely to be poor, with a poverty rate of 6.2 percent. The poverty rate for Vietnam era veterans was 5.1 percent. Korean War and World War II veterans had among the lowest

[7] Among the general population 20 and older, 61.3 percent were employed according to Census 2000.

poverty rates for veterans, 4.5 percent and 4.8 percent, respectively.

The oldest veterans had the highest disability rates in 2000.

Almost 3 out of every 10 veterans (29.1 percent) were disabled (see Table 1).[8] However, 1 in 3 Korean War veterans (33.6 percent) and almost 1 in 2 World War II veterans (45.2 percent) were disabled. Approximately 1 in 4 Vietnam veterans (24.8 percent) was disabled. The disability rates for those who served most recently, from September 1980 to July 1990 or in August 1990 or later, were the lowest, at 18.2 percent and 16.3 percent, respectively.

GEOGRAPHIC DISTRIBUTION OF VETERANS

The following discussion of the geographic distribution of veterans focuses on the civilian population 18 and older.

In 2000, the largest veteran populations lived in the South and the Midwest.[9]

The veteran population was largest in the South (9.9 million) and the Midwest (6.1 million), the two most

[8] Veterans responding to Census 2000 were considered to have a disability if they answered "yes" to having a sensory, physical, mental, or self-care disability; or they answered "yes" to having a disability affecting their ability to go outside the home; or they were under 65 years old and answered "yes" to having an employment disability.

[9] The Northeast region includes the states of Connecticut, Maine, Massachusetts, New Hampshire, New Jersey, New York, Pennsylvania, Rhode Island, and Vermont. The Midwest region includes the states of Illinois, Indiana, Iowa, Kansas, Michigan, Minnesota, Missouri, Nebraska, North Dakota, Ohio, South Dakota, and Wisconsin. The South region includes the states of Alabama, Arkansas, Delaware, Florida, Georgia, Kentucky, Louisiana, Maryland, Mississippi, North Carolina, Oklahoma, South Carolina, Tennessee, Texas, Virginia, West Virginia, and the District of Columbia, a state equivalent. The West region includes the states of Alaska, Arizona, California, Colorado, Hawaii, Idaho, Montana, Nevada, New Mexico, Oregon, Utah, Washington, and Wyoming.

populous regions of the country (see Table 2). The West and Northeast had veteran populations of 5.7 million and 4.6 million, respectively. The percentage of civilians 18 and older who were veterans varied only slightly among the regions, ranging from 11.5 percent in the Northeast to 13.4 percent in the South.

Between 1990 and 2000, the number of veterans decreased in every region except the South, where it increased from 9.3 million to 9.9 million (a 6.7 percent increase). The greatest decline was in the Northeast, where the number of veterans dropped from 5.5 million to 4.6 million or 15.4 percent. The veteran population fell 7.6 percent in the Midwest and 2.7 percent in the West.

Between 1990 and 2000, veterans declined as a percentage of the civilian population in all regions. The percentage of veterans in the West fell 2.3 percentage points, while it dropped 2.2 percentage points in the Northeast. The Midwest and the South experienced smaller declines, 1.7 percentage points and 0.9 percentage points, respectively.

The most populous state, California, had the greatest number of veterans.

California was the only state that was home to more than 2.5 million veterans in 2000. Additionally, six other states had veteran populations of one million or more: Florida, Texas, New York, Pennsylvania, Ohio, and Illinois. Together, these seven states, which contained 44.6 percent of the total U.S. population 18 and older, accounted for 11.0 million veterans or 41.6 percent of the U.S. total.

Among the 50 states and the District of Columbia, Alaska had

Table 2.
Veteran Status of the Civilian Population Aged 18 and Over for the United States, Regions, and States, and for Puerto Rico: 1990 and 2000

(Data based on sample. For information on confidentiality protection, sampling error, nonsampling error, and definitions, see www.census.gov/prod/cen2000/doc/sf3.pdf)

Area	1990*			2000						
		Veteran population			Veteran population		Veteran periods of service			
							Percentage in the following periods:			
	Total civilian population 18 and over	Number	Percent	Total civilian population 18 and over	Number	Percent	WWII	Korea	Vietnam	Gulf**
United States	190,120,343	27,481,055	14.5	208,130,352	26,403,703	12.7	21.7	15.3	31.7	11.5
Region										
Northeast............	40,048,451	5,489,799	13.7	40,513,717	4,642,102	11.5	25.8	16.1	28.7	7.5
Midwest.............	45,530,120	6,597,258	14.5	47,671,646	6,096,476	12.8	21.7	15.0	31.2	9.7
South..............	64,931,795	9,316,232	14.3	74,066,441	9,941,610	13.4	20.1	15.2	32.5	14.0
West	39,609,977	5,880,963	14.8	45,878,548	5,723,515	12.5	20.9	15.3	33.4	12.1
State										
Alabama	3,078,549	434,787	14.1	3,310,446	447,397	13.5	19.0	16.7	32.9	13.5
Alaska	368,403	68,252	18.5	419,320	71,552	17.1	8.5	8.6	41.2	21.4
Arizona	2,760,050	464,023	16.8	3,747,180	562,916	15.0	23.5	17.4	30.7	11.8
Arkansas............	1,789,273	265,055	14.8	1,987,107	281,714	14.2	21.4	15.7	32.0	11.9
California	22,516,192	3,001,905	13.3	24,501,941	2,569,340	10.5	22.5	15.7	32.4	10.8
Colorado	2,480,094	409,932	16.5	3,177,044	446,385	14.1	16.6	13.7	36.3	15.1
Connecticut	2,600,983	373,933	14.4	2,557,792	310,069	12.1	26.2	16.1	29.6	6.8
Delaware	513,564	80,909	15.8	585,855	84,289	14.4	20.1	15.7	31.7	11.8
District of Columbia	497,090	57,874	11.6	454,454	44,484	9.8	24.1	16.6	29.5	11.1
Florida	10,275,382	1,719,129	16.7	12,283,486	1,875,597	15.3	27.8	17.8	28.0	10.7
Georgia	4,865,246	693,225	14.2	5,954,362	768,675	12.9	14.6	13.0	34.4	17.3
Hawaii	801,517	119,256	14.9	878,220	120,587	13.7	18.7	15.0	34.5	15.2
Idaho	724,306	116,609	16.1	920,973	136,584	14.8	20.0	14.4	32.3	14.9
Illinois	8,759,325	1,162,158	13.3	9,158,208	1,003,572	11.0	23.0	15.0	30.1	9.7
Indiana.............	4,239,391	623,098	14.7	4,504,723	590,476	13.1	20.1	14.5	31.3	10.0
Iowa...............	2,129,083	310,122	14.6	2,192,132	292,020	13.3	23.0	16.3	31.4	9.0
Kansas	1,854,980	280,806	15.1	1,962,154	267,452	13.6	22.1	14.6	32.6	12.4
Kentucky	2,808,878	380,610	13.6	3,028,902	380,618	12.6	19.6	14.9	32.6	11.9
Louisiana...........	3,086,591	404,186	13.1	3,232,426	392,486	12.1	20.4	14.5	32.2	13.7
Maine..............	940,466	159,333	16.9	969,780	154,590	15.9	20.9	16.1	33.1	9.3
Maryland	3,689,812	558,613	15.1	3,910,942	524,230	13.4	18.8	13.8	32.1	14.0
Massachusetts.........	4,793,859	656,850	13.7	4,847,708	558,933	11.5	26.8	16.6	28.4	7.1
Michigan	7,088,397	1,005,699	14.2	7,341,880	913,573	12.4	21.6	14.5	31.4	9.0
Minnesota	3,317,776	489,498	14.8	3,630,355	464,968	12.8	20.7	15.2	32.8	8.3
Mississippi	1,892,443	237,977	12.6	2,054,721	249,431	12.1	19.9	16.1	31.0	14.8
Missouri	3,920,715	613,859	15.7	4,153,926	592,271	14.3	21.2	15.7	31.6	10.3
Montana	594,845	102,536	17.2	668,651	108,476	16.2	20.7	14.9	34.2	10.7
Nebraska...........	1,179,872	177,852	15.1	1,253,717	173,189	13.8	20.7	16.3	32.3	12.6
Nevada	925,692	182,084	19.7	1,480,440	238,128	16.1	18.1	16.8	34.8	12.2
New Hampshire.......	854,028	141,617	16.6	926,066	139,038	15.0	19.8	15.4	33.6	9.2
New Jersey	6,105,807	817,409	13.4	6,321,650	672,217	10.6	26.9	16.6	28.1	6.7
New Mexico..........	1,098,172	178,022	16.2	1,300,288	190,718	14.7	19.8	15.9	34.7	12.8
New York...........	14,151,119	1,707,476	12.1	14,278,716	1,361,164	9.5	25.7	16.0	27.7	7.6
North Carolina	5,084,798	719,458	14.1	5,997,177	792,646	13.2	18.2	14.6	32.3	14.9
North Dakota	470,571	64,772	13.8	474,210	61,365	12.9	19.8	14.8	32.7	12.7
Ohio...............	8,331,105	1,259,535	15.1	8,458,130	1,144,007	13.5	22.1	14.5	30.7	9.6
Oklahoma	2,369,564	377,148	15.9	2,536,569	376,062	14.8	20.2	15.4	34.6	12.9
Oregon	2,188,212	384,189	17.6	2,574,798	388,990	15.1	22.1	14.4	33.9	9.4
Pennsylvania	9,374,206	1,450,037	15.5	9,354,471	1,280,788	13.7	26.3	16.0	28.7	7.5
Rhode Island........	794,112	118,330	14.9	797,047	102,494	12.9	26.9	16.4	29.6	7.8
South Carolina........	2,604,958	381,691	14.7	2,967,197	420,971	14.2	17.4	14.9	34.1	15.2
South Dakota.........	510,794	76,923	15.1	548,771	79,370	14.5	20.3	17.4	31.3	12.4
Tennessee..........	3,772,465	531,723	14.1	4,274,395	560,141	13.1	18.0	14.6	33.9	12.5
Texas..............	12,525,484	1,726,617	13.8	14,871,550	1,754,809	11.8	18.6	14.3	34.6	15.0
Utah...............	1,146,986	146,630	12.8	1,510,842	161,351	10.7	22.1	15.4	31.7	13.2
Vermont............	433,871	64,814	14.9	460,487	62,809	13.6	20.3	15.4	32.2	8.2
Virginia	4,674,603	733,092	15.7	5,211,916	786,359	15.1	15.9	13.6	35.4	20.3
Washington	3,677,089	653,068	17.8	4,336,464	670,628	15.5	18.2	13.7	35.9	14.0
West Virginia	1,403,095	210,941	15.0	1,404,936	201,701	14.4	22.0	16.2	32.5	9.3
Wisconsin	3,728,111	532,936	14.3	3,993,440	514,213	12.9	21.4	15.1	30.6	9.0
Wyoming	328,419	54,457	16.6	362,387	57,860	16.0	18.0	13.9	36.2	14.4
Puerto Rico	2,491,952	138,150	5.5	2,714,765	146,001	5.4	15.1	26.8	26.8	10.1

*1990 data includes veterans aged 16 and older.
**Gulf war veterans include those who served on active duty in August 1990 or later.

Source: U.S. Census Bureau, Census 2000 Summary File 3.

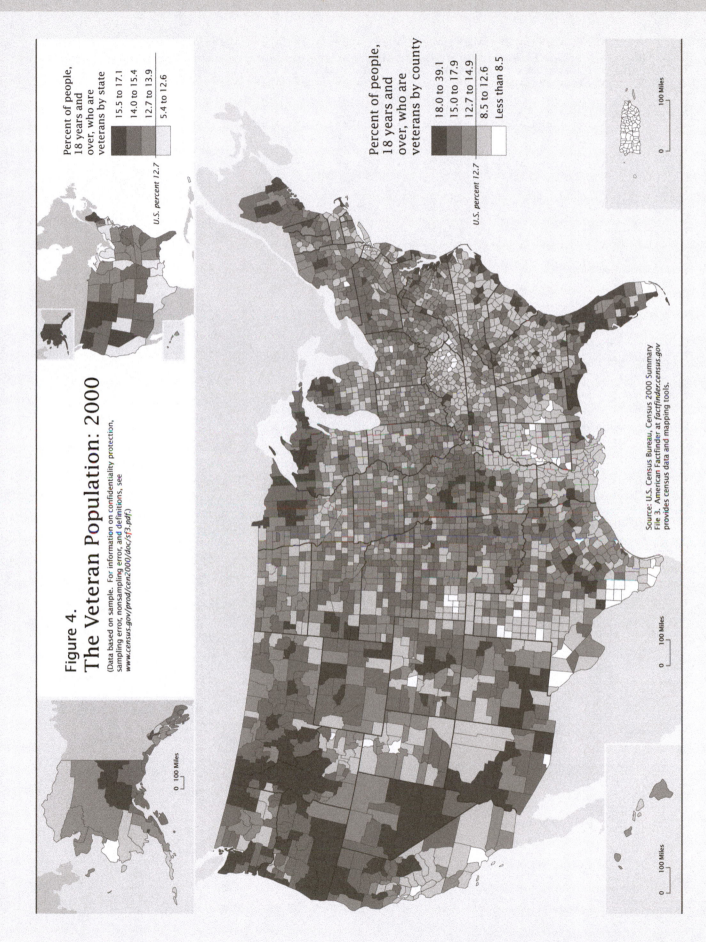

Figure 4.
The Veteran Population: 2000

(Data based on sample. For information on confidentiality protection, sampling error, nonsampling error, and definitions, see *www.census.gov/prod/cen2000/doc/sf3.pdf.*)

Percent of people, 18 years and over, who are veterans by state

15.5 to 17.1
14.0 to 15.4
12.7 to 13.9
5.4 to 12.6

U.S. percent 12.7

Percent of people, 18 years and over, who are veterans by county

18.0 to 39.1
15.0 to 17.9
12.7 to 14.9
8.5 to 12.6
Less than 8.5

U.S. percent 12.7

Source: U.S. Census Bureau, Census 2000 Summary File 3. American Factfinder at *factfinder.census.gov* provides census data and mapping tools.

0   100 Miles

0   100 Miles

0   100 Miles

Table 3.
Ten Places of 100,000 or More With the Highest Percentage of Veterans in the Civilian Population Aged 18 and Over: 2000

(Data based on sample. For information on confidentiality protection, sampling error, nonsampling error, and definitions, see *www.census.gov/prod/cen2000/doc/sf3.pdf*)

Place	Number of veterans	Percent of veterans	90-percent confidence interval
Hampton, VA	28,312	27.1	26.5 - 27.8
Clarksville, TN	15,319	24.4	23.7 - 25.1
Fayetteville, NC	19,060	23.7	23.0 - 24.4
Virginia Beach, VA	60,260	21.7	21.4 - 22.1
Colorado Springs, CO	51,609	20.2	19.9 - 20.6
Norfolk, VA	30,068	19.9	19.5 - 20.4
Newport News, VA	24,021	19.9	19.4 - 20.4
Columbus, GA*	24,984	19.6	19.1 - 20.1
Chesapeake, VA	25,621	18.9	18.4 - 19.4
Portsmouth, VA	12,955	18.4	17.8 - 19.1

*Columbus city is consolidated with Muscogee County.

Note: Because of sampling error, the estimates in this table may not be significantly different from one another or from other places not listed in this table.

Source: U.S. Census Bureau, Census 2000 Summary File 3.

the highest percentage of veterans, 17.1 percent (see Table 2). Veterans accounted for about 16.2 percent of the adult population in Montana, followed by Nevada, Wyoming, and Maine.[10] New York state (9.5 percent) and the District of Columbia (9.8 percent) had the lowest percentages of veterans in their populations.[11]

Even though the number of veterans fell nationwide between 1990 and 2000, some states saw increases. The state with the most rapidly growing veteran population was Nevada, the state with the fastest growing total population. In Nevada, veterans increased by 30.8 percent, from 182,000 to 238,000. Increases of 10 percent or more were recorded in veteran populations in Arizona, Idaho, Georgia, South Carolina, North Carolina, and Utah.

Twenty-five states and the District of Columbia recorded declines in their veteran populations during the 1990s. Among the states, New York had the largest decline — 20.3 percent. The 23.1 percent decline in the veteran population in the District of Columbia was not statistically different from declines in New York, New Jersey, or Connecticut.

The percentage of the civilian population 18 and over who were veterans fell in every state and the District of Columbia. Nevada, the state with the largest percent increase in the number of veterans, was also the state with the largest decline in veterans as a percent of the total population 18 and over. Because of rapid growth of nonveterans in Nevada, the veteran population dropped from 19.7 percent of all civilian Nevadans 18 and older to 16.1 percent, a 3.6-percentage-point decline.

The proportion of veterans fell by 2 percentage points or more in almost half of the states in the Northeast and the West. In the Midwest, most states fell by at least 1 percentage point, but less than 2 percentage points. States in

the South experienced the least decline. The decline in Texas and the District of Columbia was about 2 percentage points, but it was less than 1 percentage point in many other Southern states.

Rural and nonmetropolitan counties had the highest concentrations of veterans.

Figure 4 shows the percentage of veterans in 2000 for each county in the United States. The highest concentrations of veterans were found in many Florida counties, numerous counties of the upper Great Lakes areas, various western counties with low populations excluding California and Utah, and in scattered counties along the East Coast, all containing or near military bases. In general, Census 2000 found the highest concentrations of veterans in rural and nonmetropolitan counties. Florida was an exception, probably because of retiree migration. The lowest concentrations of veterans were found in the counties of the lower Mississippi River valley, many Appalachian counties, and several counties in the Rio Grande valley of southern Texas.

Hampton, Virginia, had the greatest concentration of veterans of any place of 100,000 or more in the United States.[12]

Among places of 100,000 or more, Hampton, Virginia, near the country's largest naval station, had the greatest concentration of veterans in 2000, 27.1 percent (see Table 3). It was followed by Clarksville, Tennessee (24.4 percent), and Fayetteville, North Carolina (23.7 percent) — whose

[10] The percentage of veterans in the population was not statistically different in Montana, Nevada, Wyoming, and Maine.
[11] The percentage of veterans in the population was not statistically different in New York and the District of Columbia.

[12] Census 2000 shows 245 places in the United States with 100,000 or more population. They include 238 incorporated places (including four city-county consolidations) and seven census designated places that are not legally incorporated. For a list of these places by state, see *www.census.gov/population/www/cen2000/phc-t6.html*.

percentages were not statistically different. Six of the 10 places with the highest concentrations of veterans were in Virginia. With the exception of Colorado Springs, Colorado, home of the Air Force Academy, all of the places with the highest concentrations were located in the Southern region of the United States.

In 2000, the concentrations of veterans in places varied depending on their period of service.

The list of places with the greatest concentrations of Gulf War veterans[13] was similar to the list of places with the greatest concentration of veterans in general (see Table 4). In both cases, Hampton, Virginia, topped the list. Gulf War veterans made up 13.4 percent of the adult civilian population in Hampton; followed by Clarksville, Tennessee, with 11.4 percent; and Fayetteville, North Carolina, with 9.0 percent.

Tables 5, 6, and 7 show the top ten places with the highest concentrations of Vietnam, Korean War, and World War II veterans, respectively. The tables suggest that the places with the highest concentrations of Vietnam veterans tend to contain or be near military facilities in the South and West, and that the highest concentrations of Korean War and World War II veterans tend to be in retirement areas in Florida, Arizona, or California, and other places with warm climates. Caution must be used in interpreting these data, since the percentages in the numbers are so close that two places may not be statistically different from one another.

Among places with populations of 100,000 or more, Hialeah, Florida,

Table 4.
Ten Places of 100,000 or More With the Highest Percentage of Gulf War Veterans in the Civilian Population Aged 18 and Over: 2000

(Data based on sample. For information on confidentiality protection, sampling error, nonsampling error, and definitions, see *www.census.gov/prod/cen2000/doc/sf3.pdf*)

Place	Number of Gulf War veterans	Percent of Gulf War veterans	90-percent confidence interval
Hampton, VA	13,981	13.4	12.9 - 13.9
Clarksville, TN	7,184	11.4	10.9 - 12.0
Fayetteville, NC	7,221	9.0	8.5 - 9.4
Virginia Beach, VA	21,176	7.6	7.4 - 7.9
Newport News, VA	8,010	6.6	6.3 - 6.9
Norfolk, VA	9,931	6.6	6.3 - 6.9
Columbus, GA*	7,373	5.8	4.9 - 6.7
Colorado Springs, CO	14,650	5.7	5.6 - 5.9
Chesapeake, VA	6,413	4.7	4.5 - 5.0
Augusta-Richmond, GA**	6,300	4.6	4.3 - 4.8

*Columbus city is consolidated with Muscogee County.
**In 2000, Richmond County and the incorporated place of Augusta-Richmond County are coextensive.

Note: Because of sampling error, the estimates in this table may not be significantly different from one another or from other places not listed in this table.

Source: U.S. Census Bureau, Census 2000 Summary File 3.

Table 5.
Ten Places of 100,000 or More With the Highest Percentage of Vietnam Era Veterans in the Civilian Population Aged 18 and Over: 2000

(Data based on sample. For information on confidentiality protection, sampling error, nonsampling error, and definitions, see *www.census.gov/prod/cen2000/doc/sf3.pdf*)

Place	Number of Vietnam era veterans	Percent of Vietnam era veterans	90-percent confidence interval
Fayetteville, NC	6,935	8.6	8.2 - 9.1
Virginia Beach, VA	22,763	8.2	8.0 - 8.4
Colorado Springs, CO	20,011	7.8	7.6 - 8.1
Clarksville, TN	4,872	7.8	7.3 - 8.2
Anchorage, AK	12,801	7.3	7.0 - 7.5
Columbus, GA*	9,245	7.3	6.9 - 7.6
Hampton, VA	7,555	7.2	6.9 - 7.6
Chesapeake, VA	9,638	7.1	6.8 - 7.4
Newport News, VA	8,115	6.7	6.4 - 7.0
Sunrise Manor, NV	7,208	6.7	6.4 - 7.0

*Columbus city is consolidated with Muscogee County.

Note: Because of sampling error, the estimates in this table may not be significantly different from one another or from other places not listed in this table.

Source: U.S. Census Bureau, Census 2000 Summary File 3.

and East Los Angeles, California (CDP),[14] had the lowest concentrations of veterans. Many of the places with low concentrations of veterans were areas with

large populations of foreign-born residents, as shown in Table 8. Some of the places with low concentrations were areas with large student populations, such as Provo, Utah, and Cambridge, Massachusetts.

---

[13] Includes veterans who served anytime in August 1990 or later, until the time of Census 2000.

[14] East Los Angeles, California, is a Census Designated Place and not an incorporated city.

Table 6.
Ten Places of 100,000 or More With the Highest Percentage of Korean War Veterans in the Civilian Population Aged 18 and Over: 2000

(Data based on sample. For information on confidentiality protection, sampling error, nonsampling error, and definitions, see *www.census.gov/prod/cen2000/doc/sf3.pdf*)

Place	Number of Korean War veterans	Percent of Korean War veterans	90-percent confidence interval
Cape Coral, FL	2,617	3.3	3.0 - 3.6
Fayetteville, NC	2,499	3.1	2.8 - 3.4
Columbus, GA*	3,773	3.0	2.8 - 3.2
Huntsville, AL	3,595	3.0	2.8 - 3.2
Scottsdale, AZ	4,685	2.9	2.7 - 3.0
Henderson, NV	3,760	2.9	2.7 - 3.1
Clearwater, FL	2,470	2.8	2.6 - 3.1
Oceanside, CA	3,145	2.8	2.6 - 3.0
Pueblo, CO	2,133	2.8	2.6 - 3.0
Las Vegas, NV	9,480	2.7	2.6 - 2.8

*Columbus city is consolidated with Muscogee County.

Note: Because of sampling error, the estimates in this table may not be significantly different from one another or from other places not listed in this table.

Source: U.S. Census Bureau, Census 2000 Summary File 3.

Table 7.
Ten Places of 100,000 or More With the Highest Percentage of World War II Veterans in the Civilian Population Aged 18 and Over: 2000

(Data based on sample. For information on confidentiality protection, sampling error, nonsampling error, and definitions, see *www.census.gov/prod/cen2000/doc/sf3.pdf*)

Place	Number of World War II veterans	Percent of World War II veterans	90-percent confidence interval
Clearwater, FL	4,744	5.4	5.1 - 5.8
Cape Coral, FL	4,013	5.1	4.7 - 5.4
Oceanside, CA	5,036	4.5	4.2 - 4.7
Pueblo, CO	3,201	4.2	3.9 - 4.5
Scottsdale, AZ	6,604	4.0	3.8 - 4.2
Metairie, LA	4,620	4.0	3.8 - 4.2
St. Petersburg, FL	7,710	4.0	3.8 - 4.2
Santa Rosa, CA	4,282	3.8	3.6 - 4.1
Mesa, AZ	10,983	3.8	3.7 - 4.0
Independence, MO	3,201	3.7	3.5 - 4.0

Note: Because of sampling error, the estimates in this table may not be significantly different from one another or from other places not listed in this table.

Source: U.S. Census Bureau, Census 2000 Summary File 3.

ADDITIONAL FINDINGS

What was the racial and ethnic makeup of veterans in 2000?

Census 2000 allowed respondents to choose more than one race. With the exception of the Two or more races group, all race groups discussed in this report refer to people who indicated only one racial identity among the six major categories: White, Black or African American, American Indian and Alaska Native, Asian, Native Hawaiian or Other Pacific Islander, and Some other race.[15] The use of

[15] For further information on each of the six major race groups and the Two or more races population, see reports from the Census 2000 Brief series (C2KBR/01), available on the Census 2000 Web site at *www.census.gov/ population/www/cen2000/briefs.html.*

the single-race population in this report does not imply that it is the preferred method of presenting or analyzing data. The Census Bureau uses a variety of approaches.[16]

Table 9 shows that, in 2000, 82.9 percent of veterans and 72.3 percent of the total civilian population 18 and older were White (and no other race), not of Hispanic origin.[17] The next largest population of veterans was in the single-race group of Black or African American, representing 9.7 percent of the veteran population. Slightly more than 11.0 percent of the general population was Black or African American. Hispanics accounted for 4.3 percent of the veteran population and 11.0 percent of the general population, and the single-race Asian population composed 1.1 percent of veterans and 3.7 percent of the general population. The smallest percentages of the veteran population were the single-race groups of American Indian and Alaska Natives, at 0.7 percent,

[16] This report draws heavily on Summary File 3, a Census 2000 product that can be accessed through American FactFinder, available from the Census Bureau's Web site, *www.census.gov.* Information on people who reported more than one race, such as "White **and** American Indian and Alaska Native" or "Asian **and** Black or African American," is forthcoming in Summary File 4, which will also be available through American FactFinder in 2003. About 2.6 percent of people reported more than one race.

[17] Hereafter this report uses the term Black to refer to people who are Black or African American, the term Pacific Islander to refer to people who are Native Hawaiian and Other Pacific Islander, and the term Hispanic to refer to people who are Hispanic or Latino.

Because Hispanics may be of any race, data in this report for Hispanics overlap with data for racial groups. Based on Census 2000 sample data, the proportion Hispanic was 8.0 percent for Whites, 1.9 percent for Blacks, 14.6 percent for American Indians and Alaska Natives, 1.0 percent for Asians, 9.5 percent for Pacific Islanders, 97.1 percent for those reporting Some other race, and 31.1 percent for those reporting Two or more races.

followed by Native Hawaiian and Other Pacific Islander, at 0.1 percent. These groups represented 0.8 percent and 0.1 percent of the general population, respectively.

The above proportions change somewhat when the population is divided into younger veterans and older veterans, as shown in Table 9. The non-Hispanic White group makes up 78.9 percent of younger veterans, but 89.9 percent of veterans 65 and older. The Black and Hispanic groups are more concentrated among veterans aged 18 to 64 (12.1 percent and 5.4 percent, respectively) than among veterans 65 and older (5.7 percent and 2.4 percent, respectively).

ABOUT CENSUS 2000

Why Census 2000 Asked About Veteran Status

Veteran status, including period of military service, is used primarily by the Department of Veterans Affairs to measure the needs of veterans and to evaluate the impact of veteran benefits programs dealing with health care, education and employment, and disability and retirement. These data are needed to conduct policy analysis, program planning, and budgeting, for federal veterans' programs, and for reports to Congress on veterans' facilities and services. Based on data about veterans, local agencies develop health care and other services for elderly veterans under the Older Americans Act.

Accuracy of the Estimates

The data contained in this report are based on the sample of households who responded to the Census 2000 long form. Nationally, approximately 1 out of every 6 housing units was included

Table 8.
Ten Places of 100,000 or More With the Lowest Percentage of Veterans in the Civilian Population Aged 18 and Over: 2000

(Data based on sample. For information on confidentiality protection, sampling error, nonsampling error, and definitions, see *www.census.gov/prod/cen2000/doc/sf3.pdf*)

Place	Number of veterans	Percent of veterans	90-percent interval
Hialeah, FL	28,312	2.1	1.9 - 2.2
East Los Angeles, CA, CDP*	15,319	3.3	3.0 - 3.6
Miami, FL	19,060	4.2	4.0 - 4.3
Santa Ana, CA	60,260	4.2	4.0 - 4.4
Provo, UT	51,609	4.4	4.1 - 4.7
El Monte, CA	30,068	4.5	4.2 - 4.9
Cambridge, MA	24,021	4.9	4.6 - 5.3
Paterson, NJ	24,984	5.0	4.7 - 5.2
Elizabeth, NJ	25,621	5.1	4.8 - 5.4
Laredo, TX	12,955	5.7	5.4 - 6.0

*East Los Angeles is a Census Designated Place (CDP) and not an incorporated city.

Note: Because of sampling error, the estimates in this table may not be significantly different from one another or from other places not listed in this table.

Source: U.S. Census Bureau, Census 2000 Summary File 3.

Table 9.
Percentage of Adults by Veterans Status, Race and Hispanic Origin and Age: 2000

(Data based on sample. For information on confidentiality protection, sampling error, nonsampling error, and definitions, see *www.census.gov/prod/cen2000/doc/sf3.pdf*)

Characteristics	Total population	Veterans		
		Total	18 to 64 years	65 years and over
Total population 18 years and over	**208,130,352**	**26,403,703**	**16,740,194**	**9,663,506**
White alone	77.7	85.5	81.9	91.7
Black or African American alone	11.3	9.7	12.1	5.7
American Indian and Alaska Native alone	0.8	0.7	1.0	0.4
Asian alone	3.7	1.1	1.2	0.9
Native Hawaiian and Other Pacific Islander alone	0.1	0.1	0.1	0.0
Some other race alone	4.8	1.4	1.9	0.5
Two or more races	2.1	1.4	1.8	0.8
Hispanic or Latino (of any race)	11.0	4.3	5.4	2.4
White alone, not Hispanic or Latino	72.3	82.9	78.9	89.9

Source: U.S. Census Bureau, Census 2000, Summary File 3.

in this sample. As a result, the sample estimates may differ somewhat from the 100-percent figures that would have been obtained if all housing units, people within those housing units, and people living in group quarters had been enumerated using the same questionnaires, instructions, enumerators, and so forth. The sample estimates also differ from the values that would have been obtained from different samples of housing units, people within those housing units, and people living in group quarters. The deviation of a sample estimate from the average of all possible samples is called the sampling error.

In addition to the variability that arises from the sampling procedures, both sample data and 100- percent data are subject to nonsampling error. Nonsampling error may be introduced during any of the various complex operations used to collect and process data. Such errors may include: not enumerating every household or every person in the population, failing to obtain all required information from the respondents, obtaining incorrect or inconsistent information, and recording information incorrectly. In addition, errors can occur during the field review of the enumerators' work, during clerical handling of the census questionnaires, or during the electronic processing of the questionnaires.

Nonsampling error may affect the data in two ways: (1) errors that are introduced randomly will increase the variability of the data and, therefore, should be reflected in the standard errors; and (2) errors that tend to be consistent in one direction will bias both sample and 100-percent data in that direction. For example, if respondents consistently tend to underreport their incomes, then the resulting estimates of households or families by income category will tend to be understated for the higher income categories and overstated for the lower income categories. Such biases are not reflected in the standard errors.

While it is impossible to completely eliminate error from an operation as large and complex as the decennial census, the Census Bureau attempts to control the sources of such error during the data collection and processing operations. The primary sources of error and the programs instituted to control error in Census 2000 are described in detail in *Summary File 3 Technical Documentation* under Chapter 8, "Accuracy of the Data," located at *www.census.gov/ prod/cen2000/doc/sf3.pdf.*

All statements in this Census 2000 Brief have undergone statistical testing and all comparisons are significant at the 90-percent confidence level, unless otherwise noted. The estimates in tables, maps, and other figures may vary from actual values due to sampling and nonsampling errors. As a result, estimates in one category may not be significantly different from estimates assigned to a different category. Further information on the accuracy of the data is located at *www.census.gov/prod/cen2000/ doc/sf3.pdf.* For further information on the computation and use of standard errors, contact the Decennial Statistical Studies Division at 301-763-4242.

For More Information

The Census 2000 Summary File 3 data are available from the American Factfinder on the Internet (*factfinder.census.gov*). They were released on a state-by-state basis during 2002. For information on confidentiality protection, nonsampling error, sampling error, and definitions, also see *www.census.gov/prod/cen2000/ doc/sf3.pdf* or contact the Customer Services Center at 301-763-INFO (4636).

Information on population and housing topics is presented in the Census 2000 Brief series, located on the Census Bureau's Web site at *www.census.gov/population/www/ cen2000/briefs.html*. This series presents information on race, Hispanic origin, age, sex, household type, housing tenure, and social, economic, and housing characteristics, such as ancestry, income, and housing costs.

To find information about the availability of data products, including reports, CD-ROMs, and DVDs, call the Customer Services Center at 301-763-INFO (4636), or e-mail *webmaster@census.gov.*

Household Income: 1999

Census 2000 Brief

Issued June 2005

C2KBR-36

By
Ed Welniak
and
Kirby Posey

Census 2000 counted 105.5 million households in the United States and collected data on income for calendar year 1999. Median household income in 1999 was $42,000, up 7.7 percent from 1989 in real terms (after adjusting for 29.8 percent inflation over the period).[1] Median income divides households into two equal groups, half having incomes above the median, the other half having incomes below. In 1999, 12.3 percent of households had incomes over $100,000, and 22.1 percent had incomes below $20,000.

[1] The estimates in this report (which may be shown in text, figures, and tables) are based on responses from a sample of the population and may differ from actual values because of sampling variability or other factors. As a result, apparent differences between the estimates for two or more groups may not be statistically significant. All comparative statements have undergone statistical testing and are significant at the 90-percent confidence level unless otherwise noted.

Figure 1.

Reproduction of the Questions on Household Income From Census 2000

31 INCOME IN 1999 — *Mark ☒ the "Yes" box for each income source received during 1999 and enter the total amount received during 1999 to a maximum of $999,999. Mark ☒ the "No" box if the income source was not received. If net income was a loss, enter the amount and mark ☒ the "Loss" box next to the dollar amount.*

For income received jointly, report, if possible, the appropriate share for each person; otherwise, report the whole amount for only one person and mark ☒ the "No" box for the other person. If exact amount is not known, please give best estimate.

a. Wages, salary, commissions, bonuses, or tips from all jobs — *Report amount before deductions for taxes, bonds, dues, or other items.*

☐ Yes   Annual amount — *Dollars*

$ ___ , ___ .00

☐ No

b. Self-employment income from own nonfarm businesses or farm businesses, including proprietorships and partnerships — *Report NET income after business expenses.*

☐ Yes   Annual amount — *Dollars*

$ ___ , ___ .00   ☐ Loss

☐ No

c. Interest, dividends, net rental income, royalty income, or income from estates and trusts — *Report even small amounts credited to an account.*

☐ Yes   Annual amount — *Dollars*

$ ___ , ___ .00   ☐ Loss

☐ No

Source: U.S. Census Bureau, Census 2000 questionnaire.

USCENSUSBUREAU

Helping You Make Informed Decisions

U.S. Department of Commerce
Economics and Statistics Administration
U.S. CENSUS BUREAU

United States Census 2000

This report, part of a series that presents population and housing data collected by Census 2000, provides information on the distribution of household income. Census 2000 income data allow more comparisons among geographic areas than do survey data. The text of this report discusses data for the United States, including regions, states, counties, and places with populations of 100,000 or more.[2]

More recent data are available from current surveys conducted by the U.S. Census Bureau. For example, the Current Population Survey's Annual Social and Economic Supplement (ASEC) estimated real median household income in 2003 to be $43,300, compared with $44,900 in 1999, a decline of 3.6 percent.[3] The ASEC showed an increase in median household income of 8.5 percent from 1989 to 1999.

The 1940 decennial census was the first to include a question about income. Later censuses expanded and refined approaches to collecting these data, most recently adding a question about

---

[2] The text of this report discusses data for the United States, including the 50 states and the District of Columbia. Information about the Commonwealth of Puerto Rico is presented in Table 2 and Figures 4 and 5 (additional information is available on the Census Bureau's Web site at <www.census.gov>). Census 2000 showed 245 places in the United States with 100,000 or more population. They included 238 incorporated places (including 4 city-county consolidations) and 7 census designated places that were not legally incorporated. For a list of these places by state, see <www.census.gov/population/www/cen2000/phc-t6.html>.

[3] The Current Population Survey's Annual Social and Economic Supplement (ASEC) is a key annual source of data on income and poverty. Annual income and poverty estimates are also available from the American Community Survey. Data from both surveys can be accessed at <www.census.gov/hhes/www/income.html>.

Figure 1.
Reproduction of the Questions on Household Income From Census 2000 — Con.

31 **d. Social Security or Railroad Retirement**
☐ Yes   Annual amount — *Dollars*
$ | | | , | | | .00
☐ No

e. Supplemental Security Income (SSI)
☐ Yes   Annual amount — *Dollars*
$ | | | , | | | .00
☐ No

f. Any public assistance or welfare payments from the state or local welfare office
☐ Yes   Annual amount — *Dollars*
$ | | | , | | | .00
☐ No

g. Retirement, survivor, or disability pensions — *Do NOT include Social Security.*
☐ Yes   Annual amount — *Dollars*
$ | | | , | | | .00
☐ No

h. Any other sources of income received regularly such as Veterans' (VA) payments, unemployment compensation, child support, or alimony — *Do NOT include lump-sum payments such as money from an inheritance or sale of a home.*
☐ Yes   Annual amount — *Dollars*
$ | | | , | | | .00
☐ No

32 **What was this person's total income in 1999?** *Add entries in questions 31a—31h; subtract any losses. If net income was a loss, enter the amount and mark ⊠ the "Loss" box next to the dollar amount.*

Annual amount — *Dollars*

☐ None   OR $ | | | , | | | .00   ☐ Loss

Source: U.S. Census Bureau, Census 2000 questionnaire.

Figure 2.

Median Household Income by Age of Householder: 1999

(In dollars. For information on confidentiality protection, sampling error, nonsampling error, and definitions, see *www.census.gov/prod/cen2000/doc/sf3.pdf*)

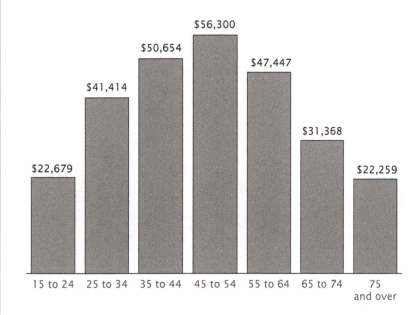

Source: U.S. Census Bureau, Census 2000.

Supplemental Security Income and combining separate farm and non-farm self-employment income questions into a single one.[4] Figure 1 shows the eight questions that Census 2000 asked of people 15 and older about different sources of income.

INCOMES OF FAMILIES AND HOUSEHOLDS

Income amounts in 1999 from wages and salary, self-employment, interest and dividends, Social Security, Supplemental Security Income, public assistance, retirement, and all other sources were aggregated for all people 15 and older in a household to form

[4] Supplemental Security Income is administered by the Social Security Administration for low income elderly and the blind and disabled population.

household income. These sources were aggregated for all related people 15 and older in the household to form family income. Most comparisons in this brief use households as the unit of analysis.

Households with a householder 45 to 54 years old had the highest median income.

The median income for this age group was $56,300 in 1999. Median income was lowest among households with a householder 75 and older ($22,300), as shown in Figure 2.

Incomes vary by type of household and family composition.

Median income was higher for families ($50,000) than for households ($42,000), as shown in Figure 3.

This result tends to occur because many households consist of people who live alone and are not included in the definition of a family. Many families have more than one earner and many people who live alone are young or elderly. Married-couple families had the highest median income of all the family types ($57,300). Households consisting of women who lived alone had the lowest median income ($19,500).

Income varies by race and ethnicity.

Respondents were asked to choose one or more races in Census 2000. With the exception of the Two or More Races group, all race groups discussed in this report refer to people who indicated only one racial identity among the six major categories: White, Black or African American, American Indian or Alaska Native, Asian, Native Hawaiian or Other Pacific Islander, and Some Other Race.[5] The use of the single-race population in this report does not imply that it is the preferred method of presenting or analyzing data. The Census Bureau uses a variety of approaches.[6]

[5] For further information on each of the six major race groups and the Two or More Races population, see reports from the Census 2000 Briefs series (C2KBR/01), available on the Census 2000 Web site at <www.census.gov/population/www /cen2000/briefs.html>. Hereafter, this report uses the term Black to refer to people who are Black or African American; the term Pacific Islander to refer to people who are Native Hawaiian or Other Pacific Islander; and the term Hispanic to refer to people who are Hispanic or Latino. Some Other Race is not a standard Office of Management and Budget race category.

[6] This report draws heavily on Summary File 3, a Census 2000 product that can be accessed through American FactFinder, available from the Census Bureau's Web site, <www.census.gov>. Information on people who reported more than one race, such as White **and** American Indian or Alaska Native or Asian **and** Black, can be found in Summary File 4, which is also available through American FactFinder. About 2.6 percent of people reported more than one race.

Figure 3.
Median Income by Household and Family Composition: 1999

(In dollars. For information on confidentiality protection, sampling error, nonsampling error, and definitions, see *www.census.gov/prod/cen2000/doc/sf3.pdf*)

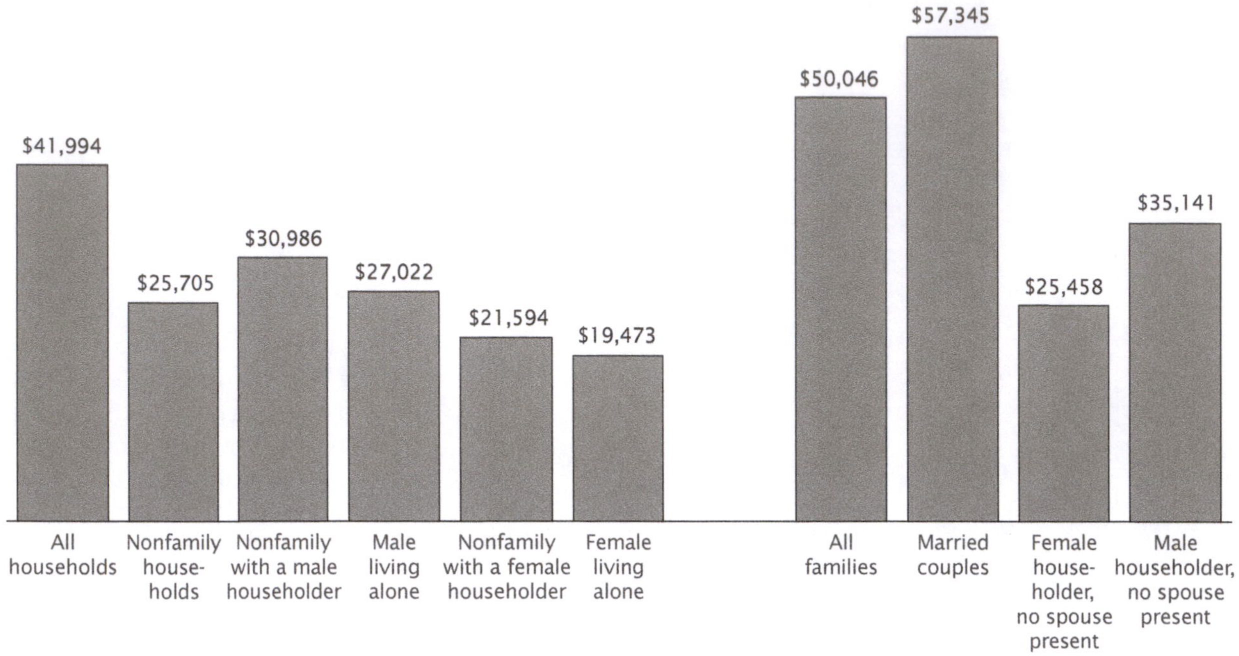

Source: U.S. Census Bureau, Census 2000.

Among the race groups shown in Table 1, median income in 1999 was highest for households with an Asian householder ($51,900) and lowest for those with a Black householder ($29,400). The median income for households with a White householder who was not Hispanic was $45,400. The median income for those with Hispanic householders was $33,700.[7]

Households with an Asian householder also had the highest percentage (19.8) of households with incomes over $100,000 and 10.0 percent reported incomes below $10,000. Households with a Black householder had the highest percentage (19.1) of households with incomes below $10,000; 5.9 percent reported incomes over $100,000.

THE GEOGRAPHIC DISTRIBUTION OF INCOME

Median income grew in each of the four regions between 1989 and 1999.

Real median household income grew more in the South and the Midwest than in the Northeast or the West—by 11.4 percent each,

compared with 3.6 percent in the Northeast and 7.6 percent in the West (see Table 2).[8] The Northeast had the highest median household income in 1999 ($45,500), followed by the West ($45,100), the Midwest ($42,400), and the South ($38,800).

---

[7] Because Hispanics may be any race, data in this report for Hispanics overlap with data for racial groups. Based on Census 2000 sample data, the proportion of respondents identified as Hispanic was 8.0 percent for Whites; 1.9 percent for Blacks; 14.6 percent for American Indians and Alaska Natives; 1.0 percent for Asians; 9.5 percent for Pacific Islanders; 97.1 percent for those reporting Some Other Race; and 31.1 percent for those reporting Two or More Races.

[8] The Northeast region includes the states of Connecticut, Maine, Massachusetts, New Hampshire, New Jersey, New York, Pennsylvania, Rhode Island, and Vermont. The Midwest region includes the states of Illinois, Indiana, Iowa, Kansas, Michigan, Minnesota, Missouri, Nebraska, North Dakota, Ohio, South Dakota, and Wisconsin. The South region includes the states of Alabama, Arkansas, Delaware, Florida, Georgia, Kentucky, Louisiana, Maryland, Mississippi, North Carolina, Oklahoma, South Carolina, Tennessee, Texas, Virginia, West Virginia, and the District of Columbia. The West region includes the states of Alaska, Arizona, California, Colorado, Hawaii, Idaho, Montana, Nevada, New Mexico, Oregon, Utah, Washington, and Wyoming.

Table 1.
Household Income by Race and Hispanic Origin of Householder: 1999

(Data based on sample. For information on confidentiality protection, sampling error, nonsampling error, and definitions, see www.census.gov/prod/cen2000/doc/sf3.pdf)

Income	All races	White	Black or African American	American Indian or Alaska Native	Asian	Native Hawaiian or Other Pacific Islander	Some Other Race alone	Two or More Races	Hispanic[1]	White, not Hispanic[1]
Total households	105,539,122	83,697,584	12,023,966	770,334	3,129,127	100,151	3,833,697	1,984,263	9,272,610	78,983,497
Percent..............	100.0	100.0	100.0	100.0	100.0	100.0	100.0	100.0	100.0	100.0
Less than $10,000	9.5	7.9	19.1	16.6	10.0	9.3	12.2	13.5	12.4	7.6
$10,000 to $14,999	6.3	5.9	8.6	8.8	4.6	5.4	7.8	7.4	7.8	5.8
$15,000 to $19,999	6.3	5.9	8.0	8.2	4.6	5.6	8.2	7.1	8.0	5.8
$20,000 to $24,999	6.6	6.3	7.8	8.1	4.9	6.7	8.6	7.3	8.3	6.2
$25,000 to $29,999	6.4	6.3	7.3	7.3	4.7	6.5	8.3	7.0	7.8	6.2
$30,000 to $34,999	6.4	6.3	6.5	7.0	5.0	6.5	7.8	6.7	7.4	6.3
$35,000 to $39,999	5.9	5.9	5.8	6.1	4.8	6.2	6.8	6.1	6.5	5.9
$40,000 to $44,999	5.7	5.7	5.2	5.5	4.9	6.0	6.1	5.6	5.9	5.7
$45,000 to $49,999	5.0	5.1	4.3	4.6	4.4	5.2	5.3	4.8	5.0	5.1
$50,000 to $59,999	9.0	9.4	7.3	7.8	8.5	9.5	8.4	8.3	8.3	9.4
$60,000 to $74,999	10.4	10.9	7.6	8.0	11.1	11.5	8.4	9.1	8.6	11.1
$75,000 to $99,999	10.2	10.9	6.6	6.6	12.7	11.2	6.7	8.3	7.4	11.1
$100,000 to $124,999	5.2	5.6	2.9	2.7	7.9	5.1	2.7	3.9	3.2	5.7
$125,000 to $149,999	2.5	2.7	1.2	1.1	4.3	2.3	1.1	1.8	1.4	2.8
$150,000 to $199,999	2.2	2.4	0.9	0.8	4.1	1.7	0.7	1.5	1.0	2.5
$200,000 or more........	2.4	2.7	0.9	0.8	3.5	1.2	0.7	1.4	1.0	2.7
Median income (dollars)...	41,994	44,687	29,423	30,599	51,908	42,717	32,694	35,587	33,676	45,367
Mean income (dollars)	56,644	59,696	39,877	40,135	67,734	53,096	41,619	47,597	44,250	60,478

[1]Hispanics may be of any race.

Source: Census 2000 Summary File 3.

Household income increased in almost all states between 1989 and 1999.

Almost all the states showed an increase in median household income; the exceptions were Alaska, Connecticut, Hawaii, and Rhode Island. The District of Columbia did not show an increase in real median household income. Colorado and South Dakota experienced the largest increase in real median household income—21 percent over the 1989–1999 period.

The relative standings of many states did not change between 1989 and 1999. The four states ranked highest in median income in 1989 (Connecticut, Alaska, New Jersey, and Maryland) remained there in 1999. New Jersey, with a 1999 median income of $55,100, replaced Connecticut as the state with the highest income. The four states with the lowest median incomes in 1989 (Mississippi, West Virginia, Arkansas, and Louisiana) remained there in 1999. West Virginia, with a 1999 median income of $29,700, replaced Mississippi as the state having the lowest income.

The highest income households were concentrated in the Northeast, West, and in large metropolitan areas.

New Jersey and Connecticut had the highest proportion of high-income households—about 30 percent over $79,700, the 80th percentile of national household income.[9] West Virginia, though not different from Arkansas, Mississippi, Montana, North Dakota, and South Dakota, had the

lowest percentage of households with incomes above $79,700—9 percent.

Figure 5 shows the percentage of high-income households by county. On the East Coast, several counties around Boston showed a high percentage of these households. The East Coast showed a nearly continuous string of high-income counties beginning north of New York City and extending through the counties around Washington, DC. On the West Coast, counties around San Francisco, Sacramento, and Los Angeles exhibited a high percentage of households with incomes above the 80th percentile. In other parts of the country, most high-income counties were part of large metropolitan areas, especially their suburban counties.

Overall, 21.1 million households had incomes higher than $79,700,

___
[9] The percentage of households with incomes above $79,663 in New Jersey (32 percent) and Connecticut (30 percent) were not statistically different.

Table 2.
Median Household Income by Region and State: 1989 and 1999

(Data based on sample. For information on confidentiality protection, sampling error, nonsampling error, and definitions, see www.census.gov/prod/cen2000/doc/sf3.pdf)

Geography	1989					1999					Percent change in real median income (1999 less 1989)
			Confidence interval					Confidence interval			
	Number	Median (1999 dollars)	Lower bound (1999 dollars)	Upper bound (1999 dollars)	Ranking	Number	Median (1999 dollars)	Lower bound (1999 dollars)	Upper bound (1999 dollars)	Ranking	
Total U.S.	91,993,582	39,009	38,994	39,024	NA	105,539,122	41,994	41,976	42,012	NA	7.7
REGIONS											
Northeast.	18,861,186	43,900	43,854	43,946	NA	20,294,648	45,481	45,443	45,519	NA	3.6
Midwest.	22,326,056	38,071	38,040	38,102	NA	24,748,799	42,414	42,379	42,449	NA	11.4
South.	31,836,124	34,824	34,799	34,849	NA	38,034,872	38,790	38,769	38,811	NA	11.4
West.	18,970,216	41,882	41,847	41,917	NA	22,460,803	45,084	45,040	45,128	NA	7.6
STATES											
Alabama	1,506,009	30,626	30,501	30,751	42-43	1,737,385	34,135	34,020	34,250	43-44	11.5
Alaska	189,700	53,742	53,388	54,096	2	221,804	51,571	51,168	51,974	4	−4.0
Arizona	1,371,885	35,743	35,598	35,888	28-29	1,901,625	40,558	40,412	40,704	26-28	13.5
Arkansas	891,665	27,446	27,341	27,551	49	1,042,807	32,182	32,059	32,305	49	17.3
California	10,399,700	46,461	46,403	46,519	9	11,512,020	47,493	47,416	47,570	8-9	2.2
Colorado	1,285,119	39,118	39,001	39,235	19	1,659,308	47,203	47,052	47,354	9-11	20.7
Connecticut	1,230,243	54,148	53,984	54,313	1	1,302,227	53,935	53,713	54,157	2	NS
Delaware	247,163	45,263	44,922	45,604	10	298,755	47,381	47,044	47,718	8-11	4.7
District of Columbia	249,034	39,879	39,545	40,213	16-18	248,590	40,127	39,693	40,561	27-30	NS
Florida	5,138,360	35,669	35,600	35,738	28-29	6,341,121	38,819	38,743	38,895	34	8.8
Georgia	2,366,575	37,665	37,551	37,779	23-24	3,007,678	42,433	42,315	42,551	20	12.7
Hawaii	356,748	50,395	50,027	50,763	5	403,572	49,820	49,494	50,146	6-7	−1.1
Idaho	361,432	32,780	32,611	32,949	39	470,133	37,572	37,378	37,766	36-37	14.6
Illinois	4,197,720	41,859	41,790	41,928	12-13	4,592,740	46,590	46,503	46,677	12-13	11.3
Indiana.	2,064,246	37,375	37,268	37,482	25-26	2,337,229	41,567	41,439	41,695	22	11.2
Iowa.	1,065,243	34,042	33,943	34,141	36-37	1,150,197	39,469	39,342	39,596	31	15.9
Kansas	946,253	35,420	35,300	35,540	30-32	1,038,940	40,624	40,478	40,770	25-27	14.7
Kentucky	1,379,610	29,246	29,136	29,356	46-47	1,591,739	33,672	33,562	33,782	45	15.1
Louisiana	1,498,371	28,487	28,383	28,591	48	1,657,107	32,566	32,444	32,688	48	14.3
Maine.	465,729	36,151	35,975	36,327	27	518,372	37,240	37,046	37,434	38-39	3.0
Maryland	1,749,342	51,118	50,963	51,273	4	1,981,795	52,868	52,687	53,049	3	3.4
Massachusetts.	2,244,406	47,959	47,836	48,082	6-7	2,444,588	50,502	50,344	50,660	5	5.3
Michigan	3,424,122	40,260	40,191	40,329	15-16	3,788,780	44,667	44,583	44,751	16-17	10.9
Minnesota	1,648,825	40,116	40,035	40,197	16-18	1,896,209	47,111	46,984	47,238	9-11	17.4
Mississippi	910,574	26,134	26,007	26,261	51	1,047,555	31,330	31,200	31,460	50	19.9
Missouri	1,961,364	34,214	34,125	34,303	35-36	2,197,214	37,934	37,835	38,033	35-36	10.9
Montana	306,919	29,835	29,626	30,044	45	359,070	33,024	32,822	33,226	47	10.7
Nebraska.	602,858	33,765	33,635	33,895	38	666,995	39,250	39,077	39,423	32-33	16.2
Nevada	467,513	40,248	40,051	40,445	15-18	751,977	44,581	44,362	44,800	16-17	10.8
New Hampshire.	411,387	47,150	46,944	47,356	8	474,750	49,467	49,220	49,714	6-7	4.9
New Jersey	2,794,316	53,118	53,009	53,227	3	3,065,774	55,146	54,998	55,294	1	3.8
New Mexico.	543,825	31,262	31,071	31,453	41	678,032	34,133	33,957	34,309	43-44	9.2
New York	6,634,434	42,784	42,698	42,870	6-7	7,060,595	43,393	43,324	43,462	19	1.4
North Carolina	2,517,098	34,584	34,503	34,665	34	3,133,282	39,184	39,094	39,274	32-33	13.3
North Dakota	241,802	30,127	29,926	30,328	44	257,234	34,604	34,408	34,800	42	14.9
Ohio	4,089,312	37,256	37,177	37,335	25-26	4,446,621	40,956	40,875	41,037	23-25	9.9
Oklahoma	1,207,235	30,600	30,477	30,723	42-43	1,343,506	33,400	33,291	33,509	46	9.2
Oregon	1,105,362	35,367	35,249	35,485	30-32	1,335,109	40,916	40,773	41,059	23-25	15.7
Pennsylvania	4,492,958	37,728	37,659	37,797	23-24	4,779,186	40,106	40,032	40,180	28-29	6.3
Rhode Island	377,080	41,766	41,509	42,023	12-13	408,412	42,090	41,771	42,409	21	NS
South Carolina.	1,258,783	34,077	33,959	34,195	35-37	1,534,334	37,082	36,954	37,210	38-39	8.8
South Dakota.	260,059	29,206	29,032	29,380	46-47	290,336	35,282	35,078	35,486	41	20.8
Tennessee	1,853,515	32,196	32,089	32,303	40	2,234,229	36,360	36,243	36,477	40	12.9
Texas.	6,079,341	35,063	35,005	35,121	32-33	7,397,294	39,927	39,864	39,990	28,30	13.9
Utah.	537,196	38,248	38,064	38,432	21-22	701,933	45,726	45,517	45,935	14-15	19.6
Vermont.	210,633	38,666	38,431	38,901	20	240,744	40,856	40,617	41,095	23-26	5.7
Virginia	2,294,722	43,255	43,128	43,382	11	2,700,335	46,677	46,545	46,809	12-13	7.9
Washington	1,875,508	40,471	40,376	40,566	14	2,272,261	45,776	45,626	45,926	14-15	13.1
West Virginia	688,727	26,989	26,859	27,119	50	737,360	29,696	29,555	29,837	51	10.0
Wisconsin	1,824,252	38,212	38,126	38,298	21-22	2,086,304	43,791	43,677	43,905	18	14.6
Wyoming	169,309	35,167	34,882	35,452	30-33	193,959	37,892	37,533	38,251	35-37	7.7
Puerto Rico	1,057,357	11,544	11,485	11,604	NA	1,261,816	14,412	14,360	14,464	NA	25.3

NA Not applicable.

NS Not statistically different from zero at the 90-percent confidence level.

Note: The estimates in this table may vary from actual values due to sampling and nonsampling error. As a result, the median income of a state with a higher rank may not be statistically different from the median income of a state with a lower rank.

Source: Census 2000 Summary File 3.

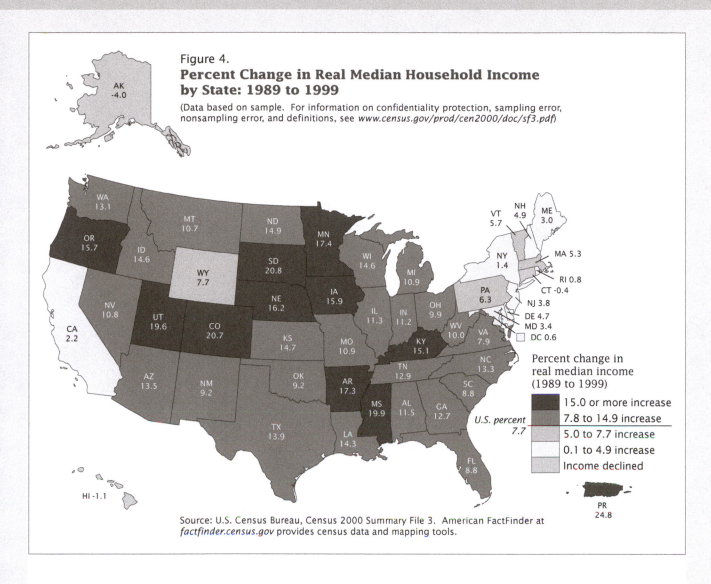

Figure 4.

Percent Change in Real Median Household Income by State: 1989 to 1999

(Data based on sample. For information on confidentiality protection, sampling error, nonsampling error, and definitions, see *www.census.gov/prod/cen2000/doc/sf3.pdf*)

AK -4.0

WA 13.1

MT 10.7

ND 14.9

MN 17.4

OR 15.7

ID 14.6

SD 20.8

WI 14.6

MI 10.9

VT 5.7

NH 4.9

ME 3.0

NY 1.4

MA 5.3

WY 7.7

IA 15.9

OH 9.9

PA 6.3

RI 0.8

CT -0.4

NV 10.8

NE 16.2

IL 11.3

IN 11.2

WV 10.0

VA 7.9

NJ 3.8

DE 4.7

MD 3.4

DC 0.6

CA 2.2

UT 19.6

CO 20.7

KS 14.7

MO 10.9

KY 15.1

NC 13.3

AZ 13.5

NM 9.2

OK 9.2

AR 17.3

TN 12.9

SC 8.8

MS 19.9

AL 11.5

GA 12.7

TX 13.9

LA 14.3

FL 8.8

HI -1.1

Percent change in real median income (1989 to 1999)

U.S. percent 7.7

- 15.0 or more increase
- 7.8 to 14.9 increase
- 5.0 to 7.7 increase
- 0.1 to 4.9 increase
- Income declined

PR 24.8

Source: U.S. Census Bureau, Census 2000 Summary File 3. American FactFinder at *factfinder.census.gov* provides census data and mapping tools.

and 13.0 million households had incomes of $100,000 or more.

California had several cities with median household incomes among the highest in the country.

Among places of 100,000 or more population, Naperville, Illinois (near Chicago) reported the highest median household income ($88,800) in 1999 (Table 3). The next highest income cities were Plano, Texas (near Dallas) and Thousand Oaks, California (near Los Angeles). Seven of the cities with the highest median incomes

were in California. Four—Sunnyvale, Simi Valley, San Jose, and Santa Clara—are in an area commonly called Silicon Valley, home to many companies that sell computer products and services.

Miami, Florida had the lowest 1999 median household income ($23,500) among places with 100,000 or more population. Five of the ten places with the lowest median household income were in the Northeast—Buffalo, New York; Hartford, Connecticut; Syracuse, New York; Providence, Rhode Island; and Newark, New Jersey.

ADDITIONAL FINDING

What are the sources of household income?

In Census 2000, households reported nearly $6.0 trillion in income in 1999. A little over 80 percent came from earnings (wages or salaries and self-employment income) with 74.6 percent coming from wages and salaries alone. Property income (interest, dividends, and rents or royalties) accounted for 6.8 percent. Social Security or Railroad Retirement provided 5.1 percent. Other retirement, survivor, or disability

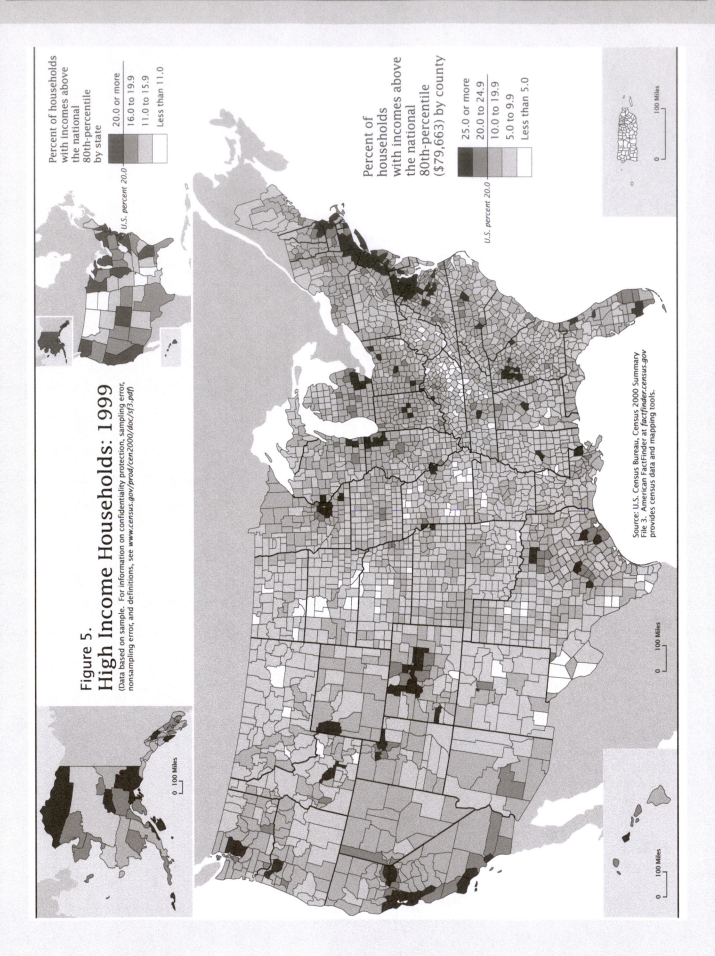

Figure 5.
High Income Households: 1999
(Data based on sample. For information on confidentiality protection, sampling error, nonsampling error, and definitions, see www.census.gov/prod/cen2000/doc/sf3.pdf)

Percent of households with incomes above the national 80th-percentile by state

20.0 or more
16.0 to 19.9
11.0 to 15.9
Less than 11.0

U.S. percent 20.0

Percent of households with incomes above the national 80th-percentile ($79,663) by county

25.0 or more
20.0 to 24.9
10.0 to 19.9
5.0 to 9.9
Less than 5.0

U.S. percent 20.0

Source: U.S. Census Bureau, Census 2000 Summary File 3. American FactFinder at factfinder.census.gov provides census data and mapping tools.

0 100 Miles

0 100 Miles

0 100 Miles

0 100 Miles

Table 3.
Ten Places of 100,000 or More Population with the Highest and Lowest Median Household Income: 1999

(Data based on sample. For information on confidentiality protection, sampling error, nonsampling error, and definitions, see *www.census.gov/prod/cen2000/doc/sf3.pdf*)

Place	Household income (dollars)			
			Confidence interval	
	Number of households	Median	Lower bound	Upper bound
Highest Median Income				
Naperville, Illinois	128,300	88,771	87,146	90,396
Plano, Texas	222,301	78,722	77,394	80,050
Thousand Oaks, California	116,725	76,815	75,010	78,620
Fremont, California	203,413	76,579	75,286	77,872
Sunnyvale, California	131,905	74,409	73,137	75,681
Irvine, California	143,034	72,057	70,532	73,582
Simi Valley, California	111,547	70,370	68,949	71,791
San Jose, California	893,889	70,243	69,669	70,817
Santa Clara, California	102,104	69,466	67,994	70,938
Gilbert, Arizona	109,936	68,032	66,905	69,159
Lowest Median Income				
Miami, Florida	362,563	23,483	23,085	23,881
Brownsville, Texas	140,075	24,468	23,812	25,124
Buffalo, New York	292,648	24,536	24,135	24,937
Hartford, Connecticut	121,578	24,820	24,193	25,447
Syracuse, New York	147,326	25,000	24,572	25,428
Cleveland, Ohio	478,393	25,928	25,635	26,221
Waco, Texas	114,032	26,264	25,509	27,019
Birmingham, Alabama	243,072	26,735	26,284	27,186
Providence, Rhode Island	173,618	26,867	26,227	27,507
Newark, New Jersey	273,546	26,913	26,390	27,436

Note: The estimates in this table may vary from actual values due to sampling and non-sampling error. As a result, the median income of a place with a higher rank may not be statistically different from the median income of a place with a lower rank.

Source: Census 2000 Summary File 3.

pension income supplied another 5.1 percent. Among the remaining categories of income asked about in Census 2000, Supplemental Security Income accounted for 0.5 percent, public assistance or welfare 0.2 percent, and 1.9 percent came from all other sources.

ABOUT CENSUS 2000

Why Census 2000 Asked About Income

The data are used to measure poverty and allocate federal funds through allocation formulas for many government programs. The questions on income also provide vital information on general economic well-being. Specific programs requiring income information include the Community Reinvestment Act of 1977 and the Enterprise Zone Development Act. The Business and Industry Guaranteed Loan Program and the Compensatory Education for the Disadvantaged Program also use income measures to direct funding.

Accuracy of the Estimates

The data contained in this report are based on the sample of households who responded to the Census 2000 long form. Nationally, approximately 1 out of every 6 addresses received that form. As a result, the sample estimates may differ somewhat from the 100-percent figures that would have been obtained if data had been collected from all housing units, people within those housing units, and people living in group quarters using the same questionnaires, instructions, personnel, and so forth. The sample estimates also differ from the values that would have been obtained from different samples of housing units, people within those housing units, and people living in group quarters. The deviation of a sample estimate from the average of all possible samples is called the sampling error.

In addition to the variability that arises from the sampling procedures, both sample data and 100-percent data are subject to nonsampling error. Nonsampling error may be introduced during any of the various complex operations used to collect and process data. Such errors may include: not enumerating every household or every person in the population, failing to obtain all required information from the respondents, obtaining incorrect or inconsistent information, and recording information incorrectly. In addition, errors can occur during the field review of the enumerators' work, during clerical handling of the census questionnaires, or during the electronic processing of the questionnaires.

Nonsampling error may affect the data in two ways: first, errors that are introduced randomly will increase the variability of the data and, therefore, should be reflected in the standard errors; and second, errors that tend to be consistent in one direction will bias estimates in that direction. For example, if respondents consistently tend to underreport their incomes, then the resulting estimates of the number of households or families in each income category will tend to be understated for the higher income categories and overstated for the lower income categories. Such biases are not reflected in the standard errors.

While it is impossible to completely eliminate error from an operation as large and complex as the decennial census, the Census Bureau attempts to control the sources of such error during the data collection and processing operations. The primary sources of error and the programs instituted to control error in Census 2000 are described in detail in *Summary File 3 Technical Documentation* under Chapter 8, "Accuracy of the Data," located at <www.census.gov /prod/cen2000/doc/sf3.pdf>.

All statements in this Census 2000 report have undergone statistical testing, and all comparisons are significant at the 90-percent confidence level unless otherwise noted. The estimates in tables, maps, and other figures may vary from actual values due to sampling and nonsampling errors. As a result, estimates in one category may not be significantly different from estimates assigned to a different category. Further information on the accuracy of the data is located at <www.census.gov/prod /cen2000/doc/sf3.pdf>. For further information on the computation and use of standard errors, contact the Decennial Statistical Studies Division at 301-763-4242.

For More Information

Census 2000 Summary Files 3 and 4 data are available from the American FactFinder on the Internet <www.factfinder.census.gov>. They were released on a state-by-state basis during 2002. For information on confidentiality protection, non-sampling error, sampling error, and definitions, also see <www.census.gov/prod/cen2000 /doc/sf3.pdf> or contact the Customer Services Center at 301-763-INFO (4636).

Information on population and housing topics is presented in the Census 2000 Brief series, located on the Census Bureau's Web site at <www.census.gov/population /www/cen2000/briefs.html>. This series presents information on race, Hispanic origin, age, sex, household type, housing tenure, and social, economic, and housing characteristics, such as ancestry, income, and housing costs.

For additional information on the income of households, families, and people, including reports and survey data, visit the Census Bureau's Internet site at <www.census.gov/hhes/www /income.html>. To find information about the availability of data products, including reports, CD-ROMs, and DVDs, call the Customer Services Center at 301-763-INFO (4636), or visit <http://ask.census.gov>.

Poverty: 1999

Census 2000 Brief

Issued May 2003

C2KBR-19

By
Alemayehu Bishaw
and
John Iceland

At the close of the 20th century, 12.4 percent of the U.S. population, or 33.9 million people, reported 1999 family incomes that were below the poverty thresholds, down from 13.1 percent in 1989.[1] The incidence of poverty varied considerably across regions, states, counties, and cities, and some groups experienced higher rates of poverty than others.

This report, which exhibits data on the poverty population, is part of a series that presents population and housing data collected by Census 2000.[2] It describes population distributions for the United States, including characteristics of regions, states, counties, and places with populations of 100,000 or more. A description of how the Census Bureau measures poverty may be found on page 2 and the poverty thresholds used are in Table 1.

Declines in poverty between 1989 and 1999 were regis-

tered for most of the age groups shown in Figure 1 and Table 2. The poverty rate for children (those under 18) declined by 1.7 percentage points, from 18.3 percent in 1989 to 16.6 percent in 1999.

Despite declines, the child poverty rate in 1999 still surpassed rates for adult age groups. In 1999, for example, the poverty rate for people 18 to 64 was 11.1 percent, and the poverty rate for people 65 to 74 and those 75 and over were 8.5 percent and 11.5 percent, respectively. Notably, people 18 to 64 experienced an increase in poverty over the decade.

[1] The estimates in this report are based on responses from a sample of the population. As with all surveys, estimates may vary from the actual values because of sampling variation or other factors. All statements made in this report have undergone statistical testing and are significant at the 90-percent confidence level unless otherwise noted.

[2] The text of this report discusses data for the United States, including the 50 states and the District of Columbia. Data for the Commonwealth of Puerto Rico are shown in Table 3 and Figure 3.

Figure 1.
Poverty Rates by Age: 1989 and 1999

(For information on confidentiality protection, sampling error, nonsampling error, and definitions, see *www.census.gov/prod/cen2000/doc/sf3.pdf*)

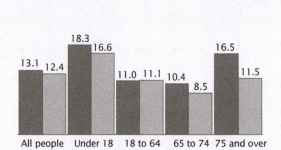

	1989	1999
All people	13.1	12.4
Under 18	18.3	16.6
18 to 64	11.0	11.1
65 to 74	10.4	8.5
75 and over	16.5	11.5

Source: U.S. Census Bureau, Census 2000 Summary File 3.

U S C E N S U S B U R E A U

Helping You Make Informed Decisions

U.S. Department of Commerce
Economics and Statistics Administration
U.S. CENSUS BUREAU

United States
Census 2000

How poverty is measured.

Poverty statistics presented in census publications use thresholds prescribed for federal agencies by Statistical Policy Directive 14, issued by the Office of Management and Budget (OMB). The original poverty measure was developed in the Social Security Administration during 1963-1964. It was adopted by the Council of Economic Advisors, and the OMB subsequently revised it slightly in 1969 and 1981.

The data on poverty status were derived in part from Census 2000 long form questionnaire items 31 and 32, which provide information on the amount of income people receive from various sources. Poverty status was determined for everyone except those in institutions, military group quarters, or college dormitories, and unrelated individuals under 15 years old.

The current official poverty measure has two components—poverty thresholds (income levels) and the family income that is compared with these thresholds. The official definition uses 48 thresholds that take into account family size (from one person to nine or more) and the presence and number of family members under 18 years old (from no children present to eight or more children present). Furthermore, unrelated individuals and two-person families are differentiated by the age of the reference person (under 65 or 65 and over). The poverty thresholds are not adjusted for regional, state, or local variation in the cost of living. The dollar amounts of the poverty thresholds used in this report are shown in Table 1.

Family income then determines who is poor. If a family's total income is less than the threshold for the family's size and composition, the family and everyone in it are considered poor. If a person is not living with anyone related by birth, marriage, or adoption, the person's own income is compared with his or her poverty threshold as an "unrelated individual." For example, the 1999 poverty threshold for a 3-person family with one member under age 18 was $13,410. If the total family income for 1999 was greater than this threshold, then the family and all members of the family were considered to be above the poverty level.

The total number of people below the poverty level is the sum of the number of people in poor families and the number of unrelated individuals with incomes below the poverty threshold. Census 2000 asked people about their income in the previous calendar year. Poverty estimates in this report compare family income in 1999 with the corresponding 1999 poverty thresholds.

Table 1.
Poverty Thresholds (Annual Dollar Amounts) by Size of Family and Number of Related Children Under 18 Years Old: 1999

Size of family unit	Weighted average threshold	Related children under 18 years								
		None	One	Two	Three	Four	Five	Six	Seven	Eight or more
One person (unrelated individual)	$8,501									
Under 65 years	8,667	8,667								
65 years and over	7,990	7,990								
Two people	10,869									
Householder under 65 years	11,214	11,156	11,483							
Householder 65 years and over	10,075	10,070	11,440							
Three people	13,290	13,032	13,410	13,423						
Four people	17,029	17,184	17,465	16,895	16,954					
Five people	20,127	20,723	21,024	20,380	19,882	19,578				
Six people	22,727	23,835	23,930	23,436	22,964	22,261	21,845			
Seven people	25,912	27,425	27,596	27,006	26,595	25,828	24,934	23,953		
Eight people	28,967	30,673	30,944	30,387	29,899	29,206	28,327	27,412	27,180	
Nine people or more	34,417	36,897	37,076	36,583	36,169	35,489	34,554	33,708	33,499	32,208

Note: The weighted average thresholds represent a summary of the poverty thresholds for a given family size. They are not used to compute official poverty statistics.

Source: U.S. Census Bureau, Current Population Survey.

Table 2.
Poverty Rates by Age: 1989 and 1999

(For information on confidentiality protection, sampling error, nonsampling error, and definitions, see www.census.gov/prod/cen2000/doc/sf3.pdf)

Characteristic	1989			1999			Percentage point change, 1999 less 1989
	Total*	Below poverty level		Total*	Below poverty level		
		Number	Percent		Number	Percent	
All people	241,977,859	31,742,864	13.1	273,882,232	33,899,812	12.4	−0.7
Under 18 years	62,605,519	11,428,916	18.3	70,925,261	11,746,858	16.6	−1.7
Under 5 years	17,978,025	3,617,099	20.1	18,726,688	3,412,025	18.2	−1.9
5 years.................	3,626,098	714,726	19.7	3,909,962	689,664	17.6	−2.1
6 to 11 years	21,187,263	3,870,105	18.3	24,587,815	4,148,573	16.9	−1.4
12 to 17 years	19,814,133	3,226,986	16.3	23,700,796	3,496,596	14.8	−1.5
18 to 64 years	149,809,693	16,533,363	11.0	169,610,423	18,865,180	11.1	0.1
65 to 74 years	17,932,656	1,857,468	10.4	18,253,226	1,550,969	8.5	−1.9
75 years and over	11,629,991	1,923,117	16.5	15,093,322	1,736,805	11.5	−5.0

* Total refers to the number of people in the poverty universe (not the total population). For more details, see the text box on how poverty is measured.

Details may not sum to totals because of rounding.

Source: 1990 census and Census 2000 Summary File 3.

GEOGRAPHIC DISTRIBUTION OF POVERTY

Poverty rates varied across regions and states.

Poverty rates varied considerably across regions (see Table 3).[3] The lowest poverty rate in 1999 was experienced in the Midwest region (10.2 percent), while the poverty rate was 11.4 percent in the Northeast and 13.0 percent in the West. Poverty rates in 1999 remained highest in the South (13.9 percent). Although 35.6 percent of the total population resided in the South, 40.0 percent of the

[3] The Northeast region includes the states of Connecticut, Maine, Massachusetts, New Hampshire, New Jersey, New York, Pennsylvania, Rhode Island, and Vermont. The Midwest region includes the states of Illinois, Indiana, Iowa, Kansas, Michigan, Minnesota, Missouri, Nebraska, North Dakota, Ohio, South Dakota, and Wisconsin. The South region includes the states of Alabama, Arkansas, Delaware, Florida, Georgia, Kentucky, Louisiana, Maryland, Mississippi, North Carolina, Oklahoma, South Carolina, Tennessee, Texas, Virginia, West Virginia, and the District of Columbia, a state equivalent. The West region includes the states of Alaska, Arizona, California, Colorado, Hawaii, Idaho, Montana, Nevada, New Mexico, Oregon, Utah, Washington, and Wyoming.

population living in poverty resided there, according to Census 2000 (see Figure 2).

The variation across the 50 states and the District of Columbia was even more pronounced (Table 3). Among the 50 states, poverty rates in 1999 ranged from a low of 6.5 percent in New Hampshire to a high of 19.9 percent in Mississippi. The estimated poverty rate for District of Columbia (20.2 percent) is not statistically different from Mississippi.

The three states with the highest poverty rates in 1989 (Mississippi, Louisiana, and New Mexico) all experienced significant declines in poverty over the 1990s, yet remained the three highest.

None of the three states with the lowest poverty rates in 1989 (New Hampshire, Connecticut, and New Jersey) experienced declines in poverty; two of them—Connecticut and New Jersey—experienced increases. Nevertheless, New Hampshire and Connecticut remained among the three states

with the lowest poverty rates in 1999, along with Minnesota.

Clusters of low and high poverty counties were evident in 1999.

Figure 3 shows how poverty rates varied among U.S. counties in 1999. The lighter-shaded counties, such as those that predominate in the Midwest, along the coast in the Northeast, and in some mountain states, had lower-than-average poverty rates. In contrast, the darker-shaded counties in the South and Southwest had higher-than-average poverty rates. High-poverty counties were clustered in Appalachia (such as in West Virginia and Eastern Kentucky), in the Mississippi delta area, along the border in Southwest Texas, and in some American Indian tribal areas in states close to the Canadian border and the Southwest.

Some places had lower poverty rates than others.

Tables 4 and 5 show the places with the lowest and highest poverty rates in 1999 among places with a

Table 3.
State and Regional Poverty Rates: 1989 and 1999

(For information on confidentiality, protection, sampling error, nonsampling error, and definitions, refer to
www.census.gov/prod/cen2000/doc/sf3.pdf)

State	1989			1999			Percentage point change 1999 less 1989
	Total*	Below poverty level		Total*	Below poverty level		
		Number	Percent		Number	Percent	
United States	241,977,859	31,742,864	13.1	273,882,232	33,899,812	12.4	−0.7
Regions							
Northeast	49,352,506	5,214,372	10.6	52,039,565	5,919,007	11.4	0.8
Midwest	58,035,788	6,971,020	12.0	62,613,918	6,360,113	10.2	−1.9
South	83,106,946	13,065,294	15.7	97,437,335	13,569,265	13.9	−1.8
West	51,482,619	6,492,178	12.6	61,791,414	8,051,427	13.0	0.4
State							
Alabama	3,945,798	723,614	18.3	4,334,919	698,097	16.1	−2.2
Alaska	532,474	47,906	9.0	612,961	57,602	9.4	0.4
Arizona	3,584,399	564,362	15.7	5,021,238	698,669	13.9	−1.8
Arkansas	2,292,037	437,089	19.1	2,600,117	411,777	15.8	−3.2
California	29,003,219	3,627,585	12.5	33,100,044	4,706,130	14.2	1.7
Colorado	3,212,550	375,214	11.7	4,202,140	388,952	9.3	−2.4
Connecticut	3,188,125	217,347	6.8	3,300,416	259,514	7.9	1.0
Delaware	645,399	56,223	8.7	759,117	69,901	9.2	0.5
District of Columbia	570,826	96,278	16.9	541,657	109,500	20.2	3.3
Florida	12,641,486	1,604,186	12.7	15,605,367	1,952,629	12.5	−0.2
Georgia	6,299,654	923,085	14.7	7,959,649	1,033,793	13.0	−1.7
Hawaii	1,071,352	88,408	8.3	1,178,795	126,154	10.7	2.4
Idaho	985,553	130,588	13.3	1,263,205	148,732	11.8	−1.5
Illinois	11,143,856	1,326,731	11.9	12,095,961	1,291,958	10.7	−1.2
Indiana	5,372,388	573,632	10.7	5,894,295	559,484	9.5	−1.2
Iowa	2,676,958	307,420	11.5	2,824,435	258,008	9.1	−2.3
Kansas	2,391,824	274,623	11.5	2,605,429	257,829	9.9	−1.6
Kentucky	3,582,459	681,827	19.0	3,927,047	621,096	15.8	−3.2
Louisiana	4,101,071	967,002	23.6	4,334,094	851,113	19.6	−3.9
Maine	1,189,534	128,466	10.8	1,240,893	135,501	10.9	NS
Maryland	4,660,591	385,296	8.3	5,164,376	438,676	8.5	0.2
Massachusetts	5,812,415	519,339	8.9	6,138,444	573,421	9.3	0.4
Michigan	9,077,016	1,190,698	13.1	9,700,622	1,021,605	10.5	−2.6
Minnesota	4,259,456	435,331	10.2	4,794,144	380,476	7.9	−2.3
Mississippi	2,502,902	631,029	25.2	2,750,677	548,079	19.9	−5.3
Missouri	4,970,573	663,075	13.3	5,433,293	637,891	11.7	−1.6
Montana	776,793	124,853	16.1	878,789	128,355	14.6	−1.5
Nebraska	1,530,947	170,616	11.1	1,660,527	161,269	9.7	−1.4
Nevada	1,178,396	119,660	10.2	1,962,948	205,685	10.5	0.3
New Hampshire	1,075,703	69,104	6.4	1,199,322	78,530	6.5	NS
New Jersey	7,563,170	573,152	7.6	8,232,588	699,668	8.5	0.9
New Mexico	1,484,339	305,934	20.6	1,783,907	328,933	18.4	−2.2
New York	17,481,762	2,277,296	13.0	18,449,899	2,692,202	14.6	1.6
North Carolina	6,397,185	829,858	13.0	7,805,328	958,667	12.3	−0.7
North Dakota	613,969	88,276	14.4	619,197	73,457	11.9	−2.5
Ohio	10,574,315	1,325,768	12.5	11,046,987	1,170,698	10.6	−1.9
Oklahoma	3,051,515	509,854	16.7	3,336,224	491,235	14.7	−2.0
Oregon	2,775,907	344,867	12.4	3,347,667	388,740	11.6	−0.8
Pennsylvania	11,536,049	1,283,629	11.1	11,879,950	1,304,117	11.0	−0.1
Rhode Island	964,376	92,670	9.6	1,010,000	120,548	11.9	2.3
South Carolina	3,368,125	517,793	15.4	3,883,329	547,869	14.1	−1.3
South Dakota	670,383	106,305	15.9	727,425	95,900	13.2	−2.7
Tennessee	4,743,685	744,941	15.7	5,539,896	746,789	13.5	−2.2
Texas	16,580,286	3,000,515	18.1	20,287,300	3,117,609	15.4	−2.7
Utah	1,694,357	192,415	11.4	2,195,034	206,328	9.4	−2.0
Vermont	541,372	53,369	9.9	588,053	55,506	9.4	−0.4
Virginia	5,968,596	611,611	10.2	6,844,372	656,641	9.6	−0.7
Washington	4,741,003	517,933	10.9	5,765,201	612,370	10.6	−0.3
West Virginia	1,755,331	345,093	19.7	1,763,866	315,794	17.9	−1.8
Wisconsin	4,754,103	508,545	10.7	5,211,603	451,538	8.7	−2.0
Wyoming	442,277	52,453	11.9	479,485	54,777	11.4	−0.4
Puerto Rico	3,494,544	2,057,377	58.9	3,769,782	1,818,687	48.2	−10.6

* Total refers to the number of people in the poverty universe (not the total populations). For more details, see the text box on how poverty is measured.
NS Not statistically different from zero at the 90-percent confidence level.
Note: Details may not sum to totals because of rounding.
Source: 1990 census and Census 2000 Summary File 3.

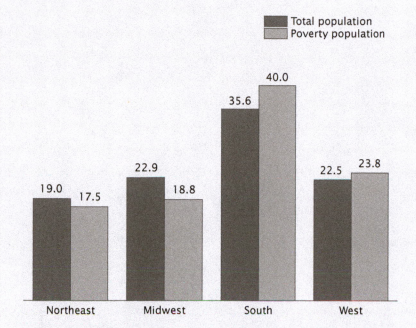

Figure 2.
Distribution of People and Poverty by Region in Census 2000

(Percent in each region. For information on confidentiality protection, sampling error, nonsampling error, and definitions, see *www.census.gov/prod/cen2000/doc/sf3.pdf*)

- Total population
- Poverty population

Region	Total population	Poverty population
Northeast	19.0	17.5
Midwest	22.9	18.8
South	35.6	40.0
West	22.5	23.8

Source: U.S. Census Bureau, Census 2000 Summary File 3.

population of 100,000 or more.[4] Naperville, Illinois, had the lowest poverty rate—2.2 percent—among these places (Table 4). Of the 10 places with the lowest poverty rates in Table 4, five were in the West (Gilbert, AZ; Westminister, CO; Thousand Oaks, CA; Arvada, CO; and Peoria, AZ), four were in the Midwest (Naperville, IL; Livonia, MI; Overland Park, KS; and Sterling Heights, MI), one was in the South (Plano, TX), and none were in the Northeast.

Brownsville, Texas, had the highest poverty rate at 36.0 percent. Five of the 10 places listed in Table 5 were in the South (Brownsville is accompanied by Laredo, TX; Miami, FL; Athens-Clarke, GA; and New Orleans, LA). Four were in the Northeast (Hartford, CT; Providence, RI; Newark, NJ; and Syracuse, NY), and only one in the West (San Bernardino, CA). None were in the Midwest.

ADDITIONAL FINDINGS ON THE POVERTY POPULATION

Poverty rates varied by race and Hispanic origin.

Census 2000 asked respondents to report one or more races. With the exception of the Two or more races group, all race groups discussed in this report refer to people who indicated only one racial identity among the six major categories: White, Black or African American, American Indian and Alaska Native, Asian, Native Hawaiian or Other Pacific Islander, and Some other race.[5] The use of the single-race population in this report does not imply that it is the preferred method of presenting or analyzing data. The Census Bureau uses a variety of approaches.[6]

Non-Hispanic Whites had the lowest poverty rate (8.1 percent) in 1999. The poverty rates for Asians (12.6 percent) and Native Hawaiians or Other Pacific Islanders (17.7 percent) were somewhat higher (see Table 6). Poverty rates were higher still among Blacks or African Americans (24.9 percent) and American Indians and Alaska Natives (25.7 percent). Poverty rates for those who were of Some other race (24.4 percent) or Two or more races (18.2 percent) were also higher than the national average (12.4 percent).[7]

People who were Hispanic or Latino (who may be of any race) also had a high poverty rate (22.6 percent) compared with the national average.[8]

[5] For further information on each of the six major race groups and the Two or more races population, see reports from the Census 2000 Brief series (C2KBR/01), available on the Census 2000 Web site at *www.census.gov/ population/www/cen2000/briefs.html*.

[6] This report draws heavily on Summary File 3, a Census 2000 product that can be accessed through *American FactFinder*, available from the Census Bureau's Web site, *www.census.gov*. Information on people who reported more than one race, such as "White and American Indian and Alaska Native" or "Asian and Black or African American," is forthcoming in Summary File 4, which will also be available through *American FactFinder* later in 2003.

[7] All the poverty rates for the race groups mentioned above differ statistically from each other except the poverty rates of Native Hawaiians and Other Pacific Islanders and people who reported Two or more races.

[8] Because Hispanics may be of any race, data in this report for Hispanics overlap with data for racial groups. Based on Census 2000 sample data, the proportion of Hispanics was 8.0 percent for Whites, 1.9 percent for Blacks, 14.6 percent for American Indians and Alaska Natives, 1.0 percent for Asians, 9.5 percent for Pacific Islanders, 97.1 percent for those reporting Some other race, and 31.1 percent for those reporting Two or more races.

[4] Census 2000 showed 245 places in the United States with 100,000 or more population. They included 238 incorporated places (including four city-county consolidations) and seven census designated places that were not legally incorporated. For a list of these places by state, see *www.census.gov/ population/www/cen2000/phc-t6.html*.

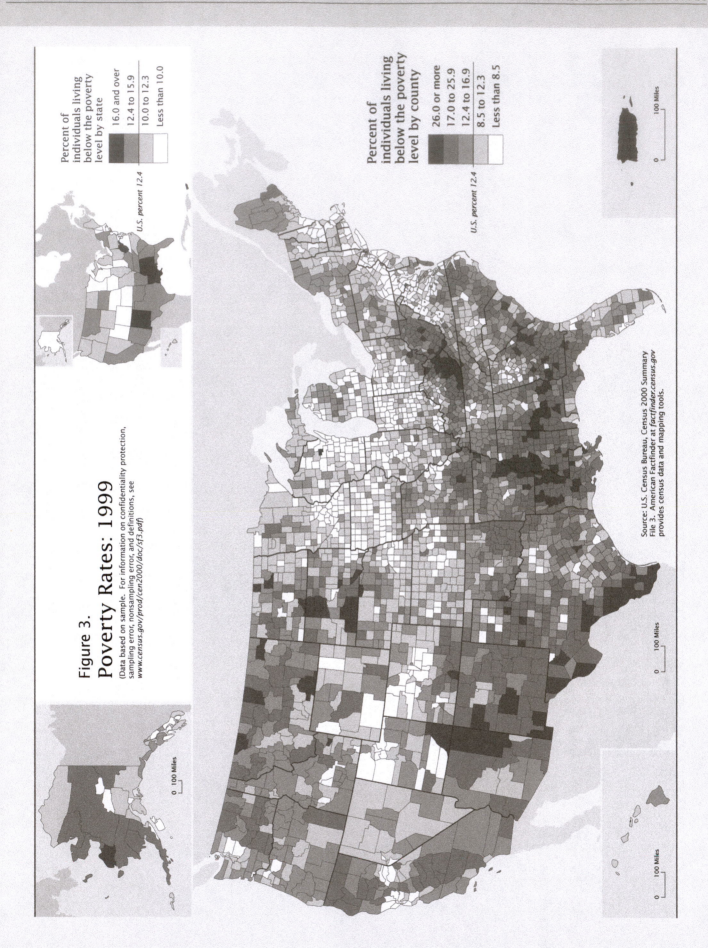

Figure 3.
Poverty Rates: 1999

(Data based on sample. For information on confidentiality protection, sampling error, nonsampling error, and definitions, see www.census.gov/prod/cen2000/doc/sf3.pdf)

Percent of individuals living below the poverty level by state

16.0 and over
12.4 to 15.9
10.0 to 12.3
Less than 10.0

U.S. percent 12.4

Percent of individuals living below the poverty level by county

26.0 or more
17.0 to 25.9
12.4 to 16.9
8.5 to 12.3
Less than 8.5

U.S. percent 12.4

Source: U.S. Census Bureau, Census 2000 Summary File 3. American Factfinder at factfinder.census.gov provides census data and mapping tools.

Table 4.
Places of 100,000 or More With the Lowest Poverty Rates: 1999

(For information on confidentiality protection, sampling error, nonsampling error, and definitions, see *www.census.gov/prod/cen2000/doc/sf3.pdf*)

Places with 100,000 or more	Total*	Below poverty level		90-percent confidence interval	
		Number	Percent	Lower	Upper
Naperville city, IL...............	126,420	2,809	2.2	2.0	2.4
Livonia city, MI..................	99,202	3,136	3.2	3.0	3.4
Overland Park city, KS..........	147,185	4,730	3.2	2.9	3.5
Gilbert town, AZ................	109,547	3,529	3.2	2.9	3.5
Plano city, TX...................	221,149	9,500	4.3	4.0	4.6
Westminster city, CO	100,436	4,726	4.7	4.3	5.1
Thousand Oaks city, CA	115,302	5,714	5.0	4.6	5.4
Arvada city, CO	101,860	5,307	5.2	4.8	5.6
Sterling Heights city, MI	123,568	6,480	5.2	4.9	5.5
Peoria city, AZ	107,094	5,627	5.3	4.9	5.7

*Total refers to the number of people in the poverty universe (not the total population). For more details, see the text box on how poverty is measured.

Note: Because of sampling error, the estimates in this table may not be significantly different from one another or from rates for other geographic areas not listed in this table.

Source: Census 2000 Summary File 3.

Table 5.
Places of 100,000 or More With the Highest Poverty Rates: 1999

(For information on confidentiality protection, sampling error, nonsampling error, and definitions, see *www.census.gov/prod/cen2000/doc/sf3.pdf*)

City and State	Total*	Below poverty level		90-percent confidence interval	
		Number	Percent	Lower	Upper
Brownsville city, TX.............	138,169	49,701	36.0	35.2	36.8
Hartford city, CT	116,756	35,741	30.6	29.9	31.3
Laredo city, TX.................	174,070	51,493	29.6	29.0	30.2
Providence city, RI	160,243	46,688	29.1	28.5	29.7
Miami city, FL..................	352,916	100,405	28.5	28.1	28.9
Newark city, NJ.................	261,451	74,263	28.4	27.9	28.9
Athens-Clarke County, GA	93,161	26,337	28.3	27.4	29.2
New Orleans city, LA	468,453	130,896	27.9	27.5	28.3
San Bernardino city, CA.........	180,100	49,691	27.6	27.0	28.2
Syracuse city, NY	137,234	37,485	27.3	26.6	28.0

*Total refers to the number of people in the poverty universe (not the total population). For more details, see the text box on how poverty is measured.

Note: Because of sampling error, the estimates in this table may not be significantly different from one another or from rates for other geographic areas not listed in this table.

Source: Census 2000 Summary File 3.

Poverty rates varied by family type and number of children.

Between 1989 and 1999, the poverty rate for all families fell from 10.0 percent to 9.2 percent, but poverty rates varied by family type and the presence of children (see Table 7).

The poverty rate for all married-couple families in 1999 (4.9 percent) was lower than the rate for male householder families with no spouse present (13.6 percent) and female householder families with no spouse present (26.5 percent). Among the latter group, the poverty rate for families with related children under 18 was higher still, at 34.3 percent in 1999, although this figure represented a decline from 42.3 percent in 1989.

ABOUT CENSUS 2000

Uses of poverty statistics

The U.S. Census Bureau's statistics on poverty provide an important measure of the country's economic well-being and are sometimes used nonstatistically to assess the need or eligibility for various types of public assistance. Funds for food, health care, and legal services are distributed to local agencies based on data about elderly people with low incomes. Data about poor children are used to apportion Title I funds to counties and school districts. Under the Low-Income Home Energy Assistance Program, income and poverty data are used to allocate funds for home energy aid among areas. Other statutory applications include the Head Start Act, the Child Welfare and Services Program, the Vocational and Applied Technology Act, and the Public Housing/Section 8 Certificate and Housing Voucher Allocation Programs.

Accuracy of the Estimates

The data contained in this report are based on the sample of households who responded to the Census 2000 long form. Nationally, approximately 1 out of every 6 housing units was included in this sample. As a result, the sample estimates may differ somewhat from the 100-percent figures that would have been obtained if all housing units, people within those housing units, and people living in group quarters had been enumerated using the same questionnaires, instructions, enumerators, and so forth. The sample estimates also differ from the values that would have been obtained from different samples of housing units, people within those housing units, and people living in group quarters. The deviation of a sample estimate from the average of all possible samples is called the sampling error.

In addition to the variability that arises from the sampling procedures, both sample data and 100-percent data are subject to nonsampling error. Nonsampling error may be introduced during any of the various complex operations used to collect and process data. Such errors may include: not enumerating every household or every person in the population, failing to obtain all required information from the respondents, obtaining incorrect or inconsistent information, and recording information incorrectly. In addition, errors can occur during the field review of the enumerators' work, during clerical handling of the census questionnaires or during the electronic processing of the questionnaires.

Nonsampling error may affect the data in two ways: (1) errors that are introduced randomly will increase the variability of the data and, therefore, should be reflected in the standard errors; and (2) errors that tend to be consistent in one direction will bias both sample and 100-percent data in that direction. For example, if respondents consistently tend to under report their incomes, then the resulting estimates of households or families by income category will tend to be understated for the higher income categories and over-stated for the lower income categories. Such biases are not reflected in the standard errors.

While it is impossible to completely eliminate error from an operation as large and complex as the decen-

Table 6.

Poverty of Individuals by Race and Hispanic Origin: 1999

(For information on confidentiality protection, sampling error, nonsampling error, and definitions, see www.census.gov/prod/cen2000/doc/sf3.pdf)

Characteristic	Total*	Below poverty level		90-percent confidence interval	
		Number	Percent	Lower	Upper
All people	273,882,232	33,899,812	12.4	12.4	12.4
Race					
White alone.	206,259,768	18,847,674	9.1	9.1	9.1
Black or African American alone. .	32,714,224	8,146,146	24.9	24.9	24.9
American Indian and Alaska Native alone	2,367,505	607,734	25.7	25.6	25.8
Asian alone.	9,979,963	1,257,237	12.6	12.5	12.7
Native Hawaiian and Other Pacific Islander alone	364,909	64,558	17.7	17.4	18.0
Some other race alone.	15,100,625	3,687,589	24.4	24.3	24.5
Two or more races	7,095,238	1,288,874	18.2	18.1	18.3
Hispanic or Latino (of any race)	34,450,868	7,797,874	22.6	22.6	22.6
White alone, not Hispanic or Latino.	189,785,997	15,414,119	8.1	8.1	8.1

*Total refers to the number of people in the poverty universe (not the total population). For more details, see the text box on how poverty is measured.

Source: Census 2000 Summary File 3.

nial census, the Census Bureau attempts to control the sources of such error during the data collection and processing operations. The primary sources of error and the programs instituted to control error in Census 2000 are described in detail in Summary File 3 Technical Documentation under Chapter 8, "Accuracy of the Data," located at www.census.gov/prod/cen2000/doc/sf3.pdf.

All statements in this Census 2000 Brief have undergone statistical testing, and all comparisons are significant at the 90-percent confidence level, unless otherwise noted. The estimates in tables maps, and other figures may vary from actual values due to sampling and nonsampling errors. As a result, estimates in one category may not be significantly different from estimates assigned to a different category. Further information on the accuracy of the data is located at www.census.gov/prod/cen2000/doc/sf3.pdf. For further information on the computation

and use of standard errors, contact the Decennial Statistical Studies Division at 301-763-4242.

For More Information

The Census 2000 Summary File 3 data are available from the American Factfinder on the Internet (factfinder.census.gov). They were released on a state-by-state basis during 2002. For information on confidentiality protection, nonsampling error, sampling error, and definitions, also see www.census.gov/prod/cen2000/doc/sf3.pdf, or contact the Customer Services Center at 301-763-INFO (4636).

Information on population and housing topics is presented in the Census 2000 Brief series, located on the Census Bureau's Web site at www.census.gov/population/www/cen2000/briefs.html. This series, which will be completed in 2003, presents information on race, Hispanic origin, age, sex, household type, housing tenure, and social, economic, and housing

Table 7.
Poverty Rates of Families by Family Type and Presence of Children: 1989 and 1999

(For information on confidentiality protection, sampling error, nonsampling error, and definitions, see
www.census.gov/prod/cen2000/doc/sf3.pdf)

Characteristic	1989			1999			Percentage point change, 1999 less 1989
	Total*	Below poverty level		Total*	Below poverty level		
		Number	Percent		Number	Percent	
All families	65,049,428	6,487,515	10.0	72,261,780	6,620,945	9.2	−0.8
Married-couple family	51,718,214	2,849,984	5.5	55,458,451	2,719,059	4.9	−0.6
With related children under 18 years	25,258,549	1,834,332	7.3	26,898,972	1,767,368	6.6	−0.7
Under 5 years only	5,578,878	377,041	6.8	5,276,884	329,946	6.3	−0.5
Under 5 years and 5 to 17 years	5,555,442	634,771	11.4	5,819,401	618,283	10.6	−0.8
5 to 17 years only	14,124,229	822,520	5.8	15,802,687	819,139	5.2	−0.6
No related children under 18 years	26,459,665	1,015,652	3.8	28,559,479	951,691	3.3	−0.5
Other family	13,331,214	3,637,531	27.3	16,803,329	3,901,886	23.2	−4.1
Male householder, no spouse present	2,949,560	407,330	13.8	4,302,568	585,970	13.6	−0.2
With related children under 18 years	1,494,956	291,572	19.5	2,526,727	448,039	17.7	−1.8
Under 5 years only	364,548	81,314	22.3	584,265	113,215	19.4	−2.9
Under 5 years and 5 to 17 years	218,849	67,882	31.0	375,284	99,326	26.5	−4.6
5 to 17 years only	911,559	142,376	15.6	1,567,178	235,498	15.0	−0.6
No related children under 18 years	1,454,604	115,758	8.0	1,775,841	137,931	7.8	−0.2
Female householder, no spouse present	10,381,654	3,230,201	31.1	12,500,761	3,315,916	26.5	−4.6
With related children under 18 years	6,783,155	2,866,941	42.3	8,575,028	2,940,459	34.3	−8.0
Under 5 years only	1,177,366	592,836	50.4	1,437,173	589,201	41.0	−9.4
Under 5 years and 5 to 17 years	1,354,965	859,782	63.5	1,583,239	812,292	51.3	−12.1
5 to 17 years only	4,250,824	1,414,323	33.3	5,554,616	1,538,966	27.7	−5.6
No related children under 18 years	3,598,499	363,260	10.1	3,925,733	375,457	9.6	−0.5

* Total refers to the number of people in the poverty universe (not the total population). For more details, see the text box on how poverty is measured.

Note: Details may not sum to totals because of rounding.

Source: 1990 census and Census 2000 Summary File 3.

characteristics such as ancestry, income, and housing costs.

For additional information on poverty, including reports and survey data, visit the Census Bureau's Internet site on at *www.census.gov/ hhes/www/poverty.html.* To find information about the availability of data products, including reports, CD-ROMs, and DVDs, call the Customer Services Center at 301-763-INFO (4636), or e-mail *webmaster@census.gov.*

Home Values: 2000

Census 2000 Brief

Issued May 2003

C2KBR-20

By
Robert L. Bennefield

The median value of a home in the United States in 2000 was $119,600, according to findings in Census 2000.[1] This value represented an increase of 18 percent over the 1990 value of $101,100, after adjusting for inflation.[2] Median value means that one-half of all homes were worth more and one-half were worth less. These values refer to specified owner-occupied housing units; that is, owner-occupied single-family homes on less than 10 acres without a business or medical office on the property. In 2000, 55.2 million of the country's 115.9 million housing units were this type. The value of a home is the owner's estimate of what the house and lot would sell for if it were on the market.

Figure 1.

Reproduction of the Question on Housing Value From Census 2000

51 **What is the value of this property; that is, how much do you think this house and lot, apartment, or mobile home and lot would sell for if it were for sale?**

- [ ] Less than $10,000
- [ ] $10,000 to $14,999
- [ ] $15,000 to $19,999
- [ ] $20,000 to $24,999
- [ ] $25,000 to $29,999
- [ ] $30,000 to $34,999
- [ ] $35,000 to $39,999
- [ ] $40,000 to $49,999
- [ ] $50,000 to $59,999
- [ ] $60,000 to $69,999
- [ ] $70,000 to $79,999
- [ ] $80,000 to $89,999
- [ ] $90,000 to $99,999
- [ ] $100,000 to $124,999
- [ ] $125,000 to $149,999
- [ ] $150,000 to $174,999
- [ ] $175,000 to $199,999
- [ ] $200,000 to $249,999
- [ ] $250,000 to $299,999
- [ ] $300,000 to $399,999
- [ ] $400,000 to $499,999
- [ ] $500,000 to $749,999
- [ ] $750,000 to $999,999
- [ ] $1,000,000 or more

Source: U.S. Census Bureau, Census 2000 questionnaire.

The specific question, reproduced in Figure 1, was asked at owner-occupied housing units and units that were being bought or were vacant and for sale at the time of enumeration.

This report, part of a series that presents population and housing data collected by Census 2000, presents data on median home values in the United States, including regions, states, counties, and places with populations of 100,000 or more. It also includes home values for householders by age, race, and Hispanic origin, as well as other findings.

---

[1] The text of this report discusses data for the United States, including the 50 states and the District of Columbia. Data for the Commonwealth of Puerto Rico are shown in Table 1 and Figure 5.

[2] The estimates in this report are based on responses from a sample of the population. As with all surveys, estimates may vary from the actual values because of sampling variation or other factors. All statements made in this report have undergone statistical testing and are significant at the 90-percent confidence level, unless otherwise noted.

USCENSUSBUREAU

Helping You Make Informed Decisions

U.S. Department of Commerce
Economics and Statistics Administration
U.S. CENSUS BUREAU

United States Census 2000

Data collection methods changed between 1990 and 2000.

In Census 2000, only a sample of households were asked the home value question, whereas all house-holds were asked that question in 1990. The 2000 question was slightly different from the one used in 1990. The wording was changed to replace "condominium unit" with "apartment" and to include "mobile home." Some of the value categories were col-lapsed while others were added, allowing respondents to indicate homes valued for $1 million or more. The highest value category in 1990 was $500,000 or more.

Median home values more than doubled between 1950 and 2000.

The median value of single-family homes in the United States rose from $44,600 in 1950 to $119,600 in 2000, after adjusting for infla-tion.[3] Median home value increased in each decade of this 50-year period, rising fastest (43 percent) in the 1970s and slowest (8.2 percent) in the 1980s. The 18-percent increase in the 1990s was higher than the rate of increase in the 1960s (11 percent) and the 1980s (8.2 percent) but below the rate of increase in the 1950s (31 percent) and the 1970s (43 percent). Figure 2 presents median home values for each cen-sus since 1950.

Homeowners aged 45 to 54 lived in the highest-priced homes.

The median value for single-family homes was lowest ($84,700) for homeowners under age 25, as shown in Figure 3. Median values

rose with age of homeowner, peak-ing for homeowners 45 to 54 at $131,100. After that, median

home values fell to $124,000 at 55 to 64, $108,300 at 65 to 74, and $95,500 at 75 and over.

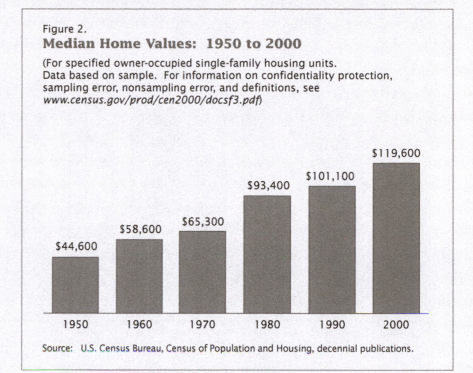

Figure 2.
Median Home Values: 1950 to 2000

(For specified owner-occupied single-family housing units. Data based on sample. For information on confidentiality protection, sampling error, nonsampling error, and definitions, see *www.census.gov/prod/cen2000/docsf3.pdf*)

Source: U.S. Census Bureau, Census of Population and Housing, decennial publications.

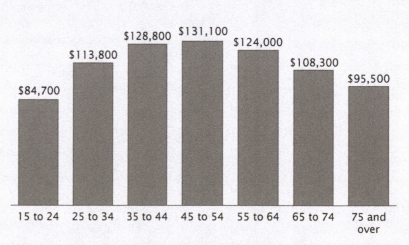

Figure 3.
Median Home Value by Age of Householder: 2000

(For specified owner-occupied single-family housing units. Data based on sample. For information on confidentiality protection, sampling error, nonsampling error, and definitions, see *www.census.gov/prod/cen2000/docsf3.pdf*)

Source: U.S. Census Bureau, Census 2000 special tabulation.

[3] Median value estimates for 1950 to 1990 were adjusted to 2000 dollars using the appropriate CPI-U-RS factors.

Figure 4.

Median Home Value by Race and Hispanic Origin of Householder: 2000

(For specified owner-occupied single-family housing units. Data based on sample. For information on confidentiality protection, sampling error, nonsampling error, and definitions, see *www.census.gov/prod/cen2000/docsf3.pdf*)

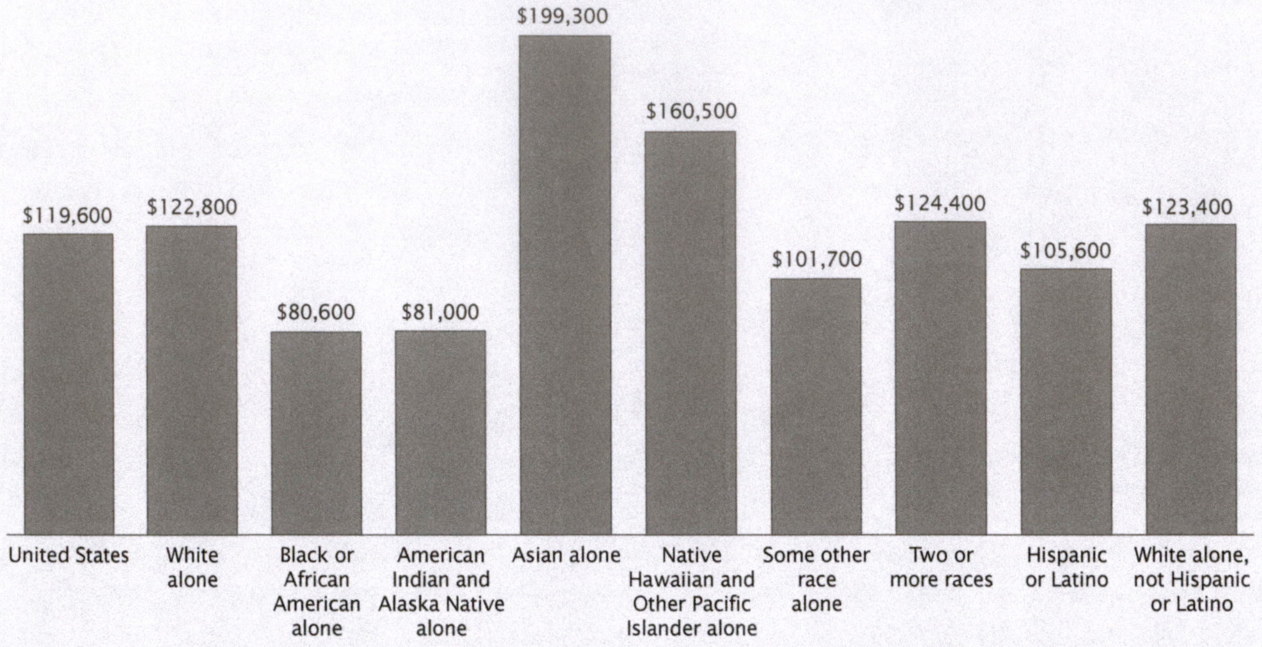

United States	$119,600
White alone	$122,800
Black or African American alone	$80,600
American Indian and Alaska Native alone	$81,000
Asian alone	$199,300
Native Hawaiian and Other Pacific Islander alone	$160,500
Some other race alone	$101,700
Two or more races	$124,400
Hispanic or Latino	$105,600
White alone, not Hispanic or Latino	$123,400

Source: U.S. Census Bureau, Census 2000 Summary File 3.

The median value of homes owned by Asian householders was more than 50 percent higher than the national median.

Census 2000 allowed respondents to choose more than one race. With the exception of the Two or more races group, all race groups discussed in this report refer to people who indicated only one racial identity among the six major categories: White, Black or African American, American Indian and Alaska Native, Asian, Native Hawaiian and Other Pacific Islander, and Some other race.[4] The use of the single-race

population in this report does not imply that it is the preferred method of presenting or analyzing data. The Census Bureau uses a variety of approaches.[5]

The median value of single-family homes for householders who identified their race as Asian was $199,300—more than 50 percent higher than the national median home value (see Figure 4). A

large proportion of these households (45 percent) were located in Hawaii or California, states that recorded the highest median home values. Householders who were Native Hawaiian and Other Pacific Islander had a median home value of $160,500, also considerably higher than the national estimate. In contrast, homeowners who were Black or African American or who were American Indian and Alaska Native had a median value of about $81,000—one-third below the national median. Among homeowners who were non-Hispanic White the median value for a single-family home was $123,400—higher than the national estimate—while among Hispanic or Latino homeowners it was $105,600—below the national

---

[4] For further information on each of the six major race groups and the Two races population, see reports from the Census 2000 Brief series (C2KBR/01), available on the Census 2000 Web site at *www.census.gov/population/www/cen2000/briefs.html*.

[5] This report draws heavily on Summary File 3, a Census 2000 product that can be accessed through American FactFinder, available from the Census Bureau's Web site, *www.census.gov*. Information on people who reported more than one race, such as "White *and* American Indian and Alaska Native" or "Asian *and* Black or African American," is forthcoming in Summary File 4, which will also be available through American FactFinder in 2003. About 2.6 percent of people reported more than one race.

estimate.[6] The median home value for people who reported two or more races was $124,400.

GEOGRAPHIC DISTRIBUTION OF HOME VALUES

Home values were highest in the West.

Median values for a single-family home were higher in the West ($171,000) than in the Northeast ($139,400), the Midwest ($105,500), or the South ($96,300) (see Table 1).[7] In the Northeast, the median value dropped between 1990 and 2000 by 12 percent, but home values increased in the other regions. The increase was greatest in the Midwest (up 33 percent), followed by the South (up 15 percent) and the West (up 6 percent).

Hawaii continued to have the highest median home value among states.

In Census 2000, as in 1990, Hawaii recorded the highest median value for single-family homes among states ($272,700)—more than twice the national median. California followed Hawaii with a

median value of $211,500 for single-family homes. Six additional states had median home values above $150,000: Massachusetts ($185,700), New Jersey ($170,800), Washington ($168,300), Connecticut ($166,900), Colorado ($166,600), and Oregon ($152,100). The District of Columbia had a similar median value at $157,200. Colorado was the only noncoastal state with a median home value above $150,000. With the exception of Maine and South Carolina, all of the states with median home values below $100,000 were adjacent and located near the middle or interior of the country (see Figure 5). The lowest median home value among the states was $70,700, recorded in Oklahoma—more than one-third below the national estimate. Four additional states in the South and Midwest had median home values below $75,000: Mississippi ($71,400), Arkansas and West Virginia (both at $72,800), and North Dakota ($74,400).[8]

Between 1990 and 2000, median home values decreased in 11 states and the District of Columbia, with Connecticut showing the sharpest drop, of 27 percent.[9] In addition to Connecticut, median values fell by more than 10 percent in eight states: Rhode Island (down 22 percent), New Hampshire (down 19 percent), New Jersey (down 18 percent), California (down 15 percent), Hawaii (down 13 percent), Maine and New York (both down 12 percent), and Massachusetts (down 11 percent). In contrast, Oregon had the

sharpest rise in median home value, up 78 percent. Other states in the West with more than a 50-percent increase in median home value were Utah (up 66 percent) and Colorado (up 58 percent). Oregon and Utah went from far under the national median in 1990 to well above it in 2000. Minnesota was the only other state to follow this path, although its gain was more modest. Maine and Vermont went in the opposite direction, from above the national median in 1990 to under by 2000. See Table 1 for values for the United States, regions, states, and Puerto Rico.

Counties with more expensive homes were primarily located in major metropolitan areas.

A band of counties with median single-family home values in excess of $150,000 extended almost continuously from the District of Columbia and its suburbs up the east coast to Boston, Massachusetts, and its suburbs (see Figure 5). Another band of homes in this price range extended along the California coast. Other counties where median single-family home values exceeded $150,000 clustered around Denver and in other Rocky Mountain areas of Colorado and in large metropolitan areas throughout the country. Counties with exceptionally high single-family median home values or those with values above $500,000 were New York County, New York (the borough of Manhattan), with a median value in excess of $1 million; Pitkin County, Colorado ($750,000); Nantucket, Massachusetts ($577,500); and Marin County, California ($514,600).[10] Counties where

---

[6] Because Hispanics may be of any race, data in this report for Hispanics overlap with data for racial groups. Based on Census 2000 sample data, the proportion Hispanic was 8.0 percent for Whites, 1.9 percent for Blacks, 14.6 percent for American Indians and Alaska Natives, 1.0 percent for Asians, 9.5 percent for Pacific Islanders, 97.1 percent for those reporting Some other race, and 31.1 percent for those reporting Two or more races.

[7] The Northeast region includes the states of Connecticut, Maine, Massachusetts, New Hampshire, New Jersey, New York, Pennsylvania, Rhode Island, and Vermont. The Midwest region includes the states of Illinois, Indiana, Iowa, Kansas, Michigan, Minnesota, Missouri, Nebraska, North Dakota, Ohio, South Dakota, and Wisconsin. The South region includes the states of Alabama, Arkansas, Delaware, Florida, Georgia, Kentucky, Louisiana, Maryland, Mississippi, North Carolina, Oklahoma, South Carolina, Tennessee, Texas, Virginia, West Virginia, and the District of Columbia, a state equivalent. The West region includes the states of Alaska, Arizona, California, Colorado, Hawaii, Idaho, Montana, Nevada, New Mexico, Oregon, Utah, Washington, and Wyoming.

[8] Because of sampling error, the estimates for geographic areas in this report may not be significantly different from one another or from estimates for other geographic areas not in this report.

[9] The decrease for the District of Columbia was not statistically significant.

[10] The single-family homes in Manhattan represented a very small proportion (1.8 percent) of all owner-occupied housing in Manhattan.

Table 1.
Median Home Values for the United States, Regions, and States, and for Puerto Rico: 1990 and 2000

(For specified owner-occupied housing units. Data based on sample. For information on confidentiality protection, sampling error, nonsampling error, and definitions, see *www.census.gov/prod/cen2000/doc/sf3.pdf*)

Area	1990 Specified owner-occupied housing units	1990 Median (dollars)	1990 Median* (dollars)	2000 Specified owner-occupied housing units	2000 Median (dollars)	Median percent change, 1990 to 2000
United States	**44,918,000**	**79,100**	**101,100**	**55,212,108**	**119,600**	**18.3**
Region						
Northeast	8,762,882	124,400	158,900	10,009,448	139,400	−12.3
Midwest	11,794,663	62,300	79,600	14,037,418	105,500	32.5
South	15,595,606	65,800	84,100	19,964,932	96,300	14.5
West	8,764,849	126,200	161,200	11,200,310	171,000	6.1
State						
Alabama	753,827	53,700	68,600	918,570	85,100	24.1
Alaska	77,527	94,400	120,600	105,620	144,200	19.6
Arizona	668,718	80,100	102,300	1,032,103	121,300	18.6
Arkansas	427,676	46,300	59,200	513,483	72,800	23.0
California	4,690,264	195,500	249,800	5,527,618	211,500	−15.3
Colorado	637,629	82,700	105,700	903,259	166,600	57.6
Connecticut	643,500	177,800	227,200	728,244	166,900	−26.5
Delaware	137,526	100,100	127,900	177,323	130,400	2.0
District of Columbia	71,532	123,900	158,300	76,289	157,200	(NS)
Florida	2,378,207	77,100	98,500	3,242,202	105,500	7.1
Georgia	1,138,775	71,300	91,100	1,596,408	111,200	22.1
Hawaii	144,431	245,300	313,400	173,861	272,700	−13.0
Idaho	177,333	58,200	74,400	255,077	106,300	42.9
Illinois	2,084,708	80,900	103,400	2,470,338	130,800	26.5
Indiana	1,137,766	53,900	68,900	1,378,878	94,300	36.9
Iowa	566,559	45,900	58,600	665,442	82,500	40.8
Kansas	500,628	52,200	66,700	581,960	83,500	25.2
Kentucky	662,174	50,500	64,500	806,461	86,700	34.4
Louisiana	733,914	58,500	74,700	864,810	85,000	13.8
Maine	214,663	87,400	111,700	254,866	98,700	−11.6
Maryland	970,864	116,500	148,800	1,178,779	146,000	−1.9
Massachusetts	1,004,573	162,800	208,000	1,187,871	185,700	−10.7
Michigan	1,916,143	60,600	77,400	2,269,175	115,600	49.4
Minnesota	894,345	74,000	94,500	1,117,489	122,400	29.5
Mississippi	441,821	45,600	58,300	532,291	71,400	22.5
Missouri	1,005,407	59,800	76,400	1,188,442	89,900	17.7
Montana	132,419	56,600	72,300	165,397	99,500	37.6
Nebraska	314,363	50,400	64,400	370,495	88,000	36.6
Nevada	183,816	95,700	122,300	363,321	142,000	16.1
New Hampshire	199,358	129,400	165,300	249,345	133,300	−19.4
New Jersey	1,466,270	162,300	207,400	1,701,732	170,800	−17.6
New Mexico	262,309	70,100	89,600	339,888	108,100	20.6
New York	2,387,606	131,600	168,100	2,689,728	148,700	−11.5
North Carolina	1,217,975	65,800	84,100	1,615,713	108,300	28.8
North Dakota	103,702	50,800	64,900	122,078	74,400	14.6
Ohio	2,241,277	63,500	81,100	2,613,123	103,700	27.9
Oklahoma	616,290	48,100	61,500	699,452	70,700	15.0
Oregon	511,829	67,100	85,700	653,869	152,100	77.5
Pennsylvania	2,581,261	69,700	89,100	2,889,484	97,000	8.9
Rhode Island	176,494	133,500	170,600	202,216	133,000	−22.0
South Carolina	615,434	61,100	78,100	783,909	94,900	21.5
South Dakota	113,057	45,200	57,700	137,531	79,600	38.0
Tennessee	938,366	58,400	74,600	1,205,931	93,000	24.7
Texas	2,949,089	59,600	76,100	3,849,585	82,500	8.4
Utah	303,724	68,900	88,000	427,244	146,100	66.0
Vermont	89,157	95,500	122,000	105,962	111,500	−8.6
Virginia	1,192,077	91,000	116,300	1,510,798	125,400	7.8
Washington	896,436	93,400	119,300	1,157,462	168,300	41.1
West Virginia	350,059	47,900	61,200	392,928	72,800	19.0
Wisconsin	916,708	62,500	79,900	1,122,467	112,200	40.4
Wyoming	78,414	61,600	78,700	95,591	96,600	22.7
Puerto Rico	**669,302**	**36,200**	**46,300**	**817,927**	**75,100**	**62.2**

*Adjusted to 2000 dollars, using CPI-U-RS factor 1.277636.
NS: Not significantly different from zero at the 90-percent confidence level.

Source: U.S. Census Bureau, Census 2000 Summary File 3 and 1990 census Summary File 1.

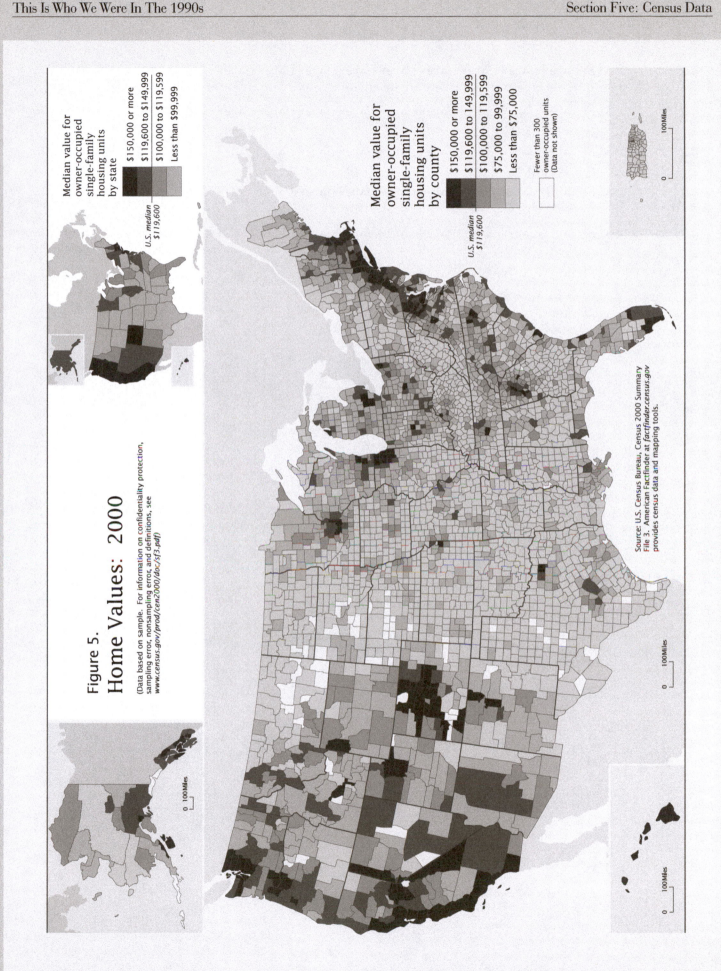

Figure 5.
Home Values: 2000

(Data based on sample. For information on confidentiality protection, sampling error, nonsampling error, and definitions, see *www.census.gov/prod/cen2000/doc/sf3.pdf*)

Median value for owner-occupied single-family housing units by state

U.S. median
$119,600

- $150,000 or more
- $119,600 to $149,999
- $100,000 to $119,599
- Less than $99,999

Median value for owner-occupied single-family housing units by county

U.S. median
$119,600

- $150,000 or more
- $119,600 to 149,999
- $100,000 to 119,599
- $75,000 to 99,999
- Less than $75,000

Fewer than 300 owner-occupied units (Data not shown)

Source: U.S. Census Bureau, Census 2000 Summary File 3. American Factfinder at *factfinder.census.gov* provides census data and mapping tools.

median home values exceeded $150,000 represented 6.2 percent of all counties. In nearly one-half of counties (49 percent) median single-family home values fell below $75,000. Most of these counties were located in the Great Plains extending from North Dakota to Texas and in the non-metropolitan South. For example, five counties with very low median single-family home values were King County, Texas ($13,800), McPherson County, South Dakota ($20,100); Corson County, South Dakota ($21,600); Kenedy County, Texas, and Boyd County, Nebraska (both at $22,500). In three counties the median home value equaled the national median of $119,600. They were Buncombe County, North Carolina, York County, South Carolina, and Whitman County, Washington.

Sunnyvale, California had the highest median home value among places of 100,000 or more.

Among places with 100,000 people or more, Sunnyvale, California recorded the highest median single-family home value, $495,200—more than four times the national median (see Table 2).[11] The remaining nine places had median single-family home values in the $300,000 to $400,000 range: Cambridge, Massachusetts ($398,500); Santa Clara, California ($396,500); San Francisco, California ($396,400); San Jose, California ($394,000); Honolulu, Hawaii ($386,700); Berkeley, California ($380,200); Fremont, California ($363,400); Stamford, Connecticut ($362,300); and Daly City, California ($335,000).[12] Seven of the ten places with the highest single-family home values were in the San Francisco Bay area and two were in the New England area.

Table 2.
Ten Places of 100,000 People or More With the Highest Median Home Values: 2000

(For specified owner-occupied housing units. Data based on sample. For information on confidentiality protection, sampling error, nonsampling error, and definitions, see www.census.gov/prod/cen2000/doc/sf3.pdf)

Area	Specified owner-occupied single-family housing units	Median value (dollars)	90-percent confidence interval
United States	55,212,108	119,600	119,500 - 119,700
Place			
Sunnyvale, CA.............	19,314	495,200	487,700 - 502,700
Cambridge, MA	4,453	398,500	377,200 - 419,800
Santa Clara, CA............	15,831	396,500	391,300 - 401,700
San Francisco, CA	79,545	396,400	393,300 - 399,500
San Jose, CA..............	146,892	394,000	392,000 - 396,000
Honolulu, HI (CDP)*	40,162	386,700	383,000 - 390,400
Berkeley, CA..............	15,869	380,200	372,100 - 388,300
Fremont, CA..............	40,429	363,400	359,900 - 366,900
Stamford, CT	18,034	362,300	355,000 - 369,600
Daly City, CA.............	15,803	335,000	331,100 - 338,900

*Honolulu is a Census Designated Place (CDP). By agreement with the state of Hawaii, the Census Bureau does not show data separately for the city of Honolulu, which is coextensive with Honolulu county.

Note: Because of sampling error, the estimates in this table may not be significantly different from one another or from estimates for other geographic areas not listed in this table.

Source: U.S. Census Bureau, Census 2000 Summary File 3.

Table 3.
Ten Places of 100,000 People or More With the Lowest Median Home Values: 2000

(For specified owner-occupied housing units. Data based on sample. For information on confidentiality protection, sampling error, nonsampling error, and definitions, see www.census.gov/prod/cen2000/doc/sf3.pdf)

Area	Specified owner-occupied single-family housing units	Median value (dollars)	90-percent confidence interval
United States	55,212,108	119,600	119,500 - 119,700
Place			
Flint, MI	26,410	49,700	48,900 - 50,500
Kansas City, KS............	31,461	52,500	51,600 - 53,400
Brownsville, TX	20,258	53,000	51,500 - 54,500
Waco, TX	18,226	53,300	51,500 - 55,100
Gary, IN..................	18,997	53,400	52,200 - 54,600
Buffalo, NY	33,030	59,300	58,600 - 60,000
Philadelphia, PA............	315,437	59,700	59,400 - 60,000
Pittsburgh, PA.............	66,568	59,700	59,300 - 60,100
Abilene, TX................	22,578	61,100	59,700 - 62,500
Rochester, NY	30,910	61,300	60,700 - 61,900

Note: Because of sampling error, the estimates in this table may not be significantly different from one another or from estimates for other geographic areas not listed in this table.

Source: U.S. Census Bureau, Census 2000 Summary File 3.

[11] Census 2000 shows 245 places in the United States with 100,000 or more population. They include 238 incorporated places (including 4 city-county consolidations) and 7 census designated places that are not legally incorporated. For a list of these places by state, see www.census.gov/population/www/cen2000phc-t6.html.
[12] See footnote 8.

Flint, Michigan recorded the lowest median home value among places of 100,000 or more.

The lowest median single-family home value among large cities (places with 100,000 people or more) was recorded in Flint, Michigan ($49,700)—more than 50 percent below the national median (see Table 3). These ten lowest median single-family home values ranged from about $50,000 to $60,000. The other nine places were Kansas City, Kansas ($52,500); Brownsville, Texas ($53,000); Waco, Texas ($53,300); Gary, Indiana ($53,400); Buffalo, New York ($59,300); Philadelphia and Pittsburgh, Pennsylvania (both at $59,700); Abilene, Texas ($61,100); and Rochester, New York ($61,300).[13]

Cambridge, Massachusetts had the highest percentage of homes valued at $1 million or more.

The city with the highest percentage of single-family homes valued at $1 million or more was Cambridge, Massachusetts with 12 percent (see Table 4). San Francisco, California followed Cambridge with 7.0 percent and Pasadena, California was next with 4.7 percent. Los Angeles, California had 3.8 percent, while the remaining six cities—Fort Lauderdale, Florida, Berkeley, California, Stamford, Connecticut, Honolulu, Hawaii, Atlanta, Georgia, and Fremont, California—all had about 3 percent. Five of the ten places were in California and two were in the New England area. None of the ten places was in the Midwest.[14]

[13] See footnote 8.
[14] See footnote 8.

Table 4.
Ten Places of 100,000 People or More With the Highest Percentage of Home Values of $1 Million or More: 2000

(For specified owner-occupied housing units. Data based on sample. For information on confidentiality protection, sampling error, nonsampling error, and definitions, see www.census.gov/prod/cen2000/doc/sf3.pdf)

Area	Specified owner-occupied single-family housing units	Homes valued at $1 million or more		90-percent confidence interval
		Number	Percent	
United States	**55,212,108**	**313,759**	**0.6**	**0.6 - 0.6**
Place				
Cambridge, MA	4,453	516	11.6	9.5 - 13.7
San Francisco, CA	79,545	5,547	7.0	6.6 - 7.4
Pasadena, CA	19,318	912	4.7	4.1 - 5.4
Los Angeles, CA	412,804	15,501	3.8	3.6 - 3.9
Fort Lauderdale, FL	22,871	765	3.3	2.8 - 3.9
Berkeley, CA................	15,869	510	3.2	2.6 - 3.8
Stamford, CT	18,034	485	2.7	2.2 - 3.2
Honolulu, HI (CDP)*	40,162	1,048	2.6	2.3 - 3.0
Atlanta, GA	61,208	1,597	2.6	2.3 - 2.9
Fremont, CA...............	40,429	1,052	2.6	2.3 - 3.0

*Honolulu is a Census Designated Place (CDP). By agreement with the state of Hawaii, the Census Bureau does not show data separately for the city of Honolulu, which is coextensive with Honolulu county.

Note: Because of sampling error, the estimates in this table may not be significantly different from one another or from estimates for other geographic areas not listed in this table.

Source: U.S. Census Bureau, Census 2000 Summary File 3.

Figure 6.
Median Home Value by Type of Structure: 2000

(For all owner-occupied housing units. Data based on sample. For information on confidentiality protection, sampling error, nonsampling error, and definitions, see www.census.gov/prod/cen2000/docsf3.pdf)

Source: U.S. Census Bureau, Census 2000 special tabulation.

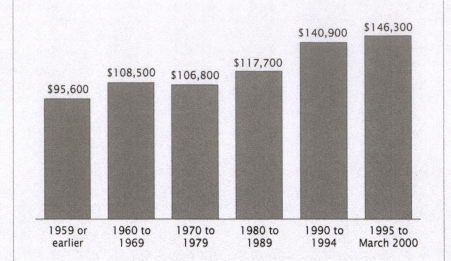

Figure 7.
Median Home Value by Year Structure Built: 2000

(For all owner-occupied housing units. Data based on sample.
For information on confidentiality protection,
sampling error, nonsampling error, and definitions, see
www.census.gov/prod/cen2000/docsf3.pdf)

$95,600 $108,500 $106,800 $117,700 $140,900 $146,300

| 1959 or earlier | 1960 to 1969 | 1970 to 1979 | 1980 to 1989 | 1990 to 1994 | 1995 to March 2000 |

Source: U.S. Census Bureau, Census 2000 special tabulation.

WHY CENSUS 2000 ASKED ABOUT HOME VALUE

The value of home and property is an important measure of neighborhood quality, housing affordability, and wealth. These data provide socioeconomic information not captured by household income and comparative information on the state of local housing markets. The federal government uses this information for the development of transportation plans, policies, and programs. It uses this information in preparing the value of housing services for the National Income and Product Accounts. Value data are incorporated in annual reports that the President sends to the Congress about housing production, occupancy, and tenure, and in analyses of housing needs.

Accuracy of the Estimates

The data contained in this report are based on the sample of households who responded to the Census 2000 long form. Nationally, approximately one out of every six housing units was included in this sample. As a result, the sample estimates may differ somewhat from the 100-percent figures that would have been obtained if all housing units, people within those housing units, and people living in group quarters had been enumerated using the same questionnaires, instructions, enumerators, and so forth. The sample estimates also differ from the values that would have been obtained from different samples of housing units, people within those housing units, and people living in group quarters. The deviation of a sample estimate from the average of all possible samples is called the sampling error.

In addition to the variability that arises from the sampling

ADDITIONAL FINDINGS

What was the median value of mortgaged homes versus nonmortgaged homes?

Of all 55.2 million specified owner-occupied homes in the United States, 70 percent were mortgaged and 30 percent were nonmortgaged. The median value of single-family homes with a mortgage ($128,800) was much higher than the median value of those without a mortgage ($96,900).

What were the median values for homes within different structures?

Among all owner-occupied housing (69.8 million), not just specified, the median home value was $111,800. For single-family detached homes (56.3 million) the median value was $121,100 (see Figure 6). This estimate was significantly higher than the $112,500 for single-family

attached units, which numbered 3.8 million and included townhouses, row houses, or duplexes. The median value for owner-occupied homes in buildings of two or more units (3.8 million) was $116,600. Finally, for mobile homes (5.9 million) it was $31,200.

What were the median values for new homes and old homes?

Of all owner-occupied homes, the 7.7 million new homes or those built between 1995 and March 2000 (median value $146,300) were much more expensive than the 24 million old homes or those built before 1960 (median value $95,600). As shown in Figure 7, the newer the home the higher the median value, except for the 12.3 million built in the 1970s ($106,800), which was lower than the 9.1 million homes built during the 1960s ($108,500).

procedures, both sample data and 100-percent data are subject to nonsampling error. Nonsampling error may be introduced during any of the various complex operations used to collect and process data. Such errors may include: not enumerating every household or every person in the population, failing to obtain all required information from the respondents, obtaining incorrect or inconsistent information, and recording information incorrectly. In addition, errors can occur during the field review of the enumerators' work, during clerical handling of the census questionnaires, or during the electronic processing of the questionnaires.

Nonsampling error may affect the data in two ways: (1) errors that are introduced randomly will increase the variability of the data and, therefore, should be reflected in the standard errors; and (2) errors that tend to be consistent in one direction will bias both sample and 100-percent data in that direction. For example, if respondents consistently tend to underreport their incomes, then the resulting estimates of households or families by income category will tend to be understated for the higher income categories and overstated for the lower income categories. Such biases are not reflected in the standard errors.

While it is impossible to completely eliminate error from an operation as large and complex as the decennial census, the Census Bureau attempts to control the sources of such error during the data collection and processing operations. The primary sources of error and the programs instituted to control error in Census 2000 are described in detail in *Summary File 3 Technical Documentation* under Chapter 8, "Accuracy of the Data," located at *www.census.gov/ prod/cen2000/doc/sf3.pdf*.

All statements in this Census 2000 Brief have undergone statistical testing and all comparisons are significant at the 90-percent confidence level, unless otherwise noted. The estimates in tables, maps, and other figures may vary from actual values due to sampling and nonsampling errors. As a result, estimates in one category may not be significantly different from estimates assigned to a different category. Further information on the accuracy of the data is located at *www.census.gov/ prod/cen2000/doc/sf3.pdf*. For further information on the computation and use of standard errors, contact the Decennial Statistical Studies Division at 301-763-4242.

For More Information

The Census 2000 Summary File 3 data are available from the American Factfinder on the Internet (*factfinder.census.gov*). They were released on a state-by-state basis during 2002. For information on confidentiality protection, nonsampling error, sampling error, and definitions, also see *www.census.gov/prod/cen2000/ doc/sf3.pdf* or contact the Customer Services Center at 301-763-INFO (4636).

Information on population and housing topics is presented in the Census 2000 Brief series, located on the Census Bureau's Web site at *www.census.gov/population/www/ cen2000/briefs.html*. This series, which will be completed in 2003, presents information on race, Hispanic origin, age, sex, household type, housing tenure, and social, economic, and housing characteristics, such as ancestry, income, and housing costs.

For additional information on housing, including reports and survey data, visit the Census Bureau's Internet site at *www.census.gov/ hhes/www/housing.html*. To find information about the availability of data products, including reports, CD-ROMs, and DVDs, call the Customer Services Center at 301-763-INFO (4636), or e-mail *webmaster@census.gov*.

Housing Characteristics: 2000

Issued October 2001

Census 2000 Brief

C2KBR/01-13

By
Jeanne Woodward
and
Bonnie Damon

According to Census 2000, there were 115.9 million housing units in the United States. Most of these housing units had people living in them (105.5 million or 91.0 percent of all housing units). The remaining 10.4 million units (9.0 percent) were vacant on Census Day. Between 1990 and 2000, the United States housing inventory increased by 13.6 million units or 13.3 percent. The South[1] (17.5 percent) and the West (16.7 percent) regions experienced higher rates of housing growth than the Midwest (10.1 percent) and the Northeast (6.6 percent).

This report, part of a series that analyzes data from Census 2000, highlights housing in 2000 and changes in housing characteristics between 1990 and 2000 in regions, states, metropolitan areas, counties, and large cities.

Housing tenure identifies a basic feature of the housing inventory, whether a unit is owner or renter occupied. It has been collected since 1890. The Census 2000 question on tenure was identical to the one used in 1990. For 1990, the response categories were expanded to allow the respondent to report whether the unit was owned with a mortgage or loan or owned free and clear (without a mortgage). The distinction between units owned with a mortgage and units owned free and clear was added in 1990 to improve the count of owner-occupied units, as research after the 1980 census indicated some respondents did not consider their units owned if they had a mortgage.

Figure 1.

Reproduction of the Question on Housing Tenure from Census 2000

2. Is this house, apartment, or mobile home —
Mark [X] ONE box.

☐ Owned by you or someone in this household with a mortgage or loan?
☐ Owned by you or someone in this household free and clear (without a mortgage or loan)?
☐ Rented for cash rent?
☐ Occupied without payment of cash rent?

Source: U.S. Census Bureau, Census 2000 questionnaire.

A housing unit is a house, an apartment, a mobile home, a group of rooms, or a single room occupied, or intended for occupancy, as separate living quarters. Separate living quarters are those in which the occupant(s) live separately from any other people in the building and which have direct access from outside the building or through a common hall.

[1] The Northeast region includes Connecticut, Maine, Massachusetts, New Hampshire, New Jersey, New York, Pennsylvania, Rhode Island, and Vermont. The Midwest includes Illinois, Indiana, Iowa, Kansas, Michigan, Minnesota, Missouri, Nebraska, North Dakota, Ohio, South Dakota, and Wisconsin. The South includes Alabama, Arkansas, Delaware, the District of Columbia, Florida, Georgia, Kentucky, Louisiana, Maryland, Mississippi, North Carolina, Oklahoma, South Carolina, Tennessee, Texas, Virginia, and West Virginia. The West includes Alaska, Arizona, California, Colorado, Hawaii, Idaho, Montana, Nevada, New Mexico, Oregon, Utah, Washington, and Wyoming.

USCENSUSBUREAU

Helping You Make Informed Decisions

U.S. Department of Commerce
Economics and Statistics Administration
U.S. CENSUS BUREAU

United States
Census 2000

Table 1.
General Housing Characteristics for the United States, Regions, and States, and for Puerto Rico: 1990 and 2000

(For information on confidentiality protection, nonsampling error, and definitions, see *www.census.gov/prod/cen2000/doc/sf1.pdf*)

Area	Total housing units in 1990	Housing units in 2000				Percent change, 1990 to 2000				
		Total	Percent vacant	Occupied	Percent owner-occupied	All housing units	Vacant units	Occupied units		
								Total	Owner	Renter
United States	102,263,678	115,904,641	9.0	105,480,101	66.2	13.3	1.0	14.7	18.3	8.3
Region										
Northeast	20,810,637	22,180,440	8.5	20,285,622	62.4	6.6	−2.2	7.5	9.3	4.6
Midwest	24,492,718	26,963,635	8.3	24,734,532	70.2	10.1	2.5	10.8	14.3	3.4
South	36,065,102	42,382,546	10.3	38,015,214	68.4	17.5	2.9	19.5	23.3	11.9
West	20,895,221	24,378,020	7.9	22,444,733	61.5	16.7	−1.4	18.5	23.5	11.4
State										
Alabama............	1,670,379	1,963,711	11.5	1,737,080	72.5	17.6	38.5	15.3	18.5	7.5
Alaska	232,608	260,978	15.1	221,600	62.5	12.2	−9.9	17.3	30.7	0.2
Arizona............	1,659,430	2,189,189	13.1	1,901,327	68.0	31.9	−0.9	38.9	47.2	24.0
Arkansas	1,000,667	1,173,043	11.1	1,042,696	69.4	17.2	19.1	17.0	16.7	17.7
California	11,182,882	12,214,549	5.8	11,502,870	56.9	9.2	−11.2	10.8	13.4	7.6
Colorado	1,477,349	1,808,037	8.3	1,658,238	67.3	22.4	−23.1	29.3	39.8	12.0
Connecticut	1,320,850	1,385,975	6.1	1,301,670	66.8	4.9	−6.7	5.8	7.7	2.1
Delaware	289,919	343,072	12.9	298,736	72.3	18.3	4.5	20.7	24.3	12.2
District of Columbia ...	278,489	274,845	9.6	248,338	40.8	−1.3	−8.1	−0.5	4.2	−3.5
Florida	6,100,262	7,302,947	13.2	6,337,929	70.1	19.7	−	23.4	28.7	12.7
Georgia	2,638,418	3,281,737	8.4	3,006,369	67.5	24.4	1.3	27.0	32.0	17.8
Hawaii	389,810	460,542	12.4	403,240	56.5	18.1	70.8	13.2	18.7	6.7
Idaho	413,327	527,824	11.0	469,645	72.4	27.7	10.6	30.2	34.5	20.1
Illinois.............	4,506,275	4,885,615	6.0	4,591,779	67.3	8.4	−3.4	9.3	14.4	−
Indiana............	2,246,046	2,532,319	7.7	2,336,306	71.4	12.7	8.5	13.1	15.0	8.6
Iowa..............	1,143,669	1,232,511	6.8	1,149,276	72.3	7.8	4.9	8.0	11.5	−0.3
Kansas............	1,044,112	1,131,200	8.2	1,037,891	69.2	8.3	−6.1	9.9	12.0	5.4
Kentucky	1,506,845	1,750,927	9.2	1,590,647	70.8	16.2	26.1	15.3	17.2	11.0
Louisiana	1,716,241	1,847,181	10.3	1,656,053	67.9	7.6	−11.9	10.5	13.9	3.8
Maine.............	587,045	651,901	20.5	518,200	71.6	11.0	9.8	11.4	13.1	7.2
Maryland	1,891,917	2,145,283	7.7	1,980,859	67.7	13.4	15.0	13.3	18.0	4.5
Massachusetts.......	2,472,711	2,621,989	6.8	2,443,580	61.7	6.0	−20.9	8.7	13.3	2.2
Michigan...........	3,847,926	4,234,279	10.6	3,785,661	73.8	10.0	4.7	10.7	15.1	0.1
Minnesota	1,848,445	2,065,946	8.3	1,895,127	74.6	11.8	−14.8	15.0	19.4	3.9
Mississippi	1,010,423	1,161,953	9.9	1,046,434	72.3	15.0	16.6	14.8	16.2	11.4
Missouri	2,199,129	2,442,017	10.1	2,194,594	70.3	11.0	4.0	11.9	14.3	6.5
Montana...........	361,155	412,633	13.1	358,667	69.1	14.3	−1.9	17.1	20.3	10.7
Nebraska	660,621	722,668	7.8	666,184	67.4	9.4	−3.0	10.6	12.2	7.4
Nevada	518,858	827,457	9.2	751,165	60.9	59.5	45.1	61.1	79.0	39.4
New Hampshire	503,904	547,024	13.2	474,606	69.7	8.6	−21.9	15.4	18.0	10.0
New Jersey	3,075,310	3,310,275	7.4	3,064,645	65.6	7.6	−12.5	9.7	10.9	7.3
New Mexico.........	632,058	780,579	13.1	677,971	70.0	23.5	14.8	24.9	29.6	15.2
New York	7,226,891	7,679,307	8.1	7,056,860	53.0	6.3	5.9	6.3	7.9	4.5
North Carolina	2,818,193	3,523,944	11.1	3,132,013	69.4	25.0	30.1	24.4	26.9	19.2
North Dakota	276,340	289,677	11.2	257,152	66.6	4.8	−8.3	6.8	8.5	3.5
Ohio..............	4,371,945	4,783,051	7.1	4,445,773	69.1	9.4	18.6	8.8	11.4	3.3
Oklahoma..........	1,406,499	1,514,400	11.4	1,342,293	68.4	7.7	−14.1	11.3	11.8	10.2
Oregon............	1,193,567	1,452,709	8.2	1,333,723	64.3	21.7	31.8	20.9	23.1	17.0
Pennsylvania	4,938,140	5,249,750	9.0	4,777,003	71.3	6.3	6.9	6.3	7.2	3.9
Rhode Island	414,572	439,837	7.1	408,424	60.0	6.1	−14.2	8.1	9.1	6.6
South Carolina.......	1,424,155	1,753,670	12.5	1,533,854	72.2	23.1	32.3	21.9	26.1	12.4
South Dakota........	292,436	323,208	10.2	290,245	68.2	10.5	−1.3	12.0	15.6	5.0
Tennessee	2,026,067	2,439,443	8.5	2,232,905	69.9	20.4	19.8	20.5	23.8	13.3
Texas	7,008,999	8,157,575	9.4	7,393,354	63.8	16.4	−18.5	21.8	27.7	12.7
Utah..............	598,388	768,594	8.8	701,281	71.5	28.4	10.1	30.5	37.0	16.6
Vermont	271,214	294,382	18.3	240,634	70.6	8.5	−11.3	14.2	16.8	8.5
Virginia............	2,496,334	2,904,192	7.1	2,699,173	68.1	16.3	0.3	17.8	21.0	11.5
Washington	2,032,378	2,451,075	7.3	2,271,398	64.6	20.6	12.3	21.3	25.2	14.8
West Virginia	781,295	844,623	12.8	736,481	75.2	8.1	16.6	7.0	8.6	2.4
Wisconsin..........	2,055,774	2,321,144	10.2	2,084,544	68.4	12.9	1.3	14.4	17.4	8.5
Wyoming	203,411	223,854	13.5	193,608	70.0	10.1	−12.5	14.7	18.3	7.0
Puerto Rico	1,188,985	1,418,476	11.1	1,261,325	72.9	19.3	17.2	19.6	21.0	15.9

− Percentage rounds 0.0.

Source: U.S. Census Bureau, 1990 Census of Population and Housing, *General Housing Characteristics,* Table 176, and Census 2000 Summary File 1.

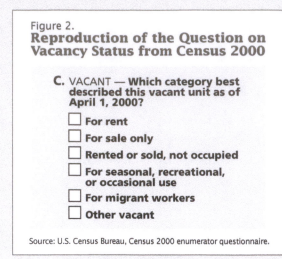

Figure 2.

Reproduction of the Question on Vacancy Status from Census 2000

C. VACANT — **Which category best described this vacant unit as of April 1, 2000?**

☐ **For rent**

☐ **For sale only**

☐ **Rented or sold, not occupied**

☐ **For seasonal, recreational, or occasional use**

☐ **For migrant workers**

☐ **Other vacant**

Source: U.S. Census Bureau, Census 2000 enumerator questionnaire.

Data on vacancy status have been collected since 1940. Vacancy status and other characteristics of vacant units were determined by enumerators obtaining information from property owners and managers, neighbors, rental agents, and others. Vacant units were subdivided into six housing market classifications: for rent; for sale only; rented or sold, not occupied; for seasonal, recreational, or occasional use; for migrant workers; and other vacant.

Owning one's home has long been considered a part of the "American Dream." Census 2000 showed that about 2 out of 3 householders (69.8 million, 66.2 percent) attained this goal.

Owner-occupied units included those with one or more mortgages as well as those owned free and clear. The remaining 35.7 million occupied units (33.8 percent) were rented or occupied without payment of cash rent. The increase in the number of owner-occupied homes in the United States (10.8 million, 18.3 percent) far outpaced the change in the rental inventory (2.7 million, 8.3 percent) during the 1990s.

In 1890, less than half of United States households owned their homes. The homeownership rate

declined from 1890 to 1920. A robust economy in the 1920s raised the homeownership rate, but the Great Depression drove the rate to its lowest level of the century — 43.6 percent in 1940. The post-World War II surge in homeownership was remarkable. A booming economy, favorable tax laws, a rejuvenated home building industry, and easier financing saw homeownership explode nationally, topping 60 percent in just two decades. In 1990, about 64 percent of U.S. households owned their homes.

In 2000, 3.8 million vacant housing units were on the market either for sale only or for rent. Another 0.7 million housing units were recently rented or sold and were awaiting occupancy at the time the census was conducted. The count of vacant housing units included 3.6 million units for seasonal, recreational, or occasional use. This vacancy category also included housing units that were temporarily

occupied at the time of enumeration entirely by people with a usual residence elsewhere; these occupants were counted at the address of their usual place of residence. A small number of vacant units (25,000 units) were intended for occupancy by migratory workers employed in farm work during the crop season. The remaining 2.3 million vacant housing units were classified as "other vacant" and included units held for personal reasons of the owner as well as units held for occupancy by a caretaker or janitor.

The majority of householders in each of the four census regions owned their homes.

In 2000, homeownership rates were 61.5 percent in the West, 62.4 percent in the Northeast, 68.4 percent in the South, and 70.2 percent in the Midwest. More than a third (26.4 million, 37.7 percent) of all owner-occupied homes were located in the South. The next largest segment was in the Midwest (17.4 million, 24.9 percent). The West (13.4 million, 19.2 percent) and the Northeast (12.7 million,

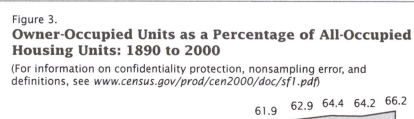

Figure 3.

Owner-Occupied Units as a Percentage of All-Occupied Housing Units: 1890 to 2000

(For information on confidentiality protection, nonsampling error, and definitions, see *www.census.gov/prod/cen2000/doc/sf1.pdf*)

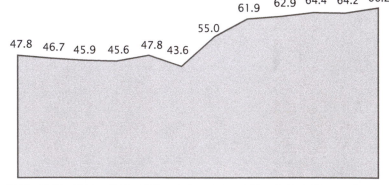

| 1890 | 1900 | 1910 | 1920 | 1930 | 1940 | 1950 | 1960 | 1970 | 1980 | 1990 | 2000 |
| 47.8 | 46.7 | 45.9 | 45.6 | 47.8 | 43.6 | 55.0 | 61.9 | 62.9 | 64.4 | 64.2 | 66.2 |

Source: U.S. Census Bureau, Census of Population and Housing, decennial volumes.

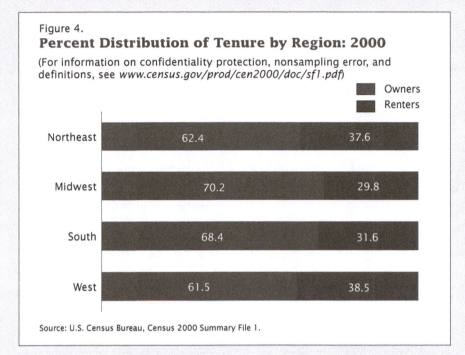

Figure 4.
Percent Distribution of Tenure by Region: 2000

(For information on confidentiality protection, nonsampling error, and definitions, see *www.census.gov/prod/cen2000/doc/sf1.pdf*)

Owners
Renters

Region	Owners	Renters
Northeast	62.4	37.6
Midwest	70.2	29.8
South	68.4	31.6
West	61.5	38.5

Source: U.S. Census Bureau, Census 2000 Summary File 1.

In 2000, as in 1990, West Virginia and Minnesota maintained their positions as the states with the highest proportions of owner-occupied housing.

While the majority of occupied units in all 50 states were owner occupied, about 3 out of 4 households in West Virginia (75.2 percent) and Minnesota (74.6 percent) owned their homes. As in 1990, New York ranked at the bottom with respect to homeownership (53.0 percent) in 2000. Renters outnumbered owners in Washington, DC, where about 2 out of 5 (40.8 percent) were homeowners.

Nevada, Arizona, and Idaho also posted high growth in their stock of rental units, adding respectively, 39.4 percent, 24.0 percent, and 20.1 percent more rental units since 1990. The rental inventories in four states (Alaska, Illinois, Iowa, and Michigan) remained relatively unchanged between 1990 and 2000, while the rental inventory in the District of Columbia declined 3.5 percent.

One in ten homes in the South were vacant on Census Day.

With 9 percent of United States housing vacant in 2000, regional rates ranged from less than 8 percent in the West to more than 10 percent in the South. Three states in the Northeast, four in the South, and six in the West had total vacancy rates that exceeded 12 percent. Housing markets were especially "tight" (less than 7 percent of units were vacant) in five states: California, Illinois, Connecticut, Iowa, and Massachusetts.

Many states with a higher-than-average proportion of vacant units had a sizeable number of homes classified as "Vacant — for seasonal, recreational, and occasional use" in Census 2000 (see Table 2). These units make up a class commonly referred to as "vacation" homes,

18.1 percent) contributed the balance of the homeowner inventory.

Among the 35.7 million renter-occupied units in the United States, about a third (12.3 million, 34.4 percent) were located in the South and about 8.4 million (23.5 percent) in the West. The remaining renter-occupied homes were about evenly distributed between the Northeast (7.6 million, 21.4 percent) and the Midwest (7.4 million, 20.6 percent).

Among the states, Nevada showed the largest percentage gain in housing units between 1990 and 2000.

The housing stock in Nevada increased 59.5 percent in the 1990s, from 519,000 to 827,000. Other western states with rapid increases in their housing inventories were Arizona (31.9 percent), Utah (28.4 percent), and Idaho (27.7 percent). California led the country in the total number of housing units in the United States in 2000 (12.2 million) and grew by more than 1.0 million units (9.2 percent) over the course of the decade.

In the South, North Carolina led the way with a 25.0 percent increase in the number of housing units, closely followed by Georgia (24.4 percent) and South Carolina (23.1 percent). Florida added 1.2 million units, the largest absolute gain among the 50 states, and increased its stock of housing by 19.7 percent between 1990 and 2000. Housing growth below the 10-percent level in the South was evident in just three states — Louisiana, Oklahoma, and West Virginia. The remaining states in the region all posted gains above the national level of 13.3 percent. The housing stock in the District of Columbia, however, declined slightly (-1.3 percent) from its 1990 level.

Housing growth in states in the Northeast (6.6 percent) and the Midwest (10.1 percent) was generally somewhat slower than the national pace (13.3 percent). Connecticut and North Dakota (both about 5 percent) were considerably below the national level.

Table 2.
Ten States With the Highest Percentage of Seasonal, Recreational, or Occasional Use Homes: 2000

(For information on confidentiality protection, nonsampling error, and definitions, see www.census.gov/prod/cen2000/doc/sf1.pdf)

Area	Total housing units	For seasonal, recreational, or occasional use	Percent
United States	**115,904,641**	**3,578,718**	**3.1**
Maine	651,901	101,470	15.6
Vermont	294,382	43,060	14.6
New Hampshire	547,024	56,413	10.3
Alaska	260,978	21,474	8.2
Delaware	343,072	25,977	7.6
Florida	7,302,947	482,944	6.6
Arizona	2,189,189	141,965	6.5
Wisconsin	2,321,144	142,313	6.1
Montana	412,633	24,213	5.9
Hawaii	460,542	25,584	5.6

Source: U.S. Census Bureau, Census 2000 Summary File 1.

which can be big summer estates on Long Island, time-sharing condos in Fort Lauderdale, or simple fishing cabins in northern Michigan. Although many analysts have used this category to estimate the number of second homes in a given area, the category also includes units occupied on an occasional basis as corporate apartments and other temporary residences where all the household members reported that their residence was elsewhere.

On a percentage basis, three northern New England states — Maine (15.6 percent), Vermont (14.6 percent), and New Hampshire (10.3 percent) — topped the list. Florida is the clear leader in the number of these seasonal, recreational, and occasional-use properties (483,000), followed by California (237,000), New York (235,000), and Michigan (234,000).

Homeowners were a majority in nearly all United States counties.

In 2000, owners outnumbered renters in all but 36 (1.1 percent) of the 3,141 counties and equivalent areas. Homeownership was fairly uncommon among households living in New York City, where only

1 in 5 households (19.6 percent) in Bronx and (20.1 percent) in New York (Manhattan) counties and about 1 in 3 (34.3 percent) in Kings County (Brooklyn) were homeowners. Other counties with homeownership rates below 30 percent were Chattahoochee in Georgia (27.0 percent), Aleutians West Census Area (a county equivalent) in Alaska (27.8 percent), and the very small county of Kalawao on the island of Molokai in Hawaii where all 115 occupied housing units were rented.

Alcona County in Michigan (89.9 percent) and Elbert County in Colorado (89.6 percent) topped the list in terms of the highest proportion of households who owned their homes. Other counties notable for their high rates of ownership (about 89 percent) were Powhatan and New Kent Counties in Virginia and Keweenaw County in Michigan.

Florida's metropolitan areas were leaders in terms of homeownership.

Five areas in the Sunshine State — Punta Gorda, Ocala, Fort Pierce-Port St. Lucie, Sarasota-Bradenton, and Fort Myers-Cape Coral — were among the top ten metropolitan areas with the largest proportions

of owner-occupied units in 2000. Two other metropolitan areas in Michigan — Jackson and Saginaw-Bay City-Midland — joined Barnstable-Yarmouth (Massachusetts), Houma (Louisiana), and Sharon (Pennsylvania) to round out the list.

In only five metropolitan areas were owners outnumbered by renters. These included the two large Northeastern primary metropolitan statistical areas (PMSAs) — Jersey City, New Jersey (30.7 percent) and New York, New York (34.7 percent) — and two PMSAs on the West Coast — Los Angeles-Long Beach (47.9 percent) and San Francisco (49.0 percent). The fifth metropolitan area where fewer households owned (45.6 percent) rather than rented was Bryan-College Station, Texas, home of Texas A&M University.

Renters outnumbered owners in many of our country's largest cities.

In the four largest United States cities in 2000, most households were renters. About 70 percent of households in New York City, 61 percent in Los Angeles, 56 per-

Table 3.
Ten Metropolitan Areas With the Highest Percentage of Owner-Occupied Units: 2000

(For information on confidentiality protection, nonsampling error, and definitions, see www.census.gov/prod/cen2000/doc/sf1.pdf)

Metropolitan area	Percent
Punta Gorda, FL	83.7
Ocala, FL	79.8
Barnstable-Yarmouth, MA	79.2
Fort Pierce–Port St. Lucie, FL . .	78.8
Sarasota–Bradenton, FL	76.8
Houma, LA	76.7
Jackson, MI	76.5
Fort Myers–Cape Coral, FL	76.5
Sharon, PA	76.3
Saginaw-Bay City-Midland, MI .	76.3

Source: U.S. Census Bureau, Census 2000 Summary File 1.

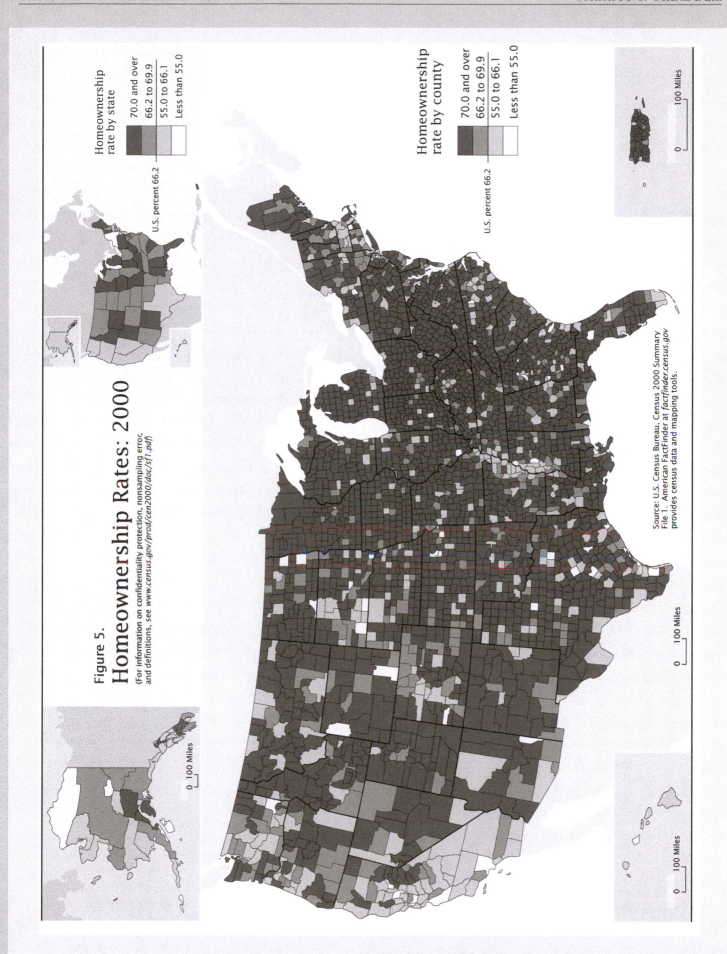

Figure 5.
Homeownership Rates: 2000
(For information on confidentiality protection, nonsampling error, and definitions, see www.census.gov/prod/cen2000/doc/sf1.pdf)

Homeownership rate by state

70.0 and over
66.2 to 69.9
55.0 to 66.1
Less than 55.0

U.S. percent 66.2

Homeownership rate by county

70.0 and over
66.2 to 69.9
55.0 to 66.1
Less than 55.0

U.S. percent 66.2

Source: U.S. Census Bureau, Census 2000 Summary File 1. American FactFinder at factfinder.census.gov provides census data and mapping tools.

0   100 Miles

0   100 Miles

0   100 Miles

0   100 Miles

Table 4.
Ten Largest Cities and Percent of Renter-Occupied Units: 2000

(For information on confidentiality protection, nonsampling error, and definitions, see www.census.gov/prod/cen2000/doc/sf1.pdf)

City	Total population	Total occupied housing units	Percent renters
New York, NY	8,008,278	3,021,588	69.8
Los Angeles, CA	3,694,820	1,275,412	61.4
Chicago, IL	2,896,016	1,061,928	56.2
Houston, TX	1,953,631	717,945	54.2
Philadelphia, PA	1,517,550	590,071	40.7
Phoenix, AZ	1,321,045	465,834	39.3
San Diego, CA	1,223,400	450,691	50.5
Dallas, TX	1,188,580	451,833	56.8
San Antonio, TX	1,144,646	405,474	41.9
Detroit, MI	951,270	336,428	45.1

Source: U.S. Census Bureau, Census 2000 Summary File 1.

cent in Chicago, and 54 percent in Houston rented their homes. Renters were also a majority (56.8 percent) of households in Dallas, the eighth largest city in 2000 (see Table 4). Households in San Diego were almost evenly split between renters (50.5 percent) and owners (49.5 percent). Homeownership was more common among the remaining largest cities in 2000 — Philadelphia, Phoenix, San Antonio, and Detroit.

Table 5.
Family Type by Tenure: 2000

(For information on confidentiality protection, nonsampling error, and definitions, see www.census.gov/prod/cen2000/doc/sf1.pdf)

Family characteristic	Occupied units			
	Total	Owner	Percent owner	Renter
Total housing units	**105,480,101**	**69,815,753**	**66.2**	**35,664,348**
Total families	71,787,347	53,071,538	73.9	18,715,809
Married-couple families	54,493,232	44,240,872	81.2	10,252,360
With children[1]	24,835,505	19,103,921	76.9	5,731,584
Without children[1]	29,657,727	25,136,951	84.8	4,520,776
Male householder, no spouse present......................	4,394,012	2,433,530	55.4	1,960,482
With children[1]	2,190,989	1,113,804	50.8	1,077,185
Without children[1]	2,203,023	1,319,726	59.9	883,297
Female householder, no spouse present..............	12,900,103	6,397,136	49.6	6,502,967
With children[1]	7,561,874	2,851,607	37.7	4,710,267
Without children[1]	5,338,229	3,545,529	66.4	1,792,700
Total nonfamily households	33,692,754	16,744,215	49.7	16,948,539
Male householder.............	15,556,103	7,004,848	45.0	8,551,255
Living alone................	11,779,106	5,530,759	47.0	6,248,347
Living with nonrelative.......	3,776,997	1,474,089	39.0	2,302,908
Female householder	18,136,651	9,739,367	53.7	8,397,284
Living alone................	15,450,969	8,659,549	56.0	6,791,420
Living with nonrelative.......	2,685,682	1,079,818	40.2	1,605,864

[1]Children represent own children under 18 years.

Source: U.S. Census Bureau, Census 2000 Summary File 1.

ADDITIONAL FINDINGS ON TENURE

Which type of family had the highest rate of homeownership?

About 4 out of 5 married-couple families owned their homes in 2000. Empty nesters and other married couples without children under the age of 18 were more likely (84.8 percent) than married couples with children (76.9 percent) to own their homes.

More than half (55.4 percent) of the families maintained by men without spouses were homeowners, compared with about half (49.6 percent) of families maintained by women without spouses.

In 2000, were people living alone more likely to own or rent their homes?

The answer depends on the gender of the householder. In 2000, more women (15.5 million) than men (11.8 million) lived alone. Approximately 8.7 million (56.0 percent) of women who lived alone owned their homes, compared with 5.5 million (47.0 percent) of the lone male householders.

What proportion of United States households were comprised of two or more unrelated people, and are these households more likely to rent or own their homes?

The Census Bureau uses the term "nonfamily households" to include people living alone as well as those householders who only live with people who are not related to the householder by birth, marriage, or adoption. In 2000, the 6.5 million householders who lived with other unrelated individuals represented about 6 percent of all United States occupied households. About 2 out of 5 (39.5 percent) of these householders owned their homes.

How likely are young house-holders to be homeowners?

Homeownership was directly related to the age of the householder. The youngest householder age group (under 25 years of age) had the lowest level of homeownership (17.9 percent). The percentage of homeowners increased to 45.6 among householders between the ages of 25 and 34 and continued to increase up to a peak of about 81 percent for householders 65 to 74 years of age.

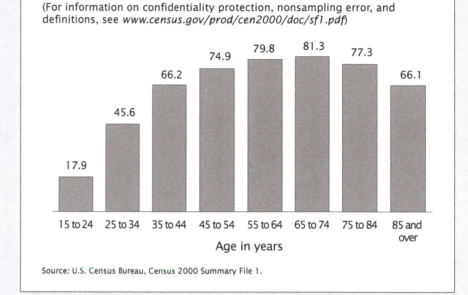

Figure 6.

Homeownership Rates by Age of Householder: 2000

(For information on confidentiality protection, nonsampling error, and definitions, see *www.census.gov/prod/cen2000/doc/sf1.pdf*)

Source: U.S. Census Bureau, Census 2000 Summary File 1.

ABOUT CENSUS 2000

Homeownership rates have served as an indicator of the health of the Nation's economy for decades. Data on vacant units are needed by federal and local agencies in order to evaluate the overall state of housing markets.

The federal government uses this information to allocate Section 8 and other housing program subsidies that assist Americans to afford decent, safe, and sanitary housing. Local organizations use the information to assess neighborhood stability and to plan road, health, and transportation improvements in their communities.

FOR MORE INFORMATION

Census 2000 data for state and local areas are available on the Internet via *factfinder.census.gov* and for purchase on CD-ROM and later on DVD. For information on housing tenure, vacancy status, and other characteristics of the housing inventory, visit the U.S. Census Bureau's Internet site at *www.census.gov* and click on Housing located next to the People icon. For more information on metropolitan areas, including concepts, definitions, and maps, go to *www.census.gov/population/www/estimates/metroarea.html*.

Information on other population and housing topics is presented in the Census 2000 Brief Series, located on the U.S. Census Bureau's Web site at *www.census.gov/population/www/cen2000/briefs.html*. This series presents information about race, Hispanic origin, age, sex, household type, housing tenure, and other social, economic, and housing characteristics.

For more information about Census 2000, including data products, call Customer Services Center at 301-763-INFO (4636) or e-mail: *webmaster@census.gov*.

Housing Costs of Homeowners: 2000

Census 2000 Brief

Issued September 2003

C2KBR-27

By
Robert Bonnette

Census 2000 counted 69.8 million owner-occupied housing units, or about two-thirds of the 105.5 million occupied housing units in the United States. Owner-occupied units included those with one or more mortgages (including home equity loans) as well as those owned free and clear.

This report, part of a series that presents population and housing data collected from Census 2000, examines mortgage status, selected monthly owner costs, and selected monthly owner costs as a percentage of household income in 1999 for specified owner-occupied housing units. The data show how these measures vary geographically (by regions, states, and large cities), by age of the householder, by race and Hispanic origin of the householder, and by some housing characteristics.

The Census Bureau collected mortgage status on the decennial censuses in 1940 and 1950, ceased collecting these data in the 1960 and 1970 censuses, then

Figure 1.

Reproduction of the Questions on Housing Showing the Components of Selected Monthly Owner Costs From Census 2000

45 **What are the annual costs of utilities and fuels for this house, apartment, or mobile home?** *If you have lived here less than 1 year, estimate the annual cost.*

a. Electricity

Annual cost — *Dollars*

$ ___ , ___ ___ .00

OR

☐ Included in rent or in condominium fee
☐ No charge or electricity not used

b. Gas

Annual cost — *Dollars*

$ ___ , ___ ___ .00

OR

☐ Included in rent or in condominium fee
☐ No charge or gas not used

c. Water and sewer

Annual cost — *Dollars*

$ ___ , ___ ___ .00

OR

☐ Included in rent or in condominium fee
☐ No charge

d. Oil, coal, kerosene, wood, etc.

Annual cost — *Dollars*

$ ___ , ___ ___ .00

OR

☐ Included in rent or in condominium fee
☐ No charge or these fuels not used

Source: U.S. Census Bureau, Census 2000 questionnaire.

USCENSUSBUREAU

Helping You Make Informed Decisions

U.S. Department of Commerce
Economics and Statistics Administration
U.S. CENSUS BUREAU

United States
Census
2000

464

Figure 1.

Reproduction of the Questions on Housing Showing the Components of Selected Monthly Owner Costs From Census 2000—Con.

47 Answer questions 47a—53 if you or someone in this household owns or is buying this house, apartment, or mobile home; otherwise, skip to questions for Person 2.

a. Do you have a mortgage, deed of trust, contract to purchase, or similar debt on THIS property?

☐ Yes, mortgage, deed of trust, or similar debt
☐ Yes, contract to purchase
☐ No → *Skip to 48a*

b. How much is your regular monthly mortgage payment on THIS property? *Include payment only on first mortgage or contract to purchase.*

Monthly amount — *Dollars*

$ ___ , ___ .00

OR

☐ No regular payment required → *Skip to 48a*

c. Does your regular monthly mortgage payment include payments for real estate taxes on THIS property?

☐ Yes, taxes included in mortgage payment
☐ No, taxes paid separately or taxes not required

d. Does your regular monthly mortgage payment include payments for fire, hazard, or flood insurance on THIS property?

☐ Yes, insurance included in mortgage payment
☐ No, insurance paid separately or no insurance

48 **a. Do you have a second mortgage or a home equity loan on THIS property?** *Mark* ☒ *all boxes that apply.*

☐ Yes, a second mortgage
☐ Yes, a home equity loan
☐ No → *Skip to 49*

b. How much is your regular monthly payment on all second or junior mortgages and all home equity loans on THIS property?

Monthly amount — *Dollars*

$ ___ , ___ .00

OR

☐ No regular payment required

49 **What were the real estate taxes on THIS property last year?**

Yearly amount — *Dollars*

$ ___ , ___ .00

OR

☐ None

50 **What was the annual payment for fire, hazard, and flood insurance on THIS property?**

Annual amount — *Dollars*

$ ___ , ___ .00

OR

☐ None

52 **Answer ONLY if this is a CONDOMINIUM —**

What is the monthly condominium fee?

Monthly amount — *Dollars*

$ ___ , ___ .00

53 **Answer ONLY if this is a MOBILE HOME —**

a. Do you have an installment loan or contract on THIS mobile home?

☐ Yes
☐ No

b. What was the total cost for installment loan payments, personal property taxes, site rent, registration fees, and license fees on THIS mobile home and its site last year? *Exclude real estate taxes.*

Yearly amount — *Dollars*

$ ___ , ___ .00

Source: U.S. Census Bureau, Census 2000 questionnaire.

resumed in 1980. The Residential Finance Survey (RFS) filled the gap in 1960 and 1970. Selected monthly owner costs include the sum of payments for mortgages, deeds of trust, or similar debts on the property (including payments for the first mortgage, second or junior mortgages, and home equity loans); real estate taxes; fire, hazard, and flood insurance on the property; utilities (electricity, gas, water, and sewer); and fuels (oil, coal, kerosene, wood, etc.). It also includes, where appropriate, monthly condominium fees. The components of selected monthly owner costs are presented in Figure 1. Selected monthly owner costs consisted of the same components in both 1990 and 2000. Medians in this report are computed for owner-occupied one-family houses on less than 10 acres with no business or commercial establishment on the property, referred to in this report as specified owner-occupied units. Census 2000 counted 55.2 million of these units, almost 80 percent of the total owner-occupied housing inventory. The Census Bureau began collecting data and tabulating data on selected monthly owner costs as a percentage of household income in 1980.

The percentage of specified owner-occupied units without a mortgage declined between 1960 and 2000.

In 2000, 30 percent of specified owner-occupied homes in the United States had no mortgage; that is, they were owned free and clear, down from about 35 percent in both 1980 and 1990.[1] This

decrease likely occurred as home-owners who had paid off their mortgages took out home equity loans. If a home equity loan was the only lien against a property, it was counted as a mortgage in both 1990 and 2000. The RFS recorded or tracked mortgage status for one-family homes as far back as 1960.[2] The RFS showed that 42 percent of owners in one-family homes reported no mortgage in 1960; this figure was 39 percent in 1970, 39 percent in 1980, and 37 percent in 1990. (The 1980 and 1990 RFS rates are provided for comparison with the 1980 and 1990 censuses.)

Housing costs were highest for Asian householders, and lowest for American Indians and Alaska Natives.

Census 2000 allowed respondents to choose more than one race. With the exception of the Two or more races group, all race groups discussed in this report refer to people who indicated only one racial identity among the six major categories: White, Black or African American, American Indian and Alaska Native, Asian, Native Hawaiian or Other Pacific Islander, and Some Other Race.[3] The use of the single-race population in this report does not imply that it is the preferred method of presenting or analyzing data. The

Census Bureau uses a variety of approaches.[4]

In 2000, Asian householders *with a mortgage* had median selected monthly costs of $1,540, far above the national median of $1,088 for all householders. Native Hawaiian and Other Pacific Islander householders, Two or more races householders, and Non-Hispanic White householders also reported medians above those of all householders ($1,261, $1,137, and $1,095, respectively). Monthly homeowner costs were lowest for American Indian and Alaska Native ($879) and Black or African American ($937). See Figure 2.

The high homeowner costs for Asian and Native Hawaiian and Other Pacific Islander householders likely occur because these two groups are concentrated in California and Hawaii, two states with very high homeowner costs and housing values for units with a mortgage. Median homeowner costs for Hispanic or Latino householders with a mortgage were $1,061.[5]

Asian householders, at $344, had the highest costs for units *without a mortgage*. Median costs were

---

[1] The estimates in this report are based on responses from a sample of the population. As with all surveys, estimates may vary from the actual values because of sampling variation or other factors. All statements made in this report have undergone statistical testing and are significant at the 90-percent confidence level, unless otherwise noted.

[2] Estimates from the RFS are considerably less reliable than those based on census data because of the much smaller sample size. Comparability is also affected by differences in the questionnaire design, data collection procedures, and other sources of nonsampling errors such as procedure differences. See the *Accuracy of the Estimates* section for further RFS references.

[3] For further information on each of the six major race groups, and the Two or more races population, see reports from the Census 2000 Brief series (C2KBR/01), available on the Census 2000 Web site at *www.census.gov/population/wwwcen2000 /briefs.html*.

[4] This report draws heavily on Summary File 3, a Census 2000 product that can be accessed through American FactFinder, available from the Census Bureau's Web site, *www.census.gov*. Information on people who reported more than one race, such as "White *and* American Indian and Alaska Native" or "Asian *and* Black or African American," is available in Summary File 4, also available through American FactFinder. About 2.6 percent of people reported more than one race.

[5] Because Hispanics may be of any race, data in this report for Hispanics overlap with data for racial groups. Based on Census 2000 sample data, the proportion Hispanic was 8.0 percent for the White alone population, 1.9 percent for the Black alone population, 14.6 percent for the American Indian and Alaska Native alone population, 1.0 percent for the Asian alone population, 9.5 percent for the Native Hawaiian and Other Pacific Islander alone population, 97.1 percent for the Some other race alone population, and 31.1 percent for the Two or more races population.

lowest for American Indian and Alaska Native households ($216), but Some other race households reported the next-lowest costs for this category, $255. Median home-owner costs for Hispanic or Latino householders without a mortgage were $263, not statistically differ-ent than the $262 reported for Black householders.

Housing costs were lowest for the youngest and the oldest homeowners.

Median selected monthly costs for homeowners 15 to 24 with a mort-gage was $833 (see Table 1). Costs were highest for those 35 to 44 ($1,158), then fell gradually as age increased to a low of $814 for householders 75 and over.

For those without a mortgage, the lowest median costs were reported by those homeowners 15 to 24 ($257) and the highest by house-holders 45 to 54 and 55 to 64 ($311 and $309, respectively).

Housing affordability can be measured by the percentage of household income in 1999 devoted to monthly owner costs.

The median monthly owner costs as a *percentage* of monthly income for homeowners with a mortgage was 21.7 percent in 2000, up slightly from the 21.0 percent reg-istered in 1990. For units without a mortgage, the percentage was lower, at 10.5 percent, down from 11.1 percent in 1990.

Housing was most affordable for the middle-aged groups.

Householders aged 15 to 24 with a mortgage spent a median of 25.7 percent of household income for monthly housing costs. This percentage declined to 22.7 per-cent for the 25-to-34 age group,

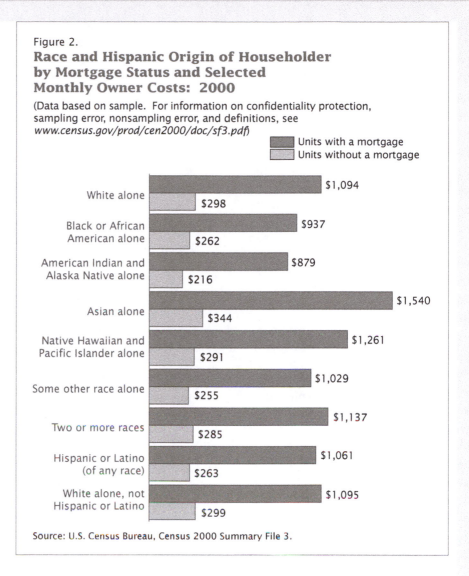

Figure 2.

Race and Hispanic Origin of Householder by Mortgage Status and Selected Monthly Owner Costs: 2000

(Data based on sample. For information on confidentiality protection, sampling error, nonsampling error, and definitions, see *www.census.gov/prod/cen2000/doc/sf3.pdf*)

Units with a mortgage
Units without a mortgage

Race/Origin	With mortgage	Without mortgage
White alone	$1,094	$298
Black or African American alone	$937	$262
American Indian and Alaska Native alone	$879	$216
Asian alone	$1,540	$344
Native Hawaiian and Pacific Islander alone	$1,261	$291
Some other race alone	$1,029	$255
Two or more races	$1,137	$285
Hispanic or Latino (of any race)	$1,061	$263
White alone, not Hispanic or Latino	$1,095	$299

Source: U.S. Census Bureau, Census 2000 Summary File 3.

Table 1.

Mortgage Status by Median Selected Monthly Owner Costs by Age of Householder: 2000

(Data based on sample. For information on confidentiality protection, sampling error, nonsampling error, and definitions, see *www.census.gov/prod/cen2000/doc/sf3.pdf*)

Age of householder	Specified owner-occupied units		Median selected monthly owner costs	
	With a mortgage	Without a mortgage	With a mortgage	Without a mortgage
Total..........................	38,663,887	16,548,221	$1,088	$295
15 to 24 years......................	483,755	79,717	$833	$257
25 to 34 years......................	5,966,933	391,342	$1,056	$273
35 to 44 years......................	11,727,506	1,128,916	$1,158	$296
45 to 54 years......................	10,863,671	2,099,326	$1,145	$311
55 to 64 years......................	5,803,296	3,163,260	$1,049	$309
65 to 74 years......................	2,683,826	4,683,524	$887	$296
75 years and over	1,134,900	5,002,136	$814	$283

Source: U.S. Census Bureau, Census 2000 Summary File 3.

21.9 percent for the 35-to-44 age group, and 19.9 percent for the 45-to-54 age group. The median then rose to 20.6 percent for householders aged 55 to 64, 25.4 percent for the 65-to-74 age group, and 32.0 percent for those aged 75 and over. Households with owner costs at 30 percent or higher are often considered to be financially burdened. By this measure, more than half of all householders aged 75 and over with a mortgage would have been considered financially burdened in Census 2000. However, over 8 in 10 householders 75 and over owned their homes outright.

The same pattern holds for units without a mortgage, but median selected monthly owner costs as a percentage of household income in 1999 were quite low compared with mortgaged units. The only age groups with medians over 10 percent were those aged 15 to 24 (12.9 percent), 65 to 74 (11.2 percent), and 75 and over (13.6 percent).

GEOGRAPHIC DISTRIBUTION OF MORTGAGE STATUS AND HOMEOWNER COSTS

Homeowners in the West were most likely to have a mortgage.[6]

Nationally, 70 percent of specified owner-occupied units were mortgaged (see Table 2). At 76.9 percent, the West was the only region with a percentage higher than the U.S. level, likely due to the fact

that this region had the highest proportion of owners who recently moved into their homes (for further information on recent movers, see the statistical brief on *Housing Structural and Occupancy Characteristics: 2000*). The other three regions reported rates with similar values: 67.7 percent in the Northeast, 69.0 percent in the Midwest, and 68.0 percent in the South (these percentages are statistically different).

Median selected monthly costs for units with a mortgage were highest in the West, and lowest in the South.

The West reported the highest median monthly costs at $1,289, closely followed by the Northeast at $1,274. The Midwest ($976) and the South ($967) enjoyed monthly owner costs far below the national median of $1,088.

Housing cost increases from 1990 to 2000 were highest in the Midwest (18.0 percent) despite the relatively low homeowner costs in this region.[7] The lowest increase was in the South (11.9 percent); as a result, the South supplanted the Midwest as the region with the lowest monthly homeowner costs between 1990 and 2000. A similar switch occurred between the Northeast and the West — the Northeast was highest in 1990 and the West in 2000. Increases were 13.1 percent for the Northeast and 15.4 percent for the West between 1990 and 2000. Nationally, median selected monthly costs increased 15.7 percent for units

with a mortgage, not significantly different from those in the West.

For units without a mortgage, monthly owner costs were above the national median only in the Northeast.

Median monthly costs were $405 in the Northeast, well above the $295 for the United States nationally, probably due to higher real estate taxes and utility costs in the region. The South reported the lowest median ($262), while the Midwest and West were both estimated at $290, close to the national level.

In general, median selected monthly owner costs increased more slowly from 1990 to 2000 for homes owned free and clear than for those with a mortgage — 10.5 percent for the nation. However, in the South and the West, the increase was greater for unmortgaged than for mortgaged homes.

Homeowners in West Virginia were more likely than those in other states to have no mortgage.

Although, nationally only 30 percent of all specified owner-occupied units were owned free and clear, this percentage varied among the states (see Table 2). West Virginia topped all states with nearly half of its homeowners (47.7 percent) owning their homes outright. North Dakota and Louisiana were the two other states reporting rates over 40 percent (41.9 and 40.3 percent, respectively).

On the other hand, homeowners in Nevada were least likely to have no mortgage (18 percent). Seven states had nonmortgage rates under 25 percent: California, Colorado, Georgia, Maryland, Nevada, Utah, and Washington.[8]

---

[6] The West region includes the states of Alaska, Arizona, California, Colorado, Hawaii, Idaho, Montana, Nevada, New Mexico, Oregon, Utah, Washington, and Wyoming. The South region includes the states of Alabama, Arkansas, Delaware, Florida, Georgia, Kentucky, Louisiana, Maryland, Mississippi, North Carolina, Oklahoma, South Carolina, Tennessee, Texas, Virginia, West Virginia, and the District of Columbia, a state

equivalent. The Northeast region includes the states of Connecticut, Maine, Massachusetts, New Hampshire, New Jersey, New York, Pennsylvania, Rhode Island, and Vermont. The Midwest region includes the states of Illinois, Indiana, Iowa, Kansas, Michigan, Minnesota, Missouri, Nebraska, North Dakota, Ohio, South Dakota, and Wisconsin.

[7] 1990 owner costs were adjusted to 2000 dollars using CPI-U-RS factor 1.277636.

[8] Virginia at 24.9 percent and Arizona at 25.1 percent, showed no statistical difference from 25.0 percent.

Table 2.
Mortgage Status for the United States, Regions, and States, and for Puerto Rico: 1990 and 2000

(Data based on a sample. For information on confidentiality protection, sampling error, nonsampling error, and definitions, see www.census.gov/prod/cen2000/doc/sf3.pdf)

| Area | Specified owner occupied, 1990 | Specified owner occupied, 2000 | Specified owner occupied with a mortgage | | | | Specified owner occupied without a mortgage | | | |
| | | | 1990 | | 2000 | | 1990 | | 2000 | |
			Number	Percent	Number	Percent	Number	Percent	Number	Percent
United States ..	45,550,059	55,212,108	29,811,735	65.4	38,663,887	70.0	15,738,324	34.6	16,548,221	30.0
Region										
Northeast.........	8,874,029	10,009,448	5,564,402	62.7	6,779,481	67.7	3,309,627	37.3	3,229,967	32.3
Midwest	11,953,114	14,037,418	7,510,776	62.8	9,692,743	69.0	4,442,338	37.2	4,344,675	31.0
South	15,831,164	19,964,932	10,118,336	63.9	13,582,882	68.0	5,712,828	36.1	6,382,050	32.0
West	8,891,752	11,200,310	6,618,221	74.4	8,608,781	76.9	2,273,531	25.6	2,591,529	23.1
State										
Alabama	764,726	918,570	458,264	59.9	587,895	64.0	306,462	40.1	330,675	36.0
Alaska	77,859	105,620	59,489	76.4	78,582	74.4	18,370	23.6	27,038	25.6
Arizona	678,958	1,032,103	498,614	73.4	773,328	74.9	180,344	26.6	258,775	25.1
Arkansas	433,048	513,483	241,412	55.7	312,244	60.8	191,636	44.3	201,239	39.2
California........	4,773,895	5,527,618	3,687,978	77.3	4,367,361	79.0	1,085,917	22.7	1,160,257	21.0
Colorado	645,565	903,259	496,121	76.9	715,493	79.2	149,444	23.1	187,766	20.8
Connecticut	649,970	728,244	449,008	69.1	520,076	71.4	200,962	30.9	208,168	28.6
Delaware	139,059	177,323	93,778	67.4	129,692	73.1	45,281	32.6	47,631	26.9
District of Columbia ..	73,658	76,289	46,967	63.8	55,138	72.3	26,691	36.2	21,151	27.7
Florida..........	2,414,406	3,242,202	1,668,542	69.1	2,323,452	71.7	745,864	30.9	918,750	28.3
Georgia	1,153,109	1,596,408	810,603	70.3	1,201,569	75.3	342,506	29.7	394,839	24.7
Hawaii	147,510	173,861	102,601	69.6	122,128	70.2	44,909	30.4	51,733	29.8
Idaho...........	178,506	255,077	119,692	67.1	186,647	73.2	58,814	32.9	68,430	26.8
Illinois	2,113,422	2,470,338	1,350,593	63.9	1,724,034	69.8	762,829	36.1	746,304	30.2
Indiana.........	1,152,343	1,378,878	742,515	64.4	978,279	70.9	409,828	35.6	400,599	29.1
Iowa...........	571,870	665,442	319,340	55.8	417,849	62.8	252,530	44.2	247,593	37.2
Kansas	507,512	581,960	306,884	60.5	382,518	65.7	200,628	39.5	199,442	34.3
Kentucky	671,433	806,461	389,536	58.0	521,748	64.7	281,897	42.0	284,713	35.3
Louisiana........	746,570	864,810	429,514	57.5	516,660	59.7	317,056	42.5	348,150	40.3
Maine..........	215,996	254,866	131,558	60.9	169,138	66.4	84,438	39.1	85,728	33.6
Maryland	984,921	1,178,779	710,691	72.2	916,046	77.7	274,230	27.8	262,733	22.3
Massachusetts......	1,014,824	1,187,871	691,108	68.1	850,347	71.6	323,716	31.9	337,524	28.4
Michigan	1,943,809	2,269,175	1,235,196	63.5	1,580,828	69.7	708,613	36.5	688,347	30.3
Minnesota	902,805	1,117,489	624,273	69.1	829,081	74.2	278,532	30.9	288,408	25.8
Mississippi........	447,954	532,291	266,664	59.5	330,697	62.1	181,290	40.5	201,594	37.9
Missouri..........	1,019,220	1,188,442	622,426	61.1	803,068	67.6	396,794	38.9	385,374	32.4
Montana	133,194	165,397	78,899	59.2	106,560	64.4	54,295	40.8	58,837	35.6
Nebraska.........	318,320	370,495	186,901	58.7	240,096	64.8	131,419	41.3	130,399	35.2
Nevada	185,935	363,321	151,185	81.3	297,994	82.0	34,750	18.7	65,327	18.0
New Hampshire.....	200,219	249,345	144,554	72.2	184,745	74.1	55,665	27.8	64,600	25.9
New Jersey	1,488,145	1,701,732	997,205	67.0	1,215,974	71.5	490,940	33.0	485,758	28.5
New Mexico.......	265,970	339,888	163,863	61.6	216,082	63.6	102,107	38.4	123,806	36.4
New York.........	2,414,482	2,689,728	1,564,131	64.8	1,824,984	67.9	850,351	35.2	864,744	32.1
North Carolina......	1,233,284	1,615,713	762,675	61.8	1,116,287	69.1	470,609	38.2	499,426	30.9
North Dakota.......	104,567	122,078	58,441	55.9	70,891	58.1	46,126	44.1	51,187	41.9
Ohio............	2,276,743	2,613,123	1,435,245	63.0	1,811,744	69.3	841,498	37.0	801,379	30.7
Oklahoma	625,647	699,452	376,922	60.2	439,410	62.8	248,725	39.8	260,042	37.2
Oregon	516,057	653,869	352,943	68.4	485,655	74.3	163,114	31.6	168,214	25.7
Pennsylvania.......	2,621,539	2,889,484	1,412,136	53.9	1,798,402	62.2	1,209,403	46.1	1,091,082	37.8
Rhode Island......	179,626	202,216	116,397	64.8	142,479	70.5	63,229	35.2	59,737	29.5
South Carolina.....	623,303	783,909	385,604	61.9	523,848	66.8	237,699	38.1	260,061	33.2
South Dakota......	114,009	137,531	62,312	54.7	83,359	60.6	51,697	45.3	54,172	39.4
Tennessee.........	949,242	1,205,931	583,674	61.5	795,765	66.0	365,568	38.5	410,166	34.0
Texas...........	3,008,039	3,849,585	1,872,449	62.2	2,471,978	64.2	1,135,590	37.8	1,377,607	35.8
Utah............	306,226	427,244	213,968	69.9	323,835	75.8	92,258	30.1	103,409	24.2
Vermont..........	89,228	105,962	58,305	65.3	73,336	69.2	30,923	34.7	32,626	30.8
Virginia	1,208,434	1,510,798	863,766	71.5	1,135,138	75.1	344,668	28.5	375,660	24.9
Washington	903,351	1,157,462	641,275	71.0	872,307	75.4	262,076	29.0	285,155	24.6
West Virginia	354,331	392,928	157,275	44.4	205,315	52.3	197,056	55.6	187,613	47.7
Wisconsin	928,494	1,122,467	566,650	61.0	770,996	68.7	361,844	39.0	351,471	31.3
Wyoming	78,726	95,591	51,593	65.5	62,809	65.7	27,133	34.5	32,782	34.3
Puerto Rico	672,696	817,927	214,598	31.9	307,109	37.5	458,098	68.1	510,818	62.5

Source: U.S. Census Bureau, 1990 census and Census 2000 Summary File 3.

Table 3.
Median Selected Monthly Owner Costs by Mortgage Status and as a Percentage of Household Income, for the United States, Regions, States, and for Puerto Rico: 1990 and 2000

(In this table, the "10–" in the last two columns represents "less than 10 percent". Data based on a sample. For information on confidentiality protection, sampling error, nonsampling error, and definitions, see *www.census.gov/prod/cen2000/doc/sf3.pdf*)

Area	Median selected monthly owner costs				Median selected monthly owner costs as a percentage of household income			
	With a mortgage		Without a mortgage		With a mortgage		Without a mortgage	
	1990	2000	1990	2000	1990	2000	1990	2000
United States	$940	$1,088	$267	$295	21.0	21.7	11.1	10.5
Region								
Northeast	$1,126	$1,274	$364	$405	21.8	22.5	13.1	13.2
Midwest.................	$827	$976	$272	$290	19.3	20.1	11.3	10.2
South	$864	$967	$229	$262	20.8	21.0	10.6	10.0–
West	$1,117	$1,289	$244	$290	23.1	24.0	10–	10.0–
State								
Alabama	$706	$816	$203	$228	19.1	19.8	10.3	10–
Alaska	$1,353	$1,315	$296	$393	21.5	22.3	10–	10–
Arizona	$983	$1,039	$240	$268	22.8	22.1	10–	10–
Arkansas	$655	$737	$221	$240	20.0	19.4	12.1	10–
California..............	$1,376	$1,478	$244	$305	24.9	25.3	10–	10–
Colorado	$1,022	$1,197	$259	$277	22.5	22.6	10.8	10–
Connecticut	$1,400	$1,426	$432	$473	22.9	22.4	12.8	13.1
Delaware	$975	$1,101	$256	$267	19.7	20.8	10–	10–
District of Columbia	$1,209	$1,291	$319	$313	20.5	22.2	10–	10–
Florida.................	$917	$1,004	$238	$306	22.3	22.8	10–	10.5
Georgia.................	$942	$1,039	$233	$259	20.9	20.8	10.5	10–
Hawaii	$1,288	$1,636	$217	$271	21.4	26.3	10–	10–
Idaho..................	$715	$887	$201	$236	19.6	21.5	10–	10–
Illinois	$979	$1,198	$308	$353	20.2	21.7	11.2	11.1
Indiana.................	$714	$869	$240	$255	18.0	19.3	10.2	10–
Iowa...................	$703	$829	$250	$268	18.5	19.1	11.5	10–
Kansas	$802	$888	$239	$273	19.5	19.3	10.9	10–
Kentucky	$684	$816	$192	$214	18.8	19.6	10–	10–
Louisiana...............	$759	$816	$215	$232	20.6	19.6	11.2	10–
Maine..................	$847	$923	$284	$299	21.4	21.4	12.2	12.1
Maryland	$1,173	$1,296	$300	$333	21.1	22.2	10.0	10–
Massachusetts...........	$1,258	$1,353	$381	$406	22.3	21.9	12.6	12.4
Michigan	$828	$972	$314	$288	18.8	19.6	12.5	10–
Minnesota	$925	$1,044	$238	$271	20.4	20.0	10.5	10–
Mississippi.............	$653	$752	$202	$232	20.8	20.4	11.8	10–
Missouri................	$767	$861	$226	$249	19.1	19.5	10.0	10–
Montana	$735	$863	$224	$261	20.2	22.2	10.9	10.4
Nebraska................	$779	$895	$244	$283	19.7	19.7	11.5	10.5
Nevada	$1,067	$1,190	$261	$294	22.4	23.8	10–	10–
New Hampshire...........	$1,278	$1,226	$410	$441	24.4	22.3	14.2	13.6
New Jersey	$1,412	$1,560	$488	$567	23.4	23.7	14.6	15.3
New Mexico..............	$833	$929	$208	$228	21.6	22.2	10–	10–
New York	$1,141	$1,357	$413	$457	21.5	23.2	13.8	13.6
North Carolina..........	$836	$985	$235	$254	20.5	21.3	10.8	10–
North Dakota	$777	$818	$245	$270	20.3	19.4	11.9	10.2
Ohio...................	$797	$963	$262	$289	19.0	20.6	11.0	10.6
Oklahoma	$731	$764	$210	$231	20.0	19.2	10.9	10–
Oregon	$828	$1,125	$289	$303	20.4	23.2	12.7	10.5
Pennsylvania............	$870	$1,010	$289	$318	20.2	21.6	12.1	12.2
Rhode Island............	$1,138	$1,205	$371	$406	22.7	22.7	13.0	13.4
South Carolina..........	$787	$894	$229	$240	19.9	20.5	10.7	10–
South Dakota............	$724	$828	$249	$279	19.9	19.7	12.6	10.5
Tennessee...............	$759	$882	$217	$240	20.1	21.1	10.2	10–
Texas..................	$908	$986	$247	$296	20.9	20.1	11.5	10.9
Utah...................	$851	$1,102	$236	$249	20.9	22.9	10–	10–
Vermont.................	$917	$1,021	$335	$378	21.9	22.4	14.1	13.9
Virginia................	$1,060	$1,144	$245	$263	21.9	21.4	10–	10–
Washington	$942	$1,268	$248	$338	20.4	23.8	10–	10.4
West Virginia	$636	$713	$183	$207	18.5	19.5	10–	10–
Wisconsin	$866	$1,024	$321	$333	20.1	20.9	12.8	11.2
Wyoming.................	$781	$825	$207	$229	19.4	19.7	10–	10–
Puerto Rico	$408	$625	$82	$124	22.3	27.9	10–	12.5

Note: 1990 owner costs were adjusted to 2000 dollars using CPI-U-RS factor 1.277636.

Source: U.S. Census Bureau, 1990 census and Census 2000 Summary File 3.

For units with a mortgage, half the states had median monthly owner costs over $1,000.

Census 2000 found 25 states (plus the District of Columbia) with median owner costs over $1,000 and 25 under that amount (see Table 3). Nationally, the median was $1,088 for owners with a mortgage; 18 states (and the District of Columbia) exceeded the U.S. median.

States with the highest median monthly costs were concentrated in the West and the Northeast. Hawaii, at $1,636, exceeded all other states. Among the ten states with the highest costs, those in the West were Alaska, California, Hawaii, and Washington. New Jersey was second among all states ($1,560); four other states in the Northeast were also among the highest ten — Connecticut, Massachusetts, New Hampshire, and New York. Maryland was the only southern state in the top ten (although the District of Columbia was not significantly different than Maryland).

Seven of the 11 states with the lowest median monthly costs (below $850) were in the South: Alabama, Arkansas, Kentucky, Louisiana, Mississippi, Oklahoma, and West Virginia. Three were in the Midwest: Iowa, North Dakota, and South Dakota. Wyoming was the only state in the West with a median below $850.

Selected monthly costs for owners with a mortgage increased in all but two states from 1990 to 2000.

Median selected monthly costs increased nationally at 15.7 percent over the last decade; only Alaska and New Hampshire experienced a decline in costs.

States with the biggest increases were in the West: Oregon (35.9 percent), Washington (34.6), Utah (29.5), Hawaii (27.0), and Idaho (24.1).

The northeastern states were the most expensive to live in for homeowners with no mortgage.

New Jersey registered the highest median monthly costs for homes owned free and clear, $567, almost double the national median of $295. In five other states, all in the Northeast, median costs exceeded $400: Connecticut, Massachusetts, New Hampshire, New York, and Rhode Island.

Of the dozen states with the lowest monthly owner costs for homes without a mortgage, nine were in the South and three in the West. The lowest medians were in West Virginia ($207) and Kentucky ($214).

Homeowner costs increased for those without a mortgage from 1990 to 2000, but not as much as for those with a mortgage.

Costs increased 15.7 percent for homeowners with a mortgage, but only 10.5 percent for those who owned their homes free and clear in the last decade. Michigan was the only state to register a decrease in owner costs for homeowners without a mortgage (although the District of Columbia experienced no statistical difference between 1990 and 2000). *Because of sampling error, the state estimates given may not be significantly different from one another or from other state estimates not listed.*

The highest cost increases were in Washington (36.3 percent), Alaska (32.8 percent), and Florida (28.6 percent). California and Hawaii also had cost increases

greater than 20 percent. Interestingly, Alaska was one of two states (New Hampshire was the other) to show a decrease in owner housing costs for units with a mortgage, but an increase for those without a mortgage.

Higher homeowner costs were concentrated in relatively few counties.

Figure 3 presents Census 2000 median selected monthly owner costs for mortgaged units for states and counties. Specified owner-occupied units at or above the national median of $1,088 tended to cluster in certain areas, such as the Boston-Washington corridor, California, south Florida, Puget Sound, the Colorado Rockies, and in some larger metropolitan areas such as Chicago, Atlanta, Minneapolis, and Dallas. Only about 300 counties (less than 10 percent) were at or above the U.S. median.

If the entire mortgaged homeowner inventory for the whole United States were divided into four equal groupings or *quartiles*, the lowest would have monthly owner costs under $773, the next one-quarter would be between $773 and the median of $1,088, another one-quarter would be between the median and $1,532, and the highest quarter would be above $1,532. Only about 50 counties had medians in this upper quartile, an indication that high homeowner costs were concentrated in a few large counties, such as Westchester, New York; Santa Clara, California; Fairfax, Virginia; and Lake, Illinois. Counties with medians under $600 were generally in Appalachia and in the center of the nation from north to south.

Figure 4 presents median selected monthly owner costs for units with

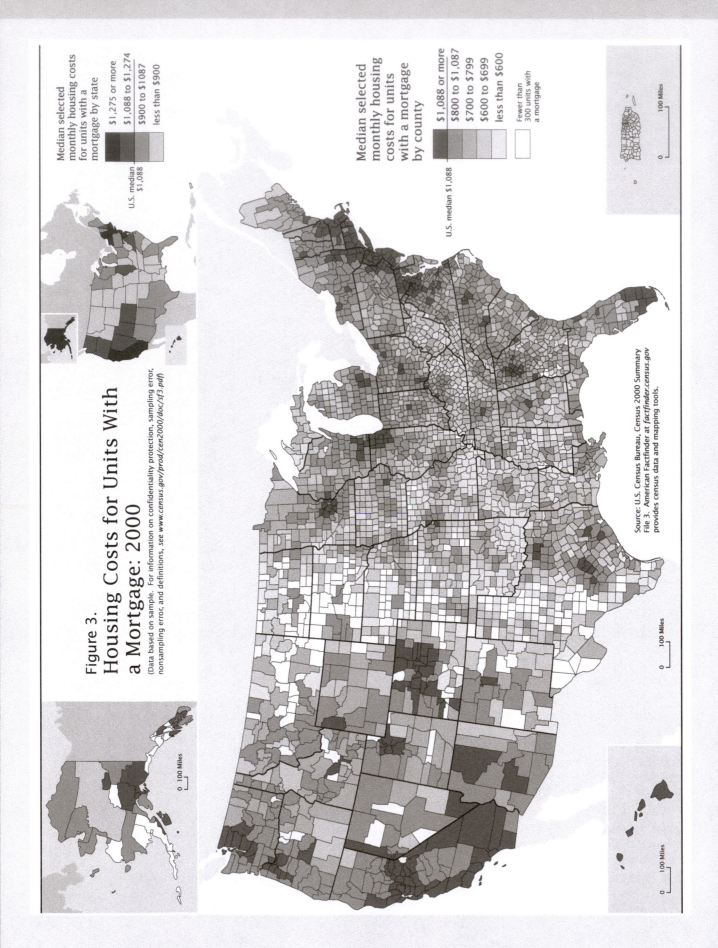

Figure 3.

Housing Costs for Units With a Mortgage: 2000

(Data based on sample. For information on confidentiality protection, sampling error, nonsampling error, and definitions, see *www.census.gov/prod/cen2000/doc/sf3.pdf*)

Median selected monthly housing costs for units with a mortgage by state

$1,275 or more
$1,088 to $1,274
$900 to $1087
less than $900

U.S. median $1,088

Median selected monthly housing costs for units with a mortgage by county

$1,088 or more
$800 to $1,087
$700 to $799
$600 to $699
less than $600
Fewer than 300 units with a mortgage

U.S. median $1,088

100 Miles

0   100 Miles

0   100 Miles

0   100 Miles

Source: U.S. Census Bureau, Census 2000 Summary File 3. American Factfinder at *factfinder.census.gov* provides census data and mapping tools.

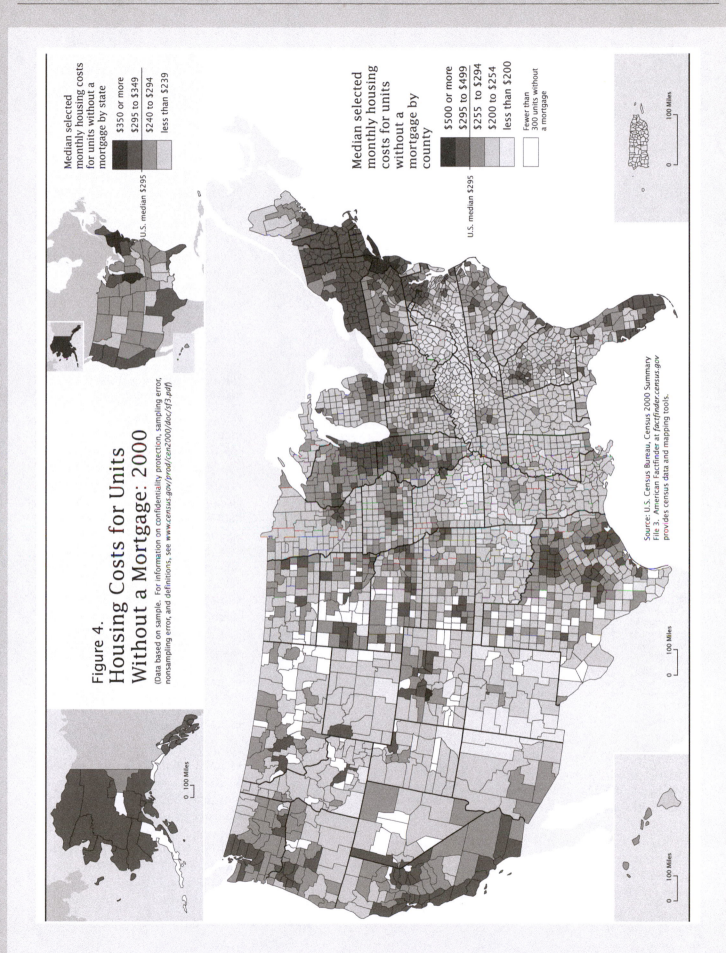

Figure 4.
Housing Costs for Units Without a Mortgage: 2000

(Data based on sample. For information on confidentiality protection, sampling error, nonsampling error, and definitions, see www.census.gov/prod/cen2000/doc/sf3.pdf)

Median selected monthly housing costs for units without a mortgage by state

$350 or more
$295 to $349
$240 to $294
less than $239

U.S. median $295

Median selected monthly housing costs for units without a mortgage by county

$500 or more
$295 to $499
$255 to $294
$200 to $254
less than $200

Fewer than 300 units without a mortgage

U.S. median $295

Source: U.S. Census Bureau, Census 2000 Summary File 3. American Factfinder at factfinder.census.gov provides census data and mapping tools.

Table 4.
Places of 100,000 or More With the Highest Median Selected Monthly Costs for Units With a Mortgage: 2000

For specified owner-occupied housing units

(Data based on a sample. For information on confidentiality protection, sampling error, nonsampling error, and definitions, see *www.census.gov/prod/cen2000/doc/sf3.pdf*)

Area	Specified owner-occupied units with a mortgage	Median selected monthly owner costs	90-percent confidence interval
Stamford, CT	12,841	$2,203	$2,152 - $2,254
Sunnyvale, CA...........	14,299	$2,051	$2,004 - $2,098
Honolulu, HI (CDP)*	23,799	$2,043	$2,005 - $2,081
San Jose, CA	122,324	$1,936	$1,924 - $1,948
Glendale, CA	16,836	$1,936	$1,901 - $1,971
Thousand Oaks, CA	24,942	$1,916	$1,890 - $1,942
Yonkers, NY	10,730	$1,906	$1,870 - $1,942
Irvine, CA	23,960	$1,897	$1,872 - $1,922
Fremont, CA.............	34,797	$1,896	$1,875 - $1,917
Cambridge, MA	2,999	$1,896	$1,796 - $1,996

*Honolulu is a Census Designated Place (CDP). By agreement with the state of Hawaii, the Census Bureau does not show data separately for the city of Honolulu, which is coextensive with Honolulu county.

Note: Because of sampling error, the estimates in this table may not be significantly different from one another or from rates for geographic areas not listed in this table.

Source: Census 2000 Summary File 3.

Table 5.
Places of 100,000 or More With the Highest Median Selected Monthly Costs for Units Without a Mortgage: 2000

For specified owner-occupied housing units

(Data based on a sample. For information on confidentiality protection, sampling error, nonsampling error, and definitions, see *www.census.gov/prod/cen2000/doc/sf3.pdf*)

Area	Specified owner-occupied units without a mortgage	Median selected monthly owner costs	90-percent confidence interval
Yonkers, NY	7,082	$704	$686 - $722
Stamford, CT	5,193	$682	$663 - $701
Paterson, NJ............	1,797	$615	$592 - $638
Jersey City, NJ..........	2,827	$569	$554 - $584
Naperville, IL	3,864	$540	$526 - $554
Cambridge, MA	1,454	$526	$480 - $572
Coral Springs, FL	2,410	$521	$502 - $540
New Haven, CT..........	2,345	$516	$495 - $537
Plano, TX	5,862	$513	$497 - $529
Elizabeth, NJ	2,159	$512	$493 - $531

Note: Because of sampling error, the estimates in this table may not be significantly different from one another or from rates for geographic areas not listed in this table.

Source: Census 2000 Summary File 3.

no mortgage. The map of these costs by county resembles the pattern of costs for homeowners with a mortgage, with a few exceptions such as Kansas, Nebraska, and the Dakotas. The lower quartile for units without a mortgage was $219, the median was $295, and the upper quartile started at $411.

Places of 100,000 or More With the Highest Median Selected Monthly Owner Costs for Units With a Mortgage Clustered in the Northeast and the West.

The places with the highest owner costs for mortgaged units are shown in Table 4. Stamford, Connecticut, led all large places

with a median of $2203. Table 5 presents places with the highest owner costs for units without a mortgage.

Flint, Michigan, recorded the lowest median selected monthly owner costs for units with a mortgage for places with 100,000 or more people (see Table 6). Flint also showed the lowest median housing values for large cities, as cited in the report *Home Values: 2000 (C2KBR-20)*. The places with the lowest median owner costs for units without a mortgage are presented in Table 7.

ADDITIONAL FINDINGS

How did the percentage of housing owned without a mortgage vary by age?

Householders under 25 were more likely to own their homes free and clear than the next two age groups, possibly the result of inheritance from parents or other older relatives. Figure 5 shows data on nonmortgaged homes by age of householder for specified owner-occupied housing units. A rate as high as that of the 15-to-24 group was not achieved until the 45-to-54 group. The rate then climbed steadily by age, reaching 81.5 percent for those 75 years and over.

In general, homeowner costs declined by age of the house, but rose slightly for the oldest homes.

For units with a mortgage, median selected monthly owner costs were $1,331 for new homes (those built between 1995 and March 2000). Medians steadily declined, reaching a low of $917 for houses built 1940 to 1949, then rose to $931 for those built before 1940. For those without a mortgage, new homes showed a median monthly cost of $330, while houses built from 1990 to 1994 had a cost of $335. Costs then declined steadily to a low of $268 for homes built between 1940 to 1949, then, like mortgaged houses, rose slightly to $277 for those built before 1940.

How did housing affordability vary among states?

Median selected monthly owner costs as a percentage of household income in 1999 for units with a mortgage exceeded 25 percent in only two states — California and Hawaii (see Table 3). The most affordable housing was in the Midwest and the South, where the median was below 20 percent for several states.

For homes without a mortgage, eight of the nine northeastern states showed medians at 12 percent or higher, while no state outside this region had a median at this level.[9] In fact, many states had median costs under 10 percent for homes owned free and clear.

In the West, median selected monthly costs as a percentage of household income were highest in the nation for houses with a mortgage (24 percent), but relatively low for homes owned free and clear (less than 10 percent). The Midwest showed an opposite trend: the median of 20.1 percent was the lowest among the regions for units with a mortgage, but, at 10.2 percent, was the second-highest for homes without a mortgage.

ABOUT CENSUS 2000

Why Census 2000 Asked About Homeowner Costs

The U.S. Census Bureau collects data on selected monthly owner costs which are the sums of

_____
[9] Maine, at 12.1 percent, showed no statistical difference from 12.0 percent.

Table 6.

Places of 100,000 or More With the Lowest Median Selected Monthly Costs for Units With a Mortgage: 2000

For specified owner-occupied housing units

(Data based on a sample. For information on confidentiality protection, sampling error, nonsampling error, and definitions, see www.census.gov/prod/cen2000/doc/sf3.pdf)

Area	Specified owner-occupied units with a mortgage	Median selected monthly owner costs	90-percent confidence interval
Flint, MI	17,371	$640	$630 - $650
Evansville, IN	18,720	$698	$688 - $708
Springfield, MO	20,193	$699	$689 - $709
South Bend, IN	16,361	$708	$696 - $720
Waco, TX	9,343	$724	$706 - $742
Birmingham, AL	32,435	$730	$722 - $738
Kansas City, KS	19,805	$731	$720 - $742
Fort Wayne, IN	34,384	$732	$724 - $740
Shreveport, LA	26,445	$747	$735 - $759
Abilene, TX	13,364	$749	$734 - $764

Note: Because of sampling error, the estimates in this table may not be significantly different from one another or from rates for geographic areas not listed in this table.

Source: Census 2000 Summary File 3.

Table 7.

Places of 100,000 or More With the Lowest Median Selected Monthly Costs for Units Without a Mortgage: 2000

For specified owner-occupied housing units

(Data based on a sample. For information on confidentiality protection, sampling error, nonsampling error, and definitions, see www.census.gov/prod/cen2000/doc/sf3.pdf)

Area	Specified owner-occupied units with a mortgage	Median selected monthly owner costs	90-percent confidence interval
Springfield, MO	11,597	$207	$203 - $211
Pueblo, CO	9,010	$212	$208 - $216
East Los Angeles, CA (CDP)	3,436	$221	$213 - $229
Norwalk, CA	3,477	$225	$218 - $232
Shreveport, LA	16,496	$231	$227 - $235
Huntsville, AL	11,384	$231	$226 - $236
Columbus, GA	9,803	$231	$226 - $236
Evansville, IN	10,100	$234	$230 - $238
Fort Wayne, IN	12,765	$235	$231 - $239
Birmingham, AL	17,041	$239	$235 - $243
Louisville, KY	19,560	$239	$236 - $242
Lafayette, LA	8,615	$239	$233 - $245
Lexington-Fayette, KY	12,909	$239	$236 - $242

Note: Because of sampling error, the estimates in this table may not be significantly different from one another or from rates for geographic areas not listed in this table.

Source: Census 2000 Summary File 3.

payments for mortgages, deeds of trust, or similar debts on the property (including payments for the first mortgage, second or junior mortgages, and home equity loans); real estate taxes; fire, hazard, and flood insurance on the property; utilities (electricity, gas, water, and sewer); and fuels (oil, coal, kerosene, wood, etc.). It also includes, where appropriate, monthly condominium fee.

Selected monthly owner costs as a percentage of household income in 1999 are also computed as a measure of housing affordability. These data are used by the Department of Housing and Urban

Figure 5.
Percentage of Homeowners Who Did Not Carry a Mortgage by Age of Householder: 2000

(Data based on sample. For information on confidentiality protection, sampling error, nonsampling error, and definitions, see *www.census.gov/prod/cen2000/doc/sf3.pdf*)

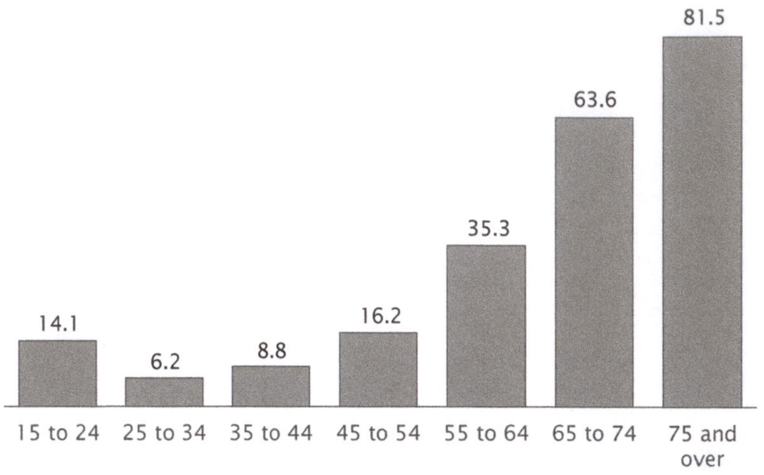

Source: U.S. Census Bureau, Census 2000 Summary File 3.

Development in many of its housing assistance programs and the Department of Health and Human Services to assess the need for housing assistance for elderly, handicapped, and low-income homeowners. These items also provide benchmark statistics to measure progress toward the Congressional declaration of goals for national housing policy: a decent home and suitable living environment for every American family.

Accuracy of the Estimates

The data contained in this report are based on the sample of households who responded to the Census 2000 long form. Nationally, approximately 1 out of every 6 housing units was included in this sample. As a result, the sample estimates may differ somewhat from the 100-percent figures that would have been obtained if

all housing units, people within those housing units, and people living in group quarters had been enumerated using the same questionnaires, instructions, enumerators, and so forth. The sample estimates also differ from the values that would have been obtained from different samples of housing units, people within those housing units, and people living in group quarters. The deviation of a sample estimate from the average of all possible samples is called the sampling error.

In addition to the variability that arises from the sampling procedures, both sample data and 100-percent data are subject to nonsampling error. Nonsampling error may be introduced during any of the various complex operations used to collect and process data. Such errors may include: not enumerating every household or every

person in the population, failing to obtain all required information from the respondents, obtaining incorrect or inconsistent information, and recording information incorrectly. In addition, errors can occur during the field review of the enumerators' work, during clerical handling of the census questionnaires, or during the electronic processing of the questionnaires.

Nonsampling error may affect the data in two ways: (1) errors that are introduced randomly will increase the variability of the data and, therefore, should be reflected in the standard errors; and (2) errors that tend to be consistent in one direction will bias both sample and 100-percent data in that direction. For example, if respondents consistently tend to underreport their incomes, then the resulting estimates of households or families by income category will tend to be understated for the higher income categories and overstated for the lower income categories. Such biases are not reflected in the standard errors.

While it is impossible to completely eliminate error from an operation as large and complex as the decennial census, the Census Bureau attempts to control the sources of such error during the data collection and processing operations. The primary sources of error and the programs instituted to control error in Census 2000 are described in detail in *Summary File 3 Technical Documentation* under Chapter 8, "Accuracy of the Data," located at *www.census.gov/prod /cen2000/doc/sf3.pdf*.

Technical documentation for the Residential Finance Survey is located in the following Census Bureau publications: 1960 Census of Housing, Volume V, Residential

Finance, Introduction, Sample Design and Sampling Variability; 1970 Census of Housing, Volume V, Residential Finance, Appendix C, Accuracy of the Data; 1980 Census of Housing, HC-80-5, Residential Finance, Appendix D, Accuracy of the Data; and 1990 Census of Housing, CH-4-1, Residential Finance, Appendix D, Source and Accuracy of the Estimates.

All statements in this Census 2000 Brief have undergone statistical testing and all comparisons are significant at the 90-percent confidence level, unless otherwise noted. The estimates in tables, maps, and other figures may vary from actual values due to sampling and non-sampling errors. As a result, estimates in one category may not be significantly different from estimates assigned to a different category. Further information on the accuracy of the data is located at *www.census.gov/prod/cen2000/doc/sf3.pdf*. For further information on the computation and use of standard errors, contact the Decennial Statistical Studies Division at 301-763-4242.

For More Information

The Census 2000 Summary File 3 data are available from the American Factfinder on the Internet (*factfinder.census.gov*). They were released on a state-by-state basis during 2002. For information on confidentiality protection, nonsampling error, sampling error, and definitions, also see *www.census.gov/prod/cen2000/doc/sf3.pdf* or contact the Customer Services Center at 301-763-INFO (4636).

Information on population and housing topics is presented in the Census 2000 Brief series, located on the Census Bureau's Web site at *www.census.gov/population/www/cen2000/briefs.html*. This series, which will be completed in 2003, presents information on race, Hispanic origin, age, sex, household type, housing tenure, and social, economic, and housing characteristics, such as ancestry, income, and housing costs.

For additional information on housing, including reports and survey data, visit the Census Bureau's Internet site on at *www.census.gov/hhes/www/housing.html*. To find information about the availability of data products, including reports, CD-ROMs, and DVDs, call the Customer Services Center at 301-763-INFO (4636), or e-mail *webmaster@census.gov*.

Housing Costs of Renters: 2000

Census 2000 Brief

Issued May 2003

C2KBR-21

By
Robert Bonnette

Census 2000 counted 35.7 million renter-occupied housing units, or about one-third of the nation's 105.5 million occupied housing units. Renter-occupied units consisted of those rented for cash payments plus those occupied by someone other than the owner without payment of cash rent; the latter usually were rent-free houses or apartments provided by friends or relatives, or for compensation for services to resident managers, ministers, and tenant farmers. Almost all rental units (95 percent) were rented for cash rent.

This report, part of a series that presents population and housing data collected from Census 2000, examines gross rent and gross rent as a percentage of household income in 1999 for specified renter-occupied housing units. It shows how these measures vary geographically (by regions, states, and large cities), by age of the householder, by race and Hispanic origin of

Figure 1.

Reproduction of the Question on Housing Utilities and Fuels From Census 2000

45 **What are the annual costs of utilities and fuels for this house, apartment, or mobile home?** *If you have lived here less than 1 year, estimate the annual cost.*

a. Electricity

Annual cost — *Dollars*

$ ____ , ____ . 00

OR

☐ Included in rent or in condominium fee
☐ No charge or electricity not used

b. Gas

Annual cost — *Dollars*

$ ____ , ____ . 00

OR

☐ Included in rent or in condominium fee
☐ No charge or gas not used

c. Water and sewer

Annual cost — *Dollars*

$ ____ , ____ . 00

OR

☐ Included in rent or in condominium fee
☐ No charge

d. Oil, coal, kerosene, wood, etc.

Annual cost — *Dollars*

$ ____ , ____ . 00

OR

☐ Included in rent or in condominium fee
☐ No charge or these fuels not used

Source: U.S. Census Bureau, Census 2000 questionnaire.

USCENSUSBUREAU

Helping You Make Informed Decisions

U.S. Department of Commerce
Economics and Statistics Administration
U.S. CENSUS BUREAU

United States
Census
2000

478

the householder, and by some housing characteristics. This brief also examines "meals included in rent," which is intended to gauge the extent of congregate housing. Congregate housing is generally considered to be housing units where the rent includes meals and other services, such as transportation to shopping and recreation.

Gross rent is the monthly amount of rent plus the estimated average monthly cost of utilities (electricity, gas, water, and sewer) and fuels (oil, coal, kerosene, wood, etc.). Figures 1 and 2 reproduce the Census 2000 questions about the components of gross rent. Medians in this report are computed for specified renter-occupied units paying cash rent, which exclude one-family houses on ten or more acres.

The Census Bureau initially collected gross rent data for renter-occupied housing units in 1940, the first Census of Housing. Beginning in 1950, the Census Bureau tabulated gross rent as a percentage of income to create a measure of affordability. From 1950 to 1970, income was defined as that of families and primary individuals; since 1980, the Census Bureau has used household income. The question of whether meals were included in rent was first asked in 1990.

Rents rose in every decade from 1950 to 2000.

According to Census 2000, the median monthly gross rent was $602 for the United States as a whole, a 5.4 percent increase over the $571 median for 1990[1], and more than double the median (adjusted for inflation) of $257 a month in 1950,

_____
[1] 1990 rent was adjusted to 2000 dollars using CPI-U-RS factor 1.277636. Rents for previous years were also adjusted to 2000 dollars using factors appropriate for those years.

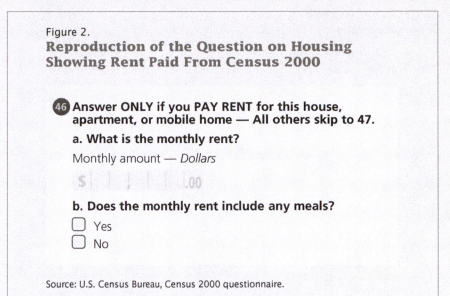

Figure 2.

Reproduction of the Question on Housing Showing Rent Paid From Census 2000

46 **Answer ONLY if you PAY RENT for this house, apartment, or mobile home — All others skip to 47.**

a. What is the monthly rent?

Monthly amount — *Dollars*

$ | | , | | | .00

b. Does the monthly rent include any meals?

☐ Yes
☐ No

Source: U.S. Census Bureau, Census 2000 questionnaire.

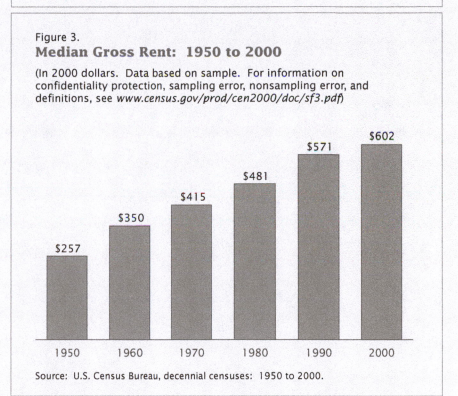

Figure 3.

Median Gross Rent: 1950 to 2000

(In 2000 dollars. Data based on sample. For information on confidentiality protection, sampling error, nonsampling error, and definitions, see *www.census.gov/prod/cen2000/doc/sf3.pdf*)

1950	1960	1970	1980	1990	2000
$257	$350	$415	$481	$571	$602

Source: U.S. Census Bureau, decennial censuses: 1950 to 2000.

as shown in Figure 3.[2] Much of this increase may be attributed to the increase in amenities included with

_____
[2] The estimates in this report are based on responses from a sample of the population. As with all surveys, estimates may vary from the actual values because of sampling variation or other factors. All statements made in this report have undergone statistical testing and are significant at the 90-percent confidence level, unless otherwise noted.

rental units. In 1960, for example, over 90 percent of all rental housing lacked air conditioning, about 40 percent lacked central heating, and 20 percent lacked complete plumbing facilities. By 1980, the last census to measure these three items, almost half of all rental units had air conditioning, slightly over 80 percent had central heating, and only 3 percent lacked complete plumbing.

Rents varied by race and Hispanic origin.

Census 2000 allowed respondents to choose more than one race. With the exception of the Two or more races group, all race groups discussed in this report refer to people who indicated only one racial identity among the six major categories: White, Black or African American, American Indian and Alaska Native, Asian, Native Hawaiian and Other Pacific Islander, and Some other race.[3] The use of the single-race population in this report does not imply that it is the preferred method of presenting or analyzing data. The Census Bureau uses a variety of approaches.[4]

Median gross rent was highest for householders who classified themselves as Asian ($734), second-highest for Pacific Islander renters ($690), and third-highest for those of Two or more races ($637).[5] Rents were high for the Asian and Native Hawaiian and Pacific Islander households because these two groups were concentrated in Hawaii and California, which registered median monthly rents far above the U.S. median. In fact, 5 of the 7 racial groups shown in Table 1 reported rents at or above the U.S. median of $602; only American Indian and Alaska Native and Black households reported rents below the national median.

Table 1.
Median Gross Rent by Race and Hispanic Origin of Householder: 2000

(Data based on sample. For information on confidentiality protection, nonsampling error, and definitions, see www.census.gov/prod/cen2000/doc/sf3.pdf)

Race and Hispanic origin of householder	Specified renter-occupied units paying cash rent	Median gross rent
Total, all households	33,386,326	$602
White alone	22,239,892	$612
Black or African American alone	6,156,870	$541
American Indian and Alaska Native alone	309,034	$518
Asian alone	1,415,812	$734
Native Hawaiian and Other Pacific Islander alone	50,694	$690
Some other race alone	2,206,431	$602
Two or more races	1,007,593	$637
Hispanic or Latino (of any race)	4,810,020	$604
White alone, not Hispanic or Latino	20,068,338	$613

Source: U.S. Census Bureau, Census 2000 Summary File 3.

Figure 4.
Median Gross Rent by Age of Householder: 2000

(Data based on sample. For information on confidentiality protection, sampling error, nonsampling error, and definitions, see www.census.gov/prod/cen2000/doc/sf3.pdf)

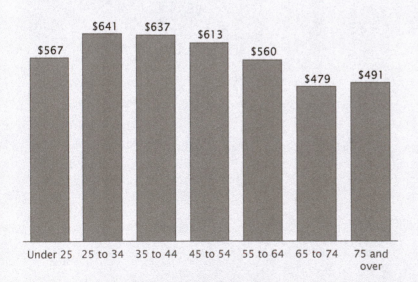

Under 25	25 to 34	35 to 44	45 to 54	55 to 64	65 to 74	75 and over
$567	$641	$637	$613	$560	$479	$491

Source: U.S. Census Bureau, Census 2000 Summary File 3.

[3] For further information on each of the six major race groups and the Two or more races population, see reports from the Census 2000 Brief series (C2KBR/01), available on the Census 2000 Web site at www.census.gov/population/www/cen2000/briefs.html.

[4] This report draws heavily on Summary File 3, a Census 2000 product that can be accessed through American FactFinder, available from the Census Bureau's Web site, www.census.gov. Information on people who reported more than one race, such as "White *and* American Indian and Alaska Native" or "Asian *and* Black or African American," is forthcoming in Summary File 4, which will also be available through American FactFinder in 2003. About 2.6 percent of people reported more than one race.

[5] Hereafter this report uses the term Black to refer to people who are Black or African American, the term Pacific Islander to refer to people who are Native Hawaiian and Other Pacific Islander, and the term Hispanic to refer to people who are Hispanic or Latino.

Because Hispanics may be of any race, data in this report for Hispanics overlap with data for racial groups. Based on Census 2000 sample data, the proportion Hispanic was 8.0 percent for Whites, 1.9 percent for Blacks, 14.6 percent for American Indians and Alaska Natives, 1.0 percent for Asians, 9.5 percent for Pacific Islanders, 97.1 percent for those reporting Some other race, and 31.1 percent for those reporting Two or more races.

Median gross rent paid by Hispanics (who can be of any race) was slightly above the national average. Rents paid by non-Hispanic Whites were also above the national median.

Householders aged 25 to 34 paid the highest rents.

Monthly rents were relatively low ($567) for householders 15 to 24, peaked among householders 25 to 34 ($641), and then declined steadily to $479 for householders 65 to 74. For older householders, aged 75 and over, rents rose slightly to $491 (see Figure 4).

The number of bedrooms was a major factor in determining rent.

Median gross rent was $522 for units with no bedroom (generally efficiencies) and then rose to $542 for one-bedroom units, $620 for two bedrooms, $698 for three bedrooms, and $786 for units with four or more bedrooms, which were almost always one-family homes.

Gross rent as a percentage of household income in 1999 is a measure of the affordability of rental housing.

Nationally, renter households spent a little over one-quarter of their pre-tax income on rent (median 25.5 percent). This value was down almost a full percentage point from the median of 26.4 percent in 1990.

When gross rent equals or exceeds 30 percent of household income, renters are often considered to be financially burdened. In all states, fewer than half of rental households paid this percentage; but certain subgroups of renter households had medians at or above the 30-percent level. These included renters where the householder was under 25 (for whom the median was 30.8 percent) and the oldest renters, those

Table 2.

Median Gross Rent and Median Gross Rent as Percentage of Household Income for the United States, Regions, and States, and for Puerto Rico: 1990 and 2000

(Data based on sample. For information on confidentiality protection, sampling error, nonsampling error, and definitions, see www.census.gov/prod/cen2000/doc/sf3.pdf)

Area	1990		2000	
	Median gross rent	Median gross rent as percentage of household income in 1989	Median gross rent	Median gross rent as percentage of household income in 1999
United States	**$571**	**26.4**	**$602**	**25.5**
Region				
Northeast...................	$638	26.4	$651	25.9
Midwest	$506	25.4	$533	24.0
South	$517	25.7	$559	25.0
West	$684	27.9	$694	27.1
State				
Alabama	$415	24.8	$447	24.8
Alaska	$714	23.8	$720	24.8
Arizona	$560	27.5	$619	26.6
Arkansas	$418	26.5	$453	24.4
California	$792	29.1	$747	27.7
Colorado	$533	26.1	$671	26.4
Connecticut	$764	26.6	$681	25.4
Delaware	$634	24.7	$639	24.3
District of Columbia	$612	25.4	$618	24.8
Florida	$613	28.0	$641	27.5
Georgia	$553	25.8	$613	24.9
Hawaii	$830	27.4	$779	27.2
Idaho	$422	23.8	$515	25.3
Illinois	$569	25.9	$605	24.4
Indiana...................	$477	24.3	$521	23.9
Iowa......................	$429	24.1	$470	23.2
Kansas	$474	24.5	$498	23.4
Kentucky	$408	24.9	$445	24.0
Louisiana.................	$450	27.9	$466	25.8
Maine.....................	$535	26.8	$497	25.3
Maryland	$700	25.4	$689	24.7
Massachusetts............	$741	26.8	$684	25.5
Michigan	$540	27.2	$546	24.4
Minnesota	$539	26.7	$566	24.7
Mississippi...............	$394	27.1	$439	25.0
Missouri..................	$470	25.2	$484	24.0
Montana	$396	25.0	$447	25.3
Nebraska.................	$445	23.7	$491	23.0
Nevada...................	$650	26.8	$699	26.5
New Hampshire...........	$701	26.4	$646	24.2
New Jersey	$756	26.3	$751	25.5
New Mexico...............	$473	26.5	$503	26.6
New York.................	$620	26.3	$672	26.8
North Carolina	$488	24.4	$548	24.3
North Dakota.............	$400	23.9	$412	22.3
Ohio......................	$483	25.3	$515	24.2
Oklahoma	$434	25.4	$456	24.3
Oregon	$521	25.5	$620	26.9
Pennsylvania..............	$516	26.1	$531	25.0
Rhode Island..............	$625	27.5	$553	25.7
South Carolina............	$482	24.4	$510	24.4
South Dakota.............	$391	24.6	$426	22.9
Tennessee................	$456	25.0	$505	24.8
Texas.....................	$505	24.6	$574	24.4
Utah......................	$471	23.8	$597	24.9
Vermont..................	$570	27.1	$553	26.2
Virginia	$632	25.8	$650	24.5
Washington	$569	25.7	$663	26.5
West Virginia	$387	26.8	$401	25.8
Wisconsin	$510	24.9	$540	23.4
Wyoming	$425	23.7	$437	22.5
Puerto Rico	$261	29.4	$297	27.0

Note: Adjusted to 2000 dollars, using CPI-U-RS factor 1.277636.

Source: U.S. Census Bureau, 1990 census and Census 2000 Summary File 3.

75 or over (33.7 percent). Two other financially burdened groups, with over half paying 30 percent or more of their household income on rent, were female householders living alone, and female householders, with no husband present, who lived with their own children under 18.

GEOGRAPHIC DISTRIBUTION OF RENTAL COSTS

Median gross rents were above the national level in the West and the Northeast, while below it in the South and the Midwest.[6]

Median monthly gross rent was highest in the West at $694, far above the national median of $602 (see Table 2). The Northeast registered the second highest median gross rent at $651, while the South ($559) and the Midwest ($533) were below the national median.

Rents rose fastest in the South and the Midwest from 1990 to 2000.

In this report, 1990 median gross rents have been adjusted to constant 2000 dollars. Interestingly, the two regions with the lowest median gross rents in 2000 had higher increases than the other two regions from 1990 to 2000. Median rent increases were highest in the South (8.1 percent) and the Midwest (5.3 percent), and lowest in the Northeast (2.0 percent) and the West (1.5 percent).

---

[6] The Northeast region includes the states of Connecticut, Maine, Massachusetts, New Hampshire, New Jersey, New York, Pennsylvania, Rhode Island, and Vermont. The Midwest region includes the states of Illinois, Indiana, Iowa, Kansas, Michigan, Minnesota, Missouri, Nebraska, North Dakota, Ohio, South Dakota, and Wisconsin. The South region includes the states of Alabama, Arkansas, Delaware, Florida, Georgia, Kentucky, Louisiana, Maryland, Mississippi, North Carolina, Oklahoma, South Carolina, Tennessee, Texas, Virginia, West Virginia, and the District of Columbia, a state equivalent. The West region includes the states of Alaska, Arizona, California, Colorado, Hawaii, Idaho, Montana, Nevada, New Mexico, Oregon, Utah, Washington, and Wyoming.

Hawaii continued to have the highest median gross rent among all states.

Median gross rent in Hawaii, at $779, surpassed that in all other states, just as it did in 1990. New Jersey ($751) edged out California ($747) for second place; California had been second-highest in 1990. In 2000, half of the ten states with the highest rents were located in the West: Alaska, Colorado, and Nevada joined California and Hawaii in this group. In the Northeast, Connecticut, Massachusetts, New York, and New Jersey, were among the ten highest-rent states nationally. Maryland was the only southern state among the national top ten.

Median monthly rents were lowest in West Virginia ($401). North Dakota and South Dakota featured the next lowest rents ($412 and $426 respectively). Six of the ten states with the lowest rents were in the South: West Virginia, Alabama, Arkansas, Kentucky, Mississippi, and Oklahoma. The other two states with the lowest monthly rents were in the West: Montana and Wyoming ($447 and $437, respectively).

From 1990 to 2000, rents rose the most in three Rocky Mountain states and decreased the most in two New England states.

In three states — Colorado, Idaho, and Utah — median gross rent increased over 20 percent between 1990 and 2000. In another four states — Arizona, Montana, Oregon, and Washington — rents increased 10 percent or more. Big increases in rents in these seven western states were offset to some degree by a 5.7-percent decline in median rents in California's huge rental inventory, so that the West as a whole registered only a small increase (1.5 percent) in median

rents between 1990 and 2000. Georgia, Mississippi, North Carolina, Tennessee, and Texas also recorded double-digit rent increases from 1990 to 2000.[7]

Ten states posted rent decreases. Seven of the nine states in the Northeast, including every one in New England, registered rent decreases, with Connecticut and Rhode Island the only states in the United States posting double-digit rent decreases. However, the sheer size of the rental inventories in New York and Pennsylvania, the two states where rents increased in the Northeast, prevented the region as a whole from decreasing. California, Hawaii, and Maryland were the three states outside the Northeast posting rent decreases from 1990 to 2000.[8]

The proportion of household income spent on rent decreased in almost every state between 1990 and 2000.

The few states registering increases were generally in the West — for example, Alaska, Idaho, Oregon, and Utah. States with large decreases in median gross rent as a percentage of household income were more widely scattered, such as Michigan in the Midwest; Arkansas, Louisiana, and Mississippi in the South; and New Hampshire in the Northeast.

Renters in California devoted the largest share of their income to rent (median 27.7 percent). Renters in Iowa, Kansas, Nebraska,

---

[7] At the 90-percent confidence level, Iowa showed an increase between 8.7 and 10.3 percent, Nebraska between 9.4 and 11.2 percent, and South Dakota between 7.7 and 10.2 percent, so these three states may also have experienced double-digit increases.

[8] At the 90-percent confidence level, Alaska showed a 1990-2000 change of -0.5 to 2.1 percent, Delaware -0.2 to 2.1 percent, and the District of Columbia -0.3 to 2.3 percent, so these states may also have experienced median rent decreases.

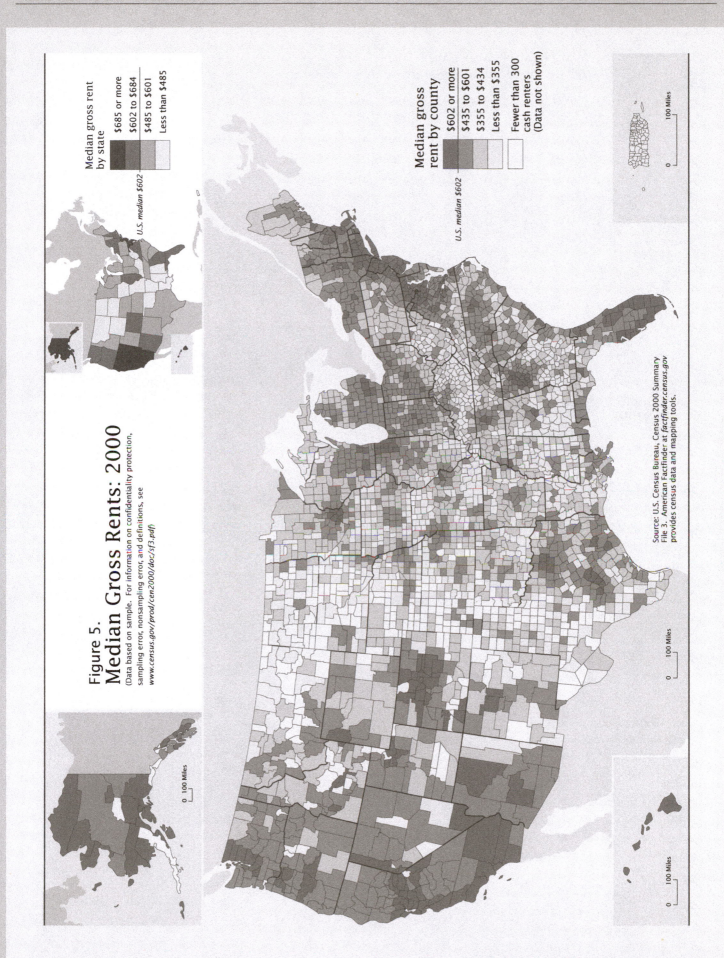

Figure 5.
Median Gross Rents: 2000

(Data based on sample. For information on confidentiality protection, sampling error, nonsampling error, and definitions, see www.census.gov/prod/cen2000/doc/sf3.pdf)

Median gross rent by state

$685 or more
$602 to $684
U.S. median $602
$485 to $601
Less than $485

Median gross rent by county

$602 or more
$435 to $601
U.S. median $602
$355 to $434
Less than $355
Fewer than 300 cash renters (Data not shown)

Source: U.S. Census Bureau, Census 2000 Summary File 3. American Factfinder at factfinder.census.gov provides census data and mapping tools.

0   100 Miles

Table 3.
Places of 100,000 or More With the Highest Median Gross Rent: 2000

(The data are for specified renter-occupied housing units. Data based on sample. For information on confidentiality protection, sampling error, nonsampling error, and definitions, see www.census.gov/prod/cen2000/doc/sf3.pdf)

Place	Specified renter-occupied units paying cash rent	Median gross rent	90-percent confidence interval
Irvine, CA	20,147	$1,272	$1,257 - $1,287
Sunnyvale, CA	27,158	$1,270	$1,256 - $1,284
Santa Clara, CA	20,337	$1,238	$1,219 - $1,257
Fremont, CA	23,782	$1,196	$1,183 - $1,209
Thousand Oaks, CA	10,007	$1,131	$1,109 - $1,153
San Jose, CA	103,317	$1,123	$1,115 - $1,131
Daly City, CA	11,964	$1,074	$1,062 - $1,086
Simi Valley, CA	7,932	$1,058	$1,037 - $1,079
Stamford, CT	19,283	$1,007	$986 - $1,028
Huntington Beach, CA	28,514	$985	$980 - $990

Note: Because of sampling error, the estimates in this table may not be significantly different from one another or from rates for geographic areas not listed in this table.

Source: U.S. Census Bureau, Census 2000 Summary File 3.

Table 4.
Places of 100,000 or More With the Lowest Median Gross Rent: 2000

(Data based on sample. For information on confidentiality protection, sampling error, nonsampling error, and definitions, see www.census.gov/prod/cen2000/doc/sf3.pdf)

Place	Specified renter-occupied units paying cash rent	Median gross rent	90-percent confidence interval
Brownsville, TX	13,633	$405	$400 - $410
Erie, PA	17,153	$424	$416 - $432
St. Louis, MO	75,581	$442	$439 - $445
Louisville, KY	51,102	$443	$438 - $448
Cincinnati, OH	88,512	$444	$441 - $447
Birmingham, AL	43,681	$446	$441 - $451
Dayton, OH	30,787	$448	$442 - $454
Springfield, MO	28,916	$452	$446 - $458
Evansville, IN	20,079	$454	$448 - $460
Laredo, TX	15,425	$454	$446 - $462

Note: Because of sampling error, the estimates in this table may not be significantly different from one another or from rates for geographic areas not listed in this table.

Source: U.S. Census Bureau, Census 2000 Summary File 3.

North Dakota, South Dakota, Wisconsin, and Wyoming spent the lowest share of their income on rent (23.4 percent or less).

High rents show distinct clusters.

Rental units at or above the national median of $602 cluster in a few areas, such as the Boston-Washington corridor, the Pacific coast of California, the southern coasts of Florida, Puget Sound, central Colorado, and around various large metropolitan areas like Chicago, Atlanta, Detroit, and Dallas. In about 10 percent of all counties the median was at or above the U.S. median. County-level data are mapped in Figure 5.

If the rental inventory were divided into four equal groupings called *quartiles*, the lowest group would have rents below $436 (the lower quartile), another one-quarter between $436 and the median ($602), another quarter between the median and the upper quartile of $804, and the highest quarter above $804. However, counties were not equally divided into these quartiles; in fact, in about 60 percent of all counties, median rents were below the lower quartile of $436. Higher rents, those at or above the U.S. median, were concentrated in a few counties which generally had a large number of renters and relatively expensive rental housing. Only about 60 counties had median rents above the upper quartile.

Nine of the ten places of 100,000 or more people with the highest rents were in California.

The only one of these ten high rent places not in California was Stamford, Connecticut (see Table 3).

The ten places with the lowest median gross rent are shown in Table 4. Unlike the top ten, these bottom ten were scattered across the nation, in every region except the West. Among places of 100,000 or more people in 2000, Brownsville, Texas, and Erie, Pennsylvania, had the lowest rents ($405 and $424, respectively).

ADDITIONAL FINDINGS

How did rents vary by type and age of structure?

Median gross rent for one-family, detached houses was $648, well above the $602 for all specified renter units. Rent was even higher for one-family, attached units ($688), which were generally townhouses and rowhouses. For units in apartment buildings of two to four units, the median gross rent was $573 and it rose to $608 for those units in buildings with five or more apartments.

Median gross rent for new housing units — those built 1995 or later — was $718. Older homes, those built before 1940, commanded much lower rents of $565.

Was rental housing more or less affordable in 2000 than it was 50 years earlier?

Median gross rent as a percentage of income from 1950 to 2000 is shown in Figure 6. The percentage rose steadily until 1990, but then declined a bit by 2000. Thus, in 2000, rental housing was less affordable than in 1950 but more affordable than in 1990. The income measure used in1980, 1990, and 2000 was household income. Income of families and primary individuals was used from 1950 through 1970. The main effect of the change was to include income of all members of the household. For example, only the income of the person designated as the householder would have been used in the earlier censuses if two or more unrelated people lived in the same apartment.

Among householders of different races and Hispanic origin, were there significant differences in the proportions of household income spent on rent and utilities?

Data on gross rent as a percentage of household income by race and Hispanic origin are presented in Figure 7. Single-race Black householders and those with a householder classified as two or more races paid the highest proportion of their income (27.6 percent) for rent. Single-race White householders, irrespective of Hispanic origin, paid the lowest (24.8 percent). Hispanic or Latino households spent a higher percentage of their household income for rent (27.0 percent) than all specified renter households nationally (25.5 percent).

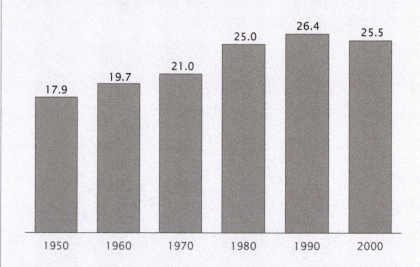

Figure 6.
Gross Rent as a Percentage of Income: 1950 to 2000

(Data based on sample. For information on confidentiality protection, sampling error, nonsampling error, and definitions, see www.census.gov/prod/cen2000/doc/sf3.pdf)

Note: Income of families and primary individuals for 1950-1970; and household income for 1980-2000.
Source: U.S. Census Bureau, Census of Population and Housing, decennial volumes.

Did the percentage of units with meals included increase during the 1990s?

The 1990 census introduced a question on whether meals were included in the rent (see Figure 2). This question was intended to measure congregate housing, generally for older households. In 1990, 3.8 percent of householders 65 and over reported meals included with the rent, and for householders 75 and over, the figure was 6.3 percent. By 2000, these percentages had increased to 8 percent for all householders 65 and over and to 13 percent for those 75 and over.

The largest number of elderly households reporting meals included in the rent in 2000 were found in California and Florida, but that was not unexpected given the size of the elderly population in those two states. The highest percent-

age of elderly reporting meals included in rent were found in Oregon and Washington.

ABOUT CENSUS 2000

Why the Census Bureau collects and tabulates rent data.

The U.S. Census Bureau collects data on gross rent, which is the sum of rent contracted for plus amounts paid for utilities (electricity, gas, water, and sewer) and fuels (oil, coal, kerosene, wood, etc.). Federal uses include establishment of Section 8 fair market rents by the Department of Housing and Urban Development and allocation of funds by the Departments of Health and Human Services and Agriculture to help low- and moderate-income families whose rents exceed 30 percent of their household income. Rent data are also used by the Bureau of Economic Analysis in its state per-capita

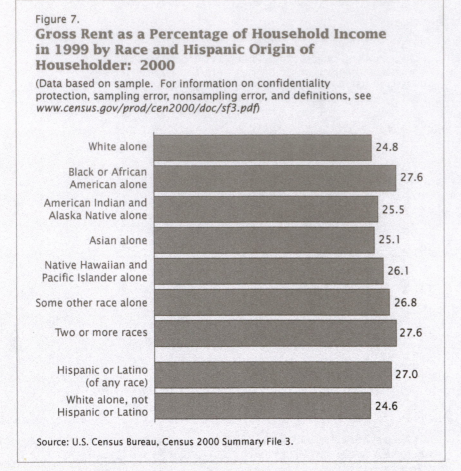

Figure 7.

Gross Rent as a Percentage of Household Income in 1999 by Race and Hispanic Origin of Householder: 2000

(Data based on sample. For information on confidentiality protection, sampling error, nonsampling error, and definitions, see *www.census.gov/prod/cen2000/doc/sf3.pdf*)

Race/Hispanic Origin	Percentage
White alone	24.8
Black or African American alone	27.6
American Indian and Alaska Native alone	25.5
Asian alone	25.1
Native Hawaiian and Pacific Islander alone	26.1
Some other race alone	26.8
Two or more races	27.6
Hispanic or Latino (of any race)	27.0
White alone, not Hispanic or Latino	24.6

Source: U.S. Census Bureau, Census 2000 Summary File 3.

income estimates, which are used in allocation formulas or eligibility criteria of more than 20 federal programs. Rent data are also needed to distribute funds for housing for low-income households under the Older Americans Act and for home energy assistance to low-income individuals and families.

Accuracy of the Estimates

The data contained in this report are based on the sample of households who responded to the Census 2000 long form. Nationally, approximately one out of every six housing units was included in this sample. As a result, the sample estimates may differ somewhat from the100-percent figures that would have been obtained if all housing units, people within those

housing units, and people living in group quarters had been enumerated using the same questionnaires, instructions, enumerators, and so forth. The sample estimates also differ from the values that would have been obtained from different samples of housing units, people within those housing units, and people living in group quarters. The deviation of a sample estimate from the average of all possible samples is called the sampling error.

In addition to the variability that arises from the sampling procedures, both sample data and 100-percent data are subject to nonsampling error. Nonsampling error may be introduced during any of the various complex operations used to collect and process data. Such errors may include: not

enumerating every household or every person in the population, failing to obtain all required information from the respondents, obtaining incorrect or inconsistent information, and recording information incorrectly. In addition, errors can occur during the field review of the enumerators' work, during clerical handling of the census questionnaires, or during the electronic processing of the questionnaires.

Nonsampling error may affect the data in two ways: (1) errors that are introduced randomly will increase the variability of the data and, therefore, should be reflected in the standard errors; and (2) errors that tend to be consistent in one direction will bias both sample and 100-percent data in that direction. For example, if respondents consistently tend to underreport their incomes, then the resulting estimates of households or families by income category will tend to be understated for the higher income categories and overstated for the lower income categories. Such biases are not reflected in the standard errors.

While it is impossible to completely eliminate error from an operation as large and complex as the decennial census, the Census Bureau attempts to control the sources of such error during the data collection and processing operations. The primary sources of error and the programs instituted to control error in Census 2000 are described in detail in *Summary File 3 Technical Documentation* under Chapter 8, "Accuracy of the Data," located at *www.census.gov/ prod/cen2000/doc/sf3.pdf.*

All statements in this Census 2000 Brief have undergone statistical testing and all comparisons are significant at the 90-percent confidence level, unless otherwise noted. The estimates in tables, maps, and other figures may vary from actual values due to sampling and nonsampling errors. As a result, estimates in one category may not be significantly different from estimates assigned to a different category. Further information on the accuracy of the data is located at *www.census.gov/ prod/cen2000/doc/sf3.pdf*. For further information on the computation and use of standard errors, contact the Decennial Statistical Studies Division at 301-763-4242.

For More Information

The Census 2000 Summary File 3 data are available from the American Factfinder on the Internet (*factfinder.census.gov*). They were released on a state-by-state basis during 2002. For information on confidentiality protection, nonsampling error, sampling error, and definitions, also see *www.census.gov/prod/cen2000/ doc/sf3.pdf* or contact the Customer Services Center at 301-763-INFO (4636).

Information on population and housing topics is presented in the Census 2000 Brief series, located on the Census Bureau's Web site at *www.census.gov/population/www/*

cen2000/briefs.html. This series, which will be completed in 2003, presents information on race, Hispanic origin, age, sex, household type, housing tenure, and social, economic, and housing characteristics, such as ancestry, income, and housing costs.

For additional information on housing, including reports and survey data, visit the Census Bureau's Internet site on at *www.census.gov/ hhes/www/housing.html*. To find information about the availability of data products, including reports, CD-ROMs, and DVDs, call the Customer Services Center at 301-763-INFO (4636), or e-mail *webmaster@census.gov*.

Employment Status: 2000

Census 2000 Brief

Issued August 2003

C2KBR-18

By
Sandra Luckett Clark
and
Mai Weismantle

Census 2000 found that 63.9 percent of the 217.2 million people aged 16 and over in the United States were in the labor force.[1] Of the 138.8 million people in the labor force, 129.7 million were employed, 7.9 million were unemployed, and 1.2 million were in the Armed Forces. The civilian unemployment rate was 5.8 percent.[2]

Note that, in general, the estimates in this report will differ from the official labor force data collected in the Current Population Survey and released by the Bureau of Labor Statistics. For further information on these differences, see the text box on page 3.

[1] The labor force includes all people classified in the civilian labor force (employed or unemployed) plus members of the U.S. Armed Forces. Employed people include civilians 16 and over who were either "at work" or were "with a job but not at work." Unemployed civilians are those who did not have a job during the reference period, were actively looking for work, or waiting to be called back to a job from which they had been laid off, and were available to go to work.

[2] This rate is defined as the number of unemployed people divided by the sum of employed plus unemployed people.

Figure 1.

Reproduction of the Questions on Employment Status From Census 2000

21 LAST WEEK, did this person do ANY work for either pay or profit? *Mark* ☒ *the "Yes" box even if the person worked only 1 hour, or helped without pay in a family business or farm for 15 hours or more, or was on active duty in the Armed Forces.*

☐ Yes
☐ No → *Skip to 25a*

25 a. LAST WEEK, was this person on layoff from a job?

☐ Yes → *Skip to 25c*
☐ No

b. LAST WEEK, was this person TEMPORARILY absent from a job or business?

☐ Yes, on vacation, temporary illness, labor dispute, etc. → *Skip to 26*
☐ No → *Skip to 25d*

c. Has this person been informed that he or she will be recalled to work within the next 6 months OR been given a date to return to work?

☐ Yes → *Skip to 25e*
☐ No

d. Has this person been looking for work during the last 4 weeks?

☐ Yes
☐ No → *Skip to 26*

e. LAST WEEK, could this person have started a job if offered one, or returned to work if recalled?

☐ Yes, could have gone to work
☐ No, because of own temporary illness
☐ No, because of all other reasons *(in school, etc.)*

Source: U.S. Census Bureau, Census 2000 questionnaire.

USCENSUSBUREAU

Helping You Make Informed Decisions

U.S. Department of Commerce
Economics and Statistics Administration
U.S. CENSUS BUREAU

United States
Census 2000

Table 1.
Employment Status of the Population 16 and Over for the United States, Regions, and States, and for Puerto Rico: 1990 and 2000

(Data based on sample. For information on confidentiality protection, nonsampling error, sampling error, and definitions, see www.census.gov/prod/cen2000/doc/sf3.pdf)

Area	1990					2000				
			Civilian labor force		Civilian			Civilian labor force		Civilian
	Population 16 and over	Percent in labor force*	Employed	Unem-ployed	unem-ployment rate	Population 16 and over	Percent in labor force*	Employed	Unem-ployed	unem-ployment rate
United States	191,829,271	65.3	115,681,202	7,792,248	6.3	217,168,077	63.9	129,721,512	7,947,286	5.8
Region										
Northeast	40,187,730	64.9	24,311,910	1,644,612	6.3	41,985,417	63.2	24,904,791	1,566,751	5.9
Midwest	45,692,769	65.7	27,985,184	1,854,073	6.2	49,639,541	66.4	31,185,231	1,676,002	5.1
South	67,133,912	64.1	39,536,681	2,634,638	6.2	77,518,144	62.7	45,226,189	2,743,409	5.7
West..............	40,127,166	66.8	24,596,907	1,693,875	6.4	48,024,975	63.9	28,405,301	1,961,124	6.5
State										
Alabama	3,103,529	61.1	1,741,794	128,587	6.9	3,450,542	59.7	1,920,189	126,911	6.2
Alaska............	393,394	74.7	245,379	23,587	8.8	458,054	71.3	281,532	27,953	9.0
Arizona	2,785,730	62.9	1,603,896	123,902	7.2	3,907,229	61.1	2,233,004	133,368	5.6
Arkansas	1,800,056	59.8	994,289	72,079	6.8	2,072,068	60.6	1,173,399	76,147	6.1
California	22,786,281	67.0	13,996,309	996,502	6.6	25,596,144	62.4	14,718,928	1,110,274	7.0
Colorado	2,518,482	70.3	1,633,281	99,438	5.7	3,325,197	70.1	2,205,194	99,260	4.3
Connecticut.......	2,616,747	69.0	1,692,874	95,819	5.4	2,652,316	66.6	1,664,440	92,668	5.3
Delaware	518,946	68.3	335,147	13,945	4.0	610,289	65.7	376,811	20,549	5.2
District of Columbia ...	503,173	66.3	303,994	23,442	7.2	469,041	63.6	263,108	31,844	10.8
Florida	10,377,252	60.4	5,810,467	356,769	5.8	12,744,825	58.6	6,995,047	412,411	5.6
Georgia..........	6,250,687	66.1	3,839,756	223,052	5.5	6,250,687	66.1	3,839,756	223,052	5.5
Hawaii............	855,518	70.4	529,059	19,288	3.5	950,055	64.5	537,909	35,886	6.3
Idaho	729,819	65.5	443,703	29,070	6.1	969,872	66.1	599,453	36,784	5.8
Illinois...........	8,796,610	66.4	5,417,967	385,040	6.6	9,530,946	65.4	5,833,185	375,412	6.0
Indiana	4,248,923	65.9	2,628,695	160,143	5.7	4,683,717	66.6	2,965,174	152,723	4.9
Iowa	2,131,703	66.0	1,340,242	63,641	4.5	2,281,274	68.2	1,489,816	64,906	4.2
Kansas	1,880,434	66.8	1,172,214	57,772	4.7	2,059,160	67.5	1,316,283	58,415	4.2
Kentucky.........	2,838,709	60.5	1,563,960	124,354	7.4	3,161,542	60.9	1,798,264	109,350	5.7
Louisiana	3,119,293	59.3	1,641,614	175,303	9.6	3,394,546	59.4	1,851,777	146,218	7.3
Maine	952,644	65.6	571,842	40,722	6.6	1,010,318	65.3	624,011	31,165	4.8
Maryland.........	3,736,830	70.6	2,481,342	111,536	4.3	4,085,942	67.8	2,608,457	128,902	4.7
Massachusetts	4,809,772	67.8	3,027,950	218,000	6.7	5,010,241	66.2	3,161,087	150,952	4.6
Michigan.........	7,102,020	64.1	4,166,196	374,341	8.2	7,630,645	64.6	4,637,461	284,992	5.8
Minnesota.........	3,321,415	69.7	2,192,417	118,919	5.1	3,781,756	71.2	2,580,046	109,069	4.1
Mississippi	1,909,851	59.7	1,028,773	94,712	8.4	2,158,941	59.4	1,173,314	93,778	7.4
Missouri	3,939,284	64.5	2,367,395	155,388	6.2	4,331,369	65.2	2,657,924	148,794	5.3
Montana	599,765	63.7	350,723	26,217	7.0	701,168	65.4	425,977	28,710	6.3
Nebraska	1,192,803	68.3	772,813	29,326	3.7	1,315,715	69.7	877,237	32,287	3.5
Nevada...........	936,050	70.3	607,437	40,083	6.2	1,538,516	65.2	933,280	61,920	6.2
New Hampshire	858,615	71.9	574,237	38,108	6.2	960,498	70.5	650,871	25,500	3.8
New Jersey.........	6,129,923	67.4	3,868,698	235,975	5.7	6,546,155	64.2	3,950,029	243,116	5.8
New Mexico	1,113,046	62.8	629,272	54,888	8.0	1,369,176	61.0	763,116	60,324	7.3
New York	14,191,044	63.6	8,370,718	618,903	6.9	14,805,912	61.1	8,382,988	640,108	7.1
North Carolina	5,203,230	67.6	3,238,414	163,081	4.8	6,290,618	65.7	3,824,741	214,991	5.3
North Dakota	480,464	65.3	287,558	16,083	5.3	502,306	67.5	316,632	15,257	4.6
Ohio.............	8,349,183	63.5	4,931,357	348,638	6.6	8,788,494	64.8	5,402,175	282,615	5.0
Oklahoma	2,398,899	62.5	1,369,138	100,931	6.9	2,666,724	62.1	1,545,296	86,832	5.3
Oregon	2,191,764	64.4	1,319,960	87,183	6.2	2,673,782	65.2	1,627,769	112,529	6.5
Pennsylvania	9,392,816	61.7	5,434,532	344,795	6.0	9,693,040	61.9	5,653,500	339,386	5.7
Rhode Island	801,625	66.1	487,913	34,690	6.6	827,797	64.6	500,731	29,859	5.6
South Carolina	2,669,383	66.0	1,603,425	94,673	5.6	3,114,016	63.4	1,824,700	113,495	5.9
South Dakota	517,032	66.2	321,891	13,983	4.2	577,129	68.4	374,373	17,221	4.4
Tennessee	3,799,725	64.0	2,250,842	154,235	6.4	4,445,909	63.5	2,651,638	153,596	5.5
Texas	12,656,267	66.0	7,634,279	584,749	7.1	15,617,373	63.6	9,234,372	596,187	6.1
Utah	1,154,039	68.0	736,059	41,389	5.3	1,600,279	69.0	1,044,362	54,561	5.0
Vermont	434,544	69.4	283,146	17,600	5.9	479,140	69.3	317,134	13,997	4.2
Virginia	4,843,182	68.9	3,028,362	142,048	4.5	5,529,980	66.8	3,412,647	151,125	4.2
Washington........	3,730,985	66.7	2,293,961	139,216	5.7	4,553,591	66.5	2,793,722	186,102	6.2
West Virginia	1,404,900	53.0	671,085	71,142	9.6	1,455,101	54.5	732,673	58,021	7.3
Wisconsin..........	3,732,898	67.6	2,386,439	130,799	5.2	4,157,030	69.1	2,734,925	134,311	4.7
Wyoming	332,293	67.7	207,868	13,112	5.9	381,912	67.5	241,055	13,453	5.3
Puerto Rico.........	2,497,078	47.3	934,736	239,940	20.4	2,842,876	40.7	930,865	220,998	19.2

*Includes members of the armed forces

Note: The armed forces population is equal to the population 16 years old and over multiplied by the percent in the labor force minus the civilian labor force. The population not in the labor force is equal to 100 minus the percent in the labor force (or the percent not in the labor force) multiplied by the population 16 years and over.

Source: U.S. Census Bureau, 1990 census and Census 2000 Summary File 3.

Differences between Census 2000 and Current Population Survey (official) estimates of the labor force

Employment and unemployment estimates from Census 2000 will, in general, differ from the official labor force data collected in the Current Population Survey (CPS) and released by the Bureau of Labor Statistics, because the design and collection methodology of the census and the CPS meet different purposes.

Census 2000 was designed to collect general information about the labor force for very small geographic areas on a one-time basis. It was primarily a mail-out/mail-back data collection that asked fewer and less precise questions than the CPS on employment and unemployment.

The CPS is specifically designed to produce the official estimates of employment and unemployment for the United States each month. Data collection consists of personal interviews of respondents by field representatives who ask numerous detailed questions on labor force participation. For example, the

CPS asks a more detailed and extensive series of questions about whether a person is "actively looking for work" than can be asked in the census.

Specifically, at the national level, Census 2000 estimates of employment were considerably below, and estimates of unemployment above, the corresponding CPS estimates. Subnational estimates from the two sources may exhibit even wider relative differences.

A known problem in Census 2000 increased the number of unemployed people for some places with relatively large numbers of people living in civilian noninstitutional group quarters, such as college dormitories, worker dormitories, and group homes, and may have affected comparisons of labor force data for higher levels of geography. For more information on this specific problem, see Data Note 4 in Chapter 9 of the technical documentation for Census 2000 Summary File 3 at *www.census.gov/prod/cen2000/doc/sf3.pdf.*

Decennial censuses have included questions on employment status since 1930. Census 2000 collected information on employment status from people aged 15 and over; however, all published tabulations of employment-status data are restricted to the population aged 16 and over. Questions 21 and 25 on the Census 2000 forms asked people about their connection to the paid workforce in the week before they filled out the questionnaire (see Figure 1). Answers to these questions were used to measure labor force participation, the unemployment rate, and other indicators of the economic activity of the population.[3]

The battery of Census 2000 questions that collected employment status information differed slightly

from the 1990 census questions. The new questions were developed in cooperation with the Bureau of Labor Statistics (BLS) of the Department of Labor. Highlights of the changes include the addition of the words "for either pay or profit" to the "work last week" item (question 21); the removal of the 1990 question "How many hours did you work last week?"; the division and expansion of the "temporary absence from a job or layoff" item into three separate questions (25a, 25b, and 25c); and the revision of the definition of "available" in the "availability to work" item (question 25e) from being able to "take a job" to being able to "start a job if offered one, or return to work if recalled."

This report is part of a series that presents population and housing data collected by Census 2000. The report provides data on the employment status of people 16

and over and how employment status varies among regions, states, counties, and places with populations of 100,000 or more.[4]

The U.S. labor force increased over the decade.

Between 1990 and 2000, the number of people in the U.S. labor force increased by 13.5 million, or 10.8 percent (see Table 1).[5] The population 16 and over increased by 25.3 million (13.2 percent), while the population not in the labor force grew 17.8 percent.

---

[3] While both questions are used to determine a person's employment status, they are not discussed individually within this report.

[4] The text of this report discusses data for the United States, including the 50 states and the District of Columbia. Data for the Commonwealth of Puerto Rico are shown in Table 1 and Figure 3.

[5] The estimates in this report are based on responses from a sample of the population. As with all surveys, estimates may vary from the actual values because of sampling variation or other factors. All statements made in this report have undergone statistical testing and are significant at the 90-percent confidence level, unless otherwise noted.

Labor force participation by women increased between 1990 and 2000, but at a slower pace than in previous decades.

In 1960, about 36 of every 100 women participated in the labor force, a figure that hit 57 in 1990, but then increased slightly to 58 in 2000 (see Figure 2). The labor force participation of men declined from 80 percent in 1960 to 71 percent in 2000.[6]

The labor force is demographically diverse.

To highlight how the economy and various groups in the population influence each other, this section concentrates on the prime working-age population, 20 to 64 year olds.[7] Of the 166.3 million people aged 20 to 64 in 2000, 118.9 million were employed, 1.0 million were in the Armed Forces, 6.2 million were unemployed, and 40.1 million were not in the labor force (see Table 2).

In 2000, women were more likely than men to be outside the labor force (30.0 percent of women, 18.1 percent of men). The gap between unemployed men and women was narrower in 2000 than in 1990 (4.0 percent and 3.5 percent, respectively, in 2000, compared with 4.9 percent and 3.9 percent, respectively, in 1990).[8]

The age categories with the largest percentage employed were those 45 to 54 years old (76.3 percent)

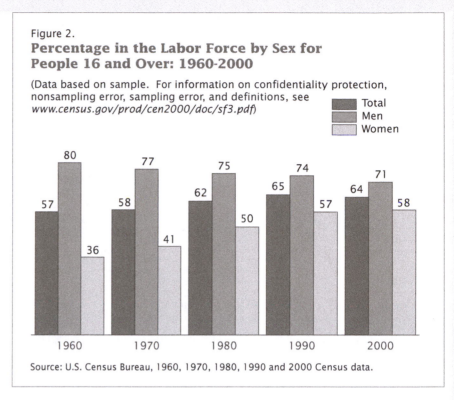

Figure 2.

Percentage in the Labor Force by Sex for People 16 and Over: 1960-2000

(Data based on sample. For information on confidentiality protection, nonsampling error, sampling error, and definitions, see *www.census.gov/prod/cen2000/doc/sf3.pdf*)

Legend: Total, Men, Women

	1960	1970	1980	1990	2000
Total	57	58	62	65	64
Men	80	77	75	74	71
Women	36	41	50	57	58

Source: U.S. Census Bureau, 1960, 1970, 1980, 1990 and 2000 Census data.

followed by those 35 to 44 years old (76.2 percent). People 20 to 21 were most likely to be unemployed (9.2 percent). The likelihood of being unemployed declined with increasing age. People 62 to 64 were most likely not to be in the labor force (59.6 percent).

People aged 20 to 64 with incomes in 1999 at or above the poverty level were almost twice as likely to be employed during the reference week as those with incomes below the poverty level (76.8 percent and 38.9 percent, respectively).[9] More than half (51.4 percent) of those with incomes below the poverty level were not in the labor force. Unemployed people were nearly

five times as likely to be in poverty as employed people (27.9 percent versus 5.8 percent).

Employment rates varied among the race and ethnic groups.

Census 2000 allowed respondents to choose more than one race. With the exception of the Two or more races group, all race groups discussed in this report refer to people who indicated only one racial identity among the six major categories: White, Black or African American, American Indian and Alaska Native, Asian, Native Hawaiian or Other Pacific Islander, and Some other race.[10] The use of the single-race population in this report does not imply that it is the preferred method of presenting or

---

[6] The labor force participation rate is defined as those people in the labor force divided by the total population aged 16 and over.

[7] The data for people in this group are less likely to reflect the influence of noneconomic factors, such as education and retirement, which cloud the data for younger and older people.

[8] These rates are the unemployed population divided by the total population; they differ from the civilian unemployment rate, which is the unemployed population divided by the total civilian labor force.

---

[9] Employment status and poverty have different reference periods. Employment status relates to calendar weeks in 2000. Poverty status is determined based on a family's income during the previous calendar year, 1999. For more information on poverty status, see *Poverty: 1999* (C2KBR-19) by Alemayehu Bishaw and John Iceland.

---

[10] For further information on each of the six major race groups and the Two or more races population, see reports from the Census 2000 Brief series (C2KBR/01), available on the Census 2000 Web site at *www.census.gov/population/www/cen2000/briefs.html*.

Table 2.
Selected Characteristics of the Population 20 to 64 by Employment Status: 2000

(Data based on sample. For information on confidentiality protection, nonsampling error, sampling error, and definitions, see www.census.gov/prod/cen2000/doc/sf3.pdf)

Characteristics	Total	In labor force						Not in labor force	
		Number	Percent of total	Civilian labor force				Number	Percent of total
				Employed		Unemployed			
				Number	Percent of total	Number	Percent of total		
All people...................	166,258,647	126,149,256	75.9	118,897,175	71.5	6,202,557	3.7	40,109,391	24.1
Sex									
Men	82,401,295	67,485,877	81.9	63,300,673	76.8	3,280,583	4.0	14,915,418	18.1
Women........................	83,857,352	58,663,379	70.0	55,596,502	66.3	2,921,974	3.5	25,193,973	30.0
Age									
20 to 21 years	7,892,819	5,672,742	71.9	4,784,870	60.6	727,264	9.2	2,220,077	28.1
22 to 24 years	11,133,161	8,576,078	77.0	7,649,427	68.7	739,624	6.6	2,557,083	23.0
25 to 29 years	19,212,244	15,219,226	79.2	14,147,042	73.6	863,772	4.5	3,993,018	20.8
30 to 34 years	20,365,113	16,101,522	79.1	15,169,436	74.5	760,117	3.7	4,263,591	20.9
35 to 44 years	45,905,471	36,776,494	80.1	34,961,987	76.2	1,552,338	3.4	9,128,977	19.9
45 to 54 years	37,578,609	29,801,024	79.3	28,671,720	76.3	1,074,811	2.9	7,777,585	20.7
55 to 59 years	13,383,251	8,972,311	67.0	8,662,391	64.7	305,528	2.3	4,410,940	33.0
60 to 61 years	4,515,448	2,497,033	55.3	2,407,126	53.3	89,469	2.0	2,018,415	44.7
62 to 64 years	6,272,531	2,532,826	40.4	2,443,176	39.0	89,634	1.4	3,739,705	59.6
Race									
White alone	125,817,324	98,071,328	77.9	93,527,883	74.3	3,800,088	3.0	27,745,996	22.1
Black or African American alone......	19,645,401	13,584,629	69.1	12,042,857	61.3	1,355,114	6.9	6,060,772	30.9
American Indian and Alaska Native alone.............................	1,409,145	961,304	68.2	844,951	60.0	106,581	7.6	447,841	31.8
Asian alone......................	6,646,456	4,764,861	71.7	4,523,302	68.1	211,899	3.2	1,881,595	28.3
Native Hawaiian and Other Pacific Islander alone....................	224,136	164,098	73.2	145,344	64.8	14,948	6.7	60,038	26.8
Some other race alone.............	8,832,789	5,977,201	67.7	5,408,955	61.2	521,358	5.9	2,855,588	32.3
Two or more races	3,683,396	2,625,835	71.3	2,403,883	65.3	192,569	5.2	1,057,561	28.7
Hispanic or Latino Origin									
Hispanic or Latino (of any race)	19,949,575	13,448,890	67.4	12,242,310	61.4	1,105,861	5.5	6,500,685	32.6
Not Hispanic or Latino	146,309,072	112,700,366	77.0	106,654,865	72.9	5,096,696	3.5	33,608,706	23.0
White alone, not Hispanic or Latino	116,216,507	91,590,295	78.8	87,573,488	75.4	3,314,303	2.9	24,626,212	21.2
Poverty*									
Income in 1999 at or above the poverty level....................	145,295,481	116,714,795	80.3	111,628,422	76.8	4,315,496	3.0	28,580,686	19.7
Income in 1999 below the poverty level	17,514,796	8,506,928	48.6	6,817,882	38.9	1,668,160	9.5	9,007,868	51.4

*Poverty status was determined for all people except institutionalized people, people in military group quarters, people in college dormitories, and unrelated individuals under 15 years old. These groups also were excluded from the numerator and denominator when calculating poverty rates.

Note: The total and in labor force estimates include those in the armed forces.

Source: U.S. Census Bureau, Census 2000 Summary File 3.

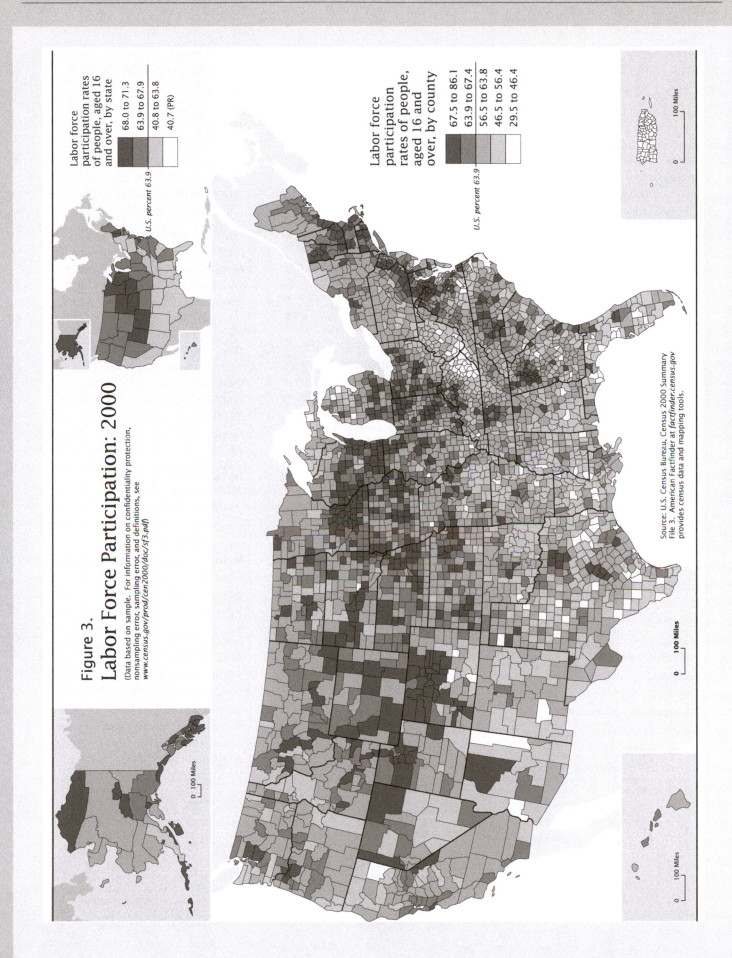

Figure 3.
Labor Force Participation: 2000

(Data based on sample. For information on confidentiality protection, nonsampling error, sampling error, and definitions, see www.census.gov/prod/cen2000/doc/sf3.pdf)

Labor force participation rates of people, aged 16 and over, by state

68.0 to 71.3
63.9 to 67.9
40.8 to 63.8
40.7 (PR)

U.S. percent 63.9

Labor force participation rates of people, aged 16 and over, by county

67.5 to 86.1
63.9 to 67.4
56.5 to 63.8
46.5 to 56.4
29.5 to 46.4

U.S. percent 63.9

Source: U.S. Census Bureau, Census 2000 Summary File 3. American Factfinder at factfinder.census.gov provides census data and mapping tools.

0   100 Miles

analyzing data. The Census Bureau uses a variety of approaches.[11]

Among the race and Hispanic or Latino origin categories in Table 2, non-Hispanic Whites (single race) were most likely to be employed (75.4 percent) and least likely to be unemployed (2.9 percent). Of the Asian population who reported only one race, 68.1 percent were employed and 3.2 percent were unemployed. The percent of people unemployed was highest for those in the American Indian and Alaska Native category, 7.6 percent.

The percentage of people of Hispanic or Latino origin between 20 and 64 years who were employed, 61.4 percent, was considerably below the corresponding 72.9 percent for those who were not Hispanic.[12] Non-Hispanic Whites accounted for 79.4 percent of the non-Hispanic population in this age group. The 5.5 percent of Hispanics who were unemployed was nearly double the 2.9 percent of non-Hispanic Whites who were unemployed.

GEOGRAPHIC DISTRIBUTION OF LABOR FORCE PARTICIPATION

More than one-third of the labor force lived in the South.[13]

Census 2000 data showed that 35.0 percent of the nation's labor force lived in the South, and 23.8 percent lived in the Midwest, percentages that closely follow the distribution of the population aged 16 and over (see Table 1). The labor force participation rate was highest in the Midwest, at 66.4 percent. The region with the lowest labor force participation was the South, at 62.7 percent. The only region where the labor force participation rate increased from 1990 to 2000 was the Midwest (65.7 percent to 66.4 percent).

Alaska and Minnesota led the states in labor force participation.

Labor force participation rates were highest in Alaska and Minnesota, at 71.3 percent and 71.2 percent, respectively (see Table 1).[14] The state map located at the top of Figure 3 also shows a cluster of states in the Midwest with high labor force participation rates. The state with the lowest rate was West Virginia, 54.5 percent, followed by Florida, at

58.6 percent. Labor force participation was also low in many other southern states.

The state with the highest civilian unemployment rate was Alaska (9.0 percent), but the District of Columbia's rate was even higher (10.8 percent). Nebraska's unemployment rate was the lowest among the states (3.5 percent).

From 1990 to 2000, Iowa was the only state with an increase in its labor force participation rate that was greater than 2 percentage points (see Table 1).[15] Hawaii was the only state who's rate decreased more than 5 percentage points from 1990 to 2000.[16] Texas experienced the largest state-level increase in the number of employed people from 1990 to 2000 (1.6 million).

Labor force participation rates were high in some counties in the Northeast and upper Midwest and low in parts of Appalachia.

Counties in the upper interior Midwest from Chicago to Minneapolis-St. Paul displayed high labor force participation rates, as did a band of counties stretching from southern Maine to northern Virginia (see Figure 3). Labor force participation rates were also high in several metropolitan areas in the South, such as Atlanta, Nashville, Dallas-Fort Worth, and Austin. In Census 2000, low labor force participation was found in many Appalachian counties and in scattered nonmetropolitan counties throughout the South.

---

[11] This report draws heavily on Summary File 3, a Census 2000 product that can be accessed through *American FactFinder,* available from the Census Bureau's Web site, *www.census.gov.* Information on people who reported more than one race, such as "White **and** American Indian and Alaska Native" or "Asian **and** Black or African American," is forthcoming in Summary File 4, which will also be available through *American FactFinder* in 2003. About 2.6 percent of people reported more than one race.

[12] Because Hispanics may be of any race, data in this report for Hispanics overlap with data for racial groups. Based on Census 2000 sample data, the proportion Hispanic was 8.0 percent for the White alone population, 1.9 percent for the Black alone population, 14.6 percent for the American Indian and Alaska Native alone population, 1.0 percent for the Asian alone population, 9.5 percent for the Native Hawaiian and Other Pacific Islander alone population, 97.1 percent for the Some other race alone population, and 31.1 percent for the Two or more races population.

[13] The Northeast region includes the states of Connecticut, Maine, Massachusetts, New Hampshire, New Jersey, New York, Pennsylvania, Rhode Island, and Vermont. The Midwest region includes the states of Illinois, Indiana, Iowa, Kansas, Michigan, Minnesota, Missouri, Nebraska, North Dakota, Ohio, South Dakota, and Wisconsin. The South region includes the states of Alabama, Arkansas, Delaware, Florida, Georgia, Kentucky, Louisiana, Maryland, Mississippi, North Carolina, Oklahoma, South Carolina, Tennessee, Texas, Virginia, West Virginia, and the District of Columbia, a state equivalent. The West region includes the states of Alaska, Arizona, California, Colorado, Hawaii, Idaho, Montana, Nevada, New Mexico, Oregon, Utah, Washington, and Wyoming.

[14] These rates are not statistically different from each other.

[15] South Dakota and North Dakota also had labor force participation rates greater than two percentage points, however they were not statistically greater than two percentage points.

[16] Nevada's labor force rate also decreased more than five percentage points, however the decrease was not statistically more than five percentage points.

Most places with the highest and lowest labor force participation rates were in the South and the West.[17]

For places of 100,000 or more population, the labor force participation rates were highest in Westminster, Colorado; Carrollton, Texas; and Gilbert, Arizona (see Table 3).[18] Among the ten places with the highest labor force participation rates, two other places were in Texas, another in Arizona, and a total of two in Virginia. Rounding out the top ten were Sioux Falls, South Dakota, and Anchorage, Alaska. The Northeast was not represented in the top ten.

Among the ten places with the lowest labor force participation rates, the top three were Miami and Hialeah, Florida, along with East Los Angeles, California (see Table 4).[19] The other seven were scattered among older industrial-era cities (Newark and Paterson, New Jersey; and Gary, Indiana) and a variety of other locations that included Brownsville and Laredo,

---

[17] Census 2000 shows 245 places in the United States with 100,000 or more population. They include 238 incorporated places (including 4 city-county consolidations) and 7 census-designated places that are not legally incorporated. For a list of these places by state, see *www.census.gov /population/www/cen2000/phc-t6.html.*

[18] The participation rates for these three places were not statistically different from each other.

[19] The labor force participation rates in these three cities are not statistically different from each other. The labor force participation rate for East Los Angeles, California, is not statistically different from that for Brownsville, Texas.

Table 3.
Ten Places of 100,000 or More With the Highest Percentage of People 16 and Over in the Labor Force: 2000

(Data based on sample. For information on confidentiality protection, nonsampling error, sampling error, and definitions, see *www.census.gov/prod/cen2000/doc/sf3.pdf*)

Place	In the labor force		Margin of error*
	Number	Percent	
Westminster, CO	59,746	77.7	0.7
Carrollton, TX	63,424	77.6	0.6
Gilbert town, AZ	58,180	76.9	0.7
Plano, TX	124,183	75.3	0.5
Arlington CDP, VA**	120,803	74.9	0.5
Sioux Falls, SD	71,988	74.8	0.6
Chandler, AZ	96,063	74.7	0.5
Alexandria, VA	80,949	74.4	0.6
Anchorage, AK	143,350	74.4	0.4
Irving, TX	109,409	74.0	0.5

*When the margin of error is added to or substracted from the estimate, it produces a 90-percent confidence interval.

**Arlington is a Census Designated Place and not an incorporated area.

Note: Because of sampling error, the estimates in this table may not be significantly different from one another or from rates for other geographic areas not listed in this table.

Source: U.S. Census Bureau, Census 2000 Summary File 3.

Table 4.
Ten Places of 100,000 or More With the Lowest Percentage of People 16 and Over in the Labor Force: 2000

(Data based on sample. For information on confidentiality protection, nonsampling error, sampling error, and definitions, see *www.census.gov/prod/cen2000/doc/sf3.pdf*)

Place	In the labor force		Margin of error*
	Number	Percent	
Miami, FL	147,356	50.3	0.4
Hialeah, FL	91,536	50.8	0.5
East Los Angeles CDP, CA**	43,538	50.9	0.8
Brownsville, TX	50,622	52.4	0.7
Newark, NJ	108,275	52.7	0.5
Laredo, TX	64,387	53.5	0.6
Paterson, NJ	60,507	55.4	0.7
Pueblo, CO	44,417	55.7	0.8
San Bernardino, CA	70,413	55.8	0.7
Gary, IN	42,206	55.9	0.8

*When the margin of error is added to or substracted from the estimate, it produces a 90-percent confidence interval.

**East Los Angeles is a Census Designated Place and not an incorporated area.

Note: Because of sampling error, the estimates in this table may not be significantly different from one another or from rates for other geographic areas not listed in this table.

Source: U.S. Census Bureau, Census 2000 Summary File 3.

Texas; Pueblo, Colorado; and San Bernardino, California. Texas had two places among the bottom ten, giving it the distinction, with

Colorado, of making both the top-ten and bottom-ten lists. At least one place from every region was in the bottom ten.

Table 5.
Five States With the Highest Percentage of People 16 to 64 in the Armed Forces: 2000

(Data based on sample. For information on confidentiality protection, nonsampling error, sampling error, and definitions, see *www.census.gov/prod/cen2000/doc/sf3.pdf*)

| State | In armed forces | | Margin of error* |
	Number	Percent	
Hawaii	39,036	4.95	0.10
Alaska	17,111	4.05	0.12
Virginia	130,891	2.76	0.03
North Dakota	7,093	1.74	0.05
North Carolina	90,847	1.71	0.02

*When the margin of error is added to or substracted from the estimate, it produces a 90-percent confidence interval.

Note: Because of sampling error, the estimates in this table may not be significantly different from one another or from rates for other geographic areas not listed in this table.

Source: U.S. Census Bureau, Census 2000 Summary File 3.

Table 6.
Ten States With the Highest Number of People 16 to 64 in the Armed Forces: 2000

(Data based on sample. For information on confidentiality protection, nonsampling error, sampling error, and definitions, see *www.census.gov/prod/cen2000/doc/sf3.pdf*)

State	Population 16 to 64 years	Number in armed forces	Margin of error*
California	22,009,350	148,677	1,840
Virginia	4,739,413	130,891	1,538
Texas	13,549,906	106,591	1,437
North Carolina	5,320,796	90,847	1,102
Georgia	5,462,781	66,858	1,137
Florida	9,938,688	64,519	1,119
Washington	3,891,429	47,910	962
Hawaii	788,914	39,036	786
South Carolina	2,628,171	36,027	834
Maryland	3,487,938	32,166	789

*When the margin of error is added to or substracted from the estimate, it produces a 90-percent confidence interval.

Note: Because of sampling error, the estimates in this table may not be significantly different from one another or from rates for other geographic areas not listed in this table.

Source: U.S. Census Bureau, Census 2000 Summary File 3.

ADDITIONAL FINDINGS

Where are people on active duty in the U.S. Armed Forces concentrated?[20]

As part of its measurement of the labor force, Census 2000 counted the number of people on active duty in the U.S. Armed Forces (United States Army, Air Force, Navy, Marine Corps, or Coast Guard), who resided in the United States.[21] Tables 5, 6, and 7 display state data on the Armed Forces population.

Hawaii was the state with the largest percent of people in the armed forces, followed by Alaska (see Table 5). The Northeast was the only region that did not have a state represented in the top five states.

The states with the highest number of people in the armed forces were coastal states located in the South and the West (see Table 6). The states in the top ten ranged from California, with an estimated 148,677 people in the armed forces, to Maryland, with an estimated 32,166 people. Vermont and New Hampshire were the two states with the lowest number of

[20] This section refers to the population 16 to 64 years, because they are in the primary age range for serving in the armed forces.
[21] People in the military assigned to military installations outside the United States and crews of military vessels with a homeport outside the United States are not included in Armed Forces figures cited in this report. They are part of the U.S. overseas population and are not counted as part of the U.S. resident population.

people in the armed forces (fewer than an estimated 1,000 people, see Table 7).[22]

ABOUT CENSUS 2000

Why Census 2000 asked about employment status.

The questions on labor force participation are key to understanding work and unemployment patterns and the availability of workers. The Department of Labor identifies service delivery areas and determines amounts to be allocated for job training based on labor markets and unemployment levels. The impact of immigration on the economy and job markets is measured partially by labor force data, which is included in required reports to Congress. Under the Job Training Partnership Act, labor force data are used to allocate funds and identify programs that create new jobs in local areas with substantial unemployment. Also, areas with substantial unemployment are targeted for housing and community development projects under the Community Development Block Grant Program.

Accuracy of the Estimates

The data contained in this report are based on the sample of households who responded to the Census 2000 long form. Nationally, approximately 1 out of every 6 housing units was included in this sample. As a result, the sample estimates may differ somewhat from the 100-percent figures that would have been obtained if all housing units, people within those housing units, and people living in group quarters had been enumerated using the same questionnaires, instructions, enumerators, and so forth. The sample estimates also differ from the

___
[22] These numbers are not statistically different from each other.

Table 7.
Ten States With the Lowest Number of People 16 to 64 in the Armed Forces: 2000

(Data based on sample. For information on confidentiality protection, nonsampling error, sampling error, and definitions, see *www.census.gov/prod/cen2000/doc/sf3.pdf*)

State	Population 16 to 64 years	Number in armed forces	Margin of error*
Vermont	401,845	761	71
New Hampshire	812,459	819	95
West Virginia	1,178,275	1,650	149
Iowa	1,844,897	1,859	159
Oregon	2,235,895	2,340	178
Minnesota	3,188,341	2,594	187
Wisconsin	3,454,362	2,868	197
Indiana	3,930,832	3,006	242
District of Columbia	398,953	3,273	273
Wyoming	324,445	3,300	211

*When the margin of error is added to or substracted from the estimate, it produces a 90-percent confidence interval.

Note: Because of sampling error, the estimates in this table may not be significantly different from one another or from rates for other geographic areas not listed in this table.

Source: U.S. Census Bureau, Census 2000 Summary File 3.

values that would have been obtained from different samples of housing units, people within those housing units, and people living in group quarters. The deviation of a sample estimate from the average of all possible samples is called the sampling error.

In addition to the variability that arises from the sampling procedures, both sample data and 100-percent data are subject to nonsampling error. Nonsampling error may be introduced during any of the various complex operations used to collect and process data. Such errors may include: not enumerating every household or every person in the population, failing to obtain all required information from the respondents, obtaining incorrect or inconsistent information, and recording information incorrectly. In addition, errors can occur during the field review of the enumerators' work, during clerical handling of the census questionnaires, or during the electronic processing of the questionnaires.

Nonsampling error may affect the data in two ways: (1) errors that are

introduced randomly will increase the variability of the data and, therefore, should be reflected in the standard errors and (2) errors that tend to be consistent in one direction will bias both sample and 100-percent data in that direction. For example, if respondents consistently tend to underreport their incomes, then the resulting estimates of households or families by income category will tend to be understated for the higher income categories and overstated for the lower income categories. Such biases are not reflected in the standard errors.

While it is impossible to completely eliminate error from an operation as large and complex as the decennial census, the Census Bureau attempts to control the sources of such error during the data collection and processing operations. The primary sources of error and the programs instituted to control error in Census 2000 are described in detail in Summary File 3 Technical Documentation under Chapter 8, "Accuracy of the Data," located at *www.census.gov/prod/cen2000/doc/sf3.pdf.*

All statements in this Census 2000 brief have undergone statistical testing and all comparisons are significant at the 90-percent confidence level, unless otherwise noted. The estimates in tables, maps, and other figures may vary from actual values due to sampling and nonsampling errors. As a result, estimates in one category may not be significantly different from estimates assigned to a different category. Further information on the accuracy of the data is located at *www.census.gov/prod /cen2000/doc/sf3.pdf.* For further information on the computation and use of standard errors, contact the Decennial Statistical Studies Division at 301-763-4242.

For More Information

The Census 2000 Summary File 3 data are available from the *American Factfinder* on the Internet (*factfinder.census.gov*). They were released on a state-by-state basis during 2002. For information on confidentiality protection, nonsampling error, sampling error, and definitions, also see *www.census.gov/prod/cen2000 /doc/sf3.pdf* or contact the Customer Services Center at 301-763-INFO (4636).

Information on population and housing topics is presented in the Census 2000 brief series, located on the Census Bureau's Web site at *www.census.gov/population/www /cen2000/briefs.html.* This series, which will be completed in 2003, presents information on race, Hispanic origin, age, sex, household type, housing tenure, and social, economic, and housing characteristics, such as ancestry, income, and housing costs.

For additional information on employment status, including reports and survey data, visit the Census Bureau's Internet site at *www.census.gov/hhes/www /laborfor.html.* To find information about the availability of data products, including reports, CD-ROMs, and DVDs, call the Customer Services Center at 301-763-INFO (4636), or e-mail *webmaster@census.gov.*

Occupations: 2000

Census 2000 Brief

Issued August 2003

C2KBR-25

By
Peter Fronczek
and
Patricia Johnson

"What do you do for a living?" is a question frequently asked in contexts ranging from social conversation to scientific research. A person's occupation has often been a defining characteristic, so much so that many of today's surnames reflect the occupation of a long ago relative.

Census 2000 counted 281.4 million people in the United States on April 1, 2000, of whom 129.7 million were employed civilians aged 16 and over (Table 1).[1] The census classifies occupations at various levels, from the least-detailed summary level — six occupational groups — to the most detailed level — 509 occupation categories. This Census 2000 Sample Brief examines occupations of the employed civilian population 16 years old and older.

Census 2000 occupation classifications were based on the government-wide 2000 Standard Occupation Classification (SOC) system, whereas the 1990 census occupations were based on the 1980

Figure 1.

Reproduction of the Questions on Occupation from Census 2000

28 Occupation

a. What kind of work was this person doing?
(For example: registered nurse, personnel manager, supervisor of order department, auto mechanic, accountant)

b. What were this person's most important activities or duties? *(For example: patient care, directing hiring policies, supervising order clerks, repairing automobiles, reconciling financial records)*

Source: U.S. Census Bureau, Census 2000 questionnaire.

SOC. The SOC was overhauled in 1998 (with additional revisions in 2000) to create a classification system that more accurately reflected the occupational structure in the United States at the time of the revisions. As a result, comparisons of occupation data from the 1990 census and Census 2000 are not recommended and therefore are not attempted in this report.

At the least-detailed summary level, the highest proportion of civilian workers 16 and older, 33.6 percent, were in

[1] The text of this report discusses data for the United States, including the 50 states and the District of Columbia. Data for the Commonwealth of Puerto Rico are shown in Table 6 and Figure 3 only.

management, professional, and related occupations, followed by 26.7 percent in sales and office occupations.[2] The occupational group made up of farming, fishing, and forestry occupations had the lowest proportion of workers (0.7 percent).[3] The proportion of workers in the other summary level occupational groups were: service occupations, 14.9 percent; production, transportation, and material moving occupations, 14.6 percent; and construction, extraction, and maintenance occupations, 9.4 percent.

This report is part of a series that presents population and housing data collected by Census 2000, and highlights the occupations of American workers in 2000 for the United States, regions, states, metropolitan areas, and counties. Because of the importance of occupation data in understanding the economy and the changes taking place in society, the Census Bureau has asked questions on occupation in every decennial census since 1850. In Census 2000, two questions on occupation (Figure 1) were asked of everyone 15 or older (with responses tabulated for those 16 and older). The first question (28a) focused on the kind of work done, while the second (28b) asked about the duties of the job. Both questions allowed respondents to write a description of their occupation

and its duties. The descriptions provided in these two questions, along with the answers to the questions on type of industry and whether an occupation was with the government, a private for-profit organization, a nonprofit organization, or a family business enabled the Census Bureau to classify the responses into one of 509 occupation categories.

Differences still exist in the jobs held by men and women.

Despite the movement into nontraditional occupations, men and women still showed differences in the types of jobs they held in 2000. For example, 36.7 percent of women but only 17.9 percent of men worked in sales and office occupations. The proportions of men and women were also substantially different in construction, extraction, and maintenance occupations where 17.1 percent of men and only 0.7 percent of women were employed; production, transportation, and material moving occupations where 20.5 percent of men and 8.0 percent of women worked; and service occupations where 12.1 percent of men were employed compared with 18.0 percent of women.

Approximately 31.4 percent of all employed men 16 and older worked in management, professional, and related occupations. The next highest categories were production, transportation, and material moving occupations with 20.5 percent; sales and office occupations at 17.9 percent; and construction, extraction, and maintenance occupations with 17.1 percent. Only 1.1 percent of men were employed in farming, fishing, and forestry occupations.

More than one-third (36.7 percent) of women 16 and older worked in sales and office occupations in

2000, closely followed by management, professional, and related occupations (36.2 percent). The only other group employing more than 10 percent of women was service occupations, at 18.0 percent. Construction, extraction, and maintenance occupations and farming, fishing, and forestry occupations employed the lowest percentage of women at 0.7 percent and 0.3 percent, respectively.

Tables 2 and 3 present the ten occupations employing the most men and the most women, based on occupations at the most detailed level available from Census 2000 — 509 occupation categories. Once again differences appear in the type of jobs held by men and women 16 and older. Only one occupation, retail salespersons, appears on both lists.

The top occupations for men included drivers/sales workers and truck drivers; first-line supervisors/managers of retail sales workers; retail salespersons; laborers and freight, stock, and material movers; carpenters; and janitors and building cleaners. For women, the top occupations included secretaries and administrative assistants; elementary and middle school teachers; registered nurses; cashiers; and retail salespersons.

The diversity of the ten most popular occupations was greater for men than for women. For men, five of the six major occupational groups are represented on their top ten list with only farming, fishing, and forestry occupations not included. In contrast, only three of the six major occupational groups are represented on the women's list of the ten most popular occupations: management, professional, and related occupations; service occupations; and sales and related occupations.

---

[2] The estimates in this report are based on responses from a sample of the population. As with all surveys, estimates may vary from the actual values because of sampling variation or other factors. All statements in this report have undergone statistical testing and are significant at the 90-percent confidence level unless otherwise noted.

[3] This surprisingly low percentage requires further explanation. Prior to the overhaul of the SOC, farm and ranch owners and renters were classified in the farming, fishing, and forestry occupations group. After the reclassification, they were put into the management, professional, and related occupations group.

Table 1.
Selected Occupational Groups and Subgroups by Sex for the United States: 2000

(Data based on a sample. For information on confidentiality protection, sampling error, nonsampling error, and definitions, see www.census.gov/prod/cen2000/doc/sf3.pdf)

Occupational groups and subgroups	Total		Men		Women	
	Number	Percent	Number	Percent	Number	Percent
Total population	281,421,906	–	137,916,186	–	143,505,720	–
Employed civilian population 16 years and over	129,721,512	100.0	69,091,443	100.0	60,630,069	100.0
Management, professional, and related occupations ...	43,646,731	33.6	21,708,758	31.4	21,937,973	36.2
Management, business, and financial operations occupations	17,448,038	13.5	10,131,223	14.7	7,316,815	12.1
Management occupations, except farmers and farm managers	11,115,046	8.6	6,910,883	10.0	4,204,163	6.9
Farmers and farm managers	773,218	0.6	661,288	1.0	111,930	0.2
Business and financial operations occupations	5,559,774	4.3	2,559,052	3.7	3,000,722	4.9
Business operations specialists	2,718,121	2.1	1,248,755	1.8	1,469,366	2.4
Financial specialists	2,841,653	2.2	1,310,297	1.9	1,531,356	2.5
Professional and related occupations	26,198,693	20.2	11,577,535	16.8	14,621,158	24.1
Computer and mathematical occupations	3,168,447	2.4	2,218,400	3.2	950,047	1.6
Architecture and engineering occupations	2,659,298	2.1	2,301,953	3.3	357,345	0.6
Architects, surveyors, cartographers, and engineers .	1,926,689	1.5	1,702,234	2.5	224,455	0.4
Drafters, engineering, and mapping technicians	732,609	0.6	599,719	0.9	132,890	0.2
Life, physical, and social science occupations	1,203,443	0.9	709,392	1.0	494,051	0.8
Community and social services occupations	1,953,184	1.5	787,587	1.1	1,165,597	1.9
Legal occupations	1,412,737	1.1	747,170	1.1	665,567	1.1
Education, training, and library occupations	7,337,276	5.7	1,930,948	2.8	5,406,328	8.9
Arts, design, entertainment, sports, and media occupations	2,484,201	1.9	1,302,419	1.9	1,181,782	1.9
Healthcare practitioners and technical occupations ...	5,980,107	4.6	1,579,666	2.3	4,400,441	7.3
Health diagnosing and treating practitioners and technical occupations	4,144,065	3.2	1,210,571	1.8	2,933,494	4.8
Health technologists and technicians	1,836,042	1.4	369,095	0.5	1,466,947	2.4
Service occupations	19,276,947	14.9	8,346,408	12.1	10,930,539	18.0
Healthcare support occupations	2,592,815	2.0	305,247	0.4	2,287,568	3.8
Protective service occupations	2,549,906	2.0	2,041,698	3.0	508,208	0.8
Fire fighting, prevention, and law enforcement workers, including supervisors	1,536,287	1.2	1,300,671	1.9	235,616	0.4
Other protective service workers, including supervisors	1,013,619	0.8	741,027	1.1	272,592	0.4
Food preparation and serving related occupations	6,251,618	4.8	2,663,418	3.9	3,588,200	5.9
Building and grounds cleaning and maintenance occupations	4,254,365	3.3	2,565,933	3.7	1,688,432	2.8
Personal care and service occupations	3,628,243	2.8	770,112	1.1	2,858,131	4.7
Sales and office occupations	34,621,390	26.7	12,341,968	17.9	22,279,422	36.7
Sales and related occupations	14,592,699	11.2	7,364,006	10.7	7,228,693	11.9
Office and administrative support occupations	20,028,691	15.4	4,977,962	7.2	15,050,729	24.8
Farming, fishing, and forestry occupations	951,810	0.7	750,915	1.1	200,895	0.3
Construction, extraction, and maintenance occupations	12,256,138	9.4	11,802,699	17.1	453,439	0.7
Construction and extraction occupations	7,149,269	5.5	6,937,857	10.0	211,412	0.3
Supervisors, construction and extraction workers	911,013	0.7	886,001	1.3	25,012	0.0
Construction trades workers	6,116,087	4.7	5,933,117	8.6	182,970	0.3
Extraction workers	122,169	0.1	118,739	0.2	3,430	0.0
Installation, maintenance, and repair occupations	5,106,869	3.9	4,864,842	7.0	242,027	0.4
Production, transportation, and material moving occupations	18,968,496	14.6	14,140,695	20.5	4,827,801	8.0
Production occupations	11,008,625	8.5	7,437,071	10.8	3,571,554	5.9
Transportation and material moving occupations	7,959,871	6.1	6,703,624	9.7	1,256,247	2.1
Supervisors, transportation and material moving workers	237,902	0.2	193,527	0.3	44,375	0.1
Aircraft and traffic control occupations	158,481	0.1	147,143	0.2	11,338	0.0
Motor vehicle operators	3,852,820	3.0	3,394,798	4.9	458,022	0.8
Rail, water and other transportation occupations	400,826	0.3	352,303	0.5	48,523	0.1
Material moving workers	3,309,842	2.6	2,615,853	3.8	693,989	1.1

– Not applicable.

Source: U.S. Census Bureau, Census 2000, Summary File 3.

501

Management, professional, and related occupations paid the most to both men and women.

At the least-detailed summary level (six occupational groups) for employed civilian men and women 16 and older, management, professional, and related occupations paid the most. The median 1999 earnings[4] in these occupations were $50,034 for men and $35,654 for women (Figure 2 and Table 4). The second highest paying occupational group for men, with a median of $35,079, was sales and office occupations; followed by construction, extraction, and maintenance occupations at $32,000; production, transportation, and material moving occupations at $30,992; and service occupations at $26,000. The lowest paying occupational group for men was farming, fishing, and forestry occupations, with a median of only $20,000 in 1999 earnings.

The second highest paying occupational group for women was construction, extraction, and maintenance occupations, where the median earnings were $29,000. This category was followed by sales and office occupations at $24,497; production, transportation, and material moving occupations at $20,850; and service occupations at $17,805. As with men, the lowest paying occupational group for women was farming, fishing, and forestry occupations, with a median earnings of only $15,996.

Women earned less than men in all occupations, but construction, extraction, and maintenance occupations was closest to parity.

In each of the summary level occupational groups, men earned more than women as measured by median earnings in 1999. The occupational group closest to parity was the traditional "blue collar" group, represented by construction, extraction, and maintenance occupations, where women earned 90.6 percent of men's earnings (Table 4). In farming, fishing, and forestry occupations, women earned 80.0 percent of their male counterparts' pay. However, both these occupational groups employed very few women in 2000. Of all employed civilians 16 and older employed in construction, extraction, and maintenance

[4] Earnings is calculated for year-round, full-time workers, defined as employed civilians 16 years and older who worked 50 weeks or more in 1999 and usually 35 hours or more a week.

Table 2.
The Ten Occupations[1] Employing the Most Men for the United States: 2000

(Data based on a sample. For information on confidentiality protection, sampling error, nonsampling error, and definitions, see www.census.gov/prod/cen2000/doc/sf3.pdf)

Occupations	Number	Percent
Employed civilian males 16 years and over......	69,091,443	100.0
Driver/sales workers and truck drivers	2,925,936	4.2
First-line supervisors/managers of retail sales workers...	1,606,310	2.3
Retail salespersons	1,605,860	2.3
Laborers and freight, stock, and material movers, hand..	1,448,035	2.1
Carpenters	1,317,690	1.9
Janitors and building cleaners	1,308,889	1.9
Managers, all other.....................................	1,253,965	1.8
Construction laborers...................................	1,066,404	1.5
Sales representatives, wholesale and manufacturing	1,026,745	1.5
First-line supervisors/managers of production and operating workers...................................	1,008,876	1.5

[1]Based on the most detailed level of occupations available in Census 2000 – 509 occupations.

Note: Confidence intervals are not displayed because they round to the percentages shown in the table.

Source: U.S. Census Bureau, Census 2000, Sample Edited Detail File.

Table 3.
The Ten Occupations[1] Employing the Most Women for the United States: 2000

(Data based on a sample. For information on confidentiality protection, sampling error, nonsampling error, and definitions, see www.census.gov/prod/cen2000/doc/sf3.pdf)

Occupations	Number	Percent
Employed civilian females 16 years and over	60,630,069	100.0
Secretaries and administrative assistants	3,597,535	5.9
Elementary and middle school teachers...............	2,442,104	4.0
Registered nurses....................................	2,065,238	3.4
Cashiers..	2,030,805	3.3
Retail salespersons	1,775,889	2.9
Bookkeeping, accounting, and auditing clerks	1,526,803	2.5
Nursing, psychiatric, and home health aides............	1,469,736	2.4
Customer service representatives.....................	1,396,105	2.3
Child care workers	1,253,306	2.1
Waiters and waitresses	1,228,977	2.0

[1]Based on the most detailed level of occupations available in Census 2000 – 509 occupations.

Note: Confidence intervals are not displayed because they round to the percentages shown in the table.

Source: U.S. Census Bureau, Census 2000, Sample Edited Detail File.

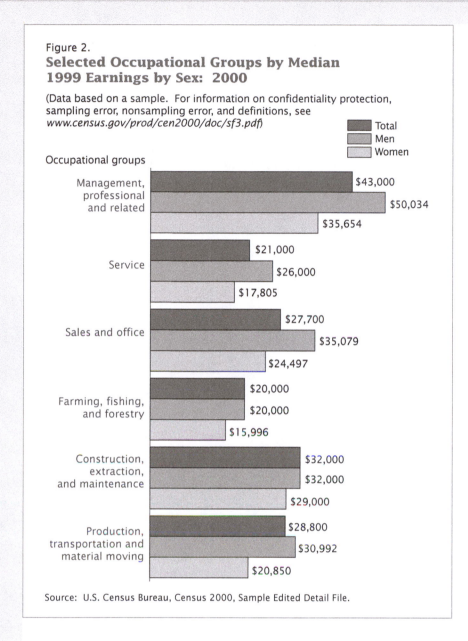

Figure 2.
Selected Occupational Groups by Median 1999 Earnings by Sex: 2000

(Data based on a sample. For information on confidentiality protection, sampling error, nonsampling error, and definitions, see *www.census.gov/prod/cen2000/doc/sf3.pdf*)

Total
Men
Women

Occupational groups

Management, professional and related
$43,000
$50,034
$35,654

Service
$21,000
$26,000
$17,805

Sales and office
$27,700
$35,079
$24,497

Farming, fishing, and forestry
$20,000
$20,000
$15,996

Construction, extraction, and maintenance
$32,000
$32,000
$29,000

Production, transportation and material moving
$28,800
$30,992
$20,850

Source: U.S. Census Bureau, Census 2000, Sample Edited Detail File.

occupations in 2000, 96.3 percent were men and only 3.7 percent were women, representing about 0.7 percent of all employed women. Similarly, only about 0.3 percent of employed women were in farming, fishing, and forestry occupations. In the occupational groups employing the most women — sales and office occupations and management, professional, and related occupations — women earned 69.8 percent and 71.3 percent compared with their male colleagues, respectively.

The occupational group where women earned the least compared to men was production, transportation, and material moving occupations, where the median earnings for women were only 67.3 percent of men's earnings.

Asians and non-Hispanic Whites (who reported no other race) were more often in management, professional, and related occupations than people reporting other races.

Census 2000 allowed respondents to choose more than one race. With the exception of the Two or more races group, all race groups discussed in this report refer to people who indicated *only one* racial identity among the six major categories:

Table 4.
Median 1999 Earnings of Men and Women and Women's Earnings as a Percentage of Men's Earnings by Selected Occupation Groups for the United States: 2000

(Data based on a sample. For information on confidentiality protection, sampling error, nonsampling error, and definitions, see www.census.gov/prod/cen2000/doc/sf3.pdf)

Occupational groups	Men	Women	
	Median earnings	Median earnings	Percent of men's earnings
Management, professional, and related occupations..............	$50,034	$35,654	71.3
Service occupations	$26,000	$17,805	68.5
Sales and office occupations	$35,079	$24,497	69.8
Farming, fishing, and forestry occupations.....................	$20,000	$15,996	80.0
Construction, extraction, and maintenance occupations	$32,000	$29,000	90.6
Production, transportation, and material moving occupations	$30,992	$20,850	67.3

Note: Confidence intervals are not displayed because they round to the percentages shown in the table.

Source: U.S. Census Bureau, Census 2000, Sample Edited Detail File.

Table 5.
Selected Occupational Groups by Race and Hispanic Origin for the United States: 2000

(Data based on a sample. For information on confidentiality protection, sampling error, nonsampling error, and definitions, see www.census.gov/prod/cen2000/doc/sf3.pdf)

Race and Hispanic or Latino Origin	Occupational groups						
	Employed civilian population 16 years and over	Management, professional, and related occupations	Service	Sales and office	Farming, fishing, and forestry	Construction, extraction, and main-tenance	Production, transportation, and material moving
Total.............................	129,721,512	33.6	14.9	26.7	0.7	9.4	14.6
White alone..........................	102,324,962	35.6	13.4	27.0	0.6	9.8	13.6
Black or African American alone..........	13,001,795	25.2	22.0	27.3	0.4	6.5	18.6
American Indian and Alaska Native alone .	914,484	24.3	20.6	24.0	1.3	12.9	16.8
Asian alone..........................	4,786,782	44.6	14.1	24.0	0.3	3.6	13.4
Native Hawaiian and Other Pacific Islander alone........................	157,119	23.3	20.8	28.8	0.9	9.6	16.5
Some other race	5,886,427	14.2	22.7	21.7	3.5	14.0	24.0
Two or more races	2,649,943	26.7	19.8	27.1	0.9	9.8	15.7
Hispanic or Latino (of any race)..........	13,347,876	18.1	21.8	23.1	2.7	13.1	21.2
White alone, not Hispanic or Latino	95,834,018	36.6	12.8	27.2	0.5	9.6	13.2

U.S. Census Bureau, Census 2000, Sample Edited Detail File.

White, Black or African American, American Indian and Alaska Native, Asian, Native Hawaiian or Other Pacific Islander, and Some other race.[5] The use of the single-race population in this report does not imply that it is the preferred method of presenting or analyzing data. The Census Bureau uses a variety of approaches.[6]

The percentage of workers employed in management, professional, and related occupations was higher (44.6 percent) for Asians (who reported no other race) than for people reporting any other race group shown in Table 5. Non-Hispanic Whites (who reported no other race) had the second highest percentage of workers in this occupational group (36.6 percent), followed by people who reported Black or African American only (25.2 percent), American Indian and Alaska Native only (24.3 percent), and Native Hawaiian and Other Pacific Islander only (23.3 percent).[7][8] About 18.1 percent of Hispanics were employed in management, professional, and related occupations.

Blacks (who reported no other race) were prominent in production, transportation, and material moving occupations.

About 18.6 percent of Black workers (who reported no other race) were employed in production, transportation, and material moving occupations. This percentage was higher than for people reporting any other race group except Some other race only (24.0 percent), a residual category used in the census to classify individuals who did not identify themselves as being in one of the other race groups. Approximately one-fifth (21.2 percent) of Hispanics were employed in production, transportation, and material moving occupations. In contrast, only 13.2 percent of non-Hispanic Whites were in this group.

---

[5] For further information on each of the six major race groups and the Two or more races population, see reports from the Census 2000 Brief series (C2KBR/01), available on the Census 2000 Web site at *www.census.gov/population/www/cen2000/briefs.html*

[6] This report draws heavily on Summary File 3, a Census 2000 product that can be accessed through American FactFinder, available from the Census Bureau's Web site, *www.census.gov*. Information on people who reported more than one race, such as "White *and* American Indian and Alaska Native" or "Asian *and* Black or African American" is forthcoming in Summary File 4, which will also be available through American FactFinder in 2003. About 2.6 percent of people reported more than one race.

[7] Hereafter this report uses the term Black to refer to people who are Black or African American, the term Pacific Islander to refer to people who are Native Hawaiian and Other Pacific Islander, and the term Hispanic to refer to people who are Hispanic or Latino.
Because Hispanics may be of any race, data in this report for Hispanics overlap with data for racial groups. Based on Census 2000 sample data, the proportion Hispanic was 8.0 percent for Whites, 1.9 percent for Blacks, 14.6 percent for American Indians and Alaska Natives, 1.0 percent for Asians, 9.5 percent for Pacific Islanders, 97.1 percent for those reporting Some other race, and 31.1 percent for those reporting Two or more races.

[8] The difference between American Indian and Alaska Natives and Native Hawaiian and Other Pacific Islanders was not statistically significant.

Blacks were also well represented in sales and office occupations, where 27.3 percent were employed in 2000. This was second only to Pacific Islanders at 28.8 percent, and about the same as non-Hispanic Whites at 27.2 percent. Sales and office occupations employed 23.1 percent of Hispanic workers.

Hispanics led in farming, fishing, and forestry occupations.

Although the percentage of people working in farming, fishing, and forestry occupations was much smaller than in the other summary level occupational groups, the percentage of each race and ethnic group in this category is interesting. These occupations claimed a higher percentage of Hispanic workers, 2.7 percent, than any of the race groups examined in this brief (except the residual Some other race category, which had 3.5 percent). This percentage was about double that of American Indians and Alaska Natives, 1.3 percent; and was far higher than the percentage of Pacific Islanders, 0.9 percent; non-Hispanic Whites, 0.5 percent; Blacks, 0.4 percent; and Asians 0.3 percent.

THE GEOGRAPHIC DISTRIBUTION OF OCCUPATIONS

The following discussion focuses on the employed civilian population 16 and over.

The four regions did not differ greatly in the distribution of occupations.

Table 6 shows occupational groups for the four census regions, the 50 states, and the District of

Columbia.[9] In each region the pattern was similar: the highest percentages of workers were in management, professional and related occupations, followed by sales and office occupations. Construction, extraction, and maintenance occupations and farming, fishing, and forestry occupations had the lowest percentage of workers. The only regional differences involved service occupations and production, transportation and material moving occupations. The percentage of workers in service occupations in the Northeast and West was higher than the percentage for production, transportation and material moving occupations, while in the Midwest and the South, the opposite was true.

The District of Columbia had the highest percentage of workers in management, professional, and related occupations.

Over half (51.1 percent) the workers in the District of Columbia were in management, professional, and related occupations in 2000, followed at some distance behind by the state of Maryland, where 41.3 percent of workers were in that occupational group. These

___

[9] The Northeast region includes the states of Connecticut, Maine, Massachusetts, New Hampshire, New Jersey, New York, Pennsylvania, Rhode Island, and Vermont. The Midwest region includes the states of Illinois, Indiana, Iowa, Kansas, Michigan, Minnesota, Missouri, Nebraska, North Dakota, Ohio, South Dakota, and Wisconsin. The South region includes the states of Alabama, Arkansas, Delaware, Florida, Georgia, Kentucky, Louisiana, Maryland, Mississippi, North Carolina, Oklahoma, South Carolina, Tennessee, Texas, Virginia, West Virginia, and the District of Columbia, a state equivalent. The West region includes the states of Alaska, Arizona, California, Colorado, Hawaii, Idaho, Montana, Nevada, New Mexico, Oregon, Utah, Washington, and Wyoming.

high percentages in the District of Columbia and Maryland likely reflect the large presence of federal workers and related support occupations in those areas. Another state with a high percentage of workers in management, professional, and related occupations was Massachusetts (41.1 percent).[10] The state with the lowest percentage of workers in this occupational group was Nevada with 25.7 percent.

Nevada and Hawaii, two states that cater to vacation and recreation travelers, led all states in the percentage of workers employed in service occupations with 24.6 percent and 20.9 percent, respectively. New Hampshire, with only 13.0 percent, had the lowest proportion of workers in this occupational group.

The range between the states with the highest and the lowest percentage values was smaller for sales and office occupations than for any other occupational group.[11] Florida led in sales and office occupations, with 29.5 percent of workers employed in this area. Only 22.8 percent of the workers in the District of Columbia were employed in these occupations.

Seven out of the ten states with the highest percentage of workers in production, transportation, and material moving occupations were in the South, although the state with the highest percentage was Indiana (21.4 percent) in the Midwest. The seven southern

___

[10] The difference between Maryland and Massachusetts was not statistically significant.

[11] Except for the farming, fishing, and forestry occupational group, which had so few workers that it is not included.

Table 6.
Selected Occupational Groups as a Percentage of the Employed Civilian Population 16 Years and Over for the United States, Regions, States, and for Puerto Rico: 2000

(Data based on a sample. For information on confidentiality protection, sampling error, nonsampling error, and definitions, see www.census.gov/prod/cen2000/doc/sf3.pdf)

Area	Occupational groups					
	Employed civilian population 16 years and over	Management, professional, and related occupations	Service	Sales and office	Farming, fishing, and forestry	Construction, extraction, and maintenance	Production, transportation, and material moving
United States	129,721,512	33.6	14.9	26.7	0.7	9.4	14.6
Region							
Northeast	24,904,791	36.5	15.1	27.0	0.4	8.0	13.0
Midwest.	31,185,231	32.1	14.4	26.3	0.6	9.0	17.6
South	45,226,189	32.4	14.7	26.7	0.7	10.6	14.9
West	28,405,301	34.8	15.4	26.8	1.2	9.4	12.3
State							
Alabama	1,920,189	29.5	13.5	25.9	0.8	11.3	19.0
Alaska.	281,532	34.4	15.6	26.1	1.5	11.6	10.8
Arizona	2,233,004	32.7	16.2	28.5	0.6	11.0	10.9
Arkansas.	1,173,399	27.7	14.1	25.1	1.5	10.6	21.0
California.	14,718,928	36.0	14.8	26.8	1.3	8.4	12.7
Colorado	2,205,194	37.4	13.9	27.2	0.6	10.5	10.5
Connecticut.	1,664,440	39.1	14.3	26.5	0.2	8.0	12.0
Delaware.	376,811	35.3	14.6	27.6	0.5	9.5	12.5
District of Columbia.	263,108	51.1	16.1	22.8	0.1	4.8	5.2
Florida.	6,995,047	31.5	16.9	29.5	0.9	10.3	10.8
Georgia.	3,839,756	32.7	13.4	26.8	0.6	10.8	15.7
Hawaii	537,909	32.2	20.9	28.1	1.3	8.6	8.9
Idaho.	599,453	31.4	15.6	25.3	2.7	10.8	14.2
Illinois	5,833,185	34.2	13.9	27.6	0.3	8.2	15.7
Indiana	2,965,174	28.7	14.2	25.3	0.4	10.0	21.4
Iowa	1,489,816	31.3	14.8	25.9	1.1	8.9	18.1
Kansas	1,316,283	33.9	14.4	25.8	1.0	9.9	15.0
Kentucky.	1,798,264	28.7	14.3	25.4	0.9	11.0	19.7
Louisiana.	1,851,777	29.9	16.7	26.8	0.8	11.7	14.1
Maine	624,011	31.5	15.3	25.9	1.7	10.3	15.3
Maryland.	2,608,457	41.3	13.9	26.4	0.3	8.6	9.5
Massachusetts	3,161,087	41.1	14.1	25.9	0.2	7.5	11.3
Michigan	4,637,461	31.5	14.8	25.6	0.5	9.2	18.5
Minnesota	2,580,046	35.8	13.7	26.5	0.7	8.4	14.9
Mississippi.	1,173,314	27.4	14.9	24.9	1.2	11.2	20.4
Missouri.	2,657,924	31.5	15.0	26.9	0.6	9.8	16.3
Montana	425,977	33.1	17.2	25.5	2.2	10.7	11.2
Nebraska.	877,237	33.0	14.6	26.4	1.6	9.3	15.1
Nevada	933,280	25.7	24.6	27.6	0.3	11.4	10.4
New Hampshire.	650,871	35.8	13.0	26.6	0.4	9.4	14.8
New Jersey	3,950,029	38.0	13.6	28.5	0.2	7.8	12.0
New Mexico	763,116	34.0	17.0	25.9	1.0	11.4	10.7
New York.	8,382,988	36.7	16.6	27.1	0.3	7.6	11.7
North Carolina.	3,824,741	31.2	13.5	24.8	0.8	11.0	18.7
North Dakota.	316,632	33.3	16.7	26.1	1.7	9.8	12.4
Ohio	5,402,175	31.0	14.6	26.4	0.3	8.7	19.0
Oklahoma	1,545,296	30.3	15.5	26.6	0.9	11.3	15.4
Oregon	1,627,769	33.1	15.3	26.1	1.7	9.1	14.7
Pennsylvania.	5,653,500	32.6	14.8	27.0	0.5	8.9	16.3
Rhode Island.	500,731	33.9	15.7	27.1	0.3	7.7	15.2
South Carolina.	1,824,700	29.1	14.7	25.2	0.6	11.5	19.0
South Dakota	374,373	32.6	15.6	26.5	1.9	9.1	14.2
Tennessee.	2,651,638	29.5	13.7	26.1	0.6	10.3	19.9
Texas	9,234,372	33.3	14.6	27.2	0.7	10.9	13.2
Utah	1,044,362	32.5	14.0	28.9	0.5	10.6	13.5
Vermont.	317,134	36.3	14.6	24.5	1.3	9.3	14.0
Virginia	3,412,647	38.2	13.7	25.5	0.5	9.6	12.5
Washington	2,793,722	35.6	14.9	25.9	1.6	9.4	12.7
West Virginia.	732,673	27.9	16.6	26.1	0.7	12.3	16.4
Wisconsin	2,734,925	31.3	14.0	25.2	0.9	8.7	19.8
Wyoming	241,055	30.0	16.7	24.2	1.5	14.8	12.8
Puerto Rico	**930,865**	**27.4**	**16.2**	**28.0**	**1.1**	**12.1**	**15.2**

Source: U.S. Census Bureau, Census 2000, Summary File 3.

states were Arkansas, Mississippi, Tennessee, Kentucky, Alabama, South Carolina, and North Carolina. The District of Columbia with 5.2 percent had the lowest percentage of production, transportation and material moving workers.

Wyoming (14.8 percent) had the highest percentage of workers in the traditional "blue collar" occupational group: construction, extraction, and maintenance occupations, followed by West Virginia at 12.3 percent. Once again, the District of Columbia had the lowest percentage of workers in this occupational group (4.8 percent). Five of the next six states with the lowest percentage were Massachusetts, New York, Rhode Island, New Jersey, and Connecticut, all in the Northeast.

Sales and office occupations were predominant in more counties than any other occupational group.

Figure 3, a graphical representation of occupations throughout the United States and Puerto Rico, shows which of the least detailed summary-level occupational groups[12] employed the most civilian workers 16 and over in each state and county in the country.

At the county level, sales and office occupations (yellow) were the primary occupational group in more

counties than any other group and every state had at least one county where this group was primary. This occupational group was most predominant in the Northeast and the West and less so in the Midwest and parts of the South.

Production, transportation and material moving occupations (brown) tended to be popular in nonmetropolitan counties in the Midwest and the South, particularly in Indiana, Ohio, Tennessee, and Arkansas. Service occupations (red) were the primary group in a small number of widely scattered counties throughout the United States. Interestingly, several of these counties were in the upper Midwest along or near the border with Canada, and in Texas and New Mexico along or near the border with Mexico, suggesting that considerable employment in these counties was in services related to our nearest neighbors.

Figure 3 also shows that professional and related occupations (purple) were predominant in several isolated counties or small groups of counties throughout the United States, many where universities or colleges are located. Examples are Dane County, Wisconsin (University of Wisconsin), Tippecanoe and Monroe Counties, Indiana (Purdue and Indiana University), and Centre County, Pennsylvania (Pennsylvania State University).

A second interesting pattern from Figure 3 appears with management, business, and financial operations occupations (blue). That this group would predominate in several rural and sparsely populated counties in states such as Montana, the Dakotas, and Nebraska might seem odd, but the pattern becomes more understandable given the overhaul

of the Standard Occupation Classification system in 1998 that moved farm and ranch owners to this group (see footnote 3).

The Washington-Baltimore and San Francisco-Oakland-San Jose metropolitan areas led in management, professional, and related occupations.

Among the ten metropolitan areas with the highest percentage of their workers in management, professional, and related occupations in 2000, two — Washington-Baltimore, DC-MD-VA-WV, and San Francisco-Oakland-San Jose, CA, — had more than 3 million employed civilians 16 and over. (Table 7).[13] Six of the remaining eight were "college towns": Corvallis, OR; Charlottesville, VA; Raleigh-Durham-Chapel Hill, NC; Madison, WI; Gainsville, FL; and Iowa City, IA.

About 26.7 percent of the workers in the Las Vegas, NV, metropolitan area were employed in service occupations in 2000, the highest percentage for any metropolitan area in the country. Several of the ten metropolitan areas shown in Table 7 with high percentages of service occupation workers cater to tourists and vacationers. These include not only Las Vegas, but also the Punta Gorda, Naples, and Panama City, FL; Reno, NV; Myrtle Beach, SC; and Honolulu, HI metropolitan areas.

Three metropolitan areas in Florida, Jacksonville, Tampa-St. Petersburg-Clearwater, and Miami-Fort Lauderdale, were among the ten with the highest percentage of sales and office occupation workers. Each of the metropolitan

---

[12] The highest level or least detailed summary level comprises six occupational groups: management, professional, and related occupations; service occupations; sales and office occupations; farming, fishing, and forestry occupations; construction, extraction, and maintenance occupations; and production, transportation, and material moving occupations. However, Figure 3 shows seven groups. The management, professional, and related occupations group was split into two sub-groups: management, business, and financial operations occupations and professional and related occupations. This was done to present a more representative picture.

[13] Because of sampling error, the estimates for the metropolitan areas shown in Table 7 may not be significantly different from one another or from metropolitan areas not shown.

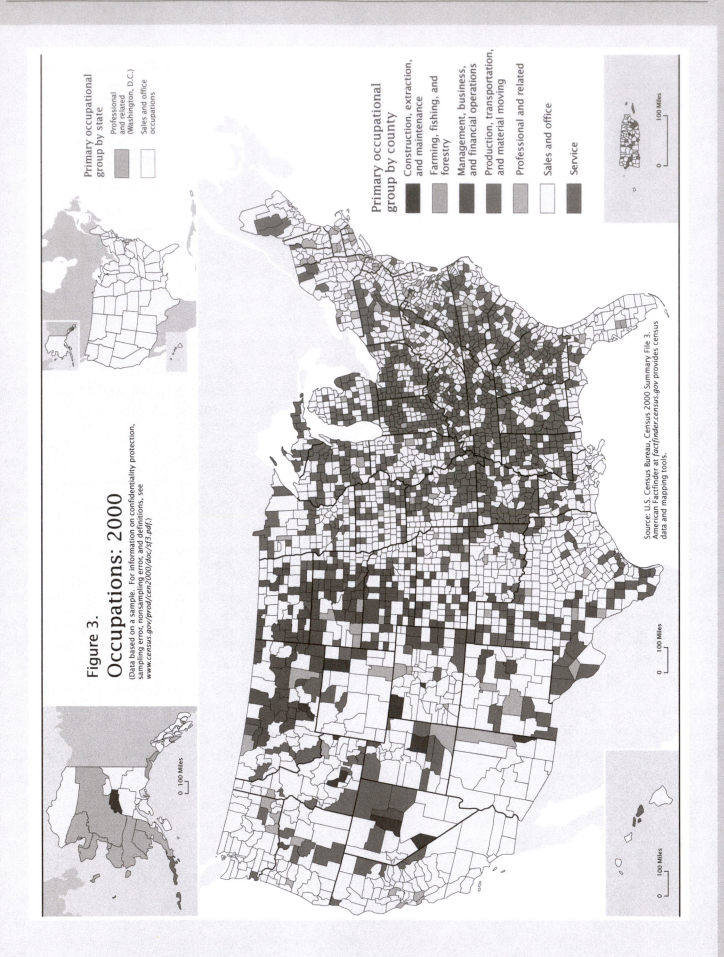

Figure 3.
Occupations: 2000

(Data based on a sample. For information on confidentiality protection, sampling error, nonsampling error, and definitions, see *www.census.gov/prod/cen2000/doc/sf3.pdf*.)

Primary occupational group by state

Professional and related (Washington, D.C.)

Sales and office occupations

Primary occupational group by county

Construction, extraction, and maintenance

Farming, fishing, and forestry

Management, business, and financial operations

Production, transportation, and material moving

Professional and related

Sales and office

Service

Source: U.S. Census Bureau, Census 2000 Summary File 3. American Factfinder at *factfinder.census.gov* provides census data and mapping tools.

0   100 Miles

0   100 Miles

0   100 Miles

0   100 Miles

Table 7.
Ten Metropolitan Areas With the Highest Percentage of Civilians Employed in Selected Occupational Groups: 2000[1]

(Data based on a sample. For information on confidentiality protection, sampling error, nonsampling error, and definitions, see www.census.gov/prod/cen2000/doc/sf3.pdf)

Metropolitan areas	Total employed civilian population 16 years and over in area	Percent in occupation group	90-percent confidence interval
Management, professional, and related occupations			
Corvallis, OR	38,356	46.9	45.7 - 48.1
Washington-Baltimore, DC-MD-VA-WV	3,843,329	45.4	45.3 - 45.5
Charlottesville, VA	78,424	45.4	44.6 - 46.3
Santa Fe, NM	74,586	45.2	44.3 - 46.1
Rochester, MN	66,973	44.5	43.7 - 45.3
Raleigh-Durham-Chapel Hill, NC	627,772	44.3	44.1 - 44.6
Gainesville, FL	105,293	44.0	43.3 - 44.7
Madison, WI	246,064	43.6	43.2 - 44.0
San Francisco-Oakland-San Jose, CA	3,495,883	43.6	43.5 - 43.7
Iowa City, IA	64,255	43.3	42.5 - 44.1
Service occupations			
Las Vegas, NV-AZ	710,179	26.7	26.5 - 27.0
Punta Gorda, FL	50,690	20.9	20.0 - 21.8
Biloxi-Gulfport-Pascagoula, MS	155,970	20.1	19.6 - 20.6
Myrtle Beach, SC	97,577	20.1	19.5 - 20.7
New London-Norwich, CT-RI	141,736	20.0	19.5 - 20.5
Naples, FL	105,436	19.9	19.3 - 20.5
Reno, NV	171,723	19.9	19.4 - 20.4
Brownsville-Harlingen-San Benito, TX	108,904	19.8	19.2 - 20.4
Panama City, FL	64,883	19.7	19.0 - 20.5
Honolulu, HI	383,148	19.6	19.3 - 19.9
Sales and office occupations			
Sioux Falls, SD	96,177	32.2	31.6 - 32.8
Jacksonville, FL	519,840	31.4	31.1 - 31.7
Tampa-St. Petersburg-Clearwater, FL	1,079,627	31.1	30.9 - 31.3
Miami-Fort Lauderdale, FL	1,680,147	31.0	30.9 - 31.3
Billings, MT	65,512	30.8	30.1 - 31.5
Salt Lake City-Ogden, UT	648,104	30.8	30.5 - 31.1
Des Moines, IA	244,649	30.6	30.2 - 31.1
Roanoke, VA	116,592	30.3	29.7 - 30.9
Charleston, WV	112,867	30.1	29.6 - 30.7
Omaha, NE-IA	368,142	30.1	29.8 - 30.4
Construction, extraction, and maintenance occupations			
Houma, LA	78,613	14.3	13.8 - 14.9
Jacksonville, NC	49,020	14.1	13.4 - 14.9
Lake Charles, LA	79,408	13.9	13.4 - 14.4
Fort Myers-Cape Coral, FL	186,417	13.5	13.1 - 13.9
Casper, WY	33,213	13.5	12.7 - 14.3
Beaumont-Port Arthur, TX	155,964	13.4	13.1 - 13.8
Victoria, TX	38,464	13.4	12.6 - 14.2
Myrtle Beach, SC	97,577	13.3	12.8 - 13.8
Biloxi-Gulfport-Pascagoula, MS	155,970	13.2	12.8 - 13.6
Wilmington, NC	113,593	13.1	12.7 - 13.5
Production, transportation, and material moving occupations			
Hickory-Morganton-Lenoir, NC	176,415	34.3	33.8 - 34.8
Elkhart-Goshen, IN	93,074	32.7	32.0 - 33.4
Sheboygan, WI	59,454	29.8	29.0 - 30.6
Danville, VA	49,261	28.7	27.9 - 29.5
Mansfield, OH	79,992	27.7	27.1 - 28.3
Kokomo, IN	47,717	26.8	26.0 - 27.6
Janesville-Beloit, WI	76,336	26.8	26.2 - 27.5
Lima, OH	71,550	26.3	25.6 - 27.0
Decatur, AL	65,388	25.6	24.9 - 26.3
Fort Smith, AR-OK	92,135	25.4	24.8 - 26.0

[1]Farming, fishing, and forestry occupations are not shown in this table because of the small number of employed people in this group.

Note: Because of sampling error, the estimates in this table may not be significantly different from one another or from rates for other geographic areas not listed in this table.

Source: U.S. Census Bureau, Census 2000, Summary File 3.

Table 8.
Occupational Groups by Industry Groups for the United States: 2000

(Data based on a sample. For information on confidentiality protection, sampling error, nonsampling error, and definitions, see www.census.gov/prod/cen2000/doc/sf3.pdf)

Industry groups	Occupational groups					
	Employed civilian population 16 years and over	Manage-ment, profes-sional and related occupa-tions	Service	Sales and office	Farming, fishing, and forestry	Con-struction, extrac-tion, and mainte-nance	Produc-tion, transpor-tation, and material moving
Totals	129,721,512	100.00	100.00	100.00	100.00	100.00	100.00
Agriculture, forestry, fishing and hunting, and mining....	2,426,053	2.2	0.4	0.4	82.2	1.9	1.2
Construction.................................	8,801,507	2.9	0.4	1.9	0.4	51.4	2.6
Manufacturing...............................	18,286,005	10.3	1.6	7.5	2.9	10.6	50.5
Wholesale trade............................	4,666,757	1.9	0.3	6.8	6.2	2.3	5.7
Retail trade..................................	15,221,716	4.1	2.9	30.0	2.4	6.1	9.0
Transportation and warehousing, and utilities	6,740,102	2.0	1.5	5.5	0.7	5.3	15.8
Information	3,996,564	4.5	0.4	3.9	0.0	3.3	1.0
Finance, insurance, real estate, and rental and leasing .	8,934,972	8.0	1.6	13.8	0.0	1.6	0.7
Professional, scientific, management, administrative, and waste management services.....................	12,061,865	14.3	9.9	8.5	2.3	2.3	3.6
Educational, health and social services	25,843,029	36.7	28.4	10.1	0.5	2.3	3.0
Arts, entertainment, recreation, accommodation and food services	10,210,295	4.2	33.5	4.0	0.6	1.2	2.0
Other services (except public administration)	6,320,632	3.3	9.7	3.0	0.3	9.9	4.0
Public administration................................	6,212,015	5.5	9.4	4.6	1.5	1.9	0.9

Source: United States Census 2000, Sample Edited Detail File.

areas in the ten highest had about 3 out of 10 workers employed in sales and office occupations.

Nine out of ten metropolitan areas with the highest percentage of construction, extraction, and maintenance workers were in the South.

Nine out of ten metropolitan areas with the highest percentage of workers in construction, extraction, and maintenance occupations were in the South in 2000. The only area not in the South was Casper, WY, which was in the West. All of the ten were relatively small, with none having more than 200,000 workers.

Similarly, each of the ten metropol-itan areas with the highest percent-age of workers in production, transportation, and material mov-ing occupations in 2000 was small: only one had more than 100,000

workers. The leading metropolitan areas in this group were Hickory-Morganton-Lenoir, NC, and Elkhart-Goshen, IN, with 34.3 percent and 32.7 percent[14] of their workforce in production, transportation, and material moving occupations.

ADDITIONAL FINDINGS

How does occupation differ from industry?

People often confuse industry and occupation data. Industry refers to the kind of business conducted by a person's employing organization; occupation describes the kind of work that person does on the job.

Some occupation groups are relat-ed closely to certain industries. Operators of transportation

[14] The difference between these two met-ropolitan areas was not statistically signifi-cant.

equipment, farm operators and workers, and health care providers account for major portions of their respective industries of transporta-tion, agriculture, and health care. However, the industry categories include people in other occupa-tions. For example, people employed in agriculture include truck drivers and bookkeepers; people employed in transportation include mechanics, freight han-dlers, and payroll clerks; and peo-ple in the health care industry include occupations such as securi-ty guard and secretary.

The industry classification system used during Census 2000 was developed for the census and con-sists of 265 categories classified into 13 major industry groups. The Census 2000 industry classification was developed from the 1997

North American Industry Classification System (NAICS), which is an industry description system that groups establishments into industries based on activities in which they are primarily engaged. Several census data products use the aggregation structure shown in this report, while others, such as Summary File 3 and Summary File 4, use more detail.

Some occupational groups have a closely related industry counterpart.

About 82.2 percent of farming, fishing, and forestry workers were employed in agriculture, forestry, fishing and hunting, and mining industries. A little more than half (51.4 percent) of construction, extraction, and maintenance occupation workers were in the construction industry. Similarly, over half (50.5 percent) of workers in production, transportation, and material moving occupations were in manufacturing industries. Service occupations was the only occupational group to have a substantial percent of workers in two industry areas — arts, entertainment, recreation, accommodation and food service, with 33.5 percent; and educational, health and social services, with 28.4 percent. More than one-third (36.7 percent) of workers in management, professional and related occupations worked in the educational, health and social services industries. About 30.0 percent of sales and office workers worked in retail trade industries.

ABOUT CENSUS 2000

Why Census 2000 asked about occupation.

The study of occupations is important because it facilitates a better understanding of the economy by tracking labor force trends and identifying new and emerging occupations, such as those related to computers or the Internet. It also provides a window on changes taking place in society, reflected by the work people do.

Specifically, information on occupations is used by a number of federal agencies to distribute funds, to develop policy, and to measure compliance with laws and regulations. For example, occupation data are required by the Bureau of Economic Analysis to develop state per capita income estimates, which are used in the allocation formulas or eligibility criteria of more than 20 federal programs. Data are used to help the Environmental Protection Agency, under the Toxic Substances Control Act, to identify occupations that expose people to harmful chemicals and that adversely affect the environment. They are also used by the Equal Employment Opportunity Commission, under the Civil Rights and Equal Pay Acts, to monitor compliance with federal law and to investigate complaints where employment discrimination is alleged. Occupation data are used by the Department of Labor to formulate policies and programs for employment, career development, and training.

Accuracy of the Estimates

The data contained in this product are based on the sample of households who reported to the Census 2000 long form. Nationally, approximately 1 out of every 6 housing units was included in this sample. As a result, the sample estimates may differ somewhat from the 100-percent figures that would have been obtained if all housing units, people within those housing units, and people living in group quarters had been enumerated using the same questionnaires, instructions, enumerators, and so forth. The sample estimates also differ from the values that would have been obtained from different samples of housing units, people within those housing units, and people living in group quarters. The deviation of a sample estimate from the average of all possible samples is called the sampling error.

In addition to the variability that arises from the sampling procedures, both sample data and 100-percent data are subject to nonsampling error. Nonsampling error may be introduced during any of the various complex operations used to collect and process census data. Such errors may include: not enumerating every household or every person in the population, failing to obtain all required information from the respondents, obtaining incorrect or inconsistent information, and recording information incorrectly. In addition, errors can occur during the field review of the enumerators' work, during clerical handling of the census questionnaires, or during the electronic processing of the questionnaires.

Nonsampling error may affect the data in two ways: (1) errors that are introduced randomly will increase the variability of the data and, therefore, should be reflected in the standard errors; and (2) errors that tend to be consistent in one direction will bias both sample and 100-percent data in that direction. For example, if respondents consistently tend to underreport their incomes, then the resulting estimates of households or families by income category will tend to be understated for the higher income categories and overstated for the lower income categories. Such biases are not reflected in the standard errors.

While it is impossible to completely eliminate error from an operation as large and complex as the decennial census, the Census Bureau attempts to control the sources of such error during the data collection and processing operations. The primary sources of error and the programs instituted to control error in Census 2000 are described in detail in *Summary File 3*

Technical Documentation under Chapter 8, "Accuracy of the Data," located at *www.census.gov /prod/cen2000/doc/sf3.pdf.*

All statements in this Census 2000 Brief have undergone statistical testing and all comparisons are significant at the 90-percent confidence level, unless otherwise noted. The estimates in tables, maps, and other figures may vary from actual values due to sampling and nonsampling errors. As a result, estimates in one category may not be significantly different from estimates assigned to a different category. Further information on the accuracy of the data is located at *www.census.gov/prod /cen2000/doc/sf3.pdf.* For further information on the computation and use of standard errors, contact the Decennial Statistical Studies Division at 301-763-4242.

For More Information.

The Census 2000 Summary File 3 data are available from the American Factfinder on the Internet (*factfinder.census.gov*). They were released on a state-by-state basis during 2002. For information on confidentiality protection,

nonsampling error, sampling error, and definitions, also see *www.census.gov/prod/cen2000 /doc/sf3.pdf* or contact the Customer Services Center at 301-763-INFO (4636).

Information on population and housing topics is presented in the Census 2000 Brief series, located on the Census Bureau's Web site at *www.census.gov/population/www /cen2000/briefs.html.* This series, which will be completed in 2003, presents information on race, Hispanic origin, age, sex, household type, housing tenure, and social, economic, and housing characteristics, such as ancestry, income, and housing costs.

For additional information on occupations in the United States, including reports and survey data, visit the Census Bureau's Internet site at *www.census.gov /hhes/www/occupation.html.*

To find information about the availability of data products, including reports, CD-ROMs, and DVDs, call the Customer Services Center at 301-763-INFO (4636), or e-mail *webmaster@census.gov.*

Journey to Work: 2000

Census 2000 Brief

Issued March 2004

C2KBR-33

By
Clara Reschovsky

Among the 128.3 million workers in the United States in 2000, 76 percent drove alone to work. In addition, 12 percent carpooled, 4.7 percent used public transportation, 3.3 percent worked at home, 2.9 percent walked to work, and 1.2 percent used other means (including motorcycle or bicycle).

This report, one of a series that presents population and housing data collected during Census 2000, provides information on the place-of-work and journey-to-work characteristics of workers 16 years and over who were employed and at work during the reference week.[1] Data are shown for the United States, regions, states, counties, and metropolitan areas.[2]

The questions on place of work and journey to work in Census 2000 ask about commuting patterns and

Figure 1.

Reproduction of the Questions on Journey to Work From Census 2000

22 **At what location did this person work LAST WEEK?** *If this person worked at more than one location, print where he or she worked most last week.*

a. Address (Number and street name)

(If the exact address is not known, give a description of the location such as the building name or the nearest street or intersection.)

b. Name of city, town, or post office

c. Is the work location inside the limits of that city or town?

☐ Yes
☐ No, outside the city/town limits

d. Name of county

e. Name of U.S. state or foreign country

f. ZIP Code

Source: U.S. Census Bureau, Census 2000 questionnaire.

characteristics of commuter travel, as illustrated in Figure 1.

Respondents' answers provide information about where people work, how they travel, what time they leave for work, and how long it takes them to get there. The place-of-work questions provide

---

[1] The reference week is the calendar week preceding the date on which the questions were answered.

[2] The text of this report discusses data for the United States, including the 50 states and the District of Columbia. Data for the Commonwealth of Puerto Rico are shown in Table 5 and Figure 4.

USCENSUSBUREAU

Helping You Make Informed Decisions

U.S. Department of Commerce
Economics and Statistics Administration
U.S. CENSUS BUREAU

United States Census 2000

information that is used to understand the geographic patterns of commuter travel and the volume of travel in "flows" between origins and destinations (e.g., home in a suburban county to work in a central city). The 1960 census was the first to ask place-of-work questions, including the name of the city or town where the work takes place, whether it is inside or outside the city limits, the name of the county, and the name of the state. Beginning with the 1970 census, the place-of-work information was expanded to include the street address and ZIP code of the work location. This information provides more precise data for transportation planners to use to address the increasing pressure on the national transportation infrastructure.

The question on usual means of transportation to work identifies the various types of transportation people use to get to their jobs. The "usual means" is defined as the one used on the most days in the previous week. The 1960 census, which was the first to include this question, asked for the one type of transportation used over the longest distance. The transportation categories changed somewhat between 1960 and 2000, but the question has remained essentially the same. The question on the number of people in the vehicle measures the extent of carpooling and the number of cars, trucks, and vans used for travel to work. This question was first introduced in its present form in the 1980 census.

Information on the time the worker leaves home to go to work is used to estimate the volume of commuter travel at different time periods during a typical day, particularly peak hours of travel when traffic congestion is most severe. The departure time question was first

Figure 1.
Reproduction of the Questions on Journey to Work From Census 2000—Con.

23 **a. How did this person usually get to work LAST WEEK?** *If this person usually used more than one method of transportation during the trip, mark* $\boxed{x}$ *the box of the one used for most of the distance.*

☐ Car, truck, or van
☐ Bus or trolley bus
☐ Streetcar or trolley car
☐ Subway or elevated
☐ Railroad
☐ Ferryboat
☐ Taxicab
☐ Motorcycle
☐ Bicycle
☐ Walked
☐ Worked at home → *Skip to 27*
☐ Other method

b. How many people, including this person, usually rode to work in the car, truck, or van LAST WEEK?

☐ Drove alone
☐ 2 people
☐ 3 people
☐ 4 people
☐ 5 or 6 people
☐ 7 or more people

If "Car, truck, or van" is marked in 23a, go to 23b. Otherwise, skip to 24a.

24 **a. What time did this person usually leave home to go to work LAST WEEK?**

☐ a.m. ☐ p.m.

b. How many minutes did it usually take this person to get from home to work LAST WEEK?

Minutes

Source: U.S. Census Bureau, Census 2000 questionnaire.

included in the 1990 census and was not changed on Census 2000.

The question on the usual travel time to work asks for the amount of time in minutes that people regularly spend commuting to their daily

job. Increases in travel time may be due to increased congestion in particular areas or on particular roads, or to people traveling greater distances between home and work. Combined with departure time data, travel time information is used by

Table 1.
Means of Transportation to Work: 1990 and 2000

(Data based on sample. For information on confidentiality protection, sampling error, nonsampling error, and definitions, see www.census.gov/prod/cen2000/doc/sf3.pdf)

Means of transportation	1990		2000		Change, 1990 to 2000	
	Number	Percent	Number	Percent	Number	Pct. point
Workers 16 years and over	115,070,274	100.0	128,279,228	100.0	13,208,954	(X)
Car, truck, or van.........................	99,592,932	86.5	112,736,101	87.9	13,143,169	1.3
Drove alone	84,215,298	73.2	97,102,050	75.7	12,886,752	2.5
Carpooled.............................	15,377,634	13.4	15,634,051	12.2	256,417	−1.2
Public transportation.....................	6,069,589	5.3	6,067,703	4.7	−1,886	−0.5
Bus or trolley bus	3,445,000	3.0	3,206,682	2.5	−238,318	−0.5
Streetcar or trolley car	78,130	0.1	72,713	0.1	−5,417	-
Subway or elevated	1,755,476	1.5	1,885,961	1.5	130,485	−0.1
Railroad..............................	574,052	0.5	658,097	0.5	84,045	-
Ferryboat............................	37,497	-	44,106	-	6,609	-
Taxicab	179,434	0.2	200,144	0.2	20,710	-
Motorcycle................................	237,404	0.2	142,424	0.1	−94,980	−0.1
Bicycle....................................	466,856	0.4	488,497	0.4	21,641	-
Walked....................................	4,488,886	3.9	3,758,982	2.9	−729,904	−1.0
Other means...............................	808,582	0.7	901,298	0.7	92,716	-
Worked at home	3,406,025	3.0	4,184,223	3.3	778,198	0.3

- Rounds to zero.
(X) Not applicable.

Source: U.S. Census Bureau, 1990 Census Summary Tape File 3 and Census 2000 Summary File 3.

transportation planners to measure the efficiency of different modes of travel during peak (rush hour) and off-peak periods. Travel time also is a factor in determining the air quality attainment status for metropolitan areas and a measure that has been required since 1991 in the Inter-modal Surface Transportation Efficiency Act (ISTEA). This question was first included in the 1980 census and was substantially the same in 1990 and 2000.

Three out of four workers drove alone to work.

The pattern of commuting to work did not change dramatically from 1990 to 2000. The vast majority of commuters drove alone to work, a trend that has been seen since the question was first asked in 1960. As illustrated in Table 1, the number of people who drove alone to work increased between 1990 and 2000, from 84 million to 97 million,

and rose from 73 percent to 76 percent of workers.[3] Carpooling rose slightly, from 15.4 million to 15.6 million, but its share of commuters decreased from 13 percent to 12 percent. The number of workers using public transportation to get to work was 6.1 million in both 1990 and 2000, but dropped from 5.3 percent to 4.7 percent of workers. The number of people walking to work decreased from 4.5 million to 3.8 million and fell below the number working at home for the first time since the question was initially asked in 1960. The number of people working at home rose from 3.4 million in 1990 to 4.2 million in 2000 and increased

[3] The estimates in this report are based on responses from a sample of the population. As with all surveys, estimates may vary from the actual values because of sampling variation or other factors. All statements made in this report have undergone statistical testing and are significant at the 90-percent confidence level unless otherwise noted.

from 3.0 percent to 3.3 percent of workers.

Means of transportation to work varies among racial and ethnic groups.

Census 2000 allowed respondents to choose more than one race. With the exception of the Two or more races group, all race groups discussed in this report refer to people who indicated *only one* racial identity among the six major categories: White, Black or African American, American Indian and Alaska Native, Asian, Native Hawaiian and Other Pacific Islander, and Some other race.[4] The use of the single-race population in this report does not imply

[4] For further information on each of the six major race groups and the Two or more races population, see reports from the Census 2000 Brief series (C2KBR/01), available on the Census 2000 Web site at *www.census.gov /population/www/cen2000/briefs.html*.

Figure 2.

Means of Transportation to Work by Race and Hispanic Origin: 2000

(Data based on sample. For information on confidentiality protection, sampling error, nonsampling error, and definitions, see *www.census.gov/prod/cen2000/doc/sf3.pdf*)

Drove alone (percent of workers 16 years and over)

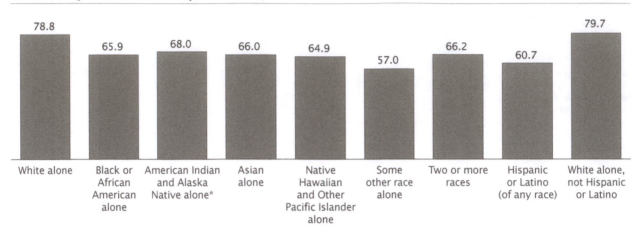

Carpool (percent of workers 16 years and over)

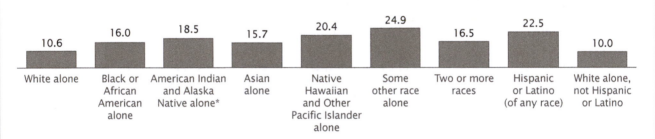

Public transportation (percent of workers 16 years and over)

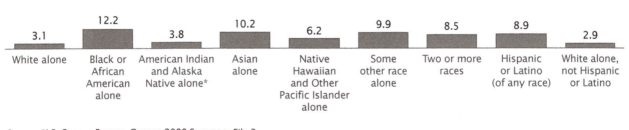

Source: U.S. Census Bureau, Census 2000 Summary File 3.

Table 2.
Travel Time to Work: 1990 and 2000

(Data based on sample. For information on confidentiality protection, sampling error, nonsampling error, and definitions, see www.census.gov/prod/cen2000/doc/sf3.pdf)

Travel time	1990		2000		Change, 1990 to 2000	
	Number	Percent	Number	Percent	Number	Pct. point
Workers 16 years and over	115,070,274	100.0	128,279,228	100.0	13,208,954	(X)
Did not work at home	111,664,249	97.0	124,095,005	96.7	12,430,756	−0.3
Worked at home	3,406,025	3.0	4,184,223	3.3	778,198	0.3
Did not work at home	111,664,249	100.0	124,095,005	100.0	12,430,756	(X)
Less than 5 minutes	4,314,682	3.9	4,180,407	3.4	−134,275	−0.5
5 to 9 minutes	13,943,239	12.5	13,687,604	11.0	−255,635	−1.5
10 to 14 minutes	17,954,128	16.1	18,618,305	15.0	664,177	−1.1
15 to 19 minutes	19,026,053	17.0	19,634,328	15.8	608,275	−1.2
20 to 24 minutes	16,243,343	14.5	17,981,756	14.5	1,738,413	−0.1
25 to 29 minutes	6,193,587	5.5	7,190,540	5.8	996,953	0.2
30 to 34 minutes	14,237,947	12.8	16,369,097	13.2	2,131,150	0.4
35 to 39 minutes	2,634,749	2.4	3,212,387	2.6	577,638	0.2
40 to 44 minutes	3,180,413	2.8	4,122,419	3.3	942,006	0.5
45 to 59 minutes	7,191,455	6.4	9,200,414	7.4	2,008,959	1.0
60 to 89 minutes	4,980,662	4.5	6,461,905	5.2	1,481,243	0.7
90 or more minutes........................	1,763,991	1.6	3,435,843	2.8	1,671,852	1.2
Average travel time (minutes)*	22.4	(X)	25.5	(X)	3.1	(X)

* Excludes workers who worked at home.
(X) Not applicable.

Source: U.S. Census Bureau, 1990 Census Summary Tape File 3 and Census 2000 Summary File 3.

that it is the preferred method of presenting or analyzing data. The Census Bureau uses a variety of approaches.[5]

Driving alone was by far the most prevalent means, followed by carpooling, regardless of race or Hispanic origin.[6] Figure 2 shows how people of different racial and ethnic groups traveled to work in 2000. A much higher proportion of non-Hispanic White workers drove alone to work than workers of other races or Hispanic origin. Hispanic workers were least likely to drive alone to work.[7] People who were non-Hispanic White were least likely to take public transportation or to carpool.

Average travel time to work was about 26 minutes in 2000.

Average travel time increased from 21.7 minutes in 1980 to 22.4 minutes in 1990, and to 25.5 minutes in 2000, as shown in Table 2.[8]

However, the averages for 1990 and 2000 are not totally comparable. About 1 minute of the 3.1 minute increase between 1990 and 2000 was due to a change in methodology.[9] The increase in average travel time between 1990 and 2000 is reflected in the changes in the percentage distribution shown in Table 2. The proportions of trips in categories below 20 minutes all declined between 1990 and 2000, while the proportions in the categories of 25 minutes or more all increased. The proportion in the category 90 or more minutes nearly doubled, from 1.6 percent to 2.8 percent.

Men took longer to get to work than women.

Figure 3 shows how travel time to work differs for men and women. Traditionally, men have had longer commutes than women, and this continued to be true in 2000, with average commutes of 27.2 minutes

[5] This report draws heavily on Summary File 3, a Census 2000 product that can be accessed through American FactFinder, available from the Census Bureau's Web site, www.census.gov. Information on people who reported more than one race, such as "White and American Indian and Alaska Native" or "Asian and Black or African American," is in Summary File 4, which is available through American FactFinder. About 2.6 percent of people reported more than one race.

[6] Because Hispanics may be of any race, data in this report for Hispanics overlap with data for racial groups. Based on Census 2000 sample data, the proportion Hispanic was 97.1 percent for those reporting Some other race, 8.0 percent for Whites, 1.9 percent for Blacks, 14.6 percent for American Indians and Alaska Natives, 1.0 percent for Asians, 9.5 percent for Pacific Islanders, and 31.1 percent for those reporting Two or more races.

[7] Hereafter, this report uses the term Black to refer to people who are Black or African American, the term Pacific Islander to refer to people who are Native Hawaiian and Other Pacific Islander, and the term Hispanic to refer to people who are Hispanic or Latino.

[8] Data on average travel time in 1980 can be found on the Journey to Work and Place of Work page of the Census Web site at www.census.gov/population/www/socdemo/journey.html.

[9] Prior to Census 2000, the questionnaire permitted respondents to mark no more than two digits for their travel time, limiting reported travel time to 99 minutes. Three digits were made available in the Census 2000 questionnaire, reflecting the greater frequency of extremely long commutes.

for men and 23.6 minutes for women. In general, a higher proportion of women than men made shorter commutes, particularly for trips that took from 5 to 24 minutes. Nearly equal proportions of men and women commuted between 25 and 29 minutes to work. For trips of 30 minutes or more, the proportion in each category was higher for men than women. The proportion working at home was also higher for men than for women: 3.7 percent compared with 2.9 percent. However, of the 4.2 million who worked at home, approximately 53 percent were women.

In 2000, about 53 percent of workers departed between 6:30 a.m. and 8:29 a.m. to go to work.

Table 3 shows the time period in which workers left home to go to work. The peak period was from 6:30 a.m. to 8:29 a.m., covering 55 percent of workers in 1990 and 53 percent in 2000. During the decade, the number departing from 12 midnight to 6:29 a.m. rose by nearly 4.8 million people, and increased from 18 percent to 20 percent of the total. Small changes occurred in the percentage of workers who left for work among the categories between 8:30 a.m. and 3:59 p.m. Additionally, the percentage did not show any statistical evidence of a change for those who departed between 4:00 p.m. and 11:59 p.m.

Fewer people worked in central cities than elsewhere in metropolitan areas in 2000.

Table 4 presents data on commuting patterns by place of residence and by place of work among central cities, the remainder of metropolitan areas (outside central cities), and nonmetropolitan areas for 1990 and 2000. The number of workers living in metropolitan areas

Figure 3.
Travel Time to Work by Sex: 2000

(Percent distribution of male workers and of female workers, 16 years and over. Data based on sample. For information on confidentiality protection, sampling error, nonsampling error, and definitions, see *www.census.gov/prod/cen2000/doc/sf3.pdf*)

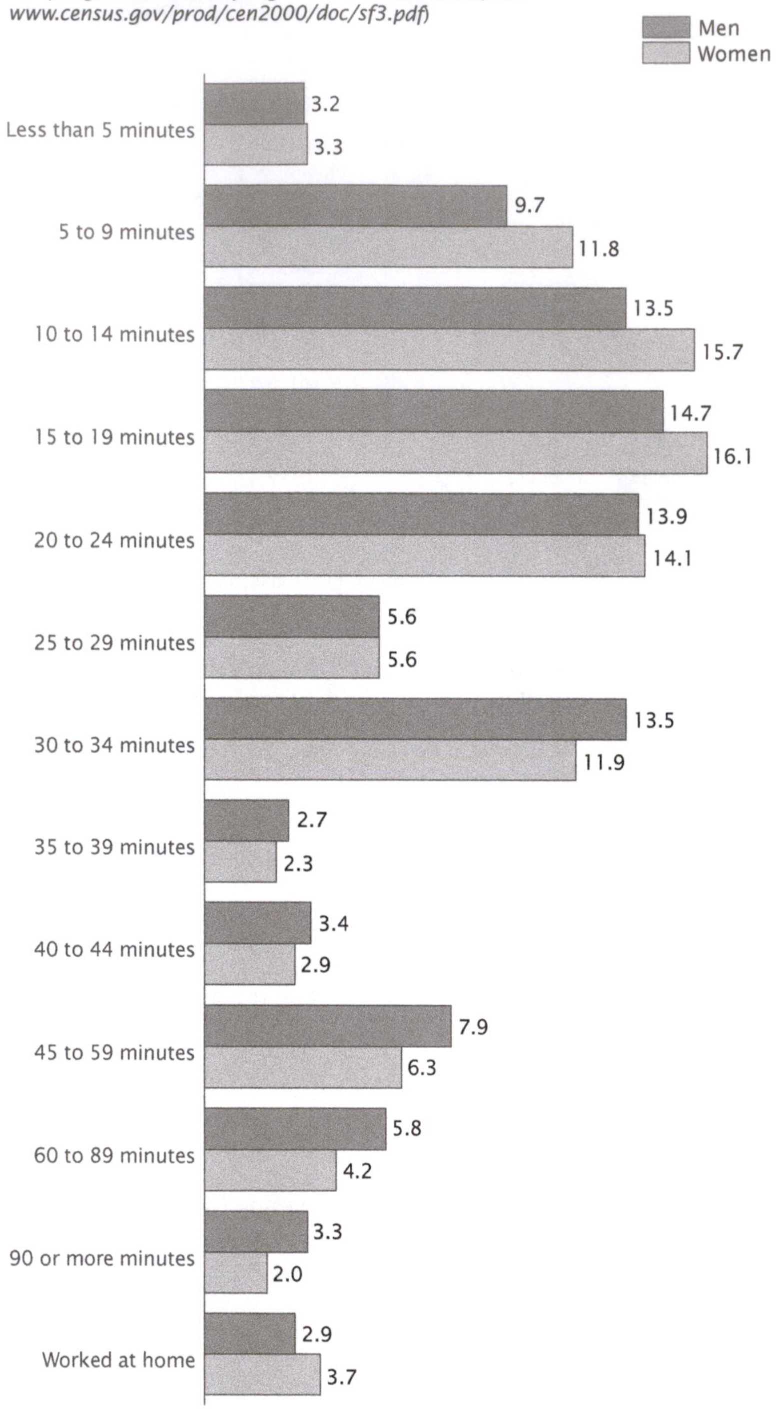

Legend: Men, Women

Travel Time	Men	Women
Less than 5 minutes	3.2	3.3
5 to 9 minutes	9.7	11.8
10 to 14 minutes	13.5	15.7
15 to 19 minutes	14.7	16.1
20 to 24 minutes	13.9	14.1
25 to 29 minutes	5.6	5.6
30 to 34 minutes	13.5	11.9
35 to 39 minutes	2.7	2.3
40 to 44 minutes	3.4	2.9
45 to 59 minutes	7.9	6.3
60 to 89 minutes	5.8	4.2
90 or more minutes	3.3	2.0
Worked at home	2.9	3.7

Average travel time* for men = 27.2 minutes, women = 23.6 minutes

*Excludes workers who worked at home.
Source: U.S. Census Bureau, Census 2000.

Table 3.
Time Leaving Home to Go to Work: 1990 and 2000

(Data based on sample. For information on confidentiality protection, sampling error, nonsampling error, and definitions, see www.census.gov/prod/cen2000/doc/sf3.pdf)

Time leaving home	1990		2000		Change, 1990 to 2000	
	Number	Percent	Number	Percent	Number	Pct. point
Workers 16 years and over	115,070,274	(X)	128,279,228	(X)	13,208,954	(X)
Did not work at home......................	111,664,249	97.0	124,095,005	96.7	12,430,756	−0.3
Worked at home	3,406,025	3.0	4,184,223	3.3	778,198	0.3
Did not work at home	111,664,249	100.0	124,095,005	100.0	12,430,756	(x)
12:00 a.m. to 6:29 a.m...................	19,699,963	17.6	24,487,991	19.7	4,788,028	2.1
12:00 a.m. to 4:59 a.m.	2,747,488	2.5	4,237,970	3.4	1,490,482	1.0
5:00 a.m. to 5:29 a.m.	2,724,375	2.4	3,763,208	3.0	1,038,833	0.6
5:30 a.m. to 5:59 a.m.	4,421,571	4.0	5,677,113	4.6	1,255,542	0.6
6:00 a.m. to 6:29 a.m.	9,806,529	8.8	10,809,700	8.7	1,003,171	−0.1
6:30 a.m. to 8:29 a.m...................	61,194,181	54.8	65,101,888	52.5	3,907,707	−2.3
6:30 a.m. to 6:59 a.m.	13,013,935	11.7	13,386,429	10.8	372,494	−0.9
7:00 a.m. to 7:29 a.m.	17,745,201	15.9	18,640,062	15.0	894,861	−0.9
7:30 a.m. to 7:59 a.m.	17,601,419	15.8	19,665,861	15.8	2,064,442	0.1
8:00 a.m. to 8:29 a.m.	12,833,626	11.5	13,409,536	10.8	575,910	−0.7
8:30 a.m. to 11:59 a.m...................	30,770,105	13.7	34,505,126	14.2	3,735,021	0.2
8:30 a.m. to 8:59 a.m.	6,033,700	5.4	6,528,339	5.3	494,639	−0.1
9:00 a.m. to 9:59 a.m.	5,792,355	5.2	6,835,549	5.5	1,043,194	0.3
10:00 a.m. to 10:59 a.m.	2,249,960	2.0	2,839,779	2.3	589,819	0.3
11:00 a.m. to 11:59 a.m.	1,167,633	1.0	1,360,775	1.1	193,142	0.1
12:00 p.m. to 3:59 p.m.	7,965,160	7.1	8,522,829	6.9	557,669	−0.3
4:00 p.m. to 11:59 p.m.	7,561,297	6.8	8,417,855	6.8	856,558	-

- Round to zero.
(X) Not applicable.

Source: U.S. Census Bureau, 1990 Census Summary Tape File 3 and Census 2000 Summary File 3.

increased by 12.9 million (from 91.5 million to 104.4 million), while the number living outside metropolitan areas increased by only 340,000 (from 23.6 million to 23.9 million). As a result, the proportion of workers residing in metropolitan areas rose from 79.5 percent to 81.4 percent.

The number of workers who worked in metropolitan areas increased from 1990 to 2000 by 13.1 million (from 93.1 million to 106.3 million). Among workers in metropolitan areas, the number who worked in central cities rose by 2.7 million (from 47.9 million to 50.6 million), while the number who worked in the remainder, or suburbs, of metropolitan areas increased by 10.4 million (from 45.3 million to 55.7 million.) The changes in the numbers of workers

who worked in central cities compared with those who worked in the remainder of metropolitan areas continued trends seen over recent decades. For the first time, however, more than half of metropolitan area resident workers worked in the noncentral city portion of metropolitan areas, as the proportion rose from 48.6 percent in 1990 to 52.4 percent in 2000.

GEOGRAPHIC DISTRIBUTION OF COMMUTERS' JOURNEY TO WORK

Public transportation use was concentrated in the Northeast, and carpooling was concentrated in the South and the West.

As shown in Table 5, the means of transportation differed noticeably among the regions of the United

States.[10] Specifically, public transportation usage was concentrated in the Northeast where about 50 percent of all workers who used public transportation resided. This group represented about 12 percent of workers in the Northeast, while less than 5 percent of workers in the other regions

_____

[10] The Northeast region includes the states of Connecticut, Maine, Massachusetts, New Hampshire, New Jersey, New York, Pennsylvania, Rhode Island, and Vermont. The Midwest region includes the states of Illinois, Indiana, Iowa, Kansas, Michigan, Minnesota, Missouri, Nebraska, North Dakota, Ohio, South Dakota, and Wisconsin. The South region includes the states of Alabama, Arkansas, Delaware, Florida, Georgia, Kentucky, Louisiana, Maryland, Mississippi, North Carolina, Oklahoma, South Carolina, Tennessee, Texas, Virginia, West Virginia, and the District of Columbia, a state equivalent. The West region includes the states of Alaska, Arizona, California, Colorado, Hawaii, Idaho, Montana, Nevada, New Mexico, Oregon, Utah, Washington, and Wyoming.

519

Table 4.
Residence and Workplace by Metropolitan Status: 1990 and 2000

(Data based on sample. For information on confidentiality protection, sampling error, nonsampling error, and definitions, see www.census.gov/prod/cen2000/doc/sf3.pdf)

Year and place of residence	Workers 16 years and older		Workplace							
			In a metropolitan area						Outside metro area	
			Total		Central city		Remainder of metro area			
	Number	Percent	Number	Percent	Number	Percent	Number	Percent	Number	Percent
1990										
Workers 16 years and over ..	115,070,274	100.0	93,117,895	80.9	47,861,224	41.6	45,256,671	39.3	21,952,379	19.1
In a metropolitan area	91,515,002	100.0	90,223,393	98.6	46,471,566	50.8	43,751,827	47.8	1,291,609	1.4
Central city	35,384,640	100.0	35,030,705	99.0	27,656,472	78.2	7,374,233	20.8	353,935	1.0
Remainder of metropolitan area..	56,130,362	100.0	55,192,688	98.3	18,815,094	33.5	36,377,594	64.8	937,674	1.7
Outside any metropolitan area	23,555,272	100.0	2,894,502	12.3	1,389,658	5.9	1,504,844	6.4	20,660,770	87.7
2000										
Workers 16 years and over ..	128,279,228	100.0	106,264,817	82.8	50,601,339	39.4	55,663,478	43.4	22,014,411	17.2
In a metropolitan area	104,383,631	100.0	102,775,810	98.5	49,028,843	47.0	53,746,967	51.5	1,607,821	1.5
Central city	37,811,559	100.0	37,389,405	98.9	28,221,936	74.6	9,167,469	24.2	422,154	1.1
Remainder of metropolitan area..	66,572,072	100.0	65,386,405	98.2	20,806,907	31.3	44,579,498	67.0	1,185,667	1.8
Outside any metropolitan area	23,895,597	100.0	3,489,007	14.6	1,572,496	6.6	1,916,511	8.0	20,406,590	85.4

Note: Workers who lived in a metropolitan area may work in any metropolitan area, whether they lived there or not. For full detail, see Table P-028 in Summary File 3.

Source: U.S. Census Bureau, 1990 Census SSTF20 Journey to Work in the United States and Census 2000 Summary File 3.

used public transportation. Lower proportions of workers drove alone to work in the Northeast (69 percent) and the West (73 percent) than in other regions. Carpooling was highest in the West and the South, used by 14.1 percent and 13.5 percent of workers respectively, and carpooling was employed the least in the Northeast, by only 9.8 percent of workers. However, 30 percent of those who walked to work lived in the Northeast, encompassing 5 percent of Northeast workers. Only 2 percent of workers in the South walked to work, but they accounted for 24 percent of walkers nationally due to the high number of workers residing in the South.

The Northeast had the longest average travel time, 28.2 minutes, nearly three minutes above the national average of 25.5 minutes. The Midwest had the shortest average travel time (23.2 minutes),

while the South and the West had travel times that were closer to the national average. Reflecting regional differences, average travel time varied from a low of 15.8 minutes in North Dakota in the Midwest to a high of 31.7 minutes in New York in the Northeast.

About one-third of all public transportation riders lived in New York State in 2000.

Additional variation across means of transportation appeared at the state level. The proportion of workers who drove alone ranged from a high of about 83 percent in Michigan, Alabama, and Ohio to a low of 56 percent in New York. Carpooling varied from 19 percent in Hawaii to 9 percent in Massachusetts. Public transportation use was highest in New York, with 24 percent of workers using public transportation to go to

work. The next highest state was New Jersey, with only 10 percent. Workers in other states with cities that offer major public transportation systems often used public transit. In the District of Columbia, 33 percent of workers used public transportation.[11] On the other hand, states not dominated by large metropolitan areas had high proportions walking to work. They included Alaska, Vermont, and Montana, with 7.3 percent, 5.6 percent, and 5.5 percent, respectively, but also high on the list was the District of Columbia (11.8 percent) and New York (6.2 percent).[12]

_____

[11] The District of Columbia has a somewhat different pattern of means of transportation to work than the states because it is more comparable to large cities than to states.

[12] The rates in Vermont and Montana are not significantly different from one another.

Table 5.
Travel to Work Characteristics for the United States, Regions, States, and for Puerto Rico: 2000

(Data based on sample. For information on confidentiality protection, sampling error, nonsampling error, and definitions, see www.census.gov/prod/cen2000/doc/sf3.pdf)

| Area | Workers 16 years and over | Means of transportation to work | | | | | | | | | | | | Average travel time (minutes) |
| | | Drove alone | | Carpooled | | Public transportaton | | Walked | | Motorcycle, bike, and other means | | Worked at home | | |
		Number	Per-cent	Number	Per-cent	Number	Per-cent	Number	Per-cent	Number	Per-cent	Number	Per-cent	
United States ...	128,279,228	97,102,050	75.7	15,634,051	12.2	6,067,703	4.7	3,758,982	2.9	1,532,219	1.2	4,184,223	3.3	25.5
Region														
Northeast..........	24,444,773	16,932,345	69.3	2,400,258	9.8	3,028,243	12.4	1,121,181	4.6	213,838	0.9	748,908	3.1	28.2
Midwest..........	30,712,260	24,441,211	79.6	3,180,627	10.4	902,656	2.9	869,013	2.8	266,002	0.9	1,052,751	3.4	23.2
South............	44,982,432	35,252,687	78.4	6,075,935	13.5	968,250	2.2	905,672	2.0	540,848	1.2	1,239,040	2.8	25.6
West	28,139,763	20,475,807	72.8	3,977,231	14.1	1,168,554	4.2	863,116	3.1	511,531	1.8	1,143,524	4.1	25.7
State														
Alabama	1,900,089	1,576,882	83.0	234,020	12.3	9,496	0.5	25,360	1.3	15,028	0.8	39,303	2.1	24.8
Alaska	290,597	193,165	66.5	45,012	15.5	5,236	1.8	21,298	7.3	13,908	4.8	11,978	4.1	19.6
Arizona	2,210,395	1,638,752	74.1	340,447	15.4	41,105	1.9	58,015	2.6	50,918	2.3	81,158	3.7	24.9
Arkansas	1,160,101	927,213	79.9	163,626	14.1	5,127	0.4	21,915	1.9	12,109	1.0	30,111	2.6	21.9
California	14,525,322	10,432,462	71.8	2,113,313	14.5	736,037	5.1	414,581	2.9	271,893	1.9	557,036	3.8	27.7
Colorado	2,191,626	1,646,454	75.1	268,168	12.2	69,515	3.2	65,668	3.0	33,689	1.5	108,132	4.9	24.3
Connecticut	1,640,823	1,312,700	80.0	154,400	9.4	65,827	4.0	44,348	2.7	12,130	0.7	51,418	3.1	24.4
Delaware	373,070	295,413	79.2	42,990	11.5	10,354	2.8	9,637	2.6	3,585	1.0	11,091	3.0	24.0
District of Columbia .	260,884	100,168	38.4	28,607	11.0	86,493	33.2	30,785	11.8	4,901	1.9	9,930	3.8	29.7
Florida...........	6,910,168	5,445,527	78.8	893,766	12.9	129,075	1.9	118,386	1.7	116,325	1.7	207,089	3.0	26.2
Georgia	3,832,803	2,968,910	77.5	557,062	14.5	90,030	2.3	65,776	1.7	42,039	1.1	108,986	2.8	27.7
Hawaii	563,154	359,916	63.9	107,191	19.0	35,368	6.3	27,134	4.8	13,349	2.4	20,196	3.6	26.1
Idaho............	594,654	457,986	77.0	73,273	12.3	6,275	1.1	20,747	3.5	8,360	1.4	28,013	4.7	20.0
Illinois	5,745,731	4,207,339	73.2	625,411	10.9	497,632	8.7	180,119	3.1	58,739	1.0	176,491	3.1	28.0
Indiana..........	2,910,612	2,379,989	81.8	320,910	11.0	29,792	1.0	69,184	2.4	26,754	0.9	83,983	2.9	22.6
Iowa............	1,469,763	1,155,008	78.6	158,699	10.8	15,021	1.0	58,088	4.0	13,163	0.9	69,784	4.7	18.5
Kansas	1,311,343	1,068,501	81.5	139,348	10.6	6,366	0.5	33,271	2.5	11,995	0.9	51,862	4.0	19.0
Kentucky	1,781,733	1,429,053	80.2	224,643	12.6	21,522	1.2	42,494	2.4	15,877	0.9	48,144	2.7	23.5
Louisiana.........	1,831,057	1,430,142	78.1	249,640	13.6	43,277	2.4	40,184	2.2	28,485	1.6	39,329	2.1	25.7
Maine............	615,144	483,317	78.6	69,208	11.3	5,217	0.8	24,700	4.0	5,740	0.9	26,962	4.4	22.7
Maryland	2,591,670	1,910,917	73.7	320,992	12.4	187,246	7.2	64,852	2.5	20,960	0.8	86,703	3.3	31.2
Massachusetts.....	3,102,837	2,290,258	73.8	279,111	9.0	270,742	8.7	134,566	4.3	30,656	1.0	97,504	3.1	27.0
Michigan	4,540,372	3,776,535	83.2	440,606	9.7	60,537	1.3	101,506	2.2	33,423	0.7	127,765	2.8	24.1
Minnesota	2,541,611	1,971,668	77.6	264,690	10.4	81,276	3.2	84,148	3.3	23,175	0.9	116,654	4.6	21.9
Mississippi........	1,164,118	924,506	79.4	176,465	15.2	6,587	0.6	21,868	1.9	12,093	1.0	22,599	1.9	24.6
Missouri..........	2,629,296	2,116,096	80.5	306,179	11.6	39,153	1.5	55,631	2.1	21,453	0.8	90,784	3.5	23.8
Montana	422,159	311,872	73.9	50,192	11.9	2,812	0.7	23,336	5.5	7,036	1.7	26,911	6.4	17.7
Nebraska.........	873,197	698,680	80.0	91,901	10.5	6,260	0.7	28,003	3.2	7,837	0.9	40,516	4.6	18.0
Nevada	923,155	687,368	74.5	135,874	14.7	36,446	3.9	24,875	2.7	14,715	1.6	23,877	2.6	23.3
New Hampshire....	638,565	522,043	81.8	62,763	9.8	4,645	0.7	18,545	2.9	5,262	0.8	25,307	4.0	25.3
New Jersey	3,876,433	2,828,303	73.0	412,299	10.6	371,514	9.6	121,305	3.1	36,456	0.9	106,556	2.7	30.0
New Mexico.......	759,177	575,187	75.8	112,489	14.8	6,074	0.8	21,435	2.8	12,019	1.6	31,973	4.2	21.9
New York	8,211,916	4,620,178	56.3	756,918	9.2	2,006,194	24.4	511,721	6.2	69,036	0.8	247,869	3.0	31.7
North Carolina	3,837,773	3,046,666	79.4	538,264	14.0	34,803	0.9	74,147	1.9	40,942	1.1	102,951	2.7	24.0
North Dakota	319,481	248,277	77.7	32,005	10.0	1,303	0.4	16,094	5.0	2,694	0.8	19,108	6.0	15.8
Ohio............	5,307,502	4,392,059	82.8	494,602	9.3	110,274	2.1	125,882	2.4	38,432	0.7	146,253	2.8	22.9
Oklahoma	1,539,792	1,231,711	80.0	203,444	13.2	7,456	0.5	32,796	2.1	16,828	1.1	47,557	3.1	21.7
Oregon	1,601,378	1,171,641	73.2	195,950	12.2	66,788	4.2	57,217	3.6	29,996	1.9	79,786	5.0	22.2
Pennsylvania......	5,556,311	4,247,836	76.5	577,364	10.4	289,699	5.2	229,725	4.1	47,041	0.8	164,646	3.0	25.2
Rhode Island	490,905	393,322	80.1	51,004	10.4	12,197	2.5	18,717	3.8	4,670	1.0	10,995	2.2	22.5
South Carolina.....	1,822,969	1,447,338	79.4	255,857	14.0	15,468	0.8	42,567	2.3	23,504	1.3	38,235	2.1	24.3
South Dakota......	372,648	288,227	77.3	38,805	10.4	1,702	0.5	16,786	4.5	2,972	0.8	24,156	6.5	16.6
Tennessee........	2,618,404	2,140,377	81.7	328,321	12.5	21,168	0.8	39,689	1.5	21,351	0.8	67,498	2.6	24.5
Texas............	9,157,875	7,115,590	77.7	1,326,012	14.5	170,268	1.9	173,670	1.9	120,311	1.3	252,024	2.8	25.4
Utah............	1,032,858	779,438	75.5	145,950	14.1	23,199	2.2	28,523	2.8	12,413	1.2	43,335	4.2	21.3
Vermont..........	311,839	234,388	75.2	37,191	11.9	2,208	0.7	17,554	5.6	2,847	0.9	17,651	5.7	21.6
Virginia	3,481,820	2,685,914	77.1	441,093	12.7	124,166	3.6	80,487	2.3	40,093	1.2	110,067	3.2	27.0
Washington	2,785,479	2,040,833	73.3	357,742	12.8	136,278	4.9	89,739	3.2	40,057	1.4	120,830	4.3	25.5
West Virginia	718,106	576,360	80.3	91,133	12.7	5,714	0.8	21,059	2.9	6,417	0.9	17,423	2.4	26.2
Wisconsin	2,690,704	2,138,832	79.5	267,471	9.9	53,340	2.0	100,301	3.7	25,365	0.9	105,395	3.9	20.8
Wyoming	239,809	180,733	75.4	31,630	13.2	3,421	1.4	10,548	4.4	3,178	1.3	10,299	4.3	17.8
Puerto Rico	908,386	626,578	69.0	163,579	18.0	48,322	5.3	36,834	4.1	17,109	1.9	15,964	1.8	29.4

Note: Because of sampling error, the estimates in this table may not be significantly different from one another or from rates for other geographic areas not listed in this table.

Source: U.S. Census Bureau, Census 2000 Summary File 3.

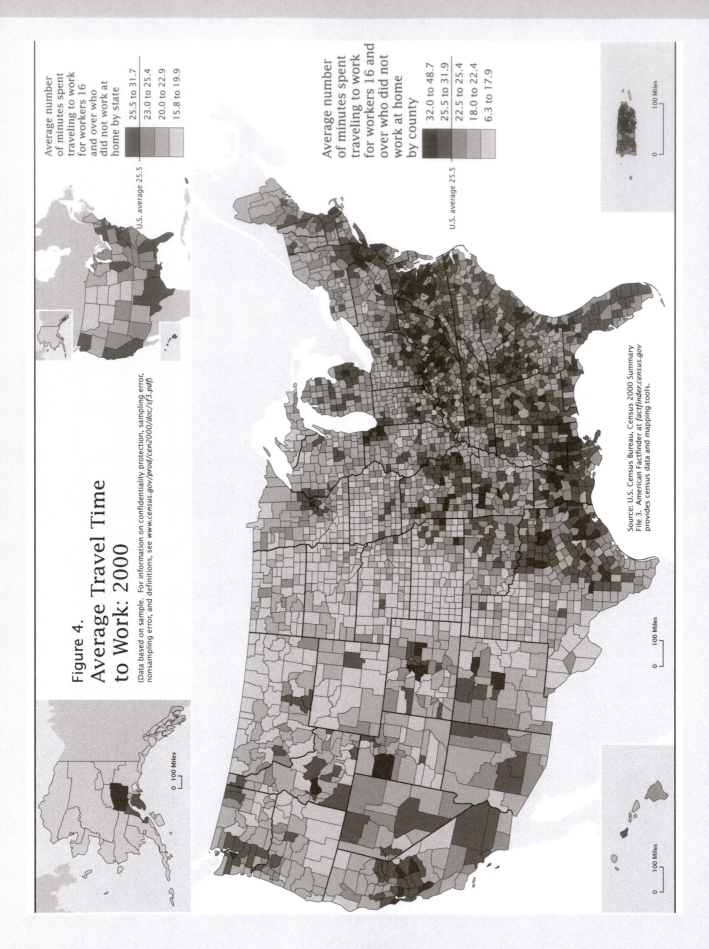

Figure 4.
Average Travel Time
to Work: 2000

(Data based on sample. For information on confidentiality protection, sampling error, nonsampling error, and definitions, see *www.census.gov/prod/cen2000/doc/sf3.pdf*)

Average number
of minutes spent
traveling to work
for workers 16
and over who
did not work at
home by state

25.5 to 31.7
23.0 to 25.4
20.0 to 22.9
15.8 to 19.9

U.S. average 25.5

Average number
of minutes spent
traveling to work
for workers 16 and
over who did not
work at home
by county

32.0 to 48.7
25.5 to 31.9
22.5 to 25.4
18.0 to 22.4
6.3 to 17.9

U.S. average 25.5

Source: U.S. Census Bureau, Census 2000 Summary
File 3. American Factfinder at *factfinder.census.gov*
provides census data and mapping tools.

0   100 Miles

Table 5 shows also that states with high and low proportions of workers working at home tended to be primarily nonmetropolitan. States with the highest proportions were Montana, North Dakota, South Dakota, and Vermont; some of the states with low proportions of workers at home are Mississippi, Alabama, South Carolina, and Louisiana.

Workers east of the Mississippi River generally took longer to go to work than those west of the Mississippi River.

Figure 4 shows the average travel time to work by counties. Travel time varies by region of the country, and a major dividing line is the Mississippi River. East of the Mississippi, very few counties fit into the lowest category of less than 18 minutes, while a large number of counties west of the Mississippi fit into that category. Even though the Northeast had the overall highest regional travel time, the South contained more counties with higher travel times, reflecting the fact that there are more counties in the Southern region of the United States. The northern Midwest also had short travel times in comparison with other parts of the country. Most of the counties in the 6.3-to-17.9 minute category were located in the Midwest. The lower average travel time generally coincides with counties that have lower population densities. In Alaska, county equivalents, known as Boroughs or Census Areas, also fit the same pattern, with shorter travel times outside of the Anchorage MSA and surrounding area.

Metropolitan areas with high rates of carpool usage were concentrated in Texas and California.

Table 6 shows ten metropolitan areas with a high proportion of

workers who used the various types of transportation to work in 2000. Ten metropolitan areas with high percentages of commuters who drove alone were all east of the Mississippi River, concentrated in Ohio and Alabama.[13] At the state level, these states also had high percentages of workers who drove alone, which contradicts the idea that driving alone to work characterizes only the newer metropolitan areas of the Southeast and the West. By contrast, the ten metropolitan areas where carpooling was frequent were located in the South and the West, primarily in Texas and California. A higher proportion of Hispanic workers than of other workers used carpools, and higher proportions of Hispanic workers reside in the South and the West than in other parts of the country.

On the other hand, different metropolitan areas have greater percentages of their workers utilizing means of transportation other than a car, truck, or van. For instance, the metropolitan areas that had a large share of people who walked to work were predominately college towns, such as the State College, PA, MSA. Two exceptions were the Jacksonville, NC, MSA and the Wichita Falls, TX, MSA, which contain large military bases. The New York-Northern New Jersey-Long Island, NY-NJ-CT-PA, CMSA, not surprisingly, had heavier-than-average use of public transportation. Most of the other areas in Table 6 that had high usage of public transportation also have large rail transit systems.

---

[13] Metropolitan areas include consolidated metropolitan statistical areas (CMSAs), primary metropolitan statistical areas (PMSAs), and metropolitan statistical areas (MSAs). CMSAs, which are made up of at least two PMSAs, were used in this analysis rather than PMSAs. MSAs were used for metropolitan areas that do not have a CMSA.

ABOUT CENSUS 2000

Why Census 2000 asked about journey to work and place of work.

Commuting data are essential for planning highway improvements and developing public transportation services, as well as designing programs to ease traffic problems during peak hours, conserve energy, and reduce pollution. These data are used by state departments of transportation and more than 350 metropolitan planning organizations responsible for comprehensive transportation planning activities required by the Transportation Equity Act for the 21st Century (TEA21). Public transit agencies use these data to plan for transit investments, identify areas in need of better service, determine the most efficient routes, and plan for services for people with disabilities. Police and fire departments use data about where people work to plan emergency services in areas of high concentration of employment.

Accuracy of the Estimates

The data contained in this report are based on the sample of households who responded to the Census 2000 long form. Nationally, approximately 1 out of every 6 housing units was included in this sample. As a result, the sample estimates may differ somewhat from the 100-percent figures that would have been obtained if all housing units, people within those housing units, and people living in group quarters had been enumerated using the same questionnaires, instructions, enumerators, and so forth. The sample estimates also differ from the values that would have been obtained from different samples of housing units, and hence of people living in those housing units, and people

Table 6.
Selected Metropolitan Areas by Means of Transportation to Work: 2000

(Data based on sample. For information on confidentiality protection, sampling error, nonsampling error, and definitions, see www.census.gov/prod/cen2000/doc/sf3.pdf)

Means of transportation and metropolitan area	Workers 16 years and over	Number	Percent	90-percent confidence interval on percent*
DROVE ALONE				
Saginaw-Bay City-Midland, MI MSA	177,490	153,396	86.4	86.1-86.8
Youngstown-Warren, OH MSA	256,048	220,686	86.2	85.9-86.5
Canton-Massillon, OH MSA	190,116	163,530	86.0	85.7-86.3
Florence, AL MSA	61,069	52,490	86.0	85.4-86.5
Steubenville-Weirton, OH-WV MSA	53,617	45,749	85.3	84.7-86.0
Decatur, AL MSA	64,248	54,762	85.2	84.7-85.8
Anniston, AL MSA	47,181	40,171	85.1	84.5-85.8
Owensboro, KY MSA	42,298	35,984	85.1	84.4-85.8
Evansville-Henderson, IN-KY MSA	143,722	122,135	85.0	84.6-85.4
Johnson City-Kingsport-Bristol, TN-VA MSA	211,953	180,091	85.0	84.7-85.3
CARPOOL				
Salinas, CA MSA	164,517	32,117	19.5	19.0-20.0
Brownsville-Harlingen-San Benito, TX MSA	106,769	20,742	19.4	18.8-20.1
Honolulu, HI MSA	412,250	80,009	19.4	19.1-19.7
Laredo, TX MSA	61,256	11,822	19.3	18.5-20.1
McAllen-Edinburg-Mission, TX MSA	176,308	33,671	19.1	18.6-19.6
Visalia-Tulare-Porterville, CA MSA	130,744	24,391	18.7	18.1-19.2
Merced, CA MSA	73,346	13,535	18.5	17.7-19.2
Bakersfield, CA MSA	229,733	42,220	18.4	18.0-18.8
Victoria, TX MSA	37,867	6,651	17.6	16.6-18.6
Jacksonville, NC MSA	79,399	13,629	17.2	16.6-17.7
PUBLIC TRANSPORTATION				
New York-Northern New Jersey-Long Island, NY-NJ-CT-PA CMSA	9,319,218	2,320,155	24.9	24.8-25.0
Chicago-Gary-Kenosha, IL-IN-WI CMSA	4,218,108	484,835	11.5	11.4-11.6
San Francisco-Oakland-San Jose, CA CMSA	3,432,157	325,212	9.5	9.4-9.6
Washington-Baltimore, DC-MD-VA-WV CMSA	3,839,052	361,877	9.4	9.3-9.5
Boston-Worcester-Lawrence, MA-NH-ME-CT CMSA	2,898,680	261,862	9.0	8.9-9.1
Philadelphia-Wilmington-Atlantic City, PA-NJ-DE-MD CMSA	2,815,405	245,909	8.7	8.6-8.8
Honolulu, HI MSA	412,250	34,250	8.3	8.1-8.5
Seattle-Tacoma-Bremerton, WA CMSA	1,776,224	119,919	6.8	6.7-6.9
Pittsburgh, PA MSA	1,057,354	65,345	6.2	6.1-6.3
Portland-Salem, OR-WA CMSA	1,105,133	63,126	5.7	5.6-5.8
WALKED				
State College, PA MSA	63,097	7,844	12.4	11.9-13.0
Jacksonville, NC MSA	79,399	8,219	10.4	9.9-10.8
Iowa City, IA MSA	63,087	6,306	10.0	9.5-10.5
Bloomington, IN MSA	60,423	5,173	8.6	8.0-9.1
Champaign-Urbana, IL MSA	91,368	7,770	8.5	8.1-8.9
Corvallis, OR MSA	37,747	2,910	7.7	7.1-8.3
Flagstaff, AZ-UT MSA	56,904	4,246	7.5	7.0-7.9
Lawton, OK MSA	51,684	3,767	7.3	6.8-7.8
Wichita Falls, TX MSA	65,448	4,594	7.0	6.5-7.5
Lawrence, KS MSA	54,496	3,659	6.7	6.2-7.3
WORKED AT HOME				
Santa Fe, NM MSA	73,129	5,064	6.9	6.5-7.3
Medford-Ashland, OR MSA	79,197	4,441	5.6	5.3-6.0
San Luis Obispo-Atascadero-Paso Robles, CA MSA	107,807	6,028	5.6	5.2-6.0
St. Cloud, MN MSA	90,105	4,978	5.5	5.2-5.8
Grand Junction, CO MSA	54,101	2,854	5.3	4.9-5.7
Fort Collins-Loveland, CO MSA	134,615	6,855	5.1	4.8-5.4
Wausau, WI MSA	65,680	3,340	5.1	4.7-5.4
Barnstable-Yarmouth, MA MSA	72,154	3,668	5.1	4.7-5.5
Eugene-Springfield, OR MSA	152,737	7,763	5.1	4.9-5.4
Bellingham, WA MSA	79,263	3,998	5.0	4.6-5.4

*For the highest percentage of commuters, the 90-percent confidence interval applies to the percent.

Note: Because of sampling error, the estimates in this table may not be significantly different from one another or from rates for other geographic areas not listed in this table.

Note: Metropolitan Statistical Areas (MSAs) are used in conjunction with Consolidated Metropolitan Statistical Areas (CMSAs) for the purposes of reporting these means of transportation to work. For more complete information on metropolitan area definitions, see http://www.census.gov/population/www/estimates/metroarea.html.

Source: U.S. Census Bureau, Census 2000 Summary File 3.

living in group quarters. The deviation of a sample estimate from the average of all possible samples is called the sampling error.

In addition to the variability that arises from the sampling procedures, both sample data and 100-percent data are subject to nonsampling error. Nonsampling error may be introduced during any of the various complex operations used to collect and process data. Such errors may include: not enumerating every household or every person in the population, failing to obtain all required information from the respondents, obtaining incorrect or inconsistent information, and recording information incorrectly. In addition, errors can occur during the field review of the enumerators' work, during clerical handling of the census questionnaires, or during the electronic processing of the questionnaires.

While it is impossible to completely eliminate error from an operation as large and complex as the decennial census, the Census Bureau attempts to control the sources of such error during the data collection and processing operations. The primary sources of error and

the programs instituted to control error in Census 2000 are described in detail in *Summary File 3 Technical Documentation* under Chapter 8, "Accuracy of the Data," located at *www.census.gov/prod /cen2000/doc/sf3.pdf.*

Nonsampling error may affect the data in two ways: (1) errors that are introduced randomly will increase the variability of the data and, therefore, should be reflected in the standard errors; and (2) errors that tend to be consistent in one direction will bias both sample and 100-percent data in that direction. For example, if respondents consistently tend to underreport their incomes, then the resulting estimates of households or families by income category will tend to be understated for the higher income categories and overstated for the lower income categories. Such biases are not reflected in the standard errors.

More Information:

The Census 2000 Summary File 3 data are available from the American Factfinder on the Internet (*factfinder.census.gov).* They were released on a state-by-state basis during 2002. For information on

confidentiality protection, nonsampling error, sampling error, and definitions, also see *www.census.gov /prod/cen2000/doc/sf3.pdf* or contact the Customer Services Center at 301-763-INFO (4636).

Information on population and housing topics is presented in the Census 2000 Brief series, located on the Census Bureau's Web site at *www.census.gov/population/www /cen2000/briefs.html.* This series presents information on race, Hispanic origin, age, sex, household type, housing tenure, and social, economic, and housing characteristics, such as ancestry, income, and housing costs.

For additional information on Journey to Work and Place of Work, including reports and survey data, visit the Census Bureau's Internet site at *www.census.gov /population/www/socdemo /journey.html.* To find information about the availability of data products, including reports, CD-ROMs, and DVDs, call the Customer Services Center at 301-763-INFO (4636), or e-mail *webmaster@census.gov.*

Congressional Apportionment

Census 2000 Brief

Issued July 2001

C2KBR/01-7

By
Karen M. Mills

The Census 2000 apportionment population was 281,424,177, as shown in Table 1. The apportionment population consists of the resident population of the 50 states plus overseas federal employees (military and civilian) and their dependents living with them, who were included in their home states. The population of the District of Columbia is excluded from the apportionment population. As required by the U.S. Supreme Court ruling (*Department of Commerce v. House of Representatives*, 525 U.S. 316, 119 S. Ct. 765 (1999)), the apportionment population counts do not reflect the use of statistical sampling to adjust for overcounting or undercounting in the census.

This report, part of a series that analyzes population and housing data collected by Census 2000, examines trends in congressional apportionment and discusses the apportionment population — what it is, who is included, what method is used to calculate it, and so forth.

Apportionment is a fundamental reason for the census.

One of the fundamental reasons for conducting the decennial census of population is to reapportion the U.S. House of Representatives. Apportionment is the process of dividing the 435 memberships or seats in the U.S. House of Representatives among the 50 states. An apportionment has been made on the basis of each decennial census from 1790 to 2000, except following the 1920 census.

The average size of a congressional district will rise.

The number of representatives or seats in the U.S. House of Representatives has remained constant at 435 since 1911, except for a temporary increase to 437 at the time of admission of Alaska and Hawaii as states in 1959 (see Table 1). However, the apportionment based on the 1960 census, which took effect for the congressional election in 1962, reverted to 435 seats.

The average size of a congressional district based on the Census 2000 apportionment population will be 646,952, more than triple the average district size of 193,167 based on the 1900 census apportionment, and about 74,486 more than the average size based on the 1990 census (572,466). Of the seven states with one seat in Census 2000, the population of the largest — Montana — was 905,316, compared with an average size of congressional district in the other

Table 1.
Apportionment Population Based on Census 2000 and Apportionment of U.S. House of Representatives: 1900 to 2000

(For information on confidentiality protection, nonsampling error, and definitions, see *www.census.gov/prod/cen2000/doc/pl94-171.pdf*)

State	2000 apportionment population[1]			Number of representatives										
	Total	Resident population	U.S. population overseas	2000	1990	1980	1970	1960	1950	1940	1930	1920[2]	1910	1900
Apportionment total	**281,424,177**	**280,849,847**	**574,330**	**435**	**435**	**435**	**435**	**435**	**[3]437**	**435**	**435**	**435**	**[3]435**	**[3]391**
Alabama	4,461,130	4,447,100	14,030	7	7	7	7	8	9	9	9	10	10	9
Alaska	628,933	626,932	2,001	1	1	1	1	1	1	(X)	(X)	(X)	(X)	(X)
Arizona	5,140,683	5,130,632	10,051	8	6	5	4	3	2	2	1	1	1	(X)
Arkansas	2,679,733	2,673,400	6,333	4	4	4	4	4	6	7	7	7	7	7
California	33,930,798	33,871,648	59,150	53	52	45	43	38	30	23	20	11	11	8
Colorado	4,311,882	4,301,261	10,621	7	6	6	5	4	4	4	4	4	4	3
Connecticut	3,409,535	3,405,565	3,970	5	6	6	6	6	6	6	6	5	5	5
Delaware	785,068	783,600	1,468	1	1	1	1	1	1	1	1	1	1	1
Florida	16,028,890	15,982,378	46,512	25	23	19	15	12	8	6	5	4	4	3
Georgia	8,206,975	8,186,453	20,522	13	11	10	10	10	10	10	10	12	12	11
Hawaii	1,216,642	1,211,537	5,105	2	2	2	2	2	1	(X)	(X)	(X)	(X)	(X)
Idaho	1,297,274	1,293,953	3,321	2	2	2	2	2	2	2	2	2	2	1
Illinois	12,439,042	12,419,293	19,749	19	20	22	24	24	25	26	27	27	27	25
Indiana	6,090,782	6,080,485	10,297	9	10	10	11	11	11	11	12	13	13	13
Iowa	2,931,923	2,926,324	5,599	5	5	6	6	7	8	8	9	11	11	11
Kansas	2,693,824	2,688,418	5,406	4	4	5	5	5	6	6	7	8	8	8
Kentucky	4,049,431	4,041,769	7,662	6	6	7	7	7	8	9	9	11	11	11
Louisiana	4,480,271	4,468,976	11,295	7	7	8	8	8	8	8	8	8	8	7
Maine	1,277,731	1,274,923	2,808	2	2	2	2	2	3	3	3	4	4	4
Maryland	5,307,886	5,296,486	11,400	8	8	8	8	8	7	6	6	6	6	6
Massachusetts	6,355,568	6,349,097	6,471	10	10	11	12	12	14	14	15	16	16	14
Michigan	9,955,829	9,938,444	17,385	15	16	18	19	19	18	17	17	13	13	12
Minnesota	4,925,670	4,919,479	6,191	8	8	8	8	8	9	9	9	10	10	9
Mississippi	2,852,927	2,844,658	8,269	4	5	5	5	5	6	7	7	8	8	8
Missouri	5,606,260	5,595,211	11,049	9	9	9	10	10	11	13	13	16	16	16
Montana	905,316	902,195	3,121	1	1	2	2	2	2	2	2	2	2	1
Nebraska	1,715,369	1,711,263	4,106	3	3	3	3	3	4	4	5	6	6	6
Nevada	2,002,032	1,998,257	3,775	3	2	2	1	1	1	1	1	1	1	1
New Hampshire	1,238,415	1,235,786	2,629	2	2	2	2	2	2	2	2	2	2	2
New Jersey	8,424,354	8,414,350	10,004	13	13	14	15	15	14	14	14	12	12	10
New Mexico	1,823,821	1,819,046	4,775	3	3	3	2	2	2	2	1	1	1	(X)
New York	19,004,973	18,976,457	28,516	29	31	34	39	41	43	45	45	43	43	37
North Carolina	8,067,673	8,049,313	18,360	13	12	11	11	11	12	12	11	10	10	10
North Dakota	643,756	642,200	1,556	1	1	1	1	2	2	2	2	3	3	2
Ohio	11,374,540	11,353,140	21,400	18	19	21	23	24	23	23	24	22	22	21
Oklahoma	3,458,819	3,450,654	8,165	5	6	6	6	6	6	8	9	8	8	5
Oregon	3,428,543	3,421,399	7,144	5	5	5	4	4	4	4	3	3	3	2
Pennsylvania	12,300,670	12,281,054	19,616	19	21	23	25	27	30	33	34	36	36	32
Rhode Island	1,049,662	1,048,319	1,343	2	2	2	2	2	2	2	2	3	3	2
South Carolina	4,025,061	4,012,012	13,049	6	6	6	6	6	6	6	6	7	7	7
South Dakota	756,874	754,844	2,030	1	1	1	2	2	2	2	2	3	3	2
Tennessee	5,700,037	5,689,283	10,754	9	9	9	8	9	9	10	9	10	10	10
Texas	20,903,994	20,851,820	52,174	32	30	27	24	23	22	21	21	18	18	16
Utah	2,236,714	2,233,169	3,545	3	3	3	2	2	2	2	2	2	2	1
Vermont	609,890	608,827	1,063	1	1	1	1	1	1	1	1	2	2	2
Virginia	7,100,702	7,078,515	22,187	11	11	10	10	10	10	9	9	10	10	10
Washington	5,908,684	5,894,121	14,563	9	9	8	7	7	7	6	6	5	5	3
West Virginia	1,813,077	1,808,344	4,733	3	3	4	4	5	6	6	6	6	6	5
Wisconsin	5,371,210	5,363,675	7,535	8	9	9	9	10	10	10	10	11	11	11
Wyoming	495,304	493,782	1,522	1	1	1	1	1	1	1	1	1	1	1

(X) Not applicable.

[1]Includes the resident population for the 50 states, as ascertained by Census 2000 under Title 13, U.S. Code, and counts of overseas U.S. military and federal civilian employees (and their dependents living with them) allocated to their home state, as reported by the employing federal agencies. The apportionment population does not include the resident or the overseas population of the District of Columbia.

[2]No reapportionment was made based on the 1920 census.

[3]Includes representatives assigned by Congress to newly admitted states after the apportionment act for that census: 1900, Oklahoma (five representatives); 1910, Arizona and New Mexico (one representative each); and 1950, Alaska and Hawaii (one representative each).

Note: As required by the U.S. Supreme Court ruling (*Department of Commerce v. House of Representatives,* 525 U.S. 316, 119 S. Ct. 765 (1999)), the Census 2000 apportionment population counts do not reflect the use of statistical sampling to adjust for overcounting or undercounting.

Source: U.S. Census Bureau, Census 2000 and earlier censuses at *www.census.gov/population/www/censusdata/apportionment.html;* and 1990 and earlier censuses also published in 1990 CPH-2-1, *Population and Housing Unit Counts, United States,* Table 3.

Figure 1.

Apportionment of the U.S. House of Representatives for the 108th Congress

(For information on confidentiality protection, nonsampling error, and definitions, see *www.census.gov/prod/cen2000/doc/pl94-171.pdf*)

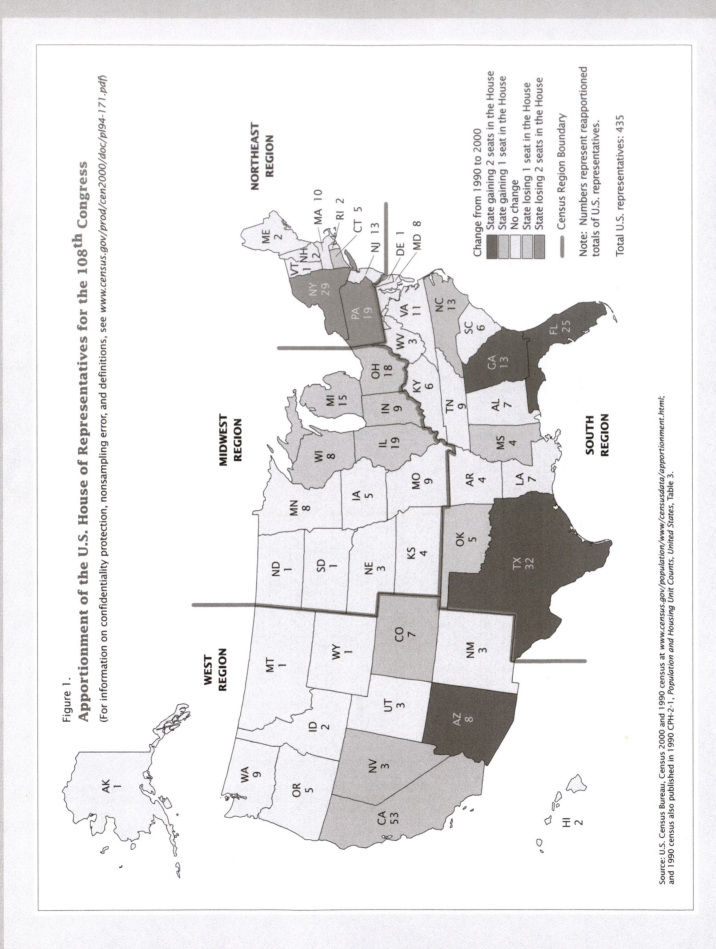

Change from 1990 to 2000

- State gaining 2 seats in the House
- State gaining 1 seat in the House
- No change
- State losing 1 seat in the House
- State losing 2 seats in the House
- Census Region Boundary

Note: Numbers represent reapportioned totals of U.S. representatives.

Total U.S. representatives: 435

Source: U.S. Census Bureau, Census 2000 and 1990 census at *www.census.gov/population/www/censusdata/apportionment.html*; and 1990 census also published in 1990 CPH-2-1, *Population and Housing Unit Counts, United States*, Table 3.

43 states of 646,259. Wyoming, also with one seat in Census 2000, had the smallest district size, with 495,304.

Twelve seats in the U.S. House of Representatives will shift from one state to another.

As a result of the apportionment based on Census 2000, 12 seats in the U.S. House of Representatives will shift among 18 states. Eight states will have more representatives in the 108th Congress, which convenes in January 2003, and ten states will have fewer representatives (see Figure 1 and Table 2).

Of the eight states gaining seats, four — Arizona, Florida, Georgia, and Texas — will each gain two seats. The other four — California, Colorado, Nevada, and North Carolina — will each gain one seat.

Of the ten states losing seats, two — New York and Pennsylvania — will each lose two seats. The other eight — Connecticut, Illinois, Indiana, Michigan, Mississippi, Ohio, Oklahoma, and Wisconsin — will each lose one seat.

The 1990 census apportionment shifted 19 seats.

Following the 1990 census, reapportionment shifted 19 seats among 21 states (see Table 2). The largest gains were in California (seven seats), Florida (four seats), and Texas (three seats). Five states gained one seat each: Arizona, Georgia, North Carolina, Virginia, and Washington.

The largest losses in seats after the 1990 census apportionment were in New York (three fewer seats); and in Illinois, Michigan, Ohio, and Pennsylvania (two fewer seats each). Eight states lost one seat each: Iowa, Kansas, Kentucky, Louisiana, Massachusetts, Montana, New Jersey, and West Virginia.

Table 2.
Change in the Number of U.S. Representatives by State: 1990 and 2000

(For information on confidentiality protection, nonsampling error, and definitions, see www.census.gov/prod/cen2000/doc/pl94-171.pdf)

State	Seats gained	State	Seats lost
BASED ON THE 1990 CENSUS			
Total gain in 8 states	**19**	**Total loss in 13 states**	**19**
California.............	7	New York................	3
Florida	4	Illinois	2
Texas	3	Michigan	2
Arizona	1	Ohio	2
Georgia	1	Pennsylvania............	2
North Carolina	1	Iowa	1
Virginia..............	1	Kansas................	1
Washington...........	1	Kentucky	1
		Louisiana..............	1
		Massachusetts	1
		Montana...............	1
		New Jersey	1
		West Virginia...........	1
BASED ON CENSUS 2000			
Total gain in 8 states	**12**	**Total loss in 10 states**	**12**
Arizona	2	New York...............	2
Florida	2	Pennsylvania...........	2
Georgia	2	Connecticut	1
Texas	2	Illinois	1
California.............	1	Indiana	1
Colorado	1	Michigan	1
Nevada	1	Mississippi.............	1
North Carolina	1	Ohio	1
		Oklahoma	1
		Wisconsin	1

Source: U.S. Census Bureau, Census 2000 and 1990 census at *www.census.gov/population/www/censusdata/apportionment.html*; and 1990 census also published in 1990 CPH-2-1, *Population and Housing Unit Counts, United States*, Table 3.

Shifts in congressional representation reflect regional trends in population.

The regional patterns of change in congressional representation between 1990 and 2000 reflect the Nation's continuing shift in population from the Northeast and Midwest to the South and West.

Based on the Census 2000 apportionment, the net increase of five seats in the South reflected a gain of seven seats in four states and a loss of two seats, one each in Mississippi and Oklahoma (see Table 3). The West gained five seats and lost none; the Northeast and Midwest each lost five seats and gained none.

Based on the 1990 census apportionment, the net increase of seven seats in the South reflected a gain of ten seats in five states and a loss of three seats, one each in Kentucky, Louisiana, and West Virginia. The net increase of eight seats in the West reflected a gain of nine seats in three states and a loss of one seat in Montana. The Northeast lost seven seats and gained none; the Midwest lost eight seats and gained none.

Figure 2 shows the percentage distribution of House seats or

Table 3.
Change in the Number of U.S. Representatives by Region: 1990 and 2000

(For information on confidentiality protection, nonsampling error, and definitions, see *www.census.gov/prod/cen2000/doc/pl94-171.pdf*)

Region	Seats changed based on the 1990 census	Seats changed based on Census 2000
Northeast (net)	**-7**	**-5**
Gained	-	-
Lost...	7	5
Midwest (net)......................................	**-8**	**-5**
Gained	-	-
Lost...	8	5
South (net)	**7**	**5**
Gained	10	7
Lost...	3	2
West (net)	**8**	**5**
Gained	9	5
Lost...	1	-

- Represents zero.

Source: U.S. Census Bureau, Census 2000 and 1990 census at *www.census.gov/ population/www/censusdata/apportionment.html*; and 1990 census also published in 1990 CPH-2-1, *Population and Housing Unit Counts, United States,* Table 3.

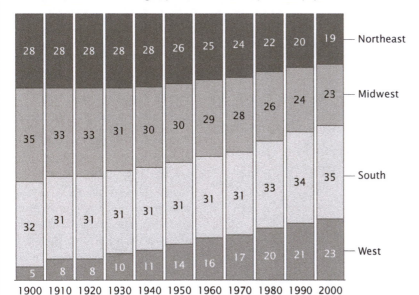

Figure 2.
Percentage Distribution of Seats in the U.S. House of Representatives by Region: 1900 to 2000

(For information on confidentiality protection, nonsampling error, and definitions, see *www.census.gov/prod/cen2000/doc/pl94-171.pdf*)

Source: U.S. Census Bureau, Census 2000 and earlier censuses at *www.census.gov/population/www/ censusdata/apportionment.html*; and 1990 and earlier censuses also published in 1990 CPH-2-1, *Population and Housing Unit Counts, United States,* Table 3.

memberships by region for each census in the 20th century. The West gradually increased its share of House seats in each decade of the last century, so that its 23-percent share in 2000 was more than four times its 5-percent share in 1900.

During the same time, the South's share of House seats, after a small initial fall between 1900 and 1910, held steady at 31 percent for seven decades, until rising to 35 percent by 2000. The South continued to hold the largest share of House seats of any of the four regions in 2000, as it has since 1940.

Meanwhile, the Midwest, which accounted for the largest regional share of House seats from 1900 to 1920, showed a gradual decline in its share to 23 percent in 2000, the same as the West.

After holding 28 percent of the House seats from 1900 to 1940, the Northeast saw a drop to 19 percent by 2000, the smallest share of House seats of any of the four regions.

The Congress decides the method to calculate the apportionment.

Several apportionment methods have been used since the first census in 1790. The apportionment for Census 2000 was calculated using the method of equal proportions, in accordance with the provisions of Title 2, U.S. Code. This method has been used in every census since the 1940 census. First, each state is assigned one congressional seat, as provided by the Constitution. Then the apportionment formula allocates the remaining 385 congressional seats one at a time among the 50 states until all 435 seats are assigned.

The goal of apportionment is to produce the most equitable distribution of congressional seats among the states. The method of equal proportions attains this by minimizing the percentage differences in the size of the congressional districts.

ADDITIONAL TOPICS ON CONGRESSIONAL APPORTIONMENT

When are the apportionment population counts given to the President? To the Congress? To the states?

To the President. Title 13, U.S. Code, requires that the apportionment population counts for each state be delivered to the President within 9 months of Census Day, which was April 1, 2000. The Census 2000 counts were delivered to the President on December 28, 2000.

To the Congress. According to Title 2, U.S. Code, within 1 week of the opening of the next session of the Congress in the new year, the President must report to the Clerk of the U.S. House of Representatives the apportionment population counts for each state and the number of representatives to which each state is entitled.

To the States. Also according to Title 2, U.S. Code, within 15 days of receiving the apportionment population counts from the President, the Clerk of the House must inform each state governor of the number of representatives to which each state is entitled.

Were undocumented residents (aliens) in the 50 states included in the Census 2000 apportionment population counts?

Yes, all people (citizens and noncitizens) with a usual residence in one of the 50 states were included in Census 2000 and thus in the apportionment counts.

Were children under 18 years old included in the Census 2000 apportionment population counts even though they cannot vote?

Yes, being old enough to vote, being registered to vote, or voting are not requirements for inclusion in the apportionment counts.

Did the Census 2000 apportionment population counts also include any Americans overseas?

Yes, as for the 1990 census, the Census 2000 apportionment counts included those overseas federal employees (military and civilian) and their dependents living with them that could be assigned to a home state. These data were provided to the Census Bureau by the employing federal departments and agencies from their administrative records. Private U.S. citizens living abroad who were not affiliated with the federal government (either as employees or their dependents) were not included in the overseas counts, which are used solely for reapportioning seats in the U.S. House of Representatives, not for redistricting (see question below).

What is the difference between apportionment and redistricting?

Population data from the decennial census provide the basis for both apportioning seats in the House of Representatives among the states and for redistricting this and other legislative bodies.

Apportionment is the process of determining the number of representatives to which each state is entitled in the U.S. House of Representatives based on the decennial census. By law, the apportionment results (the apportionment population of each state) must be submitted to the President within 9 months of the census date.

Redistricting is the process of revising the geographic boundaries of areas from which people elect representatives to the U.S. House of Representatives, a state legislature, a county or city council, a school board, and so forth. By law, redistricting data must be submitted to the states within 1 year of the census date. The Census Bureau released the redistricting population data at the census block level on a state-by-state basis during March 2001.

FOR MORE INFORMATION

Census 2000 data are available on the Internet via *factfinder.census.gov* and for purchase on CD-ROM and later on DVD. For more information on apportionment for both Census 2000 and the 1990 census, visit the U.S. Census Bureau's Internet site at *www.census.gov/ population/www/censusdata/ apportionment.html.*

Information on other population and housing topics is presented in the Census 2000 Brief series, located on the U.S. Census Bureau's Web site at *www.census.gov/ population/www/cen2000/briefs.html.* This series presents information about race, Hispanic origin, age, sex, household type, housing tenure, and other social, economic, and housing characteristics.

For more information about Census 2000, including data products, call our Customer Services Center at 301-763-INFO (4636) or e-mail *webmaster@census.gov.*

Migration by Race and Hispanic Origin: 1995 to 2000

Census 2000 Special Reports

Issued October 2003

CENSR-13

By
Jason P. Schachter

The likelihood that people move varies by race and Hispanic origin.[1] Given these differences, do the locations to and from which they move also differ? In other words, do geographic patterns of migration differ by race and Hispanic origin? The redistribution of people by race and Hispanic origin is largely a function of domestic and international migration, which strongly influence the population growth and decline of particular racial and ethnic groups in particular locations.

This report first examines and compares general mobility patterns by race and Hispanic origin — how many people moved and what types of moves they made, based on the Census 2000 question on residence in 1995. The second part of the report discusses the redistribution of people by race and Hispanic origin between 1995 and 2000 by examining net migration at the regional, division, and state levels and by considering movers from abroad. This provides an overview of geographic areas that experienced the largest net migration gain (or loss) of people of various race or Hispanic-origin groups, as well as the geographic origins and destinations of individual populations. Maps of county-level net migration rates complement the regional-, divisional-, and state-level analyses with a finer degree of geographic detail. This report helps answer questions about what areas are gaining

Census 2000 allowed respondents to choose more than one race. With the exception of the Two or more races group, all race groups discussed in this report refer to people who indicated *only one* racial identity among the six major categories: White, Black or African American, American Indian and Alaska Native, Asian, Native Hawaiian or Other Pacific Islander, and Some other race. The use of the single-race population in this report does not imply that it is the preferred method of presenting or analyzing data. The Census Bureau uses a variety of approaches.

This report also uses truncated race and Hispanic origin names. People who indicated they were "Black or African American" (single race) are simply referred to as "Blacks." People who marked the single race "White" and reported that they were not Hispanic are referred to as "non-Hispanic Whites." Hispanics may be of any race.[2] See Table 1 for the full list of race and Hispanic-origin names.

---

[1] For examples of moving rates by race and Hispanic origin, see U.S. Census Bureau, 2001, *Geographical Mobility: March 1999 to March 2000*, by Jason Schachter, Current Population Reports P20-538, Washington, DC: Government Printing Office.

[2] Because Hispanics may be of any race, data in this report for Hispanics overlap with data for racial groups. Based on Census 2000 sample data, the proportion Hispanic was 8.0 percent for Whites, 1.9 percent for Blacks, 14.6 percent for American Indians and Alaska Natives, 1.0 percent for Asians, 9.5 percent for Native Hawaiians and Other Pacific Islanders, 97.1 percent for those reporting Some other race, and 31.1 percent for those reporting Two or more races.

USCENSUSBUREAU

Helping You Make Informed Decisions

U.S. Department of Commerce
Economics and Statistics Administration
U.S. CENSUS BUREAU

United States
Census
2000

Common Migration Terms

Movers can be classified by type of move and are categorized as to whether they moved within the same county, to a different county within the same state, to a different county from a different state or region, or were movers from abroad.[3] *Migration* is commonly defined as moves that cross jurisdictional boundaries (counties in particular), while moves within a jurisdiction are referred to as *residential mobility*. Moves between counties are often referred to as *intercounty* moves, while moves within the same county are often termed *intracounty* moves. Further, migration can be differentiated as movement within the United States (*domestic* or *internal* migration) and movement into and out of the United States (*international* migration). Census 2000 did not measure the number of people who moved to locations outside the United States, hence net international migration cannot be estimated.

or losing people of various races or Hispanic origin, such as where the growth of Hispanics is occurring and the nature of Black migration to the South.[4]

GEOGRAPHIC MOBILITY

The likelihood that a person moved is related to personal characteristics. For example, people in their twenties are much more likely to move than people in their fifties. The likelihood of moving varies by race and Hispanic origin, though some of this variation is explained by age structure, housing tenure, and other characteristics.[5] The following section briefly looks at mobility rates by race and Hispanic origin, as well as the types of moves that were made.

Hispanics and Blacks were more mobile than non-Hispanic Whites.

As seen in Table 1, non-Hispanic Whites were the least mobile population, as only 43 percent changed residence between 1995 and 2000. In contrast, 49 percent of Blacks, 50 percent of American Indian and Alaska Natives, 54 percent of Asians, and 56 percent of Hispanics moved during this period. Native Hawaiians and Other Pacific Islanders were found to be as mobile as Hispanics, while those in the Two-or-more race group were slightly more mobile.

Hispanics were more likely to have made intracounty moves, while non-Hispanic Whites were more likely to have made interstate moves.

Among people who moved, non-Hispanic Whites (20.6 percent), although less mobile than other groups, were more likely to have

moved to a different state than other racial or Hispanic-origin groups. Hispanics (11.5 percent) were the least likely to have made an interstate move. Conversely, Blacks (62.9 percent) and Hispanics (57.2 percent) were more likely to have made intracounty (short-distance) moves than non-Hispanic Whites (53.1 percent). These differences to some extent reflect differences in characteristics like education, which is positively related to the likelihood of moving long-distances.[6]

Among movers, Asians (26.4 percent) were most likely to have moved to the United States, while many Hispanics (17.3 percent) were also likely to have moved from abroad. Between 1995 and 2000, non-Hispanic Whites (2.7 percent) were least likely to have moved from abroad. These findings are consistent with high proportions of immigrants coming from Asia and Latin America in recent decades.

INTERNAL MIGRATION AND MOVERS FROM ABROAD

Although non-Hispanic Whites were more likely to have moved between states than other groups, 2.3 million Blacks, 2.0 million Hispanics, and 830,000 Asians moved to a different state between 1995 and 2000. Migration is a major factor in explaining changing concentrations of people of different races and Hispanic origin in the United States. The following section examines migration patterns of the non-Hispanic White, Black, Asian, and Hispanic populations. Data on migration by detailed race and Hispanic-origin categories (as seen in Table 1) are available on the Internet at *www.census.gov/population/www /cen2000/migration.html*.

---

[3] In this report, movers from abroad include movers from foreign countries, as well as movers from Puerto Rico, U.S. Island Areas, and U.S. minor outlying islands.

[4] Due to the relatively small number of people in some race categories, discussion of migration data for all race and Hispanic origin groups is limited. Gross and net migration data for regions and states for all race groups are available on the Internet at *www.census.gov/population/www/cen2000 /migration.html*.

[5] For example, see U.S. Census Bureau, 2001, *Geographical Mobility: March 1999 to March 2000*, by Jason Schachter, Current Population Reports P20-538, Washington, DC: Government Printing Office.

The estimates in this report are based on responses from a sample of the population. As with all surveys, estimates may vary from the actual values because of sampling variation or other factors. All comparisons made in this report have undergone statistical testing and are significant at the 90-percent confidence level unless otherwise noted.

[6] Ibid.

Table 1.
Type of Move by Race and Hispanic Origin: 1995 to 2000

(Data based on a sample. For information on confidentiality protection, sampling error, nonsampling error, and definitions, see www.census.gov/prod/cen2000/doc/sf3.pdf)

Characteristic	Total, 5 years and over	Same residence (nonmovers)	Movers				
			Total	Same county	Different county, same state	Different state	From abroad[1]
NUMBER							
United States.....................	262,375,152	142,027,578	120,347,674	65,435,013	25,327,355	22,089,460	7,495,846
White alone..........................	198,544,098	111,545,820	86,998,278	46,420,436	19,785,431	17,231,876	3,560,535
Black or African American alone........	31,616,957	16,223,625	15,393,332	9,679,483	2,669,686	2,329,209	714,954
American Indian and Alaska Native alone...............................	2,243,344	1,132,387	1,110,957	594,838	279,239	196,252	40,628
Asian alone	9,520,205	4,374,003	5,146,202	2,136,373	824,565	828,709	1,356,555
Native Hawaiian and Other Pacific Islander alone......................	347,400	155,919	191,581	96,056	30,207	37,203	28,115
Some other race alone	13,802,883	5,809,056	7,993,827	4,671,217	1,076,952	865,261	1,380,397
Two or more races...................	6,300,265	2,786,768	3,513,497	1,836,610	661,275	600,950	414,662
Hispanic (of any race)	31,569,576	14,047,118	17,522,458	10,030,447	2,453,817	2,010,719	3,027,475
White alone, not Hispanic or Latino	183,342,983	104,404,231	78,938,752	41,908,074	18,648,378	16,287,499	2,094,801
PERCENT							
United States.....................	100.0	54.1	45.9	24.9	9.7	8.4	2.9
White alone..........................	100.0	56.2	43.8	23.4	10.0	8.7	1.8
Black or African American alone........	100.0	51.3	48.7	30.6	8.4	7.4	2.3
American Indian and Alaska Native alone...............................	100.0	50.5	49.5	26.5	12.4	8.7	1.8
Asian alone	100.0	45.9	54.1	22.4	8.7	8.7	14.2
Native Hawaiian and Other Pacific Islander alone......................	100.0	44.9	55.1	27.6	8.7	10.7	8.1
Some other race alone	100.0	42.1	57.9	33.8	7.8	6.3	10.0
Two or more races...................	100.0	44.2	55.8	29.2	10.5	9.5	6.6
Hispanic (of any race)	100.0	44.5	55.5	31.8	7.8	6.4	9.6
White alone, not Hispanic or Latino	100.0	56.9	43.1	22.9	10.2	8.9	1.1
PERCENT OF MOVERS							
United States.....................	(NA)	(NA)	100.0	54.4	21.0	18.4	6.2
White alone..........................	(NA)	(NA)	100.0	53.4	22.7	19.8	4.1
Black or African American alone........	(NA)	(NA)	100.0	62.9	17.3	15.1	4.6
American Indian and Alaska Native alone...............................	(NA)	(NA)	100.0	53.5	25.1	17.7	3.7
Asian alone	(NA)	(NA)	100.0	41.5	16.0	16.1	26.4
Native Hawaiian and Other Pacific Islander alone......................	(NA)	(NA)	100.0	50.1	15.8	19.4	14.7
Some other race alone	(NA)	(NA)	100.0	58.4	13.5	10.8	17.3
Two or more races...................	(NA)	(NA)	100.0	52.3	18.8	17.1	11.8
Hispanic (of any race)	(NA)	(NA)	100.0	57.2	14.0	11.5	17.3
White alone, not Hispanic or Latino	(NA)	(NA)	100.0	53.1	23.6	20.6	2.7

NA Not applicable.

[1]This category includes movers from foreign countries, as well as movers from Puerto Rico, U.S. Island Areas, and U.S. minor outlying islands.

Source: U.S. Census Bureau, Census 2000.

REGIONAL AND DIVISIONAL MIGRATION

The South experienced net inmigration of Blacks; the West had net outmigration of Hispanics to other U.S. regions.

Between 1995 and 2000, more Blacks moved to the South from other parts of the United States than left the South. Black migrants to the South totaled 680,000, and Blacks leaving the region numbered 334,000. These figures mean that for every Black person who left the South, two moved in (see Table 2A). During this same period, the West, Northeast, and Midwest experienced net outmigration of Blacks.

More Hispanics left the West to go to other parts of the United States than moved to the West from elsewhere in the United States between 1995 and 2000. In this 5-year period, 396,000 Hispanics moved from the West to other parts of the United States, and 235,000 Hispanics moved to the West from elsewhere in the United States (see Table 2B). The Northeast also experienced net outmigration of Hispanics during 1995-2000. The South and Midwest recorded net inmigration of Hispanics.

Internal migration redistributed Asians from the Northeast and Midwest to the South. Between 1995 and 2000, Asians moving to the South numbered 165,000 and those leaving for other parts of the United States totaled 120,000. The West had similar numbers of Asians moving to and from the region. The Northeast and Midwest experienced net outmigration of Asians during this period.

As non-Hispanic Whites comprise over two-thirds (69.9 percent) of the total population aged 5 years and over, interregional migration

patterns of this group generally reflected patterns of the overall population.[7]

Movers from abroad helped offset net domestic migration loss in many areas.

In terms of population distribution, movers from abroad can have a tremendous impact on an area's racial or ethnic make-up, particularly for Asians and Hispanics, who make up the majority of movers from abroad. Given the nature of census migration data, however, it is often difficult to distinguish between movers from abroad and secondary migration of immigrants. A mover from abroad may move to one location in the United States, then move once or even several times more during the same 5-year period. For example, a Hispanic person living in Georgia in 2000 who reported living abroad in 1995 could have moved to Georgia in 1999 after initially moving to California in 1996. Instead of being counted as a California-to-Georgia domestic migrant, this person would be characterized as having come to Georgia from abroad.

Movers from abroad strongly affected the Northeast. About 488,000 non-Hispanic Whites, 474,000 Hispanics, 336,000 Asians, and 200,000 Blacks moved there from abroad, offsetting the region's domestic net migration loss. Other regions were also affected, as over 1.2 million Hispanics moved to the South, 1.0 million Hispanics moved to the West, and 316,000 Hispanics moved to the Midwest from

outside the United States. It is important to keep migration from abroad in mind when interpreting the domestic migration numbers described in this report.

The South experienced the largest net migration gain of non-Hispanic Whites, Blacks, Asians, and Hispanics.

Among the four regions, the South had the highest level of net domestic migration gain (and net migration rates) for non-Hispanic Whites, Blacks, Asians, and Hispanics (see Tables 2A and 2B). Between 1995 and 2000, approximately 1.1 million more non-Hispanic Whites moved into the South than moved away. The South also experienced positive net migration of 347,000 Blacks, 256,000 Hispanics, and 45,000 Asians. Much of this net migration gain was concentrated in the South Atlantic division, in terms of numbers for non-Hispanic Whites (870,000), Blacks (299,000), Hispanics (210,000), and Asians (40,000), and in term of rates for non-Hispanic Whites (27.7), Blacks (31.2), and Asians (49.5).[8] The East South Central division actually had the highest net migration rate (149.8) for Hispanics in the South, but this can be explained partly by the relatively small number of Hispanics in that area in 1995. This net migration rate indicates that the East South Central division gained 150 Hispanics for every 1,000 Hispanics living there in 1995.

---

[7] For example, see U.S. Census Bureau, 2003, *Domestic Migration Across Regions, Divisions, and States, 1995 to 2000*, by Rachel S. Franklin, Census 2000 Special Reports, CENSR-7, Washington, DC: Government Printing Office.

[8] The net migration rate in this report is based on an approximated 1995 population, which is the sum of the respective race or Hispanic origin population in 2000 who reported living in the area in both 1995 and 2000, and those who reported living in that area in 1995 but lived elsewhere in 2000. The net migration rate divides net migration, which is inmigration minus outmigration, by the approximated 1995 population and multiplies the result by 1,000.

Table 2A.
Migration for Regions, Divisions, and States for Non-Hispanic Whites and Blacks: 1995 to 2000

(Data based on a sample. For information on confidentiality protection, sampling error, nonsampling error, and definitions, see www.census.gov/prod/cen2000/doc/sf3.pdf)

Area	Non-Hispanic White					Black				
	Domestic migration				From abroad[3]	Domestic migration				From abroad[3]
	Inmigrants[1]	Outmigrants[1]	Net	Rate[2]		Inmigrants[1]	Outmigrants[1]	Net	Rate[2]	
Northeast	1,164,467	1,996,103	-831,636	-22.2	487,975	136,780	369,665	-232,885	-41.6	199,584
New England	607,579	690,655	-83,076	-7.6	149,374	43,251	58,064	-14,813	-23.5	33,934
Maine	100,442	96,109	4,333	3.8	7,768	1,379	2,240	-861	-153.6	715
New Hampshire	149,481	122,870	26,611	24.9	9,682	2,307	3,003	-696	-84.7	721
Vermont	65,339	61,701	3,638	6.7	5,693	875	1,894	-1,019	-290.1	200
Massachusetts	350,626	405,836	-55,210	-11.3	81,980	21,519	28,057	-6,538	-21.9	18,670
Rhode Island	75,223	76,166	-943	-1.2	7,508	5,281	5,170	111	2.9	2,908
Connecticut	196,980	258,485	-61,505	-24.5	36,743	20,296	26,106	-5,810	-21.1	10,720
Middle Atlantic	924,746	1,673,306	-748,560	-28.2	338,601	125,263	343,335	-218,072	-43.9	165,650
New York	512,230	999,636	-487,406	-42.8	199,610	79,965	245,331	-165,366	-58.8	111,712
New Jersey	344,265	482,687	-138,422	-26.1	73,438	64,552	99,234	-34,682	-33.2	31,739
Pennsylvania	521,013	643,745	-122,732	-12.5	65,553	62,265	80,289	-18,024	-16.2	22,199
Midwest	1,814,349	2,336,977	-522,628	-10.6	388,827	212,076	276,090	-64,014	-10.9	100,010
East North Central	1,384,189	1,833,164	-448,975	-13.3	278,147	174,183	242,300	-68,117	-13.9	67,431
Ohio	475,779	591,436	-115,657	-12.8	52,484	59,909	62,222	-2,313	-2.0	15,877
Indiana	356,039	358,679	-2,640	-0.5	26,643	42,957	36,765	6,192	13.8	6,377
Illinois	486,177	731,656	-245,479	-30.4	105,409	72,810	128,048	-55,238	-31.8	25,185
Michigan	353,252	438,455	-85,203	-11.6	70,101	49,237	65,686	-16,449	-12.8	15,474
Wisconsin	276,636	276,632	4	-	23,510	22,096	22,405	-309	-1.2	4,518
West North Central	912,944	986,597	-73,653	-4.7	110,680	86,954	82,851	4,103	4.3	32,579
Minnesota	274,634	279,555	-4,921	-1.2	27,845	25,164	16,046	9,118	71.9	14,992
Iowa	182,010	217,529	-35,519	-13.8	16,762	8,207	8,806	-599	-11.5	2,483
Missouri	384,426	351,036	33,390	7.7	31,556	42,217	39,883	2,334	4.2	8,612
North Dakota	53,085	75,427	-22,342	-38.9	4,849	1,328	2,054	-726	-200.9	411
South Dakota	61,286	74,092	-12,806	-20.2	4,258	1,326	1,880	-554	-142.6	683
Nebraska	120,850	142,237	-21,387	-15.1	8,997	8,168	8,582	-414	-6.9	1,967
Kansas	214,200	224,268	-10,068	-4.8	16,413	19,830	24,886	-5,056	-36.3	3,431
South	3,529,784	2,402,821	1,126,963	18.7	676,428	680,131	333,585	346,546	20.8	340,028
South Atlantic	2,818,286	1,948,455	869,831	27.7	426,507	590,691	291,986	298,705	31.2	242,419
Delaware	71,228	65,533	5,695	10.8	5,102	19,633	10,559	9,074	73.0	3,626
Maryland	292,340	361,289	-68,949	-22.1	43,296	138,544	94,995	43,549	34.1	36,276
District of Columbia	60,242	63,501	-3,259	-22.2	10,212	38,572	72,690	-34,118	-98.3	7,939
Virginia	577,572	555,565	22,007	4.8	71,739	140,733	111,584	29,149	23.8	29,822
West Virginia	124,545	134,537	-9,992	-6.2	4,912	7,461	7,069	392	7.6	610
North Carolina	661,619	434,635	226,984	45.0	49,966	142,875	89,504	53,371	35.0	25,027
South Carolina	329,537	225,854	103,683	43.7	20,372	77,555	61,302	16,253	15.2	10,213
Georgia	586,179	442,736	143,443	31.1	56,570	252,237	122,488	129,749	65.7	43,659
Florida	1,403,907	953,688	450,219	48.2	164,338	168,862	117,576	51,286	25.9	85,247
East South Central	931,704	750,153	181,551	15.2	76,154	180510	154,398	26,112	8.5	32,102
Kentucky	264,445	237,402	27,043	8.1	20,178	29,599	26,985	2,614	10.0	5,365
Tennessee	451,808	340,956	110,852	27.0	27,470	68,995	49,652	19,343	23.5	9,795
Alabama	237,585	221,246	16,339	5.6	18,593	63,630	56,784	6,846	6.6	10,529
Mississippi	159,417	132,100	27,317	17.2	9,913	51,415	54,106	-2,691	-2.9	6,413
West South Central	1,170,114	1,094,533	75,581	4.4	173,767	199,246	177,517	21,729	5.4	65,507
Arkansas	197,119	163,911	33,208	17.2	11,242	25,593	27,785	-2,192	-5.8	3,695
Louisiana	168,513	220,305	-51,792	-19.5	16,323	58,075	76,149	-18,074	-13.6	9,682
Oklahoma	237,165	229,659	7,506	3.1	17,167	27,729	28,046	-317	-1.4	4,887
Texas	890,170	803,511	86,659	8.6	129,035	156,403	114,091	42,312	20.1	47,243
West	2,027,550	1,800,249	227,301	6.7	541,571	171,309	220,956	-49,647	-18.0	75,332
Mountain	1,652,381	1,161,580	490,801	42.9	155,042	88,890	66,090	22,800	53.8	18,316
Montana	101,168	104,308	-3,140	-4.1	4,951	754	1,189	-435	-178.9	148
Idaho	161,653	128,553	33,100	32.5	9,743	1,292	1,943	-651	-139.2	599
Wyoming	64,650	74,374	-9,724	-23.2	3,406	979	2,004	-1,025	-270.5	190
New Mexico	133,401	154,397	-20,996	-26.8	11,817	6,068	8,792	-2,724	-84.9	1,278
Arizona	610,112	369,507	240,605	85.5	43,286	28,071	19,162	8,909	69.7	5,388
Colorado	503,409	388,356	115,053	40.2	42,990	24,767	25,984	-1,217	-8.6	5,877
Utah	195,985	185,542	10,443	6.1	23,249	3,641	3,144	497	39.3	1,286
Nevada	303,920	178,460	125,460	115.2	15,600	31,356	11,910	19,446	197.2	3,550
Pacific	1,384,359	1,647,859	-263,500	-11.7	386,529	127,671	200,118	-72,447	-31.1	57,016
Washington	469,316	426,963	42,353	9.9	73,182	29,843	28,981	862	5.3	7,838
Oregon	324,659	271,011	53,648	20.5	27,904	7,551	7,405	146	3.2	2,131
California	1,003,615	1,302,897	-299,282	-19.9	269,407	98,713	161,893	-63,180	-30.4	44,243
Alaska	71,792	98,569	-26,777	-64.1	6,068	5,999	9,071	-3,072	-140.1	1,164
Hawaii	76,455	109,897	-33,442	-116.3	9,968	10,576	17,779	-7,203	-293.1	1,640

– Represents zero or rounds to zero.

[1]Values for in- and outmigrants for regions, divisions, and states were calculated independently. Thus, within a region, numbers for states do not sum to the number for each division, which in turn do not sum to the number for the region.

[2]The net migration rate in this report is based on an approximated 1995 population, which is the sum of the respective race or Hispanic origin population in 2000 who reported living in the area in both 1995 and 2000, and those who reported living in that area in 1995 but lived elsewhere in 2000. The net migration rate divides net migration, which is inmigration minus outmigration, by the approximated 1995 population and multiplies the result by 1,000.

[3]This category includes movers from foreign countries, as well as movers from Puerto Rico, U.S. Island Areas, and U.S. minor outlying islands.

Note: A negative value for net migration or the net migration rate is indicative of net outmigration, meaning that more migrants left an area than entered it. Positive numbers reflect net inmigration to an area.

Source: U.S. Census Bureau, Census 2000.

Table 2B.
Migration for Regions, Divisions, and States for Asians and Hispanics: 1995 to 2000

(Data based on a sample. For information on confidentiality protection, sampling error, nonsampling error, and definitions, see www.census.gov/prod/cen2000/doc/sf3.pdf)

Area	Asian					Hispanic				
	Domestic migration				From abroad[3]	Domestic migration				From abroad[3]
	Inmigrants[1]	Outmigrants[1]	Net	Rate[2]		Inmigrants[1]	Outmigrants[1]	Net	Rate[2]	
Northeast	92,601	131,108	-38,507	-23.0	335,649	105,187	256,229	-151,042	-34.0	473,590
New England	45,528	40,041	5,487	19.9	63,683	64,582	53,491	11,091	16.5	98,989
Maine	1,308	1,579	-271	-41.0	1,204	2,378	2,200	178	23.1	352
New Hampshire.	3,293	3,087	206	19.2	3,260	4,538	3,175	1,363	96.0	2,082
Vermont	675	1,323	-648	-162.2	982	,410	1,442	-32	-6.9	277
Massachusetts	31,219	25,204	6,015	34.4	40,238	32,817	30,557	2,260	6.8	48,767
Rhode Island	3,745	3,628	117	6.0	2,531	10,293	6,513	3,780	58.1	11,525
Connecticut	12,942	12,874	68	1.1	15,468	25,505	21,963	3,542	14.3	35,986
Middle Atlantic.	76,447	120,441	-43,994	-31.5	271,966	91,865	253,998	-162,133	-43.0	374,601
New York	49,754	100,280	-50,526	-57.8	156,671	67,273	225,429	-158,156	-62.0	223,033
New Jersey	51,380	43,877	7,503	20.9	78,315	64,410	79,132	-14,722	-16.0	116,588
Pennsylvania	28,548	29,519	-971	-5.9	36,980	44,410	33,665	10,745	35.4	34,980
Midwest	90,841	100,558	-9,717	-10.9	205,237	220,502	164,169	56,333	23.9	316,424
East North Central	70,558	80,011	-9,453	-14.3	155,839	136,862	126,736	10,126	5.3	240,659
Ohio	16,081	19,450	-3,369	-34.6	28,379	24,158	19,045	5,113	30.6	17,165
Indiana	10,199	10,744	-545	-13.6	13,547	32,050	15,228	16,822	118.7	26,304
Illinois	34,594	39,612	-5,018	-15.0	66,159	58,804	88,724	-29,920	-24.2	146,253
Michigan	18,848	18,788	60	0.5	36,534	33,305	22,944	10,361	42.1	27,600
Wisconsin.	10,685	11,266	-581	-9.0	11,220	20,609	12,859	7,750	57.1	23,337
West North Central. . . .	36,905	37,169	-264	-1.1	49,398	100,677	54,470	46,207	106.7	75,765
Minnesota	17,443	10,188	7,255	71.3	16,677	26,137	11,405	14,732	165.6	19,424
Iowa	4,570	7,074	-2,504	-89.0	6,619	15,417	9,333	6,084	112.7	10,068
Missouri	9,618	10,990	-1,372	-29.5	10,775	23,362	14,474	8,888	109.4	12,569
North Dakota	529	1,502	-973	-300.1	879	1,921	2,254	-333	-50.2	389
South Dakota	892	1,195	-303	-83.4	913	2,869	2,009	860	112.3	529
Nebraska	3,053	3,756	-703	-46.0	4,942	17,149	10,102	7,047	112.1	11,301
Kansas	6,237	7,901	-1,664	-48.4	8,593	26,333	17,404	8,929	67.9	21,485
South	165,229	120,051	45,178	31.9	303,806	548,330	292,235	256,095	28.7	1,215,592
South Atlantic	120,849	80,997	39,852	49.5	172,204	387,918	177,490	210,428	70.5	668,943
Delaware	3,169	3,007	162	14.3	3,367	5,514	3,323	2,191	84.4	4,801
Maryland	23,927	23,929	-2	–	31,674	29,000	22,436	6,564	39.2	30,178
District of Columbia	4,517	5,981	-1,464	-122.7	3,592	6,870	12,071	-5,201	-133.3	7,239
Virginia	31,240	24,423	6,817	35.7	41,995	51,761	36,818	14,943	65.7	51,284
West Virginia	1,745	2,541	-796	-102.7	1,874	2,368	2,386	-18	-1.8	577
North Carolina.	24,797	13,236	11,561	159.3	18,364	71,268	30,197	41,071	218.3	99,018
South Carolina	7,382	6,218	1,164	43.3	5,965	21,108	10,323	10,785	212.2	21,418
Georgia	29,085	14,769	14,316	123.8	29,731	78,567	30,954	47,613	208.9	105,951
Florida	34,707	26,613	8,094	39.6	35,642	221,534	129,054	92,480	45.2	348,477
East South Central	20,439	23,855	-3,416	-34.5	25,659	57,584	31,832	25,752	149.8	56,567
Kentucky	5,108	5,576	-468	-23.5	7,339	12,288	8,609	3,679	105.5	11,234
Tennessee	9,219	9,046	173	4.4	10,282	26,447	12,395	14,052	217.0	26,969
Alabama	4,525	6,938	-2,413	-98.9	5,715	14,039	8,254	5,785	124.8	12,281
Mississippi	3,460	4,168	-708	-47.4	2,323	7,857	5,621	2,236	86.2	6,083
West South Central . . .	62,018	53,276	8,742	17.0	105,943	251,002	231,087	19,915	3.4	490,082
Arkansas	2,831	3,430	-599	-40.2	3,459	18,924	8,170	10,754	216.2	14,143
Louisiana	6,601	9,898	-3,297	-68.5	6,602	14,094	14,804	-710	-7.7	7,693
Oklahoma	5,281	8,005	-2,724	-75.2	9,161	27,106	17,504	9,602	77.1	20,795
Texas	56,139	40,777	15,362	37.1	86,721	224,082	223,813	269	–	447,451
West	142,245	139,199	3,046	0.7	511,863	234,508	395,894	-161,386	-12.6	1,021,869
Mountain.	61,706	36,187	25,519	103.3	52,005	313,572	148,723	164,849	61.0	283,047
Montana	655	1,240	-585	-147.2	721	3,411	3,734	-323	-20.0	444
Idaho.	1,706	2,072	-366	-40.2	1,917	11,808	11,620	188	2.3	7,758
Wyoming	526	984	-458	-158.9	384	3,965	5,247	-1,282	-45.8	1,087
New Mexico	3,376	4,671	-1,295	-82.6	2,430	48,173	52,702	-4,529	-6.7	21,210
Arizona	16,297	10,578	5,719	89.1	15,138	113,081	57,611	55,470	56.9	113,527
Colorado	15,210	9,917	5,293	78.9	14,255	80,517	40,791	39,726	72.3	66,483
Utah	4,627	5,408	-781	-27.5	6,500	27,947	13,998	13,949	107.4	29,780
Nevada	23,868	5,876	17,992	323.1	10,660	87,917	26,267	61,650	255.3	42,758
Pacific	134,617	157,090	-22,473	-5.7	459,858	178,065	504,300	-326,235	-32.3	738,822
Washington	34,463	22,015	12,448	50.3	41,355	52,759	40,307	12,452	37.8	40,347
Oregon	12,916	9,483	3,433	46.3	14,467	35,819	22,250	13,569	71.7	34,399
California	127,384	151,864	-24,480	-7.9	377,408	160,374	505,947	-345,573	-36.5	660,076
Alaska.	4,685	3,593	1,092	54.7	2,782	5,794	6,754	-960	-43.9	1,546
Hawaii	13,650	28,616	-14,966	-31.5	23,846	11,179	16,902	-5,723	-71.4	2,454

– Represents zero or rounds to zero.

[1]Values for in- and outmigrants for regions, divisions, and states were calculated independently. Thus, within a region, numbers for states do not sum to the number for each division, which in turn do not sum to the number for the region.

[2]The net migration rate in this report is based on an approximated 1995 population, which is the sum of the respective race or Hispanic origin population in 2000 who reported living in the area in both 1995 and 2000, and those who reported living in that area in 1995 but lived elsewhere in 2000. The net migration rate divides net migration, which is inmigration minus outmigration, by the approximated 1995 population and multiplies the result by 1,000.

[3]This category includes movers from foreign countries, as well as movers from Puerto Rico, U.S. Island Areas, and U.S. minor outlying islands.

Note: A negative value for net migration or the net migration rate is indicative of net outmigration, meaning that more migrants left an area than entered it. Positive numbers reflect net inmigration to an area.

Source: U.S. Census Bureau, Census 2000.

What were the characteristics of Blacks who moved to the South?

According to Census 2000, more than half of the U.S. national Black population 5 years and over lived in the South. Contributing to this number was the net domestic inmigration of over 300,000 Blacks to the South between 1995 and 2000. What were the characteristics of these Black migrants? For one thing, Black inmigrants to the South had more education than southern Blacks who did not leave the region between 1995 and 2000. However, while 97,000 Blacks with college degrees moved to the South from other regions, 60,000 college educated Blacks moved away. So, while the South did gain many Blacks with higher educational attainment, they also gained many more with lower educational attainment. For instance, 137,000 Black migrants to the South had only a high school education, but only 66,000 outmigrants had this level of education.

Figure 1 shows the percentage age, sex, and education distribution of Blacks who migrated to the South, those who migrated away from the South, and those who did not leave the South between 1995 and 2000. In terms of percentages, Blacks who left the South were more likely to be college educated, male, and 25-44 years of age than those who moved into the South. Still, Black migrants to the South were more likely to be younger and more highly educated than Black noninterregional migrants. That Black inmigrants to the South tended to be older than Blacks who left the South could suggest some degree of return migration, with Blacks who left the South at younger ages now returning at older ages.

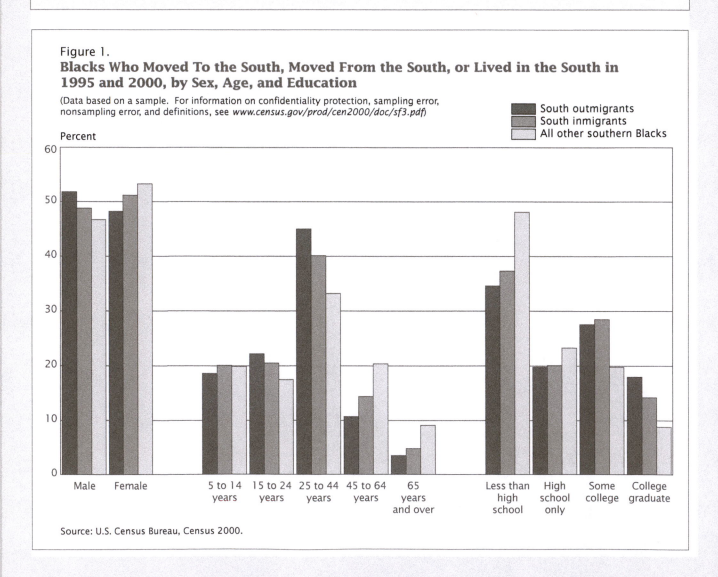

Figure 1.

Blacks Who Moved To the South, Moved From the South, or Lived in the South in 1995 and 2000, by Sex, Age, and Education

(Data based on a sample. For information on confidentiality protection, sampling error, nonsampling error, and definitions, see *www.census.gov/prod/cen2000/doc/sf3.pdf*)

■ South outmigrants
■ South inmigrants
□ All other southern Blacks

Source: U.S. Census Bureau, Census 2000.

The Northeast experienced a net migration loss of non-Hispanic Whites, Blacks, Asians, and Hispanics.

The Northeast experienced net domestic migration loss of all four race/Hispanic-origin groups and had the highest net outmigration rates of all four regions (22.2 for non-Hispanic Whites, 41.6 for Blacks, 23.0 for Asians, and 34.0 for Hispanics).[9] This means, in the case of non-Hispanic Whites, that the Northeast lost about 22 non-Hispanic Whites through migration for every 1,000 living in the region in 1995. In numerical terms, between 1995 and 2000, the Northeast had a net migration loss (from domestic sources) of 832,000 non-Hispanic Whites, 233,000 Blacks, 151,000 Hispanics, and 39,000 Asians. The majority of net outmigration from the Northeast left the Middle Atlantic division rather than New England. In fact, New England had positive net migration gain (from domestic sources) of both Hispanics (11,000) and Asians (5,000). It should also be noted that the net domestic migration loss of Hispanics (162,000) and Asians (44,000) from the Middle Atlantic division was offset by the arrival of Hispanics (375,000 — many from Puerto Rico) and Asians (272,000) from abroad.

The Midwest experienced a net migration gain of Hispanics, but had a net migration loss for all other groups.

The Midwest experienced a net domestic migration loss of non-Hispanic Whites (523,000), Blacks (64,000), and Asians (10,000), though these losses were smaller than those in the Northeast. However, the Midwest did have a positive net migration of Hispanics

(56,000), which offset a small portion of the net migration loss of the other three groups. The Hispanic net migration rate in the Midwest was 23.9, meaning that the Midwest gained about 24 Hispanics through migration for every 1,000 Hispanics living there in 1995.

The loss of non-Hispanic Whites, Asians, and Blacks was much greater in the East North Central division than in the West North Central division (see Tables 2A and 2B). Similarly, the West North Central division had a net migration gain of over 46,000 Hispanics, while the East North Central division's net gain of Hispanics was only 10,000. The West North Central division also had a net migration gain of 4,000 Blacks. It is important to remember that the Midwest gained over 300,000 Hispanics from abroad during this same period, some of whom might have been domestic inmigrants who moved to the Midwest after initially arriving at some other region in the United States. The majority of these Hispanic movers from abroad went to the East North Central Division (particularly Illinois).

The West's net migration gain was concentrated in the Mountain division.

The West experienced a net domestic migration gain of 227,000 non-Hispanic Whites, but had a net migration loss of 50,000 Blacks and 161,000 Hispanics. The region's net migration rate was highest for non-Hispanic Whites (6.7) and lowest for Blacks (-18.0). Net migration gain in the West was concentrated in the Mountain division. In fact, the Mountain division had positive net migration of non-Hispanic Whites, Asians, Blacks, and Hispanics, while the Pacific division had negative net migration for all four groups. Again, most of the net domestic outmigration of

Asians and Hispanics from the Pacific division was more than offset by movers from abroad. While the Pacific division had a net domestic migration loss of 22,000 Asians and 326,000 Hispanics, it gained 460,000 Asians and 739,000 Hispanics from abroad.

STATE-TO-STATE MIGRATION

The above analysis for regions and divisions can be extended to states. Among states, Florida had the largest net domestic migration gain of non-Hispanic Whites and Hispanics; Georgia had the highest net migration gain of Blacks; and Nevada, Texas, and Georgia had high net migration gains of Asians. In terms of net migration rates, Nevada had high rates for each of these groups.

Florida had the largest net migration gain of non-Hispanic Whites.

Florida experienced the largest net migration gain (450,000) of non-Hispanic Whites from other states, followed by Arizona and North Carolina. Nevada had the highest net migration rate for non-Hispanic Whites at 115.2, followed by Arizona (85.5). Finally, California (269,000) had the largest number of non-Hispanic White movers from abroad, followed by New York (200,000).

Georgia had the largest net migration gain of Blacks.

Black domestic migration patterns were somewhat different from those of non-Hispanic Whites, as the state with the largest net migration gain of Blacks was Georgia (130,000), followed by North Carolina (53,000), Florida (51,000), Maryland (44,000), and Texas (42,000).[10] In terms of net

---

[9] The estimated difference between non-Hispanic Whites and Asians was not statistically significant.

[10] The estimates for North Carolina and Florida were not statistically different.

Characteristics of Hispanics moving to and away from the Midwest.

As described earlier, both the South and the Midwest saw large increases in their Hispanic populations due to migration (both internal and international). While the South also experienced net migration gains of non-Hispanic Whites, Blacks, and Asians, the Midwest differed in that it had a net migration gain only of Hispanics. Did Hispanics moving to the Midwest differ from those living in the rest of the United States? Table 3 details the age, sex, nativity, and more detailed origin of Hispanic migrants who moved to and away from the Midwest, as well as the total U.S. Hispanic population 5 years and over.

Hispanic migrants to and from the Midwest were more likely to be male than the overall Hispanic population, as were Hispanics who moved from abroad. Among domestic Hispanic migrants, those who moved to the Midwest were more likely to be male than those who left the Midwest. In contrast, Hispanic migrants from the Midwest were somewhat older than Hispanic migrants to the Midwest. Hispanic outmigrants from the Midwest were more likely to be natives than domestic inmigrants, while these domestic inmigrants to the Midwest were as likely as the overall Hispanic population to be foreign born. Finally, both Hispanic movers from abroad and domestic migrants to the Midwest were more likely to be of Mexican origin than the overall U.S. Hispanic population. To summarize, Hispanics moving to the Midwest differed somewhat from the overall Hispanic population, being younger and more likely to be male and of Mexican descent, but these differences were not great.

Table 3.
Characteristics of Hispanic Migrants To and From the Midwest: 1995 to 2000

(Data based on a sample. For information on confidentiality protection, sampling error, nonsampling error, and definitions, see www.census.gov/prod/cen2000/doc/sf3.pdf)

Characteristic	U.S. Hispanics, aged 5 and over	Midwest inmigrants	Midwest outmigrants	From abroad to Midwest[1]
Total............................	31,569,576	220,502	164,169	316,424
PERCENT DISTRIBUTION				
Sex				
Male............................	51.3	55.9	54.1	58.7
Female...........................	48.8	44.1	45.9	41.3
Age				
5 to 14 years....................	21.6	22.4	20.6	14.2
15 to 24 years	20.5	23.5	22.0	38.1
25 to 44 years	37.2	44.9	43.5	39.6
45 to 64 years	15.2	8.2	10.7	6.9
65 years and over	5.4	1.1	3.2	1.4
Nativity				
Native...........................	55.8	54.7	65.9	12.6
Foreign born	44.2	45.3	34.1	87.4
Hispanic or Latino Origin				
Mexican..........................	58.6	66.5	59.2	76.9
Central American	5.3	5.6	3.6	4.8
South American	4.3	2.9	4.6	5.0
Puerto Rican......................	9.8	7.6	12.4	5.8
Cuban............................	3.8	2.0	3.3	0.9
Dominican	2.3	1.0	0.8	0.5
Other	15.9	14.4	16.1	6.2

[1]This category includes movers from foreign countries, as well as movers from Puerto Rico, U.S. Island Areas, and U.S. minor outlying islands.

Source: U.S. Census Bureau, Census 2000.

migration rates, Nevada had the highest net migration rate of Blacks at 197.2, while Delaware, Minnesota, Arizona, and Georgia also had high rates. New York (112,000) and Florida (85,000) had the largest number of Black movers from abroad, perhaps due to Caribbean and African immigrant destination choices.

Nevada had a large net migration gain of Asians.

Nevada (18,000), Texas (15,000), and Georgia (14,000) recorded large net migration gains of Asians.[11] In terms of rates, Nevada had by far the highest net migration rate for Asians at 323.1, followed by North Carolina (159.3) and Georgia (123.8).[12] California (377,000) and New York (157,000) were the top destination states of Asian movers from abroad.

[11] The estimates for Nevada, Texas, and Georgia were not statistically different.
[12] The estimates for North Carolina and Georgia, and for Georgia and Arizona were not statistically different.

Florida had the largest net domestic migration gain of Hispanics.

The states with the largest net domestic migration gains of Hispanics were similar to those for the race groups. Florida had the highest net migration gain of Hispanics (92,000), followed by Nevada, Arizona, and Georgia. High net migration rates (about 200 or more) of Hispanics were found in Nevada, North Carolina, Tennessee, Arkansas, South Carolina, and Georgia. While rates were not as high as in the southern states listed above, Hispanic net migration rates were also high (about 100 or more) in the midwestern states of Minnesota, Indiana, Nebraska, South Dakota, Iowa, and Missouri, suggesting rapid growth in those areas as well (see previous text box). It should be kept in mind that migration rates are often influenced by low population totals (in this case Hispanics) in those areas in 1995, as rates are particularly sensitive to low population bases.

The top six states in terms of the number of Hispanic movers from abroad mirrored the six immigration gateway states.[13] California was first with 660,000, followed by Texas (447,000), Florida (348,000), New York (223,000), Illinois (146,000), and New Jersey (117,000).[14]

New York and California had the highest net migration loss of all four race/Hispanic origin groups.

New York, California, and Illinois were the largest exporters of migrants among all four race/Hispanic origin groups. New York had the largest net migration loss of non-Hispanic Whites (487,000), Blacks (165,000), and Asians (51,000), and also had the second-largest loss of Hispanics (158,000).[15] California had the largest net migration loss of Hispanics (346,000), and the second-largest loss of non-Hispanic Whites (299,000) and Asians (24,000). Illinois had the third-largest loss of non-Hispanic Whites (245,000) and Hispanics (30,000). California (63,000) and Illinois (55,000) also had high net outmigration of Blacks.[16] As described earlier, much of this outmigration was moderated by large numbers of movers from abroad to these states.

Net outmigration rates varied by race and Hispanic origin.

Hawaii (116.3) had the highest net outmigration rate for non-Hispanic Whites, followed by Alaska (64.1) and New York (42.8).[17] Some of the highest net outmigration rates of Blacks were found in Hawaii (293.1), Vermont (290.1), and Wyoming (270.5).[18] North Dakota, Vermont, and Wyoming had high net outmigration rates of Asians. One of the highest Hispanic net outmigration rates was experienced by the District of Columbia (133.3), while Hawaii and New York also had high rates. The rates for Blacks and

Native Hawaiians moved to Nevada.

Of note was the extremely high state-level net migration rate (563.1) of Native Hawaiian and Other Pacific Islanders to Nevada. This means that Nevada gained 563 Native Hawaiians for every 1,000 Native Hawaiians living there in 1995. In addition, Nevada's net migration gain of 2,400 Native Hawaiian and Other Pacific Islanders was among the highest of all states, with only Washington being similar. In contrast, Hawaii and California had the largest net migration loss of Native Hawaiian and other Pacific Islanders (-7,000 and -4,000, respectively). When examining state origins of Native Hawaiian and other Pacific Islander migrants to Nevada, the largest flows came from Hawaii (1,600) and California (1,000).[19] Hawaii's economic downturn in the 1990s, combined with Nevada's rapid economic growth, may help explain this migration from Hawaii to Nevada.

Asians probably reflect low Black and Asian 1995 population totals, as rates are sensitive to low population bases.

STATE-TO-STATE MIGRATION FLOWS

Where did migrants to the top gaining states originate? What were the destinations of migrants from the top losing states? State-to-state migration flows illustrate the geographic origin of the gain

---

[13] For more discussion on "immigrant gateway states" and their effect on domestic migration patterns, see U.S. Census Bureau, 2003, *Migration of Natives and the Foreign Born: 1995 to 2000*, by Marc J. Perry and Jason P. Schachter, Census 2000 Special Reports, CENSR-11, Washington, DC: Government Printing Office.

[14] The estimates for New Jersey and Arizona were not statistically different.

---

[15] The estimates for Blacks and Hispanics were not statistically different.

[16] The estimates for California and Illinois were not statistically different.

[17] The estimates for New York, North Dakota, and the District of Columbia were not statistically different.

[18] The estimates for Hawaii, Vermont, and Wyoming, and several other states were not statistically different.

---

[19] The estimates for Hawaii and California were not statistically different.

What were the origins of Asians moving from Louisiana to Texas?

About 3,000 Asians moved from Louisiana to Texas. Disaggregating this migration flow by place of birth gives a clearer picture of the types of Asians who made this move. Figure 2 shows that a large percentage of Asian migrants who moved from Louisiana to Texas were born in Vietnam, as well as in India, Louisiana (perhaps the children of Asian immigrants), and China. These results illustrate the diversity among the Asian population and, in this case, of Asian migrants moving from Louisiana to Texas.

or loss for a particular state. [20] The following section describes some of the largest inmigration and outmigration flows, by race and Hispanic origin, for states with the largest net migration gains or losses of those populations.

Many non-Hispanic Whites moved from New York to Florida, and from California to nearby western states.

As detailed earlier, the two states with the largest net domestic migration gain of non-Hispanic Whites were Florida and Arizona. The largest inmigration flows of non-Hispanic Whites to Florida

___

[20] Tables with complete state-to-state migration flows of the White, Black, Asian, and Hispanic populations are available on the Census Bureau's Web site at *www.census.gov/population/www/cen2000/migration.html.*

came from New York (190,000), while the largest inmigration flows to Arizona of this group came from California (109,000) and Illinois (39,000). California and New York had the largest net migration loss of non-Hispanic Whites. The largest outmigration flows of non-Hispanic Whites from New York went to Florida (190,000) and the adjacent states of New Jersey (115,000) and Pennsylvania (73,000). The largest numbers of non-Hispanic White outmigrants from California moved to the western states of Arizona (109,000), Nevada (105,000), Washington (102,000), and Oregon (98,000).[21]

The destinations of outmigration flows from California were more geographically dispersed for Blacks than for non-Hispanic Whites.

As with non-Hispanic Whites, New York and California had large net migration losses of Blacks. New York's largest Black outmigration flows were to Florida (40,000), Georgia (28,000), New Jersey (26,000), and North Carolina (24,000).[22] Outmigration patterns of Blacks who left California were more geographically dispersed than those of non-Hispanic Whites, as the largest numbers moved to Texas (18,000), followed by Georgia and Nevada (14,000 each). States with large net migration gains of Blacks were Georgia and North Carolina. The largest number of Black inmigrants to Georgia came from Florida (32,000) and New York (28,000). Among Black inmigrants to North Carolina, the largest flows came from New York

Figure 2.
Place of Birth of Asian Louisiana-to-Texas Migrants: 1995 to 2000

(Only sources accounting for greater than one percent shown. Data based on a sample. For information on confidentiality protection, sampling error, nonsampling error, and definitions, see *www.census.gov/prod/cen2000/doc/sf3.pdf*)

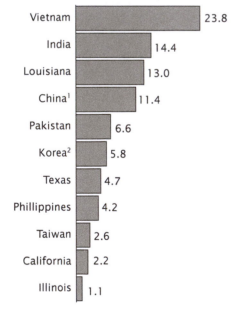

Vietnam	23.8
India	14.4
Louisiana	13.0
China[1]	11.4
Pakistan	6.6
Korea[2]	5.8
Texas	4.7
Phillippines	4.2
Taiwan	2.6
California	2.2
Illinois	1.1

[1] Excludes migrants born in Hong Kong, Taiwan, or Macau.
[2] Includes migrants born in South Korea and North Korea.
Source: U.S. Census Bureau, Census 2000.

___

[21] The estimates for Arizona and Nevada, for Nevada and Washington, and for Washington and Oregon were not statistically different.

[22] The estimates for Georgia and New Jersey, and for New Jersey and North Carolina were not statistically different.

Figure 3.

Net Migration Rates for Non-Hispanic Whites: 1995 to 2000

(Data based on a sample. For more information on confidentiality protection, sampling error, nonsampling error, and definitions, see *www.census.gov/prod/cen2000/doc/sf3.pdf*)

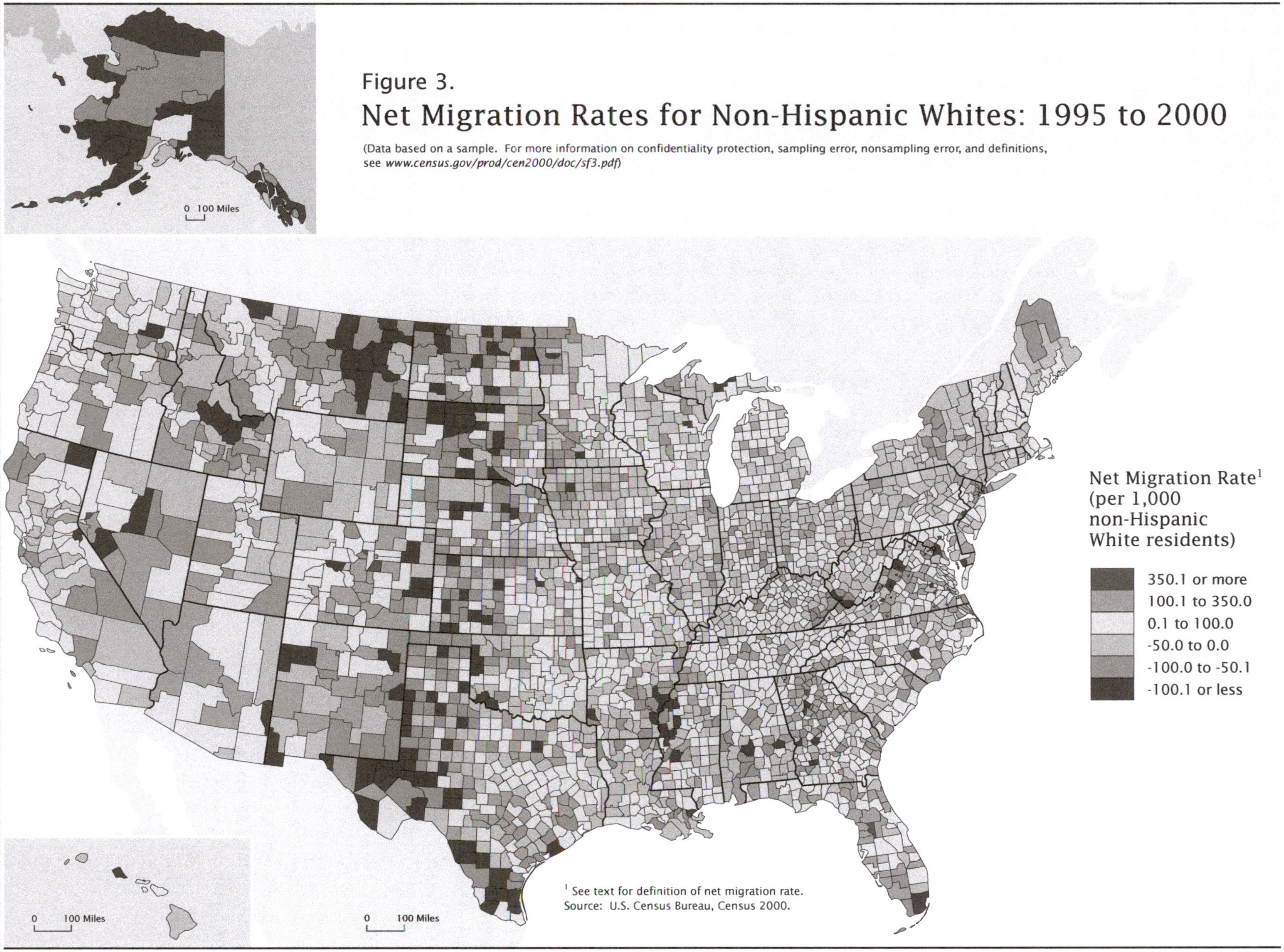

Net Migration Rate[1]
(per 1,000
non-Hispanic
White residents)

350.1 or more
100.1 to 350.0
0.1 to 100.0
-50.0 to 0.0
-100.0 to -50.1
-100.1 or less

[1] See text for definition of net migration rate.
Source: U.S. Census Bureau, Census 2000.

(24,000), Virginia (15,000), and South Carolina (14,000).[23]

Many Asian migrants to Nevada and Texas came from California.

States with large net migration gains of Asians were Nevada and Texas. The bulk of Asian inmigrants to Nevada came from California (13,000) and Hawaii (3,000), while many of Texas' Asian inmigrants came from California (12,000), as well as states like New York, Illinois, and Louisiana (see text box 6). New York and California had the largest net migration loss of Asians. The largest flows of Asians out of New York went to New Jersey (25,000), followed by California (14,000). California's three largest Asian out-migration streams were to Nevada (13,000), Texas (12,000), and Washington (12,000), two of which (Nevada and Texas) were the same as for Blacks.[24]

Hispanic state-to-state migration patterns showed many immigrant gateway states to be top origins for domestic migration.

Florida and Nevada experienced large net migration gains of Hispanics between 1995 and 2000. Large Hispanic inmigration flows to Florida came from fellow gateway states like New York (68,000), New Jersey (27,000), and California (22,000). Similarly, the vast majority of Hispanics who moved to Nevada came from California (61,000), while many also came from Texas (5,000), and Arizona (4,000).[25] California and New York had the largest net migration loss of Hispanics. The largest Hispanic

outmigration flows from California went to Texas (62,000), Nevada (61,000), and Arizona (60,000).[26] From New York, the largest outflows were to Florida (68,000), New Jersey (38,000), and Pennsylvania (17,000).

COUNTY-LEVEL MIGRATION

This section looks at county-level migration by race and Hispanic origin. Figures 3 through 5 depict county-level net migration rates for non-Hispanic Whites, Blacks, and Hispanics, respectively, providing greater geographic detail regarding the results described earlier.[27] At this scale, events like military base closings and the openings and closings of retirement homes and prisons can have substantial effects on migration patterns (especially net migration rates) for counties with small populations of particular groups.

County-level migration patterns of non-Hispanic Whites displayed patterns of continued suburbanization.

County-level migration patterns of non-Hispanic Whites confirm migration gains in the South and the West and losses in the Midwest and the Northeast. However, even within states located in these regions there were variations. For example, counties in the central and eastern parts of Texas gained migrants, while the western portion of the state experienced net losses. Also, the net migration gain of non-Hispanic Whites in north Texas counties surrounding Dallas County fits classic suburbanization patterns. Another example of suburbanization was in the Chicago area, as inner counties

had net migration losses of non-Hispanic Whites, while surrounding counties had net migration gains of this group.

Among counties nationwide, the largest gains of non-Hispanic Whites were in Maricopa County, AZ (147,000) and Clark County, NV (102,000), in the Phoenix and Las Vegas metropolitan areas, respectively. In juxtaposition, counties with large urban centers like Cook County, IL —Chicago (233,000), Los Angeles County, CA —Los Angeles (181,000), and Dallas County, TX —Dallas (104,000) had the largest losses of non-Hispanic Whites. In terms of net migration rates, among counties with a population of at least 5,000 non-Hispanic Whites in 2000, counties like Douglas County, CO (suburban Denver) (488.8), Sumter County, FL (456.4), and Forsyth County, GA (suburban Atlanta) (451.2) had high net inmigration rates, while St. Louis City, MO (322.5) and Chattahoochee County, GA (302.2) had high net outmigration rates.[28]

Many southern counties showed modest net migration gain or losses of Blacks

In general, county-level migration patterns of Blacks were similar to those of non-Hispanic Whites, but reflected greater variation in the Midwest, primarily due to the low number of Blacks living in some counties in that region. Although the South as a whole experienced net inmigration of Blacks between 1995 and 2000 (particularly in the interior of states along the eastern seaboard), many parts of the region had moderate rates of net outmigration of Blacks (see Figure 4). Relatively few southern counties had relatively high net outmigration

---

[23] The estimates for Virginia and South Carolina were not statistically different.

[24] The estimates for Nevada, Texas, and Washington were not statistically different.

[25] The estimates for Texas and Arizona were not statistically different.

[26] The estimates for Texas, Nevada, and Arizona were not statistically different.

[27] County-level migration data for Asians are not presented because of the high number of counties with very small Asian populations.

[28] The estimates for Douglas County, Sumter County, and Forsyth County, and for St Louis City and Chattahoochee County were not statistically different.

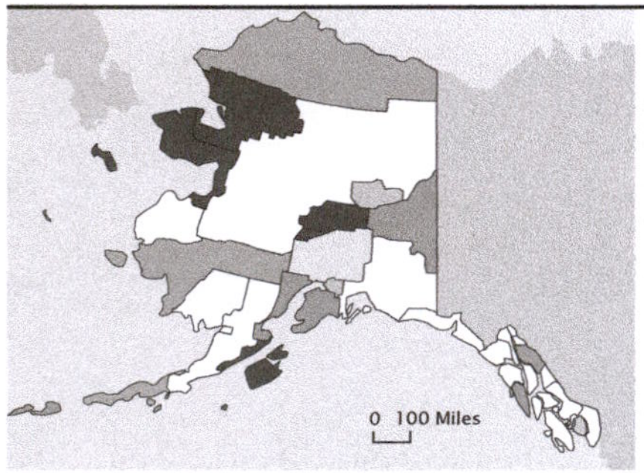

Figure 4.
Net Migration Rates for Blacks: 1995 to 2000

(Data based on a sample. For information on confidentiality protection, sampling error, nonsampling error, and definitions, see *www.census.gov/prod/cen2000/doc/sf3.pdf*)

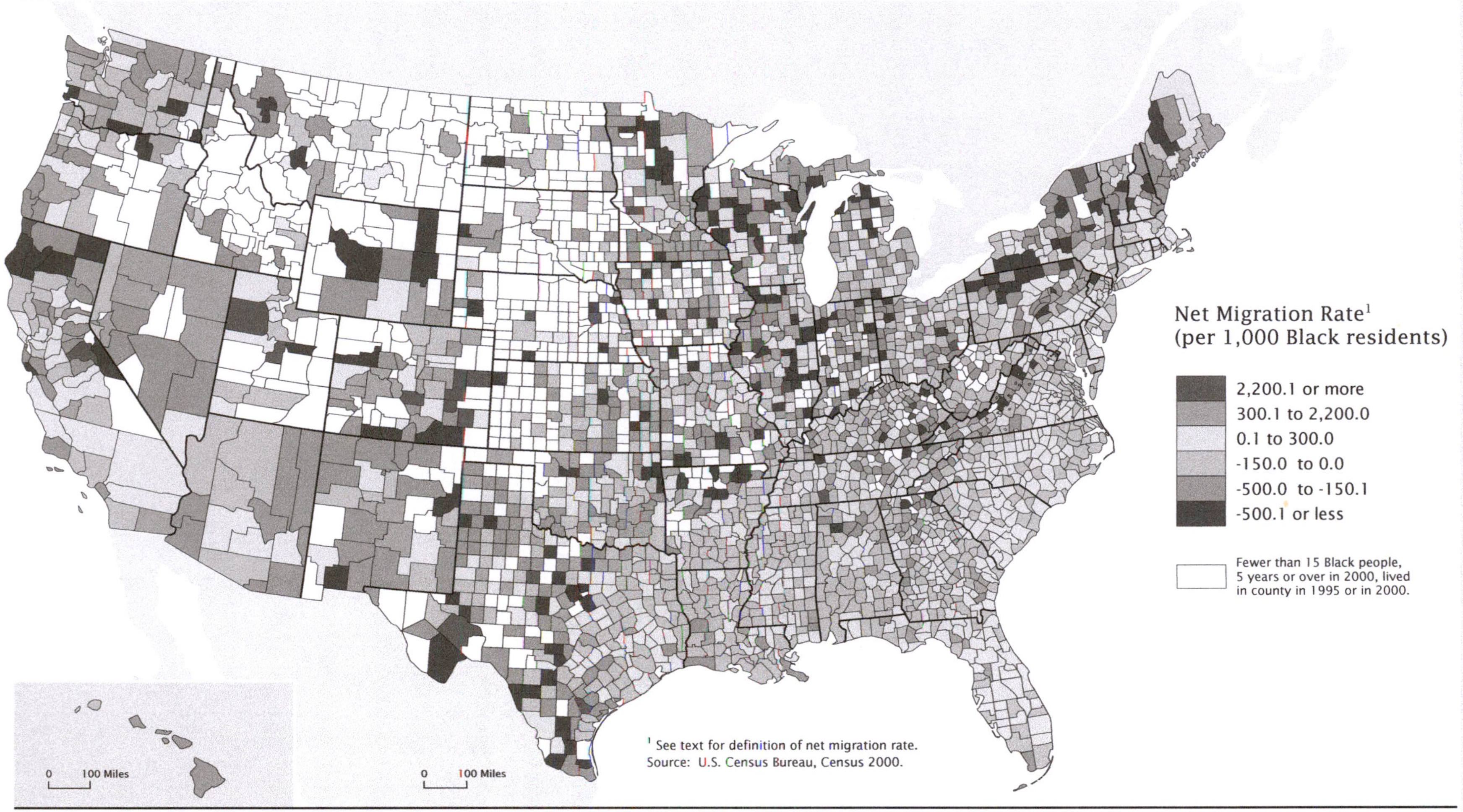

Net Migration Rate[1]
(per 1,000 Black residents)

2,200.1 or more
300.1 to 2,200.0
0.1 to 300.0
-150.0 to 0.0
-500.0 to -150.1
-500.1 or less

Fewer than 15 Black people,
5 years or over in 2000, lived
in county in 1995 or in 2000.

[1] See text for definition of net migration rate.
Source: U.S. Census Bureau, Census 2000.

0   100 Miles

0   100 Miles

0   100 Miles

rates of Blacks, partly due to the large proportion of Blacks already living in the South. Many counties that experienced high net outmigration rates of Blacks were concentrated in western parts of Texas, and in parts of Appalachia and the Midwest.

Nationally, in terms of individual county net migration gain, St. Louis County, MO, Baltimore County, MD, and Clayton County, GA (around 31,000 each) had large net gains of Blacks. Counties with the greatest volume of net migration loss were Kings County, NY (78,000), Cook County, IL (70,000), and Los Angeles County, CA (47,000). These counties encompassed considerable parts of New York City, Chicago, and Los Angeles, respectively.

Net inmigration of Hispanics extended across extensive parts of the South and Midwest.

Many counties in the South and Midwest experienced moderate to high rates of net inmigration of Hispanics (see Figure 5). These data exclude movers from outside the United States, so the extensive gains of Hispanics in the South and Midwest represent population exchanges with other parts of the United States.

Areas with net outmigration of Hispanics were areas where Hispanic immigrants traditionally

settle. Many counties along the U.S.-Mexico border experienced net outmigration of Hispanics (excluding movement of people who lived outside the United States in 1995). Other parts of Texas and many counties in New Mexico and along the California coast also experienced net outmigration of Hispanics to other parts of the United States. Quite clearly, Figure 5 depicts a redistribution of Hispanics from traditional areas of residence in the southwest to a wider variety of locations, especially in the South and Midwest.

Counties with the largest net migration gain of Hispanics were similar to those which gained non-Hispanic Whites, and included Clark County, NV (56,000), Maricopa County, AZ (47,000), and Broward County, FL (41,000).[29] As before, these numbers exclude movers from outside the United States. Conversely, counties with the greatest net migration loss of Hispanics were Los Angeles County, CA (290,000), Cook County, IL (55,000), Kings County, NY (55,000), and Miami-Dade County, FL (51,000).[30] These counties also experienced extensive net outmigration of non-Hispanic Whites and Blacks, and illustrate

the redistribution of people away from some core areas in and around some of the nation's largest cities.

SUMMARY

This report shows that U.S. migration patterns between 1995 and 2000 differed by race and Hispanic origin. In terms of mobility, Hispanics and Blacks were more mobile than non-Hispanic Whites, while non-Hispanic Whites were most likely to have moved between states. In terms of migration, regional, state, and county migration patterns differed somewhat among non-Hispanic Whites, Blacks, Hispanics, and Asians, while movers from abroad helped offset net migration losses in many areas. The South had a net migration gain and the Northeast a net migration loss of all four race or Hispanic origin groups. However, the Midwest experienced a net migration gain only of Hispanics, while having net migration losses for the other three groups. Florida had the largest net migration gain of non-Hispanic Whites and Hispanics, while Nevada had the highest net migration rate for all four groups. Conversely, New York and California had the highest net migration loss for all four race or Hispanic origin groups. Finally, state-to-state migration flows, as well as county-level migration patterns, varied among the different race or Hispanic-origin groups.

[29] The estimates for Maricopa County and Broward County were not statistically different.

[30] The estimates for Cook County, Kings County, and Miami-Dade County were not statistically different.

Figure 5.
Net Migration Rates for Hispanics: 1995 to 2000

(Data based on a sample. For information on confidentiality protection, sampling error,
nonsampling error, and definitions, see *www.census.gov/prod/cen2000/doc/sf3.pdf*)

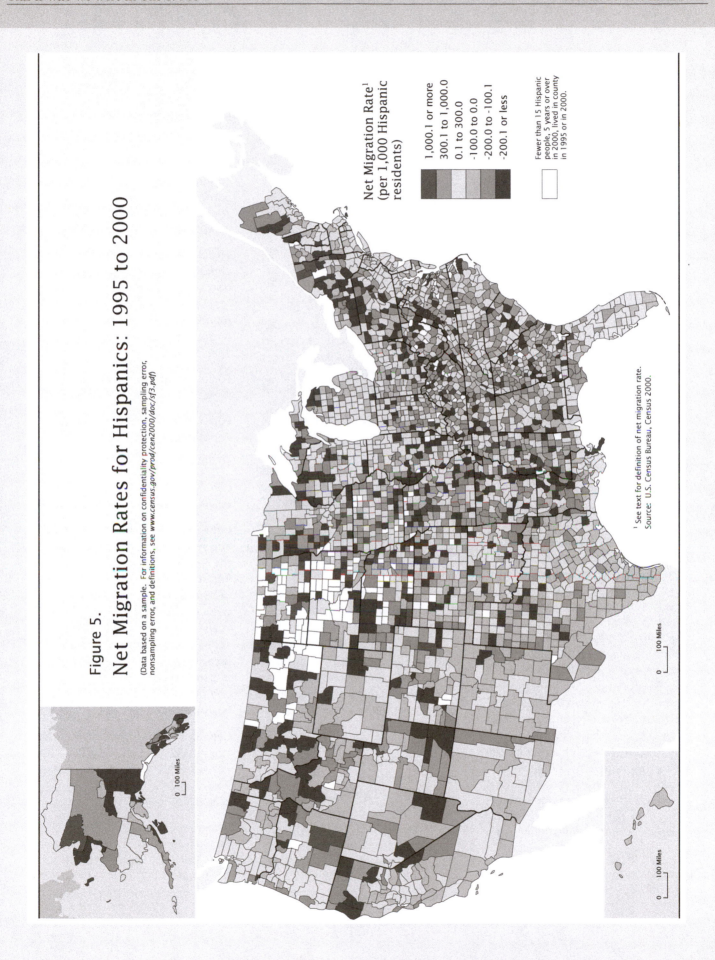

**Net Migration Rate[1]
(per 1,000 Hispanic
residents)**

1,000.1 or more
300.1 to 1,000.0
0.1 to 300.0
-100.0 to 0.0
-200.0 to -100.1
-200.1 or less

Fewer than 15 Hispanic
people, 5 years or over
in 2000, lived in county
in 1995 or in 2000.

[1] See text for definition of net migration rate.
Source: U.S. Census Bureau, Census 2000.

0   100 Miles

0   100 Miles

0   100 Miles

ACCURACY OF THE ESTIMATES

The data contained in this report are based on the sample of households who responded to the Census 2000 long form. Nationally, approximately 1 out of every 6 housing units was included in this sample. As a result, the sample estimates may differ somewhat from the 100-percent figures that would have been obtained if all housing units, people within those housing units, and people living in group quarters had been enumerated using the same questionnaires, instructions, enumerators, and so forth. The sample estimates also differ from the values that would have been obtained from different samples of housing units, people within those housing units, and people living in group quarters. The deviation of a sample estimate from the average of all possible samples is called the sampling error.

In addition to the variability that arises from the sampling procedures, both sample data and 100-percent data are subject to nonsampling error. Nonsampling error may be introduced during any of the various complex operations used to collect and process data. Such errors may include: not enumerating every household or every person in the population, failing to obtain all required information from the respondents, obtaining incorrect or inconsistent information, and recording information incorrectly. In addition, errors can occur during the field review of the enumerators' work, during clerical handling of the census questionnaires, or during the electronic processing of the questionnaires.

Nonsampling error may affect the data in two ways: (1) errors that are introduced randomly will increase the variability of the data and, therefore, should be reflected in the standard errors; and (2) errors that tend to be consistent in one direction will bias both sample and 100-percent data in that direction. For example, if respondents consistently tend to underreport their incomes, then the resulting estimates of households or families by income category will tend to be understated for the higher income categories and overstated for the lower income categories. Such biases are not reflected in the standard errors.

While it is impossible to completely eliminate error from an operation as large and complex as the decennial census, the Census Bureau attempts to control the sources of such error during the data collection and processing operations. The primary sources of error and the programs instituted to control error in Census 2000 are described in detail in Summary File 3 Technical Documentation under Chapter 8, "Accuracy of the Data," located at *www.census.gov/prod /cen2000/doc/sf3.pdf*.

All statements in this Census 2000 report have undergone statistical testing and all comparisons are significant at the 90-percent confidence level, unless otherwise noted. The estimates in tables, maps, and other figures may vary from actual values due to sampling and nonsampling errors. As a result, estimates in one category may not be significantly different from estimates assigned to a different category. Further information on the accuracy of the data is located at *www.census.gov /prod/cen2000/doc/sf3.pdf*. For further information on the computation and use of standard errors, contact the Decennial Statistical Studies Division at 301-763-4242.

FOR MORE INFORMATION

More detailed information on decennial migration products, including additional tables and other product announcements, is available on the Internet and can be accessed via the Census Bureau's decennial migration Web page at *www.census.gov /population/www/cen2000 /migration.html*.

The decennial migration Web page contains additional detailed migration tables not included in this report, a schedule of upcoming migration data releases, and migration-related Census 2000 Special Reports.

For more information on decennial migration products, please contact:

Population Distribution Branch
Population Division
U.S. Census Bureau

301-763-2419

or send e-mail to *pop@census.gov*.

Information on other population and housing topics is presented in the Census 2000 Brief and Special Reports Series, located on the U.S. Census Bureau's Web site at *www.census/gov/population/www /cen2000/briefs.html*. These series present information about race, Hispanic origin, age, sex, household type, housing tenure, and other social, economic, and housing characteristics.

Census 2000 information and data can also be accessed via the Census 2000 Gateway Web page at *www.census.gov/main/www /cen2000.html*.

For more information about Census 2000, including data products, call our Customer Services Center at 301-763-INFO (4636) or e-mail *webmaster@census.gov*.

Migration and Geographic Mobility in Metropolitan and Nonmetropolitan America: 1995 to 2000

Census 2000 Special Reports

Issued August 2003

CENSR-9

By
Jason P. Schachter,
Rachel S. Franklin,
and
Marc J. Perry

Geographic mobility has long been an important aspect of American life, directly affecting both people and geographic areas. At an individual level, moving has a number of potential impacts, such as the potential for expanding economic opportunity or raising residential satisfaction. Given the relative stability of current birth and death rates in the United States, the critical demographic factor for any area's population growth or decline is the movement of people. From the national to the local level, residential mobility, domestic migration, and international migration are paramount to explaining population growth and decline. Finally, federal, state and local governments, as well as the private sector, need to understand where people move when planning needed services, facilities, and businesses.

This report looks at 5-year mobility data from Census 2000 and focuses on migration and mobility patterns for metropolitan areas and territory outside metropolitan areas (hereafter referred to as nonmetropolitan territory) in the United States.[1] The first section addresses general

___
[1] All mobility and migration data in this report are for the population 5 years old and over. Movers are defined as those who did not live in their current house or apartment 5 years previously; thus, previous residence is measured 5 years prior to the Census and does not track any other moves made within that 5-year period. Similarly, the residence-five-years-ago question does not measure those who moved away from a place of residence and later returned to that same residence during that 5-year period.

The estimates in this report are based on responses from a sample of the population. As with all surveys, estimates may vary from the actual values because of sampling variation or other factors. All comparisons made in this report have undergone statistical testing and are significant at the 90-percent confidence level unless otherwise noted.

Common Migration Terms

Movers can be classified by type of move and are categorized as to whether they moved within the same county, to a different county within the same state, to a different county from a different state or region, or were movers from abroad. *Migration* is commonly defined as moves that cross jurisdictional boundaries (counties in particular), while moves within a jurisdiction are referred to as *residential mobility*. Moves between counties are often referred to as *intercounty* moves, while moves within the same county are often referred to as *intracounty* moves. Further, migration can be differentiated as movement within the United States (*domestic, or internal*, migration) and movement into and out of the United States (*international* migration). *Inmigration* is the number of migrants who moved into an area during a given period, while *outmigration* is the number of migrants who moved out of an area during a given period. *Net migration* is the difference between inmigration and outmigration during a given time. A positive net, or *net inmigration*, indicates that more migrants entered an area than left during that time. A negative net, or *net outmigration*, means that more migrants left an area than entered it.

USCENSUSBUREAU

Helping You Make Informed Decisions

U.S. Department of Commerce
Economics and Statistics Administration
U.S. CENSUS BUREAU

United States
Census 2000

Table 1.
Type of Move by Area of Residence in 2000: 1995 to 2000

(Data based on a sample. For information on confidentiality protection, sampling error, nonsampling error, and definitions, see www.census.gov/prod/cen2000/doc/sf3.pdf)

Residence in 2000	Total, 5 years and over	Same residence (non-movers)	Movers				
			Total	Same county	Different county, same state	Different state	From abroad[1]
NUMBER							
United States	262,375,152	142,027,478	120,347,674	65,435,013	25,327,355	22,089,460	7,495,846
Metropolitan	210,418,424	111,658,605	98,759,819	54,506,465	19,393,335	17,984,001	6,876,018
Central city	79,368,285	39,187,934	40,180,351	23,257,702	6,353,320	7,095,376	3,473,953
Suburbs	131,050,139	72,470,671	58,579,468	31,248,763	13,040,015	10,888,625	3,402,065
Nonmetropolitan	51,956,728	30,368,873	21,587,855	10,928,548	5,934,020	4,105,459	619,828
PERCENT							
Total	100.0	54.1	45.9	24.9	9.7	8.4	2.9
Metropolitan	100.0	53.1	46.9	25.9	9.2	8.5	3.3
Central city	100.0	49.4	50.6	29.3	8.0	8.9	4.4
Suburbs	100.0	55.3	44.7	23.8	10.0	8.3	2.6
Nonmetropolitan	100.0	58.5	41.5	21.0	11.4	7.9	1.2

[1]This category includes movers from foreign countries, as well as movers from Puerto Rico, U.S. Island Areas, and U.S. minor outlying islands.

Source: U.S. Census Bureau, Census 2000.

mobility patterns for those living in metropolitan areas within central cities, those living in metropolitan areas outside central cities, and those living in nonmetropolitan territory. Section two examines migration patterns for nonmetropolitan residents, and the third section looks at migration patterns to and from metropolitan areas by size, and for the twenty largest metropolitan areas (metropolitan statistical areas [MSAs] and consolidated metropolitan statistical areas [CMSAs]).[2]

GEOGRAPHIC MOBILITY BY METROPOLITAN STATUS

Residents of central cities of metropolitan areas were more mobile than suburban residents and those living in nonmetropolitan territory.

Over 120 million (45.9 percent) people 5 years old and older

This report uses metropolitan areas as defined by the Office of Management and Budget (OMB) as of June 30, 1999. Census 2000 data releases use metropolitan area definitions in existence at the time of the census. This approach ensures that data tabulations and publications associated with Census 2000 use consistent definitions. New definitions, based on Census 2000 population and commuting data were announced by OMB in 2003. The metropolitan status of some counties changed when new metropolitan area definitions were announced.

changed residence between 1995 and 2000 (see Table 1).[3] Over half (54.4 percent) of these moves were within counties, followed by moves to different counties in the same state (21.0 percent), moves between states (18.4 percent), and moves from abroad or Puerto Rico (6.2 percent).

People currently living in central cities were most likely to have moved, with 50.6 percent having changed residence within the past

5 years. Suburban residents (those living in metropolitan areas but outside central cities) were somewhat less mobile (44.7 percent), and those living in nonmetropolitan territory were the least mobile, with 41.5 percent reporting having moved within the past 5 years. That central city residents were more mobile than other metropolitan types could be attributable to the population in central cities having a younger age structure and lower homeownership rates than suburban and nonmetropolitan residents (both age and tenure are

[2]More detailed Census 2000 mobility and migration data are available on the Census Bureau's Web site www.census.gov/population/www/cen2000/migration.html.

[3]To ease the flow of the text, numbers have been rounded. Complete numbers are presented in the tables.

Table 2.
Migration Between Nonmetropolitan Territory and Metropolitan Areas: 1975 to 1980, 1985 to 1990, and 1995 to 2000[1]

(Data based on a sample. For information on confidentiality protection, sampling error, nonsampling error, and definitions, see www.census.gov/prod/cen2000/doc/sf3.pdf)

Flow	1975 to 1980	1985 to 1990	1995 to 2000
Metropolitan to Nonmetropolitan....................................	6,618,149	6,020,438	6,166,532
Nonmetropolitan to Metropolitan....................................	5,622,077	5,969,024	5,656,044
Net Migration to Nonmetropolitan territory	996,072	51,414	510,488

[1]The metropolitan status of some counties changed between censuses, as new metropolitan areas were recognized, and some metropolitan areas expanded their boundaries.

Source: U.S. Census Bureau, Decennial censuses of 1980, 1990, and 2000.

strongly correlated with the likelihood of moving).[4]

Suburban areas had the highest number of people who migrated across county borders and from abroad (27.3 million), followed by central city (16.9 million) and nonmetropolitan residents (10.7 million). However, central city residents were more likely to have made an intracounty move (29.3 percent), while nonmetropolitan residents were more likely to have moved to a different county within the state of current residence (11.4 percent). Residents of central cities were more likely to have been movers from abroad or Puerto Rico (4.4 percent) than residents in suburbs (2.6 percent) or in nonmetropolitan counties (1.2 percent).

MIGRATION PATTERNS FOR NONMETROPOLITAN AMERICA

Between 1995 and 2000, more people moved into nonmetropolitan territory from metropolitan areas than vice versa.

Nonmetropolitan-to-metropolitan migration patterns have long interested analysts, particularly during the so-called nonmetropolitan

"turnaround" of the 1970s, when inflows to nonmetropolitan territory were greater than outflows for the first time since migration data had been available. The "turnaround" abated in the 1980s, as growth in nonmetropolitan territory slowed dramatically due to modest net outmigration flows. During the 1990s this trend fluctuated, but for the period 1995 to 2000, nonmetropolitan territory showed substantial net migration gain from metropolitan areas.

Table 2 shows migration exchanges between metropolitan and nonmetropolitan territory, as recorded in the censuses of 1980, 1990, and 2000. Between 1995 and 2000, about 6.2 million people moved to nonmetropolitan territory, and about 5.7 million moved in the opposite direction (from nonmetropolitan to metropolitan areas). As a result, nonmetropolitan territory experienced net inmigration of about 500,000 people between 1995 and 2000. Between 1985 and 1990, nonmetropolitan territory experienced a net gain of only about 50,000 people in the exchange of migrants with metropolitan areas. Between 1975 and 1980, nonmetropolitan territory's gain was nearly 1 million. In addition to migration, these numbers reflect changing boundaries, as new metropolitan areas are recog-

nized and as metropolitan areas expand their boundaries.

Recent migration gains to nonmetropolitan territory, however, were not evenly distributed across all nonmetropolitan counties (see Figure 1). While Figure 1 shows that nonmetropolitan counties in a wide variety of settings showed net inmigration between 1995 and 2000, nonmetropolitan counties with high rates of net domestic migration gain were especially prominent near metropolitan areas that experienced relatively high growth rates. Examples include Dawson County, GA (adjacent to the Atlanta MSA); Elbert County, CO (southeast of the Denver CMSA); and Sumter County, FL (northeast of the Tampa-St. Petersburg MSA).[5] The nonmetropolitan county with the greatest net domestic inmigration was Yavapai County, AZ (near Phoenix), while Humboldt County, CA; Geary County, KS; and Cortland County, NY were among nonmetropolitan counties with the greatest net outmigration.[6]

---

[4]For examples of moving rates by age, see U.S. Census Bureau, 2001, *Geographical Mobility: March 1999 to March 2000,* by Jason Schachter, Current Population Report P20-538, Washington, DC: Government Printing Office.

---

[5]Abbreviated titles of metropolitan areas are used in the text of this report. See Table 4 for the full names of the twenty largest metropolitan areas.
[6]Detailed tables with mobility data for all regions, states, counties (and minor civil divisions in New England), and metropolitan areas are available on the Census Bureau's Web site at *www.census.gov/population /www/cen2000/migration.html.*

Figure 1.
Net Domestic Migration Rates for Nonmetropolitan Counties: 1995 to 2000

(Data based on a sample. For information on confidentiality protection, sampling error, nonsampling error, and definitions, see *www.census.gov/prod/cen2000/doc/sf3.pdf*)

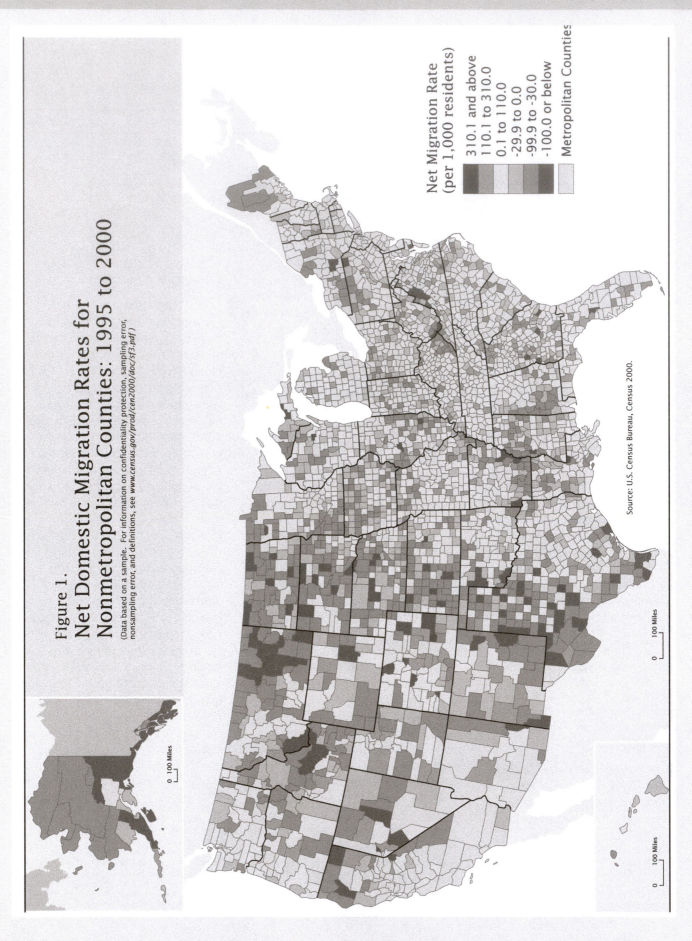

Net Migration Rate
(per 1,000 residents)

310.1 and above
110.1 to 310.0
0.1 to 110.0
-29.9 to 0.0
-99.9 to -30.0
-100.0 or below
Metropolitan Counties

Source: U.S. Census Bureau, Census 2000.

0   100 Miles

0   100 Miles

0   100 Miles

Table 3.
Net Domestic Migration and Movers From Abroad by Size Category of Metropolitan Area: 1995 to 2000

(Data based on a sample. For information on confidentiality protection, sampling error, nonsampling error, and definitions, see www.census.gov/prod/cen2000/doc/sf3.pdf)

Size of area	Net domestic migration		Movers from abroad[2]
	Number	Rate[1]	
Total for all metropolitan areas	−510,488	−2.5	6,876,018
Less than 250,000	141,551	8.0	317,739
250,000 to 999,999	217,771	5.3	880,525
1,000,000 to 1,999,999	714,246	21.7	897,506
2,000,000 to 4,999,999	526,968	14.8	1,437,974
5,000,000 or more	−2,111,024	−27.4	3,342,274

[1]The net migration rate is based on an approximated 1995 population, which is the sum of people who reported living in the area in both 1995 and 2000, and those who reported living in that area in 1995 but now live elsewhere. The net migration rate divides net migration, inmigration minus outmigration, by the approximated 1995 population and multiplies the result by 1000.

[2]This category includes movers from foreign countries, as well as movers from Puerto Rico, U.S. Island Areas, and U.S. minor outlying islands.

Note: A negative value for net migration or the net migration rate is indicative of net outmigration, meaning that more migrants left an area than entered it. Positive numbers reflect net inmigration to an area.

Source: U.S. Census Bureau, Census 2000.

MIGRATION TO METROPOLITAN AREAS

The highest levels of net inmigration were found in midsized metropolitan areas of 1 to 2 million people.

Although Census 2000 showed renewed gains in net migration for many nonmetropolitan counties, the sheer numbers of migrants into metropolitan areas remained high. Between 1995 and 2000, nearly 25.8 million individuals were inmigrants to metropolitan areas. This flow was counteracted, however, by outmigration of 26.3 million people. The result was net outmigration of around 500,000 people, or a net migration rate of −2.5 (see Table 3).[7]

When all metropolitan areas are classified by size category, a more varied picture emerges, as can be seen for five categories of metropolitan areas shown in Table 3. Net migration from other parts of the United States was positive for all size categories except the largest, which covers all areas with a total population greater than 5 million in 2000. For the largest metropolitan area category, the net migration rate was −27.4, meaning there was a net loss of 27 people from those metropolitan areas for every 1,000 residents in 1995. Metropolitan areas in all other size categories experienced net migration gains during this period, although some saw more net inmigration than others. The two size classes under 1 million, for example, gained 8.0 and 5.3 migrants for every 1,000 residents, respectively, in 1995. In comparison, the net migration rate for the 2 to 5 million class was 14.8, much higher than the size classes under 1 million. Metropolitan areas with populations between 1 and 2 million experienced the greatest net inmigration; net migration to these areas was about 700,000, or a net migration rate of 21.7. Examples in this category were Las Vegas,

NV; Orlando, FL; Austin, TX; and Charlotte, NC.

Movers from abroad are an increasingly large and important component of migration, particularly for the largest metropolitan areas. Of the 6.9 million people who moved to metropolitan areas from abroad, most went to the largest metropolitan areas (Table 3). The number of movers from abroad tended to decrease as size of the metropolitan areas decreased. Thus, metropolitan areas of 5 million or more received almost half of all people who moved from abroad to metropolitan areas. The smallest category, metropolitan areas with 250,000 or fewer residents, received over 300,000 migrants from abroad.

The net effect of domestic migration and movers from abroad varied even among the largest metropolitan areas. Migration figures for the 20 largest metropolitan areas, shown in Table 4, provide insight into migration patterns of the United States' largest metropolitan areas, the majority of which experienced net domestic outmigration

[7]The net migration rate in this report is based on an approximated 1995 population, which is the sum of people who reported living in the area in both 1995 and 2000, and those who reported living in that area in 1995 but now live elsewhere. The net migration rate divides net migration, inmigration minus outmigration, by the approximated 1995 population and multiplies the result by 1000.

Table 4.

Net Domestic Migration and Movers From Abroad for the 20 Largest Metropolitan Areas: 1995 to 2000

(Data based on a sample. For information on confidentiality protection, sampling error, nonsampling error, and definitions, see www.census.gov/prod/cen2000/doc/sf3.pdf)

Rank	Metropolitan area	Total population in 2000	Net domestic migration		Movers from abroad[1]	
			Number	Rate[2]	To central city (cities)	To suburbs
1	New York-Northern New Jersey-Long Island, NY-NJ-CT-PA CMSA.	21,199,865	−874,028	−44.4	614,057	369,602
2	Los Angeles-Riverside-Orange County, CA CMSA	16,373,645	−549,951	−36.8	324,013	375,560
3	Chicago-Gary-Kenosha, IL-IN-WI CMSA	9,157,540	−318,649	−37.6	172,597	150,422
4	Washington-Baltimore, DC-MD-VA-WV CMSA	7,608,070	−58,849	−8.6	65,837	234,429
5	San Francisco-Oakland-San Jose, CA CMSA	7,039,362	−206,670	−32.2	194,220	179,649
6	Philadelphia-Wilmington-Atlantic City, PA-NJ-DE-MD CMSA	6,188,463	−83,539	−14.5	58,131	69,790
7	Boston-Worcester-Lawrence, MA-NH-ME-CT CMSA	5,819,100	−44,973	−8.5	99,790	93,708
8	Detroit-Ann Arbor-Flint, MI CMSA.	5,456,428	−123,009	−24.2	36,179	72,796
9	Dallas-Fort Worth, TX CMSA.	5,221,801	148,644	33.6	151,679	79,815
10	Houston-Galveston-Brazoria, TX CMSA	4,669,571	−14,377	−3.5	138,826	75,442
11	Atlanta, GA MSA	4,112,198	233,303	68.4	15,975	146,997
12	Miami-Fort Lauderdale, FL CMSA	3,876,380	−93,774	−27.4	60,493	239,412
13	Seattle-Tacoma-Bremerton, WA CMSA	3,554,760	39,945	12.6	47,001	75,765
14	Phoenix-Mesa, AZ MSA	3,251,876	245,159	93.6	104,609	30,408
15	Minneapolis-St. Paul, MN-WI MSA	2,968,806	34,207	12.9	31,145	34,975
16	Cleveland-Akron, OH CMSA	2,945,831	−65,914	−23.7	13,969	22,288
17	San Diego, CA MSA	2,813,833	−6,108	−2.4	63,695	45,127
18	St. Louis, MO-IL MSA	2,603,607	−43,614	−17.9	13,915	21,432
19	Denver-Boulder-Greeley, CO CMSA	2,581,506	93,586	42.3	44,472	49,498
20	Tampa-St. Petersburg-Clearwater, FL MSA	2,395,997	103,375	49.5	24,728	42,936

[1]This category includes movers from foreign countries, as well as movers from Puerto Rico, U.S. Island Areas, and U.S. minor outlying islands.

[2]The net migration rate is based on an approximated 1995 population, which is the sum of people who reported living in the area in both 1995 and 2000, and those who reported living in that area in 1995 but now live elsewhere. The net migration rate divides net migration, inmigration minus outmigration, by the approximated 1995 population and multiplies the result by 1000.

Note: A negative value for net migration or the net migration rate is indicative of net outmigration, meaning that more migrants left an area than entered it. Positive numbers reflect net inmigration to an area.

Source: U.S. Census Bureau, Census 2000.

between 1995 and 2000. In fact, the sole exception among the ten largest metropolitan areas was Dallas-Fort Worth, which had a net domestic migration rate of 33.6. The net migration rates for the remaining top 10 metropolitan areas varied from −3.5 in Houston to −44.4 for New York, the largest metropolitan area in the country. Among the second tier of top 20 metropolitan areas, most had positive net migration, and only four experienced negative net migration during this period: Miami (-27.4), Cleveland (-23.7), St. Louis (-17.9), and San Diego (-2.4). The net migration rate for the Phoenix metropolitan area, the 14th largest

metropolitan area in the country, was 93.6, the highest net inmigration rate found in the top 20 metropolitan areas, while the second highest was for Atlanta at 68.4.

The number of movers from abroad was positively correlated with the size of the metropolitan area. As a result, of the top 20 metropolitan areas, the New York CMSA received the largest number of movers from abroad, close to 1 million (see Table 4). Movers from abroad to metropolitan areas are subdivided in Table 4 into those who moved to the central city and those who moved to the suburbs (the part of metropolitan areas outside central cities). The traditional

concept about the destinations of movers from abroad, particularly those immigrating to the United States, has been that they first settle in the central city, and then move elsewhere. In 12 of the top 20 metropolitan areas, however, more movers from abroad went to the suburbs than went to the central city between 1995 and 2000. Although this imbalance tended to be concentrated in the lower half of the top 20, several of the largest metropolitan areas, including Los Angeles (ranked 2nd) and Washington-Baltimore (ranked 4th), experienced higher numbers of movers from abroad to their suburbs than to their central cities.

SUMMARY

Although nonmetropolitan residents were less likely to change residence than metropolitan residents, nonmetropolitan counties showed substantial net migration gain from metropolitan counties. Nonmetropolitan net migration gain was particularly high in counties near metropolitan areas, while the largest metropolitan areas (over 5 million) lost population, and medium-sized metropolitan areas gained population, due to domestic migration. Movers from abroad helped offset this domestic migration loss in the largest metropolitan areas, while also contributing to the growth of other metropolitan areas. Whether movers from abroad went to central cities or suburbs varied by specific MSA/CMSA.

ACCURACY OF THE ESTIMATES

The data contained in this report are based on the sample of households who responded to the Census 2000 long form. Nationally, approximately 1 out of every 6 housing units was included in this sample. As a result, the sample estimates may differ somewhat from the 100-percent figures that would have been obtained if all housing units, people within those housing units, and people living in group quarters had been enumerated using the same questionnaires, instructions, enumerators, and so forth. The sample estimates also differ from the values that would have been obtained from different samples of housing units, people within those housing units, and people living in group quarters. The deviation of a sample estimate from the average of all possible samples is called the sampling error.

In addition to the variability that arises from the sampling procedures, both sample data and 100-percent data are subject to nonsampling error. Nonsampling error may be introduced during any of the various complex operations used to collect and process data. Such errors may include: not enumerating every household or every person in the population, failing to obtain all required information from the respondents, obtaining incorrect or inconsistent information, and recording information incorrectly. In addition, errors can occur during the field review of the enumerators' work, during clerical handling of the census questionnaires, or during the electronic processing of the questionnaires.

Nonsampling error may affect the data in two ways: (1) errors that are introduced randomly will increase the variability of the data and, therefore, should be reflected in the standard errors; and (2) errors that tend to be consistent in one direction will bias both sample and 100-percent data in that direction. For example, if respondents consistently tend to underreport their incomes, then the resulting estimates of households or families by income category will tend to be understated for the higher income categories and overstated for the lower income categories. Such biases are not reflected in the standard errors.

While it is impossible to completely eliminate error from an operation as large and complex as the decennial census, the Census Bureau attempts to control the sources of such error during the data collection and processing operations. The primary sources of error and the programs instituted to control error in Census 2000 are described in detail in Summary File 3

Technical Documentation under Chapter 8, "Accuracy of the Data," located at *www.census.gov/prod /cen2000/doc/sf3.pdf*.

All statements in this Census 2000 report have undergone statistical testing and all comparisons are significant at the 90-percent confidence level, unless otherwise noted. The estimates in tables, maps, and other figures may vary from actual values due to sampling and nonsampling errors. As a result, estimates in one category may not be significantly different from estimates assigned to a different category. The estimates in tables, maps, and other figures may vary from actual values due to sampling and nonsampling errors. As a result, estimates in one category may not be significantly different from estimates assigned to a different category. Further information on the accuracy of the data is located at *www.census.gov/prod /cen2000/doc/sf3.pdf*. For further information on the computation and use of standard errors, contact the Decennial Statistical Studies Division at 301-763-4242.

FOR MORE INFORMATION

More detailed information on decennial migration products, including additional tables and other product announcements, is available on the Internet and can be accessed via the Census Bureau's decennial migration Web page at *www.census.gov /population/www/cen2000 /migration.html*.

The decennial migration Web page contains additional detailed migration tables not included in this report, a schedule of upcoming migration data releases, and migration-related Census 2000 Special Reports.

For more information on decennial migration products, please contact:

Population Distribution Branch
Population Division
U.S. Census Bureau
301-763-2419

or send e-mail to *pop@census.gov.*

Information on other population and housing topics is presented in the Census 2000 Brief and Special Reports Series, located on the U.S. Census Bureau's Web site at *www.census.gov/population/www /cen2000/briefs.html.* These series present information about race, Hispanic origin, age, sex, household type, housing tenure, and other social, economic, and housing characteristics.

Census 2000 information and data can also be accessed via the Census 2000 Gateway Web page at *www.census.gov/main/www /cen2000.html.*

For more information about Census 2000, including data products, call our Customer Services Center at 301-763-INFO (4636) or e-mail *webmaster@census.gov.*

Married-Couple and Unmarried-Partner Households: 2000

Census 2000 Special Reports

Issued February 2003

CENSR-5

By
Tavia Simmons
and
Martin O'Connell

Introduction

Census 2000 enumerated 105.5 million households in the United States,[1] of which the majority (52 percent) were maintained by married couples (54.5 million). A reflection of changing life styles is mirrored in Census 2000's enumeration of 5.5 million couples who were living together but who were not married, up from 3.2 million in 1990.[2] These unmarried-partner households were self-identified on the census form as being maintained by people who were sharing living quarters and who also had a close personal relationship with each other.[3] The majority of these unmarried-partner households had partners of the opposite sex (4.9 million) but about 1 in 9 (594,000) had partners of the same sex.[4]

Figure 1.

Reproduction of the Question on Relationship to Householder From Census 2000

2. **How is this person related to Person 1?** *Mark* ☒ *ONE box.*
- ☐ Husband/wife
- ☐ Natural-born son/daughter
- ☐ Adopted son/daughter
- ☐ Stepson/stepdaughter
- ☐ Brother/sister
- ☐ Father/mother
- ☐ Grandchild
- ☐ Parent-in-law
- ☐ Son-in-law/daughter-in-law
- ☐ Other relative — *Print exact relationship.* →

If NOT RELATED to Person 1:
- ☐ Roomer, boarder
- ☐ Housemate, roommate
- ☐ Unmarried partner
- ☐ Foster child
- ☐ Other nonrelative

Source: U.S. Census Bureau, Census 2000 questionnaire.

Of these same-sex unmarried-partner households, 301,000 had male partners and 293,000 had female partners.

This report presents information from Census 2000 on the characteristics of the 60 million households maintained by couples (also called coupled households). These coupled households were assigned

---

[1] The text of this report discusses data for the United States, including the 50 states and the District of Columbia. Data for the Commonwealth of Puerto Rico are shown in Tables 2, 4, 5, and 6 and Figure 2.

[2] Data on unmarried partners from the 1990 census (which were based on data from the sample form) are not comparable with data from Census 2000 because of changes in the editing procedures. See www.*census.gov/population/www/cen2000 /samesex.html* for an explanation of these changes.

[3] In contrast, people who were sharing the same living quarters but were doing so just to share living expenses were offered the opportunity to identify themselves as roommates or housemates.

[4] Estimating numbers and characteristics of population groups with low probabilities of occurrence may be affected by even small reporting errors or incorrect optical reading of some questionnaires during data processing. The analysis of the number of same-sex couples and their characteristics may be susceptible to these problems if such errors were made in the relationship and sex items. For instance, if an error was made by the household respondent for the item "What is this person's sex?," an opposite-sex married-couple household could have been erroneously processed as a same-sex married-couple household. In this instance, the household would have most likely been reclassified as a same-sex unmarried-partner household. For a further explanation of the editing process, see *www.census.gov/population/www/cen2000 /samesex.html.*

USCENSUSBUREAU

Helping You Make Informed Decisions

U.S. Department of Commerce
Economics and Statistics Administration
U.S. CENSUS BUREAU

United States
Census 2000

Table 1.
Married and Unmarried-Partner Households by Metropolitan Residence Status: 2000

(For information on confidentiality protection, nonsampling error, and definitions, see *www.census.gov/prod/cen2000/doc/sf1.pdf*)

Household type and sex of householder	Total	In a metropolitan area						Not in a metropolitan area	
		Total		In central city		Not in central city			
		Number	Percent of all house-holds	Number	Percent of all house-holds	Number	Percent of all house-holds	Number	Percent of all house-holds
Total households[1]	105,480,101	84,304,885	79.9	32,753,918	31.1	51,550,967	48.9	21,175,216	20.1
Total coupled households[2] .	59,969,000	47,214,481	78.7	15,189,744	25.3	32,024,737	53.4	12,754,519	21.3
Married-couple households	54,493,232	42,757,993	78.5	13,232,903	24.3	29,525,090	54.2	11,735,239	21.5
Male householder	47,449,405	36,968,706	77.9	11,101,326	23.4	25,867,380	54.5	10,480,699	22.1
Female householder	7,043,827	5,789,287	82.2	2,131,577	30.3	3,657,710	51.9	1,254,540	17.8
Unmarried-partner households	5,475,768	4,456,488	81.4	1,956,841	35.7	2,499,647	45.6	1,019,280	18.6
Opposite-sex partners...	4,881,377	3,949,743	80.9	1,709,317	35.0	2,240,426	45.9	931,634	19.1
Male householder	2,615,119	2,083,069	79.7	849,082	32.5	1,233,987	47.2	532,050	20.3
Female householder ..	2,266,258	1,866,674	82.4	860,235	38.0	1,006,439	44.4	399,584	17.6
Same-sex partners	594,391	506,745	85.3	247,524	41.6	259,221	43.6	87,646	14.7
Male householder	301,026	259,807	86.3	135,546	45.0	124,261	41.3	41,219	13.7
Female householder ..	293,365	246,938	84.2	111,978	38.2	134,960	46.0	46,427	15.8

[1]Total includes other types of households including family and nonfamily households which do not contain either spouses or unmarried partners.

[2]Coupled households represent the total of married-couple and unmarried-partner households.

Source: U.S. Census Bureau, Census 2000 Summary File 1.

to 1 of 4 mutually exclusive groups, depending on the relationship and gender of the householder and the spouse or partner: opposite-sex married couples, opposite-sex unmarried partners, male same-sex unmarried partners, and female same-sex unmarried partners. The numbers in this report do not show a complete count of all married couples and unmarried partners but only of couples and partners where one person was the householder. If the household included more than one couple, the household designation was determined by the status of the householder. For example, if a household was maintained by an unmarried couple but also contained the son of the householder and the son's wife, the household would be tabulated only as an unmarried-partner household in this report.

The information on household type is derived from the item on the Census 2000 questionnaire (Figure 1) that asked about the relationship of each person in the household to the person on line 1, the householder (the person in whose name the house was owned or rented). The relationship item, which has been asked on the census since 1880, provides information about both individuals and the make-up of families and households. In 1990, the category "unmarried partner" was added to the relationship item to measure the growing complexity of American households and the tendency for couples to live together before getting married.[5]

_____

[5] For historical estimates of the number of unmarried partners derived from the Census Bureau's Current Population Survey, see www.*census.gov/population/socdemo /hh-fam/tabUC-1.txt*. For the results of the most recent survey, see Jason Fields and Lynne M. Casper, *America's Families and Living Arrangements: March 2000*. Current Population Reports, P20-537. U.S. Census Bureau, Washington, DC, 2001.

Unmarried partners are more likely than married couples to live in metropolitan areas.

Of the 105.5 million households in the United States, 84.3 million were located in metropolitan areas—32.8 million were within central cities and 51.6 million were located in the suburbs[6]—while the remaining 21.2 million were outside metropolitan areas (Table 1). Among the 60 million coupled households, 47.2 million were in metropolitan areas—15.2 million were in central cities and 32.0 million were in the suburbs—while the remaining 12.8 million coupled households were outside metropolitan areas.

Of the four different types of households maintained by couples,

_____

[6] In this report, two terms—suburban areas and suburbs—are used to designate that part of the metropolitan area which is not in the central city.

married-couple households had the lowest rate of metropolitan residence (79 percent), while same-sex unmarried-partner households had the highest rates: 84 percent of female same-sex households and 86 percent of male same-sex households. Opposite-sex unmarried-partner households had an intermediate rate of metropolitan residence (81 percent).

Married-couple households were less likely to be found in central cities (24 percent) than were unmarried-partner households (36 percent). Among unmarried-partner households, opposite-sex partners were less likely to reside in central cities (35 percent) than female same-sex partners (38 percent) or male same-sex partners (45 percent).

Married-couples and opposite-sex unmarried partners with female householders were more likely to be in metropolitan areas (both 82 percent) than were their counterparts with male householders (78 percent and 80 percent, respectively). Gender differences in central city residence were even more apparent: 30 percent and 38 percent for women compared with 23 percent and 33 percent, respectively, for men.[7]

About 9 percent of coupled households are unmarried-partner households.

Nationally, 57 percent of all households in 2000 were coupled households. Table 2 shows that the West and Midwest had the highest proportion (58 percent), while the Northeast had the lowest

(55 percent).[8] Overall, 9 percent of all coupled households were unmarried-partner households: the West had the highest percentage (10 percent), while the South had the lowest (8 percent).

Opposite-sex partners (4.9 million) constituted the vast majority of the 5.5 million unmarried-partner households. Nationwide, 594,000 same-sex unmarried-partner households represented 1 percent of all coupled households. On a comparative basis, the West had the highest percentage (1.2 percent) and the Midwest had the lowest (0.7 percent). Fifty-one percent of same-sex couples in the South and the West had male partners, compared with 50 percent in the Northeast and 49 percent in the Midwest.

The highest proportion of coupled households was in Utah.

Coupled households were most likely to be found in western states such as Utah (67 percent of households in that state), Idaho (64 percent), and Wyoming (60 percent), and in New England states (New Hampshire at 62 percent, and Vermont and Maine at 60 percent). Two other states, Iowa and Alaska, also had 60 percent of their households maintained by couples. New York had the lowest percentage (52 percent).

Other states with proportions under 55 percent were Massachusetts, Rhode Island, Louisiana, and Mississippi (54 percent each). In the District of Columbia, 29 percent of all households were coupled.

Unmarried-partner households are least frequently found in the central United States.

The unmarried-partner category identifies people with a close and personal relationship that goes beyond sharing household expenses. People may live together as an unmarried couple for a variety of reasons. For young men and women, it may be a precursor to an impending marriage, while for others it may represent a transitory or trial relationship. For older couples that have been formerly married, it could represent an alternative lifestyle to the one they previously experienced, especially if child bearing and child rearing activities are not anticipated.

Interesting geographic patterns emerge in the proportion of all coupled households maintained by unmarried partners. Figure 2 shows that counties with above-average proportions of unmarried-partner households were concentrated in several areas. One extends from a number of southwestern states up the Pacific coast and into Alaska. A second large cluster runs from New York through New England. Other areas include the Mississippi Valley and southern Florida. In general, the counties in the Great Plains section of the United States, from west Texas northwards, were characterized by below-average proportions of unmarried-partner households. In a previous report,[9] this area was

---

[7] On an historical note, the Census Bureau began listing wives as householders in married-couple families in surveys and the census beginning in 1980. Before that time, husbands were automatically designated as the householder in married-couple families. Beginning in 1990 when unmarried-partner households were first identified, either sex could be listed as the householder.

[8] There are four regions (Northeast, Midwest, South, and West). The Northeast includes Connecticut, Maine, Massachusetts, New Hampshire, New Jersey, New York, Pennsylvania, Rhode Island, and Vermont. The Midwest includes Illinois, Indiana, Iowa, Kansas, Michigan, Minnesota, Missouri, Nebraska, North Dakota, Ohio, South Dakota, and Wisconsin. The South includes Alabama, Arkansas, Delaware, the District of Columbia, Florida, Georgia, Kentucky, Louisiana, Maryland, Mississippi, North Carolina, Oklahoma, South Carolina, Tennessee, Texas, Virginia, and West Virginia. The West includes Alaska, Arizona, California, Colorado, Hawaii, Idaho, Montana, Nevada, New Mexico, Oregon, Utah, Washington, and Wyoming.

[9] See Tavia Simmons and Grace O'Neill, *Households and Families: 2000.* Census 2000 Brief, Series C2KBR/01-8. U.S. Census Bureau, Washington, DC, 2001.

Table 2.
Married-Couple and Unmarried-Partner Households for the United States, Regions, States, and for Puerto Rico: 2000

(For information on confidentiality protection, nonsampling error, and definitions, see *www.census.gov/prod/cen2000/doc/sf1.pdf*)

Area	Total coupled households[1] Total households	Number	Per-cent of all house-holds	Married-couple house-holds	Total unmarried-partner households Number	Per-cent of coupled house-holds	Opposite-sex unmarried partners Number	Per-cent of coupled house-holds	Same-sex unmarried partners Total Num-ber	Per-cent of coupled house-holds	Male part-ners	Female partners
United States	105,480,101	59,969,000	56.9	54,493,232	5,475,768	9.1	4,881,377	8.1	594,391	1.0	301,026	293,365
Region												
Northeast	20,285,622	11,205,641	55.2	10,127,653	1,077,988	9.6	958,742	8.6	119,246	1.1	59,328	59,918
Midwest	24,734,532	14,222,533	57.5	12,963,564	1,258,969	8.9	1,153,219	8.1	105,750	0.7	52,142	53,608
South	38,015,214	21,549,582	56.7	19,740,328	1,809,254	8.4	1,599,512	7.4	209,742	1.0	107,636	102,106
West	22,444,733	12,991,244	57.9	11,661,687	1,329,557	10.2	1,169,904	9.0	159,653	1.2	81,920	77,733
State												
Alabama	1,737,080	965,453	55.6	906,916	58,537	6.1	50,428	5.2	8,109	0.8	3,980	4,129
Alaska	221,600	132,886	60.0	116,318	16,568	12.5	15,388	11.6	1,180	0.9	483	697
Arizona	1,901,327	1,104,499	58.1	986,303	118,196	10.7	105,864	9.6	12,332	1.1	6,278	6,054
Arkansas	1,042,696	606,944	58.2	566,401	40,543	6.7	36,120	6.0	4,423	0.7	2,176	2,247
California	11,502,870	6,560,600	57.0	5,877,084	683,516	10.4	591,378	9.0	92,138	1.4	49,614	42,524
Colorado	1,658,238	949,895	57.3	858,671	91,224	9.6	81,179	8.5	10,045	1.1	4,640	5,405
Connecticut	1,301,670	745,340	57.3	676,467	68,873	9.2	61,487	8.2	7,386	1.0	3,559	3,827
Delaware	298,736	171,434	57.4	153,136	18,298	10.7	16,430	9.6	1,868	1.1	979	889
District of Columbia	248,338	71,517	28.8	56,631	14,886	20.8	11,208	15.7	3,678	5.1	2,693	985
Florida	6,337,929	3,561,888	56.2	3,192,266	369,622	10.4	328,574	9.2	41,048	1.2	22,988	18,060
Georgia	3,006,369	1,694,543	56.4	1,548,800	145,743	8.6	126,455	7.5	19,288	1.1	10,251	9,037
Hawaii	403,240	239,593	59.4	216,077	23,516	9.8	21,127	8.8	2,389	1.0	1,234	1,155
Idaho	469,645	299,075	63.7	276,511	22,564	7.5	20,691	6.9	1,873	0.6	902	971
Illinois	4,591,779	2,573,438	56.0	2,353,892	219,546	8.5	196,659	7.6	22,887	0.9	12,155	10,732
Indiana	2,336,306	1,376,309	58.9	1,251,458	124,851	9.1	114,632	8.3	10,219	0.7	5,054	5,165
Iowa	1,149,276	690,076	60.0	633,254	56,822	8.2	53,124	7.7	3,698	0.5	1,789	1,909
Kansas	1,037,891	610,223	58.8	567,924	42,299	6.9	38,326	6.3	3,973	0.7	1,888	2,085
Kentucky	1,590,647	929,210	58.4	857,944	71,266	7.7	64,152	6.9	7,114	0.8	3,310	3,804
Louisiana	1,656,053	893,061	53.9	809,498	83,563	9.4	74,755	8.4	8,808	1.0	4,180	4,628
Maine	518,200	310,033	59.8	272,152	37,881	12.2	34,487	11.1	3,394	1.1	1,493	1,901
Maryland	1,980,859	1,104,884	55.8	994,549	110,335	10.0	99,092	9.0	11,243	1.0	5,230	6,013
Massachusetts	2,443,580	1,328,836	54.4	1,197,917	130,919	9.9	113,820	8.6	17,099	1.3	7,943	9,156
Michigan	3,785,661	2,149,930	56.8	1,947,710	202,220	9.4	186,852	8.7	15,368	0.7	7,293	8,075
Minnesota	1,895,127	1,118,603	59.0	1,018,245	100,358	9.0	91,211	8.2	9,147	0.8	4,290	4,857
Mississippi	1,046,434	567,582	54.2	520,844	46,738	8.2	41,964	7.4	4,774	0.8	2,251	2,523
Missouri	2,194,594	1,251,876	57.0	1,140,866	111,010	8.9	101,582	8.1	9,428	0.8	4,684	4,744
Montana	358,667	210,008	58.6	192,067	17,941	8.5	16,723	8.0	1,218	0.6	554	664
Nebraska	666,184	390,533	58.6	360,996	29,537	7.6	27,205	7.0	2,332	0.6	1,112	1,220
Nevada	751,165	427,103	56.9	373,201	53,902	12.6	48,929	11.5	4,973	1.2	2,739	2,234
New Hampshire	474,606	294,998	62.2	262,438	32,560	11.0	29,857	10.1	2,703	0.9	1,156	1,547
New Jersey	3,064,645	1,789,640	58.4	1,638,322	151,318	8.5	134,714	7.5	16,604	0.9	8,257	8,347
New Mexico	677,971	385,360	56.8	341,818	43,542	11.3	39,046	10.1	4,496	1.2	1,901	2,595
New York	7,056,860	3,667,070	52.0	3,289,514	377,556	10.3	331,066	9.0	46,490	1.3	24,494	21,996
North Carolina	3,132,013	1,789,026	57.1	1,645,346	143,680	8.0	127,482	7.1	16,198	0.9	7,849	8,349
North Dakota	257,152	148,812	57.9	137,433	11,379	7.6	10,676	7.2	703	0.5	360	343
Ohio	4,445,773	2,514,887	56.6	2,285,798	229,089	9.1	210,152	8.4	18,937	0.8	9,266	9,671
Oklahoma	1,342,293	770,918	57.4	717,611	53,307	6.9	47,544	6.2	5,763	0.7	2,811	2,952
Oregon	1,333,723	777,166	58.3	692,532	84,634	10.9	75,702	9.7	8,932	1.1	3,846	5,086
Pennsylvania	4,777,003	2,705,295	56.6	2,467,673	237,622	8.8	216,456	8.0	21,166	0.8	10,492	10,674
Rhode Island	408,424	219,937	53.9	196,757	23,180	10.5	20,709	9.4	2,471	1.1	1,172	1,299
South Carolina	1,533,854	853,564	55.6	783,142	70,422	8.3	62,813	7.4	7,609	0.9	3,561	4,048
South Dakota	290,245	171,282	59.0	157,391	13,891	8.1	13,065	7.6	826	0.5	389	437
Tennessee	2,232,905	1,267,908	56.8	1,173,960	93,948	7.4	83,759	6.6	10,189	0.8	5,090	5,099
Texas	7,393,354	4,316,987	58.4	3,989,741	327,246	7.6	284,334	6.6	42,912	1.0	21,740	21,172
Utah	701,281	467,035	66.6	442,931	24,104	5.2	20,734	4.4	3,370	0.7	1,665	1,705
Vermont	240,634	144,492	60.0	126,413	18,079	12.5	16,146	11.2	1,933	1.3	762	1,171
Virginia	2,699,173	1,552,409	57.5	1,426,044	126,365	8.1	112,563	7.3	13,802	0.9	7,053	6,749
Washington	2,271,398	1,321,464	58.2	1,181,995	139,469	10.6	123,569	9.4	15,900	1.2	7,652	8,248
West Virginia	736,481	432,254	58.7	397,499	34,755	8.0	31,839	7.4	2,916	0.7	1,494	1,422
Wisconsin	2,084,544	1,226,564	58.8	1,108,597	117,967	9.6	109,735	8.9	8,232	0.7	3,862	4,370
Wyoming	193,608	116,560	60.2	106,179	10,381	8.9	9,574	8.2	807	0.7	412	395
Puerto Rico	1,261,325	723,042	57.3	682,804	40,238	5.6	33,420	4.6	6,818	0.9	3,122	3,696

[1]Coupled households represent total of married-couple and unmarried-partner households.

Source: U.S. Census Bureau, Census 2000 Summary File 1.

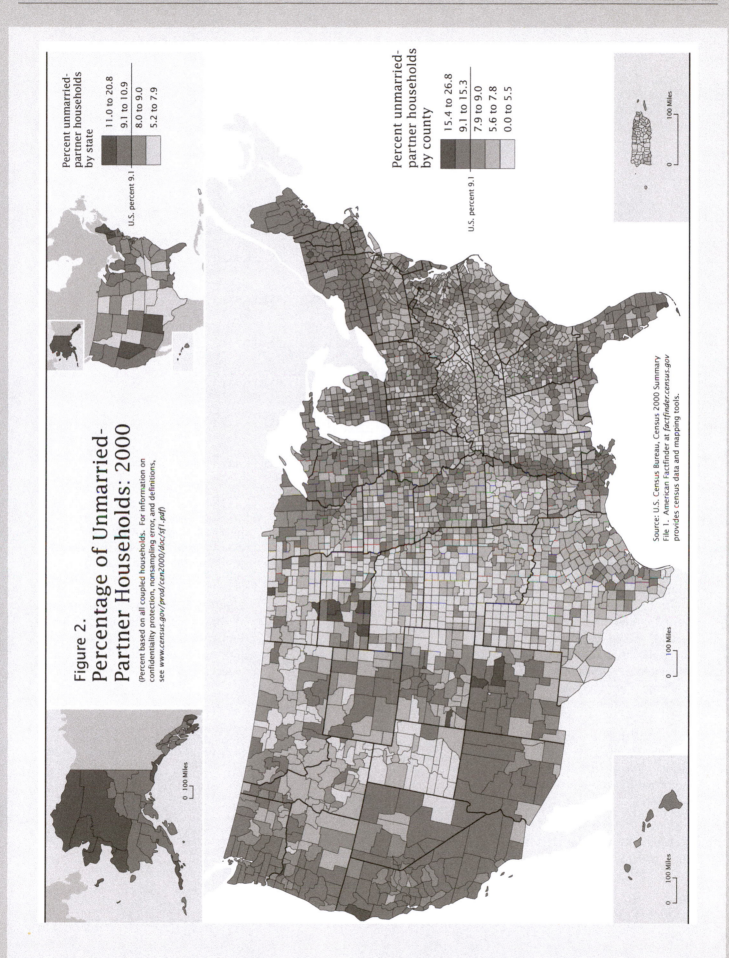

Figure 2.
Percentage of Unmarried-Partner Households: 2000

(Percent based on all coupled households. For information on confidentiality protection, nonsampling error, and definitions, see *www.census.gov/prod/cen2000/doc/sf1.pdf*)

Percent unmarried-partner households by state

11.0 to 20.8
9.1 to 10.9
8.0 to 9.0
5.2 to 7.9

U.S. percent 9.1

Percent unmarried-partner households by county

15.4 to 26.8
9.1 to 15.3
7.9 to 9.0
5.6 to 7.8
0.0 to 5.5

U.S. percent 9.1

Source: U.S. Census Bureau, Census 2000 Summary File 1. American Factfinder at *factfinder.census.gov* provides census data and mapping tools.

Figure 3.

Unmarried-Partner Households by Sex of Partners and Race and Hispanic Origin of Householder: 2000

(Percent of all coupled households. For information on confidentiality protection, nonsampling error and definitions, see *www.census.gov/prod/cen2000/docs/sf1.pdf*)

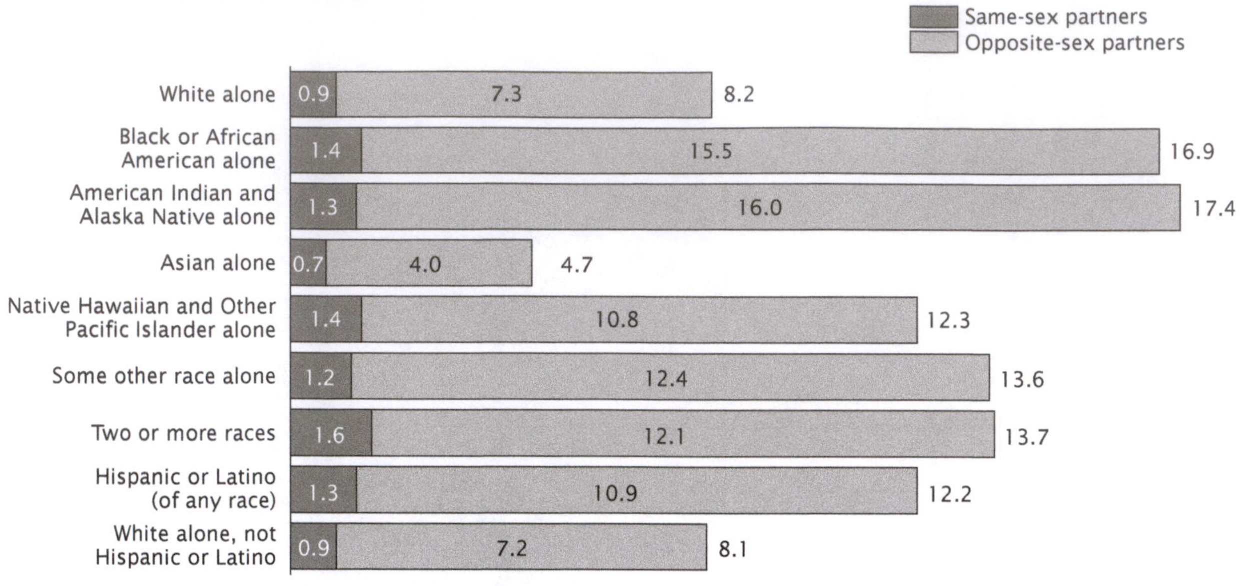

Legend:
- Same-sex partners
- Opposite-sex partners

Race/Hispanic Origin	Same-sex partners	Opposite-sex partners	Total
White alone	0.9	7.3	8.2
Black or African American alone	1.4	15.5	16.9
American Indian and Alaska Native alone	1.3	16.0	17.4
Asian alone	0.7	4.0	4.7
Native Hawaiian and Other Pacific Islander alone	1.4	10.8	12.3
Some other race alone	1.2	12.4	13.6
Two or more races	1.6	12.1	13.7
Hispanic or Latino (of any race)	1.3	10.9	12.2
White alone, not Hispanic or Latino	0.9	7.2	8.1

Note: Percent same-sex partners and percent opposite-sex partners may not add to total percent unmarried-partner households because of rounding.
Source: U.S. Census Bureau, Census 2000 Summary File 2.

found to have above-average proportions of households consisting of married couples.

Compared with a nationwide ratio of 1 in 11, approximately 1 out of every 8 coupled households in Nevada, Alaska, Vermont, and Maine was an unmarried-partner household. In the District of Columbia, the ratio was 1 out of 5. States with the lowest percentages of unmarried-partner households included Utah (5 percent) and Alabama (6 percent). Puerto Rico also had a low percentage of unmarried-partner households (6 percent).

Since marriage patterns and living arrangements differ by racial and ethnic groups, geographic patterns

of the proportions of unmarried-partner households may emerge if an area has a high proportion of a specific population group. For example, Figure 2 shows that although the majority of counties in the Great Plains had below-average proportions of unmarried-partner households, high proportions were recorded for several counties in South Dakota that are geographically coincidental with American Indian reservations.[10] Similarly, above-average proportions of unmarried couples were found in the

[10] A visual representation of the population by race and ethnicity at the county level can be found in Cynthia A. Brewer and Trudy A. Suchan, *Mapping Census 2000: The Geography of U.S. Diversity*. Census Special Reports, Series CENSR/01-1. U.S. Census Bureau, Washington, DC, 2001.

Mississippi Valley, where above-average proportions of the population reported a single race of Black.[11]

Figure 3 illustrates the wide range of differences in the proportion of unmarried-partner households to all coupled households by race and

[11] Census 2000 allowed respondents to choose more than one race. In this report, the "alone" category refers to people who indicated one race among the six primary categories: White, Black or African American, American Indian and Alaska Native, Asian, Native Hawaiian or Other Pacific Islander, and Some other race. The "alone" category is used for all of the racial groups in this report except for the Two or more race category. The use of the alone population in this section does not imply that it is the preferred method of presenting or analyzing data. In general, either the alone population or the alone or in combination population can be used, depending on the purpose of the analysis. The Census Bureau uses both approaches.

ethnicity.[12] In 2000, about 17 percent of coupled households for those reporting a single race of American Indian and Alaska Native or of Black were unmarried-partner households. The Hispanic[13] population, which is concentrated in the southwest and California, also recorded above-average proportions of unmarried-partner households (12 percent). However, none of these groups is particularly concentrated in the Pacific Northwest or the New England states, which also have high proportions of unmarried-partner households, suggesting that explanations must be found elsewhere. The lowest proportion shown in Figure 3 was for those reporting a single race of Asian (5 percent).

California contained 1 out of every 8 unmarried-partner households in the country.

California, which had 11 percent of all households, had more unmarried-partner households than any other state: 684,000, or 12 percent of the 5.5 million total. Of these, 591,000 were opposite-sex and 92,000 were same-sex couples, representing 12 percent and 16 percent, respectively, of these types of households in the nation. The majority (54 percent) of the same-sex couples in California had male partners.

States which had the highest percentage of opposite-sex unmarried partners of all coupled households were Alaska (12 percent), followed by Maine, Vermont, and Nevada (11 percent each). States, which had the lowest percentage were Utah (4.4 percent) and Alabama (5.2 percent).

Among the states, the highest percentage of same-sex unmarried partners of all coupled households was in California, with 1.4 percent, closely followed by Massachusetts, Vermont, and New York, with 1.3 percent. The lowest proportion was found in Iowa, South Dakota, and North Dakota (0.5 percent). The District of Columbia recorded relatively high percentages for both types of unmarried-partner households: 16 percent of its coupled households were composed of opposite-sex partners and 5 percent of same-sex partners.

Nationally, 51 percent of the same-sex couples had male partners. States that had the lowest proportions included Vermont (39 percent) and Alaska (41 percent). Other states under the 45-percent level were geographically dispersed from New Hampshire (43 percent) and Maine (44 percent) in New England, to New Mexico (42 percent) in the Southwest and Oregon (43 percent) in the Pacific Northwest. Only two states had higher proportions of male partners than California (54 percent)—Florida (56 percent) and Nevada (55 percent). Seventy-three percent of the same-sex couples in the District of Columbia had male partners.

Married-couple households are often found in rapidly growing suburban communities.

Table 3 shows that, as a percentage of all types of households in

an area, the ten places with the highest percentage of married-couple households were most likely to be found in rapidly growing areas outside of large cities, such as Gilbert, Arizona, which is near Phoenix; Naperville, Illinois, which is outside of Chicago; and Plano, Texas, which is close to Dallas.[14] Five of the ten highest-ranked places were in California. These findings are consistent with overall national statistics that show that the majority of married-couple households were in suburban areas of the United States (Table 1).

The three places with the highest percentage of households with opposite-sex unmarried partners were in the older industrial areas of the Northeast: Paterson, New Jersey; Manchester, New Hampshire; and Rochester, New York. However, two rapidly growing places in Nevada (Sunrise Manor and Spring Valley) also made the list.

In contrast, the highest percentage of households with same-sex unmarried partners were found in larger coastal cities such as San Francisco, California; Ft. Lauderdale, Florida; and Seattle, Washington. Four of these top ten places are in California, while only one is located in the Midwest (Minneapolis, Minnesota).

[12] Because Hispanics may be of any race, data in this report for Hispanics overlap with data for racial groups. Based on Census 2000 100 percent data, the proportion Hispanic was 8.0 percent for the White alone population, 2.0 percent for the Black alone population, 16.4 percent for the American Indian and Alaska Native alone population, 1.2 percent for the Asian alone population, 11.4 percent for the Native Hawaiian and Other Pacific Islander alone population, 97.0 percent for the Some other race alone population, and 32.6 percent for the Two or more races population.
[13] The terms "Hispanic" and "Latino" may be used interchangeably to reflect the new terminology in the standards issued by the Office of Management and Budget in 1997 that are to be implemented by January 1, 2003.

[14] Gilbert, Arizona, was the fastest growing city between 1990 and 2000 of cities with 100,000 or more people in 2000. Two other cities in Table 3 were also ranked among the top ten fastest growing: Plano, Texas (number 8) and Corona, California (number 9). Naperville, Illinois, along with Fontana, California, and Laredo, Texas, were also in the top 20 fastest growing cities. See U.S. Census Bureau, *County and City Data Book: 2000.* U.S. Census Bureau, Washington, DC, 2002, Table C-1, for a list of these cities.

Table 3.
Ten Places of 100,000 or More Population With the Highest Percentage of Married-Couple and Unmarried-Partner Households: 2000

(For information on confidentiality protection, nonsampling error, and definitions, see *www.census.gov/prod/cen2000/doc/sf1.pdf*)

Types of household and area	Total households, all types	Specified type of household	
		Number	Percent of all households
MARRIED-COUPLE HOUSEHOLD			
Gilbert, AZ..	35,405	24,613	69.5
Naperville, IL	43,751	30,256	69.2
Plano, TX	80,875	52,029	64.3
Simi Valley, CA	36,421	23,258	63.9
Corona, CA..	37,839	24,156	63.8
Livonia, MI	38,089	23,938	62.8
Fremont, CA.......................................	68,237	42,757	62.7
Fontana, CA.......................................	34,014	21,273	62.5
Thousand Oaks, CA	41,793	26,063	62.4
Laredo, TX	46,852	29,054	62.0
UNMARRIED-PARTNER HOUSEHOLD			
Opposite-sex partners			
Paterson, NJ.......................................	44,710	3,602	8.1
Manchester, NH..................................	44,247	3,498	7.9
Rochester, NY	88,999	6,817	7.7
Sunrise Manor, NV*	53,745	4,071	7.6
Allentown, PA.....................................	42,032	3,139	7.5
San Bernardino, CA	56,330	4,193	7.4
Spring Valley, NV*...............................	47,965	3,546	7.4
Hartford, CT	44,986	3,320	7.4
Lansing, MI...	49,505	3,630	7.3
Green Bay, WI	41,591	3,040	7.3
Same-sex partners			
San Francisco, CA	329,700	8,902	2.7
Fort Lauderdale, FL	68,468	1,418	2.1
Seattle, WA..	258,499	4,965	1.9
Oakland, CA.......................................	150,790	2,650	1.8
Berkeley, CA.......................................	44,955	788	1.8
Atlanta, GA	168,147	2,833	1.7
Minneapolis, MN	162,352	2,622	1.6
Washington, DC..................................	248,338	3,678	1.5
Long Beach, CA	163,088	2,266	1.4
Portland, OR.......................................	223,737	3,017	1.3

*Sunrise Manor, NV, and Spring Valley, NV, are census designated places and are not legally incorporated.

Note: Census 2000 shows 245 places in the United States with 100,000 or more population. They include 238 incorporated places (including 4 city-county consolidations) and 7 census designated places (CDPs) that are not legally incorporated. For a list of these places by states, see *www.census.gov/population/www/cen2000/phc-t6/tab04.pdf*.

Source: U.S. Census Bureau, Census 2000 Summary File 1.

Female householders are found most frequently in the Northeast.

Research has shown that opposite-sex unmarried partners tend to share household activities more equally than married couples.[15]

[15] For a discussion of the changing roles of spouses and partners in married-couple and unmarried-partner households, see Lynne M. Casper and Suzanne M. Bianchi, *Continuity and Change in the American Family* (Sage Publications: Thousand Oaks, CA, 2002), Chapter 2.

This role-sharing behavior may also be reflected in the decision of whom to designate as the householder—the man or the woman. These differences in householder designation are revealed in Table 4—only 13 percent of married-couple households had a female householder, but nearly half (46 percent) of all opposite-sex unmarried-partner households did. Regionally, the Northeast had the highest and the Midwest had the lowest percentage of householders who were women for married-couples (15 percent and 11 percent, respectively), while the Northeast had the highest percentage and the West had the lowest for unmarried-partner households (48 percent and 45 percent, respectively).

The highest percentage of married-couple households with female householders was recorded in New

Table 4.
Selected Household and Family Characteristics of Married-Couple and Unmarried-Partner Households for the United States, Regions, States, and for Puerto Rico: 2000

(For information on confidentiality protection, nonsampling error, and definitions, see *www.census.gov/prod/cen2000/doc/sf1.pdf*)

Area	Percent of householders female		Percent of households with children under 18 years						
				Unmarried-partner households					
				Opposite-sex partners		Male partners		Female partners	
	Married-couple households	Opposite-sex unmarried-partner households	Married-couple households[1]	Own children[1]	Own and/or unrelated children[2]	Own children[1]	Own and/or unrelated children[2]	Own children[1]	Own and/or unrelated children[2]
United States	12.9	46.4	45.6	38.9	43.1	21.8	22.3	32.7	34.3
Region									
Northeast	15.4	48.4	45.2	37.4	40.9	21.3	21.7	31.2	32.6
Midwest	11.1	45.8	45.1	38.7	43.9	22.3	22.9	32.8	34.7
South	12.6	46.7	44.4	39.7	44.0	22.1	23.9	34.4	36.1
West	13.4	45.0	48.5	39.2	42.7	20.6	21.1	31.5	33.1
State									
Alabama	11.7	48.2	43.1	41.6	46.1	27.8	28.3	36.8	38.1
Alaska	15.0	43.8	54.4	40.6	45.1	36.2	37.1	37.0	38.6
Arizona	12.7	44.6	43.5	40.5	44.3	22.5	23.0	33.1	35.0
Arkansas	9.9	44.4	41.9	41.8	47.6	26.1	26.7	36.2	38.2
California	14.0	45.3	50.9	41.4	44.4	19.6	20.2	32.8	34.3
Colorado	13.8	45.7	47.2	31.3	34.6	19.9	20.5	26.1	27.8
Connecticut	17.2	50.7	45.4	35.6	38.7	21.9	22.2	30.2	31.6
Delaware	14.5	48.6	42.8	39.9	44.1	18.4	18.9	29.4	31.8
District of Columbia	24.9	56.6	36.6	31.8	32.8	4.8	5.0	23.4	24.5
Florida	14.4	46.5	38.1	35.5	39.2	17.4	17.8	29.3	31.0
Georgia	14.1	48.9	47.3	42.2	46.1	21.1	21.6	34.4	36.2
Hawaii	13.9	45.2	44.8	35.8	39.0	20.7	21.3	30.6	32.6
Idaho	10.0	42.3	47.8	37.6	43.0	30.3	30.8	35.7	37.9
Illinois	11.9	46.2	47.3	38.3	42.5	23.5	24.0	35.6	37.0
Indiana	10.3	44.0	44.4	40.5	47.0	22.8	23.5	33.6	36.3
Iowa	10.0	44.6	43.4	37.5	43.0	24.9	25.4	33.8	35.5
Kansas	10.1	44.8	45.9	39.1	44.1	28.3	29.0	36.5	38.1
Kentucky	11.4	46.1	43.7	40.1	46.0	23.5	24.4	33.0	34.9
Louisiana	12.1	47.7	46.2	44.4	48.5	25.9	26.3	38.5	39.8
Maine	15.1	45.2	41.4	35.7	40.9	18.7	19.0	25.2	27.1
Maryland	15.0	49.5	46.4	38.1	42.1	23.3	24.0	31.7	33.3
Massachusetts	16.6	49.8	45.8	32.8	35.9	18.1	18.6	27.7	29.0
Michigan	11.3	46.9	44.8	40.1	45.3	22.8	23.6	33.2	35.3
Minnesota	11.4	45.7	46.9	35.4	40.2	17.2	17.9	26.8	28.5
Mississippi	12.2	48.9	45.0	49.2	53.4	30.7	31.1	42.0	43.8
Missouri	10.3	45.5	43.6	39.9	45.7	20.9	21.5	31.7	33.7
Montana	11.7	44.0	42.9	35.1	39.3	28.7	29.6	34.2	35.5
Nebraska	9.8	44.6	45.9	36.4	41.5	24.7	25.7	32.7	34.4
Nevada	13.9	41.9	44.5	36.1	40.2	24.7	25.3	35.4	37.5
New Hampshire	15.3	43.7	45.9	33.0	38.1	22.3	22.9	27.2	29.0
New Jersey	14.7	48.0	47.4	38.1	40.9	25.4	25.8	33.6	34.7
New Mexico	12.0	44.2	46.1	48.4	51.7	27.4	27.9	31.0	32.2
New York	17.5	50.1	46.4	39.2	42.2	21.3	21.7	33.1	34.3
North Carolina	12.3	46.1	43.0	38.4	42.9	25.2	25.9	33.3	34.7
North Dakota	8.8	43.0	45.1	36.9	41.5	21.4	21.7	34.4	34.7
Ohio	12.4	46.9	43.6	40.2	45.3	20.9	21.6	31.8	34.0
Oklahoma	10.6	45.1	43.4	42.1	47.2	26.7	27.3	35.0	36.9
Oregon	13.7	45.6	42.8	33.9	38.4	18.9	19.5	26.3	28.1
Pennsylvania	11.6	45.6	42.3	38.5	42.8	20.9	21.3	31.5	33.2
Rhode Island	16.6	50.4	43.6	37.1	40.1	20.5	20.6	27.3	28.6
South Carolina	14.2	47.8	42.6	41.9	45.7	26.8	27.2	37.1	38.8
South Dakota	9.9	44.2	45.2	42.1	47.4	33.2	33.9	41.4	42.3
Tennessee	11.3	46.3	42.5	39.1	44.3	23.9	24.7	33.4	35.4
Texas	11.5	45.2	50.2	42.9	46.8	26.7	27.3	39.2	40.9
Utah	8.9	41.9	55.5	42.2	47.2	29.7	30.2	40.6	42.3
Vermont	16.5	46.2	44.2	33.8	38.3	19.9	20.6	26.7	28.9
Virginia	12.6	46.5	45.3	35.0	39.6	19.8	20.3	31.2	32.7
Washington	13.3	45.9	45.8	35.1	39.7	18.1	18.6	26.7	28.2
West Virginia	9.9	43.7	39.5	40.2	45.6	27.6	27.9	34.9	36.4
Wisconsin	10.5	45.4	44.5	34.9	40.5	21.7	22.4	30.6	32.4
Wyoming	10.9	41.2	44.3	36.0	41.8	28.2	29.9	35.7	37.5
Puerto Rico	14.1	54.4	49.4	56.5	56.7	39.2	39.2	42.2	42.5

[1]Refers to own sons/daughters of the householder.
[2]Refers to own sons/daughters of the householder and other children not related to the householder.

Source: U.S. Census Bureau, Census 2000 Summary File 1; and Census 2000, special tabulation.

York (18 percent). In all the states in New England, at least 15 percent of married couples had female householders. Only two states, North Dakota and Utah, had less than 9 percent. In the District of Columbia, one-quarter of married couples had female householders.

In Connecticut, 51 percent of opposite-sex unmarried partners had female householders, followed by New York (50 percent). The state with the lowest percentage was Wyoming (41 percent). The District of Columbia (57 percent) and Puerto Rico (54 percent) also had a relatively high percentage.

Almost one-half of married-couple households include children under 18 years.

Nationally, 46 percent of married-couple households had at least one son or daughter living in the household (defined as an "own child" of the householder).[16] The West had the highest percentage with children (49 percent), while the South had the lowest (44 percent). Four states had at least 50 percent: Utah (56 percent), Alaska (54 percent), California (51 percent), and Texas (50 percent). The state with the lowest percentage was Florida (38 percent), likely a reflection of its older age distribution.

Four out of ten opposite-sex unmarried-partner households have children present.

The identification of the partner's own children in an unmarried-partner household is complicated when the child of the partner is not the biological child of the householder, because the Census

2000 questionnaire recorded only each person's relationship to the householder. In circumstances where the child of the partner was not related to the householder, an actual family unit may not be identified in the tabulation. To address this issue, Table 4 includes data that attempt to capture the presence of the partners' children in unmarried-partner households.

Using this expanded child-defined universe, the percentage of children present in opposite-sex unmarried-partner households increases from 39 percent—counting only own children—to 43 percent—including both own and/or unrelated children under 18. Similar but smaller increases of 1 or 2 percentage points are noted for same-sex couples.

The South had the highest percentage of opposite-sex unmarried-partner households with their own children.

Among opposite-sex unmarried-partner households, the South had the highest percentage with their own children (40 percent), while the Northeast had the lowest (37 percent). Among the states, Colorado had the lowest percentage (31 percent), while Mississippi had the highest (49 percent).

Although married-couple households were more likely to contain own children of the householder than were opposite-sex unmarried-partner households, households in three states (Mississippi, New Mexico, and West Virginia) were more likely to contain their own children in unmarried-partner households. In Puerto Rico, 57 percent of all opposite-sex unmarried-partner households contained own children of the householder, 7 percentage points more

than for married-couple households.[17]

One-third of female partner households and one-fifth of male partner households contain children.

Nationally, 33 percent of female same-sex householders were living with their sons and daughters under 18 years old.[18] The South had the highest percentage with own children under 18 years of age (34 percent), while the Northeast had the lowest (31 percent). In three states, 40 percent or more of these households had at least one own child living in the household (Mississippi, South Dakota, and Utah).

Overall, 22 percent of male same-sex householders had their own children present in the household. The percentage with own children ranged from 17 percent in Florida and Minnesota to 36 percent in Alaska. Other states where 30 percent or more of male same-sex households had own children present were South Dakota (33 percent), Mississippi (31 percent), and Idaho and Utah (30 percent each).

---

[16] In this report, an "own child" of the householder includes any child under the age of 18 who is a biological, adopted, or stepchild of the householder.

[17] In 2000, both Mississippi and New Mexico had the highest percentage of children born out of wedlock of all states (46 percent, compared with the national average of 33 percent), while the corresponding percentage for Puerto Rico was 50 percent. This could possibly account for the relatively high proportions of unmarried-partner households with children in these states. See Joyce A. Martin, et al., *Births: Final Data for 2000. National Vital Statistics Reports*, Vol. 50, No. 5. National Center for Health Statistics, Hyattsville, MD, 2002, Table 19.

[18] The proportions of same-sex unmarried-partner households with children shown in this report may be too high because of the possible inclusion of opposite-sex couples who had erred in marking their sex on the questionnaire or by incorrect optical reading of some questionnaires during data processing. However, research has indicated that sex was reported with extremely high consistency levels when subsequent reinterviews were made.

What circumstances may influence inter-state variations in the presence of children in same-sex unmarried-partner households? Factors could include not only geographical differences in fertility patterns of previously married partners before they entered a same-sex relationship, but also state laws related to child custody placements in cases of marital dissolution—which determine who retains custody of the child—and to adoption by same-sex couples.

Data from Census 2000 illustrate the variety of living arrangements of households with children: while the vast majority of households containing own children were married-couple households (24.8 million), over 2 million households included own children whose parents were living in nontraditional arrangements (1.9 million opposite-sex unmarried partners, 96,000 female partners, and 66,000 male partners).

Interracial couples are most prevalent in the West.

Nationally, in 6 percent of married-couple households, the householder and the spouse were of different races (Table 5).[19] Three to five percent of married couples in the Midwest, the Northeast, and the South had spouses of different races, compared with 11 percent in the West. The highest proportion was found in Hawaii (35 percent), followed by Alaska and Oklahoma (about 15 percent). Because these states have high proportions of native populations (for example, Native Hawaiian and Other Pacific Islanders, and American Indian and Alaska Natives, respectively), these states may have a greater potential for the likelihood of inter-marriage.

Unmarried-partner households consistently had higher percentages of partners of different races at the national and regional levels, and in individual states than did married-couple households.[20] Nationally, these percentages ranged from 10 percent for female unmarried partners to 12 percent for opposite-sex unmarried partners.

For opposite-sex unmarried-partner households, the West recorded the highest percentage of mixed-race partnerships (19 percent), and the Midwest the lowest (9 percent). Over one-half (56 percent) of these households in Hawaii had partners of different races, followed by Alaska (26 percent) and Oklahoma (25 percent).

The New England states of Maine, New Hampshire, and Vermont, which have very high proportions of people who reported the single race of White, had the lowest proportions of different race partnerships for all four household types (around 5 percent or less). Two other states (Mississippi and West Virginia) also had comparatively low percentages for all four household types.

Three percent of married-couple households have one Hispanic and one non-Hispanic partner.

Nationally, 3 percent of married couples had only one Hispanic partner and the other partner not of Hispanic origin, compared with about 6 percent of unmarried partners (Table 5). Similar to the geographic pattern noted for inter-racial partners, the highest percentages of Hispanic/non-Hispanic partner households for all four types of households were found in the West. The West also had the highest portion of Hispanics (24 percent) in its total population.[21] New Mexico had the highest percentage of households having only one Hispanic partner, more than 10 percent for each household type. West Virginia had the lowest proportions, with 1 percent or less for each household type.

The last four columns of Table 5 present the data for the 14 possible race/Hispanic-origin combinations, which generate 196 possible combinations per couple.[22] Overall, 7 percent of married couples had spouses of a different race or origin. Percentages for opposite-sex and male same-sex households were about 15 percent, compared with 13 percent for female same-sex households. Couples in Hawaii experienced the greatest diversity: the percentages of partners of a different race or origin for all four household types in Hawaii were more than 3 times the national average, ranging from

---

[19] The seven race groups used in this report were White alone; Black or African American alone; American Indian and Alaska Native alone; Asian alone; Native Hawaiian and Other Pacific Islander alone; Some other race alone; and Two or more races. If either spouse or partner was not in the same single race as the other spouse or partner, or if at least one spouse or partner was in a multiple-race group, then the couple was classified as an interracial couple (see Census 2000, PHC-T-19, *Hispanic Origin and Race of Coupled Households: 2000,* for detailed tabulations).

[20] Research has indicated that since unmarried-partner relationships often tend to be short-term or trial relationships, the partners may be less likely to choose partners with the same characteristics, such as race or ethnicity, than married couples. The higher proportions of mixed-race couples found among unmarried partners in Census 2000 than among married couples is consistent with this research. See Robert Schoen and Robin M. Weinick, "Partner Choice in Marriages and Cohabitations." *Journal of Marriage and Family*, Vol. 55, No. 2 (1993), pp. 408-414.

[21] For Census 2000 distributions of the population by Hispanic or Latino origin, see Betsy Guzman, *The Hispanic Population: 2000.* Census 2000 Brief, Series C2KBR/01-3. U.S. Census Bureau, Washington, DC, 2001.

[22] Since the race and Hispanic origin groups overlap, the combined percentages are always less than the sum of the individual percentages for each household type shown in Table 5.

Table 5.
Selected Race and Hispanic Origin Characteristics of Married-Couple and Unmarried-Partner Households for the United States, Regions, States, and for Puerto Rico: 2000

(For information on confidentiality protection, nonsampling error, and definitions, see *www.census.gov/prod/cen2000/doc/sf1.pdf*)

Area	Percent of households with partners of different races				Percent of households with only one partner of Hispanic origin				Percent of houholds with partners of different races or origins			
	Married-couple house-holds	Unmarried-partner households			Married-couple house-holds	Unmarried-partner households			Married-couple house-holds	Unmarried-partner households		
		Opposite-sex partners	Same-sex partners			Opposite-sex partners	Same-sex partners			Opposite-sex partners	Same-sex partners	
			Male part-ners	Female part-ners			Male part-ners	Female part-ners			Male part-ners	Female partners
United States	5.7	12.2	11.5	10.0	3.1	6.4	6.9	5.4	7.4	15.0	15.3	12.6
Region												
Northeast	4.3	10.3	10.7	8.5	2.1	5.2	5.9	4.3	5.7	12.8	14.2	10.8
Midwest	3.5	9.4	8.2	7.4	1.7	4.0	3.8	3.0	4.5	11.2	10.3	8.9
South	4.9	10.3	8.7	8.0	2.7	5.2	5.8	4.3	6.5	12.8	12.4	10.3
West	10.6	19.3	17.7	15.7	6.1	11.2	11.1	9.2	13.7	23.7	23.2	19.7
State												
Alabama	2.8	6.7	4.5	4.6	0.9	1.9	1.5	1.2	3.3	7.5	5.4	5.3
Alaska	15.4	26.0	17.4	19.4	3.6	4.9	5.4	6.0	17.1	27.7	19.3	22.1
Arizona	8.0	15.7	12.2	13.0	6.6	12.3	10.7	10.3	11.5	20.9	17.7	17.6
Arkansas	3.6	8.4	6.1	6.5	1.2	2.7	2.1	1.8	4.2	9.6	7.0	7.4
California	12.0	21.0	19.8	17.3	7.2	12.7	12.8	10.5	15.6	26.0	26.2	21.8
Colorado	7.8	15.0	13.6	11.6	6.2	11.5	11.5	9.1	11.2	20.1	19.5	15.6
Connecticut	4.2	11.8	8.4	8.1	2.3	6.6	5.2	3.9	5.7	14.6	11.6	10.2
Delaware	4.1	10.5	9.8	7.1	1.7	3.9	4.0	3.5	5.1	12.2	12.5	9.0
District of Columbia	7.8	10.4	16.0	13.3	2.9	3.9	9.4	4.1	9.6	12.6	22.5	15.0
Florida	5.2	10.4	8.6	8.4	4.1	7.3	8.5	6.7	8.3	14.9	15.0	12.8
Georgia	3.7	8.2	7.6	6.4	1.6	3.1	3.8	2.6	4.6	9.5	10.0	7.8
Hawaii	34.7	55.6	43.8	40.9	6.2	12.6	7.9	8.9	36.1	57.6	46.1	42.3
Idaho	5.3	11.0	8.0	8.1	3.0	6.7	4.9	5.4	6.8	13.8	10.4	10.2
Illinois	4.3	10.0	11.0	8.6	2.6	5.7	6.7	4.3	5.8	12.6	14.7	10.8
Indiana	2.9	8.2	5.8	6.0	1.5	3.4	2.5	2.3	3.8	9.7	7.4	7.1
Iowa	2.3	7.7	5.5	6.4	1.2	3.6	2.2	2.7	3.0	9.2	6.8	8.0
Kansas	5.4	14.5	8.4	9.2	2.8	6.9	3.7	4.2	6.8	17.1	10.2	11.1
Kentucky	2.3	7.3	4.6	5.6	0.8	1.8	1.6	1.6	2.8	8.1	5.7	6.4
Louisiana	3.3	7.2	6.5	5.2	1.8	2.9	3.7	2.9	4.5	8.8	8.8	6.9
Maine	2.3	4.9	4.2	4.0	0.7	1.1	1.5	1.5	2.8	5.6	5.4	4.9
Maryland	5.1	9.6	9.7	8.6	1.9	2.9	3.5	3.2	6.3	11.0	11.9	10.6
Massachusetts	4.1	10.3	9.9	8.1	1.5	4.4	4.6	3.5	5.1	12.3	12.7	9.9
Michigan	4.1	9.7	8.5	7.4	1.8	4.2	3.5	2.8	5.2	11.7	10.4	8.7
Minnesota	3.4	10.6	9.1	8.0	1.2	3.3	3.4	2.6	4.1	12.0	10.8	8.9
Mississippi	2.1	5.1	3.7	3.2	0.8	1.5	1.7	1.1	2.6	5.8	4.8	3.8
Missouri	3.5	8.8	7.3	7.5	1.4	2.7	2.7	2.9	4.3	10.0	8.9	9.1
Montana	5.3	11.2	8.8	8.4	1.9	4.3	4.0	3.3	6.4	13.3	11.6	10.5
Nebraska	3.4	11.2	5.7	8.3	2.0	5.9	3.1	4.4	4.4	13.5	7.3	10.5
Nevada	10.9	18.9	14.9	15.2	6.2	10.7	9.1	8.3	14.3	23.7	19.5	19.2
New Hampshire	2.6	5.2	5.3	4.2	1.0	2.0	2.1	2.3	3.3	6.3	6.7	5.4
New Jersey	5.1	12.0	11.2	8.8	3.1	7.5	6.6	5.2	7.2	15.8	14.9	11.7
New Mexico	10.8	18.6	15.8	16.4	11.2	18.4	17.6	14.7	16.9	26.3	25.4	23.2
New York	5.7	12.3	13.7	10.9	3.0	6.7	8.0	6.0	7.6	15.6	18.4	14.1
North Carolina	3.6	9.6	6.9	6.5	1.4	3.0	2.1	2.2	4.3	10.7	8.0	7.5
North Dakota	3.1	9.3	4.4	6.4	0.8	2.3	0.6	1.7	3.6	10.4	4.7	7.6
Ohio	2.9	8.5	6.9	6.7	1.2	2.9	2.4	2.0	3.6	9.8	8.4	7.7
Oklahoma	14.8	24.6	17.6	18.2	2.6	5.8	3.3	4.5	16.0	26.5	18.8	19.9
Oregon	7.4	14.1	12.4	11.7	3.0	6.4	5.6	4.6	8.9	16.7	15.0	13.5
Pennsylvania	2.4	7.5	7.1	5.6	1.1	3.2	3.1	2.2	3.1	8.9	8.8	6.8
Rhode Island	4.4	11.1	9.0	8.0	1.5	4.3	3.9	2.8	5.2	13.0	10.6	9.6
South Carolina	2.9	7.3	5.4	4.8	1.1	2.3	1.4	1.7	3.5	8.3	6.2	5.7
South Dakota	3.6	10.9	5.7	7.3	1.0	2.8	1.8	0.9	4.1	12.1	6.7	7.6
Tennessee	2.7	7.4	5.2	5.7	1.0	2.2	1.8	1.8	3.3	8.4	6.3	6.6
Texas	6.8	14.1	11.5	10.7	5.4	11.2	10.7	8.0	9.8	19.0	17.4	14.6
Utah	5.4	14.6	9.2	9.6	3.8	10.0	6.4	6.5	7.3	18.8	12.5	12.8
Vermont	2.6	4.7	4.7	4.5	0.9	1.4	1.7	0.9	3.2	5.5	5.9	5.2
Virginia	5.3	11.3	10.4	8.3	2.1	3.6	4.2	3.5	6.5	12.9	12.8	10.1
Washington	9.2	17.3	14.8	13.6	3.2	6.6	5.9	5.4	10.8	19.8	17.6	16.1
West Virginia	1.8	5.6	3.6	3.2	0.5	1.0	0.9	0.9	2.2	6.1	4.4	3.8
Wisconsin	2.9	8.7	7.2	6.8	1.4	3.9	3.3	3.0	3.7	10.4	8.9	8.2
Wyoming	5.3	10.8	7.5	7.6	4.0	8.7	5.6	5.8	7.4	14.9	10.7	10.9
Puerto Rico	12.5	18.5	13.7	13.8	1.3	1.7	1.7	1.7	13.5	19.7	14.7	15.0

Source: U.S. Census Bureau, Census 2000, special tabulation from Summary File 1.

36 percent for married-couple households to 58 percent for opposite-sex partner households.

Overall, the western region of the United States exhibited the greatest diversity in couples' living arrangements. It had both the highest percentage of its coupled households composed of unmarried partners (Table 2) and also the highest percentage of either married-couple or unmarried-partner households with partners not of the same race or origin.

Partners in opposite-sex unmarried-partner households are 12 years younger, on average, than partners in married-couple households.

Living together is often a precursor to marriage among young couples in contemporary America.[23] Table 6 shows that the average ages of the partners in opposite-sex unmarried-partner households, many of whom will ultimately marry each other, were about 12 years younger than that of their married-couple counterparts.[24] Nationally, the average age of husbands was 49 years old, 2.4 years older than their wives. Opposite-sex partners, while younger, were

only slightly closer in age—on average, male partners were 36.8 years old, 2.1 years older than their female partners.

Overall, married couples who lived in the Northeast were the oldest while those in the West were the youngest. Among the individual states, the oldest husbands and wives were in Florida (53 years and 50 years, respectively), while the youngest lived in Alaska and Utah (about 46 years and 43 years, respectively).

On average, the youngest opposite-sex partners lived in the Midwest. The Great Plains states of Kansas, Nebraska, South Dakota, and North Dakota, on average, tended to have both partners below 35 years of age. While the lowest average ages for both partners were in Utah (34 years for men and 32 years for women), Florida had the oldest opposite-sex partners (39 years and 37 years).[25]

The average age of same-sex partners was in their early forties, intermediate between that of married-couples and opposite-sex partners. In male unmarried-partner households, the householder was about 2 years older, while in female unmarried-partner households, the householder was slightly more than 1 year older. The average age of same-sex partners was lowest in the West and highest

in the Northeast for both types of households.

FOR MORE INFORMATION

Data on households and families from the Census 2000 Summary File 1 were released in 2001 and are available on the Internet via *factfinder.census.gov* and for purchase on DVD. One can also investigate household and family data from other Census Bureau surveys like the American Community Survey, the Current Population Survey, and the Survey of Income and Program Participation, and access recently released reports related to the topic, by going to *www.census.gov.*

For information on confidentiality protection, nonsampling error, and definitions, see *www.census.gov /prod/cen2000/doc/sf1.pdf* or contact our Customer Services Center at 301-763-INFO (4636).

Information on other population and housing topics is presented in the Census 2000 Brief Series, located on the U.S. Census Bureau's Web site at *www.census.gov/population /www/cen2000/briefs.html.* This series presents information about race, Hispanic origin, age, sex, household type, housing tenure, and other social, economic, and housing characteristics.

For more information about Census 2000, including data products, call our Customer Services Center at 301-763-INFO (4636) or e-mail *webmaster@census.gov.*

---

[23] For a discussion of the transition from cohabitation to marriage, see Wendy D. Manning and Pamela J. Smock, "Why Marry? Race and the Transition to Marriage Among Cohabitors," *Demography*, Vol. 32, No. 4 (November 1995), pp. 509-520; and Larry L. Bumpass and Hsien-Hen Lu, "Trends in Cohabitation and Implications for Children's Family Contexts in the United States," *Population Studies*, Vol. 54, No. 1 (March 2000), pp. 29-41.

[24] These averages refer only to those couples who are the householder and spouse or partner, and do not include those couples who may be in subfamilies or other living arrangements within the household.

[25] The ages of spouses and partners reflect the overall age composition of the population in each state. Utah had the youngest population in the United States in 2000, while Florida had the second oldest population. See Julie Meyer, *Age: 2000.* Census 2000 Brief, Series C2KBR/01-12. U.S. Census Bureau, Washington, DC, 2001.

Table 6.
Average Age in Years of Householder and Partner in Married-Couple and Unmarried-Partner Households for the United States, Regions, States, and for Puerto Rico: 2000

(For information on confidentiality protection, nonsampling error, and definitions, see *www.census.gov/prod/cen2000/doc/sf1.pdf*)

Area	Married-couple households		Unmarried-partner households					
			Opposite-sex partners		Male partners		Female partners	
	Age of husband	Age of wife	Age of male partner	Age of female partner	Age of householder	Age of partner	Age of householder	Age of partner
United States ...	49.0	46.6	36.8	34.7	44.5	42.4	43.4	42.2
Region								
Northeast.........	50.0	47.5	37.8	35.5	45.2	43.3	44.3	43.2
Midwest.........	49.2	46.8	35.8	33.7	44.8	42.8	43.1	42.0
South............	48.8	46.3	36.8	34.7	44.5	42.5	43.4	42.1
West.............	48.4	45.9	37.1	35.2	43.9	41.5	42.7	41.6
State								
Alabama	48.8	46.2	36.5	34.3	46.8	44.6	45.0	43.6
Alaska	45.5	43.0	36.9	34.6	43.9	41.7	40.8	39.9
Arizona	49.8	47.3	37.0	35.1	43.5	41.3	42.7	41.5
Arkansas.........	49.3	46.6	36.3	34.0	46.2	44.5	44.8	43.3
California.........	48.2	45.6	37.6	35.6	44.0	41.5	42.9	41.7
Colorado.........	47.4	45.2	35.5	33.7	41.9	39.9	41.3	40.2
Connecticut.......	50.1	47.7	37.6	35.5	45.7	44.0	44.4	43.5
Delaware.........	49.7	47.4	37.2	35.1	45.4	43.1	43.7	42.7
District of Columbia.	50.8	48.0	38.6	36.2	42.4	39.8	42.4	41.3
Florida	52.5	49.6	39.2	36.9	46.1	44.0	45.1	43.8
Georgia	47.1	44.7	35.8	33.8	41.8	40.1	41.7	40.4
Hawaii	50.6	47.8	38.5	36.2	47.9	45.0	46.6	44.8
Idaho	48.1	45.6	36.1	34.0	46.4	43.9	43.5	42.4
Illinois...........	48.7	46.3	36.5	34.4	43.8	41.6	42.9	41.8
Indiana...........	48.7	46.4	35.5	33.4	44.5	42.4	42.4	41.3
Iowa	50.0	47.8	34.8	32.8	46.7	44.7	43.6	42.5
Kansas...........	48.8	46.6	34.5	32.5	44.4	42.4	42.8	41.6
Kentucky	48.1	45.6	35.9	33.6	45.7	43.6	43.8	42.3
Louisiana.........	48.5	45.9	36.7	34.2	45.5	43.1	44.2	42.5
Maine............	50.2	47.8	37.2	34.8	46.4	44.9	43.5	42.7
Maryland	49.0	46.6	37.8	35.6	44.6	42.7	42.8	41.6
Massachusetts.....	49.7	47.4	37.3	35.2	44.4	42.7	43.4	42.6
Michigan	49.3	46.9	36.2	34.0	45.5	43.5	43.9	42.6
Minnesota	48.9	46.6	35.5	33.5	44.0	42.0	42.7	41.5
Mississippi........	48.5	45.9	36.6	34.2	46.8	44.6	44.7	43.3
Missouri..........	49.4	47.0	36.1	33.9	45.2	43.3	42.6	41.5
Montana	50.2	47.5	36.4	34.1	46.2	44.1	45.2	44.1
Nebraska.........	49.2	47.0	34.6	32.6	45.7	43.5	44.1	43.0
Nevada	48.5	45.7	38.2	36.1	42.9	40.8	42.2	40.6
New Hampshire....	49.0	46.7	37.3	35.1	45.2	43.8	43.7	42.6
New Jersey........	49.6	47.1	38.7	36.4	45.3	43.5	44.5	43.3
New Mexico	49.2	46.7	36.3	34.4	45.2	42.9	43.8	42.8
New York..........	49.9	47.2	38.3	35.9	44.7	42.6	44.4	43.1
North Carolina	48.2	45.9	35.6	33.6	43.9	42.2	43.2	42.0
North Dakota	50.0	47.5	33.9	31.7	52.3	50.5	47.2	46.4
Ohio..............	49.4	47.1	35.8	33.7	45.2	43.3	43.5	42.3
Oklahoma	48.9	46.4	35.5	33.4	45.2	43.1	43.2	41.8
Oregon...........	49.6	47.1	36.9	34.9	44.9	42.5	42.5	41.7
Pennsylvania	50.6	48.3	37.3	35.0	46.8	44.9	45.2	44.0
Rhode Island	50.2	47.8	36.8	34.6	44.9	43.2	43.5	42.6
South Carolina.....	48.9	46.5	36.2	34.1	45.7	43.7	44.2	42.9
South Dakota......	49.9	47.5	35.0	32.6	46.7	45.1	44.4	42.6
Tennessee........	48.4	45.9	36.4	34.2	44.8	42.7	43.1	41.8
Texas............	47.1	44.6	35.6	33.6	42.9	40.6	42.1	40.6
Utah	45.5	43.2	34.2	32.1	41.7	39.6	41.5	40.0
Vermont..........	49.9	47.4	37.4	35.0	45.7	43.9	43.8	43.1
Virginia...........	48.4	46.0	36.5	34.5	44.5	42.5	43.3	42.0
Washington........	48.6	46.2	36.6	34.7	43.3	41.2	42.3	41.3
West Virginia	50.0	47.2	36.9	34.4	47.8	45.5	46.0	44.3
Wisconsin	49.5	47.2	35.6	33.5	44.7	43.0	42.8	42.0
Wyoming..........	49.0	46.5	36.4	34.1	48.2	45.6	44.1	42.9
Puerto Rico	48.2	45.1	40.9	38.5	47.4	45.4	47.4	45.6

Source: U.S. Census Bureau, Census 2000, special tabulation from Summary File 1.

FURTHER READING

Baker Jr., Houston A. and Patricia Redmond. *Afro-American Literary Study in the 1990s*. University of Chicago Press, 1992.

Bolger, Daniel P. *Savage Peace: Americans at War in the 1990s*.

Brill, Marlene Targ. *America in the 1990s (Decades of Twentieth-Century America)*. Twenty-First Century Books, 2009.

Cashill, Jack. *Snake Handling in Mid-America: An Incite-ful Look at American Life and Work in the 1990s*. Westport Publishers, 1991.

Cooper, Gael Fashingbauer and Brian Bellmont. *The Totally Sweet 90s: From Clear Cola to Furby, and Grunge to "Whatever," the Toys, Tastes, and Trends that Defined a Decade*. TarcherPerigee, 2013.

Davidson, Telly. *Culture War: How the '90s Made Us Who We Are Today Whether We Like It or Not*. McFarland, 2016.

Farkas, E. *Fractured States and U.S. Foreign Policy: Iraq, Ethiopia, and Bosnia in the 1990s*. Palgrave Macmillian, 2003.

Farley, Reynolds. *State of the Union: America in the 1990s: Volume 1: Economic Trends*. Russell Sage Foundation, 1995.

Frankel, Jeffrey A. and Peter R. Orszag. *American Economic Policy in the 1990s*. The MIT Press, 2002.

Haines, David W. *Refugees in America in the 1990s: A Reference Handbook*. Praeger, 1997

Harrison, Colin. *American Culture in the 1990s (Twentieth-Century American Culture)*. Edinburgh University Press, 2010.

Hughes, Jane Elizabeth and Scott B. MacDonald. *Carnival on Wall Street: Global Financial Markets in the 1990s*. Wiley, 2003.

Kelly, Adam. *American Fiction in Transition: Observer-Hero Narrative, the 1990s, and Postmodernism*. Bloomsbury Academic, 2014.

Lapchick, Richard B. *Five Minutes to Midnight: Race and Sport in the 1990s*. Madison Books, 2000.

London, Herbert. *Decade of Denial: A Snapshot of America in the 1990s*. Lexington Books, 2001.

Martin, Jack and Steven T. Tuch. *Racial Attitudes in the 1990s: Continuity and Change*. Praeger, 1997.

Mayer, Martin. *Whatever Happened to Madison Avenue: Advertising in the '90s*. Little Brown & Co., 1991.

Newfield, Christopher and Ronald Strickland. *After Political Correctness: The Humanities and Society in the 1990s (Politics and Culture)*. Westview Press, 1995.

Ochoa, George. *America in the 1990s (Decades of American History)*. Facts on File, 2005.

O'Neill, William L. *A Bubble in Time: America During the Interwar Years, 1989-2001*. Ivan R. Dee, 2009.

Oxoby, Marc. *The 1990s (American Popular Culture Through History)*. Greenwood, 2003.

Rushefsky, Mark E. and Kant Patel. *Politics, Power and Policy Making: Case of Health Care Reform in the 1990s*. Routledge, 1998.

Salem Press. *The Nineties in America*. Salem Press, 2009.

Sandling, Molly and Kimberley Chandler Ph.D. *Exploring America in the 1990s: New Horizons*. Prufrock Press, 2014.

Shaiko, Ronald G. *Voices and Echoes for the Environment: Public Interest Representation in the 1990s and Beyond*. Columbia University Press, 1999.

Troy, Gil. *The Age of Clinton: America in the 1990s*. Thomas Dunne Books, 2015.

Weaver, David H. and G. Cleveland Wilhoit. *The American Journalist in the 1990s: U.S. News People at the End of An Era*. Routledge, 1996.

Weigel, George. *Idealism Without Illusions/U.S. Foreign Policy in the 1990s*. Isi Books, 1994

2017 Title List

Visit www.GreyHouse.com for Product Information, Table of Contents, and Sample Pages.

General Reference
An African Biographical Dictionary
America's College Museums
American Environmental Leaders: From Colonial Times to the Present
Encyclopedia of African-American Writing
Encyclopedia of Constitutional Amendments
An Encyclopedia of Human Rights in the United States
Encyclopedia of Invasions & Conquests
Encyclopedia of Prisoners of War & Internment
Encyclopedia of Religion & Law in America
Encyclopedia of Rural America
Encyclopedia of the Continental Congress
Encyclopedia of the United States Cabinet, 1789-2010
Encyclopedia of War Journalism
Encyclopedia of Warrior Peoples & Fighting Groups
The Environmental Debate: A Documentary History
The Evolution Wars: A Guide to the Debates
From Suffrage to the Senate: America's Political Women
Gun Debate: An Encyclopedia of Gun Control & Gun Rights
Political Corruption in America
Privacy Rights in the Digital Era
The Religious Right: A Reference Handbook
Speakers of the House of Representatives, 1789-2009
This is Who We Were: 1880-1900
This is Who We Were: A Companion to the 1940 Census
This is Who We Were: In the 1900s
This is Who We Were: In the 1910s
This is Who We Were: In the 1920s
This is Who We Were: In the 1940s
This is Who We Were: In the 1950s
This is Who We Were: In the 1960s
This is Who We Were: In the 1970s
This is Who We Were: In the 1980s
This is Who We Were: In the 1990s
U.S. Land & Natural Resource Policy
The Value of a Dollar 1600-1865: Colonial Era to the Civil War
The Value of a Dollar: 1860-2014
Working Americans 1770-1869 Vol. IX: Revolutionary War to the Civil War
Working Americans 1880-1999 Vol. I: The Working Class
Working Americans 1880-1999 Vol. II: The Middle Class
Working Americans 1880-1999 Vol. III: The Upper Class
Working Americans 1880-1999 Vol. IV: Their Children
Working Americans 1880-2015 Vol. V: Americans At War
Working Americans 1880-2005 Vol. VI: Women at Work
Working Americans 1880-2006 Vol. VII: Social Movements
Working Americans 1880-2007 Vol. VIII: Immigrants
Working Americans 1880-2009 Vol. X: Sports & Recreation
Working Americans 1880-2010 Vol. XI: Inventors & Entrepreneurs
Working Americans 1880-2011 Vol. XII: Our History through Music
Working Americans 1880-2012 Vol. XIII: Education & Educators
Working Americans 1880-2016 Vol. XIV: Industry Through the Ages
World Cultural Leaders of the 20th & 21st Centuries

Education Information
Charter School Movement
Comparative Guide to American Elementary & Secondary Schools
Complete Learning Disabilities Directory
Educators Resource Directory
Special Education: Policy and Curriculum Development

Health Information
Comparative Guide to American Hospitals
Complete Directory for Pediatric Disorders
Complete Directory for People with Chronic Illness
Complete Directory for People with Disabilities
Complete Mental Health Directory
Diabetes in America: Analysis of an Epidemic
Directory of Health Care Group Purchasing Organizations
HMO/PPO Directory
Medical Device Market Place
Older Americans Information Directory

Business Information
Complete Television, Radio & Cable Industry Directory
Directory of Business Information Resources
Directory of Mail Order Catalogs

Directory of Venture Capital & Private Equity Firms
Environmental Resource Handbook
Food & Beverage Market Place
Grey House Homeland Security Directory
Grey House Performing Arts Directory
Grey House Safety & Security Directory
Hudson's Washington News Media Contacts Directory
New York State Directory
Sports Market Place Directory

Statistics & Demographics
American Tally
America's Top-Rated Cities
America's Top-Rated Smaller Cities
Ancestry & Ethnicity in America
The Asian Databook
Comparative Guide to American Suburbs
The Hispanic Databook
Profiles of America
"Profiles of" Series – State Handbooks
Weather America

Financial Ratings Series
TheStreet Ratings' Guide to Bond & Money Market Mutual Funds
TheStreet Ratings' Guide to Common Stocks
TheStreet Ratings' Guide to Exchange-Traded Funds
TheStreet Ratings' Guide to Stock Mutual Funds
TheStreet Ratings' Ultimate Guided Tour of Stock Investing
Weiss Ratings' Consumer Guides
Weiss Ratings' Financial Literary Basic Guides
Weiss Ratings' Guide to Banks
Weiss Ratings' Guide to Credit Unions
Weiss Ratings' Guide to Health Insurers
Weiss Ratings' Guide to Life & Annuity Insurers
Weiss Ratings' Guide to Property & Casualty Insurers

Bowker's Books In Print® Titles
American Book Publishing Record® Annual
American Book Publishing Record® Monthly
Books In Print®
Books In Print® Supplement
Books Out Loud™
Bowker's Complete Video Directory™
Children's Books In Print®
El-Hi Textbooks & Serials In Print®
Forthcoming Books®
Law Books & Serials In Print™
Medical & Health Care Books In Print™
Publishers, Distributors & Wholesalers of the US™
Subject Guide to Books In Print®
Subject Guide to Children's Books In Print®

Canadian General Reference
Associations Canada
Canadian Almanac & Directory
Canadian Environmental Resource Guide
Canadian Parliamentary Guide
Canadian Venture Capital & Private Equity Firms
Financial Post Directory of Directors
Financial Services Canada
Governments Canada
Health Guide Canada
The History of Canada
Libraries Canada
Major Canadian Cities

Grey House Publishing | Salem Press | H.W. Wilson | 4919 Route, 22 PO Box 56, Amenia NY 12501-0056

2017 Title List

Visit www.SalemPress.com for Product Information, Table of Contents, and Sample Pages.

Science, Careers & Mathematics

Ancient Creatures
Applied Science
Applied Science: Engineering & Mathematics
Applied Science: Science & Medicine
Applied Science: Technology
Biomes and Ecosystems
Careers in The Arts: Fine, Performing & Visual
Careers in Building Construction
Careers in Business
Careers in Chemistry
Careers in Communications & Media
Careers in Environment & Conservation
Careers in Financial Services
Careers in Healthcare
Careers in Hospitality & Tourism
Careers in Human Services
Careers in Law, Criminal Justice & Emergency Services
Careers in Manufacturing
Careers in Overseas Jobs
Careers in Physics
Careers in Sales, Insurance & Real Estate
Careers in Science & Engineering
Careers in Sports & Fitness
Careers in Technology Services & Repair
Computer Technology Innovators
Contemporary Biographies in Business
Contemporary Biographies in Chemistry
Contemporary Biographies in Communications & Media
Contemporary Biographies in Environment & Conservation
Contemporary Biographies in Healthcare
Contemporary Biographies in Hospitality & Tourism
Contemporary Biographies in Law & Criminal Justice
Contemporary Biographies in Physics
Earth Science
Earth Science: Earth Materials & Resources
Earth Science: Earth's Surface and History
Earth Science: Physics & Chemistry of the Earth
Earth Science: Weather, Water & Atmosphere
Encyclopedia of Energy
Encyclopedia of Environmental Issues
Encyclopedia of Environmental Issues: Atmosphere and Air Pollution
Encyclopedia of Environmental Issues: Ecology and Ecosystems
Encyclopedia of Environmental Issues: Energy and Energy Use
Encyclopedia of Environmental Issues: Policy and Activism
Encyclopedia of Environmental Issues: Preservation/Wilderness Issues
Encyclopedia of Environmental Issues: Water and Water Pollution
Encyclopedia of Global Resources
Encyclopedia of Global Warming
Encyclopedia of Mathematics & Society
Encyclopedia of Mathematics & Society: Engineering, Tech, Medicine
Encyclopedia of Mathematics & Society: Great Mathematicians
Encyclopedia of Mathematics & Society: Math & Social Sciences
Encyclopedia of Mathematics & Society: Math Development/Concepts
Encyclopedia of Mathematics & Society: Math in Culture & Society
Encyclopedia of Mathematics & Society: Space, Science, Environment
Encyclopedia of the Ancient World
Forensic Science
Geography Basics
Internet Innovators
Inventions and Inventors
Magill's Encyclopedia of Science: Animal Life
Magill's Encyclopedia of Science: Plant life
Notable Natural Disasters
Principles of Astronomy
Principles of Biology
Principles of Chemistry
Principles of Physical Science
Principles of Physics
Principles of Research Methods
Principles of Sustainability
Science and Scientists
Solar System
Solar System: Great Astronomers
Solar System: Study of the Universe
Solar System: The Inner Planets
Solar System: The Moon and Other Small Bodies
Solar System: The Outer Planets
Solar System: The Sun and Other Stars
World Geography

Literature

American Ethnic Writers
Classics of Science Fiction & Fantasy Literature
Critical Approaches: Feminist
Critical Approaches: Multicultural
Critical Approaches: Moral
Critical Approaches: Psychological
Critical Insights: Authors
Critical Insights: Film
Critical Insights: Literary Collection Bundles
Critical Insights: Themes
Critical Insights: Works
Critical Survey of Drama
Critical Survey of Graphic Novels: Heroes & Super Heroes
Critical Survey of Graphic Novels: History, Theme & Technique
Critical Survey of Graphic Novels: Independents/Underground Classics
Critical Survey of Graphic Novels: Manga
Critical Survey of Long Fiction
Critical Survey of Mystery & Detective Fiction
Critical Survey of Mythology and Folklore: Heroes and Heroines
Critical Survey of Mythology and Folklore: Love, Sexuality & Desire
Critical Survey of Mythology and Folklore: World Mythology
Critical Survey of Poetry
Critical Survey of Poetry: American Poets
Critical Survey of Poetry: British, Irish & Commonwealth Poets
Critical Survey of Poetry: Cumulative Index
Critical Survey of Poetry: European Poets
Critical Survey of Poetry: Topical Essays
Critical Survey of Poetry: World Poets
Critical Survey of Science Fiction & Fantasy
Critical Survey of Shakespeare's Plays
Critical Survey of Shakespeare's Sonnets
Critical Survey of Short Fiction
Critical Survey of Short Fiction: American Writers
Critical Survey of Short Fiction: British, Irish, Commonwealth Writers
Critical Survey of Short Fiction: Cumulative Index
Critical Survey of Short Fiction: European Writers
Critical Survey of Short Fiction: Topical Essays
Critical Survey of Short Fiction: World Writers
Critical Survey of World Literature
Critical Survey of Young Adult Literature
Cyclopedia of Literary Characters
Cyclopedia of Literary Places
Holocaust Literature
Introduction to Literary Context: American Poetry of the 20th Century
Introduction to Literary Context: American Post-Modernist Novels
Introduction to Literary Context: American Short Fiction
Introduction to Literary Context: English Literature
Introduction to Literary Context: Plays
Introduction to Literary Context: World Literature
Magill's Literary Annual 2015
Magill's Survey of American Literature
Magill's Survey of World Literature
Masterplots
Masterplots II: African American Literature
Masterplots II: American Fiction Series
Masterplots II: British & Commonwealth Fiction Series
Masterplots II: Christian Literature
Masterplots II: Drama Series
Masterplots II: Juvenile & Young Adult Literature, Supplement
Masterplots II: Nonfiction Series
Masterplots II: Poetry Series
Masterplots II: Short Story Series
Masterplots II: Women's Literature Series
Notable African American Writers
Notable American Novelists
Notable Playwrights
Notable Poets
Recommended Reading: 600 Classics Reviewed
Short Story Writers

Grey House Publishing | Salem Press | H.W. Wilson | 4919 Route, 22 PO Box 56, Amenia NY 12501-0056

SALEM PRESS

SALEM PRESS

2017 Title List

Visit **www.SalemPress.com** for Product Information, Table of Contents, and Sample Pages.

History and Social Science

The 2000s in America
50 States
African American History
Agriculture in History
American First Ladies
American Heroes
American Indian Culture
American Indian History
American Indian Tribes
American Presidents
American Villains
America's Historic Sites
Ancient Greece
The Bill of Rights
The Civil Rights Movement
The Cold War
Countries, Peoples & Cultures
Countries, Peoples & Cultures: Central & South America
Countries, Peoples & Cultures: Central, South & Southeast Asia
Countries, Peoples & Cultures: East & South Africa
Countries, Peoples & Cultures: East Asia & the Pacific
Countries, Peoples & Cultures: Eastern Europe
Countries, Peoples & Cultures: Middle East & North Africa
Countries, Peoples & Cultures: North America & the Caribbean
Countries, Peoples & Cultures: West & Central Africa
Countries, Peoples & Cultures: Western Europe
Defining Documents: American Revolution
Defining Documents: American West
Defining Documents: Ancient World
Defining Documents: Civil Rights
Defining Documents: Civil War
Defining Documents: Court Cases
Defining Documents: Dissent & Protest
Defining Documents: Emergence of Modern America
Defining Documents: Exploration & Colonial America
Defining Documents: Immigration & Immigrant Communities
Defining Documents: Manifest Destiny
Defining Documents: Middle Ages
Defining Documents: Nationalism & Populism
Defining Documents: Native Americans
Defining Documents: Postwar 1940s
Defining Documents: Reconstruction
Defining Documents: Renaissance & Early Modern Era
Defining Documents: 1920s
Defining Documents: 1930s
Defining Documents: 1950s
Defining Documents: 1960s
Defining Documents: 1970s
Defining Documents: The 17th Century
Defining Documents: The 18th Century
Defining Documents: Vietnam War
Defining Documents: Women
Defining Documents: World War I
Defining Documents: World War II
The Eighties in America
Encyclopedia of American Immigration
Encyclopedia of Flight
Encyclopedia of the Ancient World
Fashion Innovators
The Fifties in America
The Forties in America
Great Athletes
Great Athletes: Baseball
Great Athletes: Basketball
Great Athletes: Boxing & Soccer
Great Athletes: Cumulative Index
Great Athletes: Football
Great Athletes: Golf & Tennis
Great Athletes: Olympics
Great Athletes: Racing & Individual Sports
Great Events from History: 17th Century
Great Events from History: 18th Century
Great Events from History: 19th Century
Great Events from History: 20th Century (1901-1940)
Great Events from History: 20th Century (1941-1970)

Great Events from History: 20th Century (1971-2000)
Great Events from History: 21st Century (2000-2016)
Great Events from History: African American History
Great Events from History: Cumulative Indexes
Great Events from History: LGBTG
Great Events from History: Middle Ages
Great Events from History: Modern Scandals
Great Events from History: Renaissance & Early Modern Era
Great Lives from History: 17th Century
Great Lives from History: 18th Century
Great Lives from History: 19th Century
Great Lives from History: 20th Century
Great Lives from History: 21st Century (2000-2016)
Great Lives from History: American Women
Great Lives from History: Ancient World
Great Lives from History: Asian & Pacific Islander Americans
Great Lives from History: Cumulative Indexes
Great Lives from History: Incredibly Wealthy
Great Lives from History: Inventors & Inventions
Great Lives from History: Jewish Americans
Great Lives from History: Latinos
Great Lives from History: Notorious Lives
Great Lives from History: Renaissance & Early Modern Era
Great Lives from History: Scientists & Science
Historical Encyclopedia of American Business
Issues in U.S. Immigration
Magill's Guide to Military History
Milestone Documents in African American History
Milestone Documents in American History
Milestone Documents in World History
Milestone Documents of American Leaders
Milestone Documents of World Religions
Music Innovators
Musicians & Composers 20th Century
The Nineties in America
The Seventies in America
The Sixties in America
Survey of American Industry and Careers
The Thirties in America
The Twenties in America
United States at War
U.S. Court Cases
U.S. Government Leaders
U.S. Laws, Acts, and Treaties
U.S. Legal System
U.S. Supreme Court
Weapons and Warfare
World Conflicts: Asia and the Middle East

Health

Addictions & Substance Abuse
Adolescent Health & Wellness
Cancer
Complementary & Alternative Medicine
Community & Family Health
Genetics & Inherited Conditions
Health Issues
Infectious Diseases & Conditions
Magill's Medical Guide
Nutrition
Nursing
Psychology & Behavioral Health
Psychology Basics

2017 Title List

Visit **www.HWWilsonInPrint.com** for Product Information, Table of Contents and Sample Pages

Current Biography

Current Biography Cumulative Index 1946-2013
Current Biography Monthly Magazine
Current Biography Yearbook: 2003
Current Biography Yearbook: 2004
Current Biography Yearbook: 2005
Current Biography Yearbook: 2006
Current Biography Yearbook: 2007
Current Biography Yearbook: 2008
Current Biography Yearbook: 2009
Current Biography Yearbook: 2010
Current Biography Yearbook: 2011
Current Biography Yearbook: 2012
Current Biography Yearbook: 2013
Current Biography Yearbook: 2014
Current Biography Yearbook: 2015
Current Biography Yearbook: 2016

Core Collections

Children's Core Collection
Fiction Core Collection
Graphic Novels Core Collection
Middle & Junior High School Core
Public Library Core Collection: Nonfiction
Senior High Core Collection
Young Adult Fiction Core Collection

The Reference Shelf

Aging in America
American Military Presence Overseas
The Arab Spring
The Brain
The Business of Food
Campaign Trends & Election Law
Conspiracy Theories
The Digital Age
Dinosaurs
Embracing New Paradigms in Education
Faith & Science
Families: Traditional and New Structures
The Future of U.S. Economic Relations: Mexico, Cuba, and Venezuela
Global Climate Change
Graphic Novels and Comic Books
Guns in America
Immigration
Immigration in the U.S.
Internet Abuses & Privacy Rights
Internet Safety
LGBTQ in the 21st Century
Marijuana Reform
The News and its Future
The Paranormal
Politics of the Ocean
Prescription Drug Abuse
Racial Tension in a "Postracial" Age
Reality Television
Representative American Speeches: 2008-2009
Representative American Speeches: 2009-2010
Representative American Speeches: 2010-2011
Representative American Speeches: 2011-2012
Representative American Speeches: 2012-2013
Representative American Speeches: 2013-2014
Representative American Speeches: 2014-2015
Representative American Speeches: 2015-2016
Representative American Speeches: 2016-2017
Rethinking Work
Revisiting Gender
Robotics
Russia
Social Networking
Social Services for the Poor
Space Exploration & Development
Sports in America

The Supreme Court
The Transformation of American Cities
U.S. Infrastructure
U.S. National Debate Topic: Educational Reform
U.S. National Debate Topic: Surveillance
U.S. National Debate Topic: The Ocean
U.S. National Debate Topic: Transportation Infrastructure
Whistleblowers

Readers' Guide

Abridged Readers' Guide to Periodical Literature
Readers' Guide to Periodical Literature

Indexes

Index to Legal Periodicals & Books
Short Story Index
Book Review Digest

Sears List

Sears List of Subject Headings
Sears: Lista de Encabezamientos de Materia

Facts About Series

Facts About American Immigration
Facts About China
Facts About the 20th Century
Facts About the Presidents
Facts About the World's Languages

Nobel Prize Winners

Nobel Prize Winners: 1901-1986
Nobel Prize Winners: 1987-1991
Nobel Prize Winners: 1992-1996
Nobel Prize Winners: 1997-2001

World Authors

World Authors: 1995-2000
World Authors: 2000-2005

Famous First Facts

Famous First Facts
Famous First Facts About American Politics
Famous First Facts About Sports
Famous First Facts About the Environment
Famous First Facts: International Edition

American Book of Days

The American Book of Days
The International Book of Days

Monographs

American Reformers
The Barnhart Dictionary of Etymology
Celebrate the World
Guide to the Ancient World
Indexing from A to Z
The Poetry Break
Radical Change: Books for Youth in a Digital Age

Wilson Chronology

Wilson Chronology of Asia and the Pacific
Wilson Chronology of Human Rights
Wilson Chronology of Ideas
Wilson Chronology of the Arts
Wilson Chronology of the World's Religions
Wilson Chronology of Women's Achievements

Grey House Publishing | Salem Press | H.W. Wilson | 4919 Route, 22 PO Box 56, Amenia NY 12501-0056